CONTEMPORARY AMERICAN BUSINESS LEADERS

CONTEMPORARY AMERICAN BUSINESS LEADERS
A Biographical Dictionary

JOHN N. INGHAM
AND
LYNNE B. FELDMAN

GREENWOOD PRESS
NEW YORK • WESTPORT, CONNECTICUT • LONDON

Library of Congress Cataloging-in-Publication Data

Ingham, John N.
  Contemporary American business leaders : a biographical dictionary
/ John N. Ingham and Lynne B. Feldman.
    p. cm.
  Includes index.
  ISBN 0–313–25743–4 (lib. bdg. : alk. paper)
  1. Businessmen—United States—Biography—Dictionaries.
I. Feldman, Lynne B.   II. Title.
HC102.5.A2I534   1990
338.092'2—dc20   89–11866
[B]

British Library Cataloguing in Publication Data is available.

Library of Congress Catalog Card Number: 89–11866
ISBN: 0–313–25743–4

First published in 1990

Greenwood Press, Inc.
88 Post Road West, Westport, Connecticut   06881

Printed in the United States of America

The paper used in this book complies with the
Permanent Paper Standard issued by the National
Information Standards Organization (Z39.48–1984).

10 9 8 7 6 5 4 3 2 1

Copyright Acknowledgments

The authors gratefully acknowledge permission to quote the following:

Poem presented by Leo Burnett to the Central Region of the Four A's in Chicago, October 13,
1955. Used with permission of Leo Burnett Company, Inc.

1940 Pepsi-Cola Company jingle. Used with permission of the Pepsi-Cola Company.

We dedicate this book to Joseph and Mae Louise ''Mickie'' Ingham
and in loving memory of Carol and Harry Feldman

"This relationship is, of course, still in progress, but in the most advanced countries of the world, and particularly in America, it is giving way to another sort of revolution— a whole range of social developments associated with the shift from an age of production to an age of consumption." (David Riesman, *The Lonely Crowd*, 1955, p. 20)

"We have chosen to consume, not invest. . . . The only way to afford and enjoy the future is to invest in it. . . . Unless a nation pays the dues required for economic progress, its politics become a mean contest over scarce resources. . . . Where are we to find the resources for a Decade of Investment? Whose consumption is to be cut?" (Peter G. Peterson, "No More Free Lunch for the Middle Class," *New York Times Magazine*, January 17, 1982, pp. 40, 41)

"This community is basically dead. People here realize this is not the thriving South Side any longer. Steeltown. I think all hope has been given up. The rate of [small] business closings, home foreclosures, the separation rate of marriages, everything around here is in a very sad state." (Michael Ally, Chicago steel worker, interviewed by Ralph Nader and William Taylor, *The Big Boys*, 1986, p. 25)

"I have a personal thing about saving smokestack America, but it won't be with the large companies. They have their heads in the sand. When you think of manufacturing, you think of these huge plants, but now, with all this technology the small guys—the job shops—might be a hell of a lot more efficient. The pendulum swings and it's swinging to the smaller shops." (John West, president of Cadlink, a Chicago-based computer-controlled design and manufacturing firm, quoted in Dan Gervitz, *The New Entrepreneurs*, 1984, p. 105)

CONTENTS

PREFACE

In the four decades following World War II American business has experienced a profound transformation. This volume addresses that transformation and the business people who played such a vital role in it. To a certain extent, *Contemporary American Business Leaders* is a companion to John Ingham's earlier *Biographical Dictionary of American Business Leaders*, published by Greenwood Press in 1983. That four-volume work, which covered American business leaders from the very earliest period of American history to the present day, included a number of post–World War II business leaders who would normally have been part of the present work. This collection, however, delves far more deeply into significant trends and developments in the postwar world. Thirty-five of the 1,159 biographical entries in the *Biographical Dictionary* focused on business leaders whose careers took place principally after World War II. Those biographies have not been reproduced in this volume, but the reader may refer to the previous work for them.[1] In *Contemporary American Business Leaders*, whenever a business leader included in the *Biographical Dictionary* is mentioned, that person's name appears with an asterisk (*). Similarly, when an individual discussed in one of the other biographies in this volume is mentioned elsewhere here, that person's name appears with a dagger (†).

In any biographical compilation, the selection process for choosing who is to be included is most critical. In the present work, we tried to define and choose those business leaders whom we deemed to be the "historically most significant." That somewhat elastic term allows a certain amount of discretion in selection. Not all leaders of *Fortune* 500 corporations are included within these pages. Nor are many very wealthy and successful business leaders. We attempted to identify the most important trends in the development of the American business system during the forty years after World War II and to identify business leaders who exemplified those trends. The biographies, as a result, are less oriented toward the personal lives of these individuals than toward the business decisions they made, and toward the impact those decisions had upon the development of the broader business system. The rationale for our selections is developed most comprehensively in the introduction, by which the reader can follow quite precisely the logic we used for determining who should be included.

Each biography is followed by a bibliography. The bibliography is divided into two parts. Part A includes writings by the subject. Part B includes secondary materials written about the subject, particularly those items that we found most helpful in compiling the biographies. We generally included, however, only materials that would be fairly readily available on a nationwide basis. We seldom included items, for example, from local newspapers or from obscure trade publications unless those were the only sources available. The goal of the bibliographies was not to be exhaustive as much as it was to be helpful to the readers in finding useful additional information about the subjects.

Included in this volume are also five appendices that allow the reader to access the biographies according to industry (Appendix 1), company (Appendix 2), place of business (Appendix 3), place of birth (Appendix 4), and black and women business leaders (Appendix 5). There is also, of course, a comprehensive index that enables the reader to pursue any number of important themes, individuals, companies, and other details.

During the three years we have worked on this volume, we have accumulated many debts to persons who have been remarkably supportive and helpful. We would like to take this opportunity to thank Lynda Pearson, public relations manager, Canada, for Kelly Services; Peter Flach, division manager for Southland Canada, Inc.; Catherine Eisner, formerly of Leo Burnett, Inc., Canada; John J. Ingham of Phoenix, Arizona; and Joseph N. Ingham of San Clemente, California for the research assistance and information they provided. We would like to thank the staffs of the following libraries for their help: Robarts Library of the University of Toronto; the Metro Central Reference Library of the Toronto Public Library System; the Public Library of Savannah, Georgia; the Main Public Library of Philadelphia, Pennsylvania; and the Business Library at the University of Western Ontario. We would also like to thank Susan Ingham for her assistance in compiling the appendices. Finally, we would like to thank our friends, who not only have shown interest in our project and given us support and encouragement but, most important, have provided an outlet of fun and relaxation away from the book when it was so desperately needed: Richard Prupas and Eva Karpati, Ralph and Joy Sheppard, Sigmund and Nancy Levy, Daniel and Carolyn Karin, Bruce and Nancy Leslie, Catherine Eisner, Richard Waxman, Janet and Lou Liebenau, and Jack and Syma Solomon.

NOTE

1. Following are the postwar business leaders included in the *Biographical Dictionary:* Walter H. Annenberg, Roy L. Ash, O. Gene Autry, Stephen D. Bechtel, Charles G. Bluhdorn, Walter E. and Roy Disney, Otto Eckstein, Henry Ford II, Harold S. Geneen, Leonard H. Goldenson, Berry Gordy Jr., Katherine Graham, Patrick E. Haggerty, Armand Hammer, Howard R. Hughes Jr., Lee A. Iacocca, James K. Jamison, John H. Johnson, Ray A. Kroc, Edwin H. Land, Samuel J. Lefrak, William J. Levitt, James J. Ling, Daniel K. Ludwig, Robert S. McNamara, Andre Meyer, Arthur C. Nielsen, Walter F. O'Malley, William W. Prince, Simon Ramo, David Rockefeller, Felix G. Rohatyn, Harland Sanders, Charles B. Thornton, Gloria M. Vanderbilt, Diane von Furstenberg, Lew R. Wasserman, Mary G. Wells, Charles Erwin Wilson, Kemmons Wilson, Dean E. Wooldridge, William Zeckendorf.

INTRODUCTION

American business after World War II was perhaps the wealthiest and most powerful the world had ever known. From 1945 to about 1970, American business, in alliance with the American state and its military power, was predominant both at home and abroad. Supremely confident, even arrogant, concerning the prodigious capacity of the American system to both produce and consume goods, it seemed to many analysts in the 1950s and 1960s to be "America's Century."

During the period from 1945 to 1970, the key words in America were abundance and affluence, and the two concepts were positively correlated. The major problem in postwar America was not the production of goods; World War II, after all, had demonstrated the country's awesome capacity to outproduce the rest of the world. Rather, the matter at hand was how to market these goods—to ensure that Americans did not hoard the savings they had accumulated during the war years and save their way right back into a depression. The magic word for young businessmen coming of age in the years just after the war was marketing—product development, advertising, selling, and a plethora of consumer services designed to urge the consumer to spend. The production concerns of earlier generations of business leaders who built "smokestack America" were smugly dismissed in the heady, exciting world of business in 1945.

For a quarter of a century, the American marketing juggernaut could do no wrong. It poured out a veritable cornucopia of goods and services, the like of which the world had never before witnessed, and provided an unparalleled standard of living for most Americans. By the 1950s, America, with just 6 percent of the world's population and 7 percent of the geographic area, was producing nearly half of the world's manufactured products. Contained within the country's borders were fully 75 percent of all the automobiles in the world, 60 percent of the telephones, and 30 percent of the televisions and radios. America also consumed nearly half the world's annual production of energy and the lion's share of most of the earth's resources. The gross national product (GNP), which had been just $91.5 billion in 1939, stood at $212 billion at the end of World War II. After that, the GNP grew rapidly, reaching a breathtaking $1 trillion in 1971.

As the American economic system achieved these stunning levels of growth, it pioneered in dramatic new areas of technology—electronics, computers, aerospace, and communications.

Nor was this, in the minds of many observers, an accident. America's economic dominance was, in their view, blessed by God, or at least by the benevolent hand of nature. Summer Slichter, an economist at Harvard, in 1948 asked "Why Is U.S. Industry So Productive?" It had less, according to Slichter, to do with technical prowess than with America's moral superiority. Business prospered because person and property were secure, because ambition was not restricted by rigid hierarchies, but most of all, because "industry in the United States is in the hands of men who desire to make money rather than to enjoy wealth."[1]

But somewhere along the way the American genius began to crumble, and after 1970 it completely fell apart. American automobiles could no longer compete with foreign imports, American electronic products were inferior in quality and more expensive than imports from Japan, and whole basic industries, such as steel and machine tools, where America had long led the world, faltered badly. The deterioration was so marked in so many industries, and so many plants were closed and so many communities devastated, that the media began referring to America's industrial heartland as the "rust-belt." Analysts pointed the finger of blame at many elements—on intrusive, over-regulatory government and greedy unions—but most laid the blame squarely on American management. *Dun's Review* put the matter bluntly in an article entitled: "Don't Blame the System, Blame the Managers."[2] The heroes of the 1950s and 1960s, those magicians of America's astonishing economic miracle, were now the villains, or at least the scapegoats, of the 1970s and 1980s.

THE AMERICAN BUSINESS SYSTEM, 1945–1970

During the quarter century after World War II, America entered a period known as "high mass consumption." As a result of this postwar boom, nearly 60 percent of Americans achieved a middle-class standard of living. That is, they owned their homes, often in the burgeoning suburbs, and they had sufficient income to afford the increasingly large number of goods (automobiles, televisions, boats, swimming pools, and so forth) that were considered an essential part of this life-style.

Despite Slichter's claims of higher morality, this postwar prosperity was in reality propelled by several mundane factors. One important element was spending by the federal government. It poured billions of dollars into the economy through subsidies for farmers, home loans for veterans, welfare programs, and foreign aid. Most important, though, was defense spending. By 1960, defense spending and veteran's benefits amounted to over $50 billion, nearly 56 percent of federal spending and 10 percent of the GNP. Then, in the late 1960s, with the onset of the war in Vietnam, defense spending increased, totaling $600 billion from 1965 to 1970.

America's fabulous economic growth during this period was also fueled (literally) by cheap and plentiful energy. The nation's petroleum industry forecast a nearly unending supply of domestic oil as part of its argument to avoid federal regulation of oil reserves. Benefiting from low prices for gasoline, electricity, and home heating oil, Americans went on an energy binge. They turned away from coal as the principal source of heat for their homes, bought gas-guzzling automobiles, and purchased electrical appliances in unprecedented numbers. To provide increasing amounts of inexpensive electricity, some oil firms like Kerr-McGee (see Robert Kerr and Dean McGee) turned to the production of nuclear energy. Viewed as a nearly limitless source of energy for future generations, nuclear power in the 1950s and 1960s carried none of the negative connotations of danger and caution that it acquired after 1970.

The prosperity of the postwar decades was also fueled by advertising. Although modern advertising had been present for decades, the years after 1945 became the era of marketing and advertising. Far more than in previous decades, even in the 1920s, the economic health of the 1950s and 1960s depended upon advertising. Since the basic needs of society were already provided for the vast majority of people, the key to economic growth lay in the consumption of luxury goods. The consumer, therefore, had to be convinced to buy these goods, goods he or she did not need, and in some cases, might not even want. Not only was vastly more money spent on advertising (from $6 billion in 1950 to $13 billion in 1965), but advertising also became more subtle and sophisticated. Advertising men like William Bernbach,[†] David Ogilvy,[†] and Leo Burnett[†] stimulated a revolution in the industry, wherein advertising copy was less direct, more humorous, and adapted itself to a fabulous new medium—television.

The biggest advertiser of all during these years was General Motors, which was significant, since the automobile, more than anything else, symbolized the new consumer society of the postwar period. Practically every American family owned at least one car by 1970, and, increasingly, the badge of middle-class status was the two-car family. Although there were many important innovations in the auto industry—with the introduction of power steering and power brakes, V–8 engines, automatic transmissions, and a host of other improvements—and although productivity increased greatly (it took 310 man-hours to produce an automobile at the end of World War II, and just half that fifteen years later), the period was remarkable primarily for excesses in size and styling. The automobiles of the 1950s and 1960s were huge, gas-guzzling behemoths, festooned with tail fins, double headlights, multiple taillights, two-tone paint jobs, and an endless array of gadgets. They were the quintessence of marketing and advertising prowess, as buyers were convinced that their status and happiness were dependent on buying "your Big Pontiac," or were persuaded that "never before [was a] Lincoln . . . so long and so longed for."

The automobile culture of the 1950s and 1960s also spawned a host of new service industries. Although service stations and repair shops had been around for some time, a more specialized phenomenon emerged at this time. Nate and Gordon Sherman[†] started their Midas Muffler Shops to provide that specialized car service primarily to the female consumer who, isolated in the new suburbs, was responsible for car repairs. Leonard Shoen[†] founded his U-Haul firm after World War II to rent trailers and trucks to increasingly mobile Americans.

Other older American industries did not progress as rapidly during this time, but, in the euphoria of the period, few noticed. The steel industry, for one, was largely stagnant. Saddled with old plants and an increasingly obsolete basic open-hearth technology, the American steel industry was protected by tariff walls and distance from competitors. So, as wages and prices rose, American consumers meekly complied. The textile industry also entered a period of relative decline; increasingly transferring their operations to the South, firms like J. P. Stevens & Company (see Stevens Family) and Deering, Milliken & Co. (see Roger Milliken) attempted to restructure themselves in the postwar world. However, they, like the steel industry, were largely protected from the most powerful competition from abroad during these years.

Nobody, however, paid much attention to stagnation and uncompetitiveness in the 1950s and 1960s. The word on most people's lips was innovation. World War II had proved America's ability to produce goods more innovatively and on a grander scale than anybody else, and the postwar decades were simply a manifestation of that formula in most people's minds. Even in the textile industry, observers were more impressed with the seemingly endless numbers of synthetic fabrics that were being introduced during these years. These synthetics, of course, came not from the labs of the textile companies, but from those of chemical companies like Du Pont. The plastics industry grew by 600 percent in the first decade and a half after the war, and products were developed to take the place of wood, metal, and glass. Man-made fibers like Orlon, Dacron, and nylon replaced cotton, wool, and silk.

Other older industries also grew and transformed during these years. The farm implement industry, in which America had world leadership for over a century, began dying out. Firms like Caterpillar Tractor[†] moved in new directions to find success. Recognizing the great expansion of construction in America and all over the world, Caterpillar specialized in new types of earth-moving equipment that were regarded as state of the art for decades. Airplanes, which had been the preserve of the wealthy in the prewar period, were made available to the masses after the war by Dwayne Wallace[†] and his Cessna Aircraft Company. By applying concepts of mass production to the industry, he turned out air pleasure craft by the thousands. The food industry, another of America's oldest, also metamorphosed. America had taken the lead in the rationalization of the food industry in the early twentieth century with the development of large concerns like Quaker Oats and General Foods, but these developments were carried still further in the 1950s and 1960s. Nathan Cummings[†] with Consolidated Foods and Sara Lee Corporation and Norton Simon[†] with Hunt Foods created food conglomerates that used new and more sophisticated techniques to advertise and market their products. Both men and their companies represented an important revolution in the eating habits of America. Before the war Americans had eaten fresh dairy products, meats, vegetables, and fruits; after the war, they turned increasingly to canned and frozen foods. Simon's company specialized in the former; Cummings' Sara Lee led in the development of frozen foods. Pharmaceuticals, one of the oldest American industries, revolutionized American culture in the early 1960s when G. D. Searle & Co., under the guidance of John G. Searle,[†] introduced the oral contraceptive, which not only made Searle very successful, but also contributed to changing the sexual mores of millions of Americans. Minnesota Mining & Manufacturing (3-M), under the leadership of William McKnight,[†] continued to bring out a plethora of innovative products, refusing to be pigeonholed into any particular area. 3-M, to many people, symbolized the essence of American inventiveness and innovation during these years.

Whole new industries, industries in which America held world leadership throughout the 1960s, were also developed during this time. The electronics industry, which had been stimulated by World War II, surged after the war to become the country's fifth-largest industry by the 1960s. Producing televisions, radios, tape recorders, hi-fi's and stereos, home appliances, and testing and measuring devices for automation, and sophisticated weaponry for the Defense Department, firms like Texas Instruments, Hewlett-Packard (see William Hewlett and David Packard), General Electric, and Motorola (see Paul and Robert Galvin) were the envy of the world.

Even more dramatic was the emergence of the computer industry. This industry also had its origins during World War II, when the federal government funded research into computers. Participating in this early research was William Norris,[†] among others. He later joined the Sperry-Rand Corporation to develop the UNI-VAC computer, the first of the huge mainframe computers. Shortly thereafter, the lead in computers was assumed by International Business Machines (IBM), which dominated the market thereafter. Norris, in turn, left Sperry-Rand to form his own computer firm, Control Data Corporation, which by the mid-1960s was the third largest computer company, after IBM and Sperry-Rand. Control Data found its niche in the market by making so-called supercomputer mainframes with power and capabilities greater than IBM's. Kenneth Olsen[†] founded another important computer firm in the late 1950s—Digital Equipment Corporation—which became the leader in developing the powerful minicomputer in the 1960s. Hewlett-Packard, which had concentrated on producing measuring equipment and scientific calculators, also began to turn out sophisticated minicomputers in the 1960s. An Wang,[†] who held important patents on the magnetic core memory, also started his own computer firm in the late 1950s. IBM, however, continued to dominate not only the domestic market, where it had two-thirds of the sales, but also practically every foreign market for computers. Providing chips and semiconductors for these computer makers were firms like Intel, founded by

Gordon Moore[†] and Robert Noyce,[†] and Motorola, under the guidance of Robert Galvin. H. Ross Perot,[†] a former IBM salesman, recognizing that large firms who installed data processing systems needed assistance in operating them efficiently, responded to this need by establishing Electronic Data Systems, and Saul Steinberg[†] established Leasco to lease computers.

America also developed new techniques for marketing goods during these years. Forrest Mars, Sr.,[†] of Mars, Inc. used television advertising innovatively to power his firm's candy bars to the top of the pyramid in the 1950s and 1960s. Whereas the traditional leader, Hershey Chocolate, disdained any form of advertising for years, Mars saturated the market with it, thereby surpassing Hershey and other rivals quite easily. Other firms developed unique ways to reach the American buying public. Earl Tupper organized "Tupperware parties" in customers' homes as a means of selling his plastic household products, and the "house party" idea caught on. It was borrowed by Mary Kay Ash,[†] who used it to market her Mary Kay Cosmetics. She also used a version of an older, but effective "pyramid" system of distributorships in her operations. That technique was utilized more effectively by Richard De Vos[†] and Jay Van Andel[†] in their Amway Corporation. Ostensibly selling household cleaning products, Amway's allure to potential distributors was actually selling distributorships in a pyramid organization. In an era when marketing was divine, De Vos and Van Andel transformed their marketing organization, Amway, into virtually a religious cult. Even banks moved into marketing with greater vigor in the postwar period. Mills Lane, Jr.,[†] head of Citizens & Southern National Bank in Savannah and Atlanta, Georgia, pioneered the use of the bank credit card.

Mary Kay Ash was not the only person in the cosmetics industry to develop powerful new marketing techniques. Charles Revson,[†] head of Revlon, Inc., used seductive advertising and marketing strategies to build his company into a powerhouse in the postwar years. Similarly, Estée Lauder[†] developed a highly successful technique for selling her cosmetics through department stores, particularly by offering free samples. Lauder also produced the first truly successful line of men's high-quality fragrances and skin-care products. Edward Gardner,[†] founder of Soft Sheen, Products, Inc., created a large national hair-care firm for blacks in a similar fashion.

The most dramatic change in postwar retailing came with the development of discount stores. For years, fair trade laws had legislated against retail chains engaging in deep price cutting. In 1951, those laws were declared unconstitutional by the United States Supreme Court, and a group of new discount stores emerged. The largest and most important of the new discounters was K mart, headed by Harry Cunningham[†] during the 1950s and 1960s who transformed the old Kresge Company into the nation's leading discounter. In the late 1970s, K mart passed J.C. Penney* as the number-two retailer, and it was threatening to surpass the national leader, Sears, Roebuck in the 1980s. Another important discount chain which emerged in the early 1960s in the specialty field was Toys "R" Us, founded by Charles Lazarus.[†] Using the discount formula, Toys "R" Us became the dominant retailing force in the toy industry. The revolution in retail merchandising brought on by discount stores like K mart was part of a major change in consumer spending practices, and it represented a profound alteration in the service sector of the economy.

An older segment of the retailing sphere which was also transformed in the decades after World War II was department stores. Older, staid, department store operations began to develop a new cachet, a new merchandising approach at this time. Led by Beatrice Fox Auerbach,[†] Stanley Marcus,[†] and Dorothy Shaver,[†] these stores became shining beacons on the American merchandising scene, carrying designer fashions and exotic imported goods for their upscale customers.

As the discount stores established themselves in suburban locations, major department stores followed suit. Unlike the discounters, though, the department stores settled into large, new shopping malls in the suburbs. Although a few shopping centers had emerged as early as the 1920s, their full development was delayed until the vast explosion of suburbs. Usually built near an expressway, most shopping centers were anchored by two department stores, along with other retail (chain) stores. As early as the mid–1950s, there were 1,800 shopping centers in the United States, and they grew ever larger and more ubiquitous in later years, until they numbered over 20,000 in the late 1970s. A pioneer in the development of shopping centers was Edward DeBartolo,[†] who opened his first one in Boardman, Ohio, just outside of Youngstown, in the late 1940s.

Edward Carter[†] was a leader in taking urban department stores into the suburban shopping malls. As head of the Carter, Hawley, Hale chain on the West Coast, he focused on the suburban shopping centers for his regional chain. At about the same time, Fred Lazarus,[†] of Federated Department Stores, welded together a number of local and regional department store chain operations into a highly successful national chain. These chain stores, like Carter's, increasingly were located in suburban shopping malls. As the department stores spearheaded the shopping center movement, specialty chain stores moved into malls around the nation. Women's clothing stores, like The Limited, founded by Leslie Wexner,[†] and other firms all developed chain outlets to take advantage of the new retailing environment.

Perhaps the most dramatic change in retailing emerged with the development of convenience store chains. The pioneer in this activity was the Thompson Family[†] and the Southland Corporation with their 7-Eleven stores. As supermarkets surfaced in the postwar years and the older mom-and-pop grocery stores disappeared, a void was left in the marketplace. The supermarket, which provided high-quality food at lower prices, was ideal for the family buying weekly groceries. But the impulse shopper, who needed a pack of cigarettes, a six-pack of beer, or a soft drink, was discouraged by long lines. 7-Eleven stores addressed that problem by providing a nationwide network of stores carrying a limited stock of high-turnover goods and ensuring that the customer could complete a purchase quickly.

A relatively new phenomenon in the postwar period was franchising. Although a few companies, like Rexall Drug, had developed franchise arrangements in the prewar years, it did not really blossom until after 1945. Among the leaders in this movement were the Shermans with their Midas Muffler shops and Leonard Shoen with his U-Haul outlets in gasoline stations around the nation. Typically, a franchiser granted an operating franchise to a small-scale operator in an exclusive territory under the direct control and assistance of the parent company. In this way, many Americans in a time of "big business" and bureaucracy could "be their own bosses" and could perpetuate, at least somewhat, the idea of small business opportunity. The quintessential franchiser was Ray Kroc* with his McDonald's chain; his business not only plugged into the franchising craze of the time, but it also revolutionized America's eating and leisure habits. Featuring clean kitchens, well-dressed employees, and standardized food, Kroc became the "Henry Ford" of the fast-food industry. The model for other fast-food franchises, which, like Thomas Monaghan's[†] Domino's Pizza, sprang up around the nation, McDonald's Golden Arches soon dominated America's suburban landscape and the diet of America's young in an unprecedented manner.

Emerging a few years later on the franchise scene was Charles Tandy[†] with his Radio Shack stores. His stores provided electronic products with a high turnover and profitable margins. Locating his franchise operations in suburban shopping malls and in small towns and cities, by 1980 Tandy had 7,500 stores, more than McDonald's. At around the same time, William Millard[†] established his chain of ComputerLand stores, which sold IBM and Apple (see Steven Jobs) computer products to the public. Other successful chain franchise operations of the time were H & R Block, Inc., started by Henry and Richard Bloch,[†] which made a successful business out of computing tax returns. These franchise operations were also part of a growing trend toward a service economy in the United States, as fewer people were employed to produce goods, and as larger numbers were hired to provide a multitude of specialized services. Another product of America's transition to a service economy was started by William Kelly.[†] He established his Kelly Girl company to provide temporary help for the burgeoning corporate bureaucracies of the time. Although it was not franchised, it resembled in most other respects those operations.

Information and entertainment were two other major industries of the 1950s and 1960s. Telecommunications witnessed a good deal of technological advancement during these years, but despite antitrust suits brought by the Justice Department, the industry remained a monopoly under the control of American Telephone and Telegraph. Television was a somewhat different story. Although television had been around almost as long as radio, it was not commercially successful until after World War II. Rapid expansion began in 1952, when the Federal Communications Commission lifted its freeze on new television stations. At that time, just 108 stations could beam their signals to 15 million households; four years later, there were over 400 stations and 35 million sets. Television came to dominate American suburban life in the 1950s and 1960s, and it became the principal medium for advertising in the new consumer economy.

Television programming, as was the case with radio, was dominated by the three great networks: the National Broadcasting Company, the Columbia Broadcasting System, and the America Broadcasting Company. The programs themselves, however, were developed by independent producers. The most popular television programs were the situation comedies, and the most popular of these in the 1950s was "I Love Lucy." The show's producer Desi Arnaz[†] developed the singularly most successful television production company, Desilu Productions, whose programs dominated the airwaves for years. Later, Merv Griffin,[†] along with Marc Goodson and Bill Todman, used the game show format to develop highly successful business empires in the television industry. By the end of the 1960s, however, new forces, including cable and syndication, were beginning to challenge the dominance of the networks.

The print medium also underwent a revolution during these years. In books, the most important change was the development of paperbacks. Born out of wartime necessity, Ian Ballantine[†] with his Ballantine Books helped create a lucrative new publishing business that was later adopted by the major publishing firms. In magazines, the most dramatic and noteworthy change came with the introduction of *Playboy* by Hugh Hefner[†] in the early 1950s. The magazine not only helped bring about a revolution in the nation's morals and attitudes during the 1950s and 1960s, but also opened a whole new genre of publishing in the country. Before, "men's magazines" had been sold surreptitiously, under the counter, and were never read in polite society. Hefner and *Playboy* changed that. Bob Guccione,[†] with his *Penthouse* magazine, took Hefner's formula, updated it, and created yet another publishing giant based on men's soft-core pornography.

As America's economy grew in world influence and power during these years, the role and number of multinational corporations vastly expanded. American firms had had overseas operations for many years prior to World War II, but it was in the postwar years that they benefited greatly from a trend toward worldwide business diversification. By 1970, at least 3,500 American firms had direct foreign investments in over 15,000 enterprises. This investment amounted to over $78 billion and was equal to 8 percent of the GNP of the United States. Prominent among these multinationals were firms that exploited the natural resources of other countries, particularly petroleum and mining companies. Such firms, however, represented a somewhat older type of multinational. In the 1950s and 1960s, with the negotiation of the General Agreement on Trade and Tariffs (GATT), trade barriers were reduced, which allowed American firms to use their marketing prowess to sell American goods and services on the world market.

Coca-Cola became a worldwide phenomenon after the war, and many other American companies and products followed suit; Procter and Gamble, Nabisco, Kellogg's, and other quintessentially American products became staples the world over. American services also expanded abroad during this time. One of the most dramatic world conquests by an American product was by Levis jeans. The Levi Strauss firm, run by the Haas Family,[†] promoted its formerly humble garment into the most sought-after piece of apparel in history. McDonald's revolutionized the landscape of foreign countries just as it had done in America. Similarly, Sears, Roebuck, Holiday Inn, Hilton Hotels, and many others became ubiquitous abroad. These developments made it possible for American tourists to travel outside the United States without having to experience the "inconveniences" of a foreign culture—America was there waiting for them.

There were other, less visible, multinational operations. The commodities market had always been international in scope, but in the period after World War II, a number of more truly global firms emerged. Cargill Co., run by John and Whitney MacMillan[†] with its vast multinational grain and food processing operations, was one of the largest private firms in the entire world. Similarly, as the international petroleum and metals markets heated up during these years, numerous American firms and individuals came to the fore. Among the wealthiest, and most notorious, was Marc Rich,[†] a genius in the formerly European-dominated metals market.

The business movement that dominated the headlines in the late 1960s was the rise of conglomerates. American industrial firms since the 1920s had been moving increasingly toward diversification and decentralization. Du Pont and General Motors had led the way in the movement in the early years. This trend in diversification, however, was into areas of related technologies and marketing practices. The conglomerate was something different. It was a company with many different divisions manufacturing and selling unrelated products and services. Among the earliest conglomerates to emerge in the 1950s were Textron and Litton Industries. Litton had started as a small electronics firm, but, after 1958, it brought in a myriad of new divisions in a bewildering variety of areas. As the head of the firm, Tex Thornton,[*] said: "We are in the business of opportunity." Teledyne, founded by Henry Singleton,[†] developed in a manner nearly identical to Litton.

The conglomerates emerged, ironically, because of more stringent antitrust legislation by the U.S. Justice Department. In 1950, Congress had passed the Celler-Kefauver Act, which stringently restricted vertical and horizontal mergers within the same industry. The message to management was clear: only expansion into totally unrelated areas would be allowed. Thus was born the conglomerate. Among these early and highly successful conglomerates was Norton Simon, Inc., which grew from a small food canning firm to a giant diversified enterprise. The Tisch brothers,[†] with Loews Theaters as a base, also created a vast conglomerate of hotels, insurance firms, and cigarettes.

The peak year of conglomerate mergers occurred in 1969, when there were over 6,000 such corporate "marriages." The practice, however, incited a good deal of controversy, as it raised visions of what Robert Reich was later to term "paper entrepreneurialism." As he later noted, "Conglomerate enterprise rarely, if ever, brings any relevant managerial, technical, or marketing skills to the enterprises they acquire."[3] They simply made profits for their creators without contributing anything to the economy. The conglomerate craze died out in the early 1970s, largely because the American stock market plunged. Heavily leveraged, and carrying large debt loads, many conglomerates performed poorly during those years. They would, however, reemerge in an altered form in the 1980s. But the stock market downturn of the early 1970s proved to be something more than a passing phenomenon; it did, in many ways indicate a profound turning point in the American economy. An era ended at about that time—American mastery of the world, and of its own economy, seemed to dissolve almost overnight. The next decade and a half were difficult years for American managers and analysts of the business scene.

THE AMERICAN BUSINESS SYSTEM SINCE 1970

The turnaround was so sudden and so dramatic that most Americans simply could not believe it had happened. The United States, the wealthiest, most powerful nation in the world, suddenly seemed nearly prostrate, economically, militarily, politically, and socially. The abundance that had symbolized the American economy for two and a half decades seemed to many observers to have ended. The 1970s became a decade of transition, one characterized by confusion, frustration, and an almost overwhelming sense that America had lost its sense of direction.

The rapid economic growth that had been the wellspring of the American dream after World War II had ground to a halt by the mid–1970s. The statistics told a stark tale: the percentage of American manufacturing capacity employed in production, which stood at 86 percent in 1965, fell to less than 70 percent in 1982. The unemployed, numbering just 3.5 percent in the mid–1960s, escalated to 11 percent in the early 1980s. The Dow-Jones industrial average, measured in constant dollars, fell from 2,624 to 1,000 over this same period. Productivity, which had stood at from 2.5 to 3.5 percent throughout the 1950s and 1960s, plunged to just over 1 percent. At the same time, Japanese productivity soared to 7 percent, with Germany at 4 percent. Even Canada, whose economy had traditionally underperformed that of the United States, had a rate of productivity almost two and a half times greater than its neighbor to the south. Double-digit inflation was rampant throughout this period, and the GNP plummeted. A new phenomenon appeared in America, a curious beast called "stagflation." Back in the "old days," when the economy made sense, if demand and production fell off there was a depression, and prices fell. But not in the 1970s. Spurred by high petroleum prices, instigated by the Arab oil embargos of 1973 and 1979, and a massive sale of wheat to the Soviet Union, prices continued to escalate even as the economy stumbled and millions of Americans were laid off. By the early 1980s, real discretionary income per worker had declined some 18 percent. As a result, America's much ballyhooed standard of living began to decline. When a worldwide recession struck in 1981 and 1982, the American economy was among the hardest hit.

The great American core industries—automobiles, steel, petrochemicals, textiles, consumer electronics, electrical machinery, and machine tools—were in deep trouble. The American economic malaise came at a time when a new international business environment began to emerge, and this worsened an already bad situation. As American firms and, indeed, as entire industries faltered, foreign competitors, particularly the Japanese, moved in to capture important markets. Ironically, American business leaders themselves had worked for years to foster a more open international marketplace, assuming that in an open-door situation, the more efficient American firms would always predominate. Suddenly, when that new international market matured, many American firms and industries had grown weak and flaccid, and Americans felt the crush of foreign competition in a way similar to that experienced by other nations when American companies overwhelmed their economies after World War II.

There were a number of reasons for this transformation, and many of them were not internal to the American system. The Japanese and European economies, which had been devastated by World War II, had been rebuilt (partially through U.S. foreign aid funds) by the 1960s. With newer and more productive industrial plants and with generally lower wage rates and more cooperative workers, these nations' economies were young and hungry, and they voraciously pursued the enormous American marketplace. Prior to 1965, few foreign imports entered the United States. By 1980, more than 22 percent of the goods Americans consumed were imported. Even worse, these imports were not concentrated in just one or two areas of the economy. Indeed, by 1980, more than 70 percent of all the goods produced in the United States were forced to compete with foreign-made imports.

In American core industries, the situation was especially trying. By the early 1980s, America was importing 26 percent of its automobiles; 25 percent of its steel; 60 percent of its television sets, radios, and tape recorders; and 43 percent of its calculators. Most distressingly, these were the high-volume, capital-intensive kinds of industries that America had staked its world economic predominance upon since the early twentieth century. America not only lost control of its home market in these areas, but was also a less effective competitor abroad, losing 40 percent of the world market in agricultural machinery; 50 percent of the market in telecommunications machinery; 55 percent of the market in metal-working machinery; and, unkindest of all, 33 percent of the world market in automobiles. By 1984, the trade deficit—the gap between imports and exports—had grown to $123 billion, and with Japan alone it stood at $37 billion.

With economic malaise came political, social, and cultural malaise. America lost the war in Vietnam, suffered the trauma of Watergate, and then watched helplessly in 1979 as the Iranians held fifty-three Americans hostage for over 400 days. To most Americans, it seemed as if their country could do nothing right—it was being humiliated and embarrassed continually. Crime, drug use, and violence increased in America, and its central cities became the habitats of what many called a new "underclass." Permanently unemployed, having generations of children out of wedlock, growing up and living on welfare, and using drugs—particularly "crack" cocaine in the 1980s—this seemed to become a way of life in these ghettos. As violence and murders escalated, other statistics seemed to indicate a new reality for America in the 1980s: with just 5 percent of the world's population, the United States consumed fully 50 percent of the world's cocaine. To many Americans, this internal disintegration was all part of America's decline. As its economy faltered, its society and culture were decaying. If businessmen were regarded as the heroes who brought the American dream to fruition in the 1950s and 1960s, they were often considered the villains in creating a selfish, hedonistic environment in America in the 1970s and 1980s, one which manifested itself in the crack dens of the ghetto at one extreme and in the massive leveraged buyouts and egocentric arbitragers at the other extreme.

As economists and sociologists attempted to find answers to America's economic decline, they focused on the rise of a professional managerial class. This was ironic. In the 1950s and 1960s, America's managers had been the envy of the world. The British adopted the American system of decentralized control, and the Japanese picked up quality control ideas from the United States. These countries, which had virtually no professionally trained managers, looked with awe upon the hordes of MBAs pouring out of Harvard and other American universities. By 1988, more than 70,000 MBAs were awarded annually in 650 schools in the United States, far more than in the rest of the world combined. For years, Americans and everybody else assumed that the country's economic predominance came from this managerial expertise. Then, suddenly, as American prosperity and productivity went into a steep decline, this same managerial class had brickbats hurled at them.

H. Edward Wrapp, who taught at Harvard Business School, took America's managers to task in a trenchant article published in *Dun's Review* in 1980:

We have created a monster. . . . The business schools have done more to insure the success of the Japanese and West German invasion of America than anything I can think of . . . [by] producing hordes of managers with . . . talents that are not in the mainstream of enterprise . . . [and] the tragedy is that these talents mask real deficiencies in overall management capabilities. These talented operators run for cover when grubby operating decisions must be made and often fail miserably.[4]

By the mid–1960s, as conglomerates became the glamour business in America, young men (and a few women) in MBA programs turned away from marketing as the favored focus and instead pointed toward Wall Street. Mergers and acquisitions, paper entrepreneurialism, became the dashing, sexy new field. The battleground of the 1970s and 1980s was no longer in the marketplace, it was on Wall Street. The new management class was no longer concerned with the fight for more customers, the real battle was now to be in the boardrooms, over control of massive blocks of stock. Corporate machismo now featured the arbitrager, that cold, fearless predator who excelled in the new field of hostile takeovers. By 1981, the unfriendly corporate takeover had become such a familiar part of the American business scene that the fear of such takeovers became the principal preoccupation of many chief executive officers (CEOs), many of whom sought to protect themselves (and perhaps their companies) by constructing elaborate and expensive "golden parachutes" which they said would deter corporate raiders but would also assure the protection of the managers themselves. Since massive amounts of money, time, and energy were devoted to these takeovers in the 1970s and since none of them enhanced the competitiveness of either the companies or their industries, many critics believed they were a key part of America's problem.

The decline of America's high-volume, standardized industries was most troubling to many commentators. They had all operated in a protected, noncompetitive environment throughout the 1950s and 1960s. With profitability almost guaranteed, they could afford to grant large wage and benefit packages to their unionized employees. But foreign imports came as a rude shock to this complacent system. In no industry was the transition more traumatic and symbolic than in the automobile industry.

There were few imported cars in America in the 1950s and 1960s. Even with the relative success of the Volkswagen "Beetle," only 5 percent of the cars sold in America in 1963 were imports. By 1970, imports had climbed to 11 percent; by the early 1980s, they stood at about 30 percent of all cars sold in America. The gasoline crisis of the 1970s, which had given a great advantage to the more fuel-efficient Japanese automobiles, opened the door, but their higher quality and lower price kept the market share for them even after gasoline prices began to decline. The severe recession of 1980 and 1981 closed scores of auto plants in America, throwing some 350,000 auto workers out of work. That crisis, in turn, spread to their suppliers, worsening the recession. The American automakers, then, had to respond to the Japanese challenge. They spent enormous amounts of money creating better, more fuel-efficient automobiles, at the very time they were losing oceans of money. As a result, American Motors and Chrysler almost went bankrupt; while Ford passed a dividend for the first time in its history. Even General Motors (GM), the world's behemoth of automaking, was struggling.

The response of the auto firms to the crisis was less than successful. Although they collectively spent over $65 billion during the early 1980s to bring out competitive new models, most were pale imitations of Japanese cars. Chrysler, under Lee Iacocca,* regained its profitability, and Ford, under the brilliant guidance of Donald Petersen,† was actually able to compete effectively with foreign imports. GM, however, under the dynamic leadership of Roger Smith,† seemed to flounder endlessly. Despite grandiose plans for new models like the Saturn, and flamboyant introductions of new model lines, most industry observers thought GM's cars were inferior in design and workmanship, and that firm's troubles seemed to epitomize the problems of the entire industry.

Steel was another ailing American industry. The huge integrated steel firms in America did little to innovate during the 1950s and 1960s. During the same period that Japanese and European steel makers were installing electric furnaces and building huge, modern integrated plants, American steel men did little more than add on to existing, largely obsolete facilities. As a result, by 1979, Japanese steel mills had a 30 to 35 percent cost advantage over American mills. Fourteen of the world's largest steel plants were in Japan, and America had only 16 percent of the world market, exporting just 3 million metric tonnes, compared to over 70 million by the Japanese. The only ray of hope in America was the so-called mini-mill. Relatively small firms with low management and capital costs and nonunion labor, these mini-mills generally did not produce their own pig iron, and they were not integrated operations. The most successful of these was Nucor, run by Kenneth Iverson.[†] U.S. Steel, the doyen of the industry, under the guidance of David Roderick, seemed to turn away from steel production, as he transformed the firm into a diversified conglomerate. Unfortunately, he diversified in the wrong direction; he bought Marathon Oil at the top of the market and then watched the bottom fall out of oil prices and stocks shortly thereafter.

The American oil industry was also struggling. After experiencing a halcyon period in the 1970s, when oil prices and profits skyrocketed, reality intruded in the 1980s. As their stocks were undervalued compared to their asset holdings, the huge American oil refining firms became the object of incessant takeover bids in the 1980s. Phillips Petroleum was "put into play" by arbitrager T. Boone Pickens.[†] Carl Icahn,[†] another "arbitrager," bought a significant stake in Texaco, making no secret of his desire to take it over. Other large oil firms disappeared entirely. Cities Service, under attack from Pickens, agreed to be taken over by Occidental Oil. Massive Gulf Oil, which had been mismanaged for decades, was taken over by Standard Oil of California, creating a new company called Chevron. Meanwhile, wildcatters like Marvin Davis[†] simply pulled out of the industry entirely, and Amerada-Hess, a massive international oil giant created by Leon Hess,[†] teetered precariously.

The electronics industry suffered several embarrassments also. American television maker Motorola had introduced solid-state circuitry in 1968, only to find itself overwhelmed in the marketplace in the 1970s by the Japanese, who had been far more aggressive in adopting the new technology. Similarly, videocassette recorders (VCRs), which had been invented in the United States in 1956, were largely ignored by RCA, Zenith, and other American electronics manufacturers. As a result, VCRs became the sole province of Japanese manufacturers, as American electronic manufacturers were virtually uncompetitive.

Not everything was dark during the 1970s and 1980s; some electronic firms were able to find profitable market niches. Motorola, under the guidance of Robert Galvin, became a leading manufacturer of semiconductors, holding its own against Japanese competition. Intel was even more successful in the field. Although the Japanese challenge was mounting by the late 1980s, those two firms continued to perform very well and were highly innovative. By 1988, the semiconductor firms united to form an industry association, Sematech, headed by Robert Noyce, intended to increase American competitiveness. The electronics market in which they were succeeding was one area where America had not lost its edge—computers and computer components.

Despite increasing competition from the Japanese, American computer makers continued to retain their world leadership. This leadership was largely the result of a breathtaking pace of innovation emerging from the "Silicon Valley" in California and from its counterparts across the country. Even though America's share of the world market in computers fell from over 47 percent in 1980 to just over 30 percent in 1986, its manufacturers were still dominant. In fact, IBM, the largest domestic manufacturer, continued to hold between 60 and 70 percent of the world's market in mainframe computers and also held a commanding position in the Japanese market. With 18,000 employees in Japan alone, it had over $6 billion in sales around the world. The big computer breakthrough in the late 1970s and 1980s was the personal computer. This innovation was brought about by Steven Jobs[†] and Steve Wozniak at Apple Computer. IBM was slow to enter the field, which allowed Apple to prosper and also allowed Charles Tandy of Radio Shack to make large inroads into the market with his Tandy computers. Then, in the 1980s, powerful new workstations became state of the art in the industry, and Wang Office Systems, Hewlett-Packard, and Digital Equipment Corporation were among the leaders in this development. The world of software was dominated by Microsoft, under the direction of youthful William Gates.[†] Americans even took the lead in publishing about computers when Patrick McGovern[†] created a huge stable of computer magazines that dominated the world market.

One area in which America experienced a surprising rebirth in the 1980s was textiles. Long among the world's least efficient producers, American textile manufacturers, due to mammoth modernization efforts, increased their productivity more than 20 percent between 1980 and 1986. Among the leaders in this transformation were Burlington Mills, along with Deering-Milliken and J. P. Stevens. Although the American apparel industry continued to shrink in the 1970s and 1980s, as Pacific Rim manufacturers took over a lion's share of the production, a number of highly successful American designers established a world presence. During this period, individuals such as Ralph Lauren,[†] Anne Klein,[†] Calvin Klein,[†] and Liz Claiborne[†] all had a dramatic impact on the worldwide sales of apparel. They used a time-worn American method—marketing—to achieve this success. In a related area—athletic shoes—Philip Knight[†] propelled his Nike running shoes to world leadership in that burgeoning market, overtaking traditional leader Adidas. Then, in the 1980s, Paul Fireman[†] caught the tail of the aerobics boom to make his Reebok company one of the fastest growing in history. Both firms used highly sophisticated marketing and advertising campaigns to propel their astonishing growth.

Marketing and structural change also came to elements of the food processing industry which had remained immune for generations. Among the oldest industries in America were meat packing, poultry raising, and grain marketing. These industries had been systematized in the nineteenth century to better serve a national marketplace. But the revolution in these industries generally did not reach the marketing stage. Although firms like Swift and Armour advertised their names and marketed a few trademarked products, such as hams and bacon, generally their output was sold somewhat anonymously through butchers and supermarkets. In the 1970s and 1980s, firms like ConAgra, under the direction of Mike Harper,[†] and Iowa Beef Processors, under Currier Holman,[†] engineered powerful food conglomerates that marketed and distributed packaged and trade-marked beef, poultry, and other products. Frank Perdue,[†] was one of the leaders in this trend with his personalized advertising for poultry, and Jack Simplot[†] created a massive empire based upon the potato. Cargill, the giant grain trader, also moved into this area with some force during these years. The result was a revolution in that segment of the food trade, one that was similar to the revolution in breakfast cereals, flour, and other products that had occurred a half century earlier.

Other areas of the food industry also went through important transformations. Robert Rich[†] revolutionized the market for frozen dairy products with a whole series of innovative products, and Margaret Rudkin[†] was one of the first to recognize America's interest in wholesome, natural products with her Pepperidge Farms products. Later, Wally Amos[†] and Debbi and Randy Fields[†] created important marketing niches with their boutique, upscale, cookie operations.

The soft-drink industry also entered a period of intense marketing wars. Al-though Coca-Cola had been America's dominant soft drink for decades, Pepsi Cola, under the direction of Alfred Steele[†] and Donald Kendall,[†] provided an increasingly serious challenge after the 1960s. Using highly sophisticated mar-keting and advertising campaigns, the two companies waged ferocious battles for shares in the rapidly expanding world soft-drink market. If many other American products were finding it difficult in world markets, that certainly was not the case with soft drinks where American firms were nearly totally dominant. To a certain extent, the battles of the Cold War were even fought through the two soft-drink firms, as Coca-Cola was given permission to market it in China and Pepsi-Cola received the exclusive franchise for the Soviet Union. A highly publicized confrontation came in the 1980s, when Coca-Cola head Robert Goi-zueta[†] introduced the "New Coke" and Pepsi retaliated under Roger Enrico with a powerful media campaign. During this time, bottlers of Coke and Pepsi were becoming some of the wealthiest individuals in America. As a result, rising black business leaders wanted a piece of the action. The largest piece was acquired by Bruce Llewellyn.[†]

The wine industry, which in earlier years had been dominated by thousands of small vineyards, also experienced an important transformation, as Ernest and Julio Gallo[†] became the world's largest wine makers. Marketing blended wines and pushing products like wine coolers, the E. and J. Gallo Winery used very subtle and effective advertising campaigns, combined with bare-knuckles mar-keting, to dominate the wine industry, like General Motors used to dominate the auto industry. Although most of America's large national brewers had dominated the scene for some time, a new competitor, the Coors Family,[†] emerged in the 1970s with the establishment of the Adolph Coors Brewing Company in Golden, Colorado. Riding a "yuppie" cachet, and without full national distribution for a number of years, Coors became one of America's leading brewers.

As the world closed in on Americans, and as American companies found it difficult to compete in the high-volume, standardized goods where they had before reigned supreme, niche marketing and advertising became the vogue. A highly successful practitioner of this was Thomas Burrell,[†] who developed the largest black-owned advertising agency in America during this time. He targeted the newly emergent, black, middle-class market for advertisers and then offered to transfer his expertise to the world arena. Focusing on potentially lucrative markets among blacks in Africa, Burrell moved his agency successfully onto the world stage in the 1980s.

Another important marketing area of the 1970s and 1980s was retailing, where a number of developments took place. One of these saw the decline of traditional department stores, as many of the mainline, older stores lapsed into old age. A major complaint against these stores was their poor service. America had virtually created the modern service economy in the 1950s, but the inflation of the 1970s, coupled with the severe recession of the early 1980s, caused department stores and other service sectors to cut back. Some newer, more aggressive department store chains, such as Nordstrom's, emerged, using service as a means to attract customers, and some of the older operators, like Macy's and Dayton-Hudson, reinvigorated themselves. At the end of the 1980s, several of the larger department stores chains, like Allied and Federated, were merged into still larger operations. The 1980s, however, were more notable for the growth of a number of specialty stores. Charles Lazarus'[†] Toys "R" Us achieved enormous growth during these years, and upscale stores such as Bloomingdale's and Neiman-Marcus grew rapidly, giving customers old-style service while selling them new-style, expensive merchandise. Chains like The Limited, The Gap, and Banana Republic, which depended on aggressive marketing more than service, also expanded greatly. Discounting remained important, and it was an area in which lack of service was part of the attraction. Sam Walton's[†] Wal-Mart stores spread throughout the American South and Southwest, but most older discount stores were replaced by new super discounters, like Sol Price's Price Club and Walton's Sam's Wholesale Clubs.

Some other service areas also grew impressively in the 1970s and 1980s. Most notable was the development of the Federal Express Corporation by Fred Smith.[†] Recognizing the need for fast, dependable parcel and letter delivery in the new economy, Smith established a complex and effective courier system. He was soon imitated by a host of other companies. Perhaps the oldest of all the service industries was the telephone. AT&T, protected by a government-sanctioned (and regulated) monopoly, prided itself on efficient service. Every day, it sent conversations back and forth on 138 million telephones, and AT&T was "Ma Bell" to millions of Americans. Then, in 1980, William McGowan[†] and his MCI

Communications Corporation won a stunning antitrust suit against AT&T, and the world of telecommunications was irretrievably changed. The industry was deregulated, and the market nexus began to operate for the first time. Although long-distance phone charges dropped as a result, AT&T felt compelled to raise the rates on basic telephone service to subscribers, and some felt that poorer Americans, many of whom had taken telephones for granted as a basic service in American life, would be deprived in the future. Service, which under the old regulated system had been taken for granted, by the late 1980s varied greatly across the nation.

The airline industry was also deregulated, with tumultuous consequences. The Airline Deregulation Act of 1978 upset a long-standing status of government protection and regulation of the industry by the Civil Aeronautics Board (CAB). Allowing fare discounting for the first time in the late 1970s, the act called for the dissolution of the CAB over a six-year period. Airlines were free to enter into routes of their own choosing and let competition determine fare structures. An early beneficiary of the new system was Frank Lorenzo[†] and his Texas Air Corp. Using discount fares, he took business away from other carriers, and later bought out Continental Airlines, Eastern Airlines, Frontier Airlines, and, finally, People Express. People Express had been started by Donald Burr[†] as the quintessential deregulated airline. Shunning all frills and services, Burr's airline grew rapidly on the basis of cheap fares. Ultimately, however, he could not sustain its operation and was forced to sell to Lorenzo. Although the consumer benefited from lower fares on some routes for a relatively short time, a major casualty of airline deregulation was service. On-time performance of airlines declined; attendants, who were overworked, became surly; and airline travel increasingly seemed like bus service to the passengers.

If deregulation brought diminished service in portions of the American economy, it also brought increased variety and service in other sectors. In television, the three networks' lockhold on the medium was broken by the introduction of cable. Entrepreneurs such as Ted Turner[†] of Turner Communications and John Kluge[†] of Metromedia used the new satellite technology to insinuate their service into American homes. Using syndicated programs provided by the likes of independent game show producer Merv Griffin, they captured an increasing number of American homes. Then, Turner invaded the sanctum sanctorum of the networks—the national news—with his CNN. As CNN became popular and profitable, providing twenty-four-hour news programming and headlines to busy two-income families, the face of television and news reporting changed commensurately.

A somewhat similar phenomenon occurred in newspaper publishing. Allen Neuharth,[†] head of the Gannett Company, brought out America's first truly national newspaper, *USA Today*. Against formidable odds, Neuharth made a success of the paper, which was often referred to as "television news in print." To complete the circle, Neuharth in the fall of 1988 brought the "USA Today" show to television. Another important publishing phenomenon of the 1970s and

1980s was the national tabloid. Led by Generoso Pope, Jr.,[†] and his *National Enquirer,* supermarket checkout stations were lined with headlines screaming lurid, sensationalist fare. In a more upscale development, Edward Lewis[†] brought out *Essence* magazine to provide a glossy new image for the emerging black middle class. Part of a broader homogenization of American life, *USA Today* and the tabloids lessened regional distinctiveness and, along with television and chain stores, loosened community bonds and individuality. As service declined and community roots dissolved, many Americans felt increasingly alienated and adrift.

For many Americans, all of this seemed to come to a head in the 1980s with the dizzying flurry of mergers and acquisitions, and of hostile takeovers and leveraged buyouts which characterized the business scene. Corporate raiders, like T. Boone Pickens, Carl Icahn, Saul Steinberg, and Henry Kravis,[†] who called themselves the champions of the small shareholder and the enemy of entrenched, professional management, pursued venerable American firms as if they were wounded deer. The key to their takeover maneuvers was the availability of abundant, high-yield, low-quality securities—the so-called junk bonds. The junk bond market was created by Michael Milken[†] of Drexel, Burnham Lambert. By using this kind of bond, a corporate raider could almost literally buy a company with its own money. Milken, through his junk bond network, could put together, on almost a moment's notice, virtually 100-percent financing at inflated prices for a company. He could do this because the junk bonds, although they were not what was considered investment quality, carried very high interest rates, and protected his investors from losses under his guidance. Pension funds, insurance companies, and other big ticket investors literally lined up to buy his bonds, which were not considered investment quality. Milken could, therefore, promise his raider clients practically unlimited funds. They, in turn, issued securities backed by the target corporation's assets to finance the purchase in a "leveraged buyout." Milken's influence was so great that he was often called the "J. P. Morgan of the 1980s."

This mechanism allowed many corporate raiders to build massive corporate empires practically overnight by using somebody else's money. Then, when the raiders took control of a firm, it was saddled with an enormous debt load. As a result, the raider more than likely had to dismantle parts of the company he had taken over and to engage in divestiture to pay down some of the massive debt. This usually brought short-term profits to shareholders, as the company's stock price soared during the bidding war, and divestiture often brought exceptional profits and dividends. The asset base of the firm, however, was diluted, and many analysts felt that the resulting companies were greatly weakened by the takeover battle. The raiders, and their investment cohorts, of course, denied this, asserting that they were forcing management to operate in the interests of the shareholder, and that divestiture and layoffs often excised unnecessary "fat" from the company.

Some raiders, of course, never intended to take over the companies they targeted. They set the company "into play" to force management to come to an agreement. Buying a less than 5-percent stake in the company, a raider like Pickens would then demand certain concessions from management. When management refused, he made an offer for the firm, backed by junk bond financing. Management would then resort to one or more of a number of defenses—the "Pac-Man defense," in which the target company tries to take over the company that initiated the takeover; a scorched-earth defense, in which the defending corporation sells off its most desirable assets, or encumbers itself with liabilities, to make it less attractive; finding a "white knight," or a "white squire" to thwart a takeover; and establishing lucrative "golden parachutes" for incumbent management to help forestall a takeover. If these maneuvers failed, and management still wanted to avoid a takeover, management often engaged in a "management leveraged buyout" using the same junk bond financing as the raider and often paying the raider "greenmail" to buy him off. The results of these maneuvers, even when they were successful in avoiding takeover, left the firm as heavily in debt as if the raider had taken them over.

This new junk bond financing was used to build enormous empires, but not everyone who resorted to this financing practiced hostile takeovers or ruined established firms. A number built solid, stable empires in which the companies they bought were greatly enhanced by inclusion in the new empires. Warren Buffett,[†] one of the most astute Wall Street speculators, built a massively successful empire through Berkshire Hathaway Inc. Also the Pritzker family[†] of Chicago and the Tisch brothers built impressive collections of industrial firms, real estate, television networks, and other entities during these years. Even some of the raiders surprised critics by running some of their target companies in a competent manner. Carl Icahn's management of TWA was viewed by virtually everyone as a major improvement over the earlier management. Also, Reginald Lewis[†] used junk bond financing and the leveraged buyout technique to take control of the most massive corporate empire ever controlled by a black in the United States. Buying Beatrice International from the Beatrice Corporation when it was forced to divest after a hostile takeover, Lewis vowed to run his new empire profitably in the interests of both shareholders and employees.

The American business establishment has generally been highly critical of this paper entrepreneurialism. Leaders of *Fortune* 500 Corporations, of older, established investment houses, and the business press have treated the raiders and their investment banker cohorts with disdain. Felix Rohatyn* of Lazard Frères has been particularly vocal in his criticism, asserting that these mergers and takeovers, by saddling the firms with such excessive debt, are severely weakening the American economy. The Business Roundtable, the principal mouthpiece for the business establishment, has been unceasing in its criticism also. The Roundtable had been founded in the early 1970s to allow leaders of major American corporations to influence government decision making. Under the direction of Irving Shapiro,[†] head of Du Pont in the 1970s, the Roundtable began taking an increasingly public role on a number of issues.

In many respects, the quintessential business leader of the 1980s was Donald Trump.[†] Taking over his father's successful, but low-profile, real estate development business, Trump transformed it into a sexy, high-profile concern. Naming his Manhattan buildings after himself, he used the whole concept of ego gratification that became such an integral part of the 1980s to create a huge corporate empire (although one that was never as large as he claimed). Trump went from Manhattan real estate to Atlantic City gambling casinos and then became a corporate raider, netting some $125 million in greenmail from his runs on Holiday Corp., Bally, and Allegis. In late 1988, he bought Eastern's shuttle service from Frank Lorenzo. More than anything, though, Trump engaged in self-promotion and, in the process, became sort of a "populist billionaire," as millions of Americans lived their hopes and dreams vicariously through Trump's excesses.

Despite Trump's glitter, and notwithstanding the luxurious life-style adopted by America's business establishment in the 1980s (skewered so deliciously in Tom Wolfe's best-selling *Bonfire of the Vanities*), most observers agreed that the American business system was in trouble. *Business Month* commissioned the research firm of Yankelovich Clancy Shulman to question 609 CEOs from leading American firms to determine their views of the future. The results were not encouraging. The vast majority were concerned about the huge corporate debt loads being carried as a result of the takeover mania and were even more worried about the massive federal deficit accumulated during the Reagan years. During his eight years in office, Ronald Reagan, by massively increasing defense spending without raising taxes, tripled the national debt. A large majority were also deeply concerned over America's growing trade deficit with other countries. Nor were many very optimistic that America was going to become an effective competitor in the world market in the very near future. They were, in fact, exceedingly pessimistic about the state of American business and the American economy. A staggering 86 percent of the CEOs interviewed believed that American management was too short-term oriented. One executive was so disgusted that he dismissed America's chances in the following curt manner: "American companies do such a lousy job in productivity and customer service."[5] What is to be done? Is there an answer to America's apparent economic malaise?

Generally, the reaction of the business community and business schools has been that the crisis is not really a crisis at all. It is simply part of a normal cyclical adjustment. Furthermore, whatever problems America has had in terms of cheap imports flooding the American market or the inability of American products to compete abroad has merely been due to an overvalued dollar. As the dollar is allowed to reach its true market level, they argue, the situation will reverse itself. There are, they assert, no structural problems in the American economy; if only government would allow the market mechanism to operate freely, would reduce its own tariff barriers, and would encourage freer and more open trade abroad, the apparent crisis would quickly dissipate. Ronald Reagan was the most visible advocate of this laissez-faire approach in the 1980s.

Other critics, like Robert Reich, disagree. America, they argue, needs an industrial policy similar to that of Japan and other nations. He and others argued that what America needed was a rational, coherent approach to its problems, one in which government would work in concert with business and labor leaders to improve the material well-being of the mass of Americans. According to Reich: "Either we will adapt to this new reality, or following our historical predecessors, the American ascendancy will needlessly come to an end."[6] Advocates of the laissez-faire approach thought the concept of an industrial policy was naive. They pointed out that it presumed the existence of a peculiarly enlightened government able to make sound, rational economic decisions for the future. The American system, however, they argued was what is called a "broker state," one in which entrenched, vested interests, precisely those most likely to oppose the making of hard economic choices, hold the greatest power. Thus, they argued, an industrial policy would in actuality be self-defeating. Whither we goest?

Sherman McCoy, the bond trader protagonist in Tom Wolfe's *Bonfire of the Vanities*, spoke bitterly of his profession toward the end of the book:

"All the takeovers, buy-outs, mergers—all done with bonds" said Sherman. "The national debt? A trillion dollars? What do you think that is? All bonds. Every time interest rates fluctuate—up or down, it doesn't matter—little crumbs fall off the bonds and lodge in the cracks of the sidewalk." . . . "The important thing is not to stick your nose up at those crumbs, because there are billions and billions of them. At Pierce & Pierce, believe me, we sweep them up very diligently."[7]

Many wondered by 1989 if that is what American business had been reduced to—sweeping up the crumbs to retain a surface prosperity. There was surface prosperity, but underneath was a deep malaise, and prevailing business practices seemed to be more concerned with simply making money than with making it better.

NOTES

1. Sumner Slichter, *The American Economy: Its Problems and Prospects,* 1948.
2. *Dun's Review*, September 1980.
3. Robert Reich, *The Last American Frontier*, 1983, p. 146.
4. *Dun's Review*, September 1980, pp. 88.
5. *Business Month*, January 1989, pp. 36–51.
6. Reich, p. 282.
7. Tom Wolfe, *Bonfire of the Vanities*, 1987, p. 582.

CONTEMPORARY AMERICAN BUSINESS LEADERS

A

AMOS, WALLACE, JR. (WALLY) (July 1, 1936–   ). Cookie company founder, Famous Amos Chocolate Chip Cookie Company. In 1944, the sociologist
Leo Lowenthal wrote a famous article in which he talked about the rise of what
he called the "idols of consumption" in America after the 1920s. In this new
framework, people were encouraged to believe, not so much that they could
become successful in a Horatio Alger–like manner, but that by eating the same
cereal, drinking the same tomato juice, or smoking the same cigarette, they could
share the celebrity status and success of a number of popular entertainers. Wally
Amos, creator of the Famous Amos Chocolate Chip Cookies, created the first
"celebrity cookie," that is, the first cookie that was merchandised and purchased
because Carol Burnett, Ann-Margaret, John Denver, Elton John, Marvin Gaye,
or any one of a number of other stars loved it. However good and unique the
taste of the cookie, it achieved popularity primarily because it had celebrity chic;
consumers wanted to share in the lives of the stars by sharing their cookie.

Wally Amos was born in the black ghetto of Tallahassee, Florida, son of Ruby
and Wallace Amos, neither of whom could read or write. Suffering miserably,
as did most blacks from the depression, the Amos family relied on prayer and
hope to get them through the hard times. But Wally Amos has happy memories
of growing up, saying in his autobiography, *The Famous Amos Story:* "My
childhood in Tallahassee was like kids everywhere; living my life to the fullest
every day, going to bed every night tired and happy." When he was twelve
years old, however, Amos received devastating news—his parents were getting
a divorce and he was moving with his mother to Orlando, Florida. A month
later, young Wally moved to New York without his mother. There he went to
stay with his Aunt Della, who lived in the Washington Heights section of the
city.

It was Aunt Della who introduced young Wally Amos to chocolate chip
cookies. It was her cookies which, years later, gave Amos the inspiration for
his own company. While living with Aunt Della, Amos attended Edwin W. Stitt
Junior High School. This was a difficult transition for him, since it was the first

integrated school he had ever attended. He also had to adjust to the tough street gangs in Harlem, who often shook him down for money. During this period Wally Amos began to work part-time, first delivering newspapers, then groceries for local supermarkets, and then ice. After junior high school, Amos decided to attend Food Trades Vocational High School, with the idea of becoming a chef, since the school's recruiter told him that "cooks make a lot of money."

Amos recalled later that he loved his time at Food Trades and especially looked forward to his second year, when he would alternate a week of school with a week of on-the-job training, which he got paid for. For his training, Amos was assigned to the pantry of the Essex House Hotel, one of the prestige hotels in the city. But as Amos recalls, "I wasn't happy about the assignment," since he found he spent most of his time preparing salads, desserts, pancakes, and waffles rather than cooking main courses. When he complained to his counselor, Amos was told the assignment was temporary, but after a year he knew this was not the case. As he reported, "I was discouraged, to say the least, and I felt that racism was the reason I didn't get what I deserved. Therefore, I started thinking again about whether I really wanted to be a cook." Amos then went through a difficult period; he dropped out of school, gambled away his Aunt Della's utilities payments, and ran away to live on the streets. When he finally returned home, Amos told his aunt that he did not want to return to school but instead wanted to join the U.S. Air Force. She agreed to sign the required papers for the seventeen-year-old to enlist in 1953. Amos was assigned to Sampson Air Force Base in Geneva, New York, where he spent two months in basic training.

After basic training, however, Amos was sent to Keesler Air Force Base in Biloxi, Mississippi, a rigidly segregated city and state in the early 1950s. He was assigned to learn to repair airplane radar and radio equipment. After nine months there, Amos was assigned to Hickham Air Force Base in Honolulu, Hawaii, which introduced him to a city and a society that he grew to love, and where he would return to live later in his life. After four years in the Air Force, Amos came back to New York, where he job hunted. He decided to get his diploma at the Collegiate Secretarial Institute and, at the same time, got a job working in the supply department of Saks Fifth Avenue department store. Amos started there as a stock clerk, unloading cartons from trucks, and receiving and storing cartons and office supplies. He worked there mornings and evenings and went to school during the afternoons.

While working at Saks, Amos impressed his supervisor, Ernie Riccio, and when he was promoted, Riccio recommended that Amos be his replacement. The store agreed, and Wally became an executive with an increase in salary. Amos then was sent to New York University's retail and merchandising course, but he had so much trouble with the math that he decided he no longer wanted to be a buyer. In 1961 Amos decided to leave Saks to look for other employment. Jobs were not easy to come by, but an employment counselor at Collegiate Secretarial got him an interview with the William Morris Talent Agency in New York City. After several interviews, Amos was hired, and he was informed that he would be given no special treatment because he was black—he would be judged solely on the quality of his work and attitude. Starting in the mailroom, in two months Amos became a substitute secretary by continuing school and practicing typing during his lunch hours. His next step on the ladder was in the music department of the firm, where Amos became one of two secretaries to Howard Hausman, one of the firm's top executives. After just over two months there, Amos was made an assistant agent at William Morris, the first black 'to be employed as an agent at the company.

While at William Morris, Amos experienced a good deal of success, booking the Supremes, the Temptations, Marvin Gaye, and Simon and Garfunkel. But, by 1967, Amos felt he was burned out with the agency. He had been booking rock and roll acts for the firm for over six years, and he felt that the music scene was changing too radically. He had trouble relating to the hard rock and acid rock emerging at that time. Also, there were a number of personnel changes in the music department at William Morris, which made Amos feel less comfortable. Worst of all was the fact that he found he would not be able to advance any further in the firm, since the executives did not think the other agents would take direction from a black. In 1967 he left to manage the career of trumpeter Hugh Masakela, but, after several months, that relationship ended. As Amos tells it, "Masakela came off the most successful tour ever and told me he didn't like the way I was managing his career. . . . It was the low point of my life."

The next months and years were difficult for Wally Amos. He went from job to job in the entertainment industry. He worked for a time for John Levy, a personal management firm, as a manager of acts for Venture Records, and he tried to go out on his own again as a personal manager. After that, he formed his own production company and a number of other short-lived ventures. During this same troubled period (when two of his marriages also dissolved), Amos turned to baking his Aunt Della's chocolate chip cookies for therapy. He often took a bag of cookies with him to parties and other engagements. With his card in the bag of cookies, it became his own unique calling card, his gimmick. Unfortunately, the cookies did not help to get his career going.

One day, while munching on his cookies with Quincy Jones' secretary at A&M Records, Amos was bemoaning his hopeless future. The secretary said, "Why don't we go into business together selling your chocolate chip cookies?" Amos smiled and said, "That's a great idea. But I don't have the money." Nonetheless, an idea had been planted in Amos' mind, and soon he became committed to the idea—the problem was finding some financing. For that, Amos turned to his friends in the music and entertainment industry. He first approached his long-time friend, singer Helen Reddy. She and her husband agreed to put up $10,000 if he found some other investors. Artie Mogull, a recording executive, put up $5,000, as did Herb Alpert, band leader and founder of A&M Records. The final $10,000 came from singer Marvin Gaye.

With his financing lined up, Amos next had to establish a business. Again, Quincy Jones' secretary suggested a name—Famous Amos—and he began to call his product "the superstar of cookies." Amos rented a storefront on the corner of Sunset Boulevard and Formosa Avenue. It was not a prime location—the business next door was the Exotica School of Massage ("Sindy's Nude, Nude, Nude Girls, Girls, Girls") and across the street was the American School of Hypnosis and the Seventh Veil Restaurant, which billed itself as "The Home of Camel Juice." But Wally Amos was determined to make his opening a celebrity event, a "happening." He sent out 2,500 invitations to his opening. It turned out to be a magnificent event: some 1,500 people showed up on March 10, 1975; many were celebrities, some arrived in chauffeured limousines. Amos provided all with free champagne and had a strolling Dixieland band on hand.

Wally Amos has a genius for promotion. Truly the showman, Amos applied all the techniques he had learned flogging musical acts to promoting his celebrity cookies. He made himself the star of the "cookie extravaganza" he was developing, and he played the role to the hilt. He appeared in various locations where there were crowds of people and sang "Fa-mous Amos!" to the tune of the "Hallelujah Chorus." With a tin of cookies in his hand, he began to chant:

Here, have a Famous Amos cookie. I am *the* Famous Amos. Whoop! Cookie time here, cookie time! I am *the* Famous Amos and there's my store right there. Oh, please take my cookies! How can I sell 'em, if I can't give 'em away? Oh me, let's talk about it! Hey, we got two left. One for you . . . (*Newsweek*)

But what really gave his cookies cachet was the fact that various stars were reported to love his cookies. These stories first ran in the Los Angeles papers and then were picked up and syndicated across the United States. As a result, the demand for his cookies became nationwide.

In 1976, a dress designer friend took some of Amos' cookies to Bloomingdale's in New York. The buyers there, having already heard something about the cookies, were excited, and they contacted Amos about carrying the cookies in their twelve New York stores. He agreed, but to do so, he had to set up a factory and wholesaling operation on the West Coast. At the same time, he also began to open other Famous Amos cookie stores in the Los Angeles area. To service his rapidly expanding East Coast business, Amos soon decided he would have to set up a factory in Nutley, New Jersey. But all of this was really just preparation for what happened in the spring of 1977, when Famous Amos Cookies skyrocketed in popularity.

Media hype had made Famous Amos Cookies reknowned as the "cookie of the jet set," and when they began to be handled by the famous Neiman-Marcus department stores, they really hit the big time in prestige. At the same time, Amos abandoned selling cookies at Bloomingdale's to sell them in the basement boutique at Macy's. The big clincher in making this move was that Macy's promised Amos that he and his cookies could be part of the great Macy's Thanksgiving Parade. Famous Amos would be visible to at least 20 million television viewers. For four years, Wally Amos appeared in the parade, becoming a true media celebrity himself.

By 1979, Wally Amos was in charge of a mammoth operation. His factories turned out 7,000 pounds of handmade cookies every day, the company had $4 million in revenue annually, and his first store in Los Angeles was included on the Grayline Sightseeing Bus Tour of Hollywood. Over the next three or four years, his cookies also began appearing on supermarket shelves, and Amos expanded his production facilities extensively. But, at the same time, a number of problems began to surface. First, Amos faced increasing competition. New cookie companies, such as Mrs. Fields (see Debra Jane Sivyer and Randy Fields) and David's, were taking much of the upscale cookie business away from Famous Amos. Also, he made the mistake of not franchising his operation when it was the leading cookie business. By 1983 he had just eight franchises; most of his business focused on wholesaling, and the newcomers were gaining momentum via specialized prestige cookie kiosks rather than in department stores or supermarkets.

Of greatest significance, however, was the fact that, although Wally Amos was perhaps the greatest cookie salesman and promoter who ever lived, he was nonetheless an ineffective businessman. He was uninterested in the mundane chores of managing the company, and he was unable to assess others who were hired to do the job for him. Further, although the company's headquarters remained in Los Angeles, in 1977 Amos moved to Hawaii, where he was able to neglect his obligations even more easily. Amos himself recognized this years later: "You can't run a business unless you're there. In 1977 I moved from Los Angeles to Hawaii. Other people tried to run the company but they really weren't qualified to do so." As a result, the firm was soon in a chaotic state and suffering from a severe cash flow problem.

As a result, in 1985, Wally Amos had to look for additional financing, and in February of that year he struck a deal with a group of private investors that included former Senator John Tunney. Amos explained: "All the money went into the company. None of it went into my pocket. We were in such bad shape it was either that or try to reorganize under Chapter 11." Amos kept just 8 percent of the firm's stock, and the new investors instituted stiff financial controls on the lax company. This was a difficult situation for Amos, but he adjusted to it after a time. With new management, the firm was revitalized and expected to reach $12 million in sales in 1987.

Wally Amos himself went back to doing what he did best—promoting the company. Like Orville Redenbacher and Colonel Sanders,* company founders who sold their concerns to others, Amos spent little time at company headquarters after the sale. He no longer ran the business, he was solely a spokesman. But as he said, "I'll always be part of the business because I *am* the business." He also commented once, "I started the cookie business just to make a living, and that's still all I'm concerned with."

Some of his most visible work in the 1980s was as a spokesman for the Literacy Volunteers of America. He told audiences about his illiterate parents, about how he never could have followed a cookie recipe if he had not been able to read, and he stressed the message: "If you can't read, you can't succeed." On November 18, 1980, however, Wally Amos achieved true immortality. On that date he was selected by the Smithsonian Institution of the National Museum of History to donate his trademark embroidered shirt and Panama hat to become part of the exhibits in the Business Americana Collection. Famous Amos was the first food company to have anything accepted at the Smithsonian, and he was the first black businessman to be represented in the collection. Wallace and Ruby Amos and Aunt Della would be very proud of him indeed. (**A.** Wally Amos with Leroy Robinson, *The Famous Amos Story: The Face that Launched a Thousand Chips*, 1983. **B.** Leo Lowenthal, "Biographies in Popular Magazines," in Paul F. Lazarsfeld and Frank Stanton, eds., *Radio Research*, 1942–43, 1944; *Time*, June 13, 1977; *Ebony*, September 1, 1979; *Black Enterprise*, January 1981, June 1987; *Essence*, December 1981; *Nation's Business*, December 1981; *Newsweek*, November 14, 1983; Joseph J. Fucini and Suzy Fucini, *Entrepreneurs*, 1985.)

ARNAZ, DESI (DESIDERIO ALBERTO ARNAZ Y DE ACHA III) (March 2, 1917–December 2, 1986). Television producer, Desilu Productions. The image is incongruous: a baby-faced Cuban-born bandleader and singer, speaking English with a thick Spanish accent as one of the most innovative and powerful producers in the history of television. Anyone who tried to sell the concept as a pilot for a television series would be hooted down. Yet the image is accurate: Desi Arnaz, for a period of a dozen years, did more to revolutionize the television industry than anyone else. As Jess Oppenheimer, the original writer-producer of "I Love Lucy," said in the late 1950s: "He was in at the birth of television, but as television matured, Desi matured with it. . . . He's the number one man in television production today. . . . The top men, the L. B. Mayers of television, come to this boy for advice."

Desi, who was born in Santiago, Cuba, was the son of the mayor of the city. The family was wealthy, and, while Desi was growing up, owned three ranches, a town house, an island in Santiago Bay, a racing stable, and several cars and speedboats. During the Cuban Revolution of 1933, however, the elder Arnaz, by then a member of Congress, supported president Machado. When Batista emerged triumphant, the Arnaz property was confiscated, and Mr. Arnaz was imprisoned. Mrs. Arnaz and her teenage son left Cuba for Miami, Florida, where young Desi entered St. Patrick's High School and worked at a number of part-time jobs. A few months later his father joined the family in Miami where he opened an import-export business.

In 1934 young Desi found employment as a guitarist in a four-piece Cuban band. He was playing guitar and singing for a larger Cuban band when he was spotted by the "rumba king" Xavier Cugat. Desi Arnaz toured for a year as the

featured vocalist in Cugat's orchestra. In 1937 Arnaz organized his own Latin
dance band, which soon became popular playing for conga lines in cities around
the United States. His success led in 1939 to a part in George Abbott's stage
musical, *Too Many Girls*. In 1940 the screen rights to the play were purchased
by RKO, and Arnaz went to California to recreate his stage role.

On the set of *Too Many Girls*, Desi Arnaz met and fell in love with the film's
leading lady, Lucille Ball. Miss Ball, five years Arnaz's senior, had come to
Hollywood in 1934. She had worked as an extra at Paramount for a time before
she finally secured a contract for $50 a week at RKO. After a few bit parts, she
was hailed as a "new find" for her performance as a burlesque queen in *Dance,
Girl, Dance*. This led to her casting as the lead in *Too Many Girls*. A whirlwind
seven-month courtship led to the marriage of Lucille Ball and Desi Arnaz on
November 30, 1940. The next decade involved a relentless effort on the part of
the couple not only to achieve professional success, but also to devote more time
to working and living together.

The basic problem the newlyweds faced during the first several years of their
marriage was that Desi Arnaz had difficulty landing parts in Hollywood films
because of his accent, while Lucille Ball was becoming a major movie star. She
starred in a series of films, particularly in the late 1940s (*Easy to Wed, Fancy
Pants*, and *Miss Grant Takes Richmond*, among many others), while Desi served
in the U.S. Army during World War II, entertaining hospitalized servicemen.
After the war, he had brief parts in a number of films, including *Cuban Pete*
and *Holiday in Havana*. He also served as musical director in 1946–1947 of the
Bob Hope radio show. Most of the time, however, he spent touring the United
States and Canada with his band. As a result, he estimated that in their first
eleven years of marriage, he and Lucy spent a total of three years together, and
spent some $29,000 on telephone calls and telegrams.

As a result, the couple decided in 1950 to form a corporation, Desilu Productions, with Desi Arnaz as president and Lucille Ball as vice president. It was
Desi, however, who handled all the organization's business affairs, particularly
promoting joint contracts that allowed them to work together in films and on
radio. Their first production was a highly successful radio program, "My Favorite
Husband." In this show, Lucille perfected many of the comedy techniques that
she later used on "I Love Lucy," as the scatterbrained redhead. She did not,
however, work on this program with Desi, who had his own music series on
the CBS network. The couple was determined to star together in their situation
comedy. They approached CBS television and outlined the concept for what
later became "I Love Lucy"—a wacky wife married to a Cuban bandleader
who would spend much of his time trying to keep Lucy out of show business.
The network was interested in the concept and wanted to snare a star of Lucille
Ball's magnitude, but it felt that because of Desi Arnaz's heavy accent, audiences
would not find him credible in the role of her husband. Even her logical argument
that he was her husband failed to persuade them.

Thus, to test their theory that they could be a successful comedy team, they
went on a nationwide vaudeville tour in the spring of 1951, playing six or seven

shows a day before enthusiastic audiences. Lucy and Desi then produced a film pilot for the series with $5,000 of their own money. CBS by then was convinced it was a good series, but still had another objection. The network wanted the show broadcast live from New York, as was then customary, but Lucy and Desi wanted to film it in Hollywood before a live audience. This was a more expensive procedure, so, as part of the deal, Desilu Productions agreed to pay for the filming, thereby owning the films and re-release rights. Desilu then contracted with Philip Morris Company to pay for advertising rights on the show at $30,000 per week. Since the episodes cost from $23,000 to $25,000 a week to shoot, Desilu made a gross profit of from $5,000 to $7,000 per week in its first season.

CBS slotted the program to run on Monday nights from 9:00 to 9:30. What followed was the greatest success story in the history of American television. First telecast in October 1951, it was an overnight sensation; during its six years of originals, it never ranked lower than third in popularity among all television programs. When combined with the phenomenal, never-ending success of the show's reruns, "I Love Lucy" was the most popular program in television history. The reasons for the show's success were clear: excellent plots, inventive gags, and the comic genius of Lucille Ball. By 1953, the series had become such an American institution that the birth of "Little Ricky" drew an estimated 44 million viewers, more than the audience for President Eisenhower's inauguration later that month.

But, the business success of "I Love Lucy" and Desilu were the result of a number of important decisions made by Desi Arnaz. The decision to film the program rather than to broadcast it live made it possible to have high-quality prints available. This made the films available for endless rebroadcasting. Thus, Desilu Productions literally created the phenomenon of reruns, which also made possible the later development of syndication. Reruns of "I Love Lucy" were shown in prime time for several years after the show ceased production; they are currently viewed almost everywhere in the world in syndication. Robert Metz wrote in *CBS: Reflection in a Bloodshot Eye* that "A mad fan with insomnia, and some kind of yet-to-be-developed television receiver that can pull in any station on the air, could have his beloved Lucy on view almost 24 hours a day— if not in English, then in Greek, Portuguese or Bantu."

The success of this technique also resulted in the wholesale shift of television production from New York to Hollywood. The decision to film it before a live audience and to film it in sequence forced Desi Arnaz to originate the now standard three-camera technique for filming that permitted motion picture–type editing afterward. The success of the Lucy show allowed Desilu to become an entertainment conglomerate in the early to mid–1950s, as it began to produce other shows. During 1952 Desilu produced the commercials for the "Red Skelton Show" and became the producer of the highly successful "Our Miss Brooks" and "Danny Thomas" shows.

All of this led in 1957 to the most daring venture of Desi Arnaz's career. Selling the rerun rights to "I Love Lucy" to CBS for between $4 and $5 million,

Desi borrowed some additional money and offered General Tire and Rubber Company $6.15 million for RKO studios, which they had purchased in 1955. The bargain bid was accepted, and Desi and Lucy became the sole owners of the largest array of television film-making facilities in the industry, including the twenty-five sound stages on the fourteen-acre RKO lot. As a result, the new company had the capacity to produce, or to assist in producing, from twenty-five to thirty television shows a year, grossing about $30 million annually in the late 1950s and early 1960s. The biggest success during the years was the hugely popular and very controversial "The Untouchables." Desi Arnaz's philosophy for making successful television shows was simple: "I've never yet made a show for the 21 Club or the Romanoff's crowd, and I'm not going to start now. The viewers have to be able to identify themselves with the characters or you're going to lose them. I've always had the guy in Omaha in mind."

During his four years as head of the enlarged and expanded Desilu Productions, Desi Arnaz participated in virtually every aspect of its operation. He redirected scenes, cut scripts, conducted the bands, and dealt with almost all the business decisions. He was a pioneer in keeping production costs down, paying his technicians scale but working them a steady six-day week, and with the RKO studios he was able to offer television networks a volume discount for every six shows Desilu made for them. Desilu was simply the largest motion picture and television studio in the world.

By the early 1960s, however, Desi Arnaz was becoming increasingly unhappy. Marital stress had caused him to develop a drinking problem, and he soon began to lose control of Desilu's sprawling and complicated operations. Also, "The Untouchables" came under attack from members of the National Italian-American League to Combat Defamation. This also took its toll on Desi Arnaz, and after a lengthy and highly publicized divorce from Lucille Ball in 1960, he sold all his stock in Desilu to her for $3 million in 1962 and retired from the business. She became the company's president and, several years later, sold Desilu to Gulf and Western for a reported $10 million.

Lucille Ball reflected on Desi Arnaz's situation after she took control: "Desi has wanted out for a long time, he's had the business bit. I honestly believe he enjoyed launching Desilu more than the actual running of it." After leaving Desilu, Desi Arnaz retired to his horse ranch, but he continued to dabble in show business as a "behind the scenes guy," writing a number of series pilots, including "The Mothers-in-Law," which ran on NBC from 1967 to 1969. Arnaz, who had been seriously ill since at least 1981, died of cancer at his home in Del Mar, California, in 1986. Reflecting on her ex-husband in 1963, Lucille Ball told *Ladies Home Journal*, "He was a great showman, a great business executive, I was very proud of him. I still am. He built an empire. It was unfortunate that he also liked to let things fall apart. But there are people like that. They build and they destroy." (**A.** Desi Arnaz, *A Book*, 1976. **B.** *Current Biography*, September 1952; *Newsweek*, January 19, 1953; *Time*, April 7, 1958; *New York Times Magazine*, April 20, 1958; *Life*, October 6, 1958; Les Brown,

The Business behind the Box, 1971; Robert Metz, *CBS: Reflections in a Bloodshot Eye*, 1975; *New York Times*, December 3, 1986.)

ASH, MARY KAY (1915?–   ). Cosmetics firm founder, Mary Kay Cosmetics. Nearly 20,000 ."beauty consultants" have paid their own way to Dallas for the four-day extravaganza put on by their company—an affair that will cost the firm a cool $4 million. They have gathered there to view the new line of eye shadows, blushes, and lip colors—but most of all—to see, and perhaps touch, May Kay! Suddenly, a hush descends on the audience as Mary Kay makes her dramatic appearance: "There she is, sheathed in sequins. Her bolero jacket is trimmed with mink; a diamond heart rests at her throat." The applause is deafening. Then, as it subsides, Mary Kay launches into her talk like a tent-meeting evangelist. "If you are here today," she tells the predominantly female audience, "you are too smart to go home and scrub floors. You are spending one dollar time on a one penny chore." This admonition not only gives them pride, but also encourages them to hire housekeepers so they can spend more time recruiting additional consultants and selling more cosmetics. "I created this company for you," she tells them, and a roar goes up from the audience. Several "queens of sales" are crowned, for which they win a variety of prizes, including Mary Kay's famous pink Cadillacs. Through tactics like these, Mary Kay has provided the inspiration for thousands of secretaries, teachers, and housewives to start their own businesses selling Mary Kay products. At the same time, she has become a cult figure for these women.

This female dynamo, who is unfailingly described in the press as "petite" and "sweet as a magnolia blossom," was born Mary Kay Wagner in Hot Wells, Texas, sometime around the outbreak of World War I. She refuses, however, to tell her age, blinking coquettishly and saying: "A woman who will tell her age will tell anything." She had a difficult childhood. Hot Wells was a tiny town about twenty-five miles from Houston, where her parents owned a small hotel. When Mary Kay (she insists to this day that everyone call her Mary Kay) was seven years old, her father came down with tuberculosis, and, after spending three years in a sanatorium, he was unable to work for the rest of his life. The repercussions on the Wagner family were enormous. Mary Kay's mother had to sell the hotel and move to Houston, where she leased a small cafe near the Southern Pacific Railway depot. There she worked long hours, cooking solid, plain meals for the railroad men. Mary Kay, the youngest of the four children, had to care for her father when he returned from the sanatorium.

Since her mother was working day and night, Mary Kay saw little of her, and she was responsible for most of the household chores and the care of her father, with only an occasional telephone call from her mother. She later recalled, however, that this worked to her advantage, since Mrs. Wagner used the situation to instill confidence and a positive outlook in her daughter. Whenever Mary Kay called her mother with a problem, Mrs. Wagner replied, "You can do it." After a time, Mary Kay became convinced she could. In the meantime, Mary Kay attended public schools in Houston and was a straight-A student. When she graduated from Reagan High School, however, there was no money to attend college, and no scholarships were offered. Deciding she needed to do something with her life, Mary Kay at eighteen years of age married Ben Rogers. Rogers, who sang and played guitar with a local Houston group called the Hawaiian Strummers, has been called "the Elvis Presley of Houston" by Mary Kay.

During the next eight years, she and Rogers had three children, but when he was drafted into the army during World War II, Rogers deserted his family, and Mary Kay ultimately obtained a divorce. Her oldest child was eight, and as Mary Kay recalls, "I was the sole support of those kids, and that was in the days before day care." She got herself a job as a secretary at the Tabernacle Baptist Church, and she also took a part-time position at Stanley Home Products as a salesperson. Her job with Stanley involved conducting demonstrations and sales parties in people's homes. Although Mary Kay did not make much money in sales initially, she found she enjoyed the work. People seemed to enjoy her company and to listen to her talk, but not many bought her merchandise.

Mary Kay realized that she needed help, and upon learning of the company's annual convention in Dallas, she borrowed $12 for the round trip by train and three days at the hotel. As she later remembered: "That didn't include food. It worried me because I liked to eat." But her experience at the convention motivated her, and when one woman was crowned "Queen of Sales," Mary Kay vowed she would be queen the next year—and she was. The previous winner had been awarded a lovely alligator purse; Mary Kay, however, was chagrined when she received her prize—an underwater flashlight. Disappointed, Mary Kay vowed if she were ever in a position to do so, she would give prizes to her employees that would inspire them. In any event, she became one of Stanley's better salespeople, but she left the company in 1953 when she was offered a better job with World Gift Company.

World Gift was a Dallas-based home accessories firm that was expanding into other parts of the United States. Mary Kay took over its Houston operation and in the first year made $1,000 a month. As a result, she began a rapid rise in the organization. Before the year was out, Mary Kay was named area manager, and then she became national training director. In the latter position she functioned as nominal sales manager of the firm, and she did an excellent job of developing business in forty-three states, traveling three out of every four weeks to perform her job. But she was becoming angry with the sexism she encountered in the company's operations. As she later recalled:

Several times I would take a man out on the road for training, and after I'd been teaching him the business for six months he'd come back to Dallas and end up being my superior at twice my salary. It always irked me when I was told that the men "had families to support," so they deserved more pay, because I had a family to support too! It seemed that a woman's brains were worth only fifty cents on the dollar in a male-run corporation. (Shook, *The Entrepreneurs*)

Nonetheless, by 1963, she was making $25,000 a year, was remarried, and had a comfortable life. Then, an efficiency expert told the company that Mary Kay's power was too great, and the strains of the previous decade erupted onto the surface. The company removed her from her position as national training director and offered her a position as a unit manager, which meant she would have had to move every six months. She turned it down and retired.

A housewife for the first time since World War II, Mary Kay at first welcomed the change. Within six weeks, however, she was bored to tears. "I quickly discovered," she said, "why they put in the obituaries, 'He retired last year.' I really believe that sometimes when you retire from your life's work, you retire from life too." Needing something to do, Mary Kay decided to write a book geared to women, about selling. To organize her thoughts, she made up two lists. The first was all the things wrong with companies dominated by males. The second was a series of recommendations on how to correct those faults. From these lists began to emerge a "dream company"—one in which everyone would be treated equally, promotions would be based upon merit, and the products sold would not only be superior to others on the market, but the sales force would fervently believe in these products. After she had done this, and read over her notes, she said: "The thought struck me, 'Wouldn't it be wonderful if somebody started a company like this instead of just talking about it?' I decided to put my money where my mouth was."

Mary Kay felt she had the formula for a successful company. All she lacked was a product. But this, too, became obvious to her on further reflection. One night in 1953, while she was still working for Stanley Home Products, she gave a demonstration party in a poor section of Dallas. She noticed that all the women there, young and old, had smooth, flawless complexions. As she later remembered: "It turned out the hostess was a cosmetologist and that she was using her guests as guinea pigs for a skin-care product she was working on." The hostess was the daughter of a tanner, and her formula was derived from a solution used to tan hides. Mary Kay took home a shoe box full of samples and was so amazed at how well the skin creams worked that she became a regular customer. When the cosmetologist died in 1961, Mary Kay purchased the formula from her heirs, more to assure herself a continuing supply of the product than anything else. These cosmetics became the basis of her new dream company.

Putting up $5,000 of her own money, Mary Kay contracted with a local cosmetics manufacturer to make the product for her, and she made plans to open a modest retail shop in Exchange Park, a development west of downtown Dallas that was beginning to boom. Things were going along smoothly until, just a month before the store was to open, her husband suddenly died of a heart attack. Mary Kay's attorney advised her that she should liquidate the business and recoup whatever she could from it or she would be left without a cent. It was a horrible period for her, but Mary Kay decided to go ahead with her plans. "After he died," she said, "I was by myself with one-half a company and no idea how to manage it alone. What do you do? You turn to God." A devout Baptist, she said that "when God closes a door, He always opens a window." The window was her twenty-year-old son Richard Rogers. He was selling life insurance at the time for Prudential, making $450 a month. Mary Kay offered him $250 a month to help her launch the new company, and he accepted the challenge. While Mary Kay concentrated on selling and on recruiting and training a sales force, Richard handled the financial and administrative side of the company. The company, called Beauty by Mary Kay and later shortened to Mary Kay Cosmetics, Inc., was founded on September 13, 1963.

From the beginning, the new venture was full of the ideas Mary Kay had been accumulating over the years. From Stanley Home Products she borrowed the house-party technique, renaming them "beauty shows." Under Mary Kay's format, these beauty shows took place in the hostess' home for not more than six people at a time. This allowed Mary Kay's salespeople, called consultants, to offer the participants a two-hour beauty-care program, plus a personalized makeup lesson. The goal of these meetings was for everyone to purchase Mary Kay's products. She also determined to pay her salespeople the highest commissions in the direct sales field, often up to 50 percent of the product's retail price. In this way, they would feel amply rewarded. A major innovation, and one executives of other companies have trouble understanding, was that no fixed territories were assigned. A salesperson could sell Mary Kay products wherever she happened to be. At a time when many women's husbands were being transferred, this was a boon to them. Mary Kay says: "Men don't usually understand our system, but it works! Everyone helps everyone else." And they seem to. Called an "adoptive system" by Mary Kay, it seems to operate on a less competitive basis than in most companies. For that reason, Mary Kay Cosmetics has often been referred to as a vast sorority.

The competition at Mary Kay Cosmetics is not over determining exclusive territories, it is over winning one of a series of prizes for selling excellence. And there is never just one prize for one "Queen of Sales." Many prizes are awarded (often as many as seventy-five pink Cadillacs alone are given out) for many different levels of accomplishment. Each year, dozens of women are called up on stage to receive a series of prizes ranging from mink coats, gold and diamond jewelry, trips to Acapulco, and the use of brand-new pink Cadillacs and Buicks. The key to all of this, in Mary Kay's eyes, is her understanding of the female psyche. "Women *need* praise," she told a reporter, "and so I praise them. If I criticize, I sandwich it between layers of praise." And the praise is not confined to once a year at the sales meetings. Each week she personally signs about 2,000 letters offering encouragement, and at the sales meetings an important element for all consultants is the applause they receive, even if they do not win one of the prizes. "We're constantly praising our representatives," Mary Kay says, "and the round of applause that our new people receive when they do a good job is probably the first applause they've ever had."

Her system worked, and it worked well. In 1964, the company's first-year sales were an impressive $198,514, and Mary Kay had recruited 318 salespeople.

In the second year, sales exploded to over $800,000, and the rate of growth quickened. Profit margins ran at about 20 percent, the firm's consultants and distributors were among the best rewarded in the industry, and in 1967 Mary Kay Cosmetics went public. Sales the following year exceeded $10 million, and by 1977 they were over $50 million. In 1969, the company, which had long been manufacturing its own products, added 102,000 square feet to its Dallas plant, which in the late 1970s was expanded again to 250,000 square feet. During the early 1970s four new distribution and training centers were set up in the United States, and the company also expanded into Canada and Australia. In 1977, the firm moved into a new corporate headquarters, a gleaming $7-million rounded structure of bronzed-gold glass and beige brick—which was paid for, in cash, when it opened. By then, Mary Kay Cosmetics had over 1,000 employees at the Dallas headquarters, along with 150,000 consultants and 3,000 directors. Sales in 1980 topped $167 million. From 1973 to 1983, the firm's stock price rose by an astonishing 670 percent, and in 1984 sales reached $278 million.

Despite the aura of riches that Mary Kay Cosmetics projects, few of the firm's consultants get rich. By the early 1980s, the typical consultant earned less than $2,000 for the year, but this was for an average nine-hour week. The company's motto, "God first, family second, career third," appeals to most of the firm's sales force. Mostly married women or divorced mothers seeking to earn extra funds for their families rather than start a full-time career, they thrived on the bonus system Mary Kay established, with the chance to win Cadillacs, free trips, or jewelry. It gave them a goal and a dream, and none seemed to resent the fact that they were not actually getting rich—it was the dream that mattered. And a few were doing very well at Mary Kay. By the early 1980s, the twenty-four national sales directors (the cream of the crop) were averaging about $144,000 a year. In that year, the most successful of them, Helen McAvoy of Dallas, made $242,000.

What is the secret of Mary Kay's success? There are a number of factors. Mary Kay stressed skin care from the very beginning, and that was the area where Avon Products, the long-time champion of door-to-door cosmetics sales, was weakest. As Americans became more concerned with skin care, as opposed to simply beautification, Mary Kay's sales increased greatly. And Mary Kay Cosmetics did better than its rivals because of the unparalleled way in which Mary Kay herself was able to motivate her sales force. One of its strengths was a relatively narrow product line. Whereas Avon sold 650 products, so that a representative could carry only a few along with her and could list just 250 in her catalog, the Mary Kay consultants could take samples of all Mary Kay's products to the home demonstrations.

Mary Kay Cosmetics was hardly the first company to use direct sales to profit. This had been done for years by firms like Fuller Brush and Avon Products. Nor was it the first to introduce the concept of the house party to sell these products; this had been pioneered by Tupperware and Stanley Home Products. Nor was it even the first to develop motivational sales techniques that bordered on cultism. These had been introduced four years before Mary Kay by Amway. Mary Kay's principal contribution has been to create a uniquely successful company by and for women. Others had exploited women's needs and strengths in the past, but Mary Kay did more than any previous entrepreneur to create a company that tried to fulfill the material and psychological needs of women. The firm's symbol from the beginning has been the bumblebee, and Mary Kay explains: "The reason our symbol is the bumble bee is that aerodynamically the bumblebee shouldn't be able to fly. But the bumblebee doesn't know it, so it goes on flying anyway." This, of course, is how Mary Kay views her company and the women who helped build it: "They come to us not knowing how to fly. Finally, with help and encouragement, they find their wings—and then they fly very well indeed." And although Mary Kay herself certainly revels in the great material comforts her successful company has brought her (a $4-million thirty-room home, luxurious automobiles, clothes, jewelry, and so on), she summed up her own feelings in the following manner: "My greatest sense of accomplishment is the unparalleled opportunity that we have provided to women. Nothing excites me more." (**A.** Mary Kay Ash, *Mary Kay Ash*, 1981; *Mary Kay on People Management*, 1985. **B.** *Nation's Business*, August 1978; *Reader's Digest*, November 1978; Robert L. Shook, *The Entrepreneurs*, 1980; *Forbes*, June 22, 1981; *Saturday Evening Post*, October 1981; *American Way*, October 1984; *Working Woman*, December 1984; A. David Silver, *Entrepreneurial Megabucks*, 1985; *People Weekly*, July 29, 1985; Robert Sobel and David B. Sicilia, *The Entrepreneurs*, 1986.)

AUERBACH, BEATRICE FOX (July 7, 1887–November 29, 1968). Retail store executive, G. Fox & Company. Beatrice Fox Auerbach had been happy in the role of wife and mother without ever contemplating a career outside of the home, much less one in business. Having received relatively little formal education as a child, she later joked that she had never received a diploma, "not even from Sunday School." After she married George Auerbach in 1911, the couple moved to Salt Lake City, Utah, where the Auerbach family ran the largest Non-Mormon department store in the city. In Utah, Beatrice Auerbach conformed to local customs and family expectations; she devoted herself to raising her two daughters, keeping house, and maintaining a "decently feminine" involvement in community affairs. The couple later moved to Hartford, Connecticut, where her husband became treasurer in the Fox family department store. Beatrice Auerbach expanded her community activities there but still maintained what was viewed as a proper feminine role. When George Auerbach died suddenly in 1927, things changed. She went to work for her father in the store, at first just part-time. As she recalled later "I just came down to be here a couple of months, but I found myself fascinated and stayed." At forty years of age, Beatrice Auerbach began her business career. For the next forty years, she was one of the most important and influential women in American business.

Beatrice Fox had been born in Hartford, Connecticut, the eldest daughter of Moses and Theresa (Stern) Fox, and part of a mercantile dynasty. Both her grandparents were German Jews who came to America prior to the Civil War and established locally important dry-goods stores. Gerson Fox had established his store as a one-room fancy-goods shop in Hartford in 1845. His son, Moses, took over in 1880. Over the next several years, Moses Fox developed the Fox & Co. dry-goods store into a full-fledged department store which came to dominate retail trade in the city.

Beatrice Fox attended local public and private schools, and she spent some time at the Benjamin Deane School in New York City, an expensive finishing school. During her later school years she traveled extensively with her family in Europe, and on one of the trips she met her future husband, George Auerbach. They lived in Salt Lake City for six years, until 1917, when the family store in Hartford burned to the ground. Devastated at the loss, and in need of help, the elder Fox asked George Auerbach for assistance. George Auerbach took a major role in managing the new and remodeled store, serving as secretary-treasurer of the company until his death ten years later.

When Beatrice Auerbach entered G. Fox & Co. in 1927, she had a great deal to learn, but she proved a bright and dynamic learner and soon assumed an ever-increasing share of the managerial responsibilities. As her father's health began to fail in the 1930s, Beatrice virtually took over complete management of the store, and when he died in 1938, she inherited the major share of stock in the firm and was named president. It is almost certain that she was the only female president of a major department store in the United States at that time, although Dorothy Shaver[†] was a powerful vice president at New York's Lord & Taylor.

As president of G. Fox & Co., Beatrice Auerbach was responsible for a number of important innovations. A pioneer in a number of fair employment practices, she introduced the five-day workweek, in which the store was closed on Sundays and Mondays, except during the Christmas season. She also instituted retirement plans, medical plans, and nonprofit lunch facilities for employees. Beatrice Fox Auerbach took an important step in creating the Theresa Stern Fox Fund, which lent employees interest-free money in times of personal emergency. Fox's was also the first large department store to hire black employees in something other than dead-end jobs. None of these things were the result of coercion or force but came about as a result of her genuine sense of concern for her 3,500 employees. As Beatrice Auerbach once commented, "Our whole approach has been a community one."

But her innovations were not just in areas of employee relations. She was also a hardworking, innovative store manager and marketer. During the twenty-seven years she ran the store, she increased its sales volume tenfold, to $60 million. In doing this, she established a statewide toll-free telephone order department, free delivery service, and fully automated billing. Attention to customers was extended to the sales counters also, as certain appliances were sold only in locales where the store's own repairmen were available to service them.

By 1959 an $8-million addition was required for floor space. By this time, Fox's was the largest privately owned department store in the country and was the largest in business volume between Boston and New York.

In 1965 Beatrice Auerbach retired as president and, at the same time, engineered the exchange of her family's privately held stock in G. Fox & Co. for $40-million worth of publicly held stock in May Company department stores. Mrs. Auerbach was a director of May Co. until her death, and her two sons-in-law continued as president and board chairman of the G. Fox & Co. subsidiary of the May Co. By the early 1980s, G. Fox had seven stores in the Hartford area, with sales of $145 million.

After her retirement from G. Fox & Co., Beatrice Auerbach became one of Hartford's most important philanthropists and civic leaders. When she sold G. Fox to May Co., realizing many millions in the transaction, she commented: "One thing you can be certain of is that I won't be spending it on yachts and horses, but for the benefit of people." She had much earlier established and provided funds for the Auerbach program in retailing and allied arts at the Connecticut College for Women in order to provide professional education for women. In 1941 she established the Beatrice Fox Auerbach Foundation, which financed educational and civic activities. One of the major beneficiaries of this foundation was the Service Bureau for Women's Organizations, which was founded in 1945. This bureau trained women's groups in techniques of community organization. In 1948 the nation's retailers honored her with their Tobe award for "distinguished contributions" to the industry. The award signified something more than simply the fact that Beatrice Fox Auerbach was a successful female executive. She was, in fact, one of the few retailers (the other was Bloomingdale's) that was able to upgrade its appeal from the broad middle classes to the upper-class consumer. (**B.** *Who Was Who*, vol. V; *Notable American Women*; *New York Times*, December 24, 1965, December 1, 1968; Irene D. Neu, "The Jewish Businesswoman in America," *American Jewish Historical Quarterly*, September 1976, 137–54.)

B

BALLANTINE, IAN KEITH (February 15, 1916–   ). Book publisher, Penguin Books, Bantam Books, Inc., Ballantine Books, Peacock Press. Ian Ballantine was not the first paperback book publisher in the United States, or the largest, or even the most successful, but he was by far the most important. Ballantine was born in New York City, the son of a Scottish-born actor and sculptor and an American-born mother who worked as a publicist for the Ben Greet Players, Jesse Lasky, and other theater groups. Ian Ballantine grew up in New York and graduated from Columbia College in 1938. He went to England, where he got his master's degree after writing what has been described as a "brilliant" thesis on the economics of the paperback industry. While researching this paper, Ballantine talked with Allen Lane, head of Penguin Books. In 1935 Lane had begun publishing paperbound books in England. By peddling his books through Woolworth's and other variety stores, rather than bookshops, Lane had achieved a great deal of success. Ballantine convinced Lane to allow him to distribute Penguin paperbacks in the United States. Borrowing $500 from his father, Ian Ballantine opened Penguin's American office in New York in July 1939. Ballantine just missed being the first "paperbounder" (his term for a publisher of paperback books) in the United States; that honor went to Robert de Graff.

Actually, paperbound books of one kind or another had been around since the nineteenth century. Several companies during that century had published series of popular fiction, often referred to as "penny dreadfuls" and "dime novels." This great publishing empire had been fed primarily by an unlimited supply of British writers whose works were published with no royalties paid. This practice ended with the passage of the international copyright law in 1891, which effectively destroyed paperback publishing in the United States. The business remained essentially dead until the 1930s, when a series of elements coalesced to revive the industry. First was the development of the high-speed, roll-fed printing press, which could inexpensively mass-produce these books. Second was the availability of reprint rights on short-term leases from hardcover publishers.

Finally, and most important, was the use of the mass-market channels of newsstand distribution that had been established by the magazine industry. It was in this area that de Graff pioneered in America.

Robert de Graff had gone to England to study Lane's operation, and he came back to America determined to publish paperbound books. Receiving financial support from Simon & Schuster Publishing, de Graff founded Pocket Books, and he brought out his first ten titles in June 1939. Similar to Penguin's books, de Graff introduced one important difference—he marketed his books through independent magazine wholesalers, who had access not only to variety stores like Woolworth's, but also to newsstands and railroad stations. Pocket Books swept the country; becoming the nation's largest paperback publisher, the name Pocket Books became synonymous with paperbacks.

Thus, Ballantine found he had unexpectedly stiff competition when he introduced Penguin paperbacks to the United States in July 1939. Further, when war broke out in September of that year, it created both inconvenience and opportunity for Ballantine. The war heightened the demand for books and paper in England and also cut off his supply of Penguin books, forcing Ballantine to become a publisher rather than merely an importer. This involved greater expense and difficulty, but it also opened up new possibilities. When de Graff began distributing his books through magazine wholesalers, he found that they needed striking, even lurid, covers in order to attract attention on the racks. Newsstand buyers were not like bookstore buyers. They neither read reviews, nor browsed. They quickly scanned the racks and grabbed a book whose cover art and blurb seemed to promise action, adventure, excitement, and sex.

But Penguin Books in England had maintained a staid, decorous appeal. Only type was used on the covers; there was no lurid art featuring half-naked women or smoking guns. Thus, Ballantine in the early months had found it difficult to compete with Pocket Books. Now that he was doing his own publishing, however, Ballantine began to supply illustrated covers. He also began to introduce books with greater interest to the American people—*Guadalcanal Diary, Thirty Seconds over Tokyo,* and *They Were Expendable.* This brought Penguin Books much success in America during the war, but it also led to a bitter break between Ballantine and Lane.

When the war ended in 1945, Allen Lane was finally able to visit his prosperous American operation. He was shocked and furious when he saw the kinds of book covers Ballantine had been producing. He felt they were terribly vulgar, and he was embarrassed to have the Penguin name associated with them. Lane demanded that Ballantine use type-only covers for Penguin Books in America. Aware that the books would never sell that way, Ballantine adamantly refused. Since their differences were irreconcilable, Ballantine was forced to resign from Penguin and to sell his 49-percent interest back to the company. With several ex-Penguin executives he then formed his own firm, Ballantine & Company, to produce paperback books.

Ballantine hired Curtis and Company, the great magazine publisher and distributor, to distribute his books, but he lacked the money to commence publishing operations. Recent developments in the business, however, gave him an opportunity. Five major book publishers (Random House, Harper's, Charles Scribners' Sons, Book-of-the-Month Club, and Little, Brown) had just purchased Grosset & Dunlop, a prominent hardback reprinter, to compete with Marshall Field III,* who had just purchased Simon & Schuster and Pocket Books. To compete effectively with Field, however, they needed a paperback publisher. Ian Ballantine approached Bennett Cerf of Random House and proposed that the Grosset & Dunlop group back him in his paperback venture. Ultimately, Grosset & Dunlop and Curtis Publishing provided 85 percent of the financing; Ballantine owned only 9 percent of the new firm, but he was elected president, publisher, and chief operating officer. Only a name remained to be chosen for the new firm. Bernard Geis, then a young editor with Grosset, suggested Bantam Books— their logo would be a bantam rooster, to do battle with Pocket Books' kangaroo. Bantam began operations in August 1945.

When Ballantine brought out Bantam's first twenty titles in January 1946, he had a very strong lineup. Along with books by Mark Twain, Zane Grey, and Booth Tarkington were such modern classics as F. Scott Fitzgerald's *The Great Gatsby* and John Steinbeck's *The Grapes of Wrath* and such popular recent bestsellers as Budd Schulberg's *What Makes Sammy Run?* They were priced at twenty-five cents each, and printings started at 200,000 copies. The books were fed into the massive Curtis distribution system and soon were filling the racks at retail stores. Four additional titles, primarily westerns and mysteries, were added each month. Some of the titles had strong sales, but others had fatally weak sales. Ironically, one of the problems was Ballantine's reluctance to use even more lurid cover art. As he later noted, "We did kind of arty and non-newsstand covers for our early Bantam titles. . . . For certain kinds of books we found we weren't getting the kind of sales we should have at all." As a result, they commissioned artist Ben Stahl to create covers that were suggestive but not as crude as those of other publishers. As Walter Pitkin Jr., Bantam's vice president commented, the covers had "a kind of sensuousness or suggestiveness but not a lot of raw meat."

Nevertheless, the cover art accentuated what were coyly dubbed the "3 S's" (sex, sadism, and the smoking gun) in the public's mind. This, in turn, tarnished the image of all paperback publishers, and it brought on government investigations of the industry in the early 1950s. In 1952 the paperback book industry found itself under investigation by the House Select Committee on Current Pornographic Materials. The committee, which found much grist for their mill, proclaimed in their report: "The so-called pocket-sized books, which originally started out as cheap reprints of standard works, have largely degenerated into media for the dissemination of artful appeals to sensuality, immorality, filth, perversion, and degeneracy." As a result, the cover art of all paperback publishers became more restrained after the mid–1950s. But governmental investigations were only part of Bantam's problems in the early years of the decade.

As the paperback business flourished in the early 1950s, it attracted a host of new competitors. The result was that too many books were being published by too many marginal competitors, and the newsstand racks were crammed with twenty-five-cent books. As a result, the returns to all publishers mounted, severely crimping profits. Meanwhile, production costs were rising, and it had become clear by 1950 that cover prices would have to rise. Ian Ballantine was the first to break the mythical twenty-five-cent barrier when he brought out a Bantam Giant for thirty-five cents. The book lost money, but Ballantine at least felt he had established an important precedent. Others at Bantam were not so certain. The company was racked by internal dissension and policy differences. As a result, Ballantine resigned in June 1952 to start his own publishing house.

The new firm, to be called Ballantine Books, brought out original fiction and nonfiction in hardbound editions, starting at $1.50, simultaneously with softcover editions at thirty-five cents. In September 1952 Ballantine announced the first four "simulprint" titles: *Executive Suite* by Cameron Hawley, *The Golden Spike* by Hal Ellson, *All My Enemies* by Stanley Wade Baron, and *Saddle by Starlight* by Luke Short. The plan was called by one industry analyst "unquestionably the most significant phenomenon of 1952 in books." The first titles did well, especially Hawley's *Executive Suite*, which became a huge best-seller and a successful motion picture.

Working closely with Ian Ballantine in his new operation was his wife, Betty (Elizabeth Norah Jones), whom he had married in 1939. She became secretary of Ballantine Books, and they worked side by side at the company for nearly twenty-five years. Despite successes, there were also some difficult times in those early years. The Hearst Corporation, which had been distributing their paperback books, cancelled their contract in 1954, and Ballantine lost a great deal of money. They had to start again, virtually from scratch, and it took them eight years to pay off their $600,000 debt. Houghton, Mifflin, the hardcover publisher, which owned 25 percent of Ballantine, did much to help them through these trying times. Ballantine began to publish science fiction in soft cover to increase sales and profits. Other publishers felt that this was too thin a market, but Ballantine showed that substantial profits could be made in this area. This interest in science fiction helped lead Ballantine Books to one of its greatest all-time sellers: J.R.R. Tolkien's Middle Earth series. Indirectly, it also led them into environmental issues and the publication of Paul Erlich's *Population Bomb*, which sold about 300,000 copies in the first two years.

Despite their success, however, the Ballantines were not finding much contentment with their publishing house. They were working fifteen-hour days and making very little money for themselves. It had become clear by the early 1970s that the only way they could enjoy the financial fruits of the empire they had built was to sell out to a larger operator. Ian Ballantine knew that Random House was interested in entering the paperback market, and in 1974 he sold Ballantine

Books to them for $6 million. The Ballantines then left their paperback "boutique," which they had run for twenty years, and watched Random House turn it into a major mass-market contender.

The Ballantines then started Peacock Press, which they still run out of their rambling old house high on a hillside in the Catskills. The firm produces a series of war books and picture books for Bantam and hardcover books like *Gnomes and Faeries* for publisher Harry N. Abrams. Ian Ballantine continues in the late 1980s to tour the country tirelessly, chatting up booksellers and authors, while Betty takes care of things at the home office. In recognition of their enormous contributions to the industry, the Ballantines were presented with the Irita Van Doren Award in 1985 by the American Booksellers Association for their "many contributions to the cause of the book as an instrument of culture in American life." Such a commendation would have shocked many Americans in the 1950s, when paperback books were viewed as a cancer on the American public. (**B.** *Publishers Weekly*, July 9, 1949, April 8, 1974, December 12, December 26, 1977, April 27, 1984; *Current Biography*, May 1954; Frank Shick, *The Paperbound Book in America*, 1958; Charles Peterson, *The Bantam Story: Thirty Years of Paperback Publishing*, 1975; John Tebbel, *A History of Book Publishing in America*, vol. 3, 1978; Geoffrey O'Brien, *Hardboiled America: The Lurid Years of Paperbacks*, 1981; Ray Walter, *Paperback Talk*, 1985.)

BERNBACH, WILLIAM (August 13, 1911–October 2, 1982). Advertising agency founder, Doyle Dane Bernbach. Bill Bernbach, called by Martin Mayer in his 1960s study of Madison Avenue "[t]he unquestioned hero of the business today," was the godfather of the creative advertising revolution of the 1960s. Bernbach however, started his own agency in the late 1940s, during the peak years of influence of research and science in the advertising trade. During the 1950s Bernbach fought a pitched battle against the research orthodoxy. "There are a lot of great technicians in advertising," he said in 1953, "and unfortunately they talk the best game. They know all the rules. . . . But there's one little rub. They forget that advertising is a persuasion, and persuasion is not a science, but an art. Advertising is the art of persuasion." And Bill Bernbach was supreme in this persuasive art.

Bernbach was born in the Bronx, New York City, the son of Jacob Bernbach, a designer of women's clothes, and Rebecca (Reiter) Bernbach. He attended public schools in the city and got his B.A. from New York University in 1932, where he majored in English. Since the depression was at its nadir at this time, Bernbach was unable to find a job in advertising, and he had to settle for a position as an office boy with Schenley Distillers. This did not curtail his ambitions and creativity, however, and while working in the mail room, he decided to write an ad for Schenley's American cream whiskey and to send it to the company's advertising department. The company ran the ad as Bernbach had written it, but it did not give him credit. Never a shrinking violet, Bernbach contacted the president of the company and informed him that he had written the ad; consequently, Bernbach got a position in the firm's advertising department.

Grover Whalen, who was chairman of the board at Schenley, took a great liking to Bernbach, and when Whalen was named president of the New York World's Fair in 1938, he took Bernbach with him. His title was "director of research," but he actually functioned as a ghost writer for a Professor Monahan of Yale, who did a history of fairs that was published by Encyclopedia Britannica, and he also wrote speeches for Whalen. When the fair ended, Bernbach joined the William H. Weintraub agency as a writer, where he worked from 1941 to 1943. While at Weintraub, Bernbach became close friends with Paul Rand, the art director of the agency, who refined Bernbach's interests in art and graphics. The seeds of the creative revolution in advertising took place in the interaction between these two men during this period. As Bernbach later commented: "The two of us began to pioneer a new look in advertising."

At this time, Bernbach enlisted in the army, but he was released early because of his age and a somewhat irregular heartbeat. Joining Coty, Inc., for a short time in their planning department, Bernbach then was hired by Grey Advertising as a copywriter. Grey at that time was what Bernbach called a "Seventh Avenue agency," with only a few large accounts. Bernbach convinced the head of Grey, Arthur Fatt, to make him vice president in charge of copy and art. He then pursued some large accounts with remarkable success. During this time, Bernbach began to work closely with Ned Doyle. Doyle, about nine years older than Bernbach, was an experienced account executive. The two men began to talk about forming their own agency where they could do the kind of advertising they wanted to do. When Bernbach found that Orbach's, the New York chain of budget-priced women's fashion stores, was willing to leave Grey to become their first client, he and Doyle decided to take the plunge.

Teaming up with Maxwell Dane, an administrator and accountant who owned a small agency and who was a friend of Doyle's, the three men pooled their resources (Bernbach invested $1,200) and formed Doyle Dane Bernbach in 1949. Joining them at their new agency were two key people from Grey: Robert Gage, the art director, and Phyllis Robinson, a copywriter who became copy chief and then vice president at Doyle Dane. Their prize account was Orbach's, and it was with its ad campaigns that William Bernbach first established his reputation. Orbach's competition included department stores that had much larger advertising budgets and stronger reputations. The tradition in retail advertising was to stress price and sales, but Bernbach refused to conform. He wanted to catch the public's eye in the most economically feasible way. He created an impression of reliable quality at low cost, and he did this with innovative, eye-catching ads. One ad showed a man carrying a woman under his arm with a caption reading: "Liberal Trade-In: bring in your wife and just a few dollars . . . and we will give you a new woman." The most famous ad showed a cat wearing a large hat, smoking a cigarette in a long holder, and remarking cattily that her friend Joan dressed well by buying cheap at Orbach's. The ad made Orbach's as famous as Macy's or Gimbel's, each of which had an advertising budget thirty times larger.

The success of the Orbach's ads brought a large number of clients to Doyle Dane. Taking on the Henry S. Levy Bakery of Brooklyn, which had only a $40,000 advertising budget, presented another challenge to Bernbach and his partners. Their most famous ads for Levy's presented a series of non-Jewish ethnics (blacks, Indians, orientals) with the caption, "You don't have to be Jewish to love Levy's." Before long, Levy's became the biggest selling rye bread in New York. Bernbach's success with these two local clients prepared the agency to take on a national client for the first time. Again, they took on a big challenge.

The Polaroid instant camera was a new product in 1954 when the company approached Doyle Dane about an advertising campaign. Doyle Dane took a sentimental approach, creating a series of vignettes of friends and families at the zoo and at weddings. Reasoning that "people take pictures of people they love," in the words of Bob Gage, Doyle Dane's Polaroid ads tried to capture those feelings without becoming too syrupy. The ads were largely successful, and soon Polaroid cameras were so well known that they could be sold without copy or headline.

In 1957, Doyle Dane developed an extremely successful campaign for El Al Airlines, in which they violated a number of advertising rules. They showed a picture of a stormy sea, which previous advertisers had feared would frighten people, with its right border ripped and rolled like a window shade. The headline announced that "Starting December 23 the Atlantic Ocean will be 20% smaller." The airline's sales tripled in the year after Doyle Dane's campaign. The fame of this campaign and others brought increasing numbers of advertisers to the agency, and billings rose from $8 million in 1954 to approximately $40 million in the early 1960s.

The great breakthrough for Bernbach and his agency, however, came in 1959, when they took on the Volkswagen account. The car's previous agency, recognizing that, at a time when America was at the height of its infatuation with bigness and tail fins, the Volkswagen looked almost "un-American," was hesitant to even show a picture of the car in its ads. Doyle Dane Bernbach decided to take a very different approach, to develop an advertising campaign which made virtues of the car's supposed deficiencies. The most famous ad in the series showed a great expanse of white space and a modest photo of the little car. The headline read, "Think Small," and went on to proclaim:

Ten years ago, the first Volkswagens were imported into the United States, these strange little cars with their beetle shapes were almost unknown. All they had to recommend them was 32 miles to the gallon . . . an aircooled engine that would go 70 mph all day without strain, sensible size for a family and a sensible price-tag too. Beetles multiply; so do Volkswagens.

Another famous ad in the series showed a picture of an apparently normal Volkswagen, with the caption: "Lemon." The copy went on to explain that this particular Volkswagen had not been exported to America because the "chrome strip on the glove compartment is blemished and must be replaced. . . . We pluck the lemons; you get the plums." The ads were phenomenally successful, and they not only established Doyle Dane Bernbach as a major national agency, but also helped give birth to the creative revolution in American advertising in the 1960s. As Stephen Fox has commented in his history of advertising, "It was easily the most admired, most influential campaign of the early 1960's, bringing the DDB style its first truly national attention."

An equally successful ad campaign by Bernbach was for Avis Rent A Car. At that time, Hertz was by far the dominant car rental agency, and Avis ranked a distant second. As with Volkswagen, Bernbach decided to make a virtue of a deficiency. The copy stated, "Avis is only No. 2 in rent a cars. So why go with us? We try harder. (When you're not the biggest, you have to.)" The phrase became an authentic part of Americana during the 1960s, as the phrase "We try harder" entered the language and showed up on lapel buttons. Avis' sales increased 28 percent in two years, and by 1966 Hertz was forced to retaliate by recognizing Avis in its ads. It also forced Avis itself to become a first-rate company, and, as its president admitted, "This is tough to do when you really aren't a first-rate company, our problem today is how to continue to deliver up to the implications of our advertisings."

The Volkswagen and Avis campaigns catapulted Doyle Dane Bernbach into the front ranks of advertising agencies. Large accounts soon began flowing to them, and in 1965 DDB moved into the top ten with $130 million in billings. It also won a number of industry polls in the 1960s as the best agency in America. DDB's success was a team effort, but everyone in the industry recognized that it was Bill Bernbach who was most responsible. He had a clear vision of what he felt advertising should be, and he stamped that vision on his agency.

It was as a teacher that Bernbach was most effective, and one of the staffers at DDB referred to the agency as an "adult Summerhill." Rather than propagating a list of rules, Bernbach attempted to put forth a series of principles to guide all his employees. First of all, he rejected the primacy of research, asserting that he considered research the "major culprit in the advertising picture" and concluding that "it has done more to perpetuate creative mediocrity than any other factor." Marketing surveys, he felt, simply led to dullness and uniformity, and they were often used as a substitute for the true creative process.

Also, unlike many advertisers, Bernbach had a fundamental faith in the intelligence of Americans, and therefore he was willing to take chances with ads that were wittier, subtler, and more honest than those of many of his competitors. As he once noted, "Don't be slick. Tell the truth." Most important, he instructed his creative department to trust their own instincts. To facilitate this, Bernbach developed the concept of the creative team. Rather than calling together brainstorming sessions or group meetings, he put together an artist and a writer and told them to work as equals, trusting that a truly creative synergism would result. If he did not actually invent the idea of the creative team, he certainly refined the concept and coaxed more creativity from it than anyone else had done previously.

Bernbach's principles, however, went beyond simple creativity. He refused to handle a product that could not live up to its advertising, stating that "Nothing makes a bad product fail faster than a great advertising campaign." Just a few years after the agency's inception, when clients were still scarce, one of DDB's larger clients had a business practice with which Bernbach strongly disagreed. He warned the company that the practice would have to be changed if their business relationship was to continue. When the firm ignored his entreaty, at the end of the year, Bernbach wrote the client a letter which offered to help them find another agency.

Bernbach was also committed to the idea of world peace, and one of the advertisements of which he was the most proud was one he did for the Committee for a Sane Nuclear Policy (SANE), which featured Dr. Benjamin Spock. The doctor was pictured with a child on his knee; a simple caption stated, "Dr. Spock is worried." Bernbach, a lifelong Democrat, also worked on the 1964 advertising campaign for Lyndon Johnson.

Doyle Dane Bernbach not only pioneered the creative revolution in advertising, it was also the first agency to put a serious dent in the formerly WASP dominance of advertising. Bernbach and most of the early creative people in the agency were Jewish, and most of the truly successful ads in the early years reflected a recognizably Jewish air and attitude. The Volkswagen and Avis ads focused on plucky, struggling newcomers who were challenging larger, more prestigious, better entrenched competition. They used their wit and humor to keep from being overwhelmed. The humor in DDB's ads was similar to the wry, ironic humor traditionally favored by Jewish comedians in the "borscht belt." Later, the agency also hired large numbers of Italians and other ethnics. Bernbach commented on this whole phenomenon later: "I found that you overcome all prejudice by making money for someone. I just happened to have had a lot of Italians and Jews on my creative staff, and when business saw that what they did worked, business wanted them too."

In 1976, at the age of sixty-five, Bernbach retired as CEO of the agency, but he was asked to remain as chairman of the executive committee. By this time, however, DDB had begun to settle into a kind of middle-aged complacency. The firm had entered the 1970s by losing its first major account, Alka Seltzer. In 1971 they lost $15 million in billings, and this was followed by the exodus of a number of clients (Lever Brothers, Whirlpool, Sara Lee, Quaker Oats, Cracker Jack, and others). DDB's status as a fresh, creative agency was no longer assured; it was now a mature, bureaucratic agency like all the others. Although the flood of clients leaving the agency slowed in the later 1970s, DDB was a stodgy, grey firm by the time of Bernbach's death in 1982.

In the two years after Bernbach's demise, the agency suffered a high degree of management turnover and account losses, losses which were high even by Madison Avenue standards. In 1984, a new CEO, Barry Loughrane, was named, and he acknowledged DDB's serious problems: "We were fat, dumb, and happy, and resting on our laurels. I don't think we had the drive we once had." Clients were also different. They were no longer small, upstart companies trying to get an edge; they were huge corporations that wanted careful, predictable ads—just the kind that Bill Bernbach had always despised. Still the eleventh largest agency in America, with $1.5 billion in billings in 1983, it was riven by antipathy between the "creatives"—Bill Bernbach's people, the artists and writers—and the account managers—the researchers and testers Bernbach had fought against for so long. For those who were dissatisfied, there was a beacon of hope—John Bernbach, Bill Bernbach's son. John Bernbach was head of DDB's international division. Trading on nostalgia for the earlier glory times, John's speech in an interview was punctuated with the phrase, "As my father used to say . . . " But he had no clear answers to the agency's problems, either. As he said, "We are no longer unique. So, my God, what's our identity? That's what we're figuring out." (**B.** Martin Mayer, *Madison Avenue*, 1958; *Printers' Ink*, July 31, 1959; *Newsweek*, June 8, 1964; *Current Biography*, 1967, November, 1982; *Advertising Age*, November 8, 1976, October 11, November 8, 1982, April 25, 1983, December 10, 1984; *Harper's*, January 1983; *Business Week*, November 5, 1984; Stephen Fox, *The Mirror Makers*, 1984.)

BLOCH, HENRY WOLLMAN (July 30, 1922–   ) and **RICHARD A. BLOCH** (1926–   ). Tax preparation and legal services chain, H & R Block, Inc., and Hyatt Legal Services. H & R Block is the nation's largest preparer of income tax returns and one of the very earliest franchisers in the country, but both of these aspects of the company evolved almost by accident. In 1946 Henry and his older brother, Leon Bloch, started the United Business Company in Kansas City, Missouri. The small firm was organized to provide advertising, bookkeeping, accounting, and legal services for small businesses that could not afford to hire in-house expertise. After a time Leon left the company, and Henry was joined by his younger brother, Richard. At first, they did tax returns for their clients solely out of courtesy to them, earning $1,800 in 1954 for computing 300 returns. They agreed, however, that it was not worth the effort, and they decided to abandon the tax preparation business. But many clients appreciated this service, and one of them persuaded the Blochs to advertise in the local paper. If the promotion failed, they could leave this aspect of their business forever. The ads were very successful—clients poured into their offices, and the Blochs made $25,000 during the short income tax season. There was no turning back: eliminating their other business services, they thenceforth concentrated on tax preparation work. They made an early decision to spell the name of the business phonetically, thereby eliminating the possibility of confusion in pronunciation, so the Bloch brothers' United Business Company became H & R Block.

The Bloch brothers' move into franchising was similarly unplanned. With the success of their Kansas City operation, they decided to open their first external office in New York City in 1956. Neither of the young men wanted to leave Kansas City, so they each alternated spending two weeks at a time in New York. The new office brought in $56,000; although it was impressive, it only allowed them to break even. To make a profit the following year, at least one brother would have to remain in New York throughout the year. Neither of them was willing to move, so they put an ad in the *New York Times* to sell their New York office. There was only one response to the ad—two New York CPAs offered $10,000 for the business. This was well below what the business was worth, but it was also all the two CPAs could afford. The Blochs accepted the $10,000 but charged them a fee of from 5 to 10 percent of the gross revenues each year. As Henry Bloch later observed, "They became, in effect, our first franchise, though at the time we didn't know what a franchise was."

Subsequently, the small tax preparation chain grew rapidly. By the mid–1980s, H & R Block had 131 offices in the New York area alone and about 9,007 offices in North America during the tax season from January 1 to April 30. Of these, the company owned 4,200, and 3,277 were satellites of company-owned stores. Another 760 were located in Sears, Roebuck & Co. stores, and some 1,570 were franchises. Approximately 10 percent of U.S. and Canadian taxpayers (nearly nine million individuals) have their returns prepared by H & R Block. The firm's total sales were nearly half a billion dollars in 1985, with earnings of over $55 million.

The Bloch brothers are members of one of Kansas City's oldest and most prestigious families. Their great-grandmother, Betty Wollman, was one of the first pioneer women to enter Kansas, and her picture hangs in the state office building in Topeka. She came from a eminent New York family which owned the brokerage firm of W. J. Wollman & Company and built the Wollman skating rink in Central Park, which Donald Trump[†] later rebuilt for the city. On their father's side, their grandfather came west as a scout for Kit Carson, and he eventually opened a general store on the Kansas-Nebraska border. Their father was a lawyer in Kansas City.

Henry Bloch was educated in the schools of Kansas City and graduated from Southwest High School. He attended the University of Kansas City (now part of the University of Missouri) and transferred to the University of Michigan because a wealthy great-aunt in New York City promised to pay for his education if he did so. Henry was a mathematics major at Michigan, but he left before graduation when he was drafted into the U.S. Army Air Corps. While in the Air Corps, however, Henry's father wrote to the president of the university requesting that the navigation courses young Bloch was taking in the service be counted toward graduation. When they answered affirmatively, Henry was able to get his degree. As part of his Air Corps training, Henry Bloch also attended the Graduate School of Business at Harvard University, where he completed courses in statistical control.

Returning from the service, Henry Bloch worked for a Kansas City stockbroker for a year, until he and his brother Leon borrowed $5,000 from a great-aunt in New York to start United Business Company. The first year of business was so disappointing that Leon left the firm to attend law school. Henry himself subsisted primarily on $50 a month from the GI bill and an extra $15 a month he received for providing bookkeeping services to the owner of a hamburger stand. Slowly the business began to expand, and, when Henry felt he could no longer handle it alone, he hired his younger brother, Richard, to help him run the business.

Richard Bloch, nearly four years younger than Henry, received a degree in economics with a concentration in finance at the University of Pennsylvania's Wharton School of Finance. In the early years, because the two brothers conferred on virtually every decision, there was no clear division of roles between the two men. As Henry Bloch has stated, however, as the firm grew,

[W]e couldn't talk over everything from the time one of us got an idea and waste a lot of precious time. So we decided that, if one of us felt strongly about something, the other could have absolute veto power, and that was it. However, once a decision was made and we did something, the other couldn't undo it. (Goldwasser, *Family Pride*)

Nevertheless, as this system evolved, there developed clearly defined areas of authority.

Richard Bloch had always been more of a go-getter, more of an entrepreneur. As a teenager he had set up a successful printing business for Kansas City–area high schools, and during college he rebuilt and sold cars to earn money for school. Thus, it was Richard who was primarily responsible for building H & R Block during its years of greatest expansion. As a business associate, Kenneth Baum, a member of the Bloch's investment banking firm, has commented: "Richard was the real builder but he wasn't too good at managing. Henry, of course, had a real hand in the growth of the company, too, but his forte was managing. They complemented each other very well." Richard Bloch retired from active management in the firm in 1978 upon learning that he had terminal lung cancer. Radiation and chemotherapy have caused the cancer to go into remission, but he has devoted his years since his departure from the company to the fight against cancer. Henry Bloch and his son, Thomas M. Bloch, have run H & R Block since 1978.

After the Bloch brothers stumbled onto tax preparation in the mid–1950s and the firm really began to take off, they encountered a great deal of opposition. Henry Bloch said that "Accountants and lawyers thought that preparing people's tax returns was strictly their domain, and they wanted us out." But the Blochs persisted, and H & R Block grew impressively throughout the 1960s and 1970s. Richard Bloch explained the reasons for such growth: "I really believe that we did the finest possible work, we charged fairly; and we stood behind our work. And believe me, these principles are just as important today as they were thirty years ago." Also operating in their favor were two national trends during these years: the steady rise in individual income and the increasing complexity of the tax laws. Operating on a massive scale at low per unit cost, H & R Block carved out a special niche for itself in the proliferating service industries.

An irony in all of this is that Henry Bloch never stops urging Americans to fill out their own tax returns. "People should really fill out their own returns when they can," he has argued, "because it'll teach them a lot about their economics. There's nothing like getting into your own tax return for teaching you where your money is going." Luckily for him, a large number of Americans don't follow this advice. One who does, however, is Henry Bloch himself. He never hires anyone else to do his taxes—not H & R Block, not a fancy tax lawyer or accountant—nobody but Henry Bloch himself does his taxes. For him, it has become an important annual ritual. Each April, he removes a foot-long gray metal box from a drawer in his home in suburban Kansas City. Having kept meticulous records all year long and placing items in envelopes marked "Taxes," "Income," "Charitable Contributions," "Medical Expenses," and so forth, he computes his own taxes and completes his own tax forms.

Implicit in the principles that Richard Bloch mentioned is the concept of quality, and H & R Block from the beginning has insisted upon quality. They train their tax preparers in a uniform way, making them take eighty-one hours of training in their first year, with refresher courses during subsequent years. Perhaps the most unusual part of this training program is that the tax preparers themselves are billed an average of $250 for the twenty-seven three-hour sessions. Nor are they paid any wages during this training period. As a result, the company in 1985 received nearly $8 million in revenue from its Basic Income Tax Course. Most of those who do become preparers are retired, semiretired, or part-time workers; many are housewives. During the mid–1980s, H & R Block employed 2,800 people year-round, but during the tax season the number swelled to 46,000 with part-timers.

The tax preparation business is a quintessential service industry, and the Bloch brothers have always been keenly aware of that. As Richard commented,

We've always had a requirement that, whenever a client left our preparer's desk, he or she would voluntarily say, "Thank you. That's the best job of tax preparation I've ever had." When that happens there's a good chance there also will be repeat business, which we depend on. (Goldwasser, *Family Pride*)

H & R Block offices contain a reception area where clients can read magazines and sip free coffee. No appointment is necessary; everyone is taken on a first-come, first-serve basis, and the mood is friendly, calm, and serious. Even as early as the 1960s, the Block offices served 8 million cups of coffee, used 55 million sheets of paper, which weighed more than 500,000 pounds, and used up 100,000 crayons and little coloring books for children who were waiting for their parents. In 1985, the average cost of an individual tax return was $45.39. The sessions took an average of 45 minutes. Although individual tax returns are H & R Block's bread and butter, they also offer an executive tax service. Directed at higher income people with more complex returns, Block did more than 55,000 of these returns in 1985, for an average fee of $95.65.

Although during the early years H & R Block depended on a great deal of word-of-mouth advertising for its growth, in the 1970s they began large-scale expenditures on national media campaigns. By the mid–1980s they were spending at least $20 million a year on advertising. Over the years, Henry Bloch has acted as the media spokesman for the company, and he has become so well known in American households that he has even been asked to appear in ads for other companies. In March 1985, he appeared in an Alka Seltzer commercial with a young mother and her twins. She is inquiring about tax deductions for child care, and he tells her there is another kind of relief—Alka Seltzer, of course.

The steady growth of H & R Block was interrupted only briefly in 1972, when the company significantly expanded its number of offices in anticipation of an increase in the number of taxpayers as a result of the economic recovery of 1971. They also began their first national advertising campaign in the same year. Both moves were disasters. For the first time since the establishment of the income tax in 1913, the total number of taxpayers actually declined. The Blochs had failed to calculate the impact of the Tax Reform Act of 1971 on their business, which lopped three million people off the tax rolls, precisely the kind of small taxpayer who tended to use H & R Block's services. This taught Richard and Henry Bloch that in order to survive they had to become less dependent on tax preparation.

Because tax preparation is such a seasonal business, it became clear to the Blochs in the 1970s that diversification was necessary for the firm's further growth and survival. Their early acquisitions—a door-to-door distributor of handbills and shopping news and several others—were unsuccessful, and they were liquidated. In 1978 they bought Personnel Pool of America, an industrial, medical, and clerical employment agency, for $23 million. With 57 owned and 259 franchised offices, this company's revenues reached $75 million in 1985. Henry Bloch also purchased Compuserve, a network for the transmission of data via computer. Over ninety data banks download information to personal computer users through Compuserve. It had revenues of $68 million in 1985 and, in that year, introduced its electronic mall service to complement and augment its discount brokerage and airline reservation and ticketing components.

Perhaps the most significant acquisition was Hyatt Legal Services. The firm, which had started in Cleveland, Ohio, in 1977, offered low-cost, fixed-price services on basic legal services, similar to what H & R Block had been doing for years in tax preparation. In fact, Joel Hyatt's colleagues dubbed him the "H & R Block of the legal profession." They did not realize how prophetic they were, since this was a natural acquisition target for H & R Block. In June 1980 H & R Block, through Block Management Company, bought 80 percent of Hyatt Legal Services. Hyatt Legal Services shared quarters nationwide with Block's tax preparation offices. Revenues reached $17 million in 1985, although Block had yet to see a profit from this operation. A year later, Joel Hyatt bought back the 80-percent stake that Block had purchased, ending the tax firm's foray into the legal profession.

Tax preparation in 1985 still accounted for 80 percent of H & R Block's business, and had an operating margin of 24.6 percent, far more profitable than the other businesses Henry and Richard Block acquired over the years. And the company's tax operations were amassing so much cash annually that company officials could not invest it all in the existing stable of businesses. With virtually no long-term debt and a cash reserve of $120 million, H & R Block might normally have been a target for a corporate raider. But H & R Block, a $700-million-dollar company, remains largely a family business, and appears likely to remain that way.

H & R Block went public in 1962, but the family kept about 45 percent of the stock. In later years family members have sold off substantial stock holdings. By the mid–1980s Henry Bloch himself held just 11.3 percent of the stock, although other family members, including his brother and son, had significant holdings. Nonetheless, H & R Block remains very much a family operation. Henry Bloch, still very much in charge of the company in the late 1980s, admitted that "I'm still a workaholic who talks to the office almost daily no matter where I am. I guess you'd call me the classic entrepreneur." Furthermore, there is little question that his son Tom will succeed him when he retires. As Henry stated,

I'll stay here as long as I can. I love it. But when I do call it quits, I am confident of two things. One, as a family business that concentrates on service, we'd be hard to take over in an unfriendly manner. Second, and most important, with Tom around and doing so well, a father knows that he can trust the business he built to the next generation. (Goldwasser, *Family Pride*)

(**B.** *Business Week*, March 25, 1967, December 8, 1980, June 17, 1987; *Forbes*, November 15, 1970; *Dun's Review*, September 1974; *People Weekly*, March 24, 1980; Stan Luxenberg, *Roadside Empires*, 1985; A. David Silver, *Entrepreneurial Megabucks*, 1985; Thomas Goldwasser, *Family Pride: Profiles of Five of America's Best-Run Family Businesses*, 1986; *Inc.*, December 1987.)

BLUMENTHAL, W(ERNER) MICHAEL (January 3, 1926–   ). Business executive and government official, Bendix Corp., Burroughs Corp., Unisys Corp., U.S. trade negotiator, secretary of the treasury. Michael Blumenthal has been described as "brash, hard-nosed, roughhewn, and sometimes abrasive," and Irving Shapiro,[†] chairman of Du Pont, said that Blumenthal was not "the guy you'd expect to meet at the bar of the club." Blumenthal became a prime specimen, however, of that unique species of businessman–government official who emerged after World War II. Although his success in government posts was not uniform, Blumenthal has perhaps combined the two roles more successfully than any other person, with the possible exception of his predecessor secretary of the treasury, William E. Simon.[†]

To say that Michael Blumenthal represents an affirmation of the Horatio Alger ideal in America would be understating the case. Perhaps no American business leader was ever faced with more disadvantageous beginnings. Although his father owned a small clothing business in Berlin when Michael was born, the ascension to power of the Nazis in 1933 plunged the twelve-year-old boy into a nightmare world. The Blumenthals were Jewish, and, although they did not practice their religion, they suffered terribly from Nazi policies. In 1938, the family business was seized, and Michael Blumenthal's father was sent to Buchenwald concentration camp. His mother sold the rest of their possessions to raise enough money to secure her husband's freedom. In 1939 they fled Germany for Shanghai, where they remained for the duration of the war. When the Japanese took control of the city, the Blumenthals spent two years in an internment camp. Blumenthal described Shanghai during those years as a "cesspool."

Michael Blumenthal attended elementary school in Germany and, for a time, was enrolled in a British private school in Shanghai, where he learned English. He also became fairly proficient in Chinese, Japanese, French and Portuguese. But the years in Shanghai were extraordinarily difficult for him. Blumenthal worked at a number of odd jobs after the Japanese closed his school, "doing everything imaginable to earn enough to eat," even pulling dead bodies off the streets after bombing raids. To make matters worse, his parents were divorced during this time, and his mother married a Jewish businessman who was also interned.

The turning point for Blumenthal came in 1945, when the U.S. Seventh Fleet liberated Shanghai. Blumenthal, who rented a sampan and made his way up the Yangtze River to meet the ships, later recalled: "We were anxious to get on—and get the hell out." The Americans, impressed by his facility with languages, made him a warehouse supervisor for the Air Transport Command in the city. But Blumenthal wanted to leave China, and he applied to the Canadian government for a visa to immigrate to Canada. When he was refused admission to Canada, he came to the United States with his sister, landing in San Francisco in 1947 with just $60 between them.

Upon his arrival, Blumenthal got a job as a billing clerk with the National Biscuit Company. After a few weeks, however, he decided to continue his education at San Francisco Junior College. He spent a year there, and then he transferred to the University of California at Berkeley, where he got his bachelor's degree in international economics in 1951. Despite the fact that he had to hold many part-time jobs to finance his schooling, Blumenthal had a brilliant record at Berkeley, and he was elected to Phi Beta Kappa. He went on to the Woodrow Wilson School of Public and International Affairs at Princeton, where he got his master's in economics and a master's in public affairs in 1953. During the next few years, Blumenthal pursued his Ph.D. in economics at Princeton while serving as a fellow of the Social Research Council and teaching economics and industrial relations at Princeton. In addition, he spent some time as a labor negotiator for the state of New Jersey. After he was awarded his doctorate in 1956, Blumenthal continued to teach at Princeton.

After a year of full-time teaching, Blumenthal felt he was wasting his time in academic life. He wanted to be involved in more critical decision-making endeavors, and, upon making the acquaintance of Herman R. Ginsberg, head of Crown Cork International Corporation in 1957 while on a cruise to England, Blumenthal was named vice president of the firm. He soon became bored with manufacturing bottle caps, and in 1961, when George W. Ball offered him the post of deputy assistant secretary of state for economic affairs in the incoming John F. Kennedy administration, Blumenthal eagerly accepted. In this position, Blumenthal inherited a number of unglamorous tariff and commodity price negotiations but nonetheless performed admirably. In 1961, he was a delegate to the conference at Punta del Este, Uruguay, which initiated the Alliance for Progress. Blumenthal also negotiated the Long-Term Cotton Textile Agreement and the International Coffee Agreement, and he served as a representative to the United Nations Commission on International Commodity Trade. In 1963 he was advanced to ambassadorial rank and became President Lyndon Johnson's special representative for trade negotiations. From 1963 to 1967, he was the chief U.S. negotiator on the General Agreement on Tariffs and Trade (GATT). The *New Republic* later commented on his work during these years: "Remarkably bright, a well-trained economist who clearly relished the subject, Blumenthal swiftly positioned himself prominently between the gray bureaucracy and the distracted glamor boys."

In 1967, having concluded the GATT talks, Blumenthal returned to Washington, where he again became restless. Wondering whether he should return to private business, Blumenthal asked Ball for advice. Ball advised Blumenthal to return to the corporate world, reasoning that, "if Mike could establish a strong base in the private sector, I knew he could always reenter government later at a much higher level." Some observers also said that Blumenthal left Washington because he disapproved of President Johnson's policy of escalation in Vietnam. In 1967, Blumenthal was appointed president of Bendix International, a subsidiary of the Bendix Corp. He served in that position for three years, when he became vice chairman of the parent company. A few months later he became president and chief operating officer.

Bendix had been founded in 1924 by Vincent Bendix, maker of the first dependable four-wheel braking system for American cars and the inventor of the Bendix starter drive, which eliminated the need to hand-crank automobilies to start them. In 1929 Bendix branched into the aviation industry by acquiring a number of small companies. But the Great Depression of the 1930s was very hard for Bendix, and in 1937 General Motors (which had helped Vincent Bendix start the company) ousted Bendix and installed their own management team. This action put the firm back on its feet, and World War II brought it into the big leagues. Military orders boosted its sales from $40 million to $90 million, and the Korean War further enhanced the situation in the 1950s. But in the late 1950s and early 1960s, Bendix found itself caught in a severe boom/bust cycle because of its overdependence on the Pentagon and the auto industry. It, therefore, began to diversify into a number of fields, until sales to the government, which amounted to 80 percent of its business in the 1950s, was reduced to 15 percent by the 1970s.

But in solving one problem, Bendix had simply created more serious ones for itself, and Blumenthal had to address these problems when he became chairman. By that time Bendix had become a gigantic conglomerate which produced a bewildering variety of products. With 86,000 employees in twenty-seven states, it was, according to *Business Week*: "a loose-knit hodge-podge, short on central control, suffering from tired management blood, and going nowhere." Blumenthal attacked these problems with his typical gusto. He sold several of the company's unprofitable divisions, generally tightened the entire operation, and doubled Bendix's sales during his tenure to more than $3 billion. By the end of 1975, *Dun's Review* identified Bendix as one of America's best managed corporations, and *New Republic* reported that Blumenthal had turned the company around "by a combination of sensible modernization, skillful internal and external policies, and plain energy and brilliance."

But Blumenthal had entered the corporate arena primarily as a means to enhance his political worth, so as the 1976 presidential election rolled around, he began to assert himself. Initially a supporter of Henry "Scoop" Jackson, Blumenthal switched his endorsement to Jimmy Carter at the Democratic Convention. As a reward for his support, Carter appointed Blumenthal Secretary of the Treasury in December 1976. He was unanimously confirmed by the Senate a month later. But Blumenthal, the streetwise, tough, highly successful entrepreneur/bureaucrat, did not fare well as secretary of the treasury. From the very beginning, he was out of his element, and he was particularly lax in assuming his role as Carter's link to the business community. Even more damaging, most critics decried the fact that he had not, even a year later, developed a coherent, comprehensible economic policy. Blumenthal's troubles in the Treasury Department soon seemed symptomatic of the problems throughout the Carter administration. Perhaps the most crippling aspect of Blumenthal's tenure in Washington, however, was his utter inability to get along with what was called the "Magnolia Mafia," those Carter confidants who had accompanied the president from Georgia. In 1978, when Blumenthal tried to arrange a compromise on a capital-gains tax cut with the House Ways and Means Committee, his position was cut out from under him by a White House spokesman, who virtually repudiated what Blumenthal was trying to do. In an interview with *Fortune* in January 1979, Blumenthal demonstrated his bitterness and disappointment: "[E]ven though I'm technically the chief executive of the Treasury, I have little real power, effective power, to influence how the thing functions."

All of this came to a head in August, 1979. The Carter administration by this time was reeling from foreign and domestic foul-ups, and, according to *Business*

Week (October 29, 1979), Carter dropped Blumenthal from the Treasury because "the White House staff thought he was not a team player." So Blumenthal left and signed on with Burroughs Corp., as vice chairman, with the proviso that he would step up to the chairman's spot in December 1980. Burroughs, by 1979, was a corporation in deep trouble. For many years, the company had been an important manufacturer of office equipment and computers, but its position had deteriorated rapidly during the 1970s. Burroughs had fallen a generation behind in mainframe computer architecture and trailed badly in desktop computer technology. As a result, sales were declining; inferior, ill-conceived products were rolling off the assembly line; the workforce was bloated; morale was low; management was poor; and profit ratios were scandalously low. Most embarrassing was the B–80, a small business computer Burroughs brought out in the late 1970s. The computer was so inferior, was such a lemon, that the company was deluged with lawsuits. Michael Blumenthal stepped out of the frying pan of bureaucratic in-fighting in Washington into the fire of corporate malaise at a critical juncture in the nation's economic history.

When Blumenthal took over at Burroughs, he estimated that it would take him about two years to turn the company around. After a few months in office, however, he realized that the job was much larger than he had estimated. Blumenthal "began to turn over one rock after another and found the landscape unattractive." But he characteristically waded into the situation with great force. Pruning redundant production facilities and projects, he replaced about one-third of the company's top executives, closed fourteen plants, and purchased Memorex and Storage Technology, formerly leading companies in the memory and storage products market. But both of these firms were also quite troubled by the time Blumenthal picked them up, and Memorex had nearly gone bankrupt in the 1970s. These acquisitions were part of a broader, long-range strategy designed by Blumenthal, one that called for Burroughs to pursue certain niche markets, such as document processing, software, and small business computers.

In 1984, Blumenthal's plan began to bear fruit at Burroughs. Having brought in a number of executives from IBM, he instilled an IBM-like sense of discipline and structure in the organization. Along with this went a strong sense of accountability—the idea that everyone had to pull his or her own weight, and, if one did not, he or she would be replaced. Net profits for 1984 reached $260 million, a remarkable improvement over the early 1980s, but still behind the record prerecession profits in 1979. Blumenthal soon realized, however, that these internal changes were not enough to retain Burroughs' position as a major player in the giant computer markets of the 1980s and 1990s. As a consequence, in 1986 he began to pursue the Sperry-Rand Corporation. When asked why he wanted to acquire Sperry-Rand, Blumenthal replied that it was an opportunity to create "another strong company, another viable competitor in the mainframe business," which would provide "formidable competition to IBM."

Industry analysts were not impressed with Blumenthal's merger plans. A market researcher said it was "like merging the *Lusitania* with the *Titanic*."

Others termed it "barely comprehensible" and "ludicrous." Both Burroughs and Sperry-Rand were old mainframe producers, the slowest growing segment of the computer industry, and neither had proved to be adept in the new desktop end of the market. How, they asked, could they expect to compete by simply pooling their resources? Some analysts compared the proposed merger to the "mating of dinosaurs."

Sperry-Rand, like Burroughs, was an old, venerable office equipment firm with a strong history and uncertain future in the computer industry. James Henry Rand* had brought together a number of small business machine ventures in 1927 with the Remington Typewriter Company to form Remington-Rand. Created to compete with firms like National Cash Register and Burroughs, it made typewriters, office machinery, furniture, and office supplies. Initially, Remington-Rand was an enormous success; its 1928 sales placed it in the number one position in the industry. It continued its leadership during the 1930s, but faced increasingly stiff competition from IBM during those years. During World War II, Remington-Rand devoted most of its resources to the manufacture of munitions, and, consequently, after the war, IBM emerged as the top office equipment firm.

James Rand, however, was not ready to give up without a struggle, and he decided to move into the newly emerging computer field. In 1950 he acquired the Eckert-Mauchly Computer Corporation and, two years later, Engineering Research Associates. These were the two leading firms in the new computer technology, and by 1952 Remington-Rand was the giant of the new computer industry. In fact, during that decade, the words UNIVAC (the name of the Remington-Rand computer) and computer were synonymous in the minds of most people. The Census Department had purchased the UNIVAC I in 1951 for $1.1 million. In 1954, General Electric became the first commercial enterprise to buy a UNIVAC, which opened up the whole corporate market in computers for Remington-Rand. Its prospects looked extraordinarily bright. Yet, by the mid–1950s, IBM's rapid product development in computers had superseded Remington-Rand's, and technological and marketing leadership in the industry slipped from its grasp. Remington-Rand developed new products too slowly, offered little service support to its customers, and used antiquated marketing techniques. In 1955, Remington-Rand merged with Sperry Corporation to form Sperry-Rand.

The Sperry Corporation was a manufacturer of military electronics when it merged with Remington-Rand. The ancestor of the firm was Sperry Gyroscope, which had been founded by Elmer Sperry.* That firm merged with several others in allied fields to form the Sperry Corporation in 1933. During the 1930s, it acquired additional small aviation companies and, by the outbreak of World War II, had revenues of $24 million. The war, of course, gave the firm an enormous boost, and sales soared to $460 million by 1944. After the war, however, they dropped sharply for several years, until the outbreak of the Korean War restored sales to their former level. Having made large profits during that war, and wishing to balance its product line in nonmilitary areas, Sperry decided to acquire Remington-Rand in 1955. Sperry-Rand was determined to take on IBM for leadership in office equipment and computers, but, by 1963, although Sperry-Rand was solidly in second place in the industry, its sales of $145 million were miniscule compared to IBM's $1.244 billion. A year later, when IBM introduced its 360 line of computers, Sperry-Rand was pushed even farther behind. Continuing as an important mainframe computer manufacturer, in 1971 Sperry-Rand bought RCA's computer division. As a result, the 1970s were golden years for Sperry. It still had a strong computer business, and its hydraulic equipment division was doing very well as were the farm equipment and defense divisions.

But all of this came unglued in the early 1980s. Sperry-Rand was by that time a confused conglomerate which had lost any focus or direction. It sold off its retail shaver and typewriter divisions but still suffered large losses. Its major mistake, however, lay in computers, where it continued to emphasize mainframe computers long after the industry had turned to powerful minicomputers and microcomputers. At the same time, it began to slip behind technologically in its mainframe market. By 1984 Sperry was a target for takeovers. Although most corporate suitors lusted after Sperry's $2.2 billion defense electronics business, they did not wish to take on the debt-laden $3.5-billion-a-year computer division. In September 1984, defying all conventional wisdom, Burroughs bought Sperry-Rand for $4.8 billion in cash, notes, and stock. It also assumed Sperry's staggering $3.5-billion debt load, which cost Burroughs its A bond rating.

Two months later, Blumenthal unveiled the merged corporation's new name—Unisys—which stood for united information systems. It soon became clear that critics of the Burroughs/Sperry-Rand merger had underestimated the determination and skill of Michael Blumenthal. Unisys' first two years under his management were impressive. During that time, he slashed more than $300 million from the firm's overhead, partly by furloughing 5,000 of the 121,000 employees, and he also reduced the long-term debt to $2.1 billion. He accomplished this largely by selling off the Memorex and Sperry Aerospace divisions. As a result, Unisys had revenues of $9.7 billion in 1987 and strong earnings growth for five straight quarters. In 1988, earnings were $680 million on nearly $10 billion in sales. The firm's operating profit margins more than doubled after the merger, going from 4.6 percent to 10.4 percent. Unisys ranked as the world's third-largest computer maker, behind IBM and Digital.

Responding to criticism of his approach with Unisys, in early 1989, Blumenthal commented:

While our industry will support many niche players, I am convinced that an industry consolidation will produce a limited number of bigger, full-line, worldwide computer companies. And we will be one of them. I am more certain that we are on the right track than at any time since the merger. (*Business Month*)

Blumenthal based much of his optimism for Unisys' future growth on the Unix operating system for computers developed by AT&T. As Blumenthal commented: "Until Unix, IBM was the standard. Unix represents a window of opportunity and we are jumping through it." Many industry experts agreed with Blumenthal on this point, feeling that nonproprietary systems like Unix were the wave of the future in the computer industry. In 1988 Unisys helped found an alliance of thirty-five computer manufacturers, called Unix International, to promote the new standard. The challenge posed by Unix became so great that both IBM and Digital were forced to produce Unix-based systems, but at the same time they were also working on a rival Unix standard.

Many times, of course, in the previous thirty years competitors have predicted that they had a new technology that would allow them to overtake IBM. No one has yet succeeded. Will Blumenthal catch lightning in a bottle at Unisys? Or will it be just another of a string of failed attempts to challenge IBM? Only time will tell. One thing most experts agree upon, though, is that Michael Blumenthal is a formidable competitor. As Frederick Withington, a management consultant, commented: "Above all else, [Blumenthal] is a man with a strong personal ambition to create a very large business entity." (**A.** W. Michael Blumenthal, *Co-Determination in the German Steel Industry,* 1956; *Disability Retirement in Industrial Pension Plans*, 1956. **B.** B. Morgan, *Total to Date: The Evolution of the Adding Machines: The Story of Burroughs*, 1953; *Fortune*, April 1972, January 30, June 29, 1979, October 5, 1981, November 24, 1986; *Current Biography*, 1977; *National Cyclopaedia of American Biography; Business Week*, January 8, October 29, 1979, October 15, 1984, November 24, 1986, October 3, 1988; Katherine D. Fishman, *The Computer Establishment*, 1981; Robert Sobel, *IBM: Colossus in Transition*, 1981; Stephen T. McClellan, *The Coming Computer Industry Shakeout*, 1984; *New York Times*, May 6, 1986; James W. Cortada, *Historical Dictionary of Data Processing Organizations*, 1987; *Forbes*, July 11, 1988; *Financial World*, July 12, 1988; *Business Month*, March 1989.)

BUFFETT, WARREN EDWARD (August 30, 1930–). Financier, investor, Berkshire Hathaway Incorporated. Donald Keough, a rich and powerful man who in the late 1980s was president of Coca-Cola, had one major regret. In the 1950s he was a young executive with Beech-Nut, who was living in Omaha, Nebraska. His next-door neighbor was Warren Buffett. He later recalled:

He [Buffett] had a marvelous hobby, model trains, and my kids used to troop over there and play with them. One day, Warren popped over and asked if I'd thought about how I was going to educate these kids. . . . I told him I planned to work hard and see what happened. Warren said that if I gave him $5,000 to invest, he'd probably be able to do better [for me]. My wife and I talked it over, but we figured we didn't know what this guy even did for a living—how could we give him $5,000? We've been kicking ourselves ever since. I mean, if we had given him the dough, we could have *owned* the college by now.

Well, not quite, but close. Five thousand dollars invested in Buffet's partnership in 1956 then shifted into Berkshire Hathaway later on with all principal and profits kept in the company for the next thirty years was worth an estimated $9 million by 1986. Just the interest on that amount of money for one year would send about fifteen students to Harvard, Yale, or Princeton for the full four years. That is why Warren Buffett is known as the "Wizard of Omaha."

Buffett was born in Omaha to a prosperous and prominent family. His maternal grandfather owned and edited the *Cuming County Democrat* in West Point, Nebraska, and his mother, the former Leila Stahl, worked on the newspaper while attending the University of Nebraska. His father, Howard Homan Buffett, the son of a grocery store owner, went to the University of Nebraska and became a stockbroker upon graduation. Howard H. Buffett later was elected as a Republican to Congress where he served four terms. A staunch fiscal conservative, the elder Buffett once returned to the treasury a raise that Congress had voted itself. While Warren was growing up in Omaha, his father hoped he would become a clergyman, but Buffett proved himself to be a wizard with numbers. At an early age he was fascinated with the stock market and making money. He had read and reread *One Thousand Ways to Make $1000* and often visualized himself as the world's youngest millionaire.

Buffett also began to follow stocks when he was very young. At eight years of age, he bought his first stock, and he experimented with a number of trading methodologies. He did a lot of "charting" of the market during his teenage years and also did some market timing. He and his sister also put out a horseracing handicap sheet. After all of that, Buffett decided at age fifteen that it was about time to do some serious business. He later recalled:

We put reconditioned pinball machines in barbershops. In Washington you were supposed to buy a tax stamp to be in the pinball business. I got the impression we were the only people who ever bought one. The first day we bought an old machine for $25 and put it out in a shop. When we came back that night it had $4 in it. I figured I had discovered the wheel. Eventually we were making $50 a week. I hadn't dreamed life could be so good. Before I got out of high school I bought myself an unimproved 40-acre farm in northeast Nebraska for $1,200. (Train, *The Money Masters*)

Besides all that, Buffett was such an eager-beaver paperboy for the *Washington Post* that he was able to cover several routes simultaneously, and he also retrieved golf balls at a suburban golf course, which he sold for a tidy profit. But there was a troubled side to Buffett during these years. He had not wanted to move to Washington when his father was elected to Congress, and he was very homesick for Omaha. As a result, he ran away from home once, and he did poorly in junior high until his father threatened to take his paper routes away from him. Once he applied himself, Buffett did better, and he graduated from Washington High School when he was just sixteen years old. He spent two years (1947 to 1949) at the University of Pennsylvania, but he transferred to the University of

Nebraska, where he got his B.A. in 1950. During his final year there, Buffett read a book that changed his life. He discovered *The Intelligent Investor* (1949), written by Benjamin Graham, and subsequently read *Security Analysis* (1934), written by Graham and David Dodd. Graham, a pioneer in the "value" approach to portfolio management, stressed the purchase of undervalued stocks, which were to be maintained patiently for long periods. This approach was contrary to the more popular "growth" approach, in which stocks were purchased with an eye to rapid growth potential and turnover. "Reading it," according to Buffett, "was like seeing the light."

Upon graduation, Buffett decided he wanted to go to the Graduate School of Business at Harvard. He was interviewed by a Harvard representative in Chicago but was rejected. Buffett remembered that what the Harvard man saw was "a scrawny 19-year-old who looked 16 and had the social poise of a 12-year-old." But it turned out to be one of the luckiest things that ever happened to Buffett because he decided to go instead to the Columbia University Business School, where Benjamin Graham was teaching. Buffett took Graham's course and became his devoted disciple. At the end of the year, however, when Buffett offered to work for Graham at his investment company, Graham-Newman, for no pay, he was rejected again. Buffett recounts the story whimsically: "Ben made his customary calculation of value to price and said no."

Buffett put his tail between his legs and headed back to Omaha, where he worked as an investment salesman for Buffett, Falk and Company, his father's investment firm. Finally, in 1954, Buffett got a call from Graham, requesting Buffett to work for him in New York City. Buffett became Graham's jack-of-all-trades and learned the investment business from Graham's point of view. Essentially, he learned the technique of looking for bargains, which Graham rigidly defined as stocks that could be bought at no more than two-thirds of their net capital. Although in later years stocks fitting those requirements would be very scarce, in the 1950s they were quite plentiful.

When Buffett returned to Omaha in 1956, at the age of twenty-five, he was ready to begin investing in earnest. Putting up $5,000 of his own money, and $100,000 he got from family members and friends, he set up a limited partnership called Buffett Partnership. He had no office or staff, just a small room in the home he and his wife had purchased when they married in 1952. But Buffett proved immediately that he had learned his lessons well, as his investment firm earned impressive profits from the start. As word spread about its success, other partners signed on, and Buffett had more money to work with. Using the criteria established by Graham, Buffett bought stocks he thought were undervalued, and by the time he liquidated the partnership in 1969, during a wildly speculative period in the market, he had $100 million under management, of which $25 million was his own. Over the thirteen years he ran the partnership, Buffett had compounded its funds at an average annual rate of 29.5 percent.

Buffett's most dramatic and profitable purchase in the 1960s was American Express. In 1963 the company was gripped by scandal. The master swindler,

Tino De Angelis, had created what was known as the "salad oil scandal" for Amex by having one of its subsidiaries issue receipts certifying the existence of massive amounts of cottonseed and soybean oil that did not exist. Since Wall Street feared the incident could bankrupt the company, Amex's shares plummeted on the exchanges. Buffett, however, assessed the firm's charge card and traveler's checks businesses and concluded that they were rich enough to allow the company to weather any financial storm. So he bought 5 percent of Amex's stock for $13 million. Although an unwritten rule that dictated the terms of Buffett partnerships allowed the company to commit no more than 25 percent of its money to one security, Buffett was so sure of Amex that his $13 million investment amounted to 40 percent of the company. It was a big gamble, but it paid off magnificently. Amex stock over the next five years rose from 35 to 189 on the stock market. Buffett had made a fortune for his partners by doing the opposite of what everyone else was doing—buying when others were selling. "Things aren't right just because they are unpopular," he said years later, "but it is a good pond in which to fish. You pay a lot on Wall Street for a cheery consensus."

Not all of Buffett's purchases during these years were successes. One, a farm implement manufacturer in Beatrice, Nebraska, seemed to be a bargain when he bought it, but it never performed well, and he sold it two years later. In 1965, Buffett bought Berkshire Hathaway, a textile manufacturing concern in New Bedford, Massachusetts. Its price had also been cheap, but even after installing new management, contrary to Buffett's principles, the company was unable to turn a profit. Later, he appended another mill in Manchester, Vermont, to it, but it remained unresponsive. Despite stockholder opposition, Buffett did not close the textile operations until 1985 because they were the largest employers in New Bedford and Manchester, and he could not find a buyer. In 1976, after many years of frustration, and much complaining from his stockholders, Buffett stated in the Berkshire Hathaway annual report: "It should be recognized that the textile business does not offer the expectation of high returns on investment. Nevertheless, we maintain a commitment to this division—a very important source of employment in New Bedford and Manchester—and believe reasonable returns on average are possible."

Despite these mistakes, human (and humane) as they might have been, Buffett's partnership outperformed the market by a good amount. As Adam Smith (Jerry Goodman) in *Supermoney* said:

No quote machines, no ticker, no Oscar's [a Wall Street bar], no chewed fingernails, no tranquilizers, no Gelusil, no backgammon after the close, no really big spectacular winners . . . [just] quiet, simple stocks, easy to understand, with a lot of time left over for the kids, for handball, for listening to the tall corn grow.

He concluded that Buffett was "easily the outstanding money manager of the generation." John Train, in his *The Money Masters,* wrote: "He [Buffett] never had a down year, even in the severe bear markets of 1957, 1962, 1966, and

1969. That achievement stands alone in modern portfolio management." The "Wizard of Omaha" was beginning to acquire a minor reputation.

Buffett really gained recognition in 1969, the year he dissolved his profitable partnership. The market was booming, and most market people were ecstatic over its prospects. Buffett, however, felt everything was overpriced, and, trained on Graham's principles of value, he could not find anything to buy. As he later commented: "When I started, the bargains were flowing like the Johnston Flood; by 1969 it was like a leaky toilet in Altoona." So he liquidated the partnership and distributed to each investor his capital plus profits, together with a pro rata interest in Berkshire Hathaway, which continued to operate as a small conglomerate with a textile division. Buffett owned 44 percent of Berkshire; his wife owned 3 percent; other former partners of Buffett Partnership had 35 percent; and outside investors held 18 percent.

For about four years, Buffett essentially stayed out of the market, while it suffered a period of one of the most severe price downturns since World War II. Buffett had made a prescient decision, and this trait soon became his trademark: he seemed to have an uncanny ability to know when to buy and when to sell, an ability that confounded most experts. As stock prices dropped drastically during these years, Buffett started picking up bargains. He bought 8 percent of Ogilvy & Mather and 15 percent of Interpublic—both advertising agencies—5 percent of Media General, and 11 percent of the *Washington Post*, and Affiliated Publishing, the parent company of the *Boston Globe*. These purchases not only racked up some big profits for Buffett and Berkshire Hathaway, but also signalled Buffett's new interest in media companies. The *Washington Post* shares alone, which he bought for $11.6 million, were worth about $250 million by the late 1980s.

Perhaps people should have seen his new interest coming. Buffett's mother's family had long been involved in publishing, and one of Buffett's most lucrative loves of his childhood was his paper route, but his new interest in media surprised many people. Buffett's first media purchase had been made in 1969, when he acquired the Sun Papers chain of Omaha, a string of weeklies. In 1973 the Sun Papers became the first weekly to win a Pulitzer Prize for an expose of Boys Town, a story Buffett himself helped develop and write. He sold the Sun Papers in 1981, and they folded two years later. Buffett knew when to get in and when to get out. In 1977, through Blue Chips Stamps of California, a Berkshire subsidiary, Buffett acquired a 100-percent interest in the Buffalo *Evening News*. This was, again, a daring move. Evening newspapers were a dying breed in the late 1970s, and the *Evening News* was a six-day publisher with no Sunday paper, competing against the *Courier-Express*, which was published every day. Buffett immediately began to publish a Sunday *News*, and the two papers competed head to head for five years, until the *Courier-Express* gave up and closed down. Buffett was victorious. He owned a profitable monopoly paper generating $39 million in pretax operating profits by the end of the 1980s.

What is significant is that Buffett made these purchases well before others recognized the value of media stocks. As an industry analyst commented:

Warren understood the concept of the media business way back then, and he was virtually alone. He saw what many of us failed to see, namely the advantage of a good franchise and the potential for growth. Furthermore, he has great potential as to what represents value. (*Current Biography*)

Beyond that, however, Buffett characteristically saw a greater significance for the media. As the *New York Times* reported: "Warren identified communications companies as the bridge between the manufacturer and the consumer. These companies—newspapers and the rest of the media—have taken the place of what was once a personal setting."

If Buffett's media purchases were beginning to attract some attention, most of his other purchases fit more clearly into the classic Buffett mold: quiet, simple, unexciting, and highly profitable. Probably the most important of these acquisitions was Government Employees' Insurance Company (Geico), an auto insurance firm. Buffett had first invested in the company in 1951, before he had established his partnership. A flyer back then, it did not fit in with Graham's principles at all. Nonetheless, Buffett bought $10,000 worth of stock, and he sold it a year later for a nifty 50-percent profit. Buffett did not buy Geico again until 1976, when the giant firm was teetering on the brink of bankruptcy. It had miscalculated its claim costs and had underpriced its policies, but Buffett felt that it still retained a sharp competitive advantage. As a result, Buffett purchased $45 million of Geico's stock over a five-year period. By the late 1980s, Geico was a solid performer, and Berkshire's stake in the firm was worth a whopping $800 million. It, along with the *Washington Post* and Capital Cities/ABC (purchased later), made up what Buffett called the "permanent" parts of Berkshire's portfolio.

Despite his success, Warren Buffett managed to maintain a fairly low profile until 1985, when he participated in the Capital Cities Communications' takeover of the American Broadcasting Company. Ending up with an 18-percent stake in Capital Cities/ABC, Buffett was suddenly thrust into the limelight as the company's largest stockholder, potentially with great power and glamour. Many were confounded by the apparent contradiction of this purchase with Graham's rules, which Buffett had followed so assiduously. It was hardly a bargain-priced, undervalued stock. Buffett invested over $500 million of Berkshire Hathaway's money, about one-quarter of the $2-billion company's liquid assets, in the media giant. This was by far the most money Buffett had ever invested in anything, and the stock was trading at about twenty times earnings, double the multiple of Standard & Poor's index. Buffett's response was: "I'm willing to pay more for a good business and for good management than I would 20 years ago." One of the problems was that there were few bargains left anymore; it was necessary for Buffett to change his strategy if he wished to remain active in the market.

But many wondered if he would continue to be as successful as he had been in the past.

During this same time Buffett continued to exhibit what many began to term his "contrarian" nature. In early 1985 he spent $139 million to buy long-term bonds issued by the Washington Public Power Supply System (WPPSS), often called "Whoops" because it had defaulted on $2.25 billion of bonds in 1983 and because the whole nuclear power system in Washington State was so trouble-ridden. In 1986, just to confound the experts further, Buffett bought another $700 million of the bonds. When he was told that the bonds' ratings were quite low, Buffett responded: "If we wanted Moody's and Standard and Poor's to run our money, we'd give it to them." In late September 1987 Buffett also put $700 million into Salomon, Inc., the parent company of Salomon Brothers, Wall Street's largest investment banking house. Buffett made the purchase at the urging of John Gutfreund, chairman of Salomon, who regarded Buffett as a "white knight." It is the only way Buffett operates; he does not do hostile takeovers. It was a dramatic purchase, and again Buffett's name appeared in the headlines. When the stock market crashed on October 19, 1987, many wondered if Buffett had made a huge mistake. Wall Street brokerage firms and investment houses went through troubled times during the next year. But as Buffett always says, he makes long-term investments.

By 1988 Berkshire Hathaway was a large, powerful investment fund. With a stock price of about $12 a share in 1965, it hit a high of $4,200 in 1987, before sliding to about $3,000 in 1988. Berkshire had more than $2 billion in revenues in 1987, and Buffett still owned 42 percent of the company, with his estranged wife holding another 3 percent. Berkshire Hathaway owned 12 percent of Geico, 20 percent of the *Washington Post*, and 29 percent of Capital Cities/ABC. In addition, it had large holdings in what Buffett called the "Sainted Seven": the Buffalo *Evening News*; Fechheimer Brothers, a maker of uniforms; Nebraska Furniture Mart, which sells more home furnishings than any other store in the country; See's Candies, a California chain; World Book; Kirby vacuum cleaners; and a diversified manufacturing operation. Considered perhaps the fourth-richest man in America, Buffett's personal fortune in 1988 was valued at $1.6 billion.

Buffett's appeal comes not only from his success, but also from his folksy, homespun charm. He has always claimed to have two rules for investors: "Rule no. 1: Never lose money. Rule no. 2: Never forget Rule no. 1." His letters in the Berkshire Hathaway annual report have become minor classics in the world of business. Straightforward and honest, they exhibit a wry humor that captures attention. Berkshire Hathaway is run with a small office and staff, but in the 1983 report Buffett announced an expansion of the small office: "In a charac-teristically rash move," he said, "we have expanded World Headquarters by 252 square feet (17 percent), coincidental with the signing of a new five-year lease." The former commissioner of the Securities Exchange Commission, A. A. Sommer, Jr., has commented on Buffett's letters: "Warren's letters are unique.

Damn few CEOs are as smart in as many ways as Warren. It would be awfully hard to require that kind of discussion from all CEOs.''

Buffett, despite deviating from Graham's principles in recent years, has remained true to another of his precepts—holding stocks for a long time. As he commented, ''The best stock to buy is one you are never going to sell.'' ''It's like dumping your wife when she gets old,'' Buffett continued. For that reason, Buffett, the supreme investor and stock market expert, is adamantly opposed to the kind of merger and acquisition mania which gripped the market in the 1980s. Unlike many who criticized it, however, he had a solution, one that coincided with Graham's principles—a 100 percent tax on all profits derived from the sale of stocks owned for less than a year—kind of a modern-day ''single tax.'' ''The substantial brain power and energy now applied to the making of investment decisions that will produce the greatest rewards in a few minutes, days, or weeks would be instantly reoriented to decisions promising the greatest long-term rewards,'' Buffett said. ''The most enticing category of inside information—that relating to takeovers—would become useless.'' The ''Wizard of Omaha'' has spoken—was anyone on Wall Street or in Washington listening? (**B.** *Forbes*, November 1, 1969, November 1, 1974, January 5, August 6, 1979, February 9, 1987; Adam Smith, *Supermoney*, 1972; *Editor & Publisher*, February 27, 1977, March 30, 1985; *Wall Street Journal*, March 31, 1977, April 23, 1985; *Fortune*, May 1977, August 22, 1983, April 29, 1985; April 27, 1987, April 11, 1988; *The Nation*, December 3, 1977; *Financial World*, December 15, 1979; John Train, *The Money Masters*, 1980, *The Midas Touch*, 1987; *Broadcasting*, March 25, 1985; *Business Week*, April 1, April 15, 1985; *Newsweek*, April 1, 1985, March 2, October 12, 1987; *New York Times*, April 22, 1985; A. David Silver, *Entrepreneurial Megabucks*, 1986; *Who's Who in America*, 1986–87; Toronto *Globe & Mail*, September 29, 1987; *Current Biography*, November 1987; *Money*, Fall 1987.)

BURNETT, LEO (October 21, 1891–June 7, 1971). Advertising executive, Leo Burnett Company, Incorporated. Leo Burnett was hardly anyone's image of an advertising man or the founder of a huge international agency. A short, pear-shaped man, with a perpetually rumpled suit, sloping shoulders, and a comfortable paunch, he had prominent lips, jowly cheeks, and heavy glasses. Further, he had a diffident manner and was almost completely inarticulate, except on paper, where it counted most. Although he was a highly creative, driven man, he was a man who could always laugh at himself, while poking fun at others. His wife, Naomi, recalled these aspects of Leo Burnett. They bought a farm at Lake Zurich, Illinois, where Leo was supposed to relax on weekends. She recounted, ''There were two swamps in the back forty and Leo wanted to dam them up to make a ten-acre lake. It seemed to me to be a major undertaking and, being practical, I suggested we sell the farm and buy another with a lake already on it. He responded with that look, familiar to many of you who worked with him, which said he didn't just want a lake, he wanted to *build* a lake.''

And build it he did, naming it Lake Naomi after his wife. The dam that created it Naomi called Dam Leo.

Leo Burnett was born in St. Johns, Michigan, a small town near Lansing, which then had about 3,800 inhabitants. The oldest of four children of a local dry-goods dealer, Burnett got his first exposure to advertising layout and copy by watching his father prepare ads for the local newspaper. His father's connections got Leo his first job as a printer's devil at the newspaper. He became a summer reporter on rural weeklies. After graduating from high school, Burnett served for a time as a rural schoolmaster and then attended the University of Michigan. Graduating from Michigan in 1914, he became a police reporter for the Peoria *Journal*. His grand plan at that time was to become the publisher of the *New York Times*. When a former classmate, O. B. Winters, told Leo that he was making $35 a week in advertising (twice what Burnett was making at the newspaper), Burnett went to Detroit, where he got a job in the advertising department of the then independent Cadillac Motor Car Company. There he edited the "Cadillac Clearing House," a company house organ, and later became the advertising director.

While in Detroit, Burnett came under the influence of Theodore MacManus, the genius of Cadillac advertising, who had developed the brilliant "Penalty of Leadership" campaigns for the firm. During this time, Burnett absorbed the best of the MacManus traditions, especially its ethical standards and polite manners. Many years later, Burnett acknowledged his debt to MacManus: "I became fascinated with his thinking and his quality-mindedness and his great power of assumptiveness that he employed in his copy."

After a six-month stint in the navy, stationed at the Great Lakes Naval Station in Chicago in 1918, Burnett joined a group of executives in 1919 who left Cadillac to form the LaFayette Motors Company in Indianapolis, Indiana. He was named advertising manager of the new firm. Shortly thereafter, when LaFayette decided to move its operations to Racine, Wisconsin, Burnett stayed in Indianapolis and joined Homer McKee Company, a local advertising agency. At Homer McKee, Burnett specialized in automobile advertising, handling the accounts of Marmon, Stutz, and Peerless. Remaining there throughout the 1920s, Burnett seemed to have entered into a safe, comfortable life, one which would bring him moderate success on a local level. As he later noted, he was "very happy there." With his fortieth birthday approaching, however, Burnett began to visualize a larger life for himself in a bigger city. He remarked: "I talked it over with my wife, I thought I'd better get the hell out of Indianapolis if I was ever going to amount to anything in the ad business." Erwin, Wasey and Company, a New York ad firm, hired Burnett as creative head for its Chicago office. Again, his classmate O. B. Winters was one of the heads of the Chicago office, and he helped Burnett secure the position there. Burnett spent five years in Erwin, Wasey's Chicago office as vice president and creative head.

The depression years, however, were difficult for advertising agencies in Chicago, as many of the best people were hired away by New York firms.

Finally, in 1935, one of his best copywriters told Burnett he was going to go to New York unless Leo started his own agency. With eight associates from Erwin, Wasey, Burnett started his own ad firm that year. These were difficult years, but as Burnett saw it, there was a crying need for a truly creative agency in the Chicago area. As he later recounted: "My associates and I saw the opportunity to offer a creative service badly needed in the Middle West. . . . I sold my house, hocked all my insurance, and took a dive off the end of the springboard."

Launched with meager capital of $50,000, an "office" that was just a suite in Chicago's Palmer House, and a handful of women's products accounts, Leo Burnett Company, Inc., opened for business on August 5, 1935. A month later, new and larger quarters were available in the London Guarantee Building. The small agency's only chance for survival was to stake out its turf as a truly creative agency in the city. As Burnett said at the time, "There is entirely too much dull advertising, pages and pages of dull, stupid, uninteresting copy that does not offer the reader anything in return for his time taken in reading it." The first year, however, was a struggle. With its largest clients The Hoover Company, The Minnesota Valley Canning Company, and Realsilk Hosiery Mills, total billing for the first year was around $900,000.

For over a decade, the Leo Burnett agency muddled along with billings under $10 million. Slowly, the firm expanded, taking over floor after floor in the London Guarantee Building. But the real expansion came after World War II, with the great burst in postwar prosperity. From $10 million in billings in 1946, it grew to $22 million in 1950, and $55 million in 1954. By the mid–1950s, the Burnett agency had become a factor with which to be reckoned on the national advertising scene. The postwar expansion was brought about partly by the efforts of Richard Heath, a handsome, affable account man who was brought in from Detroit, and partly by Burnett's brilliantly creative approach to advertising. The two men worked well together. As Draper Daniels recalled, "Leo wrote the gospel, but Dick Heath preached it to the heathen." A number of large clients came to the Burnett agency during these years, including Kellogg, Campbell Soup, and part of Procter & Gamble. It was the inventiveness of Leo Burnett's advertising that was the single most important factor in attracting these companies.

The first of the characteristic Leo Burnett advertising touches, and one which characterized perfectly his approach to advertising, was his development of the Jolly Green Giant for the Minnesota Canning Company. One of the firm's original clients, the canning company's executives had formed an association with Leo Burnett when he was still at Erwin, Wasey. Burnett had first visited the small canning company at its headquarters in Le Sueur, Minnesota, in 1931. A few weeks later, when the agency planned to send its regular account executive to call on Minnesota Canning, they protested, saying "We'd just as soon have that little guy with dandruff on his shoulders." Thus started the relationship between Burnett and Minnesota Canning, a relationship that lasted until Leo Burnett's death, and beyond.

The campaign that the Leo Burnett agency developed for Minnesota Canning exemplified perfectly Leo Burnett's principles of advertising and how he used these principles to create a highly successful agency. Burnett believed that it was the agency's task to find the "inherent drama" in the product itself and then to present it effectively, largely through the use of nonverbal archetypes and symbols. For Minnesota Canning he created the Jolly Green Giant, one of the most effective symbols in the entire history of advertising. Striking some hidden chord in the American public's subconscious, the Jolly Green Giant rapidly became part of the national folklore. The tiny Minnesota firm, with just $5 million in sales in 1935, became a giant itself in the years after World War II. Burnett's advertising campaign was so successful that in 1950 the firm changed its name to Green Giant. By the mid–1980s, Green Giant was still a Burnett client, with billings of $50 million a year. Since 1979, as part of the Pillsbury Company, Green Giant's sales have been over $400 million annually.

Because of Leo Burnett's success with Green Giant, the Philip Morris Company approached the firm in 1954 to develop a campaign for its Marlboro brand of filter cigarettes. Like other filter cigarettes, Marlboro's were marketed as women's cigarettes, with a delicately designed white package and an ad campaign stressing that they were "Mild as May." Philip Morris wanted to make the cigarette more attractive to men, and the company turned to Burnett to develop this campaign. It was Leo Burnett himself who came up with the winning idea, one which became a classic in American advertising.

Leo Burnett gathered his top creative people together at his farm outside Chicago. Deciding to create a "Marlboro Man," the question became: "What's the most masculine type of man?" Burnett remembered a dramatic black-and-white photograph of a cowboy on a *Life* magazine cover. Don Tennant, a former Burnett writer-producer, recalled: "That picture symbolized everything they wanted to represent the new Marlboro cigarette." So, although other occupations were also featured in the first series of ads for Marlboro, it was the cowboy image that soon became dominant. Leo Burnett had captured an image of how Americans liked to think of themselves, encapsulated it in a simple picture of a series of rough-hewn men, and brought Marlboro cigarettes from a market share of less than 1 percent in 1953 to the position of the largest-selling cigarette in the world.

Leo Burnett and his agency had found their métier. Following on the heels of the Marlboro Man and the Jolly Green Giant came Tony the Tiger for Kelloggs' Frosted Flakes, the Pillsbury Doughboy, Charlie the Tuna, and the phenomenally popular Morris the Cat for Starkist, the "lonely" Maytag repairman, and many others. Another highly successful campaign for the Burnett agency was conceived for United Airlines. When Burnett won the account in 1965, United was perceived as a "big, cold, stainless steel airline," said Jack Smith, Leo Burnett's vice chairman. Burnett, applying the same principles that sparked his other campaigns, added a human element to United by talking about the "friendly skies of United" in the campaign. Typical of Burnett's "warm sell" approach, it was extremely successful. Within ninety days of the first exposure of Burnett's ads, 40 percent of those polled associated that phrase with the airline. More than twenty years later, "Fly the friendly skies" was still United's theme, and it was recognized by 94 percent of the people polled by Burnett, which continued to function as the airline's agency.

Yet, despite (or perhaps because of) Burnett's tremendous success, not everyone in the advertising industry was impressed. Unlike the wryly humorous ad campaigns of Doyle Dane Bernbach, created by William Bernbach,[†] Leo Burnett's ads were often perceived as corny and unsophisticated. Many in New York felt that much of his work was too similar, too much a "menagerie" of animals; that it had become, by the 1960s, an antiquated product of the "Chicago School" of advertising. Leo Burnett responded by stressing the "friendliness quotient" found in Chicago advertising, asserting that consumers reacted better to ads that they liked than to ones they did not like. He mused further, "I like to think that we Chicago ad-makers are all working stiffs. I like to imagine that Chicago copywriters spit on their hands before picking up the big, black pencils." Stephen Fox, in *The Mirror Makers*, summed up Burnett's influence in this manner: "Simplicity, clarity, and peopletalk. Straightforward without being flat-footed. Warm without being mawkish. The lighter the touch, the heavier the wallop."

Hooper White, who worked for Leo Burnett for over twenty years, recalled in 1985 what it was like to work there. In 1959, he was with J. Walter Thompson in Chicago, but said "down the street there was a madhouse called Leo Burnett Co. It was rumored that they threw away more good ideas than the rest of the city produced." The agency was renowned as a marvelous training ground to learn the advertising business. During Leo Burnett's later years, the agency hired fifty or sixty people a year right out of college. At Leo Burnett they were given in-depth training in media or research for several years before being assigned to a client. The agency's principles were simple: "Teach young people to think in a disciplined manner, to identify problems, to think creatively." As much as Leo Burnett was respected, and even loved, by many of his staff, he was not an easy man to work for. Burnett was a stern taskmaster. Even as his agency grew to gigantic proportions, it was still run as a one-horse operation, and Leo Burnett had final approval of creative input. Art and copy had to survive harrowing sessions of the plans board, in which people learned to judge their chances of having their ideas accepted by what they called the lip protrusion index: the more Leo Burnett pursed his lips, the greater the likelihood that the ad would not be accepted.

Strother Cary, who worked for Leo Burnett, commented later that "He was not an easy boss." He drove his people hard, and he demanded a great deal from them, both in terms of the amount of work and in terms of the level of creativity. But two aspects of Burnett's personality disarmed all but his most aggravated employees. The first was his ingenuousness, his ability to see his own flaws and to make fun of himself. Draper Daniels, a copywriter at Burnett, had become so frustrated with Leo Burnett's incessant questioning at the plans board meetings that he wrote a satire of it, in which Ned Jordan's famous ad of the 1920s—"Somewhere West of Laramie"—was presented for Burnett's approval. It skewered Leo Burnett quite soundly, and his response was to use the satire for a speech before the American Association of Advertising Agencies in 1955 and to comment that "something must be done about meetings. The man with the pencil sits through far more meetings than he should."

The second reason that Leo Burnett's employees were not alienated by his demands on them was that nobody worked harder than Leo Burnett himself. The advertising agency was his entire life. He was up at 5 A.M., worked in his study for several hours before breakfast, arrived in the office at 9 A.M., kept two secretaries busy all day, and got home at midnight by taxi with papers to go through that night before bed. Then, all weekend he buried himself in his study. Burnett himself recognized his importance to the agency with a poem he wrote in 1955:

> When the day's last meeting is over,
> And the V.P.'s have left for the train,
> When account men are at bars with the client,
> and the space men have switched off the brain,
> We shall work, and, by God we shall have to—
> Get out the pencils and pads,
> For finally, after the meetings—someone
> Must get out the ads!

Leo Burnett, a simple, hardworking man, who did simple, effective advertising. (**A.** Leo Burnett, *Communications of an Advertising Man,* 1961. **B.** *Advertising Age,* October 23, October 30, 1970, June 14, June 21, 1971, August 10, 1981, August 1, 1985; *New York Times,* June 9, 1971; *Time,* June 21, 1971; *Who Was Who,* vol. VI; Stephen Fox, *The Mirror Makers,* 1984; *The Burnettwork,* August 5, 1985.)

BURR, DONALD CALVIN (May 8, 1941–). Airline company founder, People Express Airlines, Inc. Some animals cannibalize their young; if their babies are not taken from them soon after birth, they may devour them. Frank Lorenzo[†] devoured Donald Burr. Lorenzo, in effect, gave birth to Burr's career in the airline industry, nurtured him, taught him everything he knew—and then ate him alive. Donald Burr, a man who, in just a short time, was lionized by every business school in the country—which called him the prototypical 1980s executive—was hung out to dry by Lorenzo in 1986. His company, People Express, the fastest growing airline in aviation history, was teetering on the brink of bankruptcy, and Burr reluctantly had to sell out to his former boss. Donald Burr changed the face of American aviation, but at the age of forty-five he was looking for a new job.

Donald Burr was born in South Windsor, Connecticut; his father was an engineer and his mother was a social worker. He was raised in a comfortable life-style, experiencing what *Business Week* called a "Father Knows Best" middle-class upbringing. He met his future wife in the seventh grade, sang for a barbershop quartet, played saxophone in the school band, served as class treasurer, and played on the baseball, basketball, and soccer teams. His high school coach called him "an unusually versatile and very popular kid," and after graduation he went on to tiny Bowdoin College in Maine. After a year at Bowdoin, he transferred to Stanford University, where he got his B.A. in economics in 1963. After that, Burr attended the Graduate School of Business at Harvard, where he got his M.B.A. in 1965.

Burr, who had loved flying as a youngster and who got his private pilot's license, went to Wall Street for his first job, where he worked for National Aviation Corporation, a mutual fund specializing in the aerospace industry. In 1972, when he was just thirty years old, Burr became president of the company. The following year, Burr met Frank Lorenzo, who had taken over the struggling Texas International Airline in 1972. The airline was in deep trouble; Lorenzo had no experience in running an airline and needed help, badly. At Lorenzo's urging, Burr joined Texas International in 1973 as executive vice president. Lorenzo, with the help of Burr and Robert Carney, pulled Texas International out of the doldrums with a series of bold moves. The most dramatic, however, was Burr's idea. In 1977, he came up with the concept of what he called "peanuts fares" —ultradeep discount fares. He convinced a skeptical Lorenzo to apply to the Civil Aeronautics Administration (CAB) for permission to offer these fares. The permission was granted, and over the next several years Texas International was highly successful, as net income zoomed from $2.5 million in 1976 to $41.4 million in 1979. As a result, Burr was named chief operating officer of Texas International in 1978, and president in June 1979. Six months later, however, he resigned, partially out of frustration and partially because of a dream he concocted as he jogged around suburban Houston.

Burr had been disillusioned by the environment he found at Texas International. As he said: "It was grind, grind, with no better purpose than to grind out some profits. It had no vision, no excitement." He had become convinced that "there was a better way of doing things," a "better way for people to work together" within the capitalist system. "If you give people freedom," he declared, "they will produce better on balance." This discontent was united with a vision that began forming in Burr's mind—a vision of a new kind of airline. He wanted to start a low-cost carrier that would take advantage of the recently passed Airline Deregulation Act of 1978. It would have the same peanuts fares as Texas International, but, unlike that airline, it would be unconventional, with little hierarchy and much freedom. He would create a sense of "family," giving all employees a financial stake in the enterprise. Excited by his messianic fervor, fifteen of Burr's coworkers at Texas International followed him to his new airline.

Burr's first task was to finance his airline. He and George L. Gitner, who had been Texas International's vice president of planning, and Melrose Dawsey, Burr's executive assistant at Texas International, drained their savings to raise

$545,000. They applied to the CAB for permission to become the first airline to form under the new deregulated system. Burr then approached venture capitalist William R. Hambrecht and sold him on his idea. Hambrecht helped Burr raise $24 million in a public offering in November 1980, and Burr's dream was a step closer to reality. He had a daring idea. Burr planned to use the Newark terminal, across the Hudson River from New York City, as his hub. Even though Newark was an eminently logical and sound choice, Burr did not receive total support for the idea, since Newark had been unaccountably shunned by the airlines for decades. Although it was closer to downtown Manhattan than the other New York airports and although it had better and cheaper bus transportation into the city, it had been ignored by most airlines. It was uncongested, it had good parking and good transit service, and its North Terminal was available— cheap. The North Terminal was a mixed blessing. It had not been used since 1973, when newer and better terminals began to be built. Burr described it as a ghost town, saying that "what didn't fall on your head, bit you in the ankle."

Next Burr had to put together an airline. First he purchased seventeen used Boeing 737–100s from Lufthansa, the very reputable German airline. This was a shrewd move. The airplanes cost him just a little over $4 million each, as opposed to over $10 million when new. For a relatively small amount of money, Burr had a fleet of decent planes. When Lufthansa flew the planes, each had ninety seats and a galley for hot meals. Burr took out the galleys and the first-class sections and added twenty-eight seats per plane. In this way, the airline increased its passenger-carrying capacity per plane, which helped reduce People Express' costs per passenger mile.

The next step was to hire a staff. At the time Burr was starting People Express, a lot of airline employees had been laid off because of deregulation. He found many experienced personnel willing to accept nonunion wages, which were less than half the industry average. Even more important, they were willing to accept working practices that would never have been tolerated in the halcyon days of regulated airlines. Burr's secret was not simply that his new employees were desperate; recognizing the importance of good employee-management relations, he set up an innovative program of industrial relations, and he developed a messianic, almost cultlike following among his staff. Working closely with Lori L. Dubose, who had been the human resources director at Texas International, Burr developed the flat organizational structure and human resource strategy that set this airline apart from the others. There was no corporate hierarchy—only a very small officer staff, which by 1982 still totaled just fifteen people—no vice presidents, and no secretaries for anyone, not even Burr. Opting to establish just three managerial levels, the emphasis at People was on versatility, not hierarchical status. A crossover of talent was established to enable People Express to have a leaner staff complement than most airlines. In 1982, the company had about 800 full-time employees, or 57 per aircraft. In contrast, the industry as a whole had 149 per aircraft. Versatility made the difference. Other airlines, because of union work rules and established job traditions, could not move their employees around when the need occurred, but People could.

A major factor in encouraging employees to accept lower wages and greater versatility in their jobs lay in the fact that each employee was offered a real stake in the company. Every new recruit had to purchase 100 shares of People Express stock, at a 70-percent discount. (This could be accomplished through a payroll deduction plan, if necessary.) The ultimate goal, as Burr said, was "to provide an environment for all of us to do better on the same team." Since employees also had the option of buying unlimited amounts of stock, and since People Express' fortunes improved significantly during the first several years, many became quite comfortable. By 1985, "the average employee owns $60,000 worth." This created a sense of togetherness and family at People in the early years. The company's chief financial officer, Robert McAdoo, said: "We're all in this together." Employees found themselves putting in longer hours at People, but feeling good about it. One employee said: "[I]t's definitely a work-ethic company. . . . I'm here all the time. It's because I want to be." But when some commentators remarked on the "family ethic" at People, Burr cautioned that the company "is not a social experiment. It's a hard-driving capitalist business."

Equally important was Donald Burr himself. Often called the Pied Piper of People Express, he fervently preached the gospel of "worker participation" and "humanistic capitalism" at orientation sessions for new employees. As People Express met with phenomenal success, Burr became the darling of the nation's business schools. Viewed as a classic "new wave capitalist," John Naisbitt called People a "reinvented" corporation, and Thomas J. Peters in *A Passion for Excellence* praised Burr extravagantly. Burr began lecturing, writing editorial pieces, and hobnobbing with management gurus as a way of spreading his gospel. Harvard Business School chose Burr as the example for case study of 1980s-style entrepreneurship, complete with videotapes shown on 10–by–10-foot screens. When *The 100 Best Companies to Work for in America* came out, People Express was prominent among them. The authors commented: "There is a messianic quality to People Express that Donald Burr . . . does nothing to dispel when he holds orientation meetings for newcomers and tells them that one of the objectives of this company is to 'make a better world.' "

Finally, to enable People Express to offer deep discount fares in the high-density eastern seacoast corridor in which they intended to operate, Burr cut back all of what he termed the "frills." He dispensed with a lot of the services that passengers took for granted on other airlines; for example, hot meals were not provided, although passengers could buy sandwiches for $1 and coffee for 50 cents. People Express took reservations by telephone, but without computers to hook them up with other airlines or to issue tickets. Ticketing was done on the plane to save about $18 per ticket. Passengers were encouraged to carry their own bags on board; if they insisted on checking their luggage, they were charged $3 per bag. Again, checked luggage could not be transferred to other airlines. By artful scheduling, People's planes were kept in the air for ten or eleven hours a day, three or four hours more than other airlines, and pilots flew about seventy hours a month, well above the industry average of forty-five hours. The cabins were clean, the seats close together, and the attendants friendly and attentive. As *Fortune* commented, "It's like a McDonald's of the air."

As a result, People Express had the lowest cost-per-seat-mile of any airline in the early 1980s. Costs-per-seat-mile were a phenomenal 5.4 cents in 1981; competitors like USAir's costs were over 11 cents a mile, and others ran from 8 to 9 cents a mile. People could profitably offer lower fares. Passing along its economies to customers, People's passengers were charged an average of 9.3 cents a mile, while USAir charged 18.6 cents a mile, and Piedmont, 16.1 cents. Although People's reduced fares created tremendous competition for other airlines, Burr declared that he had no wish to take passengers from other airlines. He hoped, instead, to lure them from taking buses and driving their own cars— to convince people who were not used to flying to take People Express. Burr's airline broke into what *Maclean's* called the "sofa trade," that is, people who normally stayed home or who traveled long distances in the family car. Burr remarked: "We're getting people who wouldn't have traveled to New York to see a show, or buy clothes. If they did, they would have driven or taken a train."

Donald Burr and People Express had all the ingredients for success, but the route to success and profitability was not even or straight. First of all, People Express "took off" at the worst possible time. The air-traffic controllers' strike in 1981 caused the company to lose nearly $9.2 million during its first nine months of operation. Because it severely limited landing rights at Newark, the strike had a devastating impact on the young company. Burr had planned to establish what he called a "hub and spoke airline," with Newark as the hub for passengers to fly to a selected number of cities in the eastern portion of the United States. Burr, therefore, had to revamp his route system, scheduling flights from cities like Buffalo and Syracuse to various points in Florida. It was not ideal, but it was innovative—and it worked. By the end of the year, nearly one million passengers had taken advantage of People Express.

During 1982, Burr's airline was built on that base, carrying more than 2.8 million passengers. As a result, they turned a small profit on revenues of $139 million. With demand for his services growing rapidly, Burr purchased twenty Boeing 727–200 planes from Braniff Airways and arranged to lease a jumbo jet. By early 1983, People was servicing nineteen cities in the United States, mostly along the eastern corridor, and it began service to London, England. Charging a one-way fare of just $149, People's flights overnight were booked solid for months in advance. In July of that year, People's stock, which had been issued for $8, reached a high of $50, and split two for one. Burr's employees, with their 100 shares of stock, were getting rich—it all seemed too good to be true.

People's revenues continued to soar in 1984, reaching $587 million, more than double the year before. But profits took a nosedive, as the firm registered a loss in the final quarter, after seven consecutive quarters of profits. As a result, People's stock dropped as low as $8 a share during the year. The problem, industry analysts pointed out, was that People's growth in traffic did not match its accelerated expansion program. During that year, People had opened service to eight more major cities in the United States with a combined population of 40 million, and the Midwest and Great Lakes became part of its route service area. Then, too, with the vast expansion of traffic and facilities, Burr's managerial system had not kept pace. During the year, there was a sharp increase in passenger complaints concerning delayed flights, lost luggage, and overbooking. Service had deteriorated so badly that passengers began referring to it as "People Distress."

Even worse, Burr's charisma began to erode, and several severe labor and managerial problems emerged at the airline. Most significant was the firing of Lori Dubose. Dubose had been one of Burr's earliest disciples at Texas International, and she had been primarily responsible for the humanistic managerial system at People. She became a strong role model for many employees, especially the airline's customer service managers (flight attendants). But she was detested by the pilots, since they felt she undercut their status in the organization. Then, in late 1984, when the Air Line Pilots Association was pushing a solicitation drive to unionize People pilots and the airline was experiencing a loss of over $14 million for the final three months, Burr struck back. He stopped issuing profit-sharing checks to employees, froze salaries and hiring, and put the airline on an austerity program. Dubose objected, and Burr fired her. Shortly thereafter several other key employees left.

The Harvard case study ideal of a harmonious new company was crumbling. The Burr charisma was taking on a new image also. Some employees took to calling him "Guyana Jones," in reference to the Reverend Jim Jones, whose followers died after blindly heeding their leader's call to drink poisoned Kool-Aid. Burr dismissed those comments, saying: "I believe in leadership by example. That's just basic truth. If that's Kool-Aid, so be it." One of the employees who left said: "We were mesmerized by him (Burr) at first, but when we took our rose-colored glasses off, we found a masterful manipulator." Even an employee who stayed with Burr recognized this: "We lost our sense of family and gained a sense of alienation."

Despite all these problems, Burr managed to bootstrap People Express back into the black in 1985. Profits for the second quarter in that year rose to $13 million, and in the third quarter to $16.5 million. Revenues zoomed toward $1 billion. But when United Airlines, American Airlines, and Frank Lorenzo's Continental Airlines reduced their fares and began to compete head to head with People, Burr became convinced that he had to broaden the company's geographic base by buying several smaller airlines. In October 1985, Burr announced his intention of taking over Frontier Airlines, which served the southwestern United States. This acquisition forced Burr to compete with Lorenzo's Continental, which was also interested in Frontier, but Lorenzo's rigid antiunion attitudes caused Frontier's employees to favor Burr's bid. With the acquisition of Frontier for $300 million, Burr suddenly had the fifth-largest carrier in the country, behind only United, American, Delta, and Eastern. As part of the deal, Burr promised to run Frontier, a conventional unionized airline, as a separate company until 1990.

Burr felt the acquisition of Frontier was exactly what People needed in order to survive into the 1990s, but most everyone else questioned his wisdom. Even his twelve-year-old son was skeptical, saying "Dad is just doing what's popular. He's copying what everybody else was doing. The raider-type stuff." Donald Burr was devastated by the comment, saying: "He couldn't have hurt me more. . . . I bit my lip." But others recalled that Burr had always promised he would never buy another airline, since that would conflict with his most important goal—the development of People's people. The Frontier decision came as an enormous shock to People's employees. Many, especially those who had come with Burr from Texas International, wondered if he was trying to emulate Frank Lorenzo. Burr dismissed that, saying: "People call up asking, 'Does Don really want to be Frank?' That's nonsense. All I want to do is win."

But many industry analysts were unconvinced of the wisdom of the move. They pointed out that People Express, which had always thrived on a lean, simplified management structure, would become more complex with the addition of Frontier. As *Business Week* (November 25, 1985) commented: "Frontier is the opposite of Don Burr's vision of an airline. Frontier has five unions, People has none. Frontier's 737's have 106 seats; People's pack in 130. Frontier's passengers get free baggage checking, meals, and coffee; People charges extra." Burr insisted, however, that there would be no culture clash: "We can put the economies together without putting the people together. All we do is become a self-feeding mechanism. Over time, the fundamental ideas that give direction to People will find root at Frontier." But a skeptical Wall Street analyst was not convinced: "Burr thinks he can fly to the moon."

Having barely digested Frontier, Burr took out after other game in early 1986, buying Provincetown-Boston Airlines in January and Britt Airways in February. Both were small commuter lines that further expanded People's base. It soon became clear that Burr had bitten off more than he could chew. The explosive growth of the airline, coupled with its enormous debt load and increased competition from other carriers, brought about a river of red ink. In the first quarter of 1986, people had a staggering net loss of $58 million, which was partially caused by the increased competition from Continental Airlines, run by Burr's old mentor Frank Lorenzo. Burr had stolen Frontier from Lorenzo, and it was clear that Lorenzo was going to make him pay dearly. Burr reacted wildly to the situation, thrashing about for a solution. In May 1986, he announced that People Express would offer first- and business-class sections, would serve free food and drinks to full-fare passengers, and would introduce a frequent-flyer program. People Express began to look just like every other airline. Subsequently, Burr announced that he was "downsizing" People by selling some of the airline's larger planes, since the airline's average load factor had dropped significantly.

This strategy did not succeed, and Burr belatedly realized that the acquisition of Frontier had been a fatal mistake. In July 1986, he agreed to sell Frontier to United Air Lines for $146 million. Burr explained the rationale of the sale by saying that it "allows our managers to refocus their time on the business we continue to build at Newark," which, of course, was admitting how accurate much of the criticism was that was targeted at the deal. In August, however, United called off the deal because of a protracted dispute with the pilots' union. Burr was desperate. The following day, August 28, he filed for protection under Chapter 11 of the federal bankruptcy code. This was another stopgap measure. To save People, Burr needed a massive infusion of cash. He therefore began to negotiate with Frank Lorenzo to sell People and Frontier to Texas Air. On September 15, Lorenzo and Burr made a rare public appearance together to announce that Burr had agreed to sell People Express to Texas Air for about $125 million in securities, and to sell Frontier to them for an additional $176 million. Burr's dream had died a quiet, unmourned death.

Airline deregulation created Donald Burr and People Express. And it destroyed them. Burr himself recognized that, saying: "If not for deregulation there never would have been a People Express. There never would have been a goad to the system." But he also understood that People Express ultimately reached a point where it could not compete with high-tech airlines like American, with its sophisticated computer system. After leaving Texas Air management in April 1987, Burr had a good deal of time on his hands, and he occupied himself by giving speeches for $10,000 an appearance and writing a book on his airline experience. He continued to believe in the management approach he employed at People. "People Express was a lesson in freedom in corporate behavior," he told *Business Week* (January 16, 1989). "Yet people say to me all the time: 'That stuff doesn't work. That's all touchy-feely.' But that's why we came out of nowhere and grew to be the fifth-largest airline in the country."

George L. Gitner, People's cofounder and first president—and also the first to leave—commented when Burr sold the airline: "Participative management was supposed to be a means to an end: a profitable company. Burr forgot about the end. He thought management was his strong suit, but the results speak for themselves." *Maclean's* quoted an industry insider in 1983 about Burr: "Everyone admires Burr and his airline. He has done exceptionally well. . . . But over the years we have seen these cut-price people come and go. Eventually, People Express will go." And it did. (**B.** *Fortune*, March 2, 1982; *Newsweek*, April 4, 1983, October 21, 1985, July 7, September 29, 1986; *Forbes*, April 25, 1983, May 6, 1985; *Christian Science Monitor*, December 19, 1983; *New York Times*, June 5, November 2, 1983, September 9, 1984, March 9, July 11, September 23, 1986; *Maclean's*, August 8, 1983; *Inc.*, January 1984; *New York Times Magazine*, December 23, 1984; *Time*, January 7, 1985; *Business Week*, January 28, November 25, 1985, December 19, 1988, January 16, 1989; *Contemporary Newsmakers*, 1985; *Current Biography*, 1986; Robert Levering, et al., *The 100*

Best Companies to Work for in America, 1984; Charles Garfield, *Peak Performers*, 1986; Thomas J. Peters, *A Passion for Excellence*, 1986; A. David Silver, *Entrepreneurial Megabucks*, 1986; R. E. G. Davies, *Rebels and Reformers of the Airways*, 1987.)

BURRELL, THOMAS J. (March 18, 1939–). Advertising agency founder, Burrell Advertising Incorporated. The television ad for Crest toothpaste showed a black father lovingly teaching his son how to knot a tie—a simple message, one most whites would find familiar and unremarkable. But this kind of sensitivity to the emotional needs of the black market has made the Burrell Advertising Agency the largest black-owned agency in the United States. Thomas Burrell, the agency's founder, continually makes the point that white agencies do not know how to reach the black market. Since 40 percent of blacks grow up in fatherless households, it is necessary to present an image to them, not of what is, but of what it could and should be. Most white advertisers, he claimed, missed this important emotional point when dealing with blacks. Thus, emotional appeal became the hallmark of Burrell's advertising approach. He often noted that "to reach the purse strings, you must first touch the heartstrings."

Thomas Burrell was born in Chicago and educated in the city's public schools. He attended Chicago's Roosevelt University, where he graduated with a degree in English in 1961. About a year before graduating, Burrell joined the now-defunct Wade Advertising Agency of Chicago as a mailroom clerk. Burrell, who always wanted to be a writer, became a copy trainee at the agency, and after graduating he was promoted to copywriter. At the time, Wade, as was true of all other white-owned agencies, paid virtually no attention to the black market. It was, therefore, a big breakthrough for Burrell, and for the black community overall, when he landed the Toni account, which was attempting to market a hair product to black women. "There wasn't much of that going around then," he said.

In 1964, Burrell moved on to the giant Leo Burnett Company of Chicago as a copywriter. There he found that "there wasn't much acknowledgement that there was a black consumer market. The only thing they ever heard was television reaches everybody." This was characteristic of highly successful large agencies in the 1960s. They were so imbued with the magic of communications technology, so caught up in the concept of a homogeneous American marketplace, that they simply gave no thought to a segmented market approach. It was not just that the black market was ignored; there was no recognition that one needed to develop alternative approaches to market goods effectively. America was the melting pot, and television was the crucible in which everybody was reduced to a common denominator. But blacks and advertising had been a particularly nettlesome area for some time.

During the 1940s, a few pioneer black admen started their own agencies in New York, Detroit, and Chicago. They serviced a profoundly limited market— selling black products through the black media to black customers. None of these agencies achieved significant size. The major white agencies had little interest in the black market, and they hired very few blacks. The first white agency to recognize that there might be a special market niche for blacks was Batten, Barton, Durstin and Osborn in the 1950s. They started a "special markets" unit staffed by blacks to sell to blacks. The few blacks hired at other agencies during the 1950s were simply so good that their credentials outweighed their color and they were assigned to work on general accounts. By the early 1960s, when Thomas Burrell broke into advertising, a survey by the Urban League showed there were fewer than twenty-five blacks working at creative or executive jobs in the top ten agencies. Whites simply dismissed the problem by claiming they did not hire blacks because there were so few qualified black applicants.

By the mid–1960s, civil rights pressures for the hiring of blacks had intensified, resulting in a slight increase in blacks at white-owned agencies. The push by civil rights organizations in the later 1960s, though, went beyond a demand merely to hire more blacks. They began to demand that more blacks be shown in the agencies' ads and that greater sensitivity in the advertising copy be directed toward blacks. They also demanded that the old white stereotypes of blacks— Aunt Jemima, the Gold Dust twins, Cream of Wheat's smiling black chef, and Hiram Walker's butler—be erased because all of them either depicted blacks in demeaning service roles or perpetuated the image of blacks as smiling, happy "pickaninnies" in a way that was extremely offensive to the black community. The black organizations had some success in their campaign; Doyle Dane Bernbach, headed by William Bernbach,[†] led the way. DDB's ad for Levy's Jewish rye bread, showing a picture of a smiling black child with the caption "You don't have to be Jewish to love Levy's" won praise from the black community. Malcolm X, the black militant, was so impressed that he told a photographer: "Take my picture by this sign, I like it."

Heavy pressure was mounted by the Congress of Racial Equality on Proctor & Gamble, Coca-Cola, Colgate-Palmolive, and other major advertisers to develop more sensitive advertising campaigns aimed at blacks. The subtext of these demands was the necessity to hire more blacks to handle these campaigns, since only they understood the unique cultural role of blacks in America. Progress came, but it came very slowly during the 1960s. A survey of ads run in New York, monitored by the New York City Commission on Human Rights, showed that just 314 of the 7,340 commercials in the city during 1966 and 1967 had blacks represented in them—just 4 percent of the total. There was also minimal progress in securing employment of blacks in white-owned agencies. An Equal Employment Opportunity Commission study in 1966 showed that just 2.5 percent of the white-collar jobs at sixty-four New York agencies were held by blacks, even though blacks made up over 18 percent of the city's population. At the largest ad agencies, blacks fared even more poorly, where they accounted for just 1.9 percent of the total.

Consequently, Thomas Burrell, during these years, was in a lonely and often ignored situation. In 1967 he left Leo Burnett to become a copywriter in the

London office of Foote, Cone & Belding, and a year later he returned to the United States as copy supervisor at Needham, Harper & Steers. Although Burrell was advancing in a largely lily-white advertising community, he was not happy with the kind of work he was doing, nor was he impressed with the ads Needham, Harper and other white agencies were producing. Even though the murder of Martin Luther King in 1968 had brought about a characteristic surge of concern for blacks, with a flood of ads and pious statements, blacks already employed in advertising decided to organize themselves, and they started the Group for Advertising Progress. The message was clear: "You white advertising folks are a lot happier about the progress of integration than us black advertising folks."

No matter what small gains were made, by then it seemed far too little and too late for many blacks in advertising. Edgar Hopper, a former account executive at Foote, Cone & Belding said, "We have to become black Anglo Saxons to make it. If you let your hair grow out, you're Rap Brown. Speak out and you're coming on too strong." Hopper, Burrell, and others insisted that "When you hire a black creative person, hire him for his lifestyle, not because you want him to imitate the white." As this sense of nationalist pride grew in the late 1960s and early 1970s, several blacks, Thomas Burrell among them, decided to open their own agencies. In 1971, Burrell left Needham, Harper and along with two associates rented a small, one-room office in Chicago to house his Burrell McBain Advertising Agency. "We had no secretary, one telephone, and three old desks," he recalled, "which we painted red, green, and orange." He then waited six agonizing months before he got their first piece of business, which paid the agency a piddling $3,000 a month. But they were finally on their way. Burrell Advertising was one of about a dozen black-owned agencies spawned during the early 1970s to operate on a nationwide basis. Some failed, and some survived, but Burrell's became the largest, by far.

The key to Burrell's success was the pitch he used with white advertisers. He argued that blacks were "not just dark-skinned white people," but a group with a unique heritage, with distinctly different tastes and formidable buying power. Furthermore, the best way to reach this black market, he argued, was not with a sales pitch oriented toward the product, which was characteristic of most white advertising, but with a form of life-style advertising to create and celebrate a positive, uplifting image of black people which, at the same time, reflected positively upon the product. He warned advertisers who were beginning to use increasing numbers of blacks in their ads that this was a path fraught with dangers. "As soon as a black face appears on the screen," he said, "it's 'Okay. How you gonna be usin' us now?' White people don't have to go through that."

From the start, Burrell determined to go after only big clients, and his big breakthrough came in 1972 when he garnered the Coca-Cola soft-drink account for the black market. Burrell was invaluable in the early years in providing Coca-Cola with insights into the black market. In 1974 Coke decided to run a campaign entitled "Look up America and see what you've got." Burrell did not think it would work in the black community. He argued that the time had not yet come when blacks could take pride in the American experience. So he persuaded them to run ads that said, "For the real times, it's the real thing." Burrell also picked up the McDonald's black advertising account in the 1970s. At that time, McDonald's slogan in the white community was "You deserve a break today." This, argued Burrell, implied that going to McDonald's was a special dining treat. But in the black neighborhoods, "kids were running into [McDonald's] four and five times a day." As a result, Burrell substituted the theme "Mc-Donald's is good to have around" for the black market. Burrell also lined up a number of other blue chip firms, including Ford Motor Company and Stroh's Brewery. The only black-owned businesses among his client mix were Johnson Publishing, Chicago-based publisher of *Ebony* and *Jet*, and Johnson Products, a Chicago hair products manufacturer. Burrell pointed out that, although he did not pursue black businesses, he did not turn them away either.

By the early 1980s, Burrell had used this strategy to build Burrell Advertising into an agency with $30 million in bookings. It was still a midget compared to huge international agencies like J. Walter Thompson, which had U.S. billings of about $1.5 billion. Compared to most other black agencies, however, Burrell was huge. Only Uniworld, started by Byron Lewis, and Mingo-Jones, established by Frank Mingo, both in New York, even approached Burrell's size.

Despite Burrell's impressive earlier growth, 1983 was a major turning point for the agency. In that year, they began to escape the "black ghetto" in which all black agencies had been confined, and they acquired accounts to service the broad general market. The first step in this important watershed came with Burrell's acquisition of Proctor & Gamble's Crest account for the black market. Heretofore, the account had been handled by Benton & Bowles, which had argued that its ads reached the white and black markets equally well. Burrell convinced P&G's management that blacks' "behavior is different and interests are different, [and] that can certainly translate into different buying habits, different brand preference, different ways of looking at a particular product category or a particular brand." This persuasive argument was enough to win the Crest account, and Burrell was well aware of its significance: "The acquisition of [a P&G account] was the major package-goods consumer company in the U.S. saying that the black consumer market was big enough, important enough and unique enough to require a special effort. That was the first step out of the quick-service restaurant, soft-drink, and distilled-spirits categories," which along with cigarettes made up the bulk of products advertised to blacks.

More important, however, was a smaller account Burrell picked up that year: Brown-Forman's Jos. Garneau Co.'s Martell Cognac. For some time, the advertising for Martell's cognac had been split between Benton & Bowles, which produced advertising for the white market, and Burrell, which handled the black market. In late 1983, Burrell made a bid to consolidate the entire $2.5 million ad budget in his shop. He developed an integrated advertising program that changed the cognac advertising from what was called the big-bottle approach, print ads dominated by a large photo of the bottle, to Burrell's familiar life-style advertising. Burrell came up with an "I assume you drink Martell" campaign, which was originally used for the black market with great success. When Brown-Forman found that Burrell's ad tested better than B&B's in the general market, black models replaced white models, and the ad ran very successfully.

With the success of the Martell ads, Brown-Forman gave Burrell an assignment in 1984 to develop ads for its Jack Daniel Distillery. Jack Daniel, an old, white, Southern company in Lynchburg, Tennessee, was given a new image by Burrell. Whereas earlier ads had stressed models dressed in upwardly mobile attire, Burrell instead stressed Jack Daniel's lineage, its heritage, and its quality in a highly successful series of long-copy, product-oriented ads. Burrell's success in landing these general market accounts stemmed from his conviction and argument that not only are white agencies unable to understand the nuances of black culture and the black market, but that black agencies are uniquely qualified to deal with the white market. Black consumers, explained Burrell, are "a much more complex and more sensitive audience" than white consumers. "If I can sell to black consumers," he argued, "I can sell to anybody." Therefore, contrary to what had been conventional wisdom in the advertising community, Burrell felt that the special sensitivity needed to reach black consumers made it more likely that a campaign developed for a black audience could be used successfully for white, rather than the reverse. According to Burrell:

Blacks, in order to be successful, have to know the white world and culture. I had to when I worked at Leo Burnett and had to sell Robin Hood flour to whites in West Virginia. But whites can live their white lives and never know anything about the black world. And that's why we wouldn't have any problems with general-market advertising. (*Advertising Age*)

In addition to the Crest and Brown-Forman accounts, Burrell regained the Coca-Cola account in a big way in 1983. Coca-Cola had been one of his earliest accounts, but it had been lost to another agency. Burrell, however, became the beneficiary of the confluence of a number of forces in the early 1980s. Jesse Jackson's black activist Operation PUSH lobbied Coca-Cola to increase its ad spending in the black community and to use black agencies more extensively. The soft-drink company responded by naming Burrell as its worldwide agency of record for black consumer advertising for its food and soft-drink brands. The contract was worth about $7.5 million annually, which was by far the largest account Burrell had landed to that point. Part of the goal of Coca-Cola was to reach new markets—in this case, the vast black population on the African continent, especially in Nigeria.

Burrell first led a fact-finding tour through several African markets, and then he began to design a comprehensive worldwide program to meet these needs. Ira C. Herbert, Coca-Cola's executive vice president noted: "This is believed to be the first time a black-owned agency has received international agency of record status for all brands of a major consumer products company." Burrell, for his part, said he was pleased to be a pioneer in the concept of reaching blacks on a worldwide basis. "We see potential for other American marketers as well as those who do business in parts of the world populated by blacks." The Coca-Cola account, plus the other new business, pushed Burrell's billings to $40 million in 1984, one-third higher than the year before. In 1985 they went past $50 million. The plans for Coca-Cola in Nigeria, however, hit a snag when a military coup in 1984 dashed all hopes of developing a campaign for that country.

Burrell compensated for that loss by increased effective advertising for the black market in the United States. A particularly effective series of ads for Coke in 1985 featured five black kids on a Manhattan stoop singing the "Coke adds life" jingle. This spot won a Clio, the advertising industry's equivalent of an Oscar, for Burrell. He also won a Clio for his McDonald's ads. In 1985, Burrell picked up yet another new client—Beatrice Co., the giant Chicago-based food conglomerate, one of America's biggest advertisers, with total billings of some $680 million. Burrell argued that America's 30 million blacks spent about $23 billion a year on food, and no one was doing a good job of reaching that market. Beatrice, convinced by his argument, gave Burrell a large account. As a result of all these accomplishments, Burrell was named the Advertising Person of the Year by the Chicago Advertising Club in 1985.

By the late 1980s, not only was Burrell Advertising the largest black-owned agency in America, but Thomas Burrell had done much to change the nature of advertising and marketing in the United States. His effective campaigns had shown companies how to better reach the black market and in the process had greatly enhanced their market share there. A good example was McDonald's, a longtime Burrell client. His decade-long campaign to win the black community over to McDonald's was an outstanding success. Although blacks composed just 12 percent of the nation's population, they accounted for 20 percent of Mc-Donald's business by 1986. "All of a sudden," said Chuck Wimbley, Burrell's director of account services, "blacks are being talked to," and advertisers were finding an untapped gold mine. The country's 30 million blacks had an estimated annual income of $203 billion; if they were a separate nation, they would rank twelfth in buying power in the free world. For decades they were taken for granted by the white corporate world. Thomas Burrell and his black advertising cohorts were crucial in creating an awareness of this vast, important market.

Even with his success, however, Burrell often experiences frustration. Frequently, when he calls upon a potential general market client with six members of his staff to make a presentation, the client will remark, "You must have brought your whole staff." That is a common perception: since it is a black agency serving a niche market, it must be tiny. Burrell responds, "No, these are seven of our 115 employees." Burrell has great hopes for the continuing expansion of his agency and sees his own role in that expansion very clearly:

My duty is very narrow and very simple. My job, no matter what size this agency gets to be, is to be in charge of quality control for the product that we manufacture, which is advertising. I have always been inclined that way and I think it is key to the success of the agency. (*Black Enterprise*)

(**B.** *Advertising Age*, April 11, 1966, October 30, 1967, January 22, March 25, May 27, 1968, May 5, 1969, March 1, 1982, January 24, 1983, September 17, 1984, December 19, 1985; Stephen Fox, *The Mirror Makers*, 1984; *Black Enterprise*, January, December, 1985; *Fortune*, September 2, 1985; *Jet*, December 16, 1985; *Newsweek*, February 10, 1986; *Who's Who among Black Americans*, 1986.)

C

CARTER, EDWARD WILLIAM (1912?–). Chain retailer, Broadway-Hale Stores; Carter Hawley Hale. A good portion of the credit (or blame) for what America had become by the 1980s must be given to a rather obscure man: Edward Carter, head of the largest retailing chain in the American West for a number of years. Taking over the Broadway Stores in Los Angeles in 1946, he transformed them into a retailing giant—one which set important patterns of American retailing and suburban development in the postwar years. Reflecting on the situation in the late 1940s, Carter said:

I knew the nation would prosper, even though others cried depression. I was sure the affluence of the country would increase and that goods, being the symbol of affluence, would experience increased demand. Partly because I studied my statistics, and partly because of my gut feeling, I also knew California would grow faster than the rest of the country. We developed the first shopping center in 1947 because I realized the retailing consequences of the movement to the suburbs. (*Forbes*)

Personal information about Edward Carter is scarce. Born in Maryland, he graduated from UCLA in 1932, working as a clothing salesman to put himself through school. He spent a year at the Harvard Graduate School of Business, where he received his MBA cum laude in 1937. Carter joined May Department Stores, the large California department store chain, the following year. By the time he was thirty-four years old, Carter was making $60,000 annually as merchandise manager for the firm, in charge of one-third of the West Coast division's retail departments. In 1946 he took a $10,000 pay cut, in return for potentially lucrative stock options, to join the Broadway Company, a relatively stagnant Los Angeles department store chain. As Carter said at that time, the Broadway stores were ''last among Los Angeles department stores both in size and stature.''

The first Broadway store had been opened fifty years earlier, in 1896, by Arthur Lett, an English immigrant. The company built a large store in downtown Los Angeles and had two smaller branch stores by the end of World War II, with annual sales of $30 million. When Letts died, his estate sold the small chain to Blyth & Co., a San Francisco investment banking firm, who chose Carter to transform the Broadway into a significant competitive force. The first thing Carter did was to double the size (and cost) of a small new branch store then under construction and to convert it into a national prototype of the regional shopping center, with ample parking, underground deliveries, and competing stores in the same complex. This daring experiment in 1946–1947 proved to be a great success for a number of reasons: with more people moving to the suburbs, it was easier to find quality help if you were located in the suburban areas where they lived; it was possible to acquire spacious grounds for stores and parking for a lower initial outlay per acre; and taxes were less.

With the success of his suburban operation, Carter began to think in terms of what he called a regional chain. In his mind, ''[R]egional chains are the coming thing, because they have the strength of size that a big chain has, yet are responsive to local demand.'' A key ingredient in this, something that made Carter's regional chain concept so different from earlier department store chains, was his desire to downgrade the status of the downtown store. Traditionally, the downtown store was the ''anchor,'' the ''mother'' store for the chain; the outlying stores were simply satellites. In Carter's vision, however, each of these units, both downtown and suburban, should be a strong outpost with its own distinct marketing area. Furthermore, he felt that Los Angeles was an ideal area for the development of this concept. It was (and remains) probably the most suburbanized city in the world. Equally important, it was a region where tastes and buying habits were fairly uniform.

Carter felt that the regional chain had certain advantages that would give it a significant competitive edge over its rivals. Its enhanced size would allow it to have more buying and merchandising power, more efficient promotion, better command of prime money markets, the ability to acquire the talents of better trained executives, and the capacity to hire better help in the suburban areas. One of the keys for Carter's development of the Broadway chain was to centralize the warehouse facilities. He decreed in the early years that no store should be more than thirty-five miles from the chain's central warehouse. To this end, he built a 600,000-square-foot warehouse to service all the Broadway stores in the Los Angeles area. The regional chain concept, with the shopping center as its key ingredient, became enormously successful, and the Los Angeles area soon was dotted with Broadway stores. Starting with three stores in 1946, by 1957 there were eight, and a 1.15-million-square-foot ''super store'' was being built in the Del Amo shopping center. By 1980, there were forty-seven Broadway stores in the Los Angeles suburbs, the largest single department store group in the United States.

Carter wanted to expand his regional concept beyond the Los Angeles area. He particularly wanted to invade the rich northern California–San Francisco market. Unable to do so directly with his Broadway stores, Carter in 1950 engineered a merger with the Hale Bros. chain, whose operations included the

Weinstock department store in Sacramento. Although this move was successful in certain respects, in that it allowed Carter to escape the confines of the Los Angeles area and thereby become a major retailer on the American scene, it also forced him to abandon many of the principles that made the Broadway such a success in southern California. Unlike Los Angeles, San Francisco and the surrounding area was not uniform and homogeneous. Nor was it served by a single newspaper. Therefore, while the Broadway group in southern California grew and prospered greatly during the 1950s and 1960s, the Hale stores were relatively stagnant. As a result, the Hale stores ultimately were closed. Expansion in northern California was accomplished through the Weinstock stores, which had ten stores by the end of the 1970s. The chain, called Broadway-Hale Stores, had $137 million in sales by 1957.

During the 1960s, the Broadway-Hale chain continued to grow under Carter's guidance. By the mid–1960s it had become the West Coast's largest department store chain with thirty stores and sales of $220 million. Carter also suffered frustrations in the mid–1960s. After acquiring the Marston stores in San Diego, along with the Korrick group in Phoenix, the Federal Trade Commission (FTC) intervened. In 1962 the FTC ruled that Broadway-Hale had to agree not to purchase any additional department stores for five years. Carter regarded the ruling as a serious blow to his plans, since he felt that the growth of the Broadway stores in the Los Angeles area was already being curtailed by the expansion of such national chains as J. C. Penney and Sears, Roebuck. When the FTC restriction was lifted in the late 1960s, Carter brought his chain into another era of expansion, one which fundamentally changed its focus.

Carter had always had an unerring sense of the market he was attempting to reach with his stores during the twenty-two-year period from 1946 to 1968. He was so astute that his longtime partner, P. C. Hale, called him a "master of the intangibles of retailing." Carter aimed his stores squarely at the middle-income shopper who was moving to the suburbs in the 1950s and 1960s. Thus, he made sure that his stores reflected the character of the inhabitants of these new suburban developments and that his merchandise was, in his words, "not the highest fashion, but in good taste." His stores were designed to be regional equivalents of such national chains as Sears and J. C. Penney. By being regional, however, Carter tried to avoid the sense of absentee ownership. Instead, his stores were designed "not to look like a chain store, either to the customers or to the community."

By the end of the 1960s, the suburbs were changing. American society was becoming increasingly affluent, and the most promising retail market was the growing number of upper-middle-class families. Carter undertook a twofold approach in reaching this market. The first was slowly and subtly to upgrade the merchandise in his existing stores. As Carter said, "We upgrade taste and quality, right along with improvements in our customer's discretionary spending ability." It sounded simple and straightforward, but it is, in fact, one of the most difficult things for a mass retailer to accomplish. Only a few stores, such as Bloomingdale's in New York City and G. Fox & Co. in Hartford, have been able to upgrade themselves to bring in higher income customers without alienating their original clientele.

Carter purchased a controlling interest in San Francisco's Emporium Capwell, the Bay Area's largest department store chain, in 1967. Broadway-Hale had owned a portion of it since 1950, but gaining full control of it greatly increased the firm's retailing presence in that important market. Broadway-Hale's most important and controversial acquisition occurred in 1968, when it took over Neiman-Marcus, the tony Dallas specialty store. Broadway-Hale also diversified in other ways in 1968, by taking over Waldenbooks, a chain of bookstores, and establishing a mail-order business. This activity brought a great explosion in growth for the chain. Sales, which stood at $220 million in 1964, skyrocketed to $640 million in 1969.

These acquisitions were immediately successful. During the next five years, Broadway-Hale tripled its sales, growing from a regional department store chain into a major national retailer. Carter expanded Neiman-Marcus beyond its traditional Texas boundaries into Bal Harbor, Florida, and Atlanta, Georgia, in the first three years, and by the end of the 1970s had a total of nine Neiman-Marcus stores. In so doing, however, much of the unique appeal and service that had characterized the Dallas-based carriage-trade store disappeared. Its profits, on the other hand, which had languished for years under the flamboyant management of Stanley Marcus,[†] rebounded impressively under Carter. In 1972, Carter acquired Bergdorf-Goodman, a posh New York fashion emporium that had also lost its instinct for profit, with plans to establish branches of that store in other parts of the United States. In 1974 Carter bought Holt-Renfrew & Co. of Canada, that country's most prestigious retailer. Finally, Carter did something that was in many respects a contradiction of his earlier philosophy: he began construction of the Broadway's big, new flagship store in downtown Los Angeles. For the man who staked the growth of his chain on the suburbs and who built the regional department chain concept around the idea of not having a downtown flagship store, it was a stunning turnabout. The plain-Jane suburban retailer now owned some of America's most prestigious specialty stores, and he turned his major effort toward the creation of the kind of downtown department store that had characterized nineteenth-century retailing.

Built in what was called Broadway Plaza, Carter's new development covered an entire city block and contained a new 240,000-square-foot Broadway store, a 500-room Hyatt House Hotel, a 32-storied office building, a 2,000-car garage, and a two-level shopping mall. Carter cautioned, however, that "[t]his doesn't necessarily mean we're creating a whole new wave of downtown department stores, but if a similar opportunity existed in another city, we might be interested." In any event, by 1974 it was clear that the chain Carter had created had greatly changed. This was symbolized by a new name: Carter Hawley Hale Stores, made up of the names of Edward Carter, Prentis Hale, and the chain's new president, Philip M. Hawley. Asked why the change was made, Carter replied that the Broadway name, which stands for "regional and medium-priced department stores" was not appropriate for a company which owned the likes of Neiman-Marcus and Bergdorf-Goodman. A competitor, however, thought a better name might be Ego, Inc.

In 1977 Edward Carter stepped down as chief executive officer of Carter Hawley Hale (CHH), remaining chairman emeritus. The corporate reins were handed to Philip Hawley, who experienced nothing but difficulty during the following decade. He inherited a chain that no longer had the magic profitability of Carter's early years. Carter's repeated acquisitions of money-losing stores and chains, entities which had to be turned around by CHH's tight-fisted management policies, eroded profits. This was not enhanced by Hawley's acquisition of John Wanamaker's sixteen department stores in Philadelphia or the twenty-six-store Thalhimers chain in Virginia and North Carolina. The latter was just marginally profitable; the former continued to lose money at a staggering rate. By 1980, it was clear that something had to be done. Many analysts criticized CHH for "mindless expansion," and Hawley promised, in 1979, that he would cease any further acquisitions. Instead, he committed himself to making the chain's existing entities profitable and competitive. He particularly had to battle the great incursions of Macy's and Mervyn's (owned by Dayton-Hudson) into their West Coast backyard. While CHH had been occupied with expanding itself into a national chain, other firms had moved into its home market and were taking a significant portion of its business. Inventory turnover, which had been one of Edward Carter's great keys of success with the Broadway stores in the 1950s, was lagging woefully behind by 1980. Nonetheless, with sales of $2.4 billion, CHH was the nation's fourth-largest department store chain with profits of $69.7 million.

Hawley's program for the 1980s seemed to be a fulfillment of Edward Carter's blueprint in 1968. Hawley told *Business Week* magazine that he intended to cater to individuals who can afford to satisfy their "ego-gratification." Explaining, he said:

I decided to go after the mid- to upper-income customers; discounting has a place in American retailing, but it is predicated heavily on lowest price, and lowest price begins to be a contest. We think there are more opportunities to set ourselves apart via service in higher quality goods. (*Business Week*)

With the maturing of the baby boomers of the 1960s into the "yuppies" of the 1980s, Hawley appeared to have hit upon a winning idea, but the distance between concept and execution was large.

By 1982, five years into Hawley's tenure, CCH was in deep trouble. The Wanamaker chain continued to lose large sums of money, and they were facing ever greater competition from Macy's Bamberger stores. Even worse, back in its home base of California, where Edward Carter had created a retailing giant, CHH was losing market share. In northern California, their stores were under heavy siege from Macy's San Francisco and from Mervyn's. By the early 1980s, the thirty-three CHH stores in northern California were grossing about $750 million annually, versus the $900 million generated by the twenty-six Macy's stores. A far bigger problem, however, existed in southern California. There, the forty-one Broadway stores, the cornerstone of the chain, were losing market share to Robinson's, Bullock's, and May Company. The situation in the Los Angeles area illustrated well the kind of problems CHH was having. In an effort to reach the affluent consumer Hawley had decided to woo in the late 1970s, the chain had introduced lines of high-margin sportswear into their stores and virtually ignored the customers who had been at the core of their business for years—the middle class who purchased moderately priced apparel. The Broadway had marginal success in this attempt. Ironically, Bullock's and Robinson's, which had traditionally dominated the better-goods market, found it easier to move down to pick up the middle-class trade. At the same time, however, the high-fashion and specialty stores, such as Neiman-Marcus, Bergdorf-Goodman, and Holt-Renfrew, did much to justify Carter's faith in them. By 1982, the three were generating $600 million in sales annually; Neiman-Marcus alone had $450 million of that.

Hawley and CHH realized that they had to make changes if they were to survive in the supercharged retailing landscape of the 1980s. As Hawley said at the time:

In the 60's and early 70's, department stores were complacent. The retail pie was big enough for everyone, and we all sliced at it furiously. Then came inflation, recessions, high interest rates and the slowdown of shopping center construction. Everyone was forced to stop and think. (*Apparel Merchandising*)

Before he could take any concrete action, however, the CHH chain came under attack from The Limited, a chain of women's clothing stores. Leslie Wexner,[†] its founder, made a valiant effort to acquire the CHH empire for The Limited, and, in order to ward off this challenge, Hawley had to sell off many of the chain's most successful operations. Neiman-Marcus and Bergdorf-Goodman were sold to General Cinema, Holt-Renfrew to Canadian buyers and Waldenbooks to K mart. This left CHH with its five regional chains of department stores, operations which had led a troubled existence throughout the 1970s and 1980s. The stripped-down CHH in 1987 had sales of $2.77 billion (a 30-percent drop from 1986) and losses of $115 million.

Hawley claimed that CHH was finally going to turn the corner and find success again after so many troubled years. It was, in effect, going to go back to its successful strategy of the 1950s and 1960s—selling goods to middle-class consumers in plain-Jane department stores. But the retail world had changed greatly over the intervening twenty years. Discounters had emerged at the low end of the market, which is where many middle-class Americans had shopped for years.

Yet, CHH, among all major retailers, was the least likely to mark down merchandise. If these customers were to be wooed back to the department stores, it had to be on the basis of service, not price. Hawley recognized this by saying, "Service is first, middle, and last. It's the critical issue we are going to win or not win on." Yet, the CHH stores, especially the Broadway stores in Los Angeles, were infamous for their poor service—often characterized by gum-popping "Valley girl" part-timers. It would involve a wrenching change of "culture" for the chain. Even if they did change, they would have to face the incursion of the Seattle-based Nordstrom's department stores into their area, which based its success on exceptional service. The chances of success for CHH and Hawley in this area were perhaps best summarized by an ex-manager in the chain: "Carter Hawley had been in transition for an awfully long time. As a company we've been challenged for years to get profits to the bottom line."

As the 1980s came to an end, Ed Carter quietly watched the great retail empire he built disintegrate. Yet he never uttered a word of protest or criticism of his successor. Instead, he put his time and effort into civic affairs in Los Angeles. Involved as a regent of the University of California, a trustee of the Brookings Institution, and the chairman of the Los Angeles County Museum of Art, Carter served as a major fund-raiser in the city. Franklin D. Murphy, chairman of the Times-Mirror Company said of him: "If somebody wants to get something done in this city, and if he can get Ed Carter involved, then he's got a good guarantee of success." Perhaps Carter Hawley Hale should not have forced Edward Carter into mandatory retirement at the age of sixty-five. (**B.** *Business Week,* March 30, 1957, May 27, 1967, April 15, 1972, September 6, 1980, May 31, 1982, December 22, 1986, March 14, 1988; *Time*, September 24, 1965; *Forbes*, March 15, 1970, April 28, 1980, June 16, 1986; Milton Moskowitz et al., *Everybody's Business*, 1980; *Apparel Merchandising*, March 1984; *Chain Store Age*, June 1985; *Fortune*, April 27, 1987, April 11, 1988.)

CATERPILLAR TRACTOR: LOUIS BONTZ NEUMILLER (1896–?); WILLIAM BLACKIE (1906–?); LEE LAVERNE MORGAN (January 20, 1920–   ); and GEORGE ANTHONY SCHAEFER (June 13, 1928–   ).

Earth-moving equipment company executives, Caterpillar Tractor Company. Caterpillar, for over eight years, has been the dominant company in the world in its field. It has dominated the market for earth-moving equipment like General Motors once dominated the world automobile market, IBM the world computer market, and Coca-Cola the soft drink field. Its eminence was so great and its managerial expertise so widely recognized that Thomas J. Peters and Robert H. Waterman, Jr., chose Caterpillar as one of the "excellent" companies in their best-selling *In Search of Excellence.* Yet, if most people recognize the characteristically yellow Cat equipment at construction sites, few have ever heard of the company's executives. Mostly modest Midwesterners, the corporate culture at Caterpillar dictated they keep a low profile. As former Caterpillar chief executive Lee Morgan recognized: "This is no place for individual star performers. We encourage an uncommon amount of subordination of personal wishes to the good of the company." His successor as chief executive officer (CEO), George Schaefer, had an even more humbling experience. He had so low a profile that a local newspaper failed to list him among the contenders for the CEO position, and when he informed his wife that he did get the job, he found it hard to convince her that he actually had won the position. As a result, there is much information on the company itself, but far less on the men who have guided it to its present position. This entry focuses on the four men who have been in power during the times of critical transitions at Caterpillar.

Caterpillar's origins reach back to 1904 when farmers in the Sacramento Valley of California were having problems. Although the soil was remarkably fertile, it was also very soft. In order to work this land profitably, farmers wanted to use even larger farm implements, which, in turn, demanded larger and heavier steam tractors. Some of these steam tractors weighed twenty tons, and even though they were supplied with increasingly larger drive wheels, some of them still sank hopelessly into the soil. Benjamin Holt, of Holt Manufacturing, a farm implement manufacturer that had been founded in Stockton in the 1880s, decided to tackle the problem. He hit upon the idea of running the machine on tracks, like a train, except that the machine would lay its own track ahead of itself. In this way, the tractor, running on this circular track, had a continuous broad base beneath it as it moved, which distributed the weight over a much greater area than was possible with wheels. Holt developed the "Caterpillar" trademark for his new invention, and he used it for many of the items in his line.

With the success of his invention in California and elsewhere, Holt decided to expand his operations, and he wanted to find a more centrally located plant. He discovered this in Peoria, Illinois, in 1909, when his firm purchased a former steam tractor factory there. He began to manufacture gasoline-powered Caterpillar tractors in that location, and by 1915 there were more than 2,000 of them operating in twenty countries. World War I provided a big boost for Caterpillar, when it became the standard artillery and supply tractor for the Allied forces. Most important, the war opened a whole new market for Caterpillar—the construction industry—as the U.S. government turned its surplus tractors over to state and county governments for road work after the war.

The end of the war brought hard times for Holt Manufacturing. By this time old Benjamin Holt had died, the company was burdened with a good deal of short-term debt, and strong new competition had emerged. One of the most formidable of these was C. L. Best Tractor of San Leandro, California. To lessen this threat, a San Francisco stockbroker proposed and then arranged a merger between the two companies in 1925. The Caterpillar name was retained for the merged company's products, and the headquarters was moved to the Peoria plant. Raymond C. Force, one of the officers of the Best company, was named president. The newly merged company had sales of $13.8 million in its first year of operation.

Force made an important decision for Caterpillar in the late 1920s. At a time of agricultural depression, when other farm implement manufacturers were diversifying into full-line farm implement producers, Force decided to move Caterpillar's focus outside the farm industry. Honing in on construction, earthmoving, and other industrial areas, Force guided Caterpillar to great prosperity in the late 1920s. By 1929, sales had increased to $51.8 million, an almost fourfold increase. The depression of the 1930s, however, had a negative impact on construction projects, and Caterpillar's sales suffered their first decline. To reduce costs, all tractor manufacturing was moved to Peoria, and other cost-cutting measures were adopted. But the slide in sales was devastating. In 1932, sales stood at a mere $13.3 million, and the company failed to earn a profit—the only year in its history, until the 1980s, that it failed to do so.

Nonetheless, the foundation for Caterpillar's later great success was laid during this time. Force's decision to emphasize the construction industry began to bear fruit, even in the late 1930s, as various large-scale government construction projects created a demand for their product. Also, during this time Force and his successor, B. C. Heacock, decided they would not compete on the basis of price, but rather would emphasize premium quality products. This was a difficult decision at a time when the market was depressed and the temptation for price-cutting was strong. But they recognized that their customers were concerned primarily with the dependability of their product—about how much downtime there would be. So, Caterpillar began making a high-quality, premium-priced product, which would have fewer breakdowns. During this time, the company also began to lay the foundations of a dealership and parts-supply network that ultimately could deliver a spare part anywhere in the world within twenty-four hours. Its dealer organization became perhaps the best of any industry, anywhere in the world. As one of Caterpillar's competitors admitted: "The Cat dealer is the one man you have to beat everywhere. Cat's dealer organization is simply fabulous." Meanwhile, Caterpillar's interest in the farm market continued to diminish during the late 1930s, and it concentrated its energies on making machines to move earth. Caterpillar made a fundamentally important decision to specialize—to emphasize depth rather than breadth. Finally, the Caterpillar executives made one more important decision—they began to pursue overseas markets. Benefiting particularly from the five-year plans, Caterpillar sold $18 million worth of equipment to the Soviet Union; by the latter part of the decade, foreign volume made up 20 percent of sales.

By 1941, when Louis Neumiller became president of Caterpillar, the company was well developed along many lines. With sales of over $100 million that year, with a strong reputation for quality, and with a dominant position on the world market, Caterpillar was already an important company. Nonetheless, it was Neumiller who was responsible during his twenty years as chief executive for giving the company its distinctive personality. Neumiller, a local boy, was born in Peoria and left fatherless at five years of age. Like so many other Caterpillar executives, he started his career at the tractor firm and patiently worked his way up the ranks. After graduating from high school, Neumiller went to business college in Peoria for a short time and then joined Caterpillar; he worked his way to the top without ever having to leave his hometown.

Neumiller joined Caterpillar in 1915 as an engineer's clerk, just as the great World War I expansion began. Advancing to drafting-room superintendent, when Holt and Best merged in 1925, Neumiller became parts manager and later service manager. Then, in the early 1930s, Neumiller became a sales executive. Explaining his own ascent, Neumiller said that "I always tried to get the desk nearest the boss's door." After Caterpillar had endured a bitter strike with the CIO, which had won the right to represent the firm's workers, Neumiller was appointed to the sensitive job of industrial relations director. He did a good job of calming those troubled waters, and in 1941, when Caterpillar needed a new president, Neumiller was the logical choice.

As *Fortune* (July, 1963) commented toward the end of Neumiller's career, "[he] imparted to the company much of his own rather folksy idealism and modesty." Neumiller himself indirectly admitted this when he talked of his mission in the early years. "It's been a studied object," he said, "to build a 'we' organization and not an 'I' organization." In turn, he felt Caterpillar's later success "flowed from the building of an organization. Instead of talking about profit, profit, profit all the time, we talked about the atmosphere of the company, and the advantages of that kind of atmosphere. . . . I know that profits flow from able people working wholeheartedly together." Expanding on this philosophy, Neumiller proclaimed: "Product to me is almost an accident if the organization is right." So he set out over the next two decades to build one of the strongest, most successful business organizations in the world.

Caterpillar's business was given an enormous boost when America entered World War II at the end of 1941. The federal government and army ordnance people pressured Caterpillar to convert to ordnance manufacture, but Neumiller resisted, arguing that the army would need earth-moving equipment more than anything else. Then, too, Neumiller thought it was ridiculous for Caterpillar to attempt to make products with which they were unfamiliar. The company's reputation for quality was based on "sticking to its knitting," and he didn't want to disturb that stability. As it turned out, Neumiller was right. The United States desperately needed earth-moving equipment, especially in the Pacific, and Caterpillar sold almost $500 million worth of equipment, including bulldozers, to the government during the war years. But the benefits to Caterpillar went beyond those sales. Caterpillar bulldozers were seen everywhere—even routing enemy pillboxes—and Admiral William Halsey proclaimed that the bulldozer made a major contribution to winning the war in the Pacific. Furthermore, when the war was over, the government simply left thousands of pieces of Caterpillar equipment behind. When these were taken over by the locals, Caterpillar representatives provided free lessons in operating and maintaining the equipment, and they set up parts and dealer networks in the area. This provided the company with millions of dollars of free advertising, and generated a lucrative spare-parts market for the company. Thus, similar to Coca-Cola, Caterpillar and Neumiller were able to use World War II profitably to establish a powerful, worldwide distribution system.

But Caterpillar's most lucrative market in the late 1940s and 1950s was not abroad—it was at home. As America prepared to embark upon the greatest orgy of road and superhighway building in its history, Caterpillar, as the dominant firm in the industry, was ideally placed to take advantage of that boom. In order to service this rapidly growing American market, Caterpillar began building a number of new plants to supplement its facilities in Peoria and San Leandro. The first of the new factories, in Joliet, Illinois, was completed in 1951 to ensure an adequate supply of bulldozer blades, scrapers, attachments, and controls. Over the years, this plant was expanded to three times its original size. In 1955 another new plant was opened in Decatur, Illinois, to make motor graders, wheel tractors, and off-highway trucks. Over time, it also grew to over four times its original size. Three years later, Caterpillar opened another new plant near Aurora, Illinois, to produce a large number of basic machines for the company. This plant tripled in size over the years. During the 1950s, other component plants were opened in Milwaukee, Wisconsin; York, Pennsylvania; and Davenport, Iowa. In 1959, the company also set up an industrial engine plant near Peoria, the first Caterpillar factory designed to produce engines and related items.

Caterpillar's sales, which stood at $242 million at the end of the war, reached $337 million in 1950, with 25,000 employees. Ten years later, revenues were about $730 million, and in 1963, Neumiller's last year in command, Caterpillar sold $827 million worth of equipment. At that point, its nearest competitor, International Harvester, was selling less than one-third as much earth-moving equipment as Caterpillar, which accounted for about one-half of all the sales in that field in the United States. Caterpillar had increasingly become a powerhouse abroad during these years, and by 1963, $369 million of its $827 in sales were overseas. By then, it was one of the three or four biggest exporters among all U.S. companies. Throughout much of this time, nearly all of Caterpillar's foreign sales were supplied from U.S. plants.

Neumiller also instilled Caterpillar with a unique corporate ethic. He provided the company with an atmosphere of "countrified innocence and old-fashioned idealism," in the words of *Fortune* (July 1963), giving it an "industrial version of the Boy Scout law." Many Caterpillar offices were graced with a quotation from Neumiller: "There is but one Caterpillar and wherever it is, you will find it reaching for high levels of quality—standing first and foremost for the rights and dignity of the individual and wishing to make association with the Company a life-satisfying experience."

Neumiller also built an already solid dealer organization into one that was the envy of the industry. By the time he retired, Caterpillar had 258 dealers world-wide, and they employed nearly 30,000 people, just about as many as Caterpillar itself. Neumiller had built the Caterpillar dealer organization the same way in which he had built the firm's internal organization. Since Caterpillar built the most complete line of products of any company in the industry, Neumiller made it possible for Caterpillar dealers to prosper by selling their products exclusively. And prosper they did. Caterpillar products had an almost unique market acceptance, even though they sold for from 5 to 10 percent more than the products of its competitors. As a result, Caterpillar commissions for dealers were also higher, enabling them to grow significantly richer than the distributors of other earth-moving equipment manufacturers. As William Blackie, a former Caterpillar CEO commented: "Caterpillar dealers don't quit. They die rich." By the early 1970s, the average Caterpillar dealer was worth $4 million (compared to less than $1 million for an International Harvester dealer). The franchises were handed down in families, from father to son, so that many were on their third or fourth generation by the 1980s. And Neumiller developed a firm policy of selling their products only through the dealer network. Except for sales to the U.S. government, the Soviet Union, and several others, all sales are made through dealers. Caterpillar does not compete with its dealer network with direct sales outlets.

In other areas, however, Neumiller and Caterpillar were slow to respond to market demand during these years. Neumiller finally set up a sophisticated and well-funded research and development program in the mid–1950s to respond to these pressures. As a result, when Caterpillar finally entered these markets, it was with better machines with greater reliability than their competitors, and they swept the market. "We do it the second or third time," Neumiller said concerning their late entry, "and we do it better." Even though competitors derided the lack of innovation at Caterpillar, calling their products "copy-Cats," the company retained its superiority in virtually every corner of the earth-moving and construction field, selling three times as much as its nearest competitor.

Louis Neumiller was a self-confessed "country boy," and Caterpillar reflected that bucolic atmosphere with its sparse and unpretentious offices. There was no elaborate corporate symbolism, no modern art on the walls. The corporate headquarters was still located next to the factory, so that the sounds of the foundry penetrated the offices on a daily basis. Yet, Caterpillar became a highly sophisticated corporation under Neumiller's regime. Peter Drucker, the high priest of corporate management, said in his *Managing for Results* (1964): "Every business needs a core—an area where it leads. Every business must therefore specialize. But every business must also try to obtain the most from its specialization." It must, in other words, appeal to a broad enough market in order to be profitable and stable. Under Neumiller, Caterpillar made machines that performed a common function but had markets that were incredibly diverse. They were, as *Fortune* (July 1963) put it, the "Gentle Bulldozers of Peoria," and Neumiller was the chief bulldozer. After he retired, Neumiller decided to try his hand at politics, and he was elected to the park's commission in Peoria. The "home boy" never left home.

William Blackie was not a "home boy" or a "country boy" by any stretch of the imagination. Born in Glasgow, Scotland, and educated at the University of Glasgow, he was one of the very few Caterpillar executives to receive a college education. He studied accounting, business law, and economics. More than anyone else, Blackie was responsible for making Caterpillar a multinational corporation. Blackie began his business career in Scotland, but he was frustrated by his lack of advancement. In 1930, at the age of twenty-four, he came to America. Arriving in Chicago, Blackie immediately got a job with the accounting firm of Price, Waterhouse. Blackie remained there as an accountant until 1939, when Caterpillar hired him as comptroller. At that time, the firm was still fairly small, with just two manufacturing plants and sales of $58 million.

Blackie went to Europe in 1946, to check on the dealers servicing the Caterpillar machines left behind after the war. His visit resulted in the company's first overseas venture: a licensing arrangement to manufacture structural items, such as blades and weldments. But until the early 1950s, all of Caterpillar's output for both American and foreign consumption was produced at the big Peoria plant and the smaller one in San Leandro. None of the company's basic machines were manufactured abroad. But a number of circumstances forced it to reconsider its position. With a large market for Caterpillar parts after the war, some European and Brazilian producers began making parts also. They were cheaper and often were more available than genuine Caterpillar parts, but they were largely of inferior quality. This created a two-pronged problem for Caterpillar: first, the company stood to lose a large percentage of the extremely lucrative parts market and second, the profusion of what Caterpillar called "gypo" parts, which did not have Caterpillar's standards of quality, were certain to affect its own reputation. For that reason, Caterpillar began to manufacture parts outside the United States.

Caterpillar's first overseas plant operation began in England in 1950, where it established a British subsidiary to procure and stock parts made to Caterpillar specifications by British manufacturers, and to sell them to authorized dealers in Britain and Europe. In 1954, Caterpillar set up another parts facility in São Paulo, Brazil, and in 1955 one was established in Melbourne, Australia. During these years, Blackie had been intimately involved in Caterpillar's overseas expansion, but in 1954 he was made executive vice president for foreign operations, and it was under his vision and guidance during the next eight years that Caterpillar developed into a truly multinational company. Neumiller, who appointed him to the position, said Blackie was "a genius with respect to organization," and Walter D. Fackler of the University of Chicago's Graduate School of Business said that he was "one of the few businessmen who understands the economics of foreign trade."

Soon after becoming executive vice president, Blackie announced plans to build a factory in his native Glasgow to make complete tractor-crawlers. With the success of that operation, Blackie began manufacturing the machines in Australia and Brazil. In 1960, Caterpillar made its first entrance into the European Common Market, when it bought a plant at Grenoble, France, which was greatly expanded. Convinced that whenever Caterpillar operated in an advanced industrial country, a local competitor would eventually rise to challenge it, Blackie used a policy of "preemptive occupation," establishing his own plant in the area to blunt the challenge. During the early 1960s, a small plant was set up in Canada, and an even smaller one was established in Mexico. At about the same time, Caterpillar began to enter the Japanese market, after it finally got permission from the Ministry of International Trade and Industry for a joint venture with Mitsubishi. In addition, Caterpillar set up smaller joint ventures with companies in India and Belgium during these years.

To coordinate these increasingly far-flung operations, in 1956 Blackie created the Foreign Trade Group, which pulled together from various departments all elements relevant to foreign operations, allowing a high degree of coordination. The key, as far as Blackie was concerned, was the interchangeability of product and components. As a Caterpillar executive explained to *Business Week*: "We design the basic product in the U.S. and adapt it overseas to local conditions for complete functional, dimensional, and endurance interchangeability." This approach gave Caterpillar what Blackie called a "tremendous logistics advantage" since "it means the international contractor and the military can get delivery on parts, components, and product from several sources and buy it for different currencies." This extraordinary geographic flexibility was adroitly exploited by Blackie. "We aspire to work on the most favorable basis of make, buy, or import," said Blackie, "and this changes and evolves from time to time." The problem, however, was that splitting the company between foreign and domestic business was giving it an increasingly schizophrenic personality— an issue that Blackie was impatient to address. He soon got his chance.

In 1962, when Neumiller retired, Blackie was named president. It soon became clear that, although he did not have the title, he had the powers of a chief executive officer. Blackie undertook to overhaul Caterpillar's internal organization to match its multinational approach. "Because the product we make abroad," he explained, "is identical to that made at home we have an even stronger need for unified control than other companies." He established a highly centralized organization in terms of policy, but one that granted enough flexibility to respond to local conditions. "General policy is set in Peoria and centralized as much as possible," Blackie said. "Execution is decentralized and where law or custom requires departure, as in methods of compensation or pension plans, it's expected." He theorized that centralizing policy-making actually created more flexibility and freedom at the local level: "If a man has no parameters, he is more inhibited than when he knows his limitations and can work within them."

Three years after assuming the presidency, Caterpillar's sales passed the billion dollar mark, with a robust 10.7-percent profit margin. In 1966, Blackie became chairman and CEO, and sales continued growing throughout the late 1960s, though at a slower rate than earlier in the decade. At the same time, Blackie embarked upon an expensive investment program that cut into its traditionally lucrative earnings, which fell three years in a row from 1969 to 1971. By 1972, Caterpillar had the plant capacity to produce about $3 billion worth of product annually, but sales had advanced only to about $2.3 billion. During these later years, it was the vast international organization that Blackie had built that kept the company from backsliding any further. By the early 1970s, even the overseas areas were beginning to stagnate due to lagging demand and increased competition, especially from the Komatsu company of Japan. Even more ominously, Komatsu at the same time began to build a strong dealer organization on Caterpillar's home turf.

Clearly, the great highway building spree and the huge construction projects that had fueled Caterpillar's domestic profitablity in America for many years were coming to an end. The focus of the construction industry was shifting to smaller scale projects in urban areas. Those projects demanded smaller machines. Although Caterpillar made some smaller bulldozers and motor graders, they earned far less money on them and had not developed the expertise to be successful with that kind of production. As a vice president at John Deere, one of Caterpillar's major competitors in the small machine field, commented:

Caterpillar is largely a job shop. It produces a high-grade, low-volume line. We are a mass producer of farm tractors that can be converted to other uses. If we tried to challenge Caterpillar in its field, we would have to spend a lot to change our production system. By the same token, if Caterpillar tried to challenge us, it would have to retool and redesign its operations. It would be very expensive for either company to invade the other's territory. (*Fortune,* May, 1972)

But most analysts agreed that Caterpillar had no choice: there were perils in entering the smaller machine market, but there were greater dangers in ignoring it. The later years of Blackie's administration posed an enormous challenge to him and to his company.

During his final five years as head of Caterpillar, Blackie continued to maintain the company's high-profile success. He pushed Caterpillar into a daring $2.4-billion expansion program, despite the potential softness of the market, until it operated twenty-seven plants worldwide, with 85,000 employees. Ranking twenty-ninth in sales in 1976 among all American industrial companies, Caterpillar had revenues of just over $5 billion, with an annual growth in profits of 13 percent. When Lee L. Morgan took over the top spot from Blackie in 1977, he inherited what seemed to be a powerful and growing company, with some hidden flaws. First of all, although Caterpillar was one of the most intensely multinational companies in the world, it was also highly ethnocentric, or as *Fortune* (May 1972) said, "Illinoiscentric." Over two-thirds of its top executives were born in Illinois or the states bordering Illinois, and they tended to be an inbred social group who worked, lived, and socialized together.

Blackie and other Caterpillar executives tended to discount the importance of this inbreeding, saying: "At Caterpillar we make capital goods that change the face of the earth. We don't make consumer products that are here today and gone tomorrow." But it became clear to many observers that as Japan and other countries increased their market penetration in America and the rest of the world, it was precisely the kind of smug, closed attitude that Caterpillar exhibited that caused American managers so many problems in meeting these challenges. This problem was further exacerbated by Caterpillar's penchant for secrecy. In its in-house slogan, "Say nothing that will give aid and comfort to the enemy," the enemy was often defined as anyone who did not work at Caterpillar. The company even refused to supply sales data to the Construction Industry Manufacturer's Association, its own trade association, and discouraged its dealers from belonging to the Associated Equipment Distributors. This clubbiness even extended to Blackie's vaunted overseas operations. In foreign countries, Caterpillar executives were as close-mouthed as at home, and usually formed an expatriate community in the country in which they lived, known locally as "Caterpillar Village." Nor did they place many local people in positions of authority in these operations. And never did any one of them rise to the top ranks of management in Peoria.

But in the late 1970s, all of this seemed very remote. Caterpillar was still one of the world's most powerful industrial companies; its sales and profits were rising at impressive rates; and Lee Morgan, a year after taking control, smugly asserted that "Business has been good." Still garnering 40 percent of the world-wide market, with half of its sales from abroad, Caterpillar's position seemed unassailable, since it held a four-to-one lead over Komatsu, its nearest international competitor. Morgan, like his predecessors, was a Caterpillar company man, who had spent thirty-two years—his entire working life—with the firm. As he told *Dun's Review* (December 1978): "Most of us come here from college not knowing much else, and find a home."

Morgan was born and educated in the small town of Aledo, Illinois, and he graduated from the University of Illinois in 1941. Upon graduation, Morgan went into the U.S. Army, rising to captain by the time he left in 1946. Morgan had worked part-time as a clerk at John Deere and Montgomery Ward before the war, but when he joined Caterpillar in 1946, it was his first real job. Morgan rose to the top through Caterpillar's extensive and sophisticated sales organization, becoming vice president in 1961, executive vice president in 1965, and chief operating officer in 1975. Two years later he became chairman and CEO. Striving to maintain the kind of folksiness developed by Louis Neumiller, Morgan asserted that "the root of our organizational process is the ability of anyone to walk into my office."

It soon became clear, however, that not everyone could walk into Morgan's office, especially members of the United Auto Workers (UAW); and in 1979 the union struck Caterpillar for the first time since 1937. Even worse, the conflict centered not on wages, but on noneconomic matters. As *Human Resource Management* noted: "Management simply could not respond to the union's concerns over the treatment and morale of the workforce." To complicate matters further, Cat's vaunted sales and profitability suddenly hit a stone wall at the same time. The company faced extremely difficult strategic challenges. Like other "smokestack industries," Caterpillar became a rearguard defender of its market niche in the late 1970s. Sales and profits declined, and the workforce changed. The old, stable, dependable Caterpillar workforce was increasingly being replaced by newer, younger, and less pliable workers. Less imbued with the corporate ethic, they were more concerned with individual fulfillment. Yet the concept of placing "I-ness" over "we-ness" was anathema to the management philosophy developed by Neumiller and imbibed by Morgan.

Just as Caterpillar executives had become closed off from the realities of the rest of the world, they had lost touch with their own workforce. The firm made clear distinctions, as did most American companies, between managers and nonmanagers, and between the company and the union. With a long history of paternalism and a well-paid workforce, company executives initially shrugged off the workers' complaints. To meet the union's challenge, Caterpillar ultimately undertook a worldwide human resource strategy conference in 1980. The conference made a number of recommendations, many of which top management approved and incorporated into the firm's basic strategic business plan. The most important aspect of this was a company statement committing it to an integration of the needs of people and the organization. Many local plant managers refused to adopt the proposals, which resulted in another strike by the UAW. Then, massive reductions in the workforce along with technological changes slowed the implementation of a workable labor relations policy. It remained a major thorn in Caterpillar's side during these years.

Morgan, like all Caterpillar executives, was a hard worker, and was committed to returning the firm to its past glory. For a time it looked as if he had succeeded: in 1980 sales mounted to a record $8.6 billion, an increase of almost $1 billion over the year before, and profits were a near-record $565 million. It looked as if a turnaround had occurred, and one Caterpillar executive trumpeted: "There's no magic at all to Caterpillar's success; we just know our business better than anyone else, and we work harder at it." Even their major competitor, Komatsu, was impressed. An executive there commented:

They are very concentrated. It's the firms that veer off into other industrial areas that are vulnerable. Caterpillar stays in its specialty and strengthens itself by improving its products and services. They are not just buying up other companies the way so many American companies do. (*Business Week,* May 4, 1981)

Morgan felt he knew the answer to Caterpillar's future. It would be a repeat of the firm's illustrious past—growth and expansion. He made plans to pour $5 billion into more new plants over the next several years, and this was on top of $2.5 billion he had spent since 1975. To Morgan, the biggest sin was the inability to meet an order anywhere in the world and placing a customer on allocation. His strategy was to have slightly more than enough capacity to meet demand peaks. In the early 1980s, Morgan visualized Caterpillar expanding at an annual rate of 6 percent, as it had done during the previous thirty years. Some analysts, however, were less sanguine. They pointed out that Caterpillar already held 58 percent of the U.S. market for construction equipment, and spending for highway construction was likely to be reduced even further. Morgan brushed those concerns aside, asserting that the company had already changed its marketing emphasis to machines that lay pipeline and sewers. Morgan felt that Caterpillar had considerable control over its own destiny and that it would continue to find and develop lucrative new markets, just as it had in the past.

But this did not happen. When Morgan retired at the end of 1984, Caterpillar had been shaken to its roots; 1982 turned out to be Caterpillar's last profitable year in the early 1980s. By the time Morgan retired, Caterpillar was in its third consecutive year without a profit and mired in unparalleled losses. Morgan informed the firm's shareholders in 1984 that "We've examined ourselves to the very heart of the organization, questioning everything we do." He and other company officials embarked on a vast program of cost slashing, and for the first time they began to cut prices to recover lost market share. By then it was clear that Morgan's vision of growth was in error. Caterpillar had built plants, spending $836 million in 1981 alone, and then realized that they had far more capacity than necessary. With 75 percent more plant space in 1984 than in 1973, production volumes were running 25 percent below 1973 levels. Caterpillar, which had long prided itself on providing virtual lifetime employment for its workers, was forced to begin massive layoffs. By 1984, nearly one-quarter of its 82,000 workers had been furloughed, and another 4 percent (2,500 workers) were scheduled to be laid off in 1985.

To beat high labor costs, Caterpillar moved more of its production offshore and commissioned other companies to produce some of its parts and components. Daewoo, South Korea's giant producer, for example, was making lift-trucks for Cat. Also, Caterpillar continued to cut prices in order to retain some of their market share. Arguing that this was necessary because the American dollar was overvalued in world markets, the company strongly urged devaluation to help them and other multinational manufacturers. And, finally, it began to court smaller customers, and, since these customers often needed smaller machines, it was clear that Caterpillar would have to increase its production in that area.

In early 1985, George Schaefer succeeded Morgan as chairman and CEO of Caterpillar. Schaefer, a native of Covington, Kentucky, fit the patented Caterpillar executive mold. He joined the firm in 1951, shortly after graduation from St. Louis University with a commerce degree. Schaefer held a variety of auditing and accounting jobs with the company before becoming accounting manager of the Grenoble, France, operation. When he returned to Peoria in 1968, Schaefer moved to the manufacturing side, and eventually ran a heavy equipment factory before moving up the corporate ladder. Like Neumiller and Morgan, if not Blackie, Schaefer was low-key and modest. A Peoria businessman said: "He's just a nice guy." Despite his deep respect for Caterpillar traditions, Schaefer realized that the company was in deep trouble when he took over and that certain drastic actions were necessary to restore it to its former position of power and profitability.

Schaefer's first task was to cut Caterpillar costs drastically. "We are permanently reducing employment, consolidating unnecessary facilities and reducing manufacturing costs,'' he said. He planned to use Caterpillar's traditional strength in the technical and marketing spheres to rebuild market share. He announced that the firm would be entering some new businesses, primarily to support its core businesses. In late 1984, Caterpillar began to introduce a series of new products. Many of these were small machines, the very antithesis of the giant earth movers upon which it had built its reputation. But the profit margins of these smaller machines were far less than Caterpillar was used to which meant even greater cost-cutting measures were necessary. As a result, the firm began to engage heavily in robotics to cut labor costs. By 1986, Caterpillar finally began to see some results from its draconian program. Sales stood at $7.3 billion, which was still below the peak year of 1982, but profits stood at $468 million—the first profit in four years. Yet the firm's metamorphosis was hardly over.

Schaefer, in response to a rise in Caterpillar's stock price on Wall Street, cautioned in 1987 that ''I suspect there's more enthusiasm than is warranted.'' Employment had been slashed 40 percent since 1982, and nine domestic plants had been closed. More manufacturing was being done overseas to save money. All told, Caterpillar executives estimated that they had cut costs by 25 percent by these moves, but since Komatsu was underselling Caterpillar by as much as 40 percent in some markets, that was scant consolation. Schaefer and other personnel continued to try to find alternatives—through factory ''cells,'' through automation and through other kinds of incentive systems to reduce costs and increase productivity. But none of these addressed Caterpillar's principal problem: a declining market for its products. With construction markets stagnating, Schaefer considered a radical move for Caterpillar—diversification. ''Maybe we've got to change the direction of the big ship Caterpillar,'' he said. Ominously Caterpillar in 1986 dropped the word ''tractor'' from its name, signalling its plans to diversify.

Then, just when things looked most bleak, the situation began to turn around. In 1987, profits jumped nearly fourfold, and sales increased to $8.2 billion, nearly equaling the record year of 1982. Profits were still well below the record levels of that year, but it was, nonetheless, an impressive performance. And Caterpillar was still revered by most industry analysts. An industry study of 6,000 executives, outside directors, and financial analysts by *Fortune* in 1983 revealed that, even at the depth of Caterpillar's troubles, it was regarded as the most admired firm in the industrial/farm equipment area. As William Blackie once commented: ''The value of an image can't be measured in dollars and cents, but there is no doubt that our name is our biggest asset.'' (**B.** *National Cyclopaedia of American Business*, N–62, 189–190; *Business Week*, August 2, 1947, August 13, 1966, February 5, 1979, May 4, 1981, July 23, November 5, 1984, November 25, 1985, August 31, 1987, June 20, July 18, December 12, 1988; *Time*, February 7, 1949; *Fortune*, August 1954, July 1963, May 1972, April 20, 1981, January 10, 1983, October 27, 1986, April 25, 1988; Peter Drucker, *Managing for Results*, 1964; *Forbes*, April 15, 1965, December 15, 1971, May 11, 1981, May 6, 1985; *Dun's Review*, May, December 1970,

December 1978; *Nation's Business*, August 1972; *Management Accounting*, March 1977; William L. Naumann, *The Story of Caterpillar Tractor*, 1977; Milton Moskowitz et al., *Everybody's Business*, 1980; Thomas J. Peters and Robert H. Waterman, Jr., *In Search of Excellence*, 1982; *Business Marketing*, May 1985; *Human Resource Management*, Winter 1985; *Who's Who in America*, 1986–87.)

CLAIBORNE (ORTENBERG), ELISABETH (March 31, 1929–   ). Fashion designer, Liz Claiborne, Incorporated. Liz Claiborne saw her potential customer clearly: "She is a busy lady [who] has neither the time [n]or the inclination to shop the old fashioned way of visiting four or five department stores." The "Liz Claiborne lady" was the career working woman; by the mid–1980s there were 12 million working women in the United States, and the number was growing at the rate of 10 percent annually. Before Liz Claiborne came along, designers provided executive women with a steady diet of navy-blue-suit-and-bow-tie uniforms. But Claiborne had a different idea—clothes that were comfortable, colorful, and fashionable, yet managed to find the balance between femininity on the one hand and practicality and good taste on the other. Her company's success in finding this formula was responsible for one of the fastest growing companies in the history of American business. Launched in 1976, it moved onto the *Fortune* 500 list of the largest industrial companies only a decade later. It was one of the youngest companies ever to accomplish this feat.

Liz Claiborne was born of American parents in Brussels, Belgium. Her father, a banker with Morgan Guaranty Trust, later brought his family to New Orleans, to Baltimore, and then to New York City. Claiborne lived in so many places during these years that she never finished high school, and, since her father frowned on her going into either business or fashion, she went to Brussels and Paris to study painting. At twenty she won a Harper's Bazaar design contest, and a year later, Claiborne returned to the United States, where, in defiance of her father's wishes, she cut off her long hair, which her parents insisted she keep, married Time-Life Books designer Ben Schultz, and took jobs as a sketch artist and model in New York.

In the mid–1950s, while Arthur Ortenberg was running the junior dress division of a women's sportswear company, he hired Claiborne as a designer. They developed a strong attraction to one another, divorced their respective mates, went through years of psychoanalysis, and were finally wed in 1957. In the meantime, Claiborne moved on to the giant Jonathan Logan company, where she became chief designer, and Ortenberg set up the textile and consulting firm of Fashion Products Inc. In the late 1960s and early 1970s, Claiborne tried to convince her bosses at Jonathan Logan to abandon junior dresses and to create clothes for the new class of highly paid working women who were emerging in America at that time. Although her superiors made some effort in that direction, it was not enough for Liz Claiborne. She and her husband might have struck out on their own earlier, but for the fact that their youngest son was still living at home. When he turned twenty-one, they decided it was finally time to branch out: "If we were going to lose everything we had," Claiborne said, "I wanted him to be old enough to handle it."

At the end of 1975, Claiborne left Jonathan Logan, Ortenberg phased out his consulting business, and together they went into business with their entire life savings, about $50,000. They advertised for a production partner, and Leonard Boxer, who had run production for seven years at Susan Thomas, Incorporated, an apparel subsidiary of Genesco, answered the ad. With a fourth partner, Jerome Chazen, Ortenberg's college roommate who had twenty years of experience in manufacturing and retailing women's sportswear, they scraped together a total of $250,000. The business was almost an instant success. By September of the first year it was in the black, and after eighteen months of operation it was grossing $7 million a year. By 1978, revenues had leaped to $23 million.

At this point, the firm reached a major turning point in its growth. Claiborne's dream had been simple, but modest: she would design and manufacture clothes for professional women, put the Liz Claiborne name on the label, and build a small, successful business. Now, however, the firm was growing spectacularly, beyond her wildest dreams. In 1978, the four partners went on a three-day retreat to the Poconos to talk about "what success would mean, how it would change each of our lives and whether we wanted those changes to happen," Chazen recalled. Two of the partners were opposed to rapid growth, but Arthur Ortenberg and Liz Claiborne had a vision, and their arguments were persuasive and compelling. As a result, although Liz Claiborne is the firm's designing influence, her husband increasingly emerged as the business genius of the organization. To Ken Wyse, the company's former marketing director, Ortenberg was the "Wizard of Oz." As he noted, "He's the man behind the door—intellectual and godlike, Socratic and dogmatic. He makes the pronouncements." While his wife is shy and retiring, Ortenberg is outgoing. She says she manages by doing, he says he manages by teaching. Together, they have created a synergistic managerial environment that has been extraordinarily successful.

The young fashion firm, which grew with dizzying speed, decided in 1981 to go public. With $80 million in sales at the time, Merrill Lynch, which usually did not handle such small offerings, sold the stock at $19 a share, which was about ten times earnings, and raised about $6.5 million for the young company. It turned out to be one of Merrill Lynch's most successful public offerings. The first major apparel company to go public in about eight years, the stock was selling for $30 a share within six months and even retained its high value in the recession of the early 1980s. The stock has split twelve times, and in 1987 sold for about $45 a share. What was the secret of their success?

There are, first of all, the fashions and designs themselves by Liz Claiborne. Rejecting the emaciated, runway-model image of other designers, she designs for the full, even pear-shaped bodies that most American women have. But if her clothes were not high fashion, neither were they the frumpy designs often created for older or larger women. What Liz Claiborne created was a line of well-made, fashionable sportswear that could be worn to the office. The clothes were colorful, graceful, but not snobbish. As Claiborne has noted: "These are work clothes. Women don't look to us for snob appeal, but for a brand name they can trust." At the same time, her clothing—although classic in appearance, well made, and with the cachet of quality—is moderately priced. This is the second element in the firm's success. The company is able to hold down prices because it owns no factories—everything is manufactured under license in the Orient, where labor is cheap.

Also, to save distribution costs, Liz Claiborne sells primarily through large department stores. This can often be a problem for designers, since they can lose control over the way in which the product is displayed and sold. But Claiborne and her husband developed a patented concept, called "Claiboards," which were provided to retailers who stocked the line. As *Women's Wear Daily* noted: "Claiboards [are] a trademarked concept using sketches, photos, and printed explanations showing how merchandise should be displayed in groups." They told the retailer how to mix and match the merchandise in order to maximize the appearance for the consumer.

Another reason for the success of Liz Claiborne, Incorporated, is the attention they give to the ultimate consumer. Unlike other designers, they offer a constant flow of merchandise throughout the year, with six seasons rather than the traditional four. This makes it possible for a customer to find a summer outfit in July when she needs it, rather than finding only the fall collection. This also makes for better inventory turnover, allowing stores to buy merchandise in smaller "lumps," rather than at the same time as other manufacturers. The firm employs a number of fashion consultants, who spend all their time visiting stores, taking photographs, talking with customers, and giving seminars to salespeople. With a sophisticated computer system to record what styles, colors, and sizes the customer buys each week in a cross-section of stores, Liz Claiborne is able to maintain a clear, up-to-date view of her market at all times.

Having given the Liz Claiborne label a high-quality image, the Ortenbergs are obsessed with maintaining that standard. They discourage retailers from listing the Liz Claiborne label in their ads, and they rarely give any "markdown money," credits, or discounts to retailers to help them absorb the cost of clearance sales. Like the clothes of rival Calvin Klein,[†] Liz Claiborne clothes have established such an excellent selling record that they do not have to conform to the normal rules of retailing and promotion. Far more oriented to the ultimate consumer than the retailer, Liz Claiborne does not even keep a sales force on the road, forcing retailers to come to New York if they want to buy the goods. Why do they come? Annual sales per square foot, a common industry yardstick, are at from $400 to $500—about three times the average. In addition, about 60 percent of Liz Claiborne's goods are sold at full price, versus 40 percent on average.

Yet the firm has had its failures also. In the early years there were occasional problems with filling orders and with quality control. Some designs failed to make it: a pure-silk Western-style shirt had snaps that kept disintegrating. The company also had some problems with licensing agreements with the Liz Claiborne name, especially because they could not control store promotions using it. In addition, the company's men's line has not been particularly successful, since the early designs were baggy and fit poorly. Their children's line, called "LizKids," was launched in 1983, but four years later still accounted for just $15 million in annual sales.

These ventures have made Claiborne and her husband somewhat wary of diversification; as she has said: "I worry about the label being everywhere." Nonetheless, they have recently undertaken two important diversified ventures. The first was a hookup with Avon Products, the giant cosmetics manufacturer, to launch a Liz Claiborne perfume, which was eventually to lead to a full line of cosmetics. The second is even more daring—they have decided to open their own retail stores, which will sell their clothes with a different label and lower price tag to compete with stores like The Limited (see Leslie Wexner), The Gap, and Banana Republic. Although Ralph Lauren[†] has found much success with his own stores and boutiques, industry analysts are divided about the wisdom of this move.

However these new ventures turn out, there is little controversy regarding Liz Claiborne's enormous stature in the fashion industry. Called by *Fortune* (January 5, 1987) the "reluctant revolutionary of the apparel business," the firm's sales in 1987 were in excess of $1 billion, and profits were at $114 million. Both figures were about 30 percent higher than the year before. In 1988 sales increased to $1.2 billion. Wall Street analyst Edward Johnson commented about the firm: "Management is both strong and versatile—they do what they do very well, and, over the years, they've made very few mistakes." Eileen Gormley, another industry analyst, made similar comments: "It's a well-run company with a nicely diversified product line." *Fortune* called Liz Claiborne one of the "Fifty Most Fascinating Business People" in 1987, and Bernard Chaus, head of a rival sportswear firm, said: "Liz Claiborne has been a great pathfinder." What he meant was that, by her success, Liz Claiborne has become the leading role model for the next generation of fashion entrepreneurs.

Since Liz Claiborne, Incorporated, went public in 1981, its average annual growth rate has been more than 40 percent. When *Business Week* compiled its list of the top 1,000 companies in the United States, there were only three female chief executive officers: Liz Claiborne, Katharine Graham* of the Washington Post Company, and Marion O. Sandler of Golden West Financial. But from mid–1987 onward, Claiborne's company, along with the rest of the fashion industry, experienced hard times. This narrowed the firm's profit margins, so that net earnings dipped 11 percent to $102 million in 1988. Harvey L. Falk, the firm's executive vice president for operations, commented that "We've made mistakes before, but this is the first year our mistakes became evident." Some analysts believed that the source of the firm's problems lay in the fact that the nation's women's sportswear market, of which Liz Claiborne controlled 60 percent, was leveling off. Some industry observers were also dismayed when Claiborne, Ortenberg, and Chazen unloaded 500,000 shares of stock in May and June of 1988 for relatively low prices. Shortly thereafter, the company issued a disappointing earnings report for the second quarter. Despite these problems, Liz Claiborne is widely recognized as the most effective manager in the industry. "The industry has a lot of prima donnas at the top who can't tolerate management development," said one industry consultant. "Liz isn't like that."

None of this seems to have gone to the heads of Liz Claiborne and her husband. They work ten-hour days in their sleek, modern Manhattan offices (Liz's is decorated in her trademark white). They spend their weekends at their $4-million retreat on Fire Island. Avid nature lovers, she jogs and photographs, while he reads and birdwatches. Once, when asked the value of her 4.3-percent stake in the company, Liz Claiborne replied, "A couple of million?" She seemed blissfully unaware that it was worth fully $80 million. (**B.** *New York Times*, January 3, 1978, July 6, 1980, January 10, 1984, January 8, March 24, 1985; *Forbes*, January 4, 1982, March 12, 1984; *Newsweek*, February 22, 1982; *People Weekly*, March 1, 1982; *Women's Wear Daily*, June 26, 1984; *New York Times Magazine*, March 24, 1985; *USA Weekend*, September 27–29, 1985; A. David Silver, *Entrepreneurial Megabucks*, 1985; *Contemporary Newsmakers*, 1986; *Esquire*, January 12, 1986; *Fortune*, January 5, 1987, April 25, 1988; Toronto *Globe & Mail*, February 9, 1987; *Business Week*, January 16, 1989.)

COORS FAMILY: JOSEPH COORS (1917–   ), **WILLIAM K. COORS** (1916–   ), **PETER HANSON COORS** (September 20, 1946–   ). Brewers, Adolph Coors Brewing Company. It was one of the great phenomena of the late 1960s and early 1970s—Coors became a unique cult beer. Without benefit of advertising, without national distribution, a venerable brewery nestled in the Rocky Mountains of Colorado became *the* beer to drink and to serve. Paul Newman, the movie star, demanded cases of Coors be kept on ice on his movie sets. Henry Kissinger, when secretary of state, regularly brought several cases of Coors back with him from California to Washington, D.C. President Gerald Ford used to take back cases of Coors from his retreat in Colorado, and one Secret Service agent was reprimanded for loading thirty-eight cases of Coors on Air Force One for his own use. Just as suddenly as it began, just as Coors reached for the brass ring of national distribution and dreamed of challenging Anheuser-Busch for top spot among American brewers, everything came apart for the company. A victim of countless strikes and boycotts, embroiled in continual political and social controversy, the brewery almost collapsed under the weight of all the problems in the late 1970s and early 1980s.

The Coors brewery was founded in 1873 by Adolph Coors, a native of Germany who had come to America as a stowaway on a Baltimore-bound sailing ship five years earlier to avoid the draft in his native country. After working for a time in a Denver brewery, he borrowed enough money to start his own business. Ironically, the Coors firm did not again take on any debt for 102 years. Taking advantage of sixty natural springs in the area around Golden, Colorado, Adolph Coors built his tiny brewery into a thriving, but small-scale, operation. Surviving a flash flood on Clear Creek in 1886 that washed away Adolph Coors' newly built brewery, the business continued to grow cautiously and slowly as a local popular beer in the mining towns that sprang up along the Front Ridge during these years. The company was incorporated in 1914, with Adolph Coors as president, his son, Adolph Coors, Jr., as vice president and secretary, and Grover Coors as general manager. Coors suffered an indignity in that same year, when its own town of Golden voted to ban the sale of all alcoholic beverages. The action did not, however, retard the company's growth.

A great crisis for Coors, as with every other brewery in America, was Prohibition during the 1920s. The company survived by making malted milk, ceramics, and near beer. During this time, the company was run by Aldolph Coors, but he did not live to see the end of Prohibition. He suffered a fatal accidental fall from a hotel window in Virginia Beach, Virginia, in 1929. Adolph Coors, Jr., then took over the brewery. With the end of Prohibition in 1933, the Coors brewery again began to prosper. In 1933, it made 123,000 thirty-one-gallon barrels of beer, and it continued to grow over the years, making modest gains. Suddenly, in the 1960s, sales exploded, doubling between 1968 and 1973, as the brewery vaulted from twelfth to fourth place among national brewers. During this time, a third generation of the family assumed control of the company, after Adolph, Jr., died in 1970.

Joseph and William Coors were the sons of Adolph Coors, Jr. By the rights of modified primogeniture, Adolph Coors III should have taken control of the company, but he was killed in a kidnapping in 1960. In any event, the three brothers were raised from the time they were very young to adopt the mantle of leadership in the family business. As Bill Coors recalled,

There was an intense amount of sibling rivalry when we were young, and in subtle ways my father encouraged it. It was great motivation for us. But we have suppressed it. We believe in the philosophy of our grandfather and our father that we must perpetuate this great institution, and this comes first. (*Business Week,* May 8, 1978)

The three brothers, working together in a spartan, moderate-sized room, moved into management positions at the brewery while they were still quite young. After Adolph III was killed, William and Joseph continued to work as a team.

Over time, the two brothers developed certain areas of expertise: Bill handled the technical side and, after their father's death, became chairman and chief executive; and Joe, who oversaw the financial and administrative side of the business, became president. Nevertheless, as Joe Coors commented, "People know they can talk to either one of us and get decisions." The Coors brothers throughout their careers adopted a casual demeanor. Both lean men, over six feet tall, they seldom wore business suits to the office, preferring windbreakers, boots, and casual shirts without ties. An associate said, "Coors folk are dead honest about everything, and they are very proud of what they do.'' Their offices were also spartan, as both worked behind grey metal desks. Bill Coors commented, ''We don't believe in management props, there is not a private secretary in the organization.'' What they did believe in, however, was secrecy. ''We've been secretive about our affairs,'' said Bill Coors, ''that was the nature of our grandfather and our father, and it is my brother's nature and mine.''

As a result, it is difficult to ascertain how the two brothers managed the brewery during the 1960s and early 1970s. Even though they did very little advertising and had virtually no marketing strategy, Coors beer sales skyrocketed during this time. As a later vice president of marketing for the firm commented, ''You could have sold Coors beer in Glad bags.'' Coors' big problems, in fact, revolved around production—getting beer out of the plant in sufficient amounts to meet the ever rising demand. To do so, they continually expanded the brewery in Golden until it was the largest single plant in the world. By 1974, it had an output of 12 million barrels a year. Although this was only one-third as much as Anheuser-Busch, the leading brewer, Coors produced all of its output in one plant; Budweiser was brewed in eleven plants around the nation. What was the secret of Coors beer's popularity?

That is not an easy question to answer. Everyone in the industry recognized that Coors brewed a good beer but felt that it was no better than many others. The answer, many felt, was a calculated mystique, a mystique based largely on Coors' unavailability. Throughout the period of its greatest growth, Coors beer was sold only in eleven western states. Since it was unpasteurized and contained no preservatives, it had to be made, stored, and shipped in a refrigerated state. If left unrefrigerated, the beer went bad in a week, and even when refrigerated it kept just a month. For that reason, the conservative Coors family refused for years to sell their beer outside a fairly convenient radius of their Colorado plant. Bill and Joe Coors never believed that the mystique factor was very significant. As the vice president of Dillon, Read & Company, the Coors' investment firm, commented: ''They genuinely believe they simply make a better product, and that is why it sold.'' A Coors executive put it more bluntly: ''If the public likes our beer, it buys it. We don't sell them.''

Whatever the answer, it is clear that there were some unique characteristics of Coors beer. Unlike many other breweries, it did not employ a brew master. Its mild, light-bodied beer was scientifically tested and brewed, using hops, rice, Rocky Mountain spring water, and a specially developed strain of barley grown by 1,000 farmers under contract to Coors. Bill Coors said,

No stone goes unturned here in making this the best beer, the most expensive beer in the U.S. in terms of processing and raw materials . . . our top management thrust is on engineering and production. I am an engineer, my father was an engineer. We're production-oriented. Nobody knows more about production than I do. (*Business Week,* August 22, 1970)

He said at another time, "There's no mystique about Coors' popularity, it tastes better than other beers, that's all."

Although taste is a subjective matter, it is true that certain characteristics of its taste did enhance Coors beer's popularity. As a light beer, it was brewed with less malt, fewer hops, and more rice than tangier tasting beers. As a result, it tended to appeal largely to people who were not traditional beer drinkers—it was its relative lack of taste, in fact, that accounted for some of its popularity. Coors was, therefore, very popular with two burgeoning groups of consumers in the 1960s and 1970s: women and young people. Veteran beer drinkers, especially those in the West, where Coors was easily available, often referred to it as "Colorado Kool-Aid," which brings us back to the whole question of mystique and availability. Easterners, who could not get the beer easily, would pay almost any price for it, and Coors beer served at a party became a great status symbol. Westerners, on the other hand, rarely made a fuss if their local bar was out of Coors; they just ordered something else.

But, no sooner had Coors moved into a position to challenge the largest American brewers then it fell upon hard times. By 1975, Coors beer was a true phenomenon. Sold in only eleven states, it was the top-selling beer in ten of them, and in the eleventh did not have full state-wide distribution. Although it was not distributed in thirty-nine states, including some of the most populous states in America, and although it did not advertise and had no marketing strategy, it sold every can and barrel of beer it produced. Then, just as suddenly as it had begun, it ended. In 1976, for the first time since 1933, Coors did not sell all the beer it produced. Its sales slipped, and the company fell back to fifth place. During the late 1970s and early 1980s, Coors fell increasingly farther behind. What happened? Many things, but Peter H. Coors, Joe's son, perhaps put it best—"We got arrogant."

Coors had become smug in the belief that all it had to do was to make a single, superior beer, and the world would beat a path to its door. Thus, it advertised and promoted little, ignored the realities of a changing marketplace for beer, and got embroiled in union, cultural, and political controversies that negatively affected its situation. On the marketing side, Coors was blindsided by the segmentation inaugurated by Philip Morris' Miller Lite Beer, a reduced-calorie beer that was the biggest new product in beer history. With a brilliant advertising campaign, featuring such personalities as Bubba Smith, Mickey Spillane, Rodney Dangerfield, Billy Martin, Dick Butkus, and Joe Frazier, Miller featured men who were ex-athletes, "men's men," who argued over whether they liked Miller Lite because of its taste or because it was less filling. Miller, which had been the number seven brewery in 1971 but was number two by the late 1970s, took market share away from breweries like Coors rather than from the industry leader, Anheuser-Busch. Four out of every ten new light-beer drinkers switched from Coors to Miller Lite.

These marketing problems were compounded by a union boycott. In 1977, Coors was hit by a strike that was sparked, at least in part, by Coors' insistence that all prospective employees take lie-detector tests. Negotiations proceeded for a time until Joe and William Coors broke the strike. This occasioned a nationwide union boycott against Coors beer at exactly the time the company decided to send its beer into the lucrative East Coast markets. That move, in turn, was based on another fateful decision made in 1975—to issue stock to the public for the first time. Hit with a $50-million inheritance tax bill from the federal government on their parents' estates, Coors raised $127 million in the stock issue, in which they sold only nonvoting stock, and retained about 88 percent of the firm's ownership in family hands. But trying to sell the stock in the markets of the mid–1970s, particularly when Coors' sales were declining, put additional pressure on the company.

In 1976, Bill Coors explained why he felt it was necessary to take Coors national: "The others can put the heat on us too easily because we sell to only 20 percent of the U.S. beer market. We're vulnerable." But, the move to go national made Coors more vulnerable to a large-scale union boycott—a boycott that lasted for a full ten years. Bill Coors' reaction to the boycott was typical: "It was a shock to us to find that, as far as the union is concerned, anything goes. No lie is too great to tell if it accomplishes their boycott objectives. We view the boycott as a monument to immorality and dishonesty." This impassioned rhetoric, no doubt honestly felt, was hardly politic in the world of the late 1970s. Because of the intransigent attitudes of Coors, the company ranked, according to *Forbes* in 1978, "with J. P. Stevens on union hate lists." Coors had a mountain of other troubles during these years. In 1976, the Supreme Court upheld the Federal Trade Commission (FTC) in its suit against Coors. Coors, with what the *Washington Post* called an "obsession with control," had long intimidated distributors with the threat that unless bars handled Coors exclusively, they would not be allowed to handle their beer at all. They also barred certain retail chains from carrying Coors. As a consequence, the FTC charged Coors with restraint of trade, and the company had to remove its restrictions as a result of the decision. At about the same time, the Colorado Health Department charged Coors with polluting Clear Creek, in the very same valley where they got their vaunted Rocky Mountain spring water. It further tarnished the company's image.

On top of all this, the right-wing political views of Joe and Bill Coors began to cause trouble for the company. Both brothers were unreconstructed capitalists, strong believers in the free enterprise system, and bitter opponents of the federal government—once the company even refused to withhold taxes from its workers' paychecks for two months and then, in the following month, took off taxes for all three months to demonstrate just how much of a bite federal taxes took from their paychecks. But the brothers' conservative attitudes did not come to national attention until 1975, when President Nixon nominated Joe Coors to the board of the Corporation for Public Broadcasting. A key complaint against Joe Coors that emerged at the Senate hearings was that he was using his company to further his own political views. Particularly at issue was Television News Incorporated, a broadcast news agency that had been established in 1972 under the corporate umbrella of Adolph Coors Company. At the same time, Joe Coors generated headlines by his statements and activities as a regent of the University of Colorado, where he fought the distribution of birth control information to female students and opposed the existence of such organizations as the Black Students Union. In 1973 he was a cofounder of the conservative Heritage Foundation.

The company was also under siege during these years from Mexican-Americans, blacks, women, and gays. Despite the large numbers of Hispanics in Colorado, they were virtually unrepresented among Coors' workers in the 1960s. As a result, Mexican-American organizations organized a long-running strike and boycott against the company. Similarly, gays felt that the infamous lie-detector tests were used to find out, among other things, the sexual orientation of prospective workers. As a result, gay organizations effectively boycotted Coors beer, resulting in a claim that not a single gay bar in San Francisco carried Coors beer. These reactions against Coors' company policies were aided by the fact that Joe and Bill Coors did little to hide their own right-wing prejudices. Bill Coors, considered slightly more moderate than Joe, touched off a nationwide fire storm when he addressed a group of minority businessmen in Denver in 1984. Observing that Rhodesia had blossomed under white rule and that Zimbabwe was not faring nearly as well under black control, he commented:

It's a disaster, it's not that the dedication of blacks is less; in fact, it's greater. They lack the intellectual capacity to succeed, and it's taking them down the tubes. . . . One of the best things [the slave traders] did for you is to drag your ancestors over here in chains. (*Manhattan, Inc.*)

These, and similar comments, put Coors Brewery under constant siege from federal agencies like the National Labor Relations Board and the Equal Employment Opportunity Commission, along with a series of private groups, finally forcing them to begin liberalizing some of their policies in the late 1970s and early 1980s. But, even with those grudging changes, the company's fortunes did not improve. With Joe and Bill Coors continuing to fund a plethora of right-wing causes, most groups questioned the sincerity of the firm's concessions. As a result, the company's market share continued to plummet. In California, which had always been Coors' biggest market, sales dropped 43 percent from 1977 to 1984, and the decline in Colorado was almost as steep. Furthermore, Coors was having a terrible time penetrating the East, especially New York City. It became clear to all concerned that a change of management was in order. With Joe and Bill Coors in their late sixties, it was time to bring Joe's sons, Peter and Jeff, into control. With that changeover, a revolution took place at Coors.

Pete and Jeff Coors, like their father and uncle, were raised in the almost hermetically sealed environment of the family brewery. They began working at the company at an early age, and they were inculcated in the family's conservative, traditional values throughout their lives. Like the rest of the Coors, they were simple, hardworking people who revered God, family, and country. Their father was a strict disciplinarian, and both Pete and Jeff worked in the brewery during their summer vacations from Exeter. Both young men went to Cornell, where Pete studied industrial engineering. After graduating from Cornell, he then went to the University of Denver, where he got his MBA in 1970. At that point, he followed the family tradition by joining Coors Brewing full-time as an industrial trainee. Although Jeff was a year older, it soon became clear that Pete had the managerial talent, and he was rapidly pushed up the hierarchy.

A critical appointment came in 1975, when Pete Coors was named a director of the firm and head of market research. Pete, although he had obeyed his father's dictates as a youngster, was chafing at the authoritarian tactics of his father and uncle. A colleague noted that he "did all the accepting things . . . but he was always his own man and seemed eager to assert his own independence." He also had immersed himself in marketing strategy from his first months with the company. During a time when his father and uncle disdained any sort of marketing approach, Pete was honing his understanding of the competitive realities of the marketplace. Thus, when the great crunch hit the company in the 1975–1976, he had more answers than anyone else. As the director of community relations for Coors commented, "Pete's got a better sense of the real world than many of the people in this company."

The die was cast in 1975 for Pete Coors' later actions with the company when, shortly after becoming a director, he cast the sole dissenting vote in a board meeting concerning a new type of beer can lid. A stunned silence followed the vote, and Pete was informed that it was the very first time in the history of the company that a boardroom vote had not been unanimous. It was not the last. In issue after issue over the following decade, Pete and his brother Jeff disagreed with their uncle and father and the older directors on a multitude of issues. When sales began to tail off in the mid–1970s, Pete, unlike his father and uncle, did not blame the unions, or left-wing political groups, or anyone else. He blamed the company:

We got arrogant. We thought we were doing the retailers a favor to bring beer to them. We didn't have a product mix or a package mix to serve their needs. We had a hard-to-open press-tab can that we tried to force on the consumer because it was environmentally responsible. In the last three or four years, we've given the consumer no reason to stay with us. (*Forbes,* October 16, 1978)

Strong words, indeed, from a member of the Coors family.

But Joe and Bill Coors still controlled the company, and Pete and Jeff could merely mount limited campaigns for specific objectives for several years. Neither Bill nor Joe wanted to stoop to developing a light beer to compete with Miller and the others, but Pete and Jeff were adamant. Finally, the younger Coors were able to get their elders to accede reluctantly to the development of Coors Light. When the beer was finally introduced with a strong advertising campaign, Coors Light had a dramatic impact on the market, and by the late 1980s it accounted for 40 percent of Coors' sales. When Pete was appointed senior vice-president in charge of sales and marketing, he argued, with Jeff's support, that the company had to mount far more extensive, and expensive, advertising campaigns than they had used in the past. They argued that Coors could never hold its own against giants like Anheuser-Busch and Miller without it. Accepting this approach nearly caused Joe and Bill Coors to gag. Bill had boasted as late as 1976 that, "we don't need marketing, we know we make the best beer in the world." But not everybody else knew that, and Pete and Jeff were finally able to get the company to agree to greatly increased spending for advertising in the early 1980s. By 1987, Coors was spending $200 million a year.

In 1982, when Pete became president of the brewing division, he recognized the importance of distancing the company from Joe and Bill's extreme political stances. Not that Pete and Jeff were liberal—both were conservative Republicans—but they firmly believed that politics and the brewery business did not mix. One of the first things Pete had to handle when he became chief executive of the company in 1985 was the fallout from his uncle's intemperate speech about blacks in Denver. He later noted, "We needed to move aggressively to mend our fences with the black and Hispanic communities." The result was a five-year, $350-million agreement with a black coalition including the National Association for the Advancement of Colored People and Operation PUSH (People United to Save Humanity). At the same time, he signed a similar $350-million agreement with the Hispanic Association for Corporate Responsibility. Under the terms of both agreements, Coors agreed to increase its minority hiring, invest large amounts of its funds in minority-owned banks and financial institutions, and purchase goods and services from minority vendors. As part of the agreement, it was stipulated that, if sales of Coors increased among blacks and Hispanics, Coors would then increase its financial commitment. If not, it would spend no more money. The agreement eliminated much of the antagonism directed against Coors that had been festering for decades in the minority communities. It was a masterful stroke.

Pete next dealt with the long-standing union boycott of Coors products, a boycott that had done so much to frustrate the brewery's efforts to increase its sales on the East Coast, especially in New York City. A former Coors executive noted, "Both Bill and Joe harbored tremendous hostility toward the unions. In their eyes, Pete was making a tremendous mistake, but now that the brewery was his responsibility, he was determined to at least try to end the boycott." What followed was two years of negotiation with the leadership of the American Federation of Labor and Congress of Industrial Organizations (AFL-CIO). Finally, in August 1987, Coors agreed to let the AFL-CIO organize workers at the Colorado brewery and agreed to sign a union-approved contract for any future plant construction. In return, the AFL-CIO called off its boycott of Coors beer— which, at ten years, was one of the longest boycotts in recent labor history.

Pete Coors made it clear to the company and to the press that he did not want unions in the plant any more than his father or uncle had, but, as he said, "They [the workers] get to vote. We don't." By the mid–1980s, however, it was clear to Pete that concessions were necessary if Coors were to expand. In 1978, the brewery, whose beer at the time was distributed in only sixteen states, sold 12.6 million barrels of beer. In 1986, it sold 15.2 million barrels, but the beer was by then distributed in forty-seven states. If Coors was going to increase its sales, it could not expand geographically; it had to attract those beer drinkers who were not drinking Coors because of the various boycotts, or because of the political opinions of Joe Coors. All of these actions by Pete Coors were designed to undo the damage caused by the third generation of Coors executives.

While Pete was negotiating with the unions, he was also trying to get broader distribution for Coors in New York City. In July 1986, he got approval from the Coors board to proceed with the move into New York and New Jersey, along with the green light to spend $25 million in advertising. It was to be a major blitz. But Coors was met with antagonism and hostility beyond what Pete had ever imagined. As he noted, in a masterpiece of understatement, "It was all something of a shock."

First, the area unions, despite the AFL-CIO agreement, would not lift their boycott against Coors. Nor would the Hispanic and black groups rescind their boycott, despite Coors' much publicized agreement with leaders of their organizations. Pete's attempt to negotiate with these various groups in New York was not successful either. Finally, Pete had to agree to put union construction workers back on the job at Coors. With this accomplished, the New York unions finally lifted their ban, and Coors beer trucks began rolling into the city in August 1987. The AFL-CIO's David Sickler said of Pete Coors: "You've got to give Pete credit. He's probably saved Coors." He at least had the company on the right track. In 1987, beer sales amounted to $1.3 billion, just a 3-percent increase from the previous year; profits were a meager $48 million, down 19 percent from the year before. But Pete won't give up. As he commented once, "It's been beat into us that the family, the company, comes before any personal desires." (**B.** *Fortune*, March 1952, October 12, 1987, April 25, 1988; *Business Week*, August 22, 1970, November 20, 1971, September 22, 1975, May 8, July 24, 1978, December 16, 1985, September 7, 1987, July 11, 1988; *Newsweek*, September 22, 1975, August 31, 1987; *New York Times Magazine*, December 28, 1975; *Forbes*, June 1, 1976, October 16, 1978, July 19, 1982, October 24, 1983; Milton Moskowitz et al., *Everybody's Business*, 1980; *Advertising Age*, January 16, 1984; *New York Times*, April 26, 1984; *Black Enterprise*, August, December 1984; *Contemporary Newsmakers*, 1985; Joseph J. Fucini and Suzy Fucini, *Entrepreneurs*, 1985; *Who's Who in America*, 1986–87; *Los Angeles Times*, Sept. 27, 1987: *Manhattan, Inc.*, February 1988.)

CROW, (FRED) TRAMMELL (1914–). Real estate developer, Trammell Crow Company. Quick now! Who is the largest real estate developer in America? The biggest private landlord in the country? Is it Donald Trump?[†] No? Well, then, Edward DeBartolo?[†] No? Well, then, who is it? Trammell Crow. Trammell

Crow? Who in the world is Trammell Crow? Such is the usual reaction of most people when the subject is broached. Trammell Crow is so little known that sometimes visitors to his Dallas office can hear him politely spelling "C-R-O-W" into his telephone to some bewildered person. Although Donald Trump is the most highly publicized, most visible developer, and Edward DeBartolo is the largest developer of shopping malls, Trammell Crow is the biggest real estate developer in America. Period. He has developed some of America's great urban landmarks—Peachtree Center in Atlanta and the Embarcadero Center in San Francisco—and he is the largest owner of rental housing in the United States, with some 40,000 units. In the late 1980s, his real estate holdings totaled over 250 million square feet of space—including 35 million square feet of office space, 140 million square feet of industrial space, 12 million square feet of retail space—along with a variety of other concerns. Another 17 million square feet was under construction. *Texas Monthly,* in an attempt to sum up the extent of Crow's holdings, put it this way: "How big is Trammell Crow's empire? Unimaginably big." His personal worth was estimated by *Forbes* in 1988 to be at least $775 million.

Trammell Crow was born in Dallas, the fifth of eight children of a bookkeeper. When the Great Depression hit in the 1930s, Crow's father was thrown out of work, and, as a result, when Trammell Crow graduated from high school, he was not able to raise the tuition to attend college full-time. Instead, he got a job as a runner for the Mercantile National Bank and studied accounting at night at Southern Methodist University. After passing his CPA exams, Crow took a job at the Dallas office of Ernst & Ernst, an accounting firm. In 1941, he joined the U.S. Navy, where he spent most of the next five years auditing contracts in Washington, D.C. During this time, Crow made a fortuitous marriage, when he returned to Dallas to marry Margaret Doggett, the daughter of the owner of a grain-elevator business, who had inherited a substantial estate when her parents were killed in an automobile accident.

After the war, Crow got a job with Doggett Grain, a wholesale grain business that his wife's father had founded. Crow soon concluded that the company had had its day and began to wind it down while looking for other opportunities. That opportunity turned out to be the Doggett's warehouse. During the late 1940s, Crow remodeled the structure and then leased some space in it to Ray-O-Vac Company, the battery manufacturer. After a time, Ray-O-Vac decided they wanted to move to larger quarters. Rather than viewing their decision as a defeat or catastrophe, Crow convinced the firm to let him build them a new warehouse, which he would lease to them. This was Crow's first real estate deal, and it introduced him to the intricacies of finance. He persuaded Pacific Mutual Life Insurance Company to take out a $40,000 mortgage on the property, but he had to find other financing as well. Relying on his wife's credit at the bank, Crow was able to raise the needed capital. He bought the land for the warehouse from Industrial Properties Corporation, owned by the Stemmons brothers of Dallas, who would be his partners in a myriad of ventures over the years, and he leased half the building to Ray-O-Vac. The warehouse was located in a strategic area, part of a corridor of rising values along the Stemmons Freeway, which ran from downtown Dallas to the local airport.

With the success of the warehouse investment, the Stemmons family became Crow's backers and partners in a whole series of ventures. Buying land from the Stemmons brothers, but always in partnership with them, Crow built more and more warehouses in the late 1940s and early 1950s, often "on spec," assuming that tenants would be found once they were finished. The Stemmons, who were deeply conservative, were awed by Crow's audacity and success. John Stemmons commented that: "We looked upon him as our wild little brother we had to keep control of." Crow was an eternal optimist, and he leveraged everything to the hilt in order to keep building. His partners often grew timid, but Crow continued to push, and he turn out to be correct, time after time. By the early 1950s, Crow had pushed his operations into Atlanta and Denver.

With the success of these smaller ventures, the Stemmons decided to back Crow in their first sizable joint undertaking—the Homefurnishings Mart in Dallas—in the mid–1950s. A $2-million, 219,000-square-foot building to house retail furniture showrooms, the Homefurnishings Mart was also built on spec, and several local banks, assessing it as too risky, refused to provide financing. Crow successfully found a backer in his old employer Mercantile National Bank. Crow's inspiration for this venture had been Joseph P. Kennedy's* Merchandise Mart in Chicago: "I was gripped by the Merchandise Mart," he said. "Gripped by what it did for its exhibitors and for its retail attendees." But Crow brought his own innovation to the concept. Whereas the Merchandise Mart had served a diversified clientele, Crow wanted to serve a single industry—in this case, furniture retailers. Crow judged his market correctly. Furniture retailers signed up so fast that he had to double the size of the building just six months later.

Specialized trade marts thus became Crow's emblem; he built them in Atlanta, Brussels, Belgium, and a number of other cities. Crow had first ventured outside Dallas in 1952, when he built a warehouse in Atlanta, and in 1961 he made another bold move outside of Dallas. In that year he joined forces with Atlanta architect-developer, John Portman, to build the Peachtree Center in that city. This highly successful urban mixed-use project began a new series of developments for Crow. Peachtree Center was one of the very first of a new phenomenon in American cities—the suburban shopping mall transplanted downtown. Unlike the suburban malls, though, the Peachtree and its counterparts were multipurpose centers. In addition to the typical array of shops, they included hotels, theaters, and restaurants. A major factor in the revitalization of many older downtown centers, these new centers were built with ingenious combinations of private capital enticed by tax breaks and low-interest loans. With the success of Peachtree Center, Crow made plans to replicate it elsewhere.

Acquiring new backers, David Rockefeller and Winthrop Rockefeller (the Rockefeller Family*), along with David's Chase Manhattan Bank, Crow and Portman built the Embarcadero Center in San Francisco in the early 1970s.

Comprising five buildings, which cost a total of $300 million, the Embarcadero Center was Crow's biggest undertaking to that time, but unlike most of his projects, his share was only 8.3 percent. He usually owned at least one-third of any project he was involved in, but this time Prudential Insurance, which put up most of the mortgage money, owned 50 percent of it, and Portman, the Rockefellers, and their associates owned the rest. The Embarcadero was followed by the Allen Center in Houston.

By 1971, according to *Forbes*, Crow had become the biggest private landlord in the United States, with holdings of over $1 billion in real estate. Over the 1950s and 1960s, Crow had built a bewilderingly complex organization. So complex, in fact, that some doubted the term organization could even apply to it. Crow, or one of the members of his family, shared in the ownership of a staggeringly large number of corporations and partnerships, some 650 throughout the world by the early 1970s. In these, he had "money partners," like the Rockefellers, and "operating partners," who usually contributed only token amounts of their own cash but were expected to put in massive amounts of work ("sweat equity") on the projects involved. Crow did not really believe that a man on a salary would do an adequate job, so he always gave his key people a "piece of the action":

It is a highly individualistic business, not a business you can organize into levels. It just doesn't work that way. A man who is paid a salary won't do the same job as a man who owns part of the real estate. There isn't any way—he just *won't*. (*Fortune*, November 1973)

The partners were all dependent on Crow's credit and reputation with lenders. Trammell Crow Company was on all their business cards, and Crow allowed them to use his personal balance sheet in negotiating loans. Crow was also almost always willing to sign his name to a note.

Crow's method of choosing his partners was unique. Rather than seeking men (and his partners were all men) with experience, or toughness, or even brilliance, Crow instead said:

I ask myself if he's a nice person, a good human being, someone you like to see coming into the room. Has he got any brains? Is he disciplined and eager enough to get up in the morning without an alarm clock? Is he the sort of man whom other people want to succeed? (*Inc.*)

As a result, Crow's early partners described their early relationship with him in terms that suggest that he was like a fairy godfather to them. Ned Speiker, who joined Crow in 1969, recalled their first meeting: "Trammell flew out in his Learjet, and I flew back with him to Dallas. He's a very persuasive guy—warm, engaging and humorous. Trammell told me I'd be an owner, that what I built would be mine. He'd provide the capital."

Crow's transactions always demanded a lot of financing because he seldom had much cash available. Unlike many developers, whose technique was to build something, depreciate it rapidly, and then sell it, Crow held onto his property. He often commented that "you can get rich selling real estate, but you can only get wealthy owning it." As a result, he used the equity value of his existing properties to finance his next investments. This meant he was always leveraged to the limit. His extreme optimism about the real estate market, coupled with the fact that Crow was always so heavily mortgaged, brought him very close to bankruptcy in the mid–1970s. When *Fortune* profiled him in an article in 1973, Crow was riding the crest of a wave of success. *Fortune* agreed with him, and many of his partners, that the success was at least partially the result of the "creative chaos" Crow had created with his complex, anti-organization organization.

By the end of 1974, though, his 650 corporations were projecting a negative cash flow of nearly to $25 million, and Crow himself was personally liable for $151 million in borrowings and contingently liable for another $433 million. To help him out, David Rockefeller and Chase Manhattan came through with $12 million, but Crow was still severely hobbled by the recession of the time. As Crow commented in 1975: "When they write the history of the industry, this period will be described like the 1929 crash." Crow managed to ride out the recession without filing for Chapter 11 bankruptcy, but his firm's organization and his way of doing business had to be profoundly altered. A private, closely held corporation prior to his difficulties, the Crow family holdings dominated the company, but, by the 1980s, outsiders held 44 percent of the stock.

As a result, Crow found he had to rein in his enthusiasm quite a bit. "Oh, I bite my tongue a lot," he said, "but I've learned the hard way that you can't do everything yourself and get it done right. And now I hold the world's indoor record for delegation of authority." J. McDonald Williams became managing partner and Crow's designated successor in Trammell Crow Company, although Crow's children also played important roles. The most significant of these was his daughter, Lucy Billingsley, who became chief operating officer; Crow's three sons handled various divisions in the firm. Asked if a non-Crow would ever run the companies, Lucy replied: "Not in my lifetime and not in my children's. Obviously, my father didn't work all of his life—and I'm not going to work all of my life—to build this thing and let it go."

By all accounts, however, Crow faced a Hobbesian choice in the late 1970s— either save the real estate firm and see it pass out of family control, or pass it on to his familial heirs and watch it wither and die. Declaring that "my proudest accomplishment is this company. That it will endure," Crow turned over the reins to J. McDonald "Don" Williams. In the process, McDonald brought a drastically different management style to Trammell Crow and Company. A 1966 graduate of George Washington Law School, McDonald was cool, calculating, and rational, where Crow had been exuberant, optimistic, and trusting. As a result, McDonald installed tighter and more stringent financial and reporting requirements for partners and employees in the firm. The standard partnership agreement, which in the early days had been simply a verbal promise and a handshake, evolved into a twenty-five-page document bristling with all the legal signposts of mutual mistrust. Further, the down-home Trammell Crow Company of earlier years became a chic place to work in the 1980s. Attracting large numbers of MBAs from prestigious schools, in 1984 it was labeled one of the 100 Best Companies to Work for in America, and was one of seven companies "where an advanced degree from a top school helps."

If this brought a radical change to the corporate culture at Trammell Crow Company, it was a transformation which Crow himself approved. Wanting more than anything else that his firm be "evergreen" and outlive him, Crow approved the discipline and structure introduced by McDonald. Commenting on these changes, Crow said of McDonald: "He's a better man than I am. He's the guy who made this a great company. How did I know he was the man to do it? I'm that smart," Crow said with a twinkle. And the firm seemed to thrive with the combination of Trammell Crow's audacious optimism in the real estate market and McDonald's cautious, conservative approach to its internal structure. Rather than adopting a more conservative approach to real estate acquisitions, Crow continued building and buying despite a real estate glut that caused most developers to hold back. Crow chose not to think about the close shave he had experienced in the mid–1970s. Talking with a reporter in the atrium of the Dallas Trade Center, Crow said: "Whatever you do, don't make me look like a phoenix rising out of the goddam ashes. I haven't done it alone." With over $2.7 billion in assets in 1982, Trammell Crow Company started $1 billion worth of new projects in that year, far more than any other developer. "We would do better without a recession," he said, "but this business isn't a 100-yard dash. It's a marathon."

By the mid–1980s, Trammell Crow's firm had become so entrenched in Dallas, Houston, San Francisco, Chicago, and Atlanta, that it was difficult for others to challenge it effectively. When Olympia & York, the mammoth real estate development firm owned by the Reichman family of Toronto, moved into the Dallas area, they opened their office right across the street from the Crow Company headquarters. Thinking they could easily take business away from Crow, they learned a hard lesson. Finding it difficult to fill their buildings, Olympia & York's executive in charge of renting said: "Crow has what no other developer has in the Dallas market: captive tenants." Crow also began to break into the high-profile New York City real estate market in the 1980s. Named manager for a Times Square redevelopment project, the twenty-story New York Trade Mart, he even began to acquire some media visibility. When hailed by people on the street, however, they usually got an "Aw, shucks, they found me grin in return." Despite his wealth and influence, Crow remains modest and relatively unassuming. A reporter once asked Crow how many buildings he owned. "I don't know," Crow replied, "thousands." "Hell, I've never seen most of the Trammell Crow buildings.'' Unlike Donald Trump, and some other builders, Crow's name does not appear on any of his buildings. When asked about this, he replied: ''My name isn't on my buildings. Maybe they're monuments, but the public will never know it.'' Crow said the motto of his company could be described in three words—''to do good.'' ''That means *good* buildings, *good* support for our lessees, *good* civics, *good* morals, and having a *good* time.'' Don Williams, in reflecting on Trammell Crow, said: ''The day of the Lone Ranger, Trammell Crow riding into town and making deals, that's *gone.*'' Instead, he commented, ''[T]he day calls for teams of highly professional people, *disciplined* entrepreneurs.'' Trammell Crow was the last of his breed—the cowboy capitalist—as he passed from the scene, his place was taken by legions of suave, well-pressed young men from Harvard, Stanford, and Wharton. Somehow, it won't be quite the same. (**B.** *Business Week*, September 18, 1965, May 7, 1984; *Forbes*, April 15, 1971, October 15, 1975, June 7, 1982, December 17, 1984, October 24, 1988; *Fortune*, November 1973, April 13, 1987; *Newsweek*, April 30, 1984; *Esquire*, June 1985; *Inc.*, November 1988; Robert Sobel, *Trammel Crow, Master Builder*, 1989.)

CUMMINGS, NATHAN (October 14, 1896–February 19, 1985). Food Wholesaler, processor, and industrialist, Consolidated Grocers, Consolidated Foods, Sara Lee Corporation. Nathan Cummings often elicited laughter from his audience when he gave a speech by introducing himself as ''Mister Sara Lee.'' Since his company, Consolidated Foods, manufactured Sara Lee, America's number one brand of frozen pastries, it was an appropriate moniker. However, Cummings did not quite fit the cuddly image the Sara Lee name implied, as he was, by all accounts, a tough, cantankerous man. Cummings had bought the Sara Lee firm in 1956 from Charles Lubin, a neighborhood baker on Chicago's South Side, who had created the frozen dessert industry in the early 1950s. A few years later, Cummings fired Lubin when Lubin had the perceived temerity to stalk out of a board of directors meeting at Consolidated Foods when he objected to Cummings' rigorous cross-examination of him. Lubin fared well nonetheless. With resentment, he cashed in his Consolidated stock for a few million and invested a large chunk of it in Swift & Company just as the company was being converted into the modern conglomerate Esmark, and he watched his stock quadruple in the space of a few years.

That confrontation characterized Nate Cummings in many respects. He was extraordinarily confrontational with his business associates, who suffered frequent firings. A prime example of this came in 1970, when the seventy-four-year-old Cummings, by then supposedly in retirement, fired the chairman and chief executive officer of Consolidated, William Howlett. Howlett, assuming he had absolute power at Consolidated, fired Cummings' son, cut Cummings' salary in half, and removed his picture from the cover of the annual report. Cummings' retribution was lightning swift, and Howlett commented that the thought ''that hell hath no fury like a founder scorned is perhaps an accurate one.'' Cummings, often called ruthless by his critics, responded: ''A businessman can be ruthless, otherwise he's not a good businessman. Too many people are afraid of making decisions.''

Cummings was born in Saint John, New Brunswick, Canada, the son of Lithuanian Jewish immigrants (originally named Kaminsky) who owned a small shop in the city. The family later moved to Montreal where his father owned a shoe store. Young Nate worked for his father until he was fourteen, at which time he was sent to a trade school in New York, where he studied window dressing. It was during this time, according to a story Cummings often told, that he learned a great object lesson. One night, he found himself stranded without money in Brooklyn. Cold, hungry, and frightened, he vowed he would never again be caught short of money. He returned shortly afterward to Montreal, where he became his father's partner in the shoe business, and later branched into shoe wholesaling as a salesman for a manufacturer. During this same period, Cummings began to import rubber goods into Canada and began to manufacture shoes. These enterprises did reasonably well until the Great Depression of the 1930s, and Cummings was forced into bankruptcy in 1934. Somehow, he scraped together enough money to buy McCormick's Limited, a maker of biscuits and candy in London, Ontario. Cummings began building this firm into a strong competitor of the powerful British-controlled Weston, Limited, for the Canadian market. Ultimately, Weston proved to be too powerful, and in 1938 Cummings sold out for a reported half million dollars. At the age of forty-two, Cummings had made a nice fortune for himself; he had proved he was a capable businessman in two Canadian industries; and he thought it was probably time to retire. Before long, Cummings was looking for a diversion from his boredom.

In 1939, some ''friends in Dun & Bradstreet'' put Cummings on to the seventy-two-year-old C. D. Kenney Company, wholesale grocers of Baltimore. The venerable firm was limping badly, and Cummings invested a reported $200,000, deciding to shape up the company. By 1942, Cummings had Kenney operating so well that he borrowed $4.2 million to purchase Chicago's Sprague, Warner & Company, the Midwest's biggest wholesale grocer. He merged it with Kenney to create a powerful entity in the wholesale grocery business. Two years later, when the two companies were running smoothly, Cummings bought yet another. Borrowing $1.5 million, he purchased 85 percent of Western Grocery of Marshalltown, Iowa, one of the biggest wholesale grocers west of the Mississippi. With this move, Cummings' wholesale grocery operations blanketed about three-quarters of the United States. Much of the financing for these acquisitions was obtained from Baltimore's Commercial Credit Corporation; some viewed Cummings as simply a front man for that organization, but he denied it. In 1945, Cummings took control of the ninety-two-year-old Reid, Murdoch Company, and he also picked up Dannemiller Grocery of Canton, Ohio, merging all of these units into Consolidated Grocers Corporation of Chicago. At that time, he laid out his strategy to *Time* magazine: ''Acquire control of good, old, large companies and apply streamlining.''

By the end of the 1940s, Cummings and his Consolidated Grocers had become dominant forces in the wholesale grocery business. With net sales of $141 million in fiscal 1947, profits were running very well, particularly since Cummings had greatly increased the number of private label products that the firm handled. Sold under the Jack Sprat label, they carried a higher profit margin than nationally advertised brand names. Cummings' strategy was to sell primarily to independent retailers, providing discounts on the national brands, and selling large quantities of the Consolidated brand simultaneously.

In 1954, Cummings renamed his food giant Consolidated Foods, reflecting the fact that it was increasingly moving from wholesaling into manufacturing. A major acquisition in 1955 was the giant Omaha Cold Storage Company, which he operated as Ocoma Foods until it was sold in 1972. Another important acquisition during this time was the Piggly Wiggly markets, which were sold in 1969. The most significant and most profitable acquisition, however, was the Kitchens of Sara Lee. Named for Lubin's daughter, the small outfit had prospered by marketing high-quality frozen desserts, specializing in rich cheesecakes. Other important purchases during the 1950s and early 1960s were the Lawson Milk Company, a chain of Ohio convenience stores which Consolidated kept until 1985, and the Shasta Beverage Company, makers of soda pop distributed through grocery wholesalers rather than bottlers.

By the 1960s, Cummings was referring to Consolidated as a "food banker," and he was on the prowl for small manufacturing firms to add to its vault. American Tobacco had tried to purchase Consolidated in the early 1960s, but the Justice Department had disapproved of the merger. Cummings later reflected that "we will consider only those mergers in which Consolidated will be the surviving corporation"—meaning that he was looking for smaller fish. In the mid–1960s he found two such companies: Joe Lowe Corporation, a New Jersey maker of Popsicles and Fudgsicles, and Chicken Delight, a processor and supplier for a chain of nearly 500 franchised carryout and delivery chicken outlets. In 1966, Cummings acquired Idaho Frozen Foods for $3.4 million, along with a number of other small food companies. By then, Consolidated had become America's fastest growing food processor, with sales of $830 million and profits of $24 million.

But Cummings was beginning to lust after companies outside the food industry, with the idea that Consolidated could become a full-fledged conglomerate. Calling the company an "autonoplex," standing for autonomous complex, he intended to use a decentralized administrative system to allow Consolidated to purchase a wide variety of firms. Growth over the next several years was dizzying—in the 1970s alone, Cummings bought at least seventy companies and sold about the same number, sometimes the same companies. Added to the fold were the Fuller Brush Company; the Electrolux vacuum cleaner firm; a number of regional meat packers with combined sales by the end of the 1970s of $600 million; Abbey Rents, the equipment rental concern; and Tyco Industries, makers of toys; along with a large variety of other companies.

By 1975, Nate Cummings had already removed two successors who failed to please him. The first was William Howlett in 1970, and the second was William A. Buzick, Jr., in 1975. Although the second parting was more amicable than the first, Buzick had not been able to keep earnings up to the standards Nate Cummings had expected, so his resignation was requested. By this point, it did not seem that anyone but the seventy-nine-year-old Cummings was ever going to be able to run the $2-billion conglomerate. In fact, the *Wall Street Journal* commented in 1976: "The company had the simplest organization chart you ever saw. It was Nate." But changes were in the offing, and they came in the person of young John H. Bryan, Jr.

Bryan, a native of West Point, Mississippi, had earned an economics degree at the University of Virginia and then his MBA at Mississippi State, by studying evenings. During this time, he joined his family's meat-packing concern in West Point, where he installed more sophisticated financial and production control systems, modernized and expanded the plant, and engaged in a high-quality marketing and advertising program for his company's products. But, as a family business, disagreement evolved about who should run it. When the dispute proved to be unsolvable, the company was sold to Consolidated Foods in 1968 for $16 million in Consolidated shares. John Bryan continued to run the family business, now called Bryan Foods, for Consolidated until 1974, when he was made second-in-command of the parent company. A year later, when Buzick was let go, Cummings picked Bryan as his replacement.

Many observers were certain that Bryan would be totally intimidated by the legendary Cummings. As one insider said in 1975, "Now we have a situation where a 38-year-old will be coming up to cope with a septuagenarian chairman." But Bryan quite coolly and politely said, "Don't think I'm going to sit here and get instructions from Mr. Cummings." And he didn't. He started right off by telling Cummings that Cummings' vaunted autonoplex system was dead. Consolidated provided too much autonomy, and Bryan was determined to bring a greater degree of central control to its operations. He also made an important change in the board of directors. Cummings had controlled the firm (even though he had less than 5 percent of the stock) because fourteen of the seventeen directors were insiders, devoted to Cummings. Called "the barons," they made it possible for Cummings to fire two past presidents. But Bryan suggested to Cummings that seven of the barons be replaced, and Cummings agreed. As a result, only four of the directors, by the early 1980s, were insiders, and Cummings' power was broken. But Bryan was always careful to respect Cummings' accomplishments and position. As he said, "I show Nate respect because he has done some very great things, and because I was taught to treat my elders in that manner. But I also genuinely like him, even though I know some other people don't." He also respected Cummings' wishes in other ways. Cummings, who was very parsimonious, even demanded that secretaries retrieve paper clips from wastebaskets. Howlett and Buzick had attempted to curb Cummings' demands in these areas, but Bryan humored him. Bryan even eliminated the firm's only limousine to please Cummings, and he refused to decorate Consolidated's drab offices as long as Cummings was alive. After Cummings' death, the offices of the Sara Lee Corporation became among the most elegant in Chicago.

By the end of the 1970s, Consolidated Foods was a massive operation, with sales of $4.7 billion and $111 million in profits. The firm had grown at an annual compounded rate of 16.5 percent, from $2.5 billion when Bryan took over. Part of Bryan's strategy for this growth involved dealing with larger units than before. As he told *Fortune* in 1979: "It's utter foolishness to have a $10-million company in a $4-billion or $5-billion corporation." So he identified about forty-nine relatively small operations within the Consolidated empire (the largest had sales of $100 million a year) and sold them. He then used about $500 million to make some significant purchases. One of these was the Douwe Egbert company of Holland, a coffee, tea, and tobacco exporter, which gave Consolidated a presence on the European scene for the first time. Most significant, however, was the $250-million acquisition of Hanes Corporation, a Winston-Salem, North Carolina, producer of women's hosiery and men's underwear. As ruthless as Cummings appeared at times, during his tenure, Consolidated had traditionally made only friendly mergers. But Bryan showed that there was a lot of iron inside his velvet glove. When he set his sights on Hanes, nothing could stop him, not even the concerted opposition of the founding family. Bryan's victory was denounced by many, including the Hanes family. During the 1980s, Consolidated continued its impressive growth under the guidance of John Bryan, and by 1983 it had become one of the most profitable diversified food companies in the United States. The most successful unit in the firm at that time was Bryan's prize, the Hanes Corporation; with sales doubling from $450 million to $900 million, it proved to be a great bargain. Renamed Sara Lee Corporation in April 1985, Cummings' creation in 1987 had sales of over $9 billion, profits of $267 million, and over 92,000 employees. It was one of the largest food companies of any kind in the United States, and one of the most consistently profitable. Although recognizing the value in acquisition, John Bryan during the late 1980s turned his focus to a comprehensive $450-million capital investment program designed to expand facilities (new plants, warehouses, and equipment) to encourage and accommodate growth.

By that time, of course, old Nate Cummings was dead. He had gone out in style. For his eightieth birthday, in 1976, he had thrown himself a birthday party at the Waldorf Astoria. Six hundred people were invited, and Bob Hope was the emcee. During his lifetime, Cummings had become interested in art, and he had gathered one of the most impressive private collections in contemporary America. The paintings and sculptures, which filled his nine-room apartment at the Waldorf Towers, were also exhibited at the National Gallery of Art, the Metropolitan Museum of Art, the Chicago Art Institute, and the Museum of Modern Art. His gift of over 600 pieces of rare pre-Columbian art has been placed in a gallery bearing his name at the Metropolitan Museum. It was a fitting tribute to a man who said: "I used to walk by the Metropolitan Museum and ask myself, 'Do people like me go into places like that?' '' (**B.** *Who Was Who*; *Time*, February 7, 1944, June 11, 1945, June 24, 1966; *Business Week*, January 10, 1948, May 22, 1965, March 3, 1975, August 29, 1983, October 23, 1987, November 14, 1988; *Newsweek*, September 6, 1948, January 26, 1970; *Fortune*, November 1955, June 4, 1979, November 16, 1981; *Life*, October 23, 1970; Milton Moskowitz et al., *Everybody's Business*, 1980; *New York Times*, February 21, 1985; Edwin Darby, *The Fortune Builders*, 1986.)

CUNNINGHAM, HARRY BLAIR (1907–   ). Retailer, S. S. Kresge, K mart. The greatest innovation in American retailing after World War II was the emergence of the discounters, and Harry Cunningham was the most significant new retailing revolutionary. Until 1951, a series of so-called fair trade laws dominated retailing. Generally passed during the Great Depression of the 1930s, these laws sought to eliminate unfair competition by price cutting; in other words, to prevent large chain stores from engaging in deep discounting which might drive out their smaller, independent competitors. In 1951, the Supreme Court declared these laws unconstitutional, and the doors were opened for the large chains to offer discounts of from 15 to 25 percent on name brand merchandise. Out of this situation emerged a new phenomenon—the discounter. Although neither Harry Cunningham nor his company, S. S. Kresge, invented the discount approach, they brought the concept to its apotheosis.

Harry Cunningham was born in Home Camp, Pennsylvania, the youngest of eight children of a farmer. His family ran out of money after he had spent two years at Miami University in Ohio. Forced to leave school, Cunningham began to work for Kresge's in 1928 as a management trainee. His first position was as a stockboy in the sub-basement of a Kresge store in Lynchburg, Virginia. Working seventy, eighty, and even ninety hours a week, Cunningham was tagged early as a standout by Kresge brass, and promotions came quickly to the young man. He soon became a store manager and progressed from there to superintendent of stores, assistant sales manager, sales director, and general vice president and a member of the board of directors in 1957. Two years later, Cunningham became president and chief executive officer of the 717-store retail chain. He remained head of the firm until his retirement in 1972.

The retail chain Cunningham inherited at the end of the 1950s was in deep trouble. The company had been founded as a five-and-ten-cent store by Sebastian S. Kresge* in 1899. Over the next half century, it became one of the most successful retail businesses in America. By the early 1950s, however, the industry had become the victim of two phenomena: the first was the Supreme Court's decision that invalidated the fair trade laws; the second was the mass exodus of Americans from the central cities to the suburbs. The Kresge chain thus found itself caught in a twin dilemma: Kresge's stores, which were located in downtown areas, were being left behind by potential shoppers; and the new stores, being built in the suburbs, were following the discount framework. Kresge Company, before Cunningham took over, seemed unable to respond effectively to this challenge.

Cunningham began to make Kresge a discounter when he became sales director in 1953. He felt strongly that the Kresge chain had lost contact with the principles responsible for bringing it success in its early years. The five-and-dime stores of the early twentieth century had competed successfully with department stores and other competitors by stressing low profit margins with a rapid turnover of merchandise, often five or six times a year. Beginning in the 1920s, this strategy began to change. Greater gross margins became the new watchwords. Kresge, like other similar stores, began to expand the range of merchandise it carried, raised its gross margins, and reduced the number of turnovers per year to about four. When the discounters resurrected the old dime-store philosophy of low margins and high turnover in the early 1950s and began to cut deeply into Kresge's sales and profits, Cunningham knew it was time to respond.

As assistant sales manager, Cunningham became interested in the discounting operations of a new venture in Garden City, Long Island. Eugene Ferkhauf, a retailing genius, started a discount department store called E. J. Korvette. In his store, Ferkhauf offered shoppers a no-frills, mass-merchandising approach. Featuring low prices, even on nationally advertised brands, Korvette's established free-standing department stores in the suburbs with plenty of parking space. Cunningham studied Ferkhauf's operation closely and determined that he would apply the same principles to Kresge. Cunningham recognized, however, that he would have to move cautiously in the venerable and conservative company. As he commented, "Discounting at the time had a terrible odor, if I had announced my intentions ahead of time I never would have been made president."

Cunningham, as executive vice president from 1957 to 1959, slowly and carefully laid the groundwork for the changes he would later make. During these years, he traveled around the country and investigated sites for future discount operations. When he was named president in 1959, Cunningham instructed all his executives to study the discounters for two years, and he made a commitment of nearly $80 million in leases and merchandise for the first sixty discount stores. The new stores, which were called K mart to distinguish them from the tired old Kresge operations, were enormous, 60,000- to 90,000-square-foot operations, located outside existing shopping plazas, in free-standing sites with acres of parking space. The keys to the new K mart operation were low gross margins and high turnover, with a goal of eight stock turns a year, double what the Kresge stores were doing at the time. The first K mart store opened in a Detroit suburb on March 1, 1962. That store was a success, and seventeen more stores were opened during the year.

It was soon clear that Cunningham had hit upon a winning combination. The Kresge-chain sales in 1962 were $483 million, less than half that of the Woolworth chain. In a few years, Kresge overtook Woolworth, which moved slowly into discounting with its Woolco stores. By 1980, with its name changed to K mart Corporation, the chain had sales of nearly $13 billion, and profits had risen from $9 million in 1962 to over $300 million. By that time there were nearly 1,500 K marts. Cunningham had opened them at a pace of about 150 per year while he was head of the company, but after he resigned the numbers accelerated greatly. During 1976, an unprecedented 271 K marts were opened, committing the company to increase its retail space by 17 million square feet in a single year. All the K mart stores have one thing in common—Cunningham's conviction that the modern American shopper wants the nicer things in life but wants them provided in a self-service framework that results in lower prices. K mart also recognizes its limitations. As Cunningham's successor commented, "We'll never be a fashion leader, but we will be the fastest follower there ever was." K mart has been such a rapid follower that they have become the nation's second largest retailer, after Sears. It nearly passed Sears in 1984 when it had $21.1 billion in sales, leaving it just about $600 million behind. In the later 1980s, however, Sears has pulled significantly ahead by stressing a variety of nonretailing concerns, while K mart remained mired at about $25 billion in 1987. Its profits, though, were still strong at $642 million.

Cunningham has also served as president and chairman of the Variety Stores Association, and he has received a number of awards for his achievements: Marketing Executive of the Year, Pioneer Retailer Award, and the National Retail Men's Association Gold Medal in 1976. Perhaps his greatest reward came in 1977, however, when the Kresge board of directors voted to change the name of the venerable corporation to K mart Corporation. In the emotional debate which ensued, Stanley Kresge, the founder's son, argued that the company's name "should relate to the founder." But the meeting overwhelmingly supported the change, and perhaps it reflected part of the important homogenization effect that K mart has had upon America. One of Cunningham's and K mart's most enduring (and least admirable) legacies is the way in which K mart has added to the sterilization of the American suburban landscape. Except for size, all K marts are alike. They are laid out in an identical manner, the decor is undifferentiated, and the stores themselves are located in the middle of nowhere—on a highway between two places, rather than within a community. A rootless reflection of modern America, it is perhaps more symbolic than was intended that the company severed its own roots by changing its name to K mart. (**B.** *Newsweek*, May 18, 1959; *Business Week*, January 29, 1966; *Stores*, January 1976; *Fortune*, July 1977, January 30, 1978; Milton Moskowitz et al., *Everybody's Business*, 1980; *Chain Store Age Executive*, August 1985.)

D

DAVIS, MARVIN HAROLD (1925–   ). Oil wildcatter, entertainment mogul, entrepreneur, Davis Oil Company, Twentieth Century-Fox. Marvin Davis is a full-fledged Denver billionaire, and one of the most powerful entrepreneurs in America, but he gets little respect from the Denver social elite. He remains an outsider, they claim, because he lacks polish. A good example of this came in 1977 when he decided to throw a birthday party for himself. The grounds were decorated in an Old South motif, with a ministeamboat chugging around the pool. One of the guests remarked that "[t]here was enough Dom Pérignon to put out a fire in an oil field." Most astonishing, however, was the fact that Davis had hired a group of young blacks to sit on cotton bales and eat watermelon. Behind Davis' back the local notables still refer to the affair as "the pickaninny party." Sensitivity has never been one of the noted attributes of the 6-foot 4-inch, 300-pound ex-defensive tackle.

Davis was born in New Jersey, son of Jack Davis, a Jewish immigrant from England. The elder Davis had been a sailor and boxer in his home country, but he hustled a modest fortune in the garment industry in New York in the late 1930s and early 1940s. After World War II, Jack Davis started to drill for oil in Colorado, Texas, and Illinois with some success and formed the Davis Oil Company. During the 1960s, in increasingly poor health, the elder Davis turned the business over to his son. Marvin had attended Syracuse University and earned a degree in civil engineering from New York University. He joined his father's company in 1947, soon after it was organized, and the two men focused their attention on the Rocky Mountains area. At this time the Rocky Mountains were still considered a backwater of the nation's oil industry. At first, Jack Davis had precious little success with his oil drilling, and he wanted to cease operations. But Marvin, whose guru was H. L. Hunt* ("Son, the guy that drills the most has the chance of coming up with the most"), urged his father to continue buying leases, which ultimately proved to be the secret of success for Davis Oil. Throughout the 1950s and 1960s, Davis Oil bought up leases that other companies considered uneconomic. Marvin Davis then hired high-powered geologists to determine the amount of oil reserves on these leases, and when the price of oil began escalating, particularly in the 1970s, Davis Oil made windfall profits. As one analyst has commented, Davis "bought leases wholesale and sold drilling ventures retail."

Thus, by the early 1970s Davis Oil owned interests in 600 producing wells and was digging another 250 to 300 wells a year, and Marvin Davis was called "Mr. Wildcatter." Wildcatters are independent oil prospectors whose oil discoveries are then sold, refined, and distributed through the major oil companies. Davis' philosophy was to drill as many wells as possible, echoing Hunt: "This is a percentage business. The more wells you drill, the better the chances for success." Most of these wells were partnerships with major oil companies, but Davis Oil itself remained a partnership with no public ownership. As a consequence, its operations were deeply shrouded in secrecy.

With the great explosion in oil prices and profits after the Arab oil embargo in 1973, Marvin Davis became profoundly wealthy. In 1979, he was ranked the third most active driller of wildcat oil and gas wells in America, behind only Amoco and Exxon. During the twenty-five years from the mid–1950s to the end of the 1970s, it was estimated that he drilled or helped drill 10,000 wells, of which 1,500 became producers. Davis Oil's operating wells in 1979 produced as much as 100,000 barrels of oil daily. At the high price levels of that year, his personal return was somewhere between $40 and $80 million annually. His wealth at that time was estimated at anywhere between $200 and $500 million. But Davis was just getting started. The 1980s saw him move out of the oil patch and into the broader realm of mergers and acquisitions, as Davis became one of the major players in the great game of arbitrage that so characterized the decade.

With his extraordinary wealth and cash flow, Davis began investing in other ventures. During the late 1970s, he built and owned Denver's Metro Bank (assets: $168 million in 1981), and he became the city's largest real estate developer. He built four Denver office towers, which he sold to Prudential Insurance in 1982 for $500 million, just before real estate prices in the area crashed. He also built a $150-million shopping center and office complex, and in 1979, with a group of investors, he bought the 22,000-acre Phipps family estate in Littleton, Colorado, for $16 million. Six months later, the group sold it to Mission Viejo Company, a California-based developer, for $22 million. In 1978, Davis offered $12 million to Charlie Finley for the Oakland A's, but the deal fell through when the A's could not get out of their lease. All of this activity, however, merely laid the groundwork for Davis' more spectacular forays of the later 1980s.

In 1981, just before oil prices crashed, Davis sold about half of his oil properties to Hiram Walker–Consumers Home Ltd., of Toronto, for $630 million. With this money, Davis decided to pursue the movie business. Most observers felt that Davis' desire to enter the movie industry was based less on cool business calculation than on the fact that he was "starstruck." One former movie executive said: "Marvin just fell in love with the business. He got bit by the showbiz bug.'' Teaming up with the wily commodities trader Marc Rich,[†] Davis paid $720 million for Twentieth Century-Fox in June 1981. Fox, founded in 1933 by Darryl F. Zanuck, had, over the years, been one of the most successful studios in Hollywood. In the 1950s, however, it began to decline, and in 1962 it was almost destroyed by the disastrous *Cleopatra*. Richard Zanuck, son of Darryl, saved Fox with *The Sound of Music* in 1965, but was nonetheless forced out in 1970. In 1973, Alan Ladd, Jr., was hired to run the film division, and he pulled out a string of hits, culminating with *Star Wars*, which was made for $10 million in 1977 and grossed $200 million in the first two years after its release. With the money it made from *Star Wars*, Fox bought a Coca-Cola bottling plant in Minnesota; Aspen Skiing, the nation's largest ski resort operator; Magnetic Video, which sells prerecorded video cassettes; and Pebble Beach Corporation, which operates a luxury hotel, golf course, and other amenities on California's Monterey Peninsula.

With the price at fifteen times 1980 earnings, however, the ''smart money'' thought Davis and Rich had stars in their eyes, and had been victimized on their Fox purchase. The irony was that Davis ended up owning the massive movie business without having to put up a cent of his own money. Davis and Rich put up $172 million and borrowed $550 million, mostly from Chicago's Continental Illinois Bank, to pay for the film company. The banks gave them until December 31, 1981, to repay their loan. Rich then moved into the background and let Davis manipulate the assets. What followed was a complex lesson in high finance. The first step for Davis was to divide up the assets. The second was to write up the asset's values, and the third was to borrow heavily against those—what is termed ''mortgaging out.'' It was a way of making the purchase pay for itself— a classic leveraged buyout. By September of that year, Davis had broken up Fox into marketable pieces. He then sold a half interest in the bottling plant, movie-theater chain, Aspen, Pebble Beach, and posh Century City development (site of the original Fox studio) to Aetna Life & Casualty for $183 million, of which the studio immediately paid $176 million to Davis and Rich. A short time later, Fox and Aetna sold the bottling company for $70 million, which netted another $35 million for Davis and Rich. They also paid themselves $18 million out of Fox's treasury. Thus, by the end of 1981, Davis and Rich had recovered their original investment and had taken an additional $58 million from Fox.

Some of this money had to be paid to the banks as interest on the massive loan, but Davis immediately transferred the debt from him and Rich to Fox. By the end of December, Davis had pledged the assets Fox still owned against a new $300-million term loan due in 1990, and a $200-million revolving line of credit, convertible in 1985 to a four-year term loan. In the end, Davis and Rich were able to pay off their loan with the proceeds and have $7 million left over. But they had not yet mortgaged out, so in July 1982, Fox and Aetna unloaded Fox's movie theaters, and in August of that year Fox dumped its record and music publishing businesses. The two sales raised $72 million cash, of which $53 million went to Davis and Rich. At that point, Davis brought in another partner—CBS—to produce and distribute Fox films in the booming videocassette market. For this privilege, CBS paid in $45 million, $40 million of which went to Davis and Rich. In August 1983, Davis withdrew another $66 million from Fox's treasury and during the next fiscal year, $145 million more.

Thus, by the end of the 1984 fiscal year, Davis and Rich had taken out of Fox enough to repay their $550-million purchase debt, enough to cover their $172-million purchase equity, and were still $300 million ahead. The next step for Davis was to remove Marc Rich. When the two men bought Fox, only Davis had voting shares, but in the fall of 1981 Rich demanded that his shares also be given voting rights. Davis agreed, but the conversion was never carried out because the following summer Rich came under investigation by the U.S. Attorney for illegally selling price-controlled oil and for failing to pay at least $48 million in income taxes. Rich fled to Switzerland, where he continued to live as a fugitive. Davis then announced his intention of purchasing Rich's half-share in Fox. The price he paid was not disclosed, but it was about $116 million, all of which went to pay the government's claim against Rich and his companies.

Davis had won again. He was a billionaire on paper by the mid–1980s, and he was the owner of Twentieth Century-Fox, which, although heavily burdened with debt, was worth about $1.3 billion. In March 1985, however, Davis began selling off Fox to Rupert Murdoch, the Australian media baron. Davis sold half of his interest in Fox to Murdoch for $250 million. Later, Davis sold the other half for a similar amount, while retaining some real estate holdings from the Fox properties. It was estimated that Davis made about $350 million on the deal. These transactions, along with the sale of about $200 million worth of oil properties to Apache Petroleum in 1985, made him a cash billionaire. Davis took $135 million of this money and bought the Beverly Hills Hotel from Ivan Boesky in 1986, flipping it a year later for $200 million. It soon became clear that Davis had an uncanny knack for knowing when to buy and sell properties. One of the reasons for his success, according to Marvin Goldfarb, a film distributor, and one of Davis' oldest friends, is that "Marvin never marries anything. He knows when to buy and when to sell."

In 1986 Davis became a suitor for CBS. He offered $3.75 billion for the giant entertainment company, of which $600 million was reputed to be Davis' own money. By this point, however, CBS had come under the influence of its largest stockholder, Laurence Tisch[†] of Loews Corporation. Davis had badly miscalculated the situation at CBS, and he was astonished at the speed with which his offer was rejected. He had thought Tisch was simply an investor who would sell for the right price. It later became clear that Tisch wanted the firm for himself, and Davis had been fleeced by an older, more experienced operator. Davis was hardly chastened by his experience, proclaiming his interest in a number of other properties and boasting that "nobody scares me off."

Throughout his business career, Davis has always had a reputation as an extremely demanding boss, but one who pays valuable employees exceedingly well. He hires the best geologists in the business and rewards them handsomely with royalty incomes. But, as one oilman has said, "Davis tends to burn people out." Thus, in the late 1970s, both R. W. Willingham, drilling and production manager, and Marlis Smith, chief geologist, left Davis' employ, each with hundreds of thousands of dollars annually in royalty income for their retirement. Edward Lafaye, who succeeded Smith as chief geologist, earned an estimated $3 million in royalty payments in just his first year. Nonetheless, "Davis is brutal on his people," a competitor has commented, "they get Sunday phone calls at 2 A.M. His attitude is: 'They're expendable.'"

In the early 1970s, Marvin Davis was asked to provide some tips for success in the industry for small independent oil operators. He provided a two-word answer: "Be aggressive!" That philosophy has guided Davis' business career over the years. Aggressive buying of oil leases in the 1950s laid the basis for his fortune. Aggressive buying for oil in the late 1960s and early 1970s brought him mountains of cash. Selling these oil properties at the peak of oil prices brought him still more money. He then invested in the real estate boom, which he again liquidated before the market fell. Then he bought Twentieth Century-Fox with borrowed money, held it for a short time, and made a large profit. Finally, when the stock market crashed in October 1987, his assets were in cash rather than stocks, again enhancing his position.

In 1988 *Forbes* estimated that Davis was worth "at least" $1.6 billion, with about $1 billion of this in cash. His fortune rested on three pillars: tough deal making ("Marvin will get your last nickle"), keen timing, and the shrewd use of other people's money. Marvin Davis may never be accepted by the bluebloods of Denver, but he has become one of the most powerful and successful entrepreneurs of the past quarter century. (**B.** *The Oil and Gas Journal*, November 1, 1971; *Forbes*, November 26, 1979, March 12, December 31, 1984, October 24, 1988; *Newsweek*, March 2, 1981; David McClintick, *Indecent Exposure*, 1983; *Fortune*, January 7, 1985, October 12, 1987; *Business Week*, April 8, 1985, April 21, 1986; *Barron's*, November 22, 1988.)

DEBARTOLO, EDWARD JOHN (May 17, 1919?–   ). Real estate and shopping mall developer, Edward J. DeBartolo Corporation. Cruising along at 41,000 feet in his private Learjet, Edward DeBartolo experiences what for him is the ultimate joy—examining land for a proposed shopping mall. "You see that graded trapezoidal area? That's our mall. That's big, boy. That's a piece of land you can work with. See that land to the south? That's Kissimmee. Look at all that growth fanning out there from Orlando . . . and there's the Interstate connecting them. My gosh, that site has everything." DeBartolo, by far America's largest mall developer and operator, by the mid–1980s owned fifty-five major malls with over 60 million square feet. In addition, he also owned offices, hotels, condominiums, racetracks, sports teams, and much of the real estate surrounding his malls. When one talks about the "malling" of America and the great suburban explosion that has changed the landscape and social interaction of Americans so much in the postwar period, DeBartolo, as much as anyone, else, is responsible.

And he makes no apologies. When critics began bemoaning the loss of downtown cores in American cities and decried the nameless, faceless, sameness of the exploding suburban environment DeBartolo and others were creating, he was unapologetic. "Downtown is dead," he said. . . . I wouldn't put a penny downtown. It's bad. . . . Face it, why should people come [downtown]? They don't want the hassle, they don't want the danger. . . . So, what should you do? Exactly what I'm doing: stay out in the country. That's the new downtown."

Born Edward J. Parnessa in Youngstown, Ohio, he became DeBartolo after his father's death and his mother's marriage to Michael DeBartolo. Young Edward DeBartolo was educated in area schools, and he worked part-time for his stepfather, a master mason who later became a general contractor. Edward first worked on a few sidewalk and driveway jobs, but as he matured, he gradually played a more significant role in the company. Since his stepfather's primary language was Italian, Edward began to write out bids for him and conduct some of the small company's business negotiations in English while he was still in his teens.

After graduating from high school, DeBartolo evidently thought about becoming a truck driver. His mother objected vehemently. A cousin was going to Notre Dame, and she insisted Edward also go. "Jackass!" she said. "Your cousin will be a college graduate, and you will be a *truck driver!*" So, he headed for Notre Dame, with no application and no high school references, but he managed to gain admittance anyhow. DeBartolo studied civil engineering and worked his way through school with night jobs in general contracting. When he left Notre Dame, DeBartolo had big plans. Upon returning home, he convinced his stepfather to expand his business, and, subsequently, they went from building sidewalks and driveways to building roads. The roads got longer and wider, and the DeBartolo operation grew apace. In 1940 Edward made his first real estate deal. With no capital to back him, DeBartolo went to a sheriff's sale in Boardman, an exurb of Youngstown. There he bought a downtown corner of shabby buildings for $75,000. The reaction of other people was that he had bought junk, but the buildings were structurally sound, and DeBartolo knew they just needed refacing. He then went to the banks and said, "Lend me the money, I just bought that corner." His brother-in-law later commented, "I guess they admired his guts. He got the money, and then he was off and running."

Before DeBartolo could run too far, however, World War II intervened. After serving as a lieutenant in the U.S. Army, he returned to Youngstown to resume his business career. He and his stepfather began to erect supermarkets and drugstores in and around Youngstown in the late 1940s. In 1948 Edward DeBartolo established his own company. Two years later, he developed Boardman Plaza, a convenience shopping strip consisting of food and specialty stores which opened with twenty-three stores. People thought DeBartolo had made a huge mistake with this venture. As his wife, Marie, later commented, Boardman at that time was way out in the country: "I mean *country*," she said, "everyone thought he was crazy." But DeBartolo went ahead and built it and convinced others to lease stores in it. The day it opened, a proud Edward DeBartolo stood outside on the new sidewalk to admire his property, only to overhear one leading local realtor say to another: "I'll give this place six months to fold." It didn't. Boardman Plaza instead was the beginning of the suburbanization of Youngstown, and one of the first instances of suburban mall development in America. Soon, office buildings and medical centers followed the shopping center, more roads were built, Boardman became a residential suburb, and the little shopping strip continued to grow. By 1980, it continued to thrive with fifty-two stores. "We were able to lease those stores so rapidly," he said, "that we knew we were on the right track by moving out into the country, and we started to really go."

Consequently, DeBartolo began building other malls, first in Ohio and Pennsylvania, and then all over the United States. His strip malls became L-shaped malls, and these evolved into U-shapes. Then, in the 1960s, DeBartolo began enclosing those U-shaped malls, making them shiny, spacious, comfortable, affluent, and secure. These became giant regional malls, the veritable prototype of a new, suburban America. By the mid–1950s, there were over 1,800 shopping centers in the United States, and hundreds more were in the design and construction stages. No one was more important in this transformation of America than Edward DeBartolo. As the *New York Times Magazine* put it:

A shopping mall is elusively more than its parts . . . a shopping mall is consumerism transformed into social experience: a place to dress up for, meet friends in, take a leisurely browse, have a meal, see a movie, bring the kids, bring the spouse, bask in the warm, sly suggestion that families that spend money together have more fun.

During the 1960s and early 1970s, DeBartolo built about thirty of the covered supermalls—"monsters," he calls them proudly—each covering one million square feet or more. By the early 1980s, he had forty-one of them, with seven more malls under construction and twenty-six more in some stage of planning. In addition, the company owned four banks and three condominiums in Florida. In an about-face for DeBartolo, he also owned a forty-six-storied combination office and retail building in *downtown* Pittsburgh. DeBartolo's investment in Pittsburgh made economic sense because it was one of the few American cities that retained a vibrant, healthy downtown core.

It was not just luck or good timing that brought this prosperity to DeBartolo— he was a workaholic. Even as he entered his seventies, he was in the office every day at about 5:30 A.M. During the early morning hours he concentrated on reading reports and dictating letters. At around 9 A.M. he walked around headquarters, where 300 of his 3,000 employees worked, and inquired what they were doing. Every Saturday he held a staff meeting with the sixteen people who headed his divisions, but, since DeBartolo Corporation is a private, family-held company, most of the important decisions were made by Edward and his two children—Maria Denise, a graduate of St. Mary's at Notre Dame and vice president, and Edward Jr., a graduate of Notre Dame, who was co-head of the company.

DeBartolo drove his executives as hard as he drove himself, expecting them to put in six-day weeks, but the rewards were ample. He not only paid his top executives very well, but he also distributed among his employees about 35 percent of the ownership of every fifth mall he built. As a result, he has created a number of millionaires on his staff. DeBartolo kept a close watch on every detail of his operation, and he knew his staff intimately. His chief of public relations said he had a mind like a steel trap—he never forgot the name of an employee, a birthday, or a due date for a report.

Although DeBartolo was a workaholic, and a driven man, his passion was not for the organization, or for money. It was for the malls themselves. The malls were designed in what an associate called "DeBartolo Modern"—"Clean lines, functional, efficient, well-landscaped, with colors and textures that look pleasant and suit the region. . . . Our whole idea is easy maintenance, prevention of decay, keeping the place from looking seedy." To make sure they did not deteriorate, DeBartolo was a stickler for cleanliness. "Disorder is costly," he said. "Mental disorder, physical disorder, all disorder is *costly*. I take more pride in our maintenance than anything else. Our maintenance cost is 50 percent less than other developers'. Why? Because our people are trained, trained, trained." He was also famous for the speed with which he launched and finished his projects. Usually finishing a mall in a year, he said: "That's what made this company. Speed and guts." This speed was possible because the company is privately held. He could make all the decisions himself, or by consulting several family members. As he noted: "I'll tell you, the most exciting thing about this business is making my own decisions and making them fast, move, *move*. No board of directors breathing down my neck. I could never take that."

Edward DeBartolo and his son also took over the ownership of a number of sports teams. It all started for DeBartolo with racetracks. He had invested in them around 1960, purely as a real estate venture. Then, he began to grow fond of them; he owned Thistledown in Cleveland, Balmoral in Chicago, and part of several others. Later, he bought the Pittsburgh Penguins hockey team and also purchased the Pittsburgh Civic Arena, where they played. His son became owner of the San Francisco 49ers of the National Football League. When DeBartolo tried to buy the Chicago White Sox of the American Baseball League in 1980, he ran into problems. Baseball commissioner Bowie Kuhn determined there was no way he would allow DeBartolo to own the team, and he lobbied so effectively that the owners refused him the franchise by an 11–to–3 vote. The stated reason for this rejection was twofold, according to Kuhn: DeBartolo, since he lived in Youngstown, would be an absentee owner of the White Sox; and he also owned race tracks, which Kuhn felt was a detrimental interest. Of course, as many analysts pointed out, several major league club owners were absentee owners, and a number also owned racetracks. What many felt was behind Kuhn's stand was something that had dogged DeBartolo throughout his career—that he was somehow affiliated with organized crime, specifically, the Mafia. DeBartolo had refuted these charges over the years, and he had survived the continual scrutiny of the FBI and the Treasury Department. As Pete Axthelm pointed out in *Newsweek*, baseball had only succeeded in singling out DeBartolo as a "known Italian," and he felt it was a classic example of prejudice. DeBartolo, for his part, was perplexed: "Kuhn gave a speech about baseball's troubled economic picture," he said. "I want to infuse money into the game and make it more competitive—and he stops me. That's quite a contradiction."

In the 1980s, DeBartolo began to expand his interests beyond malls to the stores themselves. In 1986 he bid for Allied Stores, owners of over 200 department stores, including Jordan Marsh and Bonwit Teller. The chain, which placed many stores in DeBartolo's malls, had turned to him as a "white knight" to help foil their takeover by Robert Campeau, the Canadian real estate developer. Despite a protracted court battle, Campeau won control of the Allied chain. One result of this battle, however, was that it forged close ties between DeBartolo and Campeau for future operations. In 1987, when Campeau pursued and won the massive Federated Department store chain with over $11 billion in sales, DeBartolo backed him. Developing what Campeau called a "bang up combination," rival developers were gravely concerned over the consequences of DeBartolo using Campeau's department stores as anchor tenants in new malls he would build in the future. The potential economic might of the two men on the retailing and real estate fields was enormous.

Worth about $1.4 billion in late 1988, DeBartolo was "King of the Malls," with 84 million square feet of space under his management nationwide. He had no plans to slow down. Yet it was not really the money that motivated him. When asked why he drives himself so hard, DeBartolo replied:

I guess I'm kind of obsessive about it. Why? I don't know. Listen, it's not the money. Look at me, a suit off the rack, no big deal. It's the action, I love it. Sometimes I think I'd like to start again from scratch, to see how I'd do. Would I make it? Sure. (*New York Times*)

(**B.** *New York Times Magazine*, August 12, 1973; *Newsweek*, December 22, 1980; *Chain Store Age Executive*, May 1981; *Financial World*, November 25, 1986; *Who's Who in America*, 1986–87; Toronto *Globe & Mail, Report on Business*, July 1988, 36–45; *Forbes*, October 24, 1988.)

DELLA FEMINA, JERRY (July 22, 1936–   ). Advertising agency executive, Della Femina and Travisano. In 1967, Jerry Della Femina was the new, thirty-year-old creative director of the Ted Bates & Company advertising agency. As one of the so-called "class of '67" in American advertising, he had been hired to bring sparkle and zest to Bates' advertising. The account was Panasonic, the Japanese electronics firm. The six account, copy, and art supervisors were all engaged in a deadly serious discussion about what approach to take in the campaign. After listening in mind-numbing boredom for some time, Della Femina (it was his first day on the job) cleared his throat and proclaimed: "I've got it! How about this for a headline: 'From Those Wonderful Folks Who Gave You Pearl Harbor.' " The group sat dumbfounded, and one account executive dropped his pipe. Finally, an art director began to laugh hysterically. The rest of the group remained unsure about what had just happened. By using humor and by defying convention, Della Femina hoped to relax everyone and develop a lighter, more creative ad campaign for the client. Later, Della Femina used the line as the title for his humorous book on the advertising industry.

Jerry Della Femina was born and raised in the tough Gravesend section of Brooklyn. Commenting on his early environment, he said: "The principal product of the neighborhood was the Mafia." His father was a paper cutter for the *New York Times,* and Jerry and his parents lived with his grandparents. He grew up speaking only Italian and did not know a word of English when he started school. Della Femina went to Lafayette High School in Brooklyn, where he distinguished himself primarily by being expelled from school twice for shooting dice in the halls. Upon his graduation in 1954, Della Femina immediately married his high school sweetheart and got a job working as a messenger for the *New York Times*. During the same time, he enrolled in night courses at Brooklyn College, studying advertising. Della Femina dropped out of formal education after one year, commenting that "the losers who can't get a job in advertising teach advertising."

During the next seven years, Della Femina held an astonishing number of meaningless jobs. He knew that he desperately wanted to be a copywriter, but he had great difficulty breaking into the profession. At that time, advertising was very much a WASP preserve, and few "ethnics" were hired at the agencies. The only non-WASP group with any representation on Madison Avenue were the Jews, and they were in only a couple of agencies that had been formed with Jewish owners and staff. As Della Femina noted: "The Italians, they didn't even have this, they were nowhere. We were all working for the Sicilian Asphalt Paving Company. It wasn't that the WASP's hated us, they didn't even know we existed."

During the 1950s, things began to loosen up a bit in the advertising business. Two factors played a major role in this. The first was that the doors of industry everywhere began swinging open to non-WASP groups, and this filtered into advertising. Second, as television became the dominant advertising medium, advertising costs were driven up tremendously. When advertisers began to demand higher quality, more innovative ads for their money, many of the larger agencies, which for years had relied on the WASP "old-boy network" to bring them business, found they were threatened with new competition. A great creative revolution in American advertising, which began in the mid–1950s, came into its own in the 1960s. The leader of this movement was William Bernbach,[†] who brought a new look to advertising with his campaigns. This changed the emphasis in agency hiring, when family background became less important than creative ability. But it was, nonetheless, a long, difficult struggle for Jerry Della Femina during this time.

From 1954 to 1961, Della Femina wandered the fringes of the advertising world, working as a shipping clerk for a shirt company, a mailroom boy for an ad agency, a toy salesman at Macy's, and a bathrobe salesman in Gimbel's basement. Finally, in 1961, when Della Femina was totally down on his luck, having been out of work for six months, he sent some unsolicited sample advertisements to the agency of Daniel & Charles. After sending them for a week, he was granted an interview with the firm's president, Daniel Karsch, who hired Della Femina as a $100-a-week copywriter. At the age of twenty-six, Jerry Della Femina was finally about to start his career in advertising.

While at Daniel & Charles, Della Femina made a reputation for himself as a bizarre, but creative, individual. By the end of his first year, he had received a number of raises, but he felt he should move on to significantly better himself. Therefore, in 1963 he signed on with Fuller & Smith & Ross at $18,000 a year. Fuller & Smith was an agency that dealt primarily with industrial accounts, and until Della Femina's arrival it had maintained a strict decorum. He decided to shake up the agency, playing paddle ball in its long hallways. Within six months, he was on the move again, stopping off for a brief stay at Ashe & Engelmore. Then, in 1964, he joined the firm of Delehanty, Kurnit & Geller, which had a stronger creative bent than his previous agencies and a greater concomitant tolerance for eccentricity. At Delehanty, Kurnit & Geller, Della Femina finally had the opportunity to pour his creativity into something other than personal behavior.

One of Della Femina's most famous campaigns with that agency was for a product called Pretty Feet. His ad showed a picture of a nude woman with the headline: "What's the Ugliest Part of Your Body?" The answer, contained in the copy, was a woman's feet. It then pitched the product as a perfect cure for this imperfection. The ad elicited an incredible response; nearly 300,000 women spontaneously wrote in. But the campaign, rather than enhancing Della Femina's position at the agency, led to a series of bitter arguments with the firm's president. Shep Kurnit, head of the firm, had been reluctant to run the ad in the first place, and he only agreed to do it when Della Femina brought the entire creative staff out on strike in order to force his hand. The agency finally conceded, and the ad was a great success, but relations between Della Femina and the rest of the agency were strained. Thus, when Ted Bates & Company began looking for a creative director at their hard-sell, "claim" approach agency, Della Femina was only too willing to move on.

He was hired by the Bates agency at $50,000 a year in 1967. The Bates executives had no idea what they were letting themselves in for. Regarding the job as a lark, Della Femina played loud rock music and held parties in his office, inviting all 700 employees at the agency. Soon, difficulties began to surface at the Bates agency. The problem, as one of the Bates executives explained, was that Della Femina was a "natural rebel . . . prolific, quick, mercurial, undisciplined . . . antiestablishment.'' Della Femina fit well into the public mood of the late 1960s, but he was not regarded fondly at Bates, a bastion of conservative, grey-flannel, corporate America. He produced few creative ads at Bates, continuing to develop provocative ads which circulated in the tight-knit advertising community, thereby further enhancing his reputation, but making no money for his bosses.

In September 1967 Della Femina left Bates to start his own agency. In partnership with Ron Travisano, he founded the firm of Della Femina, Travisano & Partners. He obtained the necessary $80,000 by selling shares in the new firm to friends both in and out of advertising. The early months at the new agency were difficult, but gradually things began to improve. At the end of the first year, they made a net profit of $12,000, and Della Femina and Travisano each paid themselves salaries of $25,000. They were on their way. Over the next year or so, they brought in a number of important clients, including American Home Assurance, American International Underwriters, Geigy Chemical, McGraw-Hill Books, and Corum Watch. As Della Femina said, "We may dress funny, look funny, and sound funny, but we move the goods."

Jerry Della Femina's firm in the late 1960s represented a new type of advertising agency. Highly creative, sometimes even bizarre in both personal behavior and approaches to advertising, the partners were the cultural heirs of William Bernbach and David Ogilvy,[†] who helped blaze the creative revolution a decade earlier. Whereas Bernbach and Ogilvy, as men of the 1940s and 1950s, were relatively staid and conservative in personal taste and demeanor, Della Femina and his cohorts who started the creative "boutiques" of the 1960s were typical of the young adherents of the counterculture of the time. Della Femina expressed their cynicism and irreverence perfectly when he said, "I honestly believe that advertising is the most fun you can have with your clothes on." As an advertising industry analyst wrote at the time, Della Femina's "commercials and ads seem to be able to make themselves heard above the deafening noise-level of today's advertising." In appreciation for his innovations, Della Femina, during the first two years he ran his agency, received three ANDY'S from the Advertising Club of New York. He was also voted Advertising Executive of the Year in 1970. He was also a survivor. The same year he and Travisano founded their agency, 140 others were founded. Three years later, only ten of these continued.

By the late 1970s, Della Femina's agency was beginning to creep up on the giants of the industry. No longer an off-the-wall boutique, in 1979 it had billings of $135 million, a 50-percent increase from the year before. New accounts included some real heavyweights, like Schlitz Light Beer and Borden's dairy division. By that time, Della Femina's annual salary, not counting his 38-percent share of agency profits, was $250,000. But in many respects, he still had not changed his ways. When asked how much of this he had saved, he replied:

Absolute zippo, and that's what I'm going to save next year. People put money into savings accounts so they can take it out at 65 and spend it. I'm just doing that now. And lobster tastes a helluva lot better at 43 than at 65 because maybe by then you'll have a pain in your right side from gall-bladder trouble. (*Forbes*)

The next several years, however, were not kind to either Jerry Della Femina or his agency. The one time enfant terrible had succumbed to middle age, and as a friend commented: "Jerry seemed to go into semiretirement and he lost a lot of creative people." Della Femina also proved to be something less than successful as a manager. This is not surprising, since creative people often do not have the temperament to handle managerial chores. In 1986 he sold his agency, which by then had billings of $200 million, to the London-based Wight Collins Rutherford & Scott for $29 million. Of this amount, Della Femina himself got about $23 million (Travisano had left several years before to run his own film company). Under the terms of the deal, Della Femina continued to run the agency, but he was free to immerse himself in the creative side again. Louise McNamee was named president, and she handled the day-to-day operations that Della Femina found so onerous and distracting. As he commented, "Why do we always walk away from what we do best? I'm just a good copywriter."

Freed from other pressures, Jerry Della Femina began stirring up controversy again and exploiting that controversy for the advancement of himself and his agency. One area of dispute in which he threw himself with reckless abandon was the issue of AIDS and condoms. Print and broadcast media for years had refused ads for condoms on the grounds of good taste, but when they became the chief defense against the AIDS epidemic, Della Femina wrote an ad for Ansell-America's Lifestyles condoms. Although the ad stressed the safety issue, it also focused on sex, with a young woman saying, "I'll do a lot for love, but I'm not ready to die for it." The ad created an enormous amount of controversy and generated a good deal of free publicity for Jerry Della Femina, his agency, and his client. Appearing on a series of local and national news programs, Della Femina was at his best and most controversial, but his client felt that Della Femina's personality was detracting from the product. As a result, Della Femina's agency resigned the account.

Another Della Femina ad stirred a great deal of controversy in 1986. In an ad for Perry Ellis cologne, Della Femina had a male model with his shirt open to the waist telling readers that he hated modeling. But, he said, that he liked the Perry Ellis cologne so much that he once pocketed a bottle he was asked to use in a modeling session, saying, "(I) smiled my best f—you smile," and walked out. The "f-word," even with dashes substituting for three of the letters, had never before appeared in American advertising, and many magazines refused to run it. But it did appear in *Esquire, New York Magazine,* and *GQ.* It was vintage Della Femina. (**A.** Jerry Della Femina, *From Those Wonderful Folks Who Brought You Pearl Harbor,* 1970; **B.** *New York Times Magazine,* January 26, 1969; *Time,* June 22, 1970; *Saturday Review,* July 4, 1970; *New York,* October 22, 1978; *Forbes,* January 21, 1980; *Who's Who,* 1986–87; *Advertising Age,* March 2, 1987; *Fortune,* April 13, 1987.)

DEVOS, RICHARD MARVIN (March 4, 1926–   ) and **JAY VAN ANDEL** (June 24, 1924–   ). Founders, Amway Corporation. To many conservative Republicans DeVos and Van Andel are folk heroes who truly represent the "American way." To some others, they are evil, sadistic cultists who use the techniques of religion to seduce gullible souls into making vast sums for Amway and its founders. To the Canadian government, they are crooks, pure and simple. An official of the Canadian government said bluntly: "They [Amway] treated Canada like a banana republic then [in the 1960s and 1970s] and they're treating Canada like a banana republic now." *The Possible Dream*, written by Charles Paul Conn, views the two men and their company in the best possible light: "The dream of Rich DeVos and Jay Van Andel was to build a company that would offer all persons who seek it a chance to change their lives." Stephen Butterfield, an embittered ex-Amway distributor, saw it differently in his *Amway: The Cult of Free Enterprise:*

Amway offers to its distributors not only the dream of wealth, but a born-again religious experience, 'a faith to live by, a purpose to live for,' a new set of goals and friends and associations and beliefs, a new folklore of heroes, a total pre-packaged pursuit of happiness in which all authority comes from the top down.

Who are Rich DeVos and Jay Van Andel, and why are they saying such things about them?

DeVos and Van Andel are both descendents of Dutch immigrants who settled in Michigan. Both born in Grand Rapids, they became friends while in high school, and they attended Calvin College after World War II. Van Andel is the elder of the two, and his father ran an automobile agency in Grand Rapids. After attending local schools, Van Andel went to Calvin College in 1942–1943, joined the U.S. Army Air Corps, and again attended Calvin College after the war. Rich DeVos, the son of an electrical contractor in Grand Rapids, attended Christian parochial schools in the city and the public high school, and then joined the U.S. Army Air Corps, serving overseas in the Pacific. After he was discharged, DeVos attended Calvin College with Jay Van Andel.

The two men, from such similar backgrounds, became friends in 1940. Since Van Andel's father owned an automobile agency, Jay had a car, and he made a deal to drive DeVos to school every day. The two teenagers became fast friends and began a number of business ventures together at that early age. In the summer of 1940, they drove two used trucks from Mr. Van Andel's shop to Montana. The trip cemented a lifelong friendship between the two.

After the war, and a stint at Calvin College, the two young men went into business together. The business, called Wolverine Air Service, had actually been started in 1946 by Van Andel and James Bosscher, when they bought a small Piper Cub airplane while still in college. In 1947, Bosscher sold his interest to DeVos, and a lifelong business partnership with DeVos commenced. The Wolverine Air Service was a flying school and air charter service operating out of

Comstock Park airfield, near Grand Rapids. By 1948, they had twelve aircraft and fifteen instructors, but they found that business was slack between flights. So, the two young entrepreneurs set up a hamburger stand in a prefab building at the airstrip, where they took turns cooking and carhopping the food. That experience cured them of any further interest in the restaurant business, and having tired of the air service business, they sold it in 1948.

Taking the proceeds from the sale of the air service, DeVos and Van Andel bought an old thirty-eight-foot schooner, on which they planned to take a cruise to the West Indies and South America. Not accomplished sailors, they watched the boat sink off the coast of Cuba in March 1949. Undaunted, they continued their excursion by other means and, during this time, conceived the idea of forming a business to import items from the Caribbean. Returning to Grand Rapids in July 1949, DeVos and Van Andel created the Ja-Ri Corporation to look for other products to distribute. They found Nutrilite Products. Van Andel's cousin in Chicago had started the Nutrilite business and needed new distributors. DeVos and Van Andel signed a contract with him and began distributing the product, which was a food supplement for which the customer paid $19.50 for a month's supply of capsules.

Achieving some success with Nutrilite, the two started other businesses: Stone Mill Products, which offered customers "a home-baked stone-ground loaf of bread," and the Grand Rapids Toy Company, a less successful venture which made rocking horses. At that point they made a fateful decision. Although they had had some success selling Nutrilite through a traditional network of jobbers, wholesalers, and supermarket buyers, they recognized its limitations. They decided to try a new approach—direct sales. They began selling Nutrilite directly to customers in their homes and offices and established their own network of distributors who carried out direct sales in their designated territories. By 1955 they had created a vast distribution network of 5,000 independent salesmen pushing Nutrilite, but sales began to decline because of stiffer regulations imposed by the U.S. Food and Drug Administration on the food supplement industry.

At the same time, Ja-Ri Corporation was suffering from internal management problems with its network of distributors. DeVos and Van Andel gathered the company's top distributors into a study group to improve sagging sales. Warfare developed between members of the manufacturing and jobbing wings, and the situation simply worsened during the next four years. As a result, DeVos and Van Andel ended their association with Nutrilite and looked for new products to distribute through their network. Early in 1959, they brought their key distributors into a new organization, called the American Way Association, to evaluate new sales approaches. At the same time, Ja-Ri Corporation began to handle a number of new household products, among them a liquid cleaner and a laundry compound. They quickly realized they had found a successful new business, and in November 1959, the Amway Sales Corporation was formed to secure and inventory products, sell them to affilliated distributors, and administer the marketing plan. The new organization was set up in Ada, Michigan, a small town near Grand Rapids.

As DeVos and Van Andel developed their joint business associations, their personal lives also became increasingly intertwined. They both married young women from Grand Rapids' Dutch community within a few months of each other and moved into adjacent homes. They were both prominent members of the city's La Grave Christian Church, each had four children, and both were leading members of the Republican party, first locally, and then nationally. They were also both leading members of the Grand Rapids' Chamber of Commerce. They were so close to one another and their lives were so similar that when *Reader's Digest* did an article on them in 1982 they entitled it "Amway's Dutch Twins"; others referred to them as the "Gold Dust Twins of the New Conservatism."

The direct sales approach that DeVos and Van Andel adopted for their new Amway corporation was nothing particularly unique. After all, it had been used successfully by a number of American corporations, including the Fuller Brush Company and Avon Products. What was unique, and highly controversial, was the system of distributorships that the two men organized. Although they deny it, the Amway system is essentially what is called "pyramid sales": whereas the concept of product selling is stressed to the general public, the dreams of vast wealth promoted within the organization itself appear to be predicated upon the idea of pyramiding. The issue plagued Amway for decades, and in 1979 a Federal Trade Commission (FTC) judge concluded that Amway did not practice pyramiding. Nonetheless, it has been almost universally recognized that at least some of the firm's most successful independent distributors have set up pyramid-like organizations.

DeVos and Van Andel stress the simple, direct sales aspect of their business, and they promote the fact that Amway manufactures quality products that are easily and profitably sold on a person-to-person basis. They point out that by the 1970s Amway manufactured about 150 different household products, and to reporters they emphasize that people can become independent distributors quite easily by simply purchasing a sales kit from Amway. Asked to define a typical Amway distributor, Van Andel replied, "A husband and wife team working together to develop extra income." But the ultimate objective of Amway is for these independent distributors to become what they call direct distributors, who sign up other distributors to sell Amway products through them and thereby get a certain portion of their sales. This is where the real profits for distributors lie.

Van Andel and DeVos deny this is pyramiding, but a glance at Amway's own literature confounds the observer. Its manual, "Professional Sponsoring Step by Step," states:

Selling Amway products at retail to homes and small industries is a lucrative and rewarding business. There are, however, certain practical limits to how much dollar volume you can produce by yourself, but when you sponsor other distributors, who, in turn, sell products and sponsor other distributors, you can greatly expand the potential sales volume generated by your efforts.

To most Amway critics, if not to the FTC, this sounds like pyramiding; whatever it is called, it is the core of the "Amway Dream."

Stephen Butterfield has raised the issue most directly. In his book, he states:

The marketing system of Amway, disclaimers notwithstanding, is a legal form of pyramid sales. None of the products move over the counter in retail stores. . . . It is all person-to-person selling. To get the product you have to know a distributor. This is one of the system's greatest strengths, and also a great weakness. . . . Your business succeeds only to the extent that those people [new customers] can be recruited to sell, and recruit others to sell.

Butterfield also noted: "The goal is to keep your groups duplicating themselves, so that huge numbers of people are buying and using products through an account with your name on it, which is maintained by the great Amway Computer." Many of Amway's big distributors have gotten very wealthy indeed. A fair number in the early 1980s were making between $200,000 and $350,000 a year with their networks.

If one of the keys to the success of Amway was its intricate pyramiding of distributorship, at least as important was the unique and somewhat controversial motivational techniques they employed. This latter area was the special preserve of Rich DeVos, an exceptionally charismatic leader. According to DeVos, "To a distributor, Amway becomes a philosophical base as well as a business opportunity. The distributorship makes you an entrepreneur—and therefore a believer in the free enterprise system." These tenets are transmitted to distributors through a series of seminars, held at the rate of about 200 a year in over eighty cities in the United States and Canada. *Forbes* described one of these meetings chaired by DeVos:

The young crowd, mostly couples, is clean-cut, middle-class and enthusiastic. An organist pumps out an upbeat version of *This Is My Country*. Minutes before 8 P.M., a tanned, 49-year-old man . . . makes his way up the aisle. . . . People crush to shake his hand. Ladies kiss his cheek. . . . A charismatic politician? A revivalist? A movie star? No. The meeting is being conducted by Amway Products, whose husband-and-wife teams have come—some of them hundreds of miles—to be spellbound as Richard DeVos . . . extolls the virtues of patriotism, free enterprise, and positive thinking.

For those who believed, it was a powerful message. As Conn wrote in *The Possible Dream*, "Their [DeVos' and Van Andel's] dream was to offer to those who would work for it a chance to build their own business, set their own goals, make their own future. That, they said, was the American way." But for those who do not believe, Amway's dream seemed more like a nightmare.

It was a nightmare for Stephen Butterfield:

The Seminar and Rally is the essence of Amway: the dress code, politics, values, tech- niques, the full spirit of the business, all concentrated into a dramatic happening that lasts from early afternoon until far into the night. . . . The audience may be expected to remain in the hall for a marathon brainwash that lasts up to twelve hours at a stretch, on hard folding chairs, without eating, sleeping, or going to the restroom. . . . What the revival meeting is to evangelical Christianity, the Seminar and Rally is to the world of Amway.

Butterfield goes on to explain that most of the seminar is devoted to an evocation of the "Amway Dream": "A thoroughly consumerist and materialist craving which the leaders do everything possible to instill into their distribution force." Then, according to Butterfield, Amway distributors become part of a special way of life, an "attitude" shaped and molded by Amway itself. He claims the Amway distributor must protect this "attitude" from all negative (non-Amway) influences. In this respect, Butterfield and other critics see Amway as similar to many religious cults, such as the Unification Church and Hare Krishna.

Whatever the ethics of all of this, it was enormously successful for DeVos, Van Andel, and Amway for over two decades. In 1964, the two men reorganized and streamlined Amway's corporate structure, as the various separate organi- zations were merged into Amway Corporation. The company's growth was tremendous, and Amway soon became one of the largest direct selling companies in the world, with a line of over 150 household, personal, and auto-care products, and an extensive catalog operation. Their plant site in Ada was expanded from two to three hundred acres, and building space was increased from 2,400 to 450,000 square feet by the end of the 1960s. In 1962, they established a Canadian affiliate, Amway of Canada Ltd., in London, Ontario. By 1968, Amway had sales of over $65 million, of which $10 million were in Canada, with over 100,000 independent distributors.

The company, which continued to be privately held by DeVos and Van Andel, maintained its rapid growth rate throughout the 1970s and early 1980s. By 1977, revenues reached a reported $350 million, which peaked in 1981, when they topped $1.2 billion. By that time, Amway had become an impressive organi- zation. With subsidiaries around the world, it was truly universal in scope. By then, its complex of administration-manufacturing-laboratory-distribution facil- ities in Ada covered over one million square feet. There were over 300,000 distributors the world over, and 4,000 employees at Amway itself. It also owned a hotel in Grand Rapids, the Mutual Broadcasting radio network, and an island in the Caribbean. Amway was obviously a highly profitable operation, but since it was private, no figures were available. It was estimated, however, that DeVos and Van Andel were each worth over $300 million by the early 1980s.

These profits, according to Butterfield, come from the exploitation of the entrepreneurs who make up the company's principal labor force—its distributors.

[T]hey are every employer's dream. They work for next to nothing. They get no regular wage. Every nickel they receive is tied to productivity. They pay all their own expense accounts. . . . They have no legal standing as employees, and so cannot unionize, bargain collectively, or make importune demands on the Company for medical and insurance benefits. . . . Best of all, they are fanatically loyal to the Company and believe religiously in the system that exploits them.

But most distributors do not seem to share this sense of exploitation. A highly successful direct distributor was asked what was wrong with Amway. He replied, "I've been looking for years, and I give up. There's nothing wrong with Amway."

By the mid–1980s, however, it was clear something was wrong. Revenues had reportedly slipped badly, some said to as low as $800 million, the radio network was struggling, the Grand Rapids hotel was losing money and so was the Caribbean resort. Worst of all, the recruitment of distributors had reportedly fallen off very badly. Amway was said to be encountering trouble with their most successful distributors, the so-called black hats. Reportedly, these distributors were turning their distribution networks into pyramid-like operations. They "push their recruits to consume Amway goods, skip the retailing, and buy large amounts of non-Amway peripherals (tapes, books, suits, jewels, and even tickets to motivational rallies)." An ex-Amway executive said in 1985, "A distributor shakeout years ago would have helped Amway, but they have yet to throw out any major distributor who is violating the rules." Belatedly, DeVos recognized the problem, and he sent a memo to distributors addressing the problem: "I need your help, folks. We must clean it up." They brought in William Nicholson, formerly President Ford's appointments secretary, to reorganize the company. Nicholson cleansed the sales force and downplayed the evangelism and cultism which had formerly characterized Amway's approach. In its place, he emphasized more traditional sales training.

Amway also had enormous problems with its Canadian operation. In November 1983, Amway pleaded guilty in the Supreme Court of Ontario to an elaborate scheme by which they had defrauded the Canadian government of millions and millions of dollars. They had, in effect, created "dummy invoices" for years, which lied about the true market value of the products they were bringing into Canada, thereby reducing the amount of duties and taxes owed. With their admission, Amway paid a whopping $25-million fine to the courts, but the federal government of Canada was still after them for more than $105 million in duties, taxes, and fines it said Amway still owed them. As of 1988, Amway was still refusing to pay this latter amount, claiming that the $25-million penalty absolved them of any further obligation. Attempts by the Canadian government to get DeVos and Van Andel to appear in Canadian courts have proved fruitless, and that has stalled the entire proceeding.

The evocation of patriotism, free enterprise, and the American Way by DeVos and Van Andel has also brought them into the center of conservative Republican politics. During the 1960s they confined their political activities to the local area. But in the 1970s, with the ascendence of Republicans to national office, the two men became prominent figures in the party and in peripheral conservative organizations. Their first major effort on the national scene was to establish the Free Enterprise Institute in 1972 to foster education programs teaching the free enterprise system to schoolchildren. DeVos explained their philosophy: ''Our greater cause is human freedom—which begins with economic freedom. The only freedom, other than freedom of religion, that really counts is freedom from want. It is time for this generation of Americans to believe once more in free enterprise.''

Critics like Stephen Butterfield, however, dispute their claims. Butterfield writes: ''The underlying assumption of Amway is that private enterprise will solve all our problems, and if private enterprise won't do it, then they are insoluble and must be endured until the coming of Armageddon.'' He continues:

Quite simply, Amway threatens everything the public fought for in the last hundred years: Medicaid, Medicare, the rudiments, however inadequate, of public transportation and housing, occupational health and safety, social security, unemployment compensation, access to public education all the way up through the university level, and the right to bargain collectively, from a position of strength, over terms and conditions of employment.

However one views the political attitudes of DeVos and Van Andel, there was little question about their influence on national politics in the 1980s. They were among the most lavish personal supporters of Ronald Reagan's presidential campaigns in 1980 and 1984, and their Seminars and Rallies were often turned into occasions for campaign proganda for conservative Republicanism. In addition, DeVos himself became the chief fund-raiser for the Republican Party during these years. Van Andel, as head of the U.S. Chamber of Commerce in 1984, arranged for Reagan to address a large ''free enterprise'' rally in Atlanta. Reagan returned the favor by visiting Grand Rapids and appearing in numerous ''photo opportunities'' with members of the DeVos and Van Andel families. They remained close friends with ex-president Gerald Ford, a native of Grand Rapids. When the Canadian government began criminal proceedings against DeVos and Van Andel in 1982 (dropped in 1983 as part of Amway's agreement to plead guilty and pay a $25-million fine), DeVos told a press conference that ''influential contacts in Washington'' might be called upon to assist in the case. Later, Devos dined at the White House with Attorney General William French Smith.

Richard Louv, in *America II,* interviewed a young entrepreneur who vocalized perfectly the kind of faith and ideology represented by Ronald Reagan, Richard DeVos, and Jay Van Andel in the 1980s:

Entrepreneurialism is the whole difference between the European mentality and the American mentality. The American mentality is, ''Grab your hands onto whatever you need to do to get it done and go do it.'' The European mentality is, ''Check with the authorities first.'' That's the American dream: the independent contractor who doesn't check with the authorities first, getting rid of artificial barriers to flexibility. . . . I'd love to see the day when just about everybody is an independent contractor to everybody else.

(**B.** *National Cyclopaedia of American Biography*, K: 470–74; *Nation's Business*, October 1973; *Industry Week*, November 7, 1977; Charles Paul Conn, *The Possible Dream*, 1977, *The Winner's Circle*, 1979, *An Uncommon Freedom*, 1982, and *Promises to Keep*, 1985; *Time*, May 28, 1979; *Saturday Evening Post*, November 1979, July/August 1982; *Commonweal*, August 29, 1980; *The Reader's Digest*, April 1982; Richard Louv, *America II*, 1983; Stephen Butterfield, *Amway: The Cult of Free Enterprise*, 1985; *Forbes*, March 25, 1985; *Toronto Star*, July 31, 1988.)

F

FIELDS, DEBRA JANE SIVYER (DEBBI) (September 18, 1956–   ) and
RANDY FIELDS (1947–   ). Cookie company founders, Mrs. Fields Cookies.
The idea of the upscale chocolate chip cookie was created by Wallace Amos,
Jr.,[†] and his Famous Amos Cookies in the mid–1970s, but it was the Fields,
with their Mrs. Fields Cookies, who turned a brilliant concept into an art. Amos
had given cookies a certain cachet by linking his product to Hollywood stars
and musical artists; the Fields, along with David's Cookies and the Original
Great Chocolate Chip Cookie Company, among others, cashed in on the trendy
appeal of homemade treats in the 1980s. They made the once humble cookie a
gourmet treat, as much a part of the required "yuppie" life-style as frozen
yogurt, BMWs, and Aprica Strollers. Randy Fields understood this perfectly.
When asked by a reporter why their cookies had achieved such an exalted status,
he replied: "Well, we—this generation—we've upscaled everything from our
childhoods." Debbi Fields viewed things in a less jaded way: "We're a people
company, and what we're really selling is a feel-good feeling."

Debbi Fields was born and raised in East Oakland, California. Daughter of a
welder for the U.S. Navy, she and her four sisters were raised in a Catholic,
working-class environment, and they went to parochial elementary and high
schools. Part of this environment included learning to cook and bake at an early
age. The girls developed their own specialties; Debbi became the expert on
cookies, improving the Toll House cookie recipe that had been around since
1930. When Debbi was eighteen, she went on a trip to Denver, and in the airport
there she met Randy Fields, a young executive from Palo Alto, California, who
had his own financial management business. Just like in the storybooks, they
were instantly attracted to one another, fell in love, and married.

Randy Fields came from a comfortable, but not affluent, background. His
father owned a hardware store, and Randy went to Stanford, where he got a
B.A. and M.A. in political science. Graduating magna cum laude, he was elected
Phi Beta Kappa, and a Danforth Fellow. Randy had a keen sense of money;
even before he graduated, he was managing money for family and friends. After

a time he established his own firm, Fields Investment Group, and soon was providing financial advice for firms on the *Fortune* 500 list in the capacity of an economic futurist.

After Randy and Debbi were married, they lived in Palo Alto. Debbi attended community college, took care of the house, and served as an Oakland A's ballgirl, but she was restless. She wanted to make money. She had had a succession of jobs in her teens, and she liked earning her own money. She had continued to make chocolate chip cookies and often served them to her husband's business associates, who raved about them, telling her that she ought to open a store and sell them. They may not have been serious, but it struck a nerve with Debbi, and she began to consider the options. Finally, Debbi approached Randy and asked for a $50,000 loan to open a cookie store in Palo Alto. Randy was willing, but he was worried about how Debbi might handle failure. As he remembered, "I was concerned what failure would do to her psychologically, and I thought it would fail." Most of all, he could not understand why she wanted to open a cookie store—for a long time, all he could say to her was: "Cookies? You want to sell *cookies*?"

But Debbi kept pushing, and finally Randy gave in. On August 13, 1977, she opened Mrs. Fields Chocolate Chippery in an international food arcade. Although Randy had loaned her the money, he was still certain she would fail. He bet her she would not make $50 in her first day. Debbi opened her store in the morning— and by noon had not served a single customer. It appeared that Randy was right: trying to sell a product that people could bake at home for themselves, or buy by the bagful in a supermarket, was a poor idea. But Debbi refused to admit defeat. She piled a bunch of the cookies on a tray and took them out into the mall and gave them away. Then, she returned to the store and began to bake a fresh batch. Slowly, people started wandering in. Debbi recognized many of the people were people to whom she had given free samples. When she counted up the money at the end of the day, she had made exactly $50. Randy paid up and bet her she would not make $75 the second day. She did.

A major decision for Debbi and Randy Fields, after the success of Debbi's first store was established, was whether to open a second store. After all, the first store had been a bit of a lark. Debbi Fields wanted to prove her mettle as a businesswoman, and Randy had gone along with her to the tune of $50,000. But a second store? This meant they were serious—that the operation was going to be something more than a device to satisfy her ego. They were concerned also that the cookie craze might be limited to the Bay Area or, at most, to California. At one point, a major corporation appeared and offered them a whopping $500,000 for the rights to sell Debbi's cookies outside of California. The Fields probably would have accepted, but at the last moment the corporation backed off.

In making their decision to expand in early 1978, Randy and Debbi Fields grappled with two important elements of the fast-food industry: product quality and worker motivation. Both are crucial to the success of any fast-food operation;

both are difficult to achieve. Randi and Debbi decided the only way to guarantee quality and worker motivation was not to franchise—to own and manage all the stores in the chain themselves. This ran counter to the perceived wisdom of the time, which viewed franchised operations as the ideal mechanism to expand rapidly by making the franchises themselves provide both capital and managerial oversight. But the Fields felt this would not work with cookies. According to Randy Fields, "It's a feel-good product; it has to be sold in a feel-good way." Debbi and Randy Fields began to open stores as quickly as they could find outlets, finance the opening, and staff the store. By 1984, the firm, which was still privately owned, was earning about $45 million a year from its 160 stores in seventeen states, Hong Kong, Tokyo, Singapore, and Sydney.

Their methods of ensuring product quality and worker motivation involve an almost perfect melding of the skills and personality of the couple. Together they created a management system that combines a strong personal touch with a set of strict guidelines. Debbi Fields is the "personality" of the corporation—she *is* Mrs. Fields Cookies in a myriad of ways. Debbi involves herself personally in virtually every aspect of the stores' management. She has been known to sweep into one of her stores, inspect the cookies, and judge that they are not up to her standards. She will then take some 200 cookies, throw them in the garbage, put on an apron, and show the startled store employees how the cookies should be made. This might be a traumatic experience for the employees (and probably is), but one of Debbi's tenets is that employees must be treated with great tenderness and respect. The staff, in turn, are expected to treat customers in the same way. Debbi Fields creates an ethic, an image for the company that derives strongly from her own personality.

Debbi Fields recognizes that: "I'm the heart and soul of the company. That's my job. Sometimes when I'm frustrated or disappointed I think, well, maybe I haven't done enough good things. . . . So I do something nice for somebody and I snap right out of it." This is the attitude that infuses the entire Mrs. Fields operation and drives competitors to distraction. David Liederman, a tough, cynical New Yorker, who owns David's Cookies, found Debbi Fields' cheerleader optimism grating: "That airhead. She is really he. Randy Fields runs Mrs. Fields Cookies. Debbi Fields is a nice, good-looking blonde who doesn't make any business decisions at all." But Debbi Fields more clearly understands her importance to the company: "It's a people company. That's what it's all about . . . Mrs. Fields is in the business of selling cookies, but that's just what the customer believes. What we really do is . . . we take care of people." Debbi Fields' image is that of a "people person," and she recognizes that, as does everyone else in her company.

What, then, does Randy Fields do? Debbi Fields puts it this way: "I do rely on Randy's expertise with numbers because he's so good at it . . . I would be foolish not to." How does Randy view his role, and that of Debbi? "She started it, she runs it, and will continue to run it," he told a reporter for *The Desert News*. "She has a real talent for business, maybe not in the sense of being profit-driven, but she has a gift for knowing how to satisfy consumer demand, and she knows how to build an organization to meet that demand.'' But what does Randy do? Randy Fields, as Debbi indicated, is the numbers and systems man for the organization, and his role is equally as important as Debbi's. He set up the organizational system that has allowed Mrs. Fields Cookies—which had grown to 500 stores in thirty seven states by 1987 with 4,500 mostly young employees and sales of $87 million—to retain the personal touch and personality of Debbi Fields herself. He did it largely with a sophisticated computer system.

Because of this computer system, Mrs. Fields Cookies has one of the leanest management staffs in corporate America. The headquarters staff in Park City, Utah, in 1987 had just 115 people—one staffer for every five stores. This is far below the industry norm. For example, when Mrs. Fields bought the La Petite Boulangerie chain from Pepsi in early 1987, fifty-three headquarters people at Pepsico were assigned to administer the French bakery/sandwich shop chain's 119 stores. In four weeks, Randy cut the staff to three people. Because of his computer system and a telephone, the administrative layers, the chain of command, that exists in most companies between the store manager at the bottom of the chain and the chief executive officer are largely absent at Mrs. Fields.

Each Mrs. Fields store is equipped with a personal computer and a modem for the telephone. Every morning, 500 store managers unlock their stores; call up the day planner program on their Tandy computers; plug in the day's sales projections, which are based on earlier sales adjusted for growth; and answer several questions the computer asks. The computer then reviews the store's sales for comparable days in the recent past and spews out a printout, which tells the manager what he will have to do that day, hour by hour, product by product, to meet the sales projection. Each hour, as the day progresses, the manager keeps the computer informed of his progress. The computer, in turn, revises the hourly projections and makes various suggestions. It sounds terribly Orwellian, like something out of *1984*, but it is a personal link to Debbi Fields herself.

Most mornings, the store manager will find something on his computerized PhoneMail that are messages from Mrs. Fields herself. And this is not some general, vague statement about company policies and goals. The head office— Randy and Debbi Fields, along with chief operating officer Taylor Devine— monitors the computer reports from the individual stores. Spotting specific problems or areas to praise, by aid of computer analysis, she can then respond directly and personally to each store manager—every working day. By the same token, if the store manager has something personal to say to Debbi Fields, he uses the computer. He calls up the FormMail program and types his message; the next morning, it is on Debbi's desk. She promises an answer within forty-eight hours, either from herself or from her staff. This allows the growing chain to retain a personal and individual perspective on management. As she has said, ''The people who work in my stores are my customers. Staying in touch with them is the most important thing I can do.'' She logs about 350,000 miles a year visiting individual stores, but the most important link she has on a day-to-day basis is Randy's computer system.

The computer system also allows Mrs. Fields Cookies to delegate much more authority and decision making to the individual store level. For example, at David's Cookies, to retain product control, the cookie dough is mixed in a central plant and sent out to the stores where the cookies are baked in automatic ovens. The machines do the mixing and baking; the people just do the routine work of putting cookies in and taking cookies out of the ovens. At Mrs. Fields, individual store employees combine the ingredients, according to a company formula, and bake the cookies in the oven until they feel they are done. There are no timers, no precise directions. One of the store workers has commented, "I don't know how long they bake, I just *know* when they're done." And the computer knows when they make mistakes. The point is that the system allows for individual initiative, albeit one that is constantly monitored by the head office. According to Randy, the computer has allowed Debbi Fields to "leverage" her ability to project her influence into more stores, but without destroying the sense of personal initiative and accomplishment.

Cookies in America in the mid–1980s were a $2.5-billion-a-year business. Most of this money was spent in supermarkets on prepackaged cookies; only about $200 million was expended on freshly baked chocolate chip cookies. Into this huge market came the "boutique" operators including David's Cookies and Mrs. Fields, who carved out fairly large and profitable segments for themselves. The large corporate cookie manufacturers responded by trying to make similar sorts of cookies. For example, one of the unique features of Mrs. Fields Cookies is that they, unlike supermarket varieties, are "soft and chewy." In response, Keebler brought out their Soft Batch cookies for supermarkets, Nabisco brought out Almost Home, and Frito-Lay introduced Grandma's Rich and Chewy. These brands did little to retard the growth of Mrs. Fields and its competitors. Will they continue to grow in the future? Or are cookies a passing fad, like the hula hoop? Debbi Fields has considered that:

Most people will ask me, "Aren't cookies a fad? Isn't there a saturation point? Isn't there a product lifecycle?" I think that's all baloney. My view of the market is quite simple: Are our cookies incredibly fabulous? Yes. Do they make people happy? Yes. Are they as good as homemade? In my opinion, yes. Do people love to eat them? Yes. Are they going to give up the things they love to eat? I think that's very doubtful. . . . You grew up with cookies. Your mom made you cookies. (*Inc.*, July 1984)

For Debbi Fields, her cookies are more than simply food and not just a product— they are a psychological elixir. And as American life becomes more tense and stressful in the waning years of the twentieth century, Debbi Fields is betting that Americans will increasingly need the feel-good lift they get from a chocolate chip cookie. (**A.** Debbi Fields and Alan Furst, *One Smart Cookie*, 1987. **B.** *Glamour*, August 1981; *New York Times*, June 31, 1983; *Working Woman*,

August 1983; *Good Housekeeping*, September 1983; *Advertising Age*, April 2, 1984; *Inc.*, July 1984, October 1987, August 1988; *Esquire*, December 1984; *Rolling Stone*, March 28, 1985; A. David Silver, *Entrepreneurial Megabucks*, 1985; *Nation's Business*, April 1986; *Wall Street Journal*, May 21, 1986; *Contemporary Newsmakers*, 1987.)

FIREMAN, PAUL (February 14, 1944–   ). Athletic shoe manufacturer, Reebok International. Reebok is the great business phenomenon of the 1980s. The fastest growing company in America from 1983 to 1987, as tabulated by *Fortune* magazine, its growth rate during those years was a staggering 155 percent annually. The company, which had been founded in 1979, had just $13 million in sales in 1983. Five years later, sales had exploded to $1.389 *billion*. In 1986, Reebok toppled Nike as the top-selling maker of athletic shoes in the United States and moved into second place worldwide behind Adidas. By that point, many analysts were confidently predicting that Reebok's growth would slow down. But, in 1987, it broke all of its previous records. Sales, which had been just under $1 billion in 1986, increased by a staggering 50 percent. The firm's record of profitability was even more impressive—in a survey taken at the end of 1987, *Forbes* ranked Reebok as the most profitable of 880 companies, in terms of return on equity. It had had an average return on equity of 200 percent over the previous three years, and 52 percent return in 1987. Head of this incredibly successful firm was Paul Fireman, a failed sporting goods distributor.

A native of Brockton, Massachusetts, at the age of thirty-two Fireman took over a family fishing tackle distributorship in his hometown. Soon after, he watched the company go under when manufacturers began to deal directly with retailers. Fireman needed something else, a new endeavor. He found it at a trade show in 1979. Displayed there were some hand-sewn, leather British track shoes called Reebok, the same brand worn by the 1924 Olympians who were soon to be immortalized in the hit film *Chariots of Fire*. It took him six months, but Fireman convinced the British company to set up Reebok USA to distribute shoes in America, and Fireman gave the British parent company a portion of the American firm. Then, with his partner and cofounder, James Barclay, Fireman began to manufacture running shoes. During the first few years, they were a very modest success in a field dominated by Nike, Adidas, New Balance, and several other athletic shoemakers. Then, in the early 1980s, Fireman hit upon a new idea.

Fireman noticed that millions of women were taking aerobics classes in gyms, church basements, and health clubs. In these classes, they wore everything on their feet from running shoes, to court shoes, to socks. No athletic shoemaker was producing a product designed specifically for aerobics. Fireman decided to design such a shoe of soft, comfortable leather, with its padding primarily in the toe rather than heel area. Most important, since the vast majority of those who took aerobics classes were women, he made sure that the shoes would be fashionable—that they could be coordinated with exercise clothing so that the wearer was not only comfortable, but looked good. After all, he reasoned, if women were taking aerobics to trim their bodies to be more attractive, wouldn't they most likely want to be beautiful and fashionable while exercising? The answer was a resounding yes, as women flocked to the stores to buy the new Freestyle Reebok. As Fireman recalled,

There was a social change going on that nobody had noticed, we realized that the aerobics craze was for real and that there was a huge untapped market for women seeking both comfort and style. The industry was only focused on jogging shoes. It wasn't growing with the consumer. (*Fortune*)

The Nike shoe company, founded by Phillip H. Knight,[†] had achieved success by responding to the jogging craze of the 1970s. His company's orientation, however, was toward the male athlete, and it refused to recognize the important new female athletic market that had developed in the 1980s.

Having changed the orientation of athletic footwear from performance to fashion, Reeboks rapidly became the hot new athletic shoe of choice. And their appeal soon expanded beyond women in aerobics classes. A young "yuppie" lawyer, when quizzed as to why he wore Reeboks, responded: "I know they have a yuppie image now but I got my Reeboks before they became really trendy. I don't do aerobics. I bought them because they looked good and they felt lightweight and comfortable."

But success, even if it came quickly to Fireman and Reebok, did not come without hard work. Barclay, who is executive vice president of the athletic shoe division of the firm, recalled the early days: "We would spend about two-thirds of the day going from store to store to sell the shoes, bring the orders back to the warehouse, pack, inspect, and ship them out that day and bill the customers the same night." His boyhood friend, David Epstein, summed up Fireman's career in this manner: "His is a real Horatio Alger story, but he learned a lot of lessons along the way." Most agree that Fireman has remained largely unaffected by his great success and vast wealth (in 1986 *Forbes* estimated his stock in Reebok alone was worth $320 million). Fireman was still happily married to his high school sweetheart, still owned the same summer cottage in the New Hampshire mountains he had owned for years, and still considered his best friends those he has had since elementary school. His one concession to success in the late 1980s was to switch from his casual garb of jeans and sneakers to suits and wing-tip shoes, which he calls "corporate sneakers."

Reebok's sales rose exponentially during the first few years after Fireman developed his aerobic shoe. Accordingly, in 1984–1985 Fireman began to make significant changes in his organization. First, he took the firm public in 1985, buying out his British partners and raising a great deal of capital for further expansion. Fireman then began to change and diversify Reebok, giving it the staying power for the long haul. He expanded beyond track and aerobics shoes into tennis and basketball shoes, making the firm a leader in these fields also.

At about the same time, he also expanded into apparel, making athletic wear for such activities as aerobics and tennis. This was Fireman's only blunder during these years. The firm ran into marketing and production problems and could not fill orders. Not wishing to give up, however, Fireman changed the emphasis and marketing focus to general sportswear, making warm-up suits, sweatshirts, and other articles of clothing for a broader market.

At about the same time, Fireman ventured into children's shoes, setting up a line of expensive infant's shoes called Weeboks. The success of this venture led Fireman in 1987 to introduce a line of casual women's shoes called Metaphors. According to Fireman, that line did well also. Despite all this success, many industry experts predicted that Reebok would be a flash in the pan, that its shoes were a fad that would soon fade. They even felt that Fireman's diversifications were insufficient to sustain long-term growth. As a result, in 1987, Fireman staged an aggressive three-pronged diversification strategy: acquisitions, internal development, and international expansion. The acquisitions were the most dramatic and attracted the greatest attention.

Fireman wanted to ensure that the products and firms he acquired would add diversity to the Reebok firm, yet would continue to appeal to the same trendsetting eighteen-to-forty-five age group on which he had built all of his success. As he said, "Our whole company is set up on a consumer basis, and we spend a lot of time and money researching what the next trend will be, we try to interpret it correctly and get at what they really want." The first major acquisition came in the spring of 1987, with the purchase of Avia athletic shoes for $180 million. Avia, based in Portland, Oregon, put out a high-priced line of aerobic, running, tennis, and basketball shoes. With $70.3 million in sales in 1986, it was emerging as a major competitor to Reebok. Avia was close to becoming a new fad product, as Reebok had been a few short years before. Fireman blunted the challenge by buying the competitor while still retaining the separate name and identity.

Fireman reasoned,

Reebok is two companies, Reebok the brand and Reebok the corporation, which acquires younger companies that can connect with our image. One of the things Reebok the corporation can't get caught up in is becoming the product. That's what happened to Cadillac. They built the same product, but the customers moved on. Reebok the brand will compete with Avia the brand. I figure between the two of them, one will win. (*Business Month*)

Industry analysts were equally impressed. Jessica J. Reif, a footwear analyst said: "Avia is a great fit and captures a segment where Reebok potentially could have had some competition."

But Fireman was hardly finished. In 1986, he had purchased The Rockport Company of Marlboro, Massachusetts, for $118 million. Fireman strongly believed that walking shoes would be the next great fitness craze; 25 million Americans identify themselves as fitness walkers, and Rockport was the fastest growing walking and hiking shoe manufacturer. In 1987, Fireman picked up Marlboro's Frye Boot Company, a venerable maker of high-quality boots that was drowning in debt. He merged Frye with Rockport and planned to develop the Frye label into a line of men's and women's classic hand-sewn shoes with the look, quality, and price of the Ralph Lauren[†] line. Again, industry analysts were impressed: "Rockport's demand is so high, they can't fill the backlog. With Frye they are getting the production capability and management they need." Another perfect "fit."

Reebok intended to pursue internal development primarily in the apparel field, reasoning that "We are good at businesses that have sparkle and pizzazz, we're not interested in Tupperware or dishwashers." To this end, in 1987, Fireman purchased Ellesse International, an Italian shoe and sportswear company, for $60 million. He was also planning to invade the international market, which represented potential sales of from $7 billion to $10 billion a year, more than three times that of the United States. As of 1987, Reebok was doing only about 10 percent of its sales abroad, but with its affiliation with Reebok International and the British conglomerate, Pentland Industries, which owns 32 percent of the firm, it has the resources and expertise to engage in overseas expansion.

Many analysts still question whether Fireman and Reebok have the staying power, feeling that its success is based too much on fads (that often go out of style after a short time). Then, too, Reebok, with its rapid expansion, inevitably has had management problems. Nevertheless, industry insiders have been impressed with the manner in which Fireman has addressed these problems, dealing with the unwieldy size of the organization by separating it into five divisions just in time to avert chaos. Also, his moves to diversify Reebok's product line have been just what most observers thought necessary.

Despite all of Fireman's ingenuity and precaution, however, Reebok began slipping noticeably in the late 1980s. In 1988, Reebok lost 3-percent market share and expected its fourth-quarter profits in that year to plunge 80 percent. It stood on the brink of being overtaken by its arch competitor, Nike, which had used a series of stunning ads featuring basketball star Moses Malone hitting the boards to increase its sales dramatically. In response, Fireman hired Chiat/Day, Nike's old agency, and commissioned them to create an eye-catching, innovative $25-million ad campaign to recapture the youth market for Reeboks. Chiat/Day came up with the Let U.B.U. campaign, whose ads were so avant-garde that many analysts thought they went over the heads of their intended market. As a result, the next series of ads stressed Reebok's performance factors, but many observers thought the firm's product line was too stale to make the ads believable. Fireman himself took it all rather philosophically: "When I got into Reebok, I had no idea it would be this big, I just wanted to make a living doing something I liked." (B. *Business Week,* February 24, July 28, September 29, October 6, 1986, June 12, 1987; *Toronto Globe & Mail*, September 29, 1986, September 28, December 28, 1987; *Forbes*, October 27, 1986, October 24, 1988; *Contemporary Newsmakers*, 1987; *USA Today*, March 12, 1987; *Time*, March 23, 1987;

Business Month, August 1987; *Fortune*, May 23, 1988; *Manhattan, Inc.*, January 1989.)

FISHER, HERMAN GUY (November 2, 1898–September 26, 1975) and **IRV-ING LANOUETTE PRICE** (September 21, 1884–November 23, 1976). Toy manufacturers, Fisher-Price Toy Company. In 1930 America was in the depths of the depression, and toys seemed to be the last thing on most consumers' minds. But Herman Fisher and Irving Price (along with Helen Schelle) wanted to start their own toy company. Bringing out a series of sturdy toys made of Ponderosa pine, they were moderately successful. Then, in 1938, they introduced a new toy called Snoopy Sniffer at the Toy Fair. A loose-jointed, floppy-eared pull toy that made a woof sound when pulled and had a spring tail that wagged, it was an instant hit with the buyers and the public. Snoopy Sniffer was the beginning of a great toy empire in a small town in upstate New York.

Irving Price was born in Worcester, Massachusetts, the son of a cabinetmaker. He was educated in the public schools of his hometown and graduated from Brown University in 1905. Two years earlier, he had started his career as a part-time stockboy at F. W. Woolworth Company. After graduation, Price stayed with the firm, rising to the position of eastern district division manager. In 1920, he retired from Woolworth's and moved to the small town of East Aurora, New York. During the 1920s, he served on the school board, and in 1928 he began trying to attract new industries to the town. In his search, Price came upon Herman Fisher, who wanted to start a toy company.

Fisher had been born in Unionville, Pennsylvania, a member of a family that had lived several generations in the area. He was educated in the public schools of his hometown and in Bellefonte, Pennsylvania, and he graduated from Penn-sylvania State University in 1921. Fisher had earned his college tuition by selling Fuller Brushes and by working at a number of other jobs. After graduation, Fisher took a surety bond training course in New York City and afterward began working for a bond company. Shortly thereafter, he was transferred to the firm's Rochester, New York, office. In 1926, Fisher left the bond business to become sales promotion and advertising manager for Alderman-Fairchild Company, a manufacturer of specialty paper boxes and games in Rochester. Then, he became vice president and general manager of All Fair, Incorporated, a toy and game manufacturer, which had just separated from its parent company and moved to Churchville, New York. Fisher and a group of investors attempted to buy the All Fair company, but were unsuccessful. At that point, Fisher began making plans to start his own toy company. After he met Irving Fisher, he and Fisher decided to set up a manufacturing plant in East Aurora with Helen Schelle, a former operator of the Penny Walker Toy Shop in Binghamton, New York, as the third partner.

They established the Fisher-Price Toy Company in 1930 and converted an old frame and concrete house in East Aurora into a small factory. Fisher, as president, was the chief executive of the operation; Price, as vice president and treasurer, handled financial matters. The three partners had very little money in 1930, and it was almost impossible to raise capital in the stock market, so they turned to local businessmen and their own workers. Raising $71,600 from local business leaders, they also enticed fifteen workers with promises of shares in future profits. In 1931, a combination office and showroom was set up in New York City, and the small firm was on its way.

Fisher had a very clear idea of the kind of toys he wanted to make. He set out to make children "toys that played with them." To this end, he wanted to ensure that each toy have intrinsic play value, ingenuity, strong construction, good value for the money, and action. The company's first brochure, entitled "The Sixteen Hopefuls," featured toys such as Granny Doodle and Doctor Doodle, comical toy ducks. These and other early Fisher-Price toys were fashioned out of solid blocks of Ponderosa pine and well decorated with color lithographs. The real key to their success, however, was the fact that they were action toys. As they were pulled, the ducks quacked and their beaks moved. Designed to appeal to preschoolers, the line slowly gained acceptance. But the first few years were difficult for the partners, when they lost two-thirds of their capital.

In 1936, the company finally was able to pay out some dividends, and the loyal workers received their share of the profits in silver dollars. At the same time, Fisher-Price brought out a line of blocks, the first of their toys to receive the designation "educational." The action emphasis was still maintained: the blocks would stimulate imagination, increase ingenuity, and build muscles. Fisher-Price toys began to attain a cachet as "good" toys—that is, toys that were not only fun for the children, but also good for them. Fisher-Price's philosophy was that toys should be safe, durable, brightly colored, and affordable, and that they should entertain, educate, amuse, and engage—but, above all—should provide fun for the children. Thus, to many parents they seemed ideal. By the late 1930s, Fisher-Price was producing over 2 million action toys a year, making it a leader in the field. It also became the first toy company to be licensed by Walt Disney to make toys using Disney characters. Using slogans like "Good toys are more fun" and "Our work is child's play," Fisher-Price had found success by the end of the 1930s, with annual sales of $1.6 million.

World War II briefly interrupted this ascension. When Fisher-Price was forced to stop making toys during the war, its factory was used to turn out ship fenders, glider ailerons, and medical chests. In 1946, toy production resumed. With the return of prosperity after the war, and with the rise of a highly child-centered, suburban environment in America in the late 1940s and 1950s, Fisher-Price prospered mightily. In 1949, they made a decision of profound importance. After making toys only of Ponderosa pine for nearly twenty years, Fisher and Price decided it was necessary to begin producing them out of plastic to keep up with increasing demand. But they were determined to maintain the high level of quality of their toys. Therefore, it was essential that they use a special high-impact plastic, one which would resist breakage and splintering and which was lightweight and impervious to moisture. To this end, they contracted with the Trimold Company of Buffalo to mold various shapes and sizes for them. As sales increased, Fisher-Price became Trimold's largest customer. In 1957, Fisher-Price purchased the Trimold plant and operated it thereafter as a wholly owned subsidiary. In 1962, they built a new molding facility in Holland, New York, which became the center of all Fisher-Price molding operations, and one of the largest molding facilities in the eastern United States.

In the 1960s, with the development of discount mass marketing, toy sales increased enormously. Fisher-Price grew concurrently. A major factor in this growth was the introduction of play people as integral parts of a toy. These toys, which greatly increased the play factor involved in many traditional toys, such as cars and trucks, were extremely popular. Fisher-Price also introduced a standardized package in the 1960s which utilized bright colors and uniform graphics. It also developed a sophisticated core of marketing personnel to work with retailers in developing displays of Fisher-Price toys, and created its first planned display in 1965. Fisher-Price's revenues, which had been just $116,000 in 1932, had climbed to over $26 million in 1966.

By this time, the two founders had become tired of dealing with the day-to-day operations. Irving Price retired in 1965, and Herman Fisher stepped down as president a year later, becoming chairman of the board. The new president and chief executive officer was Henry H. Coords, who was recruited from Western Electric Company. At the same time, about $850,000 was distributed pro rata to the employees, an amount equal to about 14 percent of the annual payroll. This kind of profit sharing led Herman Fisher to seek corporate membership in the Council of Profit Sharing Industries, of which he served as a director from 1963 to 1966.

When Fisher and Coords expanded the company headquarters in 1968, space was provided in its research and development building for a nursery school, which gave the company's designers a laboratory in which to test its products. It was a great success. Robert Hicks, then head of company research and development, commented: "You'd be amazed what we learned, kids will turn toys upside down and find the smallest detail." This research and care in development of product helped make Fisher-Price the largest maker of toys for preschool children by the late 1960s. In this market it had only one major rival—Playskool, owned by the game maker, Milton Bradley Company. Because of the extreme youth of its market, Fisher-Price recognized early that it would have to advertise to parents rather than the children themselves. Thus the ads carried in *Good Housekeeping, Parent's Magazine,* and *Woman's Day* emphasized quality, enrichment, and enjoyment—a far cry from the toy ads of most manufacturers.

Despite its earlier success, Fisher-Price experienced flat sales in the latter 1960s. Without sufficient capital to develop new lines and approaches, the firm's management was frustrated, as sales inched to $39 million in 1969. In that year, they decided to sell the company to Quaker Oats, the giant cereal company, which wanted to diversify. Quaker paid $50 million for Fisher-Price. Herman

Fisher retired completely from the firm at that time, and Henry Coords remained as president. As an industry analyst commented, Fisher-Price was given "a tremendous amount of money from Quaker," and they proceeded to leave Playskool far behind over the next three years. Although Fisher-Price stuck to the market it knew best—preschoolers—it greatly increased the number of new toys introduced each year, and it stepped up its ad budget from $200,000 in 1969 to $3 million in 1973. Sales increased threefold from 1969 to 1972, reaching $112 million in 1972. Earnings alone were $25 million in 1972. At a time when other toy companies were experiencing difficulties, Fisher-Price went through a major growth phase.

By the mid–1980s, Fisher-Price had continued its phenomenal growth pattern, all achieved without deviating from its fundamental principles and target market group—preschoolers. Whereas other toy makers had either ventured into electronic and video games and monster toys or had gone into camping equipment and other areas, Fisher-Price found success by "sticking to its knitting." With sales of $353 million in 1983, it continued to dominate the market for preschool toys into the late 1980s. Herman Fisher, when asked in the mid–1960s if he would cash in on the current craze of monster models, replied: "This is the last thing we want to do," feeling that toys should not be outlets for aggression. His was a lonely voice in an industry increasingly focused on violence and aggression, but a voice that brought the firm unparalleled success. (**B.** *National Cyclopaedia of American Biography*, 58:87; 60: 293; *Business Week*, March 27, 1965, March 3, 1973, May 21, 1984; *Who Was Who in America*, vol. VI, 1974–76; *New York Times*, September 28, 1975; *Industry Week*, April 30, 1984; Joseph J. Fucini and Suzy Fucini, *Entrepreneurs*, 1985.)

G

GALLO, ERNEST (1910–) and JULIO GALLO (1911–) Vintners, E. & J. Gallo Winery. They almost did it. Ernest and Julio Gallo, the world's largest and most successful wine makers, had never had a very complimentary image. Both powerful and secretive men, they inspired as much hatred as admiration from their competitors, advertising agencies, distributors, and winegrowers. One grower said his hatred stemmed from ''getting rejected by Gallo at the crusher.'' Distributors complained of being unceremoniously dumped for failing to satisfy Ernest Gallo's stringent criteria; competitors live in mortal fear of being crushed by Gallo's marketing power. But Ernest Gallo is particularly feared by advertising men. The Gallo firm went through seventeen advertising agencies in thirty-three years, and Ernest was widely reputed to be the toughest client in the advertising business, a worthy heir to the traditions of American Tobacco's George Washington Hill* and Charles Haskell Revson† of Revlon. One advertising executive who suffered through the trials of the Gallo account for a time joked that if he wrote his autobiography the chapter dealing with that time would be called ''Sentenced to the Gallos.'' What makes this all rather ironic is that it was a highly successful advertising campaign put together for Gallo's Bartles & Jaymes wine coolers by Hal Riney that did much to change their public image.

In 1987, *Advertising Age* conducted a poll to determine the most popular commercial characters on television. Third and fifth, respectively, on the list were Frank Bartles and Ed Jaymes of Bartles & Jaymes wine coolers. Only the Pillsbury Doughboy and Nine Lives' Morris the Cat were more popular than Ed. Frank and Ed were, indeed, appealing characters. A humorous, bucolic duo, they sat on their sagging front porch and spun yarns about their wine coolers to the delight of the national television audience. In one of the first spots, Frank, who did all the talking while Ed just sat there whittlin', asked viewers to suggest new names for their product. Later on, however, he announced that they had decided to stick with Bartles & Jaymes. ''If you don't like it,'' he said, ''please don't tell us, because we've already printed up our labels.'' In a later ad, Frank urged viewers to buy more Bartles & Jaymes because Ed had to make a big balloon payment on the second mortgage he took out to start the company. Many viewers were convinced; dozens wrote in offering financial help. The image portrayed in the ads is that of a small, underfinanced winery taking on the giants of the wine cooler trade. In fact, it amounted to what in many respects was a complex, double "sting" operation on the American public.

Nowhere did the ads mention that Bartles & Jaymes was made by the Gallo wine company, a firm that makes about one-third of all the wine in America, a company so large and so dominant that *Time* called it the "General Motors of American Wine." Members of America's media gleefully pounced on that omission and exposed Bartles & Jaymes wine cooler as a product of the giant E. & J. Gallo Winery. In the process, some were seduced into an even greater mistake, thinking that the two men were actually Ernest and Julio Gallo. *Newsweek* (August 5, 1985) went so far as to call it "[a] quirky campaign by two Gallos in disguise." They were not, nor were the parts of Ed and Frank played by professional actors. In real life, Frank was an Oregon farmer; Ed, a Santa Rosa building contractor. The series was recognized as one of the most successful advertising campaigns of recent years, and it helped give the Gallo brothers a more cuddly image. Reality, however, did not change. When Hal Riney, who also did the narration for the ads, learned that the Gallos wished to replace his voice on certain ads, he thought he was going to be fired and promptly resigned the account. Ernest Gallo went looking for his eighteenth advertising agency.

Ernest and Julio Gallo, who were born near Modesto, California, were the sons of Italian immigrants who owned a small vineyard there. The family was struck by catastrophe in 1933 when their father, Joseph Gallo, Sr., went beserk, shot his wife and chased his sons across the fields with a shotgun. After they escaped, he turned the gun on himself and committed suicide. The brothers decided to use their small inheritance of about $6,000 to produce their own bulk commercial wine. They faced enormous odds—it was during the depths of the depression, and 700 wineries were competing for the market. Even worse, they did not know how to make wine. To solve that elementary problem, they went to the Modesto Public Library, where they found two thin pamphlets of instructions on the topic. Julio used them to learn how to make the wine, while Ernest concentrated on marketing the product and keeping the books. They made a good business partnership. With Julio producing wine in a shed, and Ernest's wife working to save labor costs, Ernest managed to sell his wine at half the going rate of $1 a gallon. He then headed east and convinced a Chicago distributor to order 6,000 gallons at 50 cents a gallon. Thus encouraged, he continued east, signing up enough distributors to sell the company's entire annual production. Their profits for the first year were $34,000, and they have never looked back.

Each year the Gallos poured every penny of profits back into their business. They expanded their facilities each year, largely without the aid of bankers, who snubbed them. Until 1938 the Gallos sold their wine in bulk to bottlers, but in that year they decided to do their own bottling under the Gallo label. This was a far more profitable operation, and, as sales continued to rise during World

War II, the Gallo winery became increasingly profitable. Ernest, reflecting on those early years, said, "My confidence was unlimited." After World War II, the bulk wine price hit $1.50 a gallon, and the Gallos sold all they could to the large liquor distillers, who were determined to exploit the market of returning servicemen. The wine boom went bust in 1947, and the Gallos bought their wine back for about 50 cents a gallon. As Ernest said, "Every winery in the state lost money that year, as far as I can determine—except one." That one, of course, was E. & J. Gallo Winery, which, according to Ernest, has never lost money.

It was during the 1950s that the Gallos built the foundation for growth that allowed the once tiny Gallo winery to dominate the American wine industry. The Gallos built a vertically integrated winery that controlled production from growing the grapes to placing the finished product on the retailer's shelf. The key contributing element was the erection of an ultramodern winery with stainless-steel storage tanks rather than the old wooden or cement vats, used in other wineries, which can breed bacteria. It made E. & J. Gallo look more like an oil refinery than a traditional winery, but it allowed the brothers to maintain more rigorous standards. Julio, responsible for that end of the business, personally tasted the wine every morning at 11 o'clock. The Gallos also constructed a bottling plant, which churned out two million bottles a day, and they also owned the Midcal Aluminum Company, which manufactured the screw tops for those bottles. They developed their own trucking company, Fairbanks Trucking, with 200 semis and 500 trailers, to deliver wine throughout California. Finally, the Gallo firm created a corps of captive distributors in about a dozen markets. They would have had more except for the laws in many states that forbid the practice.

The Gallos' principle secret for their success, however, is Ernest's uncanny knack for predicting consumer tastes. In the early 1950s, most of the California vintners were located in the Napa Valley—small operators who prided themselves on making high-quality, distinctive wines. Ernest had no patience for these wineries or their customers, calling them "wine snobs." Instead, he targeted his products at the low end of the market. In the 1940s he had brought out a number of cheap sherries and muscatels under the Gallo name. In the 1950s, Ernest noticed that ghetto blacks bought 40-proof white port wine, and then cut the cloying taste by mixing in lemon juice. With Ernest's instructions, Julio and his wine makers developed a wine called Thunderbird—a mixture of white port and citric acid. Using a catchy advertising campaign aimed at ghetto blacks— "What's the word? Thunderbird. How's it sold? Good and cold. What's the jive? Bird's alive. What's the price? Thirty twice"—the company sold an unprecedented 2.5 million cases of Thunderbird in less than a year. Thunderbird has been a staple of ghetto drinkers and winos ever since. But Thunderbird also left Gallo with a tainted image—the image of a cut-rate maker of cheap wines drunk out of paper bags. It has been difficult for the company to shake that image over the years.

Nonetheless, with the profits from Thunderbird, Gallo was able to afford more salesmen, to demand more shelf space, and to push a whole array of new innovative wines well into the 1960s. One of these wines, Ripple, became enormously popular in its own right, and it even inherited a place in American folklore, as Redd Foxx, on his television show "Sanford and Son," talked about the attractions of a "good bottle of Ripple." Although this was valuable free advertising for the Gallo firm, it did little to enhance its image with upscale wine drinkers.

The Gallos' next big attraction arrived when they added carbonation to the company's old slow-selling Boone's Farm apple wine. Overnight, Boone's Farm increased its sales from 30,000 cases a year to 720,000 cases a month in early 1971. When the "pop wine" craze peaked in 1972, Gallo was selling 16 million cases a year and had a whopping 88 percent of that market. Then, at the very peak of the pop wine craze in 1972, when other wineries were rushing into the market with new wines and massive advertising, Ernest Gallo stopped all advertising of Boone's Farm and watched sales of the wine dwindle rapidly. From 1971 to 1974, Gallo saw its pop wine sales drop from 16 million cases to 6 million annually. By saving money on advertising, the Gallos made a greater profit on each case, and by then the pop wine market had dried up anyway.

With those profits, Ernest Gallo moved the company into premium wines for the first time. He pushed the company's new higher priced Hearty Burgundy wine and watched sales climb from 4 million cases to 13.5 million. Since the more expensive wine had a higher profit margin, the Gallos made even more money on this transaction. As Jack Dadum of competitor Guild Wine commented, "What can I say? Ernest is a genius." Despite that success, the Gallos found it difficult to convince many wine drinkers of the value of their new product. Julio insisted that "We have varietals we think are the very best," and many wine experts agree. But the Thunderbird, screw-top image has been difficult for the company to shake. In his office, Ernest has a framed New Yorker cartoon that reads: "Surprisingly good, isn't it? It's Gallo. Mort and I simply got tired of being snobs."

The Gallos' next challenge came with wine coolers in the 1980s. By 1980 Gallo wine was a giant, privately owned company with an estimated $475 million in annual sales. Of the 314 million gallons of wine shipped from California in 1979, Gallo's share was 104 million, and it had about 25 percent of the total wine market in the United States. Then, out of the blue came something even Ernest Gallo had not foreseen—"California Cooler." In the early 1980s, two young men, Michael Crete and Stewart Bewley, concocted a mixture of Chablis wine, citrus juices, sweeteners, preservatives, and carbonation, which they marketed as California Cooler. Rather than sell California Cooler through the traditional wine outlets, Bewley and Crete marketed it through beer distributors. As Crete noted: "It is packaged just like beer, it can be warehoused and handled on trucks just like beer. There was nothing they [the beer distributors] had to do differently." Using beer distributors opened up a vast market to the cooler product, since beer distributors call on every outlet, from local, mom-and-pop stores to huge supermarket chains. Also, since coolers sell better if refrigerated, beer distributors were ideal to handle the product, since their forte was the "cold box" or refrigerated case.

California Cooler sales skyrocketed. *Impact*, a beverage industry newsletter, commented: "This is the fastest-growing beverage category I've ever seen. Five years ago this category didn't exist. Today it's the most explosive happening in the beverage industry." What was the secret of California Cooler's phenomenal success? Bewley and Crete tapped a number of emerging trends in the 1980s. Wine coolers appeal most to people in their twenties and thirties, especially to women, who make up about 65 percent of the market. The typical cooler consumer is twenty-six years old, white, and middle class—in other words, the prototypical "yuppie" of the 1980s. Yet the appeal of the wine cooler is broader than that. Many people who became concerned about health and fitness in the 1980s, believed that switching from hard liquor to coolers, with their lower alcohol content and fruit juice, would result in a better, healthier diet. Also, the sweetness appealed to an entire generation of young people who had grown up on sweet carbonated sodas, allowing them to make an easy transition to an "adult" drink. As a result, coolers were often called "adult soft drinks," "alcoholic Kool-Aid," and "Gatorade with a kick."

By 1985, Bewley and Crete's company had sales of $100 million a year, and it was evident that the Gallos were going to have to enter this lucrative new market. What must have made the whole affair galling to Ernest Gallo was that his company had long dominated the market for pop wines, with citrus juices and sweeteners, and, furthermore coolers had been popular in California for years. Ernest Gallo may have missed an important trend in popular consumption with wine coolers, but it did not take him long to use the power and muscle of Gallo wine to carve out a powerful market position. Bewley and Crete's brand, which had been the market leader for five years, was simply overwhelmed by Gallo's Bartles & Jaymes wine coolers, and they had to sell their company to Brown-Forman. In explaining how he was driven out of the market, Bewley commented about Gallo, "They aim all their guns at once."

Using its high-power advertising campaign for Bartles & Jaymes, in just three months in 1985, Gallo sold 2 million cases of the cooler; by 1986, they overtook California Cooler as the country's top seller, capturing 30 percent of the market. Although it later surrendered the top position to Seagrams, which used Bruce Willis from the popular television show "Moonlighting" to represent its Golden Wine Cooler, Gallo has, nonetheless, had a tardy, but significant success with wine coolers. This, in turn, got its products into beer refrigerators in mom-and-pop stores and a number of other outlets that even their powerful merchandising techniques had not previously opened to them.

Everything has not worked out perfectly for the Gallos, however. There have been nagging problems over the years. One problem has concerned Gallo's reputed strong-arm tactics with distributors. As a result, the Federal Trade Commission began an investigation of the company in 1971. In 1976, they determined that Gallo had used its "dominant position, size, and power to lessen . . . competition in the sales and distribution of wines in the U.S. by engaging in unfair acts." Gallo also encountered major problems with Cesar Chavez's United Farm Workers Union (UFW). In many ways, this was ironic because Ernest Gallo is a lifelong liberal who originally welcomed the union in 1967. By 1973, however, relations had become bitter, and Gallo signed a contract with the Teamsters. The result was a nationwide boycott of Gallo's products until 1978, when the UFW returned as the representative of the field workers.

The final problem concerned an internecine family quarrel. Ernest and Julio's younger brother Joseph, who had never owned shares in the family wine company, brought suit against his brothers in 1986, charging that they had defrauded him of his one-third share in the billion-dollar family empire. The feud began in 1983 when Joseph Gallo began marketing "Joseph Gallo" cheddar cheese. Ernest and Julio, after some negotiation, sued Joseph for trademark infringement and forbade him to use the Gallo name on his cheese. The case was still in the courts at this writing.

The personalities of Ernest and Julio Gallo are very different. Julio is an easygoing, gregarious man who enjoys making wine and having a good time; Ernest is a grim, unsmiling, tough businessman. Ernest has been the heart and soul of the firm; he has charted its direction and given it its drive for over fifty years. He also gave Gallo its passion for secrecy and its ferocious competitiveness. Ernest is known as a ruthless perfectionist, a fiercely driven, supersecretive man; and the firm is known within the industry for its secrecy, superb marketing skills, and occasional ruthless tactics with distributors and labor unions. All of this has helped create a massive empire. Gallo's sales probably exceeded $1 billion in 1985, and Ernest and Julio share a family fortune, which, in 1986 the *Forbes* 400 estimated at well over $700 million. Both in their late seventies, the brothers continue to run the giant winery with an iron hand, giving no evidence of stepping down. Commenting on the lack of a clear successor to the seventy-seven-year-old Ernest Gallo in 1986, *Fortune* commented: "Rest assured, though, Ernest has figured out how to sell Gallo products from the grave. He is probably well along on a manual outlining every conceivable war that could break out in the wine world and ten steps to win each one." (**B.** Leon Adams, *The Wines of America*, 1973; *Time*, November 3, 1961; *Forbes*, October 1, 1975, October 24, 1988; Milton Moskowitz et al., *Everybody's Business*, 1980; *Business Week*, October 4, 1984, October 26, 1987; *Newsweek*, November 5, 1984, August 5, 1985, August 18, 1986; *Inc.*, January 1985; *Nation's Business*, October 1985; *Fortune*, September 1, 1986, January 5, 1987; *USAir*, March 1987; Toronto *Globe & Mail*, May 6, 1988.)

GALVIN, PAUL V. (June 29, 1895–November 5, 1959) and **ROBERT WILLIAM GALVIN** (October 9, 1922–   ). Electronics company founder and executives, Motorola, Incorporated. Motorola, one of the giants in the world of electronics, was started by a man, Paul Galvin, who had already failed several times in business. He had begun to manufacture automobile storage batteries in the early 1920's, but failed twice at it. In the later years of the decade, he began making home radio batteries with some success, but in 1929 he hit pay dirt with the introduction of radios for automobiles. During World War II Motorola did a great deal of defense work in electronics, including the invention and production of walkie-talkies. After the war, his son Robert Galvin joined the firm, and Motorola began to produce advanced electronic components. In the 1950s, it began making semiconductors and soon became one of America's top producers. For a time, Motorola also manufactured televisions and stereos. In the 1960s, before the rise of several Japanese firms, Motorola was known as the world's largest exclusive electronics manufacturer. Never a leader in technology, Motorola was usually regarded as a fast follower, but by the late 1980s many analysts questioned whether it had the youth and vigor to continue to compete with dynamic Japanese electronics companies.

Paul Galvin, the founder of Motorola, was born in the small town of Harvard, Illinois. His father, of Irish farming stock, ran a saloon. Educated in local schools, Paul Galvin got his first job stripping the stems from large tobacco leaves in a small tobacco factory in the town, where he worked for two summers. After graduating from Harvard High School, Galvin went to the University of Illinois, where he studied business administration for two years until he enlisted in the U.S. Army in 1917. Commissioned as a second lieutenant, Galvin spent a year in France before being mustered out in 1919.

After his discharge, Galvin took a job with the D & G Storage Battery Company in Chicago. The growth of the automobile market in the early 1920s, combined with the development of radio, opened new opportunities for Galvin. He had earlier formed a friendship with Edward Stewart, who had been active in the infant radio field for a number of years. In 1921, Galvin and Stewart joined to form the Stewart Battery Company, establishing a manufacturing plant in Marshfield, Wisconsin. Their venture was ill-starred from the beginning: neither man had much experience, the battery field was highly competitive, and their plant was located far from transportation and markets. Coupled with a sharp depression in 1921–1922, the young company was unable to endure and went bankrupt in 1923. Paul Galvin took a job as a salesman for the Brach Candy Company, where he remained for three years, when he again joined in a partnership with Stewart to produce batteries.

This time, Galvin and Stewart decided to specialize in radio batteries. At that time, radios could be powered only by direct-current storage batteries, although everyone was certain that eventually some method would be found to make them operate on alternating current (AC). Galvin came up with an ingenious device, which he called the "A-Eliminator." The owner could plug the A-Eliminator into an electrical outlet and then plug his radio into the eliminator. The alternating current from the home would keep the battery charged, while the radio ran on direct current from the battery. It was a good idea for the time, and the market seemed to be within reach, but again, Galvin and Stewart were undercapitalized and went bankrupt.

But Paul Galvin was nothing if not determined. Convinced that he had a marketable item, he and his brother Joseph attended his own auction and with $750 bought back the battery eliminator portion of the business. This marked the beginning of Galvin Manufacturing Corporation, which, established on September 25, 1928, with five employees, focused on the production of eliminators rather than batteries. Soon after Galvin started his company, however, AC radio sets began to enter the market, threatening his young business. Galvin realized the necessity to develop other products if his company were going to survive. He began to manufacture a nine-tube AC home radio, which he sold on a private-label basis to about twenty suppliers. After the Great Depression struck in the fall of 1929, competition in the home radio field became intense. Galvin realized that he needed something unique, something that would guarantee his company a place in the business establishment.

What Galvin hit upon was the idea of car radios. These were already being installed on a custom basis in cars in small, backyard garage operations, but Galvin wanted to begin mass producing a radio that could easily fit into the dashboard of any model car. To develop this, he turned to William P. Lear, a brilliant inventor, who operated his own company (Radio Coil & Wire) but had also done consulting for Galvin Manufacturing. Lear invented the prototype of the car radio for Galvin and sold him rights to the patent. Although it still operated on a separate battery system, Lear's design was a winner, and Galvin, despite the onset of the Great Depression and the efforts of some states to ban car radios because they constituted a hazardous distraction for the driver, began to sell increasing numbers of the radios. In 1931, a Galvin Manufacturing engineer, Ray Yoder, invented a vibrator-type power supply to replace the B-batteries. This made Galvin Manufacturing the most advanced firm in the industry technologically, and it soon overwhelmed the competition, becoming the premier producer of car radios during the 1930s, using the name Motorola.

During the 1930s, Galvin also set up a separate division in his company that concentrated on producing police radios, which operated on higher frequencies so that dispatchers could contact police and emergency vehicles. As Galvin commented, "There was a need and I could see it was a market that nobody owned." While pursuing this technology, Galvin read an article in an academic journal by Daniel E. Noble, a professor at the University of Connecticut. Noble had created a frequency-modulated (FM) mobile communications system for the state police in Connecticut, and he described it in the article. Galvin contacted Noble and the latter agreed to take a year's sabbatical to work at Galvin Manufacturing on the new technology for police communications. Noble never left the firm; he remained as one of several dynamic geniuses in the research arm of the company in the years during and after World War II.

During the 1930s, the U.S. Army, which was using heavy, cumbersome, backpack radios, complained to Galvin about its communications problems. In response, Galvin sent his chief engineer, Don Mitchell, to investigate. Mitchell developed something he called the "Handie-Talkie," which was designed to provide better two-way portable radio communication. Noble then worked with Mitchell on the device; substituting FM for amplitude modulation (AM) and reducing its size and weight, they devised what became known during World War II as the walkie-talkie. Nearly 40,000 of them were in use during the war, which helped cement Galvin Manufacturing's reputation as the leader in mobile and portable communications equipment. Also at this time, the company produced radar equipment and, at its peak in 1944, was making more than $80 million worth of military equipment annually. The firm's largest volume prior to the war had been $17 million.

Like so many other firms that rapidly expanded as a result of military orders, Galvin Manufacturing faced a severe downturn at the end of the war. As a consequence, the company had to adapt as it faced the postwar years. First of all, in 1943, it went public, after being privately held during its first fifteen years. Second, Joseph Galvin, who had handled production, credit, and labor relations, died in 1944. Consequently, Paul Galvin had to bring a new management team to the fore and to find new products and markets for the company at the same time. On the management side, Galvin gave increased responsibility to Daniel Noble, and he brought his son, Robert Galvin, onto the management scene.

Robert Galvin was born in Marshfield, Wisconsin, but was educated in the public schools in Chicago. When he was in seventh grade, the family moved from Chicago to suburban Evanston, where Robert was elected president of his high school class. After high school, he attended the University of Chicago and the University of Notre Dame. In 1940, at eighteen years of age, Robert Galvin went to work in the family enterprise, starting as an apprentice in the stockroom. Except for a brief period in the Army Signal Corps during World War II, Galvin spent the rest of his career at Motorola, where he worked in a variety of positions during his early years. In 1945, he was named a director of the company, and in 1946 he was given a voice in executive decision-making when the firm's sales dropped off sharply to $23 million.

In that year, the company's name was changed to Motorola, Incorporated, to reflect the importance of the car radio to its business. At the same time, Paul and Robert Galvin recognized that television was the field of the future. They decided to enter the field, and in 1947 Motorola introduced the first workable television set priced at under $200, which helped increase company sales to $47 million. The following year, after acquiring a number of car-radio contracts, sales increased to $62 million. Motorola was on the road to recovery. It then entered the luxury television field, further increasing sales and profits. But the company's move into these areas increased its dependence on vacuum tubes, which it was purchasing from other companies, especially RCA, a competitor. Paul Galvin, wishing to reduce the dependence on RCA, planned to acquire a company that made these tubes. David Noble, who was by then director of research for Motorola, opposed the move. He felt that this was an obsolete technology and that a solid-state component would soon replace the vacuum tube. Noble was able to convince Paul Galvin to let him develop these components.

In 1952, Noble secured licensing rights to the transistor from Bell Laboratories, and he set up a research station in Phoenix, Arizona, where he and his staff spent the next several years trying to develop the first germanium power transistors. Lacking quality materials, adequate manufacturing technology, and sufficient knowledge, it was an almost impossible task, but by the mid–1950s Noble's team had developed transistors that could be used in car radios. An important new area of technology with a great deal of market potential, development of these transistors involved many production problems in the early years. By the late 1950s, the team had mastered transistors, and they were now ready to move on to the new important phase for the company—semiconductors—which in the late 1950s were a new, crude product. Motorola was a rather late entrant into this field in the late 1950s, but demand was still small. Since the materials used often became contaminated, the product was unreliable, which forced up costs and prices. Nonetheless, it was a market with unlimited potential, and it was important that Motorola persevere. It was Robert Galvin who took the major gamble involved for the company to continue this costly, risky venture.

Robert Galvin had advanced to the post of executive vice president in 1949. A year later, the Korean War broke out, bringing Motorola huge military orders. As a result, sales in 1950 shot up to a staggering $177 million, and in response the company set up a separate national defense division headquarters in Chicago in 1952. During the early 1950s, Motorola manufactured more mobile radio equipment than RCA, GE, Westinghouse, and ITT combined, and it also led in the production of microwave relay communications systems. By 1956, sales at the mammoth company had reached $227 million. In that year Paul Galvin moved up to chairman of the board, and Robert was elected president and chief executive officer of the firm. Together, the two men still controlled about 25 percent of the stock in the company. Three years later, in 1959, Paul Galvin died of leukemia.

Robert Galvin inherited a company with a number of problems. In 1954, while still under the leadership of Paul Galvin, Motorola tried to enter the new world of color television, but failed miserably. It withdrew from that market, but began to experience increasing problems with its black and white sets. Motorola had chosen to market its black and white sets based on price and, as a result, cut a number of corners in manufacturing, affecting the quality of the product adversely. Consequently, it lost a number of dealerships and lost its third-place position in the television industry. The first thing Robert Galvin had to do when he took over in 1956 was to reestablish a sense of quality and reliability in its consumer television products. Motorola was able to reestablish its position in the marketplace by the late 1950s, since, as a marketing man stated: "Fortunately, the consumer has a short memory." It took longer, however, for Galvin to bring

Motorola back into color television. It did not start making them again until 1963—a very late entrant in the field. But, when Robert Galvin decided to reenter the color television market, he did it dramatically and successfully. He introduced a twenty-three-inch rectangular color tube that outflanked the competition and allowed Motorola to regain third place among television makers.

Galvin also pursued the new semiconductor field with vigor. Noble demanded to be supplied with "first-class brainpower and first-class materials" for this project, and Robert Galvin complied. Motorola experienced losses in its first year of production of semiconductors, broke even the second year, and began to make a profit in the third year. By the mid–1960s, Motorola was the second largest semiconductor maker in America, with 14,000 workers at its Phoenix plant.

By the mid–1960s, Robert Galvin had recognized and reestablished Motorola as a major competitor on the electronics scene. Discontinuing his father's old one-man-rule, Robert Galvin moved to decentralize the company. Galvin also tried to establish a relaxed, but productive atmosphere at the massive company. There was strong emphasis on the idea of the Motorola Family, in which white-shirted executives stood in line for lunch at the company cafeteria, like everyone else, and all wore name tags, including Galvin. He continued the profit-sharing program his father had set up in 1947, and he belonged to the Council of Profit-Sharing Industries.

Although Galvin's changes and reforms brought prosperity to Motorola in the early– and mid–1960s, by the later years of that decade, problems began to reemerge. Profits declined, largely because Galvin was not able to get more than 6 percent of the color television market. The consumer products division, of which televisions were a part, operated at a loss during most of these years. The desertion of the head of their semiconductor division, C. Lester Hogan, to Fairchild Semiconductor in 1968, severely crippled Motorola's progress in that area. Galvin's response was typically aggressive. To shed the stodgy image Motorola had developed over the years in television, he adopted a new space-age name for his products—Quasar—which featured an all-transistor television set featuring all electronic parts in a easy-to-service pull out drawer.

It was a valiant, but unsuccessful, attempt. By the mid–1970s, it was clear to Galvin that Motorola simply was not equipped to cope with consumer markets anymore. Although the Quasar sets were regarded as the class of the market, they made little headway against either the older American producers or the new Japanese competitors. As a result, in 1974 he sold the Quasar division to Matsushita, the Japanese electronics firm. Significantly, however, Matsushita continued to purchase Motorola components for the sets, since these components were cost-effective and reliable. Galvin continued to hang on to the last of Motorola's consumer products—the car radio—until 1984. By this time, Motorola was a world-class semiconductor manufacturer, with $2.5 billion in sales in that product alone. Moving beyond consumer products, Galvin wanted to position Motorola in new communications markets, like mobile telephones, and into the computer-run electronic office business. As he said at the time, "Data, communications, and semiconductors are our three legs." Although Motorola fell behind in the production of integrated circuits (several components on one chip) in the late 1960s, it achieved enormous success in the 1970s and 1980s with the production of microprocessors. Among American companies, only Intel produced more of these. The big breakthrough came in 1974, with the introduction of the 6800 microprocessors with 5,000 components on one chip. That was succeeded in 1979 by the 68000, with 200,000 components, which became a particularly important base for the new supercomputers of the 1980s. In 1984 Motorola had sales of $5.53 billion, an increase of 28 percent over the year before. Profits were $571 million, up a whopping 50 percent over the previous year.

Despite this success, the firm again faced problems in the latter years of the 1980s. Never a leader in technology, Motorola suffered the consequences of its inability to keep pace with rapid changes in the semiconductor industry during these years. It lagged in the development of discrete semiconductors—chips containing just one device rather than thousands on an integrated circuit. It also lagged behind Texas Instruments and Japan in the production of 256-K DRAMs (dynamic random access memory chips). Where it continued to succeed, however, was in its 32-bit microprocessers.

Robert Galvin's most significant contribution to American industry in the 1980s, however, transcended his giant electronics company. Becoming gravely concerned about the impact of Japanese competition in the electronics and semiconductor fields, he became the chief spokesman in an angry crusade against Japan's trading practices. Galvin called for a three-year, 20-percent surcharge on all imported manufactured goods. He was not optimistic that the government would respond favorably, so he began to make plans to move a number of Motorola's operations closer to Asia. Although this practice drew criticism, Galvin responded by saying that he had no choice: "We will do what we have to do in order to survive. But that survival includes a strategy of defection. We are defecting from this country."

In this process of streamlining and restructuring his company, Galvin trimmed 8,500 from the 45,000-strong semiconductor workforce. He also pulled out of the 64-K DRAM market when the prices fell too low to make a profit, and he began discussions with Toshiba concerning a joint venture in chip manufacturing in Japan—a venture which ultimately bore fruit for both companies. In 1987, Motorola established a fifty-fifty joint venture with Toshiba to swap Motorola's microprocessor designs for Toshiba's know-how in producing computer memory chips. Together, they set up the Tohoku Semiconductor Company, which began shipping their first microprocessors and megabit DRAMs in 1988. It was a dramatic and important venture.

By 1986, semiconductor sales had recovered, and the division, which had experienced two years of losses, rebounded with nearly $100 million in profits. Motorola also performed well in other areas: the company continued to dominate the two-way radio market for fire and police departments and developed a hot new market for pagers. Perhaps Galvin's most significant achievement in the late 1980s, however, was the role he played in the United States–Japan semiconductor trade agreement in 1986. He was a major architect of that plan, which finally opened the large Japanese semiconductor market to American manufacturers. Under the agreement, Japan agreed to increase its purchases of U.S. semiconductors from 8 percent to 20 percent over the next five years. It also agreed to stop dumping computer chips onto the U.S. market. In return, the Reagan administration agreed to suspend its pending antidumping duties against Japan. The agreement capped many years of involvement by Galvin in trade issues. Robert Galvin in 1986 relinquished his role as chief executive of the company, remaining chairman, but playing a less active role.

Motorola has continued to try to improve its production record in semiconductors at home. The company, which had been second in worldwide sales of semiconductors in 1982 (behind only Texas Instruments), had fallen to fourth by 1987. With worldwide sales of about $2.5 billion in chips, Motorola was the largest American manufacturer, but was well behind NEC, Toshiba, and Hitachi on the world scene. Galvin, before he relinquished control of the firm, decided that education of Motorola's workforce was the key to recovering its position in world sales of semiconductors. In 1982, he mandated that at least 1.5 percent of each manager's payroll be devoted to training. The aim was to transform the entire corporate culture to focus on total customer satisfaction. Another goal was to break down the walls of the company that divided department from department, and managers from workers. A company which had once prided itself on its informality had become a huge, bloated bureaucratic lump. These communication difficulties led to internal problems. A company spokesman said: "We were actually beating the Japanese in manufacturing quality and manufacturing time, but our design time took twice as long."

Motorola's 1987 sales reached $6.7 billion, an increase of 14 percent over the year before. Profits were $308 million, up nearly 60 percent. It was the seventh largest electronics firm in America in terms of sales, and had over 97,000 employees. Spending over a half billion dollars on research and development, it finally realized that its traditionally conservative and sluggish attitude on that score had to change. As George M. C. Fisher, Galvin's successor, said, "Now we have to improve faster than the competition." And the more Motorola improved, the richer Robert Galvin became. Owner of 7 percent of the company's stock, he had a fortune of nearly $400 million in the late 1980s. (**B.** *Who Was Who*, vol. 3; *New York Times*, November 6, 1959; *Current Biography*, 1960; Harry M. Petrakis, *The Founder's Touch: The Life of Paul Galvin of Motorola*, 1965; *Nation's Business*, January 1966; *Business Week*, April 23, 1966, April 15, 1985, March 14, June 6, June 20, July 4, 1988; *Dun's Review*, June 1969; *Forbes*, January 30, 1984, August 11, 1986, October 24, 1988; Daniel I. Okimoto et al., *Competitive Edge: The Semiconductor*

158

GARDNER, EDWARD G.

Industry in the U.S. & Japan, 1984; *Financial World*, March 20–April 2, 1986; *Industry Week*, October 13, 1986; Robert Sobel, *IBM vs. Japan*, 1986; Robert Sobel and David B. Sicilia, *The Entrepreneurs*, 1986; *Fortune*, April 25, 1988; *Business Month*, July 1989.)

GARDNER, EDWARD G. (February 15, 1925–   ). Founder of hair products company, Soft Sheen Products, Incorporated. Edward Gardner is almost the prototypical contemporary black American business leader. He was born and raised in a time of severe racial discrimination and came into his adulthood at the end of World War II, at a time when black Americans were beginning to demand a "bigger piece of the pie" as a result of their "Double V" campaign. Taking advantage of the relative openness of education during these years, Gardner went to college, obtained advanced degrees, and worked his way up within the educational establishment. Then, in the 1960s, when pressures for greater economic opportunities for blacks intensified, Gardner began operating his own business. Unlike most of the blacks who started small businesses during those years, however, Gardner's grew into an enormous national concern, the sixth largest black-owned business in the United States, in terms of sales.

Born in Chicago, Edward Gardner grew up in the city during the years when it was being made famous as the "Black Metropolis" of America. In the words of St. Clair Drake and Horace R. Cayton, authors of that classic sociological document,

Black Metropolis is the second largest Negro city in the world, only New York's Harlem exceeding it in size. It is a city within a city—a narrow tongue of land, seven miles in length and one and one-half in width, where more than 300,000 Negroes are packed solidly.

It was a city with a tradition of violence against blacks, one in which the patterns of segregation and discrimination were firmly established and clearly delineated. Further, the depression years of the 1930s worsened the economic condition of blacks in Chicago; they were often the first to be fired or laid off from increasingly scarce positions. Although no information is available on Edward Gardner's life during these early years, one can presume that his situation did not deviate much from the norm for Chicago blacks.

During World War II, Gardner was able to go to college and received his B.A. from Chicago Teachers College. In 1945 he got a job as an elementary school assistant principal in the Chicago school system. Although it would be gratifying to think that Gardner achieved this position purely on merit, understanding of the nature of the Chicago school system would tend to raise suspicions on that regard. Since the Chicago school system was notorious for the political connections needed to get jobs and to advance to administrative positions, one must presume Gardner cultivated those connections. Sometime during the next decade he received his master's degree at the University of Chicago. During these same years, Gardner set up the E. G. Gardner Beauty Products Company, which he ran from his basement.

Entrance into business activities in the early postwar years was difficult for blacks in Chicago and elsewhere. As Drake and Cayton point out, although success for blacks was inevitably measured in terms of their ability to attain positions of power in the city's business world, these same positions were almost universally closed to them. Those few which were open tended to be small-scale, retail operations. That is, it was much more likely for a black to be a barber or a beautician than a manufacturer of beauty products. Yet blacks had particular needs as far as hair care was concerned, needs that were little understood by whites and almost totally ignored by them. As a consequence, the hair care and hair "straightening" field had long been lucrative for blacks in America. Madame C. J. Walker* was one black entrepreneur who made a sizable fortune catering to these needs of the black market. She was also a great hero and role model for a generation of blacks growing up in the 1920s and 1930s.

As a result, there were a number of small-scale hair-care manufacturers like Edward Gardner, who mixed products in their basements and distributed them from the trunks of their cars. By 1945, Drake and Cayton report that fifteen such companies in the black ghetto of Chicago constituted one-third of all black manufacturing enterprises in the city. During the late 1950s or early 1960s, Gardner also worked for another black beauty supply company, and, when that firm went bankrupt, Gardner took over its customers and began producing his own line of products. Calling his new company Soft Sheen Products, he began to mix a number of hair-care products for blacks in his basement. With the help of his wife and four children, Gardner hawked his products out of his car, going from block to block and from store to store in his South Side Chicago neighborhood.

At that time, however, Gardner's company was merely the copycat of an emerging giant in the black hair-care field in Chicago. George Johnson, a sharecropper's grandson, had founded Johnson Products in 1954 to market a hair product called Afro Sheen. When the Afro hairstyle became a great fad among blacks in the 1960s, Johnson Products was able to garner 80 percent of the black hair-care market in the United States. Gardner's Soft Sheen, along with a number of other manufacturers, divided up the remainder. In the 1970s, as the Afro hairstyle lost its allure, Johnson Products began to lose market share, and Soft Sheen captured an ever-larger share of the market. Its big breakthrough came with the introduction of Care Free Curl in 1979. In 1978, the curl, which was a loose-perm look popularized by black stars like Michael Jackson that required many hair maintenance products, burst on the scene. From 1978 to 1982 the new hairstyle spurred the growth of the black hair-care industry at a 32-percent annual rate. Soft Sheen, as the first of the black-owned hair products firms to enter this new market niche, quickly reaped huge revenue increases. Before long, it surpassed Johnson Products as the largest and most profitable black hair products manufacturer. By 1987, Soft Sheen had sales of over $81 million; Johnson Products, only $38 million.

In the mid–1980s, however, Soft Sheen was faced with a challenge from white hair products manufacturers. Revlon, Incorporated (see Charles Revson), one of the industry giants, began packaging a number of "ethnic" hair-care products that were similar to Soft Sheen's Care Free Curl. Gardner was determined that massive white-owned conglomerates would not displace him from his hard-won market. "I heard that the people at Revlon say, 'We don't want just part of the market, we want *all* of it,' " Gardner said. "Well, they're not going to get it." But the black hair-care market, which by 1988 was worth $1 billion, was very attractive to large white-owned cosmetics companies which found their growth stymied in other areas. It was particularly so because blacks spend significantly more on hair and skin products per capita than whites, and as a larger, more prosperous black middle class emerged in the 1980s, it represented an increasingly attractive market. By 1988, white-owned businesses owned 50 percent of the ethnic hair-care market and had plans to take all of it from the far smaller, struggling, black-owned businesses.

But the black-owned hair-care businesses were not about to roll over and play dead to the white conglomerates. When Irving Bottner, head of Revlon's professional products division, told a reporter that companies like his would take over all black-owned firms because the black firms produced poor-quality products, the black business community united as seldom before. Gardner, along with his cohorts, mounted an intensive campaign against this penetration. Rev. Jesse Jackson's Operation PUSH (People United to Save Humanity) launched a boycott of Revlon products, and Edward T. Lewis[†] of *Essence* refused to accept any of the company's advertising, as did John H. Johnson[*] of *Jet* and *Ebony*. Picketers marched in front of a Chicago store selling Revlon's products. The boycott galvanized the membership of the American Health and Beauty Aids Institute (AHBAI), a twenty-two-member minority trade association of which Edward Gardner was a prominent member. They kicked off a $3-million campaign to induce black consumers to buy black products, all of which were marked with the AHBAI "proud lady" logo. It generated a remarkable response, but it was not Gardner's only strategy to ensure his firm's survival in turbulent times.

Gardner's other response was to diversify his operations. During a period of eighteen months, from mid–1986 to early 1988, Soft Sheen made a number of important moves. It first sold a company—Perfect Pinch, a condiment manufacturer—on the grounds that it did not fit in with the new approach the company was taking. Edward Gardner, chief executive officer, and his son Gary, who was president and chief operating officer, devised a strategy for Soft Sheen whereby they would create and manage a portfolio of companies that did business in related areas. They set up Brainstorm Communications, an advertising agency that promoted Soft Sheen's products, among others. They also set up Bottlewerks, which packaged Soft Sheen products, and *Shoptalk,* a trade magazine. In addition, they purchased Dyke and Dryden, the largest black-owned importer, manufacturer, and distributor of black personal care products in Great Britain. With the growth of the black population in Britain, the Gardners felt that Dyke and Dryden had great potential, and they also viewed it as a gateway to the African market. Dyke and Dryden had a great deal of experience selling to Africa, which gave Gardner access to a market of about 600 million blacks. Soft Sheen also purchased Alaion Products, a manufacturer of lower priced, black men's, hair-care products, in Newark, New Jersey.

In recent years, Edward Gardner has moved out of day-to-day management of Soft Sheen, leaving that to his son Gary and other family members. Daughter Denise is vice president of marketing, another daughter Terri heads the advertising agency, and son Guy manages the bottling operation. Edward Gardner and his wife, meanwhile, have become intimately involved in community development in Chicago. Their roles were especially important in the $5-million renovation of the Regal Theater on Chicago's South Side. During the 1950s and 1960s, the Regal rivaled Harlem's Apollo Theater as a showcase for black talent, and it represented in the 1980s a major investment in community concerns on the part of Gardner and Soft Sheen.

But Edward Gardner worries about the next generation of black business leaders. When he was growing up, black business served a black market, and they tended to have important roots in the black community itself. Bright and talented young blacks in the 1980s, however, "get the MBA and go right to work for the major corporation and forget about building their own businesses." As a result, he argues that blacks will never break the cycle of poverty, that the black underclass will have an increasingly bleak future. Many black leaders concur. Alice Bussey, an Atlanta florist, and once head of the mostly black Atlanta Business League, saw it in much the same way. "After integration, a lot of blacks got into the system and made it," she said. "But now they have become so individualized that they forget they are supposed to be active in the community. That's why we're not as cohesive as we need to be." Tony Brown, host of a popular television show about blacks, put it more bluntly:

You can talk about the other problems of our community, but the real cause is that we have failed to get into business. We have to do something to shore up our economic institutions, to generate jobs within the community. When we take care of that, the other stuff—the family problems, crime, our political needs—will start taking care of itself. (*Inc.*)

The head of the black cosmetics industry trade group echoed the sentiment: "It's the younger blacks, who didn't live through the civil-rights movement, who don't understand why they should care." To most blacks and whites in America, Edward Gardner's Soft Sheen products are just yellow and red bottles that cater to particular black cosmetic needs. To many black leaders, however, they represent the future. (**B.** St. Clair Drake and Horace R. Cayton, *Black Metropolis: A Study of Negro Life in a Northern City*, 1945; *Inc.*, September 1986; *Newsweek*,

October 13, 1986; *Black Enterprise*, June 1987, June 1988; *Who's Who among Black Americans*, 1988.)

GATES, WILLIAM HENRY, III (October 27, 1955–   ). Computer software company founder, Microsoft, Incorporated. Picture this scene: A highly agitated screenwriter rushes into a film producer's office. He proclaims, "I've got the script for a wonderful movie for you! It's all about this kid who is born into a wealthy family, excels in school, and is recognized as a genius in mathematics at an early age. In his early teens he becomes infatuated with computers, and at fourteen he is hired by a major manufacturer to debug computer programs. He graduates from a posh private high school and goes to Harvard, but he is bored by the lack of intellectual challenge there and drops out after a year. He founds a company to develop the operating software system that is used for the vast majority of personal computers sold in America. Just nineteen when he starts the company, by the time he is thirty-one he is a billionaire—having made more money than anybody his age in the *entire history of business*." The producer, of course, shakes his head and replies, "That story is just too fantastic, too unreal. Come back when you have something people can believe and identify with." But that story, fantastic as it may seem, is the true-life story of Bill Gates.

Born in Seattle, Washington, Gates' father was a partner in a prominent law firm in the city, and his mother taught school for a time, when she became a major figure in the social services directorate of the city. Bill Gates attended local schools, and then went to Lakeside School, a private middle and high school renowned for its academic rigor. In this environment, Bill Gates' abilities came to the fore. Highly intelligent—an Intel vice president said of Gates that he has "an IQ that would peg up the IQ meter"—and highly motivated, Gates excelled at Lakeside. When he was fourteen, the Lakeside Mother's Club put on a rummage sale to buy a terminal linked to a computer at a local company, and Gates became, in his father's words, "completely engrossed" with computers. He and three friends started the Lakeside Programming Group, and he and Paul Allen became early "computer hackers," breaking into systems via software. Gates grew so adept at the black art of what was called "computer crashing," that he was able to defeat the security systems of many of the leading firms in the country. At this time, computer crashing had not yet achieved the notoriety it later attained when movies such as *War Games* showed its destructive potential.

He and Allen got their first jobs with computers when they were just fourteen. A local firm had just purchased a computer from Digital Equipment (DEC), with the proviso that as long as there were bugs in the system they did not have to start paying for the computer. The firm hired Gates and Allen to find these bugs, and find them they did. Riding their bicycles to work each day from school, they performed so well that ultimately DEC canceled its original agreement with the company. A year later, Gates and Allen were hired by TRW to work as troubleshooters in the DEC computer system they used to control the electrical power generated by the Bonneville Dam on the Columbia River. Still riding their bicycles to work, the two young computer wizards were already living a life that most computer freaks could only fantasize about.

With the enormous experience gained at TRW, Gates and Allen decided to start their own company. Earlier, the Lakeside Programming Group had developed two programs: one to handle payroll for the school and the other to count the holes punched in cards by machines that monitored highway traffic. Gates and Allen formed a company called Traf-O-Data, and sold their service to various municipalities. Gates became president of the company, because he was the only one who read business magazines. Feeling he had at least some nascent business talent, the computer freaks elected him head of the company. Traf-O-Data had revenues in its first year of $20,000. By this time, Gates was in his last year of high school, and Allen was studying at Washington State University. That summer, the two young men worked for another computer giant—Honeywell. Allen decided to stay with Honeywell at the end of the summer instead of returning to school, and he was transferred to the firm's Boston office.

Gates, meanwhile, had taken the Scholastic Aptitude Test and had scored a perfect 800 on the math portion. With his pick of virtually any college in the country, he chose Harvard, because of its prestige and because he would be near his friend, Paul Allen. At Harvard, Gates rapidly became bored with his studies, and he spent most of his time playing in late-night poker games or engaging in hard-core computer hacking with Allen. Then, in 1975, Allen brought Gates an issue of *Popular Electronics*, which featured an ad for the Altair build-it-yourself microcomputer kit. Fascinated by its possibilities, Gates and Allen called the president of MITS, manufacturers of the computer, and offered to deliver a BASIC interpreter for the Altair to him in four weeks. The purpose of such a program—an operating system for the computer—was to make it easier for programmers to write programs for specific applications, such as word processing. They took the program to the MITS headquarters in Albuquerque, and despite the fact they had not had an Altair computer on which to test it, the program ran perfectly the first time. The head of Altair was tremendously impressed and immediately hired Paul Allen away from Honeywell to become software director of MITS. Although Gates remained at Harvard, he and Allen still controlled Traf-O-Data, and they decided to convert it into a software company, changing its name to Traf-O-Data Microsoft, later shortening it to Microsoft. At that point, Gates took a leave of absence from Harvard (never to return) and moved to Albuquerque, where he established the headquarters of his firm.

At Microsoft, Gates wrote the disk operating system program for the first Altair disk drives in February 1976. In that same year, new microcomputer kits were brought out by other manufacturers, thus further expanding the market for Microsoft's program. At this point, however, Gates made a significant break with his computer hacker brethren. In an "Open Letter to Hobbyists" in the *Homebrew Computer Club Newsletter* (the Homebrew Computer Club in Palo Alto, California, was perhaps the most important club for hackers and computer freaks), Gates criticized them for copying Microsoft software, establishing a code of ethics that he himself had not followed when he had been on the other side of the fence. But the nineteen-year-old programmer was now well on his way to becoming one of the most successful entrepreneurs in the history of American business. As the use of microcomputers expanded exponentially over the next few years, Microsoft grew apace, becoming one of the most successful companies in the chaotic, infant software industry. By 1980, it was a solid success, with eighty employees and $8 million in revenues. Even so, Gates was hardly ready for what happened next.

In 1979, Gates and Allen moved the headquarters of Microsoft from Albuquerque to their hometown of Seattle and set up corporate offices in the suburb of Bellevue. In July, 1980, Gates received a call from IBM, requesting an appointment with him. Of course, Gates was elated to comply, but he was surprised when he found out they planned to fly up from Florida that very day. Upon meeting with the blue-suited representatives of the computer giant, Gates learned that they wanted Microsoft to develop an operating system for a highly secret microcomputer, the IBM personal computer (PC), they were developing. IBM had first contacted Digital Research, Incorporated to develop the system, but they had balked at IBM's rigid nondisclosure agreement. Gates, having no such problem, signed the agreement. Gates, however, had a bigger problem— he had never written an operating system before. He spent $50,000 to buy a system from Seattle Computer Products, Incorporated and reworked and polished it to fit the specifications of IBM's new personal computer. Calling it the PC-DOS, Gates and Allen presented it to IBM brass in Boca Raton, Florida. They were impressed with the program, and in November 1980, Microsoft signed a contract with IBM. The contract catapulted Microsoft and Bill Gates into the big leagues. In August 1981, the IBM PC was introduced to the public, and within a year it dominated the market for personal computers. As the IBM PC became the standard for the microcomputer industry, nearly all other manufacturers of personal computers felt that their PCs had to operate on a compatible system. Thus, they also bought Microsoft's system, called MS-DOS for the general public, which generated enormous revenues for the young firm. Within a couple of years, Microsoft was supplying the operating systems for about 90 percent of the IBM personal computers and IBM-compatible equipment sold in America. Microsoft passed $100 million in revenues in 1984, with profits of about $15 million.

In the meantime, Paul Allen became ill with Hodgkin's disease, and he had to leave Microsoft for radiation therapy in 1983. After successfully combatting the disease, he set up Asymetrix Corporation in 1985 to develop application software for business. Gates continued to run Microsoft himself, but it was clear that he needed help. Although he was chief executive officer of the company,

Gates wanted to concentrate on technology, and he needed a president to manage the day-to-day affairs. In 1982 he recruited James C. Towne as president, but severed the relationship after eleven months because he felt Towne was not enough of a "technoid." Towne's replacement was Jon A. Shirley, who deserted Tandy Corporation. Gates and Shirley worked well together, but it was always clear who was the major force at Microsoft. Gates describes himself as a hands-on manager with a passion for excellence. As he admits, "I give people a hard time." Intel vice president David L. House says of Gates: "There are a lot of geniuses who can't affect the direction of the world. Bill can, because he's a shrewd businessman." This shrewdness is evidenced in Gates' marketing acumen and in the work environment he has created at Microsoft.

Despite his enormous success with operating systems, Gates was not content to rest on his laurels. Recognizing that the life of new products in the computer industry was often not much more than eighteen months, he felt compelled to push Microsoft into applications software. Designed to sell at computer retailers for between $50 and $500, they cost the software manufacturer only about $10 per unit to manufacture and thus carry enormously lucrative profit margins. Microsoft's first application, introduced in 1982, was called Multiplan. A spreadsheet, Multiplan did well, but it ran into stiff competition five months later, when Lotus Development introduced its phenomenally successful Lotus 1–2–3. Gates' next big application was Microsoft Word, a word processing program, which was exceptionally capable, but difficult to use, causing it to run behind in sales to WordStar. Microsoft's next major software development was called Windows, which, in April 1987, IBM chose as a key piece of software for the new generation of machines it was introducing. Windows, which uses graphics similar to those of Apple's Macintosh, made IBM PCs much easier to use by simplifying the commands needed to operate them. Bill Gates had done it again. His astute sense of the market caused Greg Couch in *Money* magazine to proclaim that Gates was "not only a technological visionary who can dream of software applications years ahead but a marketing strategist who prices his products for the mass market."

Gates also established a powerful work ethic at Microsoft. By 1987 the 1,500-employee company was an extension of Gates himself. The median age was thirty-one (Gates' own age at the time), and most talked in the same "techie" vocabulary as Gates. Like Gates, the employees worked long hours under a great deal of pressure. But he also maintained a highly paternalistic, family atmosphere, with lots of picnics and parties, and free membership in a nearby health club. All, even the executives, dressed casually, many in jeans, and many set their own hours. But Gates was a perfectionist who placed stern demands on all his employees. As one manager has commented: "Bill has toughened us up. He used to beat us up and we went away feeling bad. You have to be able to take this abuse and fight back. If you back down, he loses respect. It's all part of the game." But it was a game that worked remarkably well.

In 1986 Microsoft went public. The stock sale was successful, and Gates' 40 percent of the company was worth $390 million. A year later, it was worth $550 million, and by October 1987, Gates was worth an estimated $1.2 billion—one of just four people who had become billionaires in the computer industry. The others were David Packard[†] and William Hewlett,[†] cofounders of Hewlett-Packard, and H. Ross Perot,[†] founder of Electronic Data Systems. Packard and Hewlett were both in their mid-seventies when they achieved this status. Perot, at fifty-seven, was younger, but no one had ever made a billion dollars as quickly or at such a young age as Bill Gates. By 1987, Microsoft had sales of nearly a half billion dollars a year, and profits were $93 million. Sales were up 75 percent over the previous year, and profits were 61 percent higher. Over the period from 1983 to 1987, Microsoft averaged an annual increase of 66 percent in sales and 82 percent in profits. By 1988, it was second in software sales only to Computer Associates International, which had grown by merging many smaller software firms into one company. In every other respect, Microsoft dominated the software market.

Fortune said this about Gates in 1984:

Gates is a remarkable piece of software in his own right. He is childishly awkward at times, throws things when angry, and fidgets uncontrollably when he speaks. But he is an extraordinarily intelligent master programmer steeped in technical knowledge about his complicated business. At the same time, he is monstrously competitive.

David Bunnell, publisher of *PC World,* said, ''When the history of the microcomputer industry is written, Bill Gates will be remembered as the guy who wrote the first successful program for the mass market.'' *People* magazine put Gates in esteemed company: ''Gates is to software what Edison was to the light bulb—part inventor, part entrepreneur, part salesman and full-time genius.'' **(B.** *Business Week,* May 9, 1983, April 16, 1984, July 22, 1985, February 17, 1986, April 13, 1987, March 14, June 20, July 11, September 12, 1988; *Newsweek,* July 11, 1983; *PC World,* November 29, 1983, September 18, September 25, 1984, August 27, 1985, August 5, October 21, 1986; *People Weekly,* January 2, 1984; *Fortune,* January 23, 1984, July 21, 1986, January 5, October 12, 1987; *Time,* April 14, 1984, February 17, 1986; *Esquire,* December 1984; Paul Freiberger and Michael Swaine, *Fire in the Valley,* 1984; Robert Levering et al., *The Computer Entrepreneurs,* 1984; *New York Times,* September 4, 1985; Douglas G. Carlston, *Software People,* 1985; A. David Silver, *Entrepreneurial Megabucks,* 1985; *Wall Street Journal,* April 7, June 16, August 27, 1986; *Money,* July 1986; *U.S. News & World Report,* July 21, 1986, July 6, 1987; *Contemporary Newsmakers,* 1986; James W. Cortada, *Historical Dictionary of Data Processing Organizations,* 1987; *Forbes,* July 11, October 24, 1988.)

GOIZUETA, ROBERTO CRISPULO (November 18, 1931–). Soft drink company executive, Coca-Cola, Incorporated. On April 23, 1985, Roberto Goizueta, chairman and chief executive officer of Coca-Cola, stunned the world with his announcement that he was making a major change in the composition and flavor of the firm's flagship drink, Coke. In making the news release, Goizueta said that the "best has been made even better, we have changed the taste of the most universally enjoyed consumer product around the world." It is difficult to know what he expected, but Goizueta was greeted with a storm of protest virtually unprecedented for an American consumer product—and the protest came even before anyone had tasted the "new and improved" Coke. Why such a violent reaction? In large measure it was because Coke had become an American institution, an important part of American culture and identity—it played, by the 1980s, a mythic role in America's identity, a role that had been carefully nurtured by Coca-Cola's advertising over the years.

Many years before, William Allen White, the famous Kansas newspaper editor, had articulated this: "Coca-Cola is the sublimated essence of all that America stands for. A decent thing, honestly made, [and] universally distributed." When Goizueta announced he was changing Coke's formula, the company was deluged with remarkably impassioned letters from people, pleading with him not to do it: "Changing Coke is like God making the grass purple or putting toes on our ears or teeth on our knees." "You have fouled up by changing the only perfect thing in the world." "I don't think I could be more upset if you were to burn the flag in our front yard." "Changing the flavor of Coca-Cola would be like tearing down the White House." "Coke has always been like apple pie, mom, etc., something you could count on. I'm glad the person who came up with this dumb idea wasn't around when the Mona Lisa was painted, he probably would have said her smile wasn't big enough." *Advertising Age,* noting that the three people involved in making this decision were Goizueta, a Cuban, Brian Dyson, an Argentinian, and Sergio Zyman, a Mexican, commented: "[T]hey just don't understand America." How did such a thing come to pass?

Coca-Cola was invented in Atlanta, Georgia, in 1886 by John S. Pemberton, a pharmacist. Just before he died in 1888, he sold the business, and it changed hands again in the next year. Finally, in 1891 it came into the possession of Asa Briggs Candler,* another Atlanta druggist, for $2,000. It was Candler who laid the foundations for Coca-Cola to become a major enterprise. He sent salesmen across the country, selling kegs of Coca-Cola syrup to other druggists, along with instructions for making the fountain drink. He began the tradition of spending a considerable amount of money on advertising, putting up painted Coca-Cola signs on barns across the country. He also put Coca-Cola symbols on hundreds of other items, like glasses and ashtrays. By 1895, Coke was sold in every state and territory in America, and it was one of the earliest nationally distributed, brand-name consumer food products. In 1899, Candler signed a contract with two Chattanooga, Tennessee, lawyers, giving them the rights to bottle Coca-Cola. They bought syrup from Coca-Cola Company and sold it to local bottlers around the country. This was the beginning of the franchise system, which remains the basis of Coca-Cola's operations.

In 1916, when Candler was elected mayor of Atlanta, he gave all but 1 percent of his stock to members of his family. Three years later, without informing him, his family sold the company to Georgia financier Ernest Woodruff and his allies for $25 million, the largest financial transaction that had taken place in the South to that date. Woodruff installed his son, Robert W. Woodruff,* as operating head of the firm. Young Woodruff was chairman of the firm until 1955, but he continued to serve as chairman of the finance committee and had a powerful influence on company policies and decisions until his death in 1985. Under Woodruff, Coca-Cola became one of the marketing and merchandising wonders of twentieth-century America. As one Coca-Cola executive remarked, "Asa Candler gave us feet, but Woodruff gave us wings."

One of the major devices Woodruff used to accomplish this hegemony for Coke in the soft-drink industry was advertising. Woodruff hooked up with Archie Lee, who was with Coca-Cola's longtime advertising agency–D'Arcy Advertising Agency of St. Louis. Lee was at that time just a young copywriter, but he understood the attraction of Coke in a changing, urbanizing world. Both Woodruff and Lee recognized that as America became increasingly industrial and urbanized, Americans hankered after older traditions and the verities of the rural past, but, nevertheless, Americans did not really want to be old-fashioned or out of step. Coca-Cola advertising focused on capturing that essence—that borderline area that seized upon elements of the old folk culture that still survived in the city. Working with Woodruff, Archie Lee devised one brilliant advertising campaign after another. Over the years, they captured the spirit of America in their ads as no other campaign had ever done, and Lee penned the company's most famous advertising slogan, "The pause that refreshes." Coke became an indelible part of America's cultural fabric—it became something more than a consumer product. As a Coca-Cola executive told writer E. J. Kahn,

You want to know what makes Coke so romantic to so many people? Well, maybe that starry-eyed kid who lives next door to you was sitting in a drugstore booth with his girl one night, and maybe they were drinking Coke, and maybe while they were drinking that Coke was the first time that girl let the boy put his hand on her leg. (*The Big Drink*)

With the outbreak of World War II, Coca-Cola became an indelible part of American life. Woodruff, exploiting his close ties with the Democratic administration, and with the blessings of General Dwight Eisenhower, a confirmed Coke drinker, made Coca-Cola part of every soldier's life. Vowing that "We will see that every man in uniform gets a bottle of Coca-Cola for 5¢ wherever he is and whatever it costs," Woodruff got government help to set up Coca-Cola bottling plants worldwide. At home, Coke's advertisements strongly linked Coca-Cola with the war effort.

Coca-Cola emerged from World War II as the overwhelmingly popular soft drink in America, one that had attained the status of an icon of popular culture and patriotism. Its cultural role was so pronounced that communist countries during the Cold War often attacked Coca-Cola as the very symbol of America and capitalism. To most people, both in America and overseas, the two were virtually inseparable. Yet, much to Coca-Cola's chagrin, this supremacy did not go unchallenged in the postwar years. Pepsi-Cola emerged from the ashes of bankruptcy in 1949 to mount increasingly powerful challenges to Coke's dominance.

By the mid–1950s, when Woodruff stepped down as chairman, Coke's sales and profits were beginning to slip. Although sales were $144 million in 1955, with profits of nearly $28 million, Pepsi-Cola was growing far more rapidly than Coke, which was a great cause for concern at the older firm. According to a senior vice president, at that point, Coke executives "rolled up our sleeves and went to work" to stave off the Pepsi offensive, and Woodruff, although he was ostensibly retired, directed the company's fortunes until the 1970s. A major turning point for Coca-Cola came in the late 1950s, when Woodruff diversified into beverage markets other than colas. This was a traumatic change. Coca-Cola had been a one-beverage company for seventy-five years, but in 1960, Woodruff bought Minute Maid, the country's largest producer of concentrated fruit drinks. Coke then proceeded to greatly expand its influence, and subsequent profits, in the fruit juice industry by increased advertising expenditures for the product.

In 1962 Woodruff acquired a powerful and important ally in running Coca-Cola, John Paul Austin. Son of a cotton mill executive in LaGrange, Georgia, Austin was a Harvard graduate who came up through the ranks at Coke before becoming president in 1962. In many ways, Austin marked a new era in leadership at Coca-Cola. Woodruff and earlier Coke executives had been primarily sales and marketing people, but Austin was an internal manager—for him management was a cool, efficient science. Using the facilities of the business schools at Harvard, Stanford, and others, he reshaped the management cadre at Coke in his own image.

In 1964, Austin and Woodruff diversified Coca-Cola still further. In that year the company purchased Duncan Foods, which processed and distributed several coffee brands. They brought out their Fanta lines of non-cola drinks to compete in other segments of the soft-drink market, and they introduced Sprite, their answer to 7-Up and Pepsi's Teem. At about the same time, Royal Crown introduced the first diet cola, and Coke responded with the introduction of Tab, which was never terribly successful. In 1966, Coca-Cola brought out Fresca, a citrus-based soft-drink developed by its Minute Maid subsidiary. By 1967, Coca-Cola still had 30 percent of the soft-drink market, compared with Pepsi's 14 percent. During these same years, Coke's sales outside the United States exploded. From 1955 to 1975, foreign sales rose a staggering 2,700 percent, while profits increased an even more impressive 3,600 percent. As stated in *The Cola Wars,* "The Coca-Cola Company was perhaps the first consumer-focused multinational because it marketed not only a retail product, but values and even lifestyles. It sought to encourage all peoples, regardless of their needs, to find meaning and gratification in the consumption of soft drinks."

The 1970s, however, brought troubles for the giant firm. The Federal Trade Commission had taken Coca-Cola to court in 1971, charging that the bottlers' contracts granting territorial exclusivity restricted competition. Coca-Cola viewed this action as a direct attack on the whole franchise nature of Coke's business—one of the key factors that had made the firm so powerful over the years. Coca-Cola executives, therefore, began to spend more time fighting government allegations during the 1970s than they did worrying about marketing and selling their key product—Coke. Donald R. Keough, who was by then president of Coca-Cola USA, admitted as much when he said, "Our system was immobilized. . . . Looking back, I made a mistake. I should have hired a roomful of lawyers and told them to deal with it and we could have gotten on with business." But they did not, and, consequently, Coca-Cola suffered. In 1975, Pepsi-Cola pulled ahead of Coke in supermarket sales, using a catchy "Pepsi Generation" advertising campaign. At the same time, Coca-Cola officials became embroiled in a bitter controversy with their bottlers.

When Woodruff had signed a contract with Coke's bottlers in 1923, they were given a guaranteed price in perpetuity on syrup. It would only be adjusted according to the price of sugar, the largest single ingredient in the product. This had worked well for a half century, but, by the 1970s, escalating labor, transportation, and other material costs were eating into the parent company's profits. They then tried to persuade their bottlers to sign a new contract that geared the price of syrup to general rises in inflation. In return, Coke promised to spend more money on marketing. The bottlers opposed any change in the contract, and Coke had to continue selling syrup to them at 1923 prices. Coke finally persuaded enough bottlers to agree to the amendment, but in the process alienated many of them. By the end of the 1970s, it was clear that new management was needed at Coke. Woodruff, the aging king, was nearing his ninetieth birthday, and the average age of the board of directors was seventy. The company's annual rate of growth, which had been 13 percent in earlier years, dropped to just 2 percent from 1976 to 1979. Profits between 1978 and 1981 grew at a compound rate of just 7 percent, also a significant drop from previous years. Everybody recognized the need for new management; a clean sweep was required in order for Coca-Cola to resume its "rightful place" as America's premier soft drink. No one thought the new head of Coke would be Bob Goizueta.

Roberto Goizueta was born in Havana, Cuba, the son of a well-to-do architect and businessman. Young Goizueta grew up in a privileged environment, and, like his father, was educated in the United States. He came to America to attend Cheshire Academy in Connecticut. Not knowing a word of English when he arrived, "after many sleepless nights studying the dictionary," Goizueta completed his prep school studies. He then went on to study chemical engineering at Yale. After his graduation in 1953, Goizueta returned to Havana, where he became a quality-control chemist at Coca-Cola. After Fidel Castro came to power, the situation became increasingly uncomfortable for Goizueta and his family, so they fled the country in 1961, just before Castro announced the nationalization of Coca-Cola's operations in that country.

Goizueta then transferred to Coke's operations in Nassau, where he became staff assistant to the senior vice president in charge of Latin America. In 1965, he was transferred to Atlanta, and in 1966 he was made, at the age of thirty-five, Coke's youngest vice president, responsible for research and quality. In 1975 Goizueta was promoted to executive vice president in charge of the technical division, and in 1978 his duties were expanded to include administration, legal affairs, and external relations. When the struggle began after 1978 to find a successor to Austin and Woodruff, no one paid much attention to Goizueta. In a company dominated by marketing men, he was a quiet, introspective technocrat. As he himself acknowledged, "I've always preferred working in the background." But when a potentially devastating struggle for power developed among several of the Coke "old boys," Austin and Woodruff pushed Goizueta forward as a dark horse. Goizueta had gained a reputation as an astute corporate politician whose ability to listen to the ideas of others offset his lack of experience in operations and marketing. Goizueta also had the immense advantage of a close relationship with the elderly Woodruff, who viewed him almost as a son. Nonetheless, many Coca-Cola officials, along with many members of Atlanta's old-line families, were shocked at Goizueta's appointment. He was a foreign national, who spoke with a heavy accent, who was heading a company that was quintessentially American, a technocrat leading a firm that had found success through marketing and advertising. Then, too, many saw him as an interim leader—a safe choice—who would soon be deposed by a "rightful" leader. They could not have been more wrong.

Goizueta realized he had inherited a wealthy, powerful, tradition-laden, but troubled, firm in Coca-Cola, and he set about to develop a clear strategy to deal with the situation. First of all, recognizing that Coca-Cola's return on assets was declining, he determined to get rid of those parts of the business that were not productive. Second, he wanted to cut back on dividends, to free up capital that could be used to finance needed investments. Third, and most important, he planned to develop an innovative and aggressive campaign to vault Coke back into first place among buyers of soft drinks at supermarkets. Pepsi, with its effective "Pepsi Challenge" ad campaign, had displaced Coke from first place in supermarket sales after 1977. Since supermarket sales accounted for 40 percent of all soft-drink sales, this was a vitally important area of concern. Goizueta called all Coca-Cola executives together for an intense five-day meeting in March 1981 in Palm Springs, California. There he laid out his strategy and chided them on their complacency, on what he viewed as the organization's corporate culture. Goizueta's strategic statement became, in *Industry Week*'s view, Coca-Cola's "Ten Commandments" over the next several years, and Donald Keough, Coca-Cola's chief operating officer, called it "the most important thing Roberto has done." The 1,200-word statement was printed up in a pocket-sized folder; a copy was placed on the desk of every Coke manager. Goizueta promised that

Coca-Cola in the future would take risks, would make changes, would shake itself out of its doldrums. Over the next several years he was as good as his word.

Over a short period of time, Goizueta pulled Coke out of industrial markets where it had little expertise, including the sale of the Aqua-Chem division, which made water-purification equipment. He also appointed Bryan Dyson head of Coca-Cola USA to counter the "Pepsi Challenge" with innovative new marketing and advertising campaigns. In addition, Goizueta adopted a new corporate slogan— "Coke is it!"—which became part of a revised advertising campaign. He overhauled the firm's organizational structure, centralizing the food, wine, and plastics businesses under a new Foods & Wine Group, and he opened up communications in the company, developing a more participative management style. Goizueta also developed a controversial program to restructure Coca-Cola's network of bottlers. As a fallout of Coke's difficulties with bottlers over syrup prices in the 1970s, he began buying out bottlers in key markets where he deemed they were not "sufficiently aggressive." This expensive operation was financed, at least partly, by the reduction of dividend payments Goizueta had promised in his strategy statement.

Goizueta's most stunning, and most highly publicized move, however, was his purchase of Columbia Pictures in 1982 for $750 million in cash and stocks. There was an immediate torrent of adverse publicity that truly shocked Goizueta. Many analysts were sharply critical of the move, feeling that motion pictures were a risky, quixotic business that would do little to improve Coke's profitability. Besides, they believed that Coke had paid far too much for the company. In a word, Goizueta had been fleeced by Hollywood sharpies. Goizueta responded, however, by saying, "We don't view Columbia as a motion picture company. We view it as an *entertainment* company." Within six months after the purchase, nearly everyone agreed that Goizueta had made a remarkably astute deal. By 1985, the motion picture company was contributing 14 percent of Coca-Cola's operating income, edging out the Foods Division as the number two contributor. In terms of profits, the entertainment division was the largest in the country, surpassing Gulf & Western, Warner, and MCA.

By 1985, Coke and Goizueta seemed to be on top of the world. Coke, which had had $5 billion in sales in 1979, along with profits of $420 million, five years later had a 50 percent increase in both areas. What's more, Coke's return on equity reached 22 percent, its greatest in eleven years. Most significantly, the firm's share of the American soft-drink market in 1984 was 36 percent, an all-time high. Goizueta's acquisitions, such as Columbia Pictures, had proved stunningly successful. Things looked so positive at Coke that in March 1984, the *New York Times* ran a story on the company headlined: "Putting the Daring Back into Coke." The article credited Goizueta with most of the company's recent changes and successes. There was just one nagging area of concern—the sales of the firm's flagship product—Coke. The Coca-Cola company's increase in market share had not come because Coke itself was besting Pepsi in the battle of the colas, rather it was due to the extraordinary success of Diet Coke and, to a lesser extent, Cherry Coke. Diet Coke had climbed rapidly up the charts to become the third most popular soft drink in America, but old Coke itself continued to lose market share to Pepsi, dropping yet another 1 percent of the market to Pepsi in 1984, a continuation of a long-range and troublesome trend. Goizueta remarked somewhat ominously in early 1985: "We will soon be unfolding what is probably the strongest marketing program in the history of the company behind our brand, Coca-Cola."

Shortly thereafter, Roberto Goizueta made the announcement that shook America to the core—he was changing the formula of Coca-Cola, to make it better able to compete with Pepsi-Cola in the new markets of the 1980s and 1990s. The company had analyzed the competitive situation between Coke and Pepsi from every angle, and always it had come up with the same conclusion: Coke spent more money on advertising than Pepsi, and it had a more effective distribution system. But Pepsi's taste was deemed superior. Ironically, the "Pepsi Challenge" had been right on target all along, and Coke executives knew it. When Coke conducted its own taste tests, for those cola drinkers who professed a preference, Pepsi was the preferred choice by a narrow margin. Coke executives felt that the only reason Coke continued to have a lead in total sales was because it was more widely available in soda fountains and the like. If Pepsi were ever to be carried in as many venues as Coke, it would beat out Coke as America's favorite soft drink. This would be a crushing blow for the "American Drink."

Coke's marketing research expert, Dr. Roy Stout, was blunt about the reason for Coke's decline. "You look at the Pepsi Challenge," he said, "and you have to begin asking about taste." Bryan Dyson, Coca-Cola USA's new president, was also convinced: "Maybe the principal characteristics that made Coke distinctive, like its bite, consumers now describe as harsh. And when you mention words like 'rounded' and 'smooth,' they say 'Pepsi.' Maybe the way we assuage our thirst has changed." Another time, he was even more emphatic: "If you want to be the leading brand, you can't have a taste disadvantage that is proclaimable." Thus, Dyson became an important cog in a vigorous campaign to change the century-old Coke formula. He chose Sergio Zyman, the senior vice president for marketing at Coca-Cola USA, to head the project (called Project Kansas) to develop a new taste for Coke.

In September 1984, Coke's technical division told the firm's higher executives that they had finally developed a new taste for Coke. The marketing research department conducted numerous blind taste tests, and the new formula beat Pepsi by a margin of from 6 to 8 points; the old Coke was beaten by Pepsi by from 12 to 15 points in earlier tests. Even more important, 70 percent of committed Pepsi drinkers, who had heretofore always been more brand loyal than Coke drinkers, preferred the new Coke in these tests. Dyson and Zyman were convinced they had the right product, and they wanted to proceed with a rapid and total replacement of the old Coke with the new, in order to begin the demolition of

Pepsi. They presented their data to Goizueta, and he agreed to introduce a new Coke formula to replace the venerable Coke product.

The problem was how to introduce the new product without either denigrating the old Coke, or alienating the public. Goizueta and the others realized there would be some negative response (just as there had been when Coke bought Columbia Pictures), but the company underestimated how intense it would be. They thought that, as soon as the public had a chance to taste the new Coke formula, they would be convinced that Coke's management was correct yet one more time. Goizueta and Coke's management had fallen into the very trap Goizueta had warned against when the *New York Times* praised the company in 1984: "There is a danger when a company is doing as well as we are. And that is, to think we can do no wrong."

The new Coke was much more like Pepsi than the old Coke had been. It was sweeter, smoother, and, in the minds of many Coke loyalists, a flatter cola than before. Roy Stout later confessed, "New Coke was more different from old Coke, more than I realized at the time." And this difference, this similarity to Pepsi, caused the company problems after the introduction of the new Coke. Coca-Cola had been running a series of ads featuring television star Bill Cosby during this time in which Cosby praised Coke for being less sweet than Pepsi. In its campaign to launch the new Coke, Coca-Cola and its ad agency designed some new Cosby commercials in which he appeared and solemnly intoned:

The words I am about to say will change the course of history. Coca-Cola has a new taste and it's the best-tasting Coca-Cola ever. You like Coke the way it is? Me too. Always did. I like this one better. . . . You're a Pepsi drinker? Ah, well, maybe that'll be history too after you try the new taste of Coke. Now more than ever, "Coke is it."

After Goizueta announced the new Coke on April 23, Pepsi-Cola counterattacked. Roger Enrico, who had become president of Pepsi in 1983, was responsible for masterminding the attack. Enrico admitted that "I was shocked," but nonetheless felt that he had a golden opportunity to mount a devastating attack on Coke. He did this in the form of a letter to Pepsi bottlers, which ran as a full-page ad on the day of the Goizueta news conference. The letter said, in part:

It gives me great pleasure to offer each of you my heartiest congratulations. After 87 years of going at it eyeball to eyeball, the other guy just blinked. Coca-Cola is withdrawing their product from the marketplace, and is reformulating brand Coke to be more like Pepsi . . . victory is sweet, and we have earned a celebration. We're going to declare a holiday on Friday. Enjoy!

A brilliant move, it shook the Coke organization to its boots.

What was to follow was even more disquieting, as the switchboard at Coke's headquarters was hit with over 1,000 calls a day from around the country; most of the callers expressed how shocked and upset they were that Coke had been changed. Furthermore, the media, almost universally against the new Coke, greatly preferred the older formulation and questioned how Goizueta and other Coke officials could possibly have made such a mistake. On April 25, *Newsday*'s headline said: "What Have They Done to My Coke?" The answer was: "The new drink will be smoother, sweeter, and a threat to a way of life." This was typical of the fare newspapers and news weeklies ran concerning the change. Pepsi-Cola continued to exploit Coke's change in a similar vein. It ran a commercial featuring three elderly, working-class Southern whites. One, Wilbur, was forlorn, and one of his friends asked him what was the matter. "They changed my Coke," he told them. "I stuck with them through three wars and a couple of dust storms, but this is too much." Wilbur then speculated that it must have been something big to make Coke change after so many years. His friend replied, "Right big," and then offered Wilbur a can of Pepsi. Wilbur drank the Pepsi, and nodded his head in approval. It was devastatingly effective.

By June, the anger and resentment of the public was actually disrupting the personal lives of Coke officials at every level. Old friends displayed remarkable hostility toward them; they were no longer invited to parties, they were accosted by strangers on the street. By that time also, sales volume for Coke was beginning to decline. This prompted Goizueta to action. As he said at the time, "I can put up with flak with sales up, flak doesn't bother me, but I can't when sales are down." By early July, Goizueta and the other officials realized they were going to have to bring back the old Coke, but they were not willing to admit they had made a mistake with the new Coke. Henceforth there would be two Cokes— the regular, or "new" Coke, and the old Coke, which would be called "Coca-Cola Classic," with its own packaging and advertising.

Goizueta made the announcement that the old Coke was coming back in the following way:

Today, we have two messages to deliver to the American consumer. First, to those of you who are drinking Coca-Cola with its great new taste, our thanks. . . . But there is a second group of consumers to whom we want to speak today and our message to this group is simple: We have heard you. (Oliver, *The Real Coke*®)

Donald Keough followed with his message, which got closer to the essence of what had happened:

The simple fact is that all the time and money and skill poured into consumer research on the new Coca-Cola could not measure or reveal the deep and abiding emotional attachment to original Coca-Cola felt by so many people . . . the passion for original Coca-Cola—and that is the word for it: passion—was something that caught us by surprise. (*Fortune*, August 5, 1985)

Goizueta closed by looking at the audience and saying, "It's nice to be loved again." He was referring to the incredible outpouring of thanks the company

had received since it had been learned the old Coke was being brought back—
one day it received 18,000 calls. One Coke executive said, "You would have
thought we had invented a cure for cancer."

By 1986, Coke Classic was outselling the "new" Coke in nearly every major
market. Only in Detroit was new Coke outselling Classic; in the South, always
the heartland of Coke loyalists, Classic Coke was outselling new Coke by rates
ranging from 9 to 1 to 33 to 1. Although the introduction of the new Coke had
been perceived as one of the greatest marketing mistakes of all time, the end
result, ironically, strengthened Coca-Cola's market position by giving it a "two-
cola" policy—with Coke Classic for the legions of old Coke drinkers, and new
Coke left free to challenge Pepsi for its market. Using the smug and smarmy
computer-generated Max Headroom, Coca-Cola launched a highly successful
campaign against Pepsi, using new Coke as their cola vehicle. He extolled
"Cokeologists" to "catch the wave" and cautioned them not to mention the
"P-word."

In 1986, Classic Coke not only outsold new Coke, but also beat out Pepsi as
the best-selling soft drink in America. With 39.9 percent of the $38 billion
American soft-drink market, it was four-tenths of a percentage point ahead of
Pepsi, which was down one-tenth of one percent from the year before. Diet
Coke, with 7.1 percent, was up from 6 percent the year before, and was still
the third best-selling soft drink. Diet Pepsi, with 4.3 percent was fourth. New
Coke only had 2.3 percent of the market, but the total lineup of Coca-Cola soft
drinks gave the firm 39.9 percent of the American soft-drink market, up almost
4 percentage points from 1984—the first major advance Coca-Cola had made
on Pepsi-Cola in decades. In January 1986, Coca-Cola's centennial year, *Industry
Week* voted Roberto Goizueta one of the "most-admired CEO's" in America,
and noted that he scored ahead of Pepsi-Cola's Donald McIntosh Kendall.[†] They
did comment, however, that he was given the vote "in spite of the 'New Coke'
fiasco," saying, "What appeared to be a real goof now appears to be a marketing
coup." (**B**. E. J. Kahn, *The Big Drink*, 1959; J. C. Louis and Harvey Z. Yazijian,
The Cola Wars, 1980; Milton Moskowitz et al., *Everybody's Business*, 1980;
Fortune, September 8, 1980, June 1, 1981, August 5, 1985; *Forbes*, December
22, 1980, March 25, November 18, 1985; *Industry Week*, November 1, 1982,
January 6, 1986; *Nation's Business*, March 1984; *New York Times*, March 4,
1984; *International Management*, October 1984; *Financial World*, April 3–16,
1985; The Coca-Cola Company, *News Release*, April 23, 1985; *Newsday*, April
25, 1985; *Advertising Age*, April 29, 1985; *USA Today*, July 12, 1985; *Business
Week*, July 29, 1985, October 13, 1986, March 16, 1987; Thomas Oliver, *The
Real Coke®, The Real Story*, 1986; *Who's Who in America*, 1986–1987; Carl
L. Kell, "The Rhetoric of the New Coke," paper delivered to Conference on
American Popular Culture in Canada, University of Western Ontario, May 4–
6, 1988; Toronto *Globe & Mail*, January 28 1988.)

GRIFFEY, DICK (November 16, 1943–   ). Recording company founder, Dick Griffey Productions and Solar Records. Most whites would just dismiss Dick Griffey as a good A & R (artists and repertory) man and record producer. Successful at what he does, and wealthy, the attitude of the business press is generally that his activities are better handled in *Variety*, or, better yet, *Ebony* or *Jet*. There is a tendency to trivialize music and popular culture as the stepchild of real business and real culture. Dick Griffey disagrees. He views himself as a man with an important mission:

I want to see the world give credit to black people for the heritage and art that they have given to the world musically. . . . When it comes to our art form, nobody has really stood up and said black people have given something beautiful to the world. Black music is the most widely accepted music there is, it's not only being done by black people. The largest selling album in history, "Saturday Night Fever," was the Bee Gees doing black music. (*Black Enterprise*, July 1982)

Griffey is not the first black man to bring his music to the broader public in a major way—Berry Gordy* preceded him with Motown Records in the 1960s—but Griffey has built his firm into one of the most important and fastest growing black entertainment enterprises in the 1980s. It was also the eleventh largest black-owned firm in the United States, with sales in 1987 of nearly $44 million.

Dick Griffey was born in Nashville, Tennessee, the home of country western music in the United States, and one of the centers of the recording industry in the country. No information is available about his father, but his mother is Juanita Hines, one of the most prominent gospel music singers in America, and later one of Griffey's record artists. Griffey was raised and educated in Nashville, and attended Tennessee State University, where he played defensive lineman on the football team. Unlike many blacks, who view athletics as a means to instant fame and fortune, Griffey was what he calls "entrepreneur-minded" from the very beginning. His mother says that even when he was a small boy he never wanted to work for white people, and when he was at Tennessee State this idea became further crystalized. As he later recalled:

When I was in school, I never wanted to play on the football team as much as I wanted to own it. Look at Gale Sayers. He was a great player for the Chicago Bears, but when he hurt his knees after six years, he was out of football. But George Halas is almost 90 years old and he still owns the team. (*Black Enterprise,* July 1982)

After Tennessee State, Griffey went into the Air Force. When he came out in 1966 he began to think about a career in the entertainment field. A classmate of his from Tennessee State, Dick Barnett, was then a player-coach for the New York Knicks basketball team, and they decided to become coowners of a black nightclub in Los Angeles called Guys and Dolls. Griffey was responsible for booking acts into the club. Bringing in renowned black groups like the Temptations, the Impressions, and the Four Tops, Griffey helped build the nightclub into a popular institution for blacks in the city. After a time, he decided to become a music promoter on a broader level. "By the time I decided I wanted to be a show promoter," he said, "I already was one. Instead of trying to get 500 people into the club seven nights a week, I found myself thinking I'd rather rent a big place and fill it with people for just one night." Beyond that, some of the old ideas he had when he played football at Tennessee State returned: "As I got older, I kept thinking how entertainers come and go, but the promoters are always here. And the promoters were usually white. I felt it was time for black promoters to make their mark."

By the early 1970s, Griffey had established himself as one of the major promoters in the Los Angeles area, and he was beginning to have an impact on the national scene. He was one of the founding members of the Black Concert Promoters Association, and he forged strong alliances with such black superstars as Stevie Wonder, for whom he arranged a highly successful world tour in 1974. A year earlier, Griffey was approached by Don Cornelius, producer and host of television's "Soul Train," who asked him to handle booking responsibilities for the series. Two years later, they cooperated in the founding of Soul Train Records. They secured a limited distributing deal with RCA Records, which at the time was very weak in its black music division. Griffey and Cornelius, however, did not have great success with their record ventures. Their first attempt, "Soul Train '75" by the Soul Train Gang, never went higher than seventy-fifth spot on the pop record charts; an album by the same group fared worse.

Griffey, however, was not disillusioned. He bought the recording rights to a group he managed called the Whispers from Chess/Janus records and started recording tracks for their next album. RCA liked what they heard, and, despite the failure of Soul Train Records' first attempt, they distributed the Whispers' album with moderate success. The big breakthrough for Griffey and Soul Train Records, however, came with two very popular disco singles: "I Gotta Keep Dancin' " by Carrie Lucas and "Uptown Festival," a medly of disco-ized Motown tunes by Shalamar. Disco was a curious phenomenon of the mid– to late–1970s. It was, in the words of *Rolling Stone*'s writers, "the most self-contained genre in the history of pop, the most clearly defined, and the most despised." A great generator of disco music in the 1970s was Philadelphia International Records, but it was picked up by all the major recording companies and became a world sensation. Griffey's company was a very minor player in this massive, highly profitable, but relatively empty, largely studio-created dance music. The profits he made from these records, however, allowed him to consider bigger things.

In 1978, Griffey and Cornelius amicably parted company, and Griffey took sole control of the record company. He first changed the name to Solar (Sounds of Los Angeles Records), and signed another distribution contract with RCA. Recognizing that disco was dying out, Griffey had to find a new sound, one that would appeal to both black and white audiences, but mainly to the former.

Synthesizing pop, soul, funk, and disco, he arrived at a formula that other black producers such as Quincy Jones and Maurice White also found highly successful. He continued making successful records with Shalamar, but also signed a group called Lakeside, with which he had several moderate hits. Lakeside was what was called a "funk band." Funk was a less accessible music than disco. With the rougher edges that disco usually smoothed over, funk had closer ties with the older traditions of rhythm and blues and pre-Motown soul music in its gritty instrumentation and studio production. Lakeside, whose best funk record was "Fantastic Voyage" in 1980, changed their wardrobe for every album—appearing as cowboys for one, and as pirates for the next. To a certain extent critics viewed Griffey as attempting to create a "Los Angeles sound" similar to early manifestations of a "Motown" or "Philadelphia" sound, but he denied it. In large measure he was correct, since the music has tended to resist any geographic identification.

But Griffey's company was successful, and at least a fair portion of his records were popular. If he did not have any of the enormous, worldwide hits of the 1980s, he did have a fair number of records with respectable sales. This prompted *Rolling Stone* to comment that "Solar is becoming to the Eighties what Philadelphia International was to the Seventies and Motown was to the Sixties—a veritable pop factory." Griffey also expanded into the gospel area, not only recording his mother, but also signing some other gospel artists. Griffey announced plans to bring out jazz records, although he would not say much about the venture other than the fact that it would not be called jazz, since jazz records seldom make a profit.

In 1981, Griffey switched his distribution contract from RCA to Elektra-Asylum records. He was able to get a highly lucrative contract with Elektra because, as *Black Enterprise* (July 1982) said, "it is a well-known axiom in the business that blacks buy records regardless of what the economic climate may be." As the vice president of marketing at Solar commented: "RCA never lost money on any Solar record they distributed. Black music accounts for one-third of all money generated by the entire record business, so a good black company is necessary to ensure corporate success." The Solar sound is very much a middle-of-the-road sound within the spectrum of black music. It is not overly smoothed-over as it is in much of the white disco music, neither does it have the truly rough edges of real funk and rhythm and blues. It is commercial music, but commercial music that attempts to retain some sense of its roots in the black community. Griffey also demands that all his groups maintain a "squeaky-clean" image. "I won't deal with self-destructive artists," he has said. "There's enough negativity going around and I don't want to perpetuate it."

Griffey has also had a major impact as a promoter; he serves as president of the United Black Concert Promoters, and as head of Dick Griffey Productions. The key to the success of the company is Griffey's knowledge of his product: "I know what's good. When it comes to black music I think I'm probably the best A & R man in the country. I know how to recognize a good act and how to pick out a good song.'' By the late 1980s Griffey's company provided employment for nearly 100 individuals, and it did its share in providing a fund of money coming into the black community.

One of the problems in the black ghettos in the 1980s has been the fact that black-owned businesses have been dying out and that bright, well-educated blacks have been moving into the mainstream of white-owned corporations. As a result, the black community has been losing its institutional business base. Dick Griffey, like Edward G. Gardner[†] and other black business leaders, is keenly aware of this problem. As he commented in the early 1980s:

The reason the ghetto is a ghetto is because black folks spend the dollar once and that's it. The money doesn't circulate, it evaporates. I'm concerned with more money from black concerts being donated to the United Negro College Fund. I want to see more black ushers, ticket-takers, and caterers, so that more of us can profit from the money our music generates.

Although Motown Industries remained the largest black-owned entertainment firm in the late–1980s, with revenues in excess of $100 million, it was no longer profitable, and Berry Gordy ultimately sold his record business to MCA. Other black firms in the media field, like Inner City Communications, which owned radio stations and the Apollo Theater in Harlem, were also experiencing difficult times. Dick Griffey Productions, however, continued to grow and be profitable. As a result, Griffey was viewed as somewhat of a ''miracle man'' in the music business, finding success where others were experiencing difficulty. Called ''one of the most powerful new figures to emerge in black music in years,'' Griffey does not belittle the importance of his role. ''I hold firm in my belief that black music is the only national resource black people in America have,'' he said. ''Black music generates more dollars for black people than any other industry in America, and I think we should use our music in the same way that the Arabs use their oil.'' (**B.** *Rolling Stone*, June 12, 1980; *Black Enterprise*, July 1982, June 1987, June 1988; Ed Ward et al., *Rock of Ages: The Rolling Stone History of Rock & Roll*, 1986; *Who's Who among Black Americans*, 1988.)

GRIFFIN, MERVYN EDWARD, JR. (July 6, 1925–   ). Television producer, real estate tycoon, entrepreneur, Griffin Productions, Griffin Company. As a young man of twenty-two, Merv Griffin was billed as ''America's Romantic Singing Star'' by radio station KFRC in San Francisco, where he did a daily radio show. Graced with a lush, Perry Como–like voice, Griffin was also grossly overweight, with 240 pounds layered onto his five-foot, nine-inch frame. With a forty-four-inch waist, he was anything but romantic in person. Once, in 1948, a visitor to the studio was searching for the singing star. When she heard a secretary call him by name, she stared incredulously at the fat young man. *''You're* Merv Griffin?'' she cried. *''You're* the 'Romantic Singing Star'?'' Merv blushed, and the woman began to laugh uncontrollably. Merv recalled the incident in his autobiography, saying, "She laughed until the tears rolled down her face. And the tears started to roll down *my* face. And then I went on a diet and lost 80 pounds in four months." Nobody laughs at Merv Griffin any longer. Owner of a production company that syndicates two of the most popular shows on television, and of a company that owns radio and television stations, a tape film company, a mail-order firm, an airplane charter service, a building in New York City, the Beverly Hills Hilton, and Resorts International, Merv Griffin is worth close to $300 million and is one of the most powerful men in the entertainment industry.

Merv Griffin was born in San Mateo, California, a suburb of San Francisco. His father, a stock broker and tennis pro, provided a comfortable life for his family until the Great Depression hit. In 1930 they lost their home and moved in with relatives. Griffin's mother's family, who were amateur musicians, encouraged him at an early age to develop his musical talent. Griffin became quite accomplished on the piano, and during high school he began playing at local dances. While in high school, Merv Griffin was a poor student, focusing instead completely on his music. He managed to graduate, however, and spent several years wandering aimlessly at San Mateo Junior College and the University of San Francisco.

In 1943, Griffin applied for a job as a staff musician at radio station KFRC. They asked him to sing for them, liked what they heard, and hired him as a vocalist rather than a piano player. Merv Griffin's career in show business had been launched. He became a phenomenally popular radio singer in the San Francisco area, and by 1946 was making as much as $5,000 a month. After losing a good deal of weight, Griffin was approached by the band leader, Freddy Martin, to join his band as lead vocalist. Although Griffin had to take a significant pay cut to accept the job, Martin could provide something Griffin lacked— national exposure. Griffin agreed to take the position, and a profitable four-year association followed. Their partnership climaxed in 1951 when they made a hit recording of the novelty tune, "I've Got a Lovely Bunch of Cocoanuts." The song exploded to number one on the Hit Parade, and sold three million copies. On the strength of that hit, Griffin ended his association with the Martin band and signed a recording contract with RCA Victor in 1951 and, at the same time, embarked on the nightclub circuit as a solo performer.

This, in turn, opened Hollywood to Merv Griffin. Catching his act at the Last Frontier in Las Vegas, Doris Day recommended that Warner Brothers Studio sign him to a contract. He passed the screen test and became a contract player at the studio. Although he had a series of bit parts at the studio, Griffin was never cast in a singing role. His only notable role was in *So This Is Love* with Kathryn Grayson, but only because they did the first on-screen "french kiss" in movie history, which generated a fair amount of controversy. Shortly afterward, however, Griffin became discouraged and left Warner Brothers, accepting an offer to headline a fifteen-minute, twice-weekly, musical telecast for CBS-TV. He also resumed his nightclub singing tours and made his stage debut in

New York in *Finian's Rainbow*. During the next several years, Griffin hosted or made guest appearances on a number of other television shows, and in 1957 he hosted his own radio show on the ABC network.

A major turning point came for Merv Griffin in 1958. In that year, Mark Goodson and Bill Todman, the most successful game show producers in television, chose Griffin to host their new daytime "Play Your Hunch" show. It gained in popularity over the next several years, and most critics agreed it was due more to the entertainment Griffin provided as host than to the questions and answers themselves. It also introduced Griffin to the television game show medium, an area that would provide him with the bulk of his fortune in later years. His work on this show, which lasted until 1961, also led Griffin to his next big break—guest host on NBC-TV's "Tonight Show" as a replacement for Jack Parr. He was so successful that he was booked to substitute for Parr again a month later. That, in turn, brought Griffin a short stint as moderator of one of Goodson and Todman's most successful quiz shows, "To Tell the Truth."

By this time, Merv Griffin had become one of the most sought-after television personalities in America, and when Jack Parr left the "Tonight Show," Griffin was one of the leading replacement candidates. When Johnny Carson was chosen instead, NBC announced it would place Griffin in a daytime replica of the "Tonight Show." Debuting in October 1962, "The Merv Griffin Show" was a big hit with the critics, but fared poorly in the ratings. As a result, NBC cancelled the show as of April 1963. At that point, Griffin had to reassess his career.

When NBC cancelled his talk show, it had promised to find something else for Griffin; this turned out to be a game show called "Word for Word." Griffin was not enthusiastic about hosting another game show, but NBC sweetened the offer—he would not be just the host of the show, but also the producer. Griffin formed Griffin Productions and televised "Word for Word" for one season. It was not a particularly successful operation, but it helped get Griffin's production company off the ground, and it gave him and his wife the idea for a phenomenally successful game show—"Jeopardy."

Merv Griffin described the process in his autobiography by which his wife suggested the show's concept:

Julann and I were flying home from a visit to Ironwood one weekend. I was scribbling on a new game idea and bemoaning the absence of good quiz shows since the scandals of the fifties. My wife, as a joke, said, "Why don't you do a show where you give the contestants the answers?"

"Sure, and I'll end up in the slammer."

Then she said, "Five thousand two hundred eighty feet."

I answered, "How many feet in a mile?"

"Right. Seventy Nine Wistful Vista."

I questioned, "What was Fibber McGee and Molly's address?"

Griffin put this together into a game show concept and sold it to NBC. The show, with Art Fleming as host, was a resounding success and made Griffin Productions a great deal of money. As Griffin has commented, "The profit margin for a game show is attractive, to say the very least."

Despite his great success as a producer of game shows, Griffin wanted to get back into the talk show game. The opportunity came in 1965 in the form of yet another new concept—a *syndicated* talk show. At that time, only a few shows, such as "I Love Lucy" and "Dick Van Dyke," were in syndication, and it was not the big business it later became. When Westinghouse Broadcasting, owner of a number of independent, non-network television stations, approached Griffin about doing a ninety-minute program of talk, to be syndicated to stations through-out the United States and Canada, he was at first not terribly enthusiastic. But they offered him a great deal of money, and, most important, allowed him to coproduce and own the show. Griffin agreed to the deal, and soon 150 stations were carrying the show.

In 1968, however, Westinghouse was slow in coming up with a new contract. Merv Griffin was disillusioned until CBS offered him the opportunity to host a late night talk show on their network. Griffin was not keen about being a network employee again, but he named what he thought was an outlandish salary demand of $80,000 a week. To his surprise, CBS accepted his salary proposal, and "The Merv Griffin Show" debuted on CBS in 1969 to do battle with ABC's "Joey Bishop Show" and NBC's "Tonight Show." It was a fierce struggle for ratings and guests, which took a severe toll on Merv Griffin's health and personal life. By the end of 1970, he had gained thirty pounds, was smoking two packs of cigarettes a day, was in an emotional crisis, and was watching his marriage of a dozen years deteriorate into divorce.

In 1971, Westinghouse approached Griffin about returning to them. He was still under contract to CBS, but in December 1971, when his show was cancelled, he was paid $250,000 for the privilege. It was the first time Griffin was elated to be cancelled—he received a huge severance settlement, escaped the pressures at CBS, and was able to return to Westinghouse and the syndicated show which had made him rich and happy. By the early 1980s, "The Merv Griffin Show" was shown on 115 stations in the United States and Canada, and it stayed on the air until 1986. With the profits from that show, Griffin Productions launched a number of new projects in the communications industry.

Griffin set up studio facilities with his Trans-American Video Company (TAV) at Hollywood and Vine in Los Angeles. In addition to two television studios, TAV operates complete video-tape editing, dubbing, and tape-transfer facilities, a distribution department, and a fleet of mobile units for use at sporting events and other television specials. His Teleview Racing Patrol, Incorporated is a Florida-based firm which supplies closed-circuit cameras and projection screens for horse- and dog-racing tracks in North and South America. He also owns three radio stations. The various Griffin Productions, along with other shows, are telecast at the TAV studios.

One of Griffin's productions in the late 1970s was "Dance Fever," which was designed to capitalize on the disco craze of the time. The most successful show in the Griffin stable, however, is "Wheel of Fortune." Griffin conceived "Wheel" in 1973, which he sold to NBC later that year. It ran on that network for a number of years, but really hit it big when Griffin syndicated it in 1983. An incredibly elementary word puzzle game, Griffin had trouble making a hit of it until two things occurred. The first was the replacement of the original host, Chuck Woolery, with Pat Sajak, a Los Angeles newscaster, along with the choice of Vanna White to turn over the letters. The second was his association with King World Productions to handle syndication of the show. Other syndicators had trouble selling the show to stations, but King World was able to get fifty-nine stations to pick it up. This paid $32,700 per episode, of which Griffin Productions took two-thirds. By 1984, "Wheel" was appearing on 181 stations, and earning $92,000 per episode. That earned Griffin's company a total of about $16 million from the show that year, and "Wheel" was the number-one syndicated show in America. Because of this success, Griffin also decided to put his longtime hit, "Jeopardy," into syndication with King World in 1984. It earned about $10 million for Griffin from its first 260 episodes. By 1987, "Wheel," which cost $7 million a year to produce, was grossing $120 million, and "Jeopardy" was not too far behind. As a result of this success, Griffin sold both his creations along with his Hollywood studios to the Coca-Cola Company in 1985 for about $250 million, agreeing to run the company for five years.

Although Griffin claimed that he sold Griffin Productions because he was tired of business, claiming "It makes my brain go dead," he has made some spectacular business dealings since then. Forming the Griffin Company, in November 1987, Merv Griffin purchased the Beverly Hills Hilton for $100.2 million from the Hilton Hotels Corporation, which, he announced, would continue to manage it. In April 1988, Griffin won a fierce battle with real estate developer Donald Trump[†] for control of Resorts International, which owned and operated casinos in Atlantic City, New Jersey, and the Bahamas. Relying on advice from close friends Marvin Davis[†] of Twentieth Century-Fox and Metromedia's John Kluge,[†] Griffin said, "I saw what Donald Trump was doing, that he was stealing resorts, so I went after him." Under the agreement, Griffin won control of the existing Resorts International Hotel Casino in Atlantic City and all Paradise Island operations in the Bahamas, and Trump is required to purchase the 1,250-room Taj Mahal casino under construction in Atlantic City from Resorts for about $940 million. Griffin's offer amounted to about $325 million. By early 1989, Griffin's investment began to look less stable. He had gathered a good deal of junk-bond financing to make his offer, and then he watched the bond market tighten up in November 1988, thereby increasing the interest rates he had to pay. At the same time, Resorts' revenues continued to shrink, making that firm's paper more difficult to market. When a number of industry analysts criticized Griffin for the deal, he replied: "Analysts don't know sh——. Let their mothers worry about them. I'm not going to."

Griffin, who had grown tired of the business end of television, thrived under the challenge of real estate development and corporate takeovers. "What I am doing now is fun," he told reporters. "I love the gamesmanship," he said. "This may sound strange, but it parallels the game shows I've been involved in." Griffin also thought that he might have contributed his part toward shifting the balance of economic power in America from the East to the West. "Now they have new respect for the Southern California financial community," he said. "I think they're getting a little nervous, beginning to tremble a little back there in New York, wondering what the next move by any of us out here is going to be. Now they know we don't do business out of the Jacuzzi."

So the once fat-boy singer turned talk show host ends his career as a real estate and casino mogul. And perhaps that should not be surprising. Asked in 1987 about his interests, Griffin replied: "The things I would put ahead of my business interests are my family, my friends, my own life, the creative aspects of inventing TV shows, eating and real estate. All my life I've loved real estate." (**A.** Merv Griffin with Peter Barsocchini, *Merv: An Autobiography*, 1980. **B.** *Current Biography*, September 1967; *The Saturday Evening Post*, October 1979; *Forbes*, April 8, 1985; *New York Times*, February 7, February 19, April 5, May 6, 1986; *Newsweek*, February 9, 1987; *Good Housekeeping*, May 1987; Toronto *Globe & Mail*, March 18, April 15, July 6, 1988; *Business Month*, June 1988; *Los Angeles*, December 1988; *Business Week*, January 16, 1989.)

GUCCIONE, ROBERT (CHARLES JOSEPH EDWARD SABATINI) (December 17, 1930–). Publisher, *Penthouse* Magazine.

When Bob Guccione enters a room, heads invariably turn. Decked out in a suede jacket, velveteen slacks, and beige Italian boots, his shirt is open to the waist, ostentatiously displaying a number of gold chains with medallions. To complement the image, a gold bracelet dangles from his right wrist and a gold Piaget watch adorns his left. His hair has been artificially colored, and his skin sports a year-round tan. Guccione evidently likes this style, but to most observers he is the very antithesis of well-groomed sophistication. As *Maclean's* noted: "On a first meeting he gives the impression of being a man who has had a lifelong love affair with himself." Guccione was aware of this personal reaction, telling *Money* that "I'm the only one who can stand me full time, so working for myself was the only way I could hold down a job."

Guccione was born in Brooklyn, New York, in the teeth of the Great Depression, and he has retained a deep, gutteral Brooklyn patois throughout his life. His father was an accountant, and the family was able to live in middle-class comfort and respectability through the depression years and after. Raised a Roman Catholic and serving as an altar boy, Guccione spent three months in a seminary which convinced him that the life of a priest was not for him. He attended Blair Academy, a fashionable prep school, and received a number of scholarship offers when he graduated in 1948. Wanting to become a painter, however, Guccione turned them down to go to Los Angeles. He married at eighteen and had a child a year later, whereupon the marriage broke up. Guccione then went to Europe, where he met an English girl, Muriel Hudson. They drifted around Europe for a time, and in 1954 were married, with a child following a year later. Three more children were born in succeeding years.

During this time, Guccione worked at a number of jobs, but in the late 1950s he went to Paris to paint. He was not a successful artist, and, as *Money* reported, "he received checks from home and worked at an assortment of odd jobs" during these years. Guccione moved to London in 1960, where he got involved in journalism with the *London American*. Before long he was appointed managing editor of the paper, whereupon the entire staff resigned in a body. Unfazed by this, Guccione hired a tiny staff and ran a bare-bones operation until a lack of advertising revenues forced the paper into receivership. This short and unhappy apprenticeship in the publishing business, however, served him well. He learned from this experience the importance of newsstand sales, and this, in turn, prompted him to examine areas of publishing where there was little competition. *Playboy* magazine immediately caught his eye. With this magazine, Hugh Hefner[†] had pioneered the whole area of men's soft-core pornography magazines. Having fought many censorship battles over the publication of *Playboy*, by the early 1960s, Hefner had a vast market, with impressive newsstand sales and advertising revenues, to himself.

Guccione was determined to bring out a magazine to compete with *Playboy*, but he knew that it would require a great deal of capital. With a few thousand dollars supplied by his father, Guccione started in a small way with a mail-order business, selling American girlie magazines and pinups in England. For the next three years, he was so preoccupied with finding additional financial backing for his proposed magazine that the mail-order business folded. While he was deeply in debt and under great stress, his wife left him and took the children with her. He finally scraped together a modest amount of money and brought out the first issue of his new magazine, called *Penthouse*, in 1965. It was, as he recalls, "a guerrilla operation from the word go." Police had gotten word of his operation, and efforts were made to close him down. Nonetheless, the first issue appeared in London with a print run of 120,000 copies and was sold out in five days.

Success, however, was not immediate. Although Guccione could sell ample quantities of the magazine, he was able to lure few advertisers, who were reticent about having their products displayed in a magazine featuring nudes. At that point, Guccione met Kathy Keeton, then an exotic dancer in a London nightclub, who took over the job of selling advertising space during the day while continuing her dancing at night. Within three years she had built a solid base of advertising support for the magazine. The couple began to live together and continued to do so in the late 1980s. The big turning point for *Penthouse* came in 1967, when, in the words of Bob Guccione, it "went pubic" for the first time. That is, Penthouse achieved a good deal of fame and notoriety as the first widely distributed men's magazine to show the pubic hair of its models.

By 1969 *Penthouse*, with 180,000 copies in newsstand sales in England and a solid core of advertisers, was a success. But, this was not enough for Guccione. He wanted to challenge *Playboy* on its home turf in the United States, and he inaugurated an aggressive advertising campaign to do so. Taking out a full-page ad in the *New York Times*, he declared that *Penthouse* was "going rabbit hunting." The ad showed the famous *Playboy* bunny symbol in the crosshairs of a rifle sight. Guccione boasted that the English edition of *Penthouse* outsold *Playboy* three to one, and that "If you can catch a rabbit once, you can catch him again." This challenge hardly struck fear in the hearts of the Hefner empire. One executive there dismissed Guccione's claims by pointing out that *Playboy* was edited for an American audience and could not be expected to sell as well in England. On the surface, it seemed their confidence was well placed. *Playboy* had been around for sixteen years, and it had a circulation of over five million. Nonetheless, within fifteen months *Penthouse* had a circulation of 500,000, and by 1973 it stood at a staggering 3.8 million. By the early 1980s, the two magazines were running neck and neck in circulation, with *Penthouse* the clear leader in newsstand sales. Its success was so stunning that in August 1978 *Forbes* said *Penthouse* was the single most profitable magazine in publishing history, with the possible exception of *Reader's Digest* or *TV Guide*. Why was *Penthouse* so successful?

Recognizing that the much vaunted sexual revolution of the 1960s had made the once daring *Playboy* passé, Guccione made a bold move with *Penthouse*, explaining, "*Playboy* has become part of the Establishment, *Penthouse* is in tune with today's permissive society." Where *Playboy* had shocked America by baring breasts in the mid–1950s, *Penthouse* pioneered in the display of pubic hair. But Guccione's excursion into sexual permissiveness went well beyond that. He knew that the vast majority of his readers were young males from eighteen to thirty-four years of age, and that they were buying *Penthouse* for the nudes. Whereas *Playboy* tried to pretend that the nudes were incidental to the editorial content of the magazine, which reflected the attitudes of its somewhat older readership, *Penthouse* targeted its magazine to reach the young male who was purchasing his copy at the newsstand rather than receiving it by subscription. (Ninety-six percent of *Penthouse* sales were made at newsstands, compared to 60 percent of *Playboy*. This has some important implications for comparative profit returns. All newsstand sales are at full price, whereas many subscription sales are at a discount. Further, mailing costs are higher to subscription readers, thus *Penthouse* has continually shown higher profit ratios than *Playboy*.)

Newsweek agreed with Guccione's assessment of the buying public:

Latecomer *Penthouse* has prospered by never losing sight of what a skin-book is really selling. Its "Pets of the Month" leave little work for the libido. The girls flash their tongues, pose with animals and whips and fondle their bodies as though they were looking for lumps.

When *Time* asked Guccione what, besides the introduction of pubic hair, he had contributed to the industry, Guccione replied, "with the air of a man who might have invented first penicillin and then Aureomycin, 'Lesbians, threes, full-frontal male nudity, erect penis.' " Guccione also presented letters from readers (which later were published in a separate magazine called *Penthouse Forum*) that recounted their sexual experiences (or fantasies) in extraordinary detail. The letters often expounded the delights of bondage, incest, sadomasochism, and sexual devices. As society became more liberal, Guccione skirted the very margins of acceptability with his magazine, showing scenes of simulated group sex, female masturbation, and other once-taboo subjects. Yet, this was always presented in such a manner that kept *Penthouse* from being labeled hard-core pornography. All of this was very well planned by Guccione. As he recalled:

I studied *Playboy* very carefully and I thought that a lot of things they were doing was very puerile, immature. . . . *Penthouse* never used airbrushes. Our philosophy was different from the beginning. *Playboy* was a great believer in promoting the innocent girl next door look, whereas we felt that the girl next door didn't really exist. . . . We presented what we believed to be the real women in our society. *(Globe and Mail)*

Yet what readers encountered in *Penthouse* was anything but reality. The women in the photos were extraordinarily beautiful and sexually voracious, while the men portrayed in the letters to *Penthouse Forum* were exceptionally well endowed and capable of multiple orgasms. Both *Playboy* and *Penthouse* catered to the sexual fantasies of the North American male; Guccione's magazine just did it more explicitly for a younger, more hip audience.

Guccione's prescience about what his males readers wanted, and what the broader public will allow, has enabled him to build a massive publishing empire, which came to include a host of publications: *Penthouse, Penthouse Forum, Variations, Omni* (a science magazine), and *New Look*, which attempted to move into a new generation of men's magazines. Guccione also backed his son, Bob Guccione, Jr., for a time in *Spin*, a rock and roll magazine similar to *Rolling Stone*. Since *Penthouse* is privately held, it is difficult to acquire exact figures on its worth or that of Guccione. In the late 1970s, the *Penthouse* empire was judged to be worth from about $250 to $300 million. It has gone up since that time, and Guccione, according to *Forbes*, was worth about $300 million in 1988 and earned around $25 million annually in pre-tax income. Guccione has also made investments in feature films; he had a large financial stake in such hit films as *Chinatown* and *The Longest Yard*. He also made the infamous *Caligula*. There have been failures also. The Penthouse Club in London was a financial disaster, and a slick men's fashion magazine called *Lords* survived only a year, as did *Photoworld*. *Viva*, a women's magazine, somewhat more successful, lasted from 1973 to 1978.

A workaholic, Guccione does not smoke or drink, and he does most of his work at night, rising late in the morning. He lives on diet soft drinks all day until dinner at 9 P.M. His management style is equally demanding of his staff. He expects complete and total loyalty from his staff, but pays remarkably low salaries. As a consequence, staff turnover is high, many are abruptly fired, and morale is often low. But the end result has been success for Guccione. He has not only made a great deal of money, but he has also made a significant impact on American popular culture, and it is apparent that the latter is more important to him. As he has commented: "Clearly the best thing about having money is that you can do just about whatever you want, but the greatest aphrodisiac is power." Most gratifying for Guccione was the fact that he had beaten *Playboy* in the "Pubic Wars." In September 1977, when Penthouse finally surpassed *Playboy* as the best-selling men's magazine in America, Guccione took out a full-page ad in the *New York Times*. The ad reproduced *Penthouse*'s original "rabbit hunting" ad with the target; below, in big bold letters, it read: BANG! WE GOTCHA! (**B.** *Business Week*, August 9, 1969, December 6, 1982; *Time*, November 7, 1969, July 30, 1973, June 24, 1974, January 3, July 4, 1977, December 6, 1982; *Newsweek*, March 2, 1970, June 24, 1974, February 23, 1981, July 30, 1984; *Forbes*, March 1, 1971, August 7, 1978, May 25, 1981, October 28, 1985, October 24, 1988; *Fortune*, January 1975; *Maclean's*, February 6, 1978; *Money*, February 1980; Toronto *Globe and Mail*, November 7, 1985; *Contemporary Newsmakers*, 1986; *Manhattan, Inc.*, October 1987; Douglas K. Ramsey, *The Corporate Warriors*, 1987.)

H

HAAS FAMILY: WALTER A. HAAS (1889–December 7, 1979); **DANIEL EDWARD KOSHLAND** (March 16, 1892–December 10, 1979); **WALTER A. HAAS, JR.** (January 24, 1916–   ); **PETER E. HAAS** (December 20, 1918–   ); **ROBERT DOUGLAS HAAS** (April 3, 1942–   ). Apparel manufacturers, Levi Strauss & Company. America has made a number of contributions to world culture during the twentieth century: Coca-Cola, jazz and rock music, the mass-produced automobile, the computer, the copying machine, polio vaccine, and others. But none has had any greater impact, or has become more ubiquitous, than the phenomenon of wearing blue jeans. John Brooks, writing in the *New Yorker*, went so far as to call it ''an event without precedent in the history of human attire.'' The Levi Strauss Company was the principal beneficiary of the fashion revolution—becoming the largest maker of apparel in America as a result of it. As a measure of its popularity and as a perverse form of flattery, Levi's have been imitated and copied—illegally—more than any other piece of clothing. In America, jeans are the third most popular item for highjackers, after cigarettes and liquor. And when Levi's are shipped overseas, the company has to send them in plain brown boxes to avoid theft. The Soviet Union was one of the few European countries that did not allow the importation of Levi's, but even there, the black market was so strong that authorities arrested a teenage gang in the late 1970s that was selling Levi's for $200 a pair! Levi's have been ensconced in the Smithsonian Institution, and they have been presented a special Coty Fashion Award as ''America's most significant contribution to international fashion.''

The giant clothing manufacturer was founded by Levi Strauss, a Bavarian-born Jew who came to New York City at age nineteen in 1848. Finding life in the young country difficult, Strauss eked out a meager living as a peddler, lugging around a 180-pound assortment of sundries door to door in the rural towns and villages of New York. In 1850, when his married sister, who was living in San Francisco, offered to pay his way West, Strauss jumped at the opportunity, taking with him a bolt of canvas that he planned to sell for tenting.

It turned out to be the wrong kind of canvas for tenting, but Strauss learned from a miner that pants that would stand up to the rigors of prospecting were hard to find. Measuring the man with a piece of string, Strauss fashioned him a pair of pants from the sturdy canvas, charging him $6 in gold dust. Fame soon spread around the mining areas about "those pants of Levi's" (which is why the company continues to use the apostrophe in its trademark), and soon he was doing a booming business. When he ran out of canvas, Strauss wrote to his two brothers in New York to send him more. Instead, they sent him denim, a tough, brown cotton cloth made in Nîmes, France (*serge de Nîmes*, shortened to denim). Strauss dyed the cloth an indigo blue, which became its identifying color over the years. The pants sold well, and Strauss became a successful and respected San Francisco merchant and manufacturer during the following twenty years. But the great popularity and uniqueness of his product was not established until the 1870s, when copper rivets were added to the pockets.

Those copper rivets came about in a curious fashion. Jacob Davis, a tailor in Nevada, received complaints from miners that the pockets of their jeans tore when they stuffed them with ore samples. As a bit of a lark, Davis took a pair of pants to the local blacksmith, who put rivets at the stress points. The miners were elated with the results, and Davis soon had a thriving little cottage industry refashioning blue jeans. In 1872, Davis wrote to the Levi Strauss firm, suggesting it patent the product, and, in return, agree to share the resulting profits with him. As he told them in his phonetic English: "The secratt of them Pents is the Rivits that I put in those Pockots and I found the demand so large that I cannot make them up fast enough. . . . I knew you can make a very large amount of money on it." And so they did. Upon being granted the patent in May 1873, Levi Strauss began making riveted garments of various kinds. In appreciation, Davis not only shared in the profits, but was also made a regional manager in the firm.

One of the most amusing and revealing anecdotes about the Levi firm concerns those rivets. In addition to affixing rivets to the pockets, the firm put in a "crotch rivet." For years, cowboys and others had complained privately about the danger of standing too close to the campfire in their Levi's. There were many stories about tired cowboys who were huddled around a campfire when suddenly one of them would let out a bellow of pain and begin dancing in agony. The firm, however, took no note of the problem until 1933, when company president Walter A. Haas went on a camping trip. Haas, after crouching too close to the campfire, suffered the common fate. When he inquired of the professional wranglers in the party if they had ever had the same problem, they answered affirmatively. The next day, Haas called the board of directors together, and the crotch rivet was gone. Other rivets disappeared in succeeding years. In 1937, yielding to complaints of schools in the West that the rivets were scratching desks and chairs, the Levi company concealed the rear rivets on the inside of the pockets. A few years later, a refinement in the needle trade made it possible to stitch the jeans more securely than was possible with rivets, which made the rivets technologically obsolete. By then, however, they were a key element in the whole distinct look of Levi's—in effect, they had become part of their trademark. So the rear rivets were eliminated entirely, but the front ones were retained for purely stylistic reasons.

The product known the world over as Levi's, or simply as blue jeans, was known inside the company after the 1870s as the "501 Double X blue demin waist overall''—501 was the lot number; Double X was used to denote the extra-strength denim being used; and waist overall was the description of the garment preferred by Levi Strauss, who did not like the term "jeans.'' In 1886, he added the brand patch, still attached to the pants, which shows two horses, each urged on by a farmer, trying to pull apart a pair of Levi's. The last major identifying mark on the pants came in 1936, when a red tab, about one-fourth by five-eighths of an inch, bearing the name Levi's in white letters, was stitched to the right rear pocket. Since that time, all 501 Levi's have been virtually identical.

Levi Strauss built a highly successful business, with a number of dry-goods stores in San Francisco, along with the jeans manufacturing outlet, which sold Levi's to Western miners and cowboys over the years. Each year, sales increased modestly, but they never became much more than a sideline for the ex-peddler. A bachelor when he died in 1902, Strauss left the bulk of his $6-million estate to four nephews: Jacob, Sigmund, Louis, and Abraham Stern. They continued to run the fairly small, conservative company for the next several years, with Jacob as nominal head of the company until 1927, when he was succeeded by Sigmund. The key executive in the firm from the early 1920s onward, however, was Walter A. Haas, who had married Sigmund's daughter, Elise Stern, in 1914.

Walter Haas was born into a prominent San Francisco mercantile family, which had wholesale grocery outlets in both that city and in Los Angeles. They also owned a utility concern in Los Angeles. Walter graduated from the University of California at Berkeley in 1910, and he worked in the family business until he entered the U.S. Army in 1917. When he mustered out in 1919, his father-in-law convinced him to join the Levi Strauss firm. The company then was at a critical juncture. Both Jacob and Sigmund, who had been with the firm for about fifty years, wanted to retire from active management. They told Haas that if he did not like the work or saw no future in the company, it would be liquidated at the end of that year. Haas liked it and recognized that it had more of a future than the declining grocery trade.

To assist him in administering the company, Haas recruited his brother-in-law, Daniel E. Koshland, to join the firm in 1922. Although Haas was president, and Koshland was nominally second-in-command during the next thirty-five years, those titles were largely meaningless, since the two men worked closely and successfully together. Koshland graduated from the University of California in 1913, and went to New York City, where he was assistant manager of the foreign department of Equitable Trust from 1914 to 1916, and an executive at Lazard Frères, bankers, until 1922. Having tired of his financial focus by 1922, when Haas called him back to San Francisco, he put his primary concern in the areas of production and personnel, labor relations, and the field of corporate social responsibility. Haas, on the other hand, had general oversight of the firm, with his own special interests in finance, marketing, and promotion. On nearly every issue, though, there was consultation, with a common approach.

One of the most important and unique elements of the firm in these early years was its enlightened sense of social responsibility. Koshland, having inherited a deeply ingrained Levi Strauss tradition, was primarily responsible for implementing the social policy over the years. Not that Levi Strauss himself had been particularly enlightened. The company keeps on file in its History Room a copy of a late-nineteenth-century advertisement, in which Strauss boasts: "[O]ur riveted goods . . . are made up in our factory, under our direct supervision, and by WHITE LABOR only, and therefore not likely being infected by a disease." The Sterns had established a more benign policy during their tenure. When the great earthquake and fire leveled San Francisco in 1906, destroying the Levi Strauss facilities, the firm took out ads in the city papers, informing their 350 employees that their salaries would be continued until further notice. They also informed retail merchants whose stores had been destroyed that Levi Strauss would provide them with interest-free loans until they were back on their feet.

Haas and Koshland continued this tradition during the years they ran the company. To maintain and expand employment, the two men adopted a number of innovative policies. In the early 1920s, they established a Christmas cash bonus which produced a hysterical response when first issued, but soon became a generalized tradition. They were also among the first employers in the garment industry to provide their employees with year-round jobs. This policy was sorely tested during the Great Depression in the 1930s, when sales fell off drastically. At first, when production was stopped, the company had employees re-laying plant floors to keep them working. When the depression continued, and this kind of work was not possible, Haas and Koshland still refused to lay off workers. Instead, they put them on a three-day week, so that the diminished amount of work could be shared. In return, Levi's workers became almost fanatically devoted to the company, allowing management to place high expectations for quality work upon the workers.

These practices were not introduced out of any sense that they should be "do-gooders" or that they should attempt to act as models for enlightened employers. Haas and Koshland believed that ethical fulfillment and business success should go together, and for years it worked as such for the company. As was stated in the *California Management Review*: "[They] were not social visionaries but hardheaded businessmen with a social vision and humane concerns." These practices continued after World War II. By the time the Truman adminstration passed the Fair Employment Practices Act in 1946, the Levi Strauss company was a relatively old hand at minority hiring. The "white labor only" dictum of the nineteenth century had long since passed, and the firm led the way in hiring various minority groups. Later these principles were extended to the hard-core unemployed and the handicapped. As a result, Daniel Koshland took a leadership role in the Council for Civic Unity, the National Alliance of Businessmen, and a number of other organizations for socially conscious businessmen.

During the early years, the Levi Strauss firm conducted most of its business as a wholesale jobber rather than a jeans manufacturer. Gradually, in the 1920s and 1930s, jeans became a larger entity in their operations. During the 1920s, the 501's became the firm's major money-maker, and during the 1930s Levi's became known outside the West for the first time. During the depression decade, "dude" ranches were very popular with Easterners, and the vacationers often returned home with a pair of 501's, raving about their fit, comfort, and durability. At that time, Haas and Koshland realized that there was a far greater potential market for Levi's than they had supposed.

As a result, Haas increased national advertising for the product, stressing the sense of tradition and quality that went with the Levi's name. The rivets, the trademark leather back patch, the new red Levi's tag—all became part of Americana, part of the frontier tradition and the American West in Levi's advertisments. As Walter Haas noted: "The Levi's brand . . . is probably the most important item we have besides personnel . . . bricks and stones make the factories, but do not make a business. Good, honest merchandising and brand value are most important." To illustrate this approach, Haas placed an ad in fashionable *Vogue* magazine in 1935. The ad showed two debonair Eastern women wearing Levi's on a ranch vacation. The text read: "True Western chic was invented by cowboys, and the moment you veer from their tenets, you are lost."

Blue jeans were given an added boost in popularity during World War II, when the federal government declared them to be "essential commodities," to be sold only to war workers. This, of course, made jeans scarce, and therefore more desirable for many people. Pictures began appearing in national magazines of coeds at prestigious Bennington College and elsewhere dressed in "bobby-soxer" outfits, an essential ingredient of which was a well-worn pair of blue jeans. During this period, whether to war workers or coeds, the Levi's company could sell all the jeans it could make, but it was still a small outfit, with fifteen salespeople, two plants, sales of $8 million, and no business east of the Mississippi. When the Bennington coeds wore jeans, they were more likely Lee jeans than Levi's.

All this popularity, and the huge potential market it represented, made Haas and Koshland bullish on blue jeans after the war. They decided to close down the firm's wholesaling operations in 1948 and concentrate on the manufacture of 501's. This marked the beginning of an important transformation in leadership during these years. Even though Walter Haas and Daniel Koshland continued as official heads of the company until the late 1950s, their reign actually ended ten years earlier.

It was the decision of young Walter Haas, Jr., to concentrate on blue jeans that generated the changeover. Having graduated from the University of California in 1937, he received his MBA from Harvard two years later. In retrospect, the decision to concentrate on blue jeans seems axiomatic, but at the time, blue jeans accounted for only one-fourth of Levi's business. As Walter Haas, Jr., says of that time: "We had a reputation for honesty, integrity, and quality, but we were thought of as good, gray Levi Strauss." Young Walter set out to change that image and helping him to transform the company was his brother, Peter Haas. Like Walter, Peter graduated from Berkeley in 1940, and got his MBA from Harvard in 1943. Although he began working as an apprentice in an advertising agency, and subsequently became a riveter and then a scheduler in an aircraft plant, in 1945 Peter joined Levi Strauss.

Young Walter and Peter faced a difficult situation in the blue jean market in the late 1940s and early 1950s. First of all, the market was highly segmented regionally. Although Levi's were very strong in the West, it sold few garments in other parts of the United States. Dominating the Southeast was Wrangler jeans, made by Blue Bell, and Lee jeans were strongest in the Midwest. Nationwide, Blue Bell sold more jeans than Levi's, but Levi's had more cachet and more of a reputation, which the two young businessmen were determined to cash in on. They began extending the market for their product to the East, beefing up its sales force and expanding the number of plants. Even more important was a profound change in marketing strategy. As Walter Haas, Jr., noted, "We also did something very basic, we decided to concentrate on the teenage market."

As the 1940s gave way to the 1950s, blue jeans increasingly became an important element in teen dress. But this was not achieved without a struggle. During these years, makers of blue jeans had to withstand a furious attack on their product from a number of sources. The American Institute of Men's and Boy's Wear launched a nationwide "Dress Right" campaign aimed directly at blue jeans. Several municipalities, school systems, and even one state (Wisconsin) passed regulations prohibiting the wearing of blue jeans to school by teenagers. But Levi's slowly increased their sales, reaching $12 million by 1950. By the end of that decade, sales were nearly $50 million, and a great cultural revolution, which created a new teen market for the first time, was instrumental for much of this increase.

The great transformation began around 1954. In that year, James Dean in *East of Eden* and Marlon Brando in *The Wild One* made blue jeans enormously popular cult items for young people. A year later, in *Rebel without a Cause*, Dean made them even more popular, by associating blue jeans with a sense of middle-class teenage rebelliousness. With the emergence of rock and roll music and other phenomena in the mid–1950s, blue jeans became an authentic part of a teen culture. What made them so popular with young people? First of all, wearing jeans was a quiet, nonviolent way of rebelling against the conformity of the decade. As Peter Beagle wrote in his book, *American Denim* (cited in *New Yorker* article), the traditional clothing styles of the decade represented "a strangled, constipated idea of a normal life." Blue jeans, on the other hand, exemplified a marvelous amalgam of rebellion and tradition which was very appealing to young people.

The great explosion in the popularity of blue jeans came in the 1960s. During the decade, Levi's sales doubled every three or four years, and between 1962 and 1970, sales and net profits more than quintupled. The key to this phenomenal growth was the continuing growth in youth consciousness and the emergence of a counterculture, of which blue jeans were an integral part. Levi Strauss also began consciously linking its jeans with rock music and the youth culture. It took its first fling at radio advertising in 1966, hooking up with a then unknown rock group called the Jefferson Airplane. Making commercials for the blue jean company, the group in 1967 became a phenomenal nationwide hit, as a result of the "Human Be-In" in San Francisco's Golden Gate Park. As the "Airplane" began to have a succession of hit songs and were playing at sold-out concerts around America, they were amazed when teenagers in the audience began requesting "the Levi song" at the concerts. As the rock group became an integral part of the emerging counterculture based on "sex, 'n' drugs, 'n' rock 'n' roll," Levi's found itself intimately associated with the same phenomenon. As the popularity of the "hippie culture" grew, blue jeans, and especially Levi's, grew apace.

The association of blue jeans with nonconformity came about for a number of reasons. For a generation of young people who were rejecting the materialism, the perceived hypocrisy, the racism, and the sexism of their parents, blue jeans seemed to be the ideal clothing. Classless, ageless, and sexless, as the traditional garb of working people, blue jeans were in tune with the egalitarian ideals of the decade. Walter Haas, Jr., himself recognized the nature of this appeal. Once, when asked if it bothered him, as a conservative businessman, that his garments were being adopted as a symbol of rebellion and revolution, he replied: "It bothered me at times. But look, jeans are worn by young and old, radical and conservative. The real point is their classlessness." Tom Kasten, president of Levi's jeans division, was more prosaic: "We don't try to analyze the sociology. Our job is to get a line ready and hit the market on time."

While the Levi Strauss firm grew during these decades, it did not forget its traditions of social responsibility. Following the dictum of Walter Haas, Sr., that "We owe responsibility to the communities in which we do business," the Levi firm expressed that concern in a number of ways. They donated returned merchandise to the Red Cross, participated in United Way campaigns, and established the Levi Strauss Foundation to engage in wide-ranging philanthropic ventures. Beyond that, they did much to promote employment of visible minorities and the hard-core unemployed. These ventures were not always successful, but they were almost always noble in intent.

Levi Strauss Company soon learned that many problems accompany success. Just as blue jeans exploded in popularity in the United States, they suddenly also became enormously popular in Europe. Levi Strauss had opened an office in Antwerp, Belgium, in 1962, but sales in Europe soared after 1965. Between that year and 1971, sales rose 800 percent, and the Levi firm scrambled to take advantage of this new market. To meet the demand, Levi Strauss rapidly expanded its factories in Europe, and by 1973 it was doing $100 million worth of business a year there. But as often happens in such situations, the company misjudged the strength of the market and soon was faced with overcapacity and bulging inventories. By 1973, more than eight million Levi's jeans were packing European warehouses. The European division began racking up heavy losses, and, consequently, operations had to be trimmed.

Walter and Peter Haas tried to take the European debacle philosophically. Walter Haas accepted the blame: "I put the blame right here at home for trying to grow too fast, and for not having the proper information and controls." Yet, he also felt that, "the experience was good for us, we had always talked about controlled growth. This reminded us that we need to have controls and accurate reports." Despite the necessity to cut back operations and to reorganize, however, Levi's executives were determined to maintain their time-honored approach to employment and social responsibility. Feeling that the fault lay with top management rather than with the workers, the Haas brothers vowed there would be no permanent layoffs at the European plants.

The 1970s and 1980s were difficult decades for the venerable jeans firm. The 1970s started out in a euphoric manner, but certain portents of trouble existed even then. To deal with the great expansion of the Levi firm in the late 1960s, Walter Haas, Jr., and Peter Haas took the company public in 1970, raising $45 million for future expansion. For a time, it seemed that Levi's could do no wrong. Even the European fiasco did not significantly curtail the company's growth. In 1975, sales passed the $1 billion mark for the first time. Walter Haas, Sr., then in his eighties, commented on that milestone:

The whole of my life until it happened, a billion-dollar company was beyond my wildest dreams. My ambition was to show an annual *profit* of a *million*, and I was with the company thirty years before we did that. We were lucky all right, but I guess you have to say we took advantage of the situation. I give my sons all the credit. (*New Yorker*)

Walter, Jr., mused quizzically: "I don't think we realized what was happening. We just knew we had a bear by the tail and were trying to hang on." In 1979, the firm's sales soared past the $2 billion mark. In appreciation, the company gave all of its 42,000 employees cash awards, ranging from $50 for the newly hired to $350 for more seasoned employees. Little did anyone guess that they had seen the last of the good times for the foreseeable future.

In the late 1970s and early 1980s, the Levi company made a series of unfortunate mistakes which brought about a severe decline in earnings. First of all, they introduced the David Hunter line of clothing, which was designed to compete against designer labels, such as Ralph Lauren's[†] Polo line. It was an unmitigated disaster. Similarly, a line of sports clothing intended to compete against Nike and Adidas was unsuccessful. As a result, in 1981 Walter, Jr., and Peter Haas were eased out of their position of control and were replaced by Robert T. Grohman, the first nonfamily member to head the firm.

During the three years he was president of the company, Grohman made a number of fateful decisions. First of all, in an attempt to shore up the sagging sales of blue jeans, he signed agreements to sell Levi's to Sears and J. C. Penney's for the first time. Although this greatly increased the short-term sales and earnings of the company, it alienated the specialty and department stores with whom Levi's had traditionally done business. As the demand for jeans further slackened in the 1980s, Levi's lacked a loyal retail customer base with which to launch new products to compete in the changing marketplace. Grohman also made other changes. In 1982, he violated Levi's proud tradition of lifetime employment and trimmed 2,400 people—including middle managers—from its payroll. None of this worked, however, and the earnings slide continued. In 1984, after being groomed for the job, Robert Haas, son of Walter Haas, Jr., took over as chief executive of the firm.

Robert Haas, like other family members, graduated from Berkeley in 1964. He then joined the Peace Corps and spent two years in the Ivory Coast. When he returned, he got an MBA from Harvard and also worked on Eugene Mc-Carthy's presidential campaign in 1968. He then worked with a management consulting firm and joined Levi Strauss in 1973. In 1985 Robert took the giant blue jeans firm private again, in a $1.7-billion leveraged buyout. He began repairing damaged relationships with the company's traditional retailers, expanding the local advertising budget, and engaging in special promotions. As he noted, "we earned a reputation for arrogance and insensitivity to our retail accounts."

But if Robert Haas was attempting to return Levi's to their traditional retail roots, he was violating many of the other company traditions. By taking the firm private, Haas incurred a heavy debt with the bankers, especially California's Wells Fargo. In order to repay the long-term debt, Haas began heavy cutbacks in the company. Over a short space of time, he closed twenty-five plants worldwide and cut 6,500 people from a workforce of 44,000. In doing so, Haas also eliminated much of the diversification that had characterized earlier efforts. As in the 1950s and early 1960s, jeans, not designer clothing, were seen by Haas as the company's future. For the first time since the 1950s, the firm was also targeting adults as their principal market. "For the first time, Levi Strauss's advertising is being aimed squarely at men in their 30's and 40's—the baby boomers who first adopted denim as the unofficial uniform of youth." The latest campaign showed a father teaching his son to fish, a middle-aged man mending a fence—no streetwise teenagers, hunky young men and blues music in these ads. Levi's were no longer aimed at the young and rebellious.

The late 1970s and 1980s demonstrated the best and worst aspects of the Haas family's traditions of social responsibility. On one hand, when Charles Finley wanted to sell the Oakland A's, and there were rumblings they would be moved elsewhere, Walter Haas, Jr., purchased the team to keep it in the Bay Area. As part of Levi's strong sense of community commitment, the A's have become increasingly more successful and better run under the direction of Walter J. Haas, Robert's brother. Robert, on the other hand, has not done as well with the Levi Strauss firm. Despite the firm's slogan, "Levi's is people," Haas laid off one-quarter of the 48,000 workers in 1980 and closed forty factories. In response to criticism of his actions, Robert Haas said, "Maintaining employment for the sake of employment isn't paternalistic, it's irresponsible if it jeopardizes the welfare of all employees."

His grandfather, Walter Haas, Sr., had feared just such an occurrence. In an interview toward the end of his life, he commented: "After I'm long gone, I hope that Levi's will hold its head up with great American industries. . . . If the contrary should occur, I'll look down from Cloud Seven and be a very unhappy ghost." Ernest Gaines, manager of employee benefits, perhaps captured best the trauma taking place: "Levi Strauss is a classic example of the old-line, paternalistic company coming of age in an impersonal, modern world. The family's desire to relate to the good old days is like two people trying to pull a horse through a knothole." (**B.** *Business Week*, February 21, 1953, November 1, 1969, July 4, 1970, July 21, 1973, January 19, 1976, September 5, 1977, December 5, 1983, November 5, 1984, July 25, 1985, December 21, 1987; *Coronet*, June 1956; *Who Was Who*, vol. VII; *Time*, April 25, 1969; *Nation's Business*, November 1971; *Life*, November 24, 1972; *Fortune*, April 1974, March 26, 1979, March 22, 1982, December 26, 1983, August 19, 1985; *Financial World*, March 15, 1976, March 15, 1981; *Management Today*, January 1977; *California Management Review*, Fall 1977; *New York Times*, November 25, 1977, June 30, December 8, 1979, October 27, 1980, November 19, 1983, April 15, May 26, September 19, October 17, 1984, January 31, July 31, 1985; *American Heritage*, April 1978; *International Management*, June 1978; *Forbes*, August 21, 1978, August 11, 1986; Ed Cray, *Levi's*, 1978; *New Yorker*, November 12, 1979; Milton Moskowitz et al., *Everybody's Business*, 1980; *Contemporary Newsmakers*, 1986; *Who's Who in America*, 1986–1987; Michael Patrick Allen, *The Founding Families*, 1987; *Who's Who in the West*, 1987–1988; Toronto *Globe & Mail*, November 29, 1988.)

HANDLER, ELLIOT (1916–   ) and **RUTH HANDLER** (November 4, 1916–   ). Toy company founders, Mattel, Incorporated. At the Toy Fair in New York City in 1959, the Mattel catalog proudly introduced its new creation:

New for '59, the BARBIE DOLL: A shapely teenage fashion model! Retail price $3.00. . . . An exciting all-new kind of doll (She's grown up!) with fashion apparel authentic in every detail! This is Barbie—one of Mattel's proudest achievements for '59. Girls of all ages will thrill to the fascination of her miniature wardrobe of fine-fabric fashions: tiny zippers that really zip . . . coats with luxurious linings . . . jeweled earrings and necklaces . . . and every girl can be the star. There's never been a doll like Barbie.

For once, the ads were right: there never *had* been a doll like Barbie. For that reason, toy buyers were skeptical. Some were brutally blunt: "You're out of your mind. It won't sell." Others just politely expressed uneasiness about the idea of giving children a woman's body to play with, or expressed concern about carrying a broad line of accessories that were difficult to keep in stock. As a result, only about 20 percent of the retailers first exposed to Barbie ordered the doll. But, from the moment Barbie hit the dealer's shelves, she was an enormous success; by the late 1980s, more than 250 million had been sold. Far and away the most popular doll ever made, she has her own Barbie Doll Collectors Club, which publishes the *International Barbie Doll Collectors Gazette*. Barbie is not just a toy, not even simply a commercial item; it is one of the most remarkable fixtures of American popular culture in the late twentieth century.

Ruth and Elliot Handler were childhood sweethearts in Denver, Colorado, where both of them were born. Elliot was an aspiring artist, Ruth a business-oriented student. By the late 1930s, both of them had moved to California, where Elliot started his professional career, while still attending art school, by designing lighting fixtures, and Ruth gained employment as a secretary at Paramount Studios. In 1938, the two were married, and two years later they moved to an unfurnished apartment which they furnished with Elliot's designs. Ruth was so impressed with these that she urged Elliot to manufacture them commercially. Purchasing some home workshop equipment from Sears, he soon was producing a variety of items. Organized with a number of other partners, Elliot Handler's firm was doing about $2 million in sales annually by the end of World War II.

At this time, Elliot recognized the importance of changing the company's approach and product lines to compete more effectively. When his partners objected, Elliot sold his interest at a loss and, together with an old friend, Harold Matson, started Mattel Creations (MATT for Matson, EL for Elliot). Shortly afterward, Matson sold out due to ill health, and Ruth Handler became a member of the firm. They first produced picture frames made of scrap plastic and wood. After filling a large order, they were left with flocked wood strips and scrap plastic sheet, which Elliot designed into doll house furniture. Ruth then set up a simple sales organization, and the young firm had an excellent year, selling $100,000 worth of goods, and making an extraordinary profit of $30,000. They had almost inadvertently entered a new industry—the toy business—one they revolutionized and dominated unlike any previous firm.

The toy industry in the United States had been a small-scale affair since its origins. Toy sales in 1912 reached $30 million at the retail level; only 60 percent came from domestic manufacturers. In the early 1920s, many of the toy firms that had emerged in response to the cessation of imports during World War I, went bankrupt. In the 1920s and 1930s, however, the toy industry experienced a resurgence, and American manufacturers came to dominate the market, holding 95 percent of it by 1939. During the thirty years from 1920 to 1950, while the American population was increasing by 43 percent, its industrial production went up 150 percent, electricity consumption went up 700 percent, and the retail sales of toys and games increased a whopping 2,000 percent. In the thirty years after 1950, toy spending increased at an even more rapid rate. As America became more child centered, the importance of toys gained momentum, and the willingness of parents to spend large amounts of money on their children increased in like measure. The Handlers unknowingly entered the ground floor of one of the great growth industries of postwar America.

In 1946, they expanded their doll furniture line and added some plastic toys, but a rival manufacturer came out with an injected molded-plastic line of doll furniture with perfect detail at a lower price, which totally destroyed the Handler's doll furniture business. To survive, the Handlers had to develop new products. In 1947, they introduced their first big hit—the "Uke-a-Doodle"—a miniature plastic ukelele. Orders for the toy were enormous, but when the Toy Show arrived in March, four other companies were using the Handler's product as a sample and were quoting lower prices. The Handlers cut their own prices to compete and managed to eke out a modest profit by the end of the year. They learned an important lesson—if Mattel were to avoid the hazards of obsolescent products and price competition and if it were to achieve any kind of stability, it would have to design toys that were unique, original, and different in appearance and operation. They refused to copy other toy makers, and, at the same time, they wanted to ensure that it would be difficult for others to copy them.

In 1948, they designed a radical, new, all-plastic piano with raised black keys. The first toy piano of its kind, it was difficult and expensive for other manufacturers to copy. The item was highly successful in the marketplace, but the Handlers realized that they had miscalculated the cost of producing the piano— it was the only year in their first quarter century that they failed to make a profit. They also incorporated their firm in California in that year and began to develop a revolutionary new music box using wires in a die casting with a rubber belt to pluck the wires. Since the developmental costs of this item were high, they had to find new sources of capital. When several banks turned them down, Ruth Handler's brother-in-law in Denver, Harry Paul, loaned them $20,000. Rather than taking repayment, Paul took stock in the company and became one of its major stockholders.

The new music box had a patented mechanism and a continuous play value since it operated only when the child turned a crank. With the success of the music box, 1949 was a profitable year for Mattel, and over the next five years the firm continued a steady and stable pattern of growth. Priced below the imported music boxes which had dominated the market, it continued to enjoy great popularity year after year. By the end of the 1960s, Mattel had sold over 50 million units of music box toys.

Mattel, indeed the entire toy industry, was profoundly changed in 1955. Mattel's annual sales at that time were running about $5 million. Their advertising agency approached them about the possibility of sponsoring a fifteen-minute segment of the new Mickey Mouse Club, to be produced by Walt Disney.* To secure the show, they had to sign for fifty-two weeks, at a cost of $500,000—

an amount about equal to their net worth at that time. Ruth and Elliot Handler recognized that it was a big gamble, but they decided to proceed. Mattel had a product, an automatic cap gun called a Burp Gun, which was not selling well, but when they advertised it on the Mickey Mouse Club, sales skyrocketed. The success of these ads had far-reaching implications. Previously, since most toys were purchased by parents, advertising was aimed at them. Now, however, Mattel was pitching its ads directly to the ultimate consumer—the child. As Elliot Handler commented: "It was the beginning of a marketing revolution." Mattel's sales hit $9 million in 1957, and $14 million in 1958, nearly three times more than before they began television advertising.

However much Mattel had grown to that point, however, it was nothing compared to what transpired in 1959, the year they introduced Barbie to the nation. The idea for Barbie was Ruth Handler's, who had spent many years watching their daughter, Barbie, play with dolls. Elliot Handler recalled that "my wife noted that she invariably passed by dolls of her own age group, favoring instead teenage dolls with fashion accessories. At the time, the only such teenage dolls were paper cutouts." Ruth recommended they create an authentic teenage doll, a model for authentic clothing and accessories, which would fulfill a little girl's fantasies about growing up. Ruth even had a clear idea of how this doll should look. While traveling in Europe, she had been exposed to "Lilli," a German doll being produced in the mid–1950s. Instantly recognizing the popularity of Lilli, Ruth was certain an American version would be equally successful.

Although the initial reaction of buyers was negative at the 1959 New York Toy Show, Barbie soon caught on, and she quickly became the most famous doll of all time. Eight years later, millions had been sold, and revenues from Barbie alone totaled $500 million; Barbie catapulted Mattel into the front ranks of the toy industry. The secret of Barbie's appeal has been the topic of tremendous debate over the years. Since Barbie has become a cultural icon, representing images of childhood, teenagers, women, and consumerism to millions of Americans, she has become a highly controversial figure.

Probably the most controversial aspect of Barbie has been her figure. Twelve inches tall, Barbie was wasp waisted, large breasted, button nosed, and doe eyed. To some, she represented the very ideal of womanhood and the perfect, all-American teenager. To others, she represented a sex object, a dangerous model of sexuality and a trivialization of women's role in society. An editor in the *Village Voice* expressed it most directly: "It was the TITS. After all that's what being an adult meant, wasn't it? I loved Barbies so much. Whenever I put another outfit on her it was just to see how they'd look in it." And no one could deny that Barbie had quite a figure. If she were blown up to human size, her measurements would be 39–21–33. Even the centerfolds in *Playboy* and *Penthouse* paled in comparison to those dimensions. Other commentators, however, have been less sanguine. In a recent court case, Barbie was used as a scapegoat by a clinical psychologist, who claimed that many women suffer mentally and physically while trying to achieve a Barbie-like figure. Betty Friedan, one of the founders of the contemporary woman's movement, however, said that the issue was "not very serious," and Ruth Handler said, "In my opinion people make too much of breasts. They are just part of the body."

However that may be, at least part of the reason for Barbie's popularity was sexual. As Joyce Maynard, in an article in *Across the Board*, commented: " . . . for me Barbie was, from the start, clearly teenage—or older, even—and clearly sexual." And this sexual aspect was a very important learning device for most young girls. It was a safe and familiar way for them to experiment with their fantasies, about being grown up, about their own sexuality, about the possibilities of their future relationships with other women, and with men. Barbie allowed a child to relate her child-size hopes and needs to the world of adults— to try out ideas floating around in her mind in a situation which mirrored some kind of reality. As one young woman commented: "When you're a young girl, this is all new to you. Dressing your Barbie doll helped you to figure it out; all the private or embarrassing questions found simple and elegant answers at a pace suited to your curiosity."

As that comment implies, part of this experimentation and fantasy/reality was related to Barbie's wardrobe. Many young girls, and certainly many adult critics, felt that the best thing about Barbie was her wardrobe. The quality of her garments and their attention to detail are legendary. Her dresses came with tiny buttons and zippers, her belts had real buckles, linings were real silk or cotton full linings. Even more important, Barbie's wardrobe followed real fashion with a deadly accuracy. Portrayed by Mattel as a "teenage fashion model," clothes seemed to be the central feature of Barbie's life (and for parents, the most expensive aspect of Barbie ownership). The first twenty-one outfits created at Mattel for Barbie were developed by Charlotte Johnson and her staff, who traveled each season to Paris to view the collections of Dior, Fath, Heim, Balenciaga, Givenchy, Grès, Schiaparelli, Carven, Balmain, and Saint Laurent.

Another key to Barbie's popularity was her personality, which transcended the high-fashion-model image. Given an all-American, suburban-girl personality, Barbie soon had a host of emotions, professions, likes and dislikes, and hobbies. Perhaps the most important aspect of this was the development of an entire Barbie family tree. The first to appear was a boy friend, Ken, who was also named after one of the Handlers' children. Developed in 1962, Ken exuded a rather boyish masculinity, somewhat like Dwayne Hickman of the "Dobie Gillis" show. *Barbie Magazine* ran stories which developed the relationship between Ken and Barbie in much detail. Stories, like "Barbie's First Prom," and others made her appear like a real person to the young girls who played with her. Over the years, Barbie's family tree continued to expand. She got a last name (Roberts) and a mother (Margaret), and other mundane details were developed about her. Mattel also brought out a doll to be her little sister (Skipper, in 1964) and a cousin (Francie, in 1966). A number of doll friends were also created for Barbie.

Perhaps, however, the secret of Barbie's popularity is less complex than all of this. For a child who was looking apprehensively at a more grownup world, it was a way to try things out and experiment, to be sure. But also, for a child, whose life was continually shaped by adults, there was an important dimension to Barbie dolls. Joyce Maynard, interviewing a ten-year-old, who no longer played with Barbie, recorded this comment: " 'The thing is, about a Barbie, when you're young,' she explained, sagely chewing the end of a magic marker, 'that you can boss them.' "

With the enormous success of Barbie and her cohorts, Mattel began to bring out other dolls and toys—Chatty Cathy and Baby-First-Step, which were successes, and Charmin' Chatty and Baby Alive (a doll which defecated), which were total flops. By the late 1960s, the Handlers were astute enough to recognize that they needed something more than dolls if Mattel were to continue growing in the future. Their great breakthrough came in 1968, with the introduction of Hot Wheels, a line that initially used gravity and later a power plant to propel tiny cars around curves and down straightaways of plastic track. Like Barbie, Hot Wheels, which was directed at boys, had enormous follow-up potential. There were always more and different cars, more track, and other accessories to purchase. But the Handlers did not seem to be aware of the enormity of the product's appeal. They manufactured just three million Hot Wheels sets in the initial year. Then, when they met with a major department store buyer who requested three million sets or more just for his chain, they knew they had miscalculated. In response, Mattel went overboard, building a huge production facility just to make Hot Wheels. The plant was so large that if it had been a separate entity, it would have been the nation's second-largest toy maker, second only to Mattel itself. From 1968 to 1970, as Mattel sold all the Hot Wheels it could make, its annual sales soared from $180 million in 1968 to $345 million two years later. Hot Wheels alone made up $88 million in sales in 1970. Suddenly, Hot Wheels' sales fizzled. Toy departments were jammed with the product, and strong competition hurt even more. Mattel found that they could move Hot Wheels only by offering deep discounts, unloading its huge inventory at distress prices over the next several years. Nobody at the time paid much attention to this, since the company was still making a nice profit. But, it was a storm warning for Mattel.

In the late 1960s and early 1970s, it had seemed as though Mattel could do no wrong. Its stock reached a high of $52.50 on the New York Stock Exchange in 1971, and an official Mattel publication boasted that "the impossible is really possible." It was the "little toy company that could." The Handlers, especially Ruth, were overly optimistic; a former member of Mattel's marketing department recalled: "Ruth thought there was no limit to what Mattel could accomplish. She'd encourage unbelievably optimistic projections. It was a game of hyperbole with us, but I think she really fell for it." And most of Wall Street and the investment public did too—at least for a time.

Mattel's decline actually began in 1970, but neither the company nor the bankers were aware of it. Their first big problem, a fire in the Mexico plant that year, was followed the next year by a shipping strike which cut off the flow of toys from the Hong Kong plant. These setbacks affected sales, but when the firm's report came out, it claimed a profit of $17 million for 1971. The claim was a lie. The company had recorded $14 million in fictional or tentative sales and had conveniently pushed ahead about $5 million in expenses. Beyond that, the diversification strategy of the late 1960s was coming unraveled. The Handlers appreciated the enormous success that toys had brought their firm, but they had wanted to smooth out the boom-and-bust cycles of that industry by bringing Mattel into the leisure-time and entertainment fields. They hired Seymour Rosenberg, formerly of Litton Industries, one of America's first conglomerates, as executive vice president. Rosenberg was hired to find acquisitions for Mattel. He picked up a film production company; Ringling Brothers, Barnum & Bailey Circus; Metaframe, an aquarium manufacturer; and Monogram, a maker of hobbyist kits. In 1972 Mattel began to build a $50-million Circus World theme park in Florida. Many of these acquisitions were unsuccessful, at least in the short run.

Vast amounts were being spent on mergers and acquisitions, sales were declining, and profits were dropping. Mattel's management, which had always been lean, became bloated, as layer after layer of middle management was added. As a result, Mattel could not even bring out the kind of simple, ingenious toys that had made them successful in the past. But Ruth Handler and the other executives refused to admit the obvious. Bankers and Wall Street investors were becoming increasingly skeptical. In February 1973, Mattel finally admitted a "substantial loss"—which came to some $32.4 million. Worse, it was discovered that Rosenberg and Ruth Handler, while reassuring the public that everything was rosy at Mattel, were secretly unloading their stock—80,000 shares by Rosenberg and 16,600 by Ruth Handler. The Securities and Exchange Commission (SEC) brought suit against Mattel, Elliot and Ruth Handler, and Seymour Rosenberg. In analyzing the situation, the *Wall Street Journal* (June 20, 1973) made the following snide comment: "Have you heard about Mattel, Inc.'s latest talking doll? Wind it up and it forecasts a 100 percent increase in sales and profits. Then it falls flat on its face." Mattel's stock was selling for $2 a share.

In September 1974, the Handlers, despite their 29-percent holding in Mattel, were thrown out of the company. The firm's bankers and creditors took control of Mattel and slowly began to coax it back into the black. They brought in Arthur S. Spear, a former Revlon executive, to head up the company. For about four years he patiently rebuilt Mattel into a profitable unit through electronic toys. Mattel emphasized games involving major spectator sports—football, baseball, hockey, and soccer—but its most promising product was Intellivision. Spear made a number of acquisitions to strengthen the company. In 1979, he bought Western Publishing, a book publisher with $300 million in sales. As one industry analyst said about Spear's efforts: "This is a company that's come back from the dead.'' Another said Spear's rescue efforts with Mattel were like the ''reassembly of a doll after it had been flattened by a truck.''

In the meantime, the Handlers faced five class action suits and an investigation by the SEC. After the investigation, Elliot Handler was not indicted, but Ruth was. In 1978 she pleaded nolo contendere to charges of false reporting to the SEC, fraud, and conspiracy. She received a suspended sentence of forty-one years in prison, was fined $57,000, and was ordered to perform 2,500 hours of community service. Ruth Handler claimed she made the plea because ''I wanted to put the whole thing behind me,'' but she was bitter and felt that ''they went after the wrong people.'' She refused to name the ''right people,'' but she declared little love for Arthur Spear.

Ruth Handler bounced back from the SEC investigation and its repercussions and then some. In 1970, she had lost a breast to cancer. She remembered feeling at the time: ''I looked at the shapeless blob that lay in the bottom of my brassiere and thought, ''My God, the people in this business are men who don't have to wear these damn things.'' So, she started a new company—Ruthton, Inc.—in 1974 with Peyton Massey, a Los Angeles sculptor who specialized in custom-made prosthetics, to make artificial breasts. A unique product—her breast form was a liquid silicone enclosed in polyurethane with a rigid foam backing—it became what has been called ''the Cadillac of the business,'' and Ruthton was very successful, if small. Ruth Handler seemed to have few regrets. ''I don't want a mahogany row with its back stabbing and power struggles,'' she said. ''I had a big fat dream for Mattel and I watched it turn into a nightmare. I'm not going to let that happen again.''

Mattel itself continued to grow in the 1980s, but not fast enough; it was soon eclipsed by Hasbro Toys (see Stephen Hassenfeld). With sales of over $1 billion in 1987, Mattel suffered a 4-percent drop, along with a loss in earnings of $133 million, nearly four times the loss suffered by the Handlers in 1972–1973. Its growth rate from 1983 to 1987 was only 2.1 percent, compared to nearly 80 percent over this same period for Hasbro. Little girls were not playing with Barbie as much or for as many years as before. Hot Wheels had a lot of competition, and hand-held electronic games had been battered by video and computer versions.

Somehow, the image of Barbie seems to hang over the firm—Mattel is the ''Barbie Company.'' And maybe that image is all wrong for the 1980s. Joyce Maynard talked about what Barbie represented:

Barbie may always have represented everything in American culture that its critics hated— accessorizing life, as her costumers did, in terms of football games and proms and trips to the beauty parlor, tantalizing little girls with more and more things to buy, and all of them outdated, if not downright broken, by the following Christmas. I always knew, when I played with my Barbie, that if she were a real girl she would be the kind of girl who passed notes about me in study hall, who glided past me on the dance floor while I sat partnerless, . . . In real life, I knew Barbie would never have been my friend.

(**A.** Elliot Handler, *The Impossible Really Is Possible*, 1968. **B.** Inez McClintock, *Toys in America*, 1961; *Business Week*, August 2, 1969, May 16, 1977, June 20, 1988; *Who's Who in America*, 1970–71, 1974; Marvin Kay, *The Story of Monopoly, Silly Putty, Bingo, Twister, Frisbee, Scrabble, Etc.*, 1973; *Wall Street Journal*, June 20, 1973, March 14, 1985, May 26, July 7, October 20, 1987, June 4, 1988; *Who's Who in Finance & Industry*, 1975; *Forbes*, March 1, 1976, July 11, 1988; *Across the Board*, December 1976; *Financial World*, September 15, 1979; *Fortune*, September 8, 1980, April 25, 1988; Thomas E. Hudgeons, ed., *The Official 1985 Price Guide to Antique and Modern Dolls*, 1985; *Theriault's Presents Barbie: A Value Guide and Description*, 1985; Toronto *Globe & Mail*, October 7, 1985; *The Atlantic Monthly*, October 1986; Billy Boy, *Barbie: Her Life and Times*, 1987; Charles J. Jordan, *The Official Guide to Collectibles of the '50's & '60's*, 1987; *Toronto Star*, July 31, 1988; Ethlie Ann Vare and Greg Ptacek, *Mothers of Invention: From the Bra to the Bomb*, 1988.)

HARPER, CHARLES MICHAEL (MIKE) (September 26, 1926–   ). Food processor, ConAgra, Incorporated. Big, six-foot-six-inch Mike Harper is no shrinking violet. Yet after spending twenty years working his way to the top of the poultry division at Pillsbury, he sold it off in 1974, thus eliminating his own position. Although Pillsbury offered him another division to run, Harper demurred. Harper put the word out in the food industry—he wanted his own company to run. Before long he got it—ailing ConAgra, Incorporated, which was in debt to the tune of $136 million, and which most analysts felt would slip into bankruptcy. Harper joined the firm in 1974 as executive vice president, but he moved up to the presidency within a year. He thereupon began a dizzying overhaul of ConAgra's operations. With sales of $636 million in 1974, it had lost $12 million. By 1987 ConAgra had sales of $9 billion, an increase of 1,315 percent in thirteen years, an average of more than 100 percent annually. Profits in 1987 were $149 million, up 41 percent from the year before, and the firm had averaged a 17-percent annual growth rate of earnings per share during the previous several years. In 1983, Harper commented to skeptics about his plans for ConAgra: "You can laugh all the way home about a bunch of damn nuts who wanted to become the best food company in the country, but we knew we had a very good pattern in place."

Mike Harper was born in Lansing, Michigan, attended Purdue University, where he got a degree in mechanical engineering in 1949, and then went to the University of Chicago for his MBA in 1950. Upon graduation he spent four years at the Oldsmobile division of General Motors in the engineering department before he joined Pillsbury. Harper worked his way up through the ranks at Pillsbury, becoming vice president of research, development, and new products in 1965. In 1970, he became group vice president of the poultry division where he served until he liquidated it. In 1974 he moved to the Omaha, Nebraska, headquarters of ConAgra.

ConAgra originated in 1919 as Nebraska Consolidated Mills, an amalgamation of four Nebraska flour mills. For the next twenty-two years it operated only in Nebraska, but in the 1940s it added new product lines and expanded into other states. Long a flour miller with no consumer products, under the guidance of J. Allan Mactier it obtained the license to use the Duncan Hines label in the early 1950s for a line of cake mixes that was very successful. After Nebraska Consolidated rose to the number two position in cake mixes, Procter & Gamble, which wanted to enter the cake mix field, bought the Duncan Hines division in 1956 for $5 million. With that money, Mactier took the firm into new fields, such as fresh poultry and eggs, and catfish farming. But, by 1974, the firm (by then called ConAgra) was in deep trouble because of poor judgment. ConAgra had made several questionable acquisitions, but its most serious error was in massive speculation, especially in soybeans. These overwhelming losses forced out Mactier as head of the firm and paved the way for Mike Harper to take over.

Harper reflected that, in the first year at ConAgra, "the challenge was survival." In order to survive, he had to move ruthlessly. Real estate that was not absolutely essential to the firm's operations was sold off, as was a promising grocery distribution business. By the end of the year, some twenty-five different assets had been divested, reducing the total debt by $35 million, and sophisticated financial controls had been instituted. By 1976, said Harper, "We had gone through hell and won." At that point Harper embarked upon his strategy for building the company by acquisition. He looked for bargain-basement acquisitions in the food industry. Picking up commodity food producers, Harper plunged into grain distribution, and built it into a 400-million-bushel business. In 1979, he bought an agricultural chemical distribution company for just $14 million, and over the next several years he built the fertilizer distribution business into a significant entity.

Besides these critical, short-term solutions, Harper instituted a new corporate culture at ConAgra. He hired the best managers available, recruiting several people from Pillsbury. He commented on the situation at ConAgra: "Environment is critical. We ask our people regularly: 'Do you feel free to tell your boss to go to hell?' " By 1980, Harper had stabilized ConAgra sufficiently that he was ready to reshape the firm totally through key acquisitions.

Harper's first major purchase was Banquet Frozen Foods from RCA. The giant electronics firm had bought Banquet in 1970 for $116.5 million, but had managed it very poorly over the decade, and had not introduced a new food product during its ten years of ownership. RCA asked $250 million for Banquet, which was still the number-one-selling frozen-food brand, but found no interested parties. Harper offered RCA $50 million. With no other buyers in sight, RCA accepted the offer. Harper recruited the president of Campbell Soup's Swanson frozen-food division, John B. Phillips, to overhaul Banquet. Phillips revamped the packaging, halted discounting procedures, established Banquet as a solid, mid-priced dinner, and introduced dozens of new products. By 1986, Phillips had brought out ninety new products, and Banquet dominated what is called the "value" side of the frozen-dinner business, that is, good quality but cheap dinners. As a Banquet executive commented: "When you ask consumers what brand they buy, they usually mention high-priced brands. But people put on raincoats and hats and sneak out to load up on Banquet pot pies." Furthermore, the timely Banquet acquisition came just as America's habits and life-styles were changing. Between 1979 and 1985, frozen-food sales at supermarkets increased 60 percent, as smaller families with two incomes and microwave ovens created a greater demand for such products.

By 1983, Banquet was earning $25 million on sales of $400 million, and, in the words of an industry analyst, "That acquisition paid for itself in three years." With that company producing well, Harper, in 1982, pursued Peavey Company, a massive Minneapolis flour-milling company. Purchasing it for $165 million, Harper began to integrate Peavey's system of eighty grain elevators in fourteen Midwestern and Western states into ConAgra's system. The purchase of Peavey also gave ConAgra access to the grain export market for the first time, and it made ConAgra the number-one flour miller in the United States, with 18 percent of the market. By the mid–1980s ConAgra's Peavey division was also the nation's largest publicly held grain trader (which was important for securing the lowest possible feed prices for its poultry operations). Although Peavey remained one of the weakest links in the ConAgra system, Harper moved to offset its deficiencies in the domestic market by buying a number of international trading houses, like San Francisco's Berger & Company and Woodward & Dickerson of Bryn Mawr, Pennsylvania. This allowed ConAgra to move grain abroad when sales and prices were sluggish at home.

In 1982, Harper created Country Poultry, Incorporated with British-based Imperial Foods, Ltd., in a fifty-fifty venture, which cost ConAgra just $18 million. Two years later, ConAgra bought out Imperial's half for an additional $18 million. This was, ironically, the poultry unit Harper had run at Pillsbury, and had sold to Imperial for $20 million in 1974. Country Poultry was, by that time, the largest poultry producer in the United States, and as an industry source commented on the acquisition: "It wasn't a steal, it was a holdup." Harper built up the poultry business by stressing a brand name, following the precedent set by Frank Perdue[†] and his poultry business in the New York City area. Whereas in 1980 ConAgra has concentrated on selling unidentified chickens as a commodity in the market, which accounted for 80 percent of its poultry sales, by 1985 only 15 percent of its poultry sales were unbranded. An official noted "We've become more of a food manufacturer than a processor," as they sold larger and larger numbers of packaged chicken parts, chicken hot dogs, and chicken for fast-food chains, especially Burger King. ConAgra's Country Pride brand became the sales leader in New England and the Middle West, but it avoided head-to-head competition with Perdue in New York because of the high advertising costs involved. In 1985, ConAgra's poultry business earned about $95 million; it had about 10 percent of the market and processed about 1.2 billion pounds of chicken.

One of Harper's most significant and daring acquisitions came in 1983, when he bought Armour Foods from Greyhound Corporation. As usual, Harper bought Armour at a bargain price. The company was in a down cycle, as was the entire red-meat industry, and Harper paid just $182 million for the firm, a price just slightly above book value. Although the red-meat industry was a business fraught with high costs and labor problems, it balanced the poultry cycle well, and Harper subtly dealt with some of the labor problems—he waited for Greyhound to shut down some of its high-wage, unionized plants before closing the deal. In this way, Harper not only eliminated about 40 percent of the unionized workers in one stroke, but also avoided a master contract on wages and work rules for the plants. Harper then set about refashioning Armour in the ConAgra image. He split Armour's brands into five groups. Although sales of some of the products declined, profits rose significantly. The Armour acquisition also gave ConAgra another established frozen-dinner line, the Dinner Classics brand, which was the second-best seller in the high-quality end of the business. Not all the Armour groups did equally well; the processed meats unit suffered losses for several years. By the late 1980s Harper had still not succeeded in turning this area around.

In the summer of 1986, Harper made another important acquisition. He picked up Del Monte Frozen Foods, which added three more important brands to ConAgra's roster—Chun King Chinese Foods, Patio Mexican Food, and Morton's, a frozen-dinner competitor of Banquet. Del Monte also had a much better distribution system for these frozen-food products in the East than ConAgra, which was very beneficial. Harper's next big acquisition was Monfort of Colorado, Incorporated, the third-largest beef producer in the United States, in March 1987. Purchased for $365 million in stock, Monfort had sales of $2 billion in 1986, and, as *Business Week* (May 18, 1987) commented, with this purchase, "Harper has pushed ConAgra into the big leagues." A number of analysts, however, were skeptical, since the beef industry was declining as consumers' tastes were changing. That was the reason, in fact, why Monfort was willing to sell to ConAgra, feeling it could cushion itself against cyclical changes in the beef market if it were positioned within a large food conglomerate like ConAgra. And Harper's goal for ConAgra was to have a broad spectrum of businesses to cushion the company against problems in any one sector.

Harper continued his bold policy of acquisitions in 1988. In November he offered to acquire Holly Farms, the massive Memphis-based producer of processed chicken, with a stock exchange valued at $1 billion. Management at Holly Farms, who had approached ConAgra as a "white knight" to protect it from a hostile takeover, was receptive, but the board did not give its decision until January 1989. In December 1988, Harper purchased Pillsbury's grain merchandising division, which consisted of fifty grain elevators and about 200 river barges. These acquisitions made ConAgra, with nearly $10 billion in revenues, one of the premier food consolidations in America.

From the very beginning, Harper stressed to everyone at ConAgra that he wanted them to be the "best damn food company in the United States." By 1988 he had pretty well achieved that objective by following a number of important policies. The first was decentralization. Although Harper made the big strategic decisions for ConAgra, he left day-to-day decision making to the unit managers. As one of the ConAgra executives has commented: "The corporate culture stresses individual growth of people and delegates to operators a lot of responsibility. Our people run these businesses and make decisions themselves, but it's done within an overall structure of agreed goals." Harper also runs a lean, no-frills operation. There are no fancy titles, no large staffs, and none of the other forms of bureaucracy at ConAgra. As Harper has said, "When people surround themselves with huge staffs, they start craving power. That's not what we're about."

Although ConAgra is, as one executive said, "acquisition-driven," it also "sticks to its knitting" in some fundamental respects. The most important principle is that the proposed acquisition must be in (or closely related to) the food industry. This is the business they know, and they are comfortable making decisions about it. The vice president of corporate planning for ConAgra has explained that, although the company's acquisitions might look quite diffuse, "We look for a good fit within the broad food industry's spectrum or allied product lines." He hastened to add, however, that, "Basically, we will look at the food business from the farmer's gate to the consumer's stomach," which gives a lot of latitude.

Almost everyone agrees, however, that ConAgra's most important asset in its climb to the top of the food industry has been the remarkable skills of Mike Harper. Affable, but hard-driving, he has generally been considered a maverick in the industry. But all recognize his talent and genius. As the head of mergers and acquisitions for Morgan Stanley & Corporated of New York commented about Harper, "He has no peers when it comes to dealmaking." An official at ConAgra stated emphatically, "Much of ConAgra's success has to be credited to Mike Harper." Ken Monfort, head of Monfort of Colorado, said when he sold his firm to ConAgra: "The man knows how to do business, they're the 'big friend' I was looking for." Quite a transformation for a low-profile maker of feed, flour, and poultry. As the food industry analyst for Goldman, Sachs commented, "By the time Harper's through, he'll be running one of the largest food companies in the world." (B. Milton Moskowitz et al., *Everybody's Business*, 1980; *Business Week*, December 1, 1980, December 19, 1983, May 18, 1987; *Forbes*, December 8, 1980, October 24, 1983; *Prepared Foods*, September 1985; *Fortune*, October 27, 1986; Toronto *Globe & Mail*, November 18, December 3, 1988.)

HASSENFELD, STEPHEN DAVID (January 19, 1942–June 25, 1989). Toy manufacturer, Hasbro Toys. Most toy manufacturers either come into the business by accident, or come into it from another occupation. Few grow up totally immersed in toys. But Stephen Hassenfeld, the third generation of his family in the business, lived his entire life surrounded by toys. His father, Merrill Hassenfeld, head of Hasbro Toys throughout his working life, was a widely admired man in the toy industry. As a result, Stephen and his brother, Alan, had lots of toys when they were growing up. Other toy manufacturers, to show respect for their father, showered the Hassenfeld boys with toys. The head of Lionel, the famous maker of electric trains, listed young Stephen as one of his salesmen, so that every time a new train or accessory came out, Stephen received a sample. Stephen soon had one of the world's most spectacular train sets in his basement. Little wonder that he knew from the time he was very young exactly what he wanted to be—a toy maker.

Hasbro (the name stands for Hassenfeld Brothers) had a unique beginning. The business was founded in 1923 by two brothers, Henry and Hillel Hassenfeld. They had started out in the rag trade, selling what could charitably be called "textile by-products." Soon, however, Henry Hassenfeld found that he could make more money with his rags if he wrapped them around pencil boxes, so he began to make and sell pencil cases. This was a success for a number of years. When pencil suppliers began raising the price of pencils, the Hassenfelds started their own pencil company, called Empire Pencil. They sold their pencils and pencil cases primarily to buyers of school supplies.

During World War II, it was difficult for toy manufacturers to get manufacturing supplies, so Hasbro, which called on the same buyers, seized the opportunity to begin making toys. It brought out a number of successful lines of toys during these early years; the most popular was Mr. Potato Head. But the brothers had very distinct differences as to which end of the business each preferred. One wanted to emphasize the pencil side; the other wanted to stress toys. The result was a long-term clash between the two sides of the family about goals, financing, and operational details. Empire Pencil, which became the nation's largest pencil manufacturer, understandably wanted Hasbro to concentrate its resources on protecting Empire's position in the pencil market. Hasbro Toy, on the other hand, as one of the smaller toy makers, felt it was necessary to spend a good deal of money on research, development, and acquisition if it were to compete successfully in that volatile business. A huge argument erupted at one point, for example, when the pencil company wanted funds to develop a plastic pencil, and the toy group demanded funds be spent on their product.

Nonetheless, the firm's founder, Henry Hassenfeld, was able to keep relative peace between the two feuding factions until his death in 1960. After that, the bickering intensified. Harold L. Hassenfeld, chairman of Hasbro and head of Empire Pencil, had long resented the fact that the pencil company earned greater profits than the toy firm, but he saw a significant percentage of these spent on developing toys. Merrill Hassenfeld, head of the toy company, tried hard to keep peace in the family for a number of years. Suddenly, in 1964, Hasbro's world was turned upside down. In that year, the toy company had a new toy that was a resounding success. The new toy was G.I. Joe, which virtually created the action-figure market. It was also the first doll successfully developed for boys, rivaling the phenomenal success of Mattel's Barbie doll for girls (see Elliot and Ruth Handler). Representing some 65 percent of Hasbro Toy's sales, G.I. Joe catapulted the company into the ranks of the major toy companies for the first time.

But in the 1970s, G.I. Joe became a victim of the war in Vietnam; more precisely, it ran afoul of the antiwar sentiment created by the war. Toy guns and soldiers, along with other war toys, had long been part of the toy scene. Since most people felt toys were just toys and that playing with dolls or guns was essentially harmless, few gave much thought to the implications. In the early 1970s, however, the idea took root that toys had a deeper meaning, that they were a reflection of evil elements of American culture. The theory went that if young boys played with guns and war toys they would grow up with a war lust. So retailers were pressured to remove G.I. Joe and other war toys from their shelves, and G.I. Joe's sales fell from $23 million in 1965 to just $7.5 million in 1970. At about the same time, the Arab oil embargo drastically increased the price of plastic, and in 1978 Hasbro announced that G.I. Joe was being "furloughed," and it took him off the market for four years.

In an attempt to diversify its offerings in the face of growing antiwar sentiment, Hasbro, in 1969, purchased the "Romper Room" television show, and began turning out a line of Romper Room toys and furniture to appeal to the preschool market, a market which until this time had been almost totally dominated by Fisher-Price (see Herman Fisher and Irving Price) and Playskool. Stephen Hassenfeld, at that time a twenty-nine-year-old vice president of the firm, was put in charge of pushing the Romper Room line. He recognized that it was a difficult situation: "This is a fiercely competitive industry, and promotion is one very important key." With sales of $45 million in 1970, Hasbro lost nearly $1 million, primarily because of distribution problems. Strife between the two sides of the family nearly caused a split between the pencil company and the toy firm in 1970, and it greatly interfered with Hassenfeld's ability to pursue his goals.

Stephen Hassenfeld had dropped out of Johns Hopkins University in 1963 to join his father's toy company, and he was given positions of increasing responsibility during the later 1960s, culminating in his assignment with the Romper Room division. In 1974 Merrill Hassenfeld appointed Stephen president of Hasbro Toy, and the younger Hassenfeld made a number of nearly fatal mistakes in running the company during these years. Two of his worst decisions involved moving Hasbro into day-care centers and housewares. Both ventures were closed down within a few years. *Business Week* (September 22, 1986) noted that, from 1975 to 1978, Hassenfeld "hobbled the company with strict rules, including a return-on-investment analysis for each proposed toy. Not many of the toys got into production." Stephen, recognizing that he had made a number of mistakes, told *Esquire*:

I'm firmly convinced that if my father had operated the business as a father normally would, with him making the decisions, we would have done better through the 1970s.

But he wanted to make sure we learned, so he threw Alan and me in over our heads and let us make mistakes. I made some pretty significant ones.

When Merrill Hassenfeld died in 1979, Harold Hassenfeld, who was still running the family's Empire Pencil firm in Shelbyville, Tennessee, refused to recognize Stephen as chief executive of Hasbro Industries. Stephen Hassenfeld went to the Toy Fair in 1979 and was treated with disdain by toy retailers and other toy manufacturers. He recalled, "You could see it in their eyes . . . Hasbro is a has-been." Hasbro did not have a single electronic game in their catalog, at a time when those games were the most innovative products in the industry, and it had lost $2.5 million on sales of $74 million the year before. But young Hassenfeld was determined to change that state of affairs. The following decade witnessed one of the greatest success stories in the history of American industry.

Even before the crisis in 1979, Hassenfeld had resolved that he would turn the company around. In 1977, he took account of himself and the company he was going to inherit: "I was 35 years old and I thought to myself: 'You've been at this for 20 years now and it's not better. Is this where you want to spend the rest of your professional career? If it's going to be a roller coaster maybe you should cash in your chips now.' " He decided to persevere, but having made that decision, he had to articulate a coherent policy. He asked himself the toughest question of all: why were other firms successful in the toy industry, while Hasbro was not? The answer was that Hasbro lacked discipline. It was trying to compete in too many areas, and trying to bring out too many products each year, to compete in every corner of the toy market. Hassenfeld recognized that "firms of our size, in this industry, can't bring this many products to market and give each element of every product the kind of tender, loving care it must have."

Hassenfeld took his analysis even further. He noted that the most successful firms in the industry, like Fisher-Price, specialized in product lines. Hasbro, on the other hand, had tried to bring out every kind of toy for every age child. Hassenfeld decided to limit Hasbro's product line to three sharply defined niches—preschool toys, 3-D skill and action games, and design toys like Lite-Brite. Marginal toys were eliminated. This action precipitated dramatic results. In the three years after 1978, Hassenfeld reduced the product line from 180 to 120, and new product introductions were cut in half. By 1980, Hasbro was prosperous, earning $4.6 million on sales of $104 million. Amazingly, this was accomplished without ever entering the electronic game market—a segment of the industry that went bust in the early 1980s.

Once the toy company was on an even footing Stephen Hassenfeld could approach his uncle, Harold Hassenfeld, and propose that the pencil company and the toy company pursue separate paths. Whenever this had been proposed in the past, the problem had always been the weakness of the toy firm's sales and profit position vis-à-vis the pencil company. From 1975 to 1979, the pencil company had grown at an annual rate of 14 percent, compared to just 8 percent for the toy company. Furthermore, Empire contributed a much larger proportion of the profits (43 percent) compared to its percentage of sales (27 percent). Consequently, Harold Hassenfeld and his family allies had never accepted such a proposal. But Stephen Hassenfeld made Hasbro Toy into a consistent profit maker, which by September 1980 had experienced six straight quarters of profits. As a result, Harold Hassenfeld agreed to tender all his Hasbro shares for Stephen's shares in the new Empire Pencil Company, and the two companies were finally divided. Hasbro Toy would no longer have the consistent profits of the pencil company to fall back on, but Stephen Hassenfeld was now free to pursue the policies that he felt would benefit the firm.

By the mid–1980s his achievements were astoundingly successful, and analysts considered Hasbro Toy to be the fastest growing and best-managed firm in the toy industry. It was also one of the most profitable firms in America. With growth from 1979 to 1988 at an astounding 85 percent annually, a $1,000 investment in Hasbro stock in 1976 would have been worth $152,633 in June 1986. Only two *Fortune* 500 companies have achieved such a high rate of profits. As Thomas R. Kully, a toy industry analyst, said, "Forget size, Hasbro [which was then seventh largest in sales] is a far better company with a lot more momentum than many of its competitors with larger sales." With sales of over $300 million in 1984, it was three times larger than it had been when Hassenfeld began his rescue program five years before.

Hassenfeld's first big success was his 1982 reintroduction of G.I. Joe. It had originally been marketed in 1964 as a World War II–era infantryman; in 1970, it was turned into a cadre of quasi-military "adventurers." When Hassenfeld reintroduced the doll, it returned as a smaller, less militaristic figure. No longer billed as "a fighting man from head to toe," it was now called just "a real American hero." The new G.I. Joe racked up $49 million in sales the first year, and had become the nation's best-selling toy in the second half of the year. Sales of the doll continued to increase in successive years—to $86 million in 1983, $132 million in 1984, and $136 million in 1985. At the same time, however, Hassenfeld was determined that Hasbro would not become as dependent on G.I. Joe as it had been in the 1960s. Consequently, he expanded Hasbro's business so much that G.I. Joe's sales, which represented 36 percent of the company's revenue in 1982, had dropped to just 11 percent in 1985, even though its sales were over three times greater. Hassenfeld accomplished this transition in a number of ways.

In 1983, he sold 37 percent of the company to Warner Communications for $36 million. As part of the deal, Hasbro got $14.5 million in cash and the rights to licenses from Warner's Knickerbocker Toys subsidiary. This brought Hasbro the venerable Raggedy Ann (then about seventy years old) and Raggedy Andy dolls for their line. Hasbro entered the "plush" toy field for the first time, whereupon a whole new area of sales, amounting to some $24 million in 1984, emerged. This was achieved without diluting Hassenfeld's control of the firm, since the Warner shares were put into a trust controlled by Stephen and his brother Alan, which the brothers voted for the next seven years.

Hassenfeld took an even more dramatic step in 1984, however, when he purchased the Milton Bradley Company for $360 million. The maker of such games as Candyland, Chutes and Ladders, and the Game of Life, it also owned the Playskool line, which gave Hasbro far greater market penetration in the preschool field than before. Raymond Wagner, head of Mattel's toy business, was impressed: "You're putting together the two companies in the industry with the strongest balance sheets." The merger rocketed Hasbro's sales to $760 million, vaulting it past longtime industry leader Mattel. Hassenfeld also picked up Glenco Infant Items in 1983 for $13 million, giving the firm products such as spill-proof cups and bibs.

Not all of Hasbro's success came from acquisitions. Important products were developed internally. The most successful of these were the Transformers—an array of robots that could be reshaped into cars and trucks, and back into robots. This gave Hasbro a more balanced range of products. As a result, profits surged by 117 percent in 1983 to $15.2 million. Hassenfeld commented at the time: "I had always thought we were big league, now I know that we were just triple-A baseball, and we've only just become major league." As a result of the merger with Milton Bradley, Hassenfeld split Hasbro into three divisions: Hasbro Toy, Milton Bradley, and Playskool, giving each of the divisions what he called "almost total autonomy."

One of Hassenfeld's most daring moves came in 1986 when he introduced Jem, a rock star doll that directly challenged Mattel's fabulously successful Barbie doll. Jem was aimed at the younger kids who were watching rock videos on MTV. Feeling that these videos had introduced these young girls to a whole new way of thinking about fashion, Jem was designed to reflect that interest. The Jem dolls and the commercials that promoted them, became so popular that Hasbro developed Jem's own regular Saturday morning cartoon series; each show contained its own original songs presented in the form of "videos." After this initial success, in which 7 million dolls were sold, however, the Jem doll was removed from the shelves after two years. Barbie had beaten off yet another contender. As Daniel Leibowitz, an industry analyst commented: "Don't go head-to-head with Barbie unless you have a product that's clearly delineated, clearly differentiated."

Nonetheless, in 1988, Hassenfeld brought out Maxie, a virtual Barbie clone, to compete with Barbie. Maxie was designed to be seventeen, beautiful, with blonde hair. As *Business Week* (July 18, 1988) noted: "She's into the beach, shopping malls, and her husky California boyfriend, Rob." Hasbro executives admitted that Maxie was a clear concession to the Barbie standard, but many people in the industry thought it was too much like Barbie. A nine-year-old girl in Miami raised a disquieting point about Maxie when it was introduced: "I love Barbie dolls, and I want more. I want Maxie, but Mom might think 'Why spend money on a doll that's just like Barbie?' " A risky strategy, perhaps, but one designed to reverse a downward slide in Hasbro's profits. In 1987, after a decade of remarkable performance, Hasbro's profits were cut in half, from $99 million to $48 million. Sales remained flat, at $1.3 billion. It was clear that something had to be done, but no one was convinced that Maxie was the answer to Hasbro's woes. But Hassenfeld, who grew up surrounded by a wonderful world of toys, remained committed to them: "Whenever the investment community asks what I'm going to do next, I've replied: 'The grass isn't greener elsewhere; it's greenest right here.' "

To Stephen Hassenfeld, toys and games were not fun; they were part of a grim battle. He was a workaholic who rose at 5:30 A.M. and rarely quit work before midnight. He left the "playing" to parents, teachers, and children who volunteer to test his new products. An exceedingly driven man, Hassenfeld always felt he was being tested. A bachelor, he found "his challenges—and his joys—in generating profits for Hasbro." He told the *New York Times*: "I won't say I've been tested as a manager in the last five years. The test for me is in the future."

On February 13, 1989, the New Toy Fair kicked off its festivities with a thirtieth anniversary gala honoring Barbie. Held at Lincoln Center, it was a black-tie affair with champagne for 700 guests. Even though it was the twenty-fifth anniversary of G.I. Joe, neither he nor Hassenfeld were invited since G.I. Joe had not put in twenty-five years of continuous service. A Hasbro executive sniffed: "Frivolous. . . . We asked Joe; he said he just wanted to go out drinking with his buddies." For both G.I. Joe and Stephen Hassenfeld, the toy business was war. But for Hassenfeld, the war was over, as he died four months later in New York City at age forty-seven. (**B.** *Business Week*, March 13, 1971, September 15, 1980, May 21, 1984, September 22, 1986, March 14, June 20, July 18, 1988, February 13, 1989; *Forbes*, May 25, 1981; *Industry Week*, April 30, 1984; *New York Times*, February 2, August 4, 1985; *Chain Store Age*, March 1985; *Financial World*, April 30, 1985; *Atlantic Monthly*, October 1986; *Esquire*, December 1986; *Contemporary Newsmakers*, 1987; *Supplement to Who's Who in America*, 1987–88; *Fortune*, April 25, 1988; *Toronto Star*, July 31, 1988; *Newsweek*, February 20, 1989.)

HEFNER, HUGH MARSTON (April 9, 1926–   ) and **CHRISTINE ANN (CHRISTIE) HEFNER** (November 8, 1952–   ). Publishers, entrepreneurs, and business executives, Playboy Enterprises. Bill Davidson interviewed Hugh Hefner for an article in *Saturday Evening Post* in 1962. While visiting Hefner in his office, Davidson watched him review pictures of prospective centerfolds. Davidson commented, "I saw him leafing through dozens of these portfolios. He kept grunting and commenting, 'Too flat,' or 'Too big in the rear.' The scene had all the warmth of a restaurant proprietor selecting sides of beef for his establishment." Davidson noted that this scene was all part of a coherent whole, one that reflected the rather mindless sexism of the 1950s and 1960s. He said that Hefner's mansion had "the total effect . . . of a love temple in the last days of ancient Rome, as Cecil B. DeMille might have conceived it." Hefner, who had never been gregarious, withdrew increasingly to his bedroom as he became more successful. Shunning the daylight hours, he appeared at night, clad only in silk pajamas. Hefner exuded a smarmy sex appeal. Clenching a pipe between his teeth, with a youthful, adoring "bunny" on each arm, Hefner escorted guests into his bedroom, which was a technological wonderland. Filled with stereo equipment, a motion picture theater, eight television monitors, and a large round bed that revolved or vibrated at the touch of a button. "On top of the headboard," said Russell Miller in *Bunny*, "are four 'Magic Wand' vibrators by General Electric, all plugged in and ready to go." In a refrigerator nearby were champagne and Hefner's favorite drink—Pepsi Cola—of which he drank more than a dozen bottles daily. This life-style was designed to appeal to the adolescent fantasies of *Playboy*'s male readers.

Playboy magazine is one of the great publishing phenomena of the twentieth century. The first of what author Tom Wolfe has called "one-hand magazines," it began offering pictures of nude women to respectable middle-class readers in the 1950s. From these beginnings, Hugh Hefner built an enormous and profitable business empire, one that he handed over to his daughter, Christie, in 1982. A major reason for the success of *Playboy* was that Hefner linked sex with upward mobility. Previously, nudes and girlie magazines were the stuff of back alleys and disrepute, but Hefner consciously sought to make it part of a new, urbane, sophisticated, middle-class respectability. As he stated early on, "Our philosophy is that you should work hard and play hard, and strive to get into the sophisticated upper crust." Hugh Hefner and *Playboy* helped bring about a sexual revolution in America in the 1950s and 1960s, but he did not do this as a political or cultural radical. Rather, Hefner was an entrepreneur who simply extended the philosophy of consumer capitalism to the realm of sex.

Hefner himself spent his first twenty-six years in a dour, rather puritanical environment. He was born in Chicago, Illinois, the son of Glen and Grace (Swanson) Hefner, who had moved to the big city from Nebraska. Hefner's father was an accountant for an aluminum company, and both parents were strict Methodists who imposed rigid fundamentalist ethics on Hugh and his brother. There was no drinking, no smoking, no swearing, and no going to movies on Sunday. Most difficult for Hefner was their attitude toward sex, which was considered a dirty thing not to be mentioned in polite conversation. He commented, "My whole early life was a telescoping of the puritanical, unproductive years that the entire country went through. . . . I was never really free until the day my magazine was born. Before then I had lived through one series of restrictions after another."

As a result, Hugh Hefner entered adolescence as an introvert, occupying his time collecting butterflies and drawing comic strips. Only in his senior year of high school did Hefner begin to date girls and gain some popularity as a cartoonist for the school newspaper. Hefner graduated from high school in 1944 and immediately entered the U.S. Army, where he served as a company clerk until his discharge in 1946. He then enrolled at the University of Illinois, where he majored in psychology and contributed cartoons and articles to student publications. He married his college sweetheart upon graduation, but the marriage, according to Hefner, was a disaster from the beginning: "We had three unhappy years and two children, and the walls around me grew higher."

In the meantime, Hefner had to find a job to support himself and his new family. He worked as a personnel director for a small Chicago cardboard cartoon company, then as an advertising copywriter for a Chicago department store, and finally as a writer of subscription promotion copy for *Esquire* magazine. In 1952 *Esquire* asked him to move to New York and offered him a raise of $20 a week. Hefner's demand for an additional $5 weekly to make the move was refused by Clay Felker, editor of *Esquire*, and Hefner went out on his own. What happened next was one of the most successful, yet least predictable, experiments in journalism. Hefner decided that America was ready for a new kind of men's magazine, one which, like *Esquire*, catered to urbane tastes, but which would be more daring, especially in the area of sexuality. Hefner was broke and knew little about sex or the symbols of the good life, such as hi-fi's, sports cars, good food, and drink. Furthermore, it was not at all clear in 1952 that America, at the height of the political and cultural repression of McCarthyism, was ready for this kind of experiment. But Hefner was undaunted. In fact, he attacked the whole project with a messianic zeal, saying: "I began to work on it with everything I had, and for the first time in my life I felt free. It was like a mission—to publish a magazine that would thumb its nose at all the restrictions that had bound me."

Hefner financed the project with $600 of his own money (his entire life savings), and $10,000 raised by selling stock to friends. Working with his friend, Art Paul, who remained art director of *Playboy* for decades, they brought out the first issue of the magazine in December 1953, featuring the famous nude calendar photo of Marilyn Monroe, which Hefner had purchased the rights to for just $200. The issue quickly sold out its press run of 53,991 copies. Succeeding issues also sold out, and Hefner was on his way upward. *Playboy* moved to an office in downtown Chicago, where Hefner slept on a cot and spent nearly every waking hour getting the magazine out.

By 1960, Hefner had a budding publishing giant on his hands. Circulation exceeded one million, and *Playboy* had more than $2.3 million in advertising revenue. It had also taken on its characteristic form—nudes combined with intellectually significant articles and reviews of music, movies, food, and wine. In the early years, fiction in *Playboy* was limited to old, previously published stories. But as the magazine achieved success, it began to buy original short stories from some of America's leading literary figures. This gave a measure of intellectual cachet and sophistication to *Playboy* and greatly helped magazine sales. After all, if James Baldwin or Isaac Singer or Ken Purdy deigned to have their writings appear alongside pictures of nude women, could anyone begrudge a man reading the same material?

Then, too, Hefner's presentation of *Playboy*'s nudes was different from what had gone before. Whereas earlier "girlie" magazines featured women who epitomized a lower class, sleazy life-style, Hefner insisted upon beauty combined with freshness, wholesomeness, and the look of the "girl next door." All blemishes were airbrushed, and flattering lighting was used to create an illusion of perfection, a perfection that reflected the fantasies of both Hefner and his readers. That, of course, was the key. Hefner was not really selling either sex or nudes; he was selling fantasy. It appealed to the middle-class American male's twin daydream—easy, uncomplicated sex with beautiful, undemanding women, and upward mobility with all the accompanying creature comforts. Thus, not only did *Playboy* airbrush its centerfolds, it also refused ads for acne or other products that might suggest to its readers their shortcomings. As *Forbes* commented in 1971, "*Playboy* wants to sell its fantasy as a way of life."

Gay Talese, in *Thy Neighbor's Wife*, talked about the kind of men who were attracted to *Playboy* and its fantasy life:

They were the road salesmen in motel rooms, soldiers on bivouac, college boys in dormitories, airborne executives in whose attaché cases the magazine traveled like a covert companion. They were unfulfilled married men of moderate means and aspirations who were bored with their jobs, and who sought temporary escape through sexual adventure with more women than they had the ability to get.

Prior to *Playboy,* Talese noted, these men had seldom, if ever, seen a color photograph of a nude woman, and they were "overwhelmed and embarrassed as they bought *Playboy* at the newsstand." However embarrassed they might have been, these men continued to buy *Playboy*. Circulation increased from 60,000 copies a month to 400,000 in just two years. Hefner became, Talese said, "the first man to become rich by openly marketing masturbatory love through the illusion of an available alluring woman." Hefner wished to carry this fantasy to the ultimate, for himself and his readers.

To do so, Hefner soon branched into fields beyond publishing. His most stunning success came with Playboy Clubs International, a chain of nightclub-restaurants. The principal attraction at these clubs were the "bunnies," a play on the rabbit symbol adopted by *Playboy* from the very beginning. The bunnies were waitresses who dressed in flimsy costumes with exaggerated push-up bras and bunny tails. The bunnies were chosen, like centerfolds, for their beauty and wholesome appearance. And the code in the clubs, as with the magazine, was look but do not touch. A rigid (one is tempted to say puritanical) code of decorum was laid down for the bunnies. Thus, the customer entered yet another fantasy world when he was admitted to the Playboy Clubs. He was surrounded by beautiful women, whose costume suggested easy availability, yet it was nothing more than a fantasy—he was not allowed to do anything about it without the risk of being thrown out of the club. By the early 1970s, Hefner had a string of seventeen of what were then the world's most successful nightclubs.

Increasingly during this period, Hefner himself began living the fantasy life he pictured on *Playboy*'s pages. Heralding this as an "alternate life-style," some twenty-five to thirty bunnies lived at Hefner's mansions in both Chicago and Los Angeles, and rumors abounded of Hefner's sexual liaisons with them. Hefner never denied the rumors, and, by all accounts, they were most likely true. Hefner, in his "*Playboy* Philosophy," encouraged his readers to "enjoy the pleasures the female has to offer without becoming emotionally involved." He viewed marriage as a trap, and he urged his readers to spend their money on self-indulgence and luxurious living, rather than become one of the "sorry, regimented husbands trudging down every woman-dominated street in this woman-dominated land." Although nearly all of his readers did marry, *Playboy*, nonetheless, provided a fantasy life-style for them, and Hefner himself lived this fantasy to the fullest well into his sixties.

In the early 1970s, things began to sour for Hefner and the Playboy empire. First, there was the challenge of Robert Guccione[†] and his *Penthouse* magazine. Founded in Britain in the early 1960s, in 1969 Guccione's *Penthouse* invaded *Playboy*'s home turf. At that point *Playboy* had a circulation of five million, and had the men's magazine field virtually to itself. *Penthouse* made a huge dent in *Playboy*'s hegemony. Within a few years it had a circulation of nearly four million, and by the end of the seventies the two magazines were virtually tied. Furthermore, since *Penthouse* sold 95 percent of its magazines at the newsstand, while *Playboy* sold 40 percent by subscription (which entailed higher costs), Guccione's magazine earned higher profits. *Penthouse* challenged *Playboy* by being more daring in its pictures, showing pubic hair, and not airbrushing its models to make them look perfect. As America went through the throes of a sexual revolution that Hugh Hefner had played a major role in starting and publicizing, *Playboy* soon found it had been left by the wayside.

Hefner and *Playboy* at first refused to respond to the *Penthouse* challenge. But the full frontal nudity and generally more erotic tone of the latter publication was making huge inroads into *Playboy*'s circulation. Finally, in January 1972, Hefner decided to respond by showing pubic hair on *Playboy*'s centerfold. The changes in *Playboy* during the early 1970s amounted to a wrenching social revolution. After peace had been negotiated in Vietnam, and American prisoners of war had returned home, they were asked by reporters what changes they observed in America while they had been away. The reporters, undoubtedly expecting comments on profound social and cultural issues, were amazed when the ex-POWs, one after another, proclaimed that the most dramatic change they had noticed was that pubic hair could be seen on the *Playboy* centerfold.

The pubic wars were on. But, it was a war Hefner could not win. The erstwhile champion of sexual freedom in America had established his own standards of taste and decorum. Suddenly he was violating them. These were not some prudish Victorian restrictions, but principles Hefner himself had dictated. The reaction was swift. *Atlantic Monthly* wrote: "*Playboy* needs desperately to be accepted by reader and advertiser alike as an unobtrusive, overground publication that is part of the system." Since, they argued, it was *Playboy*'s central marketing strategy "to sell fantasies of women as powerless, grateful sexual slaves to men,'' displaying their pubic hair made them all too real and threatening to its readers. For two years, *Playboy* and *Penthouse* tried to outdo one another with increasingly explicit photographs. Finally, after *Playboy* ran a particularly explicit cover photo that received disapproving coverage in the media, Hefner conceded the contest. In *Playboy*'s Annual Report in 1975, he stated:

At present there are some 37 publications vying for a share of the male market.... Generally, they focus on only one of those [male] interests—sex—often exceeding the bounds of the most liberal of contemporary tastes. In these matters, our standard will be our own and will not be dictated by competitive pressures.

Deciding to stick to its 1950s definition of sexuality and eroticism, *Playboy* began to diversify further. This trend, which had begun in the 1960s with the Playboy clubs, continued in the 1970s with ventures into cable television with the Playboy channel, movies, and record production. None of these diversions were successful. The recession of the 1970s hit the Playboy hotels and nightclubs very hard, and only the proceeds from their five casinos curtailed the losses from being greater. The film ventures (Roman Polanski's *MacBeth* and a second film called the *Naked Ape*) lost millions, as did the record company. Pretax profits at Playboy Enterprises, which were running at $20 million in 1973, sank to just $2 million in 1975, before recovering slightly to $5 million in 1976. To put this in perspective, Playboy's four British gambling casinos earned $12 million in pretax profit in 1976, and the magazine earned $4 million (down from $23 million in 1973), as the rest of Playboy's concerns (hotels, clubs, movies, records) swam in oceans of red ink.

Hefner blamed these problems on the fact that he had stopped running the firm in 1968, entrusting its management to a number of associates. Many business analysts, however, felt the fault lay with Hefner himself and his idiosyncratic management style. In any event, it was clear that many of Playboy's operations had primitive accounting systems, so much so that their filings for the Securities and Exchange Commission were always late. Audits that took other businesses six weeks to prepare took Playboy three months. Hefner finally realized that he only really cared about the magazine and its content. He moved his mansion from Chicago to Los Angeles, where he spent his time clad in pajamas choosing centerfold pictures and reviewing editorial content. In 1977, when Hefner recognized that he needed help, he chose Derick Daniels, former vice president of Knight-Ridder Newspapers, as president and chief executive officer (CEO) of the Playboy empire. At the same time, Hefner's daughter, Christie, was promoted to vice president.

Daniels immediately set to work to jettison unprofitable segments of the bloated Playboy organization. The record business and several of the clubs and hotels were sold. This helped Playboy become profitable again, but then, lulled by continuing profits from gambling, the firm returned to its profligate ways. From 1976 to 1982, corporate overhead more than doubled, to $22 million. Then, in

1979, British police raided the London casino, where they discovered violations of the country's gaming laws and Playboy was forced to sell its British casino operations for $31 million. As a result, Playboy was refused a gaming license in Atlantic City, New Jersey.

The debacle had a devastating impact on Playboy, and it profoundly changed the management and operations of the company. At that point, Christie Hefner approached her father and pointed out to him that during Daniels' tenure the company had lost money steadily, except for the magazine and the casinos, neither of which was under Daniels' direct control. What, then, would happen now that the gambling revenues were gone? Hugh Hefner had an answer—he fired Daniels, and replaced him with his daughter. In making the announcement to the press, Hefner said: "She is simply the most remarkable twenty-nine-year-old I've ever met. We think very much alike." The elder Hefner remained as chairman of the board, and CEO, although it was clear to most observers that Christie would be piloting the craft.

Christie Hefner barely knew her father while she was growing up. Her mother and father had separated when she was only two years old, and in 1960 her mother had remarried. She visited her father for just brief periods at his mansion four or five times a year. After completing high school in Wilmette, Illinois, she entered Brandeis University. There she distinguished herself as a top notch student, being elected Phi Beta Kappa and graduating summa cum laude with a bachelor's degree in English and American literature in 1974. One of her professors remarked that she was "among the best students I've had in twenty-three years. . . . She was marvelously intelligent, sensitive, likable." While attending the university, she visited her father at the Playboy mansion in Los Angeles, and during these years their relationship grew closer. She had taken her step-father's name as a child, but, after her junior year in college, she told her father that she was taking the Hefner name again. She reported that he "got tears in his eyes and was real touched."

Following her graduation from Brandeis, Christie worked for a year at the Boston *Phoenix*, an alternative press newspaper, before joining Playboy Enterprises in 1975. Named a special assistant, she worked as her father's aide in the first few years. In her first assignment she was given charge of a boutique on the ground floor of the Playboy Building, selling clothing and records. It was, as Christie herself admitted, a "disaster," but primarily because the concept itself was flawed. She then worked for a while on magazine acquisitions, until she was promoted to vice president in 1977. In this position, Christie was told to concentrate on public relations, heading the promotion of *Playboy*'s twenty-fifth anniversary activities. In this capacity she was resoundingly successful, and an effective spokeswoman for the company. At a time when both Hugh Hefner and *Playboy* were suffering from a great deal of adverse publicity due to the suicide of Hefner's longtime aide Bobbie Arnstein after her conviction on a drug charge, Christie provided a more positive image.

Her next major project was overseeing the *Playboy* guides—periodic issues on men's fashions and other topics. These were sent free to subscribers and were sold on the newstands. Designed to appeal to advertisers who wished to reach *Playboy*'s rather upscale readership, but who were reticent to advertise in a magazine featuring nudes, they were not successful. The guides were partly a victim of the recession, but many analysts felt that Christie was also at fault. One company executive thought the guides were poorly conceived, and a *Playboy* editor went even further when he said, "The guides are a piece of s—t. Everything Christie has tried has failed."

In any event, on April 28, 1982, Christie became president of the firm, and in 1984 she received the additional title of chief operating officer. Her primary task was to cut Playboy's staggering costs. The bloated firm suffered a loss of $51.7 million in fiscal 1982, which she cut to $17.5 million in 1983. No dividends were paid to stockholders (including Hugh Hefner) during these years, and in 1983 the company withdrew from its money-losing casino operations in the Bahamas. Christie also sold the Playboy building, leasing back its own space, and gave use of the Chicago Playboy mansion to the Art Institute of Chicago. This allowed the corporation to report modest profits in 1984 and 1985. But things had not significantly improved. Christie tried to revive the sagging fortunes of the Playboy clubs by reopening the New York club with male "rabbits" as well as bunnies, but this too failed, and in 1986 Playboy Enterprises closed the three remaining company-owned Playboy clubs. In the fiscal year the firm reported a record $62.2 million loss.

Problems continued to surface in other areas also. *Playboy* magazine, long the corporation's bellwether and source of 77 percent of the sales in fiscal 1985, saw its circulation decline to 3.4 million, less than half of what it had been in 1972. Pressures by the federal government, in the form of the Attorney General's Commission on Pornography, which had pressured convenience and drug stores to not handle the magazine, had hurt, as did the decision of the 7–Eleven stores to discontinue sales of *Playboy*. Furthermore, Playboy's venture into cable television, earlier viewed with great optimism, had proved unprofitable. Although much of this was due to pressure from feminist and fundamentalist religious groups, it was also due to its loss of impact. Those who desired eroticism found *Playboy*'s fare rather tame. But Christie Hefner's decision to adapt magazine material in the form of video cassettes has been more successful.

An area in which Christie Hefner has continued to maintain a high profile has been in her defense of *Playboy* to feminist groups. She defines herself as a feminist, and she feels that feminist groups that attack *Playboy* are either ignorant or out for the publicity. She described her position to the Washington Chapter of Women in Communications as an oxymoron, "Like jumbo shrimp. Or for those who travel alot, airline food." But she pointed out that Playboy is "a company that has a pretty good track record on women's issues." She feels, most of all, that female nudity is neither offensive nor an objectification of women. Nor does she feel women are being exploited in this manner; after all, centerfold models are paid $12,000 for their appearance. Furthermore, she has persuaded her father to donate money to feminist causes, and she has continued that practice. Using that as her opening wedge, she brings the battle to feminist groups: "Playboy has been more supportive of feminist policies and philosophies than most other companies I know of—in its attitude toward hiring and promotion of women, through its editorial and financial support of the Equal Rights Amendment and abortion." Yet, to most feminists, these arguments ring hollow and ignore *Playboy*'s rather blatant insensitivity to women as full human beings.

In November 1988, Christie replaced her father as chairman and CEO of Playboy Enterprises. In her six years as president, she has eliminated the company's massive debt and has amassed $34 million in cash and investments. But the company she inherited from her father in 1988 was a pale imitation of the publishing phenomenon of the 1950s and 1960s. Magazine circulation was stagnant at 3.4 million. Sales were flat at $159.8 million, and profits were just $2.6 million. Christie recognized the problem and forecast that time would be better in the future, saying that "My becoming CEO marks the coming of a new era—an era of growth." She planned to accomplish this turnaround by improving the magazine and the cable channel, marketing new products, and acquiring specialized publications. Many analysts were skeptical. One said, "I think Christie is brilliant, but *Playboy* has become somewhat of an anachronism, and the best she can do is maintain the magazine where it is today."

Meanwhile, Hugh Hefner eased into retirement by telling reporters a story of his childhood. Just as *Citizen Kane* had his Rosebud, Hefner had a childhood possession that symbolized his yearnings. Calling it his "bunny blanket," Hefner recounted that when he was a child one of his great treasures was a blanket "with bunnies all over it." "It was what Charles Shultz calls a security blanket," he said. "I called it my bunny blanket." When his pet dog died, though, the dog was laid out on the blanket. A short time later, the blanket was burned. "When the blanket went up in flames, the bunny empire began," he said. Just think, had his dog not died, had his blanket not been burned, perhaps Hefner would have peacefully ended his career as an editor for *Esquire*. (**B.** *Fortune*, May 1957, August 23, 1982, October 3, 1983; *Saturday Evening Post*, April 28, 1962, April 23, 1966; *Life*, October 29, 1965; *Current Biography*, September 1968; *Time*, February 14, 1969, January 27, 1975, July 4, 1977, May 10, 1982; T. L. Gross ed., *Representative Men*, 1970; *Forbes*, March 1, 1971, June 1, 1977, March 26, 1984; *New York Times Magazine*, June 11, 1972; Frank Brady, *Hefner*, 1974; *Dun's*, February 1974, February 1984; *Newsweek*, June 24, 1974, January 1, 1979, May 10, October 25, 1982; *Maclean's*, December 4, 1978, April 25, 1983; *Publishers Weekly*, January 22, 1979; *Esquire*, November, December, 1979, June, 1986; Gay Talese, *Thy Neighbor's Wife*, 1980; *New York*, June 21, 1982; *Business Week*, December 6, 1982, April 15, 1985, November 14, 1988; *International Management*, February 1984; *New York Times*, March 25, 1984; Russell Miller, *Bunny*, 1984; *People Weekly*, February 25, 1985; *Rolling Stone*, March 27, 1986; *Newsweek*, August 4, 1986; *Current*

Biography Yearbook, 1986; Douglas K. Ramsey, *The Corporate Warriors*, 1987; Toronto *Globe & Mail*, April 30, May 13, 1988; *Toronto Star*, July 31, 1988; John D'Emilio and Estelle B. Freedman, *Intimate Matters*, 1988.)

HESS, LEON (March 14, 1914–   ). Oil company founder, Hess Oil & Chemical Company, Amerada Hess Corporation. John H. Shaughnessy, an oil industry analyst, borrowed a line from Winston Churchill when he described Leon Hess' oil company: "It is a riddle wrapped in a mystery inside an enigma." This statement refers to Hess' obsession with privacy; Hess has granted only one interview in a career spanning six decades. Once, when declining a request for an interview, he told *Business Week* (July 16, 1979): "I have always shunned publicity. I've been brought up all my life to stay out of the limelight and I'm never going to change." In this, and in many other respects, Leon Hess is a throwback to the hard-driving, secretive entrepreneurs of the nineteenth century. He has been a classic aggressive, resourceful, self-made entrepreneur throughout his business career—a man from humble origins who took on the giants of the international oil industry and became a giant himself. He did this by exploiting previously ignored market niches, by relying on fortuitous political connections, and by running exceedingly efficient operations. He was also a gambler and a risk taker.

Hess was born in Asbury Park, New Jersey, the son of Mores Hess, a Lithuanian immigrant who had come to the United States in 1904. The elder Hess was trained as a kosher butcher, and he plied that trade in America for nearly two decades. In 1925, he started to deliver fuel to customers near his Asbury Park home. In March 1933, however, the rigors of the depression drove the small firm into bankruptcy. When Mores Hess reorganized the firm later that year, he recruited his youngest son, Leon, who was just nineteen, to take charge of the operation. Leon Hess had grown up in Asbury Park and had graduated from high school in the trough of the depression. His two older brothers and sister had attended college, but there was no money for Leon; instead, he inherited his father's struggling fuel business.

The Hess oil operation in 1933 was not very promising. It was quartered in a single room of an old building in Asbury Park, and its major piece of equipment was a small, heavily mortgaged truck. But Hess had the instincts of an entrepreneur, and he soon made the firm a minor success. He achieved this at first simply by hard work. He spent countless hours bumping along the roads of New Jersey in the truck, selling oil and coal to retail marketers, and returning at night along the same route, delivering the fuel he had sold. In the 1940s, coal was dropped from the company's line. Hess many years later explained the decision was made because "I was basically lazy . . . . I didn't want to carry 100-lb. bags of coal for my father." The decision actually had much more to do with the fact that Hess had found more profitable lines on which to concentrate.

In any event, Hess made a success of the little firm. Within a short time, he made the final payment on the original 1929 Dodge truck, and he began to expand his operations. In the late 1930s, Leon Hess focused the firm's resources on No. 6 residual fuel, known in the oil industry as "resid" or "six oil." It was what was left at the bottom of the barrel—a "tarry, gunky ooze that remains after refining." The major oil companies generally treated it as a nuisance. It was only good as fuel for the big boilers used in large public utility operations. The large oil firms would reluctantly truck some to nearby power plants, but mostly they just wanted to be rid of it. Hess realized that as more and more of the electric utilities and other large consumers switched from coal to oil (and since his firm also sold coal, he knew that its sales were declining), residual oil would become more profitable.

One night in the late 1930s, after spending all day delivering ordinary heating oil to homes, he loaded up his truck with hot residual oil at a New Jersey refinery and drove to the Asbury Carlton Hotel in Asbury Park to deliver it. Although residual oil flows while it is still hot, once it cools, it is so viscous that one can practically walk on it. By the time Hess got to the Asbury Carlton with his load, the oil had cooled. To get it out, Hess had to stand there with a blowtorch on the drainpipe practically the entire next day. "Lord," he later told *Business Week* (June 29, 1987), "today I'd kill someone if they tried that." But Hess was still certain that residual oil was the road to riches. He built a fleet of tank trucks designed to get the residual oil to the customer before it cooled. Adding distribution depots, Hess pursued increasingly more distant markets, captured more and more customers, and developed a thriving operation. When Hess had trouble getting sufficient supplies of oil, he built his first "terminal" shortly before World War II by buying nine secondhand 20,000 barrel tankers and floating them to an abandoned brickyard in Perth Amboy, where he lashed them together. At the same time, Hess began to underbid competitors for federal contracts; he still operated on a shoestring—his bids were the only handwritten ones submitted—and Hess wrote them himself.

When World War II brought severe oil rationing, Hess asked his older brother, Henry, to run the family's oil operations, and Leon Hess joined the army as a second lieutenant in 1942. Before long, Hess was shipped to Europe, where he became a petroleum supply officer with General George Patton's armies. It was complex, difficult, and sometimes even hazardous work (Hess was slightly wounded and won a Bronze Star), and he was mustered out in 1945 as a major. The army experience, however, also taught him a great deal about organization and about running a large business in a more disciplined manner. One of Hess' friends commented about his army experience: "It taught him all about planning. He became very orderly in his way of going about any problem."

After the war, Hess rejoined the family business and began to expand its operations in an impressive manner, sending his tank trucks as far away as Binghamton, New York. As these markets grew, he built a network of terminals to service them, and also began buying his own oil tankers at a time when the large oil companies were simply making delivered-cargo supply contracts with others. During these years in the late 1940s, Hess also made another decision that was to have vast repercussions for his business—he got married. In 1947 he married Norma Wilentz, the only daughter of David T. Wilentz, a native of Lithuania who had been attorney general of New Jersey during the Lindbergh kidnapping trial and who remained leader of the Middlesex County Democratic Committee (where Perth Amboy and Hess Oil were located) into the 1980s. Wilentz was also a very powerful figure in state politics, and he gave Hess entrée to powerful Democratic politicians on the national level. As *Fortune* commented: "No one would suggest that Leon Hess made a poor choice of a father-in-law. Middlesex County is Hess country." His competitors have long suggested that much of Hess' competitive advantage has come from his successful wheeling and dealing in Washington, D.C., and that it was Wilentz who provided the political contacts during the 1960s that helped Hess win exceptionally favorable concessions in many of his operations. All analysts agree that this marriage certainly never hurt him.

In any event, Hess' operations really took off in the late 1940s, as he began to profit enormously from sales of residual oil. With the switch from coal to oil, Hess was able to get a number of prize customers, the most important of which was Public Service Electric & Gas, which served more than three-quarters of the New Jersey population. Hess imported much of his supply from Asiatic Petroleum, a subsidiary of Royal Dutch Shell. Importing about 1,000 barrels a day in 1949, by 1957 he was bringing in 38,000 barrels daily, and he was Asiatic's largest customer. Then, in 1958, Hess built his first refinery, at Port Reading near Perth Amboy. Two years later, Hess began to market gasoline under his own name. This brought him into a highly competitive stage of the industry, one in which the profit margins were notoriously low. But Hess, by this point, had developed his "grand design"—which visualized the creation of a large, integrated oil company—and retailing gasoline was an important part of that design.

Hess competed on the basis of price. The other New Jersey stations had a fair-trade pact whereby they agreed to keep their retail gasoline prices above a certain floor. Hess refused to comply. Since his refinery was close to his stations, he could save a few cents on costs there, and he decided to set up huge stations at prime locations, to sell only gasoline (no oil changes, lubrications, repairs or tires) and undersell his competitors. The tactic worked. By the end of 1961, Hess had twenty-eight gas stations in New Jersey; by the end of the 1970s he had 500, covering much of the Northeast. His stations pumped an average of 100,000 gallons a month, five times the volume of an average station.

During this time, Hess had been financing his expansion through debt, but by the early 1960s he was close to being overextended. With sales of $245 million in 1961, and earnings of just over $7 million, the firm had a long-term debt of $33 million, an extraordinarily high ratio of debt to equity for the oil industry. It was clear by then that Hess would have to take his firm public if he wanted to expand any further. He found an ingenious way to accomplish this. A friend of his owned Cletrac Corporation, which by then was really just a corporate shell. With net assets of $35 million, almost all of which were liquid, it also had an $18-million tax-loss carry forward. Under the terms of the merger in May 1962, the new company took the name of Hess Oil & Chemical Company, with Hess taking 69 percent of the voting stock and becoming chief executive officer. The firm also got an immediate listing on the New York Stock Exchange.

By the mid–1960s, although Hess Oil was profitable, it was still what is referred to in the oil industry as a "downstream" company. That is, all of its operations were in the refining, transportation, distribution, and retailing phases of the industry; it had not integrated backward into the raw material or crude oil phase. This made Hess Oil vulnerable. With only one small crude operation in Mississippi, capable of producing just 3,500 barrels a day, the firm would be crippled if the oil majors cut off supplies in a time of crisis. Besides, Hess still had his "grand design" of an integrated oil company, and Hess Oil could never be considered an integrated firm until it obtained sufficient supplies of its own crude. So, in 1966, Hess took off after Amerada Petroleum.

Amerada was a large, highly profitable entity, with revenues of $208 million in 1965, and profits of $57 million, an exceptional 27-percent margin. And it had no debt. Most important, by the time of the merger, Amerada had proven reserves totaling 582 million barrels in the United States, and a half interest in 777 million barrels in Libya. Able to pump 220,000 barrels of crude daily, Amerada was a prize that Hess coveted, and he pursued it with the tenacity and daring that became his trademarks. At the same time, he set up a mammoth refining operation in St. Croix in the Virgin Islands. In combination, these two enormously risky and expensive ventures catapulted Hess into the ranks of the major integrated oil firms, and resulted in extraordinary profits during the 1970s.

The problem with Amerada was that its autocratic chairman, Alfred Jacobsen, did not want his firm to be taken over by Hess, whom he regarded as an outsider and whom he believed wanted control of the entire operation. Hess had purchased a 9.8-percent share in Amerada from the British government in 1966 for $100 million. To stop Hess' takeover, Jacobsen arranged a merger with Ashland Oil, but Hess managed to persuade the board to stop it. Shortly thereafter, Jacobsen died of a heart attack, and the way was opened for Hess. First, he was appointed to the board, and within a few months he had largely negotiated an agreement. Out of the blue, however, came an offer from Phillips Petroleum, which had a higher dollar value than the merger with Hess. Although the board sided with Hess, he feared a proxy fight for control of the company, so he offered $125 a share for the outstanding shares, about $9 over market price. The Amerada directors agreed to allow the merged company, Amerada Hess, to assume the loans required to finance the tender offer, provided the merger succeeded. If not, Hess Oil would have to foot the entire bill itself and would be left with $250 million worth of Amerada stock. It was, as *Fortune* commented, "one of Hess's most dangerous gambles." And it paid off. In March 1969, Phillips announced it was pulling out of the contest, and Amerada's shareholders approved the merger by an overwhelming margin.

In the meantime, Hess was busy building the world's largest refinery in the Virgin Islands. Hess made a brilliant decision to locate his refinery in this tropical paradise, but the route to completion was complex and filled with political machinations. He knew he needed a large new refinery to handle the vast residual oil market he had developed in the Northeast, in addition to the gasoline needs of his own stations. Furthermore, the federal government was about to raise the amount of heavy oil (residual oil) that could be imported to the mainland from offshore refineries. Since it was much cheaper to construct refineries in the Caribbean, Hess had decided to build in the Bahamas. Hess went to see David Rockefeller* of Chase Manhattan Bank, one of his principal backers, but Rockefeller discouraged him from building on foreign soil. Rockefeller advised Hess that it would be safer to build on domestic soil and told Hess to look into the Virgin Islands, an independently governed U.S. territory, where Rockefeller's family just happened to own a good deal of property. Besides the fact that the refinery would be on American soil, and thus at an advantage with respect to import quotas, there were other advantages. There was, for example, the Jones Act of 1920, which exempted the Virgin Islands from the requirement that only U.S.-flag vessels could be used between U.S. ports. This would allow Hess to contract with much cheaper foreign tankers to carry products to the United States. Finally, construction and labor costs would be lower there, and, if Hess were able to use his political influence skillfully, there was a possibility of securing an exceptionally good deal in terms of taxes and other duties from the government of the Virgin Islands.

To achieve this, Hess went to David Wilentz, who put him in touch with Richard J. Hughes, the Democratic governor of New Jersey. Hughes, in turn, telephoned Ralph M. Paiewonsky, who was then Democratic governor of the Islands. Paiewonsky first helped Hess secure land at bargain rates, by telling the sellers they were getting a fair price. Most important, Hess got a highly favorable package of tax exemptions and subsidies from the government to persuade him to build the giant refinery there. Hess agreed to strict pollution controls and to hire mostly legal residents of the island, but the refinery was to be exempt from all local taxes for sixteen years, and the territorial government agreed to rebate three-quarters of the refinery's federal income taxes over the same period. Next, Hess had to obtain from the U.S. government partial exemption from the existing quotas to send his foreign-produced, but Virgin Island–refined, petroleum products other than residual oil to the mainland. The Virgin Island government gave him strong support, but, after his request had lain dormant at the Department of Interior for months, Hess announced he would contribute a royalty of 50 cents a barrel to the Virgin Islands and pay U.S. customs duties on the imports. A few months later, Interior Secretary Stewart L. Udall, who became closely identified with Hess in later years and received large campaign donations from him, granted Hess the quota.

A former high-level State Department official later charged that the Interior Department had granted Hess this import allocation without State Department approval:

They were obliged not to change any part of the import program without consulting State. I tried very hard to block Hess's exemption because his allocation meant he could switch from the Western Hemisphere to Libya for crude. We were seeking more imports from the Western Hemisphere and less dependence on Libya. But Libyan crude was far more profitable for him. (*Business Week,* July 16, 1979)

Hess had learned well the importance of political connections, and much of his success in later years hinged at least partially on this lesson. Always a large contributor to the Democratic party, he also became an important backer of Senator Henry M. Jackson of Washington, to whom he contributed $225,000 when Jackson made a bid for the presidency in 1972. Coincidently, Jackson was chairman of the Senate Energy Committee during the 1970s and thus in a position to have considerable influence over the nation's oil policies.

Hess built a magnificent 200,000-barrel-a-day refinery in St. Croix in the Virgin Islands, which began operation in a breathtaking ten months. Over the next few years, new refinery operations were added there, until by the late 1970s it had a capacity for 700,000 barrels a day, and had cost more than $600 million to build. The refinery was established on what is called a "European" basis; that is, because of Hess' special market needs, it focused on the low-margin residual oils for the institutional market, with that taking up between 50 to 60 percent of its production. Most American refineries produce only about 15 percent residual oil. The combination of favorable tax and rebate rules, efficient operating expenses, and cheap transportation gave Hess significant advantages in the marketplace. His competitors have claimed that he had a cost advantage that ranged as high as $2.50 a barrel, which enabled him to undersell them by one or two cents a gallon on residual fuel, and as much as by five cents on home heating oil. Others, however, gave him grudging admiration. William P. Tavoulareas, former president of Mobil Oil, and an old friend, said, "He taught us how to run a refinery. Where we'd have 800 people working, he'd have 400. He knows how to do things well with the least overhead."

A former federal official made the following observation about Hess' operations in the late 1970s:

Hess had an efficient refinery. His shipping costs to the U.S. were lower than Gulf Coast refineries, and his lightering costs were considerably less. Of course, with the entitlements he had whipped the tail off the rest of the Caribbean refiners. Everyone was so outraged that pressure grew to clean his clock. Even his political pull wasn't great enough to save him this time. (*Business Week,* July 16, 1979)

The entitlements referred to a program set up by the U.S. Energy Department in 1974 to equalize costs between domestic refineries supplied mostly by lower-priced domestic crude, and those dependent on higher-priced foreign crude. Under the program, Amerada Hess enjoyed what an industry lawyer called "the best of both worlds," as it got $881.6 million in subsidies during the first five years from a fund supplied by the owners of domestic crude oil—Hess' competitors. They were not happy. In the late 1970s Hess' entitlements were sharply reduced when he shipped refined products in a foreign tanker. This cut into his profits somewhat, but Hess still retained some important cost advantages over other producers.

All of this, as inferred above, brought enormous growth and profitability to Amerada Hess. By 1969, a year after the merger, its revenues had grown to about $900 million. But profits, which had been $94 million in 1968, were down in 1969 because of the massive amounts of money Hess poured into the development of prospective oil reserves on Alaska's North Slope. Entering into a consortium with Hunt Oil, Getty Oil, and Louisiana Land, Hess invested $272 million in the North Slope, making it the largest of all bidders in the $900-million auction. Leon Hess, by then the owner of a massive integrated oil company, was still the entrepreneur, the gambler.

The big turning point for Amerada Hess, as for so much of the petroleum industry, came with the Arab oil embargo in 1973, when all of Hess' planning and investments, all the decisions that had seemed so risky and impulsive in the 1960s, fell into place. Import quotas were abolished in face of the Arab boycott, so Hess could bring in every last barrel of refined products he wished from his massive refinery. With over 68 million barrels of mainland storage capacity, Hess was among the few operators who could satisfy the needs of a fuel-starved America. With crude oil prices tripling in a matter of months, and free to use cheaper foreign tankers, Amerada Hess earned enormous profits. Net earnings, which stood at $133 million in 1971, jumped to $246 million in 1973. Then, after 1974, with the entitlements program, Hess made even more money. But Hess was still not content to rest on his laurels. From 1973 to 1979, Amerada Hess invested $1.2 billion in exploration and production, 47 percent more than the company's net income during this period. With the prices of crude going steadily upward, all the money Hess spent to find new sources of crude were paying substantial dividends.

The late 1980s, however, were tough years for Amerada Hess, as they were for the petroleum industry generally. Amerada Hess' peak year came in 1981, when it had earnings of $213 million on revenues of nearly $10 billion. After that, its fortunes reversed, and the nadir came in 1986, when the company lost a staggering $219 million on sales of only $4 billion. Although Hess had built the company into the thirteenth largest oil firm, and the 173rd largest company in America, Amerada Hess was in trouble. Many critics insisted that the trouble with Amerada Hess was Hess himself. At seventy-three, he was still the classic hands-on manager, who ran virtually every detail of the operation from his office at the company's New York headquarters. But he was not about to give up: "As long as I live, have my health, and can justify my existence, I expect to stay." Industry analysts were not impressed; one commented, "This is a company with most of its history behind it. I think it will be put in play." And the raiders began to circle the company when its stock fell from a high of almost $4 billion in 1981 to $1.3 billion. In late 1988, the company's future remained uncertain. Profits in 1987 had rebounded to $220 million, on sales of $4.8 billion, but its five-year average growth and profit record had been just about the lowest in the industry.

Besides Amerada Hess, Leon Hess owned the New York Jets of the National Football League. He purchased a 25-percent interest for $250,000 in the early 1960s to help out his friend, Sonny Werblin; by the late 1980s, he was the sole owner of the club, which by then played their games in New Jersey. As a boss, Hess has a reputation as someone to be feared. Although he was known to be generous to employees with medical problems and he gave much to charity, a longtime acquaintance viewed him as a paternalistic tyrant: "No one dares cross him." He was also infamous in the industry as a formidable and notoriously stubborn competitor, but one who is trustworthy. He often made deals on the telephone or with a handshake, and an industry analyst claimed, "In a day when integrity is in short supply, his word is his bond." Earlier in his career, however, a veteran investment banker perhaps best summed up Leon Hess: "In all my experience in business, I have never seen anything so closely approaching a Napoleonic ability—a projection of an ego into concrete accomplishments, a force of will that can really move mountains." (**B.** *Forbes*, October 15, 1969, August 1, 1977, January 11, 1988; *Fortune*, January 1970; *Business Week*, July 16, 1979, June 29, 1987, March 14, 1988; *National Petroleum News*, July 1982.)

HEWLETT, WILLIAM REDINGTON (May 20, 1913–   ) and **DAVID PACKARD** (September 12, 1912–   ). Electronics and computer company founders, Hewlett-Packard Company. Hewlett-Packard has long had the reputation of being the best-managed company in the electronics industry. In 1976 *Fortune* magazine, impressed with the company's more than thirty-five years of sustained growth and profitability, talked about "The Gospel According to Hewlett and Packard." Six years later, Thomas J. Peters and Robert H. Waterman, Jr.'s, *In Search of Excellence*, the runaway best-seller on American management techniques, chose Hewlett-Packard as one of America's "best-run companies." They became so caught up in the company's atmosphere, in fact, that they could barely contain their enthusiasm: "Wherever you go in the HP empire, you find people talking about product quality, feeling proud of their division's achievements in that area. . . . We ourselves tried to remain sober, not become fans. But it proved impossible."

David Packard, whose father was a prosperous lawyer, was born in Pueblo, Colorado. He attended public schools in his hometown and graduated from Centennial High School in 1930. He went to Stanford University in Palo Alto,

California, where he majored in electrical engineering. A track star there, he also lettered in football and basketball. While at Stanford, he became friends with William Hewlett, a fellow electrical engineering student. Hewlett, who had been born in Ann Arbor, Michigan, was the son of a professor of medicine at the University of Michigan. When William was three years old, his father took a position at Stanford's medical school, and the family moved to the West Coast. Bill Hewlett's father died when he was twelve, but that tragedy did not impede his genius in the physics of electricity and radio wave progression. Although everyone recognized his ability, he was not a particularly good student. Hewlett later admitted that the only reason he was admitted to Stanford was because his father was an alumnus.

After Packard got his degree in 1934, he took a job in 1935 with the vacuum tube engineering department of General Electric in Schenectady, New York. After spending three years there, Packard made what many considered a rash decision—he returned to Stanford on a fellowship to continue his studies in electrical engineering. He was lured back to Stanford by his old friend Bill Hewlett. Hewlett had also graduated from Stanford in 1934 and then went to the Massachusetts Institute of Technology (MIT) for his master's degree, which he obtained in 1936. Upon his graduation from MIT, Professor Frederick A. Terman of Stanford, who would play such a major role in the early careers of the two young men, secured a contract for Hewlett to make an electroence-phalograph.

While at Stanford, Packard had taken Terman's graduate radio course and had impressed the professor with his ability. When Hewlett told Terman that Packard wanted to return to the West Coast, Terman arranged a fellowship for Packard to conduct research for a colleague. With his two brilliant protégés in place, Terman began to convince them of the importance of the negative feedback principle for amplifiers. After arousing their minds sufficiently, Terman pressured Hewlett and Packard to start their own electronics business in the Santa Clara Valley.

Together, the two young men worked in Packard's garage on an oscillator and on other products. Putting together $538 in capital, they bought a secondhand Sears press and in a short time invented a weight-reducing machine, an electronic harmonica tuner, and a bowling alley foul-line indicator. Their biggest item, however, was Hewlett's radio oscillator. They made their first commercial sale in 1939, when Walt Disney* ordered eight of them at $71.50 each for the sound track of *Fantasia*. With the success of that sale and others, Hewlett and Packard grossed $5,369, with profits of $1,653 in their first year. They could now consider moving out of Packard's garage into a new plant. At this point, Terman, who had been monitoring and encouraging their progress, persuaded them to build the plant in Stanford's 8,000-acre industrial park. As a result, Hewlett-Packard (H-P) became one of the first electronics firms to set up shop in what later became known as Silicon Valley. By the early 1980s, the 25-mile-long area had become the home of over 1,000 electronics and computer firms, including branches of IBM, Memorex, National Semiconductor, Intel, and Syntex.

By the time of America's entry into World War II, H-P had sales of $100,000 a year and seventeen employees. The company suffered a blow in 1942 when Hewlett, their chief technician, was called up for active duty and served for the duration of the war. In other respects, the war was a great boon for Hewlett-Packard. World War II was the first high-technology war, the first war to emphasize the use of electronics. A multitude of orders began pouring into the small plant for radio, radar, sonar, and nautical and aviation devices. The firm was also aided by the fact that during the war Professor Terman was in charge of the government's antiradar project at Harvard, and he arranged for Hewlett-Packard to build microwave generators for his project. In any event, David Packard was forced to run the enterprise by himself during the war years, and by the time Bill Hewlett returned in 1946, H-P was a $2-million company with 200 employees.

The two young men faced a difficult situation at the end of the war. Hewlett-Packard had been almost totally dependent upon government orders during the war, and the cessation of the fighting brought an end to the lucrative contracts. With the great slump in demand, H-P was forced to do something it never did again—lay off employees. They cut their workforce in half, and the experience strengthened Hewlett and Packard's resolve to never again be dependent upon government defense contracts. Packard later recalled his thoughts about it:

It was a rough dip. But we kept going even so. . . . I recall being very worried at that time about the future. So we designed (our new building) so it would be an all-purpose building. I remember thinking if we can't keep the company together we can at least lease it out to a supermarket or something. (Malone, *The Big Score*)

They managed to weather the hard times, and by 1950 the work force again reached 200, and the firm had revenues of $2 million on the sales of some seventy products. It was also during this time that Hewlett and Packard began to develop a set of business principles that became articulated as the "H-P Way." It was a new kind of corporate culture, an organizational morality that was seldom seen in large firms. Some aspects of the philosophy were markedly conservative; others were exceptionally liberal. On the conservative side was their determination to refrain from any long-term borrowing. This was an extraordinary decision for a research-oriented, high-technology firm. In an industry where development costs are traditionally very high, it was normal to secure financing to engage in it. But H-P was determined to use current earnings to finance research. They also decided to stay clear of large government contracts that could cause abrupt swings in employment. This was the exact opposite of the plans and ideas of most high-technology firms, which framed long-term goals around the idea of large government contracts. H-P also was determined that it would never, under any circumstances, enter businesses that they did not truly understand. This meant that the few acquisitions it did make were of companies whose products could be easily integrated into H-P's line.

But more than anything else, the H-P Way included an intense orientation toward employees. This philosophy includes one of the most complete employee benefit programs available in American industry, along with a powerful sense of job security. It made a promise to its employees after the 1946 crisis that it would never again impose layoffs, and it has kept that promise for more than forty years. Even during times of recession, when worker's wages were reduced, and work hours were shortened, employees were never laid off. Early on, the company also instituted a generous profit-sharing program. Beyond that, there was a low-key, professional, and democratic tone to the company. Packard and Hewlett always worked in shirtsleeves and were referred to by almost everyone as "Bill" and "Dave," illustrating that distinctions of rank and title in the company were very muted indeed. It was all part of what H-P employees amusingly nicknamed "management by walking around." Managers, especially William Hewlett and David Packard, were always present, on the floor, walking around, offering advice, and helping out. As vice president John Doyle later remarked: "There's a marked lack of status differentiations between different functions and divisions." Yet, it was also a very paternalistic environment, one in which there were no unions and where an atmosphere of pure capitalism pervades the company, one which hews very closely to the ideas expressed by Ayn Rand in *The Fountainhead*. Bill Hewlett reflected about this H-P Way atmosphere:

You can't describe it in numbers or statistics. In the last analysis it is a spirit, a point of view. There is the feeling that everyone is part of a team, and that team is H-P. As I said at the beginning, it is an idea based on the individual. It exists because people have seen that it works, and they believe that this feeling makes H-P what it is. (Peters and Waterman, *In Search of Excellence*)

With Hewlett the technological innovator and Packard the managerial and financial expert, H-P grew rapidly during the 1950s. It broadened its product line to include a high-speed electronic counter, a calibrated laboratory oscilloscope, and a number of other instruments. By the late 1950s the company was manufacturing about 300 different products. It also began selectively buying other companies during this time, always ensuring that the new business and products were well understood. H-P also helped some of its employees start firms that retained intimate connections with their mentor. In the early 1950s it assisted in the founding of Palo Alto Engineering, which built special-purpose transformers for H-P and other customers and, later, helped other employees set up Dynac, Incorporated, which built complete electronic instrumentation systems.

By the 1960s, H-P was beginning to face the problems of a large firm. Bureaucracy was becoming more endemic. It began to impede entrepreneurial activity, which was only partially compensated for by the sense of fellowship and group activity fostered by the H-P Way. Increased size also meant the necessity of locating newer and larger markets. An important step in this direction came in 1961, when H-P created a division to develop solid-state components. Then, in 1966, the company announced its first processor, called the Instrumentation Computer, which was intended to work with earlier instruments to provide computational support.

By the end of 1968, H-P had 13,340 employees and handled a line of 2,163 products, which included heart-monitoring equipment and atomic clocks for the Apollo spacecraft. With sales of over $280 million a year, its profits exceeded $20 million. Hewlett-Packard was the giant of Silicon Valley and one of the largest, most important firms in the American electronics industry. Then, in January 1969, David Packard left the firm to become deputy secretary of defense. His appointment stirred a great deal of controversy on Capitol Hill over potential conflicts of interest. As a result, he was forced to place his H-P stock, then worth about $300 million, into a blind charitable trust. He spent three years in Washington, D.C., but his career there was not particularly distinguished. When asked later what his biggest accomplishment had been while in Washington, Packard replied, "I gave up smoking."

While Packard was in Washington, Bill Hewlett ran H-P. During those three years, the company underwent extensive internal diversification, and sales rose substantially—to $379 million in 1971—an increase of 35 percent since 1968. Profits, however, began to slide and were 9 percent less in 1971, primarily because of problems H-P was experiencing in transferring its vaunted technological prowess to the marketplace, especially in the minicomputer and electronic calculator businesses. Profits were also affected by the ironic fact, given Packard's position in the Pentagon, that government contracts dipped from 40 percent of sales to 25 percent of sales.

H-P had introduced minicomputers in 1967 and had at first achieved success with them, since the company sold primarily to the educational, scientific, and engineering markets, where it had an established reputation. But, upon entering the general computer market, H-P found it had trouble keeping pace with the changing marketplace. On one hand, this was a venerable H-P tradition; since the company was very cautious and did not like to incur long-term debt, it was seldom first on the market with any innovation or new device. H-P was, rather, a highly skilled "counterpuncher" who waited until a technology had proved itself and then entered the market with a better product.

In the general market for minicomputers, H-P was competing with a number of aggressive manufacturers, especially DEC, which not only was an innovative company, but was also one that was willing to saddle itself with a good deal of long-term debt in order to pursue technological changes. H-P quickly found itself outfoxed, outflanked, and outgunned with its minicomputers, and its sales began to slide in the early 1970s. Still, H-P was slow to respond, and its improved minicomputer did not reach the shelves until late 1971 because of design problems. This opened the way for yet another aggressive company, Data General, to surge past H-P as the number two minicomputer maker in the country.

At that point, H-P decided to change its strategy on minicomputers—to pursue the time-sharing market rather than to compete in the larger mass market. Therefore, in early 1972, it brought out the HP–3000, a minicomputer system that performed general-purpose computation. It could do time-sharing, multiprogramming, and batch or on-line processing. Optimism about the product pervaded, but H-P was plagued with a number of design and production problems during the next four years, and it suffered from a faltering time-sharing market at about the same time, which caused significant profit reversals. The HP–3000, however, was to play an important role in the company's resurgence in the late 1970s.

Prior to the early 1970s, Hewlett-Packard produced virtually nothing that could be termed a consumer product. Even their foray into the general minicomputer market took place in a highly specialized milieu. But in January 1972, with the announcement of the HP–35 scientific calculator, nicknamed the "electronic slide rule," H-P had a legitimate mass-market product for the first time. H-P had been contenders in the electronic desk calculator market with Wang Laboratories (see An Wang) in the 1960s but had not fared particularly well. Conversely, the hand-held calculator had an explosive impact. As ubiquitous as the hand-held calculator is today, it is difficult to comprehend that there was a time when everyone did not have at least one. And it was H-P that led the way with this product.

Bill Hewlett was the driving force behind the introduction of the HP–35. An outside firm was hired to conduct a market research study which advised H-P not to make the product, calling it a toy. Also, many H-P executives were opposed to making a product which appeared to violate many of the company's traditions. But Hewlett was determined. The introduction of the HP–35 had a traumatic impact: the slide rule, companion of engineers for decades, disappeared almost overnight. Students scraped together the $400 needed to buy one, and the HP–65 programmable calculator, the top of the line, became the most stolen item of equipment in labs. Advertising and sales strategy quickly shifted to this enormous new market, which brought H-P into the previously uncharted waters of mass consumerism, which H-P found to be teeming with sharks.

The biggest shark was Texas Instruments (TI), a sophisticated veteran of mass-market electronics. It introduced inexpensive hand-held calculators that could add, subtract, multiply, and divide, which completely dominated the low end of the calculator market by 1973–1974. Then TI took off after H-P's scientific calculator. TI built lower quality imitations of the H-P calculator and sold them at half the price. H-P had always stressed the fact that it did not engage in price competition—it made quality products and charged a premium for them. As long as H-P was selling to its specialized market, the strategy worked well. But with students, engineers, and scientists it did not work as well. These people wanted an H-P calculator, but if they could not afford one, they bought a cheaper TI model instead. H-P did not know how to react. Totally misunderstanding the mass market, they decided to combat TI with the HP–01 wrist calculator. A magnificent piece of engineering, it was a calculator and watch combined—that is, a time calculator—that was virtually indestructible. But it cost a staggering $795, and it was so big and bulky that buyers would have had to have their shirt cuffs retailored in order to wear it. Hardly anyone bought the HP–01.

Hewlett-Packard not only survived these miscues, it prospered in spite of them. In 1978, Bill Hewlett stepped down as chief executive officer, handing the reins to John A. Young, a longtime veteran of the firm. After this time, neither Hewlett nor David Packard played any significant role in the day-to-day operations of the company, but they left behind them a firm in robust shape with a legacy of management that boded well for the future. Sales had surpassed the $1-billion mark in 1976, and in 1978 reached $1.7 billion. A major factor in the company's resurgence in the late 1970s was the HP–3000 computer. Finally having debugged the device, the computers were sold successfully for such applications as order entry, production control, and warehousing. It was in manufacturing plants that the HP–3000's were most attractive, and here Hewlett-Packard successfully competed with IBM, Sperry, and several other major computer vendors. Rather than emphasizing price, H-P returned to its old formula with the HP–3000—reliability and customer service. It was a winning combination again.

Both Bill Hewlett and Dave Packard left their firm with great dignity in 1978. Buying an Idaho cattle ranch together, they rode the range and gathered their cattle with the HP-Bar brand. Packard functioned as part of President Reagan's "kitchen cabinet" and chaired a blue ribbon commission on defense management which monitored Pentagon spending. David Packard recently gave more than $2 billion, the bulk of his fortune, to charity. Starting in 1988, he gradually donated his 450,000 shares of H-P to the David and Lucille Packard Foundation which he and his wife set up in 1964 to support scientific and health research and to tackle a broad range of social problems.

Hewlett-Packard, in the meantime, has continued to grow and remain profitable under the guidance of John Young. In 1980 the company brought out a $120,000 laser printer which, by using microprocessors, can turn digital information into charts, tables, and business forms and then send them on to computers in remote locations. In January 1981, H-P entered the upper levels of the new personal computer market with a new personal computer. This was all part of a grand new strategy to enter the lucrative, but highly competitive, office automation market. Although the company experienced some difficulties in these markets, its efforts were generally successful. By 1984, revenues were $6.3 billion, of which $3.4 billion came from data processing products. At that point, Hewlett-Packard, which had started in such a modest manner in the 1960s, was the eighth largest company in the data processing industry. With 80,000 employees in eighty countries, it had a staggeringly large product line of 9,700 different items related to data processing.

Then, in 1985, H-P began to work on an entirely new computer line based on a new technology called RISC (Reduced Instruction Set Computer). The RISC system was designed to eliminate extraneous instructions so that the computer could execute the most common jobs more quickly. This would make it possible to produce more powerful computers at a lower cost. There was an urgency for a new system, because H-P's market share in computers began to slide in the 1980s, from 7.3 percent in 1982 to 5.9 percent in 1986. As DEC and other computer manufacturers introduced more powerful machines, H-P characteristically held back. The two-year delay in introducing its new machines alienated many of the firm's top managers so much that several left the company and H-P's stock dropped to an all-time low of 28 in 1985. Earnings also fell for the first time in a decade.

When the Spectrum (RISC) computer line entered the market, however, the situation turned around dramatically for H-P. Revenues rose 14 percent in 1987, to over $8 billion, and market share in computers shot back up to 7 percent. Profits stood at $614 million, a 25-percent increase over the year before. Craig Symons, an industry analyst, declared that "Clearly, H-P is now the only mid-range company that has a legitimate shot at Digital and IBM." By the late 1980s H-P was primarily a computer company, with computers accounting for 65 percent of its revenues. With its research and development spending at nearly $1 billion, representing over 11 percent of its sales, H-P intended to stay on top. Only DEC approached H-P in the percentage of revenues devoted to research and development.

In the 1920s Frederick Terman had a dream—a grand vision of an industrial park that would surround Stanford University. When it officially opened in 1956, its first resident was the Hewlett-Packard Company. By the 1980s, it was glittering spectacle of green valleys crammed with more than 1,000 high-technology firms. Even by 1960, its reknown was so great that when General Charles de Gaulle visited California, there were only two places he wanted to visit: Disneyland and Silicon Valley.

Nor did David Packard and William Hewlett ever forget how Fred Terman helped them. Terman sat on the board of H-P for more than forty years; always he was treated with respect and admiration by his two former students. In the late 1970s, Hewlett and Packard donated millions to Stanford to build a new electrical engineering building, called the Frederick Terman, Jr., Building. On hand the day it was dedicated, Terman, old and infirm, listened to the glowing speeches made by his two former students about his contributions. Hewlett, Packard, and Terman, the three pioneers of California's Silicon Valley. Terman's vision gave it its start; Hewlett and Packard's management style gave the valley its distinctive ethic—the Hewlett-Packard model—the H-P Way. (**B.** *Business Week,* December 14, 1957, January 29, 1972, June 1, 1987, March 7, March 14, 1988; *Time,* January 25, 1963, May 9, 1988; *Newsweek,* January 25, 1969; *Current Biography,* 1969; *Fortune,* October 1976, October 1, 1984, April 25, 1988; *Management Today,* August 1977; *Financial World,* April 1, 1979, February 9, 1988; Milton Moskowitz et al. *Everybody's Business*, 1980; *Forbes*, March 2, 1981; Thomas J. Peters and Robert H. Waterman, Jr., *In Search of Excellence*, 1982; Hewlett-Packard Company, *Hewlett-Packard: A Company History*, 1983; Stephen T. McClellan, *The Coming Computer Industry Shakeout*, 1984; Everett M. Rogers and Judith K. Larson, *Silicon Valley Fever: Growth of High Technology Culture*, 1984; Joseph J. Fucini and Suzy Fucini, *Entrepreneurs*, 1985; Michael S. Malone, *The Big Score, 1985; A. David Silver, Entrepreneurial Megabucks*, 1985; *Who's Who in America*, 1986–87; Michael Patrick Allen, *The Founding Families*, 1987; James W. Cordata, *Historical Dictionary of Data Processing Organizations*, 1987.)

HOLMAN, CURRIER J. (1911–February 16, 1977). Beef processor, Iowa Beef Processors. It was an incongruous sight—a shabby Manhattan courtroom, usually the habitat of shady, underworld characters, petty crooks, and prostitutes—but standing there that day in October 1974 was a dignified sixty-three-year-old man, dressed in a tailored brown suit, with matching shirt and tie. He had just been convicted by the judge on two counts each of conspiring to bribe supermarket butchers' union officials and supermarket chain executives to get his company's boxed beef products into New York area supermarkets. Worse, the bribes were given to one Moe Steinman, reputed to be a highly placed Mafia figure. The judge, however, sympathized with the man, saying "There are few people in American business who would have acted differently in these circumstances." The judge continued, "Sadly, like a modern-day Dr. Faustus, Currier J. Holman sold his soul to Moe Steinman." He then gave Holman an unconditional discharge without a sentence, saying to Holman, "I like you and was tempted to acquit you." Before sentencing, Currier Holman had said to the court, "If I'm as guilty as you say I am, then I should pay whatever penalty that requires. But I disagree with your assessment of the facts. I disagree that I'm guilty." Later, Holman was to say in a more general way, "Business as we pursue it here at IBP is very much like waging war." The *Wall Street Journal* (December 17, 1976) was less certain about the contrition of Holman or Iowa Beef, commenting that the "company's history is laced with criminals, gangland figures, civil wrongdoers, brazen conflicts of interest, and possible violations of antitrust and labor law."

Currier Holman was born in Sioux City, Iowa, educated in area schools, and attended Notre Dame University. He began his career in the meat-packing industry as a slaughterhouse butcher for Swift & Company in the 1930s, and then he spent many years as an independent cattle dealer and order buyer in the Sioux City stockyards. In 1960, with a $300,000 loan from the Small Business Administration, he and Andy Anderson founded the Iowa Beef Processing (IBP) Company, with a single beef slaughterhouse and processing plant in Denison, Iowa. Although the firm started in a small way, it helped revolutionize the meat-packing industry in the United States. Anderson was particularly responsible for the technical innovations; Holman provided the managerial stability in the early years.

The Iowa Beef system was ingenious. First of all, its plants were set up in small towns, first Denison, then West Point, Nebraska, and Emporia, Kansas. Previously, live cattle had been shipped to Kansas City, Omaha, or Chicago, losing weight the longer they traveled. The cattle were then sold to one of the big beef processing firms, whose plants were staffed by high-wage workers. At Iowa Beef, from the beginning, the plants were highly automated, and wages, therefore, were kept comparatively low. IBP's cattle buyers (known as the Iowa Boys' Patrol because of their radio-equipped cars) bought cattle directly from the farmers, cutting out middlemen at the stockyards, and coordinating their purchases with the needs of their nearby plant. Iowa Beef paid farmers about as much as they would have received in Chicago or Kansas City, but it saved them transportation costs, yard expenses, and commissions. Naturally, farmers were elated to sell to Iowa Beef, and Iowa Beef got cattle that were fully fattened and would not lose weight in transportation. IBP then used truck transport, not railroads, to bring the cattle to its plants—and to ship the final product to its customers.

When they arrived at the plant, the cattle were slaughtered in a different manner at Iowa Beef. Under the old meat-packing system, cattle were taken to the fifth floor of an old packinghouse, where skilled, highly paid cattle butchers killed and reduced each steer to a carcass, in effect working individually or in small groups, very much in the older craft tradition. Under the system devised by Anderson and Holman, an animal was taken to a large, single-storey building, where it was stunned, lifted by one hoof onto a moving chain, killed, halved, and quartered. This process was not undertaken by highly skilled, highly paid butchers, but by laborers who performed a series of simple, specialized tasks— removing the hoofs or tail, slitting open the abdomen, or halving the carcass— that reduced the steer to boxed, plastic, vacuum-wrapped cuts of meat. These cuts, of course, were the same as those produced by individual neighborhood butchers, but Iowa Beef did it faster and more efficiently and could save supermarkets time and labor costs. Furthermore, the shelf life of the vacuum- wrapped boxed beef was about one month, compared to from three to seven days for the carcass. This boxed-beef product was then sold to 2,500 supermarket chains, meat brokers, wholesalers, and restaurant and hotel chains. Since only relatively light boxes of high-priced meat were shipped, the per-pound freight costs were lower. The remainder of the meat, which could not be cut into these boxed assortments, was sold to other manufacturers for use in shoe leather, dog food, laundry detergent, cosmetics, and chewing gum. Although other packers also practiced this, the scale of operations at Iowa Beef allowed it to make even more money on what is called the drop. According to one Iowa Beef official, "Our drop can get as high as $50 a head, and our kill costs are less than that."

These cost-cutting innovations gave Iowa Beef great advantages over its competitors in the marketplace, and it soon became the dominant meat-packing firm in the country. Even with the automation Holman introduced, beef slaughtering remained a highly labor-intensive business, but Holman successfully divided that labor into its simplest elements, just as scientific management people had divided labor in other factory settings years earlier, and he significantly reduced the cost of slaughter. At Holman's first plant in Denison, he had a kill cost of $10 a head, whereas the cost for conventional packers was from $15 to $20 a head. Since the profit margin on a head of beef was often only about $5 or $6, Iowa Beef obviously had an immediate advantage. Holman also had advantages of economies of scale—the original Denison plant could slaughter 500 cattle a day, and twenty years later could slaughter 1,500 a day. The Dakota City, Nebraska, plant initially could slaughter 1,600 head a day; by 1980, 3,500. This gave the IBP plants a capacity to slaughter between 300,000 and 1 million cattle a year. Although far less well known than the established "barons" of the beef industry—Swift & Company, Armour, Wilson, Morrell, and Cudahy—IBP soon surpassed them in sales, as it soared from total obscurity in 1960 to sales in the billions by the early 1970s. Its market share, which was zero in 1961, rose to 8 percent by 1973, and by 1980 was 16 percent. Although this was a far cry from the kind of market domination IBM or AT&T enjoyed, IBP's competitors nonetheless often raised cries of monopoly. But, in fact, by the mid–1970s Iowa Beef was bigger than the five giant beef barons combined. Sales in 1980 amounted to a whopping $4.6 billion. Holman's achievement with Iowa Beef was so original in conception, so daring in implementation, that *Forbes* in 1981 commented that it should "rank with Alfred Sloan's* reorganization of General Motors in the twenties or the evolution of IBM's long-term marketing strategy in the fifties." Officials at Iowa Beef viewed the situation in more elementary terms: "We are only out to be the lowest-cost producer in the industry."

But these innovations ran afoul of several powerful vested interests in the industry. The meat-packing industry had been governed for some time by nationwide master agreements with the United Food and Commercial Workers International Union (UFCW), which represented 80 percent of the industry's 158,000 employees. Holman systematically demolished this arrangement and, consequently, withstood a series of bitter and violent strikes in his plants. The major points of contention between IBP and UFCW were wages and benefits. The UFCW wanted skilled butcher rates for assembly-line labor, which IBP steadfastly refused to pay. IBP bucked the union's demands by organizing its plants without unions, by signing with other unions, like the Teamsters, or by signing separate agreements with UFCW locals. According to an IBP official, Holman was prepared to have one of every three IBP plants out on strike at any given time, and still continue processing enough beef for its markets. The system worked. The success of Holman and IBP in resisting union demands had a devastating ripple effect throughout the industry.

Armour complained that its average $16 hourly cost of wages and benefits was from 40 to 60 percent higher than the cost at Iowa Beef. The union, for its part, promised the old-line packers that wages at IBP would be increased to meet the industry level. But, as the president of Swift & Company said, "Not only did they fail, they couldn't even organize a lot of these companies, and their membership started dwindling." As a result, the old firms found themselves stuck with high-cost labor and restrictive work rules. This impeded their entrance into the areas where IBP succeeded. Specifically, they did not begin producing boxed beef to compete with IBP, since, as the Swift president said, "When you're at a noncompetitive cost, the more you do to the animal, the more noncompetitive you get." During the 1970s, at least 350 meat-packing firms closed down. Venerable Wilson got out of beef slaughter entirely, as did Hormel and Cudahy; by the early 1980s, Armour and Morrell had only a couple of plants left; and Esmark sold off its Swift meat-packing holdings to the public in 1980. Iowa Beef was unsympathetic. In fact, that was a central part of its overall strategy. An internal memo in 1975 called for price cuts "deep enough to force some of our competitors out of the product/market segment and some of our competitors out of business." This was the reason many meat-packers accused IBP of monopoly practices.

But Iowa Beef's victory over the union was not without its costs to all sides. An especially violent strike in Iowa in 1969 and 1970 was marked by a number of shootings and several murders. The home of Holman's next-door neighbor, who was also IBP's general counsel, was destroyed by a radio-controlled incendiary bomb. In spite of everything, Iowa Beef achieved its goal, and the union was left out in the cold. As a result, the pressures on the workers increased tremendously, and IBP went through workers almost as fast as carcasses. The union claimed that IBP went through 20,000 workers in ten years to fill the 2,000 positions in the Dakota City plant. As an IBP official said, after taking a reporter on a tour of IBP's Dakota City plant: "What you saw down there was a factory. None of us are really in the meat business. We're in the tonnage business. Beef just happens to be our raw material." The result of IBP's antiunion campaign was devastating for both the workers and the union. By 1988, unions represented only 65 percent of the industry's 130,000 employees, down from the 90 percent of the early 1970s. Wages also fell drastically as IBP and other employers undercut union pay scales. In the summer of 1988, the UFCW discovered a new weapon. The union mounted a highly sophisticated campaign designed to spotlight unsafe practices in IBP's plants. As a result, in the summer of 1988, the Occupational Safety and Health Administration fined IBP a staggering $5.6 million, the largest fine ever levied by the agency. To ward off further challenges, IBP finally recognized the UFCW at its Joliet, Illinois, plant. It was a stunning symbolic victory for the union.

Holman and Iowa Beef had other union problems, which placed him and the company in hot water. Holman's system of producing boxed beef not only threatened union jobs in the packing industry, but also put thousands of local butchers and meat cutters out of work. Thus, in order for IBP's boxed beef to find acceptance, Holman had to reorganize the market, and that was a massive undertaking. The only market big enough to absorb the enormous output churned out by IBP at its giant, new Dakota City plant was metropolitan New York City, which consumed one-quarter of the nation's meat production. But the city's supermarket distribution system was heavily influenced by organized crime figures, and the city's unions were tightly interlaced into that complex structure. It was clear that some extraordinary measures would have to be taken. As *Forbes* commented in 1981, "Though IBP's executives may have been barefoot boys from the cornfields of Iowa, they weren't born yesterday, and they could hardly have been unaware that getting boxed beef into New York City was going to take some heavy payoffs in the right places." One IBP official even commented, "It was a common practice that people paid off other people to do business in New York City."

The union that controlled the New York butchers, the UFCW, was the same union that Holman was battling at his packing plants. Thus, he knew they would not be receptive to his boxed beef, even if only because of the company's bitter history of labor relations in the Midwest. But the battle entailed more than that. IBP's boxed beef threatened to put a lot of member butchers of the UFCW in New York out of a job. So, the situation for Iowa Beef in 1969 was very tense. They had a huge new plant at Dakota City geared up to send out 40,000 boxed carcasses a week, but they could not gain entrance into the New York market. Also, in August of that year, the union struck the Dakota City plant, and an especially bitter and violent strike soon spread to IBP's other plants.

In 1970, Holman was introduced to Moe Steinman, a labor consultant who had ties with both the New York meat-cutters union and the beef-buyers at most New York supermarkets. Steinman also had close ties with organized crime figures such as Johnny Dioguardi and Paul Castellano, both of whom were deeply involved in the city's meat and supermarket businesses. Holman said that Steinman told him, "Maybe I can help you in New York City. Maybe I can help you with your labor problems." Holman replied, "We can sure use all the help we can get." In April, Steinman brought Holman together with union officials in New York, and Holman was told that if he wanted to get his beef into New York City, he would have to settle the strike in Dakota City. Shortly thereafter, the strike was settled, and IBP agreed to drop a $4.5-million damage suit against the union. In return, the union agreed to suspend its boycott of IBP's boxed meat in the New York area.

But Steinman was not finished. He set up a sales agency known as C.P. Sales, into which IBP paid a penny for every pound of beef it sold in New York. It was clear to Holman and other IBP officials that this money was to be used to bribe union officials, supermarket buyers, and Steinman himself. They were galled at this arrangement and mortified that they had to conduct business with someone like Steinman. When the judge later passed sentence on this case, he described Steinman in colorful terms:

Steinman's appearance was, by all accounts, one that engendered immediate distrust. As one witness put it, "He was a furtive-looking character out of *Guys and Dolls*. I thought he was a messenger or a coffee-getter, some greasy, sleazy-looking fellow who never looked you in the eye." (*Farm Journal*, December 1974)

One of IBP's executives at the time referred to Steinman as "raunchy" and "low class." But Holman simply said, "Do you want to get your meat in New York City, or don't you? It's the largest meat market in the world." C.P. Sales, which did not handle the meat and did not have to handle any of the administrative details, received commissions of more than $1 million a year from IBP. Ultimately, however, the whole affair was exposed, and both Holman and Steinman were convicted of conspiring to bribe union officials and supermarket executives. Holman was freed on an unconditional discharge, and IBP was fined a paltry $7,000. Iowa Beef continued to pay millions in commissions to C.P. Sales, which was then run by Walter Bodenstein, a lawyer who happened to be Steinman's son-in-law, until the relationship finally ended in December 1977.

By this time, Holman had died, Robert Peterson had taken his place as chief executive, and Iowa Beef had sales of $2.1 billion, employed about 7,500 people, and slaughtered about 10 percent of the beef in the United States. And IBP had the New York market in its pocket. In succeeding years, under the guidance of Peterson, IBP opened up one city after another to boxed beef. By the early 1980s, only one major city—St. Louis—still remained closed to boxed beef. Peterson also continued Holman's policy of building ever-larger meat-packing facilities and, by the early 1980s, had four such plants in operation—all with capacities of at least 500,000 head of cattle a year. In 1981, IBP was in the process of building a massive $100-million plant in Finney County, Kansas, with the capacity to process 1.2 million head of cattle, making it the largest boxed-beef plant in the world. With that plant, IBP planned to invade the West for the first time, tackling the country's second largest market, Los Angeles. Peterson commented at the time, "We see no end of growth opportunities." An important area of expansion being considered by Peterson—one that would have a revolutionary impact on the American meat industry—was pork. Peterson felt he had to wait until his Finney plant was operating efficiently, but then he had plans to bring the same efficiencies to pork production that Holman had brought to beef. The old-line pork producers were terrified at the prospect, and Peterson said that IBP's cost advantages through automation and lower wage workers would be so overwhelming that it would be able to deliver pork to the packers more cheaply than they could do it for themselves. As a former executive said, "Iowa Beef is absolutely driven to be the lowest-cost producer. It's going to apply that to the pork business."

Before those plans could be actualized, however, a more important transformation took place at Iowa Beef. It merged with Armand Hammer's* Occidental Petroleum. With sales of $4.6 billion and revenues of $53 million, Iowa Beef was sold to Occidental for $800 million. Peterson, in announcing Iowa Beef's approval of the merger, said it "provides unlimited potential for economies of scale as well as expanded sales of U.S. meat products abroad." He also said the merger would allow Iowa Beef to speed up "somewhat" the company's plans to move into pork packing. Occidental, with revenues of $12.5 billion in 1980, surprised analysts by its purchase of Iowa Beef, but a spokesman said, "We've wanted Oxy to be a significant factor in food. This didn't just come out of the blue, but we had no idea that a company of Iowa Beef's stature would be available." Soon after the merger, Iowa Beef began to process pork, and it negotiated for the purchase of Wilson & Company's large pork slaughtering operations. By 1986 IBP was opening its third plant for hog slaughtering. A former market researcher at Iowa Beef commented about his ex-company: "There's no frivolity at IBP. They're like the University of Texas football team— they never stop." (**B.** *Farm Journal*, April 1973, December 1974; *Wall Street Journal*, October 8, 1974, December 17, 1976, February 18, 1977, August 13, 1981, October 4, 1984, May 21, 1986; *New York Times,* February 18, 1977; *Who Was Who*, vol. VII; *Business Week*, July 14, 1980; *The Insider's Chronicle*, August 25, 1980; Milton Moskowitz et al., *Everybody's Business*, 1980; *Forbes*, June 22, 1981; *Fortune*, June 29, 1981; *Business Week*, August 29, 1988.)

I

ICAHN, CARL CELIAN (1936–   ). Financier, corporate raider, airline executive, Icahn & Company, TWA. Carl Icahn is the corporate raider and greenmailer par excellence. If Saul Steinberg† invented greenmail, and if T. Boone Pickens† became an accomplished, if perhaps somewhat unwilling, practitioner of the art, Carl Icahn was its virtuoso. During his early years, at least, Icahn made little pretense or excuse for his greenmailing activities, beyond the rather standard corporate raider line that he was acting in the interest of the small shareholder by cleaning up inept management.

Unlike the often pious protestations of Pickens, Icahn always insisted he was "no Robin Hood," that he was in the game primarily for the profit. It came as a great shock, then, in 1986 when Carl Icahn, the great raider, ended up owning TWA. Icahn, the great scourge of American management, ended up as a manager himself. What was perhaps even more astounding was that Icahn was ultimately invited to take control of TWA—by the company's unions. Carl Icahn, the "Darth Vader of Wall Street," was in 1986 presented as the savior of a great, but troubled, American airline.

Carl Icahn was born in the Bayswater section of Queens, New York, one of the so-called outer boroughs of New York City. His father, Michael Icahn, was a lawyer, but apparently he lacked ambition and was a bit of a dreamer. In any event, he hated being a lawyer, so he resigned and began teaching chemistry. He also detested teaching, and professed that his great love and ambition was to be an opera singer, like Enrico Caruso. The closest he got to achieving that ambition was when he was employed as a cantor in a nearby synagogue. Ultimately, Michael Icahn developed a "heart condition" in the early 1940s and stopped working entirely until his death in 1978. A friend recalled, "He read Schopenhauer and listened to records, day and night." Carl Icahn's mother was responsible for supporting the family during these years by teaching school. Despite these problems, the Icahn life-style was comfortable. As M. Elliott Schnall, Icahn's uncle, recalled: "There weren't that many luxuries, but he didn't grow up poor. New York schoolteachers had nice salaries then. Theirs was a very nice lifestyle.''

Carl Icahn was educated in local public schools and graduated from Far Rockaway High School in 1953, where he did well enough to be accepted at Princeton University. There he majored in philosophy and developed an intense passion for chess—a passion that gave him the tactical grounding for many of his later raids. Icahn graduated from Princeton in 1957 without much direction. To satisfy his mother's wishes, Icahn enrolled in the New York University School of Medicine. He hated that probably as much as his father hated practicing law, but he stayed with it for three years. Icahn finally quit, partly because he feared he was becoming a hypochondriac. He then joined the U.S. Army, where he learned a new game—poker. He found this game had all the fun and tactical challenge of chess, but it had an added thrill—he could make money at it, lots of it. Gambling for fun and profit became an obsession he carried over into the business world with great success. And he gambled at all games—he even played Monopoly for real money. A friend recalled: "I walked into Carl's apartment, and there he was with this enormous pile of cash, buying Boardwalk for $500.''

When Icahn got out of the army in 1961, he wanted to work where the money was, so Elliott Schnall got him a job as an trainee stockbroker with Dreyfus & Company. Confident that he had a magic touch with money, Icahn began investing his poker winnings in the stock market. Before long, he had made $50,000 in a bull market, which he reinvested, only to lose it all when the market fell in 1962. In 1980 Icahn told the *New York Times*, "It was so bad that I sold my white convertible Galaxie to get enough money to eat and pay the rent. That's what hurt the most; I really loved that car." "I was so upset," Icahn told *Business Week*, "that I've really worked like crazy ever since."

Icahn decided he needed a niche; he wanted to find an area where few others were involved. He found this in option trading, which was still in its infancy in the early 1960s. Few brokers understood them at the time, but Icahn became a master; by 1963, he was manager of the Option Department at Tessel, Patrick & Company. A year later, he took a similar position at Gruntel & Company. Since information on options was not available at that time, Icahn began to publish the *Mid-Week Option Report*, and he built a strong base of options sellers. By 1968, his department was earning gross commissions of nearly $1.5 million weekly, making it one of the most profitable at Gruntel. Icahn decided he wanted to open his own brokerage firm.

Again Icahn turned to his uncle, Elliott Schnall, from whom he got a loan of $400,000 to purchase a seat on the New York Stock Exchange. This was not just largesse on Schnall's part. Icahn had made a fortune for his uncle on the option market, sending him about $100,000 a year during the late 1960s. For Schnall this was like manna from heaven since, as he told *Fortune*, "To be honest, I still don't know the difference between a put and a call." What Schnall did understand was that Carl Icahn knew how to make money, and he was investing in his nephew's future. Icahn opened an office at 42 Broadway and brought with him an associate, Alfred Kingsley, who was a brilliant market analyst. Kingsley has generally been credited with being a major factor in Icahn's success, but he has never shared significantly in Icahn's winnings. Kingsley left Icahn for two years, from 1973 to 1975, according to a friend, because Icahn was "paying him spit." Kingsley found, however, that despite his talent he could not find a better position on Wall Street, so he returned to Icahn. But he was never made a partner. Carl Icahn does not like partners; he does not want to have to answer to anyone. "I've learned over the years," he said, "a dollar bill is a better partner than a partner." A former employee also felt that it was because Icahn was just plain tightfisted: "He is a keen valuer of assets, and that's how he judges people too—how profitable you are to him. It's somewhat cold."

In any event, after founding Icahn & Company, Icahn and Kingsley began mixing arbitrage with options. It was a complicated operation, but Icahn mastered it. "There were great opportunities to make money," he said. He particularly relished a cool profit of $1.5 million he made in arbitraging Polaroid stock. In 1973, the Chicago Options Board opened, but the field soon became too crowded for Icahn's taste. "Always, I looked for a spot that was not too popular," he said. "You want to be in something other people don't see—and which makes the eminent sense."

Looking for a way to make money, Icahn began to buy large amounts of stock in companies he and Kingsley felt were undervalued. They then held onto these stocks until they rose in value and could be sold. The first of these was a mutual fund named Highland. Icahn and an investment group bought about 30 percent of it at $2, and sold it two years later at $6. After that, he bought 4.9 percent of several other closed-end funds—at 5 percent he was required to report the purchase to the Securities Exchange Commission (SEC)—and then he sold out for a premium each time. At no point was there any attempt at takeover or greenmail. Following these techniques, Icahn had built his firm into one of the most profitable on Wall Street. An $80,000 investment in Icahn & Company when it was founded was worth $4 million a decade later. But too many people were entering the risk-arbitrage game, and he felt the field was getting crowded. So, again, he sought alternatives. That turned out to be the whole cat-and-mouse game of corporate takeovers, which Icahn entered almost by accident.

In 1978, Icahn had started another risk-arbitrage action with the Tappan Company, a well-known manufacturer of household appliances. As usual in these risk-arbitrage cases, Tappan's stock was in a depressed state, and it stood a good chance of rising when Icahn started buying it. By mid–1978, Icahn had invested about $3 million in some 292,000 shares of Tappan's stock. His plan was to wait quietly for someone to take over the company, at which point the stock price would rise, and Icahn's company would reap a substantial profit. However, even after Icahn waited many months, no takeover was imminent. When Tappan's board learned that Icahn had begun prospecting for a buyer, they brought out a new issue of preferred stock, making a takeover more difficult to achieve.

At that point, Icahn decided to campaign for a seat on the board, arguing that he was trying to find a buyer who would pay shareholders a price well in excess of the current market price. Icahn was elected to the board, and, bowing to pressure from him and other shareholders, the board voted to accept a $18-per-share offer from Electrolux to take over Tappan. Icahn immediately sold his Tappan shares, reaping a profit of $2.8 million, since he had paid just $8 for his shares.

Encouraged by his success with Tappan and with the prospects of large and quick profits, Icahn began to look for other takeover/greenmail targets. Before 1979 was over he had zeroed in on Saxon Industries: he bought its stock at $7, sold it back several months later for $10.50, and made a profit of $1.9 million. During the same year, Icahn also made a run at Baird & Warner Real Estate Investment Trust (REIT). When confronted by Icahn, the REIT tried to liquidate itself rather than fall into his conniving hands, but Icahn thwarted the liquidation scheme, won a proxy fight, and ended up in full control of the company. This was not quite the way these things were supposed to turn out, but Icahn renamed the company Bayswater Realty & Capital, took it private, and used the firm to hold shares in companies that Icahn was raiding.

These ventures were so easily accomplished that Icahn pursued Hammermill Paper Company in 1980. But Hammermill's board fought back with a vengeance. After extensive litigation, the company won a proxy fight with Icahn, which enabled it to decrease the number of seats on the board. In a heated meeting, Icahn faced off with Albert Duvall, Hammermill's chief executive officer (CEO). One of Icahn's former partners recalled the confrontation:

Here's this poor guy from Hammermill, a real Ivy League guy, and he's sitting there thinking that the world works the way it always has, with his golf clubs and his graduating class, and he never raises his voice—and all of a sudden, he's got Carl, who is such a fighter. It's terrible. Carl was a scourge in those days. (*Manhattan, Inc.*)

But Duval called Icahn's bluff. He said, "I'm not putting you on the board, I'm not buying you out, I'm not selling the company right now." He knew Icahn did not have the financial resources to back up his raid on Hammermill. Icahn got a $750,000 payment for agreeing to the new board structure and for promising to mount no raids for a year. Furthermore, his capital was still tied up in Hammermill. Finally, after a year, Hammermill bought back Icahn's shares, on which he reaped a profit of $9.6 million. This was big money for Icahn, but it did little for his reputation on Wall Street—he was still regarded as a lightweight. "The guy was a laughing stock in the late 1970's," recalled a rival arbitrager. "My boss wouldn't return his calls."

By 1981, when Icahn had finally extricated his money from Hammermill, he was ready to attack Simplicity Pattern Company. Although Simplicity found a "white knight" to buy the company, Icahn made a tidy profit of $7.3 million on his four-month operation. But he still generated little interest on Wall Street or on the business pages. Such was not the case with his next target—Marshall Field & Company, the giant retailer, and one of the American Establishment's prize entities. In late 1981, Icahn began to buy Marshall Field stock at $15 per share; by early February 1982, he owned close to 15 percent of the company. He then approached Field's management and offered a "standstill agreement"— he would cease purchasing stock if they would give him a seat on the board and a chance to participate in decisions of the company's investments. Field responded by suing Icahn under the Racketeer Influenced and Corrupt Organization Act (RICO) and by branding him a "notorious corporate opportunist," who made his money from a "pattern of racketeering." An old friend of Icahn's said, "To have a conversation with them one day and then be called a racketeer by them the next really upset Carl, but I don't think he took it personally." Icahn retaliated by accusing Field of violating federal securities law and by buying additional stock. By March he held close to 30 percent. At that point, Marshall Field announced it had found a white knight—Batus, the U.S. unit of British American Tobacco, which was buying Field stock at $25.50. Icahn, who had paid an average of $15 for his shares, cried foul and asked a federal judge to block the tender offer. Ultimately, Batus offered $30 a share, and the bid was accepted. Icahn walked out of the fight with a profit of $17.6 million. Other Field's stockholders had seen the price of their shares double.

By this point, Icahn had more than $100 million at his disposal and had become a far more feared raider. He began to behave even more aggressively. His next victim was Anchor Hocking Company, in which Icahn purchased a 6-percent stake; he managed to coerce the company to buy him out a month later for double his investment. Icahn made $3 million on this maneuver. Immediately he went after the American Can Company, and he forced that firm to buy back one million shares at a price 30 percent above the market. But then Icahn got caught in another bitter confrontation that helped cement his reputation as the most rapacious of the corporate raiders. In late 1982 he began to buy shares in the Dan River Company, a South Carolina textile firm. Dan River had just successfully fought off two raids when Icahn struck in September, announcing that his group had purchased 6.9 percent of its shares and were interested in "gaining control" or possibly splitting up the company. Dan River, like its unfortunate predecessors Hammerhill and Marshall Field, fought back vehemently. On October 6 it filed suit charging Icahn with violations of securities laws. The company also announced that it was issuing a new series of preferred shares. In response, Icahn sued in federal court and filed with the SEC. Dan River then used Marshall Field's ploy—it charged Icahn with racketeering. Dan River charged that Icahn made his money through "extortion," and that "Dan River is only the latest victim of Icahn's tactics. . . . Icahn and his group have already successfully dislodged $83 million from various American corporations in the last two months alone."

Icahn was furious: "I consider it an abomination that company's management should resort to these gutter and smear tactics." He then doubled his tender offer for the company, but management again rejected the offer. Icahn then upped his bid to $18, and Dan River began to look for white knights. He again upped his offer—this time to $21, offering to buy all of Dan River's shares. The management at Dan River responded by offering to pay $22.50 a share for all the company's shares by setting up an Employee Stock Option Plan (ESOP). Dan River had decided to go "private." Icahn, however, would not surrender, and, in January 1983, the two opponents finally signed an agreement. Dan River borrowed $149 million to complete its internal buyout, and Icahn made a profit of $8.5 million after expenses, in just six months. Icahn was by this time regarded as one of the preeminent raiders on Wall Street, a new status that increased the amount of acrimony he received.

A resident of Danville, Virginia, where Dan River is located, was blunt in her assessment of Icahn: "Icahn has raped this community," she said. Icahn became associated in the public's mind with a handful of prominent corporate raiders. Andrew Sigler, head of Champion International, said of these raiders: "The robber barons look like corner muggers in comparison to the amounts now being made." According to Senator William Proxmire, "The rising tide of hostile takeovers threatens the very foundation of our American business system." The executive vice president of Phillips Petroleum, under siege from the raiders, said, "Corporate raiders, like Boone Pickens and Carl Icahn, have bent the plowshares of free enterprise into the swords of economic chaos."

Strong words these, but Icahn, like other raiders, developed a rationale for his actions. He was not a raider—he was a "corporate dissident," the "champion of the ordinary shareholder"—and he was battling against lazy, entrenched management. Icahn had accused the managers of large public corporations of becoming the "new aristocracy," a group answerable to no one until he and others began standing up for the rights of the individual shareholder. Icahn has been caustic in his condemnation of management:

American management today is what I call a pernicious type of nepotism, where you have a CEO that gets there sort of like the fraternity brother in college. The fellow you elected to be president of the fraternity in college was certainly not necessarily the best and the brightest. . . . He was the good guy, the guy you liked to go drinking with. And that is the guy who gets into the corporation . . . works his way up, likable guy. . . . It's what I call the anti-Darwinian theory, the survival of the unfittest. In a lot of corporations, a guy gets to the top by kowtowing, and then picks somebody to succeed him who has done the same. (Allison, *The Raiders of Wall Street*)

In any event, by 1983 Icahn was a major league raider—the mere mention of his name set company management aquiver. When he bought three million shares in Gulf & Western, he did not even have to approach the company. As soon as people became aware Icahn had bought into the company, they assumed the stock price would go up dramatically—so everybody began buying. This pushed the price of G&W's stock up from $22, where Icahn bought it, to $29, where he sold it two months later. He had made a profit of $19 million in two months and had not even attempted a takeover, had not even hinted at greenmail. He just bought the stock, sat back and waited two months, and sold it for a handsome profit.

Icahn did something else in 1983—he bought a company. He did not threaten to buy a company; he bought it. He went after ACF Industries, a railroad car manufacturing and leasing company. Icahn paid about $32 a share for a stake in the company, then, when management attempted a buyout, he refused to sell his stock to them, instead making a tender offer of $54.50 for all its shares. It cost Icahn $410 million to buy ACF and to pay for it he floated a loan of $225 million and paid for the balance by selling off parts of the company. It was a classic leveraged buyout, but it surprised many analysts, since this had not been Icahn's pattern. Most observers thought he would just gut the company—sell off its component parts, close whatever did not sell—and walk off with the profits. Although he had never expressed much interest in becoming a manager, Icahn proved an able administrator at ACF. Although he sold off some unprofitable units and laid off a number of workers, ACF's first-half profits for 1985 increased by 40 percent.

As 1984 dawned, Icahn was ready to ascend to higher plateaus. He was approached by an executive at Drexel, Burnham, Lambert, who offered Icahn a war chest for future acquisition assembled through junk-bond financing. Michael Milken† of Drexel had developed a superb network of junk-bond buyers, and was thus able to raise massive amounts of money virtually overnight. For a raider like Icahn, who liked the element of surprise and speed, it was an ideal arrangement. Icahn, however, was less compliant than Milken's other clients. Whereas Drexel always took equity as part of their payment in these deals, Icahn refused to give them any. As a result, Milken only raised about half as much for Icahn as he might have. Nonetheless, Icahn and Milken became close associates in various deals over the next several years. During 1984, Icahn took runs at Chesebrough-Ponds, Uniroyal, and Goodrich Tire. These activities resulted in Icahn's reaping a total profit of $29 million.

In 1985, Drexel financed Icahn in an attempt to take over Phillips Petroleum. Just a few months before, they had bankrolled T. Boone Pickens in his takeover attempt at the giant oil firm, but he had taken greenmail and pulled out. Now Icahn agreed to make a proxy fight and tender offer for Phillips. This was the largest deal either Icahn or Drexel had been involved in. It was also a historic occasion. It was the first tender offer ever launched without the financing in place and without the participation of any bank. This was the first wholly junk-bond-financed deal. Milken provided Icahn with a letter saying that Drexel was "highly confident" it could raise the funds, which became the most famous phrase in junk-bond financing. Icahn offered Phillips an $8.1-billion deal that was part cash and part securities. The $4-billion debt load was to be paid with Phillips' own cash flow and asset sales. Ultimately, Phillips voted to restructure the corporation, and Icahn agreed to sell his stock back to them for a profit of

$52.5 million, more than twice the amount he had made in any previous deal. This deal secured Drexel's reputation in the financial community. In Icahn's next deal, he and Drexel were opponents.

Icahn went after TWA in May 1985. He and a group of investors bought a 20.5-percent share in the company for about $95 million. When that became public knowledge, TWA's stock began inching upward. Meanwhile, TWA's board took actions to protect themselves from a takeover by Icahn. They filed a number of suits against him, but Icahn was undeterred, and he offered to buy the rest of the TWA's stock for $18 a share for a total of $600 million. TWA was a troubled company. Its losses for 1985 were estimated at $140 million, and it suffered from poor labor relations. TWA's board members realized that the only way they could protect themselves from Icahn was to find a white knight. They appealed to their employees for support, and they were rewarded with an outpouring of resentment against Icahn's raider tactics. Flight attendants even wore "Stop Carl Icahn" buttons. When the identity of the white knight was discovered, however, their mood changed overnight.

TWA had convinced Frank Lorenzo,[†] the head of Texas Air and a man who was vehemently hated by the airline unions as a union buster, to purchase control of the airline. The unions reacted with outrage over the deal, and they immediately announced their support for Icahn; they even agreed to a number of wage concessions in return for stock ownership and profit participation. Suddenly, Icahn was back at the bargaining table, this time with the support of the airline's unions. Texas Air pulled out, and the board agreed to sell to Icahn. He was so excited when he heard the news that he shouted, "We got ourselves an airline!" and donned a pilot's jacket and danced around the office. Many analysts thought Icahn had been outfoxed in this deal—as *Newsweek* headlined: "How to Lose by Winning." Most felt the problem-ridden airline couldn't possibly be profitable, and that Icahn wouldn't even be able to recoup his investment by selling it off in parcels. But, it was by all accounts another historic deal engineered by Icahn. As noted in the *New York Times*: "The alliance is being hailed as a benchmark in modern labor history, one that other unions in bitter acquisition contests are expected to emulate. In effect the unions bargained with the bidder who guaranteed them the best deal."

But Icahn had inherited a tricky situation at TWA. The airline's losses continued to be very heavy, stock prices began to nosedive, and he began revising his bid downward in order to survive under the new circumstances. The board agreed to several revisions, largely because they had no other choice. In January 1986, Icahn assumed the chairmanship of TWA. A daunting task faced him, but over the next eight months Icahn took strides toward solving TWA's problems. He had managed to staunch the airline's staggering losses by the wage concession he was granted by pilots and mechanics, and when the flight attendants overtly opposed his demands, he broke their strike. In February 1986 he purchased Ozark Airlines, which gave TWA increased power in the important St. Louis–Chicago corridor. In 1987 he unsuccessfully bid for USAir and Piedmont

Air. Icahn's ability to turn TWA around not only was a financial boon for him, but it earned him a new legitimacy. He was now a manager, he had saved a troubled airline, and he had at least not exacerbated a situation of bad labor relations that he had inherited.

In his new role, Icahn began to pose as an aristocrat of the business community, publishing homilies in business magazines which told America what was wrong with the business system. Just because he had become respectable, it did not mean that Icahn had given up his raids. In October 1986 he made an audacious $8-billion junk-bond-financed bid for all the shares of USX, the struggling steel and oil giant once known as U.S. Steel. Although many doubted that Icahn was serious about taking over USX, after TWA they could not be sure. And he again appeared to have the unions on his side. Although the United Steel Workers had no love for Icahn, they hated USX CEO David Roderick about as much as the airline unions hated Frank Lorenzo. USX asked Icahn for time to consider the deal, while he just sat back and waited. By late 1988, he still held his shares, the offer was still on the table, and no one was sure what was going to happen.

Even his dramatic try for USX was not enough for Icahn. In 1987 he purchased 14.9 percent of Texaco's shares, and in June of that year he demanded five seats on its board of directors. With that victory, he hoped to force the company's sale. When he lost the crucial proxy vote, he began to try to get Texaco to sweeten its restructuring offer to him so that he could sell out at a profit. In other words, the "business aristocrat" was back doing his greenmail again. Again, no one was certain just what Icahn planned to do. But that, of course, had always been the secret of his success.

Carl Icahn is the classic corporate raider, and one suspects he was at least partially the model for Gordon Gekko, Michael Douglas' character in the hit film *Wall Street*. Gekko's most famous speech in the film came during a takeover attempt when he lectured the shareholders' meeting on the virtues of greed. Icahn said virtually the same thing, if a bit less eloquently, to a Chicago business group: "We all have to have a little greed to progress. That's a virtue in business." And Icahn's greed may know no bounds. When a friend said to him in 1988, "You know, Carl, before too long you're going to be worth a billion dollars. What will you do if you're not happy then?" Icahn reflected and said, "I will know I made a big mistake. It will mean I picked too low a number." In 1989, Icahn sold his 42 million shares of TWA for $2 billion in cash. Since he still owned 29 million shares of USX, one billion was obviously too low a number. (**B**. *Forbes*, November 12, 1979, April 14, 1980; *New York Times*, April 27, 1980, February 6, 1985; *Fortune*, March 22, 1982, March 18, May 13, 1985, February 17, 1986, January 5, 1987; *Institutional Investor*, October 1982; *Business Week*, December 12, 1983, August 19, September 2, 1985, October 6, 13, 20, 27, 1986, March 16, 1987, June 20, July 11, 1988; *Time*, April 22, 1985; *People Weekly*, June 17, 1985; Eric W. Allison, *The Raiders of Wall Street*, 1986; Moira Johnston, *Takeover: The New Wall Street Warriors*,

1986; *Current Biography*, 1986; *Newsweek*, September 8, October 20, 1986, March 16, 1987; Connie Bruck, *The Predator's Ball*, 1988; *Manhattan, Inc.*, May 1988.)

IVERSON, F(RANCIS) KENNETH (September 18, 1925–   ). Steel industry executive, Nucor Corporation. Ken Iverson was a young metallurgy student at Purdue University when he went on a field trip with his class to visit one of the huge, integrated steel producers in the Chicago-Gary area. What must have been intended to have been an impressive journey for the future executives had the opposite effect on Iverson. He later recalled, "We took a field trip to a big, integrated producer. This was the late afternoon. We were going through the plant and we actually had to step over workers who were sleeping there. I decided then that I didn't ever want to work for a big steel company." And he never did. Instead, he become the "father of the minimill" and, in the process, essentially "reinvented the steel industry," in the words of Donald F. Barnett and Louis Schorsch in *Steel: Upheaval in a Basic Industry*.

Ken Iverson was born and grew up in rural Downers Grove, Illinois. He went to local schools there, and then attended Northwestern University in 1943–1944. He transferred to Cornell, where he got his bachelor's degree in engineering in 1946; a year later, he received his master's in metallurgy from Purdue. Iverson then took various jobs in the metals industry—he worked as a research physicist for International Harvester in Chicago from 1947 to 1952, and as technical director of Illium Corporation in Freeport, Illinois, from 1952 to 1954. In 1954 he became director of marketing for Cannon-Muskegon Corporation in Michigan, and then executive vice president at Coast Metals in Little Ferry, New Jersey.

In 1962, Iverson joined the Nuclear Corporation of America (Nucor), as general manager of its Vulcraft Division. Located in Florence, South Carolina, the Vulcraft Division made steel joists and girders. Iverson's was a successful, moneymaking division, within a parent company which produced diodes, leasing equipment, and radiation detectors—with continual losses. With sales of $22 million in 1965, Nuclear Corporation lost $2 million and was moving toward a Chapter 11 bankruptcy. With nowhere else to turn, the parent company appointed Iverson chief executive. As he said, "I got the job by default."

After he assumed control, Iverson conducted salvage operations to keep the firm afloat. He sold off or shut down more than half the divisions, he reduced the corporate staff from twelve to two—himself and the vice president of finance—and he moved the headquarters from Phoenix, Arizona, to Charlotte, North Carolina. His surgery worked wonders: within a year the company showed pretax profits of $1.3 million, and it remained in the black for the next two decades. Under Iverson's leadership the company reached the top of the joist manufacturing field two years later, but it was spending 56 percent of every sales dollar on steel costs. It was purchasing 80 percent of its steel from European steel makers, who were using scrap metal to manufacture steel in minimills with electric-arc furnaces and other new technological advances. Iverson was convinced that if he built a minimill he could make his own steel, and make it more cheaply.

This was a momentous decision. Virtually all steel made in America at that time was produced in huge integrated mills, following the time-honored American patterns of achieving economies of scale in a high-throughput, mass-production industry. Walter Adams, writing in 1961, said "America's steel industry is the most powerful on earth. . . . Its product is the basic ingredient of our industrial civilization." Although he worried a bit about the size of American steel plants, his concerns were political, not economic—a concern over what impact their size and oligopolistic position had on American traditions of free enterprise democracy. To Adams and nearly everyone else, the integrated framework seemed to be the most efficient and sensible for the making of steel.

An integrated steel firm was characteristically dependent upon the blast furnaces that combined iron ore, coal, and limestone to produce the pig iron or "hot metal." An efficient blast furnace had a capacity of at least 1.5 million tons a year, and most plants required two such furnaces, so the minimum optimal capacity of an integrated steel mill was about 3 million tons. The pig iron was then converted into molten steel in a basic oxygen, or less often, an open hearth, furnace. At that point, the molten steel was poured into ingots, which were sent on to primary mills for rolling into semifinished shapes. The minimill that Iverson wanted to build was a very different type of operation. Tiny, in comparison to the industry giants, minimills typically produced only billets, the smallest semifinished shapes, which were suitable for rolling into bars, small structural shapes, and rods. They could not, at that time, produce the slabs and sheets that were the mainstays of the integrated mills. The minimills simply charged scrap metal into an electric furnace to produce molten steel. Then, unlike the integrated mills of the 1960s, they used continuous casting for all of their output. The continuous caster not only bypassed the reheating before the primary rolling of ingots, but also produced steel with more consistent metallurical properties than the ingot process. Many integrated mills in Europe, and especially in Japan, were using continuous casting in the 1960s, but America's large mills were notoriously slow to adopt the process.

Iverson modeled his new plant after those run by the Bresciani, a group of northern Italian minimill operators who sprang up after World War II. They had used cheap scrap steel and electric-arc technology to carve out a significant portion of the European steel market for themselves. Nucor, serving as its own general contractor, broke ground for its new minimill in rural Darlington, South Carolina, in September 1968. Nine months later, the mill was ready to pour steel. "I don't remember it as a difficult decision," Iverson later remarked. "It just seemed like a logical thing to do. But once we had the fat in the fire, that's when we got a little scared. We had to bet the company, yessiree." More difficult than building the plant was putting together a work force.

With no experienced steelworkers in the area, Iverson recruited whatever local talent was available—sharecroppers, grocery clerks, schoolteachers, and carpenters. None had ever been in a steel plant before, which was a mixed blessing. On the one hand, they were nonunion and they were willing to work for lower wages and with fewer work rules than their counterparts in the integrated mills. On the other hand, when the furnace was first tapped and the molten steel came pouring out, they were so frightened that they ran from the building. After a time, however, these workers developed the necessary skills, and, by the early 1980s, Nucor had grown into the most profitable carbon-steel manufacturing operation in the world. In 1984, it produced 1.5 million tons of steel, with sales of $660 million and profits of $44.5 million. How has Nucor achieved this status?

First and foremost there is technology. As Barnett and Schorsch commented, "Mini-mills now occupy the 'fast lane' for steel production." It is in the minimills where the most important technological advances for the industry have been forged. One of the major technological advances is in the area of electric-arc furnaces. Using water-cooled furnaces, ultra-high power, oxygen enrichment, ladle metallurgy, and a host of other improvements, the minimills have significantly improved electric furnace technology. In addition, through the use of continuous-billet casting they have made significant gains. With better sequential pouring, improved water cooling, and other refinements, the minimill's throughput has been greatly enhanced, which has helped reduce costs. In addition, minimills, and especially Nucor, have pioneered the direct rolling of finished shapes, a goal long desired by integrated steel producers. The motto of the minimills has been to "build tight, build quick, and build cheap" in order to get the best technology on line as quickly and as cheaply as possible. This has also led to the development of smaller plants with narrower product lines and fewer redundancies, enhancing the profitability of their operations.

Another area of critical importance for minimills is labor. In 1981, it cost an American integrated steel plant $393 a ton to ship wire rods. At the same time, it cost the average minimill $284. Of that $109 difference, $71 was accounted for in labor costs. The key difference was not wage rates, because Nucor workers, for example, on an average earned about 20 percent more than their counterparts in unionized, integrated mills. The greatest variation occurred in the number of man-hours it took to produce each ton of steel. Nucor, one of the most productive firms in the industry, was producing almost twice as much steel per man-hour as the large plants. Most analysts have pointed to the fact that Nucor and many other minimills are not unionized to explain the difference in production. Iverson does not agree: "I've heard people say that Nucor is proof that unions per se have a negative impact on worker productivity. That's nonsense! . . . The real impediment to producing higher-quality product more efficiently isn't the workers, union or non-union; it's management." Iverson introduced a system of incentives to boost productivity which, in one form or another, includes all employees, manager and worker alike.

Iverson's plan for Nucor workers is simple in outline: the more steel they produce, the more money they make. The base pay for workers at Nucor is less than they can make at unionized steel plants, but the key to productivity is a bonus plan paid regularly to all production workers. Not long after Iverson first established the bonus program, he learned that a production team had earned a 100-percent bonus. "I thought I had created a monster," he recalled, but he stuck to his principles and retained the program. "If a person produces, you can afford to pay him a lot. If he doesn't, you can't afford to pay him anything." Iverson also established a system of job security similar to that found in Japanese industry. Once hired, if a person works hard and well at Nucor, he is guaranteed a lifetime job. Iverson valiantly attempts to avert layoffs, to assure the workers of stability. Programs like these, and others, build very high loyalty among Nucor's work force, and even Japanese visitors have been impressed. As one Japanese steel executive commented, "I'm not used to seeing that in an American steel mill."

Another important factor at Nucor is that *all* employees, including Iverson, are treated as equally as possible. At lunchtime, Iverson and his fellow executives eat in their "executive dining room"—the S&W cafeteria in a nearby shopping mall. The firm's headquarters is a few thousand feet of drab office space in a leased building in Charlotte, and there are no company planes or cars. As Iverson has said, "We try very consciously to eliminate any differentiation between management and everybody else. That's the reason we don't have assigned parking places, no executive dining rooms. Everybody wears the same colored hard hat. Green is the color you wear. No gold hats for the president."

For this reason, Nucor executives, including Iverson, are on essentially the same bonus system as the production workers. Executive salaries at Nucor run only about 70 percent of those at other steel firms. For an employee to earn more money, the company must first achieve a minimum 11-percent return on equity. Ten percent of pretax earnings above that amount goes into an annual incentive pool, a portion of which serves as the executive's sole source of retirement income (production employees share in a conventional profit-sharing plan). "If the company does well," said Iverson, "the officers will do very well, and they'll have enough for their retirement. If it doesn't, they won't."

As Nucor came to dominate the markets in its limited product areas, it began to expand into other products. In 1977, it began to manufacture the steel deck used in the floors and roofs that its joists supported. Then, in 1979, Nucor became the first, and for a few years the only, minimill to manufacture cold-finished bars, a specialty product used to make shafts and machined precision parts. Iverson's biggest breakthrough, however, came in the development of a new technology for making thin, two-inch slabs at his mills. Nucor invested over $235 million in a new mill at its Indiana plant which allowed the company to move beyond being strictly a minimill producer of low-end products to becoming a supplier of flat-rolled steel, like that used by the auto companies. Such technology and product development put Nucor in the big leagues of steel producers for the first time.

Nucor's new technology in this area gave it tremendous advantages over integrated mills. Using a casting machine developed by a West German company, the new technology allows the steel to be taken directly from the mill to where it is rolled into products, thereby saving energy, time, and capital. Furthermore, the slab does not have to be cooled and reheated, as is the case at large, integrated plants. Therefore, according to Iverson, Nucor will save from $50 to $75 a ton; "The average integrated steelmaker produces around 400 tons of steel per employee, per year. We're looking for this technology to do some 1,200 to 1,500 tons per employee." The mill was scheduled to open in 1989, with a capacity to produce about 800,000 tons annually. Not enough, as one of the Nucor executives said, "to get auto companies too excited right away." Nonetheless, it kept Nucor on the cutting edge of the newest technology in the industry. As Iverson commented, "We're not seeing the demise of the steel industry, we're seeing its transformation into a high-tech business."

And Iverson is, as one person commented, the "paladin" of this trend. Tom Sigler, head of Continental Steel, a Nucor competitor, has said, "Right now Ken Iverson is 'The Force' in steel. He's shown that the small companies with the new technology are paving the way—not the Inlands or the U.S. Steels. He's shown that despite all you hear, there's still a future in steel." (**B**. Walter Adams, *The Structure of American Industry*, 1961; *Institute for Iron & Steel Studies*, April 1981; *Fortune*, April 6, 1981; *Personnel Administrator*, August 1981; *Time*, January 24, 1983; *Wall Street Journal*, May 27, 1983; Donald F. Barnett and Louis Schorsch, *Steel: Upheaval in a Basic Industry*, 1983; *Inc.*, April 1984, April 1986; Don Gervitz, *The New Entrepreneurs*, 1984; *Business Week*, January 21, 1985, March 14, 1988; *Reader's Digest*, August 1985; *Iron Age*, October 4, 1985; Donald F. Barnett and Robert W. Crandall, *Up from the Ashes: The Rise of the Steel Minimill in the United States*, 1986; *Who's Who in America*, 1986–87; Toronto *Globe & Mail*, October 26, 1987; *Forbes*, July 11, 1988.)

J

JOBS, STEVEN PAUL (1955–). Computer company founder, Apple Computer, Incorporated, and Next, Incorporated.

The July 1982 issue of *California* magazine hit the nail on the head. Its cover story was entitled "Revenge of the Nerds," and the cover depicted a nerdy young man in a white shirt with the top button buttoned, wearing horn-rimmed glasses with tape at the bridge, with unkempt hair, a plastic pocket protector full of pens, and a stupid grin on his face. While he sat at his Apple II computer, two beautiful women tousled his hair and played with his pens. The caption for the photo read: "Remember me? I'm one of those guys everybody laughed at in high school. Well, today I design computers and I'm worth millions. So who's laughing now?" Steven Jobs and his friend and cofounder, Stephen Wozniak, were perfect representations of this new phenomenon. Members of the "techie" underground of computer freaks and eccentric electronic geniuses, they represented a new element in the computer industry of the late 1970s. They were the first generation of Silicon Valley natives—born at about the time that Professor Frederick Terman's massive industrial park south of Stanford University became a reality—at just about the time Professor William Shockley, inventor of the transistor, set up his semiconductor firm, the first in the valley, and Hewlett-Packard became the first major electronics firm to become a tenant in Terman's industrial park. They grew up with that new culture, and they brought it to fruition in the 1970s. They revolutionized the computer industry, and the process of change and innovation which went with it.

Steven Jobs was born an orphan, but he was adopted shortly after his birth by Paul and Clara Jobs, who then lived in San Francisco. Paul Jobs worked in number of different jobs during his life, with just modest success. When Steven was still quite young, the finance company that Paul Jobs worked for transferred him to Palo Alto, and he bought a house in nearby Mountainview. Steven had a rather difficult childhood: he was troublesome in elementary school, and he was not always well-liked by his peers. He was expelled from one class for misbehaving when he was nine years old, although he did demonstrate that he was very bright and able. His biggest problems stemmed from the behavior of his fellow students—he was the kind of kid others taunted and picked on. Mark Wozniak, younger brother of Stephen, recalled: "He was pretty much of a crybaby. He'd lose a (swimming) race and go off and cry. He didn't quite fit in with everybody else. He wasn't one of the guys." Part of the reason for this was that his parents doted on him excessively. According to another former playmate, "They absolutely doted on him. He was a golden boy who could do no wrong. They instilled that in him, and I think that's where he gets all his confidence."

A good example of the way in which Steven Jobs' parents indulged him occurred after he had attended Crittenden School for a year. The school was located in a tough, lower-class neighborhood, and Steven suffered the fate of an outcast there for the year he attended. At the end of the year, Jobs informed his parents that he would not return to that school. His parents sold their home and moved closer to the Palo Alto and Cupertino school districts, so that Steven could attend a better school.

While he was in junior high school, Jobs met Stephen Wozniak, who was four years older. Wozniak was, as Michael Malone said in *The Big Score*, the "King of the Nerds." Known as "Woz from Oz," he was the prototype of the eccentric, socially maladjusted genius. Very much a loner, like Jobs, Wozniak was totally engrossed in electronics, probably influenced by his father, who was an engineer at Lockheed. At thirteen, Wozniak had won first place in the Bay Area Science Fair by building a crude computer. Jobs and Wozniak became part of a small network of "techies" and computer freaks who were constantly experimenting with electronic devices.

Jobs was not Wozniak's equal in electronics. When he got to Homestead High School, Jobs took the same electronics course in which Wozniak had been a star pupil a few years before, but he did not do well. Jobs dropped out of the class after a year, and the teacher remembered him only as "a loner" who "always had a different way of looking at things." But whatever Jobs lacked on the technical side of electronics he made up for by a superior understanding of what the products could do, and, ultimately, how they could be marketed. Wozniak, who could invent almost anything, seldom had a clear sense of the significance of his inventions. Together, the two young men had a talent which would ultimately bring them success in computers. Before that happened, however, they made their first foray into the commercial possibilities for electronics with an illegal product.

The product was something called a "blue box." An enormous fad item among techies (blue box users were called "phone phreaks") at that time, the blue box was an electronic device that duplicated the function of telephone switching systems, allowing the users to make free long-distance calls anywhere in the world. Wozniak built a superior digital blue box, and Jobs began to market it and to organize the business side of the operation. But when Bell Telephone and the FBI began to crack down on "blue boxers," Wozniak and Jobs got out of the business. It made them the only self-confessed (but unconvicted) felons to found and run a *Fortune* 500 corporation.

Throughout his late adolescence and early adulthood, Jobs wandered rather aimlessly. When he graduated from high school and prepared to enter college, he searched for spiritual meaning, but he had no concrete goals. After graduation, he rejected both Berkeley and Stanford, and he insisted on going to liberal Reed College in Portland, Oregon. Jobs, who by this time had become a prototypical hippie of the early 1970s, was attracted to Reed's ultraliberal, antiestablishment attitudes. Also, it was a way station for an army of hippies, poets, and antiestablishment activists, which gave it an exotic, exciting flavor. As one student commented at the time, Reed was a campus peopled by "loners and freaks." Jobs, who had always been viewed as being quite different and unusual in high school, had found his element.

The attractions of Reed for Jobs were social and cultural, not academic. He dropped out of school after one semester but continued to live in Portland, where he immersed himself in the counterculture. He frequented the Hare Krishna center, practiced meditation, and learned to use the I Ching. He also became deeply involved in the drug culture. After a year, money was scarce, and, because he and a friend were planning to take a trip to India, he looked for a job.

Early in 1974 Jobs noticed that Atari, Incorporated, the video game manufacturer, was looking for someone to help design video games. He got the job by declaring that he was working at Hewlett-Packard (which was not true—he had worked there on the assembly line one summer). Atari did not check his references, and the fast-talking Jobs was hired. Because he lacked electronics experience, Jobs made no real contribution at Atari, but he did save enough money to go to India. He and his friend from Reed arrived in India, where they shaved their heads and searched for spiritual peace and fulfillment. The friend told a reporter later, "It was kind of an ascetic pilgrimage, except we didn't know where we were going." When Jobs returned from India near the end of 1974, he had no ideas for his future. The aimless search continued—he took primal scream therapy, and he went to live on a farm commune for a short time. At that point, he renewed his friendship with Stephen Wozniak. The next five years witnessed one of the most dizzying and incredible transformations imaginable.

When Jobs returned from India, he started hanging around Atari, playing the games that were still on the assembly line. Nolan Bushnell, the firm's founder, offered to pay Jobs a bonus if he could develop a new kind of video game. Since he had managed to convince everyone at Atari that he was an electronic wizard, Jobs did not confess that it was beyond his abilities. Instead, he looked up Wozniak and offered to pay him half the $700 fee from Atari if he designed a game for the firm. Wozniak created a game that Bushnell was eager to buy, and Jobs paid Wozniak $350. It was much later that Wozniak found out that Jobs had been paid $7,000 for the game. The countercultural hippie was becoming an entrepreneur.

With his ties with Wozniak reestablished, Jobs began to hang around with him at the Homebrew Computer Club. Homebrew was a gathering place for computer and electronic freaks in the Silicon Valley area. Loosely organized, it was used primarily as a means to share information about fast-breaking new developments in the field. Having dropped out of Berkeley, Wozniak was working at Hewlett-Packard and was regarded by many at Homebrew as the resident genius. By 1975 many members of the club were trying to develop micro or personal computers. Wozniak got caught up in the thrill and the competition of trying to build a better computer than anyone else, and soon, with his genius and a Motorola 6800 microprocessor, he was able to put together a working prototype. He offered the computer to Hewlett-Packard, but the firm, which was used to servicing the scientific market with sophisticated computers, could see no future in making personal computers and turned him down. Wozniak took his computer to Homebrew, but the members were not enthusiastic about it either, since it used the Motorola microprocessor rather than the Intel 8800, which was the rage then. The only person who recognized the possibilities in Wozniak's rudimentary little computer was Steven Jobs.

Jobs, who had only an average aptitude in electronics, was a genius at understanding the marketing possibilities for these products. When Wozniak demonstrated his computer, Jobs saw nothing but dollar signs. He had to use all his wiles on Wozniak to convince him to pursue the project, since Wozniak had little interest in the monetary or commercial side of electronics. The two young men raised $1,300 when Jobs sold his Volkswagen bus and Wozniak sold his HP–65 programmable calculator. Jobs named the resulting prototype computer the Apple, which also became the name of the company, in recognition of the commune in Oregon where he had worked in an apple orchard. It proved to be an inspired choice for the name of a personal computer designed to be sold to the computer-illiterate masses. Whereas most companies chose intimidating, highly technical, space-age names for their firms and products, the name Apple connoted friendliness, naturalness, and all the good, wholesome things the baby-boomers of the 1970s believed in. It was an inspired, perfect name for the product.

While Wozniak was busy perfecting the prototype machine in Jobs' garage, Jobs was handling the marketing and business activities. Jobs approached the Byte Shop, a small chain of computer stores in California, and convinced them to order fifty of the new machines. Jobs and Wozniak were thunderstruck at the ease of the sale, and both men in later years felt this was the major turning point for the young company. Jobs then began to think in terms of a larger operation, and how to deal with the manufacturing and merchandising problems of such an operation. They set up what was, in effect, a family assembly line at the Jobs' home: stuffing the printed circuit boards and preparing them for delivery. Jobs and Wozniak decided on a retail price of $666.66 for the new Apple computer.

The Apple I, which they introduced in 1976, was the first single-board computer with an on-board read-only-memory (ROM) to tell the machine how to load other programs from an external source and a built-in video interface. Chiefly of interest to hobbyists, it was sold largely as a naked circuit board to which a variety of peripherals had to be added. Although they sold 600 of them, Jobs wanted to create a computer that would have an appeal that transcended the computer freak underworld. With a remarkably clear insight into the changing tastes of the consumer market in computers, he began working with Wozniak to create a new computer—a computer which would become the Apple II. The Apple I was Wozniak's creation, but the Apple II, one of the most phenomenal products ever introduced in the computer industry, was a result of both their talents—a unique example of synergism at work. Apple Computer was officially founded in January 1977.

In Jobs' vision, the Apple II had to be something more than a board stuffed with chips like the Apple I. He wanted a fully self-contained computer, one that was equipped with its own keyboard and video screen, and one that would take little or no expertise to operate. Jobs wanted to move beyond the world of hush puppies and pocket protectors where the Apple I had found success and appeal to the emerging "yuppie" generation of the late 1970s. Lots of money was required to accomplish this goal. The question was where and how to get financing. Although the Apple I was a good product and had made money, the blunt fact was that Apple Computer at this point was a garage manufacturing operation, an entity which generally does not appeal to venture capitalists. Steven Jobs' work was cut out for him.

It was a truism in Silicon Valley, that if you wanted to be successful it was important not only to have a good product, but also to have good public and press relations. Regis McKenna epitomized these qualities. With Intel and a number of other large and powerful companies for clients, McKenna did not need any small, struggling outfits, but Jobs was determined to have the best, and he would not settle for less. Jobs had long before developed a form of persistence designed to wear people down that was as extraordinary as it was alienating. His aggression and persistence often paid off, but usually at the expense of alienating everyone around him. Even Jobs himself recognized this, saying to a writer at one point, "People think I'm an asshole, don't they?"

In any event, McKenna finally signed on with Apple. Jobs then had to allocate financing. He went to Nolan Bushnell, who recommended that Jobs meet with Don Valentine, a Silicon Valley venture capitalist. McKenna also put in a good word for Jobs with Valentine, and a meeting was subsequently set up between the two. When Jobs showed up at Valentine's office, dressed in sandals and cutoffs with long hair and a beard, Valentine was unimpressed and he commented to McKenna, "Why did you send me this renegade from the human race?" Valentine refused to back the project. He did, however, connect Jobs with Armas Clifford (Mike) Markkula, a former marketing manager at Intel, who had just retired at the age of forty with millions of dollars to invest in new ventures.

Although Markkula was very much a Silicon Valley straight-arrow, he immediately saw the commercial possibilities of the new computer product, and he agreed to join forces with Jobs and Wozniak. Markkula, whose net worth was about $22 million, put up $250,000 of his own money and underwrote a line of credit at the bank to start a company and pay the cost of developing and manufacturing the Apple II. But, in order to be successful, Apple needed even more. As a result, Markkula convinced the legendary Arthur Rock, who had backed Max Palevsky's[†] Scientific Data Systems and was reputed to have a Midas touch with Silicon Valley start-ups, to support the venture. Arthur Rock, Don Valentine, the Rockefellers,[*] and Henry Singleton formed a consortium that put $600,000 into Apple in early 1977.

In the meantime, in June 1977, Markkula (who had taken the title of chairman but remained uninvolved in the daily administrative duties) appointed Michael Scott president of the firm. Scott who had been the director of manufacturing at Semi-Conductor, Incorporated, was slated to deal with the manufacturing problems of the young company. Wozniak, clearly, was the technical genius, and Markkula was the business expert who was hiring managerial and manufacturing talent, leasing facilities, negotiating contracts, and so on. This left Jobs without any clear function, a situation that created opportunities for him to influence the project in a myriad of ways, but which also led to problems later.

In publicizing Apple, Regis McKenna decided to focus on the idea that Apple was the invention of two poor teenagers, who had created a personal computer company in their garage. America loved rags-to-riches stories, and the stories of the "Two Steves," which McKenna began filtering to the press, were very popular. Wozniak was too shy to respond to this, but Jobs was in his element. When the press made it sound as if he had created the computers by himself and was solely responsible for the company, Jobs did nothing to dispel those assumptions. As Jobs' persona aroused the public's attention, McKenna started to play up Jobs' role. Jobs struck a chord in America in the late 1970s. The young people who were making money, starting homes and families, and buying personal computers, were people who had gone through the political and cultural turmoil of the late 1960s and early 1970s. They were the Woodstock generation, the flower children, who had enjoyed rock music, smoked good dope, and dreamed of revolution and community. By the late 1970s, they had cut their hair, put on suits, and become part of the establishment. Yet, they were not entirely comfortable with their BMWs and suits—they did not like the idea that they might have sold out. This is where the image of Steven Jobs was so potent and so effective. He seemed to be one of them. He was a long-haired hippie, who had changed neither his dress nor his beliefs, and yet he was the founder of an enormously successful computer company. As Michael Malone related, they would see a photo of Jobs in his beard and "wicked smirk" and think: "That bastard did it. He stuck by his principles and still made so many millions he can tell the establishment to kiss his ass." To them, it meant the revolution had not been lost after all—the "campus guerrillas had just evolved into corporate freedom fighters."

But Jobs' role in the early years was not just corporate image-making, he also contributed to the design of Apple II. Wozniak, of course, designed the technical parts, the innards of the computer, but Jobs was responsible for the housing. As Wozniak later commented: "Steve had a great deal to do with designing the computer housing, I was more interested in making a small, powerful computer, and didn't think much about its case." The covering of most microcomputers was sheet metal, which was inexpensive, but also boxy and inelegant. Jobs wanted a plastic case that would be smoother and, thus, more aesthetically pleasing. The resulting box was sleek and classy-looking, with its logo, an apple with a bite (byte) out of it, affixed to it. At the time it got little recognition, but it is clear now that this was one of the most successful industrial designs of all time, one that would grow to be admired with time. As Malone has commented, it looked about as intimidating as a Granola bar, which is exactly what Jobs intended.

The product that emerged from their shop—the Apple II—revolutionized the computer industry. Stan Augarten, in his history of computing, called it the "Volkswagen of personal computers" and he was right. It was the computer that invaded the home, that brought computing to the masses of Americans for the first time. With just 16K of memory and a price tag of $1,195, the Apple II sold like hotcakes. Sales in 1977 were $775,000; in 1980, they exceeded $100 million and were continuing to triple annually. The Apple II had, in effect, created the personal computer industry, and was the major benefactor of it. As more and more Americans decided they wanted a computer in their home, they bought Apples, and the plant was soon shipping 25,000 of them a month.

But the incredible demand for Apple II's greatly strained the manufacturing resources of the company. In order to get circuit boards stuffed, Apple was setting up sweatshops around Silicon Valley, which lead to inevitable problems. In order to raise more capital in 1980, the firm went public. The underwriters offered Apple at $22 a share, and by the end of the first day it was selling at $29. The price increase brought the market value of Apple Computer to $1.2 billion, and made Jobs and Wozniak instant multimillionaires. Jobs, just twenty-five years old, held 15 percent of Apple's stock and was worth, at least on paper, a cool $256.4 million. Two years later, Apple Computer broke into the ranks of the *Fortune* 500—five years after its birth—the fastest any company had ever accomplished such a feat.

But in the early 1980s, although Apple continued to grow and show impressive profits, problems emerged. Some of these problems were technological. The life span of products in the computer industry is not long, even for products as popular and trendsetting as the Apple II. In 1980, Apple still had the personal computer market virtually to itself, but it was clear that new competition was on the horizon, and, if Apple were to survive, it was essential to create a follow-up product to the Apple II. The computer of the future was designated the Apple

III. It was a project doomed from the start—even Apple employees referred to it as a "fiasco," a "mistake," or a "disaster." Introduced nearly a year late, when it did appear, it was a design nightmare. Some 14,000 Apple III's were recalled. Besides hardware glitches, there were major problems with the software.

These problems might not have been critical, but IBM had finally entered the personal computer sweepstakes in 1981 with its IBM PC. Although it was not a great machine technically, the PC had IBM's name on it, and it began to have a major impact on the personal computer market. Jobs made much of the fact that Apple thrived on this kind of competition, and he even ran an ad which said, "Welcome, IBM, Seriously." Jobs toughed it out, predicting they would sell more Apple III's in 1982 than IBM would sell PCs. But, by the end of the year, IBM had sold 200,000 PCs compared to just 50,000 Apple III's. Apple, which had 80 percent of the personal computer market in 1980, saw it dwindle to 29 percent in 1982 and 24 percent in 1983. It was clear that Apple was going to have to develop newer and better products if it were to survive the 1980s.

In 1981 Apple began work on a new computer, called Lisa, which was to include state-of-the-art technology. Its most unique features were extensive graphics potential and a "mouse," a hand-held device causing commands to be executed when pointed at various functions on the video screen. The purpose of the mouse was to make the computer even easier to use than before so that one could learn to use the computer in minutes rather than in days or weeks. In this way, Apple hoped to use the Lisa to crack the business market. Although minicomputers had long been used in offices, they were complicated and used only by skilled personnel. Upper level executives refused to use them. Apple hoped the Lisa would open up computing to business executives in the same way that the Apple II had opened up computing to the family. In this way, Apple could steal the office market from IBM. But the Lisa was not a success because of the limited amount of available software and because of its price.

At about the same time, Apple began to work on another computer—the Macintosh—which was to be the fulfillment of Steven Jobs' personal vision of what a computer should be. He was given control of this project, and he saw it through from beginning to end. Somewhat of a scaled-down Lisa, the "Mac" used the mouse; it had impressive graphics; and it cost just one-third as much as the Lisa. Although it was technically sophisticated in many respects, the Mac was underpowered; it could not run most of the business software packages then available; it had a limited memory; and it did not come with a letter-quality printer. This made it a rather problematic product. Steven Jobs had always had a keen sense of the market, but it was never quite clear just who he thought would purchase the Mac. Priced at $2,500, it was too expensive for the home market, but too underpowered for commercial customers. As recorded by Butcher, "The Macintosh was the first attempt Jobs had made at creating a computer—and it was a failure." It was introduced to great fanfare in January 1984, and initial sales were brisk but then began to slide.

All of this brought on management problems at Apple. President Michael Scott, in what has been called "Black Wednesday," fired about forty managerial employees in 1982 in an attempt to bring some order to the chaos that had characterized Apple from the beginning. In the early years, when Apple was doing well, the chaos was seen as a source of creativity, but by 1982 it was viewed as a major source of Apple's problems. Although Markkula and Jobs had approved the firings, it increased Scott's unpopularity at the firm, and he was soon let go. Markkula assumed the presidency. Since Markkula did not want to continue in the post, and Jobs, who wanted the position, clearly could not handle it, they turned to an outsider—John Sculley, chief executive officer of Pepsi-Cola, a reputed marketing wizard—to fill the vacant office.

Sculley was not sure he wanted the position, but over a period of months he met with Jobs, and it was soon reported that a loving relationship had been established between the two men. Some of the press referred to their relationship as brotherly; others saw them as father and son. In May 1983 Sculley announced he was assuming the presidency of Apple, saying of Jobs: "We just spent a lot of time in blue jeans getting to know one another." Jobs responded, "I hired someone I could learn from." Despite the facade of brotherhood and love, there were some very real and serious problems beneath the surface at Apple, and many of these problems related specifically to Steven Jobs.

Although Jobs was charismatic, and although a strong core of people at Apple were almost fanatically devoted to him, he had also alienated a lot of people there. He was viewed by many as being arrogant, rude, unpredictable, and vindictive. Jeff Raskin, an early employee of the firm, recalled that "[Jobs] would try to push himself into everything, no matter what you were doing, he had to have something to do with it." Another early employee said,

He could reduce me to tears in a minute. . . . When he was charming, he was *so* charming, and when he was crazy, he was really terrible . . . he can be really sadistic and, if he feels the least bit threatened at all, he's so smart that he can turn the tables on anyone. What he does then is attack, attack, attack. . . . I just think he's spoiled. (Butcher, *Accidental Millionaire*)

In 1981, Jobs had been involved in the start-up of the Lisa computer, but he had been so disruptive of the project when he disagreed with the way in which it was being developed, that he was ousted from the team. Convinced that Apple should not be developing a high-priced business machine, he stomped off and set up the Macintosh division to turn out his visionary product—a low-cost, easy-to-use computer for the masses. He had been correct about the Lisa, but he was wrong about the Macintosh. Further, he had been so headstrong that, although the Mac was based upon the Lisa design, it could not run the Lisa software, and he did almost anything he could to sabotage the success of the Lisa, thus adversely affecting morale throughout the company.

When Sculley took over, he was faced with a company lurching erratically from product to product, and rent with internal dissension. Although sales had reached $1.5 billion in 1984, Apple was suffering from declining profits. To solve these problems, Sculley eliminated the profit-sharing program, terminated several unprofitable operations, laid off hundreds of workers, and reorganized top management. Most significantly, Jobs was put in charge of the Macintosh division. Sculley ordered Jobs to make changes and improvements in the Mac in 1984, and to make it compatible with IBM software. This Jobs was loath to do, and he resisted with every fiber. By late 1984, Arthur Rock and several other powerful shareholders were counseling Sculley to get rid of Jobs, but this would not be easy or pleasant; Jobs had become something of a folk hero for many employees at Apple and for many people in America. To many, Steven Jobs *was* Apple Computer.

In the spring of 1985, Sculley relieved Jobs of all managerial responsibilities at Apple, and he relegated him to a remote office in an auxiliary building that Jobs called "Siberia." Jobs tried to hide his hurt and confusion by telling the press, "I'm not bitter, I'm not bitter," but it was clear that his involvement with Apple was at an end. At the age of thirty, it appeared that Jobs was going to have to start over. He returned to his $2-million mansion, which was still barren of furniture, and contemplated his future. According to one acquaintance, "He considered himself washed up, he thought he was finished. He said he would be a fool to try and top what he did at Apple." By then, of course, he was a multimillionaire, worth close to $200 million. It was not exactly like starting over in his parents' garage.

Apple recovered nicely under Sculley's management after Jobs was let go. In 1986, sales climbed to $1.9 billion with a comfortable net income of $154 million. Although morale was a problem, the introduction of the Macintosh Plus, to replace the Macintosh, was successful; international sales were strong; and Sculley's austerity program kept the firm lean and profitable. The Mac Plus opened the business market for Apple and led to greatly enhanced sales. Newer, and even more powerful products, like the Macintosh SE and the Macintosh Two further enhanced the situation. Because of the continuing sympathy from the public for Jobs, Sculley felt compelled to deal with the whole situation of Jobs' firing at great length. This was done first through extensive interviews with business magazines, and then with a best-selling business autobiography called *Odyssey*. Sculley had told *Inc.* (October 1987) that he had "never understood what a genuine folk hero [Jobs] was." A spokesman for the Regis McKenna firm said, "We've realized the book will be very good for Apple."

Jobs, meanwhile, has moved ahead. In 1986 he formed Next, Incorporated to develop a powerful computer for universities. Most observers felt it was a rather quixotic venture, far removed from the kinds of things Jobs had done at Apple and more akin to the kinds of computers that Control Data and Hewlett-Packard were accustomed to producing. But the same observers began to change their minds in 1987 when H. Ross Perot,[†] the founder of Electronic Data Systems, and one of America's most successful and astute entrepreneurs, invested $20 million in the project. Stanford and Carnegie-Mellon universities also made smaller investments. The computer was supposed to be unveiled in June 1988 but, reminiscent of Jobs' problems at Apple, did not arrive on time. Nevertheless, Perot remained optimistic: "Here is a 33-year-old with 50 years worth of business experience. I can't wait for his product to hit the market."

With typical panache, Jobs introduced his Next computer in October 1988. Dresed in blue jeans and a red flannel workshirt, Jobs himself put the computer through its paces in a packed high-school gym in Berkeley, California. By all accounts, his new machine was a technological wonder; it had a high-resolution black-and-white monitor; a Motorola chip which allowed the computer to record and play back music and voices with the fidelity of a compact disk; a system of storing memory on a removable, erasable optical-disk drive, thereby eliminating floppy disks; and a strong software base. The price tag of $6,500 was low, considering what was included, and many computer analysts predicted great success for Jobs' product. Others, like Microsoft's William Gates,[†] were less enthusiastic. Gates said, "He's put a microprocessor in a box, so what? It's got a graphic interface, like everything these days, and a mouse, like everything these days." Gates dismissed the machine as "a 48[sic]-rpm record." In the end, it is the consumer who will decide if Jobs' great gamble is a success.

In the meantime, the mythic presence of Steven Jobs hovers over Apple and the personal computer industry. Apple, with sales of $2.661 billion in 1987, a 40-percent increase over the year before, also saw its profits go up an astounding 40 percent. The eighth largest firm in the computer industry, Sculley has done a remarkable job of restoring its health. In September 1988, Sculley announced a new business strategy for Apple, one based on a new generation of input devices—the keyboards, mice, and scanners that allow users to transmit data or to control the computer. He believed this would give Apple greater access to the large business and institutional market. Yet, in many people's minds, it was still Steve Jobs' company. As Esther Dyson, publisher of *Release 1.0* said of Apple: "The religion is still Steve's but its voice is John's [Sculley]. Steve is still the Messiah, but John's the Pope." Sculley responded: "You can't change history." (**B**. *Forbes*, April 13, 1981; *Current Biography*, 1983; *Venture*, March 1984; *Inc.*, April 1984, October 1987; *Business Week*, November 26, 1984, April 18, 1986, September 28, 1987; Stan Augarten, *Bit by Bit: An Illustrated History of Computers*, 1984; Paul Freisberger and Michael Swaine, *Fire in the Valley: The Making of the Personal Computer*, 1984; Doug Garr, *Woz: The Prodigal Son of the Silicon Valley*, 1984; Robert Levering et al., *The Computer Industry Entrepreneurs*, 1984; Stephen T. McClellan, *The Coming Computer Industry Shakeout*, 1984; Michael Moritz, *The Little Kingdom: The Private Story of Apple Computer*, 1984; *Wall Street Journal*, June 3, 1985; *Newsweek*, September 23, September 30, 1985, February 9, 1987, October 24, 1988; Michael S. Malone, *The Big Score*, 1985; Charles Garfield, *Peak Performers*, 1986;

Robert Sobel, *IBM vs. Japan*, 1986; *Fortune*, September 14, 1987, April 25, May 23, 1988; James W. Cortada, *Historical Dictionary of Data Processing Organizations*, 1987; John Sculley (with John A. Byrne), *Odyssey*, 1987; Toronto *Globe & Mail*, September 6, 1988; Lee Butcher, *Accidental Millionaire: The Rise and Fall of Steven Jobs at Apple Computer*, 1988; Jeffrey Young, *Steven Jobs: The Journey Is the Reward*, 1988; Frank Rose, *West of Eden: The End of Innocence at Apple Computer*, 1989.)

K

KATZ, LILLIAN MENASCHE (March 18, 1927–   ). Mail-order firm founder, Vernon Specialties, Lillian Vernon Corporation. Critics call her "Lillian Kitsch," and the stuffy *New Yorker* magazine once rejected a Lillian Vernon advertisement as "too downmarket" for its readership. These reactions were based on the fact that many view the 1,000 items in her ninety-six-page catalog as horrid examples of bad taste—products marketed to appeal to America's unwashed, uncultured masses. Crammed with hand-crocheted pillows from China, nail-polish blow dryers, rubber dishwashing gloves with carmine fingernails, reindeer-patterned men's boxer shorts, and stuffed bears dressed in pink tutus, her catalogs have provoked the disdain of America's trendsetters. Lillian Katz, one of the real powers of mail-order marketing, bristled at those slights. "My house in Greenwich is filled with things from my catalog," she told *Working Woman* (June 1986), "things I've also given as gifts. I've done the best I know how, and they don't have to like my taste." But they had better accept her ads. Her son, David Hochberg, later remarked: "They're such elitists. They said we were too downmarket for them. . . . *Well*, when you say no to Lillian. . . . We did some massive demographic studies. . . . Our customers are much more upscale than anyone expects." When she found out that the typical customer had a household income of over $38,000 and an average order of $34, Lillian Katz took the *New Yorker*'s publisher out to dinner, showed him the figures, and got her ad placed in his magazine.

Lillian Katz was born Lillian Menasche in Leipzig, Germany. Her father, who was a successful industrialist in Leipzig, began to find his life and business increasingly threatened by the Nazis. In the mid–1930s, the family was forced to flee to Holland, and in 1937 they sailed for the United States, where they settled in New York City. Young Lillian, ten years old at the time, attended public schools and learned English by working as a usherette at a local movie theater. There she also learned to become a typical American teenager, devouring *True Confessions* and falling in love with the movie stars she saw on the screen. Meanwhile, her father prospered in America. He opened a zipper reconditioning business, which did very well during the war, when new zippers were scarce, and after the war, he expanded into leather goods, making camera cases, handbags, and belts.

In 1949, the twenty-two-year-old Lillian Menasche married Sam Hochberg, a retailer. She was expected to conform to the "cult of domesticity" of the 1950s—stay at home, raise her children, keep house, and lovingly make meals for her family. But Lillian could not stay at home. She worked at a clerical job until she got pregnant with her first child. Later, she attended classes in psychology at New York University, but dropped out when she became pregnant with her second child. At loose ends, she wanted to find something to do and she wanted to find a way to supplement the $75 a week her husband was bringing home. As she later told *Nation's Business*: "I liked the stimulation of work, and I wasn't prepared to do only child care. I chose the mailorder business simply because it was the only thing I could think of that would allow me to work at home and be with my children." All of this befuddled Sam Hochberg: "When we were first married, she took a clerical job. She never showed any drive or ambition. Never before had she felt she had it in her to run her own business." Like many men, he thought of her business interest as a hobby, something to be tolerated and patronized. That was a mistake.

Lillian convinced her father to supply her with some leather goods from his factory. Her idea was to offer the merchandise through mail order. The hook, the selling point, was that the products would be personalized with the customer's initials. Taking $2,000 of their wedding gift money, Lillian bought the necessary supplies and spent $500 to place an ad in *Seventeen* magazine. The ad urged women to "be the FIRST to sport that *personalized* look on your bag and belt." The handbags, which sold for $2.99, and the belts, for $1.99, had two initials, embossed free, in 24-karat gold. Lillian designed the bag and belt for her father to manufacture, and she sat back and waited for what she thought would be a small number of orders. She was overwhelmed with the response. Six weeks after placing the ad, she had received $16,000 worth of orders, which she filled from her kitchen table in Mt. Vernon, New York (after which she had named the company—Vernon Specialties). "I typed, packed, shipped," she said later. "I couldn't afford an adding machine, so once a week I'd go to the bank and sit at the vice-president's desk and add up the checks that had come in."

Lillian Katz was on a roll. Before long, $32,000 worth of orders had arrived in response to the first ad. She next placed ads in *Redbook* and *Vogue*, and the company expanded. Sam Hochberg still thought this was a lark, and he jokingly told Lillian that he would close up his business and join her business if her sales ever reached $40,000 a year. They did. The next year. Lillian Katz was not one to be trifled with—Sam Hochberg closed his business and reluctantly joined her mail-order operations. She turned Sam's store into a warehouse and rented the adjacent building for monogramming; and the business just kept expanding, taking on manufacturing orders from such cosmetics giants as Max Factor, Elizabeth Arden, Avon, and Revlon. By 1955, the company was bringing in

$150,000 in orders, a year later they were up to $198,000. It was clear that additional manufacturing facilities were needed. Lillian Katz and her husband opened a small manufacturing concern in Providence, Rhode Island, to make many of the items she sold, such as jewelry and Christmas ornaments.

In 1960, Lillian Katz took a giant step—she brought out her first mail-order catalog. A sixteen-page, black-and-white brochure, mailed to 125,000 customers, it offered combs, blazer buttons, collar pins, and cuff links. At the same time, she changed the name of the company to Lillian Vernon Corporation. During the 1960s, the company grew by leaps and bounds, but every increment of growth for the firm was a setback for the Hochbergs' increasingly tense marriage. Not only did Sam Hochberg resent Lillian's working—perhaps he had adjusted to that—but the two had totally different work ethics. Hochberg recalled several years later: "I'm more the playboy at heart, while she's the hard worker. I just wanted to earn enough money to live the good life. I would have retired 25 years ago." When the couple divorced in 1969, Sam Hochberg kept the manufacturing operation, with revenues of about $5 million, while Lillian kept the mail-order business, with revenues of $1 million. But, as she explained, "That's the business I really wanted." Later, she repurchased the factory, called New Company, Incorporated. The following year she married Robert Katz, a display fixture manufacturer. By this time, her two sons were in prep school and college, and Lillian felt she could devote more time to the business.

Lillian Katz went on extended buying trips to Europe and Asia, and she expanded her distribution warehouses to Port Chester and Elmsford, both near her Mt. Vernon base. Before long, the company was receiving 30,000 telephone orders each week, so she installed a sophisticated, high-tech communications center in New Rochelle. In 1974, she became one of the first wave of Americans to do business with mainland China; by the mid–1980s, she was importing items from thirty-three countries. About 85 percent of the items in Lillian Katz's catalog are imported. And it is her uncanny knack as a buyer that most impresses catalog industry analysts. "Lillian goes to a great deal of trouble to stay in touch with her customers," one commented. "She does more than just find products; she researches, designs, and actually produces products that her customers want." About 96 percent of her customers are women, and Lillian Katz understands their needs and wants very clearly. According to one industry writer, "Her customers are fiercely loyal. She seems to know what the American woman will buy."

As both a buyer and a boss, Lillian Katz has another trait that is found in most successful entrepreneurs: "She's a tough cookie," says a consultant. "I think that's what keeps her running. But you don't have to be loved to be held in high regard in this business. She's a brilliant merchant and a tough negotiator, and she's not necessarily kissing you on both cheeks while she's doing it." Even her son recognizes this: "She's a tough boss, you need to hit the ground running. She tends to move very fast." Lillian Katz knows she has few friends among her colleagues, and she tends to hold herself aloof from the chummy, highly politicized, direct-market industry. Much of this, she feels, stems from the attitudes she encountered in the early years of her business. Salesmen and suppliers would arrive at Lillian Vernon headquarters, and, when she came out to greet them, they would ask her to "show me to the boss' office."

Lillian Katz is also infamous for her temper, which has often been unleashed on her employees and associates. Despite the growth of her operations, she has maintained a hands-on style of management, a style that many have termed autocratic. One former employee said, "It's a maternalistic company, obviously, with an owner-founder who runs the show." Katz replies, "It's my company, I built it. I'll do what I want with it." Part of the problem, says her son David, is that his mother is a typical entrepreneur who is totally committed to the business. "Her business is such a major part of her life. How can anybody else have that deep commitment? How can anybody else do anything as well as she can? Her greatest flaw may be her hands-on, close-to-the-chest way of operating." As far as her temper is concerned, Lillian Katz claims she has learned to control it somewhat in recent years. In any event, she contends she never would have been branded as hot-tempered had she been male: "It's okay for a man to lose his temper, it's not okay for a woman."

There is also a nurturing side to Lillian Vernon as an employer. A former personnel manager at the company has said: "You're talking about someone who would shower you with affection one moment and in the next breath tell you off. Her creativity and intelligence have to be approached very carefully." And she has done a lot to look for hidden talents among her hourly workers, and promote them to executive positions. "Our company is totally devoted to women," Lillian said. "If I'm not gonna give them a chance, who is?" By the late 1980s, there were 1,000 employees at Lillian Vernon, and sales had reached $130 million. She and her son took the firm public in 1987, fulfilling what Lillian Katz called a "lifelong dream." Sending out 6,500 catalogs a year, she has built a new distribution center in Virginia Beach, Virginia, and has opened her first retail store in New Rochelle.

Although Lillian Katz often calls herself a "typical housewife," it is hard to imagine anyone less typical. A driven, hardworking entrepreneur, as she has admitted, "I'm a woman who has gone far beyond her wildest dreams." Her son David viewed her philosophically, if a bit wistfully: "She'll die at her desk," he said, "She'll never retire—it's out of the question." (**B.** *Family Circle*, September 11, 1984; *Marketing Communications*, February 1985; *New York Times*, August 18, 1985; *Chain Store Age Executive*, April 1986; *Working Woman*, June 1986, November 1986; *Contemporary Newsmakers*, 1987; *Nation's Business*, February 1987.)

KELLY, WILLIAM RUSSELL (1906–   ). Founder, temporary office services company, Kelly Girl Services, Incorporated, Kelly Services, Incorporated. It is such an established part of the American business scene that it is hard to imagine a time when temporary office services did not exist. The concept, which had its birth following World War II, was the creation of William Russell Kelly. It happened almost by accident. Kelly had a business that performed typing, calculating, duplicating, and other related services for companies. The firms dropped off their business at Kelly's office and picked it up when it was completed. One day, a frantic customer pleaded with Kelly to send one of his typists over to help out in an emergency. Kelly complied, and that was the start of a new industry—the temporary help industry—and a new company—Kelly Girl Services.

Born in British Columbia, Canada, Kelly was the son of an international oil pioneer. His family lived in many parts of the world, but settled down when Kelly's father died in 1928, leaving no estate. After completing his education, Kelly worked as an auto salesman and then as an accountant for the Great Atlantic and Pacific Tea Company. When World War II broke out, Kelly, in his mid-thirties, volunteered and was given a position as a fiscal management analyst. He helped establish a centralized system for expediting food delivery and prompt invoice payment. The system worked so well that an associate during those days said, "Russ moved food the way Gen. Patton rolled his tanks."

After the war, Kelly went into business for himself. He foresaw a tremendous boom in American industry after the war, and he predicted that an enormous amount of paperwork would be generated by this increased activity. Having learned a great deal about efficiency and modern office technology during the previous five years, Kelly decided to put that knowledge to profitable use. He selected what he felt was the best location, Detroit, Michigan, the center of America's automobile industry. Anticipating an enormous pent-up demand for new automobiles, he felt the amount of resulting paperwork would be overwhelming. "I thought the automobile business would require a mass of paperwork," he commented. "There are thousands of parts in a car and each part requires a piece of paper." He used $10,000 in personal savings to move to Detroit, rent an office, and hire two employees. Calling his new business "Russell Kelly's Office Service," he proceeded to drum up business from those companies needing typing, duplicating, mailing, and other services.

Kelly ran virtually a one-man operation during these early months, functioning as president, handyman, recruiter, and trainer. Despite his efforts, the firm was not a rousing success. Total sales for the first three months in 1946 amounted to just $847.72. Although Kelly had correctly forecast that businesses would be virtually strangled by the mountain of paperwork in the postwar world, he had not foreseen the fact that these companies would purchase their own office equipment, in hopes of solving their problems internally. After the first harried call for temporary help, which he supplied complimentarily, Kelly realized that the real need in the postwar market was not for sophisticated office machines and procedures—these were being supplied internally by companies such as IBM and Xerox—but rather for people qualified to operate these machines. Realizing this was the trend of the future, Kelly gradually shifted the emphasis of his business from service bureau to temporary help. As businesses increasingly asked him to send over one of "those Kelly Girls," he changed the name of the company in response to these requests.

Kelly had stumbled onto an extraordinarily profitable niche in the market. Not only was there an almost ceaselessly growing demand for his temporary workers, but also he had uncovered an enthusiastic pool of potential employees. Although women had been lectured throughout the 1930s on the virtues of staying at home to save jobs for male breadwinners, the wartime manpower crisis forced the government to engage in a powerful propaganda campaign around "Rosie the Riveter," who called on women to join the ranks of the employed. Between 1940 and 1945, female workers increased by more than 50 percent; three-quarters of them were married. At the end of the war, there was an equally powerful movement to return women to their traditional roles within the home, leaving the paid work scene to the returning veterans.

This movement nurtured a new "cult of domesticity," whereby the virtues of motherhood and housewifery were passionately extolled. It was the new American dream—the great suburban ideal. Most women acquiesced to this dream, but, nevertheless, retained a strong desire to work. Temporary service was a convenient way to square the dream with the reality. Still treating housework and motherhood as her "career," a middle-aged woman could take a "job" as a temporary clerical worker without disrupting her responsibilities to her husband and children. She could always refuse an assignment if her children were sick or if the demands of her household became too great and thus be able to view herself as having put her family first. For women who suffered what William H. Chafe has called the "cultural schizophrenia" of the postwar period, with "attitudes going one way and behavior another," temporary clerical work was an ideal, if seldom recognized, way to cope with this pervasive problem.

The needs of industry for clerical workers were enormous in the postwar world. From 1950 to 1974, the number of clerical workers in the United States doubled, from 7,632,000 to 14,845,000, and most of them were women. In 1950, there were 3 million male clerical workers and 4.6 million females; in 1974, the number of males had increased to just 3.4 million, but the number of female clerical workers had exploded to 11.5 million, an increase of 250 percent. Whereas women made up about 60 percent of the clerical workers in 1950, they made up over 75 percent of the total in 1974. Of the increase in clerical workers from 1950 to 1974, women accounted for 95 percent of the total. It was obvious that industries needing bank tellers, bookkeepers, file clerks, typists, stenographers, and other personnel were dependent on women, and although some of these women workers were young and single, the overwhelming majority were married. The number of working mothers increased 400 percent during the postwar decades, and although most of these working women took full-time, permanent jobs in the work force, an important number became temporary service workers. Comprising about 13 percent of all clerical workers, the temporary office workers were overwhelmingly female.

Kelly Girls typically fit the above profile. By the mid–1960s, the 84,000 Kelly Girls were mostly housewives, averaging 37.5 years of age with 2.5 children.

And Kelly Services quite self-consciously recruited this typical worker. A career guidebook that the company published in the early 1970s, which was intended to lure women into its employ, graphically outlined the approach:

You are in your thirties, or maybe your forties or fifties, and you've been off the job scene for a number of years now. Or maybe you've never worked—you've been a wife and a mother, and a darn good one. But let's face it, popping a batch of cookies into the oven and wiping junior's nose is a lot different from stepping into an office environment.

Now you're thinking of taking a big step. Going back to work. . . . But will you fit in? Do you have any remnants at all of those old skills that once seemed like second nature to you? . . . Oh, certainly it isn't as though you've been completely housebound for these years. There has been that volunteer work . . . for the church, a political candidate, your social club . . . the point is, you can convert those skills of everyday life into job skills. . . . We at Kelly Girl have found that one-third of our employees are over forty years of age, two-thirds are married, and nearly two-thirds of these married women have children or grandchildren.

It was an honest, straightforward, sensitive, and successful pitch. By the mid–1980s, William Russell Kelly had more than 750 offices in the United States, Canada, Europe, and Puerto Rico. In 1986, in its fortieth year of operation, Kelly Services became the first temporary help company to exceed $1 billion in revenues, and in 1987 it reached $1.6 billion. It had a roster of 525,000 temporary employees, ranging in age from eighteen to eighty-five, and it paid more than $6 billion in wages to its employees. The business had been kind to Russell Kelly also, as he had a fortune estimated in excess of $380 million.

What about his "temps," his Kelly Girls? The Kelly Girls, like all temporary workers, have mixed experiences. The industry, which Russell Kelly virtually created in 1946, by 1970 had more than a thousand firms competing for business. Placing more than a million employees in that year, they had cumulative revenues of $1.5 billion. Kelly Services, garnering about 8 percent of these revenues, was one of the largest. Kelly Services, like other temporary service agencies, employed counselors to conduct face-to-face interviews with potential employees to evaluate the employee's dress, demeanor, and clerical skills. Once the "temporary" was listed in Kelly's files, she could either wait for the counselor to call her with an appropriate job assignment, or call herself to ask for assignments. A job assignment might last for as short as a day, or as long as several months, although either the employee or the employer may terminate the assignment if it is not working out satisfactorily. Kelly Services charges the client a certain amount per hour for the temporary's services, and pays the employee about 75 percent of that amount. A unique feature of Kelly Services is that it guarantees its services 100 percent.

Many analysts, who have viewed temporary clerical work as the most un-desirable occupation, contend that it reflects the lack of leverage and mobility women have in the work force. According to one such commentator, "A tem-porary clerical worker in many situations seems to be merely another type of movable office equipment. When work is characterized by such alienating qual-ities, what place does it have in the lives of the workers?" And the attitudes of some temporary workers reflect that same sentiment: "I'm just the temporary employee, not to be taken seriously, and not even known by name, just 'that's one of the temporaries.' They don't show me things they show regular em-ployees." Most, however, do appreciate the fact that they have some control over their work as temporaries. One asserted, "In my kind of [work] life you don't have much power, but one of the powers you do have is the right to give yourself where you want or to take yourself away." An extensive sociological study of temporary workers agreed: "Temporaries could say no with less risk. Autonomy was thus not absent from the temporary worker's life. This contrasts sharply with findings of powerlessness among clerical workers." Another tem-porary worker summed it up well: "As long as I have to work and I'm dealing with jobs that are really nothing, no challenge, no interest, it's better to do it on a temporary basis."

Russell Kelly had identified a market niche and an industry with a steadily rising demand. He also found a large stock of relatively compliant and satisfied workers who would not unionize or make extensive wage and benefit demands. By 1952, Kelly's Detroit business was flourishing, and he opened his first branch office—in Louisville, Kentucky—to test the feasibility of expanding his business. It worked well, and by 1955 his business had grown to twenty-nine cities. By 1959, the name Kelly Girl had become so completely identified with his business (temporary workers introduced themselves on their assignments by saying, "Hello, I'm your Kelly Girl") that he changed the name of the firm to Kelly Girl Services, Incorporated. By the mid–1950s, his company was grossing $7 million annually, and he placed between 18,000 and 20,000 women in temporary jobs each year. His brother, Richard Kelly, became an executive in the firm during these years, serving as executive vice president.

By the early 1960s, Kelly was convinced that there was room to offer other services in the temporary labor market. After careful test marketing, he intro-duced three new divisions—Kelly Marketing in 1962, and Kelly Labor and Kelly Technical in 1964. With the new divisions established in the 1960s, increasing numbers of men began to infiltrate the Kelly work force. The new divisions provided businesses with technicians, many of whom were retired professionals or graduate students, and unskilled and semiskilled workers for temporary as-signments. By the mid–1960s, revenues had increased to $46 million, and profits were a solid $1.4 million. Because of the increasingly heterogeneous nature of Kelly Girl's work force and work assignments, Kelly changed the firm's name again in 1966, this time to Kelly Services, Incorporated. Richard Kelly, who by that time was president and chief operating officer, while his brother was chairman and chief executive officer, pointed out that, in 1965, 19,000 of the firm's placements were men: "Naturally, these people don't particularly enjoy being called Kelly Girls."

Kelly took the company public in 1962. Putting shares on the NASDAQ market at $12.50, dividends were paid in every quarter from that time until the late 1980s. During that same period, the stock split eleven times. A person purchasing 100 shares of Kelly Services stock in 1962 would have had 4,942 shares in 1987, worth more than $200,000. In addition, they would have earned more than $13,000 in dividends on the stock over the years.

The company's training procedures, fairly rudimentary in the early years, had also become far more sophisticated by the 1980s. In the early 1980s, Kelly Services was among the first to maintain its own video studio and staff to create its own video training network. Kelly Services president, Terrence F. Adderley, Russell Kelly's stepson, discovered when he took over the company that training varied considerably from branch to branch, resulting in a lack of unity in training methods for an organization that prided itself on the quality of its service. By opening an in-house video training facility, Adderley found he could save two-thirds of the labor costs, and standardize training procedures. In 1985, the Kelly Dexterity Indexer System was introduced to evaluate the skills of light industrial workers, and two years later it brought out the Kelly PC-Pro System to test, train, and support temporary employees on a variety of computer word processing and spreadsheet software packages. The latter development, of course, recognized the increasing importance of personal computers in industry, and the necessity for temporary clerical employees to possess these new skills. In 1987, Kelly Services also launched its Encore Program, which was designed to lure mature, recently retired workers back into temporary service. Kelly also set up its Assisted Living Services, which provides in-house home care to the disabled and elderly.

In 1988, William Russell Kelly, well into his eighties, continued to serve as chairman of Kelly Services, and Terrence Adderley as president. The company remained highly centralized from its Detroit head office, and, since Kelly still owned 44 percent of the stock, he remained a powerful presence in its operations. With profits of over $91 million in 1987, Kelly Services remained a highly profitable enterprise. Part of the secret of its success has been a willingness to change with the times. Just as Russell Kelly stumbled into a lucrative market niche in 1946, the company has continually researched its status and introduced changes to remain abreast of changing times. As Terrence Adderley said of his stepfather: "He became a pioneer and innovator in this industry because he was willing to be flexible in his approach to the service of business." (**B**. *Newsweek*, April 23, 1956, April 18, 1966; *Business Week*, May 18, 1963; Mack A. Moore, "The Temporary Help Service Industry: Historical Development, Operation and Scope," *Industrial and Labor Relations Review*, 1965; *New York Times*, January 4, 1970; Michael Crozier, *The World of the Office Worker*,1971; *Nation's Business*, January 1971; Mary Kathleen Benet, *The Secretarial Ghetto*, 1972; William

H. Chafe, *The American Woman*, 1972; Kelly Services Inc., *The Kelly Girl Second Career Guidebook*, 1973; *Annual Report*, 1987; *Looking for the Perfect Job?*, 1988; "The Kelly Story," press release (n.d.); Martin J. Gannon, "A Profile of the Temporary Help Industry and Its Workers," *Monthly Labor Review*, May 1974; *Forbes*, May 1, 1975; Louise Kapp Howe, *Pink Collar Workers*, 1977; Virginia L. Olesen and Frances Katsuranis, "Urban Nomads: Women in Temporary Clerical Services," in *Women Working*, ed., Ann H. Stromberg and Shirley Harkess, 1978; *Management Review*, January 1981; Susan M. Hartmann, *The Homefront and Beyond: American Women in the 1940s*, 1982; Alice Kessler-Harris, *Out to Work*, 1982; Eugenia Kaledin, *Mothers and More: American Women in the 1950s*, 1984; *Forbes*, October 24, 1988.)

KENDALL, DONALD MCINTOSH (1921–   ) and **ALFRED NU STEELE** (April 24, 1901–April 19, 1959). Soft-drink company executives, Pepsi-Cola and PepsiCo. Max Headroom, the computer-enhanced star of Coca-Cola's popular television ad campaign, delights viewers by exhorting his young fans (members of the Pepsi Generation?) never to say Pepsi by name. He tells his fellow "Cokeologists" instead to refer to Pepsi as the "P-word." The very fact that Coca-Cola (see Roberto Goizueta), the august doyen of the world of soft drinks, deigned to even acknowledge the existence of Pepsi was largely the result of the efforts of two men—Alfred Steele and Donald Kendall.

Pepsi, like Coke, had its origins in the new South after the Civil War. Caleb B. Brabham's pharmacy in New Bern, North Carolina, prospered primarily because of its popular soda fountain. One of his concoctions was a cola syrup modeled on Atlanta's Coca-Cola, which he called Pepsi-Cola. Formulated to relieve dyspepsia (upset stomach) and peptic ulcers, it became so popular that by 1902 Brabham decided to drop the drugstore business entirely. In that year he registered the Pepsi-Cola name and incorporated the firm, using the backroom of his drugstore as headquarters. By 1904 Brabham was able to move to larger quarters; five years later, 250 bottlers in twenty-four states were selling the product. It was well on its way to becoming a multimillion-dollar business. One of the secrets of Brabham's success was advertising. One ad he ran said, in part: "Pepsi-Cola is the Original Pure Food Drink. . . . Beware of imitations."

World War I put an end to Brabham's dreams and ambitions. The price of sugar increased 400 percent during the war years, catching Pepsi and other bottlers in a squeeze. Brabham bought a large amount of sugar at the inflated price of 22 cents a pound, only to watch it plummet to 3 cents a pound at the end of the war. As Lawrence Dietz wrote in *Soda Pop*: "When a man sits with a warehouse full of 22¢ sugar in a 3¢ market, he inevitably is sitting with corporate books that are written in blood-red ink." Brabham's move cost Pepsi $150,000 at a time when the firm was already crippled. Brabham went bankrupt and returned to his drugstore in 1922, while Pepsi struggled valiantly to secure a future.

It was at that point that some Eastern money men appeared at Pepsi's door. The first of the Wall Street financiers to attempt to save Pepsi was Roy C. Megargel. Pepsi had enjoyed great success as a largely regional product, but Megargel envisioned it as a national brand that would compete head to head with Coke. For several years he tried to revive the firm with investment capital, but he could never raise a sufficient amount, which particularly limited advertising efforts. In 1932, Pepsi went bankrupt again. This time, Charles Guth, head of Loft's Incorporated, a New York–based candy store chain, took over the company. He established a new Pepsi-Cola company, slightly altered the drink's taste, and began to manufacture concentrate at Loft's Long Island City laboratory. At this time, the Loft's stores were Pepsi's only outlet, and the company was sinking steadily. Guth decided he was backing a losing venture, and he wanted out of the operation. He even offered to sell Pepsi to Coca-Cola, which turned down the offer, one of the greatest corporate blunders in history.

Foiled in his attempt to jettison his dying soft-drink firm, Guth decided to do something creative to make it more successful. A used bottle dealer had suggested the Pepsi be put in used beer bottles. Although the beer bottles were 12 ounces, compared to Coke's six and a half, the bottles were cheap, and the cost for the extra beverage was minimal. Besides, it gave Pepsi a unique marketing ploy during the depression years. Recognizing that many families were having trouble making ends meet, Guth advertised that consumers got twice as much Pepsi as Coke for the same amount of money. This hit a responsive chord in depression America, and sales began to boom. Guth then tightened relations with existing bottlers, and he began to aggressively seek new ones.

In the midst of this success with Pepsi, however, Guth lost control of Loft's. When new management took over, they found that Guth had wantonly used Loft's money and resources to acquire and build Pepsi, even though Guth owned all the stock in the latter firm. A complicated legal battle ensued, in which Loft's got control of Pepsi-Cola and Loft's was in turn taken over by Phoenix Securities, a Wall Street consulting and investment firm, in 1939. Walter Staunton Mack, Jr., emerged as the new head of Pepsi-Cola. Mack was a creative and free-wheeling showman who gave the struggling cola company a much needed sense of style and identity.

Mack increased Pepsi's sales 39 percent in 1939, with net earnings of $5.6 million. He divested the candy business from Pepsi and began an impressive expansion program. He scoured the country for prospective bottlers, but found only small and underfinanced companies were generally available; most of the others were under Coke's domination. Nonetheless, he instilled new confidence in the operations, and Pepsi's sales rose faster than ever. Although World War II marked the transition point whereby Coca-Cola went from being simply a consumer product to a national icon owing to some extraordinarily ingenious techniques practiced by Robert W. Woodruff,* Pepsi-Cola held its own surprisingly well.

Walter Mack was not one to minimize the symbolic significance of Pepsi's fight with Coke during World War II: "The fight between Coca-Cola and us is a fundamental American struggle." Pepsi's strategy during the 1930s had been successful among the poorer classes, but it had not done much to expand into other markets. Mack heard what he felt was a catchy adaptation of the traditional "John Peel" English hunting song with Pepsi-Cola lyrics, and he bought the jingle for $2,500. He ordered the jingle to be played on the radio, in fifteen-second spots, with no overvoice or other message. The jingle,

> Pepsi-Cola hits the spot
> Twelve full ounces, that's a lot
> Twice as much for a nickle too
> Pepsi-Cola is the drink for you.

was a phenomenal success. At a time when most radio commercials were spoken in bland voices, the song was a great hit. It was played an estimated six million times over 469 radio stations and was sent to owners of juke boxes. A survey conducted in 1942 determined it was the best-known popular tune in America. And 1942, remember, was the year in which the film *Holiday Inn* with Bing Crosby made "White Christmas" a national obsession.

Pepsi's successful World War II campaign has been called the "most famous oral trademark of all time." At one and the same time, Mack revolutionized radio advertising and gave Pepsi a new image and cachet. But he realized he had to go farther. The jingle still stressed the whole idea of price and quantity, which tended to make Pepsi a "poor man's drink" in the eyes of many. So Mack decided to emphasize quality. He introduced a "More Bounce to the Ounce" campaign, which extolled Pepsi's purity. Despite the relative success of these ad campaigns, however, Mack was not able to turn World War II into the kind of marketing bonanza that Coke had garnered. Pepsi's major accomplishment was that it survived the massive Coke juggernaut relatively unscathed. It had become, by the end of the war, a fully national soft drink, and was solidly number two in sales to Coke, having surpassed Dr. Pepper, Royal Crown, and other "pretenders." Mack had been particularly successful in the area of home sales with its twelve-ounce bottles, selling one-third more than Coke, but he was completely overwhelmed in fountain sales. Pepsi began to expand abroad, first to Canada in 1934 and then to England and especially Latin America, still one of Pepsi's strongest markets.

With the end of the war and the rise of a burgeoning new middle class, Pepsi's successful depression-era advertising began to ring hollow. Still considered a poor man's drink, Pepsi found it difficult to generate appeal among the new middle class. In addition, Mack was unsuccessful in contesting Coke in the soda-fountain business. Further, when inflation hit after the war, it forced the price of Pepsi upward—first six cents, then seven cents. Mack tried to convince the public that six cents for twelve ounces was a great deal, compared to five cents for six ounces of Coke, but the campaign fell flat. Furthermore, Coke had developed a whole new generation of vending machines after the war that would not take the larger Pepsi bottles. So Pepsi found itself closed out of a potentially lucrative new market.

The result was continually declining Pepsi sales and profits after the war. Sales stagnated and net income began a rapid decline in the postwar years. Sales, $56 million in 1947, dropped to $47 million in 1948. In 1949, they leveled off at $45 million. Earnings, which had been $15 million in 1942, fell off 70 percent in 1946. The following year they were down to $6.7 million, to $5 million in 1948, and by 1950 had dropped to $1.6 million. By 1949, Pepsi-Cola again teetered on the brink of bankruptcy. Mack, who had handled Pepsi's problems so brilliantly before the war, could not seem to get a handle on them after the war. He, therefore, brought in Alfred N. Steele, an advertising and marketing whiz from Coca-Cola, as executive vice president. A year later, Mack, over his strenuous objections, was bumped up to board chairman, and Steele was installed as president. Mack resigned in a huff a short time later. Alfred Steele vowed that Pepsi would someday outsell Coca-Cola, and his war cry became "Beat Coke."

Steele was born in Nashville, Tennessee, but remained there only a short time. His father, who was an international secretary of the YMCA, had postings all over the world, so Alfred Steele grew up in locations from London to Manila. When it was time to attend college, Steele chose Northwestern University, from which he graduated in 1923. He then worked with a metal broker, and within two years became special merchandising representative for a manufacturer of furniture hardware. In 1926, Steele shifted into publishing, becoming merchandising manager of the Chicago *Tribune*. Two years later, he became an account executive with a Milwaukee advertising agency, thus beginning a long and successful career in that field. Over the next several years, Steele held various jobs as sales manager or advertising director of one large company after another; ultimately, he became vice president of D'Arcy Advertising, Coca-Cola's long-time ad agency. The agency, located in St. Louis, had taken over Coke's advertising in 1904. Under the direction of Archie Lee, a rather ordinary brown beverage was transformed into a venerable national institution. In 1945, Coca-Cola hired Steele away from D'Arcy, making him a vice president of marketing and advertising. But Steele, who one Coke executive said could "talk the horns off a brass bull," was too flamboyant for the stern, staid Woodruff. As a result, by the late 1940s, Steele had been isolated from virtually all company decisions, and his future with the company was dead. At that point, Walter Mack approached him with an offer of $85,000 a year in stock and options to join Pepsi. It was not an easy move for Steele to make: it was an action akin to treason in the soft-drink industry, and Steele knew that he could never return to Coke if Pepsi went under. And there was every possibility, in 1949, that the company would not make it. Nonetheless, Steele made the move to Pepsi.

When Steele arrived at Pepsi, Coke controlled a whopping 67 percent of the soft-drink market in the United States, and the management system at Pepsi was a mess. Accounting was so slipshod that management did not even know the production figures of some of its biggest bottlers, or the breakdown of its costs. As Steele commented: "They were operating by gazing into a crystal ball." Further, bringing in Steele simply made things worse, because as he said, "When I arrived at Pepsi, the other vice presidents figured I had come to liquidate the company," and many left. Realizing the firm was in much worse shape than he had thought, Steele demanded complete control of the company—and he got it.

Steele, who was a veritable dynamo, proceeded to assault the status quo at Pepsi. Feeling the firm needed new blood—a Pepsi employee once said that "Al Steele told me that the whole trick in hiring executives is to find a good man and turn him into a prick"—Steele brought in young, ambitious men just back from the war, along with about fifteen defectors from Coke. Steele then began to decentralize Pepsi's operations, which had been almost completely centralized in New York. He divided the country into eight districts, assigning responsibility for each district to a divisional vice president. He altered the Pepsi formula, making it less sweet, and he standardized the company's logo, truck fleet, and signs. In addition, he sold a Cuban sugar plantation for $6 million, twice what the firm had paid for it, and he got rid of a bottle cap factory, reasoning that "our business is selling Pepsi."

Most of all, Steele set about to alter Pepsi's image. The company's bottlers were particularly bitter about the parent firm's prospects, and Steele wanted to win back their confidence. In an attempt to lure the burgeoning middle class away from Coke to Pepsi, Steele began a series of sophisticated television commercials featuring the actress Faye Emerson. As a way of enhancing the drink's cachet, Steele invariably had it brought in on silver trays, creating a more formal and elegant atmosphere. To support this stepped-up advertising campaign, Steele convinced the bottlers to invest more heavily in it, so that the budget rose each year, until it reached $14 million in 1955. The new Pepsi ads tried to eradicate the poor man image by running the theme, "Be Sociable, with Light Refreshment."

Steele also changed important features of Pepsi's bottle and label. He had a new, sleeker bottle designed, and, most important, he replaced the old paper labels with new baked-on labels. Paper labels had been used on its recycled beer bottles, but Steele felt it was time to develop a tonier image. The new baked-on label had an elegant swirl pattern with subdued lettering, all of which gave both the company and the drink a more permanent and stable appearance.

A significant decision was also made in regard to the bottle size. Pepsi had long had a twelve-ounce bottle, which gave it an advantage over Coke in supermarket sales for home consumption. During the 1940s, because of its more economical twelve-ounce size, Pepsi was outselling Coke by two-and-one-half times in the New York City market, and it had substantial leads in most of the northern urban markets. Steele recognized that the middle-class consumer in the 1950s would be buying increasing amounts of their soft drinks in supermarkets rather than soda fountains or corner stores. With the right advertising campaign,

Pepsi stood a good chance of substantially gaining on Coke during the decade. To be totally successful, however, Pepsi was going to have to make changes in other areas.

Pepsi had been suffering badly in the new vending machine field. After the war, Coke had placed a million new machines on the market, which soon accounted for 20 percent of that firm's volume, but Pepsi's twelve-ounce bottle was too big to fit in the machines. Mack had resisted any attempts to change Pepsi's bottle size in order to enter this new market, so Pepsi fell well behind Coke. Pepsi's large size also worked against it at concession stands at ballparks and other venues, since the prevailing sentiment was that the large drink filled people up too quickly, resulting in decreased purchases of peanuts and popcorn. Coke tended to dominate that market, as they did at soda fountains. In response, Steele brought out a new eight-ounce bottle and, in, cooperation with the bottlers, invested $15 million annually in vending machines. Sales from vending machines, which had been nonexistant in the 1940s, and were only 5 percent by 1952, climbed to 11 percent by Steele's death in 1959. He kept the twelve-ounce bottle for home purchases, but the smaller bottle was used for vending machines, ballparks, racetracks, and so on.

The results of Steele's innovations were spectacular. In the five years between 1950 and 1955, sales increased 112 percent, compared to 29 percent for the entire industry. At the time of Steele's death in 1959, revenues had virtually doubled again since 1955. Net profits were also increased dramatically, from $1.6 million in 1950 to $11.5 million in 1958, as Steele enhanced the efficiency of the organization, slashing administrative costs, installing new accounting techniques, and moving more aggressively into foreign markets. By 1960, Pepsi had 237 bottling plants in eighty-six countries, a vast increase from the 67 plants in thirty-one countries when Steele took over. Foreign sales by 1959 accounted for half the company's total revenue. Steele also made a deal with Schweppes Ltd., of England, by which Schweppes bottled and distributed Pepsi in England and Pepsi bottled and sold the Schweppes beverages in America, giving Pepsi bottlers a more extended line to offer to dealers. Pepsi had become a lean, mean dynamo, whose small size and aggressive leadership allowed it to move rapidly in the marketplace, often outflanking the more cumbersome King Coke. For the first time in the 1950s, Coke's market share began slipping, and Pepsi became a serious competitor. In 1954, one Coke official remarked that Pepsi was "coming up like a scalded cat," and Coke was beginning to worry.

More than anything else, what Steele gave to Pepsi during the decade he ran the company was a sense of vitality and dynamism which infected the entire firm. A former Pepsi public relations man once commented about Steele:

Every time a Pepsi bottler did anything in terms of expansion, it became a "plant opening." Hell, the guy could have put a new garage onto his plant and there'd be a ribbon-cutting, star-spangled-banner ceremony. The size of the opening, of course, would determine how much of an effort he put behind it. The local bottler would be king for a day. (Louis and Yazijian, *The Cola Wars*)

In 1955, Steele married the film star Joan Crawford, and the two of them drew massive media attention wherever they went. She became the company's "first lady," and, as J. C. Louis and Harvey Z. Yazijian commented in *The Cola Wars,* "She complemented the Pepsi-Cola Company, whose loud and showy style was akin to the make-believe, tinsel, and glamor of the movie industry of the fifties."

Steele's sudden death in 1959 was a great blow to the company, but he left the firm in much better shape than he had found it. Pepsi's share of the market had increased from under 20 percent to nearly 30 percent, with virtually all of that increase coming at the expense of Coke. Coke, which outsold Pepsi five to one at the beginning of the decade, had a two and a half to one advantage by the end of it. After Steele's death, Joan Crawford was elected a director of Pepsi, and she remained an important cheerleader and image maker for the company thereafter. Management, however, devolved upon Herbert Barnett, a competent but colorless man who lacked Steele's dynamic style of leadership. As a result, Pepsi lost some of its momentum during the next four years. Pepsi needed another savior, and this time he was waiting in the wings: head of the firm's international operations, he was a young, bluff, fast-talking outdoorsman by the name of Donald M. Kendall.

Kendall grew up on a dairy farm in Sequim, Washington. A star tackle in high school, he entered Western Kentucky State College on a football scholarship, where he distinguished himself more on the football field than in the classroom. Kendall made it through three semesters before he joined the U.S. Navy in 1942. During his service in World War II, Kendall was twice awarded the Distinguished Flying Cross as a bomber pilot in the Pacific. As a result, he came to the attention of his base commander, Vice Admiral Edward Orrick McDonnell, a general partner in the investment firm of Hornblower & Weeks, and a director of Hertz, Pan-Am, and Pepsi-Cola. In 1945 Kendall married McDonnell's daughter, and his father-in-law secured a forty-dollar-a-week job with Pepsi, selling fountain syrup in the New York City area.

Kendall promptly established himself as one of the firm's star salesmen, and he attracted the attention of Alfred Steele after Steele took control of the company in 1950. Kendall was named a sales manager, and in 1951 he became assistant national sales manager, in 1952 vice president in charge of sales, and in 1956 vice president in charge of marketing with responsibility for all sales, advertising, and promotions. Most people recognized Kendall as a born salesman for Pepsi, similar to Steele himself. One person commented:

Steele recognized that the company needed a swinging salesman to talk to theater owners, circus owners—you name it—and Kendall was the guy. Kendall could travel all day, screw all night, drink all night, stay out all night with those bums, but would come and bring in the business. (Louis and Yazijian, *The Cola Wars*)

Kendall himself had a more refined view of his role as a salesman. To be a great salesman, he said,

[Y]ou have to know and have confidence in your product, and you have to know the person you're selling to and what he wants and what his problems are. And then, once you get in the door, you have to work at keeping that relationship, do the follow-up work. I think that's where a lot of people lose out. (*Fortune,* April 13, 1987)

Whatever made Kendall a great salesman, he began to rise like a meteor in the Pepsi organization. Steele decided that Kendall's talents could best be used to boost overseas sales, and in 1957 he was made president of Pepsi-Cola International. During the six years of Kendall's leadership, Pepsi's overseas business tripled and profits increased 500 percent, accounting for 30 percent and 40 percent, respectively, of the company's totals. Kendall's most astounding victory, and one which illuminated his talents, came in the Soviet Union in 1959. An American International Exposition, sponsored by the State Department and the U.S. Information Agency was being held in Moscow. Despite some opposition within the company, Kendall managed to make Pepsi one of the 200 American firms, and the only soft-drink company, represented there. Kendall had a dramatic incident in mind for Pepsi. As he later recalled: "My one purpose was to get a bottle of Pepsi in the hands of (Nikita) Krushchev." The Pepsi company had long had close ties with the Republican party, especially Richard Nixon, who, then vice president, was in charge of Krushchev's visit at the exposition. Nixon told Kendall, "Don't worry, I'll bring him by." True to his word, Nixon brought the Soviet leader to the Pepsi booth, and cajoled him to try the soft drink. Kendall handed Krushchev a bottle of Pepsi that had been bottled in Russia, and the premier accepted. Krushchev had one Pepsi, then another; he drank seven bottles of Pepsi that day. It was a major public relations coup for Kendall and Pepsi; photos of the leader of the Communist bloc consuming an American soft drink went out all over the world. Many years later, in 1974, Kendall opened a Pepsi bottling plant in the Soviet Union, making Pepsi the first American company to produce a consumer product in that country. The groundwork had been laid in 1959.

In 1963, when Kendall was brought in as chief executive of Pepsi, he proceeded to inject new life and vitality into the firm's domestic operations. He gave the company some much-needed marketing energy, and made fence-mending visits to the firm's bottlers, who had been rebelling against price rises and the firm's lack of leadership after Steele's death. Most important, however, Kendall began to assemble a crack management team at Pepsi. Another of the company's most important moves came in 1965, when Kendall merged Pepsi with the Frito-Lay Company of Dallas, a leading manufacturer of potato chips and snack foods. With sales of $184 million and profits of $7.8 million in 1964, Frito-Lay made the firm, now called PepsiCo, the largest producer of snack food in the United States. It was also a natural match for a soft-drink firm. As Kendall noted, "Potato Chips make you thirsty; Pepsi satisfies thirst." Pepsi's international distribution network was also ideal for Frito-Lay, since Pepsi had developed, as one executive noted, the machinery to market "anything that goes down the gullet." Herman W. Lay, head of Frito-Lay, became PepsiCo's new chairman of the board and the largest stockholder. Donald Kendall continued as chief executive officer and the most powerful force in the firm.

After Kendall took control of Pepsi in 1963, he announced that a whopping $36 million would be spent on advertising in the following year. He planned to beef up the firm's existing "Think Young" campaign, which was aimed largely at the teenage market. In September 1964, Pepsi unveiled its seminal slogan for the campaign—"Come Alive, You're in the Pepsi Generation"—sung by Joannie Summers. An instant hit, the "Pepsi Generation" became one of the buzzwords of the 1960s, satirized by comedians and eulogized by *Time* magazine.

By the early 1970s, Pepsi had become a highly diversified food conglomerate, whose components were knitted together by common policy, leadership, and fiscal control. Kendall's dynamic leadership and marketing acumen had pushed Pepsi closer and closer to Coke. Pepsi's sales in 1969 were $940 million, double what they had been in 1965, and close to Coke's $1.3 billion. Although sales of Pepsi-Cola itself had continued to grow during this time, its mergers primarily fueled Pepsi's dynamic growth. Yet Coke continued to be far more profitable than Pepsi, as it earned three times more than its rival in 1969, and also managed to actually increase its market share slightly.

Kendall had long been close friends with Richard Nixon, and when the latter ascended to the White House in 1969, Kendall's influence in the business and political communities increased commensurately. Nixon appointed him chairman of the National Alliance of Businessmen (NAB), which had been set up during the Johnson administration to deal with unemployment. Kendall expanded the operations of the NAB from 50 to 131 cities, but hard-core unemployment, nonetheless, had doubled by 1970. As Kendall's star rose in the Nixon administration, Pepsi's did also, since all of Kendall's political initiatives were geared to fashioning an international economic system that would serve corporate growth and enhance Pepsi's place within that system. In 1969, Kendall was named chairman of the Emergency Committee for American Trade (ECAT), the top lobbying group for multinational corporations organized to fight protectionist sentiment. The great pinnacle of Kendall's action in this area for Pepsi came in 1974 when he signed an agreement with Soviet trade officials whereby Pepsi was to supply all the technology, engineers, and managerial know-how to install a new bottling plant in the Soviet Union. An executive at Coke grumbled that "there isn't any doubt that Nixon played a role" in Pepsi's coup. The White House denied the accusation, but a Soviet diplomat said that Nixon's friendship with Kendall "didn't hurt" Pepsi's position. Pepsi and Kendall continued to be among Nixon's strongest allies, sticking with him even through his bitter Watergate denouement.

In 1975, Pepsi decided to try a new marketing and advertising strategy—the "Pepsi Challenge." Pepsi executives had discovered that in blind taste tests slightly more people preferred Pepsi to Coke. Pepsi ran an ad campaign based on these tests in areas where Pepsi was weak, such as the South. The campaign was a success, but Coke reacted with ferocity. Attacking Pepsi in markets where Pepsi had been strong, Coke asserted that consumers preferred Coke over Pepsi by a two-to-one ratio. The marketing warfare between the two cola companies reached a fevered pitch, and by 1983 the Pepsi Challenge had become a highly successful national campaign. Although it did not significantly affect Coke's sales, it did boost Pepsi's sales, and therefore increased its relative market share slightly at the expense of other soft drinks. Nonetheless, Pepsi's aggressive, belittling campaign shook Coke greatly. Coke was forced to bring in aggressive new management in 1981; consequently, they made a number of important acquisitions and introduced several new soft-drink products. These actions increased Coca-Cola's overall sales and profitability, but Coke itself continued to slip slightly, losing one percent of its market share in 1984, while Pepsi picked up one and a half points. Then, in April 1985, Coke shocked the world by scrapping its ninety-nine-year-old formula in favor of a "new" Coke. The action was a major blunder, and Coke was forced to bring back the old formula under the "Classic Coke" label. But Coke's drastic, unprecedented action had been precipitated by the fact that the Pepsi Challenge had shaken the confidence of Coke's hierarchy.

Kendall increased Pepsi's sales and market share enormously during the 1970s and 1980s. As Pepsi entered the 1980s, Kendall had bulldozed Pepsi through the competition to finally pull even with Coke, boosting Pepsi's sales some 400 percent in the process. He reshaped Pepsi into one of the world's foremost multinational corporations and created a massive food and drink conglomerate. In addition to Pepsi-Cola and Frito-Lay snack foods, the firm makes Diet Pepsi, Pepsi Light, and it bought out Mountain Dew, Teem, and Aspen. In 1986 Pepsi purchased America's third-largest soft-drink firm—7-Up—for $380 million. This move increased Pepsi's overall share of the soft-drink market from 28 percent to 35 percent, bringing it a very close second to Coca-Cola's 39 percent. In response, Coke bought the Dr. Pepper Company for $470 million a few weeks later, thereby raising its market share to 46 percent. Kendall's expansionist activities, however, went well beyond soft drinks and snack foods. He bought the Pizza Hut chain of restaurants (with over 4,000 outlets in 1980) and purchased the Taco Bell Mexican restaurants with more than 1,000 outlets. In addition, he bought North American Van Lines and Wilson Sporting Goods. In 1986, PepsiCo's revenues exceeded Coca-Cola's—$9.3 billion to $8.7 billion—and in 1987 sales were up 26 percent to $11.5 billion. From 1983 to 1987, PepsiCo's average annual increase in sales was 12 percent. It was America's twenty-ninth largest industrial corporation, with profits of nearly $600 million. Profits went up an average of 23 percent a year from 1983 to 1987. With 225,000 employees, it was a massive enterprise.

Kendall, who was chosen for *Fortune* magazine's Business Hall of Fame in 1987, was a dominant force at Pepsi for a quarter of a century. He was so charismatic that the firm and its products tended to take on his aura. An abrasive, pugnacious, white-haired executive, who was known as "White Fang" within the company for his ruthlessness, Kendall gave his company's products the image of robustness, athleticism, competitiveness, and machismo. Pepsi's rise to parity with Coke was in most respects similar to Kendall's own rise in the corporate hierarchy. As the *New York Times* once commented, Kendall "has scaled the corporate ladder not so much by virtue of cerebral accomplishment as by sheer drive and ambition." (**B**. *Fortune*, June 1950, June 1, 1981, April 13, 1987, April 25, 1988; *Time* April 14, 1952, May 19, 1958; *Business Week*, July 5, 1952, March 16, 1987, March 14, June 20, 1988; *New York Times*, April 20, 1959; Lawrence Dietz, *Soda Pop*, 1973; *Who Was Who*, vol. 3; J. C. Louis and Harvey Z. Yazijian, *The Cola Wars*, 1980; Milton Moskowitz et al., *Everybody's Business*, 1980; *Financial World*, April 3, 1985; *New York*, July 29, 1985; *AdWeek*, August 19, 1985; Thomas Oliver, *The Real Coke, The Real Story*, 1986; *Who's Who in America*, 1986–87.)

KERR, ROBERT SAMUEL (September 11, 1896–January 1, 1963) and **DEAN ANDERSON MCGEE** (March 20, 1904–   ). Oil and energy company executives, Kerr-McGee Corp. For nearly half a century it was a charmed company. One of its founders, Robert S. Kerr, was a highly charismatic politician who was governor of Oklahoma, a United States senator, and even ran for the presidency. While in Washington, D.C., he carefully nurtured and protected the interests of the oil industry and his own company. The company's chief executive, Dean McGee, was reputed to be one of the most brilliant petroleum geologists of his generation, and was, in the bargain, an amazingly gifted organizational man. Together, there was a creative synergism that, by 1974, had brought Kerr-McGee to the billion-dollar mark in revenues. Three years later its proceeds topped $2 billion. Then came Karen Silkwood. It was the sort of thing that neither Kerr nor McGee could ever have imagined. Silkwood made allegations against the company about the unsafe handling of nuclear materials. She was killed mysteriously in an automobile accident that was investigated by several levels of government. Kerr-McGee was sued by Silkwood's family, and had to pay $10.5 million. A movie was made about Silkwood, who became a hero and martyr for the antinuclear forces in the United States. Kerr-McGee became the stereotypical corporate villain of the late 1970s and 1980s, the head of an "evil empire" bent on the destruction of America's environment and way of life. The irony was that nuclear production accounted for only 2.5 percent of Kerr-McGee's revenues by the late 1980s. Nonetheless, the once quiet, profitable company would never be the same.

Bob Kerr was born in what was then Indian Territory, near what is now Ada, Oklahoma. His parents had moved from Texas to the Chickasaw Nation a year before his birth. While the elder Kerr worked at a variety of jobs, the family tended a farm. Bob Kerr completed a rather rudimentary high school education, and then took a teaching job to earn money for his family and to further his own education. Kerr's great dream was to get his law degree, and then enter politics. He took a two-year correspondence course at East Central Normal School in Ada, and then went on to the University of Oklahoma in Norman. Ultimately, however, he depleted his funds and left school. Kerr got a job as a magazine salesman, and then as a clerk and messenger for a Missouri attorney, while he continued to read law on the side. When World War I broke out, Kerr joined the U.S. Army and served as a second lieutenant in a field artillery unit, but he never saw combat. His military service, however, provided invaluable contacts that he later used to great effect.

After the war, Kerr returned home, borrowed some money, and became a partner in the Kerr-Dandridge Produce House. In 1921 a fire destroyed the business and left him $10,000 in debt. A year before, his twin daughters had died at birth, and in 1924 his wife and infant son both died in childbirth. Kerr was alone, grieving, and deeply in debt, and he turned to law in utmost seriousness, studying in the local office of Judge J. F. McKeel. In 1922, he passed the state bar exam and commenced a law practice that endured for the next ten years. In the meantime, Kerr had involved himself in state Democratic politics, serving as a delegate in 1919 to county and state conventions and later as a precinct committeeman and inspector for the election board. He also joined the American Legion after the war, and he used this as an important political base, holding a number of important posts in the organization over the next several years.

A major turning point in Kerr's life came when his sister married James Leroy Anderson, a hard-bitten, practical oil man. Anderson, a dozen years older than Kerr, had been one of the pioneer oil drillers in Oklahoma, and in 1919 he became superintendent of a local oil company. Kerr joined Anderson at the oil company in 1926, and in 1928 the former owners sold out to Kerr and Anderson for $5,000 in cash and $25,000 in IOU's. Renamed the Anderson & Kerr Drilling Company, it was one of hundreds of oil-related firms in Oklahoma in predepression 1929. Anderson supervised the drilling, and Kerr abandoned his law practice and scouted for people to sign contracts permitting the oil firm to drill on their property. This resulted in a "Mr. Inside" and "Mr. Outside" arrangement in the firm that continued when Dean McGee was hired. Robert Kerr remained until his death the contact man, a persuasive, witty, and vigorous glad-hander. Anderson, and later McGee, was more technically oriented, less inclined to take risks, and less comfortable in the public eye.

Despite the depression, Anderson & Kerr did well, making their first breakthrough into the big money in 1932 as a result of a daring speculation. Shortly before then it had been discovered that there were extensive oil reserves within the city limits of Oklahoma City, but most oil companies refused to engage in "town lot" drilling because of the danger and expense involved, since the city required drillers to post a $200,000 bond. Nonetheless, Anderson and Kerr borrowed the money to get four such leases, and they went into partnership with Continental Oil on the leases, on the condition that Continental put up the money for the bonds and drilling—a total of $450,000. All the wells came in, and Anderson and Kerr paid back Continental and cleared close to $2 million. Their next big break came when Kerr made a deal with Phillips Petroleum. Kerr agreed to use his political contacts and wiles to get permits to allow drilling on certain town lots Phillips owned, if Anderson & Kerr got the contract for drilling. This was Kerr's first big venture into politics, and he ran a whirlwind campaign that managed to secure a vote in favor of drilling. Anderson & Kerr made another small fortune drilling these lots. Increasingly, however, the two men were unable to agree on many issues, and in 1936 Kerr bought out Anderson. At the same time, Kerr became president, for the first of his six terms, of the Mid-Continent Oil & Gas Association, an important trade association and lobby group for oil firms in the area. With Anderson's departure, Kerr had a desperate need to find someone who could fill Anderson's shoes.

Kerr found just the man at Phillips Petroleum, Dean McGee. Born in Humboldt, Kansas, McGee, whose father had held numerous jobs in the oil industry and had even tried wildcatting until he went broke, had grown up to "the smell and rhythm of the oil field." Deciding to become a petroleum geologist, McGee went to the University of Kansas, where he took the closest thing he could find—mining engineering. After he graduated in 1926, McGee did a year of graduate work and then joined Phillips Petroleum. McGee proved a tireless worker and an expert geologist, and in 1935 was advanced to the position of Phillips' chief geologist. Becoming frustrated when Phillips would not allow him to acquire equity in the firm, McGee accepted Kerr's offer to become vice president and director at Anderson & Kerr Petroleum.

During the late 1930s, Kerr and McGee continued to work together (along with Robert H. Lynn, who had also come over from Phillips) to make their oil firm a success. Increasingly, however, Kerr's interest shifted to politics. In 1940, he was reelected to another term as president of the Mid-Continent Oil & Gas Association, and was also elected Democratic national committeeman from Oklahoma. Two years later, Kerr decided to fulfill a lifelong dream—he announced his candidacy for the Democratic gubernatorial nomination. He ran as a Roosevelt Democrat and won the nomination, beating other contenders by a narrow margin. In the November election, he was elected governor by the smallest margin given any Democratic governor in twenty-eight years, reflecting the anti-Roosevelt and isolationist sentiment in the state. From then on, Kerr's role in the firm's operation changed. A new partnership was established—Kerr-McGee & Co.—and McGee became the head of the business. Kerr's role, on the other hand, gradually decreased, particularly after he went to Washington, D.C. Many years later, upon Kerr's death, McGee was asked what Kerr's role was after 1942. "Mainly to provide optimism,'' McGee replied, ''but that is an asset every business could use.''

There was no question that Kerr, an inveterate risk taker and gambler, provided a needed boost of enthusiasm and optimism for the company, but most observers agree that he played another essential role—he used his vast political influence for the benefit of the oil industry generally, and Kerr-McGee specifically. As governor, Kerr performed in a manner that brought him much praise and national attention. During his term of office, he lowered the level of state expenditures and reduced the state debt, and there was little pork barreling or corruption. He also distinguished himself as a stem-winding orator, and in 1944 President Roosevelt picked him for keynote speaker at the Democratic National Convention. This experience gave Kerr national visibility and national aspirations, and when his term as governor ended in 1947, he decided to run for the U.S. Senate. He easily won the nomination in 1948 and the election just as handily. He remained senator from Oklahoma until his death in 1963.

Kerr had a curious reputation as a senator. On the one hand, he was viewed by nearly everyone as a man whose business and political interests were so tightly interwoven they were virtually inseparable. He was one of the staunchest defenders of the oil-depletion allowance in the Senate, which was of direct benefit to the industry, and to his own firm. In addition, he first gained prominence as a freshman senator when he led the congressional forces trying to exempt independent oil and gas producers from Federal Power Commission regulation. He voted on nominees to the Atomic Energy Commission, with which Kerr-McGee did business, and he sat on the Joint Committee on Atomic Energy. He owned radio and television stations, but voted on nominees to the Federal Communications Commission. The conflict-of-interest issue was continually raised concerning Kerr, and he always cheerfully dismissed it. He always reminded people that any Oklahoma senator would have voted as he did on the oil-depletion allowance; the fact that he happened to own an oil firm was just coincidental. Besides, he pointed out, his interests were out in the open; if the people of Oklahoma thought there was a conflict of interest, they could vote him out of office. Many northern, liberal Democrats, however, were uncomfortable with the easy ethics of oil-state senators like Kerr and Lyndon Johnson on issues like the oil depletion allowance. It did cost Kerr in one way: when he tried for the Democratic presidential nomination in 1952, he could not shake his image as a parochial, special-interest politician, and he was denied the nomination. In sum, Kerr's political stance was primarily ''protectionist''—in that he viewed his role as that of someone who had to protect the interests of Oklahoma, the oil and gas industry, and his own company.

While Kerr was away in Washington protecting the interests of state, industry, and company, McGee stayed home and ran Kerr-McGee. In combination, their efforts took Kerr-McGee from being just one of many small, regional oil firms in the 1940s, to a giant of the energy industry by 1963. Besides protecting the oil-depletion allowance, the proceeds of which Kerr-McGee used to expand its operations and diversify into other areas, Kerr's political actions also opened up other opportunities for the firm. In the early 1950s, when the government decided to promote atoms for peace, Kerr-McGee purchased uranium mines and landed lucrative contracts from the Atomic Energy Commission. Nuclear power seemed like a pat hand for Kerr-McGee in 1952; there did not seem to be any way the company could err, with Kerr in Washington and McGee directing expansion from their Oklahoma City headquarters. The company also moved into coal in 1957, buying huge deposits in Oklahoma, Wyoming, and elsewhere. To aid them in this venture, Kerr pushed a $1.2-billion appropriation through Congress to make the Arkansas River navigable from the Mississippi to Tulsa, an area that just happened to be right next to Kerr-McGee's coal deposits.

But Kerr-McGee's expansion and success was not simply due to Bob Kerr's aggressive presence in Congress, although that was certainly a factor. Dean McGee's brilliant and innovative management of the firm's operations also played a significant part. Under his leadership, Kerr-McGee became a trailblazer in the energy field. McGee's first remarkable innovation came in 1947, when he tackled the problems of exploring, drilling, and producing oil hundreds of feet below the water. Confident that salt domes contained massive oil reserves that would make such a risky and expensive operation profitable, McGee forged ahead and brought in the world's first offshore oil well in the Gulf of Mexico. As McGee noted, "To drill this discovery well, the company devised new drilling concepts and equipment," the most important of which was the fixed platform and tender. An extraordinary and daring achievement, it paid handsome dividends to the firm in a myriad of ways. By 1949, Kerr-McGee had grown to a medium-sized firm in the oil industry.

In the early 1950s, however, fewer offshore possibilities for Kerr-McGee forced McGee to look for sources of revenue outside of petroleum. This resulted in a series of acquisitions that were made throughout the 1950s that significantly changed the structure and direction of the firm. The most notable venture came in 1952, when the company bought the Navajo Uranium Company, making Kerr-McGee the first oil company to enter this field of exploration. By the 1960s, it had the largest uranium-ore processing plant in the United States. In 1954, Kerr-McGee moved into the potash industry, due to Kerr's urging. In the same year, Kerr was elected to his second term as senator and moved up to board chairman at Kerr-McGee, and Dean McGee was appointed president of the company. In 1956, Kerr-McGee's stock was first offered on the New York Stock Exchange, and the company could now advertise itself in its stock prospectus as "a fully integrated oil company. It operates in every phase of the petroleum industry from the production of oil and gas to the delivery of the finished product to the consumer." It had at that time purchased Deep Rock Oil, which had retail gasoline stations, and operated all its refining, marketing, and pipeline activities.

In 1962, Kerr-McGee took yet another important, and ultimately fateful, step in diversifying its activities. In that year it purchased a plant that enabled it to produce nuclear-reactor fuel materials that were sold to nuclear power plants. It was a dangerous industry and later caused untold troubles for the company. A few months later, Robert Kerr died and McGee became chairman and chief executive officer of the company. During the next five years, McGee vigorously pursued the company's diversification policies, and he achieved a significant position in the production and marketing of fertilizers. In 1968–1969, Kerr-McGee undertook a $15-million building program for downtown Oklahoma City, setting up Kerr-McGee Center, with the McGee Tower. All of these investments were financed largely by the oil-depletion allowance. As *Forbes* explained in 1963: "McGee's system is simplicity itself: He uses the depletion allowance from one natural resource the company owns to finance the development of another. Then he uses the depletion allowance from the latter resource to finance the development of a third."

By 1973, Kerr-McGee was a large, powerful, and exceptionally profitable company. Sales in that year amounted to a whopping $728 million, and its return on equity was 15.5 percent, which put it near the top of the integrated oil companies. *Dun's Review* (May 1974) felt that Kerr-McGee's success was due to "a combination of vigorous exploration of new land and new techniques and a canny sense of where and when to diversify." Also, the Arab oil embargo of that year did not hurt the company any. Since virtually all Kerr-McGee's gas and oil were located in the United States, it still had ample supplies during the embargo, but got to enjoy the fruits of enforced scarcity, as prices were driven to unprecedented levels. As a result, McGee rather undiplomatically referred to the embargo as a "godsend." In 1974, revenues soared past the $1-billion mark.

Then the wheels began to fall off Dean McGee's well-oiled wagon. A young woman by the name of Karen Silkwood was a lab technician in Kerr-McGee's Cimarron, Oklahoma, plutonium processing plant. A member of the Oil, Chemical, and Atomic Workers Union (OCAW), she had been involved in a strike at the plant in 1972–1973. Six months later, in 1974, she was subjected to a minor degree of radioactive contamination while at work. The incident was reported to the Atomic Energy Commission (AEC), and she and two other union officials went to Washington, D.C., to report alleged improprieties in operations at the plant and unsafe working conditions. She also accused Kerr-McGee of falsifying some records of fuel rods by deliberately fogging the pictures taken as a production control. The AEC was not greatly impressed, but Silkwood promised to document her allegations.

After Silkwood returned to the plant in November, 1974, a series of bizarre occurrences took place. When she went in for a radiation check, she was found to be contaminated from an unexplained source. She was "cleansed," only to have the same thing happen again for the next two days. With her consent, company inspectors searched her apartment and found contamination in several areas. The suspicion was that someone had planted radioactive materials there. A few days later, Silkwood left in her car for Oklahoma City, allegedly to file documents to a representative of OCAW and a reporter from the *New York Times*. She never reached her destination because her car left the road and struck a culvert. An autopsy showed she had had a heavier than usual amount of sedative in her blood. An ensuing investigation showed that plutonium was missing from the plant, evidently smuggled out and left at Silkwood's apartment. Many felt that this had been done by the security forces at Kerr-McGee, with the compliance of upper management.

In any event, Silkwood's relatives sued Kerr-McGee for negligence, and in 1979 a federal district court in Oklahoma found the corporation strictly liable for the contamination under the provisions of the Price-Anderson Act and awarded punitive damages to the Silkwood estate of $10.5 million, the largest single damage award given for a nuclear mishap. Kerr-McGee appealed the decision on a number of grounds, but in 1984 the United States Supreme Court affirmed the lower-court ruling. Through a series of articles in *Rolling Stone*, and a number of books, along with the movie, Karen Silkwood became a martyr for the antinuclear movement, and Kerr-McGee acquired a reputation as, at best, a negligent firm, and, at worst, an evil one. This reputation bedeviled it in later years, as did its association with the nuclear industry.

In the meantime, Kerr-McGee continued to grow, seemingly oblivious and impervious to the accusations and commotion surrounding it. By 1977, it had revenues of $2 billion, and although earnings slipped somewhat, Kerr-McGee, nonetheless, remained an exceptionally profitable company. But as it moved into the 1980s, it found it difficult to shake off the deleterious effects of its involvement with nuclear energy. Although Dean McGee remained an enthusiastic promoter of nuclear power, the firm moved rapidly to reduce its involvement in the industry, so that the percentage of its revenues from nuclear energy dropped from 5 percent in 1979 to just 2.5 percent in 1986. In 1985, Kerr-McGee's revenues peaked at $3.5 billion, but profits were elusive. The company's return on equity had slid to just 8 percent, well below the 12 to 15 percent of its competitors. Kerr-McGee's big problem was its uranium processing; from 1982 to 1985, these operations had losses totalling $72 million. In the meantime, the company was hounded with a succession of accidents and lawsuits that dragged down the price of its stock and diverted management attention from its principal oil and gas operations.

The greatest disaster occurred on January 4, 1986, when an overfilled cylinder of uranium hexafluoride burst at the company's nuclear fuel processing plant near Gore, Oklahoma, killing one worker and injuring thirty-four. Despite the fact that the plant had been cited fifteen times in the previous eight years for infractions, it had retained its license. By the time of the accident, however, many company executives wanted simply to abandon the whole nuclear and uranium end of the business. Virtually every industry analyst agreed, pointing out that Kerr-McGee's preoccupation with diversification and its record of nuclear problems had weakened its core business of finding and producing oil and natural gas. By 1986, its estimated average cost for finding a barrel of oil was $13.03, compared to $7.35 for its competitors. But Dean McGee remained a nuclear loyalist, and most industry observers felt he thwarted every attempt to get out of the industry, despite the fact he was only honorary chairman and head of the executive committee. McGee downplayed his own influence, claiming, "I am just a figurehead."

But Kerr-McGee, like much of the oil industry, was having problems finding its way in the late 1980s. In 1987, its revenues amounted to just $2.6 billion, a remarkable decline from its peak two years earlier. Profits remained below normal, at just $81 million, and over a five-year period were well below the industry average. The *New York Times*, writing about Kerr-McGee, described the early years of the firm very well: "a colorful name in the history of the energy business," one that had been long associated with "power politics and rawboned wildcatters." But in later years, as it diversified, and especially as it became ensnared in the nuclear industry, the words of James A. Ikard, attorney for the Silkwood family, seemed more apropos: "No one wants to think badly of Kerr-McGee. But the company has earned the distrust and dislike of the public." (**B**. *Time*, July 30, 1956, June 6, 1960, March 9, 1979; *Fortune*, March 1959, February 3, 1986; *New York Times*, January 2, 1963, January 12, 1984; *Forbes*, November 1, 1963, June 15, 1973, October 16, 1978, January 11, 1988; *Dictionary of American Biography*; *National Cyclopaedia of American Biography*, F:107; *Dun's Review*, May, December, 1974; Anne Hodges Morgan, *Robert S. Kerr: The Senate Years*, 1977; *Newsweek*, October 9, 1978; *Who's Who in America*, 1978–79; John Z. Ezell, *Innovations in Energy: The Story of Kerr-McGee*, 1979; Milton Moskowitz et al., *Everybody's Business*, 1980; Howard Kohn, *Who Killed Karen Silkwood*, 1981; Richard Rashke, *The Killing of Karen Silkwood*, 1981; John W. Johnson, *Insuring against Disaster: The Nuclear Industry on Trial*, 1986; *Business Week*, February 3, 1986, January 20, March 14, 1988; *Standard & Poor's Register of Directors and Executives*, 1988.)

KLEIN, ANNE (June 7, 1923?–March 19, 1974). Fashion designer, Anne Klein & Company. Anne Klein was not an easy woman to work for. Imperious and high strung, workdays were long and tension-filled. An assistant once said: "Anne never picks up a thing she drops; she walks away, and someone else picks it up." But she had a brilliant eye for fashion and design, and she was particularly adept at coordinating her collection. As a longtime Anne Klein customer commented: "Klein clothes are great, but Anne's real genius lies in creating a total package."

Anne Klein was born Hannah Golofsky in Brooklyn, New York, the daughter of a businessman. She changed her first name to Anne for "esthetic reasons," and she acquired a new last name when she married her first husband, Ben Klein. She was educated in Brooklyn's public schools, and she went to Girl's Commercial High School, where she studied fine arts and drawing. Winning a scholarship to the Traphagen School of Fashion in New York, Anne Klein also began, at the age of fifteen, working as a free-lance sketcher at a wholesale house. A short time later, she took a full-time job as a designer at Varden Petites. After working there for about three years, she became a ladies clothing designer for

Maurice Rentner. In 1947, with her husband, Anne Klein founded Junior Sophisticates, of which she was a partner until 1966. In the meantime, in 1958, she and her first husband were divorced. The firm was a success, and over the years it succeeded in taking business away from other junior houses. During these early years, Anne Klein gained attention for pioneering the transformation of junior clothing from frilly buttons-and-bows to a sleeker, more sophisticated look. She later made these classic lines the hallmark of her own company.

In 1968, together with her second husband, Matthew N. Rubenstein, Klein started her own manufacturing company, Anne Klein & Co. She was president of the firm from its inception until her death six years later. During this short period of time, Anne Klein played a major role in the transformation of the fashion and women's wear industry in the United States. She has been credited within the industry for having inspired a new school of contemporary dress, by putting separates and sportswear into more sophisticated urban use. Her style and concepts were later adapted by Calvin Klein,[†] Ralph Lauren,[†] and Liz Claiborne,[†] but Anne Klein did it first.

As her styles caught on in the late 1960s and early 1970s, Anne Klein designed ski and tennis clothes for the Anne Klein Supersport division, and she created furs, jewelry, belts, handbags, scarves, and other items with her label for other companies. In all of these endeavors, she was a leader in creating a wholly new American look, one made up of interchangeable separates that could be combined to create a finished look. Liz Claiborne, a few years later, took this concept, which Anne Klein had developed for the haute couture trade, and applied it to moderately priced clothing for working women. By 1974, Anne Klein's collections were carried by 800 department and specialty stores in America. Many of these stores had separate Anne Klein boutiques complete with clothing and accessories so that customers could achieve the total "Anne Klein look." Carrie Donovan, senior fashion editor of *Harper's Bazaar*, said of Klein's designs: Anne Klein is "one of the few people who really understands what the American woman wants and has the sense of style to produce it."

Anne Klein's accomplishments did not go unnoticed by the fashion industry. She was one of the few designers to win three Coty American Fashion Critics Awards, the Oscars of the fashion industry, and, as a result, she was inducted into the American Fashion Awards Hall of Fame in 1971. She twice won the prestigious Neiman-Marcus Award—the first American designer to do so—and in 1973 she was one of five American designers whose styles were shown in a special fashion show at Versailles. She was also a founding member of the Council of Fashion Designers. In 1965, she and her second husband established the Anne Klein Studio in New York City, which acted as consultants and designers in various parts of the industry and also sponsored new designers. Anne Klein also had a number of inventions in the industry, including a girdle she patented in 1967 that was designed for miniskirt wearers.

In 1973, all of Anne Klein's enterprises became affiliated with Takihyo Co., Ltd., of Japan when it purchased 49.5 percent of Anne Klein & Co. With her death in the following year, the Takihyo textile firm assumed operational control of the Anne Klein company. In 1984, to compete more successfully with such designers as Liz Claiborne, Takihyo brought out the Anne Klein II line, to bring Anne Klein's haute couture design to working women at less-than-haute prices. With prices from 30 to 60 percent below those in the designer collection, the new line brought in $50 million in the first year after its introduction, twice the revenue of the more expensive collection.

Even immortals are often prophets without honor in their own country. At the height of her career, Anne Klein mused about her stepdaughter's lack of recognition for her accomplishments:

My kids think absolutely nothing of the fact that I am Anne Klein, big deal designer. . . . The other day [my stepdaughter] tried on a pair of pants and said, "Wow, they're great, they're real bell-bottoms." I said she could have them in a while. "Can't I have them now?" she asked, "they fit me perfectly." I said, "Donna, I can't see your feet." I mean, the pants were dragging on the floor. She said, "You don't know anything about pants, Anne."

(**B**. *National Cyclopaedia of American Biography*, 58: 580; *McCall's*, October 1971; *Harper's Bazaar*, April 1972; *New York Times*, March 20, 1974; *Fortune*, June 10, 1985.)

KLEIN, CALVIN RICHARD (November 19, 1942–) and **BARRY SCHWARTZ** (1942–). Fashion designers, Calvin Klein, Incorporated. The premise was perfect—it established a humorous comparison of past and present. In the hit film, *Back to the Future*, Michael J. Fox awakens from his time travels in the 1950s and is addressed as "Calvin" by the teenage girl who has helped nurse him. Puzzled as to why she should call him by this name, she replies that it is on his underwear—his name, naturally, is "Calvin Klein." In the 1950s, before designers like Calvin Klein began putting their names on jeans, it would have made sense that the name on clothing identified the wearer. By the 1980s, however, it simply gave a sense of borrowed cachet. Not your own name, it made a statement about who you were in terms of status and aspiration. Two men, boyhood friends, were behind the billion-dollar fashion empire known as Calvin Klein, Incorporated.

Calvin Klein and Barry Schwartz were born in the same neighborhood in the Bronx, and both their families owned grocery stores. Calvin early displayed a talent for fashion and style, and when Barry's mother took her son shopping for clothes, she always took Calvin along, since she truly valued Calvin's advice about clothing. Even at ten and twelve years of age, he seemed to have a knack for putting together outfits that looked just right on Barry. Barry, on the other hand, had a head for business. Klein has recounted: "When we were only five, my best friend Barry Schwartz and I wanted to open a pet shop. I was going to find the fauna and Barry was going to keep us from going broke." This division of interest continued as the two boys grew older. As Barry grew into a forceful, conventional young man who planned to enter the family's food business, Calvin was busy sketching clothes, sewing, and visiting stores to observe fashions.

Young Calvin attended the Fashion Institute of Technology, graduating in 1962, and then served an apprenticeship in the garment industry, earning $75 a week as an apprentice designer for Dan Millstein. Barry, in the meantime, attended New York University and took over his family's supermarket in Harlem. This had come about in the most tragic circumstances. In October 1964, while he was taking basic training at Fort Dix, New Jersey, he was notified that his father had been killed during a stickup in the family store. Barry was released on a hardship discharge, and he transformed the store into a highly profitable enterprise. In 1968, he offered his old friend Calvin Klein a 50-percent stake in the business.

Calvin was sorely tempted. In six years in the fashion industry, he had experienced little financial success. But this had been his boyhood dream—he just could not give it up. Calvin had an alternative suggestion. He invited Barry to enter his business. Using $2,000 of his savings, and $10,000 from Schwartz, the two friends started Calvin Klein, Limited. A few weeks later, Dr. Martin Luther King was assassinated, Harlem erupted in riots, and Schwartz's Harlem store was destroyed by looters. Barry thus moved full time into the fashion business. For five years, the small firm operated out of a suite at the York Hotel on Seventh Avenue, until Klein and Schwartz bought out Millstein, and moved Calvin Klein, Limited into a site on West Thirty-Ninth Street. During these years, Barry handled the sales and administrative ends of the company; Calvin devoted his time and creative energy to designing.

The late 1960s and early 1970s were not good years for the fashion industry, since, under the hippie influence, "dressing down" was the trend. One area of the market where there was still some interest in style was in women's coats. Calvin concentrated on that item, sewing and designing a number of models, until finally creating a classic and understated version of the trench coat. Calvin Klein's big breakthrough came with Bonwit Teller. Personally wheeling his samples to the office of Mildred Custin, president of the firm, Calvin came away with a $50,000 sale. Custin recalls: "What impressed me most was the purity of his line and the simplicity of his designs. 'Young man,' I said to him 'you better raise your prices by ten dollars or you'll never make any money.' "

When an excited Calvin Klein returned to the office to tell Barry Schwartz they had a $50,000 order from Bonwit Teller, Barry replied, "What's Bonwit Teller?" But Barry Schwartz learned fast, and as the sales of Calvin Klein, Inc. increased by about a million a year over the next few years, it was the exceptional synergism between the two men that brought them success. Calvin's sense of design and style helped bring about a transition in the early 1970s from the miniskirt to longer lengths of coats and dresses. Calvin designed mostly two-piece suits and coats until 1972, when he began to concentrate on sportswear. This was highly successful, as he created a line that allowed women to mix and match their outfits to suit the occasion. This innovation perfectly fit the emerging mood of feminism. As Calvin commented at the time:

I felt that the American lifestyle had changed and that there was certainly a need for clothing to express and relate to that change, women could no longer be dictated to. For the most part, women of today spend their time and energy working, participating in all aspects of home, community, and business. Their lives have changed, and there is little time for wardrobe planning. (*Current Biography*)

It would be easy to view all of this as Calvin's show during this time, but nothing could be farther from the truth. Without Barry Schwartz's tough business sense it might never have happened. In the early 1970s, the clothing business was still highly segmented; buyers often would not buy sportswear from a coat maker, or vice versa. When they expanded their line into sportswear, several buyers announced they would not take the line. Barry reacted in a typical manner: "I'm a very, very stubborn man. I decided that even with our best accounts that if they wouldn't buy our sportswear, we wouldn't sell them our coats." It was a bold move, one someone who had been acculturated to the ethics of the fashion business might not have dared to make. But it was characteristic of Barry Schwartz's business style. As *Fortune* commented in 1980, Barry is Calvin's "mailed fist, considered one of the harshest bargainers and most leathery bosses in a trade scarcely noted for tenderness." Calvin recognized Barry's worth. As he noted: "We're not in the business to win friends, but to make money. Barry runs the business in a tough, tight way, and I support him." Another time he said: "I give Barry a collection and he turns it into money."

During the 1970s, while European designers were still emphasizing the layered look, which tended to hide a woman's body, Calvin Klein was aware of the fitness craze surging throughout America. Understanding that fit American women who worked hard at keeping a slim figure would want to display it, he brought out youthful designs that showed off the figure and fit comfortably into the active life-style of the 1970s. Creating a clean, classic line, he emphasized the perfect coordination of the pieces by having models exchange coats and jackets as they passed on the runway. As he told the *New York Post* in 1973, "I believe in classic clothes—not the faddishness that looks right this season, and is dead the next." To a large extent, this came to epitomize what was called the Calvin Klein "look."

It was Calvin Klein, more than anyone else, who made America the leading fashion center in the world. He did this by making fashionable clothing part of the mass or popular culture. Haute couture in Europe epitomizes the sense of class distinction and privilege; Klein's designs emphasize that quality is available to everyone. His fashion is accessible; it can be obtained by the masses, but it is not cheap. In that sense, Calvin Klein, along with a few others, has Americanized fashion in the same way America has dominated popular music and film worldwide. By the 1980s, Europe was copying American mass culture in fashion in the same way as it did in music and movies. The Europeans even began reinterpreting it and successfully reimporting it to the United States. The success of Giorgio Armani is a good example of this trend. The American fashion industry recognized Calvin Klein's contribution by awarding him an unprecedented three consecutive Coty American Fashion Critics Awards in the 1970s. In 1975 he was elected into the American Hall of Fame of Fashion.

As Calvin Klein achieved success and recognition, his clothing began creeping upscale. His earlier clothes had been priced for a relatively inexpensive market, and he supplied about 1,000 stores with fashions that included a good deal of polyester fabrics. In 1973, however, he and Barry Schwartz became more selective; thus they ruthlessly cut back their stores to 250 and raised their prices. At the same time, Calvin announced that he would no longer use man-made fabrics. "Polyester feels slimy," he told one reporter. Their great breakthrough in mass marketing came in 1975, with the development of designer jeans.

This successful product was the result of a suggestion from Bloomingdale's buyer, Connie Dowling. Until then, jeans were the lowliest garment imaginable, but they were hugely popular during the 1960s and early 1970s. With the return of fashion, their popularity was waning, but Ms. Dowling thought they could be marketed as a high-fashion item. She suggested that Calvin rework the jeans into a shapelier, more stylish garment, and then sell them under his name, along with the rest of his line. Calvin liked the idea, and one year later introduced a new, sleeker blue jean. Despite a price tag of $50, which was more than twice what regular blue jeans were selling for, Calvin Klein's jeans were an instant hit.

In 1977, Puritan Fashions, which had made its living from low-priced dresses—for what Madison Avenue calls "the masses with fat asses"—approached Calvin Klein about a licensing arrangement to manufacture his designer jeans. Calvin had a three word answer: "Talk to Barry." Barry Schwartz met with Carl Rosen, head of Puritan, and drove a typically tough bargain. Rosen later recalled the negotiations:

The sharpest guy I ever met, he wanted more than 5 percent royalty on wholesale, which would give them about a dollar a garment with a minimum guarantee of a million dollars for five years. And the control they asked for was outrageous. All I can say is an angel came down from heaven and told me to do it. Now we pay them a million in royalties almost every *six weeks,* and sales are still headed up. (*Fortune,* November 17, 1980)

Using the fifteen-year-old movie star, Brooke Shields, as a model, Calvin Klein created a sensation with his ads for the jeans. Seductively declaring that "Nothing comes between me and my Calvin's," Ms. Shields had America buzzing over the ads. The more people talked and were scandalized, the more the jeans sold, and they, in turn, sparked a wave in designer apparel that swept America in the late 1970s. For many Americans, Calvin Klein jeans were the first designer garment they had ever owned, and, having been introduced to high fashion, they became more name conscious when shopping for other clothes. In that way, Calvin Klein still further made fashion an item of mass culture.

By the late 1970s, Calvin Klein revenues were in excess of $30 million, and could have been higher, but neither he nor Barry Schwartz had any wish to dilute the exclusive allure of their label. Their high profits came from the fact that Schwartz rigorously held down costs. The entire company was housed at two low-rent locations on West 39th Street, and the company subcontracted the manufacture of all its clothing. As a rival explained: "At Calvin Klein there's just no overhead; that's why the place is a money machine." The firm employed just 135 people, and Barry Schwartz was notorious for the close scrutiny he kept on them. He was also demanding with retailers. If a store irritated him, he dropped it, and that even included prestigious and important chains like I. Magnin. As he explained, "When we have the slightest trouble—returns, complaints, other aggravations—I say 'Don't sell to them,' and I don't share markdown costs with them either. . . . To us, the ultimate consumer is more important than the retailer."

These profits made both partners and Calvin Klein, Incorporated exceedingly wealthy. Calvin and Barry had developed a close working relationship with Carl Rosen, head of Puritan Fashions, and over the years they had bought 185,000 shares of Puritan's stock. When Rosen brought in Warren Hirsh in 1980 as president of Puritan with a $7-million contract, Hirsh was ousted after just three months when he had a run-in with Klein. Rosen died in August 1983, and he was replaced by his twenty-seven-year-old son, Andrew. Sales remained strong, but profits dropped 62 percent in the third quarter at Puritan, and Klein and Schwartz bought the 3.5 million shares of Puritan stock they did not already own and took control of the manufacturing firm. They borrowed only $105 million of the $612 million to make the deal. Schwartz explained:

We wanted control of the company that produces at retail $500 million worth of product annually with the Calvin Klein name on it. Up to this point, we've had a lot of input in advertising and we design the product. But it became a very, very important part of the overall business, and we felt we could do a better job than the current management. (*Forbes*, January 21, 1984)

Calvin Klein's most recent excursion was into the field of women's lingerie. His idea seemed almost perverse—to design men's underwear for women. Taking a design that many felt looked remarkably like the classic Jockey men's brief, he made it into a huge hit. A large part of the reason for its success came from the provocative advertising campaign developed for the product. Taking his cue from Brooke Shields' sexy and scandalous ads for blue jeans, Calvin Klein himself created a series of kinky ads for his underwear. Barry Day, vice-president of McCann-Erickson advertising agency, said, "Klein's the creative leader of the new eroticism in ads, but he makes the public think about sex and their own sexuality—and that's very disturbing to a lot of people.'' Klein followed this with equally sexy ads for his new perfume, Obsession, which featured three naked young men kissing a nude woman. Calvin Klein receives hundreds of angry calls every time one of his ads runs, but sales for 1984 reached nearly $1 billion worldwide, a 10-percent increase over the previous year.

The two Bronx buddies seemed very different by the late 1980s. Barry Schwartz, the classic dark-suited, suburban businessman, lived in Westchester County, New York, with his wife and three children where he devoted much of his time to stamp collecting until he remembered his youthful passion—horses. He recalls, ''I thought, gee, I can buy a horse if I want.'' Before long he had one hundred thoroughbreds on a 700-acre horse farm. Calvin Klein, on the other hand, continued to come to work dressed in slacks, a sweater, and a tieless shirt. Tall and slim, he married Jayne Centre in 1964 and they were divorced ten years later. Calvin then led the life of a Manhattan playboy for the next decade, frequenting Studio 54 and other discotheques, maintaining his youthful good looks with regular visits to health clubs and biweekly trips to a dermatologist for silicon injections to smooth out wrinkles. He became ''the leader of an androgynous disco brat pack who never seemed to care who knew about his wild life.'' In 1984, he told *Playboy*: ''Anyone I've wanted to be with I've had.'' But that hedonistic life-style took its toll on Calvin Klein, and, to a lesser extent, on his company. Klein had become cross-addicted to Valium and vodka, and he had deteriorated to such an extent that he had to enter a rigorous chemical-dependency program. At the end of treatment, he moved in with his second wife, whom he married two years earlier.

Klein's decision to clean up his personal life was reflected in a dramatic change of approach in the firm's product line and advertising. Gone was the provocative, nearly decadent approach of earlier years. Calvin Klein's new perfume, Eternity, launched in 1988, was a ''clean, floral, romantic'' perfume, and Klein commented that ''I don't think the thing to be is provocative anymore. I've done everything I could do in a provocative sense without being arrested.''

Calvin Klein has been compared to one of his major competitiors, Ralph Lauren,[†] in many ways. Both have created looks that reek of old money classicism, which are snapped up by the newly rich. But there are differences between the two. Richard Shapiro of Bloomingdale's said: ''Lauren's look is somehow WASPy, Klein is not so severe. . . . Above all, Klein's clothes are sexy.'' Though perhaps not quite so sexy anymore. (**B**. *New York Post*, October 11, 1973; *Vogue*, November 1975; *Newsweek*, November 3, 1975, May 8, 1978, March 11, 1985; *New York Times Magazine*, January 30, 1977; *Current Biography*, 1978; Barbara Walz and Bernadine Morris, *Fashion Makers*, 1978; Andrew Kopkind, ''Calvin Klein—Superstar,'' *Village Voice*, 1979; Anne Stegemeyer, *Who's Who in Fashion*, 1980; *Fortune*, November 17, 1980, October 1, 1984; *Forbes*, January 2, 1984; Joseph J. Fucini and Suzy Fucini, *Entrepreneurs*, 1985; *Toronto Star*, October 9, 1988.)

KLUGE, JOHN WERNER (September 21, 1914–   ). Media executive and entrepreneur, Metromedia. Throughout most of his long business career, analysts have confidently predicted Kluge's failure. Yet, both *Forbes* and *Fortune* in the late 1980s agreed that he was worth between $2 and $3 billion. How could so many bright and informed people be so consistently wrong, for so many years, about a businessman? Much of it has to do with Kluge's personality and his daring tactics. Excitable and often inarticulate, he is frequently unable to explain his plans and ideas to others. His plans are often extremely daring and very unorthodox. Kluge does the opposite of what the "smart money" says you should do. *Fortune* (April 5, 1982) commented that Kluge was guided as much by his own "instincts as by his own peculiar cerebrations." As a result, he is an inveterate gambler who makes many mistakes, but one who cashes in big when he is right.

Kluge's technique is to buy what are known in the trade as "dogs"—run-down operations that can be had fairly cheaply. Furthermore, the acquisition is financed with debt, so that the investment must be recouped fairly quickly—almost always within ten years. As a result, Kluge has to engage in a fast rebuilding job to turn the company around, and, at the same time, pay back the large debt. Not an easy task, but one which Kluge has mastered more times than not.

Kluge was born in Chemnitz, Germany, the son of Fritz and Gertrude (Donj) Kluge. His father, an engineer, was reportedly killed during World War I, and his mother married an American-born man who took the family to Detroit in 1922. Kluge was educated in the city's public schools, but he left home while still an adolescent during the depression, supporting himself with a number of jobs, including work on a Ford assembly line. He attended Wayne State University in 1933–1934, and then he got a scholarship to Columbia University in New York, where he graduated with a degree in economics in 1937. After graduation, Kluge joined a small paper company in Holyoke, Massachusetts, as a sales manager. In four years he doubled the company's sales and was given one-third of the equity in the firm. During World War II, Kluge served in army intelligence and was discharged a captain at the war's end in 1945.

Returning home, Kluge decided to sell his interest in the paper company and to invest his money in the burgeoning radio industry. With a partner he founded station WGAY in Silver Springs, Maryland. This was followed by the purchase of eight other radio stations during the next decade. But radio was not Kluge's only business interest. In 1947, he formed the New England Fritos Corporation to manufacture and distribute the cocktail snacks, Fritos and Chitos, which was a successful operation. He also acquired a distributorship in the same area for Standard Brands, Thomas Richardson (candy makers), and Simon & Schuster. The success of these operations resulted, in 1951, in his organization of the food brokerage firm of Kluge & Company. This turned out to be the ideal Kluge business investment. Food brokers contract with manufacturers to sell their products to supermarkets on commission, usually 3 percent. Since the broker carries no inventory, capital needs are low, and energetic salesmen who know their market can make a great deal of money. Kluge knew his market and he made a small fortune; he still owned 25 percent of the firm (the largest in the Baltimore-Washington market) in the early 1980s.

In 1959, however, Kluge ended his active participation in the food business to concentrate on the broadcasting industry. In that year, he and some friends bought a controlling interest in Metropolitan Broadcasting Corporation. They paid $4 million for Paramount Picture's 24-percent interest in the company; Kluge got 12 percent and was named president. The firm owned television stations in New York and Washington and two radio outlets, but it was a real dog, since it had earned practically nothing in 1958 on revenues of $12.4 million. Most industry experts thought Kluge was crazy since the television stations were not affiliated with networks, which was thought, at the time, to be the principal key to success in the field. Kluge thought differently, believing that it was possible to make big money with independents if they were in major markets. Soon after the purchase, Kluge set out on the road to expansion, paying top dollar for independent television stations in cities like Los Angeles and Houston.

Metromedia, which began in 1948 as the Du Mont Television Network, the broadcasting division of Allen B. Du Mont Laboratories, Incorporated, became Du Mont Broadcasting in 1955 and Metropolitan Broadcasting in 1958. In 1961, when Kluge diversified into outdoor advertising, he changed the name of the company to Metromedia. Despite the gloomy predictions of many in the business, he had made Metromedia into a profitable operation by the mid–1960s. Revenues by that time had climbed to $100 million (from $14 million), and net income was well above $5 million. This had been achieved both by expansion in the television field and by diversification, as 38 percent of its revenues came from television, 33 percent from billboards, and 17 percent from radio. The greatest profits, however, were from the broadcasting operations.

But broadcasting was a tightly controlled industry, with the Federal Communications Commission (FCC) allowing only a certain amount of chain ownership. Kluge began to look for new areas in which to expand. Many of these new avenues of investment were in the entertainment field. In 1963, Kluge bought Ice Capades, which in 1980 had three touring companies performing before audiences in ninety American and Canadian cities. It also opened seventeen Ice Capade Chalets, indoor ice-skating facilities. Through Metromedia Producers Corporation, Kluge syndicated his own and other companies' entertainment and documentary television programs, including "The Merv Griffin Show," "Crosswits," and other popular shows. This same diversification, however, brought Kluge and Metromedia a host of problems.

Kluge's Metromedia empire peaked in 1968, when it had revenues of $160 million and profits of $9.1 million. After that, the empire came unglued, prompting one industry analyst to comment that Kluge had turned a "helluva company into a shelluva company." By the early 1970s, revenues were stagnant, and profits were about half of what they had been in 1968; most of the remaining profit existed because of heavy staff cuts which saved millions per year. Part of the problem stemmed from Kluge's personal life. In 1968 he divorced his wife of twenty years, and it became increasingly difficult for associates to contact him. At about the same time, Kluge also began hobnobbing with executives of *Fortune* 500 corporations. As a result, in October 1968, he sold Metromedia to Transamerica Corporation, headed by his new friend John Beckett. Kluge explained that he wanted a closer association with "my friend John Beckett." The deal was made without telling a single executive at Metromedia, and Kluge declined to accept Transamerica's offer of employment contracts for anyone at Metromedia—except himself. But the merger never came off. It had to be approved by the FCC, which dragged its feet on the issue for eight months. During this time, Kluge and Metromedia demonstrated a perfect example of "Murphy's Law," that is, everything that can go wrong, will go wrong.

In early 1969, Metromedia lost its top-rated "Merv Griffin Show" to CBS. This disaster for the firm reflected badly on management. As a former television executive said, "Losing Griffin was bad luck, but not having a replacement ready was bad management." During the same time, radio revenues slipped badly, largely because Kluge forced his West Coast AM stations to drop their all-talk formats. Also, a direct-mail business Kluge had purchased hemorrhaged red ink, with losses of $4 million in 1969. To cope with these losses, Kluge had a single answer—drastic, devastating staff cuts. There was a lot of fat to trim at Metromedia, but Kluge's knife cut deeply. During 1970 Metromedia cut expenses by nearly $600,000 a month. The first of six very rough years was 1969, and when the recession came in 1974, Metromedia really hit bottom. Hidden in all the gloom of these years, though, was one positive factor. Kluge had made Metromedia into a "lean, mean, fighting machine." When good times returned, the company was going to be in a position to make extraordinary profits.

Kluge did not have long to wait. Just about the time he finished retrenching in 1976, advertisers suddenly began pouring oceans of money into television. Metromedia sales jumped 25 percent in that year and its earnings doubled. With its staff accustomed to a severely tightened environment, Metromedia blossomed in the late 1970s as never before. Kluge's independents in this environment attracted viewers through what is called "counterprogramming," that is, by offering different kinds of shows from whatever the network affiliates were airing. For example, when the networks are showing news, Metromedia stations offer reruns of "M*A*S*H," and then run their own news at 10 P.M. Throughout the day, his stations run old network shows, sports events, and old movies of various quality to attract viewers. Unimpressive to reviewers, they nevertheless garner impressive audience shares—from 8 to 25 percent of the total viewers. Furthermore, they attract a host of local advertisers since they offer television time at a discount.

By the early 1980s, Kluge and Metromedia had created an enormous cash machine. The company's stock, which had hit bottom in 1974 at $4.25 a share, exploded in value, growing at an annual rate of 70 percent. By 1982, it was trading at $175, far and away its highest level. The reason for this increase was the enormous return on equity at Metromedia: in 1981, it returned 42 percent on equity, the fourth year in a row it exceeded 30 percent. The richest profits came in the television business, where Kluge's seven stations reached an incredible 20 percent of the U.S. populace, and contributed 45 percent of the firm's $462 million in revenue. Most of the rest of the profits came from its fourteen radio stations and 42,000 billboards. The other entertainment items, like the Harlem Globetrotters, which were acquired in 1976, made modest amounts of money.

Because of this ability to make massive amounts of money, Kluge began buying in Metromedia's stock. By the early 1980s, he owned 17 percent of Metromedia's shares, worth at that time about $120 million. Shortly thereafter, Kluge organized a consortium of investors, which offered $1.3 billion for all of Metromedia's shares, to take the firm private. In June 1984, Kluge leveraged a buyout, with the use of bank credit. By means of this astute, complicated arrangement, he ended up owning 75 percent of Metromedia's stock. Less than six months after completing that leveraged buyout, Kluge turned to Michael Milken,[†] the leveraged buyout (LBO) and junk-bond king of Drexel Burnham Lambert, to leverage the leveraged buyout. That is, Kluge and Milken replaced the bank debt with $1.3 billion raised through a variety of securities, with Kluge accepting a high interest rate to escape the banks.

By the end of 1984, Kluge, through these complicated financial operations, had become fantastically wealthy. He took more than $100 million in cash out of the operation, owned 75.5 percent of the company, and had options to increase his ownership to more than 90 percent. In the mid–1980s, that 90 percent was worth over $1 billion. At that point, Kluge again confounded the experts—he began to sell off his carefully accumulated properties. At the very time that Warren Buffett,[†] one of the most astute investors in America, decided to plunge into the television market, Kluge began to get out. When Buffett, with his Capital Cities Communications, began buying television stations in 1985, competitor Rupert Murdoch desperately needed stations to counter his moves. Kluge was more than happy to sell off his well-run, profitable stations to Murdoch for top dollar. The deal he struck called for Murdoch to pay Metromedia more than $2 billion for its seven stations. This amounted to twelve or thirteen times the station's cash flow, above the industry average of ten times cash flow. This made it possible for Kluge to pull Metromedia out from under its $1.3-billion junk-bond debt, and to invest in a variety of new ventures.

The new venture which most interested Kluge was the cellular mobile telephone. He had actually gotten involved in this product several years earlier. In 1982, a friend informed him that companies were flooding the FCC with applications for cellular mobile telephone service. The FCC had announced that they would issue two mobile phone licenses per city—one to the local telephone company, and one to somebody else. Many of these other applicants were radio-paging companies. Wishing to get in on this newly developing business, Kluge took $270 million of Metromedia's money to acquire many of these small radio-paging businesses which held licenses to operate cellular radio systems. The prices Metromedia paid were unheard of at the time and shocked many industry experts, but by the late 1980s they looked like bargains. The paging business alone boomed, growing by more than 20 percent annually, and on the heels of that came an enormous explosion in the use of cellular phones for automobiles—the great "yuppie" toy of the late 1980s.

No sooner had he accumulated this booming business then Kluge sold it off and began to liquidate most of the rest of Metromedia. He sold the majority of his cellular telephone interests to Southwestern Bell for $1.2 billion in 1986, and in the same year he sold eleven radio stations for $285 million and his share in the outdoor advertising business for $300 million. He also sold the Ice Capades and Harlem Globetrotters for $30 million. The result of all this divestment was that Kluge was reported by both *Forbes* and *Fortune* to be worth in excess of $3 billion, making him the second wealthiest man in America, just behind Sam Walton.[†]

With that huge mound of cash, Kluge went on the prowl for new acquisitions. He acquired 70 percent of Orion Pictures, started a computerized billboard company, and bought 14 percent of Advanced Telecommunications. He also purchased the Ponderosa steak house chain, with sales of $500 million in 1988, reasoning that "if things get worse, we've always got a place to eat." Kluge was hardly finished after these conquests. Along with partners Stuart Subotnick and Jack Perkowski, Kluge put $100 million of his own money into a $1-billion LBO fund called Kluge Subotnick Perkowski & Company. Kluge remarked: "There are many opportunities, it's awesome."

When Kluge married a former magazine model in 1981, he converted to Catholicism. It was just the sort of move in the past that had caused many to laugh disdainfully at Kluge. Nobody was laughing any more. All those industry analysts and other experts, who had laughed at Kluge's emotionalism and in-articulateness over the years and had criticized his seemingly inept moves, have been silenced by his stunning success. As more than one commentator has noted, *klug* is German for "clever." (**B**. *National Cyclopaedia of American Biography*, N–63:179; *Business Week*, September 18, 1965, December 19, 1983, July 8, 1985; *Forbes*, April 1, 1971, June 8, 1981, April 23, December 17, 1984, June 3, 1985, October 24, 1988; *Fortune*, April 5, 1982, October 12, 1987; *Advertising Age*, July 7, 1986; *Newsweek*, July 14, 1986; Toronto *Globe & Mail*, June 7, 1988; *U.S. News & World Report*, June 27, 1988.)

KNIGHT, PHILIP H. (February 24, 1938–   ). Running shoe manufacturer, Nike Incorporated. Once, they were just sneakers—dirty, smelly sneakers. When the great revolution of the 1960s and 1970s arrived, they became running shoes. Led by the German makers of Adidas and Puma shoes, athletic footwear became increasingly sophisticated and expensive, but it was Philip Knight with his Nike running shoes who caught the updraft of the jogging movement of the 1970s, and, in the process, made his shoes an essential part of the official uniform of the "Me Decade." For a number of years no self-respecting weekend runner, or those affecting that look, would appear in leisure situations without Nike's. The popularity of his shoes helped Knight's company grow from $2 million in 1972 to over a billion dollars in 1986.

Philip H. Knight was born to William W. and Lota (Hatfield) Knight in Portland, Oregon. He was educated in local schools and then attended the University of Oregon in the 1950s. As an undergraduate, Knight was a member of the school's track team. An accomplished miler, his best time was 4:13. His coach was the renowned Bob Bowerman, who for many years had been trying to design a better track shoe. Bowerman later recalled that "American shoes were just awful" because they were very heavy and lacked the proper cushioning. Knight went on to Stanford for his MBA. While there, he formulated a thesis for a student term paper: as Americans turned increasingly toward health care and physical fitness, there would be an enhanced interest in running and recreation. He surmised that if a manufacturer could produce a high-quality, low-cost shoe for professional athletes, the large mass market for the product would be tapped simultaneously.

After graduating from Stanford in 1963, Knight joined the accounting firm of Coopers & Lybrand, but he continued to think about running shoes and their potential in a business framework. He became convinced that if the Japanese could manufacture higher quality electronic products more cheaply than American or European manufacturers, they could also produce better and cheaper running shoes. Knight contacted his old coach, and they each invested $500 and created Blue Ribbon Sports to import Tiger running shoes from Japan. With that money, they brought over their first 300 pairs of the shoes. Knight continued to work for Coopers & Lybrand by day, but at night and on the weekends he peddled the shoes to school athletic teams. The company grew comfortably, and its future looked promising when they became national distributors for Tiger Shoes. Suddenly, disaster struck. Onitsuka, the Japanese company which manufactured Tiger shoes, suddenly demanded a 51-percent ownership in Blue Ribbon Sports in early 1972 and threatened to revoke its franchise. Knight refused the ultimatum, and suddenly he and Bowerman were faced with a crisis: finding a replacement shoe in time for the Olympics of that year.

Knight desperately lined up an alternative manufacturer of his shoes in Japan, and he came up with a new name. The name was courtesy of the company's first full-time employee, Jeff Johnson, who claimed it had come to him in a dream the night before the first shoe boxes were to be printed. The shoe was named for the Greek goddess of victory, Nike, and a distinctive "swoosh" logo was adopted for the shoes. Luckily for the young firm, the trials for the 1972 Olympics were held at the University of Oregon in Eugene. Knight and Bowerman persuaded several marathon runners to wear Nike shoes. Although marathoners wearing Adidas shoes finished in the first three places, the next four runners wore the new Nikes. Knight immediately began advertising that "four of the top seven finishers" wore Nike shoes, whereupon serious athletes began requesting Nike shoes for themselves. That success convinced Knight that an emphasis on research and development as well as advertising was essential to the continued growth of the firm.

Fortunately, Bowerman had continued experimenting with the design of running shoes. His great breakthrough finally came in 1975, when he developed Nike's famous "waffle sole" design. He had been trying for years to design a shoe that would wear properly and have sufficient traction. Bowerman later recalled the breakthrough: "We had bored holes in molds and everything else and nothing was working until one Sunday I saw [his wife's] waffle iron and waited until my wife went to church and made the mold. I wrecked the waffle iron, but it made a great running sole." The sole with the tiny rubber studs was very springy, and when it entered the market that year, it was "soon grabbed up by the army of weekend runners who had been suffering from bruised feet." As running increasingly became the great fitness craze of the late 1970s, the Nike company experienced phenomenal growth. Sales, which were just $2 million in 1972, reached $29 million in 1976, rose beyond $200 million in 1979, and exceeded $1 billion in 1984.

To service this incredible expansion in sales, Knight identified new suppliers in the Far East. With 85 percent of its shoes in the early years coming through its Far East pipeline, Knight saved money on plant investment and equipment, while still keeping production headaches to a minimum. It was not until the early 1980s that Nike began manufacturing some of its shoes in the United States. It also continued to view its connection with athletes as a fundamental part of its advertising and promotion campaign. High-profile tennis stars like John McEnroe were paid as much as $100,000 a year to wear Nike shoes and to serve as a spokesman for the company. Nike also continued to promote its shoes by using athletes with lower profiles. Depending upon what they called "word of foot" advertising, Nike supported track clubs and paid individual athletes large sums of money to wear its shoes. As Knight explained to *Forbes* in 1981, "The secret to the business is to build the kind of shoe professional athletes will wear, then put them on the pros. The rest of the market will follow." This philosophy is an extension of what is often referred to as trickle-down fashion.

The whole process worked extraordinarily well for Knight and Nike until the mid–1980s. In 1980, in order to raise capital for expansion, the firm went public, leaving Knight with 46 percent of the company and Bowerman with 2 percent. Nike also began diversifying into children's shoes and into sports and casual apparel. In 1982, the firm's growth, which until that point seemed recession proof, began slipping ever so slightly. From 1975 to 1980, the company's average annual growth rate was 100 percent, and it handily deposed Adidas as the top-selling athletic shoe in America. But in the early 1980s, as the jogging boom in the United States began slowing down, Nike found itself somewhat directionless. To a certain extent the company was a victim of its own success. Nike shoes had become popular because they seemed "authentic" to many amateur athletes—that, is, they were the shoes of the pros. Nike had achieved that image largely because most of the executives, including Knight himself, were ex-athletes and dedicated joggers themselves. As Knight said at one point, "We are just a bunch of guys selling sneakers." But as the market changed in the early 1980s, Nike executives did not have the knowledge or experience to respond to it. Although sales of children's shoes were fairly successful in the early 1980s, Nike's foray into apparel failed. It mistakenly aimed its line at lower-middle-class consumers, and when it tried to upgrade its appeal to an upper-level market, it was too late.

Knight's big error in the 1980s was to overlook the significance of the aerobics boom. To the old, conventional jocks at Nike, aerobics probably did not really seem like athletics. After all, it appealed mostly to women, and they seemed overly absorbed with adorning their lithe young bodies with tights and leg warmers, rather than appropriate footwear. They were not perceived to be serious athletes by Nike executives. Knight and his cohorts probably assumed (incorrectly) that these women would wear the same kinds of shoes as did other recreational athletes. But aerobics demands cushioning primarily in the toe area of the shoe, whereas running shoes have most of the cushioning in the heel, the main impact point. Thus, when Paul Fireman[†] brought his Reebok aerobic shoes on the market in the early 1980s, he completely overwhelmed Nike in this huge and expanding new market.

Philip Knight tried to minimize the importance of Reebok's great popularity by calling Americans "brand crazy." He commented, "It is a heady but short ride (for Reeboks) after which a brand must compete segment by segment, which is a big transition from automatic acceptance across the board." Of course, Knight should know all about it, since Nike's were the first beneficiary of that brand craze. In the mid–1980s Nike began to take aerobics seriously, visiting aerobics championships to examine the fittest feet and develop a new line to compete with Reebok. Nike also began to adjust to a shoe market whose emphasis went beyond athletics. Since walking shoes and all-purpose shoes for casual wear made up a large segment of the market, Nike had to make large-scale adjustments in response to declining profits. Its revenues from running shoes were cut drastically, falling from $240 million in 1984 to just $150 million in 1985. Overall sales remained static in the late 1980s, hovering around a billion dollars a year, while Fireman's Reebok firm became the fastest growing company of the half decade from 1982 to 1987, with an average annual growth of 155 percent. By 1987, Reebok's sales were 40 percent higher than Nike's. Nike's profits, which were as high as $60 million in 1985, disappeared in 1986, and struggled to just $18.5 million in 1987.

Just when it looked as if Philip Knight was down, he and Nike responded with a dynamic advertising campaign. Concentrating on their highly successful Air Jordon basketball shoe, and the AirMax running shoe, Nike's ads stressed the point that they made better shoes than Reebok. "We sell authentic athletic footwear," said a Nike spokesperson, "While we were creating a technically better shoe, Reebok was painting theirs orange." As a result, Nike's earnings rebounded impressively in the first quarter of 1988. A poster at the firm's Beaverton, Oregon, headquarters proclaimed: "How to profit from the sweat of others." Philip Knight had learned his lessons well; he had accumulated a fortune of $400 million from the perspiration of others by 1988. Still working sixty hours a week, and still jogging, Knight said, "It's what I've chosen to do with my life." (**B**. *New York Times*, August 19, 1979, September 24, 1984; *Time*, June 30, 1980, February 15, 1982; *Forbes*, November 23, 1981, October 22, 1984, October 24, 1988; *Fortune*, November 1, 1982, November 12, 1984, May 23, 1988; *Wall Street Journal*, September 21, November 6, 1984; *Contemporary Newsmakers*, 1985; A. David Silver, *Entrepreneurial Megabucks*, 1985; Charles Garfield, *Peak Performers*, 1986; Toronto *Globe & Mail*, September 29, 1986; *Who's Who in America*, 1986–87; *Business Week*, March 14, October 3, 1988; *Newsweek*, October 3, 1988.)

KRAVIS, HENRY R. (January 6, 1944?–   ) and **GEORGE R. ROBERTS** (1943?–   ). Financiers, Kohlberg, Kravis Roberts & Company. In the 1980s Kravis and Roberts became the "Kings of the Leveraged Buyout": they were foremost among a new group of financiers who *Fortune* in February 1988 called "the New J. P. Morgans."* The kings of the deal makers, Kravis and Roberts, along with their former partner Jerome Kohlberg, helped change the face of corporate America. In the process, they also generated much controversy. Critics contended that, by burdening their target companies and the American economy generally with so much debt, the firms would be less competitive and less stable in the future. Supporters of leveraged buyouts (LBOs), on the other hand, counter that because the newly leveraged companies take on so much debt, they must, of necessity, become more competitive, "leaner and meaner," to survive.

Henry Kravis and George Roberts were first cousins who remained remarkably close in many respects, and startlingly different in others. Both men were born in Oil Patch country, the sons of a brother and sister. Kravis grew up in Tulsa, Oklahoma; Roberts came of age in Houston, Texas. Henry Kravis' father was the owner of a well-known geologic survey firm. Both attended Claremont Men's College in Claremont, California, where they majored in economics. Kravis was captain of the golf team; Roberts was a soccer star. During the summers they worked at Bear Stearns whose senior partner at the time was Salim "Cy" Lewis, who was a friend of Kravis' father. After graduating from Claremont, Roberts went on to get a law degree at the University of California in San Francisco, and Kravis went to Columbia University, where he got his MBA.

By that point, their lives began to take on a kind of mirror parallelism that would be characteristic during their later years. The two young men had almost identical career patterns, at the same company to boot, but lived on separate coasts. Conversely, their personal lives increasingly diverged as they experienced success. George Roberts went to work for Bear Stearns on a full-time basis in the San Francisco office; Kravis, on the other hand, joined the New York office of the company. Roberts liked San Francisco because it was beyond the glow of media and publicity. A quiet, family man, he lived a comfortable but unostentatious life-style in suburban San Francisco. Kravis, on the other hand, seemed to thrive in the high-profile, jet-set atmosphere of Manhattan. After his first marriage ended in divorce he married the glamorous fashion designer, Carolyn Roehm. They became flashily prominent in New York society, attending charity balls and donating $10 million to open the Henry R. Kravis wing of the Metropolitan Museum of Art. Kravis was, as *Newsweek* (November 7, 1988) commented, the very "image of high finance and high society conjured up in Tom Wolfe's recent novel of manners and mores, *The Bonfire of the Vanities.*"

When Kravis and Roberts joined Bear Stearns, they settled into its investment banking department, which had just been taken over by Jerome Kohlberg. Kohlberg had joined Bear Stearns in 1955, after getting his law degree and an MBA. Shortly after taking over the department, Kohlberg undertook his first leveraged buyout, at a time when the term was nonexistant; at that time, it was called a "bootstrap" or management acquisition. Whatever the name, the technique was the same, and it became increasingly prevalent on the American economic landscape. In a leveraged buyout, a company is taken private (or taken over) by issuing securities backed by the target company's assets to finance the purchase. When Kohlberg's first leveraged buyout worked out well for all concerned, he decided to pursue other such deals. Three more followed in 1966 and another in 1969. Kravis and Roberts began to work intimately with Kohlberg on these deals, and in 1972 they engineered their first major success.

In that year, Kohlberg, Kravis, and Roberts bought the Vapor Corporation, a manufacturer of valve and pumps, for $36.5 million from the Singer Corporation. The deal was highly leveraged, with 88-percent long-term debt to 12-percent equity. The interest rates were high for the time, but the company had a good cash flow, and the three men in short order turned the firm around, so that shares, for which they had paid $2.80 in 1972, went for $33 when they sold the firm in 1978. In 1975, they had another, even more successful deal, when they paid $1 a share for Incom, a subsidiary of Rockwell. They got $22 a share when they sold it in 1981. By the time they purchased Incom, however, the three men had decided they wanted to be independent. Casting themselves as a specialized leveraged buyout firm, they pursued mature companies with dependable cash flows that could be leveraged to the very limit. They also wanted to locate well-run companies whose management wanted a share of the equity and would encourage the takeover. Finally, they wanted companies in secure market niches, which faced little direct competition.

When Kohlberg, Kravis Roberts & Company (KKR) started out, there was nothing particularly remarkable about the company. It was conducting leveraged buyouts, which were relatively new, but other firms were doing them also. Ultimately, KKR's reputation was made when they proved that increasingly larger transactions were feasible. It was KKR, through the late 1970s and 1980s, that increasingly pushed the outer margins of what the market would bear in terms of the size of transactions and the degree of leverage involved. Almost like trapeze artists performing death-defying stunts, at each increment of increased risk, the crowd (Wall Street) would gasp and swear they could not make it. But KKR would prove them wrong. No sooner had the crowd grown accustomed to that level of risk, than KKR would push yet another notch higher, with the same reactions as before. As they pushed the limits farther and farther during the 1980s, experts kept asking if they were finally "headed for a fall." By 1988, with their aerial act soaring, they announced plans for their most fantastic trick of all, one that was nearly three times bigger than anything they had done before.

Prior to 1979, no one had orchestrated a leveraged buyout for much more than $100 million. That was, in effect, an informal benchmark in most experts' view of the limits of leveraged buyouts. Then, in the spring of 1979, KKR announced a $355 million LBO of Houdaille Industries, an unglamorous manufacturer of pumps, machine tools, and automotive products in Ft. Lauderdale, Florida. As lenders, KKR lined up twenty-three institutions, which were given a big "equity kicker" of over half the voting stock of the company. KKR and its venture partners got the balance of $48.4 million in equity. Over the next five years, Houdaille slowly paid off its debt and began to show respectable earnings. People who had been certain that KKR had bitten off more than it could chew had to admit that they were wrong. Wall Street began to change its mind about leveraged buyouts. In 1981, KKR and its partners bought seven companies in a similar manner. Three of these were for over $400 million each; a fourth, for $381 million. Each deal fared well for KKR and the investors, and the concept and practice of the LBO became increasingly accepted on Wall Street.

Between its founding in 1976 and 1982, KKR three times raised pools of money to finance takeovers. With this total pool of $543 million, KKR was able to earn profits of $1.5 billion for itself and its investors. The compounded annual returns on these three funds by the end of the 1980s stood respectively at 31 percent, 32 percent, and 44 percent. Of the $1.5 billion in profits, KKR itself earned about $300 million. By 1983, many believed that the limits of LBO's had finally been reached—$400 million. KKR and a number of other investment firms had done several LBOs at that amount, and no one seemed to see any reason or justification for going higher. Then, in September 1983, KKR announced a leveraged buyout of Wometco Enterprises, Incorporated, a Miami-based broadcasting and soft-drink bottling company. Again, the market was stunned. The amount was almost twice what financiers had tried to raise in the market. By then, however, KKR's reputation had been established, and other investment firms followed suit in short order. Analysts had more faith in KKR this time because the firm had just managed to put together its fourth equity pool, and it was the largest ever. Amounting to $1 billion, it could support LBOs ranging up to about $10 billion. Obviously, the Wometco buyout was by then just a drop in the bucket for KKR. Larger and larger deals lay just over the horizon.

A critical turning point for KKR came in early 1984, when Jerry Kohlberg learned he had a brain tumor. He underwent a critical series of operations for the ailment, and he had to convalesce for several months thereafter. Kohlberg, nearly twenty years older than his two partners, had been their mentor and guide, and he had served as a restraining influence on some of their dreams and ambitions. With Kohlberg on the sidelines, Kravis and Roberts ran the firm, and they took it in an even more aggressive direction, one which resulted in Kohlberg's resignation from the firm. The first big deal that Kravis and Roberts engineered alone in 1984 stunned Wall Street—they proposed a more than $12-billion buyout of Gulf Oil. The giant oil company was being pursued by corporate raider T. Boone Pickens,[†] and management turned to KKR to act as its "white knight" in the situation; to help it pull off a management buyout of the company. The buyout fell through when Chevron topped that bid and paid $13.2 billion for Gulf.

By the mid–1980s, KKR had significantly more competition for LBO deals than they had had in the past. Kohlberg's technique had always been to wait for management to approach him, which was followed by a casual discussion of the matter, until both management and investor were comfortable with the plan. But as *Fortune* (July 4, 1988) remarked: "By the mid–1980's the competition for deals was feverish and the time for shmoozing had disappeared." KKR, if it was going to continue to play the white knight in takeover situations, was going to have to pursue deals aggressively. It was a situation that Kravis and Roberts relished, and one that Kohlberg abhorred. To gear itself up for the competition, KKR raised its fifth LBO fund, which totalled $1.8 billion.

Kravis and Roberts concluded several large and highly successful deals during this time, but the one that raised yet again the limits of what was possible, one that astounded and confounded the skeptics, was their complicated $6.2-billion takeover of Beatrice Company. Not only was this deal more than three times larger than any previous successful LBO, but it also marked the first time KKR was involved in something less than a friendly takeover. It was also the first deal they conducted with the aid of money generated by Michael Milken's junk-bond financing machine at Drexel Burnham Lambert. Through Milken, KKR raised a whopping $2.5 billion in junk-bond financing, and it was the biggest and riskiest LBO yet, since it rested on a slim $417 million in equity. The key man in this deal was Donald P. Kelly, who had been head of Esmark (the old Swift & Company) when it was sold to Beatrice in 1984 for $2.7 billion. He then teamed with Kravis and Roberts in their takeover of Beatrice two years later. The whole situation was rather tangled and complex.

After Beatrice's chairman, James L. Dutt, had taken over Esmark, the acquisition dragged down the merged firm's earnings, and he was fired by the board. Former Chairman William Granger came back to take over the company, but a number of disgruntled executives left and joined Kelly on the sidelines.

At that point Kelly put together his own management team and joined with Kravis and Roberts to take over Beatrice. In-place management was not pleased with the takeover, but after a long series of tense negotiations, Beatrice's board finally acquiesced in what some called called KKR's "bear hug." Not quite a hostile takeover, neither was it a friendly LBO done in the interests of existing management. Kohlberg was greatly upset over this turn of events, and what transpired later in the year did nothing to soothe his fears.

In the fall of 1986, KKR did a large $4.1-billion white-knight deal, rescuing Safeway Stores from the raiders, Herbert and Robert Haft. Although this was a deal in the classic KKR tradition, the next one was more marginal. In early 1987, KKR took over Owens-Illinois (O-I) Glass Company. Claims and rumors of a hostile raider lurking in the bushes were circulated around this deal, but no raider ever appeared. Further, several of O-I's outside directors were opposed to KKR's takeover; they wanted O-I to remain independent and fought KKR bitterly. This was the straw that broke the camel's back for Kohlberg. A few weeks after the deal was completed, he resigned as general partner and left to start his own LBO firm. Although neither Kohlberg nor Kravis and Roberts would comment on why Kohlberg had left, most assumed it was because the firm had become too aggressive for his taste. "I guess you could say I'm too old not to do things my way," Kohlberg obliquely commented to the *New York Times*.

With Kohlberg gone, Kravis and Roberts went on a tear. They made a $2.4-billion bid for Jim Walter Corporation in July 1987, a $1.2-billion bid for Stop & Shop, and a $1.8-billion bid for Duracell Battery Company. By this point, KKR had become so completely identified with the LBO that J. Ira Harris, managing director of Lazard Frères, said the firm had become "to the leveraged buy-out business what Kleenex is to the tissue business." By that time, Kravis and Roberts had managed to orchestrate one of the largest privately held corporate empires in history. In late 1987, Kravis and Roberts lined up yet another pool of money for takeovers—this time a cool $5.6 billion. That amount of money gave KKR the capacity to do corporate takeovers ranging in value up to about $55 billion. Yet they held back. The stock market crash of "Black Monday," October 19, 1987, made investors skittish, so KKR patiently played the waiting game for several months. When they finally decided to move, Kravis and Roberts again exploded the former limits and set tongues wagging about whether they had finally gone too far.

In October 1988, F. Ross Johnson, the dynamic head of RJR Nabisco, the recently merged tobacco and food giant, announced a bid to take the company private at $75 a share. It was a staggering proposal, one that amounted to a total of $17.6 billion—almost three times more than had ever been spent on an LBO. A year earlier, Kravis and Roberts had approached Johnson to discuss an LBO. Johnson listened, but decided to go ahead on his own, with the backing of his investment bank, Shearson Lehman Hutton. Kravis, by all accounts, was furious. Almost immediately he announced a bid of $90 a share for RJR Nabisco, for a total of $20.6 billion. Was it barely a decade before that KKR's $330-million LBO had shocked Wall Street? Many now assumed Kravis was acting out of pique. One RJR executive commented: "Henry Kravis considers this his game," he said. "He's not going to let you play in his sandbox." A short time later, Kravis told Peter Cohen of Shearson that he considered LBOs his "franchise," and indicated he was determined to protect it. A week later, management came back with a $92 a share bid for the company, racheting the total bid up another notch to $21.2 billion. KKR insisted its bid was not hostile, but it was increasingly clear to observers that RJR's management had not invited them in, and, if KKR were to succeed, it would have to do so in the guise of a hostile takeover.

Wall Street and America's business press were stunned by Kravis and Roberts' move. "We all thought we were doing big deals," said one investment banker, "but this one sets a new standard." Another commented, "What's next? IBM? General Motors?" The proposed deal also brought into focus a mounting criticism of the highly leveraged empires being created by financiers like Kravis and Roberts in the 1980s. Even some of the financiers who had been key participants in the LBO craze of the early 1980s began to reconsider. Theodore J. Forstmann, senior partner of the large LBO firm of Forstmann Little, commented that the binge of the late 1980s resembled "the heated Third World lending of the '70's and the thrift crisis of the 1980's." James Grant, publisher of *Grant's Interest Rate Observer*, concurred, saying that "LBO debt today is as creditworthy as Brazil was in 1978."

For many critics, the clearest example of what could happen to KKR's empire lay with one of the first companies it took over, the Pittsburgh oil service firm of L. B. Foster. In 1977, the company was in trouble, and KKR took it over for $57 million, a small-change deal by later standards. In 1981, KKR and its backers sold a 19-percent stake in the company to the public for $17 a share, a total market value of $165 million. Yet KKR and its investors had acquired 81 percent of the company for just $57 million four years before. From that point onward, however, the history of L. B. Foster was dismal. When a prolonged depression hit the oil industry, Foster's stock rapidly plummeted from $17 to just over $2. KKR's industry analysts decided that, in order to survive, Foster must diversify its operations. As its oil industry sales fell from $367 million in 1981 to just $176 million in 1985, Edward Mabbs, KKR's manager of the company, paid $302 million for five architectural hardware and banking equipment businesses. These acquisitions, however, did not fit with Foster's existing operations, and debt was piling up rapidly. With annual interest payments of $42 million, new management in 1987 sold off the recent acquisitions, losing about $15 million in the process. The company's stock in late 1987 hovered around $4.25, and the only one that had made money on the company was KKR, which had earned handsome fees for its advice and operations. For many analysts, this was the fate of many heavily leveraged companies, and it could be the case with RJR Nabisco. With KKR's bid, the company was saddled with a staggering $24-billion debt load. The annual interest payment on that debt was around $2.8

billion. RJR's cash flow in 1987 was just $2.1 billion, raising doubts as to whether the company could survive. The answer, of course, is that Kravis and Roberts would sell off large chunks of the firm, as they did with Beatrice, to pay down that debt. But many food industry analysts felt the market in 1988 would not support these sales. Only time will tell what the result would be.

Whatever the impact of KKR's leveraged buyouts on the economy, it is clear they have been extraordinarily profitable for their firm, and for the two partners personally. By 1988, even before the RJR Nabisco deal, KKR controlled at least twenty-three companies with combined revenues of some $38 billion. If combined into one operation, it would make KKR the seventh-largest firm on the *Fortune* 500 list. KKR makes its mountain of money in three ways, in what is called in the trade a "triple-dip." First of all, they charge a management fee of 1.5 percent on the investment pool that is entrusted to them. That pool in 1988 stood at $5.6 billion, so the management fee on that pool for the year was $84 million, and would continue until the pool was liquidated in about 1992. Next, they collect transaction fees, which is essentially the same as an investment banking fee that it gets for arranging a deal. This can involve enormous amounts of money—for three deals in 1986 it came to about $165 million. Finally, there is what is called the "carry," which is 20 percent of the profits from an LBO deal. This amount varies from deal to deal and from year to year, but it can be enormous. In 1987, it was estimated that Kravis and Roberts each took home about $70 million. The result was that both men, along with Kohlberg, who remained a limited partner in the firm, were worth about $330 million apiece, according to *Forbes* in 1988.

A comment often heard during the first dozen years of KKR's operation was, "crazy." Every time Kravis and Roberts put forward a bid that exceeded by two or three times that which was considered prudent, competitors and analysts called them crazy. Yet, nearly every time the critics were proved wrong. As America looked toward the 1990s it was clear that men like Kravis and Roberts had created the corporate structure of the future. America would consist of a group of corporations that rested upon a mountain of debt, controlled by a government itself teetering under a crushing debt load. Crazy? Or crazy like a fox? Only time would tell. (**B.** *Fortune*, January 22, 1984, February 29, July 4, 1988, January 2, 1989; *Financial World*, July 22, 1986; *Forbes*, November 2, 1987, October 24, 1988; *U.S. News & World Report*, February 7, 1988; *New York Times*, August 24, 1988; *Newsweek*, November 7, November 14, 1988; *Business Week*, November 14, 1988; *Current Biography*, March 1989.)

L

LANE, MILLS BEE, JR. (January 29, 1912–   ). Banker, Citizens & Southern National Bank. The phone rings in Mills Lane's elegant, paneled first-floor office in the Citizens & Southern (C & S) National Bank in Atlanta, Georgia. He picks it up and roars into the mouthpiece: "It's a wonderful world! Can I sell you any money?" "It's a wonderful world!" became Lane's trademark. He wore ties imprinted with the logo, greeted everyone with the salutation, had it printed on matchbook covers, and posted signs proclaiming it in his banks. But that was hardly the extent of it. Mills Lane was an unorthodox banker, to say the least. His personality and antics so captivated the public and media that *Saturday Evening Post* ran an article on him entitled "The Case of the Comical Banker." He was known to dress in garb that can only be described as outlandish. He appeared at credit meetings at his bank in a crazy quilt of clashing colors; he was the first man in Atlanta to appear at a symphony concert in a plaid dinner jacket; and once, on a sultry July 4, he dressed up as George Washington, in wig, tricornered hat, knee breeches, and buckled shoes. Sweating profusely, he proceeded to read the Declaration of Independence to neighborhood children. He conducted bank meetings dressed in a football suit or a baseball uniform, and at a banking convention he showed up at formal receptions wearing a red dinner jacket, printed with facsimiles of beer-bottle labels.

Lane's unorthodox ways have brought him heavy criticism from industry stalwarts. One competitor sniffed, "Mills would stand on his head on the top of the C&S flagpole if he thought it would get him a new savings account." And there was some truth to that, because all these antics were designed, in one way or another, to increase his bank's visibility and business. "Banking is fun," he said. "Most bankers take themselves too seriously, and I refuse to do that. Of course I'm a promoter. That was the one thing the banking industry needed." And he must have been right. When Lane took over C&S in 1946, it was running a slow second to the massive First National Bank in Georgia. By the time he retired, C&S was the largest bank in the Southeast in total capital funds, and it had spread its influence throughout the entire area. In addition, Mills Lane introduced the bank credit card, along with the idea of instant credit, in the late 1950s, well in advance of other banks in the nation.

Mills B. Lane, Jr., was born in Savannah, Georgia, the son of Mills B. Lane and the grandson of Remer Y. Lane, both bankers in the area. The Lane family had been in Georgia for generations, and his ancestors had been planters before the Civil War. Remer Lane, born in 1826, was closely connected with the Central Railway of Georgia prior to the war but, after the conflict, found that most of his investments were in ruin. He chose as his reconstruction project the establishment of a private banking house in the small town of Valdosta. Mills Lane, Sr., who was born in Lowndes County, near Valdosta in 1860, received his early training in his father's bank. After spending two years at Vanderbilt, Mills, Sr., worked for about ten years in his father's bank, which in 1881 they had reorganized as the Merchants Bank of Valdosta, with $100,000 in capital. In 1891, Mills, Sr., decided Valdosta was too small to support the ambitions of all of Remer Lane's sons, and he accepted an offer to become vice president of the Citizens Bank of Savannah. A far larger bank, with capital of $500,000, Citizens Bank erected the first fireproof building in Savannah in 1895. In 1901, Mills, Sr., became president of the bank, and four years later he bought the Southern Bank of the State of Georgia, which increased its capital to $700,000. The new bank became known as the Citizens & Southern Bank of Savannah, with Mills, Sr., as president.

Mills Lane, Sr., a pioneer in the development of statewide branch banking, established in 1912 the first C&S Bank outside of Savannah, in Augusta. Other branches were opened in rapid succession in Atlanta, Macon, Athens, Valdosta, and elsewhere. By the time Mills, Sr., died in 1945, the capital of C&S Bank had been expanded to $350 million. Mills, Sr., however, had retired as president of the bank in 1928, but he served as chairman of the board of what was by then the Citizens & Southern National Bank of Savannah. As a banker, Mills, Sr., gained renown for his support of a number of important projects and industries in Georgia. His bank was instrumental in bringing the Union Bag and Paper Company to Savannah, and he took a keen personal interest in farming matters. In 1921 he played a crucial role in saving the state's cotton economy. The price of cotton in that year had fallen to four cents a pound, but instead of foreclosing on the farmers, Mills, Sr., used the bank's resources and went to New York to borrow $30 million to tide the farmers over and finance the next year's crop. He set up a chain of warehouses where the cotton could be stored while the farmers waited for the price to rise. In six months, when the price rose to twelve cents, the farmers marketed their crop and paid off Lane, and he paid off the New York bankers. This gesture catapulted C&S to the enviable position of the "bank of choice" for farmers throughout Georgia. Lane was also instrumental in helping to found the state's beef industry when he bought 7,000 head of cattle and distributed them to young farm boys on no security except their father's promises that they would feed the cattle and pay Lane off when they sold them. The plan worked well, and Georgia became a major cattle producer for the first time. Mills, Sr., also became the father of the state's huge tobacco crop, when he imported four experienced tobacco-growing families from North Carolina and set them up on South Georgia farms as a demonstration project.

But both Remer Lane and Mills Lane, Sr., had their idiosyncracies. Remer Lane had an ingenious method for breaking runs on his bank. When frightened citizens lined up at the bank for their money, he had the teller pay them off in silver dollars which Grandpa Lane had heated on a kerosene stove. It worked wonders. Mills, Sr., had financed construction of a bridge on the Suwannee River, and when county officials did not repay the loan, Mills, Sr., went out to the bridge with a shotgun and began collecting tolls from astonished drivers. He also had a unique way of determining whether a bank he was stalking was a solid property. As Mills, Jr. tells the story: "Papa Lane had a funny way of looking over a bank to tell what sort of shape it was in," he said. "First thing he'd do, he'd go to the toilet. 'Son,' he used to tell me, 'if the toilet is clean, the loans are in good shape.' " So, Mills Lane, Jr., came by his unique approach to banking honestly— he was born into it.

Mills Lane, Jr., was educated in the local schools in Savannah, and at age twelve, his father sent him off to Middlesex School in Concord, Massachusetts. Elected president of his class in the first year, two years later, he recalled, "the student body held an election to select the least popular SOB in school, and I won. They threw me in the pond." Even as a grown man, the experience still caused Lane some pain, and it was probably the main reason he did not follow his classmates to Harvard; he went instead to Yale. At Yale, he mostly took courses in psychology and architecture, and after graduating Lane worked at a variety of positions in some of his father's smaller banks. Then his father sent him to the big C&S branch in Atlanta to receive his final polishing under the tutelage of an old gentleman named H. Lane Young. Young, who was president, and Mills, Jr., who was vice president of the branch, clashed constantly. Mills, Jr., was brimful of new ideas on how to run the bank; Young thought most of his ideas were half-baked. For seven years, the two men warred with one another, with the younger officers backing Lane and the older ones siding with Young.

Finally, in 1946, Lane quit. His father had died the year before, and Lane decided to spend his time in travel while looking for a new field to conquer. While he was away, his mother held a meeting of the Lane clan, and they booted Young up to chairman of the board, making Mills, Jr., president. For the next thirty years, Lane stirred up the banking scene in Atlanta in a way it had never seen before, with the result that Atlanta became perhaps the most fiercely competitive banking city in the country. The C&S Bank grew enormously during the years Lane ran it. In less than twenty years, its size quadrupled, until it held more deposits than any other bank in the Southeast. With nearly one-fifth of all the deposits in the state by 1970, C&S was nearly as large as its two largest Georgia competitors combined. By that time, it ranked thirty-eighth on *Fortune*'s list of the nation's largest banks, and its earnings rose at a rate of 12 percent annually during the 1960s. Whenever anyone praised Lane for his success, he replied, ''Hell, my old man owned the joint!''

But no one can deny the changes Mills Lane brought to banking in Atlanta. When he took over C&S in 1946 at the age of thirty-four, he brought a sense of boundless optimism to the position, confident that the country was going to enjoy a tremendous postwar boom. The heads of the other Atlanta banks, on the other hand, were elderly men, still scarred (and scared) by their memories of the depression. Worried that the country was going to slide back into a deep depression, they counseled cautious, conservative policies. To them, Lane was a rash, misguided fool. Clarence Haverty, an Atlanta business and civic leader at that time, commented, ''In the next ten years, he [Lane] will either be one of the biggest leaders [Atlanta] has ever known, or he will be its biggest damn fool.'' There was little question that Haverty thought the latter was the greater possibility.

By the time the other Atlanta bankers discovered their mistake—discovered that there was not going to be a severe recession—Lane was off and running. Shouting ''It's a wonderful world,'' he passed his competitors in loans, deposits, and total capitalization by 1950, and they spent the next twenty years struggling to catch and overtake him. As one observer of the Atlanta banking scene commented: ''Banking here for the last ten years has been like a pack of beagles chasing a rabbit, every time it looks like they are closing in on old Mills, they see his white tail bobbing up a hundred yards ahead.'' And what Lane understood was that, although Atlanta and Georgia were changing—were growing and modernizing—and his bank was growing and changing along with them, in many ways the state retained much of the rural ''good ole boy'' culture of Bible Belt preachers and politicians. And this is the culture that Lane played on so successfully with his gimmicks and unorthodox approach. Unpretentious, Lane exudes showmanship, the same formula that was used successfully by generations of backwoods preachers and politicians. The cosmopolitan urbanites of Atlanta may have sniffed at Lane's methods, but they were designed to play to a less sophisticated rural audience. And play well they did indeed.

Lane spurred C&S's growth by accentuating retail or consumer banking. Although the bank always did well with commercial accounts, it based its growth on the retail business. A key ingredient of this was the introduction in the late 1950s of its bank credit card. Under its credit card system (later adopted by nearly all banks in America), the holder could shop at any one of about 2,500 stores in Georgia and buy what he needed, simply by presenting the card and walking out with the purchase. The store then sent the bills to the bank each day, and the bank deducted 4 percent and paid the remainder to the store. The cardholder, who was billed monthly, was expected to pay at least 15 percent of the total and was charged 1 percent per month on the unpaid balance. It was a unique idea that worked wonderfully for all concerned. But Mills Lane added yet another element to the system. Reasoning that if C&S credit-card customers could buy everything else with the card, why not cash too? With this in mind,

C&S developed the concept of "instant money." That is, a cardholder could simply show up at the bank with his or her card and get an instant loan, no questions asked. As a C&S official commented: "Other banks with credit cards said we were stupid. Now just about all of them do the same thing."

Lane also made a major effort to attract consumer savings accounts to C&S by merchandising new 4-1/2-percent certificates of deposit. C&S had much success with this endeavor, which provided a steady cash flow of deposits that helped the bank to grow rapidly during the 1960s, a time when many other banks experienced stagnation. But Lane did not neglect other elements in the Georgia economy either. After the war, many ex-GIs wanted to get into the trucking business, but other bankers were reluctant to back them. They thought that the railroads would remain the dominant means of transporting goods, and they believed that the trucking ventures were too risky. Lane, however, gave the ex-GIs financial backing, and as the truckers began to prosper, C&S prospered along with them.

Lane also pushed agricultural loans during these years. In the mid–1950s, when he was urging Georgia farmers to get into sheep raising, he penned up a flock of sheep on the main floor of the bank's Atlanta headquarters. Competitors were mortified, but the public was delighted, and in many parts of rural Georgia C&S was identified as the bank with sheep in its lobby. It helped generate a lot of business for farm equipment loans and other items. Lane's whole approach to banking was shaped by the axiom that what's good for Georgia was good for C&S. "I've got a missionary philosophy," he said. "I want to help society, and the bank is how I do it. People don't believe it. But banking is part of making this a better world to live in."

To live up to those ideals, Lane was also intimately involved in a number of community issues in Atlanta and in Georgia. Called a kingmaker by many in Atlanta, Lane was generally credited with being a major factor in the election of Ivan Allen as mayor of Atlanta in 1961. He and Allen then worked closely together on a number of civic projects for the city during these years. The first of these was the downtown Commerce Club in Atlanta. Lane recalled:

The thing was, there was no cohesive businessman's organization, no forum . . . we were building a garage downtown, and the president of the Chamber of Commerce came to me and said, "how about sticking another floor or two floors on it and get all the groups together that have anything to do with the Chamber?" I said, "Sure, we'll call it the 'Commerce Building.' " (*Atlanta Journal and Constitution*)

In this club, he brought together the heavyweights in the Atlanta business community—Robert W. Woodruff* of Coca-Cola; Richard Rich of Rich's Department stores; Ben Gilmer, head of Southern Bell; Mayor Allen; Jack Tarver, head of Atlanta Newspapers; and a number of others. As Lane commented, "What the Commerce Club did was, for the first time, people who had been arch competitors were together as friends."

Next Lane spearheaded the drive to build a stadium in Atlanta to attract a major league baseball team. With no help from the city or from the Fulton County Commission, Lane forged ahead, paying out $650,000 himself for architectural engineering fees. The stadium was built in two years by the county, and it soon attracted a team—the Milwaukee Braves—to the city.

Lane's most important contributions, however, came in the area of race relations. Like most old-line white families in the South, Lane originally had little sympathy for the position of blacks in the state, and he was appalled at the demands being made by the Civil Rights and Black Power movements during the 1950s and 1960s. To a certain extent, he was never able to come to terms with the polarization and rhetoric which developed, but he did set up a comprehensive program that was highly praised in many quarters. Lane's Georgia Plan, which was aimed at raising the standard of living of the state's poorest citizens, most of whom were black, was kicked off in his hometown of Savannah. Starting a large-scale cleanup of slums in the city in 1968, Lane put together an army of 10,000 volunteers to aid in the task. As part of the plan, C&S offered special mortgages and home improvement loans to make it possible for slum dwellers to buy and fix up their own homes. Slum landlords were also given loans if they promised to upgrade their properties. Since many of the home buyers did not even have the money for a down payment, Lane and the bank set up a subsidiary Community Development Corporation to advance them that initial outlay. C&S also financed a thirty-unit town-house project in Savannah as a pilot project to provide decent housing, and set up a program to provide small business loans to blacks to assist them in starting their own businesses. The results of these programs were less successful than anyone had anticipated in the beginning. Lane commented about the Community Development Corporation: "We have lost 171 loans and $1,487,000 trying to help help them in business. That's the record. . . . I'm having each one of these loans analyzed, and I want to show the Action Forum [a biracial group of business and civic leaders] what has happened. It is distressing." Lane, nonetheless, felt this kind of involvement was important: "My father was of the old school that thought the least you fooled with politics the better off you were." But his mother counseled him to broaden his involvements, and soon after taking over the bank in 1946 he "began to evolve a philosophy that only with good government could you have good business."

Lane, who had been at the center of controversy for the thirty years he ran the bank, bowed out quietly in 1974. When a spokesman at the bank was asked about Lane's quiet exit, he said that was "how Mr. Lane wanted it." There was a shy and modest side to Lane that did not often manifest itself. One of the few times anyone had ever seen him at a loss for words had been on the occasion of his forty-sixth birthday. To mark the event, twenty pretty girls were lined up outside his office. While he peered around in bewilderment, each of them handed him a red rose and kissed him on his bald spot. Finally, he was able to blurt out: "By golly, it *is* a wonderful world." (**B**. *Savannah Evening Press*, July

13, 1944, August 8, 1945, May 6, 1958; *Fortune*, December 1954, November 1969; *Newsweek*, June 27, 1955; *Saturday Evening Post*, June 10, 1961; *Business Week*, February 2, 1964, May 24, 1969, July 25, 1970; *Time*, March 8, 1968, May 23, 1969; *Atlanta Journal and Constitution*, January 18, 1970; *Reader's Digest*, February 1970; *Savannah Morning News*, June 16, 1971, July 11, 1973.)

LAUDER, ESTÉE (July 1, 1908?–). Cosmetics manufacturer, Estée Lauder, Incorporated. When Prince Charles and Lady Diana visited America in the 1980s, Lady Di named the three people she wanted to attend a White House dinner in her honor: Bruce Springsteen, Robert Redford, and Estée Lauder. It was perhaps the ultimate accolade for a woman who has combined equal amounts of charm, chutzpah, and rapacious ambition to create one of the all-time great empires in perfume and cosmetics. In 1986 the huge, privately held company sold about $1.3 billion worth of products. Its products were number 1 in department stores, accounting for 37 percent of all cosmetics and fragrances sold. More than anything, though, Estée Lauder was always the hardest worker at her own company. As her eldest son, Leonard, has commented: "She is the company; the company is she."

Throughout her life Estée Lauder has retained an air of mystery about her background and origins. She created an image of elegance for her cosmetic products, and then she made every effort to identify her own life with that image. Hobnobbing with royalty and the wealthy in New York, Palm Beach, and Europe, most Americans assumed that Estée Lauder was the elegant woman who was pictured in her company's ads. She did nothing to dispel this misconception. As an executive at her firm commented: "You somehow know that her closets are impeccable, her children well behaved, her husband devoted, and her guests pampered." When she published her autobiography, *Estée: A Success Story*, in 1985, she finally told the truth about everything but her birth date. Estée Lauder was born in Corona, in the New York City borough of Queens as Josephine Esther Mentzer, the youngest child in a large family of recent Hungarian immigrants to America. Her father had led a privileged life in Hungary, but he had few marketable skills in America. He, therefore, bounced from profession to profession for a number of years, before finally opening a neighborhood hardware store. The family lived above the store during the years Estée Lauder was growing up.

Mrs. Lauder admits to being ashamed of her immigrant parents' "old country ways" as a child, and she tried desperately to be "100 percent American." Perhaps for this reason, when she enrolled in school she was receptive to an enterprising teacher, who decided to "add a little romantic French to the Hungarian-Czechoslovakian-Milanese name in her roll book." Thus, Estée Mentzer was born. In 1930, she met and married Joseph Lauter, a moderately successful garment center businessman. His family name had originally been Lauder in Austria, but it had been altered by immigration officials when the Lauders came to America. Shortly after their marriage, the young couple decided to return to the original spelling, and Josephine "Esty" Mentzer became Estée Lauder. At about the same time she discovered the magic of facial creams, and in conjunction with her new "European" name, she went on to build a massive cosmetics empire.

While she was still living at home, her mother's brother, John Schotz, came to visit from Hungary. A skin specialist in the old country, Mrs. Lauder's uncle set up a makeshift laboratory in the tiny stable behind the Mentzer's home. There young Estée watched in fascination as he created a secret formula, a "magic cream potion." As she recounted in her autobiography:

He captured my imagination as no one else ever had. . . . It was a precious velvety cream . . . that magically made you sweetly scented, made your face feel like spun silk. . . . Maybe I'm glorifying the memories, but I believe today that I recognized in my Uncle John my true path.

Soon she was creating her own creams under Uncle John's direction and trying them out on her high school friends. "I didn't have a single friend at Newtown High School who wasn't slathered in our creams," she recalled.

After she married, Estée Lauder began to sell her creams to various beauty parlors in the area. Developing an increasingly successful cottage industry, she spent every spare moment cooking up "little pots of cream for faces" in her kitchen. Among her earliest customers were the proprietor and customers of the House of Ash Blondes salon on Manhattan's Upper West Side. Eventually, the salon's owner asked Mrs. Lauder to run the beauty concession in a new salon she was opening in an exclusive neighborhood on the Upper East Side. Here Lauder gave out free samples and sold her product to an increasing number of women. These contacts helped her to develop her reputation and that of her products, and soon Mrs. Lauder was offering free demonstrations during the summers at resort hotels throughout the New York metropolitan area. In the winter months she visited these women at their homes, encouraged them to have a bridge party for their friends, and sold more creams to these women. Soon Mrs. Lauder became a fixture on the guest lists of the city's most influential hostesses, and as her social contacts grew, so did her business.

Her great business success, and the single-minded ambition with which she pursued it, put strains on her marriage, and in 1939 Estée and Joseph Lauder divorced. Soon after, she went to Miami Beach, Florida, where she peddled her skin creams to affluent vacationers in the area. Her eldest son's illness in 1942, however, reunited the two Lauders, and they remarried in 1942. Together they began to run Estée Lauder's line of creams as a family business. In 1946 it was incorporated as Estée Lauder Incorporated, with Estée and Joseph as the only two employees, and with just four basic skin-care products and a few items of makeup. To display her wares, Mrs. Lauder developed her own distinctive packaging in a delicate shade of greenish blue, which came to be known as

"Lauder Blue" in the trade. In later years, she also often dressed in that color, and came to be known as the "Blue Lady."

Estée Lauder's big breakthrough came after World War II, when she finally convinced Saks Fifth Avenue to place a sizable order for her products. She and Joseph had recently renovated a "factory" in a converted restaurant, and the two scrambled to fill the order. She recounts in her autobiography: "On the restaurant's gas burners we cooked our creams, mixed them, sterilized our pretty jars with boiling water, poured and filled and planned and packaged. . . . Every bit of the work was done by hand—four hands, Joe's and mine." Their work paid off; Saks sold out in two days.

With the prestigious Saks aiding her expansion, Mrs. Lauder endeavored to get her products into other department stores. At that point she made a crucial decision. The other large cosmetic giants, Helena Rubinstein, Revlon, and Max Factor, achieved their great expansion after World War II by moving into drug stores and beauty salons where the high turnover and big dollars were. Estée Lauder decided to remain exclusively in department stores. At the time, the decision was made largely out of necessity because she did not have the sales force to service the drugstores. But the company was able to turn necessity into a virtue by offering department stores something unique. Since the Estée Lauder line could not be purchased in drugstores, it gave it a cachet, and exclusivity that the other cosmetic lines could not match. This gave her company enormous power with the department stores in years to come.

During the years of expansion in the late 1940s and early 1950s, Estée Lauder traveled around the country promoting her products, while her husband stayed home and managed the plant. At every store, she selected and trained the sales force herself. She recognized these saleswomen as her firm's "most important asset" and a "walking advertisement" for her products. A very important part of the sales promotion entailed giving out free samples. Mrs. Lauder had developed this technique when she started her company, and she continued it as it expanded, and it became another of Estée Lauder's trademarks—customers expected to receive a little free sample of her products when they made a purchase. This "gift with a purchase" proved to be an irresistible lure, and it was widely copied by her competitors.

By the early 1950s, Mrs. Lauder's struggles were paying off. Estée Lauder counters could be found all over the country in branches of prestigious stores like Marshall Field, I. Magnin, Neiman-Marcus, Bonwit Teller, and, of course, Saks Fifth Avenue. The company's next big step came in 1953 when Estée Lauder introduced her first fragrance—Youth Dew. She had wanted to introduce a perfume for some time, but she was concerned that perfume sales in America were traditionally sluggish. She recalls:

I knew what the trouble was. Perfume was the perfect gift. That was killing it. Only a rare woman would go into a department store and buy for herself. . . . How could I get American women to buy [their] own perfume? *I would not call it perfume.* I would call it Youth Dew. A *bath oil* that doubled as a skin perfume. That would be acceptable to buy, because it was feminine, all-American, very girl-next-door to take baths wasn't it?

Priced at $8.95, it was an affordable luxury, and it soon became a very popular product for the company. By the mid–1950s, Youth Dew accounted for 80 percent of Estéc Lauder's business at Saks Fifth Avenue. Even as late as 1984 the highly popular product, despite the revolution in the fragrance industry in the 1970s and 1980s, continued to rack up over $150 million in sales.

By the late 1950s, Estée Lauder, Incorporated was a large and successful company, and both the Lauders were determined it would remain a family enterprise. To that end, their eldest son, Leonard Lauder, entered the firm in 1958 after completing studies at Columbia University's Graduate School of Business. Soon a major factor in the firm, he set up a sales force, established a research and development laboratory, expanded advertising, recruited professional managers at all levels, and was responsible for overseas expansion in the 1960s. The younger son, Ronald Lauder, also joined the staff for a number of years and ran the foreign operations. His interests were more along political lines, however, and in 1983 he left to become assistant secretary of defense and then U.S. ambassador to Austria.

The 1960s saw a number of changes in the company, in addition to overseas expansion. New makeup and skin-care products were introduced, and imaginative promotional campaigns were devised to enhance their competitive position. The most significant of these was the creation, in 1962, of the "Estée Lauder Woman." Over the next fifteen years, just five models were used for this role, which personified a timeless, elegant beauty for the company's products. Equally significant, was Estée Lauder's move in 1967 into men's toiletries with the introduction of Aramis. A year later came Clinique, the first complete line of fashion-oriented, allergy-tested cosmetics. Estée Lauder became the most successful purveyor of men's toiletries in the cosmetics trade.

These changes not only helped the company grow enormously, but they also brought it into direct and serious competition for the first time with the giants of the cosmetics industry. A particularly heated and bitter battle, with personal overtones, developed between Estée Lauder and Revlon, and between Mrs. Lauder and Charles Revson,[†] head of Revlon. To counter Aramis, Revlon brought out Braggi, and when Mrs. Lauder introduced a sophisticated new fragrance called, with some egoism, Estée, Charles Revson countered with Charlie. All of this also involved a good deal of industrial espionage on both parts. Mrs. Lauder recalled her version of some of these battles:

Charles Revson tried to market our ideas. Sophisticated spying equipment was Charles's specialty . . . I retaliated on only one occasion, just to let Mr. Revson know that we were quite aware of his "interest" in our products. . . . Inside information told us that Etherea (a new hypo-allegenic line of cosmetics for Revlon) was going to give Clinique a run for its money. . . . We took out ads in *Women's Wear Daily*. In the ads, we used phrases that were admittedly Revson's own phrases from his Etherea campaign, which would be running soon. Phrases like "personal skin index" and "biologically correct" were sprinkled through our copy. Our purpose was to send a message to Revson saying, "Two can play at the same game, so be careful."

Despite Mrs. Lauder's demure, innocent protestations, Charles Revson was never able to get the best of her. As Andrew Tobias observed in his biography of Revson, *Fire and Ice* (1976), "She was the one competitor he set out to beat but couldn't."

It took several years for Aramis and Clinique to earn a profit, but by 1980 Clinique accounted for more than one-third of the company's profits. Since the firm was privately owned, it was possible to stay with these products longer than otherwise would have been possible. Clinique lost nearly $20 million over four years, at a time when the firm's total sales were only about $30 million annually. Leonard Lauder has commented about this period: "We would not be where we are today if this was not a family business, if we had been publicly held, I don't think we could have gone through the bleeding Clinique and Prescriptives took to get started."

Although Mrs. Lauder turned over a good portion of the operations of the firm to her son Leonard in 1973, she remained closely involved with the company, and was particularly responsible for developing new scents. Renowned for having one of the best "noses" in the industry, she brought out Azurée in 1969; Aliage, the company's first "sport" fragrance, in 1972; Private Collection in 1973; White Linen, a clean and crisp scent, and the exotic Cinnabar in 1978; and Beautiful in 1985. Because the complete formula for these scents is known only to a member of the Lauder family, their perfumes and colognes cannot be copied by cut-rate manufacturers, which has been true with many other designer fragrances.

Despite these creations, and her involvements in the company in the 1970s and 1980s, Estée Lauder increasingly turned her attention to the social whirl. With lavish homes in New York, London, Palm Beach, and on the Riviera, she developed a circle of friends that included the Duke and Duchess of Windsor, Princess Grace of Monaco, the Aga Khan, and socialites C. Z. Guest and Marjorie Merriweather Post. She developed a splendid social persona during these years, lunching at all the "in" places, attending all the "right" functions, and giving some of the most opulent parties in both Europe and America. Yet, as Mrs. Lauder recognizes, her business and social lives are intimately connected: "Each feeds into the other and enriches the other, and all this happens in every corner of the world, where I travel to touch base with people and business developments." Using the society pages to promote herself, Estée Lauder by the same process promotes her products as elegant and aristocratic. Developing this image did much to help her firm beat out Revlon in the 1970s and 1980s. According to Leonard Lauder, "Elizabeth Arden's style was one of Waspy restraint, Charles Revson's style was one of glitz." His mother's style, at least according to him, was one of "Elegance. A panache."

But it was panache with a difference. Estée Lauder has never managed to break free of her roots in Queens. And perhaps this is what has made her such a successful entrepreneur. A shrewd risk taker who subordinated her life to business, some of her employees irreverently refer to her as "the old lady." Lee Israel, author of her unauthorized biography, called her the "Gracie Allen of the beauty field. She always says the most outrageous things." This includes stopping women in elevators or on the street to tell them that their clothes or cosmetics make them look old. The funny thing is, that although this pushiness often borders on the extreme, she rarely offends. As industry spokespersons have noted for decades, she has a way with women, and this has helped her create such a successful company. Perhaps the last word on Estée Lauder comes from that repository of haute couture, *Vogue* magazine. Settling on one word to characterize her in 1973, they came closest to the mark when they said, "Estée Lauder is a tycoon." (**A.** Estée Lauder, *Estée: A Success Story*, 1985. **B.** *Vogue*, January 1973, January 1986; Andrew Tobias, *Fire and Ice*, 1976; Lee Israel, *Estée Lauder: Beyond the Magic*, 1985; *Business Week*, September 23, 1985; *New York Times Magazine*, October 13, 1985, November 29, 1987; *New York*, October 21, 1985; *Forbes*, November 18, 1985; *Current Biography*, 1986; *Fortune*, October 12, 1987.)

LAUREN, RALPH (October 14, 1939–   ). Fashion designer, Polo, Ralph Lauren, Incorporated. When Saks department store asked Ralph Lauren to appear in one of its newspaper ads in 1974, it was the first time he had done so. He showed up for the shooting wearing worn, faded jeans and a tweed jacket. The executives and ad men were somewhat nonplussed; they had expected the head of one of America's trendiest and toniest fashion companies to dress the part. But Lauren commented, "I wanted to be myself." Since that time, Ralph Lauren, rugged and perpetually tanned, has been his own best model. But his choice of clothing reflects his early ambitions. In response to a reporter's queries he said:

I wanted to be a history teacher. I liked the gum-soled shoes and the tweed jackets and the pipes. I was always very atmosphere-conscious. I never thought I liked the business world, because I wanted a life that was free of not being honest or straightforward. (*New York,* October 21, 1985)

Ralph Lauren has parlayed that image of honesty into a billion-dollar fashion empire.

Lauren was born Ralph Lifshitz in the Bronx, New York, but his family changed their last name in the mid–1950s. His father was an artist and house painter who painted murals in buildings and showrooms in the garment district. Both parents were rather religious, and Ralph Lauren received strong training in Hebrew and the Torah at Yeshiva University High School and Yeshiva University. He attended public schools during this same period, graduated from

DeWitt Clinton High School, and attended New York City College for a time. While in high school, Lauren worked part-time as a stockboy at Alexander's department store. A few years earlier, he had become interested in clothes, and spent most of his earnings on clothes. He was especially attracted to the expensive, conservative fashions at Brooks Brothers.

After graduating from high school in 1957, Lauren became a full-time salesman at Alexander's and took night courses in business at City College. Bored with school, he dropped out after a few months. After serving a stint in the U.S. Army, Lauren became an assistant buyer for Allied Stores. During this time, Lauren tried without success to get into the fashion end of the business. As he commented, "I had no portfolio, no sketches. All I had was taste." Finally, in 1967, he was hired by Beau Brummel Ties, Incorporated. At Beau Brummel, Lauren soon had his first great fashion breakthrough. Working with unusual fabrics, he designed ties that were four or five inches wide, compared with the standard three inches. The ties were wildly successful, and Lauren persuaded Beau Brummel to let him start his own division, which he called Polo. Shortly thereafter, Lauren left Beau Brummel altogether to start his own company, also called Polo.

Lauren chose the name Polo because of its aristocratic image, and it was on the basis of his wider tie that he began to build his great fashion empire. As he noted several years later:

It couldn't happen today. . . . You couldn't start a business based on the shape of a tie. But then men weren't used to having too much happen in the style of their clothes. The tie was a big change, but not so bizarre that men couldn't accept it. (*New York,* October 21, 1985)

Because his wider ties made a larger knot, Lauren found he had to design shirts with larger collars in 1968. These shirts caught on quickly, as Bloomingdale's, Neiman-Marcus, and other prestigious stores picked them up. Ralph Lauren was on his way. Next came suit jackets with wider lapels, and over the next several years he added the Polo line of casual shirts, suits, knitwear, coats, shoes, and luggage.

The clothes he designed had a clearly American look, but had more shape than those of other American menswear designers. As he noted, "I designed for America—Pierre Cardin was European, very spiffy; mine was more Ivy League, more elegant and traditional." This sense of style and class became the hallmark of Lauren's fashions. Commenting on its appeal, he said, "All I want is the old money look." This has been recognized by fashion commentators. Bill Cunningham of the *Los Angeles Times* wrote, "The Ralph Lauren look exudes the snobbish aristocratic formula for dressing that securely establishes the wearer as a special breed belonging to the right clubs, the right ethnic background, and the right side of the tracks."

Critics of this look, however, have been vicious in their attacks. He has been derided by many of his competitors for not having gone to design school and for not being able to draw at all. Many critics view Lauren, in his attempts to ape the "old money look," as a parvenu. Some feel that a Jew from the lower middle classes is not entitled to create the style of the Connecticut gentry. As an executive of a fashionable New York men's store commented: "We are what Ralph Lauren is trying to be." Lauren himself seems to be little affected by this sort of criticism. Discussing what he admires, Lauren described well the impression his clothing gives: "Style and not flamboyance, but sophistication, class, and an aristocratic demeanor that you can see in people like Cary Grant and Fred Astaire. They were my inspiration." The fashion industry early on agreed with this assessment, awarding Lauren the 1970 Coty Menswear Award, and he has picked up innumerable fashion awards since that time and has won more Cotys than any other designer. By everyone's admission, Ralph Lauren has been a dynamic and creative force on the American fashion scene, and he, along with Calvin Klein[†] and Perry Ellis, has helped make the American sportswear industry the most exciting in the world.

Having established himself as a menswear designer by the early 1970s with Polo grossing $10 million, Lauren branched into women's clothing in 1971. Like his men's fashions, Lauren's women's clothing was softly tailored and conservative. As he noted, he created clothes for "the young suburban woman in the so-called horsey set." Designed more for comfort than slinky style, Lauren said that "my clothes are a combination of the narrow French fit . . . with the tweedy English look." The new line was tremendously successful, as was a new men's line in 1972; by the end of 1973, Ralph Lauren's business volume had doubled. But this was not accomplished without some pain. Lauren's lack of strategic planning had his company on the verge of bankruptcy in 1972. As Jeffery A. Trachtenberg noted in his biography of Ralph Lauren, this was a time "when Ralph Lauren, master designer, was almost destroyed by Ralph Lauren, unskilled businessman."

Lauren had been furnished with $50,000 by Norman Hilton in 1968, which had allowed him to go into business on his own account. In return, Hilton received a half ownership of the business. Lauren chafed under this arrangement for four years, and in 1972 decided Hilton would have to go. Hilton asked for $750,000 for his share of the business, a reasonable amount, given its growth. Sales, which stood at $3.6 million in 1972, rose to $8 million in 1973. Lauren pressured Hilton to give up his stock, and Hilton finally sold out for $633,000. Although this brought Lauren the sole control he craved, it severely strained the company's resources. Finally, Lauren realized that he had to reorganize the company quickly and radically to avoid losing it. He brought in Peter Strom, a former executive with Norman Hilton, to provide the management expertise necessary to turn the operation around. It was Strom who decided to switch from direct manufacturing to licensing, a system in which the manufacturer finances production, shipping, and part of the promotional costs. This gave Lauren himself greater freedom to concentrate on design and marketing. He did, however, continue to manufacture his top-of-the-line Polo menswear in a rehabilitated brick mill in Lawrence, Massachusetts. By making the garments he knew best, Ralph Lauren could retain a larger profit margin and keep a closer eye on quality.

Lauren had already revolutionized much of the fashion industry by this time. When he started Polo, there were clear lines of demarcation in the industry. In menswear, tie makers made ties, shirtmakers made shirts, suit makers made suits, and so on. There was no crossover. Even more forbidding was the great wall that separated men's and women's clothing. Very few ever crossed over, and those who did were women's designers who added a few men's items. Lauren was the first to produce an entire line of men's clothing and then also make women's clothing. Nor was Lauren oblivious to what he had accomplished: "I changed the entire industry. . . . I loved Garbo and Hepburn, and I wanted to see my wife in good, tasteful clothes."

Lauren continued his conservative lines of clothing with relatively little change until 1977, when he brought out a new line for women. Denouncing the mannish styles for women he had built his collection around, he brought out a more elegant, softer, layered look. The success of the new line was clinched when Woody Allen and Diane Keaton, in choosing clothes for the title character in *Annie Hall*, assembled them from Lauren's collection. The style became the rage in 1977, but Lauren performed another about-face in 1978, when he returned to masculine tailoring for women. At the same time, Lauren brought out contemporary Western styles for men and women—a look he has continued to display into the late 1980s. Amy Yates, fashion director of Filene's called it "old L. L. Bean elevated to a new fashion significance." Since Lauren's prices for these goods were about three times those of equivalent merchandise at L. L. Bean, it was clear that the elevation was not simply aesthetic.

Ralph Lauren's great impact on America's fashion industry was recognized in 1979 when, along with Geoffrey Beene, Calvin Klein, and Halston, he was awarded the first Coty group award for Hall of Fame members. The three designers were lauded for developing an American look and for establishing New York City as a fashion rival to Paris. At about the same time, Lauren purchased Lapham Clothing and became the only American designer at that time to manufacture as well as license his designs. In addition, he brought out a moderately priced line of clothing for men, called Chaps, which was manufactured by L. Greif & Company and Hathaway Shirt Company. In association with Warner Communications, Lauren brought out his own line of men's and women's fragrances, and shortly thereafter he came out with a line of home furnishings manufactured by J. P. Stevens (see Stevens Family). At first this venture was a disaster, suffering from problems of delivery to retail stores and uneven quality control, but by 1986 it was grossing $50 million a year and making a nice profit.

Lauren's clothing lines were first carried by the most prestigious department stores, but then he began franchising free-standing Ralph Lauren stores in various parts of the United States. By 1986, there were forty-eight Polo/Ralph Lauren stores in posh locations from Beverly Hills to Palm Beach, along with 132 department store boutiques and sixteen discount outlets. Despite this, he did not have a store in the heart of the fashion district of New York City. Lauren himself felt this was the reason he was ignored by the establishment: "When I got two Coty awards, that was like Mickey Mantle, and what happened? They wrote about everybody else." He thought he knew why: "I have Polo shops all over, but I don't have a store on Madison Avenue. If I did, people would have a totally different sense of what I do."

To remedy that, in April 1987, Lauren spent $30 million to lease and renovate his own 20,000-square-foot retail store in the elegant old Rhinelander mansion on Madison Avenue. The first retail store Ralph Lauren has owned outright, his company called it the world's largest one-designer store. Dubbed the "Polo Palace," almost overnight, this magnificent shrine to "yuppie" fashion became a major tourist attraction in the city, drawing huge crowds. Tourists overheard planning their rounds of the Upper East Side museums often included the Polo store on their rounds: "Today we're doing the Whitney, Ralph Lauren, and the Frick . . . " While there, they dawdle equally over displays of antique Waterford crystal, art deco green glass panels etched with polo players, relics of the West-bury Hotel's Polo Lounge, model racing cars strewn on the bottom of an armoire in the boy's department, and the company's line of clothing itself. It had become, in the words of Jeffery Trachtenberg, "a tony theme park: Laurenland." Bloom-ingdale's and Saks, which had carried his clothing for years, were not pleased with the new competition, understandably feeling that it was bad taste for Lauren to compete with his own customers.

By this time, however, Ralph Lauren and Polo were so large, were so much of an American institution, that it did not seem to matter. They were grossing over $600 million from sales and licenses, and at the retail level his products generated over $1 billion in sales. It has been estimated that more than 10 million Ralph Lauren products are sold annually, one for every seventeen adults over the age of eighteen in America. Ralph Lauren himself was estimated to earn $27 million a year in profits, and had a fortune of $400 million in his privately held company. Furthermore, all these free-standing stores gave Ralph Lauren a degree of independence and clout unusual for a designer. He was, by 1986, the un-contested king of American sportswear, the natural successor to Bill Blass and John Weitz, the first generation of American celebrity designers. In addition, Lauren had gone multinational, a feat that many European designers achieved decades ago. But as Patrick McCarthy, editor of *Women's Wear Daily* (as cited in *Time*, September 1, 1986) noted, "He is the first American designer to seize the potential for the American look in Europe."

Lauren gives the appearance of patrician leisure, and he does, in fact, spend most of his free time relaxing with his wife and three children. But at Polo there is no question who is the boss. He works closely every day with fashion assistants and corporate colleagues. Lauren pays his employees well and demands and repays loyalty, but he is a tough taskmaster. Polo's vice president says, "He is absolutely terrible about hiding his feelings,'' and he often takes out his frustrations on his coworkers. Generally, he has retained much of his humility, though in recent years some have noted a touch of imperiousness has crept into his personality.

Ralph Lauren is a man of average height with curly gray hair and a year-round tennis tan. His favorite dress remains worn, faded jeans, a tweed jacket, and boots. He avoids the frenetic night life often associated with the fashion world. "I don't live in that world of 'Daaahling!' I can't stand it," Lauren says. Instead, he tends to his ranch in Colorado, drives a collection of antique racing cars, and jogs three or four miles each morning. Despite his success, or probably because of it, the controversy concerning Ralph Lauren's influence on American fashion continues. Lauren himself sees his contribution clearly: "My customers want quality, to look stylish without being trendy. They want the brand because of its consistency. You don't build a business unless people come back.'' Jerry Magnin, owner of the first Polo/Lauren store on Rodeo Drive in Beverly Hills, says:

In a society that doesn't communicate with itself, wearing a Lauren logo or suit is a way of identifying yourself, one of the ways of breaking down barriers is to put a message on yourself that lets people know who you are. That's what the Polo logo is all about. (*Forbes*, April 26, 1986)

As Ralph Lauren says, "We don't sell an item. We sell a way of life."

Eleanor Lambert, an industry publicist, explains Lauren's popularity: "He has grasped the solidity and the worth and the drive of American life. He is a very stabilizing influence on American fashion.'' To his critics, however, Lauren is a shameless plagiarist who appropriates styles, objects, and eras and signs his own name to them. The true answer, however, is that Lauren is the quintessential designer for the newly rich, for those who desire the cachet of old money through the acquisition of traditions obtained through possessions. They do not have style themselves, they do not know or understand these traditions; they depend upon Ralph Lauren to supply them with it. And he does not let them down. In that sense, Lauren is less a designer than a connoisseur, someone who has acquired a sufficient sense of taste to purchase and display goods with class, with snob appeal. Lauren himself recognizes that when he says, "My clothes sell because I'm the consumer, and I haven't lost touch with that."

Ralph Lauren, the man who exudes a tweedy informality and says he always wanted to be a history professor, is one of the greatest success stories in business and fashion in the last half of the twentieth century, and he has become one of the richest self-made men in the United States. He often reacts in rather bemused fashion to this success, acting as if it had been thrust upon him. Yet, in his high school yearbook, Lauren confidently listed his ambition as "millionaire." Today, Ralph Lauren claims it was a joke, but his older brother Jerry remembers that Ralph had "a constant urge to make something happen. He was always reaching for more.'' In 1987, *The Atlantic* viewed Ralph Lauren's life as a bit of an allegory for America itself:

We look at Lauren in his various poses and think, Oh, come off it, but all the while some sentimental voice in our head is saying, Well, good for you. And the moral to be drawn from his story is reassuring: if he has acquired all this for himself, then it's accessible to us too.

(**B.** *Los Angeles Times*, April 27, 1972; *New York*, October 29, 1973, October 21, 1985; Eleanor Lambert, *World of Fashion*, 1976; *People Weekly*, February 6, 1978; Barbara Walz and Bernadine Morris, *Fashion Makers*, 1978; *Forbes*, June 26, 1978, April 26, 1986; *Current Biography*, 1980; Ann Stegemeyer, *Who's Who in Fashion*, 1980; *Newsweek*, September 21, 1981; *Vogue*, August 1982; *New York Times Magazine*, September 18, 1983; *Time*, September 1, 1986; *The Atlantic Monthly*, August 1987; *Vanity Fair*, February 1988; *Manhattan, Inc.*, September 1988; Jeffery A. Trachtenberg, *Ralph Lauren: The Man behind the Mystique*, 1988.)

LAZARUS, CHARLES (1923–   ). Chain toy store founder, Toys ''R'' Us. Charles Lazarus was running a small children's furniture store in Washington, D.C., in the late 1940s. When a customer suggested he also stock some toys, he complied. Not long after, Lazarus made a simple, but profound, revelation. Parents who bought cribs and other furniture at his stores were one-time buyers—furniture, an item that had to last only a few years, did not wear out or break and did not have to be replaced. But when a customer returned to the store to replace a toy her baby had smashed, Lazarus had one of those ideas which give birth to empires: ''When I realized that toys broke, I knew it was a good business.'' Good is an understatement. With over $3 billion in sales in its 313 U.S. stores, and profits of $204 million, Toys ''R'' Us is one of the fastest growing and most profitable firms in the history of American retailing.

Charles Lazarus was born in the backroom of his father's small, second-hand bicycle shop. There, his father bought broken bicycles, which he rebuilt and sold. Lazarus later recalled, ''I always wondered why we didn't sell new bicycles, my father said it was because the big chain stores could sell them so much cheaper than we could.'' Lazarus never forgot that, but it was many years before he was able to act on that knowledge. He served in the army during World War II as a cryptographer and, after the war, returned to his father's bicycle shop. He considered attending college on the GI Bill, but decided, at twenty-four, he was too old. In 1948, he decided to clear out the bicycles and fill his father's shop with baby furniture instead. It was a wise decision. With the war's end, the returning soldiers were having large families, and there was an overwhelming demand for baby furniture. When Lazarus made his discovery about toys, they became the mainstay of his business. Changing the name of his store to the

Children's Supermarket (with Rs printed backward to increase word recognition), he became involved in the toy business full-time.

As his business grew, Lazarus realized he would have to make some changes. First of all, the name of the store was all wrong. There were too many letters in the name, and therefore the letters had to be small. Deciding that a smaller name with larger letters would make a more effective sign, Lazarus changed the name to Toys "R" Us, retaining the backward R. Other changes were also in the offing. The 1950s ushered in a new era of American retailing—the era of discounting. Fair trade laws had recently been declared unconstitutional by the Supreme Court, and several spartan discount operations were appearing on the scene. One of these was E. J. Korvette founded by Eugene Ferkauf. Ferkauf was drawing huge crowds to a Manhattan loft by offering luggage at deeply discounted prices. Recognizing that discounting was the key to E. J. Korvette's success, Lazarus closely studied Ferkauf's operation, and decided that he would employ a similar strategy for his future business. When he opened his second store, Lazarus made it a cash-and-carry, self-serve, discount operation. It was enormously successful, and by the time he opened store number three, Lazarus had settled upon the strategy that later became synonymous with Toys "R" Us. By 1966, Lazarus had four stores, which were doing an annual $12-million business. He sold the operation to Interstate Stores, thereby garnering $7.5 million in cash and capital support for the future growth of Toys "R" Us. Although this worked well for the toy chain itself (Lazarus expanded it to forty-seven stores during the next eight years), Interstate was a poorly managed hodgepodge of department stores. When it embarked upon a poorly planned expansion into discounting, it was driven into bankruptcy in 1974.

Charles Lazarus thus faced a crisis—he could either pull out, or he could try to salvage his toy-store chain. He chose the latter option. In 1975, the Interstate trustees appointed Lazarus chief executive officer, at a time when Toys "R" Us was providing 85 percent of Interstate's sales and 90 percent of its profits. He began to sell off the other units of Interstate, while continuing to build the toy-store chain. When Interstate finally emerged from bankruptcy in 1978, it was reorganized under the Toys "R" Us name, with Lazarus as its chief executive officer. With $200 million in sales in 1975, Toys "R" Us had over $2 billion in revenue ten years later. What were the secrets of its success? One of the key elements is its one-price discount policy. Toy "R" Us runs no sales, except when it wants to clear out slow-moving items. Generally, its prices are 20 percent to 50 percent below retail, which helps the chain build a loyal customer base. Since its pricing is consistent, the customer never has to wonder whether next week the price will be even less. The chain also has an extremely liberal, "no questions asked" return policy. It can do this because of its volume buying. Toys "R" Us simply will not place an order with a manufacturer unless it will agree to accept returns at no cost to Toys "R" Us.

Another important feature of the Toys "R" Us chain is its "cookie-cutter" uniformity. To facilitate its rapid growth, the stores are nearly identical: 18,000 square feet, located near, but not in, high-traffic shopping malls (to save rent), the stores look like warehouses. Toys are stacked almost to the ceiling, and there are some 18,000 items in each store. Charles Lazarus expressed his wish for uniformity most succinctly: "I should be able to close my eyes and walk 130 feet and put my hand down and touch the very same stack in each store. If not, there's something wrong." The stores are operated on a low-service concept, that is, employees are given narrow, nonjudgemental tasks, such as stocking or arranging shelves. These two factors, along with a third major element of the chain—its extraordinary deep inventory of 18,000 individual items—have elicited a common complaint from customers. A cry frequently heard in the aisles from frustrated shoppers is: "Doesn't *anybody* work here? I can't find anything in this store!" Employees, generally high school students working for minimum wage, are rarely helpful; their main responsibility is to keep the shelves stocked.

Toys "R" Us also benefits from early buy-in incentives. Since, unlike most other toys sellers (such as department stores), Toys "R" Us maintains a full stock year-round and maintains huge warehouses to store goods, it is able to get significant discounts from suppliers. As Stephen David Hassenfeld,[†] president of Hasbro Toys, said when questioned about the discounts, "Why not? We're transferring warehouse responsibility, better it should be in somebody else's warehouse than ours." Also, since toy manufacturers will often defer payment for up to twelve months on goods shipped, about two-thirds of Toys "R" Us' massive inventory is actually financed by the vendors in this fashion.

Another key to the success of Toys "R" Us is the high degree of centralization in the organization. One reason for the uniformity of the operation is that sales data from the stores are scrutinized daily with an electronic point of sale (EPOS) system which is used to transmit data directly from the cash register to central headquarters. Rated as one of the top computer systems in the country, EPOS helps Toys "R" Us decide which products to buy and which to eliminate before they get stale. All of these decisions are strongly influenced by the computer, and all are made at central headquarters. As Charles Lazarus has stated, "*Nothing* is done in the stores."

The final factor in the chain's success is what *Chain Store Age* (1981) has called the "Lazarus Factor." Two things are universally recognized about Charles Lazarus—he is very bright and creative, and he *loves* the toy business. Even Lazarus himself realizes there is some truth to this. He once commented, in discussing the failure of competitor Lionel Leisure to compete successfully: "They had no purpose in business. They had no aim, no ambition, no goal. They kept fumbling around. Someone in that company once said to me, 'You have a tremendous advantage. You love what you do. I only do it to earn a living.' " It is not that Lazarus loves toys; he loves building a business. His wife, Helen Singer Kaplan, a noted psychiatrist and specialist in human sexuality, believes Lazarus suffers from what she calls an "edifice complex." Lazarus does not disagree. "I like to have an expanding kind of business," he has admitted. "I like opening stores."

Toys "R" Us has profoundly changed the nature of the toy business itself. Because of the uniformity of the stores, and because the toys are stacked to the ceiling, toy packaging was redesigned with regard to how it would look, and whether it would fit, on the shelves at Toys "R" Us. The manufacturers also ensure that their packages will stack properly, so that they can obtain the desired space in the giant chain. So important is the receptivity of the chain to their total sales that manufacturers will even test new toys in the Toys "R" Us stores before taking them into final production. By the mid–1980s, close to 16 percent of all the money spent on toys was spent at Toys "R" Us, and many analysts predicted that the figure could go as high as 40 percent. With figures like that, manufacturers can ill afford to ignore Lazarus' clout. As *Business Week* commented: "If you are a toymaker these days, you can't ignore Toys "R" Us."

The chain has also sold children's clothing since the mid–1970s, but not seriously until 1981. Two years later it opened Kids "R" Us stores, to do with chiidren's clothing what it had achieved with toys. The approach is similar— large stores with enormous selections, stocked in depth, with good quality, name-brand merchandise at discount prices, usually about 25 percent below department store prices. Although these stores require better trained personnel and a higher degree of service than the toy stores, they were quite successful. By early 1988, there were 112 Kids "R" Us stores doing a $300-million business annually. Lazarus vowed, "We intend this to be a very large business." No one was betting against him.

In late 1988, however, a few cracks began to appear in the lean, mean Toys "R" Us management style. During the all-important Christmas season in 1988, the company's sales rose by only 5 percent, a significant slowdown from the 12-percent increase during the same period the year before. As a result, some of the gleam came off the Toys "R" Us stock. Long a favorite of institutional investors, with no fewer than 463 pension funds and other institutions holding about two-thirds of its stock, they began shying away in the early months of 1989. As a result, while Wall Street boomed in January 1989, Toys "R" Us stock barely held its own.

Although Lazarus drives his employees and executives as hard as he drives himself, he rewards them very well. The best store managers are given rapid promotions and stock options, and few ever leave the firm. In an age when executives move from one company to another with great alacrity, Toys "R" Us is almost monotonous in its stability; the top executives stay with the firm throughout their entire business lives. In 1988, Charles Lazarus viewed his store managers and executives as the key to further growth for his company:

No matter how big we get, the key unit in this company is the store. We want our store managers to take the business home in their stomach. We want them to think that their store is the only store in the world. We reward them with bonuses and stock options, and we've made a lot of millionaires. (*Fortune,* May 23, 1988)

He made it clear that he expected further change and growth—"The only thing I know how to manage is growth. We're in the growth business. What we sell is toys." (**B**. *Fortune*, June 1, 1981, November 26, 1984, May 23, 1988; *Chain Store Age*, September 1981, March 1988; *Forbes*, March 28, 1983, February 22, 1988; A. David Silver, *Entrepreneurial Megabucks*, 1985; *The Atlantic Monthly*, October 1986; *Business Week*, December 19, 1988; *Business Month*, March 1989.)

LAZARUS, FRED R., JR. (October 29, 1884–May 27, 1973). Department store chain executive, Federated Department Stores. As every American knows, Thanksgiving falls on the fourth Thursday of November. What most Americans may not know is that it was not always so. Few recall that on August 14, 1939, Franklin D. Roosevelt proclaimed from his estate at Campobello that Thanksgiving would no longer be the last Thursday of November, but would fall on the fourth Thursday. Conservative traditionalists lambasted FDR for defaming this "sacred" holiday. Thanksgiving football games had to be rescheduled, and other holiday plans had to be altered to adjust to the sudden change. What most Americans do not know is that the change came about because of a campaign mounted by Fred Lazarus, Jr., head of the F. & R. Lazarus Department store in Columbus, Ohio, and of the Federated Department Stores chain. Lazarus had noted that Thanksgiving would fall on November 30 that year, leaving only twenty shopping days until Christmas, thus severely shortening the traditional Christmas shopping season. Establishing Thanksgiving on the fourth Thursday of the month, then, ensured a longer pre-Christmas shopping season.

Fred Lazarus, Jr., built a reputation as one of the toughest, most aggressive, and most powerful men in American retailing, a reputation that was largely deserved. Yet, in personal appearance he was highly deceptive. He was barely five-feet tall, and childhood bouts of scarlet fever and the measles had left him with a permanent tremor in his hands, and when he became excited his entire body shook uncontrollably. These characteristics along with his cherubic pink jowls and gentle, diffident manner might lead one to think that he was a pushover. But in 1972, on the occasion of his eighty-eighth birthday, Lazarus told a story that illustrated just how tough he was. He recalled that when he and his brother Simon were boys in Columbus and walked through a rough neighborhood, "Si carried a loaded revolver and I a blackjack and neither of us would have hesitated to use them." Similarly, in 1929, after his nine-year-old son, Richard, was killed in an auto accident, Lazarus and his wife made a point of taking a stroll every evening on fashionable Dixon Avenue, just to prove that he was tough and had not been defeated by the tragedy.

The Lazarus store in Columbus had been founded in 1851 by Simon Lazarus, who had immigrated from Germany a year earlier. He opened a one-room men's clothing store, and with his sons over the years converted it into a department store that was a comfortable but not spectacular success. After Simon died, his two sons, Fred, Sr., and Ralph, renamed it F. & R. Lazarus. Throughout the store's first half-century of operation, the family had been content with moderate growth and success. When Fred Lazarus, Jr., joined the firm in 1902, however, things began to change dramatically. Young Fred, who had attended Ohio State University for just three months, left school to work in the family firm because of the illness of both his father and uncle. At that time, the family store had sales of less than $500,000, and except for lines of women's shoes and hose, still sold only men's clothing. In 1907, however, Fred, Jr., went to his father and persuaded him, in the midst of the panic of that year, to undertake a major expansion. Fred, Sr., at that time, retired from active control of the business, and he allowed Fred, Jr., and his older brother, Simon, to undertake the desired changes. The result was the completion in 1909 of an imposing six-storied building which would soon become a full-fledged department store. The existing Lazarus business could fill only three floors of the building; the rest was held for expansion.

The way in which Fred, Jr., handled that first expansion set the tone for the rest of his business life. Each new department was nursed into a position of solid dominance before another one was opened. To achieve that dominance, young Fred was willing to take long-term risks. By World War I, the Lazarus store had grown to dominate its central Ohio market area, and customers came from as far away as 150 miles to shop. Finally, in 1926, Fred Lazarus had added enough departments to make F. & R. Lazarus a full-fledged department store. With total dominance of the central Ohio market, and the department store finally completed, it might be expected that Fred, Jr., by then in his mid-forties, might want to rest on his laurels. But nothing could have been farther from the truth— he had just begun what would become one of the most fabulous careers in American retailing.

In 1928, Lazarus set his sights on the John Shillito & Company department store in Cincinnati. Founded in 1830, Shillito's had prestige as the oldest store west of the Alleghenies. But, the store had slipped badly in recent years, falling from first to fourth place among the city's retailers, with a volume of $4 million in 1927. Lazarus bought the store for a hefty $2.5 million, and then poured another $750,000 into it. The goal was to build a Cincinnati equivalent of F. & R. Lazarus. Many in the city thought he was crazy to attempt this, but by 1929 Shillito's sales had jumped 50 percent, and even during the depression years it never fell back to the levels experienced in the 1920s. Within a decade, under the most adverse conditions imaginable, Fred Lazarus had achieved his objective: by 1939 Shillito's was the number-one store in Cincinnati. In its wake it left the other Cincinnati merchants, who admitted sheepishly that they had been caught sleeping by Fred Lazarus. As one competitor said, they had made many fumbles, "[a]nd every ball we fumbled he [Fred Lazarus] picked up and ran with." By the end of World War II, Shillito's had sales of $30 million, more than one-third the total volume of the city's department store sales, and probably more than its next two competitors combined.

These aggressive retailing tactics and this willingness to ignore older traditions of doing business brought about as much criticism as success to Fred Lazarus. The older Jewish families in Cincinnati were particularly irked at his brashness. As Mrs. David Weston, one of the leaders of the city's Jewish community remarked:

When various Lazari began moving to Cincinnati from Columbus, they were looked down on by the best Jewish families here, the Wachtmans and Seasongoods and Stixes, and they still are. None of them ever knew or cared anything for music. I can't remember one of them giving a penny personally—only through their store. Up at Charlevoix [an upper-class summer resort in Michigan] too, they were not a blessing to the community. (Harris, *Merchant Princes*)

Fred Lazarus was hardly deterred by this kind of criticism or lack of acceptance. He just built his alliances in the non-Jewish community in Cincinnati, with the Procters, the Gambles, and the Krogers, and he went about seizing control of the retailing market in the city. He used this same aggressiveness to establish a nationwide dominance in department stores.

The foundations for a nationwide chain of department stores had their roots in 1916. In that year, the Retail Research Association was established under the leadership of Lincoln Filene.* Consisting of fourteen competitive stores, including F. & R. Lazarus, it engaged in the then unheard of practice of exchanging information on costs, prices, markups, volumes, and other operating concerns. This was, of course, possible only if the stores involved were in different communities and not in competition. In 1921, Fred Lazarus suggested that the organization be tightened to ensure greater uniformity. His ideas were accepted, and the organization was renamed the Associated Merchandising Corporation (ACM). This brought Lazarus into contact with powerful department store merchants from several cities in the United States, and, as the 1920s brought on waves of mergers and acquisitions in industries all across America, it was natural that many of the merchants who had intimate contact with one another in ACM began to think in terms of creating a nationwide department store chain. In 1929, on S. F. Rothschild's yacht in Long Island Sound, the Federated Department Store chain was created. With Federated acting merely as a holding company, the chain included F. & R. Lazarus, Shillito's in Cincinnati, Rothschild's Abraham & Strauss stores in Brooklyn, Filene's of Boston, and Bloomingdale's of New York. Created as a means to spread risk, the individual department stores traded their stock for shares in Federated on the basis of past earnings, but Federated itself was to have no management authority over the stores themselves. The seeds for an authentic national department store chain had been sown.

At the end of World War II, Lazarus decided that the Federated format had to be changed. Feeling that the existing arrangement was inadequate for the future, he concluded that the arrangement should be either abandoned or strengthened for several reasons. First, there was the problem of how Federated could profitably reinvest its wartime earnings. These could be best used to build new stores or to invest in areas outside the department store field, but under the existing form of organization, this was impossible. Second, Lazarus' two Ohio stores had grown much more rapidly and profitably than their eastern counterparts. In 1929, Lazarus' Ohio stores had made up 16 percent of the volume and 22 percent of Federated's profits; by 1945, they accounted for 28 percent of the volume and nearly a third of the profits. Yet, the Lazarus family had already converted its shares on a less advantageous basis. So, in June 1945, Fred Lazarus proposed establishing a new and stronger Federated office. When some of the others objected, he threatened to pull his two stores out of the chain, doing irreparable damage to it. As a result, the rest of the store owners agreed to go along, and Fred Lazarus became chief executive officer of the new national chain. He then set Federated on a breathtaking program of expansion.

To achieve this, Lazarus recognized that too much of the chain's money was tied up in real estate and in financing credit purchases. To solve the first problem, he sold the real estate where the various stores were located to insurance companies and foundations, and then he leased back the stores on a long-term basis. Next, Federated sold to local banks about $6-million worth of installment accounts receivable. These actions provided Lazarus with a large war chest with which he could pursue growth and expansion. His first expansion came in 1945, with the purchase of Foley's, the dominant department store in Houston, Texas. Although the large store was limping along in 1943 with sales of just $7 million, Lazarus still had to assemble a package of $3.5 million in Federated stock to gain control of the ailing giant. By October 1947, Lazarus had pushed the store's volume up to $17 million by cramming it with personnel and merchandise. This was just the beginning of Lazarus' plans for Foley's and for Houston.

In October 1947, Lazarus completed the building of a new $10-million Foley's department store in the city, the first big, new department store to be built in America since 1929. This was Lazarus' "dream store," and it became the prototype for much later department store development. One of the first reinforced, poured-concrete department store structures, it had no windows, which allowed the air-conditioning units to better withstand the brutal Houston summers. Most important, however, was what was hidden from the customers' view—a conveyer belt that moved incoming goods from the receiving dock to the marking and examining room; the unattended wheeler-lift elevators that carried a hand truck of merchandise to the proper floor and to automatically roll off onto it; perimeter stockrooms next to the building's skin; and chute-delivery systems that moved wrapped packages from any selling floor to the delivery trucks. What Lazarus had created in Houston was an efficient *machine* for the selling of department store merchandise. As he noted, "Don't get me wrong, we tried to add the looks afterward, and I think we did. But we didn't sacrifice one single bit of efficiency for the sake of looks." The new age of department stores was at hand.

With the success of the Foley acquisition and the new building, Lazarus stepped up expansion for Federated. In 1948 he bought Milwaukee's Boston Store, and in 1957, he picked up the Burdine and Goldsmith stores in the South. Rike's in Dayton, Ohio, was acquired two years later; and Bullocks, the California department store chain, was purchased in 1964, bringing with it the prestigious I. Magnin chain. The last major acquisition was Rich's, the largest department store in Atlanta, in 1976. Federated paid their entire 1975 earnings, $157 million, to acquire Rich's, the venerable belle of Southern retailing. By this time, Federated was by far the largest department store chain in America, with 340 stores and 117,151 employees. What was the secret of Federated's success? The "Lazarus approach."

The Lazarus approach was developed at F. & R. Lazarus in Columbus, perfected at Shillito's in Cincinnati, and brought to fruition at Foley's in Houston. It was then applied to nearly every other Federated store in the chain. The Lazarus approach first dictates that the store must be the dominant one in its market. Second, in order to have that size and strength, it must service an essentially middle-class market. Fred Lazarus always set his sights on the exact middle of the American marketplace, never attempting to elevate general taste levels, as specialty store merchants like Neiman-Marcus or Lord & Taylor did. As Fred Lazarus once said, "You can't be a dominant store the Lord & Taylor way." And dominance was what Lazarus was after.

A rival executive commented, "The Lazarus approach is one of sheer force. They use no tricks, no finesse. Like Macy's, they want a bigger tent than anyone else, and more monkeys and elephants. The bigger the better—that's Fred! Big!" Lazarus' chief weapon in establishing this dominance and in gaining the loyalty of the vast middle-class market was to ensure that he carried the largest, most complete stock of merchandise. He had first done this with the family store in Columbus. His goal was to convince the shopper to come to F. & R. Lazarus first, since he or she would end up there eventually anyway. Once he had made the store dominant in the consumers' mind, he could cut back his advertising expenditures. Lazarus' stores has always spent a lower percentage of their sales dollar on advertising than their rivals.

Lazarus brought these concepts to Federated after World War II. Whenever he could, he bought the dominant store in the area, or, when that was not possible, he purchased once-dominant stores that had fallen on hard times, as he had done with Shillito's in Cincinnati, Foley's in Houston, and Sanger's in Dallas. Then he hired a team of experts for his chain that no individual store could afford. He brought in real estate experts, tax experts, and experts on architecture, store fixtures, and consumer credit.

But bigness and dominance had a price. Lazarus' stores had achieved the kind of dominance that forced them to compete with everyone, including other department stores, specialty shops, and discounters. To ensure that it had as full a range of goods as possible, it often had to maintain departments at a loss. But these disadvantages were more than offset by the advantages. Being the largest, most dominant store in an area meant that it had its choice among the national brands and that it could assure exclusive agreements with many manufacturers, thereby shutting competitors out of potentially lucractive markets. To make money, however, Lazarus did something else, something which had a long-term impact on the department store trade in the United States—he cut back on service. Department stores had developed in America, at least partially, on the basis of the kinds of service they provided to the customer. But in the early 1950s, Lazarus began cutting back at Federated. As he said in 1950, "Every service which the customers don't really want must be eliminated. We must also find out the way to give the services the customers do want at the lowest possible cost." The result, however, was a profound deterioration in department store service, a deterioration which opened the way for specialty retailers like Neiman-Marcus and others to take a larger share of this business away from the Federated chain in the 1960s and 1970s.

But for a long time, prospects for the Federated chain were extraordinarily bright under the management of Fred Lazarus. In 1957, Federated passed Allied Stores in department store sales, thereby becoming America's largest department store chain for the first time—an honor it would not relinquish for some thirty years. At the same time, Fred Lazarus became chairman of the firm, and his son, Ralph, assumed the presidency. The elder Lazarus, however, continued to be the chief executive officer.

Federated continued to expand rapidly under Fred Lazarus' leadership during the 1960s. Despite the fact that he was then in his late seventies, his drive and ambition had not diminished by one iota. When asked why he continued to push himself so hard, he responded, "Because it's fun!" But a number of fateful decisions were made during that decade, decisions which would later create problems for the retailing giant. After Lazarus bought Burdines and I. Magnin for Federated in 1964, a consent decree was forced upon it by the Federal Trade Commission. Under its terms, Federated was prohibited from acquiring any more department stores for five years. Lazarus still had his expansionist ambitions, so he began to branch into other retailing areas. In 1967 he purchased Ralph's, the large California chain of supermarkets, and at about the same time he created the Gold Circle chain of discount stores. Since both units did very well in the late 1960s and 1970s, it appeared to have been another stroke of genius for the elderly retailing genius.

Finally, in 1966, at the age of eighty-one, Fred Lazarus relinquished his title of chief executive officer to his son Ralph, but he retained the titles of board chairman and chairman of the executive committee. This transition barely affected the reality of decision making at Federated. As the fifty-two-year-old Ralph Lazarus commented at the time, "Actually, this is only a change in title." Until Fred died in 1973, at eighty-eight years of age, Federated remained under his iron grip. With his passing, Ralph Lazarus finally came out from under his father's shadow. Yet the many years of serving as a figurehead for his father probably had diminished the younger Lazarus' ability to command respect.

Throughout the nine years he headed Federated, Ralph worked in tandem with another chief executive. During the first few years he worked with Harold Krensky and then with Howard Goldfeder. Jack Goldsmith, who sold his family's Memphis department store to Fred Lazarus in 1969, probably summed it up best: "Ralph ought to have learned *something* sitting on Mr. Fred's lap for twenty-five years."

In any event, Ralph Lazarus inherited a powerful, profitable entity in the mid–1970s. Federated had sales of $3.7 billion in 1975, earning profits of $157.4 million. It had fifteen department store divisions, along with Ralph's Supermarkets (with $688 million in sales) and a $277-million discount operation with Gold Circle. Its stores operated in eighteen states, on the East Coast, the West Coast, the Southeast, and the Southwest. Furthermore, Ralph Lazarus and Harold Krensky together had a reputation as a tough team—a competitor commented: "They are among the roughest in the business, they chew you up and spit you out." By 1980, things seemed quite rosy for the giant chain. With sales of $5.8 billion in 1979, and profits of $203 million, it was still the largest chain in America, with 354 stores in twenty-five states and more than 50 million square feet of selling space. In that year Krensky retired as president and was succeeded by Goldfeder. At the same time, Federated began to go into a tailspin.

In the early 1980s, discounters and specialty stores began cutting heavily into Federated's department store profits. Although sales continued to rise during these years, earnings at first leveled off, and then began dropping after the mid–1980s. Federated found itself under constant siege from two fronts—the Dayton-Hudson chain of Minneapolis and R. H. Macy's of New York. Dayton-Hudson focused on discounting, with its very successful Mervyn's stores. In response, Federated started the Gold Circle line of stores, and then, in 1984, began to set up the Mainstreet chain, a slightly more upscale version of Mervyn's. At the same time, the R. H. Macy chain of department stores took a different tack. Macy's eliminated budget basements in their stores, and they turned the space into fashionable boutiques. The chain developed a successful technique for moving large inventories through aggressive merchandising. It took Federated ten years to institute similar changes in its stores, and by then it was too late. By the early 1980s, Federated had settled into a rather uncomfortable mediocrity. As *Forbes* commented, the old Columbus maxim, "We're going to wind up at Lazarus eventually anyway, so we may as well go there first," no longer held true. As a result, Ralph Lazarus resigned as chief executive officer in 1982, and turned the reins over to Howard Goldfeder.

By 1985, Federated was a stagnating giant. With sales of $9.7 billion in the previous year, its profits had declined from $312 million in 1983 to $287 million in 1984. Floundering, but still valuable, Federated became a favorite target for corporate raiders, since it would be worth more broken up into constituent pieces. Management took a number of costly anti-takeover positions in the mid–1980s, including staggered terms for directors and a 40-percent increase in authorized shares. Federated's problem, according to most industry analysts, was that it was trying to cover all the bases (department stores, discounters, specialty stores, and supermarkets) and was unable to successfully focus itself to meet the challenges in anyone of these areas. Many advocated that Federated divest itself and concentrate on department stores, but Goldfeder refused to heed that advice. As a result, the chain became the target of a successful hostile takeover in 1988.

In 1986, Robert Campeau, a Canadian real estate developer, shocked the American retailing world by purchasing the giant Allied Stores chain for $3.6 billion. Allied, owners of such department stores as Jordan Marsh, Bonwit Teller, Bon Marché, Joske's, Pomeroy's, Stern's, and others, made Campeau an instant power in American retailing. By October 1987, Campeau had sold off sixteen of Allied's twenty-four divisions, reducing the company's $4.2-billion debt to $2.7 billion. He then set his sights on Federated. When the stock market crash of October 19, 1988, knocked Federated's price down to a bargain level, he made his move. Other powerful players, determined to keep Federated out of Campeau's hands, also entered the fray.

Although Goldfeder had allowed Federated to become a bloated, mediocre collection of fiefdoms, he was still a member of the American retailing elite, and Campeau was a despised outsider. Goldfeder turned to Edward Finkelstein, chairman of the R. H. Macy's chain. Macy's entered the fray as a "white knight" on the behalf of Federated's management, which drove up the price of Federated's stock. When Campeau finally emerged victorious April 1, 1988, he paid $73.50 a share for the company, slightly more than the twice what the stock was selling for when the bidding began. Campeau paid a staggering $6.6 billion to Federated stockholders for the firm, and he incurred an additional debt of $2.2 billion, which gave him a total indebtedness of a whopping $8.8 billion as a result of the purchase. It was the biggest non-oil takeover in American history. The terms of the deal were complicated and required Campeau to sell off various divisions of Federated. For $1.1 billion, he sold I. Magnin and Bullock's department stores to the Macy chain. In addition, Filene's and Foley's were sold by Campeau to May Department Stores Company for $1.5 billion; Allied's Brooks Brothers unit was sold to Britain's Marks and Spenser for $750 million; the Filene's Basement unit of Federated was sold to a group of investors led by company management; and Ralph's Grocery was restructured as a separate, indirect subsidiary of Campeau. These final two transactions, along with the others previously completed, brought Campeau $4.4 billion, allowing him to shave his Federated debt in half.

Campeau moved immediately to reduce employment at Federated to help finance the $320 million in annual interest payments. Federated in 1987 had over $11 billion in sales, generating profits of over $300 million, but the key for Campeau was the real estate. As a real estate developer, he had acquired a large amount of valuable property, and subsequently he teamed up with Edward DeBartolo,[†] America's largest builder of shopping malls, in what Campeau calls a "bang-up combination." There is no question that this partnership will have a major impact on U.S. retailing and real estate. Using Campeau's own department stores as anchor tenants in their new malls, he and DeBartolo have frightened rival mall developers.

When Campeau raided Federated, the retailing community was horrified. A Wall Street analyst remarked: "Mr. Campeau is an outsider, culturally the Federated management didn't feel comfortable with those real estate people." But in many respects, Campeau is much like old Fred Lazarus, Jr. Both men, outsiders in many respects, used that marginality as a tool and an incentive to drive to the top of American retailing. A French Canadian from a poor family, Campeau learned to be tough and to defend himself from the WASP kids while he was growing up in Sudbury, Ontario. Just as Lazarus was rebuked by the elite Jewish community in Cincinnati, Campeau was rejected by the WASP elite in Toronto, and even his later success has not much changed their attitudes toward him. Just as Fred Lazarus made his alliances with the non-Jewish elite in Cincinnati, the Catholic Campeau has allied himself with the Reichman family of Canada, multibillionaire real estate developers and orthodox Jews. Fred Lazarus, Jr., might have been greatly disturbed that this Federated chain was wrenched out of his family's hands, but he might also have been secretly pleased that his ultimate successor was an outsider just as he had been. (**B**. *Time*, July 16, 1945; *Business Week*, October 18, 1947, June 15, 1950, June 22, 1959, October 19, 1963, July 26, October 18, 1976, November 5, 1984, April 18, 1988; *Fortune*, March 1948; *Saturday Evening Post*, November 18, 1950; *Dun's Review*, November 1970; Alfred Gottschalk, *Fred Lazarus Jr.*, 1973; *New York Times*, May 28, 1973; *Who Was Who*, vol. 6; Leon Harris, *Merchant Princes*, 1979; Milton Moskowitz et al., *Everybody's Business*, 1980; Robert Shook, *The Chief Executive Officers*, 1981; *Forbes*, April 8, 1985; Toronto *Globe & Mail*, June 10, 1988; *Los Angeles Times*, June 12, 1988; Toronto *Globe & Mail Report on Business*, July 1988: 36–45; *Current Biography*, March 1989.)

LEWIS, EDWARD T. (May 15, 1940–   ). Publisher, Essence Communications, Incorporated. For generations, blacks were relegated to the fringes of the American economy. Black business, as understood from the time of Booker T. Washington until the 1960s, was small, local, and often marginal. Characteristic black business activities included funeral parlors, ethnic hair-care products, barber and beauty shops, and so on. After World War II, a few blacks began to achieve more substantial success in new areas. One area in which blacks had attained some measure of success was the media; a number of highly successful newspapers served the local and national black communities. These too, however, remained fairly small. The one exception emerged after World War II when John H. Johnson* developed the phenomenally successful Johnson Publishing Company, a vast media and manufacturing empire, which published *Ebony* and *Jet*, and had nearly 2,000 employees and sales of over $2,000,000 in 1987. For a long time, people assumed there was no room for other black publications. Johnson had cornered the market. Then, in 1969, Edward Lewis and three other young blacks had an idea for a new black-oriented magazine; from that, they built from scratch a massive, rapidly growing black media empire.

Edward Lewis, who was born in the Bronx, went to college at the University of New Mexico from which he graduated in 1964. In 1963 he had lectured in the Peace Corps program at UNM, and he worked for two years in the city manager's office as an administrative analyst. He then went back to the University of New Mexico and got his master's in 1966. The same year Lewis headed for New York City, where he became a financial analyst for the First National City Bank. By 1969, Lewis was regarded as one of the "bright young blacks" on his way up in the New York financial world. As a result, he was one of fifty young blacks invited to a local black capitalism conference sponsored by the prestigious Shearson, Hammill & Company brokerage firm. Shearson, Hammill called the conference to encourage the development of initiative in black capitalism. That incentive, in turn, had been prompted by the Nixon administration and Maurice Stans of the Commerce Department, who viewed it as an antidote to the violence and radicalism then coursing through the black ghettos of America.

The idea of a slick new magazine to appeal especially to black women was advanced by Jonathon Blount, a twenty-four-year-old ad salesman for New Jersey Bell Telephone Company. The Shearson, Hammill advisor got Blount together with Cecil Hollingsworth, a black with experience in the printing industry, Clarence Smith, a salesman for Prudential Insurance, and Ed Lewis, who was well trained in financial planning. The four young men met in the evenings after their regular jobs and made plans for their new magazine. The mood of white America in 1969–1970 was one of absolute panic over the possibility of a black revolution in America, so the men found a great deal of help and support for their project among the denizens of Madison and Sixth Avenues. Providing assistance by way of advice and training were *Time-Life, Newsweek, Psychology Today, New York* magazine, CBS, Young & Rubicam, J. K. Lasser Tax Institute, Cowles Communications, McCann-Erickson, and Lorillard Corporation, among others.

The young men came back to Shearson, Hammill with their first budget proposal—for a whopping $5 million. The brokerage company, telling them it would be impossible to raise that much, advised cutbacks. Finally, they came forward with a more modest $1.5-million proposal. Even this was optimistic. Just as they hit the money markets, the steep recession of 1970 brought things to a halt. Ultimately, they were able to collect only $130,000 in cash, and 52 percent of that represented their own funds. They were able, however, to get commitments to cover the balance up to $1.5 million (and ultimately $2 million) from a consortium of investors that included First National City Bank, Chase National Bank, and Morgan Guaranty Bank. They also approached Playboy Enterprises for support in this initial period, but they were turned down.

In any event, the four young men allocated enough money to finance publication of the first and several subsequent issues of a magazine named *Essence*. The first issue came out in May 1970 amidst great fanfare. It was a slick, glossy,

stylish magazine, what *Time* called "*Vogue*-cum-*Ramparts*" in style, referring
to the rather uneasy combination of two disparate elements in the magazine. The
first was some twenty pages of high-fashion color photography, similar to that
found in *Vogue*. The second was seen in an article entitled "Five Shades of
Militancy," which ran throughout the magazine's text. In response to the heightened black activism of the time, the new magazine tried to strike a note of
revolution and militancy. Most of all, however, what *Essence* presented was
something new in black magazines. The dazzling full-page color photos of
gorgeous black models clad in bikinis and miniskirts had seldom been seen
previously. White magazines, of course, almost never used black models, and
Ebony and *Jet* were generally more sedate and dignified in their presentation of
blacks. Then, too, there were pointed articles that one did not find elsewhere:
"Sensual, sexy black man. . . . What are you doing with that white woman?"

Essence was new, exciting, and different. And it was black. But it almost
folded early on. Lewis and his three partners had an optimistic initial press run
of 200,000 copies, which were distributed to 145 cities. Of these, they sold just
50,000. Worse still, *Essence* had managed to sell only thirteen pages of advertising. The infant enterprise was teetering and was further being torn apart by
editorial and managerial dissension. A major bone of contention was the strident
political tone of the magazine. Because of that, the editor of the first issue, Ruth
Ross, left when she believed her editorial independence was being undercut.
During the first year, Ross was followed by two more editors, each of whom
quickly came and went. By the second year, a number of important changes had
been made. First of all, Marcia Gillespie was installed as editor-in-chief, and
she stabilized the magazine and provided a clear, successful focus. Most important, however, Edward Lewis and Clarence Smith ousted their two partners
from control of the operation; Lewis became publisher and chairman of Essence
Communications, and Smith was named president of the corporation. The two
men, along with Marcia Gillespie, battled hard to bring *Essence* to respectability
and profitability.

By 1975, *Essence* was a success. When interviewed by *Advertising Age* that
year, however, Ed Lewis seemed more relieved than ecstatic. "We've survived,"
he told them. He also recalled that their investors "took a helluva risk with us."
By 1975, though, *Essence* was still the only black women's service magazine,
and it had experienced a 40-percent circulation gain from 1973 to 1974, a larger
increase than any other women's magazine. Its ad volume also grew by a respectable 13 percent. The first profitable issue came out in 1974, and for fiscal
1975 *Essence* earned a tiny but significant profit of $90,000 on $3.4 million in
revenues. By this point, circulation had climbed to 450,000, and it was expected
to rise another 50,000 in the following year. *Essence* also moved to new and
more spacious offices at 1500 Broadway. A critical intervention had been made
on *Essence*'s behalf during its first year, when it almost went under. Playboy
Enterprises, which had earlier refused to help, came up with much-needed backing, as did a number of other mainstream companies. All told, Lewis collected

about $2 million from investors before the magazine began showing a small profit.

Edward Lewis and *Essence* hit a snag in 1977 when his former partners, Blount and Hollingsworth in coalition with filmmaker Gordon Parks, who had provided early editorial supervision for the magazine, sued for control of the magazine. At this time, *Essence* was a profitable operation, having shown a second full year of profit, and its circulation was projected at 600,000. Parks, speaking for his group, said he thought Lewis, Smith, and Gillespie had done a marvelous job, but he thought that he and his group could do better. The battle went on for two years before Lewis finally took the company private and settled with his ex-partners. During those two years, *Essence* operated in the red, but as soon as the dispute was over it returned to profitability. In 1980, Essence Communications showed a profit of $300,000, about the same as it had had in 1979. As Lewis remarked at the time: "I'm not hearing any complaints these days." He credited the profitability to an "extraordinarily better job of controlling expenses," especially by ending the magazine's dependence on Publisher's Clearing House, which saved it 90 percent on new subscriptions.

By this point, *Essence*, which was ten years old, had a circulation of 600,000 and ran an all-time high of 109 ad pages in its tenth anniversary issue. At a time when ad pages in women's magazines were decreasing at an alarming rate, *Essence*'s were increasing. This was due in large measure to two interrelated factors: the increasing affluence of an important segment of the black population, and the ability of *Essence* to reach a huge proportion of this group. Lewis claimed it reached 46 percent of all black women between the ages of eighteen and forty-nine, and that most of these women were in the black upper-income group. *Essence* was a unique and dependable way for advertisers to reach an increasingly important market. To build on this profitability, Lewis took an important step in 1980—he set up a direct marketing operation in conjunction with the magazine. Called Essence Direct Mail, it began with an eighteen-page catalog mailed at random to a sample of 20,000 *Essence* subscribers. As Lewis noted, "Direct Mail is a booming market, and, to my knowledge, there are no other specifically black mail order houses operating now." Lewis had found another potentially important niche in the black market.

By 1988, Lewis had built a rather robust little communications empire. Circulation of *Essence* had climbed to 850,000, and profits remained very high. The mail-order business was a success, and Lewis had also purchased television station WKBW, the ABC affiliate in Buffalo, New York, for $65 million. It was the largest of about a dozen television stations owned by blacks in the United States. Years before, Lewis had expressed a dream of creating a black-owned media giant, and by 1988 he was well on his way to achieving that goal. Essence Communications had revenues of $31 million in 1987, and Lewis expected them to be between $45 and $50 million in 1988. It was the twentieth largest black business in America in 1987, and if Lewis' projections were accurate, it would climb to about tenth largest in 1988. Edward Lewis had come a long way from the young management trainee in New York City twenty years before. No wonder he could say: "I'm a capitalist. I believe in the system." (**B**. *Time*, May 4, 1970; *Newsweek*, May 11, 1970; *National Review*, November 8, 1974; *Advertising Age*, July 28, 1975, April 9, 1977, August 11, 1980; *Essence*, May 1980; *Black Enterprise*, June 1980, June 1988; *Who's Who among Black Americans*, 1986; Toronto *Globe & Mail*, May 24, 1988.)

LEWIS, REGINALD F. (December 7, 1942–   ). Arbitrager and conglomerate executive, TLC Group, Incorporated. Move over Donald Trump,[†] look out Carl Icahn,[†] here comes Reginald Lewis. Wall Street and black America were stunned in 1987 when Lewis, a black attorney and hitherto bit player in the high-stakes game of arbitrage and deal making, netted the largest offshore leveraged buyout (LBO) in business history. His TLC Group first sold its holdings in McCall Pattern Company for a staggering 90-to-1 return on its original investment and then invested the proceeds and more to finance the $985-million purchase of Beatrice International Food Company. In the twinkling of an eye, TLC Group became by far the largest firm owned by a black American, with revenues of $2.5 billion. In the previous year, the largest black-owned firm, the venerable Johnson Publishing Company, owners of *Ebony, Jet*, and a number of other interests, had sales of $173.5 million. TLC Group, the sixth largest black company that year, had revenues of just $63 million. As Lewis later commented: "It was something like the gnat swallowing the elephant, which frankly appealed to me."

Lewis was born in Baltimore, Maryland, and raised along with five half-brothers and sisters in what Lewis called a "tough but stimulating neighborhood" in the city. His mother and her children lived for many years with Lewis' grandparents, who played an influential role in his upbringing. Lewis went to neighborhood schools, where he excelled in baseball, football, and basketball. Until he was fifteen, Lewis assumed that he would make a career in professional sports, retire when he was thirty, and then become a lawyer or businessman. That summer, however, he got a high-paying job as a waiter in a Baltimore country club, and he was able to play less and less baseball. Realizing that money was more important to him than athletics, he gave up his earlier dreams. Even as a teenager he had an eye for value. His mother later recalled that when Lewis was sixteen he wanted to buy an expensive pair of loafers. His mother demurred, but Lewis insisted, saying, "Mother, they are worth every penny I'm going to pay for them." The shoes, it turned out, lasted Lewis through the rest of high school, four years of college, and three years of law school.

Lewis went on to Virginia State University, where he played quarterback on the football team for a year, until he injured his shoulder. What really captivated him, what was, in his own words "love at first sight," was, of all things, basic economics. He thereupon focused all his energies on studying, and he compiled an enviable record at Virginia State. From there, Lewis went on to Harvard Law School, where he specialized in securities law. After graduating in 1968, he worked for the New York firm of Paul Weiss Rifkind Wharton & Garrison. He did well, but the work did little to fuel Lewis' entrepreneurial ambitions. He left in 1970, before finding out whether he would become a partner and before his pay got so high he would not be able to afford to leave. In that year he became a partner in Murphy, Thorp & Lewis, the first black law firm on Wall Street.

After three years with that firm, Lewis decided to start his own company— Lewis & Clarkson—to specialize in venture capital work. In that role Lewis was very successful, helping corporations such as Aetna, Equitable, and General Foods lend money to minority-owned firms. Lewis felt in later years that this work sharpened his appreciation for the "quantitative aspects of business and how businesses are analyzed." He had received no formal business training, and he felt his interaction with a number of bright MBA's, both in the minority businesses and in the large corporations, gave him an invaluable education. After a decade of this, however, Lewis became bored. "There was not a lot I could do with the law firm besides making a good living unless I did the deals myself," he recalled.

In 1983 Lewis started TLC Group, and a year later, he took $1 million in cash and a $24-million loan and bought the McCall Pattern Company, a 113-year-old sewing-pattern firm that was suffering from a shrinking market and rapidly declining profitability. Most analysts at the time thought it was a poor move on Lewis' part, but he proved them wrong. As he later said, "A lot of people had written off [McCall Pattern Company] as not having much of a future. The more I researched the facts, the more I thought it had a great future." The biggest advantage Lewis saw for McCall was that the shrinking market left it free of serious competition, an aspect he intended to capitalize upon. He developed a line of knitting patterns and began plans to export them to China, and he branched into greeting cards, using McCall's distribution network. After Lewis had run the company for three and a half years, it showed a profit of $14 million. In all its previous years of operation, the profits had never exceeded $6.5 million. Then, in a recapitalization plan in December 1986, McCall paid stockholders $19 million. All of this activity made the formerly weak concern a target for takeover. In the summer of 1987, Lewis sold McCall Pattern to Britain's John Crowther Group for $63 million in cash, at which time it also absorbed $32 million in debt. Lewis, who had invested $1 million in McCall, had sold it for ninety times what he had paid for it. This astonishing achievement caught the notice of Wall Street, in particular Michael Milken,[†] Drexel Burnham Lambert's mastermind of leveraged buyout financing.

Without batting an eye, Lewis set out after bigger game. He found that Beatrice International Food Company was available, and he determined to make a bid for it. He put the deal together, arranged much of the financing, and submitted a bid to Beatrice. At that point, Milken invited Lewis out to his office in Beverly Hills, where, upon his arrival, Milken suggested they work on something together. Lewis replied, "Mike, I just bid $950 million for Beatrice. How about that?'' Milken's precise reaction is not recorded, but he and Drexel Burnham quickly took 35 percent of the action on Beatrice. Although Lewis welcomed Milken's assistance, all connected with the deal agree that Lewis himself masterminded it. Before submitting the bid, Lewis already had signed agreements to dispose of three of Beatrice International's units for nearly $430 million. He financed the rest of the deal with a $450-million line of credit from Manufacturers Hanover Trust and the profits from the McCall sale.

When the deal went through in August 1987, Lewis acquired a massive operation. With sixty-four separate companies in thirty-one countries, it had over 20,000 employees. To put that latter figure in some perspective, Johnson Publishing, previously the largest black-owned firm, had just over 1,800 employees. Lewis had acquired one of the giants of world food production, and Lewis found himself running an empire that ranged from the manufacture of ice cream in Italy to the making of potato chips in Ireland. And it was another venerable, mainstream American firm that Lewis had acquired. Beatrice Foods, the parent firm of Beatrice International, the thirty-sixth largest industrial corporation in America, manufactured over 8,000 product lines under more than 200 different brand names. In the early 1980s Beatrice had acquired other food giants, picking up Northwest Industries in 1981 and the giant Esmark (formerly Swift & Company) in 1984. Esmark had in 1983 acquired another food giant, Norton Simon, Incorporated. Beatrice had used the LBO technique to acquire these various firms and had, in the process, accumulated an enormous debt load. In a complex series of maneuvers, Donald P. Kelly, formerly head of Esmark joined with the Wall Street firm of Kohlberg, Kravis[†] and Roberts[†] to engineer a leveraged buyout of Esmark. As a result, Beatrice needed to sell off some portion of these recent acquisitions to finance the purchases. This opened the door for Lewis' acquisition.

Some observers questioned whether Lewis had the background or ability to run an operation like Beatrice International, but others were confident he did. A managing director at Drexel Burnham said, "Reg is a tough, aggressive guy. He's going to be a highly successful fellow." Most agree that he is strong willed and that he pursues what he wants with utter confidence. Lewis approached the job as a corporate strategist, leaving the day-to-day operations to the managers already in place. As *Fortune* (January 4, 1988) commented, "Lewis is expert at getting people to devote their best energies to a problem they may not have recognized." A partner in one of TLC Group's law firms concurred, "He has a way of making people set their goals a little higher, and helps them see what is possible if they spend a little more energy."

Lewis was obviously very proud of his successful buyout of Beatrice, but the subsequent media focus on his skin color made him very uncomfortable. There was a tendency for both the black and white media to refer to him as the "Jackie Robinson of Wall Street," the man who broke the color barrier in large-scale mergers and acquisitions and leveraged buyouts. In an interview with *Black Enterprise* (June 1988), Lewis said in response to the above description, "I really don't spend a lot of time thinking about that." At another time he said,

"I'm trying not to take that too seriously, it's tough enough to operate without the added pressure that if I make a mistake, I let down 30 million people."

Yet Lewis is very concerned with the fate of blacks in America, and he was one of Reverend Jesse Jackson's largest contributors in his run for the presidency in 1988. Lewis had first encountered Jackson in 1984, when Lewis was engineering the McCall deal and Jackson was making his first try at the presidency. They became close friends, and Jackson even claimed that Lewis got his courage to tackle Wall Street from watching Jackson try for the presidency. "It came to Reg that if I could function in that environment against those odds," Jackson said, "then he could function in the Wall Street environment against *those* odds." Whether or not that was true, Lewis did develop a deep admiration for Jackson:

I believe in the man. I also believe that the country really needs leadership. [Jackson] has a vision of what the country should be. That's not to say I agree with everything Jackson says—I don't. But he has a clear vision of the direction in which he wants to take the country, and it's one that I share. (*Black Enterprise*, January 1988)

Whether Lewis' vision is exactly like Jackson's "rainbow coalition" is not clear. What is clear is that Lewis' vision of the future for blacks in American business is quite different from that of other prominent black business leaders like Edward Gardner[†] and Dick Griffey.[†] Both Gardner and Griffey feel that black-owned businesses are the lifeblood of the black community, and they fear that the tendency of the most talented of young blacks to enter mainstream corporations will doom the residents of the black ghetto to remain an underclass in America. In response to this view, Lewis pointed out that, in the 1940s and later, "you had great men like John Johnson[†] and later Berry Gordy,[†] and many, many others who started their businesses from scratch. That was fine. In fact, that was the way most companies were built in those days, black or white." But now, Lewis thinks, there are new and greater opportunities for blacks. Discussing his ability to obtain financing for massive takeovers of large corporations, Lewis said, "It's reassuring to know that the market will reward performance notwithstanding the problems that our society continues to have with Americans of African descent moving into the mainstream." Yet, he did not feel these "problems" were of great consequence. As far as whether it was possible for blacks to achieve success in the white corporate world, he said, "I think the sky is the limit. When it comes to African-Americans, I think our experience in this country puts us in a position to know that you achieve through very, very hard work, and that's very much in vogue these days." Horatio Alger wrote popular stories in the nineteenth century which extolled the ability of bright and plucky young men to achieve fame and fortune in the capitalist system. With Reginald Lewis, it seems that Alger has been reborn a black man. (**B.** *Business Week*, June 3, 1985, August 24, 1987; Harry C. McDean, "Beatrice: The Historical Profile of an American-Styled Conglomerate," in H. C. Dethloff and C. J. Pusateri, eds., *American Business History Case Studies*, 1987; *Black Enterprise*, June 1987, June 1988; *Fortune*, September 14, 1987, January 4, 1988; *Who's Who among Black Americans*, 1988.)

LLEWELLYN, JAMES BRUCE (July 16, 1927–   ). Entrepreneur and public official, Fedco Stores, Coca-Cola Bottling Company of Philadelphia, Queen City Broadcasting, Overseas Private Investment Corporation. In the 1980s, rock star Bruce Springsteen was often known simply by his sobriquet—"The Boss." For many blacks in the 1970s and 1980s, there was another Bruce who was known to them as "the Boss"—J. Bruce Llewellyn. And with good reason. Perhaps no other black businessmen has ever had a career to rival Llewellyn's. True, there were magnificently powerful older black businessmen like John H. Johnson* and even Berry Gordy,* who made a fortune from merchandising aspects of black culture to white America, and to blacks themselves. There was also a younger generation of black business leaders—Edward Lewis,[†] Reginald Lewis,[†] and Thomas Burrell[†]—who were making a fortune as blacks moved into the mainstream of white America. But Llewellyn, well there has never been anybody else quite like him. A successful businessman, he made fortunes with businesses that served the black community along with ones that served the broader public. He was also a public official who served in important, sometimes high-profile, positions. He was as close as the black business community has come to a Business Roundtable–type businessman. Llewellyn even had a bit of show business in him. In several of his economic endeavors he collaborated with Julius Erving, the charismatic "Dr. J" of professional basketball, and Bill Cosby, the most popular television star and performer in America. This "boss" did it all.

Bruce Llewellyn was born in Harlem, New York City, the son of recent immigrants to America from Jamaica. His parents, who came to the United States in 1921, were ambitious, highly motivated people, who wanted the best for themselves and their two children. During these years, his father worked as a Linotype operator for the old *New York Herald Tribune*. After two years, they moved from Harlem to suburban Westchester County, where they settled in White Plains, a predominantly white, middle-class environ. Llewellyn recalled, "Basically I grew up like everybody else in a segregated section of an integrated neighborhood." That is, although White Plains had a few blacks, and those who lived there were not segregated in a black area, they, nonetheless, tended to congregate near one another. But Llewellyn went to integrated schools, and he felt this was an important reason for his later success. "It's important that you have no sense of inferiority about what you're learning or about your abilities," he said. "In the real world you're up against everybody, so you ought to know if you can play or not."

Llewellyn's parents were great believers in the work ethic, and they instilled this in Bruce and his sister, who became a New York District Supreme Court judge. Even in his early years, Bruce Llewellyn worked in his father's bar and restaurant in White Plains and sold magazines and Fuller Brush products. "My father used to tell me that this is a great country with great opportunity but that you're going to have to work twice as hard to get half as much.'' In 1943, when he was sixteen, Llewellyn joined the U.S. Army and pursued advancement there with the same determination and zeal he demonstrated in later life. By the time he was nineteen, he had made company commander, and when he came home in 1948, at just twenty-one years of age, he took his severance pay from the army and opened and operated a liquor store in Harlem while he attended medical school. He wanted to become a hospital administrator, but he soon changed his mind and decided to pursue a career in law. After getting his B.A. from the City University of New York, he continued on at New York Law School, where he received his J.D. in 1960. In the meantime, Llewellyn also picked up an MBA degree at Columbia University and a degree in public administration from New York University.

When he got his law degree in 1960, Llewellyn decided to go into politics and government service, feeling he would have his best career advancement in that area. As he later noted, ''You got involved in politics, which in turn got you a job in city, state, or federal government. You weren't going to get a job with some major Wall Street firm, that's for sure.'' This was before the civil rights movement began to put pressure on the white establishment in the North to open up career opportunities to blacks; the most Llewellyn believed he could hope for was to be appointed a judge. He entered New York government in 1961 in the District Attorney's office, where he had worked as a student assistant while attending law school. He also was a partner in his own small law firm during this time. He then moved on to the city's Housing and Redevelopment Board in the mid–1960s. From there, Llewellyn went on to become regional director for the Small Business Administration and later executive director of the Upper Manhattan Small Business Development Corporation. Then, in 1968, he became deputy commissioner of the city's Housing Commission. Llewellyn had come a long way, and it was clear that a judgeship was within his grasp by that point. It was also clear to him, however, from his work in the Small Business Administration, that the business world had opened up for blacks in ways that had not been true a decade earlier. Llewellyn determined to take advantage of this new, more favorable business climate.

He had also become frustrated with the public sector and its leviathan bureaucracy:

Most of the time, I found the places loaded with bureaucratic red tape and with a bunch of dumb people who retired from the moment they got the job. And they sure didn't want to hear a new idea about doing something. That really threw them into a tizzy. I decided the first chance I got, I was getting out of this. (*Black Enterprise,* September 1986)

His chance came in 1969, when a former legal client told him that Fedco Foods Corporation, a chain of ten food stores in the economically devastated South

Bronx, was for sale. Although the store chain was quite profitable and had experienced significant growth, buyers shied away because of the stores' location. Llewellyn was undeterred. The main problem he had, however, was raising the $3-million asking price for the chain. Llewellyn went to a long-time friend, Robert Towbin, who was a managing partner with the investment banking firm of L. F. Rothchild, Unterberg, Towbin. What Llewellyn proposed was, in effect, a leveraged buyout before leveraged buyouts became the rage. A leveraged buyout is a method of taking over a company by issuing securities backed by the target corporation's assets to finance the purchase. Towbin remarked that "Fedco was really one of the first leveraged buyouts that was ever done, before they became popular." He arranged for Llewellyn to meet with the Prudential Insurance Company to arrange financing. "It was a cooperative effort between the buyer, seller, and lender," Towbin recalled.

It was still not easy. Llewellyn had to mortgage his house and cash in everything he owned, but Prudential did give him a $2.5-million loan to make the purchase. They also gave him a piece of advice: "They told me," said Llewellyn, "if it doesn't work we can guarantee that it will hurt you a hell of a lot more than it will hurt us." He reflected, "You had to learn or go out of business." Llewellyn was determined he would not fail. He kept the existing management at Fedco, including the former owner. As Fedco became more and more profitable—by 1983 it had sales of $85 million and had expanded to twenty-seven stores—Llewellyn's success greatly affected both the black and white business communities. Very few blacks, prior to this, had gotten multimillion-dollar financing, and Llewellyn showed that blacks could be successful. Towbin said, "Bruce established for a lot of people the fact that you back a black businessman and it could be successful." Llewellyn's success helped open up opportunities for the next generation of black business leaders.

As Llewellyn became a success with Fedco, he was called upon to assume greater visibility in the black business community. One of these roles involved the troubled Freedom National Bank in Harlem. The bank, founded by Hall of Fame baseball star Jackie Robinson was, by 1971, in desperate need of help. It was $1.9 million in the red and facing bankruptcy. Robinson asked Llewellyn to join the board of Freedom National, then, when Robinson died two years later, Llewellyn succeeded him as chairman. Llewellyn, while still running Fedco, beefed up the bank's management staff and loan portfolio, and got the backing of such heavyweights in the white business community as Goldman, Sachs, Morgan Stanley, and the Ford Foundation to help recapitalize the bank. By the early 1980s, Llewellyn looked to move in a new business direction. He had long been impressed with the business possibilities of becoming a bottler for one of the major soft-drink manufacturers. "I knew back in 1974 that I wanted to own a bottling company," Llewellyn said.

The problem was getting one. They were highly profitable enterprises, and very scarce. Llewellyn initially pursued his interest with officials at Coca-Cola, but when that did not seem to be going anywhere, he made a bid for a Pepsi-

Cola franchise that covered practically the whole state of Connecticut. Three days before closing, however, the seller backed down, and Llewellyn was forced to continue playing the waiting game. During this time, he had a number of other interesting and attractive offers. In 1978, President Carter asked Llewellyn to become secretary of the army, but Llewellyn declined, suggesting that Carter appoint Clifford Alexander, his former law partner. A short time later, Carter called back and offered Llewellyn a job with the Overseas Private Investment Corporation (OPIC), a fifteen-year-old institution which had been started under the Nixon administration to provide insurance underwriting for American corporations conducting industrial operations in foreign countries. Llewellyn accepted the attractive offer. It was, first of all, in the business field, which would enhance Llewellyn's own profile in that area, and, second, it was a challenge that few blacks had ever been offered. The job involved negotiating with the heads of state and foreign ministers on some twenty foreign projects. Llewellyn made the organization far more efficient than it had been in the past, distributing $65 million in financing for projects and issuing $1.12 billion in risk insurance to corporations. The agency took in record profits during the years Llewellyn headed it.

With the Reagan administration coming to power in 1981, Llewellyn had to leave the OPIC post, but he was even more determined to make his dream a reality. When he returned to the South Bronx, Llewellyn teamed with Julius Erving and Bill Cosby, and the three of them began to push for a Coca-Cola bottling franchise. They were immeasurably helped in their quest by a month-long boycott staged in 1981 by Reverend Jesse Jackson and his Operation PUSH (People United to Save Humanity). In its settlement with PUSH, Coca-Cola agreed to increase the participation of blacks in the company's business. Still, things did not happen overnight. It took two more years, but finally Llewellyn got his bottling company—or at least a piece of one. In a summer of 1983, Llewellyn, Erving, and Cosby purchased 36 percent of the Coca-Cola Bottling Company of New York. This made the group the largest single stockholder in the company, and it secured Llewellyn a seat on the board and the chairmanship of its subsidiary, the Philadelphia Coca-Cola Bottling Company.

In 1984, Llewellyn sold the Fedco stores, getting $20 million for the chain. With that money, Llewellyn made his first move toward media ownership; he headed an investment group of black businessmen who joined with other minority investors to build Channel 36, KTTY-TV in San Diego, California. The investors, however, did not see eye to eye, and after a time the group of blacks from the East Coast, including Llewellyn, pulled out. "I don't like having a lot of partners," he said. "The fewer the better." The following year, however, was to be a red-letter one for Llewellyn.

In 1985, Bruce Llewellyn fulfilled two goals: he got his own bottling plant and he finally controlled a major-market, network-affiliated television station. Ever since Llewellyn had bought into New York Coke, he had been negotiating with officials of the parent company to take over the Philadelphia bottling subsidiary. By the end of 1985, the terms for the purchase of the Philadelphia Coca-Cola Bottling Company were set. The three men converted their New York Coke shares, got a loan of $75 million from various financial institutions, and bought out the Philadelphia operation. It was at the time the fifteenth largest Coke bottling plant in the country, and the fourth largest black business in America. Over the next several years, Llewellyn increased business at the plant 300 percent as a result of adding thirty-six new routes and also as a result of the enormous popularity of Julius Erving in Philadelphia, where he played basketball. In 1987, with sales of $166 million, Philadelphia Coca-Cola Bottling had moved up to the eighth largest bottler in the Coke system, and it was now the third largest black-owned business.

In 1985, there were already eight other black-owned television stations in America, but most were small, independent UHF operations. The station Llewellyn pursued was different. When Capital Cities Communications had purchased the ABC Television network, the Federal Communications Commission had required that it divest itself of WKBW-TV (Channel 7), the ABC-affiliate station in Buffalo, New York. Putting together a coalition of investors to buy the station, Llewellyn enlisted Edward Lewis[†] of Essence Communications, Julius Erving, former U.S. Ambassador McDonald Henry, auto dealer Dick Gideon, executive recruiter Richard Clarke, and several others in a new company called Queen City Broadcasting. They put in a highly leveraged bid of $65 million for the station, but another bidder had already offered over $90 million. The one advantage Llewellyn and his group had going for them was that if Capital Cities–ABC sold to a group of minority businessmen it would get a tax certificate worth $30 million. Llewellyn and his group got the station. Two years later, WBKW-TV ranked first among the seven non-cable stations in its market, and was a highly profitable entity.

When the sale was consummated, there was some criticism, most of it focusing on the highly leveraged nature of the buyout. Some businessmen said they felt Llewellyn and his group were getting in over their heads with the purchase, but Llewellyn dismissed the idea. "That whole notion is ridiculous," he said. "In the first place, we bought the station for $30 million less than it was worth at the time. The leverage is not really important." In 1987, Llewellyn arranged with Goldman, Sachs and Company to help him raise $55 million by selling debentures to private investors for Queen City Broadcasting. He said the cash would be used to acquire new stations and to pay off debt.

Bruce Llewellyn, an almost larger-than-life—six-foot-five-and-one-half-inches tall and 250-pound—man, effects a casual and modest appearance, but he is a tremendously driven and ambitious man. Richard Clarke, a longtime friend, said of Llewellyn, "When you eat with Bruce, as soon as you are done, he'll grab the plates, wash them, and come back with the brandy and cigars. He's always anxious to get on to the next step." Llewellyn's outlook is tough and determined, but decidedly upbeat. "My father always told me," he told *Business Week*, "that brains and education can defeat prejudice within society."

Edward Lewis, another business associate and friend, said of Llewellyn, "He's a very, very smart guy who can get to the heart of whatever the problem or situation is." Bruce Llewellyn, in the 1980s, was leading black businessmen into an area that was relatively new to them—the general market. Llewellyn himself was keenly aware of what he was doing: "In the old days black business people had to be based in the black community," he said. "You had generations of the John Johnsons and the Berry Gordys who expanded the black community from local neighborhoods to the national community. Now we're dealing with the entire community. I've never really been a general marketer." But by 1988 he was, and a highly successful one to boot. (**B**. *Who's Who among Black Americans*, 1986; *Black Enterprise*, March, September, 1986, June 1987, June 1988; *Forbes*, May 5, 1986; *Business Week*, November 16, 1987.)

LORENZO, FRANCISCO ANTHONY (FRANK) (May 19, 1940–   ). Airline company executive, Texas Air Corporation, Continental Airlines, Eastern Airlines, People Express, New York Air. They either love Frank Lorenzo or they hate him. His admirers, largely from the business press in the United States, shower him with praise: he "led the industry into a new competitive era," said one. Another wrote that Lorenzo's Texas International was "the airline that pioneered the discount revolution in fares." *Time* said, "Lorenzo has become the flying ace in the new era of unregulated airline routes and prices." Carl R. Pohlad, a Minneapolis banker and a director of Texas Air, called him "one of the most able business leaders I've met." A Wall Street banker put it even more succinctly in the *Wall Street Journal*, "Frank Lorenzo is as smart as they come."

Others, particularly labor leaders, have a very different view of Lorenzo. Captain Henry A. Duffy, head of the Air Line Pilots Association, said, "We don't trust him, frankly, we think he's a little short on corporate integrity." An airline attendant at Continental said, "We're treated like cattle, just like the passengers are." A ticket agent at Continental Airlines said about him, "Lorenzo is a snake in the grass. He's in this to make money and destroy our airline." John Pincavage, an airline analyst for Paine Webber said about labor leaders and Lorenzo's employees, "They view Lorenzo as Darth Vader, no matter what this man does, he is perceived as being up to no good." Lorenzo himself merely shrugged when asked about all of these comments, "I don't think I'm controversial. I'm a convenient symbol. Deregulation is controversial."

Frank Lorenzo was born in the Queens section of New York City to parents who had earlier immigrated to America from Spain. His father was a hairdresser who later owned his own beauty parlor in Manhattan. Frank was educated in the Rego Park section of Queens where he grew up, and after graduation from high school he studied economics at Columbia University. Lorenzo put himself through school by working as a part-time salesman at Macy's and by driving a Coca-Cola truck. For the latter job he had to join the Teamster's Union, an experience Lorenzo has used endlessly to prove he was not antiunion. After graduating from Columbia in 1961, Lorenzo went to Harvard's Graduate School of Business where he got an MBA in 1963.

Although Lorenzo has had a lifelong love of flying and airplanes—he took his first airplane trip on TWA to London when he was fifteen—his interest has always been financially oriented. When he returned from London, for example, he used his savings to buy stock in TWA; only later did he invest in flying lessons to get his private pilot's license. Lorenzo was able to combine his interest in finance and flying with his first job after he left Harvard. Taking a position as a financial analyst for his old love, TWA, he remained there from 1963 to 1965. He then worked for a year in the financial analysis department at Eastern Airlines. These jobs did not satisfy Lorenzo's enterpreneurial urges, so in 1966 he left Eastern to join with Robert Carney, an old classmate from Harvard, in setting up a small financial advisory firm: Lorenzo, Carney & Company, with Lorenzo as chairman. Carney, who had more experience on Wall Street, nonetheless deferred to Lorenzo in this venture. As he later remarked, the firm was "not Carney Lorenzo" because Carney was "shyer, more conservative, and less confrontational" than Lorenzo. Each invested $1,000 in the tiny venture, which was designed to bring Wall Street together with needy airlines. It was not a rousing success, but it did well enough to encourage Lorenzo to become more adventuresome.

Their next step, in 1969, was to form a holding company, Jet Capital Corporation, in which they each invested $35,000. Their announced goal was to become involved in aircraft leasing, but no sooner had they set up the business then a downturn came in the airline industry. As a result, few airlines were interested in leasing planes. As Carney put it, "[B]asically we were selling ourselves," rather than planes. This did not deter them, and in 1971 they had a public stock offering and raised about $1.5 million. As they sold themselves in the depressed airline market of the early 1970s, the two young men found that their best investment opportunities lay with the small, regional carriers, which had suffered more from the economic downturn than the majors. Deciding that they wanted to take over one of these regional airlines, Lorenzo and Carney set their sights on Mohawk Airlines in Utica, New York, but they were rebuffed in their attempts. Nevertheless, they had impressed the banking community, if not the airlines, with their activities over a number of years, and, as a result, Chase Manhattan Bank literally dropped a regional carrier right in their laps.

Texas International Airlines (TXI), a small, regional carrier in Texas, owed Chase Manhattan a good deal of money. Chase, in turn, called in Lorenzo, Carney & Company as $15,000-a-month consultants to see what could be done about the situation. The airline had been the butt of a great deal of sarcasm in Texas for a number of years. It had started out in 1947 as Trans-Texas Airways (TTA), flying a bunch of obsolete planes on low-density routes. Because TTA flew a lot of DC-3's, which were unpressurized and had to fly at low altitudes, Texans developed a series of uncomplimentary nicknames for the airline. Keying on the initials, they called it Tree Top Airlines, Tinker Toy Airways, Try Try

Again, and Thankful to Arrive, among others. Because of this unfavorable image, TTA contributed to the later Lorenzo myth. According to that myth, Lorenzo took over an airline whose planes were held together with baling wire and spit, and transformed it into a modern carrier. But Lorenzo, speaking of his and Carney's impression of TXI when they examined it, said, "Our feeling was that it was not a hopeless situation at all. It had basically a very good route structure, good people, and good equipment." What had gotten TXI into trouble, in truth, was the fact that they had upgraded the airline too quickly in the late 1960s, they were hit by the sharp recession of the early 1970s, and they lost over $20 million in a period of five years, a massive amount for a company with just $6 million in stockholders' equity.

Generally TXI had been profitable, with the support of generous subsidies from the Civil Aeronautics Board (CAB) until 1967, when it was acquired by Minnesota Enterprises (MEI), a midwestern bus-line operator. MEI undertook a highly optimistic and very expensive expansion plan. By 1971, TXI had a new fleet of fifteen DC–9's, and a whopping debt service. Losing money at a rate of from $6 to $7 million a year, by 1971 it had a negative net worth of $4.5 million. Lorenzo and Carney's solution was to put together an investment package that revolved around Lorenzo's pet tactics—leverage and control. Building around Jet Capital's $1.5 million in cash, they put together a $35-million equity-financing plan that gave Jet Capital's 24 percent of TXI's stock, and 58 percent of its voting power. In January 1972, Jet Capital applied to the CAB for approval to take control of TXI. The CAB granted its approval in August, and Lorenzo became president and chief executive officer of TXI, and Carney became executive vice president.

Lorenzo now had to put TXI's tottering house of cards in order. It was no mean task, but he had certain advantages many analysts failed to recognize. A major difficulty for Lorenzo was that he had absolutely no experience in the day-to-day operations of an airline, but he pushed forward with characteristic alacrity, nonetheless. Over a short period of time, Lorenzo restructured the company's debt, eliminated unprofitable routes, added more lucrative flights, and purchased additional planes to complete the modernization of TXI's fleet. From 1973 to 1975, TXI earned modest profits, but then a four-and-a-half-month strike in 1975 totally shut down the airline at a critical juncture. At about the same time, TXI found itself embroiled in antitrust litigation, a case which carried over from the previous management. Still, Lorenzo was not deterred, and in 1977 he boldly instituted what he referred to as "peanuts fares," offering deep discounts of up to 50 percent on a number of low-density routes. As a result, TXI's earnings mushroomed, doubling in 1977 and nearly doubling again in 1978. In 1978 the company paid its first dividend in eleven years. Everyone was agog at Lorenzo's acumen, brilliance, and daring. He was viewed as a pioneer of discount fares, and the champion competitor in the new deregulated American airline system. Although there was some veracity to this myth, it also masked some important truths.

TXI's profitability during the early years of Lorenzo's administration was not based on some sort of alchemy he performed. In fact, he took over TXI at a very propitious time. Just before he took over, the outlook for regional airlines improved markedly partly because air travel picked up significantly, but mostly because the CAB voted to double the $24 million in annual subsidies that it was paying to nine regional airlines for their losses on short-haul routes. By 1978, when the CAB voted to discontinue TXI's payments, it had forked out some $50 million to TXI, which had declared about $20 million in profits during this same time. Without the subsidies TXI under Lorenzo would not have been profitable. During the strike in 1975, TXI was kept afloat, not by Lorenzo's brilliance, but by industry strike-aid payments. It was during this time that Lorenzo trimmed unprofitable routes, laid off a good portion of the work force, and refinanced TXI's debt. TXI emerged from the strike stronger than before, and there was no mystery why. Next, Lorenzo went to the CAB for permission to reduce his fares on certain low-density routes. The CAB, under chairman John Robson, had wanted to deregulate the airline industry for several years, and he jumped at the chance to suspend its rules for Lorenzo. So, as Dallas writer Michael Innis has stated, "With a CAB subsidy in one hand and a CAB dispensation to explore the free market in the other, Lorenzo and Texas International earned more than $20 million over the next two years." Lorenzo's cozy ties with the CAB, the main government regulatory body for the industry, infuriated many other industry executives. This fury heightened in 1980 when Philip Bakes, Jr., who had been general counsel for the CAB when Lorenzo got his dispensation, joined TXI as executive vice president and chief operating officer.

Some characteristic traits of the airlines controlled by Lorenzo began to surface during the late 1970s. Although TXI was profitable, its service, safety, and on-time record were poor. Lorenzo achieved a remarkably high utilization of his fleet; the average daily operation of TXI's DC-9's rose to 10 hours, the highest in the industry. But its service to customers was notoriously poor, which resulted from Lorenzo's perception of service as being less important than fares. The Federal Aviation Administration's (FAA) complaint record on TXI was high: two-and-a-half times as many complaints as Continental between 1978 and 1980. In a poll of business travelers, TXI placed last in hospitality, and second to last in overall performance. In its Denver–Salt Lake City run, TXI's ontime record was dead last among seven competing airlines. These same complaints surfaced in each airline Lorenzo took over in the 1980s.

Lorenzo, who increasingly dreamed of creating an "empire in the sky," was not satisfied with controlling merely a regional carrier. As a result, in 1978, flush with profits from his peanuts fares, he pursued National Airlines, an airline three times the size of TXI. Industry observers were so shocked that *Forbes* (October 30, 1978) ran an article calling him "Lorenzo the Presumptuous." His try for National hinged on an important CAB move. Early in 1978, Congress passed the Airline Deregulation Act, giving the CAB the option to approve mergers between major carriers. With his pipeline to CAB officials, Lorenzo could be fairly certain of approval, but he was the first to test the new regulations, and this caused a tremendous stir in business circles. The *Wall Street Journal* commented that this was "the first case in regulated airline history in which a certificated airline sought approval of a non-negotiated acquisition of control of another certificated airline." Lorenzo had bought 9.2 percent of the stock in National by the summer of 1978, and he announced his intention of buying all the stock he could. Before long, TXI had 25 percent of National's stock. This frightened the larger airline's management, who sought the protection of both the CAB and a "white knight."

Lewis B. Maytag,* National's chairman, was furious at Lorenzo's temerity in attempting to take over his airline. The situation became increasingly tense when National's employees, who had gone through two lengthy strikes in four years, refused to support management. They, in fact, pleaded with Lorenzo to take over the airline. The airline machinists' newsletter summed up prevailing sentiment among National's employees that summer when it ran the following headline: "Texas International, Take Us, We're Yours." A National pilot was less sanguine, but he put the matter clearly: "It isn't that we think so much of Texas International, it's just that almost anybody else would be better than Maytag." Never again would a labor union welcome Lorenzo aboard. Maytag turned to Pan American Airways, which had long coveted National's domestic routes to supplement its international ones, as a white knight. Pan Am bid $350 million for National, which ended Lorenzo's takeover attempt. Lorenzo and TXI came out winners, though, since the merger battle had driven up the price of National's shares, and he was able to sell them back to the company for a hefty pretax profit of $46 million. Of TXI's $41 million in net income that year, less than $7 million came from operations. Nonetheless, this provided TXI and Lorenzo with cash reserves to tackle even bigger game.

Lorenzo was determined to take over one of the nation's larger airlines, reasoning that the new, deregulated world of the airways would ultimately result in what was called the two-airline theory. This theory had been formulated by academicians at CAB, many of whom were by then working for Lorenzo. They theorized that to survive, an airline had to achieve a "critical mass," and this would ultimately lead to two "ultra-efficient leviathans" which would dominate the industry. Lorenzo wanted to ensure that he was one of those leviathans. His next target was even more ambitious: TWA, fully ten times the size of TXI. In early 1979, Lorenzo purchased 4 percent of TWA's stock, and then he invited TWA chairman, Edwin Smart, to breakfast at the Hotel Carlyle. There, Lorenzo boldly proposed a takeover of TWA. Smart was so enraged that he stomped out of the Carlyle without eating. Lorenzo was undeterred—there were plenty of other airlines, and he had big plans.

Lorenzo's next step was to set up a holding company, called Texas Air Corporation, in September 1980. This firm established a subsidiary Lorenzo called New York Air to run a short-hop shuttle service to compete with Eastern

Airlines in the busy corridor between New York City and Washington, D.C. Again, success depended on getting approval from the CAB, and, as before, cooperation from the CAB was forthcoming. In December of that year, New York Air began offering $49 fares on weekdays, and $29 fares on weekends— only 55 cents more than a Greyhound bus fare. Lorenzo solidified his reputation as the nation's leading discounter. This was accomplished largely by driving down labor costs. New York Air recruited pilots, offering to pay about half the going rate, and the *Airline Pilot* magazine asserted that New York Air was "rotten to the core." But Lorenzo wanted more. Even though he possessed only a relatively weak regional carrier and an unproven, low-cost subsidiary, he still wanted to build his giant carrier, and he had the mammoth cash reserves to do so. Rumors circulated that a much bigger airline deal was in the works. This time the rumors were accurate.

In early 1981, Lorenzo and Texas Air purchased a 9.5-percent interest in Continental Airlines, the nation's tenth largest carrier. Continental had been developed under the innovative leadership of Robert Six, who had been one of the original rebels chafing under CAB regulations. The airline had prospered under Six's innovative, somewhat idiosyncratic, leadership, and it was renowned as one of the "premier service" airlines in America and a favorite of business travelers. But the Airline Deregulation Act of 1978 undermined the airline, as hordes of new competitors emerged to snipe at Continental's heels. Its financial situation continued to deteriorate in the late 1970s, when Six appointed Alvin L. Feldman, formerly of Frontier Airlines, as president. Feldman tried to trim Continental's costs, but to no avail. Lorenzo bought more and more of Continental's stock, and the airline's management felt it was under siege, a feeling shared by Continental's employees and their unions. Lorenzo's establishment of New York Air as a nonunion airline had been a red flag for the industry's unions, and when he attempted to take over Continental, they struck back with full fury. A massive battle was in the offing.

By early 1981, Lorenzo had acquired 48.5 percent of Continental's stock, and he stood ready to take control of the company. Alvin L. Feldman and the unions fought back with an unusual instrument—an Employee Stock Ownership Plan (ESOP). The pilots' union, which had a wealthy benefit fund with $115 million in assets, was behind the idea, and it would act as Continental's white knight in its fight with Lorenzo. Lorenzo fought back, calling the ESOP a "management-enrichment scheme." Suits and countersuits followed, in what *Fortune* called a "Wild West battle." Continental, meanwhile, was sustaining enormous losses, and the airline's bankers were becoming restive with the situation. Feldman, whose wife had died during these bitter negotiations, became depressed at the impending loss, and, after drafting a press release announcing the merger, he committed suicide in his office. In 1982 TXI was merged into Continental, which, in turn, was controlled by Texas Air.

When Lorenzo took control of Continental, it was not clear how much of a prize he had won. In its first year of operation, the newly merged airline generated a staggering $100 million in losses. Lorenzo, not without some justification, blamed high labor costs for these losses and was determined to wring concessions from the unions. In an effort to reduce labor costs, Lorenzo laid off 15 percent of the carrier's work force in March 1983. The pilots' union agreed to accept a number of significant concessions, amounting to $91 million, in their next contract. Lorenzo's response was that it was not enough, and he demanded further concessions. The first quarter of 1983 brought even more ruinous losses: $15 million on revenues of $318 million. The most critical situation, however, involved the machinists' union. Bitter negotiations ensued between the two sides, and the union ultimately walked out in August 1983. Lorenzo's response was to hire nonunion personnel and to keep the airline flying about 93 percent of its routes. As negotiations continued during the strike, Lorenzo took the unusual tactic of reducing his offer to the union each time they met, thereby ensuring there could be no settlement. Lorenzo had an audacious business plan in mind— on September 24, 1983, he announced that Continental was seeking reorganization under Chapter 11 of the federal bankruptcy laws.

This move automatically voided the existent labor contracts, and Lorenzo casually fired all 12,000 employees. He thereupon invited 4,000 of them to return to the fold, but he offered them wages at anywhere from 40 to 60 percent of their previous levels. The airline shut down for three days, and when it staggered back into operation it reduced the number of cities it serviced from seventy-eight to twenty-five with decreased fares, but it retained all the "frills" of full-service flights. Continental had emerged phoenix-like from the ashes, and it was viewed by many as the classic deregulation flying machine—nonunion with low labor costs and cheap fares, with a focus on more profitable, high-density routes. It was a stunning success. The new Continental Airlines flew under the protection of Chapter 11 for nearly three years, and it earned more than $150 million in profits during this time. Furthermore, with only 105 airplanes when it had declared bankruptcy, it had 147 three years later. Protected from its creditors and excused from union contracts, Continental could make massive profits and engage in significant growth and expansion. Widely hailed as another "Lorenzo miracle," Continental faced trouble when it reentered the postbankruptcy "real world."

Even before Continental emerged from the protection of bankruptcy, Lorenzo took further steps to create his leviathan "mega-carrier." In the summer of 1985 he bid for the mammoth TWA, but this time the airline unions were prepared. They clearly viewed Lorenzo as a union buster, and although he protested that "the enemy isn't Frank Lorenzo, but the new competitive environment," they ignored him. Consequently, when Carl Icahn,[†] the notorious corporate raider made a grab for TWA, both management and unions were receptive. Management agreed in principle to the merger, and the unions agreed to massive wage concessions to thwart Lorenzo. In August 1985, TWA's board unanimously rejected Lorenzo's bid and threw their lot in with Icahn. Several months later, Lorenzo tried to take over Frontier Airlines, but again he ran into extraordinarily strong union resistance. As a result, the airline was sold to People Express, owned by Donald C. Burr,[†] once the head of TXI.

It looked as if Lorenzo might be closed out by the unions wherever he turned, but in 1986 he found an airline whose employees hated their own president more than they feared Lorenzo—Eastern Airlines. Eastern was run by Frank Borman, a former astronaut who viewed himself as a charismatic leader. Borman, however, had been able to keep Eastern's head above water only by exacting large wage and salary concessions from his employees, with the promise that they were temporary. When he could not turn the airline around and he insisted on making the concessions permanent, he incurred the enmity of Charles Bryan, head of the machinists' union. Even though the machinists had, in effect, been locked out at Continental, Bryan announced that "I'd just as soon take my chances with Lorenzo," rather than deal with the hated Borman. In February 1986, Lorenzo put together a $640-million deal to acquire Eastern, with its fleet of 300 aircraft and its invaluable System One computer reservation system—a crucial tool for fare-juggling in the deregulated skies of the late 1980s.

Lorenzo's deal was generally regarded as a steal, as Eastern had a cash balance of $463 million, which was more than the amount of cash Texas Air had to put up to take it over. But Eastern was heavily in debt, with more than $3 billion in obligations, and Lorenzo was inheriting a bitter, highly unionized labor situation. Charles Bryan's hopes that Lorenzo would be easier to deal with than Borman were soon dashed. When he asked for a personal audience with Lorenzo after the takeover, Lorenzo rebuffed him, saying, "I do not talk to labor leaders," and he announced that he was determined to reduce the machinists' wages sharply and to alter what he considered counterproductive work rules. The new Eastern president, Philip Bakes, called the airline's labor costs a "cancer" that had to be reduced by 29 percent. Bryan declared an all-out-war on Lorenzo, saying, "This isn't union-busting 101, this is advanced union busting." The two sides were in for a long, bitter struggle.

None of this was working out as Lorenzo had hoped it would. For one thing, he could not yet build his mega-carrier. Since Eastern was strongly unionized and Lorenzo had broken the union at Continental, he could not physically merge the two airlines, because Eastern's unions would then be allowed to bargain for Continental's employees also. It was imperative for Lorenzo to break the union at Eastern if he was to achieve his dream. In the meantime, an ideal mate for Continental literally fell into Lorenzo's hands. People Express, the employee-owned, discount airline owned by Donald Burr, had been battered into bankruptcy by competition from Continental. In September 1986, Burr was forced to accept Lorenzo's offer of $300 million in cash and stock for People Express and its subsidiary, Frontier Airlines. This made Continental, with a massive fleet of 352 planes, a bonafide mega-carrier for the first time: the largest carrier in the United States, it accounted for about 20 percent of all American air travel. In addition, Lorenzo owned Eastern, with its 270 planes, and a large share of the American air-travel market.

But the war with Eastern's unions was a headline grabber. For over two years, the two sides went at each other in a manner not often seen in America since the 1930s. Lorenzo, demanding cuts of up to 60 percent in wages from the machinists, seemed intent on provoking a strike, perhaps to create the same situation as he had at Continental, when he took advantage of Chapter 11 to destroy the unions. Lorenzo, when questioned about this, casually dismissed it as "the figment of somebody's imagination." In the meantime, to cut back on what Lorenzo viewed as excessively high labor costs at Eastern, he continued to transfer Eastern assets to other portions of the Texas Air empire and to cut back on Eastern flights while building up Continental's service on the same routes. The most controversial of Lorenzo's moves was the sale of the System One computer system to Texas Air for just $100 million in paper payable in 2012. Since most analysts put a value of from $200 to $250 million on the system, and since Eastern's employees owned about 20 percent of a class of preferred stock, they complained that their interests were being ill-served by that transaction. When Lorenzo tried to spin off Eastern's highly lucrative Air Shuttle system, which linked New York with Boston and Washington, D.C., to another Texas Air subsidiary for $125 million in cash and a $100-million note, Bryan and the machinists' union went to federal court and blocked the move.

Fortune, in a 1988 article on Eastern's labor troubles, said it had become "perhaps the most troubled carrier in the often troubled industry." In 1987, Eastern posted losses of $182 million on revenues of $4.4 billion, and deficits were expected to be even bigger in 1988. Furthermore, characteristic of Lorenzo's airlines, Eastern finished dead last in on-time performance, and had the highest rate of passenger complaints of any airline except Continental—another Lorenzo airline. Most analysts agreed that the extraordinarily hostile labor-management relations at Eastern were at the heart of its problems. By 1988, 500 disgruntled pilots had left the organization, giving up their cherished seniority, and an additional 250 gave notice in the early months of that year. This caused the cancellation of hundreds of flights. The horrid situation at Eastern was simply a reflection of a generally demoralized airline empire. Texas Air, with sales of $8.5 billion in 1987, an increase of fully 92 percent from the previous year, suffered staggering losses of $466 million. Its shares, which had sold for as high as $47.75 in 1987, plunged to under $9. By July 1988, with his moves to break off large chunks of Eastern and sell them to other parts of Texas Air blocked, Lorenzo began to make more conciliatory moves toward the unions; he even requested a meeting with Charles Bryan. But he also began to hint about the possibility of filing for Chapter 11, since Eastern lost over $64 million in the first quarter of the year.

Lorenzo, whom *Fortune* in 1987 called "The New Master of the Skies" and *Business Month* called "Sky King," was looking much more vulnerable a year later. Not only was Eastern doing poorly, at least partially because of labor strife, but the nonunion Continental was underperforming even Eastern, losing a stunning $80 million in the first quarter of 1988. Since many had viewed

Continental as the ultimate deregulation flying machine, the logical question was: why was it not making money? The answers are many and complex, but part of the problem was Lorenzo's management style. Practicing what he calls "eclectic" management, Lorenzo gave a great deal of freedom to his lieutenants. But this did not work well with airlines, which need much day-to-day supervision and responsibility. Nor have Lorenzo's vicious attacks on unions been constructive in the long run, since they have tended to alienate his workers from management, making it very difficult to achieve the kinds of productivity that come from "labor entrepreneurship," the Japanese management style which has become so popular in America. But, perhaps at the heart of Lorenzo's problems has been his cavalier attitude toward passenger service. Continuing to believe that airline sales are primarily price-driven rather than service-driven, passenger service has deteriorated badly on all of Lorenzo's lines. As brand loyalty erodes, he attempts to win them back with further fare reductions; the most recent of these have been his Mas$aver fares in 1987, which were a full 40 percent lower than his competitors' "supersaver" fares. He won back some passengers, but he had to carry them at a loss, which meant he had to further reduce labor costs. A vicious cycle had been set in motion. As a further attempt to salvage his airline empire, Lorenzo was forced to sell Eastern's prized shuttle service to Donald Trump[†] in the fall of 1988 for $365 million. A short time later, Lorenzo jolted the flying public by announcing sudden and drastic increases in fares and by eliminating whole classes of discounts at Continental and Eastern. The original airline discounter, Lorenzo was the last holdout. When he announced his higher fares, the marketing chief at Delta Airlines commented, "You won't see any more bloodbaths in fares."

The result was a demoralized, dispirited airline empire. Continental's pilots are paid about half the industry average. Company veterans complain of the fatigue and stress of flying up to 90 hours a month. One pilot complained, "If I continue, I'll be do so fatigued I won't make it to age 60." The flight attendants fared no better. Another pilot commented, "Continental knows it can get good-looking, hard-working bodies. It expects that they'll do the job for one or two years, then burn out and leave." The exodus of personnel from Continental and Eastern was enormous in 1987 and 1988, and most analysts did not think it would improve. Labor-management relations at Eastern remained so bitter that there were serious questions about its effect on the safety of the airline. Although the FAA gave Texas Air a clean bill of health in a extraordinary six-week inquiry into the safety of Eastern and Continental, Transportation Secretary James Burnley warned that because of the labor strife, "I don't think there's any basis for characterizing (the FAA report) as a clean bill of health for Eastern Air Lines."

Nor was Eastern winning any prizes from the public for its customer service. An angry Ross Lawrence, president of a Toronto, Canada firm, wrote Lorenzo to complain about his treatment on what he expected to be a pleasant, leisurely flight from Toronto to Ft. Lauderdale, Florida:

In order to make the flight it was necessary for me to leave the office at 5 P.M. I arrived at my destination at about 11:30 P.M. Total elapsed time—6 1/2 hours. During this period I was served one bag of peanuts. The flight attendant suggested I eat them one at a time. (Toronto *Globe & Mail,* October 1, 1988)

In 1989, the great confrontation commenced between Lorenzo's Eastern Air Lines and the striking machinists' union after fifteen months of fruitless talks. Lorenzo had been unyielding in the negotiations, largely because Texas Air posted a staggering $718.6-million loss in 1988, while other airlines were recording large gains. When Eastern's airline pilots' union honored the machinists' picket lines, Eastern was, in effect, shut down in March 1989. Lorenzo's response was to file for Chapter 11 bankruptcy, which had served him so well at Continental in 1983. By this point, however, the confrontation had taken on the "dimensions of a holy war," in the words of Eastern's counsel, and most business analysts believed there would be no winner. The unions, they thought, would lose their jobs, since there would be little left of Eastern when the strike ended. And Frank Lorenzo, who visualized himself as a great airline builder, seemed bent on the destruction of Eastern in order to destroy the unions and save Texas Air. As *Business Week* (March 27, 1989) commented, "Frank Lorenzo, visionary airline builder, is zooming toward earth at too steep an angle, way too fast."

Early on, in 1985, when everybody thought Frank Lorenzo was some kind of magician who had discovered a secret formula for running airlines successfully and profitably, an attorney for the Air Line Pilots Association issued a note of caution. "He reminds me of Rex Barney," Bruce Simon said. The former Brooklyn Dodger pitcher, who was acclaimed for his devastating fastball, "was wild and he burned out quickly." "Maybe Frank's drive is a fatal flaw," said one of Lorenzo's defenders, "but stay tuned." (**B**. *Newsweek,* August 14, 1978, September 29, 1986, February 2, 1987; *Forbes,* October 30, 1978, March 5, 1979; *Business Week,* August 20, 1979, November 7, 1983, July 1, 1985, March 16, May 18, 1987, February 8, June 13, July 11, December 19, 1988, March 27, 1989; *Wall Street Journal,* September 18, 1979, February 18, 1982, September 8, 1983; *Airline Pilot,* February 1981; *New York Times,* October 4, 1983, July 14, 1985, March 9, December 26, 1986; *Fortune,* January 9, 1984, July 5, 1987, April 11, 1988, February 27, 1989; *Barron's,* May 3, 1986; Moira Johnston, *Takeover: The New Wall Street Warriors,* 1986; Michael E. Murphy, *The Airline That Pride Almost Bought,* 1986; *Who's Who in America,* 1986–87; *Current Biography,* February 1987; R. E. G. Davies, *Rebels and Reformers of the Airways,* 1987; *Business Month,* September 1988; Toronto *Globe & Mail,* October 1, October 12, 1988.)

M

MCGOVERN, PATRICK JOSEPH (1938?–). Publisher, International Data Group. In many companies, the employees cannot wait until the boss is gone, wishing fervently he would take a trip so they could have a respite from his incessant harping and spying. But at International Data Group. Patrick McGovern's employees once created a papier-mâché dummy and named it Chairman Pat so that they could have the boss around even when he was not there. What is it about Pat McGovern? How does he instill this kind of sentiment in his employees and executives? For one thing, his senior officials call him "one of the nicest men on the face of the earth," and, although he no longer knows each of his employees by name, McGovern spends two days a year personally signing Christmas cards to all 2,500 of them. A typical entrepreneur in many respects— he sleeps very little and works relentlessly—McGovern is a handsoff manager who thinks his job is to nourish and support his employees, not to tell them what to do. Oh yes, one more thing, he is giving them control of the company. By 1985, he had already sold them 15 percent of the firm, and he promised to turn over 51 percent to a profit-sharing employee trust when sales hit $1 billion, probably in 1990. As McGovern has said, "As you give, so shall you receive."

Patrick McGovern, an exceedingly modest and private man, was raised in Philadelphia, the son of a construction manager. When he was fifteen years old, he caught the computer bug after reading *Giant Brains: Or, Machines That Think,* by Edmund Berkeley. As a result, McGovern decided he wanted to build a computer of his own. "I spent about $20 of my newspaper route money and wired up a computer system with carpet tacks and bell wire, plywood boards, and flashlight bulbs . . . and made a machine that played tic-tac-toe in a way that was unbeatable." The problem with that, however, was that "I found people didn't like to be unsuccessful continually," McGovern recalled, "so I made it make a mistake every 40th move, so in a somewhat unpredictable style, they could win occasionally." That early episode is revealing about McGovern—he has a unique creative ability, but he also has the sensitivity to temper that to correspond to the needs of others. That unusual combination has been characteristic of McGovern throughout his career.

His little computer may have been beatable at tic-tac-toe occasionally, but it was unbeatable in other ways. It attracted the attention of an alumni group from Massachusetts Institute of Technology (MIT), who offered him a scholarship to that prestigious school. At MIT, McGovern studied biophysics and he got a job at one of the first computer magazines, *Computers and Automation*, which was edited by Edmund Berkeley, the man who had written the book about giant brains. After graduation, McGovern continued at the computer magazine, moving up to the position of associate editor. While working there for six years, McGovern honed his reporting skills, and he became aware of what seemed to him to be a gaping hole in the market. At that time, IBM controlled about 73 percent of the computer market, and the other vendors (the so-called Seven Dwarfs) had no way of knowing what interested computer users. This fact had been driven home most graphically to McGovern in 1964, when he attended a press conference in which RCA unveiled a novel computer memory technology— but one for which they confessed they knew of no practical application.

After thinking about the problem for a time, McGovern started a market research firm, which would provide information about current and potential customers for the computer makers. He decided to approach the head of Univac with his proposal to "organize a market research program and create a census that [would indicate] where all the computers are and how they're being used." The executive was intrigued with the idea and agreed it fulfilled a real need in the industry. He asked McGovern how much it would cost, and McGovern replied, "$7,000 or $8,000." "That's completely unrealistic," replied the Univac executive. Worried, McGovern lowered the price to $5,000, but the Univac executive hastened to assure him his first price had not been too high—it was too low: "You don't understand. I couldn't get anyone to use information that was too cheap. Charge at least $12,000 and sell it to a lot of other companies too." McGovern had just learned a very important business lesson—image can be as important as reality.

McGovern sent out letters to the various computer companies. Within a week, Univac, Xerox, and Burroughs had agreed to pay for his research, and before long he had received $75,000 in advance payments. With that money in hand, McGovern founded International Data Group and hired a group of high school students to count the computers in the United States. Within three years, his company was taking in $600,000 annually. One of the surveys McGovern's company did in 1967 found that the growth of the computer market was dependent on how much the people who used their computers knew about available computer products. McGovern "thought it would be useful for [managers of computer systems] to get rapid-access information about the new products and services."

Therefore, McGovern decided to launch a computer industry weekly shortly before the big Boston trade show in 1967. Faced with a two-week deadline,

McGovern scraped together $50,000, and he and his staff scrambled to produce a sixteen-page tabloid. He had originally intended to call the magazine *Computer World News*, but when the typographer could not fit the entire name across the page, McGovern shortened it to *Computerworld*. At the trade show, McGovern attracted sufficient subscribers to begin publication, getting his money up front before he ever went into production. McGovern made an important decision about *Computerworld*. The other publications in the computer field acted essentially as cheerleaders for the industry. Not *Computerworld*—it would provide balanced industry news and critical product reviews right from the start. Thus, at least at the beginning, his publication would be more dependent upon subscribers than advertisers.

Experienced industry publishers thought McGovern was crazy. They told him, first of all, that he needed at least $500,000 to launch a magazine, and secondly, that he would need the support of advertisers—he could not bite the hand that was feeding him. Nonetheless, they watched him carefully. McGovern characterized their attitude: "If you do very well, we'll come in and do a big, professional launch and wipe you off the map. And if you don't succeed, then we'll know you've saved us a lot of money because the market wasn't there." McGovern succeeded, and he made it big, and the experienced publishers fell short when they tried to match his success.

By the 1980s, *Computerworld* was the largest specialty publication of its kind, and the fortieth largest magazine of any type, with a circulation of 150,000 in the United States alone. Due to its success in America, McGovern launched editions of it in twenty other countries. The first foreign edition, naturally enough in Japan, was followed by editions in West Germany, Britain, Australia, Brazil, and even China and Hungary. With the success of that magazine, McGovern put out other, more specialized, computer industry magazines. By 1987, McGovern was publishing more than seventy computer industry publications in twenty-eight countries. Total circulation of these magazines was about 1.4 million, and revenues were more than $250 million annually. Other than *Computerworld*, his most popular magazines are *Micro Marketwork, Network World, Infoworld, PC World, MacWorld, 80 Micro, inCider, Run*, and *Amiga World. Computerworld*, which had trouble attracting advertisers in its early issues, was such a giant in the industry that it had twice as many advertising pages as its closest rival, *Datamation* (5,340 versus 2,511). All of this made Patrick McGovern a very rich man, with a fortune estimated at $370 million by *Forbes* in 1988.

Yet McGovern, a confirmed workaholic, who ignored almost everything except business, seemed little concerned about wealth. When he flies, which is often, he flies coach, with a seventy-pound sack filled with books and papers. He owns a Mercedes Benz, but it is nine years old. He has a modest home in Nashua, New Hampshire, and another one with his second wife in Hillsborough, California. He sees no reason to flaunt his wealth: "I think living ostentatiously means just putting other people down, and that is not what appeals to me." The one thing McGovern does not like to do with his money is provide venture capital for other people in the computer publishing field. He and his second wife, Lore Harp, cofounder of Vector Graphic, run a venture capital concern, and an industry analyst has said that "anybody who needs money in the computer publishing field is at McGovern's door."

"What will you do after you turn your company over to your employees?" asked *Forbes* (April 29, 1985). He told them he plans to retire to Japan, where he has already established himself as one of the earliest government-approved venture capitalists. By 1985, he had invested about $5 million in ten computer start-ups through his Pacific Technology Venture Fund. He also talks of helping mankind by bringing countries together in an interdependent world market. "I have a feeling that as people get more of a chance to intercommunicate together they gain more understanding of each other," he said. "That will result in more world harmony."

That may all sound rather utopian, but McGovern has always put his money where his mouth is. Many people are shocked at McGovern's apparently idiosyncratic wish to turn his company over to his employees when sales reach $1 billion. To McGovern, however, it makes perfect sense:

I won't have at IDG what has happened in so many other businesses, where the owner dies or sells and a new team replaces the people who have given so much blood, sweat, toil, and tears. . . . I wanted to make sure that the future control and direction of the company would be in the hands of the people who built it, the current employees. (*Inc.*)

(**B**. *Business New Hampshire*, August 1984; *Forbes*, April 29, 1985, October 24, 1988; A. David Silver, *Entrepreneurial Megabucks*, 1986; *Advertising Age*, June 30, 1986; Toronto *Globe & Mail*, March 3, 1987; *Inc.*, August 1988.)

MCGOWAN, WILLIAM GEORGE (December 10, 1927–   ). Telecommunications company founder, MCI Communications, Corporation. He sounded like a populist when he spoke, attacking the biggest trust of them all—American Telephone and Telegraph Company (AT&T)—a "regulated monopoly" that had been granted complete dominion over the nation's phone service for nearly three-quarters of a century. And it was enormous. With assets of about $155 billion in the early 1980s, revenues alone in that year amounted to nearly $50 billion, and profits were nearly $6 billion, the largest for any company in the world. With over 1 million employees, it was the nation's largest private employer, and with 3 million people holding stock in the company, it was the world's largest public company. Every day, more than half a billion conversations traveled back and forth between the 138 million telephones in the Bell System. The company, in fact, was so big that hardly anyone could even figure out how it worked, just keeping it functioning was a major organizational feat. William McGowan was not impressed; he cast himself in the role of a "giant killer."

McGowan's views of big business sounded like standard-issue, left-wing populism: "The *Fortune* 100 had, over the past five, ten, fifteen years, had a net decrease of jobs in this country . . . a decrease in productivity. They have made no contributions to the economy at all." Speaking to a group of young, liberal lawyers and economists, many of whom had been educated on the radicalized campuses of the 1960s, McGowan said of AT&T: "AT&T is an outrageous monopoly, they're holding back technology. Maybe this system made sense thirty years ago, but today they're hurting my company and a lot of others. And they're doing it in complicity with the FCC. It's crazy." Irving Kristol, the former socialist turned neoconservative, called McGowan's fight against AT&T a "modern day variant on classical Marxist class warfare theories." Yet McGowan was no "Sockless" Jerry Simpson, no William Jennings Bryan, not even a Robert LaFollette. Whatever the tone of his rhetoric, his spirit was not akin to that of the nineteenth-century farmers who fought the power of Eastern banks and railroads. He was not spawning a political movement or protesting the maldistribution of wealth in the United States. McGowan was trying to get rich. And it worked. His actions not only resulted in the breakup of AT&T in 1984, but by the mid–1980s his company, MCI Communications, was a giant, with revenues of nearly $4 billion, and profits of $85 million. As chairman and chief executive officer, McGowan had a compensation package of $2 million a year. And he owned in addition a large chunk of MCI's stock. He was a very rich man indeed.

McGowan had the background of a populist and antimonopolist. He was born in Ashley, Pennsylvania, the son of a railroad union organizer. Ashley was a small working-class community outside of Wilkes-Barre, in the coal mining regions of eastern Pennsylvania. The middle child of five children, McGowan was raised in a staunch Roman Catholic environment (his brother Andrew is a prominent priest in the Scranton area). As befit an Irish-Catholic, labor-union household, the McGowans were also passionately Democratic in their political allegiance. When McGowan was in his second year of high school, he persuaded his father to get him a job with the Central Railroad of New Jersey. An anthracite coal carrier, the Central was a consistent money loser. From 1931 to 1955, except during the war years, the Central had earned a profit in only one year. McGowan later commented on the lessons he had learned at the railroad: "Most executives at the Central Railroad of New Jersey taught me an awful lot. How not to do things. How not to deal with people. That's helpful, when you see bad examples. How not to run a railroad." It probably also gave him a distaste for large, bureaucratic organizations that helped propel his battle against AT&T many years later.

McGowan then joined another bureaucratic institution—the U.S. Army. He arrived in Europe shortly after hostilities ended in 1945, and he spent two years there, largely assisting in the relocation of concentration camp survivors. After his military service, McGowan returned to Ashley and used the GI Bill to finance his education at tiny King's College, which had recently opened its doors in Wilkes-Barre. There he majored in chemical engineering, thinking that it was a good way not only to get a job, but also to become an executive. As he prepared to graduate, McGowan was disabused of this notion:

I drove around to chemical factories in New Jersey and I would say, 'Who runs this place?' I never met a chemist who ran it. Then I would say, 'Where are the chemists?' They would point to a guy in a white smock somewhere. I couldn't see doing that for the rest of my life.'' (Nader and Taylor, *The Big Boys*)

McGowan then went to the Graduate School of Business at Harvard, where he was named a Baker Scholar, which meant that he ranked among the top 5 percent in his class. It also meant that he got a scholarship and caught the eye of several large, *Fortune* 500 corporations who were ever on the lookout for bright, ambitious young men to staff their growing executive ranks.

To that end, Shell Oil hired McGowan to work for the company as an analyst in the summer between his first and second year. He hated it:

Business can be one of the most boring professions that God ever created the way it's run in most corporations. My God, there's no spark, no motivation. . . . A lot of people working there were in their thirties. And they had retired. . . . We would go out and look at the pretty girls at noon. They would talk about crabgrass and kids and sports. No one ever talked about business. They had no more interest. They had retired. . . . I was thinking, this is deadly, this is bad. . . . That's one reason I never went to work for one of those guys. (Nader and Taylor, *The Big Boys*)

So, McGowan's antibureaucratic odyssey was launched. Little could anyone imagine it would have such a traumatic impact upon American business.

Desiring an entrepreneurial challenge and wanting to work someplace that was not boring, McGowan headed to Hollywood in 1954 after he got his MBA. There he landed a job with Magna Theater Corporation, which had been formed by the dynamic Broadway and Hollywood impressario Mike Todd. Magna was formed to market Todd-AO, a new wide-screen process developed by Todd, and to distribute films that used the process. McGowan loved it, especially when he was able to help Todd produce *Oklahoma* and to hobnob with Shirley Jones and Elizabeth Taylor. Glamorous as it was, though, there was little entrepreneurial challenge for McGowan. He was making about $35,00 a year, but he had little responsibility for running the company. McGowan left and went to New York, where he traded the glitter of Hollywood for the more earthly excitement of working as a management consultant and venture capitalist.

McGowan took over troubled companies and worked to revive them by addressing the various business problems himself. His most successful venture during these early years was with Powertron Ultrasonic Corporation. A defense contractor, Powertron manufactured components for control systems of aircraft and guided missiles, and produced devices to measure extremely cold materials. A tiny, struggling firm when McGowan started it with $25,000 in 1959, he sold it three years later for nearly $3 million. With the proceeds, William McGowan became a millionaire at age thirty-five. He invested the money in a number of other electronics and computer firms during the 1960s. He seemed to have a unique talent for rescuing these firms and restoring them to profitability. By 1966, when he was just thirty-nine, McGowan decided to retire from business—a very rich man. Not knowing what to do with himself, McGowan took a trip around the world one way. Still not satisfied, he turned around and took a trip around the world in the other direction. Still, his restless energy would not abate. It was clear to him that only another business challenge would truly satisfy him.

In 1968, a lawyer in Chicago told McGowan about a company called Microwave Communications, Inc., which was in desperate need of both managerial and financial assistance. McGowan investigated and found a tiny operation with no full-time employees, whose principal asset was a five-year-old application to the Federal Communications Commission (FCC) to provide private-line phone service over microwaves between St. Louis and Chicago. Most prudent capitalists probably would have walked away from the hapless concern, but McGowan was intrigued, and then captivated. He put $50,000 into the company, got half the shares, renamed it MCI Communications, and was appointed the firm's chairman and chief executive officer. He later recalled that it wasn't the financial or technological condition of the company that won him over—it was the chance to challenge AT&T. As he told *Time*, "Challenging the monopoly had one irresistible element, it had never been done before." Ralph Nader and William Taylor, in their study of McGowan and MCI, concurred:

The key to McGowan's motivation can be found in the restlessness and drift that characterized his life prior to MCI. McGowan needs to be challenged. . . . What kept him at MCI was the exhilaration of taking on—and the prospect of dismantling—an institution as powerful as AT&T.

MCI was founded by John D. "Jack" Goeken, then a thirty-two-year-old operator of a mobile radio business based outside of Chicago. Wishing to increase sales of citizens band radios to truckers who traveled between St.Louis and Chicago, he applied to the FCC in December 1963 to construct eleven microwave towers between the two cities. A five-year battle transpired, in which Goeken's application was vigorously opposed by AT&T, which argued, among other things, that his company lacked the financial resources to do what it promised. On that score they were right. Microwave Communications was so far in debt by the late 1960s, and Goeken was so poor, that when he lost his overcoat one winter, he could not afford a new one. The battle seemed a classic mismatch. Goeken recalled later: "The AT&T attorneys were sharp, really spiffy. Unintentionally, I looked the other part. I had holes in my shoes. I didn't have any money. I had cardboard boxes instead of briefcases." Nonetheless, Goeken managed to get an FCC hearing in October 1967, and it was this potential that made Goeken's sorry company attractive to McGowan in 1968.

McGowan provided the badly needed capital and later provided the managerial expertise Goeken lacked, but he entered the picture after the most difficult regulatory struggles had already been waged by Goeken. Shortly after McGowan became head of the company, in August 1969, the full commission of the FCC, in a vote of four to three, upheld the hearing examiner's opinion in what became known as "the MCI decision." In this decision, the FCC approved MCI's application to enter the intercity private-line business between St. Louis and Chicago. It was a devastating defeat for AT&T, the second one in as many years. A year earlier, the FCC, in the "Carterfone" decision, had ruled that AT&T could no longer forbid customers to use telephones that had been manufactured by other companies on the Bell lines. Taken together, these decisions had severely dented the comfortable monopoly AT&T had enjoyed for many years.

AT&T, under the leadership of Theodore Vail* in the early twentieth century, had argued that the telephone industry was a "natural monopoly," stating that there was no advantage for the public to have competition in this field. Instead, he said that AT&T would gladly submit to being a "regulated monopoly," whereby public oversight over its operations would be given to a regulatory commission. This commission ultimately turned out to be the FCC. This privileged status for AT&T was challenged over the years. In 1949, the Justice Department brought suit against it, charging its subsidiary, Western Electric, with exercising monopolistic control of the telephone equipment market, and attempted to separate the subsidiary from its parent. The case dragged on until 1956, when AT&T signed a consent decree in which it was allowed to retain Western Electric, but it had to make available its 8,000 patents to all comers on a royalty-free basis, and it had to promise not to engage in any business outside communications (that is, computers). The telephone industry changed little over the next two decades, but when McGowan and MCI began to exert pressure after 1973, a profound transformation took place. As late as 1974, the Bell System controlled 80 percent of all telephone service in the United States, about the same as it had in 1939. By the time McGowan emerged victorious ten years later, the industry was virtually unrecognizable.

By the time the FCC gave its final approval to the St. Louis–Chicago system in 1969, McGowan had already expanded his sights to building a nationwide network. Fearing that further dealings with the FCC could cause years of delay, he set up a series of separate companies, always with a play on the MCI name— MCI New York West or MCI Texas Pacific. Each of these firms then applied to the FCC to build a leg of a national network. All of this was going to cost money, and financing became McGowan's first priority. Goeken and McGowan went to the canyons of Wall Street to drum up financing. Goeken was a neophyte at this, but he had the technical expertise that McGowan lacked. Initially unimpressed with McGowan, Goeken changed his opinion after seeing McGowan operate on Wall Street. McGowan ultimately put together a complex financing package amounting to a whopping $110 million from private investors. It was an awesome deal, far beyond Goeken's capabilities. Goeken said about their relationship,

It was a good marriage. We did almost everything together. Every time we went to raise money, we went together. He appealed to those people. Other people thought he was too smooth. Those people liked me. Between the two of us we got enough people trusting us to put the money in. (Nader and Taylor, *The Big Boys*)

Having raised the money, McGowan began construction in January 1971 of a $4-million national network of forty-four relay towers. A year later, they were complete, and a number of corporate clients had been signed up. MCI's midwestern route was in operation, but it still had to build a national system and battle AT&T on a bewildering number of fronts. To raise additional money, in June 1972, McGowan took MCI public, selling 3.3 million shares of common stock at $10 a share, which netted the company $30 million after commissions. These early years were heady ones for MCI, ones in which an almost magical bond was formed between McGowan and his early employees. A man of enormous energy and enthusiasm, he had exceptional leadership qualities. One executive in those early years recalled those times with pleasure, saying of McGowan he was "a fucker and a fighter and a wild horse rider." Never having married, McGowan gave all of himself to the company during those years. There were all-night strategy sessions, weekend meetings, hours and hours spent at the Black Rooster, a tavern near MCI headquarters, and a "roller coaster of despair and exhilaration that is recalled today with great fondness." McGowan worked seven days a week. His idea of a vacation was to show up at a friend's home with a suitcase full of reading material, plop himself in a floating chair in the pool, and yell out to anyone within earshot the interesting details of his negotiations and reading materials. Another executive recalled that in the early years he never had McGowan's home phone number—he never needed it—McGowan was never at home, he was always at the office. Then, too, it was not just business—it was war—they were taking on "Ma Bell."

By early 1973, McGowan had taken MCI public, had completed construction of a good portion of his microwave network, had moved into his new Washington, D.C. offices, and had laid plans for a nationwide network of towers. Nevertheless, things were not going well. The problem was, as usual, AT&T: it still owned, maintained, and controlled the nation's vast telephone network. What MCI had to do, if it was going to be successful, was to interconnect with that network in the major cities where it planned to sell its private-line service. It was financially impossible for MCI to build its own private phone network in all these cities simply to handle MCI's long-distance calls. MCI had to negotiate with AT&T for the use of these lines, and AT&T had no intention of giving MCI free use of them. AT&T, announcing that it was not going to let MCI skim the cream off their system, planned to charge MCI exorbitant rental fees to cover what they called "capital contribution"—that is, to help pay for the maintenance and upkeep of the nation's basic phone system.

McGowan decided to file antitrust charges against AT&T, citing the "essential facilities" doctrine of the antitrust law. By this doctrine, if one company controlled exclusive facilities that were essential to the business of another firm, then the first company was required to give access to the second company. It was a bold move, and one McGowan had anticipated ever since he had taken over MCI, which was the reason for moving the firm's headquarters to Washington, D.C.—to be close to the scene of what would prove to be an intense lobbying campaign. If McGowan was to be successful, he would to have to lure AT&T onto a new battlefield—that of politics. As Steve Coll commented in his book on the case, "He must ruthlessly attack the delicate coalition in Washington that allowed AT&T to control the telephone industry." To succeed, McGowan had to get all three governmental institutions—Congress, the FCC, and the courts—to join his crusade. McGowan had to hire legions of lawyers: lawyers to lobby Congress, lawyers to prepare his antitrust briefs for the courts, lawyers to work with the FCC, and lawyers to tell him what all the other lawyers were doing. For these tasks he needed specialists, some of the most expensive insider Washington lawyers who knew the power configuration in that city and how to work with it. It would cost a fortune—a large fortune. But if he won, the payoff could be enormous. MCI at this point had a puny operation. Revenues for 1974 amounted to just $6.8 million, and during its entire history to that point, it had earned less than $1 million from the sale of long-distance services. MCI was, in the words of Bill McGowan, "a flea crawling up the leg of an elephant."

Nonetheless, McGowan and MCI commenced a many-pronged battle against Bell in 1974 that is complicated and difficult to describe. First of all, McGowan appeared before Senator Philip A. Hart's Senate judiciary subcommittee on antitrust activity, explained to them how AT&T was violating antitrust law and told them the company was attempting to put MCI out of business. It was a good place to start, because Hart believed strongly that the Sherman and Clayton Antitrust Acts had become outmoded in the age of multinational corporations and technological change. He wanted to fight with the "corporate state," and McGowan's crusade against AT&T seemed like a perfect fit. McGowan urged Hart and his committee to consider breaking up AT&T, and they began to listen. McGowan filed suit in Philadelphia. There he asked the courts to force AT&T's regional companies to provide hookups for MCI customers. To get support for this effort, McGowan sent letters to more than 2,000 businesses around the country, only a few of which were MCI's customers. He did so to provide information to the courts that a broad range of companies felt aggrieved by AT&T's monopoly on equipment and services.

These moves provoked the Justice Department into action, and in December 1973, it demanded that AT&T provide documents, going as far back as 1967, relating to its policies on private-line pricing and contracting. Just a few days later, a Philadelphia judge granted MCI's request for an injunction requiring AT&T to provide local hookups. Obviously the noose was beginning to tighten around AT&T, and it was becoming concerned. Then, in March 1974, came MCI's own antitrust suit against AT&T. Obviously trying to piggyback on the Justice Department's own antitrust probe, McGowan charged that AT&T was "monopolizing the business and data-communications market in the violation of the Sherman Antitrust Act." AT&T called the suit "ridiculous," and countered with an antitrust suit of its own against MCI. In its suit, AT&T charged that MCI had submitted "sham tariffs and pleadings before the FCC," "opposed tariffs and applications" unreasonably, and had filed "unreasonably low" rates that did not meet the cost of providing service. To most observers, AT&T's suit seemed ridiculous, and a company spokesman later replied that the date they were filed, April Fool's Day, 1974, was "the only explanation we have for AT&T's claim."

MCI's victories over AT&T continued to mount during these early years. Later that same April, the FCC ruled that AT&T had to provide hookups for MCI customers, and to provide the service at "reasonable terms and conditions." In response, AT&T began to compete with MCI on prices, establishing what it called a Hi-Lo Tariff system, lowering its rates on many of the lines also served by MCI. McGowan's next step was his boldest. In September 1974, he asked the FCC for permission to establish what he called Execunet. In a complex manner, Execunet would allow MCI's customers to dial an MCI computer with a seven-digit number and a five-digit identification number, and, once identified, to dial the area code and number desired. In other words, it would provide long-distance service by using MCI's computers and microwave relays and by avoiding Bell's lines entirely. It would work only between the cities serviced by MCI, but it opened up a vast new market for MCI in long distance. The FCC approved the program, and McGowan viewed this decision as a tremendously important landmark, telling other company executives that it was "the first day of the rest of our life." Bell complained to the FCC that Execunet did not actually work, and on two occasions the FCC withdrew its permission to MCI to offer the service. This had a devastating effect on MCI: executives resigned, workers were fired, and lenders refused to extend any new loans. Finally, in July 1975, the court ruled that MCI could continue to offer the service.

The decision came at a critical time. In fiscal 1975, MCI lost $28 million, and of this, more than $15 million went to the banks to pay interest on MCI's enormous debt. For two years, McGowan was being driven to distraction, trying to divide his time between lobbying the FCC and drumming up financial support on Wall Street. But 1975 was the turning point, as far as MCI's fortunes were concerned: from 1975 to 1978, MCI revenues increased tenfold. Consequently, McGowan was able to convince lenders to provide him with additional capital to continue what, by then, seemed to be an increasingly victorious fight against AT&T. In 1976, an FCC hearing again ruled against Execunet, but in July 1977, a U.S. District judge upheld Execunet's legitimacy, and also ruled that MCI and other carriers could offer any long-distance service they wished. The FCC appealed the decision to the U.S. Supreme Court, but that body declined to hear the appeal. The dam had broken, and the era of free competition in the telecommunications industry had finally been inaugurated.

By this time the FCC, once McGowan's ally, was furious with him and MCI. As a result, the commission began to side openly with AT&T, and when Bell in 1978 adopted a policy of delay and obstruction to fight MCI, the FCC cooperated. In January 1978, AT&T again refused to allow customers to tap into the MCI network from their own phones. Although this was in direct defiance of an earlier decision, the FCC supported AT&T. Once again, McGowan took AT&T to court, and it overruled the FCC, calling AT&T's position "strikingly unfair." With these victories, McGowan was determined to expand MCI's services as rapidly as he could to head off new competitors, such as ITT and Sprint, who had recently entered the new market that MCI had opened. An essential ingredient of this new strategy was to engage in an expensive advertising campaign, aimed at both the corporate and residential markets. To this end, MCI hired the advertising agency of Ally & Gargano, which had succeeded in making Fred Smith's[†] Federal Express a household name.

As the advertising campaign was being launched, Bill McGowan was back in court—this time for the antitrust case he had filed against AT&T in 1974. The trial got under way in February 1980, with McGowan as the star of the proceedings—with his irreverent humor, his self-effacing style, and his ringing denouncements of AT&T. Finally, after fifty-four days of testimony, with some seventy witnesses having taken the stand, resulting in 12,000 pages of transcript, the jurors on June 13 delivered their verdict—AT&T, the jury said, was guilty on ten of the fifteen counts brought against it. The award was a staggering $600 million, just one-third less than MCI had requested. Since, in antitrust cases, plantiffs are awarded treble damages, the judge gave MCI $1.8 billion, the largest settlement in American antitrust history.

The verdict made headlines throughout the country. Suddenly, MCI was a household word, and when it was coupled with its new advertising campaign, it immediately gained credibility. Deciding to expand its services still further in the wake of the antitrust decision, MCI found customers far more receptive than they had been previously. MCI's stock rose from $5 a share to $14 during the next six months, and by the end of the year, revenues were $90 million, two-thirds greater than the year before. Profits were also surging, reaching $9.2 million in the first six months of 1980. AT&T called the judgement "inconceivable," and immediately appealed the verdict. McGowan himself was elated, and he struck a suitably populist pose for the media: "Smaller companies that get stepped on by larger companies will come to realize that it is not true that nothing can be done. Big companies can no longer beat them by deep-pocketing them." Later, he told the *New York Times*, "We see in this award the jury saying that they will not allow the largest corporation in the world to use its power to stifle competition."

Antitrust activities continued for another three years between MCI and AT&T. In January 1983, the appellate court granted a retrial to AT&T on the amount of damages levied in MCI's suit. McGowan was devastated by the court's ruling in May 1985: The jury, disenchanted by the size of the claim, awarded MCI only $37 million before trebling. MCI also had another antitrust suit against AT&T before the courts, and MCI finally got about $200 million in cash, plus products and services, as its award in the cases. A substantial amount, but not nearly the "$2 or $3 billion" that McGowan had predicted. But if AT&T had won a battle, it had lost the war. In January 1982, after eight years of litigation and $360 million in legal fees, AT&T signed a consent decree with the Justice Department to end its antitrust suit. It was a stunning agreement. The pact was extremely complex, but in it, AT&T agreed to divest itself of its twenty-two regional companies, reducing its assets from $155 billion to about $43 billion. It was allowed to retain its Long-Lines (long-distance) Division, Western Electric, and Bell Labs. In addition, AT&T would be allowed to enter new fields, such as computers and office systems, from which it had been barred previously. The *Wall Street Journal* called it "the most important antitrust development since the Supreme Court ordered the dissolution of the Standard Oil Trust in 1911." Charles L. Brown, chairman of AT&T, admitted that "the divestiture has been a cultural trauma for us." AT&T was no longer "America's phone company," it had, as the *Wall Street Journal* commented, entered a "new and largely uncharted course as a high-technology, innovative competitor in the marketplace."

McGowan won some enormous battles in the courtroom, but these victories opened up further challenges for him and MCI in the late 1980s. The marketplace had become more crowded, as more and more firms emerged to compete for the consumers' long-distance dollar. To keep pace with this, McGowan had to spend an enormous amount of money for new technology. During 1984, he pumped $20 million a week into new equipment to open up new cities, and he planned to spend $1 billion a year in the late 1980s. He also brought MCI into new areas, such as cellular radio, electronic mail, and nationwide paging. The most daring of these was the introduction of MCI Mail in 1983, an electronic mail service. The key to success of the system was to supply a better product at a lower price than the competitors, but by 1986 it had recorded massive losses and had little hope of reaching the large market McGowan had forecast for it when it was introduced.

William McGowan and MCI by 1988 had a twenty-year history of titanic battles, exhilarating highs, and devastating lows. The scrawny little company that he took over in 1968 was a $4-billion giant in 1988. But it had been a brutal, difficult climb, both for McGowan and for his associates at MCI. McGowan himself, the quintessential workaholic, suffered a massive heart attack in April 1987, and he had to have a delicate heart transplant operation. It came at a terrible time for MCI. Despite its revenues of $4 billion, it had posted a huge loss in 1986, and its stock price was at an all-time low. It was no picnic for the people who worked at MCI either. Despite McGowan's enormous charisma and his ability to motivate his associates and employees, he was hardly an easy man to work for. McGowan admits that. He emphasized time and again that MCI was not a family, and that it did not guarantee job security. The firm did not provide the plethora of human and social services that many feel are necessary for modern corporations. There were no exercise facilities, no employee credit union, and no counseling services. It did not even have a retirement program until 1981. And McGowan, son of a union official, wants no union at MCI. To keep his workers loyal, McGowan set up an employee stock-ownership program. When asked about all of this, McGowan responded, "We are a very individualistic company." He regarded the individual challenges, the lack of boredom, as the major benefit his company offered many of the people who work there.

And what about the American consumer—John and Jane Q. Public—the ostensible reasons for all this fighting? How have they fared under the new system? Not nearly as well as McGowan and many of the advocates of deregulation promised. *Rolling Stone*, in an article entitled "Reach Out and Crunch Someone," made a stinging attack on the whole new system. AT&T, it turns out, had indeed been overcharging the consumer for long-distance service over the years. But this had been done for a purpose, to help subsidize local service to the subscriber. The result was that basic telephone bills were abnormally low, 90 percent of all households in America had a phone, and it was viewed as one of the common necessities of life that even the poorest could afford. With deregulation and divestiture, it was announced by Bell that basic local phone rates would be doubled. This forced a significant percentage of poorer Americans to discontinue their phone service. (Estimates have placed it at about 6 percent of the households.) Congressman Timothy Wirth of Colorado foresaw the creation of a two-class system in phone service, in which most Americans would enjoy the excitements of high-tech communications, while others would be denied basic access to the system. *Rolling Stone* concluded its argument by saying that "breaking up Ma Bell, the one monopoly that really worked, and creating diverse private competition in telecommunications" was a mistake. "Whatever its fault," they claimed, "AT&T as a regulated monopoly did deliver an extraordinarily efficient telephone system over the years, and I am not sure we will be better off without it." William McGowan destroyed AT&T and, in the process, built MCI to massive proportions, but the result—the system of free market capitalism that he inaugurated in the telecommunications industry—may make Americans long for the day when "Mother Bell" took care of them in her maternalistic way. (**B**. *Business Week*, November 30, 1974, March 15, 1976, January 25, 1982, October 10, 1983, November 5, December 3, 1984, December 15, 1986, May 18, 1987; *New York Times*, October 8, 1976, July 18, 1979, June 13, June 16, 1980, February 12, 1984; Robert Shook, *The Entrepreneurs*, 1980; *Forbes*, January 30, 1980; *Newsweek*, June 23, 1980, July 25, 1983; *Time*, February 23, 1981, January 7, 1985; *Wall Street Journal*, January 11, January

19, 1982, November 4, 1983, May 29, 1985; *Fortune*, January 24, June 27, 1983, August 20, 1984, April 1, 1985; *Broadcasting*, April 25, 1983; *Institutional Investor*, September 1983; *Rolling Stone*, September 15, 1983; *Financial World*, May 30–June 12, 1984; *Contemporary Newsmakers*, 1985; Steve Coll, *The Deal of the Century: The Breakup of AT&T*, 1986; *Inc.*, August 1986; Larry Kahaner, *On the Line*, 1986; Ralph Nader and William Taylor, *The Big Boys*, 1986; Paul W. Henck and Bernard Strassburg, *A Slippery Slope: The Long Road to the Breakup of AT&T*, 1987; Douglas K. Ramsey, *The Corporate Warriors*, 1987.)

MCKNIGHT, WILLIAM LESTER (November 11, 1887–March 4, 1978). Diversified manufacturing executive, Minnesota Mining & Manufacturing. It may seem illogical, but Minnesota Mining & Manufacturing (3-M), one of the most successful, innovative, and profitable companies in American industry, was built on mistakes, or at least on a tolerance for mistakes. Most people are familiar with 3-M's great successes—Scotch tape, Post-it Notes, Scotchguard fabric protector, and so on—but 3-M people often talk about their tolerance for failure as the key to their corporate success. Thomas J. Peters and Robert H. Waterman, Jr., in their best-selling *In Search of Excellence,* commented that "tolerance for failure is a very specific part of the excellent company culture—and that lesson comes directly from the top." William McKnight understood that well. When he became chairman of the board in 1949, he said:

Mistakes will be made, but if the man is essentially right himself, I think the mistakes he makes are not so serious in the long run as the mistakes management makes if it is dictatorial and undertakes to tell men under its authority . . . exactly how they must do their job. If management is intolerant and destructively critical when mistakes are made I think it kills initiative and it is essential we have many men with initiative if we are to continue to grow. (Huck, *Brand of the Tartan*)

William McKnight was born in a sod hut on a farm on the South Dakota prairie. His parents, natives of Scotland, had left the settled East Coast of the United States in the 1880s to settle on the barren, windswept prairies. Homesteading in Brookings County near the Minnesota border, they lived two and a half miles from the tiny settlement of White, with a population of 580. The youngest of three children, William McKnight attended primary school in a one-room schoolhouse, and at fourteen he went to high school in White. Like other farm boys, McKnight was expected to carry a heavy load of chores on the farm, but unlike many of them, he did not develop a love of farming. In fact, at an early age, he decided that he was not going to be a farmer like his father. Yet, McKnight did not have the slightest idea what he would do once he finished high school.

He decided to go to business school, but found when he graduated from high school that there were no funds available. So, he helped his father on the farm for a while, and then moved to Duluth, Minnesota, where he lived with relatives and entered Duluth Business University in January 1907. McKnight enjoyed school and did well in his classes, but he never finished the six-month course. He heard in May of that year that a new sandpaper factory in the city, called 3-M, was looking for an assistant bookkeeper. He decided to apply, but he recalled, "I was the scaredest boy that ever lived when I applied for that job." Despite his fears, he was hired, and he went to work in what he thought was a magnificent business opportunity for a raw, young, farm boy. Little was he aware that the 3-M company, which billed itself as the "largest manufacturer of sandpaper in the world," was in a precarious financial condition. Even less could he dream that he would be the person to transform it into one of the world's most successful industrial enterprises.

Minnesota Mining & Manufacturing had gotten its start in 1902 when four men—a doctor, a lawyer, and two railroad executives—in Two Harbors, Minnesota, pooled $1,000 each to start a mining business. They were planning to mine a substance called corundum, a common material used for abrasives. It took the group longer than expected to get the first load of corundum out of the ground, but they sold one ton of it in March 1904, which, as it turned out, was the last sale of corundum the company ever made. Silicon carbide came on the market at just about the same time they began to mine their material, and interest in corundum was virtually nil. With expenses mounting daily, the firm's founders were unsure what to do. One option they considered was manufacturing their own sandpaper.

Already deeply in debt, with manufacturing operations costing them another $25,000, the founders of 3-M had to find additional investors. They went to Lucius P. Ordway, a wealthy St. Paul plumbing supplier, and got him to invest enough money not only to keep the firm afloat, but also to allow it to start a sandpaper manufacturing operation. In June 1905, 3-M began building its sandpaper plant in Duluth in an abandoned flour mill. But troubles mounted, and it was not until January 1906 that the factory first began to turn out sandpaper. Before long, sales were running about $2,500 a month. Unfortunately, expenses were $9,000 a month, and the company was on the edge of bankruptcy. Ordway had by this time poured $100,000 into the firm, and he was serving as its president. This was the unstable enterprise Bill McKnight joined in 1907.

McKnight, in the meantime, was delighted with his salary of $11.50 a week. He impressed the small company's officials, who made McKnight cost accountant in 1909. From 1909 to 1914, 3-M managed to get a precarious foothold in the abrasives industry. Ordway continued to pour money into the firm until the amount reached nearly $250,000, when he became anxious to have the manufacturing operations moved from Duluth to his home in St. Paul. This was done in 1910. With new production facilities and an enlarged sales force, the fortunes of 3-M began to take a turn for the better. But quality control problems continued, which finally caused the firm's sales manager to resign. William McKnight was chosen to take his place. Although this seemed an unusual move, since McKnight had no sales experience, it was, as the company's historian commented, "the turning point in the nine-year struggle to get ahead."

The twenty-four-year-old McKnight had a new idea for selling abrasives. Instead of just going to the buyer's office, he told his salesmen to go into the shop, to talk to the workmen, and to demonstrate the superiority of 3-M products right on the floor. To set an example, McKnight personally called on the Rockford, Illinois, furniture firms every month to sell them sandpaper. He quickly learned, however, to his dismay, that 3-M sandpaper was inferior to its competitors' products. McKnight pleaded for improved quality control, and he worked to develop greater coordination and communication between the factory and the sales force. After three years of pushing this coordination without success, McKnight suggested to the firm's president that a general manager be appointed to oversee both sales and production. The president, Eugene Ober, accepted the suggestion and appointed McKnight to the position.

It was 1916, and the twenty-nine-year-old McKnight now had the reins of the company in his hands. He first established a research laboratory to engage in testing and hopefully to introduce improved quality control. Although the small laboratory cost just $500, for a company whose entire career and reputation were ultimately made through research and development, it was a fateful decision. The small, crude laboratory remained a one-man, one-room operation for years, but it established an important precedent.

As America tooled up for war production after 1916, demand for abrasives of all kinds increased dramatically, and 3-M's fortunes improved along with it. The high earnings continued after the armistice since, during 1919 and 1920, spending levels remained high. The nation's consumption of abrasives increased 49 percent between 1914 and 1919, and 3-M's profits increased commensurately. But William McKnight was not content to let the company rest on its laurels. During this period he established a set of guidelines that continue to influence the firm to this day. He wanted the company to diversify beyond sandpaper into other abrasives and, later, even further afield; he wished to minimize the risk of information leakage by limiting board membership to company officers; he wanted to patent new products carefully and to license these patents; he wanted to increase sales by at least 10 percent annually; and he wished to expand production facilities; to keep employee morale high; and to continue to maintain quality control.

McKnight's emphasis on diversification led to a number of new products in the 1920s. First there was waterproof sandpaper, a product that, over time, revolutionized the abrasives industry. In the early years, however, 3-M had a hard time finding a market for the product. The automobile industry became the first big customer for waterproof sandpaper. At the same time, its connection with the automobile industry inspired 3-M to find another new product, its first outside the abrasives industry. Whenever he delivered sandpaper samples to the auto companies, Richard Drew, a young laboratory assistant at 3-M, heard tales of woe from the men who had to do two-tone paint jobs. He decided he could make a masking tape that would do the job far better than anything then on the market. He developed Scotch masking tape, which, over time, formed the nucleus from which more than a hundred pressure-sensitive industrial tapes evolved.

With the success of masking tape, Drew began working on another product—cellophane tape—in response to a manufacturer's packaging problem. The product was put on the market in 1930, the first year of the depression, and 3-M was characteristically cautious and conservative about it. Initially 3-M marketed the product purely in the packaging field to industrial users, but the American public as a whole soon began to find uses for the product that went beyond anything 3-M had ever dreamed. The depression had forced Americans to practice thrift, and they began to repair items that previously might have been thrown out. The new cellophane tape, "Scotch Tape," proved ideal for a multitude of uses—mending broken toys, sealing opened cans of food, attaching labels to home-canned foods, and mending a multitude of paper products.

The cellophane tape became so popular that 3-M recognized the need for a completely separate sales force to call on the commercial outlets where it would be sold. As it became popular for home use, it became clear to 3-M that a practical dispenser was necessary for it to be used properly. 3-M's research department set to work developing the product, and soon had it perfected. The resultant product continues to be used to the present day. The cellophane tape was also the first major product introduced under William McKnight's long regime as president of the company, a position he assumed in 1929. At the same time, the firm was reorganized as a Delaware corporation.

Throughout the 1930s, McKnight continued to push for more diversification. In 1934, 3-M began to manufacture colored roofing granules made from mined quartz that was ceramically processed to give them color and weather-resistant properties. A year later, the production of resin, rubber, and synthetic adhesives was begun, as well as the fabrication of a reflective material used for commercial advertising signs and highway and other safety markers in the late 1930s. When McKnight found that advertisers were not rushing to buy his new product, he bought three outdoor-advertising companies for $4.5 million. The product, called Scotchlite, did not begin to earn its own way until 1947, but after the 1950s it became a very big seller.

During the 1930s, McKnight also established a pioneering employee relations program by introducing, on an experimental basis, an unemployment insurance program for 3-M's employees to be financed out of earnings. The plan drew reactions from business and labor circles, since McKnight openly asserted that unemployment was at least partially the employer's responsibility. Since the company had few layoffs and a federal plan was started in 1935, no payments were made under 3-M's program. Nevertheless, it represented an innovative and progressive stance in the early 1930s.

From 1929 to 1940, despite the terrible economic downturn the country was experiencing, McKnight watched 3-M's sales increase from $5.5 million to $15 million. A raft of important inventions poured out of the company's plants during these years, and they all helped to increase sales volume and profitability. As a result, McKnight, in 1937, launched a more comprehensive research program, and he planned to pour millions of dollars into product development and engineering research. Many of these products failed during the next decade, but enough succeeded to maintain growth and profitability for 3-M. During World War II, 3-M plunged full force into the war effort, developing a product called "Safety-Walk" to make walking safe on decks, airplane wings, and so forth. Scotchlite was also used extensively during the war. The war and immediate postwar years brought enormous expansion to 3-M. By 1949, when McKnight moved up to board chairman, 3-M had 8,750 employees and sales of $114 million, and was capitalized at $73 million. The tiny, faltering firm McKnight had joined forty-two years before was by 1949 an industrial giant.

During the twenty years of his presidency, McKnight maintained tight, highly centralized control. But in 1949, when the firm was reorganized, he announced that a new, more decentralized system was going into operation. This was necessary, he announced, because of the company's successful diversification program. 3-M, by then, had so many different products and serviced so many different markets that it was no longer possible for a chief executive to maintain day-to-day, intimate control of operations. By 1949, William McKnight was sixty-two years old and no longer the chief operations officer, but he was a long way from retirement. He continued to be the principal figure in the firm until his retirement in 1966, at the age of seventy-nine.

By the early 1960s, 3-M's sales were $700 million annually, and new products continued to pour out of the company's doors. By that time, the firm had thirty product laboratories, and, in the words of a technical director at the company, "We eat, drink, dream, and sweat new products." The research and development at 3-M under McKnight's guidance had a clear focus. As the vice president of research and development in the 1960s stated, "It is a tradition of 3-M research to look constantly for wider applications for new products as well as to probe for additional products."

One element of the genius of 3-M has been that all its employees, not just the laboratory scientists, are encouraged to come up with new product ideas. William McKnight himself contributed to this process. He was a passionate fan of horse racing, and during the 1950s he developed the Tartan Stables. One day, he was sitting in his clubhouse box at Hialeah racetrack with trainer John Nerud. Nerud mentioned casually that there had been no improvements in racetracks "since George Washington's day." He went on to add, "What we need is a rubberized track that will be the same in all weather at all tracks—rain or shine, hot or cold, summer or winter." Immediately interested, McKnight set the 3-M laboratories to work on it. They developed a product known as Tartan—a drip-dry, all-weather, no-dirt track surfacing material. It was first installed at a harness-racing track in Washington, Pennsylvania, in 1963, and was well received. As he waited in the stands for the first race that day, McKnight grinned and commented, "This is either going to be a howling success or it will be known as 'McKnight's Folly.'' He had no need to worry. Tartan was soon used for a number of other surfaces, including the tracks for the Olympic Games in Mexico City and then increasingly for tracks and playgrounds across America. It even began to be used on farms, to line the floors of cow stalls.

Another important innovation for the 3-M company was a product called Post-it. Arthur Fry, a 3-M chemical engineer, had heard that another scientist at 3-M had accidentally developed an adhesive with very low sticking power. Normally, for an adhesives company this would not be a good thing, but Fry had an idea. He had long been irritated by the fact that when he was in church he would mark his hymnal with pieces of paper, and then, when he stood up to sing, the little papers always fell out. He figured that if he could make small markers with a little strip of low-power adhesive on the back—something that would stick lightly and then pull right off—it might be useful in other situations. He had the secretaries at 3-M try it out, and eventually the firm began to sell the product under the name of Post-it. By 1984 sales of that item alone totaled $100 million.

Finally, in 1966, McKnight retired, although he continued to serve on the board of directors until 1973 when he received the title of director emeritus, which he held until his death in 1978. In his later years, McKnight was almost as active in the world of racing as he had earlier been with 3-M. Besides his Tartan Stables, he bought Hialeah Park with John W. Galbreath in 1972. Two years later, they sold the 219-acre landscaped park with its flock of 600 flamingos when Gulfstream Park cut deeply into Hialeah's midwinter racing handle. McKnight also served as chairman of Miami's Calder Race Course and Tropical Park. In addition, McKnight became very active in the world of theater, and he backed a number of Broadway shows, including *Hello Dolly, The Music Man, Auntie Mame, How to Succeed in Business without Really Trying*, and *Barefoot in the Park*. He also owned the Martin Beck and St. James theaters in New York, the Colonial in Boston, and the Shubert in Philadelphia. In 1953, William McKnight and his wife established the McKnight Foundation, which was devoted to funding a number of social service causes.

3-M continued to grow to mammoth proportions in the years after McKnight left the firm. By the time of his death, the company produced 84,000 products, and had annual sales of over $5 billion. Its profits in 1979 were over $600 million, and it ranked as the sixty-eighth largest company on the *Fortune* 500 list. A former 3-M executive characterized the firm as ''a nickle and dime business,'' but noted that ''fortunately, it all adds up.'' 3-M produces, in addition to the previously mentioned products, photocopiers, carbonless paper, microfilm, more than 500 kinds of pressure-sensitive tapes, graphic paper, x-ray film, motion picture film, plastic lenses for glasses, surgical masks, videocassettes, magnetic recording tape, and thousands of other products.

3-M's record over the years was so exceptional, that Thomas J. Peters and Robert H. Waterman, Jr., singled them out for special attention in *In Search of Excellence*, published in 1982. In the later years of the decade, however,

3-M began to experience some difficulties. The company was unable to reach its oftstated goal of a 10-percent growth in earnings per share throughout the 1980s, and, in fact, it even experienced some declines. Heavy dependence on slow-growing industrial customers and a price war, which put a squeeze on its profits in the videocassette and computer-diskette businesses, left 3-M uncharacteristically unsure of itself. An industry consultant made a remarkable statement about 3-M in the mid–1980s: "I view 3M at this moment as essentially in chaos." Perhaps not since the years before William McKnight took control of the firm could that sort of statement have been made about 3-M.

The company's response, though, was true to form—it immediately and significantly increased the firm's R&D budget from 4.5 percent of income in 1981 to nearly 6.5 percent in 1985. Rather than spreading this out to fund the development of hundreds of new products, the money was focused on projects with bigger potential payoffs. By 1988, 3-M had already shown significant recovery. Sales in 1987 were $9.5 billion, an increase of nearly 10 percent from the previous year; profits were $918 million, up a whopping 17.8 percent. With 82,000 employees, it was the thirty-seventh largest company on the *Fortune* list. 3-M spent in excess of $600 million for R&D, a figure that represented over 6 percent of sales. 3-M's turnaround was so rapid and so complete that by 1989 Thomas J. Peters was able to say: "It is far more entrepreneurial than any $10 billion company I've come across, and probably more entrepreneurial than a majority of those one-tenth its size." The modest South Dakota bookkeeper who transformed 3-M into a giant of American business must have been resting comfortably once again. (**B**. *Business Week*, September 29, 1949, July 21, 1986, June 20, 1988, April 10, 1989; *Newsweek*, April 7, 1952; Virginia Huck, *Brand of the Tartan: The 3M Story*, 1955; Mildred H. Comfort, *William L. McKnight: Industrialist*, c.1962; *Dun's Review*, August 1963; *National Cyclopaedia of American Biography*, H:211; *New York Times*, March 5, 1978; Milton Moskowitz et al., *Everybody's Business*, 1980; *Fortune*, October 20, 1980, April 25, 1988; *Who Was Who in America*, vol. III; Thomas J. Peters and Robert H. Waterman, Jr., *In Search of Excellence*, 1982; Charles Garfield, *Peak Performers*, 1986.)

MACMILLAN, JOHN HUGH, JR. (December 1, 1895–December 23, 1960) and **WHITNEY MACMILLAN** (1929–   ). Grain trading and food processing executives, Cargill, Inc.. It was just a small thing. The president of the Winneshick County (Iowa) Historical Society wrote a polite letter to the president of Cargill, Inc., in 1982, telling him that the society planned to place a historical marker at the site of the first Cargill facility in Conover, Iowa. A tasteful plaque, made of "good quality material of a metal alloy," it would briefly recount the founding of the great grain trading firm by Will W. Cargill on that site in August

1865. After some time, an official from Cargill, Inc., wrote back: "I regret to say that the consensus here is against our participation in establishing the marker. It is difficult for me to explain why, but the feeling seems to be that it's inappropriate for a business to erect monuments to itself." How very like the giant Cargill, Inc. Secretive and introverted, it often attempted to downplay its importance. Once a Cargill official even said of the firm, "We're just a little old grain company in the woods." A little grain company with revenues of over $30 billion annually, and earnings of over $200 million. A little grain company worth about $5 billion. How did Cargill grow so large? And why is Cargill so secretive?

William Wallace Cargill was one of five sons of a Scottish sea captain who had lived on Long Island, but in the late 1850s, he moved his family to a small farm near Janesville, Wisconsin. Will worked on his father's farm, and at the end of the Civil War, he and two of his brothers followed the frontier across the Mississippi River and settled in the small town of Conover, Iowa. There, he and his brothers purchased an interest in a small wooden grain elevator. Before long, Conover, a typical frontier boomtown, sported 300 people, thirty-two saloons, three hotels, and eleven other grain storage warehouses. When the Southern Minnesota Railroad began to build its line, however, Conover lost its marketing advantage and died out. Cargill and his brothers did not mourn their loss, but they followed the railroad, building or buying grain elevators along its line. When the Panic of 1873 bankrupted a number of elevator operators, Will Cargill bought them out at distress prices. This daring move established Cargill as a major factor in the grain trade of the upper Midwest. In 1874, he established his headquarters in La Crosse, Wisconsin, and he purchased a picturesque Victorian mansion in the small city. From this base, Cargill pioneered the system of "integration" that made his company such a powerful presence in the grain trade.

Cargill's integrated system established a "moving belt" of grain that transported wheat from the farms to small country depots, and on to large, urban terminals. There were two keys to the system. The first was to establish credit, since a grain trader had to have ready access to a massive amount of short-term credit and be able to get financing for expanding its own operations. The second was to work out an equitable system with the railroads. This usually involved establishing a system in which rebates were granted for large customers. As a result, Cargill could often move grain at lower rates than most of his competitors, a practice that incurred the wrath of farm organizations like the Grange. But it was a practical necessity in a business that operated on small profit margins and dealt with a highly cyclical price structure.

During this same period, Will Cargill's brother, J. F. Cargill, was developing (with Will's backing) another grain company headquartered in Minneapolis. It had elevators that ran along James J. Hill's* Great Northern Railway, concentrating on the fertile grain-growing regions of the Red River Valley of western Minnesota and eastern North Dakota. The Cargill family, in fact, established a close rapport with Hill and his family, thereby gaining favored positions for Cargill elevators alongside Hill's railroad. When J. F. Cargill fell ill, yet another Cargill brother, S. D., took his place. In 1903, when S. D. Cargill died, there was no Cargill to replace him, but Will Cargill had the right man at hand—John H. MacMillan.

When Will Cargill had moved to La Crosse, he had bought a home right across the street from another Scots-Presbyterian family—the MacMillans. Duncan D. MacMillan, who had been born in Quebec, Canada, was the son of a Scottish immigrant who came to La Crosse in the 1850s. Over a period of twenty years, the children of the two families became very close, and in 1895 John Hugh MacMillan married Will Cargill's eldest daughter, and Will's eldest son married a MacMillan. Young John MacMillan went to work for his father-in-law, and learned the ropes of the grain trade. When Will sent him to manage the Minneapolis operation in 1903, MacMillan viewed it as a golden opportunity to achieve a more highly integrated organization—one that did *both* grain merchandising and grain warehousing over a much larger area. In this fashion, the Cargill operations could make money in prosperous years through merchandising activities, and in less prosperous years by storing grain for others. This concept became a basic Cargill policy that has been slightly amended and updated, but never changed.

While MacMillan was putting the Minneapolis operations into fine running order, the La Crosse end of the business was in real trouble. Old Will Cargill was a very rich man and an astute businessman, but in the several years preceding his death in 1909, he had allowed his son, William S. Cargill, to make a number of unfortunate business decisions. These included building a railroad that was said to start nowhere and end nowhere, assembling a vast irrigation project in Montana, starting a lumber business, and so on. When Will Cargill died intestate, the entire Cargill operation was caught up in massive legal wranglings between relatives and creditors, and the company teetered on the brink of bankruptcy from 1909 to 1916. A creditors' committee sold off holdings in land and timber, and a virtual clan war ensued between the Cargills and the MacMillans for control of the enterprise. Ultimately, the MacMillans emerged triumphant, and the Cargills settled for cash, notes, and a minority interest in the business.

By the time he emerged in control of the grain firm, John MacMillan faced enormous challenges. Paramount was the fact that large, European grain companies had secured a large toehold in the Midwest while the Cargill firm was crippled. Clearly MacMillan had to fight back with every weapon at his disposal if Cargill were to maintain its position as even a regional power in the grain trade. First he merged the Minneapolis and La Crosse ends of the grain business into one unit, called the Cargill Elevator Company. Then he disposed of any other property he could to obtain much needed operating capital. These decisions allowed the firm to survive the hectic war years, but severe new challenges lay ahead in the 1920s.

John MacMillan recalled those years, "A revolution took place in the method of marketing midwestern grain in the East" during the 1920s. In 1919, a large

Buffalo wheat broker formed his own company to lease space in Duluth terminals, so that he could buy spring wheat in Minneapolis and Duluth. Soon after, two Eastern exporters began buying spot grain in the Midwest and selling to other exporters, free on board (FOB) to Eastern shipping points. To compete, MacMillan set up Cargill's own Eastern sales organization. To do so, he picked up a bankrupt Milwaukee grain firm with branches in several Eastern cities. Cargill could change its business to an FOB Buffalo basis, which gave the firm a great deal of wholesale grain business out of that port to the East, and in 1922 he set up a sales organization in New York City. The next step was to set up an export business, and MacMillan, who had to start from scratch, established Cargill's own offices in Europe and Argentina in 1929. For several years, the company funneled its export business through Montreal, but Cargill had the opportunity to jump ahead of its competitors with a huge new grain elevator in Albany, New York. The city's port commission wanted to build a 3.5-million-bushel elevator there for $1.5 million, but no one seemed able to do it. Cargill, which had just built a bushel elevator with a radical design in Omaha, Nebraska, proposed building one of at least 12 million bushels in Albany for $1.5 million. The man responsible for this design was John MacMillan's son, John H. MacMillan, Jr., a brilliant, irascible engineer and an abrupt, abrasive advocate of free enterprise. It was ''John Junior'' who was primarily responsible for building Cargill into a massive giant of the grain trade.

John Junior was born in Ft. Worth, Texas, received his elementary education at Blake School in Minneapolis, and then went to Phillips Academy in Andover, Massachusetts. After young MacMillan got his B.A. from Yale in 1918, he entered the U.S. Army as an officer. He served in the American Expeditionary Force in France and rose to the rank of major. Upon returning to the United States in 1919, John Junior joined Cargill Elevator, working for the family's lumbering operations in British Columbia. He then became a grain buyer and a trader for the company's Duluth office. In 1926 he was elected a director in the company, and he moved to the headquarters' office. During the late 1920s, he assumed increasing executive responsibilities, and then, with the onset of the depression in 1929, he was faced with a worsening situation.

Although it is not clear just how bad things were for Cargill during the depression, it is evident that the company was severely squeezed by the downturn. As a result, a new creditors' committee was appointed to monitor its operations, and in 1932 the company was reorganized as Cargill, Inc. With the reorganization, John Junior became vice president and general manager of the company, and John Peterson, a vice president of Chase National Bank, Cargill's longtime banking ally, was brought in to guide the firm during this difficult period. Although the elder John MacMillan remained president until 1936, John Junior and Peterson were responsible for Cargill's transformation during the 1930s.

MacMillan and Peterson scraped up every cent they could during the 1930s to invest heavily in basic transportation and storage facilities for Cargill. The massive grain elevator they built at Albany, New York, was a prime example of their ambitious approach. MacMillan, who was a self-taught engineer, designed a huge, 10-million-bushel elevator in Omaha, with a tabernacle-style roof whose slant followed the slope of the grain. With the successful completion of that elevator, Cargill had the lock on a new technology that no one else could match. They were able to build the massive 12-million-bushel elevator in Albany for the port authority with public money, and then take a long-term lease on it. It was a perfect arrangement for Cargill, since it gave the company massive storage facilities at bargain-basement prices, and access to New York City's export facilities.

Cargill had a similar experience with the barges that carried grain on the New York State Barge Canal from Buffalo to Albany. The grain barges were falling apart, and MacMillan designed a new kind of articulated barge that could be lashed together to form huge, single units. Later, Cargill also designed and built its own oceangoing vessels, which cost one-quarter less than those from conventional shipyards. These actions brought Cargill into the shipping field, thereby decreasing its dependence on other agencies.

But MacMillan's free-enterprise, buccaneering spirit also got Cargill into a lot of trouble during these years. He engaged in a long and bitter fight with the Chicago Board of Trade and the federal Commodity Exchange Authority during the 1930s. Because of severe drought conditions, corn was a very scarce commodity; the 1936 crop had been a failure, and the 1937 crop had yet to be harvested. Cargill began to buy up corn "futures" for delivery in September 1937, but people who had sold these contracts to Cargill soon found they could not get enough supplies to meet their contracts. The Chicago Board of Trade ordered Cargill to sell some of its own holdings of corn to alleviate the "squeeze," but MacMillan refused, claiming this would severely depress the corn market. In retaliation, the board suspended trading in corn for three days, and the customers who could not deliver on their contracts were ordered to pay Cargill at the rate of $1.10 a bushel. The Board of Trade expelled Cargill, denying it trading rights on the floor. At that point, Secretary of Agriculture Henry Wallace intervened and accused Cargill of trying to corner the market in corn. That action was settled in 1940 by a stipulation in which the government accepted Cargill's plea of not guilty, and MacMillan and the firm were given pro forma punishments.

During World War II, MacMillan moved into two nongrain areas—vegetable oils and animal feeds—because the international trade part of his business, which made up about 60 percent of Cargill's operations, had been shut down by the war. By the late 1940s, Cargill had become a large, diversified agricultural processor. In 1945, MacMillan had bought Nutrena Mills, Inc., a large producer of animal and poultry feed, and also purchased a large soybean-crushing mill to make vegetable oil. Corn and soybean processing became the "glamour" processing industries of the 1950s and 1960s, and MacMillan had urged Cargill into these operations at an early stage. He also began to push Cargill onto the international grain stage to a degree far surpassing anything it had done previously.

MacMillan's first step was to build a $2-million grain storage and processing plant in Puerto Rico. He then entered into a joint venture with the International Basic Economy Corporation, which was backed by the Rockefellers, to build grain elevators in São Paulo and Paraná, Brazil. This brought Cargill into territory traditionally controlled by the Bunge Corporation of Europe. Next, Cargill set up an overseas subsidiary, Tradax, in Geneva, which became one of Europe's largest grain companies in its own right. In 1957, Cargill and MacMillan reached an important milestone—they topped the $1-billion mark in sales for the first time, by handling 14 million tons of grain. A year later, it took yet another massively important step—it built an enormous 13-million-ton grain elevator at Baie-Comeau, Quebec, an ice-free port at the mouth of the St. Lawrence River. Grain was hauled there cheaply by lake vessels which could then haul back Labrador iron ore to lake ports. This two-way hauling process allowed MacMillan to shave costs and undercut the competition in a critical area. John Junior had built Cargill into a massive company, estimated to be about the thirtieth largest in the United States in terms of sales, and seventh among the big merchandising operations.

When John MacMillan, Jr., died in 1960, the firm was left without a competent MacMillan or Cargill to run the company for the first time in its ninety-five-year history. Erwin Kelm became Cargill's president, and young Whitney MacMillan, the nephew of John, Jr., then just thirty-one-years-old, served as Kelm's understudy. As Whitney MacMillan stated at the time, "We knew we needed brains to run a company of this size, and there weren't enough brains in the family to do it." In 1976, Kelm retired, and Whitney MacMillan stepped in as head of the giant grain firm.

Whitney MacMillan was educated at Yale, and he served his apprenticeship in various aspects of the Cargill operation during the summers. After graduation from Yale, Whitney went to work full time at the family firm, working as a vegetable oil merchant in several areas, and then supervising the merchandising of barley and oats. By 1959, he had become assistant superintendent in the grain division, and three years later he became assistant to Kelm, the president. In 1966 Whitney was named to the board of directors, and two years later he became a group vice president. He became executive vice president in 1971, president in 1975, chief executive officer in 1976, and chairman in 1977.

The sixteen years of Kelm's management were good to Cargill. By the time Whitney MacMillan took over in 1976, Cargill's revenues were over $10 billion a year, with earnings in excess of $100 million, and the company handled more than 25 percent of America's grain exports. It was operating about 600 various plants and offices in thirty-eight countries; employed more than 24,000 people; and had 175 grain elevators in the United States, 165 in Canada, and 5 in Europe and Japan, which gave Cargill a storage capacity of nearly 300 million bushels of grain. To haul the grain to markets, Cargill used about 5,000 railcars, 500 river barges, and fourteen transoceanic liners.

One of the Cargill traditions continued by Kelm and Cargill family members was what John MacMillan called the "negative dividend," that is, the practice of plowing virtually all earnings back into the firm. Meager dividends, if any, were paid, and as a result, the firm's net worth, which stood at about $100 million in 1965, was in excess of $1 billion in 1977. During the early 1970s, Kelm took another important step—he began quietly inching Cargill into consumer markets. He developed a large-scale broiler chicken business under the Paramount label, and he began to sell turkeys under a variety of labels. Its Burrus Mills in Texas sold flour to consumers under the Light Crust brand, and it marketed soybean-based artificial bacon chips and a soybean-based imitation chocolate. Cargill Investor Services was established to help people speculate in commodities, and Summit National Life Insurance offered life and group insurance programs.

Whitney MacMillan built on this massive base when he took over Cargill. By the mid–1980s, the firm had become the most powerful force in the world grain economy, outstripping its once mammoth European rivals. Cargill's revenues in 1985 were $32.3 billion, and its net income was $280 million. In that year, Cargill exported from the United States nearly 6 million tons of wheat in a six-month period, almost one-quarter of the total wheat exports from America. It also handled between 15 and 18 percent of all grain shipments from France, and it is the largest agricultural exporter on the European continent. The hub of Cargill's international operations continued to be the Tradax Corporation, which by then was headquartered in Panama, but its center of operations remained in Geneva. From there, it moved grain all over the world, even into the Soviet-bloc countries.

The extent of Cargill's operations is difficult to ascertain, since as a private corporation it is not obliged to publicize such information. But by the mid–1980s, the company had nearly 800 plants and offices in fifty-two countries around the world. It ran an armada of 420 barges and eleven towboats on American inland waterways, had two huge vessels that ply the Great Lakes, and twelve oceangoing ships. It also ran some 2,000 railroad hopper cars and 2,000 tank cars. It picked up a bewildering number of subsidiaries and affiliates worldwide, and it could process 300 million bushels of corn every year. It was the second largest miller of flour in the United States with thirteen plants, with the capacity to produce 4.5 billion pounds of flour annually. It sold layer chicks to egg producers in ninety different countries, and it owned a huge orange-juice plant in Brazil. Cargill has dedicated 87 percent of its cash flow to making new investments and to buying troubled agricultural companies. In 1974, Cargill acquired Caprock Industries, one of the largest cattle feedlot operations in the United States, and in 1979 Whitney MacMillan masterminded the purchase of MBPXL, a billion-dollar meat packer in Wichita, Kansas, which created a ready market for the Caprock operations.

By the mid–1980s, Whitney and his brother Cargill MacMillan together were worth about $3 billion. Other family members controlled an equal amount of wealth. The family and company remained intensely private and secretive about operations. *Forbes* magazine in 1986 called Whitney MacMillan "an unknown," and said he wanted it that way. In 1985, Cargill made an extremely rare disclosure of some financial data in the course of a European debt offering. As a result, they suddenly found themselves in the media spotlight—and they did not like it one bit. Whitney MacMillan told a reporter who appeared at the baronial sixty-three-room Cargill headquarters in suburban Minnetonka, Minnesota, "We would have preferred you were not here. This was an experiment. We didn't realize the reporting requirements. If we did, we wouldn't have done it." Nobody really knows why Cargill is so secretive, but you can bet they will not go public again. (**B**. *Business Week*, April 16, 1949, January 4, 1964, September 14, 1981; *Newsweek*, October 14, 1957; *National Cyclopaedia of American Biography*, 49:629; *Who Was Who*, vol. 4; *New York Times*, December 24, 1960; John L. Work, *Cargill Beginnings, An Account of the Early Years*, 1965; *Fortune*, December 1965, October 12, 1987; James Trager, *The Great Grain Robbery*, 1975; *Wall Street Journal*, November 7, 1975, May 7, 1982; *Forbes*, November 1, 1976, September 18, 1978, November 5, 1984, November 17, 1986; Dan Morgan, *The Grain Merchants*, 1980; Milton Moskowitz et al., *Everybody's Business*, 1980; *New Yorker*, June 18, November 12, December 17, 1984, March 4, March 11, 1985; Ralph Nader and William Taylor, *The Big Boys*, 1986.)

MARCUS, (HAROLD) STANLEY (April 20, 1905–   ). Retail chain store executive, Neiman-Marcus Company. Stanley Marcus, in an article entitled "Fashion Is My Business," which was published in *Atlantic Monthly* in 1948, clearly recognized what had enabled his family's luxury specialty store to succeed so famously. He describes how in 1930 one of the great oil fields in the world "blew in," instantly creating a new crop of millionaires in Texas. These new millionaires were classic nouveaux riches, people who lacked the elementals of good taste, but now had ample money to clothe their bodies and furnish their homes in the most opulent manner. As he noted, "[a] few spent their money blatantly and in poor taste," but the majority turned to Neiman-Marcus for help. He noted modestly, "Their tastes began to be molded and shaped by the clothes they wore and the furniture and decor selected for their homes, and in a relatively brief time it was difficult to distinguish them from any 'old' money group in America." Neiman-Marcus was soon recognized as the arbiter of taste for the entire American Southwest. Of course, not everyone was converted. A Texas cattleman who visited Neiman-Marcus summed up the store's merchandising approach when he said, "In all my time I never saw so many things a body kin get along without."

The famous Dallas store was founded in 1907 by Stanley Marcus' father Herbert Marcus, Herbert's sister, Carrie Marcus Neiman, and her husband, A. L. Neiman. Herbert and Carrie Marcus were born in Louisville, Kentucky, in 1878, of Jewish parents who had recently immigrated to America from Russia. The Marcus children grew up in Louisville, but they moved to Hillsboro, Texas with their parents. Herbert never finished grammar school. He moved to Dallas in 1896 to work as a shoe clerk at Sanger Brothers store in Dallas. At that time, Sanger Brothers was the leading department store in the Southwest, and Herbert rose quickly to become a buyer for the boy's department. Carrie Marcus followed her brother to Dallas, and into retailing, working at A. Harris, Sanger's leading competitor. While working there, she met A. L. Neiman, a flamboyant department store sales promoter from Cleveland, Ohio. They were married in 1905.

The store that Herbert Marcus and the two Neimans opened in Dallas was a risky, even foolhardy, venture for the time. They proposed to open a frankly expensive store catering exclusively to women in a city that in the days before the big oil booms was far from rich. Furthermore, they planned to sell expensive ready-to-wear, not custom, clothing for women at a time when wealthy women were ordering their clothes custom-made from New York City or from the best local dressmakers. But Herbert and Carrie put their efforts into buying the very finest clothing available, and A. L. Neiman proved a wizard at advertising and promotion. Most important, however, all three ensured that their customers were given the utmost in personal attention by the owners. This has been a major trademark of the store throughout its history.

Despite some early problems, the Neiman-Marcus store prospered, so much so that when fire struck in 1913, the owners decided to move to larger quarters. In September 1914, the new store was established at its present quarters at the corner of Main and Ervay. A few months later, it was a glittering congeries of twenty-five specialty shops in one building. In the first years of operation in the new building, Neiman-Marcus made a profit of $40,000 on sales of $700,000. The store continued to operate at a profit during the war years, and in 1918 and 1919 there was a great surge in sales, reaching almost $2.2 million in the later year. Much of this great increase (nearly 100 percent from 1918 to 1919) came as a result of the discovery of oil in the West Texas fields. This brought a vast new source of wealth to the area, and a new breed of customer into the Neiman-Marcus store. As Don M. Coerver and Linda B. Hall have noted, "It was a linking of rapid wealth and conspicuous consumption that would remain an essential part of the Neiman-Marcus 'image' down to the present."

Sales and profits continued to climb throughout the 1920s, and Herbert Marcus greatly expanded the store. During these years, Stanley Marcus, after graduating from Harvard and spending a year at the Harvard Business School, joined the family store in the shoe department. Just twenty-one when he joined the business in 1926, Stanley had originally intended to pursue a career in the publishing business, but he succumbed to his father's urgings to enter retailing. During his first year on the job, Stanley Marcus introduced the weekly fashion show, which made Neiman-Marcus the first specialty store in the United States to do so on a regular basis. Two years later, he became secretary-treasurer of the company.

A great turning point in Neiman-Marcus' history came in 1926. The first significant event was the bankruptcy and sale of Sanger Brothers department store to a Kansas City promoter. The promoter discontinued Sanger's expensive lines of merchandise and fired many of the firm's oldest and best employees. Neiman-Marcus snapped up these lines, hired the terminated salespeople, and won over many of Sanger's once-loyal and devoted customers. A second turning point came two years later, with the breakup of the marriage between A. L. Neiman and Carrie Marcus Neiman, and Herbert's purchase of A. L. Neiman's share in the store for $250,000. Stanley Marcus took over many of Neiman's responsibilities after he left. Shortly thereafter, the Great Depression struck, and Neiman-Marcus suffered a decline in sales during the early 1930s, although the store showed a profit in every year except 1931 and 1932. After 1935, sales and profits rose. Neiman-Marcus' ability to weather the depression was due largely to the discovery of the giant East Texas oil field in 1930, which created yet another new crop of millionaires in the region.

As Neiman-Marcus expanded during the 1930s, Stanley Marcus came into his own in the store's management. He had been meticulously trained for these duties. In fact, he received such thorough training in the store during the 1920s that Emerson Brewer commented in the *Southerner* that Stanley and his brothers were "as carefully and stringently groomed for their careers in retailing as a European diplomat for foreign service." Carrie Marcus Neiman was primarily responsible for the selection of merchandise in the store during the 1930s, but it was Stanley who assumed his uncle's role as a great promoter for himself and his family's store. Neiman-Marcus certainly had fine merchandise—Carrie Neiman saw to that—but it was no better than that carried by a number of other stores. The great success of Neiman-Marcus was that none of these stores, not in New York City or anywhere else, achieved the kind of reputation Stanley Marcus created for the Dallas store. In 1934, he began a national advertising campaign for the store, not because he thought shoppers from New York or elsewhere would visit, but because he reasoned that affluent Dallas shoppers would be more attracted to the store if it advertised in *Vogue* and *Harper's Bazaar*. He also helped set up an innovative credit policy during this time, designed to attract customers of "moderate circumstances." This was a roaring success, as Neiman-Marcus came to conduct an unusually high percentage of its business on a credit basis, and by 1936 it had 20,000 charge accounts. One of Stanley Marcus' great coups was to convince hundreds of manufacturers, both large and small, to sell exclusively to Neiman-Marcus in Dallas, so that their merchandise was not available in any other Dallas store. This also greatly added to the image of privilege at Neiman-Marcus.

Beyond that, Stanley Marcus—inspired by the great expert in public relations Benjamin Sonnenberg, whom Marcus had met as a young man—undertook one of the most ingenious and successful public relations campaigns ever conducted. Marcus sent out literally thousands of letters to persons all across the country— to anyone who might conceivably help enhance Neiman-Marcus' image. Then, in 1938, Stanley Marcus instituted the "Neiman-Marcus Awards for Distinguished Service in Fashion," which rapidly came to be recognized as the Oscars of the fashion industry, thereby solidifying his store's connection with the best and most tasteful fashion. It also greatly enhanced the Neiman-Marcus cachet.

The store's most sensational publicity, however, came from tales (real or apocryphal) of oil millionaires who demanded original and extravagant gifts for their wives or mistresses. Thus, as tales of diamond-studded cashmere sweaters and solid-gold bathroom fixtures became known, the national media's demand for these juicy stories soon exceeded their supply. Therefore, Stanley began to build into his annual Christmas catalog the most extravagant gift suggestions the world had ever seen. For example, some "gifts" from recent Neiman-Marcus catalogs have been his and her volcanic craters, imported from Greece, at $5,000 each; a sterling silver "think tank" or privacy capsule for $800,000; a pure-gold omelette pan with a stainless steel core and rosewood handle, along with a supply of truffles and eggs, for $30,000.

Stanley Marcus in 1935 took on the duties of executive vice president. During the war, Stanley had been called to Washington, D.C., to serve on the War Production Board. His assignment was to meet with representatives of the textile industry in an effort to conserve textiles. This role gave him the power to establish guidelines for women's fashions in the interest of conserving national resources. Eliminating ruffles and frills on women's clothing, Marcus dubbed the new styles "patriotic chic." The new, more masculine fashions became very popular with many women during the war years, as part of a broader "Rosie the Riveter" campaign designed to enhance women's wartime labor force participation. In 1944 Marcus returned to Dallas, where he became executive vice president at the family store. At that time, he and other family members began to prepare for the boom years they thought would come when the war ended.

By this time, there was little doubt that Stanley Marcus was the dominant force in the concern; this was particularly true in the years immediately following World War II. In 1946 Marcus announced plans to spend $2 million to enlarge the Dallas store, providing an even more magnificent setting for the sale of its luxury items. The Neiman-Marcus formula had been firmly established: limited lines of merchandise, higher prices, heavy promotional and advertising expenses, and luxurious surroundings that entailed substantial maintenance expense. The store, which had $2.6 million in sales when Stanley Marcus joined it in 1926, had grown to $20 million when he succeeded his father as president in 1950. By that time the store had about 100,000 charge accounts, which accounted for 65 percent of its sales. Despite Neiman-Marcus' deserved reputation as an expensive store that catered to the very rich, most of the charge customers were not wealthy. This was a major element in Stanley Marcus' success during this time: he expanded the store's customer base dramatically, without ever losing its cherished image as an upscale retailer.

Important also was the fact that half the charge accounts were outside of Dallas. These were mail-order customers who sent in orders from all over the

United States. Stanley Marcus, however, always made sure that the mail-order business did not deflect them from the primary job—serving the wealthy in-store consumer. As he put it:

We strive to provide the top 5 percent of our customers with the kind of service they want. These are the discerning ones, the tough ones, the ones who really know what they want. If we can please them, we will have pleased all our other customers. (*Business Week,* December 21, 1946)

During the years from World War II to the late 1960s, Stanley Marcus was probably the most important retailer in America; certainly, he was the most famous. At Neiman-Marcus, his influence was awesome. As one observer noted, "He has never been able to give up entirely any job he has held in the store. His shadow is cast across every department. Everybody knows that Stanley Marcus is the boss." He also had a tremendous flair for public relations, a trait instilled in him by Sonnenberg. As Walter Hoving, president of Tiffany's commented, "I think he's a top showman of the business. He's got a great sense of the theater and energy." One of Marcus' most important innovations in this area was the annual "fortnight." In 1957, he decided to stage a French fortnight at the store. Not simply limited to an exposition of French merchandise, it included cultural events with a French theme. Not just an in-store event, the Dallas Museum of Fine Arts held an exhibition of Toulouse-Lautrec paintings, the Municipal Auditorium displayed French tapestries, and local theaters showed French films. It was a stunning success—even the French ambassador to the United States attended—and it made huge profits for the store. It was the first of many such fortnights.

By the late 1960s, Stanley Marcus had increased the number of Neiman-Marcus stores from one to four, the volume of sales from $20 million in 1950 to $58.5 million, and the profits from $879,000 to $2.1 million, without ever destroying its reputation for uniqueness. He had opened the first new store in a Dallas suburb in 1951, and in 1955 he moved into Houston. The latter, however, was a public relations flop, as Neiman-Marcus had taken over an established retailer in the Houston area. It was one of the few times Marcus stumbled in public relations, and the Houston store did not capture the loyalty of Houston shoppers until it moved to a new suburban location. The Houston stores were followed by a suburban store in the Dallas–Ft. Worth area. The major disaster he had to deal with was a fire in the main Dallas store in 1964, the costliest fire in department store history. Marcus predicted that the store would "rise out of the ashes like a phoenix," and in a few months it was again open for business. Although many thought he should abandon downtown Dallas and relocate the main store in the suburbs, as Edward Carter[†] was doing with his California chain of department stores, Marcus rebuilt the old store to be more beautiful than ever, spending $1.7 million of its own money in addition to the $8.7-million insurance settlement. Years later, Marcus thought this was the most critical business decision he made in his entire career.

The expansion of Neiman-Marcus into the suburbs during the 1950s and 1960s opened up a new market for it to exploit. Before it had catered to the truly rich, and those who aspired to be, in its downtown Dallas store. The suburban stores, however, were pegged more to the upper-middle-class consumer. Those stores, then, also began stocking lines of more moderately priced merchandise. As Marcus explained the strategy, "We want to sell the millionaire, his young daughter, and his secretary." To a large extent the formula worked, as evidenced by the company's growing sales and profits during these years. By the late 1960s, Neiman-Marcus had four stores in operation—two in Dallas, one in Houston, and one in Ft. Worth—but further expansion seemed to be stymied because of shortage of capital. Since the Marcus family refused to sell stock in their company to raise the money, many in Dallas became concerned that Marcus would sell out to a large chain.

Marcus assured those concerned, however, that this was impossible. He pointed out that only 25 percent of the stock was publicly held, and that he and his brothers, along with his son, intended to keep running the company. Thus, the shock was great when, in 1969, Marcus announced that Neiman-Marcus had been sold to Carter, Hawley, Hale, the California chain of middle-America-style department stores. The worst fear of the old Dallas denizens was realized: under Carter, Hawley, Hale, Neiman-Marcus opened nine branches around the United States and became just another "cookie cutter" women's specialty store. It had lost most of its uniqueness by the 1980s, and in 1987 it was spun off from the larger chain.

Stanley Marcus continued as chairman of the board at Neiman-Marcus until 1975, when he became executive vice president with the parent company. Most felt, however, that Marcus' influence with the family firm was greatly reduced after the sale. When he joined Carter, Hawley, Hale in 1975, Richard Hauser, the first outsider, became chief executive of Neiman-Marcus. After 1975, Marcus could only watch helplessly in Dallas as Neiman's lost much of the fine-fashion business it once monopolized to small specialty stores that provided the small services Neiman's was no longer willing to give. There was something infinitely sad in May 1985 when, at the Ringling Brothers, Barnum & Bailey Circus show at Madison Square Garden in New York City, one of the heavily grease-painted clowns who popped out of the old Model T was none other than the eighty-year-old Stanley Marcus. It had been arranged as a gift to fulfill a lifelong dream for Marcus, but it seemed to accentuate a sad decline in his power, status, and, of course, taste. The family, however, seemed to take it in stride. His wife just dismissed it by saying, "[H]e's a ham"; and his brother commented, "He's been putting on a show his whole life, this is just the first time he's done it for Ringling Brothers." (A. Stanley Marcus, "America Is in Fashion," *Fortune*, November 1940; "While We Were Minding the Store, the State of Texas Grew Up," *Saturday Evening Post*, Winter 1971; *Minding the Store*, 1974; *Quest for the Best*, 1979. **B**. *Fortune*, November 1937; *New York Times Magazine*, September 13, 1942; *Business Week*, December 21, 1946, September 19, 1953, October 21, 1967; *The Atlantic Monthly*, December 1948; *Current Biography*, 1949; *Southerner*, January 1949; *Time*, September 21, 1953; Linda Hall, "Neiman-Marcus: The Beginning," *Western States Jewish Historical Quarterly*, II, 2 (January 1975); Don M. Coerver and Linda B. Hall, "Neiman-Marcus: Innovators in Fashion and Merchandising," *American Jewish Historical Quarterly*, 66, 1 (1976); Leon Harris, *Merchant Princes*, 1979; Robert Hendrickson, *The Grand Emporiums*, 1979; *People Weekly*, May 13, 1985.)

MARS, FORREST EDWARD, SR. (1904–   ). Candy manufacturer and food processor, Food Manufacturers, Incorporated, Mars, Incorporated. Forrest Mars is so reclusive that he is often referred to as the "Howard Hughes"* of the candy industry. No one outside his firm and family knows his birth date (a company spokesman remarked, "Nobody's got the courage to find out how old he is") or any other details about his life. There are few photographs of him, and he has only given one interview in his life—in 1966, to a confectionary trade paper. It took the editor five years to finally set up the interview, and when the article came out, Mars was so upset with what he felt were its inaccuracies that he vowed never again to talk to the press. If a reporter calls Mars, Incorporated headquarters, officials there will not even tell the caller if Mars is still alive. The firm's headquarters are located in McLean, Virginia,—also the home of the Central Intelligence Agency, and the security measures there are so tight—with signs all over the place saying, "Warning! These premises under constant electronic surveillance"—that B. Robert Kill, president of Beatrice Food's confectionary and snack division, commented, "They may *be* the CIA for all I know." A former sales manager with the Mars company said more seriously, "It is a very secretive, low-key, low-profile company—except in the marketplace." The family has explained that they avoid publicity primarily so as not to distract attention from the Mars brands. This relatively harmless trait has evolved, according to *Fortune,* into a cult among family members.

Forrest Mars was born in Minnesota, the son of Frank C. Mars, a native of Pennsylvania, and his young wife, Ethel G. Kissack. Not a great deal is known about either Frank or Forrest Mars in these early years, but a few facts seem clear. First of all, Frank Mars worked for a number of years as a candy salesman in Minnesota, and then in Washington State. In 1910, Ethel Mars divorced Frank on the grounds of nonsupport, and she was awarded custody of six-year-old Forrest. During the remaining years of his childhood, Forrest rarely saw his father, who often was not even able to send his $20-a-month support payments. Forrest Mars attended public schools in Seattle, Washington; North Battleford, Saskatchewan; and Lethbridge, Alberta. In 1923, he enrolled in the School of Mines at the University of California at Berkeley. In his junior year, Mars transferred to Yale University, where he enrolled in the industrial engineering program at the Sheffield Scientific School. He graduated from Yale in 1928, and then he joined his father at the latter's candy-manufacturing concern in Chicago.

Frank Mars had had an eventful eighteen years after his divorce from Forrest's mother. He had remarried soon after the divorce—to another Ethel. He also went into business for himself as a candy maker in Seattle, but the business failed, and the creditors even took his personal belongings in settlement. Frank started another candy company in Tacoma, but again he had to declare bankruptcy in 1914. The war years were difficult for him; he suffered one failure after another, and in 1920 he and his wife returned to Minnesota with $400 in cash. Settling in the Minneapolis–St. Paul area, he set up yet another candy business. Living upstairs in a one-room apartment over the factory, the two worked long hours making and distributing candy to local stores. At the same time, Frank began to experiment with candy bars. In 1923, he developed the recipe for the Milky Way bar, and in one year sales skyrocketed from $72,800 to $792,900. Forrest Mars' role in all this is coated in legend, but supposedly young Forrest suggested the basic Milky Way ingredients—malted milk with a chocolate coating—and advised his father to concentrate on a limited product line. Whatever the case, during the mid–1920s, Forrest Mars was at college, and Frank Mars built Milky Way into a nationally distributed candy bar. By 1930, shortly after Forrest joined the firm, Mars, Incorporated was one of the largest candy-bar makers in the country, with sales of $24 million, and profits of about $2.3 million.

In 1929, Mars, Incorporated moved from the Minneapolis area to Oak Park, Illinois, a suburb of Chicago, where a new plant was built. It was at this spanking new facility that Forrest Mars joined his father's thriving business. Forrest arrived with his engineering degree, and an ample supply of arrogance and brashness. He immediately began to criticize his father's running of the business, and carried on about how he could run it better. By 1932, according to legend, Frank Mars had had it with his son. Remarking that "[t]his company isn't big enough for both of us," the elder Mars supposedly gave Forrest $50,000, the recipe for Milky Way, and the foreign rights to the product.

Frank Mars continued to run a prosperous company in Chicago after his son's departure, even though the depression cut his sales by nearly two-thirds. He built a huge estate in Wisconsin, and had a 2,700-acre showplace for raising race horses in Tennessee, called Milky Way Farms. In 1934, at fifty years of age, Frank Mars died, and the control of Mars, Incorporated passed to his second wife. She was more interested in the racing stable, however, and she left the running of the candy business to her half-brother, William L. (Slip) Kruppenbacher. Kruppenbacher ran a profitable operation throughout the 1930s, and in 1939 he greatly enlarged the advertising budget and began to sponsor "Dr. I.Q.," a popular radio show. It had a dramatically positive impact on sales, which continued to grow during the war years. The death of Ethel Mars in 1945 opened up an opportunity for Forrest Mars to gain control of his father's firm.

When he arrived in England after being banished by his father, Forrest Mars set up manufacturing facilities in an old building in Slough, an industrial town near London. The facilities there were very rudimentary, and he was almost ruined once when rain leaked through the roof onto his supplies of raw materials and stacks of candy awaiting shipment. But he persevered. When he arrived in England, he slightly changed the chocolate coating of Milky Way, sweetening it to suit the tastes of the English. Sales soon took off. As he commented in the only interview he ever granted, "If you make a really good product that people want and are willing to pay for, money will come." And come it did, as Mars, Limited soon became one of the leading candy firms in England.

With the success of Milky Way, Forrest Mars began to diversify. He saw a huge potential market for pet food in England. Dogs and cats there were still fed table scraps, and so he set up Petfoods, Limited shortly after establishing Mars, Incorporated. With little or no competition, he soon dominated the British pet food industry. In fact, the firm remained so strong that even fifty years later, the British Office of Fair Trading alleged the firm still controlled 55 percent of the market.

At the outbreak of war in 1939, Forrest Mars returned to the United States, leaving a trusted associate in charge of his English operations. Mars planned to enter the American candy industry, and he brought with him the right to make a version of a British candy called Smarties, a sugar-coated pellet with a chocolate center. He had made the deal with Rowntree Mackintosh, the British candy manufacturer, in exchange for allowing them to make Snickers in Britain and Europe. His new candy, called M&M's was the first candy of that type to be sold in the United States. The candy was called M&M's because Forrest Mars' partner in the venture was R. Bruce Murrie, one of the adopted sons of Milton S. Hershey,* the founder of Hershey's Chocolate. This was an example of the kind of strategic planning that Mars used so well throughout his career. Aware that the war might well disrupt supplies of cocoa and chocolate for his new product, Mars recognized that having Hershey's son for a partner would guarantee his firm preferential treatment from the giant chocolate concern, and he was right. Murrie, who sold his 20-percent interest to Mars in 1949, said, "We had tremendous help from my father—an assured supply of chocolate and a lot of technical help." The Hersheys lived to profoundly regret all that help in later years.

At the same time he started to make M&M's, Mars set up another business to begin producing a new kind of rice. He had discovered a new method of processing rice that improved its storability, its nutritive value retention, and enhanced its cooking properties. Naming the new rice "Uncle Ben's," Mars began producing and marketing it in the early 1940s. Like M&M's, it was an instant hit. He started with a small plant in Houston, Texas, but as sales grew, he expanded the company, and with the help of some government loans, he built a large manufacturing complex. In the 1980s, Uncle Ben's still ranked among the five top-selling rice products in the United States.

By 1945, then, Forrest Mars had a thriving operation. His British companies had suffered during the war, but were in a strong position for recovery and expansion. In the United States, Forrest had built a company secured by two strong bases—candy and processed rice. But he had an almost obsessive desire to gain control of his father's highly successful candy company. One close friend of the Mars family recalled that Forrest Mars "was frantic at the notion that anyone except a Mars should control the company." With the death of his stepmother in 1945, a window of opportunity opened for him to gain control. Forrest Mars at that point owned about one-third of his father's company's stock, his half-sister owned another third, and Kruppenbacher and a group of old employees of the firm owned the remaining third. Forrest Mars approached his half-sister, telling her that the current management of Mars, Incorporated was not operating the company efficiently, and that the size of her dividend (which was the only thing his extravagant sister had much interest in) would be increased if she supported his attempt to take control. In 1946, he took over an office in the Chicago headquarters of the firm, and he began his move to take control. But Kruppenbacher, who was acting chairman and president, convinced Mars' sister to side with him, and he started a pass system at Mars, Incorporated that barred Forrest Mars from the plant because he had not been issued a pass. In 1947, Kruppenbacher and Mars signed a truce of sorts, and Mars was given control of three of the nine seats on the board. For the next fifteen years, Mars kept the board in turmoil with his constant suggestions for change, until he finally won control of the firm.

In 1947, Mars, Incorporated had sales of $30 million, while Forrest Mars' own firm had sales of about half that much. But Mars had great plans for his own company, and over the next several decades it expanded at a much faster rate than Mars, Incorporated. Much of the reason for this rapid expansion had to do with Forrest Mars' adroit use of advertising. When M&M's were introduced into the United States, one of the selling strategies had been aimed at the American GI. Arguing that the GIs could carry the new candy in their K-rations, and it would not melt like block chocolate, Mars had developed an effective advertising slogan: "The milk chocolate that melts in your mouth—not in your hand." After the war, this kind of advertising ploy made little sense for adults, and at first Mars had difficulty adjusting to the postwar market, until he aimed the product primarily at children. He started a massive television advertising campaign, using the "Melts in your mouth—not in your hand" gambit, and M&M's became extraordinarily successful. Since advertising worked for candy, Mars began to use it effectively with Uncle Ben's. By the early 1960s, Forrest Mars' company, called Food Manufacturers, had grown enormously. With sales of about $200 million in 1962, it was four times larger than Mars, Incorporated. Of this amount, about 15 percent represented sales of Uncle Ben's rice, and the rest was the result of the phenomenally successful M&M's. In the process,

Forrest Mars' M&M's had not only overwhelmed his father's old candy company, but had also overrun Hershey's, long the unchallenged leader of the candy and chocolate industry.

At Mars, Incorporated, sales began to decline in the late 1950s, and in 1962 Kruppenbacher and his family sold their shares back to the company for $5.5 million. Forrest Mars and his half-sister, then, each owned 41 percent of the company; the remainder was held by a small group of employees. In 1964, Forrest Mars was finally able to purchase his half-sister's shares, and he merged his company into Mars, Incorporated. Sixty years old, Forrest Mars had finally gained control of the family company. Because of the bitter relations between Mars, Incorporated officials and Forrest Mars for so many years, he had seldom showed his face at the headquarters or plant. Few of the employees there had ever even laid eyes on him. Now that he owned the company, Forrest Mars summoned many of them for a meeting.

Forrest Mars charged into the meeting, where the anxious staff had gathered to meet him. Nearly bald, with a ring of silver-grey hair around his scalp, he wore an English suit with wide lapels and an unfashionably wide tie. He proceeded to tell the group a bit about his plans for the new Chicago division of his company. Then, he paused and said, "I'm a religious man." There was another long pause, as the assembled group struggled with what to make of this statement. All of a sudden, Mars dropped to his knees at the head of the conference table and began to pray to what now appeared to be the God Mammon: "I pray for Milky Way. I pray for Snickers." This, of course, totally unnerved the executives, but Mars' showmanship had a purpose—all members of the organization must be zealously and religiously devoted to a single objective— the pursuit of profit. If the point was missed at that meeting, it did not take long for Mars to drive it home.

Almost immediately, Mars began to change the way in which Mars, Incorporated conducted business—to make it conform to the principles he had developed in creating the hugely successful M&M's and Uncle Ben's. Although Forrest Mars was always highly autocratic in many respects, he nonetheless believed in an egalitarian corporate culture, where all employees are called associates. Upon taking over Mars, Incorporated, Mars dismantled the executive dining room, so that all employees, regardless of rank, would eat together in the cafeteria; he removed the partitions between the formerly lavish executive offices and installed glass panels, because he felt that office walls were "barriers to communication"; he eliminated all reserved parking places; and he made everyone, even the top executives, punch a time clock. One quirky Mars concept is the payment of a 10-percent bonus for executives and blue-collar workers with perfect records of punctuality.

Forrest Mars also was fanatical about quality. Legend has it that while visiting a store, Mars found an improperly wrapped candy bar. Furious, he returned to his plant, hunted around in boxes in the plant for more poorly wrapped bars, and then called the entire office staff to the boardroom. There, Mars took the candy bars, and one by one hurled them against the glass panel set in one boardroom wall. The employees got the message—Mars would allow no inferior products to leave his plant. Forrest Mars instilled this same concern for quality at his newly acquired operation in America, and in the process he created a mystique among its peers in the candy industry. The director of a confectionary wholesaler's association said, "They do everything right to keep the quality of the product up." A former employee commented, "When Mars finds a way to make the product better, even if it's more expensive for them, they do it." This concern for quality also extends to a virtual fetish for cleanliness. A former executive at one of Mars' highly automated plants said, "There is no place in that plant that is dirtier than the cleanest spot in my house. You can eat off the floor in the boiler room." Technicians even take samples of the carpet in the reception room of the main plant to determine whether visitors have deposited unwanted germs there. In his quest for quality, Mars also had Mars, Incorporated begin to manufacture its own chocolate, as he had done with M&M's for years, rather than rely on outside suppliers like Hershey's and Baker's for the product. Most important, however, Mars installed his own powerful system of management at Mars, Incorporated.

Trained as an engineer, Forrest Mars was a foremost practitioner of the concepts of scientific management. To his mind, management involved "applying mathematics to economic problems." As a result, he controlled his company from the headquarters in Virginia with a small central staff. Armed with an intricate system of charts, tables, and terse memos, he developed a highly individualistic management style which was, nonetheless, extraordinarily effective. Each manager, for example, was given a certain set of goals when he was hired and told to sign a letter of resignation at the same time. He was then given three years to meet those goals. If he failed, Mars exercised the prerogative of accepting the resignation. Mars also liked to hire highly educated people for his management slots; several of them have doctorates. To attract and keep high-quality personnel, Mars paid wages 10 percent above the industry norm. As one Mars alumnus put it, "Mars wants good people and hard work, and he feels confident that he can get both because he is paying top money."

Both general-staff and divisional executives were guided by a constantly revised and updated organizational manual that summarized Mars' management system. Set up essentially in the multidivisional, decentralized system pioneered at Du Pont, the system has a number of controls along the line that allowed Forrest Mars total access to all information about significant aspects of any operation. His principal instrument to measure performance was the return on total assets generated by each division, and the career of each executive was dependent upon his performance in this area. Mars generally expected a 22-percent return on assets—no more and no less. Year-to-year fluctuations were permitted, but, as a former executive has said, "Forrest gets his 22 percent in the long run." Mars was also determined to run a nonunion company, and no Mars plant has ever been organized. To keep the unions out, he paid his line workers 10 percent more than comparable jobs elsewhere, and an elaborate grievance system and a generous benefits plan were established.

Forrest Mars set up a mammoth advertising program for all of Mars' candies, just as he had been doing with M&M's for years. He spent about $30 million a year on advertising for all his products, which was far more than any one of his competitors. Also, trying to pattern the success he had found in England, Mars purchased Kal Kan, a pet food company, in 1968, and gave it a large advertising push, spending between $3 and $4 million a year on it in the early 1970s. He also opened a line of franchised Puppy Palaces in the late 1960s, but it was unsuccessful.

By the early 1970s, Forrest Mars had built an impressive empire. His candy business in the United States alone amounted to about $200 million, with an additional $55 million in Britain. All together, his company's sales of all products, in both the United States and abroad, amounted to about $500 million in 1970. Although in the early 1970s Hershey still had a somewhat larger share of the U.S. market (even though Mars was undoubtedly the world's largest candy maker at that point), by the late 1970s, Mars had between 30 and 32 percent of the domestic market, and was well ahead of Hershey. In 1980, Mars pulled off a marketing coup. Accompanied by a massive advertising blitz, Mars increased its candy-bar weight by about 10 percent without increasing the price. Hershey and other candy makers kept their bars at the same weight, and Mars clobbered them in the marketplace. Mars, which already had 37 percent of the market in 1979, saw that percentage increase to a whopping 46 percent in 1980. Hershey, once the most powerful American candy company, had its share drop from 28 percent to 26 percent. Other candy makers, like D. L. Clark, Curtiss, and Peter Paul Cadbury, suffered even greater losses. Then, having garnered that huge market share, Mars, a year later, quietly raised the price of its candy bars from 25 cents to 30 cents. That meant an additional $200 million in revenues for the giant company, with little loss of market share, since they still had the largest candy bar, even if it was slightly more expensive than the others. By this point, sales from candy products made up $1 billion of the $2 billion in total sales of Mars, Incorporated. Of the ten top-selling candy bars in the United States, five were sold by Mars: Snickers was number one; M&M peanut, number three; M&M plain, number 4; Three Musketeers, number 6; and Milky Way, number 9. Mars did suffer some casualties as well; his introduction of Sprint, Mars Double Crunch, and Snicker's Peanut Butter Crunch were all failures.

The Mars company was responsible for a number of important innovations in the candy industry. As *Business Week* noted, it was the first company in the industry to date its products, and the first to take back unsold items after four months. In fact, few competitors even attempted to follow their lead on this since, as one commented, "This is very risky unless you have Mars' turnover." But the policy made Mars very popular with retailers, and as a result they gave the company more "facings" in their retail outlets. Since candy purchases are mostly impulse purchases, the more shelf space a company has, the more likely the consumer is to pick that product. So, the rich got richer.

By the mid–1980s Forrest Mars and his two sons controlled a family fortune estimated by *Fortune* at $12.5 billion, making them one of the richest families in America. In 1973, Forrest Mars turned the day-to-day management of Mars, Incorporated over to his two sons, Forrest, Jr., and John, who became copresidents. Both graduates of Yale like their father, they were expected to divide management chores between them. But their father continued to take an active concern in every aspect of the plant's management for a number of years. Only in about 1980, as far as anyone can tell, did he finally allow his sons more autonomy in management. Problems at Mars, Incorporated escalated after that time. The two young men engage in constant rivalry and have conflicting management styles. Young Forrest, although more congenial and sociable, is secretive and eccentric, given to voluble tirades. John, considered the brighter of the two, is brusque, strong-willed, and combative, and, according to *Fortune*, has a "propensity to belch, pick his nose, or take off his socks and shoes during meetings." The rivalry between the two sons has been divisive and Mars, as well as the company's penchant for secrecy, has made it difficult for the company to make acquisitions. *Fortune* said Forrest, Jr., and John Mars' "slightly nutty leadership seems to lack vision," and a former Mars manager said, "Whatever their abilities, neither of these guys is equipped to run a multi-billion-dollar company."

Soon after leaving Mars, Incorporated in 1980, Forrest, Sr., decided that "retirement is the beginning of death," and he started his own small business. Taking $6 million, he set up the Ethel M (named for his mother) candy company in Las Vegas, Nevada, one of the few states that allows the manufacture of liquor-and liqueur-filled chocolates. Mars began to put out a locally distributed line of fine, boxed chocolates. He remarked that he did not want to leave Snickers and the like as his only monument, so this would show he could also produce fine, European-style quality chocolates. Mars lives in seclusion in a penthouse above the factory, and the plant is, of course, kept spotlessly clean. All employees, including all the executives, wear white uniforms and punch a time clock. There are no executive parking places and no offices. Sound familiar?

In the meantime, with the removal of Forrest Mars' influence, Mars, Incorporated has encountered difficulties. Hershey, which had been almost prostrate before Mars by 1980, came roaring back in the early years of that decade. Hershey accomplished its resurrection by becoming a fearless product innovator. Bringing out a staggering number of new candy products, by 1985 it had seventeen of the sixty top-selling candy bars, versus just nine for Mars. Mars, of course, still had its big five among the top ten, but by then Hershey also had five. Then, Hershey stunned Mars by buying the U.S. confectionary division of Cadbury Schweppes in August 1988. This increased Hershey's share of the U.S. candy market to 46 percent, versus 37 percent for Mars. Mars, on the other hand, continued to devote its advertising and marketing efforts to its established brands. Their only successful new products were the Twix bar, introduced in 1976, and Skittles, which came out in 1982.

Those few acquisitions Mars, Incorporated made in the 1980s did not turn out well. They picked up Snackmaster, a salty food snack, but it did not do well because Mars had no experience in distributing this kind of product. Their Mars Electronics, originally a manufacturer of coin changers, branched unsuccessfully into a number of electronics areas. Its most recent acquisition, of the highly profitable Dove International in 1986, also failed. Dove, the manufacturer of an upscale ice-cream-on-a-stick, was viewed by Mars as a potential big seller. It found, however, that fighting for freezer space at the supermarket was different from fighting for shelf space, and Mars was not able to expand the market. As one analyst commented, "It is not a Mars business." Although Mars had a much larger international business than Hershey, and had worldwide sales of about $6 billion—three times more than its rival—its dominance in that area was also being challenged. In the summer of 1988, the giant Nestlé Company of Switzerland bought Britain's Rowntree, giving it about 24 percent of Britain's candy market. Nestlé also had a larger share of candy sales in the rapidly growing European Economic Community. At home, Mars, Incorporated's pet food division continued to suffer losses. With 9 percent of the market in the United States, it watched Quaker Oats pass Kal Kan as the number two pet food maker when it acquired Gaines Pet Food. Only in Europe did Mars' pet food companies continue to dominate.

In the opinion of many analysts, Mars, Incorporated, by the mid–1980s, suffered from a bloated bureaucracy. Unlike the lean, taut management style of their father, the two sons had allowed the company to become too cumbersome and unwieldy. A competitor remarked, "Mars was always a company where line managers could make a decision. Now there are more committees, more memos, and too many meetings." Illustrative of this trend, in 1982, the producers of Steven Spielberg's hit film, *E.T.*, contacted Mars, Incorporated to see whether it wanted M&M's to be used as the candy that cements the relationship between E.T. and young Elliott. Mars was not interested. So, the producers went to Hershey, and received permission to use Reese's Pieces in the film instead. Hershey was astute enough and aggressive enough to recognize the marketing possibilities of this, and the company put up a million dollars for a tie-in promotion with the film. *E.T.* was an enormous success at the box office, and the sales of Reese's Pieces soared 70 percent in the month after the film's release. Two months later, more than 800 movie theaters carried Reese's Pieces, whereas none had carried it before. It was a terrible blow to M&M's and the Mars candy company. No reporter was able to reach Forrest Mars, Sr., for his reaction. (**B**. *Fortune*, May 1967, May 31, 1982, April 2, 1984, July 8, 1985, September 26, 1988; *Dun's Review*, February 1971; *Business Week*, August 14, 1978; Milton Moskowitz et al., *Everybody's Business*, 1980; *Forbes*, November 9, 1981; *Advertising Age*, July 19, 1982; Molly Wade McGrath, *Top Sellers, USA*,

1983; Michael Schudson, *Advertising: The Uneasy Persuasion*, 1984; Joseph J. Fucini and Suzy Fucini, *Entrepreneurs*, 1985.)

MILKEN, MICHAEL R. (1946–   ). Financier, Drexel Burnham Lambert. Two images of Michael Milken and his junk-bond operations have been purveyed extensively in the press. The first derives from what is unofficially called the "Predator's Ball." Held annually at the Beverly Hilton Hotel, in Beverly Hills, California, and hosted by Michael Milken and Drexel Burnham Lambert for the edification of 2,500 major junk-bond clients, it has been a dazzling extravaganza, part industry convention, and part lavish party. But the most important part of the event took place elsewhere. Not far away, at the posh and exclusive Beverly Hills Hotel, Milken threw smaller, more intimate cocktail parties in the evenings for the firm's most prized clients. In 1985, one of those parties catered to T. Boone Pickens,[†] Asher Adelman, Ron Perelman, Carl C. Icahn,[†] Sir James Goldsmith, Rupert Murdoch, Irwin Jacobs, Saul Steinberg,[†] Marvin Davis,[†] Samuel Belzberg, and the soon-to-be-infamous Ivan Boesky. Many of these movers and shakers had not met before, but they represented a select group of American capitalists, who had collectively put into play corporations with a total market value of over $80 billion. These were the "predators," the corporate raiders most feared by corporate America. And they were all Michael Milken's clients.

The other image of Milken was even more captivating: Milken at work in his Beverly Hills office. Having arrived at the office by 5 A.M., he sat at the center of an X-shaped group of desks, with his 300 or so colleagues surrounding him. From that strategic position, he could see each and hear all. A former Drexel bond trader recalled, "Everybody would be yelling at him, he'd be holding six conversations at once—two on the phone, three across the room, and [one] with me. I'd have to try to figure out when he was talking to me." From this vantage point (Milken has never had a private office), according to Connie Bruck, Milken developed a cultlike relationship with his employees. She stated in her exposé of Milken that his staff was "not unlike a cult: intensely secret, insular, led by a charismatic and messianic leader whom many of his followers came to see as larger than life." Although Milken might have disputed this, many of his most loyal subordinates did not. They called him the "King," and in their office hung a framed quote from *Barron's*, "Drexel is like a god, and a god can do anything it wants." Milken and his minions were, in the words of the bond trader hero in Tom Wolfe's *The Bonfire of the Vanities*, "Masters of the Universe." With the junk bond as their tool, they were not only becoming rich beyond their wildest dreams, they were also transforming the face of corporate America. They were making a revolution.

This "svengali of the junk bond," called the "grand sorcerer of finance" by *Institutional Investor* and the "mystery man of mergers" by *Fortune*, started modestly enough. Since he keeps his personal life very private, it is difficult to uncover many details of his life. Born in 1946 in California, the son of an accountant, Milken was raised in the prosperous Los Angeles suburb of Van Nuys. There he attended Birmingham High School, where he dominated several of the organizations he joined. He was made head cheerleader in 1964, and he was king of the senior prom. Milken went on to the University of California at Berkeley, where he majored in business and economics. Named head of his fraternity pledge group, in his senior year, he was president of his fraternity. One of his fraternity brothers later said that these accomplishments did not result from his popularity with his peers. "I don't think you would say he was popular in the fraternity," he said. "It wasn't charisma. He campaigned very hard and gathered people's respect. It was like running for political office—kind of Machiavellian. He worked at it. He was as driven to succeed as anybody." Virtually a straight-A student, Milken was also elected to Phi Beta Kappa.

Milken proved to be a driven man in college, and one with a good deal of financial acumen. He played poker all night long at Berkeley, and then went off to a stockbroker's office at dawn to watch the stock market. Classes were fit in later in the day. "Mike has always gotten by on three or four hours of sleep," said one of his closest friends. He was winning regularly at poker, investing those winnings in the stock market, and doing very well with his investments. A fraternity brother who invested along with him said, "He was monomaniacal about making money. To be a millionaire by age 30 was his goal. I thought I shared the same goal, but Mike was different. He wanted to be *rich*."

After graduating from Berkeley in 1968, Milken married his high school sweetheart and headed east to attend Pennsylvania's Wharton School of Finance. It took him ten years to get his MBA, but not because he was slow. While in his first year at Wharton, Milken discovered junk bonds, and his grand vision began to take shape. Studying with finance professor James E. Walter, Milken began to analyze the default rates and the yields on these junk bonds, and he found that they were much less risky than people had thought. In 1973, Milken and Walter coauthored a forty-six page paper titled "Managing the Corporate Financial Structure" which Milken delivered at a Financial Management Association conference that year.

Junk bond is a derisive Wall Street term for corporate bonds of "less than investment quality." That textbook definition hardly scratches the surface of their significance. Two companies have dominated the bond-rating system in the United States for most of the twentieth century: Standard & Poor's and Moody's. They have assigned letter-grade ratings to corporate bonds that descend from AAA to C. "Investment quality bonds" were defined as those with a rating of BB or better. Anything below that was termed "junk." In the way the market operated at the time, these junk bonds were not considered suitable investments for the large, institutional investor—insurance companies, pension funds, many mutual funds, and so on. The reasoning was that, although these bonds carried a higher interest rate, they were too risky, too liable to default for someone seeking a prudent investment. They were, in effect, the equivalent in many institutional investors' eyes of gold-mining stocks, or penny stocks on the Denver Exchange.

Not so, claimed Michael Milken. His studies demonstrated that the rate of default of these corporations was hardly greater than that of blue-chip firms. Milken pointed out that the standard ratings system was done on the basis of how large a company was, as well as its historical stability. The only companies to qualify for a rating of BB or above were those with assets of over $200 million that had been in business for decades. Therefore, they were the only firms which had access to the massive investment funds of the insurance companies, pension plans, college endowments, and the like. "This was a half-trillion dollar market," said Milken, that was closed to the "other twenty-two thousand corporations." Milken wanted to open that up and to destroy the grip on investment capital that the *Fortune* 500 firms had maintained for so long. So, while still working on his MBA at Wharton, Milken went to work for Drexel Firestone in Philadelphia, one of the forerunners of Drexel Burnham Lambert. There, he slowly and painfully began to work his revolution on corporate America.

Soon after Milken arrived, Drexel Firestone, a rather faded banking firm, was merged with Burnham & Company, a sleepy but profitable retail brokerage house. Milken's first job was to attack the back-office crunch affecting most of the brokerage houses at that time. Milken, who was studying operations research at Wharton, offered several down-to-earth, nonmathematical solutions to Drexel's problems. But this was all just a means to an end. Milken's mind was focused on junk bonds, and he was merely biding his time until he got a spot in the bond trading department. Eventually, that came to pass when he was given a corner in the bond department where he could begin to sell his ideas. Ernest Widmann, who was then director of Drexel's research, recalled; "He was brilliant, but he wasn't the typical egghead. He could talk to clients without scaring them."

Milken arrived at the right place at the right time. As he began to spread his enthusiastic gospel of the junk bond, he found an enthusiastic ally in Meshelam Riklis, chairman of Rapid-American Corporation, a conglomerate put together with vast quantities of junk bonds. Since Riklis was about the only person who had used these bonds on a large scale, Milken had him appear before groups of skeptical investors. "He wanted me to show why my company was highly leveraged and still highly profitable," said Riklis. The junk bonds were attractive to Drexel Burnham Lambert also. Frederick Joseph was appointed head of the new firm's bond trading department, and he knew there was no way to compete, head to head, with Wall Street's established firms. He decided that Drexel would have to do what no one else was doing. This made him uniquely receptive to new people and new ideas, that is, to outsiders with what seemed at first to be outlandish ideas. Joseph, in fact, cultivated this outsider status at Drexel. He took pride in the firm's ability to attract the misfits, those who did not feel comfortable at the more established houses. He once boasted that Drexel bankers included more "fat women and ugly men" than any other firm. And Milken was an outsider. He was, in the words of Myron Magnet in *Fortune*, "The Jewish junk bond expert banished to a remote corner of the trading floor of white-shoe Drexel Firestone." Milken told Joseph, "I don't know if I am smarter than anyone else, but I can work 25 percent harder." Drexel wanted to consciously thumb its nose at the establishment, and do things differently ("It's a conscious form of reverse snobbery," said an ex-Drexel banker). What could be more unorthodox, more challenging to the establishment than junk bonds? So Michael Milken was given permission to pursue his dream at Drexel, to the great enrichment of both parties.

At first Milken just peddled the junk bonds of what were called "fallen angels." These were older, once gilt-edged companies, whose bonds had fallen below investment grade in recent years. They seemed safer, somewhat more attractive to the institutional investor. When those became acceptable, Milken began to push the bonds of companies that were low-rated from the first. Many of the conservative institutional investors avoided them, but Milken began to gather around him a coterie of devoted investors, people who trusted his word on these issues because he had brought them profit in the past. This was the beginning of the phenomenal junk-bond network that Milken developed, the great key to his later success. The network was so important that he regarded it as a proprietary preserve. He cultivated close personal and business friendships among a group of money managers with "$1 billion checks in their pockets." As these money managers found that the junk bonds gave them an edge of over 4 percent over investment-grade bonds—an extra $40 million a year on a $1-billion portfolio—they, in turn, were able to attract more institutions to their funds. When other money managers, even those with more conservative institutions, realized what was happening, they also joined the ranks of the converted; they became part of Milken's network. By 1976, Milken was an independent power in Drexel, and he was earning over 100 percent on the capital he was given to trade his exotic fallen angels. As a reward, Milken was awarded a $5-million bonus, which he immediately reinvested. Joesph at that time realized that Milken "understood credit better than anyone else in the country." As a result of his growing influence, Milken was able to convince Joseph and Robert E. Linton, then the chief executive officer (CEO) of Drexel, to move his junk trading operation to Beverly Hills. Although a highly unusual and unorthodox move, it simply validated the Drexel culture. With an organization of over 10,000 employees and $4 billion in revenues by the mid–1980s, Drexel Burnham Lambert was remarkably unstructured, a loose, decentralized confederation of 550 independent profit centers, each of which had its own compensation deal, devised its own business plan, and recruited its own people. In that context, Milken's request was not out of the ordinary; he was just asking for a bit more independence than all the others. "We don't want to let bureaucracy stifle people's creativity," said Joseph. "We want to let people run their own businesses to the maximum extent possible."

But Milken's move to Los Angeles in 1978 symbolized a major break with the establishment. He could now turn his tight little junk-bond network into a broader crusade to make junk bonds an integral part of the American financial scene, and, in the process, transform the nature of American capitalism. Edward Jay Epstein called Milken "Wall Street's version of the Pied Piper, leading wayward fund managers from their traditional village." Milken piled up large profits for himself and for Drexel, not by arbitrage, which is the buying and selling of securities in order to make a profit on price discrepancies, in this case between junk and investment bonds, but from the large fees he received for selling previously unsalable corporate bonds. Meanwhile, at the same time he was giving the pitch to money managers, Milken began to develop a series of alliances with larger financiers who personally controlled other finance companies. Among the important allies Milken made during this early period were Saul Steinberg of Reliance Group Holdings, Fred Carr of First Executive Life Insurance, Carl Lindner of American Financial Corporation, Victor Posner of Chesapeake Financial Corporation, and the Belzberg brothers of First City Financial Corporation. Milken also became partners with some of these individuals in various joint ventures during this time. Most important, Milken acted as their financier when they needed to raise their own money to acquire other firms. Milken viewed himself as somewhat of a marriage broker, "bringing about kind of a marriage between institutions" and aggressive new corporations.

All of this, however, took place for many years without attracting much notice on Wall Street. For one thing, the junk-bond market was still small; the volume of new public issues ranged from $1 billion to $2 billion as recently as 1982. But, more important, it was, as one Wall Street man said, "a different mind set." A veteran junk-bond executive agreed: "It seemed like a real scuzzy business, lots of weird Vesco types running around." Wall Street, and the rest of America, took notice of junk bonds and Michael Milken in 1984. Early that year, when Drexel decided to assist T. Boone Pickens in his takeover of Gulf Oil, Milken and Joseph devised a new strategy using Milken's vast junk-bond network to finance the deal. Even some of the Drexel people were astounded when Milken was able to round up $1.7 billion in commitments for Pickens within a few days. It soon became apparent that Drexel's secret weapon was not junk bonds per se, but Milken's extraordinarily effective network. It was that network which stood behind Drexel's famous letter saying it was "highly confident" that it could arrange financing for a particular deal. It soon became evident to all that the phrase "highly confident" was virtually a 100-percent guarantee—Milken's ensemble was that fanatically committed to his advice on these deals. What emerged at Drexel, then, was a rare monopoly—not on junk bonds—but on a unique and highly personalized network developed by Milken.

As a result, power and influence within Drexel began shifting away from New York to Beverly Hills. Although Milken worked closely with top executives in New York, especially Joseph after he became CEO, it was clear that Milken was the lead player. Some of Drexel's New York bankers were unhappy with the arrangement. One commented: "Mike would say, 'Here's the deal, now get it done.' We were being relegated to being processing machines." Milken himself, along with a number of his employees, had become *very* wealthy by this time. Investing in Drexel's own junk bonds, Milken had a personal trading account in 1984 estimated at over $150 million, and the Milken family foundation had over $100 million. He also had a half-dozen partnerships with employees in which they reinvested much of the profits and bonuses they received at Drexel. Not only that, Milken and a few top aides had a controlling interest in First Stratford, which had over $500 million in assets. Milken was also a partner in Bass Limited Investment, with $2 billion in holdings, and in Pacific Asset Holdings, which had about $1 billion in capital. Finally, as its third largest shareholder, Milken had a strong voice, if not control, over Drexel's own $3-billion bond portfolio. Altogether, these funds represented about $7 billion!

After 1984, Milken became something more than a bond trader. His Beverly Hills office became the epicenter of the entire junk-bond market. His office handled 250,000 transactions a month, and Milken's operation accounted for half or more of all of Drexel's profits. Milken thus became unbelievably powerful at Drexel and on Wall Street. As even his brother, Drexel attorney Lowell Milken, admits; "Mike was putting so much money in everyone's pockets that nobody wanted to question him." But if money was the source of Milken's power, it was not his own personal goal. Although he is fabulously wealthy—he earned as much as $200 million in 1986 and had a total fortune approaching $1 billion—Milken lives modestly and seems to care little for money itself. He has a comfortable, but unpretentious, four-bedroom home in suburban Encino. There is a small swimming pool in the backyard, the same as all the neighbors have. When asked if he had other residences, some visible perks of his great wealth, he replied, "I have one house, one wife, one cat, and one car." The driving force for Milken, according to his ex-boss Robert Linton, is power. Linton told *Institutional Investor*,

I don't think money has anything to do with what he does. He's been beyond that for a long time. With Michael it's different. Michael wants to win the game. Michael wants to have it all. Michael wants to do every piece of business and every deal and make every dollar.

What game was Milken trying to win? Milken had started his crusade to poke a hole in the dam that kept the half-trillion-dollar reservoir of funds as a "private fishing pond for *Fortune* 500 and utility companies." Having broken that dam, Milken began channeling it into a whole new group of industries, companies, and entrepreneurs. He set out to alter irreversibly the balance of power in corporate America. By 1986, he had gone a long way toward accomplishing this. Entire industries, such as cable television and regional airlines, had been financed through junk bonds. In the process, a whole new class of entrepreneurs had emerged—the arbitragers, the leveraged buyout artists, the empire builders. Some of these included Henry Kravis,[†] whose firm, Kohlberg, Kravis Roberts & Company organized over $30 billion in leveraged buyouts (LBOs) through Milken; Rupert Murdoch, who built a massive media empire in America using Milken's services; William McGowan,[†] who was able to create MCI Communications Corporation and to destroy the AT&T monopoly on the telephone industry in the process, with the help of junk bonds; and Frank Lorenzo,[†] who put together the world's largest airline system with the help of junk bonds.

Milken's influence transcended even these areas. As more and more money poured into Drexel, he and his associates began to finance the corporate raiders, people like Carl Icahn, Ronald Perelman, T. Boone Pickens, and, most fatefully of all, Ivan Boesky. Perelman used Milken and his junk-bond network to raise $9 billion for three different companies (Pantry Pride, Revlon, and Disney). Icahn used Milken in his takeover of TWA and his raid on U.S. Steel. Pickens attacked Gulf Oil, Phillips Petroleum, and Unocal with Milken's help. Milken justified his support of the raiders in two ways. First, he pointed out that the entrepreneurs using his junk bonds owned 30 percent of their companies, whereas the managers and directors of the companies being attacked usually owned less than 1 percent. The second point, closely connected to the first, was that the managers were not running those companies effectively, nor were they looking after the shareholders' interests as well as they should have been.

Michael Milken, then, was trying to bring about a revolution in corporate America, but even he seemed reticent to recognize that. "I never saw myself as a revolutionary," he said. "All the revolutionaries I know are dead." But Sir James Goldsmith, the British arbitrager and LBO expert, disagrees, "I don't know whether or not Mike Milken realized at the time that he had found a way of financing an immense revolution in America." But, he added, when Milken began to feel the full power of the American establishment arrayed against him, "As a European I witnessed the same alliance trying to avoid change and neutralizing those responsible for it." One of America's leading industrialists agreed, calling it "nothing short of total war." The war really concerned the nature of the American corporation and the capitalist system to which it belonged. The defenders of the status quo were those who viewed the large corporation as not just a private, profit-making institution, but also a public one. In this view, the managers and directors were there to serve not just the interests of the shareholders, but also the interests of labor, consumers, and the general public. Milken and his raider allies posit a different kind of corporation. They argue that corporations best serve others by serving the interests of their shareholders. Only corporations that are accountable to shareholders can make the kind of hard choices necessary to survive in the economy of the 1980s: closing inefficient plants, laying off workers, and moving plants offshore.

The vested interests came after Milken and the junk-bond raiders with a vengeance. By November 1986, around thirty bills had been proposed in Congress, and a dozen states had either passed, or were thinking of passing, anti-takeover laws. The voices of the establishment were shrill with condemnations and warnings. The Business Roundtable, the political voice of the *Fortune* 500 corporations, warned that junk-bond takeovers would bring on the 1929 depression again. Felix Rohatyn,* the quintessential establishment banker, issued similar dire warnings in a series of articles entitled "Junk Bonds and Other Swill" in the *Wall Street Journal* in 1985 and 1986. The New York State Insurance Department strictly limited investment in junk bonds, and several congressmen called for restrictions on their purchase. Milken responded to these attacks with a baseball metaphor:

Just imagine there was a baseball team—like the New York Yankees—that won all the time. It even came to believe it had a divine right to win. Then a new team came along whose pitchers knew how to throw curveballs and sliders which its hitters couldn't hit. It began to lose. So its manager decided, rather than teaching them how to hit these pitches, to go to the commissioner—and have them banned. (*Manhattan, Inc.*, September 1987)

But the warnings were not working. Junk-bond financing was too attractive. Even Lazard Frères, Rohatyn's banking firm, set up its own junk-bond department, as did Morgan Stanley, Salomon Brothers, and other members of the Old Guard. Although Drexel and Milken were still the dominant players in the junk-bond market, it was, in the words of a market manager, "not a one-firm market anymore." Drexel Burnham's share of the junk-bond market, which stood at 67.7 percent in 1984, had dropped to 45.2 percent in 1986. Huge Merrill Lynch by then handled 10 percent of the junk-bond financing, Salomon and Morgan Stanley about 7 percent each, and Shearson Lehman had 6 percent. Junk-bond financing was no longer rebel financing; it had attained at least a veneer of respectability by 1986. It looked as if Milken was well on the way to accomplishing his revolution. Then came Ivan Boesky.

On November 14, 1986, Boesky, who had been intimately associated with Milken and Drexel Lambert on many of his deals, settled civil charges of insider trading by paying a massive $100-million fine and agreeing to cooperate with a burgeoning government investigation into crime on Wall Street. Boesky, in turn, had been implicated by Dennis Levine, a mergers and acquisitions specialist at Drexel. Those stunning events brought to a screeching halt Drexel's rollicking decade on Wall Street. There was little question in most observers' minds that Milken and Drexel would be implicated in further government investigations. For months, rumors circulated wildly on Wall Street and in the business press, to the point where it began wilting Drexel's ability to do business, and even damaged, to a limited extent, Milken's standing with some of his network. The vast majority, however, remained fanatically loyal to him. As *Newsweek* (September 19, 1988) commented, "To his network of steadfast supporters, Milken . . . is a modern-day Tucker, a financial entrepreneur who is now the victim of a vendetta. To Milken's fans, he simply popularized a product—the junk bond—that changed corporate America forever." In June, 1989, Milken was honored at a meeting of "100 Black Men of America," becoming the first recipient of the Marcus Garvey Award for Economic Freedom. At the meeting Reginald Lewis* of TLC Beatrice said: "As far as I'm concerned, Michael walks on water." One of Milken's raiders said, "I just think the big boys don't like Milken and want to put him out of business." Some, however, could not buy this. Connie Bruck, in her devastating exposé of Milken and Drexel, called Drexel "the brass-knuckles, threatening, market-manipulating Cosa Nostra of the securities world."

Finally, in September 1988, the Securities and Exchange Commission (SEC) brought civil charges against Drexel and Milken. On September 7, they announced that "Drexel Burham Lambert, Michael Milken and others devised and carried out a fraudulent scheme involving insider trading, stock manipulation, fraud on Drexel's own clients, failure to disclose beneficial ownership of securities as required, and numerous other violations of the securities laws." Milken, who had pleaded the Fifth Amendment when called to appear before a congressional subcommittee, claimed to be pleased that the whole affair was finally out of the closet: "No one likes to be sued, but I welcome the opportunity to have, at long last, a full and open hearing . . . in an unbiased forum." There was also the possibility that U.S. Attorney Rudolph Giuliani, who had been outspoken in his criticism of Milken and Drexel, would lay criminal charges. The charges would be essentially the same as those in the civil suits. In December 1988, Drexel Burnham Lambert agreed to a settlement package with the U.S. government, in which it agreed to pay a staggering fine of $650 million and plead guilty to six counts of fraud. Although Drexel announced that the deal was "in the best interests of our firm and employees," it appeared to leave Milken open to further prosecution.

Drexel Burnham moved to distance itself from Milken and his operation. In February 1989, Milken was fired, and it was clear that Milken would be left to face the music alone. Whatever the end result, none could doubt the profound influence Milken has had upon the American financial system. As Myron Magnet remarked in *Fortune*,

The power that so intoxicated this generation of Wall Streeters is the power to boss around the bosses: to tell chief executives how to run their business, to threaten and scare these pillars of the establishment, to make them crawl, to take away their companies, their perks, their authority. That's a power the Wall Streeters got from the junk bond–financed takeover perfected and presided over by Michael Milken. . . . For all that, the revolution was real, changing America's society and economy: Corporations are more efficient and competitive, rust-belt towns are altered, Milken clients . . . are social lions. Milken was a driving force of this revolution, an individual of historical significance.

Business Week concurred, "His standing as perhaps the most innovative financier since J. P. Morgan* and the incalculable impact he has had on the restructuring of Corporate America will endure regardless." He was a "Master of the Universe.'' (**B**. *Forbes*, December 5, 1983, July 11, 1988; *Business Week*, March 4, April 1, 1985, February 16, April 13, August 10, September 7, 1987, June 20, July 4, November 28, 1988, January 2, February 13, April 10, 1989; Moira Johnston, *Takeover: The New Wall Street Warriors*, 1986; *Institutional Investor*, August 1986; *Fortune*, January 5, 1987, October 10, 1988; *Newsweek*, February 16, September 21, 1987, May 30, September 19, 1988; *Los Angeles Times Magazine*, August 30, 1987; *Manhattan, Inc.*, September 1987, August 1988; Connie Bruck, *The Predators' Ball: The Junk-Bond Raiders and the Man Who Staked Them*, 1988; *New York Times*, April 22, 1988; Toronto *Globe & Mail*, September 6, September 8, September 9, December 22, 1988, June 23, 1989; *Time*, September 19, December 5, 1988.)

MILLARD, WILLIAM H. (1932–). Computer store franchiser, ComputerLand Corporation. In 1983, shortly after Bill Millard took active control of ComputerLand, the huge chain of computer stores he had founded in 1976, an executive made an appointment with him to announce his resignation. Millard set aside three hours for the appointment. The executive's recitation of his reasons for quitting took less than an hour. He then offered to leave Millard's office so they could both return to work. Millard told him to sit still, and he used the final two hours to sit silently and stare at the man. William Millard, and most of his employees at ComputerLand, were ''est'' graduates—that is, they had gone through the training seminars of pop psychologist Werner Erhard. This popular human potential movement of the 1970s had become a corporate cult at ComputerLand, and intense stares were evidently one of its features. As another of his former employees commented, ''Bill would just wear you down, he would just not let you out of his office until you saw it his way.''

Bill Millard was born in Denver, Colorado during the depths of the depression into a family that had seen hard times. His father managed to get a job as a clerk for the Southern Pacific Railroad, where he remained throughout his life, gladly trading career advancement for the security of a union job and a seniority system. His mother worked part time for Montgomery Ward. When Millard was three, the family moved to Oakland, California where they struggled during these years but never went without the essentials. As Millard said, ''We never went hungry, we never had a lot of extra things.'' He contributed to the family earnings by delivering the *Oakland Tribune* from the time he was twelve until he was a senior in high school. He also worked as a drugstore clerk, and he held other summer jobs to make ends meet while he attended parochial school.

After graduating from high school, where he was interested in technology, science, and mathematics, Millard got his first real job, as a switchman for the Southern Pacific Railroad. He then bounced around from one blue-collar job to another—laboring as a ditchdigger, working on an assembly line in an ammunition depot at the start of the Korean War, and working in a mill where he shoveled gravel into a cement mixer. He later drove a truck and was a welder's helper. Finally, Millard decided to attend the University of San Francisco, but he had to drop out after three semesters, when he was unable to meet the expenses of college.

In 1954, Millard got a job as a lending officer for Pacific Finance Corporation, and he worked his way up to branch manager. Then, in 1958, the company decided to set up a central electronic data processing facility in Los Angeles to handle transactions from branch offices around the country. This was, as Millard has commented, during the "dinosaur age" of computers, when few people had degrees in computer science. Thus, since Millard had a head for numbers, Pacific Finance gave him a job as a field representative for its electronic data processing system. There he was introduced to the Univac I, an enormous room-size computer, filled with vacuum tubes and wires. Because of the newness of everything, Millard was able to work during these years as a computer programmer, a systems analyst, and a supervisor of data processing. As he later commented, "I had no ticket," that is, no college degree, no family money, no family networks, to get him started. Indeed, he felt that the "absence of all those things was what I needed in order to never rest, never relax."

Millard had received a number of promotions in the data processing department, and he had proved his mettle at every step. When he was told that the next highest job, that of controller, could not be his because he did not have a college degree, Millard left to become a salesman at International Business Machines (IBM). Millard traveled the world as a representative for IBM from 1961 to 1965, when he left to become director of data processing for Alameda County, California. While there, Millard conceived and managed the world's first computerized police information network. He later replicated the project for the city and county of San Francisco, and his expertise was sought by cities around the world.

With this wealth of experience and contacts, Millard decided in 1969 to start his own company. Organizing the software firm Systems Dynamics, Incorporated, he sought to write better software than IBM. As usual, Millard threw himself into the operation with a great deal of enthusiasm, and little caution. Consequently, the firm failed three years later, owing the bank $25,000. That amount exceeded the value of the Millard family home, leaving them technically bankrupt. Millard was down, but not out. Learning that Los Angeles County was seeking bids for the design of an on-line information retrieval system, Millard formed a new company called Information Management Systems (IMS) Associates and submitted a bid jointly with TRW. They won the contract. At the same time Millard discovered Werner Erhard and est.

As IMS grew and became more successful, est became increasingly central to Millard's business, and his business became increasingly central to his life. He spent long hours during these years teaching his employees to "go to the center of their fear" and to tap new wellsprings of energy. He encouraged— even demanded—that his executives take est training. It soon became clear that the aim of Millard and his company was not just to sell lots of computers and computer programs, but to change the way in which business was done. As a former salesman recalls, "We were on a mission from God. We were out to prove to the world that we could do 10 times more than anyone thought we could do. We were in the business of helping business transform itself."

Things began happening quickly for Millard during this time. In 1973, IMS underbid for a contract with a General Motors dealer, and Millard had to find the cheapest possible components for a computer system to keep from again going bankrupt as a result of his unrealistically low bid. He learned of Intel's 8080 microprocessor, and he found that a firm in Albuquerque, New Mexico, had built a small computer using the 8080. That led Millard to begin tinkering with the microprocessor chips that were becoming available in the early 1970s. By 1975, Millard had put together one of the first personal computers (PCs), which he called the IMSAI 8080. These were first sold in kits to hobbyists via advertising in magazines like *Popular Electronics*. When orders came in, Millard, his wife, and their three daughters would gather in the kitchen, hand sorting parts into plastic bags, which were then sent off with instructions to the purchasers.

With the success of this operation, Millard in 1976 decided to manufacture and market the IMSAI 8080 as a finished product in stores. For a time, Millard's computer was at the leading edge of the PC revolution. The window of opportunity was narrow, however, and in 1977 Steven Jobs[†] and Stephen Wozniak entered the market with the Apple computer. In the meantime, Millard needed lots of capital to pursue his dream. As a result, in January 1976, Millard turned to Philip Reed III for additional capital. Reed, a Harvard-educated Bostonian whose family owned a venture capital firm, Marriner & Company, had joined IMS in 1975. Marriner & Company was headed by Philip Reed's father and he arranged a $250,000 loan for Millard.

In the meantime, Millard's interests were shifting from the manufacture to the sale of computers. He had become aware that marketing other people's computers was more profitable than making his own. Thus, in September 1976, with $10,000 of the money borrowed from Marriner & Company, Millard opened a store he called Computer Shack in Hayward, California. The store was a success, but after the Tandy Corporation, owners of Radio Shack, challenged the name, Millard changed the name to ComputerLand. The concept was an instant success, and Millard began setting up a franchised chain of stores. This was one of the hottest franchise start-ups in history, and one of the fastest growing enterprises in the annals of American business. With 24 stores and $1.5 million in sales in 1977, it grew to 145 stores and $75 million in sales three years later. The big breakthrough came with the introduction of IBM's PC computer. That giant firm made the decision to market its computer only in its own stores, at Sears, Roebuck & Company, and at ComputerLand. By 1984, there were 800 franchised ComputerLand stores with revenues of $1.4 billion.

In the meantime, the IMSAI manufacturing subsidiary of Millard's parent company, IMS Associates, was doing very poorly. It finally went bankrupt in 1979 with debts of $1.9 million. Among those debts was the $250,000 loan from Marriner & Company. That loan returned to haunt Millard and ComputerLand a few years later. In the meantime, Millard adopted an arms-length approach to the management of ComputerLand. Although he owned about 96 percent of the company's stock, Millard was not the formal head of the firm. Instead, he installed Ed Faber, an ex-marine and ex–sales manager for IBM, who had been ComputerLand's first employee, as chief executive. Like Millard, Faber had taken the est training, but he viewed it more as a useful motivational tool and less as a way of life or a religion.

Faber may have been ComputerLand's head, whether real or titular, but Millard was making the money from it. ComputerLand's gross margins were estimated to be around 40 percent, and much of the aftertax profit was paid out in dividends, so, since Millard owned 96 percent of the stock, it is clear that he was becoming very wealthy. However, because the firm was private, there are no public records available on this score. But Millard was not wholly satisfied. He wanted wealth, yes, but he also wanted the clear public recognition as an entrepreneur and manager that accompanied success. As a result, he spent additional time at ComputerLand's offices, and he became a more dominant factor in the firm's management. Finally, in August 1983, a frustrated Faber resigned as president, and Millard annointed himself chief executive officer.

When Millard assumed the reins at ComputerLand, he began to reemphasize est. Faber had been downplaying its importance, but Millard greatly strengthened the ties between Erhard's organization and his own, elevating former est leaders and managers to important positions within his company. As an employee commented, "People were picked for their ideological compatibility with Bill rather than for their competence." Similarly, Millard reinstilled the kind of missionary zeal he had fostered at IMS. Gordon Starr, a former est trainer who became Millard's chief of staff, said,

Bill had a vision that extended way beyond managing stores and profits, he wanted to create a worldwide network, with the intention that it would contribute to worldwide peace. Individual franchising would transcend political boundaries, and you'd have a network of people all linked commonly with ComputerLand.

Within a year after Millard took over, things were beginning to become unglued at ComputerLand. First of all, ComputerLand's monopoly on computer sales was ending. Up to that point, the firm's success had rested upon its massive buying power, which had enabled it to get very favorable arrangements with IBM and Apple. Suddenly, fierce price competition hit the computer industry when a slew of IBM clones radically undercut prices. IBM was forced to begin offering discounts of up to 30 percent to ComputerLand's competitors, giving them the same kind of deal Millard's company had been enjoying for some time. As a result, some 500 newly franchised computer chain stores entered the marketplace in 1984, many of which were exceedingly well financed. When the bottom fell out of the personal computer market in 1984, things got even worse for ComputerLand and its franchisees.

With deteriorating market conditions, holders of ComputerLand franchises were not willing to tolerate what many regarded as the exorbitant fees charged by Millard—amounting to a 9-percent combination royalty and advertising fee each month. This was well above that charged by many other franchise operations. McDonald's, for example, charged 11.5 percent, but this included rent on the building, which was owned by the parent corporation. Kentucky Fried Chicken charged 4-percent royalties and 1.5 percent for advertising, although most also paid another 3 percent for promotion, location, and other advantages. In any event, many ComputerLand franchises did not think their arrangements with the home office justified the amount of money they were sending it each month. When they complained to the head office, the response, in typical est language, was "thank you for sharing that with me," but nothing was done to rectify the situation.

All that est vocabulary was beginning to drive many of ComputerLand's employees and franchise holders crazy. Many non-est employees grumbled that the firm and all their meetings were filled with jargon, but they were told by the est "true believers" to "get in touch with [their] own negativity." More discouraging to many on the staff was Millard's attempt to root out this "unalignedness" by creating thick policy manuals that prescribed permissable colors for tablecloths and executives' cars, and detailed the height of doors and the angles of walls allowed at franchise stores. An example of how extreme things became along this line came when Millard hired an est expert—a South American professor of communications—to give the office staff a weekend pep rally and seminar. Those who attended the two-day seminar found that the man spoke only one word of English that was understandable to them—"clear." He ended every sentence with it. Bored staffers made a pool of how many times he would utter the word during the two days. The winning guess was 13,000 times.

Service also became much worse when Millard assumed control. Whereas under Faber it had taken only several days to process and ship orders to the franchise stores, under Millard it often took weeks because he was trying to save money by keeping inventories low. Anger reached a boiling point in 1985, when Barbara Millard, Bill's daughter, who had been named chief operating officer the year before, announced ComputerLand's Hunger Initiative, designed to end world hunger by 2000. However noble the goal, the fact was that Millard took $1 million of ComputerLand's advertising money, money that was raised by docking each franchise 1 percent of its sales, and gave it to the hunger project. No matter how much they complained, Millard refused to roll back the fees, or to abandon the hunger project.

The final problem for Millard and ComputerLand, however, was not in the marketplace but in the courtroom. That nearly forgotten $250,000 loan to IMS in 1976 finally came back to haunt them. And it cost Bill Millard control of ComputerLand. Therein lies a tangled and complex tale. In 1977, Philip Reed's father found that Millard was using the $250,000 loaned to IMS to develop ComputerLand. Enraged, he declared "I don't know what you call it out there, but back in Boston . . . we got a name for it, and that's theft." After much arguing back and forth, Millard finally agreed to make the original $250,000 loan repayable in ComputerLand stock. Later, the Reeds and a disgruntled former ComputerLand employee and stockholder, John Martin-Musemeci, joined forces and informed Millard that they intended to invoke their stock conversion option, giving them 20 percent of ComputerLand's stock. To Millard, this represented the ultimate horror. He had devoted his effort to keeping ComputerLand under his strict control, and now it threatened to slip away from him. Worse still, it was going to men who neither knew nor cared anything about ComputerLand, its employees, or its future. The trial began in the Alameda County courtroom in January 1986, and dragged on until March. On March 11, the jurors returned their verdict: they ruled in favor of the plaintiffs and their claim to 20 percent of ComputerLand's stock, and, in a separate decision, they awarded them $125 million in damages—$115 million from the Millards and $10 million from ComputerLand. It was a staggering, devastating defeat for Bill Millard.

Millard was ordered to remove himself from active management of ComputerLand and to do what he had promised never to do—to allow ComputerLand to be taken public. From that point on, the company was in the hands of its top employees, its franchisees, and thousands of outside investors. Ed Faber was chosen to replace Millard as head of ComputerLand, much to the delight of franchise owners and most employees, and when they heard the chain was being sold, most breathed a sigh of relief.

Millard left America for the small island of Saipan, near Guam, where he announced that he would listen to offers for the assets of IMS Associates, the holding company through which he controlled ComputerLand stock. He also was looking for new business ventures, as he said, "Something global, involving world trade, that will be the multiple of everything I've ever done." But his fortune was greatly diminished. Millard was estimated in 1985 to be a billionaire, on the strength of his 96 percent of ComputerLand. In 1987 the New York investment firm of E. M. Warburg, Pincus & Company offered $200 million for the firm, making Millard's share $144 million. A tidy sum to be sure, but a far cry from a billion dollars. Most at ComputerLand fervently hoped Millard would find something else to occupy his time. As San Francisco franchisee Charles R. Orr said, until then, "there was always the fear of Bill coming back, it's very positive that he's out for good." (**B**. Robert Levering, Michael Katz, and Milton Moskowitz, *The Computer Entrepreneurs*, 1984; *Forbes*, July 2, 1984, August 26, 1985; *Personal Computing*, August 1984; *Contemporary Newsmakers*, 1985; *Fortune*, April 15, 1985; A. David Silver, *Megabucks*, 1985; *Business Week*, September 2, October 14, 1985, June 15, 1987; *Inc.*, August 1986; Jonathon Littman, *Once upon a Time in ComputerLand: The Amazing Billion Dollar Tale of Bill Millard's ComputerLand Empire*, 1987.)

MILLIKEN, ROGER (October 24, 1915–). Textile company executive, Deering, Milliken & Company, Milliken & Company. In 1967, Xerox Corporation ran a documentary on civil rights. Coming at a time when national concern about the plight of blacks in the South was at a peak, the program was a liberal and well-considered analysis. But Roger Milliken was furious. Enraged at what he felt was a biased presentation (a former executive at Milliken & Company said, "Roger thought it was kind of pink"), the next day he ordered his offices to remove all Xerox copiers, and he forbade his purchasing agents to ever buy them again. At least fifteen years later, the order was still in effect. In many respects, the episode illustrates some important characteristics of Roger Milliken—a fervent and militant right-winger in politics and on social issues, he ran his company as a "benevolent dictator," tolerating little in the way of dissent or disagreement.

Roger Milliken was not a self-made man. He inherited a prosperous firm that had been started by his grandfather and carried forward by his father. The original company was founded in 1865 as a dry-goods jobber in Portland, Maine, by his grandfather, Seth M. Milliken and William Deering. Although Deering left four years later to become one of the founders of the International Harvester Company, the original company continued under the name, Deering, Milliken & Company, until it was changed to Milliken & Company in 1976. Deering, Milliken was a selling house, that is, it specialized in marketing the output of numerous mills. The role of the selling house in the textile industry has been to find customers for the produce of the mills they have under contract, to guarantee their credit and aid in their financing, and to advise the mills on the types of cloth to produce. The selling house rarely assumed ownership of the cloth, but rather sold it either as "grey" or unfinished cloth which they then sold to "converters," or as finished and printed cloth to apparel manufacturers.

Seth Milliken, during the late nineteenth century, had helped finance the expansion of Southern textile manufacture by advancing money to local manufacturers. When textiles were first established in America, most mills were located in the New England area; at the start of the Civil War, almost 75 percent of the spindles were located there. Beginning in the late nineteenth century and intensifying throughout the twentieth century, the center of textile production moved increasingly to the South. By 1960, 80 percent of the spindles were located in Southern states. The cotton cloth market, however, remained centered in the North, primarily in New York City, and secondarily in Boston. Seth Milliken moved the headquarters of Deering, Milliken to New York in the early twentieth century.

The attractions of the South, compared to the North, for textile manufacture were manifold. Labor costs were lower, attitudes toward unions were less friendly, Southern communities offered lower tax rates, and they often provided water power, electricity, and rail facilities at very low costs. But, because the South lacked capital, local communities and entrepreneurs had to look to Northerners, especially many of the New York selling houses, to provide the needed financing to build their mills and help finance their operations. Deering, Milliken was one of the most important houses in providing these financial services, especially in South Carolina. The company formed an alliance with the Lockwood-Greene interests and the Montgomery, Walter, Fleming groups, first with the Pacolet mill, and then with other operations in Spartanburg and elsewhere.

By 1905, Deering, Milliken sold cloth for thirteen mills in South Carolina, most of which had some connection with various Spartanburg interests. Seth Milliken took advantage of his position to begin taking control of these mills, and he engaged in a significant movement of backward vertical integration for his firm. His most spectacular takeover occurred in 1905–1906, when Milliken, aided by its Spartanburg allies, ousted the president of the Darlington and Laurens mills following a widely publicized proxy and court battle. The defeated opponent referred to Milliken and his allies as "the coldest blooded lot that ever lived." The role of such selling houses as Deering, Milliken—controlled by Northerners like Seth Milliken—lent credence to the oft-repeated Southern claim that the selling houses were the instruments of the "colonial oppression of the South by the North." On the other hand, they did provide the capital that aided the transfer of the industry from the North to the South, a transfer which probably could not have taken place without their aid.

By the time of his death in 1920, Seth Milliken had acquired interests in forty-two Southern mills. Nonetheless, Deering, Milliken remained more a selling house than a manufacturer. After his grandfather's death, Roger's father, Gerrish Milliken, took control of the company. After a few good years, the cotton textile industry began to slide into what one scholar called its own "private depression," before American industry in general "took to its bed in 1930." Then, with the onset of the nationwide depression in the 1930s, things only worsened. As a result, many Southern mills could not pay their debts to selling houses. As many of these mills went bankrupt, Gerrish Milliken picked them up for virtually nothing. At about the same time and under similar circumstances, Deering, Milliken took over Mercantile Stores Company, a department store chain.

With the return of prosperity to the United States during World War II, Deering, Milliken, like the rest of the textile industry, operated at full capacity with high profits. Rising consumer incomes and large government purchases helped to keep textile demand at peak levels, as cloth production during the war years was 34 percent higher than it had been from 1935 to 1939. By the end of the war, Deering, Milliken was a profitable operation, but, like the rest of the textile industry, it faced an uncertain future. Demand was certain to decline somewhat, imports from abroad were destined to increase greatly, and innovations in machinery and fabrics would occur. Before he could make any concrete plans to deal with these problems, however, Gerrish Milliken died of a heart attack while playing golf with his son Roger in 1947. Roger, just thirty-one years old at the time, succeeded his father as president of Deering, Milliken.

Roger Milliken was born in New York City, he was educated in area schools, and he graduated from Yale in 1937. Upon graduation, he joined the family textile concern and learned various aspects of production, finance, and marketing. The firm Roger inherited from his father had picked up interests in a large number of textile mills over the years, but it still operated primarily as a selling house. Roger Milliken decided to change that. He shifted the headquarters from New York to Spartanburg, South Carolina, to be closer to the mills, and, subsequently, he and his family moved there also. A big, husky man, with flaming red hair, Milliken was called, much to his dismay, "Big Red" by the locals upon his arrival in the South.

Milliken next integrated the firm's mills into a more solid organization. Although his father and grandfather had acquired interest or control in a number of mills, they had all been incorporated as separate companies, many with outside shareholders. Roger Milliken proceeded to buy out thirty-six of them completely and to consolidate them into a single corporation. Although the development of these integrated manufacturing operations enhanced Deering, Milliken's position in the textile industry, it did not give the company the stature of a giant. Burlington Mills was the industry leader, Berkshire was the second largest, and J. P. Stevens (see Stevens Family) was third. Beyond that were a number of firms—Cone Mills, Pacific Mills, Dan River Mills, Cannon Mills, Mount Vernon–Woodberry, and Deering, Milliken—of somewhat equal size. A major step forward into the status of a giant firm for Deering, Milliken came in 1963, when Roger Milliken purchased the textile manufacturing properties of Textron, the emerging conglomerate developed by Royal Little.* Deering, Milliken was soon vaulted into third place, behind Burlington and J. P. Stevens. By the early 1980s, the firm operated at least sixty mills in five states, ten of which were located in the Greenville-Spartanburg area.

With a narrower product line than either Burlington or J. P. Stevens, Deering Milliken was more highly integrated than those companies; it texturized its own yarn and finished its own fabric. It also produced yarns for its own use and for sale to knitting companies. One product area Milliken never entered, which many competitors regarded as the firm's major blunder, was denims and corduroys. A former executive explained, "[Roger] always felt denims and corduroys [were] too cyclical, although the current up cycle has lasted longer than he ever thought." In the 1970s, Milliken phased out a number of products such as woolens, worsteds, towels, and linens. Although as a private company Milliken does not need to issue any sales figures (and does not), industry sources estimate that slightly more than half the firm's sales were in finished goods— knitted fabrics, wovens, and spun yarn—while grey or unfinished goods sold to converters made up about 20 percent. Of the balance, 14 percent were industrial textiles, 6 percent carpets, 3 percent decorative fabrics for upholstery, and 3 percent chemicals, primarily to treat fabrics and clean carpets. More than most textile manufacturers, Milliken shifted away from natural fibers, using far more synthetic materials.

In restructuring his company, Roger Milliken borrowed heavily from General Electric (GE) and Minnesota Mining and Manufacturing (3-M). From GE, he developed an organizational format based on product line or end market. He established four major operating divisions, each headed by a president who reported directly to Milliken, the only one who had access to consolidated financial results. Milliken was one of the first in the textile industry to establish computerized management information systems, which allowed him and his aides to analyze production costs and return on investment more meaningfully and to improve inventory controls. Roger Milliken learned how 3-M managed product development, and soon Deering, Milliken became the industry leader in research and development (R&D).

During the more than forty years that he has run Milliken & Company, Roger Milliken has been a leader in transforming an antiquated industry, suspicious of change and hesitant to adopt new techniques, into a more professional business that has become comfortable with modern managerial techniques and updated technological devices. Milliken has had a virtual passion for science and technology during his years in control of the family company. Since the firm is privately owned, he has not had the constraints that have hampered most textile executives. Studies of the textile industry in the 1950s showed that the firms did not regard research and development as a necessary business expense, but rather, something which could only come out of profit margins, and only after the shareholders had received their dividends. Thus, in the bleak years of the 1930s, textile companies spent only 0.0017 cents of each sales dollar on R&D, which was increased to just 0.12 cents of every dollar in the 1950s. Not having to answer to shareholders, Roger Milliken was able to pour more money into product development. Since his firm is private and since he is extraordinarily secretive about its operations, it is very difficult to know just how much is devoted to R&D.

Nonetheless, some basic outlines are clear. At the 600-acre company headquarters, Milliken operates a huge R&D facility that over the years has developed a large number of new yarns and fabrics, and several advanced manufacturing, dyeing, and finishing techniques. The company's slogan is "Textile leadership through research," and one of Roger Milliken's great joys is visiting textile machinery shows, where he can minutely inspect new pieces of equipment. He is reputed to have placed large orders for new kinds of machinery, simply to tie up the manufacturer's capacity so that rivals cannot get access to the new technology. Milliken & Company was also among the first in the industry to install equipment to make double-knit fabrics in the 1960s, and to automate its yarn mills. Several industry analysts, however, feel the firm went too deeply into the double-knits, and when sales of the fabric began falling off, Milliken was left with excess capacity. Milliken also became one of the first major producers of textured woven fabrics, which demand such a highly capital-intensive manufacturing process that many smaller manufacturers have not been able to adopt the technology. He was also among the first to purchase high-speed looms which required only about 40 percent of the floor space and less than half the workers of the older units. A former Milliken official commented, "Since [Roger Milliken] is not interested in growth just for the sake of growth, he invests for quality, to improve efficiency.''

Roger Milliken has also made a number of important innovations in marketing, not all of which have been appreciated by his customers or by industry analysts. Milliken & Company's most innovative and impressive marketing effort was its annual Breakfast Show. Begun in 1953 by Roger Milliken, it evolved over the years into a Broadway musical-style showcase for the firm's products. In the late 1970s and early 1980s, the show was put on in New York's Waldorf Astoria Hotel to a standing-room-only crowd of some 30,000 department store executives, fashion buyers, and garment manufacturers. Constituting the bulk of Milliken & Company's $2-million advertising budget, it was a seventy-minute advertisement for Milliken's fabrics. The talent for the shows was first-rate, and included over the years Cyd Charisse, Phyllis Diller, Donna McKechnie, Gloria Swanson, Bert Lahr, Van Johnson, and Nancy Walker.

At 8 A.M. the lights in the hall dimmed, the spotlights went on, and the sixty members of the cast sang and danced as they modeled the latest styles, all made with Milliken's fabrics. At each show were 450 of Milliken's sales and marketing people, along with Roger Milliken himself. As Milliken's general manager has said, ''The result is that we have the absolutely undivided attention of our primary sales targets for roughly two hours.'' A producer of the industrial shows commented, ''There's nothing like it in the field, unless you start considering a Walt Disney or General Motors spectacular for a World's Fair.'' A buyer for tony Bloomingdale's said, ''It's fabulous, and it makes the presentations of the other fabric companies—no matter what they do—look pared down by comparison.''

Yet, all that having been said, it is the general consensus among industry people that Milliken & Company has been less market-oriented than firms like Burlington. Critics have blamed this on Roger Milliken. ''One reason,'' says a former Milliken executive, is that ''Roger Milliken has a love for machinery and bricks and mortar. He has a distrust for the marketplace in allowing his customers to determine too much what his direction is going to be.'' The company, under Milliken's leadership, has become more production-driven than market-driven. As a result, Milliken has adopted a number of policies that have not endeared him to apparel makers. For one thing, he discontinued the policy of not billing his customers until delivery of the fabric. Instead, he issued an invoice and expected to be paid, even if delivery was not until much later. Even more important, he has refused to produce many of the kinds of fabrics and styles demanded by a fashion-conscious industry. Since these often involve short production runs of a particular style or color, they are often not very profitable. An industry consultant has said, ''If you want to be in the fashion end of the business, you have to do some things in small runs. Milliken is never going to do that.'' What keeps them up front, in spite of these policies, however, is Milliken's insistence on quality, delivery performance, new products, and aggressive pricing.

The corporate culture at Milliken & Company has been a reflection of Roger Milliken's beliefs and personality over the years. It has not been an easy or a particularly pleasant place to work for most people, whether production workers or executives. As *Business Week* commented in 1981, "Many Milliken executives have a love-hate relationship with their boss." On the one hand, he paid salaries at the upper end of the industry's executive scale; on the other, he was highly despotic toward all his employees. In 1967, suddenly deciding that his firm was beset with "Parkinson's Law," that is, too many executives were not performing necessary functions in the organization, he fired 600 middle-management personnel without warning. Subsequently, the creation of any new salaried jobs required his personal approval. He was also famous for demanding instant reports on matters that came to his attention, and for scheduling meetings with little advance notice.

But Milliken's despotic attitudes have been seen most graphically in his attitudes toward labor unions. In 1956, at the company's plant at Darlington, South Carolina, the workers voted for union representation. In response, Milliken simply closed down the mill rather than negotiate with the union. Six years later, the National Labor Relations Board filed an unfair labor practice suit and ruled that Milliken & Company was liable for back pay to more than 500 workers at the plant. Still, Roger Milliken would not concede, and he appealed the case all the way to the Supreme Court. Finally, in 1980, the high court ruled that the company was at fault and had to disperse more than $5 million in back pay to the workers. One of the longest, most celebrated cases in labor history, Milliken was adjudged to have "chilled" unionism in the South for decades because of its intransigence. The decision, however, did nothing to change Milliken's attitudes toward unionization, nor to enhance the union's ability to organize his mills.

A major element of the corporate culture at Milliken & Company is the tight secrecy and mystique which surround the entire operation. As a privately held company, it need not file most of the reports and information required of public companies. But Roger Milliken's passion for privacy goes well beyond that. He seldom grants interviews to reporters or allows them access to his plants and offices. As he commented in 1981, "I have been very consistent in trying to keep our company accomplishments . . . and plans confidential, and have considered it one of the advantages of being a private company." Edward F. Johnson, a textile industry analyst, has said, "He makes a clam seem like an open mouth."

One of the freedoms that Milliken enjoys as a private company extends to how Roger Milliken's own political ideas govern company policy. A militant Republican and a strong supporter of the conservative wing of the party, Milliken in 1964 was one of Barry Goldwater's financial angels. He has served as a South Carolina delegate to several Republican conventions, and he has developed strong ties to Strom Thurmond, the ultraright-wing Republican Senator from South Carolina. What is unusual about Roger Milliken's political beliefs is the degree to which they determine company policy. He has long held a strong distaste for any kind of governmental interference or red tape. That is not unusual among business executives. What is unique is that he refuses to bid on any defense contracts as a result, thereby foregoing potentially highly lucrative business. A fervent anticommunist, he also refused to meet with a trade delegation from the People's Republic of China, thereby losing a chance to bid on a contract for more than 15 million yards of textured woven fabric, which they ultimately purchased from Burlington and Texfi Industries.

In only one area have his conservative political beliefs and his business interests come into apparent conflict. Milliken has long been an impassioned advocate of protectionism for the textile industry, saying bluntly that "Protectionism is the inevitable response" to imports, and that "the days of free capitalism are gone." This ultimately put him in conflict with the free enterprise ideas of the Reagan administration. Becoming a public spokesman for the Crafted with Pride Council, an industry-union coalition, observers were shocked to see Milliken join hands with trade union leaders to criticize sharply the conservative economic policies of the Reagan administration. Objecting strenuously to its policies of free trade and its willingness to adopt a hands-off policy on textile and apparel imports, Milliken said, "We are sacrificing our industrial base on the altar of free trade— a god no other nation worships."

As a result of these and other efforts, Roger Milliken in 1986 was chosen as Textile Leader of the Year by *Textile World*. The venerable publication pointed out that in its one hundred years of operation it had never before singled out an individual for this honor. Ellison McKissick, president of Alice Manufacturing Company, and past president of the American Textile Manufacturers Association, said, "I don't know of anyone who has contributed more to preserve the future of the American textile industry than Roger Milliken." In his role as head of Crafted with Pride, Milliken toured the country constantly, often appearing wearing an "Uncle Sam" hat, and stressing the patriotism involved in buying American-made goods.

It was a remarkable image for those who had observed Roger Milliken over the years. Often called an innovative genius, a ruthless competitor, and an iron-fisted tyrant, who flew into tirades against unions and communism, many in the late 1980s claimed he had "mellowed." But the mellowing was caused at least partially by hard times for Milliken & Company, which had closed twelve mills since 1983. Since the veil of secrecy remains in place, no one knows for sure what the firm's earnings have been, but estimates range around $2 billion a year, making it the third largest textile firm. But no one in the industry really knows what will happen to Milliken & Company after Roger Milliken is gone. One former Milliken executive compared his old firm to the Green Bay Packers when it was coached by Vince Lombardi. Like the Packers, Milliken & Company, he noted, was a superbly tuned organization that projected an aura of superiority in what it did, and it was led by an autocrat who overshadowed his subordinates. But he completed his analogy ominously by commenting, "And look what happened to the Packers when Lombardi was gone." In the meantime, however, the family shares a fortune estimated at $1 billion, and Milliken & Company remains the world's largest private textile firm. (**B**. Melvin T. Copeland, *The Cotton Manufacturing Industry of the United States*, 1917; Stephen Jay Kennedy, *Profits and Losses in Cotton Textiles*, 1936; Solomon Barkin, "The Regional Significance of the Integration Movement in the Southern Textile Industry," *Southern Economic Journal*, April 1949; Jesse W. Markham, "Vertical Integration in the Textile Industry," *Harvard Business Review*, 1950; E. C. Bancroft, et al., *Textiles: A Dynamic Industry*, 1951; Walter Adams, ed., *The Structure of American Industry*, 1962; *Reporter*, January 3, 1963; Bill Arthur, "The Darlington Mills Case: Or 17 Years before the Courts," *New South*, 1973; *Business Week*, June 5, 1978, December 15, 1980, January 19, 1981, September 16, 1985; Laurence A. Christianson, Jr., ed., *Leaders in the Textile Industry*, 1979; David L. Carlton, *Mill & Town in South Carolina, 1880–1920*, 1977; *Forbes*, March 25, 1985, October 24, 1988; James A. Hodges, *New Deal Labor Policy and the Southern Cotton Textile Industry, 1933–1941*, 1986; *Textile World*, September 1986; *Who's Who in America*, 1986–87; *Fortune*, October 12, 1987.)

MONAGHAN, THOMAS S. (March 25, 1937–   ). Founder of pizza delivery chain, baseball team owner, Domino's Pizza, Detroit Tigers. Observing Tom Monaghan's rise from rags to riches inevitably conjures up images of Benjamin Franklin, of the heroes in Horatio Alger's novels, of, dare we say, Jay Gatsby in F. Scott Fitzgerald's *The Great Gatsby*. Like Monaghan, Fitzgerald's Gatsby (originally James Gatz) came from obscure origins, had a brief fling at college, and then began to pursue his "main chance" with an unflagging vigor and determination. Both men learned early the rigors of self-control—they neither smoked nor drank—and both marshalled every fiber of their being to achieve success. Unlike Jay Gatsby, however, who, coarse, vulgar, and ostentatious, made his money as part of the underworld during Prohibition, Monaghan, modest and unassuming, is a devout Catholic who tries to attend Mass daily.

Monaghan was born in Ann Arbor, Michigan. He evidently had a warm and loving childhood until he was four years old, when, on Christmas Eve, 1941, his much-beloved, doting father died of a bleeding ulcer. His mother, who also had an older son, needed to find a career for herself, and she decided to go to nursing school. Not feeling she could handle the raising of the two boys at the same time, she placed them with a German family. That accommodation did not work out, and Tom and his brother Jim were then placed in a Roman Catholic orphanage for what was supposed to be a year. In fact, they remained at St. Joseph's Home for Boys in Jackson, Michigan, for six years.

These were tough times for Monaghan. Later, he embellished all of this into a riveting after-dinner autobiography that he presented to audiences around America in the 1980s. At St. Joseph's, his story went, he endured strap-beatings, poor, starchy meals, and a general feeling of neglect. This was somewhat mitigated by the kindly attention of Sister Bernarda, who was his savior in several ways. First, she gave him a rosary that he still treasures, and second, she introduced him to baseball and the Detroit Tigers. Soon, Monaghan was listening to their broadcasts every day, and once a year he attended an actual game, courtesy of the Knights of Columbus. He later recalled, "To me, that team was bigger than life."

When Tom was ten, his mother fetched him and his brother from the orphanage, and for two years they lived together as a family. Deciding again that she could not raise them, she sent them to a work farm in northern Michigan. There Monaghan did farm chores, but he also had a chance to make money on the outside, working as a soda jerk and setting bowling pins. At seventeen, Monaghan enrolled in a preparatory seminary, with the idea that he might become a priest, but he was soon expelled for misbehaving. His crimes evidently were engaging in pillow fights and talking during study hall. After that, Monaghan attended a regular high school, where his great love was playing baseball and learning about Frank Lloyd Wright. These two things—baseball and architecture—fueled his dreams and ambitions. As a school-yard ball player, who played shortstop, he recalled that he "was very good at scooping up the ball, anticipating—but . . . was no power hitter." He had discovered Frank Lloyd Wright and architecture in the local library when he was twelve, and as a young marine stationed in Tokyo, Japan, he spent leave memorizing every detail of Wright's design of the magnificent Imperial Hotel.

After graduating from high school, Monaghan joined the Marine Corps, and upon his return he entered the University of Michigan in his hometown, where he intended to study architecture, but financial problems soon took him away from his studies. Monaghan attended college six different times but never advanced beyond his freshman year. This was a crushing disappointment for him. But his brother Jim, who was working at the time as a mailman in Ypsilanti, Michigan, opened up a new career for Tom. Jim Monaghan had noticed a failing pizzeria, named Dominick's, that was on his route. He told Tom about it, who put up $500 to become a coowner, and they bought the struggling concern for $900. The two young men poured heart and soul into the new venture, with Tom working some 100 hours a week. At the end of a year, Jim had had enough and wanted to get out. Tom bought his brother's share of the business for the price of a used Volkswagen. Jim returned to the security of the post office, but later became a consultant in his brother's business.

Meantime, Tom Monaghan needed more money and help with his venture. He took on a new partner who proved to be not only incompetent, but also dishonest when he embezzled money from the struggling company. Monaghan booted him out and resumed the business alone, but he continued to have problems. In 1968, a fire wiped out the corporate headquarters in Ypsilanti, destroying all the firm's records. Even worse, the damage cost Monaghan $150,000 because he had neglected to pay his insurance premium. At about this same time, the former owner of the pizzeria wanted part of the action if his name was going to be used, so Monaghan changed the company's name to Domino's. This move, however, only intensified his problems. Monaghan was hit with a suit brought by Domino Sugar Company, which tried to force him to give up the name. The case was fought all the way up to the Supreme Court before Monaghan finally won the rights to the name. The legal battle, which lasted until 1980, cost him $1.5 million.

These problems and others were the price of success because, after struggling with the business for some time, Tom Monaghan discovered a marvelously simple, but effective new formula for pizza, which still works for Domino's. He simplified the menu, limiting the toppings and pizza sizes, and then he concentrated on making deliveries in record time. He began to advertise that he would get his pizzas to the customers in 30 minutes, or they would not have to pay—and he guaranteed the pizzas would be hot. These had been the two main problems with delivered pizzas: delivery was undependable, and the pizzas were often stone-cold when they reached their destination. Monaghan solved the latter problem by installing warming ovens in his delivery vans. Suddenly, his pizza delivery caught on with the dormitory students at Central State University, and Monaghan's Ypsilanti store was soon doing a booming business. As he later remembered,

My first store was legendary. It became the busiest pizzeria in the country. I'd have been so much better off, and it would have been so much easier to stay in that first store and make it a *great* store. It would have been doing $5 or $6 million a year, easily $100,000 a week. (*Saturday Evening Post*)

But, after the success of his first store, Monaghan opened a second, then he had four; by 1969, he had a dozen.

At that point, Monaghan's driving ambition outran his business sense. In 1969, he decided to undertake a massive expansion, from twelve to forty-four stores. In the process, Monaghan let Domino's become top-heavy with management, and he lost sight of the bottom line. Before he knew it, Domino's was behind in its payments to the bank and to a massive list of 1,500 creditors, in addition to the Internal Revenue Service. As a result, the bank took over 49 percent of the company, and the creditors filed a string of lawsuits. On top of this, Monaghan was still fighting Domino Sugar over use of the name. As a result, the company almost toppled completely in the early 1970s. As Monaghan later commented, "We fell flat on our faces, in one year I went from being the wonder boy of Ypsilanti to a laughingstock." But he said it taught him a valuable lesson: "Always keep your eye on the operation."

By 1971, Monaghan had regained control of the company, but he was hardly chastened by his experience, as he again pursued rapid growth. During this time, he focused his growth primarily on college and military towns, places with large numbers of young, single persons, those most likely to order a pizza to go. By 1975 the chain numbered one hundred stores; seven years later, 750. By the mid–1980s, Domino's was growing at the rate of more than one store per day, and by 1984 had 1,200 stores. By this point, Domino's was the second largest pizza chain in the country (second only to Pizza Hut), was the fastest growing chain, and was the largest pizza delivery outfit. With revenues of $182 million in that year, it had grown at the rate of 40 percent annually since 1978. By that time, despite rapid expansion (since about 65 percent of the stores were franchised, it took relatively little of Domino's capital to achieve this growth), its long-term debt was a mere $20 million, and profits were a healthy $5.5 million in 1983. Monaghan's personal fortune was estimated at $300 million by *Forbes*. During all this time, Monaghan had achieved success by "sticking to his knitting"—running small, low-rent operations, with no tables, a limited menu, and delivery guaranteed in 30 minutes. It worked like a charm. But just as Monaghan could not be happy with only one pizza place, he could not be happy with just a pizza chain. He wanted to fulfill his childhood dream, and now he had the money to do it.

In 1982, Monaghan approached Jim Campbell, president of the Detroit Tigers, because he had heard the club's aging owner, John E. Fetzer, might be interested in selling to the right buyer. Campbell gave Monaghan the quick brushoff, but later called "Bo" Schembechler, the University of Michigan's football coach and one of Monaghan's closest friends and a member of Domino's board. Campbell asked Schembechler, "Is this character for real?" (At that time, Monaghan was not well known outside of Ypsilanti and Ann Arbor.) Schembechler replied, "Jim, if Tom Monaghan says he's got that kind of money, *believe* him." So, Campbell secured Monaghan an audience with Fetzer. Fetzer, however, was at first not much impressed with the eager young man. "As long as you're here," Fetzer said, "tell me about yourself." Monaghan launched into his patented after-dinner, rags-to-riches story, but he embellished it into a three-hour saga. Fetzer was fascinated. He, too, it turned out, had lost his father when he was young, and he had also lived a hardscrabble life as a young man. The two hit it off famously.

At that point, Monaghan asked Fetzer if he would sell the club, but he indicated that he would not negotiate with him over the price. "On our second meeting," Monaghan recalled, "he said the Tigers were worth $45 million or $50 million, and I said I'd give him $50 million, and that was it." Well, not quite. The price actually came to $53 million, and Fetzer placed all sorts of "poison pill" restrictions on the purchase—no press, no leaks, no lawyers—or there would be no deal. Monaghan also had to agree to allow Fetzer and Campbell to continue running the club for two years, while he got only one seat on the three-man board of directors. Finally, however, in October 1983, Monaghan, with the help of a long-term note from the National Bank of Detroit, purchased the Tigers from Fetzer. It was by far the highest price paid for a ball team to that time, and many felt he had paid too much for the club. When *Forbes* asked Monaghan if he thought he had paid too much, he responded, "No, not for a lifetime dream. There is nothing in this world of a material nature that I wanted more than to own the Detroit Tigers." Of course, some dreams never come true, even with money. Monaghan told Sparky Anderson, manager of the Tigers, that he had always wanted to play shortstop for the Tigers. Sparky replied, "Listen Tom, I love my mother too, but she's not gonna pitch for me."

In every other respect, though, owning the Tigers was a dream come true for Monaghan. The Tigers came out of spring training in 1984 and promptly won the first nine games of the season before losing. Then they won thirty-five of their first forty games for the best start in major league history. The team remained in first place every day of the 1984 season, won the league championship series, and then won the World Series. Attendance at Tiger Stadium went up over 800,000, and the club made an estimated profit of $8 million, in a year when most baseball teams recorded losses. It was a "Walter Mitty" sort of experience, and it captured the imagination of the press and the American people. Monaghan, who was barely known in Detroit in 1982, became a well-known national figure as the freshman owner of a World Champion baseball team. And it also helped his pizza business. As he told *Forbes* in October 1984, "It helped our pizza sales in Detroit, which are up. And it's helped us in signing leases countrywide because it gives Domino's credibility. Our timing was right. Domino's isn't a household word, but it's on the verge of being one."

Monaghan was being hailed by many in the press and the public as a managerial messiah—owner of a championship team in his first try, developer of one of the fast-food industry's most spectacular growth companies, and a man worth more than $300 million. As a result, Monaghan received even more invitations to give his inspirational talk. *Inc.* magazine commented that by then "he [had] refined the basic Domino's/Tom Monaghan biography into a riveting half-hour morality play that practically walks off the podium flapping the cloak of the American flag." Some longtime Domino's people began to feel this was all becoming too much. One nineteen-year company veteran commented,

To be honest, there are people here who're sick of hearing yet another version of the Tom Monaghan Rags-to-Riches Story. I mean, it's not that it didn't happen or anything. It's just that some parts seem to get embellished and the rest sounds pretty old. For a long time, you know, people read this "orphanage" stuff and didn't think he even *had* a mother—even though she lives right near here. I worry sometimes that Tom may have lost some perspective on the folks who stuck by him when times were tough. (*Inc.*, February 1986)

In the *Detroit Free Press*, Monaghan's mother said she felt like a "nonentity." But none of this stopped Monaghan's relentless quest for his dreams.

With the huge fortune and the fame he had accumulated, Monaghan could also nurture his other ambition. If he could not actually become an architect, any more than he could play shortstop for the Tigers, he could begin to purchase Frank Lloyd Wright's buildings; and he created what was, in effect, a massive monument to Wright's architectural genius. In 1984, he bought the dismantled pieces of a Wright model home that had stood on the site of the Guggenheim

Museum in New York City, and he began to reassemble the house on a 300-acre site near Ann Arbor. On the same site, he began construction of a new $150-million headquarters for Domino's, based on Wright's 1950s design called the Golden Beacon, which was later adapted for the concept of Broadacre City. Often referred to derisively as "Pizza Tower," the thirty-storied building was to be part of a complex that included a working farm, museums open to the public, and a mime center directed by Marcel Marceau. Monaghan also scoured the country for Wright-designed furniture to fill his buildings, and he put together an $18-million collection of classic cars.

All of this made many of Domino's franchisees nervous. Was Monaghan becoming too obsessed with his own dreams at the expense of the simple vision that had propelled the pizza firm to success? One franchisee complained, "Tom's always been impressed by 'the best' this and 'the most' that, and now he's getting the most expensive office complex in the state, maybe the whole country. It's hard to believe my costs won't rise to subsidize all that." But Monaghan responded, "I'm allowed to have hobbies, so are the franshisees. I think I've done a pretty good job of having my hobbies complement Domino's." No one could deny that. While Monaghan's personal fortune had grown to $480 million in 1988, according to *Forbes*, the pizza chain had grown apace. With 4,280 outlets in 1988, Domino's was just slightly behind Pizza Hut's 4,800, and sales jumped 35 percent in 1987, to $1.9 billion. The company continued to be privately held, with 95 percent of it in Monaghan's hands. Profits, however, fell off 24 percent that year, and the average weekly sales per store remained stagnant in an industry that was growing by about 20 percent annually.

And Tom Monaghan was having too much fun to stop. He was fulfilling all his dreams, and was enjoying himself too much. To celebrate Halloween in 1987, he and his wife dressed as raccoons and spent the entire day scampering around Domino's offices. Later, he threw a three-day Halloween extravaganza at Domino's island in northern Michigan. The seventy guests starred in their own movie, were given play money printed with a picture of Monaghan and his wife with which to buy real gifts, and dined on lobster and Russian caviar. Finally, he handed out Gucci and Tiffany trinkets to all as an early celebration of Christmas. The estimated cost was $1 million. In *The Great Gatsby*, Jay Gatsby used to throw parties like that all the time. (**A.** Thomas Monaghan and Robert Anderson, *Pizza Tiger*, 1986. **B.** F. Scott Fitzgerald, *The Great Gatsby*, 1925; *Forbes*, February 13, October 1, 1984, October 24, 1988; *People Weekly*, May 7, 1984; *New York Times*, June 6, June 12, 1984; *Time*, June 25, 1984; *Newsweek*, October 15, 1984, February 8, 1988; *Contemporary Newsmakers*, 1985; *Saturday Evening Post*, April 1985; *Inc.*, February 1986; *Who's Who in America*, 1986–87; Toronto *Globe & Mail*, July 18, 1988.)

MOORE, GORDON E. (January 3, 1929–) and **ROBERT N. NOYCE** (December 12, 1927–) Semiconductor company founders, Fairchild Semiconductor, Incorporated and Intel, Incorporated. Robert Noyce is, for most journalists and much of the public, the very image of the Silicon Valley. For these people, Noyce is also too good to be true. A graduate of Grinnell College in Iowa, ruggedly handsome and quietly charismatic, he reminded most people of Grinnell's other famous graduate, Gary Cooper. Gordon Moore, on the other hand, was "white bread," a scientist and technician of great ability who always stood in Noyce's giant shadow. A quiet, bespectacled man, Moore started out to be a chemistry professor, and he could never quite understand how he became a businessman. As he said years later, "I didn't have an entrepreneurial urge, and I still don't." But these two men, as a wonderfully matched team, founded and ran two of the earliest, largest, and most innovative companies in the Silicon Valley. And, in large measure, they created the semiconductor industry and the resulting revolution in microelectronics.

Robert Noyce was born in the tiny town of Denmark in southeastern Iowa. His father, a Congregational minister, was transferred to a number of different congregations in the state, so during his early years, Noyce lived in Atlantic, Decorah, Webster City, and Rennow. When Robert was about twelve, the Noyce family finally settled down. Reverend Noyce was awarded the associate super-intendency of the Iowa Conference of Congregational Churches, and he was stationed in Grinnell, Iowa. A college town, it became Robert Noyce's first real "home," and he began to weave himself into the fabric of the community. He attended the local high school, where he was a good athlete and a top-notch student, and he graduated at the head of his class. As he noted later, "My last year I took college courses, specifically in physics, just simply because I was relatively bored with the stuff that was going on in high school."

When it came time to go to college, Noyce's marks gave him a choice of many top-notch schools, but he chose to stay "home" and attend Grinnell College. During his last year of high school, he had developed a good relationship with the head of the physics department at Grinnell, and Noyce felt he wanted to continue there. In most instances, this sort of decision is a big mistake. Ironically, however, there was perhaps no better place in the country for Noyce to study physics at that time than Grinnell. His physics professor, Grant Gale, had been a classmate of John Bardeen, who, along with William Shockley and Walter Brattain, had recently invented the transistor. Bardeen sent Gale two of the first transistors ever produced, so while Noyce was at Grinnell, he had the unique opportunity of being introduced to the cutting edge of new technology and developments in physics. He became infatuated with the transistor and its implications:

By my junior year I began to look at [the transistor] as being one of the great phenomena of the time. And that it would be something good to exploit—well, maybe 'exploit' is the wrong way to put it—but I saw it as something that would be fun to work with. (Malone, *The Big Score*)

Upon graduation from Grinnell in 1949, Noyce enrolled in the doctoral pro-gram in physics at the Massachusetts Institute of Technology (MIT). Nominally the greatest source of technological expertise in the country, in Noyce's words, "there were no professors around who knew anything about transistors." So Noyce went into physical electronics, which could be used as a background in the study of transistors. His thesis—"Photoelectric Study of Surface States on Insulators"—was not central to solid-state electronics. Nonetheless, when Noyce finished his doctorate, he had his pick of the great electronics firms—Bell Laboratories, IBM, RCA, GE—but he chose Philco, one of the very weakest, because "the way I put it to myself at the time," Noyce recalled, "was that they really needed me. At the other places they knew what was going on, they knew what they were doing." He also felt he would not be pigeonholed at Philco, that he could wear many hats, especially those of scientist and businessman. Furthermore, Philco was just entering the solid-state field, and it had chosen the unique area of high-frequency transistors, which were used mostly in hearing aids. Before long, with Noyce's help, Philco took the industry lead in this area. Noyce soon discovered, however, that there were severe limits to Philco's interest in research and development. Philco wanted to be good enough to keep its foot in the door of transistors, but it did not want to spend a lot of money or to take many risks in that area. Noyce soon became bored. In 1956, after Noyce had been at Philco for three years, he gave a technical paper in Washington, D.C. Sitting in the audience was William Shockley, who introduced himself after the presentation. Recalls Noyce,

A month or so later he called me up and said he was starting this thing out here on the West Coast, and that he'd like to talk to me about joining him. Well, Shockley of course was the "daddy" of the transistor. And so that was very flattering. And I had the feeling that I'd done my stint in the minor leagues and now it was time to get into the majors. (Malone, *The Big Score*)

After Shockley received his Ph.D. on the behavior of electrons in crystals in 1936, he had joined the technical staff of Bell Labs. While there, Shockley began to think about the creation of switching devices which depended upon solid-state, not vacuum-state, physics. He particularly focused his attention on a group of materials referred to as semiconductors. The war interfered with his research, but after the war, he and Brattain and Bardeen discovered the "transistor effect," for which they shared the Noble Prize in physics in 1956. Few people at the time, even at Bell Labs, grasped the full potential of the transistor. Shockley left Bell in 1955 to return to Palo Alto, California, where he established his own company, Shockley Semiconductor Laboratory, with capital provided by Arnold Beckman of Beckman Instruments. He began to gather a group of highly trained scientists and technicians to aid him in creating the transistor and semiconductor industry in California. When Shockley invited Noyce out for an interview in 1956, Noyce displayed the kind of easy confidence that was so characteristic of his later career. Having arrived in San Francisco at 6 A.M., he drove out to the "Valley," bought a house by noon, and then met with Shockley in the afternoon.

Shockley offered Noyce the position of research scientist, and Noyce accepted. Noyce was not the only bright young man hired in the early months; Shockley, in fact, assembled a truly brilliant group of talented, creative men for his fledgling company. One of these was Gordon Moore.

Moore, born in San Francisco, graduated with a degree in chemistry from the University of California at Berkeley in 1950 and then earned his Ph.D. in chemistry and physics, in 1954, at the California Institute for Technology. Shortly thereafter, Moore was approached by Shockley to join him at his new semiconductor firm, and he accepted. At first it was a wonderful experience for the young scientist. Here were a dozen bright young Ph.D.s coming to work every day on topics at the leading edge of American technology. Further, Shockley was an absolute genius in electronics, and a great research director. But in terms of management techniques he had a great deal to learn. Moore, Noyce, and Jean Hoerni wanted to work on transistors, but Shockley favored developing a so-called four-layer diode. Finally, in the summer of 1957, Moore, Hoerni, and five other engineers—but not Noyce—agreed to leave Shockley. They realized that their brainpower was really the major capital asset at Shockley Semiconductor, and they were tired of being treated like children. They decided to start their own company, but were in need of capital. They went to the investment firm of Hayden Stone, where they linked up with Arthur Rock, soon to become the king of venture capitalists in the Silicon Valley. Rock had difficulty finding backers for the young scientists, but finally he was able to interest the Fairchild Camera and Instrument Company of New York. The Fairchild firm was greatly impressed with the brilliance of the seven young scientists, but it was unwilling to cooperate until the scientists had found a manager, someone to serve as an articulate spokesman to the business and financial community. The seven dissidents had the ideal candidate—Robert Noyce—Shockley's favorite. Noyce had long bristled at the cavalier treatment he was accorded by Shockley, and he was receptive to the seven dissidents' offer to join them.

A new company was formed—Fairchild Semiconductor—with the twenty-nine-year-old Noyce as its head. Fairchild Camera reserved an option to buy out the new company for $3 million any time within the next three years—an option they did in fact exercise in 1959. The new company pursued something that Shockley had put on the back burner in his firm—the 2N696—a double-diffused-base silicon transistor. This was significant because the traditional material for transistors was germanium. The young company's first goal was to make this new product commercially feasible.

In December 1983, when *Esquire* ran an issue called "50 Who Made a Difference," they commissioned Tom Wolfe to do a profile of Bob Noyce. In his essay, Wolfe talked about Noyce's curious magnetism: "Bob Noyce projected what people call the halo effect. People with the halo effect seem to know exactly what they're doing and, moreover, make you want to admire them for it. They make you see the halo over their heads." People naturally gravitated toward Noyce. He had an effortless way of taking charge that alienated no one, but made everyone feel that he was indispensible to the operation. And, since they thought he was indispensible, it was a self-fulfilling prophecy.

The early months at Fairchild Semiconductor were hardly glamorous. At first the cofounders worked in their respective garages, but in October 1957, they took over a two-storied warehouse built of tilt-up concrete slabs. It was a raw, crude environment, and it did much to shape the democratic, egalitarian atmosphere which later characterized both Fairchild and Intel. They worked without electricity in the early weeks, they put together their own workbenches, they had no offices, there was no real rank and no hierarchy. This was a joint venture, and they all contributed to make it a success. Fairchild's start-up could not have come at a better time. There were a few other semiconductor manufacturers in the country—Texas Instruments in Dallas, Motorola in Phoenix, Raytheon in Boston, and Shockley Semiconductor in the Silicon Valley—enough to supply the demands from radio and machine manufacturers. Then, suddenly, the Russians launched *Sputnik I* in 1957, and the space race was on. This linked the computer with the transistor, and greatly magnified the importance of both. Demand skyrocketed.

The first big break for Fairchild came in January 1958, when IBM ordered 100 mesa silicon transistors to use as memory drivers in their computers. This was the beginning of a long and intimate relationship between IBM and the Silicon Valley, particularly between IBM and Noyce and Moore. By the end of 1958, Fairchild had half a million dollars in sales and a hundred employees. One of the fastest growing firms the Silicon Valley ever produced, it soon began to experience profound growing pains. A classic technology-driven company, Fairchild was in need of an effective sales and marketing arm. It also began to suffer the endemic disease of the Silicon Valley—managerial employees spinning off to start their own firms. Although the "dissident eight" had, in fact, started the tradition when they left Shockley, they were, nonetheless, shaken when prominent members of Fairchild began to leave to start their own companies after 1959.

In 1959, Noyce, despite his perceived managerial abilities, was named director of research and development. He and his research team began working on what he viewed as the "horribly inefficient" business of wiring together arrays of transistors by hand after production. Jean Hoerni had been working on the problem for a number of months, but when Noyce joined the team a new level of synergism emerged. The Fairchild team soon realized that photolithography allowed them to repeat the same transistor over and over again on the surface of a silicon chip in a systematic manner, and with built-in connections between them. In the meantime, Jack Kilby of Texas Instruments had filed for a patent for what they called miniaturized electronic circuits. Noyce did not file for his patent until six months later. The Fairchild version, however, which featured a planar design, was far more practical and became the basis for the subsequent microelectronics revolution. The courts ruled that Fairchild and Texas Instruments should split the royalties from all the new semiconductor companies which began springing up at that time. It was, perhaps, the most significant invention of the past quarter century. The integrated circuit made it possible to create miniature computers, and opened up every field imaginable to the influence of electronics. It was so dramatic and so important that it has been given a number of tags: "the second industrial revolution," "the age of the computer," "the microchip universe."

Fairchild's biggest cause for celebration in 1959 came when it secured the contract to provide transistors to the Minute Man I missile program. At about the same time, Fairchild Camera exercised its option to buy Fairchild Semiconductor. Noyce, Moore, and the other six founders were each $250,000 richer as a result, but they found themselves in a new situation. They were no longer entrepreneurs, but rather employees. The casual, democratic, technology-driven Silicon Valley culture they had done so much to create would run head on into a conservative, autocratic, status-driven Eastern corporate culture. Ultimately, this cultural clash ended the glory days of Fairchild Semiconductor. But that lay in the future. Fairchild still had nine heady, hectic, dizzying years of growth ahead of it.

During these years, Noyce and Moore were the dominant forces at Fairchild, and they complemented one another beautifully. Noyce, an impulsive visionary with great charisma, and a need for publicity and people, very much needed the steadying influence of Gordon Moore, a quieter, far more cautious, highly organized man. Together, they built Fairchild into a $150-million business, but it was not easy. Noyce more than Moore had to deal directly with management problems, since he had been appointed general manager of the company when Fairchild Camera took it over.

Noyce had learned an important lesson from William Shockley—how not to run a company. Never wanting to alienate his staff as Shockley had, Noyce developed an atmosphere of trust and respect at Fairchild. Believing in the natural nobility of people, he gave employees room to operate, but he ensured that they took responsibility for their actions. As Tom Wolfe told it in *Esquire*, when a subordinate came to Noyce for direction, he would lay out the various options available to the employees and "then he would turn on the Gary Cooper smile: 'But if you think I'm going to make your decision for you, you're mistaken. Hey . . . it's your ass.' " As part of this system of trust, Noyce established what he called the short circuit paper route. This meant that any engineer, no matter how lowly, could make any purchase he wanted, unless someone else objected strongly enough to stop it. Thus, there was only one piece of paper involved— the purchase order form the engineer took to the purchasing department. He did not need the approval of layers of bureaucrats to proceed with a project.

Despite Noyce's great charisma, and despite his halo effect, he was not a great production manager. This began to hamper Fairchild's efforts in the late 1960s, as did the rash of defections from the company. Jean Hoerni, the great engineer, left with two of the other original founders to start Amelco in 1960. Later that year, four others left to found Signetics. But in the early 1960s equally talented replacements were readily available. By the mid–1960s Fairchild had sales of $130 million and 12,000 employees. It was still the hottest company in the Valley.

But the conflict with Fairchild Camera's head office in New York, which became increasingly tense, alienated many executives at the semiconductor division. This clash of cultures was brought into sharp relief when, according to Tom Wolfe, John Carter, the parent company's president, came to Silicon Valley for a visit. As befitting an Eastern businessman, he had a limousine and liveried chauffeur pick him up at the airport and bring him to the Valley. The chauffeur was "wearing the complete chauffeur's uniform—the black suit, the white shirt, the black necktie, and the black visored cap." That somewhat rankled the shirt-sleeve, democratic atmosphere at Fairchild Semiconductor, but what really got them was

the fact that the driver stayed out there for almost eight hours *doing nothing*. He stayed out there in his uniform, with his visored hat on, in the front seat of the limousine, all day, doing nothing but waiting for a man who was somewhere inside. . . . It seemed bizarre. Here was a serf who did *nothing all day* but wait outside a door in order to be at the service of the haunches of his master instantly, whenever those haunches, and the paunch and the jowls might decide to reappear . . . it seemed *terribly wrong*.

Noyce, Moore, and the others realized how much they hated the Eastern corporate system with its layers of bureaucrats, its baroque corporate etiquette. Rejecting the idea of a social hierarchy at Fairchild Semiconductor, they did not appreciate having one imposed upon them from New York.

When Charlie Sporck, who had been production manager at Fairchild, left to join National Semiconductor, Noyce, Moore, and others at Fairchild were devastated. It was the single most important blow to the company's position as the dominant chip manufacturer. One of the executives later recalled, "So we were plowing along at Fairchild, you know, number one in the world in integrated circuits. And then Charlie Sporck did something that shocked me to my boots. Charlie Sporck resigned. I couldn't believe it. I remember it so well. I couldn't believe it." Noyce had similar feelings: "Charlie was well-liked. Very well-liked. He was a straight-forward person. And I suppose I essentially cried when he left. I just felt that things were falling apart, and I just felt a great personal loss, frankly."

From that point onward, Fairchild began to fall apart. For three years, from 1965 to 1968, sales were flat, between $120 and $130 million. The company was unprofitable for a year and a half, and during this time both Texas Instruments and Motorola passed Fairchild in sales and profits. Meanwhile, Sporck's National Semiconductor was raiding talent at Fairchild almost daily. Finally, in June 1968, Noyce announced his resignation from Fairchild—from the company he had founded and brought to the top of the Silicon Valley. Leaving with him was Gordon Moore, head of research and development at Fairchild, and Andrew

Grove, a process development expert. The three men then announced they were founding a new company, to be called Intel, Incorporated. Fairchild Semiconductor, the company which established the freewheeling, pedal-to-the-metal, Silicon Valley style of management, research, and development, was as good as dead. And in its place was a new pretender. The king was dead. Long live the king.

When they left Fairchild, everybody paid attention to Noyce. But, just as in the case with Shockley Semiconductor, it was Moore, not Noyce, who first began the push to leave the firm. Although Noyce had become as frustrated with the Eastern management style as Moore, it was the latter, as director of research and development, who worried most about its impact on technological change. As Moore watched the various spin-offs from Fairchild achieve success, he began to feel that the restraints that the parent corporation were putting on the semiconductor division would be fatal to the company. He began talking about starting up a new, small company to specialize in the making of integrated circuits for computer memory. It was only later that he was able to convince Noyce, the Valley Sun God, to leave. To create a new company, Noyce was essential.

He was essential, first of all, for financing. Noyce and Moore approached Arthur Rock, who had provided financing for Fairchild, and, without even writing up a proposal, told him they were each willing to put up $250,000 of their own money to start the firm. Rock responded by rounding up $2.5 million to start the company, and then, a short time later, Grinnell College, where Noyce was by then a trustee, put up another $300,000. At Intel, Moore and Noyce decided to move into one of the most backward areas of computer technology—that of data storage of memory. Since the inception of computers in the late 1940s, memory had been stored in ceramic ringlets called cores. Noyce and Moore wanted to develop a memory chip, and within two years they had perfected their 1103 memory chip. The size of two typewritten letters in a word, the tiny silicon chips contained 4,000 transistors, and did the work of 1,000 ceramic ringlets, and did it faster.

The 1103 memory chip revolutionized the computer and semiconductor industries. Becoming the industry standard overnight, other firms like Fairchild had to struggle just to be number two. Nobody could surpass Intel. The young company had devoted its first year almost entirely to research, with sales of just $3,000 that year and forty-two employees. In 1972, with the introduction of the 1103 chip, sales went up to $23.4 million, and employees numbered 1,002. A year later, sales skyrocketed to $66 million, and the work force increased to 2,528. About $50 million of those sales came directly from the memory chips.

At about the time when some new semiconductor firms were beginning to take a larger share of the memory chip market, Intel introduced yet another revolutionary development—the microprocessor, or "computer on a chip." In 1969 a Japanese company asked Intel to design chips for a new family of calculators. An engineer at Intel, Ted Hoff, came up with an idea. Noyce recalls, "We'd build a small computer on a collection of four chips and program them to look like a calculator. And that idea was presented to the Japanese and they accepted it.'' The capabilities of that microprogrammable central processing unit on a set of chips was later integrated into a single, advanced form of integrated circuit—called the 8008—and was soon known simply as the microprocessor. Introduced in 1971, the microprocessor tripled the price of Intel's stock over a two-year period. Even Moore was a little overwhelmed. Normally taciturn and reticent, he became positively loquacious with *Fortune* in 1973: "We are really the revolutionaries in the world today—not the kids with long hair and beards who were wrecking our schools a few years ago.''

At Intel, Noyce and Moore created what became the classic Silicon Valley management style. The two men ran the company together in a partnership which Noyce called a "two-headed monster.'' In this arrangement, Noyce dealt with external affairs, and Moore concerned himself mainly with internal affairs. They were also evenly divided in terms of temperament—Noyce the optimist and Moore the realist. "It makes a good foil,'' Noyce said. "We can argue the advantages and disadvantages of a project.'' It was obvious to everyone at Intel that Noyce and Moore ran the show, but below them there was a great deal of autonomy. There is no evident social hierarchy at Intel—no executive suites, reserved parking places, or any other visible symbols of authority. Noyce and Moore felt that the stock option they gave all the engineers and most of the office workers acted as a strong incentive for innovation in the company. Most important, everyone at Intel—Noyce and Moore included—was expected to attend sessions on "Intel Culture.'' At these meetings the corporate culture was outlined and discussed. Running these seminars was the province of Andrew Grove, who would later expand this philosophy into a series of best-selling books on management.

In 1974, Noyce kicked himself upstairs to chairman of the board and turned the running of Intel over to Gordon Moore and Andy Grove. In this position, Noyce's role became more expansive. Many called him the "Mayor of the Silicon Valley,'' and he certainly acted more as a spokesman for an entire industry and for the advancement of electronic technology itself than as a representative for Intel. He was awarded the National Medal of Science in a White House ceremony in 1980, and he was elected to the Inventors Hall of Fame in 1983. By that time Noyce was a legend, and when a member of a major underwriting firm was asked about him, he replied, "Noyce is a national treasure.'' Perhaps Noyce's crowning glory came in August 1988, when he was appointed chief executive officer of Sematech, a consortium created in 1987 by the semiconductor industry to restore the United States to a competitive position against the Japanese. Noyce commented, "It wasn't quite in my lifeplan, but I just decided this was a higher priority than the other commitments I had.''

Meantime, back on earth, Gordon Moore had to steer Intel through the rough waters of the high-technology frontier of the late 1970s and early 1980s. As he had reflected a few years earlier, "This business lives on the brink of disaster. As soon as you can make a device with high yield, you calculate that you can decrease costs by trying to make something four times as complex, which brings your yield down again.'' The breakneck pace of technological innovation made products obsolete almost before they had been absorbed into the marketplace and had a chance to make a profit. And Moore and Grove had to face a situation in which the pace of change was increasing at an almost exponential rate. By 1974, this pace had begun to tell on the six-year-old Intel. Sales began to level off, and profits fell off sharply that year.

What happened? To summarize, by 1975 there were at least twenty other microprocessors on the market, and although none of them could challenge Intel's lead, the cumulative effect reduced the company's market share. Then, too, Intel made the mistake of entering a consumer market for the first time with a digital watch. It was a disaster, and it significantly drained the firm's profits. When Noyce became chairman and Moore became president, Grove was put in charge of production. Grove realized that the old research-oriented approach at Intel was not enough. Insisting that Intel adopt production procedures similar to McDonald's in the food industry, the company soon began to be referred to as ''McIntel'' by the employees. But this was necessary if Intel were to remain a profitable concern in the industry.

Grove's highly organized production processes were highly beneficial to Intel, but profits continued to sag in the late 1970s, and the market share dropped every year. Even though sales were in excess of $320 million in 1976, compared to just $23 million in 1972, Intel found itself in a relatively worse situation each year as far as profitability and market share were concerned. Gordon Moore reflected in 1977, ''A lead in this business is six months, two years if you are fortunate.'' By 1979, revenues reached $650 million, and employees numbered 14,000, and demand for the microprocessor seemed almost insatiable; even so, Intel found it difficult to sustain the hectic pace. Moore said,

We're in a major growth industry, but at the same time we have a high rate of technological obsolescence. The price of our products drops rapidly, at an average of 30 percent a year over the product life cycle. The next generation product will do the job much cheaper than the present product. So if you fall too far behind technologically, you soon become non-competitive in price. That fact drives us to keep up with the technology. (*Financial World*, March 15, 1981)

As a result, Intel has spent about 10 percent of its revenues each year on research and development.

The frustration for Intel and its executives was apparent in the early 1980s. Intel continued to grow (by 1981 it had revenues of $855 million), but its levels of profitability were never anything close to what they had been in the early years. The worldwide market for semiconductors was enormous—about $13 billion annually—but competition grew more intense each year, especially from the Japanese. And Intel, which had been the industry leader in innovations in the early years, showed signs of age and lethargy in the early 1980s. They were late in developing the 64K Dynamic Random Access Memory (DRAM) chip, and found they were well behind several domestic producers. This tardiness resulted partially from Intel's admission that it could no longer compete effectively (especially against the Japanese) in the lower end of the memory chip market. Instead, it moved toward producing higher margined items, such as the multichip boards that served as the electronic brains of industrial-process controllers and other systems. The research and development was very costly, and the payoff was slow and uncertain. In 1981 the company was forced to take on $150 million in long-term debt for the first time.

The more Intel grew in the mid- to late 1980s, the more the red ink flowed. By 1985, with sales of $1.4 billion, the firm just barely managed to break even, and that was an accomplishment considering the losses of previous years. And the company, once the largest and most powerful producer of semiconductors in the world, ranked just seventh in 1984. Moore was forced to lay off 2,600 workers, a tenth of the company's work force, and he announced in 1986 that the firm would cease production of DRAMs. It was a striking move. Intel had started in memory chips in 1970, and sixteen years later was admitting defeat in the industry they had pioneered. It was a tragic symbol for many in America of how the United States was losing its technological and production superiority to the Japanese.

But there remained a ray of hope. Moore announced that Intel had developed a new microprocessor—the 80386—a 32-bit microprocessor with the power of a medium-sized computer. Developed with the staggering cost of $100 million, it was a miracle of miniaturization. It was an enormous gamble. Would it be accepted? Would it be able to make enough money to pay back its investment? Would it bring Intel back to the top of the Silicon Valley? To the top, perhaps, of the world of semiconductors? The 80236, a 16-bit microprocessor, sold well and became the heart of IBM's new line of AT computers, but Intel desperately needed a product for the next generation. Critics were beginning to write the firm's epitaph. An executive at a smaller semiconductor company commented, "Intel is a monolith, it can't move as fast as it used to." The implication was that it had grown too large and was too ossified to continue to compete effectively in the turbulent high-technology markets.

The first breakthrough for the 32-bit 80386 came when Ford Motor Company ordered large numbers of them for use as engine-control devices. By 1988, it was clear that Intel again had a winner on its hands. Different versions of the chip—called embedded controllers—were designed to handle tasks inside appliances, automobiles, and airplanes, and they were also used with computer peripherals such as laser printers. The results were staggering. The company's profits tripled in the first quarter of 1988, resulting in a new image on Wall Street. One investment analyst commented, "Clearly they have exceeded the high range of the Street estimates." Then, in February 1989, Intel shocked the computer world with the introduction of its N–10, a superchip that could handle 64-bit-long instructions, double the length of its 32-bit processor. The N–10 was, in effect, a mainframe computer on a chip. One of Intel's scientists boasted that the N–10 was "like putting a Cray [supercomputer] on a chip." With the ability to pack the capacity of 1,000 transistors on a single chip, the N–10 was viewed by everyone in the computer industry as an enormous breakthrough for Intel. Eric Kronstadt of IBM's Thomas J. Watson Research Center was so impressed that he announced, "It's a magic number. It's like reaching 1,000 for the first time on the Dow Jones." Intel, which had become an also-ran in the computer workstation market, fervently hoped that the new chip would begin a turnaround in its fortunes. Some critics, however, felt the N–10 would jeopardize the market for Intel's next chip, the 80486, which was developed to replace the fabulously successful 80386. Only time would tell.

At about the same time, Hitachi Limited of Japan, the world's largest producer of memory chips, announced that it would begin importing microprocessors made by Intel—it seemed to many like carrying coals to Newcastle, but was, in fact, recognition of Intel's success in this area of more sophisticated semiconductor technology. Compaq Computer of Houston, one of America's fastest growing computer companies, also announced it was making the 80386 the basis of two of its new microcomputers. Intel had gambled and won, at least for the present. It all recalled in some ways the day Intel went public in 1971. On the same day they made their offering, Playboy Enterprises also went public. By the early 1980s Intel's stock was selling for about ten times that of Playboy's. Wall Street analyst Ben Rosen commented, "Wall Street has spoken—it's memories over mammaries." (**A.** Robert N. Noyce, "Innovation: The Fruit of Success," *Technology Review*, February, 1978; **B.** *Fortune*, November 1973, December 31, 1979, April 25, 1988; *Business Week*, December 14, 1974, March 1, 1976, April 18, 1983, January 21, September 2, 1985, October 20, 1986, March 16, 1987, March 14, June 20, July 4, August 15, September 26, 1988, March 6, March 13, 1989; *Forbes*, April 15, 1977, March 30, 1981, January 4, 1982, June 14, 1986; *The Economist*, December 27, 1980; *Financial World*, March 15, 1981; *Management Today*, July 1981, February 1985; Dirk Hanson, *The New Alchemists*, 1982; *Esquire*, December 1983; Glynnis Thompson Kaye, ed., *A Revolution in Progress: A History of Intel to Date*, 1984; Everett M. Rogers and Judith K. Larson, *Silicon Valley Fever*, 1984; T. T. Reid, *The Chip: How Two Americans Invented the Microchip and Launched a Revolution*, 1984; Daniel I. Okimoto et. al., eds., *Competitive Edge: The Semiconductor Industry in the U.S. & Japan*, 1984; *Electronic Business*, February 1984; *Electronics Week*, September 3, 1984; *Contemporary Newsmakers*, 1985; Thomas Mahon, *Charged Bodies: People, Power & Paradox in Silicon Valley*, 1985; Michael S. Malone, *The Big Score*, 1985; James W. Cortada, *Historical Dictionary of Data Processing Organization*, 1987; *Business Month*, August 1987; *Who's Who in America*, Supplement, 1987–88; Toronto *Globe & Mail*, April 14, July 13, 1988; *Washington Post*, February 26, 1989.)

N

NEUHARTH, ALLEN HAROLD (March 22, 1924–   ). Newspaper publisher, Gannett Company. Allen Neuharth is a throwback to the autocratic, dictatorial business tycoons of a bygone era. As he has said, "I'm a hands-on manager. I will use whatever methods seem most likely to bring results. Sometimes its bantering, sometimes its badgering." His employees have experienced his thoroughness and his wrath on more than one occasion. A circulation executive spent a long weekend preparing an exhaustive presentation for Neuharth, but when the executive finished delivering his spiel, Neuharth had just one question "How come we don't sell papers at the airport in Missoula, Montana?" Peter Prichard in *The Making of McPaper,* tells of a meeting of *USA Today's* editorial staff. That day's issue of the newspaper, displayed in a newsrack in the room, showed the smiling face of a leaping cheerleader above the fold on page one. Without saying a word, Neuharth went over to the newsrack and began slamming the door violently shut, time after time. The assembled editors were dumbstruck. Having gotten their attention, Neuharth announced, "When you run a picture of a nice, clean-cut, all-American girl like this, *get her tits above the fold.*" This kind of management, according to the experts, is not supposed to work today; today, managers are supposed to be more refined and restrained. But it cannot be denied that Allen Neuharth has transformed the Gannett Company into the largest, most successful newspaper publisher in America.

Neuharth was born in Eureka, South Dakota, the youngest child of Daniel J. Neuharth, a farmer, and his wife Christina. When Allen was two years old, his father was killed in a farm accident. As a result, his mother had to work as a waitress in an Alpena, South Dakota, restaurant, and she also took in sewing and washing to supplement her income to take care of Allen and his older brother. Because of family poverty, Allen at an early age also had to help support the family. When he was eleven, Neuharth began to deliver the *Minneapolis Tribune.* Two years later, in 1937, he got a part-time job as a printer's devil in the composing room of the *Alpena Journal.* Neuharth's first full-time job was as a butcher boy in a meat market in his hometown. Earning just $1 a week, he worked six days a week, before and after school, and on Saturdays. Consequently, Neuharth had little time for extracurricular activities, but he found time to be a staff member on the school newspaper, the *Echo*, and eventually became the editor.

After graduation, Neuharth entered Northern State Teachers College in Aberdeen, South Dakota, enrolled in a prelaw course. World War II interrupted, and in 1943, after just one quarter in school, he enlisted in the U.S. Army. After serving as an infantryman in Europe and the South Pacific, where he was awarded the Bronze Star for valor, he was discharged in 1946. Upon returning home, Neuharth entered the University of South Dakota on the GI bill, where he majored in journalism and minored in political science. He became editor of the school paper, the *Volante*, and had summer internships with a number of newspapers in the state. He graduated in 1950, cum laude and Phi Beta Kappa.

Shortly after graduation, Neuharth got a job as a general assignment reporter with the Associated Press bureau in Sioux Falls, South Dakota. Two years later, he resigned this position to launch *SoDak Sports*, a statewide weekly sports tabloid patterned after *Sporting News*. Although *SoDak Sports* was well written and innovative, the venture was an ignominious financial failure. Neuharth accepted the blame, "I was the one who mismanaged." In 1954, deeply in debt and terribly humiliated, Neuharth wanted to escape from South Dakota. He accepted a job as a reporter with the *Miami Herald*, later part of the Knight-Ridder chain. Neuharth proved to be aggressive and resourceful, and he won local acclaim for his investigative reporting. He quickly rose through the ranks, and began to display the kind of ruthlessness and political maneuvering that characterized his later career. In 1958 he was promoted to executive city editor, but he asked that no one be told for a time, so that he could "get the feel of the newsroom." A writer for the *Miami Herald* described the situation: "The circumstances were classic Neuharth. He asked that it be kept secret for several months, and worked those months as a reporter and assistant city editor, observing at elbow range a staff unaware that management was among it, planning changes." The reporter continued, "Few who were there describe those early days at the *Herald* without resorting to a cliche: He left the field littered with dead."

In 1960 Neuharth became an assistant executive editor of Knight-Ridder's Detroit *Free Press*. His three years in Detroit were what are often referred to as a "character building" experience. Despite having to contend with crippling strikes and unsuccessful bargaining with the union, Neuharth's management was praised by most at the paper. As the paper's senior managing editor later commented, "He put us on the road to running the place in a more businesslike manner." Neuharth's work at the *Free Press* was so well regarded that Paul Miller, then head of the Gannett newspaper chain, hired him as general manager of that chain's two flagship newpapers in Rochester, New York, in 1963.

The Gannett chain had been started by Frank E. Gannett* in 1906, when he merged four small New York state papers. Fifty years later, he controlled a chain of thirty newspapers and a string of radio and television stations. It was the monster of newspaper chains, one that had achieved its success by taking over existing mom-and-pop dailies in one-newspaper towns, giving Gannett a monopoly in most of its markets. As a result, it has been one of the most profitable newspaper operations in North America for decades. Gannett's strategy was to buy out going operations and transform them into little money machines with the assistance of managerial expertise. In 1966, Neuharth was named vice president of the Gannett chain and president of Gannett Florida. He rapidly put his imprint on the huge and venerable publishing giant. Almost as soon as Neuharth was given control of the Florida market, he broke Gannett's rule. He started a newspaper from scratch—*Cocoa Today*. This was a first for the chain, and it made many in the organization nervous. Within two years, however, the paper was turning a profit, and gaining a reputation "as perhaps the best newspaper of its size in the country." Neuharth was rewarded in 1970 with a promotion to president and chief operating officer of the parent company, and three years later he took full control as chief executive officer.

During his early years as head of the company, especially between 1970 and 1975, Neuharth concentrated on building the company and increasing its profit margin. He acquired about twenty newspapers in various geographical locations, and he set about making these as profitable as all the other units in the chain. Success seemed almost too easy. Since Gannett went public in 1967, it had reported year-to-year gains in earnings per share for an unprecedented period of time. Neuharth continued this impressive record, and the firm's stock was routinely selling at from twenty to thirty times earnings. Since virtually all the company's papers held a monopoly in their respective markets, making money seemed easy for Neuharth. He was free to raise advertising and subscription rates without fear of competition, which kept a large cash flow pouring in. As Rupert Murdoch, rival publishing tycoon and owner of the *New York Post* commented, running a monopoly newspaper was a "license to steal money forever."

Neuharth, however, was not content to simply allow Gannett to rest on its comfortable laurels. He instituted a rigorous program of technological and managerial innovation to cut costs and increase profits even further. He hired a staff of management experts to oversee Gannett's far-flung operations, set up a central purchasing subsidiary to keep costs down, and developed a new system for budgeting and planning. More significantly, Neuharth undertook to enhance the editorial quality of the Gannett papers. Profitable as it had been for years, the Gannett chain was the only big chain without a single prestigious newspaper, and generally the papers relied overwhelmingly on the wire services for their stories, rather than developing a large in-house staff. Neuharth increased editorial budgets of the local newspapers, upgraded the Gannett Wire Service, and acquired the Louis Harris & Associates polling agency. Although many in the journalism trade continued to be contemptuous of the Gannett papers, they began to win awards, and in 1980 Gannett News Service won the Pulitzer Prize for public service, giving the chain a total of thirteen Pulitzers.

In addition, Neuharth himself took strong stands on a number of controversial issues. He became a champion of civil rights for blacks, and his hiring practices illustrated his moral commitment. He recruited large numbers of blacks and Hispanics, making the chain an acknowledged leader in minority hiring. He also hired large numbers of women, until Gannett had more female employees than any other publishing chain. Neuharth also fought as president and chairman of the American Newspaper Publishers Association to implement fair hiring practices in the industry, and to retain First Amendment rights for newspapers in the face of severe court challenges.

In 1979 Paul Miller retired from Gannett, and Neuharth added the title of chairman to his collection. His first task was to complete Gannett's biggest merger, thus far, with Combined Communications. As a result, Gannett acquired two large city dailies, the *Cincinnati Enquirer* and the *Oakland Tribune*, a number of radio and television stations, and a large outdoor-advertising business. The newspaper giant was an astounding success. It had revenues of over $1 billion and a net income of $152 million. Its stock price stood at more than 500 percent of its initial offering price in 1967, and it was still trading at fifteen times earnings. Not only that, Neuharth himself was chosen newspaper publishing Chief Executive of the Year by the *Wall Street Transcript*.

Yet the situation by 1980 was strangely disquieting. There seemed to be little additional room for growth. Antitrust regulations prohibited Gannett from buying additional newspapers, broadcasting stations, or outdoor-advertising operations. Also, there were few independent newpapers left in the country. Of some 1,750 dailies in the United States in 1980, only about 600 had not been absorbed by chains. As a result, Wall Street began to lose interest in Gannett. Neuharth recognized this problem. When he met with financial analysts, they would ask him, "Don't you have any interesting news for us?" All he could reply was, "Just another quarter of earnings gains." Neuharth began to search for new ventures. At the end of 1980 he announced the establishment of Gannett Satellite Information Network, to explore the commercial use of communications satellites. Neuharth delivered his biggest bombshell at the year-end executive meeting in December 1980: Gannett was going to introduce a national, general-interest newspaper.

The idea was greeted by hoots of derision by most industry analysts who noted that only business-oriented publications like the *Wall Street Journal* had ever been successful on the national level. The *New York Times* sniffed that the venture was an ego-trip for Neuharth, who was tired of just making money. But Neuharth was undeterred. He pressed ahead with plans for his paper. Modeled on his Florida paper, it was to be called *USA Today*, and it was designed to be a supplement, rather than a substitute, for local newspapers. Neuharth recognized that Gannett had unique advantages for bringing out a national paper. It had printing plants in thirty-five states, most of which produced evening papers, which meant that they were idle in the early hours of the morning when *USA Today* was to be produced. Gannett's only major investment was in satellite receiving stations. Neuharth recognized that a circulation of 2.5 million nationally was necessary to break even, but most analysts felt that the *New York Times* and the *Washington Post* had already sewed up the upscale, young professional audience that Neuharth was after. However, Neuharth planned to offer something the establishment papers did not. His new paper would make bold use of color and graphics; it would have an arresting page layout; and it would present exceptionally detailed and comprehensive weather and sports coverage. Neuharth planned to take all the lessons he had learned running small-town newspapers and apply them on the national level. As one of Gannett's executives commented, "He thought the time was right for a small-town paper covering the nation."

The first issue of *USA Today* came off the presses on September 15, 1982. Dubbed "McPaper" by critics, since they felt it represented fast-food journalism, or was the journalistic equivalent of ABC-TV's upbeat "Good Morning America," the new paper caught the public's fancy. Within a few months its paid circulation was 222,000; by the end of the first year, it stood at 1.15 million. By September 1984 *USA Today* was the nation's third largest daily, behind the *Wall Street Journal* and the New York *Daily News*. Why had *USA Today* succeeded? Ironically, clues to its success were hidden in the criticism leveled at it by establishment journalists. Jonathon Yardley of the *Washington Post* called *USA Today* the newspaper junk food of the television generation, and he said that "the information it imparts is generally what the people want to know, rather than what they ought to know." Neuharth had approached his national newspaper project as a form of popular culture rather than elite journalism. True, the *New York Times* and *Washington Post* had captured the upscale market, but there were far larger numbers of potential readers who were not looking for an intellectual challenge with their daily news.

Although *USA Today* was very popular with readers, advertisers were staying away in droves, and it was losing oceans of money. In 1983 the average issue had less than seven ad pages. To solve this problem, Neuharth recruited as publisher Cathleen P. Black, who had greatly increased advertising revenues at *Ms* and *New York* magazines. By November 1985, *USA Today* had an average of 12.56 pages of advertising, and shortly before that, the newsstand price was raised from twenty-five to fifty cents to help defray losses. When he launched *USA Today* in 1982, Neuharth predicted it would begin to turn a profit after five years. Although by 1988 circulation had leveled off at 1.6 million, well below the 2.5 million considered necessary to make a profit, Neuharth announced *USA Today's* first profit just in time for the paper's fifth anniversary. That made it a stunning success compared to other comparable publishing ventures. *Sports Illustrated* took ten years to become profitable, *Money* magazine took eight years, and *Newsweek* took nine years. Only *People* magazine has turned a profit more rapidly. *USA Today* was also one of the most widely imitated newspapers in the world, with papers as far away as Greece and Turkey copying its format. But

Gannett in the first four years of *USA Today* rang up astounding losses of about $458 million. Only a corporation with revenues and profits as high as Gannett's and only someone as powerful and driven as Neuharth could have weathered such a traumatic birth and genesis.

Despite his obsession with *USA Today* during this period, Neuharth still found time to engage in more traditional Gannett pursuits. He bought the *Des Moines Register* with a stunning bid of $200 million; in March 1985 he purchased from CBS a Sunday newspaper insert, which he renamed *USA Weekend*; and shortly thereafter he also obtained the Triangle Sign Company of Chicago, making Gannett the largest outdoor-advertising company in North America. Five months later he also negotiated the purchase of the Evening News Association, publisher of the *Detroit News* and owner of several profitable television stations, for $717 million. In 1986 he masterminded the purchase of the Louisville, Kentucky, *Courier-Journal* and the Louisville *Times* for $300 million. In 1987, the Gannett Company had profits of $319 million on revenues of $3 billion.

Perhaps Neuharth's greatest gamble came in the fall of 1988, when he announced that in conjunction with Grant Tinker, formerly head of NBC, and Steven Friedman, former executive producer of NBC's "Today" show, he was bringing out a television version of *USA Today*. To be syndicated to stations around the country, it involved what Friedman called an "ironic task," of turning *USA Today*, the first daily newspaper inspired by television, into a daily television program. The reaction of the critics, even before seeing the show, was predictably scathing. Ron Powers called the new show "Nanoid News," meaning that the information on the program was compressed into bits so small as to become meaningless. When the new show went on the air on September 12, 1988, it was aired on 156 stations across the United States and Canada. Operating with a $40-million budget, "USA Today," the television show, was designed to be similar to its tabloid parent with four sections on news, sports, life, and money. It also used the latest, most dazzling graphics available in the industry. Although it was an expensive venture, and although many analysts predicted failure, some felt that the real key was the impact the television show would have on the tabloid's circulation. As a media analyst at Paine Webber commented, "I'm inclined to think *USA Today* will provide a boost for circulation. Essentially circulation is what gives them the ability to raise ad rates." And this, of course, would make the newspaper consistently profitable.

A self-confessed workaholic, who has been called obsessive-compulsive by Peter Prichard in his recent book, Neuharth dresses in black and white, wears mounds of gold jewelry, and has a bronze bust of himself in his office that looks "like a conquering Caesar." He owns four palatial homes, and can often be found hobnobbing with the rich and famous. Just as often, however, he can be found drinking beer in poolrooms, surrounded by seedy-looking characters. Neuharth is, in the words of *People*, a "street fighter, a sturdy little man with wavy gray hair that looks like it has been given a blue rinse." Although many who have dealt with Neuharth have found him "utterly charming," *Fortune* recently called him "fiercely competitive and at times seemingly ruthless." In 1987, however, Neuharth announced a BusCapade across America to discover the "secret of his success and to reaffirm his roots among the little people." Many of his employees were just relieved he would no longer be stalking the halls of Gannett's headquarters, "pounding his fists on employee's desks . . . ridiculing them with caustic memos, raging after them as they flee down the hall and driving them to tears and emotional fits." The other side of Neuharth was shown on the BusCapade. When he interviewed an elderly couple in Cape Canaveral, Florida, the husband asked Neuharth, "And who are you?" "Me?" replied Neuharth, "I'm just the paper boy." (**A**. Al Neuharth, *Confessions of an S.O.B.*, 1989; **B**. *National Cyclopaedia of American Biography*, N, 63:19; Nixon Smiley, *Knights of the Fourth Estate: The Story of the Miami Herald*, 1974; *Editor and Publisher*, March 17, 1975, April 29, 1978, March 30, 1985; *New York Times*, February 5, September 11, 1978, April 11, September 16, 1983, March 29, 1984; *New York Times Magazine*, April 8, 1979; *Esquire*, September 1979; *Time*, April 28, 1980, September 20, 1982, July 9, 1984; *Dun's Review*, December 1980; *Newsweek*, December 29, 1980, September 20, 1982, January 17, 1983, February 11, April 1, 1985, September 9, 1986, September 1, 1987; *New York*, March 1, 1981; *Fortune*, April 20, 1981, September 3, 1984, March 18, 1985, January 5, 1987; *Forbes*, February 15, 1982, January 14, 1985; *New Republic*, October 25, 1982; *Business Week*, February 7, 1983, October 15, 1984, September 30, 1985, September 15, 1988; *Financial World*, April 4–17, 1984; *Playboy*, January 1985; *Contemporary Newsmakers*, 1986; *Current Biography Yearbook*, 1986; Peter Prichard, *The Making of McPaper*, 1987; *People Weekly*, September 28, 1987; *Manhattan, Inc.*, September 1987, September 1988; *Business Month*, February 1989.)

NORRIS, WILLIAM CHARLES (July 14, 1911–   ). Computer company founder, Control Data Corporation. Ralph Nader and William Taylor, in *The Big Boys,* refer to William Norris as a "Revolutionary without a Movement." It is a fitting appellation for a man who, since the late 1960s, has been one of the most unconventional and controversial business leaders in America. One former Control Data Corporation executive, who left the firm because he profoundly disagreed with Norris' policies, nonetheless viewed him as an exceptional individual:

We're talking about a very complex character. He is a highly intelligent, hard-working guy. He doesn't give a damn about money. He wears old suits. He drives old cars. I used to think it was an affectation, but it is genuine. He looks like Carl Sandburg, he acts like Carl Sandburg. He's a farm boy. He doesn't want anything to do with people from New York. He has a dislike for securities analysts, MBA's. (Nader and Taylor, *The Big Boys*)

This iconoclast of the computer industry was born on his father's 1,000-acre farm in Inavale, Nebraska, in an area known as Cather Country (after the novelist

Willa Cather). The farm was evidently prosperous during the early years of Norris' life. Norris was educated in a one-room school in Inavale, and then attended high school in neighboring Red Cloud. As a young boy, he became enthralled with electronics and ham radios, and his favorite reading was *The Boy Mechanic,* a how-to guide for building model airplanes, boats, and other gadgets. Norris graduated from high school and went to the University of Nebraska, where he studied electrical engineering. While a student, Norris worked as a radio repairman for Walt's Music Store in Lincoln. He was just one month away from graduation in 1932 when disaster struck. The dust bowl years were creating enormous problems for farmers in the Great Plains, and Norris' father finally collapsed and died from a heart attack. Norris earned his engineering degree by accelerating the remaining requirements into a few days and returned to help his desperate mother rescue the family farm. The once profitable farm had only one salvageable asset in 1932—its cattle, which Norris preserved by feeding them thistle. When the farm was once more operating efficiently in 1934, Norris left to take a job with Westinghouse. The farm remained in Norris' family at least into the 1980s, and the lessons Norris learned during the depression always stayed with him. At Westinghouse, Norris sold x-ray equipment, first in Omaha, then in Chicago. In 1941, he left Westinghouse to join the U.S. Navy, and it was during World War II that Norris encountered the various factors that helped shape his future business career. With the navy, he was stationed in Washington, D.C., as an electrical engineer, and he was assigned to the Communications Supplementary Activity (CSAW), or "seesaw" as it was called. CSAW was a select team of cryptologists, chess masters, bridge masters, physicists, and engineers whose task was to break enemy codes. A predecessor of the National Security Agency, CSAW coordinated its activities with civilians working on state-of-the-art computer activities during the war. This introduced William Norris to computer research at the time of its genesis. Furthermore, it placed Norris at the nexus of important business and government relationships which became fundamentally important to him.

When World War II ended, the Defense Department, realizing the importance of retaining this assemblage of technical talent, informed Norris and his colleagues that if they arranged for private financing to set up a computer research and development company, the government might supply them with lucrative contracts. So Norris and Howard Engstrom went out to look for financing for their venture. This first experience with Wall Street in 1945–1946 profoundly alienated Norris from all it represented. Norris and Engstrom discovered that there was no interest on Wall Street in financing any computer ventures. As he later recalled,

We made many trips to Wall Street and we banged on a lot of doors. I remember that we tried Glore Forgan. We thought we had a deal with Kuhn Loeb, but it fell through. If there had been a deal, it would have changed the course of the industry. (*Datamation,* February 1981)

But there was no deal, and Norris and Engstrom had to try something else.

That something else turned out to be John Parker, an investment banker who had some experience in small, technological companies. He agreed to put up $200,000 for a 50-percent ownership in the new concern. The company, called Engineering Research Associates (ERA), was set up to design and develop computers. Members of the tiny firm included some of the future giants of the computer industry: Seymour Cray, Bill Keye, and Frank Mullaney. Cray was an especially gifted genius in computer design, and shortly thereafter, ERA computers became known for their sophisticated engineering features, careful design, and reliability. Further, the young team's intimate connections with the Pentagon brought it a number of juicy military contracts. In fact, it did so well that it became the target of some investigations for impropriety.

In the meantime, however, the Remington Rand Corporation was expanding its reach into computers. The giant business machine corporation purchased the Eckert-Mauchly Computer Corporation, which had developed the UNIVAC computer, and was now casting its eye on the talent-rich, but cash-poor ERA. Norris and his cohorts had no interest in selling out to a giant corporation, but John Parker had entered this venture to make money. He began shopping his shares to International Business Machines (IBM), Honeywell, National Cash Register (NCR), and Remington Rand; James Rand* of Remington Rand ultimately made the winning offer. Parker sold his share of the firm for 73,000 shares of Remington Rand stock, worth about $1.7 million (a better than eightfold increase on Parker's investment in 1946). Parker had arrived at the sum by multiplying the total number of engineers in the firm (340) by $5,000. Computer historians Erwin Tomash and Arnold Cohen commented that this "may have been one of the few times since the Civil War that individuals have been sold by the head outside of the professional sports world."

When Parker told Norris and his colleagues in December 1951 that ERA had been sold to Remington Rand, they were shocked and dismayed, since they knew they would lose their creative freedom. Having no choice, they became cogs in an organization whose corporate attention was focused upon electric shavers and typewriters. Four years later, in 1955, Norris received another shock—Remington Rand had been acquired by the Sperry Corporation. Although Norris was put in charge of all computer-related activities for the new Sperry-Rand Company, he soon learned that Sperry's senior management had little knowledge of, or interest in, furthering the firm's position in the industry, and it cut off capital in each of Norris' areas of responsibility, one by one. By 1957, Norris was intensely frustrated and ready to move on.

Arnold Ryden, a financial consultant, Byron Smith, a UNIVAC executive, and Willis K. Drake, Norris' assistant, approached Norris about forming their own computer company. Norris resigned from Sperry-Rand, and hired Drake as the first employee of the new Control Data Corporation (CDC). Norris and Drake had to raise capital for the new firm, but they refused to approach Wall Street, since the financial community had been the source of many of their problems.

Instead, they sold Control Data stock directly to the public, without the backing of an underwriter. The method was so unusual and so risky that the Minnesota State Securities Commission (Control Data was to be located in a suburb of Minneapolis) required the firm to furnish a presubscription list of people who had read the prospectus and would buy the stock if it became available. As Drake reflected later, "The idea that we could sell stock in a company with no product, no employees, and no facility seemed totally preposterous to him." Norris and his colleagues (who, by this time, included Seymour Cray, Frank Mullaney, William Keye, James Miles, and others from Sperry-Rand) had taken shares themselves and had convinced friends and relatives to also invest. Norris himself mortgaged his home to buy 75,000 shares at a dollar a share. Their objective was to distribute Control Data stock as widely as possible, so that no single stockholder, like John Parker, could ever again determine the fate of the company.

The stock sold surprisingly well—615,000 shares at $1 a share in less than two weeks. It was bought up by about 300 people, mostly UNIVAC employees and personal friends of the Control Data officers. But Norris and his colleagues were treading on thin ice, since they "stole" many of Sperry-Rand's most skilled computer personnel, and they took many of its trade secrets with them. The chairman of Minnesota Mining & Manufacturing recognized this when Norris asked him to buy stock in the venture. He replied, "Hell, if I were 20 years younger, I'd invest. And I'll tell you this too, sonny: If I were UNIVAC, I'd sue your ass." And it did, and it forced Norris to sign a consent decree. In the meantime, however, he had launched his computer company and was on his way.

Norris had two guiding ideas when he founded Control Data in 1957. The first was that multimarket companies like Sperry-Rand could never succeed in computers. As he said ten years later, "To run a computer company, it's necessary to have top executives who understand computers. People are afraid of what they don't understand, and losing money makes a man doubly afraid." Second, he would not compete with IBM, the giant of the computer industry, in the areas where "Big Blue" was strong. Instead, he adopted a strategy of "hitting IBM where they are weakest," which Norris calculated to be large-scale computers for scientific uses. These were primarily nonbusiness customers, especially government and universities, with whom Norris and his colleagues from ERA already had marketing experience. These customers, furthermore, did not require the kind of service that IBM had used to carve out its massive market share. Finally, Control Data had Seymour Cray, who had an intense desire (and a commensurate talent) to build the world's most powerful computers. Without Cray's immense talent, it is doubtful whether Norris would have been so confident about challenging IBM in this area.

An aloof, brooding genius, Cray refused to work at the company's headquarters in Bloomington, but he took a staff of fewer than thirty-five with him to a remote laboratory built for him near Chippewa Falls, Wisconsin, hundreds of miles away. Cray began designing and building the 1604, a highly compact, but powerful computer for the day, and one which would be priced at about half the cost of the competitive IBM computer. A so-called second-generation computer, the 1604 operated on transistors, unlike first-generation computers which operated on vacuum tubes, and it was designed with complex printed circuit cards, which Cray called "printed building blocks."

Cray's "supercomputer" was a tremendous success when it was unveiled eight months after Control Data was incorporated, but its development almost caused the young company to go under. Two months after the 1604 was introduced, the first order arrived—a $1.5-million sale to the U.S. Navy Bureau of Ships. That gave the computer status and respectability, and orders began rolling in from the scientific community. The success of the computer was so great that CDC reported its first profits after just two years of operating, an almost unheard of feat for a mainframe computer company. With this success and Cray's desire to continue bringing out state-of-the-art computers, CDC in 1959 brought out its Model 160, a desk-sized computer that sold for $90,000. The success of this small and relatively inexpensive, but powerful machine further enhanced the company's reputation for innovation. But Cray was not finished. A year later he began to work on the 6600—which was to be twenty times more powerful than the 1600, and three times more powerful than IBM's STRETCH, the supercomputer the giant firm had killed a few years earlier.

The first model of the 6600 was due for delivery to the Atomic Energy Commission's Livermore Laboratory in 1964, but debugging the massive machine, with its 350,000 transistors, took longer than anticipated. By this time IBM had announced its System 360, and its top-of-the-line Model 90 was to be faster than CDC's 6600. Although no prototype of IBM's machine existed, the announcement cut heavily into CDC's potential orders, and Norris, in a panic, cut fully $2 million off the scheduled $7-million price tag on the 6600.

Norris had acquired twenty-one companies, mostly manufacturers of equipment to be used in support of CDC's big machines, in 1963, when CDC was on the upswing. By 1965, several of these acquisitions were in precarious positions. Also, many of Control Data's customers, such as the government, had now decided to begin leasing computers rather than buying them, forcing the company to tie up a lot of money in leased equipment. So Control Data, which had gone from $626,000 in sales in its initial year to $121.4 million in 1964, was in serious trouble. As a result, there was a great deal of management dissension; four vice presidents and the firm's treasurer all left within the space of four months.

But Norris was determined to hold on. In 1966 he got a two-year, $120-million revolving credit from a ten-bank consortium led by Continental Illinois National Bank & Trust. The banks pressured Norris to add George A. Strichman, head of Colt Industries, to CDC's board, to replace the moody Cray. Norris also signed a contract with Saul P. Steinberg's[†] Leasco Data Processing Equipment Corporation, to ease the leasing situation with customers.

Most important, however, the 6600s worked. By the end of 1967 sixty-three debugged supercomputers had been sent out to CDC's blue-chip customers, and IBM's Model 90, promised for 1967, had still not been delivered. Later that year, IBM announced that it was abandoning the series, and that it would deliver only those machines currently on order. That meant that CDC virtually had the scientific supercomputer market to itself. In 1967 Control Data began showing significant profits, at a level second only to IBM, and Norris decided he would try to crack into the business market, which theretofore had been IBM's preserve. By 1968 Norris had already placed CDC systems in Dow Chemical, Hornblower & Weeks, and at a Martin Marietta plant in Denver. These were relatively small sales, but they gave Norris hope for the future. In an expansive mood, he told *Fortune* in 1968: "Take the *Fortune* 500 list, add the 200 largest foreign companies, the utilities, and the financial houses, and you've got your number— 1,500 to 2,000 customers." But Norris had an even bigger card up his sleeve.

Norris' experiences with IBM in 1965 had left him bitter. He felt he was fighting a mythical enemy, one whose machines existed only on paper, and whose salesmen would promise customers anything, forcing CDC to promise more for the 6600, which in turn put greater pressure on engineers and programmers. The mere suggestion that IBM was working on a new machine caused customers to hold off from ordering a 6600. "IBM really hurt us," he recalled in the early 1980s, "We couldn't get an order for almost a year." Therefore, in 1965, Norris asked CDC's lawyers to begin gathering evidence of IBM's antitrust violations. A year later they began submitting memos to the Justice Department on the alleged violations, but the government took no action. In December CDC filed a suit against IBM, charging thirty-seven instances of monopolistic practices. The most important charge involved IBM's marketing of "paper machines and phantom computers." Suits and countersuits followed, and the two giant computer firms were locked in a struggle to the death. Many of Norris' colleagues at CDC were opposed to continuing the suit, but Norris persevered. Finally, in January 1973, IBM approached him about an out-of-court settlement.

Norris, by this time, was interested in settling for the right price. The price turned out to be exceedingly steep for IBM. As part of the deal, IBM sold its potentially lucrative Service Bureau Corporation for its book value of $16 million. (On the open market it would have brought from $45 to $50 million.) Control Data also got a package of subsidies from IBM worth $101 million, including the payment of CDC's very expensive legal fees by IBM. Norris felt the whole package was worth about $1 billion to Control Data, especially since Service Bureau Corporation turned out to be worth more than anyone had realized, having established a leading position in time-sharing and data services. With forty data processing centers, 1,700 highly trained employees, and some well-developed computer programs, it turned out to be a steal for Control Data and William Norris.

Throughout its controversy with IBM, Control Data continued to grow. With its computer sales soaring to $570 million in 1969, and its stock prices reaching new heights, Norris began to make additional acquisitions. His biggest purchase was Commercial Credit Corporation, a finance company with assets nearly ten times greater than Control Data's. The acquisition fit perfectly into Norris' plans. As more and more customers were now leasing their big computers, Commercial Credit could finance these transactions. It could also lend money to students at Control Data's newly established computer schools, and most important, it would provide a steady cash flow for the firm, allowing it to ride out fluctuations in the computer market. Commercial Credit fulfilled its promise perfectly in the recession of 1970–1971, which hit supercomputers very hard. While Control Data's computer operations lost $46 million, Commercial Credit's $38 million in earnings kept losses to a manageable $2.7 million.

After his suit was settled with IBM in 1973, Norris began to pursue joint ventures with a number of firms. Control Data, with Seymour Cray still heading up the research end, had developed the 7600, which was by far the largest and most costly engineering and production effort the firm had ever undertaken, and at the same time, Cray was also developing two other supercomputers, the Star–100 and the 8600. Control Data spent at least $75 million and seven years developing the Star computer, and it was also pouring large amounts of money into the 8600, which was to be from four to eight times more powerful than the 7600. But Norris began to feel these investments were too costly, and he wanted to slow down development. As a result, Seymour Cray resigned from CDC in 1973, and the vaunted research facility in Chippewa Falls was closed. Norris moved Control Data away from production of large and expensive mainframe supercomputers, and moved, instead, in the direction of joint ventures in the production of computer peripherals.

Control Data and National Cash Register formed the jointly owned Computer Peripherals, Incorporated, which developed and manufactured high-speed computer printers, magnetic tape systems, and punch card equipment. CDC also bought NCR's disk-memory manufacturing operations, agreeing to fulfill NCR's disk requirements. Then, in 1973, Norris picked up a number of other data processing companies, giving Control Data a highly accelerated program in that area. He also purchased Ticketron, Incorporated, the computerized ticket service, and later picked up Auditron, a television and radio audience rating service. As CDC dropped out of supercomputers in the early 1970s, it became the industry leader in computer services and peripherals. By 1979, CDC made $725 million in sales of peripherals, and $600 million from services, consulting, and education. By then, it had begun limited production of supercomputers, but characterized mainframes as support for the services. Mainframe sales amounted to $500 million in 1979.

During this time, William Norris took a profound step—one that set him and his company apart from the rest of corporate America, and brought them an abundance of both praise and criticism. In 1966–1967, Minneapolis was torn by riots in its Northside black ghetto. The city's business and political leaders were stunned and worried, but William Norris was profoundly affected. Unwilling to rely simply on platitudes, Control Data constructed a major manufacturing facility in the riot-torn area. The Northside assembly plant, which began operation in 1968, was the first of seven CDC manufacturing facilities established in hard-core poverty areas. Employing about 2,000 people, the plants were designed to provide the same levels of efficiency and quality as the firm's other facilities. Norris said about this initiative, "You can't be effective if you're just giving money away. But if you focus on (your connections with the community) as business opportunities, then you're really making the capitalist system work." This successful attempt at a form of enlightened capitalism caused Norris to become far more expansive in his goals.

Becoming convinced that doing well was compatible with doing good, Norris placed Control Data at the forefront of a number of innovative and controversial ventures. The most innovative and expensive of these ventures was PLATO—Programmed Logic for Automatic Teaching Operations—a sophisticated, computer-based education system that Control Data made available through leased display terminals at colleges, high schools, prisons, and corporations. Control Data's cumulative investment in this project by the mid–1980s was about $1 billion. Few were optimistic by that time that CDC would ever reap a return on this investment.

Norris also launched Rural Venture at Control Data in 1980. A consortium with several other corporations, it went against the grain of American agriculture. Fueled by Norris' faith in the small family farm, it aimed to promote viable, small-scale agriculture. At the center of the project were computerized data bases designed to promote more sophisticated financial management by small farmers. A pilot project was established in Princeton, Minnesota, with the goal that the participating families would be successful enough to purchase their own farms. Four years later, none had achieved that goal.

Norris also set up City Venture Corporation in 1978, which was designed to rehabilitate slum buildings in Toledo, Ohio, Minneapolis, and other cities. Although well-intentioned, the program drew fire from experts in the field, and from community groups, who objected to the gentrification and commercialization which so often accompanied City Venture's programs. These programs, and the drain they put on Control Data's resources at critical periods in the 1970s and 1980s, brought a great deal of criticism of William Norris both inside and outside the company. One former executive of the firm said, "The social programs clearly took tens, probably hundreds, of millions of dollars out of the company over a period of years." But William Norris, in a speech in 1984, gave an impassioned defense of his initiatives: "Corporate social responsibility, as generally perceived at present, is on the periphery of these and other major unmet societal needs. Hence, corporations are addressing symptoms more than their root causes and doing so with a miniscule proportion of their vast resources." Time did little to lessen the ardor about Norris. After he was interviewed by *Inc.* in May 1988, the magazine was deluged with diametrically opposed responses from its readers.

By 1984 there was great pressure on William Norris to step down as chief executive of Control Data. Although sales were up $192 to $4.3 billion, earnings were off by 10 percent that year at $155 million. Many areas that had brought profits to Control Data throughout the 1970s and early 1980s, such as peripherals and data services, were suffering from intense competition. They had brought out the successful Cyber 205 computer, but in 1982 decided to spin off the supercomputer operations to a subsidiary, in order to save about $60 million in development costs. Decisions such as this made many executives at Control Data feel that research needs were being subordinated to what they viewed as Norris' rather wild and fanciful social visions. As one former executive sniped, "Bill doesn't just want to be in business, he wants to save the world, too."

In early 1986, Bill Norris stepped down as chief executive of Control Data, and he was replaced by Robert M. Price, his longtime right-hand man. By that point, Control Data was a very troubled firm, and Price immediately began to undo much of Norris' legacy. Saying, "We don't have any visions, we have a damn job to do, that's to make the company profitable," he slashed employment by 35 percent, and sold off 82 percent of Commercial Credit Corporation. Price also wrote off a number of other enterprises, including most of Norris' prized social programs. He intended to focus CDC's energies and money on computer manufacturing, disk-drives, and service businesses, which brought in about 95 percent of the company's revenues. Said one insider, "We used to be a culture-driven business. Now we're a business-driven culture."

But Price's changes did not significantly enhance Control Data's fortunes. Although it managed to show a small profit of $19 million (on nearly $3.4 billion in sales) in 1987, which was better than the combined $832 million in losses in 1985 and 1986, Price had merely succeeded in making CDC a ripe takeover target for a number of corporate raiders. Since the firm's breakup value was far greater than its market value, analysts were not optimistic that the thirty-year-old computer firm was going to be able to remain independent.

Many at Control Data undoubtedly cursed William Norris for this turn of events. But they forgot much of the innovation, success, and growth he had generated at the firm during the years in which he ran it as a nearly one-man operation. Then, too, Norris did have a profound social vision, a vision that he attempted to bring to fruition. Perhaps the greatest tribute to William Norris was given to him by his employees after they bested IBM in 1973. Giving him the steering wheel of a large sailing ship, which he hung outside his office, it was dedicated to "Our Helmsman":

> He chose a course that had no charter
> No other Helmsman dared be the martyr
> He steered the ship and brought us through
> This Wheel for him—is from his crew.

(**A.** William C. Norris, "A Risk-Avoiding, Selfish Society," *Business Week*, October 28, 1980; "Doing Well—and Doing Good—in the Inner City," *Christian Science Monitor*, March 12, 1982; *New Frontiers for Business Leadership*, 1983. **B.** *Forbes*, June 1, 1964, September 15, 1965, March 1, 1967, March 1, 1971, November 15, 1974; *Time*, August 14, 1964, April 3, 1978, January 20, 1986; *Fortune*, April 1966, February 1968, November 19, 1979, January 23, 1984, April 25, 1988; *Business Week*, July 30, 1966, November 10, 1973, June 25, 1979, October 17, 1983, October 8, October 22, 1984, February 16, 1987, March 14, June 20, 1988; *National Cyclopaedia of American Biography*, M:399; *Datamation*, September 1976, February 1981; *Corporate Report*, June 1978, June 1979; Erwin Tomash and Arnold A. Cohen, "The Birth of ERA . . . ," *Annals of the History of Computing*, October 1979; Milton Moskowitz et al., *Everybody's Business*, 1980; Katherine Davis Fishman, *The Computer Establishment*, 1981; *Harvard Business Review*, July–August 1981; *U.S. News & World Report*, September 21, 1981, October 22, 1984; Carol Pine and Susan Mundale, *Self-Made*, 1982; Robert Sobel, *I.B.M.: Colossus in Transition*, 1983; James C. Worthy, "An Entrepreneurial Approach to Social Problem-Solving: William C. Norris and Control Data Corporation," in Jeremy Atack, ed., *Business and Economic History*, 1983; James C. Worthy, *William C. Norris: Portrait of a Maverick*, 1987; *Computerworld*, September 12, 1983, July 15, 1985; *Wall Street Journal*, December 22, 1983; Stephen T. McClellan, *The Coming Computer Industry Shakeout: Winners, Losers, and Survivors*, 1984; *American Educator*, October 1984; A. David Silver, *Entrepreneurial Megabucks*, 1985; *New York Times*, February 17, 1985; Charles Garfield, *Peak Performers: The New Heros of American Business*, 1986; Ralph Nader and William Taylor, *The Big Boys: Power & Position in American Business*, 1986; *Inc.*, May 1988, August 1988; Toronto *Globe & Mail*, May 23, 1988.)

O

OGILVY, DAVID MACKENZIE (June 23, 1911–). Advertising agency executive, Ogilvy & Mather. No advertising executive in recent years has received more accolades than David Ogilvy. In 1958, the New York advertising magazine *Madison Avenue* called him ''one of the last of the really creative agency heads,'' who had ''done more to shape the look of advertising in the last 20 years.'' Rosser Reeves, the leading proponent of the hard-sell technique in the 1950s, and a general critic of Ogilvy's creative soft-sell approach, rated Ogilvy ''the most spectacular man in the agency business today'' in 1960. Dubbed the ''Samuel Johnson of advertising'' by *Fortune* in 1987 because of the two books he has written on the profession, Ogilvy has received more attention recently for his literary talents than for his advertising acumen. In fact, as early as 1965, *Fortune* profiled Ogilvy in an article entitled, ''Is Ogilvy a Genius?'' David Ogilvy, only partially tongue in cheek, remarked, ''I nearly sued them for the question mark.'' As influential as Ogilvy has been for the advertising profession, the success of his work, oddly, has been more muted.

David Ogilvy was born in West Horsley, England, the son of a classics scholar who had been a wealthy stockbroker, but who had lost his fortune during World War I. Although well connected (he was a cousin of British author Rebecca West), Ogilvy grew up in genteel poverty. Nonetheless, he was able to attend Fettes, a fine public school in Edinburgh, and he won a scholarship to Christ Church at Oxford. There, he failed and was expelled for poor marks. At that time, Britain was in the depths of the depression, and Ogilvy was unable to secure a job. His father had a key contact with the Hotel Majestic, a prestigious Parisian hotel, and Ogilvy got a job as an apprentice in the kitchen. After a year, his family summoned him home, and he became a door-to-door salesman for cooking stoves in Scotland.

While he was selling stoves, Ogilvy's flair for advertising and writing began to emerge. When he was asked by the company to put together a sales manual for the company's other salesmen, he wrote ''The Theory and Practice of Selling the Aga Cooker.'' *Fortune* (April 1965) later commented that it ''may well be the liveliest and most engaging sales manual ever written.'' Partly because of the success of the manual, and partly because his older brother Francis was an account executive there, Ogilvy got a job with the London advertising firm of Mather & Crowther.

Here, Ogilvy found his place in life. As he later noted, "I loved advertising. I devoured it. I studied, and read, and took it desperately seriously.'' Realizing the great opportunity that lay before him, Ogilvy took advantage of it. Ever since he had read *Huckleberry Finn* in boarding school, Ogilvy had been infatuated with America. Putting this interest in America to good use at Mather, he copied ads from the United States for his British clients. He was highly successful as an account executive for the firm, and in 1938 Ogilvy persuaded the firm's executives to send him to the United States for a year to study American advertising techniques. It was a wonderous year for Ogilvy. He made the rounds of Madison Avenue, picking everyone's brains and making friends along the way. One of the most significant contacts for his future was Rosser Reeves, who was then a young copywriter. Reeves later recalled their first meeting: "This beautiful boy appeared, in those days David looked just like Lord Byron. Since he didn't represent any competition, we all opened our doors to him and told him what we knew.''

Reeves introduced Ogilvy to the hard-sell techniques of Claude Hopkins, who had written the book, *Scientific Advertising*. Ogilvy read the book, and found himself torn between the British, soft-sell approach, and the research-based hard sell. As Ogilvy later recalled, "My admiration for these two opposite schools tore me apart, it took me a long time to reconcile what I learned from both of them.'' Deciding to stay in America at the end of the year, Ogilvy resigned from Mather & Crowther in 1939 and began looking for a job. He soon joined George Gallup's Audience Research Institute in Princeton, New Jersey, as an associate director. The agency had been set up to advise Hollywood producers as to whether the pictures they were planning to make would be hits. At Gallup, Ogilvy conducted 439 nationwide surveys, gaining a solid grounding in opinion research and deepening his respect for research as an advertising tool. It also gave him an opportunity to learn more about American mores and folkways than most Americans knew.

Ogilvy left Gallup in 1942 to work for British intelligence in the United States, and later he served as second secretary of the British Embassy in Washington, D.C. When the war ended, Ogilvy decided to become, of all things, a farmer. And not just any farmer, but an Amish farmer. Purchasing a farm in Lancaster County, Pennsylvania, Ogilvy grew a full Amish beard, wore a wide-brimmed Amish hat and grew cigar tobacco. Ogilvy soon realized that he was not cut out to be a farmer; he did not have sufficient strength, he was mechanically inept, and he knew nothing about animal husbandry. So, he sold his farm and returned to advertising in 1948. But David Ogilvy decided he was not going to work for an advertising agency; he was going to own one. This decision was made despite the fact that he had been out of the business for ten years, and had rather limited experience. Nonetheless, he got Mather & Crowther and another London advertising firm, S. H. Benson, to sponsor him with $45,000, and he persuaded Anderson F. Hewitt, an account supervisor with J. Walter Thompson in Chicago, to join him as president. The new firm of Hewitt, Ogilvy, Benson & Mather opened in New York in 1948 with a few clients. It was not an auspicious beginning for an agency that later became one of the world's largest.

At first, most of the young agency's clients were British firms. The first client, in fact, was Josiah Wedgewood & Sons, Limited, the famous maker of chinaware. The agency also handled the American business of Arthur Guinness & Sons and the British Travel Association. These firms had small advertising budgets for the United States, and Ogilvy commented, "We think we are pretty good at using *small* spaces—we have to be." Although Ogilvy was the firm's research director, he began to write copy and found that he had a real flair for it, whereupon he took over the job of copy chief as well. Over the next several years, billings grew slowly and the agency experienced moderate success. The great breakthrough came when it garnered the Hathaway shirt account.

In 1951, Hathaway was a small, Maine clothing company with a miniscule advertising budget. Ogilvy wanted to create something different—an ad that would convey to the reader a sense of atmosphere and class about a moderately priced line of shirts. To do this, he decided, the right model was needed, one who looked distinguished, like William Faulkner or Ernest Hemingway. At the last moment, Ogilvy had an idea—the model should wear a black eye patch. As his model, Ogilvy chose George Wrangel, a White Russian who looked a bit like Faulkner. They shot a series of photos, and Ogilvy took them to the client, saying, "I have done something outrageously unorthodox." With some persuasion, the client agreed to the photos, and the Hathaway ad appeared in *New Yorker* on September 22, 1951. For some reason, it caused an enormous sensation among readers, and sales of Hathaway shirts increased significantly. For four years, the Hathaway man appeared in the *New Yorker*, gaining, by association, a further boost up the status scale. With the success of that ad campaign, other clients were attracted to Ogilvy's agency, and by 1953 billings had risen to $10 million.

The Hathaway success was followed soon after by the "man from Schweppes" ad campaign. Ogilvy got the Schweppes quinine water account by way of Mather & Crowther, and at first it was billing only about $15,000. Ogilvy decided to feature the firm's American advertising manager, Commander Edward Whitehead, a bearded, unorthodox-looking man, as the model for Schweppes in America. Again, Ogilvy ran a series of ads in the *New Yorker* which were a big hit, and Whitehead remained Schweppes' symbol in America for many years after.

These two ad campaigns established the young firm's reputation as one of the "hot" creative agencies in the budding creative revolution of the 1950s and 1960s. Although David Ogilvy himself was trained in the research school, and never lost his attraction or affiliation with that approach, he became, along with William Bernbach[†] and Leo Burnett,[†] one of the founders in America of the softer, creative school of advertising which came to dominate the scene in the 1960s. As *Printer's Ink* commented about David Ogilvy, "His place among the great advertising writers of all time is practically assured." Martin Mayer, in his book, *Madison Avenue U.S.A.*, written in 1958, stated that Ogilvy's "ads give a brand prestige value." By 1956, for example, Ogilvy, Benson and Mather was only the forty-fifth largest agency in America, but it bought more space in the upscale *New Yorker* magazine than any other agency except the massive Batten, Barton, Durstine & Osborn.

This critical acclaim did not necessarily ensure financial success for the agency. Although his fellow copywriters rushed toward David Ogilvy as the creative genius of the era, his most famous ad campaigns either barely paid their way or lost money. Hathaway in four years spent only $300,000 on advertising, and the agency lost money each year on the Schweppes account. Furthermore, although it gained new accounts, it also lost several. Ogilvy had trouble convincing his clients that his agency could sell to the masses as well as it did to the elite; consequently, he lost the Campbell's Franco-American Spaghetti account and also Rinso, the largest, most lucrative of his Lever accounts. The result was a stagnation in billings in 1954, followed by a very slow recovery over the next several years. These problems were intensified by a simmering feud between Ogilvy and Anderson Hewitt. It became clear that one of them would have to go; Hewitt left for another agency, and David Ogilvy became chief executive of the reorganized firm.

Things did not improve for Ogilvy's agency. Ogilvy was very good at soft, image advertising, but the real money lay with harder edged "claim" advertising. Therefore, in 1956, Ogilvy approached Esty Stowell, who had just resigned as executive vice president at Benton & Bowles (B&B). Stowell had made his reputation as an exponent of hard-sell techniques. In enticing Stowell to join Ogilvy, Benson & Mather (OBM), David Ogilvy told Stowell, "Our media is awful. Our research is terrible. Our account executives are the most extraordinary collection of bums you ever saw. I'll take the creative part, and you take all the rest." Stowell joined OBM as executive vice president in 1956, and he succeeded Ogilvy as president in 1961. Billings soared as OBM took a harder approach in most of its ads, and Stowell himself brought in the giant General Foods' Maxwell House Coffee business, which he had supervised for years at B&B. In addition, his reputation and experience enhanced the image of OBM for other, more conservative clients.

David Ogilvy himself continued to concentrate on the imaginative, soft-sell ads that brought the agency much recognition, but few billings. The most famous of these in later years, and the ones in which Ogilvy himself took the most pride, were those for Rolls-Royce automobiles. The prestigious British automaker first approached OBM in 1957, but Stowell persuaded Ogilvy to turn them down because the account would only enhance the elite image they were attempting to change, and would not bring in much money. A few months later, Rolls-Royce returned with a better offer, and Ogilvy was determined to take the account. The initial billing was just $200,000, and Ogilvy himself took charge of the copywriting. After trying different approaches, Ogilvy finally wrote a headline that read, "At 60 miles an hour the loudest noise in this new Rolls-Royce comes from the electric clock." The ad was another big hit for Ogilvy, and Rolls-Royce sold 50 percent more cars in 1958. But, as with Hathaway and Schweppes, the Rolls-Royce account made money for the client but did little for OBM. Billings never exceeded $250,000 a year, and the agency lost a total of $26,000 on the account before they resigned it.

Nonetheless, OBM's billings kept progressing in a slow but steady manner during these years, and it reached $58.5 million in 1963. Then, David Ogilvy did another of those idiosyncratic things that brought him so much notoriety. This time, it brought his agency a wealth of new business, too. He had spent his vacation in the summer of 1962 writing a book about advertising. Published in 1963 as *Confessions of an Advertising Man*, the book offered ten clear how-to chapters on advertising; the final chapter was addressed to the question "Should Advertising be Abolished?" Concluding that "television advertising has made Madison Avenue the archsymbol of tasteless materialism," his book caused a mild sensation in intellectual circles. It also helped attract new business. OBM's domestic billings shot up one-third in the following year, to $77 million.

In 1964, Ogilvy's agency merged with Mather & Crowther to form Ogilvy & Mather (O&M), with David Ogilvy as chairman and chief executive, holding 31 percent of the stock. The new organization had combined billings of $130 million, and it ranked among the top agencies in the world. Ogilvy planned to use its combined power to invade the European market, saying, "We felt it would be tremendous fun to go into Europe, if God is on the side of the big battalion—and that seems to be the case—the path of wisdom lies in becoming one of the big battalions." In fact, the Ogilvy & Mather empire grew enormously. Soon it had twenty-nine offices in sixteen foreign countries. Although it was then just the twelfth largest agency in the United States in billings, it ranked ninth worldwide. About 35 percent of its $260 million in billings in 1970 came from abroad.

The irony was, however, that just as Ogilvy & Mather reached the top echelon of advertising, David Ogilvy began to lose his interest in the advertising business. Describing himself as "an almost extinct volcano," he entertained the idea of retirement in the mid–1960s. In 1967, he purchased a French chateau, and he began to spend increasing amounts of time there. Ogilvy declared, "I have developed an almost uncontrollable distaste for my job, the unappreciative clients, the perpetual fire-fighting, the humbug." He spent less and less time at the agency in the early 1970s, and finally, in 1975, he officially retired to his chateau. Ogilvy retained a seat on the board of directors, and gave himself the title of "Creative Head." Even though he was known as the "Holy Spook" at the agency because of his oversight of operations, his role was greatly diminished. In 1978, probably just to keep his hand in, Ogilvy took charge of the agency's German office, but only temporarily. He sold off most of his stock, so that by the early 1980s he owned just about 3 percent. He also grumbled about the name of the company saying, "They keep the name Mather as an historical pain in the ass."

Nonetheless, by that time, Ogilvy & Mather was one of the true giants of advertising. With domestic billings of $712 million in 1979, it was America's third largest agency. Among its major clients were Shake 'n' Bake, Maxwell House Coffee, Contac, Avon Products, TWA, and American Express. There was not a "cute," "soft," or whimsical commercial in the bunch. David Ogilvy was, paradoxically, the maverick who built one of the largest, most traditional agencies in the world. Yet this did not happen simply by accident.

What set Ogilvy apart from many of his colleagues was the taste and imagination he brought to the trade, along with his unique ability as a copywriter and his diligence in researching his product. During the years when the advertising community was deeply split between soft-sell, creative advertising and hard-sell, research-oriented, claim advertising, Ogilvy successfully combined the two in his own agency. At the age of seventy-two, he published a second book on advertising. Coming out in 1983, his *Ogilvy on Advertising* was, as he said, "my last will and testament." His desire to be viewed as the dean and guru of the advertising industry made his second book less successful than the first. *New York* magazine dismissed it as "whiny and old-biddyish, and full of unseemly self-congratulation—embarrassing stuff." Their final judgement was that *Ogilvy on Advertising* was "an advertisement for Ogilvy himself."

Yet, that is perhaps what David Ogilvy always did best. In the 1950s and 1960s, he was bigger by far than the agency he ran. While industry associations showered him with prizes and young copywriters adopted him as their hero, the American public, accepting him as the conscience of American advertising, bought 800,000 copies of *Confessions of an Advertising Man*. Queen Elizabeth II even gave him the Order of the British Empire (although she did ask him what he did for a living). He was—first, last, and always—a showman. But this often blinded others to the fact that he was an exceptionally solid businessman who engaged in bold and successful innovations in the financial relations between agencies and clients. The most important of these was his espousal of the fee system, which paid off handsomely for the Ogilvy & Mather agency, representing some 60 percent of its billings by the mid–1960s. Traditionally, advertising agencies received their pay in the form of a straight 15-percent commission on the cost of all space or time. In 1960, however, Ogilvy was able to wrest the Shell Oil account from J. Walter Thompson by taking a flat fee for handling its business. With the success of that relationship, the fee system spread to other agencies, without negatively affecting agency profits as so many admen had feared.

By the late 1980s, David Ogilvy remained involved in his agency's operations, but his was an increasingly distant voice. The agency itself was also suffering: plagued by declining growth of U.S. ad spending, O&M began to diversify in the early 1980s. These new interests took them far afield from traditional advertising. Taking up such firms as Research International in London and Decisions Center Incorporated in New York City, two market survey firms, it also bought Thompson-Leeds Company, a manufacturer of in-store displays, and Alert Marketing, which assembled displays and conducted in-store demonstrations. These acquisitions fared poorly, and agency profits and revenues limped along. O&M's operating margin in 1987 was 7.8 percent, well below the 11.2 percent it had posted in 1983, and also below the industry average of 10 percent. Further, the agency's European billings were declining as a percentage of total billings. And this is where David Ogilvy himself succeeded most; his *Confessions of an Advertising Man*, which enjoyed tremendous success in Europe, caused Europeans to look upon David Ogilvy with awe and respect. They viewed him as a precious hybrid, a man who could uniquely combine the practical know-how of Madison Avenue with the civilized outlook of Oxford. This was captured well by a leading French publisher who introduced David Ogilvy to an audience in Paris: "That is certainly your secret, M. Ogilvy—the alliance of a precise and detailed knowledge of a specific technique with the elevated viewpoint that stems only from great culture." Perhaps that was the secret ingredient missing from Ogilvy & Mather in the late 1980s. (**A.** David Ogilvy, *Confessions of an Advertising Man*, 1963, *Blood, Brains & Beer*, 1978, *Ogilvy on Advertising*, 1983. **B.** *Printer's Ink*, November 20, 1953; Martin Mayer, *Madison Avenue U.S.A.*, 1958; *Madison Avenue*, December 1958, July 1983; *Current Biography*, 1961; *Saturday Review*, December 14, 1963; *Fortune*, April 1965, March 26, 1979; *Dun's Review*, February 1971; *Advertising Age*, February 3, 1964, November 23, 1964, March 16, 1983; *New York*, August 22, 1983; *People Weekly*, October 10, 1983; Stephen Fox, *The Mirror Makers*, 1984; *Business Week*, February 22, 1988.)

OLSEN, KENNETH HARRY (February 20, 1928–   ). Computer company founder, Digital Equipment Corporation. Although Digital Equipment Corporation (DEC) and Control Data Corporation, two major rivals of International Business Machines (IBM) in the computer business, were both started in 1957, the companies and their founders could not differ more. William Norris,[†] founder of Control Data, was renowned as one of the most charismatic, visionary, revolutionary, dictatorial, complex, and unique businessmen of his era. Kenneth Olsen, on the other hand, has been viewed as a quiet, conservative, cautious engineer and businessman, who has fostered a sense of democracy and participation at his company. When he graduated from high school, his yearbook called Olsen "calm and modest, steady and sure," and a former teacher recalled years later that he was "quiet, dreary, and smart." To most people, that pretty well summarized the later Kenneth Olsen also.

Nor were the two companies they founded very much alike. Control Data grew by challenging IBM in the mainframe computer market, and by developing computers in areas where IBM was weakest. It was closely wedded to government sales and research help, and much of its later growth came by way of acquisitions.

It also leased rather than sold most of its computers in the later years. Finally, William Norris implanted Control Data with his social vision, involving the firm in a variety of radical and controversial social experiments. Olsen's DEC, on the other hand, was founded with a very different set of principles. He would not accept any government funding for research, so the company's emphasis remained on manufacturing for the marketplace. DEC never became involved with mergers or acquisitions. It did not lease even its largest machines; it paid no commissions to its sales force; and its profits were plowed back into expansion. Perhaps his most significant policy regarded involvement in community affairs. Whereas Norris immersed CDC in the nation's social problems, Olsen had a very different attitude. In 1968, when the nation's cities were wracked with turmoil, he explained his firm's noninvolvement:

This may sound trivial, but it's important. There are all kinds of pressures on senior people in organizations to do things peripheral to their business. Right now, for example, there is tremendous pressure to solve the Negro problem. After a while, these demands can take up approximately 300 percent of your time. It's somewhat unfair of society to expect people running a business responsible for thousands of jobs to also solve these other problems. The thing that destroys business management is working on these other things. (*Business Week*, September 21, 1965)

Since then, however, Olsen has become more socially responsible.

The withdrawn, somewhat introspective Kenneth Olsen was born in Bridgeport, Connecticut, but he grew up during the 1930s in a working-class neighborhood in Stratford, Connecticut. His family, however, was middle class; his father designed factory equipment, for example, a safety pin machine and a machine for making universal joints for cars, and he held several patents. Of Scandinavian background, Olsen's parents were intensely religious fundamentalists and strict disciplinarians. Kenneth Olsen grew up in a secure, highly structured, extended-family environment (his grandparents lived right next door to his parents). Not a rebellious child, he conformed naturally to his parents' wishes and desires. As a boyhood friend remembers: "Ken was down-the-path. He didn't do anything that would raise your eyebrows."

Olsen displayed an impressive early technical interest and ability. His brother reported that Ken was always more interested in technical manuals than in comic books. An electrical engineer who was a family friend kept Olsen supplied with technical literature during the early years. He was inspired also by his father's tinkering in the basement. As he recalled, "I grew up with an affection for machine tools and a love for building things." Soon, Kenneth Olsen was tinkering in the basement on his own, and he gained a reputation as the neighborhood Edison by fixing radios for free. At fourteen, he and his younger brother Stanley (who later became DEC's first employee and was a marketing executive for twenty-five years with the firm) built a radio station and broke in on local broadcasts.

Olsen graduated from Stratford High School, and then joined the U.S. Navy and served during World War II, from 1944 to 1946. During this time, he obtained his first formal training in electrical engineering and was able to enter the Massachusetts Institute of Technology (MIT) in 1947. He raced through the curriculum in three years and obtained his degree in electrical engineering in 1950. This was at the very dawn of the computer age, and MIT was in the process of building the Whirlwind computer for the Office of Naval Research and the Air Force. This highly innovative project put Olsen at the cutting edge of computer technology. While doing his Master's degree at MIT, Olsen was recruited to work on the Whirlwind project. Unlike the pioneering UNIVAC computer of a few years before, the Whirlwind was transistor driven and an interactive machine. Designed as a flight simulator, its unique feature was the computer's immediate response to the questions and commands of the operator. Using small, fast, simple circuits designed to respond quickly, the Whirlwind established what was, in effect, a dialogue with the programmer. This was the wave of the future for computers, and Olsen established a reputation with his work on it as a first-class practical engineer.

Before Olsen had finished his master's studies in 1952, MIT was awarded the contract to develop the Semi-Automatic Ground Environment (SAGE), an early-warning system, and Olsen had the opportunity to work on that project also. SAGE, the nation's first air-defense system, was intended to coordinate radar stations, fighter squadrons, and antiaircraft batteries in the event of a Russian attack. The project director, Professor Jay Forrester, was impressed with Olsen's work on SAGE, and when actual production began at IBM, he sent Olsen to IBM's headquarters in Poughkeepsie, New York, where he stayed for two and a half years. It was an extraordinary experience for the young man. He was shocked at the regimentation and insularity of the environment created by Thomas Watson Jr.* "It was like going to a Communist state," he later recalled. "They knew nothing about the rest of the world, and the world knew nothing about what went on inside." He was also shocked at the production inefficiencies at IBM, and he left convinced that he could "beat these guys at their own game."

Upon returning to MIT, Olsen directed the building of the first transistorized research computer. Although this was an important and innovative project, Olsen felt that "it wasn't really fun unless you affected the outside world." Olsen increasingly began to feel that there was a market for a small computer to do simple computing jobs, and he decided to start a new computer company. Neither he nor an MIT associate, Harlan Anderson, knew much about management, but they read about managerial theory in the Lexington Public Library, and Olsen practiced the theories by serving as the superintendent of Boston's Park Street Church Sunday School.

By 1957, the two men were ready to strike out on their own. They rented some space in an old, ramshackle woolen mill in Maynard, Massachusetts, they hired three employees, and they began to manufacture printed circuit boards in small quantities, hoping that the profits from this would help finance the building of their first computer. In the meantime, Olsen was spending most of his time trying to interest outside capital. He met retired General Georges Doriot, who, then teaching some business courses at Harvard, was head of America's oldest and best-regarded small business investment company, American Research and Development Company (ARD). Experienced in backing high-technology ventures, Doriot was intrigued enough to offer Olsen $70,000. He did advise Olsen and Anderson to focus on building components, at least for a while, since he felt that their dreams of building a computer to compete with IBM, which had just passed $1 billion in sales that year, "didn't sound quite modest."

Olsen got 13 percent of the stock of the newly organized Digital Equipment Corporation, Anderson got 9 percent, and ARD got 77 percent. Serving as a longtime director of DEC, Doriot became a friend and mentor of Olsen, without interfering in DEC's management. Of course, this was one of the most astute venture capital investments of all time. By the time ARD sold and distributed its holdings in 1972, its original investment was worth nearly $400 million. In the meantime, Olsen honed his strategy to a fine edge. He continued making circuit boards, but he made plans to begin producing his dream computer—a machine simple enough to be employed by technicians in a matter of days, and to be mastered in weeks.

The early days were difficult. Their capital of $70,000 allowed few frills. They bought some lawn furniture, an old rolltop desk, and, as Olsen said in a *New York Times* article (January 14, 1979), "We did everything ourselves; we cleaned the johns and swept the floors. We did the photography in my basement; we made our printed circuit boards with real silk on wooden frames and etched them in aquarium tanks. Since I was the closest thing to a toolmaker, I made the tools." Beyond that, Anderson recalled, Olsen had "thousands of ideas for making things cheap and simple." He had determined, for example, that although office partitions were cheap, doors were expensive, so DEC had no doors—not even on the bathrooms.

DEC made a small profit at the end of the first year, and Olsen had managed to put together a prototype minicomputer. When he presented it to ARD, Doriot was impressed that not only could it perform many of the functions of IBM's large, expensive mainframe computers, but also it could be produced for about 20 percent of its cost. He, therefore, advanced DEC another million dollars to begin production. Using DEC's circuit modules as building blocks for the computer, they had the first production model, called the PDP–1, ready in 1960. Called a programmed data processor, rather than a computer, it sold for $120,000 rather than the $1 million IBM and others charged for their mainframes, and it was relatively small—about the size of a small refrigerator. Furthermore, it did not require sterilized environments like the mainframes; it could be installed anywhere. It was designed to appeal to scientists, technicians, and engineers, all of whom needed relatively little in the way of service. Service was always IBM's major selling point, and by selling to a highly skilled market, DEC was able to maintain a leaner organization.

When International Telephone and Telegraph bought the PDP–1s in great quantities for message switching, it became standard equipment for a number of applications. By this point, the computer, which was being made to order for customers, could go into regular production for inventory. In 1963 DEC brought out the PDP–4, an instant success, which attracted a lucrative and previously untapped market of original equipment manufacturers who added their own software to the powerful machines and resold them in new markets under new names.

During these early years, DEC was known as an "engineer's paradise." With no formal corporate structure, small bands of engineers were allowed to form fluidly around projects. It was like a playground for technicians, a highly synergistic environment that fostered the creation of increasingly more inventive projects. After seven years, revenues exceeded $10 million, and there were several minicomputer models under development, all competing for scarce funds. Olsen was loath to lose the creativity of the early years, or to become ossified like the IBM he had observed in the early 1950s, but he knew something had to be done. He had to design a management structure that would maximize creativity, yet would allow some sense of overall direction and control. His solution made him a guru for advocates of managerial science, and won him a place of prominence in Thomas J. Peters and Robert H. Waterman, Jr.'s, *In Search of Excellence*.

One of the attributes that Peters and Waterman prized most in their book was what they called "simultaneous loose-tight properties": "The excellent companies are both centralized and decentralized. For the most part . . . they had pushed autonomy down to the shop floor or the product development team. On the other hand, they are fanatic centralists around the few core values they hold dear." DEC was virtually a prototype of this kind of firm for Peters and Waterman: "At Digital the chaos is so rampant that one executive noted, 'Damn few people know who they work for.' Yet Digital's fetish for reliability is more rigidly adhered to than any outsider could imagine." What had Olsen done to create this managerial nirvana?

Olsen proposed that each senior person should take very broad responsibility for one product line—developing it, marketing it, making the money. By "breaking the company into pieces," Olsen in effect created a series of companies within the company, each headed by a senior manager who was also an entrepreneur. Each submitted an annual budget and product line plan to a central committee chaired by Olsen, the only senior manager who oversaw the entire company. In this manner, DEC gradually spawned more than thirty-one semi-autonomous companies that jockeyed for money and power in what has been called the "matrix" or "bubble-up" style of management. The structure created a corporate culture at DEC that has been called "amazingly democratic" and "sternly patriarchal." And it was phenomenally successful, generating nearly two decades of 30-percent annual growth, which got DEC on the "best managed" lists of every major American business publication. Some of the old engineering fraternity at DEC, including Anderson, however, missed the old anarchy and left the firm for smaller or greener pastures.

In the meantime, in 1965, DEC brought out the PDP–8, the first true mini-computer. It took advantage of the arrival of integrated circuits to reduce the price to just $18,000. DEC's sales skyrocketed with the PDP–8, which revolutionized the way in which entire industries conducted their business. No longer having to wait for time on the large mainframe computer, technicians could now perform a computing job immediately. The PDP–8's were used for a wide variety of things, ranging from typesetters to medical scanners. Faster, cheaper, more compact circuitry, and new manufacturing techniques were bringing the prices of minicomputers down by about 20 percent a year. Hundreds of small start-up companies began making the mini's, but DEC's head start on the technology enabled it to drive most of them out of the market. Some analysts even began to speak of DEC in terms usually reserved for IBM. Olsen replied that "people say that we had the market hands down because we didn't have any competition. But we didn't have any market either."

Kenneth Olsen and DEC had managed, just as they had envisioned in 1957, to change the way in which people thought about computers. Previously, people had believed that the most economical way to process data was by sharing the power of a large computer among a variety of jobs. This was the "computer utility" theory upon which Norris had built his company. But the idea of the mini was for a small machine to take over the work of just one particular job. First used to gather data and perform experiments in laboratories, it next moved into factory automation and record keeping. It also began to be used in business data processing, in networks used with a large mainframe computer. The mini's job was to assume some of the complex tasks of managing the networks, freeing the central machine to compute. Soon, mini's began to appear everywhere—on submarines, in coal mines, in schools, and in prisons.

By this time, DEC had taken over nearly all of the old woolen mill, had 1,000 employees, and had sales of $57 million and earnings of nearly $7 million. Following its great success with small computers, Olsen brought out the PDP–10 in 1968 to compete with IBM in the mainframe market. Designed for time-sharing systems, the PDP–10, which sold for between $300,000 and $400,000, allowed multiple users to plug into the same central computer. Although it did not threaten IBM's dominance, the PDP–10 was a success for DEC. Two years later, in 1970, DEC came roaring back into the ever-changing minicomputer field, with the introduction of the 16-bit PDP–11, the most popular minicomputer line in history. The next stage was to use DECnet software to link the PDP–11s with a PDP–10, or some other large machine, in what were called distributed processing networks. This innovation, which became increasingly popular during the 1970s, put DEC squarely in competition with IBM, which theretofore had controlled over two thirds of the traditional electronic data processing (EDP) market. Soon, the PDP–11s, combined with a big computer, were monitoring the processes in automotive assembly lines and the working of oil refineries.

IBM, which had grown complacent because of its massive market share, was caught, in the words of one analyst, "asleep at the switch," and did not enter the mini market until late 1976. By this point, DEC had 37 percent of the market, Hewlett-Packard had 17.4 percent, Data General (started by ex-DEC engineers) had 8.4 percent, and others had smaller amounts. By 1980, IBM had climbed to fifth place in minicomputers, but it still was given little chance of passing DEC in that area.

DEC continued moving forward. If setting up networks of minicomputers to a large computer worked, why not link networks to each other? To this end, DEC introduced Virtual Address Extension (VAX) technology in 1974. Ranging from small desktop computers to large mainframes, DEC's VAXes all had the same architecture, which would enable them to run on the same software, share data bases, and communicate with ease. This was followed shortly thereafter by the VAX–11/780, the first supermini, which was as powerful as the IBM 370, at just one-fourth the price. The entire VAX system became an exceptional success, and by 1979 the package had secured 40 percent of the worldwide minicomputer market for DEC. Olsen and DEC were on top of the world. In 1980, sales reached $2.4 billion, and the profit margins were staggeringly high. Then, suddenly, came the microcomputer—the PC, or personal computer.

While DEC was spending millions of dollars developing the upper end of the small-computer market, a number of small start-ups were creating small, easy-to-use computers for the low end of the market. The movement began in 1971, when an engineer at Intel (see Gordon Moore and Robert Noyce) developed the first " computer on a chip," the microprocessor. At first used in large computers to handle certain functions, many thought microprocessors could become the basis of a small computer, called the microcomputer. A number of these microcomputers were sold in kits to hobbyists in the late 1970s, but it was Apple Computer (see Steven Jobs) that provided the mass-market breakthrough. The small computers took the country by storm in the late 1970s, and soon hundreds of other firms were also making micros. They were the hottest item in the computer industry. Thousands of white-collar workers who lacked the expertise to use DEC's sophisticated computers flocked to the microcomputer.

At first Olsen and the engineers at DEC paid little attention to the weak and unsophisticated "toys" the microcomputer makers were producing. But before long, the micros became more powerful and the software more sophisticated, and DEC found itself in the same position IBM had been in twenty years before— makers of a larger, more expensive, and powerful series of computers which were being challenged by smaller, cheaper, and ever more powerful computers. At the same time this was happening, IBM began to drop the prices on their mainframe computers, enticing buyers away from DEC at the high end of the market. Then, in 1982, when IBM introduced the PC, its own best-selling micro, DEC found its market share rapidly deteriorating.

All of this led to "Black Tuesday," October 18, 1983, when DEC's stock fell 21 points on the market. The story of DEC between 1980 and 1984 is not a happy one. Faced with challenges at both the high and low ends of the market, it did not perform well at either level. Its struggles were mute evidence of the difficulties faced by a company whose cultures and skills were honed for a specific market, in adapting to rapid and fundamental change. As long as the name of the game was technological evolution and nurture of an existing customer base, DEC did very well. But when the game changed to one of technological revolution and development of a more sensitive marketing approach, DEC failed miserably. Long a believer that if you "built a better mousetrap, the world would beat a path to your door," DEC had not developed aggressive marketing techniques. As a result, its earnings began falling during the early 1980s, reaching a low of $284 million in 1983.

This crisis caused Olsen to realize that he had to reorganize his company fundamentally—that he had to scrap his vaunted product line groups and make the company a more highly centralized, market-driven organization. As *Fortune* reported, "Olsen reshaped DEC by teasing, goading, and teaching employees, by sermonizing—and by remorselessly pilloring those who stood in his way." The painful, difficult, and expensive reorganization was finally completed in 1986. While this was going on, Olsen refocused DEC on minicomputers, and he brought out the VAX 8600 or "Venus" superminicomputer in 1984. A year later, the MicroVAX II workstation, which put the VAX 780 on a tiny chip, was highly praised by the industry, which called it "the most important new product since the IBM PC." Finally, in 1986, Olsen brought out the VAXmate, and IBM-PC-compatible system, with an all-in-one software package, which allowed IBM-PC users to retrieve data instantly from any VAX computer.

All of this catapulted DEC back into the realm of exceptional profitability. Although the computer industry as a whole suffered from a sharp recession in 1986, DEC's sales reached $7.6 billion, and even more significant, its profits, which had been slipping for some time, rose by 38 percent to $617.4 million. DEC was successfully invading many of IBM's traditional EDP markets in banking, insurance, and pharmaceuticals, and it was doing very well in Europe, traditionally the domain of "Big Blue." As *Newsweek* reported that year, "DEC Belts a Home Run." In the fall of that year, *Fortune* magazine called Olsen "America's most successful entrepreneur," saying a bit hyperbolically that he was "arguably the most successful entrepreneur in the history of American business."

DEC's fortunes continued their heady growth in 1987, when sales reached $9.4 billion, a 24-percent increase over the year before. Profits kept rising also, at an even more incredible rate. They reached $1.137 *billion* in 1987, a phenomenal 84-percent increase over the profoundly prosperous 1986. With 110,000 employees, DEC was second only to IBM in profits and employees, and third in the industry in sales. *Business Week* in October 1987 called DEC one of America's "leanest and meanest corporations." DEC spent over $1 billion on research and development that year, the seventh greatest amount of any corporation in America. In January 1989, Olsen and DEC took yet another daring step into the future. After a long internal battle at the company, in which the more conservative Eastern forces contested the more daring Western forces, the latter won out. As a result, DEC announced the pending release of its new P-Max workstation, the fastest, least expensive on the market. Designed to counter the massive lead built up in that area by Sun Microsystems, it used the innovative RISC technology, which shortly before Olsen had dismissed as merely a fad. Most computer industry analysts were impressed with DEC's plans.

Olsen, who had accumulated a fortune of well over $300 million just in DEC stock over the years he ran the company, began to soften somewhat in his attitudes toward social responsibility. He donated about half of his 4-percent share of DEC stock to a foundation that supports Christian philanthropies, and he began to participate, in the mid–1970s, in a prayer breakfast on the first Tuesday of each month with a number of other Boston chief executive officers. Still a simple man, he and his wife continued to live in the same home in suburban Boston that they bought shortly after DEC was founded. A director of Ford Motor Company, Olsen drives a Ford Escort station wagon, and he loathes being seen in his wife's Mercedes. The couple tend their own garden, do their own dishes, and paint their own walls.

One other thing: William Norris and Control Data made a great deal of noise and a major commitment to social responsibility for corporations in the 1970s and 1980s, but Olsen rejected the whole idea. By 1988, Control Data's social program had been almost completely dismantled, judged by nearly all to be an abject failure. Olsen and DEC, on the other hand, had quietly set up several inner-city plants (in the Roxbury section of Boston, and in Springfield, Massachusetts) to employ poor, minority workers. As was the case with so many other ghetto plants, the DEC facility in Springfield started out as a make-work project. Its 160 black and Hispanic workers made power supplies that could easily have been purchased elsewhere. One DEC manager, however, believed that the plant would be closed when things got tough. So, when DEC came out with its new VAX computers in 1976, the manager, Henry A. Burnett, along with some other black executives, proposed to Olsen that the Springfield plant be made the sole supplier of tape-drive memory devices for the VAX line. Olsen hesitantly agreed (he is, after all, a conservative man), and the Springfield facility over the next dozen years was expanded fifteenfold, and its work force has grown to 800. By 1987, it was one of the largest minority-managed businesses in the United States, with a yearly output of about $700 million. As one of Olsen's prayer-breakfast friends once commented, "The good Lord's hand is on the guy, and He's going to prosper him until He sends for him." (**B**. *Business Week*, September 21, 1968, April 26, 1976, May 2, September 5, 1983, January 3, January 30, November 5, 1984, February 25, November 25, 1985, April 21, 1986, February 16, October 5, 1987, June 20, 1988, January 16, 1989; *Forbes*, September 1, 1973, May 2, May 21, 1984, October 24, 1988; Katherine Davis Fishman, *The Computer Establishment*, 1981; Robert Heller, *The Business of Business: Managing with Style*, 1981; Robert Sobel, *I.B.M.: Colossus in Tran-*

sition, 1981; Thomas J. Peters and Robert H. Waterman, Jr., *In Search of Excellence*, 1982; *Fortune*, May 3, 1982, December 12, 1983, October 27, 1986, April 25, 1988; *New York Times*, January 14, 1979, September 4, 1983, May 14, 1985, September 4, 1986; *Management Today*, December 1983; Stephen McClellan, *The Coming Computer Industry Shakeout*, 1984; A. David Silver, *Entrepreneurial Megabucks*, 1985; *Financial World*, July 10–23, 1985; *Computerworld*, August 19, 1985, September 24, 1986; *Contemporary Newsmakers*, 1986; *Wall Street Journal*, April 3, 1986; *Newsweek*, October 27, 1986; *Dun's Business Monthly*, December 1986; *Current Biography*, March 1987; Glenn Rifkin and George Harrar, *The Ultimate Entrepreneur: The Story of Ken Olsen and DEC*, 1988; Toronto *Globe and Mail*, April 26, 1988.)

P

PALEVSKY, MAX (July 24, 1924–   ). Computer company founder and independent movie producer, Scientific Data Systems. Many founders of computer companies have been characterized by their extreme individuality and nonconformity. Technical geniuses, they often lack the social skills and discipline necessary to be effective long-term entrepreneurs. Max Palevsky may not have been the most quixotic of the company founders, but he certainly was the most successful of the more nonconformist founders. After he left the computer industry, his pockets stuffed with money, Palevsky ventured into moviemaking in Hollywood, where he produced such quality films as Costa-Gavra's *State of Siege,* but he is better remembered for such turkeys as *Fun with Dick and Jane* and *Islands in the Stream.*

Max Palevsky was born in Chicago, the son of a Polish immigrant house painter. He was educated in the city's schools, and he went to the University of Chicago, where he earned two bachelor's degrees, in philosophy and mathematics. He then did graduate work in both fields, and in 1948 he left Chicago to take a teaching position in philosophy at the University of California, Los Angeles. Palevsky had expected to get his doctorate and make a career of university teaching, but he found after a short time that scholarly life made him restive. Without the temperament to do plodding academic studies, Palevsky became interested in computer logic. In 1951, he got a job as a staff mathematician with Bendix Corporation, which had just purchased Northrop Aviation's computer division. Commenting on the fact that a number of philosophers had found positions in the infant computer industry, Palevsky said: "It's the first time a philosopher can make an honest living since Socrates."

Palevsky was intoxicated with the prospects of the young industry. He and a group of cohorts at Bendix began to design a new kind of computer by taking advantage of the latest advances in circuitry. But upper management at Bendix refused to provide support for further development. Palevsky was one of the very first individuals to recognize that a huge gap existed in the marketplace, that not everyone wanted or needed the massive "number crunching" machines that Remington Rand and IBM were producing. Although Palevsky later reflected that Bendix was probably right to refuse them support, given the state of technology at the time, he was bitterly hurt and disappointed. Thus, in 1957—the same year William Norris[†] left Remington Rand to form Control Data Corporation (CDC) and Kenneth Olsen[†] set up Digital Equipment Corporation (DEC)—Palevsky left Bendix looking for someone to back his computer project. He took an aggressive, but unscientific approach: he contacted every electronics firm in the Los Angeles phone book. He finally convinced Packard Bell to set up a computer division to produce his machine.

After getting a prototype of the new, smaller computer under way, Palevsky persuaded Dr. Wernher von Braun to use it for his Redstone Arsenal program. When this worked successfully, Palevsky was able to sell computers to a number of other satisfied users. He became executive vice president at Packard Bell, and he proceeded with his next idea, which was to build a small, cheap computer to serve the growing scientific community. Packard Bell was very supportive, and this machine was built and marketed with even greater success than the first. By this time, however, Packard Bell was in the midst of severe financial difficulties. When Palevsky, worried that Packard Bell's problems would jeopardize his computer division, asked the company to establish the division as a separate entity, issuing its own stock, he was fired. Palevsky was back on the street again, with plans for magnificent computers to serve new, untapped markets, but without financial backing.

When Palevsky approached various Wall Street investment firms, it quickly became clear that, as far as they were concerned, no company could ever compete with IBM, and they were not about to finance anyone foolish enough to try. Palevsky later reflected, "They didn't realize there was a new market that IBM didn't serve." By 1961, Silicon Valley was being born in California, and venture capitalists there were on the look out for high-technology and computer projects. Palevsky contacted Arthur Rock, a young venture capitalist formerly with Hayden Stone. With some associates, Rock put up $900,000 to match the $100,000 raised by Palevsky and Bob Beck, a Packard Bell colleague who would head the technical side of the business. Joined by eleven other Packard Bell executives, Palevsky called the new firm Scientific Data Systems (SDS) and prepared to set the computer industry on its ear.

Palevsky ran SDS for only seven years, and the firm itself did not last any longer, but he was one of the truly legendary figures in the pioneer period of the computer industry. Years after Palevsky had gone, and SDS was dismantled, a former associate recalled, "We didn't work for SDS, we worked for Max Palevsky. SDS was the personification of Max Palevsky. We were his amplification and fulfillment." An SDS engineer at the height of the firm's success put it more succinctly, if less poetically, "SDS *is* Max. We feel his presence all the time."

Palevsky had no intention of competing with IBM when he established SDS. Instead, he wanted to continue pursuing the lucrative scientific market for small-to medium-sized computers. There were many advantages to focusing on this market: entry was easy, little capital was required for start-up manufacturing, and the computers were placed with knowledgeable users who needed little of the expensive service that IBM customers demanded. This market was, in fact, two separate markets. There were the computers for scientific research, which Control Data and DEC had found success in servicing. But, there was also what was called the real-time user, that is, units meant to monitor industrial processes or medical patients, or designed to help guide missiles. Although SDS would successfully sell machines to both markets, it had its greatest success in the latter market.

The first SDS machine, the SDS 910, came on the market in 1962. The first second-generation, that is, transistorized, computer, it was made possible by the fact that Palevsky literally bought the components off the suppliers' shelves and fabricated, rather than manufactured, the machine. But it was a tremendous success. By the end of 1963, SDS had erased its deficit, and showed an astounding profit of $1.4 million on sales of $7.7 million. At the end of its third year of operation, profits reached $2 million, and about 200 SDS computers had been installed around the world. DEC had been founded four years earlier, but SDS already had twice the sales.

Much of the success in the early years must be attributed to Palevsky; his timing in the fields of finance, technology, and marketing reflected a touch of genius. Then, too, luck played a part. As a former SDS employee commented, "God gave us the silicon transistor. It became available just at the time we were founded, and brought a big improvement in reliability and speed. We delivered the first computer with all silicon transistors." He reflected further, "The market was just right for a premium grade scientific computer. The space program was getting under way—without Apollo there would have been no SDS."

All this success was heady stuff. In 1965, Palevsky began to work on the Sigma line of third-generation, integrated-circuit, computers. Unlike his earlier models, these were designed to compete with IBM's 360 line of computers. The Sigma 7 and 2 came out in 1966, and others followed soon after. Far faster than the 360, it was also cheaper, since it was cobbled together from parts purchased from others. At first sold only to scientific users, by 1967 the Sigma line was also being picked up by businesses, IBM's traditional customers.

The key to the success of the Sigma line, as was true of all SDS computers from the very beginning, was that Palevsky had insisted that they be designed on the modular, or building-block, approach. All of the 9-Series computers, and all the Sigma family of computers, were designed to be logically, electronically, and mechanically compatible. Therefore, these computers were ideal for networking and time-sharing. The primary benefit of time-sharing is that it drastically cuts the costs of computing. As many as thirty-two clients could use an SDS 940 simultaneously, and the Sigma 7, largest of the third-generation computers, allowed 200 users at once under a networking system of hardware and software. This was a great boon in marketing SDS computers in the mid- to late

1960s, when other companies' computers (including IBM's) were not able to function in a network arrangement. But it was largely serendipity which brought this about. As an SDS official noted at the time, "I don't know of a computer that was designed originally for time-sharing. Our advantage is that we don't have to adjust the hardware to fit the market. It gives us a real edge."

By the late 1960s, SDS was competing with IBM across a wide spectrum of computer products, certainly wider than either CDC or DEC, other recent start-ups. By 1968, SDS had $113 million in assets, a work force of over 4,000, and sales of over $100 million. Many industry analysts thought that a major reason for SDS's success was the management philosophy of Palevsky. First of all, he refused to train his own managers. Reasoning that SDS had only about 2 percent of the market, Palevsky hired away already trained managers from other companies. Thus, he refused to hire recent college graduates; instead he offered experienced personnel higher salaries and stock and bonus programs to join SDS. By all accounts, it was a highly successful program, and it made millionaires of several SDS executives.

Palevsky tried to foster a freewheeling, individualistic work environment, so that creativity would not be thwarted. Yet, he was also a very tough boss. An ex-employee recalled, "Max could always find the one thing you hadn't prepared. He was a complete bastard to work for; he demanded total performance or he'd make your life miserable. I was on the rack many times. But he was usually right and I respected him." He also checked the employees every morning to make sure they had arrived by 8 A.M. He explained, "I feel very strongly about this. If you make ridiculous rules, you have a ridiculous company. On the other hand, sensible rules should be lived up to. After a while, you can visit a plant and tell what they're up to simply by the atmosphere."

Palevsky, like so many of the other early computer founders, enjoyed the initial years of growth in his organization. But after 1964, when SDS had experienced phenomenal growth (and after it had gone public), Palevsky found he became more of an administrator and less of an entrepreneur. He recognized that this reduced the degree of freedom and inventiveness in the organization, but he felt it was inevitable. Personally, though, Palevsky did not cope well with the day-to-day tasks of administration, so he turned those chores over to Robert Beck. But Beck found himself under continual attack from Dan McGurk, vice president of marketing, and ultimately Beck retired to his ranch.

By 1966, the infighting at SDS had intensified, especially over the development of the new Sigma line of computers. The organization was in shambles, programming was six months behind schedule, the new plant was totally disorganized, and everything else was also going wrong. Nonetheless, the firm made money in 1968, exceeding $100 million in revenues for the first time. All of this took its toll on Palevsky. Described as having a short attention span in the best of times, Palevsky found the continual chaos at SDS profoundly distracting. He began to feel that he was stagnating there, that he needed new challenges, new goals for his life. Palevsky commented more than once that he thought it was obscene when people were highly successful early in life, and then took refuge in their first triumphs and kept on doing the same thing. Palevsky became increasingly involved in politics, particularly in Robert Kennedy's presidential campaign in 1968. During a time when America was plunged into deep turmoil over issues of race and the war in Vietnam, Palevsky, a committed political liberal, immersed himself in such causes. He also began producing movies, and by 1969 he was coming to the office only a couple of days a week—he had tired of the computer business and wanted to get out. In a short time, he got his wish.

The Xerox Corporation, by 1969, wanted desperately to become a major factor in the computer business. Having almost totally dominated the copier field since its inception, Xerox now faced increased competition and felt it was important to become a more generalized office equipment manufacturer. A key to success in that area, it thought, was computers. Peter McColough, the chief executive officer of Xerox, called on Palevsky, and they began to arrange for the sale of SDS to Xerox. After lengthy negotiations, Palevsky and Rock sold the computer firm to Xerox for $920 million. It was an enormously steep price, about four times what Honeywell had paid for General Electric's computer division in 1970. Palevsky received about $100 million for his share in SDS, and although he was named chairman of the executive committee at Xerox, he had lost interest in computer management, and he remained remote from its operations.

Before long it was clear that Xerox had made a big mistake when it bought SDS. The first blow to Xerox's dreams of combating IBM came in early 1970, when the entire marketplace collapsed, and a severe recession ensued, which hit business equipment manufacturers particularly hard. Then, too, about 40 percent of SDS's contracts during the 1960s had come from government, particularly from NASA's space program. Little did anyone realize it at the time, but when man stepped foot on the moon in 1969, it was the beginning of a long decline in spending on space exploration. Since the space program had virtually all the computers it needed, that great market dried up almost overnight. Other problems also developed. Xerox, as king of the copier market, had thought of its salesmen primarily as order takers, and had forbade them any discounting. SDS's salesmen, on the other hand, were not only highly trained on the technical side, but they were also accustomed to more freewheeling practices as far as discounts were concerned. The two corporate cultures did not mesh smoothly, and when the Xerox head office insisted upon an end to discounting to preserve organizational uniformity, there was a sharp drop-off in computer sales and profits. Over the next three years, the old SDS, now called Xerox Data Systems, lost a staggering $100 million. Finally, in 1975, Xerox announced it was getting out of the mainframe computer business, and it took an aftertax write-off of $84 million. McColough admitted that the acquisition of SDS had been "a mistake."

Meanwhile, Palevsky, his pockets bulging with cash, went on to other things, particularly moviemaking. He made a number of forgettable films during the 1970s, and soon soured on the Hollywood scene. "It's very bizarre," he commented in 1980. "Every time you start to make a movie it's like reinventing the wheel. It's an industry where most of the people are unhappy and complain an enormous amount. No, it's not the kind of place where I want to spend my time.'' But he had a number of other ventures to pursue, liberal politics for one. He was deeply involved in the George McGovern political campaign in 1972, pumping some $320,000 into it. He was also a major backer of Jimmy Carter in his presidential campaign in 1976. In the early 1980s, Palevsky took it upon himself to ''revitalize liberalism in America.'' He bankrolled a new magazine called *democracy*, which was edited by Princeton political theorist Sheldon S. Wolin, whose publication he hoped would counter the influence of a number of conservative journals that had emerged in the 1980s. However, *democracy* was not very successful.

With his $100 million from Xerox, Palevsky became an important venture capitalist, and he served for many years on the board of Intel Corporation. In his venture capital operations, Palevsky raised about $4 million to start a firm called Silicon Systems, which designed specialized integrated circuits. He also founded a new Scientific Data Systems in 1980. Promising that ''we'll have the best equipment, designed by people who have been over the track many times,'' he got his old backer, Arthur Rock, and Houston money man, Fayez Sarofim, to invest. They raised only about $2 million, however, and the idea was stillborn. But, Palevsky seemed to be able to continue making money—in 1988, *Forbes* estimated his fortune to be worth $240 million.

By that time Palevsky, in his mid-sixties, had gone Hollywood. Living in opulent Beverly Hills, he was no longer the rotund, balding, no-nonsense computer executive of the 1960s. Having trimmed off much of his girth and wearing a dark-brown toupee, Palevsky had a perpetual tan, and he dressed in the elegantly casual style of the Hollywood jet set. As *Forbes* commented when it interviewed him in 1980, ''He looks ready for a remake of *American Gigolo*.'' (**B**. *Business Week*, March 20, 1965; *Dun's Review*, November 1965, September 1968; *Time*, February 24, 1967; *Newsweek*, March 28, 1968, September 18, 1972, January 12, 1981; *Forbes*, June 15, 1976, November 24, 1980, October 24, 1988; Katherine Davis Fishman, *The Computer Establishment*, 1981; Robert Sobel, *I.B.M.: Colossus in Transition*, 1981.)

PAULUCCI, JENO FRANCISCO (July 7, 1918–   ). Food processor, Chun King, Jeno's Frozen Pizza. When Jeno Paulucci was fourteen, he got a job as a barker on Duluth, Minnesota's produce row. He proved such a loud and aggressive barker that the city passed an ordinance against fruit stand barking. Paulucci used that talent to unique advantage in his later years. Just five feet, five inches tall, the pugnacious Paulucci sent out notices of meetings to the other executives of his company on cards with a picture of him dressed in boxing gear. The notice said: ''New Production Meeting 7 A.M. Bring your own gloves!'' And he was not kidding. At both Chun King and Jeno's Pizza, Paulucci was known to jump onto the conference table, stare down at his vice presidents, and terrorize them. At one meeting, which had lasted well into the evening,

Paulucci stood up and announced, "We're really getting to the heart of our coming here now. If you guys need to, call home for more laundry, because you're not going to leave until we get this damned thing settled." And so they went on and on into the wee hours of the morning.

Paulucci was born in Aurora, Minnesota, the son of Ettore Paulucci, an Italian immigrant who had come to America to work in the iron mines. The work, however, was very irregular, and the elder Paulucci made little money during the years Jeno was growing up. Consequently, Jeno and his brothers and sisters were forced to scrounge for food and money. Young Jeno often walked along the railroad tracks looking for fallen lumps of coal, which he put into his little red wagon held together with discarded parts. He also gathered cardboard boxes which he sold to the Pauluccis' landlord for a penny each. The incident that had the greatest impact on him as a child, however, occurred when he went down to the local soup kitchen for a handout. "Once, I stood in a long, slow-moving relief line to get a handout," he recalled later. "I couldn't stomach it, so I just stepped out of line and never returned. Today I'm still adamantly against any type of dole or relief for the helpless indigent."

By the time Paulucci was twelve years old, he was ready to begin hustling for a living in earnest. He unloaded boxcars for $1 a car, sold ore samples to tourists, and conducted guided tours of the mines. He also sold wine his family made in the basement. The impact of the Great Depression finally became too great for Paulucci's father; he abandoned his family and did not return until after Jeno Paulucci was successful. In 1933, Paulucci's mother opened a grocery store in the family living room, and he got a job with the City Markets in Hibbing. At this job, and in subsequent ones as well, Paulucci developed an awe-inspiring reputation for hard work. Even as a teenager, he put in sixteen-hour days, and he demonstrated a unique flair for salesmanship. His regimen included work after school each day, and from 5 A.M. to midnight on Saturdays.

Paulucci's heavy workload caused him problems in high school, and he led two student protests against school policies: One against long homework assignments for students who held jobs, and the other against having to learn poetry, which he felt was irrelevant. At sixteen years of age, Paulucci was already well along in his future career. In that year, he became a sales representative for Minnesota Markets, a food wholesaler. He negotiated a deal with them whereby he got 50 percent of the profits. In 1936, Paulucci became the Minnesota representative for the Hancock-Nelson grocery company of St. Paul. He attempted to attend Hibbing junior college while working there, but found the requisite travel made it impossible. Paulucci remained with this firm until 1945.

In the meantime, Paulucci had noticed during World War II that, when vegetables were in short supply, Oriental families were growing bean sprouts in hydroponic gardens. Paulucci went into the bean sprout business himself, and he formed a partnership with David Persha, one of his former bosses, in the Bean Sprouts Growers Association. "I don't suppose I'll ever forget the look on the banker's face when I told him I wanted to borrow $2,500 to grow sprouts from mung beans,'' Paulucci later recounted. Nevertheless, they got the money and struggled for two years with the business; they even attempted unsuccessfully to market soybeans and package ground garlic.

Jeno Paulucci, however, was not a man to admit defeat. Although people were unwilling to buy bean sprouts and soybeans, he reasoned that they would buy fully prepared Chinese food. He later told the *New York Times* that the retailers he sold to "never seemed to have any canned Chinese food," so he decided to make chow mein. His chow mein, however, would be different. He noted that the only Chinese food available "was so bland it was tasteless." Paulucci made sure his Chinese food was not. He named his company Chun King, his version of the first Chinese name that came to his mind. The odds seemed to be stacked against the new enterprise: because of their northern location, the farms in the area had too short a growing season to supply the necessary vegetables for the product; the company was distant from any major markets; and it was not ideally located for transportation. Finally, an Italian making Chinese food? In Duluth? It was hard to imagine.

But as he would do time and again, Paulucci turned disadvantage into advantage. Deciding he would make Chun King a low-cost producer, Paulucci knew that he would have to reduce the cost of the celery used in the product, which was the single most costly ingredient. He first tried growing his own, but early frosts killed the project. Paulucci knew then that he would have to buy his celery in Florida like everyone else. But even here he found a cost advantage. He recalled,

I had watched this farmer cut the celery into even bunches so he could fit them on a truck or freight car. I found out he was using all this cut-off celery (the outside stalks) as feed for cattle. So, I brought my own truck and asked the farmer if I could take the leftover celery at $10 a ton. We settled for $20. But I didn't care. Everybody else was probably paying at least four or five times as much for their celery. (*Forbes,* April 9, 1984)

That deal meant a difference of eight cents for each can of chow mein. Instead of lowering his price to the consumer, however, Paulucci took a different route. Being the low-cost producer meant that he had more money to spend on advertising, which Chun King could use to increase demand for the product. Also, Paulucci could afford to give the retailer a somewhat higher markup than other manufacturers, which enabled him to get additional shelf space. Chun King and Jeno Paulucci were on their way.

Initially, the canning was done in a quonset hut in Grand Rapids, Minnesota, but a year later Paulucci relocated in Duluth. By 1951, the business had grown sufficiently to require larger quarters. The firm continued to grow steadily throughout the 1950s, and it achieved national prominence in 1960 when Paulucci hired comedian Stan Freberg to do a series of commercials. Chun King became a household word after one of the commercials featured a voice-over (by Freberg) saying that nine out of ten doctors recommended Chun King. While another voice loudly protested this claim, the camera slowly panned along the line of white-coated doctors, all but one of whom were Chinese. The public was charmed by the subtle, self-deprecating humor in the commercial, and sales boomed. It was not long before Chun King was the number-one producer of Chinese-style food products in the United States.

The press began to refer to Paulucci as an overnight success, since he and his firm had seemingly come out of nowhere to dominate the market. Paulucci had no patience for this point of view: "This overnight success had been getting up at 4:00 or 4:30 every morning for 15 years and fighting competitors, financiers, government agencies, some railroads and airlines, a union or two, and the TV networks, among others." By the mid–1960s, the privately held Chun King had sales of $50 million a year and distribution in nearly 87,000 retail outlets across the nation. In 1963, the company purchased the Chun Wong firm of Los Angeles, and, in 1964, Oriental Commerce, both producers of frozen Chinese foods.

This expansion did not come without its share of problems. Once, when Chun King's largest customer, the Food Fair chain, threatened to discontinue handling the line because of problems of quality control, Paulucci flew to the chain's Philadelphia office to meet with the company's chief buyer. To demonstrate the quality of his firm's products, Paulucci opened a can of chow mein in front of the buyer, looked in, and found a huge grasshopper staring back at him. Paulucci reached in, pulled out the grasshopper and ate it, before the buyer even noticed. Paulucci's quick action saved the account for Chun King.

Chun King's success began to attract acquisition interest in the early 1960s. First, Chef Boy-Ar-Dee offered $4 million for the company and was turned down. Then, several years later, Paulucci nearly sold the company to R. J. Reynolds Tobacco for $40 million, but he pulled out during the negotiations. In 1966, however, Reynolds came knocking again, and Paulucci gave a price of $63 million—in cash—and he got it. As part of the deal, Paulucci became chairman of the board of R. J. Reynolds Foods, Incorporated. The arrangement did not work out. The more casual work environment did not suit Paulucci's taste: "When I showed up for work at my usual time the first morning, the guard wouldn't let me into the building. I suddenly realized that I was in a different world! These people came to work at nine in the morning. I thought I was late walking in at six!" In 1967 Paulucci set up Jeno's Pizza to market a frozen pizza he had begun making a few years before. Reynolds, objecting strenuously, argued that its purchase had blocked Paulucci from reentering the frozen-food field. Paulucci calmly pointed to a clause in the contract that exempted pizza from the ban. Jeno Paulucci was on his way again, this time with $63 million in capital, rather than $2,500.

Paulucci had again correctly gauged the market. Figuring that a large market for frozen pizza was going to develop, and that only local and regional brands were available at the time, he decided to develop Jeno's into the leading national brand using the same techniques that he had used with Chun King. Again, he developed a low-cost baking process, had a low-wage work force, and engaged in an extensive national advertising campaign. By 1972, Jeno's had become the national market leader in frozen pizza. But Jeno's profitability did not endure as long as Chun King's. Stiff competition emerged shortly in the frozen pizza market, with brands like Totino's from Pillsbury, Ellio's by Purex, and Celeste by Quaker Oats, all of which cut into Jeno's market share. With better distribution systems, automated production, and deep discounting to retailers, they were rapidly displacing Jeno's.

In response, Paulucci retaliated with methods characteristic of his approach and personality, but were troubling for him in later years. Realizing that operating out of Duluth entailed the same disadvantages it had entailed with Chun King, Paulucci bought a 400,000-square-foot frozen-food plant from Banquet Foods in Wellston, Ohio, for $4 million in 1981. He next invested an additional $17 million into installing an automated pizza assembly system that could produce one million frozen pizzas daily. A year later, he closed down Jeno's operations in Duluth and laid off 1,300 workers in an already badly depressed local economy. Paulucci was bitterly criticized for the move by the citizens of his hometown, and he was deeply hurt and upset by their anger. "It was the toughest decision I ever had to make because it was like leaving family behind. But I didn't have any choice. If we hadn't moved our operations to Ohio, today we'd be in trouble. Our plants were small and inefficient, and we were situated too far from our major markets," he said at the time. "Now, we're going to be a survivor, and a profitable one." Shortly thereafter, he also moved the headquarters of the firm out of Duluth—this time to Casselberry, Florida.

Much of Paulucci's time since 1982 has been spent trying to revive the fortunes of Duluth. When he left the city, Paulucci made a pledge that he would replace every job he had taken from the area. To do so, Paulucci engaged in a relentless, but only marginally successful, campaign to attract other businesses to the area. "Taking jobs crushed my ego," he said five years later. "I have something to prove to the people who wrote the hate letters, the people who said I'd cut and run." In an attempt to lure companies to the area, he offered rent-free accommodations in his Duluth terminals for two years. Stung by criticism from Duluth's civic leaders over the years, he helped build a new arena, a recreation center, and a downtown retail center. Even his strongest critics in Duluth were impressed with the energy and determination Paulucci put into the project. As a Minneapolis columnist commented, "Paulucci deals with restraint the way a tornado deals with lawn chairs."

After five years, though, Paulucci had experienced relatively little success with his Duluth plans. Just five companies had relocated in Paulucci's Duluth warehouses, and they employed just 200 workers. Another 1,500 of Jeno's former employees were either still without jobs in the area, or had had to move elsewhere. As a result, the anger began to escalate. Workers sprayed graffiti on Paulucci's old pizza plant: "Please, Jeno, Don't Come Back." And although Paulucci said the sign "tears me apart," many felt his ego and irascible style were largely responsible for failing to lure more jobs to the area. He canceled his plans to build a carpet mill in the Iron Range when the United Steel Workers refused to promise that they would never try to organize the plant. In 1986, Paulucci sold Jeno's to arch rival Pillsbury for $150 million, and decided to devote his time to real estate developments in Florida, and to a last, vain attempt to resurrect Duluth's fortunes.

Perhaps the nadir of Paulucci's relations with Duluth came one night after a hockey game in the Duluth civic center, which he had helped to build. In his typical impatient manner, Paulucci had raced to beat the crowd out of the arena, only to find his illegally parked car blocked by buses. When he tried to get the bus drivers, who were playing cards, to move the buses, they refused. An angry Paulucci pulled himself up to full height and is said to have roared: "Do you know who I am?" At that point, one bus driver just turned to the others and said, "Hey, fellas, we got a guy here who doesn't know who is he."

Paulucci had little success with Duluth, nor was a venture with *Attenzione*, a magazine he founded for Italian-Americans, any more successful. After losing $4 million on the publication over a four-year period, Paulucci disbanded the project. His real estate project in Florida was also suffering. He created a 3,000-acre development near Orlando called Heathrow, which was the most grandiose project of his career. By 1988, Paulucci estimated he had invested $100 million in it, and he announced plans for a $1-billion business district in the area. But the community of exclusive homes, which were to sell for between $300,000 and $1 million each, was having trouble finding buyers, so Paulucci opened the development to more modest units and managed to sell 1,200 of them. But if he is ever to recoup his massive investment, he will have to sell the high-priced commercial land at good prices. The entire venture remained questionable in 1988. A Chamber of Commerce official in the area, however, was still optimistic: "The man is a visionary, I don't know anyone who is betting against Jeno."

But Paulucci's Florida ventures in the fast-food business were also uncharacteristic failures. In 1986, after eighteen months of planning and preparation, Paulucci opened twenty Pizza Kwik stores to enter the pizza home delivery market, and he planned to expand to 250 stores within a year. He also started a chain called China Kwik, to do the same thing for Chinese food, for which he had high hopes. By 1988, however, both ventures were failures and had to be closed. The Paulucci magic seemed to have failed him.

Meanwhile, at seventy years of age, Jeno Paulucci retained his extraordinary vigor and energy. Spending much of his time trying to find businesses to locate either in Duluth or Heathrow, he went to extremes to make a sale. Once, when he had a 9 A.M. meeting with the American Automobile Association, who were thinking of locating at Heathrow, Paulucci realized the driver of his limousine was headed in the wrong direction on the freeway—and there was no exit for miles. He ordered the driver to pull over, and he jumped out of the car and ran across the highway, down into a ditch, and up a grassy embankment. He then scaled a barbed wire fence, and arrived at the AAA headquarters just a few minutes late. He announced, "Do you want to know how badly I want your business?" He pointed out the window to the freeway: "That is how I came." The company executives were impressed, and AAA became the first major tenant at Heathrow.

When asked several years earlier about his boundless energy and enthusiasm, he said, "I'm something like *What Makes Sammy Run?* I never learned to relax and stop. I guess it's from my circumstances in the Depression when we had to sell wine and tarblocks on the street to survive." All that running and vision made Paulucci a very wealthy man. *Forbes* estimated his wealth to be in excess of $550 million in 1988, and Paulucci admitted the pursuit of wealth was a major factor for him, "You bet I'm out to make a buck. That's the name of the game, isn't it?" (**B**. *Business Week*, November 15, 1958, March 6, 1965, September 30, 1972, February 29, 1988; *Time*, August 7, 1972; *Nation's Business*, March 1976; *New York Times*, September 1, November 7, 1976, March 9, March 21, 1979, October 7, 1984; Carol Pine and Susan Mundale, *Self-Made*, 1982; *Forbes*, August 29, 1983, April 9, 1984, October 25, 1985, January 27, 1986, October 24, 1988; Joseph J. Fucini and Suzy Fucini, *Entrepreneurs*, 1985; A. David Silver, *Entrepreneurial Megabucks*, 1985; *Contemporary Newsmakers*, 1986; *Newsweek*, March 17, 1986; *U.S. News & World Report*, March 17, 1986; *Inc.*, June 1986; *Who's Who in America*, 1986–87.)

PERDUE, FRANKLIN PARSONS (1920–   ). Food processor, Perdue Farms, Incorporated. Frank Perdue was an unlikely celebrity, but certainly a memorable one—television viewers observed a mostly bald head, a furrowed brow, shrewdly intense eyes, a beaked nose, a thin neck, and, when he started to speak, they heard an incredibly squawky voice. What was he advertising? Chickens? Why, the man looked just like a—well—a chicken himself. That was the whole point. Frank Perdue was one of the very first chief executives of a company to do television commercials. Long before Lee Iacocca* of Chrysler or Victor Kiam of Remington became familiar faces on television, there was Frank Perdue, who was chosen to do the commercials, not just because he was the head of the company, but also because he looked disconcertingly like a chicken. As the head of his advertising agency commented,

This was advertising in which Perdue had a personality that lent credibility to the product. If Frank Perdue didn't look and sound like a chicken, he wouldn't be in the commercials. There's nothing straight-out spokesman about him. He always appears a little bit off the wall, a little bit irregular. (*New Yorker*)

Frank Perdue was born in Salisbury, Maryland, in the area of Maryland called the Delmarva Peninsula. He was the only child of Arthur W. Perdue, a Railway Express agent, who quit the firm when he was informed that he was being transferred to another station. After he resigned, Arthur Perdue built a small coop and filled it with fifty Leghorn chickens. Soon, he and his wife were selling table eggs. Before long, he added more chickens and expanded his market; he began to ship eggs to New York City and other urban centers on the eastern seaboard. During the depression years, he mixed his own feed and salvaged leather from his old shoes to make hinges for the coops, and he managed to stay out of debt and even prosper. For the first twenty years that he ran the business, Arthur Perdue developed important principles that he passed on to his son: he monitored costs carefully because of the slim margins in the business; he refused to borrow money or take on partners, fearing an inability to repay loans and fearing the loss of independence; and he took great pride in his eggs, proclaiming their superiority to anyone who came within earshot.

Young Frank Perdue attended one-room schools in the area and went on to high school in Salisbury, Maryland. He also spent two years at Salisbury State College, a small teacher's college, but, an indifferent student, he was more concerned with his dreams of becoming a professional baseball player. When Perdue recognized in 1939 that his dream was unrealizable, he quit school and went into the family egg business. Young Frank had been given responsibilities on the farm at an early age; when was still quite young, his father had given him some culls, and soon Frank's small flock was outproducing his father's. Frank later said, "We couldn't figure it out . . . (but) I had concluded that the larger the pen the happier the chickens." Generally, however, Frank was not a terribly enthusiastic farmer in his early years and, like most children, had to be hounded to feed the chickens, clean the coops, dig the cesspools, and perform all the other tedious tasks.

Shortly after Frank Perdue had joined his father's business full time, however, disaster struck. In 1940, their 2,000 Leghorn chickens were hit with leukosis, a highly infectious disease. They made an important decision then to switch from eggs to chickens and bought 800 of the hardier New Hampshire Reds. Now producing broilers, the Perdues had to find new distribution outlets. It might have been a daunting task, but the outbreak of World War II greatly increased the demand for all farm products, and prices soared. The Perdue family expanded their operations significantly during this time and made greater profits than they had in the past decade. They hatched their own chicks by the thousands, raised them to maturity on a special feed mixture they had developed which was superior to anything else that was on the market, and sold them at the broiler auction in nearby Selbyville, Delaware. Many Perdue chickens were purchased by Armour & Company and Swift & Company.

In 1953, Frank Perdue, at thirty-three years of age, succeeded his father as president of the company. By then, Perdue Farms, Incorporated had become a large operation. With revenues of about $8 million annually from the sales of 2.6 million broilers, and forty employees, it earned a comfortable, but not spectacular profit. The business continued to grow at a modest rate throughout the 1950s, but tremendous technological changes were beginning to impact the poultry industry, and Frank Perdue finally convinced his father to make some important changes. But it was many years before Perdue became a leader in the industry.

The poultry industry was undergoing a staggering technological revolution in the postwar years. In the 1940s, it had taken sixteen man-hours to raise 100 birds, by the early 1950s this had been reduced to eight hours. By the late 1950s it was only four. Chicken raising, which had been largely labor intensive prior to the war, became almost totally automated in the two decades after the war. By the 1960s, 100,000 fluffy baby chicks would be born at about the same time in a huge incubator, and they rode a conveyor belt out of the incubator to spend the next eight weeks of their lives crammed by the tens of thousands into automated chicken houses equipped with an array of electronically controlled feeding, watering, and ventilating devices. They grew to maturity virtually untouched by human hands. Then, a final ride on a conveyor belt took them to the automatic killing knife. They were indecorously strung up, clothesline fashion, by their ankles from the conveyor belt. An electric current knocked them out, and the knife painlessly slit their throats. The killed chickens then progressed to a "bleed tunnel," where the liquid was drained from the carcasses, and they were showered with hot water to loosen the feathers, which were removed by passing them through a series of revolving, vibrating rubber fingers. Next, hairs were singed by blowtorch machines, heads and feet were severed, and, at an eviserating counter, the innards were removed. Lungs were sucked out by vacuum cleaners; crops and windpipes were pulled out by hand, one of the few manual operations in the entire procedure. Finally, the chickens passed through another water bath to lower their temperature, and they were packed in ice for final shipment. Nothing was wasted. Ground feathers and offal, which are rich in protein, were mixed into chicken feed; damaged parts of imperfect chickens were removed and the rest was ground into "chicken product," which was sold to fast-food outlets, to become chicken nuggets.

It is not a pleasant concept, but automatic poultry raising has had a dramatic effect upon the industry and upon the American consumer. Even as late as 1957, it took sixteen weeks and ten pounds of feed to rear a four-pound broiler; twenty years later, it took half that time and less than eight pounds of computer-formulated feed. As a result, the price of chicken rose only 17 percent between 1950 and 1979, while beef and pork prices both tripled. In the 1920s and 1930s, chicken was a luxury food, so esteemed that Huey Long talked about a "chicken in every pot." Even as late as the 1940s, chicken was reserved for special Sunday dinners. Because of this luxury status, and because of the increasing popularity of chicken for dietary reasons, the market for chicken in the United States expanded tremendously. By the late 1970s, the mechanized broiler industry was producing 13 billion pounds of chicken annually, enough to provide every man, woman, and child in the United States with sixty pounds of chicken a year. Chicken raising, which just a short time before had been the province of the small family farm (in 1910 there were 5.5 million farms in America, with an average of eighty chickens each), was now big business. Frank Perdue wanted to ensure that Perdue Farms had a piece of the action.

The firm's growth surged ahead in 1958 with the changes Frank Perdue implemented. He built a huge new complex at Salisbury, which included a large feed mill for mixing grain, machinery to manufacture meal and oil from soybeans, and enormous storage capacity. The feed mill could process about 16 million bushels of soybeans and corn each year, and it had a storage capacity for 11.2 million bushels. Meal not used at Perdue Farms was sold to other producers. As Perdue recalled, "That was a red-letter day in the history of the company, because it gave the farmers confidence in us." The company's annual revenues continued to climb during the 1960s, until by 1967 they exceeded $35 million. Perdue Farms still continued to sell live chickens; it had not yet moved into fully automated operations. In 1967 Frank Perdue decided to enter the retail chicken market in New York City, and he convinced his father to do the unthinkable—to borrow $500,000 to expand the business and technologically update the company's operations.

In 1968, Perdue constructed an additional feed mill, and he bought a plant in Salisbury, which had once housed a Swift & Company operation. He renovated it and equipped it with machines capable of processing 14,000 broilers an hour. Computers were installed to handle the feeding operations, geneticists were hired to help breed chickens with larger breasts, and veterinarians were employed to provide a regimen of antibiotics to ward off disease and to boost growth. By the end of that year, Perdue was selling 800,000 broilers a week, and was beginning to advertise conservatively Perdue Farms chickens in a small way in order to expand his market. He hired a professional agency, and spent about $30,000 in the first year for radio commercials. In 1969, he spent twice as much, and the following year doubled the amount again.

In 1971, Perdue expanded his operations again. He invested at least $7 million on a new, larger poultry processing plant in Accomoc, on Virginia's Eastern Shore, which was capable of processing 26,000 birds an hour. With this increased capacity, he decided in that same year to increase his advertising budget to $200,000, but he felt it was time to look for a new advertising agency. He proceeded in a characteristically Perdue fashion. Interviewing various advertising agencies, Perdue narrowed his list to nine. He then made an appointment with a tenth agency, not on the list, and had lunch with its representatives at the Plaza Hotel. He recalled the incident:

I said, "You're not one of my finalists, but you've been nice to me, so I'm going to buy you lunch. The reason you're not one of my finalists is you've got too much turnover in personnel and too much turnover in clients, so I don't want to start with you and lose my creative team. But I have my list of nine finalists. I'd like you to rank them in preference, one through nine." One of the partners said, "I'm damned if I'm going to rank your list." The other partner said, "Give me the list." (New Yorker)

From that meeting, Perdue got his agency, Scali, McCabe, Sloves, a relatively new agency with billings of $12 million. Since one of the partners was a copywriter, which Perdue felt was necessary to give him continuity of approach, the agency was ideal for his purposes.

Although Perdue's billings were just $250,000 in 1971, the agency recognized the firm had great potential for growth, and, in fact, by 1978 billings had grown to $18 million. But in 1971 the Scali, McCabe agency had to find a gimmick. One of the agency partners commented, "Chickens had always been considered simply a commodity in the merchandising process . . . there was no way anybody could distinguish one fresh chicken from another. Our job was to figure out a reason consumers should buy a Perdue chicken rather than other chickens." Also there had never been any "brand advertising of chickens whatever on television that we were aware of." Members of the agency team traveled to Perdue's Salisbury operations to glean whatever insights they could.

The first thing that struck them was the markedly yellow color of Perdue's chickens, which was caused by the unusually high level of xanthophyll in the chicken's feed. Perdue achieved this coloration by adding marigold petals and extract to the feed, and it had been done for several years because it was possible to get a three-cent-a-pound premium for yellow chickens, even though it was really just a cosmetic difference. Nonetheless, the yellow skin color had become associated in the consumer's mind with high quality, and the agency determined to play that up in their ads. The other thing that struck the agency men in their visit to the plant was that Frank Perdue seemed to be everywhere, supervising operations very closely. As one of the advertising teams recalled, "Frank was very, very involved in *everything* to do with his company . . . . So we realized that what really set Perdue chickens apart from other chickens was Frank Perdue." The head copywriter of the agency recalled, "He looked a little like a chicken himself, and sounded a little like one, and he squawked a lot." So they decided to feature Frank Perdue himself in the ads—he would be the spokesperson for Perdue Farms chickens.

When they approached Frank Perdue with the idea, he was at first reluctant. "My reaction was really not positive," he remembers, "because I'm basically somewhat shy and somewhat retiring." But he finally agreed, and the first series of commercials went on the air. They were instantly successful, and within a year Perdue Farms quadrupled its television-advertising budget. At the same time, sales of Perdue chickens in the New York metropolitan area skyrocketed. It turned out to be a surefire strategy—Perdue's homely appeal captured the public's imagination, and the agency's copywriters penned some of the most memorable lines in advertising history, which Perdue delivered in the ads: "It takes a tough man to make a tender chicken"; "If you can find a better chicken, buy it"; "A chicken is what he eats, and my chickens eat better than people do"; "Don't wonder why my chickens are so yellow, wonder why some chickens are so white"; "My chickens even get cookies for dessert"; "If your husband is a breast or leg man, ask for my chicken parts"; "The Perdue Rooster is the master race of chickens''; and, probably most famous, "Baldness: handsome in a man, beautiful in a chicken.''

Annual revenues of Perdue's company rose from $58 million in 1971 to more than half a billion in 1983. By that time, his ads reached 22 percent of the market in the United States, his company dominated New York and the Eastern seaboard, and he was earmarking one cent per pound of every chicken sold for advertising. But a number of competitors were beginning to challenge Perdue Farms for a share of the market. Cargill, Incorporated of Minneapolis had started the barrage in the mid–1970s with a series of ads by singer Pearl Bailey for their Paramount chickens. In 1982 Showell Farms ran a series of ads that openly jeered Frank Perdue and asserted that their chickens, called Cookin' Good, were chosen for their superior taste in a series of tests. That same year, giant Holly Farms entered the fray. The second largest chicken producer in the country, Holly Farms had not competed in the New York area previously. Hiring Dinah Shore as spokesperson, it claimed that its chickens had a "healthier color" than one that was either too yellow or too white, that its chickens had a more "lifelike, more chickenlike" yellow. Then, Pilgrim's Pride chickens came on the market and advertised that its chickens had less fat; many consumers began to associate a yellow color with fatness in a chicken. As a result, Frank Perdue had to counterattack on many fronts during the early- and mid–1980s in what came to be known as the "Great American Chicken War.''

In the meantime, Perdue vigorously expanded his facilities to keep up with constantly increasing sales. In 1976, at a cost of $17 million, he opened a hatchery and a third processing plant in Lewiston, North Carolina. By then, the company had more than 3,000 employees, and the combined production from their three plants reached 1.9 million broilers a week. A year later, a fourth processing plant was opened in Felton, Delaware, and a plant to process just roasters was opened in Georgetown, Delaware, in 1979. In succeeding years, Perdue added more plants and a trucking concern, and he continued to upgrade all his operations. By the late 1980s, Perdue Farms, the nation's third largest chicken producer, was one of the largest privately owned corporations in America, with annual sales of about $1 billion. Since it was a private concern, profit levels are unknown, but profits have been so good that, despite the enormous expansion Perdue has undertaken, he has not had to resort to outside financing.

But, all has not been roses for Frank Perdue; he has had his share of problems along the way. One problem area has been his brushes with organized crime— something that confronts most producers of fresh foods. Several of the largest distributors to supermarkets in the New York City area have been reputed to have ties to organized crime, and Perdue inevitably became slightly tainted by his associations. In 1985, in a deposition Perdue made to investigators for the President's Commission on Organized Crime, Perdue indicated that he had refused to deal with Dial Meat Purveyors of Brooklyn because "Dial was owned or run by or operated by Paul Castellano, Jr., and that he was associated in some way . . . with the Mafia.'' Nonetheless, the crime commission found that Perdue dealt with another firm run by Pasquale Conte, who, in their words, "is also a *capo* in the . . . Gambino family." Although Perdue ended up conducting business with Dial Poultry, which helped him get his chickens into a larger number of New York supermarkets, the commission absolved Perdue of any wrongdoing in this regard.

Perdue has also experienced a number of labor problems. Not enthusiastic about labor unions, he has opposed their efforts to organize his plants. As a result, the United Food and Commercial Workers International Union called for a boycott of Perdue's products. Most of Perdue's plant workers are black women who make just above the minimum wage. Given their lack of options in the local economy, and the isolated nature of Perdue's plants, the unions have had difficulty organizing the workers. Perdue has also run afoul of the Department of Agriculture at times for his strong desire to retain total control of all operations. The government filed a lawsuit against him in 1981, charging that he threatened to withhold his chickens from retailers who also sold other brands. Carol Tucker Foreman, who had served as assistant secretary for food and consumer services in the Department of Agriculture under the Carter administration said of him, "Perdue does run a clean operation, in terms of sanitation—as these things go, he's topnotch." But she also said that she found him to be "not a pleasant fellow."

In early 1981, Perdue took a small step into retailing for the first time. He opened an upscale, cafeteria-style, fast-food restaurant in Queens, New York. The main feature on the menu, of course, was chicken, and unlike almost every other fast-food restaurant, the chicken was never frozen. Whole Perdue chickens, packed in ice, were delivered to the restaurant every two days, where they were put into a large number of chicken dishes. While a reporter was at the Perdue Chicken Restaurant, "the boss himself, Frank Perdue, kept a taxi waiting outside while he checked the progress of his new venture, then departed almost as swiftly as he had arrived." All of this attention to detail has made Frank Perdue a very rich man. In 1988, when Perdue retired as chief executive officer of the enterprise, *Forbes* estimated that he had accumulated a fortune of at least $350 million. That is not, well, chicken feed. (**B**. *Business Week*, September 16, 1972; *Newsweek*, October 16, 1972; *Esquire*, April 1973; *Wall Street Journal*, May 13, 1974; *New York Times*, September 12, 1976; *Current Biography*, 1979; *Quick Frozen Foods*, April 1981; *Nation's Business*, August 1982; *People Weekly*, August 30, 1982; *New York*, July 25, 1983; Robert Sobel and David B. Sicilia, *The Entrepreneurs*, 1986; *New Yorker*, July 6, 1987; *Time*, September 28, 1987; *Forbes*, October 24, 1988.)

PEROT, H(ENRY) ROSS (June 27, 1930–). Computer systems founder, entrepreneur, industrialist, philanthropist, Electronic Data Systems, F.I. duPont, Glore Forgan, duPont & Walston, General Motors, Perot Systems. *Reader's Digest* called Ross Perot the "world's first populist billionaire," and it may not have been far from the mark. He is living proof that legends and charisma can come in curious packages. A little man with a broken nose and close-cropped hair, he spouts an ideology and a rhetoric from a bygone era in his high-pitched, twangy, Texarkana speech. One of his favorite books is the *Boy Scout Handbook*, which he feels provides the kind of clear, direct, and practical code for an idealized American life. He has a love for the paintings of Norman Rockwell, who, he said, "painted what I strived to be." Somehow Perot strikes a chord of patriotism, of forthright honesty, of individualism that is in tune with many Americans. As *Fortune* said; "there is something undeniably appealing about the pint-size Jimmy Stewart who awakens some dormant Americanism that Americans are a bit too timid, or embarrassed to reveal without prompting." Others are not so certain; one General Motors executive commented, "I truly believe this guy needs causes. Everything has to be a religion. He can inspire and mobilize, and people will die for him. You've got a demagogue on your hands."

Ross Perot was born in Texarkana, Texas, the son of a cotton broker and part-time horse trader. Ross began to help his father break horses when he was six years old, and the broken nose is a legacy of that activity. The family was comfortable, but not wealthy, and Ross Perot learned a good deal about business from his father. Ross was educated in the public schools of his home town, and began promoting himself at an early age. He sold Christmas cards, saddles, the *Saturday Evening Post*, and the Texarkana *Gazette*, with which Perot early displayed an entrepreneurial bent. When he was twelve, he approached the *Gazette* for a job, and, when he was told there were none, he offered to deliver papers in the black slum called New Town. No one had done that before. Perot demanded a commission of 70 percent instead of the usual 30 percent, to which the management at the paper agreed. Probably, Perot said later, because "they figured folks in New Town couldn't read." Young Ross rose before dawn to make his deliveries on horseback, and subscriptions bloomed. The circulation manager tried to cut back on Perot's commission, but Perot protested to the paper's publisher. "Sir," Perot recalled saying, "we made a deal. We should keep to it, I believe." He did, and from then on, Perot said, "I always went straight to the top with a problem."

In elementary school and high school, Perot was never more than a middling student, but he found his métier in the Boy Scouts. He loved all things concerning the Scouts, and he rose to become an Eagle Scout. He noted, "The day I made Eagle Scout was more important to me than the day I discovered I was a billionaire." After graduating from high school, Perot attended Texarkana Junior College, where he took a two-year prelaw course. His real ambition, however, was to enroll at the United States Naval Academy, and in 1949 he succeeded in getting an appointment to Annapolis. After being commissioned in 1953, Perot shipped out on the destroyer USS *Sigourney* bound for Korea. While en route, a truce was declared in Korea, so the jubilant crew called at several Asian and European ports before returning home. Perot served the rest of his duty as assistant navigator aboard the USS *Leyte*, and he was discharged in 1957 with the rank of lieutenant. His navy years had a profound influence on Perot in later years, "I loved the Navy, loved the sea, loved ships," he later told a reporter. Ex-military men always had an advantage in applying for jobs with Perot's companies.

After leaving the navy, Perot had to find a career. While serving on the *Leyte*, he had met a visiting executive from International Business Machines (IBM) who told Perot to contact him about a job when he was discharged. Perot did so, and he was given a post selling computers in Dallas. IBM had sales quotas for their salesmen, and Perot, who was becoming increasingly bored with his job, found he was filling his quotas earlier and earlier each year. Finally, in his fifth year, he filled his year's quota in the first three weeks of January. IBM, which preferred to spread the commissions out among the salesmen so that no one salesman earned too much, transferred him to a desk job in Dallas. Perot thought his individual initiative was being stifled, and he was becoming increasingly frustrated. At about this time, he said, he came across a line by Henry David Thoreau, "The mass of men lead lives of quiet desperation," which he felt accurately summed up his existence at IBM.

Perot began to examine innovative ventures that might challenge his energy and imagination. He noticed that although IBM did a good job of making and installing computers, it was not terribly concerned with how customers used them. Perot realized that there was a niche in the market for a company that could design, install, and operate a data processing system, eliminating the need for the customer to do much more than pay a fee. When IBM transferred him to a desk job at White Plains, New York, in 1962, Perot quit and started his own firm. On his thirty-second birthday, in that year, he incorporated Electronic Data Systems (EDS) with $1,000 in savings, with his wife, mother, and sister as charter directors.

Perot had a phobia about going into debt, so he was determined not to invest money in hardware for his business. Since he needed sophisticated computer facilities for his operation, he rented time on a computer owned by a Dallas insurance company. Then he began to search frantically for customers. He finally sold computer time to Collins Radio in Cedar Rapids, Iowa. The sale gave Perot enough money to hire his first two salesmen, an ex-IBM systems engineer, and an ex-IBM secretary. One of these salesmen, Thomas J. Marquez, landed EDS' first real account—Frito-Lay Incorporated. Marquez later recalled how he convinced Frito-Lay's founder, Herman Lay, that it was customary for the customer to pay in advance and to provide office space. Lay complied, and EDS was off and running.

EDS' main clients, however, were large insurance companies, particularly Blue Cross, which had large amounts of insurance claim work that required systematization and computerization. The business grew rapidly, and by spring 1963, there were seven employees working eighteen-hour days. It was during this hectic time that Perot established his reputation as a hard-driving, but compassionate, boss. One afternoon, Perot disappeared without warning. His employees were frantic, and when he finally showed up at about 5 P.M., Perot refused to answer any questions about where he had been. Later that evening they found out. During the afternoon, Perot had visited the wives of each of his hardworking employees, told each how grateful he was for her husband's hard work, and gave each of them 100 shares of stock. He apologized that it was not much of a gift, but, by the late 1980s, those 100 shares were worth $200,000. That became the hallmark of Perot's management style—the personal touch.

What really launched EDS, though, was the passage of national Medicare legislation in 1965, which vastly increased the volume of claims that had to be processed by the entire health care system. Throughout the 1960s, Perot's company grew rapidly and proved to be a profitable entity. It was virtually unnoticed in the great computer field, however, until 1968. With revenues of just $7.7 million, and a net income of $1.55 million, it was what *Fortune* (November 1968) called a "pip-squeak" in the industry. At that point, Perot did something that changed the fortunes of EDS—he took it public. But it was the manner in which he did so that created tremendous interest and enthusiasm. He first recapitalized the firm, so that there were 12 million shares, each with a par value of 20 cents. Of the new shares, he offered only 650,000 for sale, so that he could personally retain the vast majority of stock. He finally chose R. W. Presspich & Company to sponsor the issue, which they brought out at $16.50 a share, representing a near-record price-to-earnings ratio of 118 to one. By the close of the first day of trading in September 1968, EDS stock was selling at $23, giving Perot a net worth of $200 million for his 9 million shares. Subsequently, the stock kept climbing, until it reached $150 in the great bull market of 1969–1970, which made Perot a billionaire, at least on paper. Awed by all of this, *Fortune* in 1968 called Perot "The Fastest Richest Texan Ever."

Having achieved a modicum of notoriety, Perot seemed to feast on ever greater doses. In the fall of 1969, he began a highly publicized project to free American prisoners of war in North Vietnam. At the request of the Nixon White House, Perot hired two jets and tried to airlift 30 tons of supplies to the American POWs. When the North Vietnamese thwarted his efforts, Perot arranged public confrontations all over Southeast Asia, and in Laos he himself stood outside the North Vietnamese Embassy shouting "Let us have our men!" In 1970, he offered $100 million as ransom for the prisoners, but was rebuffed. The mission was an ostensible failure, but it awoke Americans to the plight of the POWs, and according to American prisoners who returned after the war, Perot's mission did have a noticeable impact on their treatment in prison. Then, too, they no longer felt as if they were forgotten men.

Having achieved media attention beyond his wildest dreams, the outwardly modest and unassuming Perot seemed to thrive on ever more daring ventures. The most dramatic of these, by far, came in 1979. Perot had been a hero to his employees for a long time. In 1969, his employees took him out to the parking lot and made him don a suit of armor and mount a white horse. But not even they were prepared for what happened in 1979. Two EDS employees had been

thrown in an Iranian jail without charges by the Ayatollah Khomeini. Perot first
contacted U.S. government officials, but when they were unable to do anything,
Perot flew to Iran in disguise to tell his employees that he would get them out.
He organized a team of private commandos—EDS employees led by a former
Army colonel—who went in and rescued the two employees in the teeth of the
Iranian revolution. At a time when the Iranians were holding fifty-six American
consulate employees hostage, with the American government unable to effect
their release, this was a dramatic achievement. So dramatic that the mystery
writer, Ken Follett, wrote a best-seller, *On Wings of Eagles*, based on the
incident, which was later made into a television miniseries.

Meanwhile, Perot had EDS marching in lockstep during these years. His
"hands on" charismatic approach to management achieved remarkable success.
Highly righteous and moralistic, Perot had strict dress codes for his employees.
He warned employees that marital infidelity would result in immediate dismissal,
and he urged that they follow his example of abstinence from drink and smoking.
These rules were designed to promote efficiency. Supervisors were trained to
look for and remedy any wasted time or motion, and Perot tried to create a sense
of family at his company. "I wanted people who are smart, tough, self-reliant,
have a history of success since childhood, of being the best at what they've
done, people who love to win," Perot said. Outsiders most often remarked about
what they perceived as excessive militarism at EDS—there was an abundance
of fences, guards, and American flags at EDS—and EDS employees were often
called Perot's clones because they were expected to dress like their boss. But
Inc. pointed out that EDS was always more democratic than militaristic. "The
team operated," it said, "like a loose band of guerillas, with Perot as the leader.
. . . There were no class distinctions, no private parking spaces, or executive
dining rooms." As a result, the system bred "a kind of unity and loyalty that
is rare in any organization."

Perot also developed an important and unique new way of doing business
called facilities management. EDS called on customers and offered to manage
their data processing facilities under contract. EDS then bought its computers
and equipment, assumed the salaries of their employees, and contracted to deliver
the solutions for the amount of the customers' budget. EDS then sold off excess
equipment, laid off excess people, and earned a strong profit of from 30 to 40
percent. EDS became, in effect, the client's data processing department, working
under long-term contracts—usually five years. It was a solid business, and it
grew at a phenomenal rate of 100 percent a year during the 1960s. In the 1970s,
however, both Perot and EDS encountered difficulties.

The exceedingly rapid growth of the 1960s had outstripped Perot's centralized,
hands-on management technique. He insisted on making all of the decisions,
but that was becoming increasingly impossible. Also, some of EDS' long-term
contracts came due, and several of these companies moved on to competitors.
This had a traumatic effect on EDS' revenues and profits. Then Perot blundered—
he tackled Wall Street. In 1971 Perot took over the troubled Wall Street brokerage

house of F. I. duPont, Glore Forgan & Company. The firm had been on the verge of collapse, and Perot tried to save the company with an infusion of $40 million. At the time, Wall Street leaders were ecstatic—Perot had come to the rescue again. New York Stock Exchange chairman Bernard J. Lasker was effusive in his praise of Perot, "I think Ross Perot did something for the country, for the economy, for the investor, for confidence, for the industry, for the stock exchange, and for the firm's 180,000 customers." "I for one," he added, "will be, as long as I live, forever grateful." The euphoria did not last.

Although, in the short term, most viewed Perot's venture onto Wall Street as another of his crusades, it was clear from the beginning that more was involved. EDS had gotten involved with duPont, Glore Forgan in 1970 when the huge firm was in the midst of computerizing its back office operations. EDS assumed the job of cleaning up the back office, a very large operation. When it became clear that the brokerage house was going to go under, Perot moved in, partially to save a valued client. In November 1970, Perot lent Du Pont $5 million, and then, in March 1971, he agreed to pump another $35 million into the firm in return for 80 percent of its equity. A little over a year later, in July 1972, Perot lent another troubled Wall Street client, Walston & Company, $15 million. In July 1973, he arranged for the partial consolidation of duPont and Walston & Company, creating the new "front office" firm of duPont, Walston & Co. If some of the Wall Street old guard had initially viewed Perot as a savior, this attitude was not shared by the people at duPont, Glore or at Walston. For most Wall Streeters, Perot appeared to be a "homily-and-grits-spouting outsider" whose presence rankled them greatly, according to *Business Week*. Perot was also hit by lawsuits from former partners at both firms for improprieties and a breech of fiduciary relationship of the old partnership with EDS. Perot was convinced he could not only save the two troubled brokerage firms, but also that he could reform Wall Street in the bargain. Perot began to deliver the kind of evangelistic messages and dress codes he had used to such great effect at EDS, but they did not sit well with Wall Street. One Wall Street executive commented, "There's no doubt that Perot saved duPont from certain failure and maybe averted a major crisis in the industry, what I'm tired of, though, is his holier-than-thou attitude. He acts like he's going to save the industry, but he doesn't know beans about Wall Street." But Perot was determined. He brought in a cadre of ex-EDS people to help him ramrod the firms into a tighter sense of discipline. From the beginning, there was enormous friction between the two groups. An ex-duPonter recalled: "The duPont people were afraid of the EDS people." Then, as Perot began hiring new people to replace the hordes of duPont and Walston people who were leaving, he hired ex-military men, just as he had at EDS. A former duPont broker scoffed at the practice, commenting, "The whole intention is to train people their way, so they won't think for themselves. They want a cadre of trained robots."

Finally, to add insult to injury, in 1973 Perot began a splashy advertising campaign for his brokerage house. The ads featured a drawing of Perot's face, which Perot justified by saying that "Wall Street needs flesh and blood identification. They have to identify with someone." The ads were aimed at the individual investor, the person who Perot, in his populist rhetoric, always imagined he was championing. But none of it worked. In January 1974, Perot announced that he was finally throwing in the towel. DuPont, Walston & Company had suffered losses in six straight quarters, and was floundering badly. Perot had but one choice—put the business up for sale and hope someone would buy it. The venture cost him and his associates an estimated $80 million. Perot in 1979 reached an out-of-court settlement on the two lawsuits which were bedeviling him, settling for $6.7 million, but not admitting any guilt. And to complete the picture, while Perot was fiddling away in Wall Street, EDS was burning. From 1974 to 1976 the once high-flying company watched its earnings actually decline. Perot had to return to Dallas to concentrate his full attention on the salvation of EDS.

EDS' stock, which had been selling at a high of $160 in the late 1960s, had plunged to just $15 in 1975, even below its 1968 offering price of $16.50. But in the late 1970s, Perot turned EDS around in a dramatic manner. Perot named Morton H. Meyerson, who had served as head of duPont, Walston, as president of EDS, and granted him the authority to run the firm's day-to-day operation. Meyerson pursued a series of new medical-claims-processing contracts from Blue Cross and others, and pushed the company into new areas. It moved dynamically into the banking sector, and became the largest processor of credit union accounts in the United States. The customer base, which stood at 47 in 1974, was expanded to 122 by 1980, and actual contracts increased from 55 to 140. Revenue growth, which averaged only 6 percent in 1974–1976, expanded to 25 percent thereafter. The biggest change came in the early 1980s, when EDS changed its focus from private industry to Washington, D.C., going after a series of what were termed "megacontracts."

As late as 1983, the federal government was still the smallest revenue contributor at EDS, accounting for just 25 percent of the total. But their contributions grew at the rate of 50 percent per year thereafter. These megacontracts involved enormous amounts of money, and ran over long periods of time. The breakthrough came in 1981, when EDS procured a contract for Project Viable, a $656-million, ten-year program to overhaul the computer systems at the forty-seven army bases in the United States. Traditionally, computer manufacturers had secured contracts like this, and then subcontracted for the software and support systems. Project Viable was the first major federal data processing contract with a software and services company as the prime contractor. EDS agreed to train 60,000 army personnel as part of the contract. Perot next shifted his attention to the U.S. Postal Service, bidding for a system called Prism, with a possible revenue of $3 billion, and he began to talk to the Social Security Administration, the Defense Logistics Agency, and a number of others. All of this propelled EDS back into the ranks of the big operators in the computer field. It not only came close to regaining its spot as the top data processing firm, but was also moving toward a place in the top ten of all computer companies.

Ross Perot could never rest on his laurels. He thrived on media attention. On his fifty-fourth birthday, on June 27, 1984, twenty-two years to the day since he had started EDS, he and General Motors (GM) chairman Roger Smith[†] made a startling announcement: GM was buying EDS for $2.5 billion worth of special-issue GM stock. Perot would become the largest individual stockholder at GM and a member of the board of directors. It soon became clear that it was Perot's intention to "reform" GM, just as he had tried to reform Wall Street. Another crusade commenced. At first, GM people thought Perot would stick to what he knew best—data processing—and leave the running of the auto firm to the experts. But, at his first GM board meeting Perot informed the other directors that he would not be a silent partner. He planned, he said, to be an advocate on the board for the car buyer, the dealer, the worker, and the stockholder.

At first Roger Smith tolerated all of Perot's antics with a rather bemused attitude. When questioned by reporters about his reaction to Perot, Smith parried with,

He doesn't come to the meetings in purple suits or anything. He's a good, solid American businessman. He's working his buns off to help us. That's good. That's what we needed. He's poking the organization. He wants the best for us, and he wants the best for his own company. I have no complaints. (*Business Week*, October 6, 1986)

Just wait, Roger—just wait.

GM was Wall Street all over again. From the very beginning, EDS's fired-up 15,000 employees clashed with GM's entrenched bureaucrats. After the first clashes, however, much of the tension between the two groups dissipated. Over a period of two years, EDS managed to streamline GM's disparate and ill-organized data processing systems, and a GM engineer was able to say, "To a large extent, the EDS arrogance has gone away." Not quite the same thing could be said about Ross Perot. As he watched GM's market share decline and its profits slide, Perot decided to launch a one-man crusade to change GM's corporate culture. Claiming that "Revitalizing GM is like teaching an elephant to tap dance," Perot advised, "You find the sensitive spots and start poking." And poke he did. Claiming that GM was engaged in economic war with Japan, and was losing, Perot developed his own plan to get GM moving.

The first item on Perot's agenda was to scrap Alfred P. Sloan, Jr.'s* much-vaunted decentralized managerial system. He believed Sloan had established the system to give GM more flexible, more responsive management, but that it was no longer serving that purpose. GM had developed such a cumbersome bureaucracy under the system that it could no longer service the needs and desires of its customers. Perot illustrated his point with a homily: "The first EDSer to see a snake kills it," he told reporters. "At GM, first thing you do is organize a committee on killing snakes. Then you bring in a consultant who knows a lot about snakes. Third thing you do is talk about it for a year.'' Smith had developed the Saturn project as his plan for producing a car that could compete with Japanese imports, but the car was not scheduled for delivery until 1990—five years after its announcement. "We won World War II in four and a half," Perot snorted.

By 1986, Perot was visiting factories, having lunch with line workers, preaching his populist message. He was also meeting with dealers, and receiving standing ovations at meetings when he said GM was not building the kinds of cars customers wanted. Finally, Roger Smith and the other GM executives could take no more. In December 1986, they bought out Perot's 11 million shares in GM for $62.50 a share, about double the market price. In effect, GM had paid Perot a cool $700 million to get out and shut up. In the deal he lost his seat on the board at GM and his chairmanship of EDS, but he retained the title of "founder" at the latter firm. If Perot continued to criticize GM, he could be fined up to $7.5 million. Most analysts felt GM paid an enormous price for Perot's silence, but nearly all also felt Perot was a disruptive, not a creative, influence in the huge corporation. Roy Herberger, dean of the business school at Southern Methodist University, said, "The day the deal was struck, the faculty said it wouldn't work. History is full of monstrous egos that thrive in an entrepreneurial format. Put them in a bureaucracy and it's a disaster." Others were equally critical.

When he left GM, Perot promised he would refrain from competing with EDS for eighteen months. On June 1, 1988, eighteen months to the day after leaving GM, Perot announced the formation of a new firm to compete with EDS. Called Perot Systems, it clearly aimed to engage in head-to-head combat with his former company. Since he had also promised that he would only operate on a nonprofit basis until 1989, Perot's options appeared limited. Touting the idea of employee ownership, Perot supplied $20 million of his own money to the new firm, which represented all its capital. Perot, however, took only 40 percent of the stock, with the remaining 60 percent reserved for employees. He then used the idea of employee ownership to entice eight former EDS employees to join his firm, five of whom were senior executives. Perot announced his first contract was with the U.S. Postal Service, a modest $500,000 nonprofit cost-cutting study. The contract had not been let on a competitive bidding basis, and EDS and other competitors cried foul. As a result, Perot's new firm was ultimately stripped of the contract.

Perot was after other companies as well, and he bragged that he would wrest a $1-billion contract to process the Texas medicaid claims. Perhaps nothing better revealed Perot's hubris. EDS had held the lucrative contract for eleven years, and when the contract came up for bid in 1988, EDS submitted eleven boxes of material to support its bid. Perot Systems had the temerity to submit six pages supporting its bid. Texas awarded the $1.1-billion contract to EDS, and said that Perot's bid failed to meet the basic requirements. Despite these setbacks, Perot believed that Perot Systems would be a $1-billion performer by the end of the 1990s. Most Wall Street observers felt Perot's motives in founding this new firm were highly personal. "It's revenge, pure and simple," said an analyst with Prudential-Bache. "He wants to get back at Roger Smith."

Perot also backed Steven Jobs[†] in his new computer venture, called Next, Incorporated. He invested $20 million in the computer whiz's project in 1987, and the first working model was introduced to the public in October 1988. Although critics were generally ecstatic about the product, it was far too early to tell whether it would catch on with the public, or whether Perot's investment would bear fruit. Certainly he could afford it. Perot had become exceptionally wealthy through his crusades. With a fortune estimated by *Forbes* at $3 billion, he could easily have relaxed. Or perhaps tried his hand at politics.

Long an advocate of a right-wing, super-patriotic Republicanism, Perot has espoused the kinds of ideals that Ronald Reagan put forth during his adminis-tration—initiative, hard work, old-fashioned reverence for home, country, and religion, and a profound distrust of bureaucracy. And Perot had that populist knack. But Perot always claimed he would make a bad politician, since he had no patience for "the red tape and the inactivity." That came across very clearly when Perot clashed with the Reagan administration. In 1987 he had traveled to Hanoi for secret talks with Vietnamese officials about U.S. soldiers missing in action. When he returned, he accused the Reagan administration of "arrogance," and he reneged on a $2-million pledge for the Reagan library. *Fortune* gave Perot its grudging admiration, calling him "A Billionaire for the Common Man." In their eyes, "He's the straight-talking cowboy willing to go it alone, fighting the nation's enemies both military and economic." Striking a similar pose, *Inc.* called Perot a "Cowboy Capitalist," but Perot was uncharacteristically subdued as 1989 dawned. He told *Newsweek* that his days of doing "huge jobs like the IRS or the Postal Service" were probably over. Furthermore, "I don't see myself as someone who can save the United States." (**B**. *Fortune*, November 1968, October 31, 1983, January 5, 1987; *New York Times*, November 28, 1969, December 26, 1986; *Newsweek*, April 13, 1970, December 15, 1986, February 9, 1987, October 24, 1988, January 9, 1989; *Current Biography*, 1971; *New York Times Magazine*, February 28, 1971; *Business Week*, March 27, 1971, March 28, 1973, January 26, 1974, October 6, 1986, June 20, July 11, September 26, 1988; *Forbes*, June 15, 1972, October 24, 1988; *Dun's Review*, March 1973; *Financial World*, January 9, 1974, February 15, 1975; Ken Follett, *On Wings of Eagles*, 1983; Stephen T. McClellan, *The Coming Computer Industry Shake-out*, 1984; *Wall Street Journal*, August 15, 1984; A. David Silver, *Entrepre-neurial Megabucks*, 1986; *Time*, December 8, 1986; *Reader's Digest*, September 1987; Toronto *Globe & Mail*, June 10, 1988; *Inc.*, January 1989.)

PETERSEN, DONALD EUGENE (September 4, 1926–). Automobile com-pany executive, Ford Motor Company. Headlining its article, "A Humble Hero," *Fortune* called Donald Petersen "Detroit's first Japanese-style chief executive." That at first seems a strange appellation for someone of Danish descent, born in Pipestone, Minnesota. What did *Fortune* mean? Robert Sobel, in his book *Car Wars: The Untold Story*, made the following comment about Japanese management compared to American: "Whereas Americans seem to strive to stand out from the crowd, their Japanese counterparts try to blend into their milieu. American executives often utilize the corporation as a vehicle for self-realization; the Japanese believe executives should serve the larger entity." Petersen, who adheres to the principle of participatory management, lives in less than baronial splendor in a condominium complex in a suburb of Detroit. He once said that he "figured if he ever made a couple of hundred dollars a month, [he would] really have it made." In 1987, his total compensation was a very un-Japanese $4 million.

Donald Petersen's father was a wheat farmer. Since his father suffered from asthma, when Donald was two years old, the family moved to the drier climate of Long Beach, California. The elder Petersen drifted from job to job, struggling to make ends meet in California, a process that became increasingly difficult with the onset of the Great Depression. Finally, in about 1937, the family settled in Portland, Oregon, where Mr. Petersen found a job selling service-station equipment on a commission basis. Donald went to high school in Portland, where he played football and basketball, and he also proved to be an exceptional student. But all those years of moving around, of economic deprivation and uncertainty, had affected Petersen. More than anything, it caused him to embrace the imperatives of the Protestant work ethic, and to find a job with a large corporation that would offer economic security, rather than become involved in his own business venture.

In any event, Donald "Pete" Petersen went to the University of Washington, where he graduated with a degree in mechanical engineering and a Phi Beta Kappa key in 1946. During this same time, he had served a stint in the U.S. Marine Corps in World War II. After graduating, Petersen worked on a farm to earn some money, and then he enrolled in the MBA program at Stanford University. After he graduated in 1949, he traveled to Dearborn, Michigan, for an interview with the Ford Motor Company. He tells a story of missing the bus stop and convincing the bus driver to drop him off by the side of the highway. Petersen then hurled his suitcase over a fence and walked to the Ford administration building. He recalled, "I was dusty, but they liked me." They liked him enough to offer him $300 a month, an exceptionally high salary for the time, and they put him to work as a product planner.

Ford Motor Company was quite an environment for a young engineer in the late 1940s and early 1950s. Henry Ford II* in 1945 had taken over the company from his grandfather, Henry Ford.* The firm had just gone through a horrendous two decades. Jack Davis, a young Ford executive, said the company was not just dying, "It was already completely dead, and *rigor mortis* was setting in." Henry Ford, the greatest pioneer in the American auto industry, watched his company begin to fall behind General Motors (GM) in the 1920s. In the early years of the decade, Ford made about half of all the cars sold in America, and GM about one-quarter. By the mid–1930s, the proportions were reversed, and

Ford even fell behind Chrysler to become the number three automaker. World War II brought expansion and profits to Ford by making war materials, but the end of the war boded ill for the company.

Ford Motor was losing $9.5 million a month when Henry II took over, and there had never been an audit in the company's history. It had been run as a personal fiefdom of Harry Bennett, the elder Ford's assistant, and it had a horrible record of productivity and labor relations. Addressing himself to these problems, Henry Ford II fired 1,000 Ford executives, many of them Bennett's cronies, sold the Brazilian rubber plantations, soybean farms, and timber tracts, and began to concentrate on building cars. To do this, he brought in a new president, Ernest R. Breech, an ex-GM man from Bendix Corporation, along with a bright group of young men who were called the "Whiz Kids." They reorganized and decentralized the highly autocratic company (although not to the extreme that GM did), set up an audit system, and began to automate the plants, which raised productivity and efficiency greatly. In 1946, the company also signed an agreement with the United Auto Workers (UAW), getting a union guarantee against illegal strikes, and granting a number of important concessions to the workers. Most important, in 1947, Breech and Henry II decided to bring out an all-new car in 1949, the first major postwar innovation in the industry. The model sold over 800,000 units in 1949, giving Ford its biggest year since 1929, and the firm made a profit of $265 million. So Donald Petersen arrived at Ford at the flood tide, a time of enormous optimism and excitement for the future, a time when new blood was being infused into the management structure, and, most important, a time when a dramatic and innovative new car, one that was strikingly more aerodynamic than the competition, brought great profits, thereby saving the company's future.

But when Petersen joined Ford, the organization was still in its rudimentary stages in many respects. One reason he was hired initially was that he had said he was interested in what he called "product planning." Ford's own planning department at this time barely existed, so when he was hired, the young engineer was given the responsibility for creating a far more sophisticated product planning office. As a product planner, he was what *Fortune* called "a kind of conductor who orchestrated Ford's future cars by coordinating design, engineering, and finance." It was heady stuff for a twenty-three-year-old. He found strong pockets of resistance to his ideas from many of the entrenched staff, particularly from those in engineering, who were employees during the pre-war Ford days. As Petersen later recalled, "At that time, most of the engineers were master mechanics from the shop floor. They decided what was needed for the next year, did it, and told the sales department: 'This is the new model.' "

On Petersen's side, against this old guard of craftsmen-engineers were the whiz kids—Charles "Tex" Thornton,* Arjay Miller, "Ed" Lundy, Francis Reith, Robert MacNamara,* Wilbur Anderson, Charles Bosworth, Ben Davis Mills, George Moore, and James Wright, all veterans of the Office of Statistical Control in the army during World War II. With the support of Ernest Breech, these young men revolutionized Ford during the decade after the war, and Petersen, although a very junior, fringe member of the group, was given increasing responsibility and control. But the most important man for Petersen's career was neither young nor a whiz kid. He was Lewis D. Crusoe, a nearly legendary GM executive whom Breech had lured out of semiretirement. As one young executive at the time said of Crusoe, "He inspired great loyalty because unlike so many other executives he wasn't just pushing himself forward. When you worked for him, you were *making cars*." Not insignificantly, many people used this same line for Donald Petersen years later.

Crusoe was responsible for keeping the whiz kids in line. While Thornton pushed his ideas of organization and systematization at Ford, Crusoe always tempered that with what he called the "realities" of the auto business. When Thornton pushed too hard, Breech fired him, and Crusoe was given more power when he was appointed head of a new Ford division and made responsible for the development and sales of all Ford cars. The division had its own engineering and finance people, and its own sales staff. That made Crusoe, in some respects, the most powerful man in the company in the late 1940s and early 1950s. He then set up an executive training program for a number of bright young recruits, including Donald Petersen and Philip Caldwell, another future head of Ford. Crusoe created a special sense of élan with the young men he gathered around him.

Crusoe's group in these early years were "product" men, who were allied against the "bean counters" like Robert MacNamara. Whereas men like MacNamara had little feel for the product, Petersen and other members of Crusoe's group were taught to have "gasoline in their veins." As Gene Bordinat, a member of this group who later became a great Ford stylist, said, "To be a good product man you have to be ruled in part by your emotions. We assume that all cars *work*. But people *buy* cars, the product man understands, because they see in them *something that turns them on*."

As America entered the 1950s, a great consumer culture was emerging, and the automobile was a seminal part of it. The era was an automan's heaven, what Robert Sobel has called the "Age of Detroit Baroque," replete with chrome, gadgets, and every option imaginable. Although cars still had to be functional, it was now far more important that they be status symbols of the wealth and power of American society. It was a triumph of style over function, of sizzle over steak. It was in this environment that Petersen, after a short stint in the Marines during the Korean War, had his biggest thrill to that time. He became part of the team that created the legendary Ford Thunderbird.

Ford had been created, and had grown and prospered, by making cars for the masses. But Americans in the 1950s wanted something more than just utilitarian; they wanted luxury, power, speed—or, more to the point—they at least wanted the illusion of these things. Crusoe understood that well, and when he learned that Chevrolet was building a sports car called the Corvette, he challenged it. Arguing that his dream car would never pay for itself with mass sales, but rather it should be seen as an "apple in the window," Crusoe wanted to create a stunning machine that would cause stampedes into dealers' showrooms. But unlike the Corvette, which was designed and built by GM from the ground up, the Thunderbird was built as inexpensively as possible—it was a great triumph of illusion over substance. As Crusoe insisted, the car was not really a sports car at all, but "a boulevard car for the customer who insists on comfort and yet would like to own a prestige vehicle that incorporates the flair and performance characteristics of a sports car." Crusoe was right, and the car was a great success as a small car; it sold 15,000 units in 1955. Then, with Crusoe's consent, it was made longer and wider, until it became more of a jazzed-up two-door sedan than a sports car. Because of this success, Petersen and his colleagues came to be known as the "legendary team" who built the Thunderbird at Ford, and it propelled him rapidly up the corporate ladder.

In the early 1960s, when Lee Iacocca,* Henry II's "fair-haired boy," was given responsibility to develop a new model for Ford in the wake of the Edsel debacle, he carefully constructed what was called his "Mustang Team," in recognition of the car they ultimately created. Because of his great success with the Thunderbird, Petersen was chosen for the Mustang team. When the Mustang was introduced, it was a phenomenal success; it sold over 418,000 units in the first year and added over half a billion dollars to the company's sales. It went on to become Ford's all-time most successful car model. When Iacocca wanted to bring out a compact car to compete with the small Japanese cars, he again chose Petersen for the team to create the Maverick. This car was also very successful. In addition, Petersen helped design the LTD, a large, six-passenger family sedan. Finally, he held a number of positions in marketing planning, and headed the product planning and design staff during the 1960s.

During the latter half of the 1960s, Petersen began to receive promotions to positions that gave him a wide variety of managerial experience. He first served as vice president of car planning and research from 1969 to 1971, and then was vice president and manager of the truck and recreational vehicle products division from 1971 to 1975. Although Petersen was accomplished, and was moving to positions of high authority, he despised the highly charged political atmosphere at Ford. A company made up of colorful personalities and large egos, headed by an increasingly autocratic Henry Ford II, fear and envy were the ruling emotions. Petersen later recalled, "Those days built into me a strong desire to see things work differently, a strong desire to stop all the fighting, backbiting, and working to prove the other guy is wrong." These feelings were so strong in Petersen that he twice quit the company during this time, when he felt his bosses were more concerned with office politics than with building good cars.

In April 1979, Petersen was named executive vice president of the powerful International Automotive Operations Division, and later in the year was also elected to Ford's board of directors. Ford Motor Company had put a great deal of effort into building a powerful base in the European market after World War II, and as a result, it became the dominant American auto company there. Because of that, the executive vice presidency for international operations was always considered a stepping-stone to the presidency of Ford. Petersen was on the fast track, and his accomplishments there, in 1979, did nothing to tarnish his reputation. At a time when the parent company was floundering and losing oceans of money, Petersen was running the only profitable division in the firm.

Henry Ford II had fired his heir apparent, Lee Iacocca, in 1978, who in turn took many Ford executives with him to Chrysler. During the next two years, Ford stumbled badly. The problems started in 1978, with the $40-million "voluntary" recall of 1.7 million Ford Pintos, just ahead of proposed government action. Because the Pinto had a tendency to explode if struck from behind by another car, the recall made modifications to the gas filler neck and cap. That incident was simply symptomatic of fundamental problems. As one Ford executive commented, "Our quality was so bad, it was getting embarrassing to go to cocktail parties and tell them where you worked." Ford cars were getting a reputation for being unsafe and being of poor quality, and as a result, domestic sales tapered off badly. In February 1981, the company announced that its losses for 1980 totaled $1.5 billion, the largest ever for an American corporation. Suddenly placed in a situation where it had to play catch-up in developing smaller, fuel-efficient cars, Ford also had to double its debt in 1980, while working capital declined by a whopping 79 percent. Ford's market share, traditionally around 23 percent, dropped to a low of 16 percent in 1981. The future looked terribly grim for Ford Motor when Henry II finally retired as chairman on March 13, 1980. A new era was about to begin at the company, the first in which the firm was not to be run by members of the Ford family.

Chosen as new chairman and chief executive of Ford was Philip Caldwell, and the new president and chief operating officer was Donald Petersen. There was no question that the two men would have their hands full, and most industry analysts were not optimistic that they would be able to turn the company around. But Caldwell and Petersen geared up to effect one of the most dramatic restructuring programs in American industrial history. The first part of this turnaround was a $3-billion gamble on a new line of cars. Since the 1960s Petersen had been pushing Ford to make smaller, more fuel-efficient automobiles, but no one had listened to him. Now, with the company on the ropes, there was little choice but to make a dramatic move. Petersen, fresh from his experience in the European market, visualized a wholly new line of Ford cars that would be sleeker, more aerodynamic, and more European looking. Pledging full corporate backing to Ford's designers, he urged them to produce cars that they themselves would be proud to own.

The changeover took a number of years, but the first fruits of it came in 1983, when Ford redesigned the Thunderbird. Although it was originally a sleek-looking car in the 1950s, by the early 1980s it had become, like most other American cars, large and boxy. The new Thunderbird was smaller, sleeker, and much more European in styling. The reaction of other industry executives was contemptuous; they derided the Thunderbird's "jellybean" shape and claimed the American consumer would never go for anything so radically different. But *Fortune* in December 1985 commented that the Thunderbird was a virtually "new model that reversed the long slide for the [T-Bird] nameplate." Thunderbird's sales jumped dramatically, and it was becoming increasingly clear that Petersen and his staff had a winner.

Petersen's next step was to take the Ford Escort, a subcompact that was a big seller in the European market, and begin pushing it in America. Escort soon became the world's best-selling car, and it helped set the stage for greater company sales and profits. Then, in 1985, Petersen brought out the crown jewels of his new line of "Eurostyled" cars—the Ford Taurus and Mercury Sable—to replace the boxy Ford LTD and Mercury Marquis. Industry response was ecstatic. *Car and Driver* called them "the most agile and capable sedan Detroit has ever produced" and the equivalent of "the best German sedans."

Ford's reputation for producing poor-quality cars began to change dramatically under Petersen. He stressed to other company officials that productivity and quality were not antithetical, but must, in fact, go hand in hand. "In so many ways you can see how quality and productivity go together," he said. "The poorest productivity operations in any manufacturing set-up are those that have quality problems." Adopting the slogan, "Quality Is Job One," for Ford's advertising, Petersen made it a reality on the shop floor. He met almost endlessly with managers, giving them sermons on teamwork and quality. He also visited factories to hear workers' ideas on what Ford should do, and he stressed that management was receptive to ideas that trickled up from the rank and file. Significantly, Peterson hired quality and productivity guru W. Edwards Demming, who had been a prophet without honor in his own country, but had gone to Japan to work with industry there. Demming was given the assignment of reversing Ford's sagging productivity. As Philip Caldwell told *Fortune*, "We stopped shipping products if an employee on the floor said they weren't right, and stopped penalizing people if they didn't make their quotas because of worries about quality. That was a radical departure for Ford." As a result, the *Wall Street Journal* (February 24) in 1987 reported that "Independent ratings of automobile quality now rank Ford first among domestic automakers."

But Petersen and Caldwell also had to take drastic action to cut costs during the first few years. They closed fifteen plants worldwide, laid off 50,000 blue-collar workers, and eliminated many white-collar jobs. Over a five-year period, these cuts saved the company about $4.5 billion. Consequently, both Ford's sales and earnings began to climb dramatically. In 1984, Ford had sales of $52 billion worldwide, with earnings of $2.9 billion, its best year ever. Shortly after that announcement, Donald Petersen advanced to the positions of chairman and chief executive officer of Ford. The results of his first two years of operating the firm were impressive. In 1986, Ford had profits of $3.3 billion on sales of $63 billion. Since GM's earnings were just $2.9 billion, it marked the first time since 1924 that Ford had recorded higher profits than GM. In 1987, Ford had worldwide sales of $71.6 billion, up 14 percent from 1986, and earnings of $4.6

billion. That was 41 percent higher than the record earnings of 1986, and more than $1 billion greater than GM's. With 70 percent of GM's sales, Ford had less than one-half as many employees, and far higher profits. Furthermore, the $4.6 billion in earnings was the best ever for any automobile company. It was an extraordinary success story.

But Petersen had even more dramatic plans in store for Ford in the future. By the time he reaches mandatory retirement age in 1991, he hopes to set up what he calls "centers of excellence," which will be designed to bring about global integration of the company's widespread factories and design studios. The principal concept is that each Ford operating group should be allowed to do what it does best. In that way, duplication of design will be avoided, and truly "world cars" will be produced. Some industry analysts, however, remain skeptical of the program, feeling that there are too many different markets, with too many different needs, for the plan to work effectively.

As far as the domestic market is concerned, Petersen has adopted a cautious strategy. Despite the great popularity of the Taurus and the Sable, and the general boom in auto sales in 1986 and 1987, Petersen refused to expand facilities. Instead, he continued to pare costs and keep production facilities to the minimum. A number of analysts were surprised at this, but Petersen commented,

I hate losing share, to me it's like drops of blood on the floor. When you consider all that's happening and all that is going to happen and the extraordinary explosion of competition, I think first it's valid for us to aspire to be a 20 percent company in the car business. . . . I think anything beyond that on a just-in-case basis, with all the uncertainties, would be unsound. (*Forbes*, December 15, 1986)

The attitude and the strategy are very different from the egoistic approaches of earlier Ford heads, and very different from GM under Roger Smith.† Smith consciously sacrificed profitability to maintain high production levels and market share. By 1989, as the automobile market began to cool down, GM faced a massive production glut. Ford, although it also had some excess capacity, was in far better shape for the early 1990s, according to *Business Week*.

Donald Petersen, modest and unassuming, made Ford Motor Company into the world's most profitable car company—a feat almost everyone agrees was the comeback story of the decade. A reporter for the Detroit *Free Press* has called Petersen a "shirt-sleeves populist who spends long hours visiting factories, huddling with designers and encouraging employee suggestions on everything from assembly-line changes to dashboard design." Petersen reminds one of what Whitney Young, head of the National Urban League, said of Henry Ford II: "He's not your typical great man. His greatness—if you could call it that—sort of sneaks up on you." (**B**. *Business Week*, March 31, 1980, November 12, 1984, February 11, 1985, March 16, 1987, February 13, March 6, 1989; *Motor Trend*, October 1980; Victor Lasky, *Never Complain, Never Explain: The Story of Henry Ford II*, 1981; *Automotive Industries*, February 1982; Brock Yates,

The Decline and Fall of the American Automobile Industry, 1983; John B. Rae, *The American Automobile Industry*, 1984; Robert Sobel, *Car Wars: The Untold Story*, 1984; *Wall Street Journal*, October 26, 1984, February 24, 1987; *Automotive News*, November 5, 1984; *Fortune*, November 26, 1984, December 23, 1985, August 3, 1987, January 4, 1988; *Contemporary Newsmakers*, 1985; *Car Magazine*, January 1985; *Ward's Auto World*, March 1985; Car and Driver, October 1985; Robert Lacey, *Ford: The Men and the Machine*, 1986; *Forbes*, December 15, 1986, December 28, 1987; Peter Collier and David Horowitz, *The Fords: An American Epic*, 1987; Davis Dyer et al., *Changing Alliances*, 1987; Douglas K. Ramsey, *The Corporate Warriors*, 1987; *Current Biography*, 1988; *New York Times*, February 19, 1988; *Newsweek*, February 20, 1989.)

PICKENS, THOMAS BOONE (May 22, 1928–). Oil company executive, corporate raider, Mesa Petroleum Company. Eric W. Allison, in his book on corporate raiders, calls T. Boone Pickens the "Wolf of the Oil Patch," and that is one of the nicer names he's been called in recent years. Harold Hammer, executive vice president of Gulf Oil snorted, "Who is Pickens anyway? Everything he says is horse—and hot air." Fred Hartley, chairman of Unocal Oil, which Pickens tried to take over in 1985, treated him as if he had leprosy. The two men met outside a congressional hearing room; Pickens extended his hand to Hartley. "Go away," Hartley snarled. Pickens blandly replied, "Fred, you're talkin' to your largest stockholder." Not impressed, Hartley growled back at him, "Isn't that a shame." Later, Hartley vented his spleen to the press: "He's an investor not because he thinks we're a good company, but because he thinks he's gonna rape us one way or the other." But Pickens always seems to get the last laugh. Usually failing to acquire companies he attempts to take over, Pickens and Mesa Petroleum wind up with enormous "greenmail" payments. Pickens responded to the "Good Ol' Boys" of the Oil Patch and their vitriolic condemnation of him by writing his autobiography. In it, Pickens presents himself as the champion of the small shareholder in his takeover attempts, and he condemns the executives of the big oil companies for doing little for their operations other than to demand expensive perks. Pickens' book became a best-seller, the most successful of that year's crop of business books.

Pickens was born in the small cattle town of Holdenville, Oklahoma, the son of Thomas Boone Pickens, Sr., and a distant descendant of Daniel Boone. Holdenville was a tough place during the 1930s when young Pickens was growing up. In east central Oklahoma, it was the land of the dust bowl in those years, the place the "Okies" were leaving. But there was also oil around Holdenville, and Pickens' father was an independent oil man. He bought and sold oil leases, making and losing a fortune in the process. He always had a gambling instinct, but the necessity to feed and clothe his family during the depression forced him to take a job as a lease broker for Phillips Petroleum. Pickens' mother, on the other hand, was a supremely rational individual, who helped maintain a practical balance in the family. As a result, young Pickens said, "I was very fortunate in my gene mix, the gambling instincts I inherited from my father were matched by my mother's gift for analysis.''

In the mid–1940s, when Pickens was in high school, his family moved to Amarillo, Texas. There, Pickens made a name for himself as a basketball player, which got him an athletic scholarship to Texas A&M University. His career in basketball and his studies at Texas A&M were short lived. He broke his elbow, lost his scholarship, and left school after only one year. He transferred to Oklahoma State University, where he majored in geology and spent two years on the dean's list. After he got his bachelor's in 1951, Pickens landed a job at Phillips Petroleum, no doubt aided by the fact that his father worked there. ''Boone'' and his young wife headed for Bartlesville, Oklahoma, the home of Phillips' head office. A small city of about 40,000, Bartlesville was essentially a company town, and Pickens soon felt stifled there. No one would listen to his ideas, and he was enormously frustrated with the company's conservatism. After four years, Pickens abruptly quit. He used the lump-sum payment of $1,300 he received from Philips' profit-sharing plan to buy a station wagon, which he loaded up with oil exploration equipment, and he struck out on his own.

The first year was very rough, since Pickens was unable to get any financial backing. But, in 1956, his wife's uncle came up with a $50,000 line of credit, and Pickens negotiated another $50,000 line of credit from other sources, which he added to $2,500 of his own money. He founded what he then called the Petroleum Exploration Company, based in Amarillo. What Pickens possessed was what a *New York Times* reporter called ''an uncanny ability to find oil and gas.'' The more oil and gas Pickens found, the more investors he attracted, and the harder and longer he worked each day. During this time, the company continued to grow, and in 1964 Pickens incorporated it as Mesa Petroleum.

Mesa concentrated on what is called the ''upstream'' aspect of the oil industry—the drilling, exploration, and production of crude oil, which was sold to other refining and distribution companies. Some of Pickens' oil finds during these years are legendary. One was a $35,000 investment in some Canadian drilling sites in 1959 that turned into an enormous field of gushers. He used the money from the first wells to finance the drilling of new wells, and after twenty years of continual profits, Pickens sold his Canadian operations to Dome Petroleum for $600 million. People were not only impressed at the profit Pickens made on this deal, but they were even more impressed with his timing. At the time Pickens sold, Canada was regarded as an ideal area for investment in oil and gas properties, and many could not understand why Pickens wanted to sell. A few months later, the Canadian government announced a new energy policy, which severely restricted American investment in the Canadian oil industry. Pickens was the only American oil man to get out before the announcement.

The Canadian operations were just part of a highly profitable company Pickens had created, and by 1969 Mesa had grown large and powerful enough to pursue its first acquisition. In that year, Pickens successfully bid for Hugoton Production Oil Company, which was twenty times the size of Mesa. With a vast gas field north of Amarillo, Hugoton greatly expanded Mesa's exploration and production operations. A year later, Pickens went after the Southland Royalty Company, but he was unsuccessful. In 1973, he took over another small oil company, Pubco Petroleum. In 1976, Pickens tried to acquire Aztec Corporation, a natural gas producer that he coveted. He was doubly stung in this deal. Not only did Pickens not get Aztec, but he lost it to Southland Royalty, his takeover target of six years earlier. By the end of the 1970s, Mesa was, to the extent it was known at all outside the Oil Patch, recognized as a profitable oil and gas company, but certainly not one of the majors.

In 1979, an important turning point for Pickens and Mesa, Mesa had made a good deal of money by pulling out of some operations. In addition to getting $600 million for his Canadian operations, Pickens sold Mesa's North Sea finds for $65 million. Pickens was convinced that the oil industry was on the verge of entering a down cycle, and he wanted to protect Mesa in this new environment. He believed that the costs of oil and gas exploration had become prohibitive, and that Mesa was going to have to gain new oil reserves in another way. As he told the *New York Times* in 1982, "We're not going to commit big dollars to exploration. We're going to commit big dollars to acquisition." As a first step in this direction, Pickens created a unique and complex instrument—Mesa Royalty Trust—a "brand new wrinkle in an old business."

On November 1, 1979, every Mesa shareholder received a unit of Royalty Trust for each Mesa share owned; Mesa retained 10 percent of the trust units. When producing properties are put in a trust, the company's management is no longer able to decide how to spend the cash flow from those properties. As a result, the company's reserves rapidly deplete, without replacement by exploration, which also means that the firm is far more profitable, at least in the short run. The royalty trust is also a way of avoiding double taxation, since the proceeds are taxed only in the shareholders' hands; there are no corporate taxes. It was an ingenious way for Pickens to get at least some of the profits of Mesa directly into the hands of the shareholders, and at the same time to pose as a great champion of the small shareholder. This latter factor would be of great benefit to him in his later takeover attempts. Over the next several years, Mesa earned extraordinarily high profits; its stock price was nearly 50 percent higher three months later. By 1982 Pickens was ready to make his first run at one of the industry giants.

On May 31, 1982, Pickens made a bid for Cities Service Company, an Oklahoma-based oil company about twenty times the size of Mesa. The raid made Pickens' name well known on Wall Street and on the business pages of America, but he was still considered a bit of a neophyte. At the time of his bid, Mesa already owned 5 percent of Cities Service's shares and offered $50 a share for enough additional shares to raise Mesa's holdings to 51 percent. Cities Service countered with what is called a "Pac-Man" defense—that is, it began to buy up shares in Mesa. With assets far in excess of Mesa's it looked for a time as if Pickens' first attempt at a large-scale takeover would result in his losing control of Mesa. At the last moment, however, a "white knight" appeared, when Gulf Oil agreed to take over Cities Service. This deal fell through, but Occidental Petroleum stepped in as the new white knight. Pickens and Mesa made a profit of $44 million on an investment of $182 million in this attempted takeover. It had been touch and go for a time, but Pickens learned how much profit could be made in these takeover deals—even if you "lost."

Despite the impressive profits, however, Pickens had not succeeded in picking up any fresh oil reserves for Mesa. So, in December 1982, he made his second takeover attempt. Pickens made a $520-million bid for 51 percent of General American Oil Company, a firm just slightly smaller than Mesa, but one that had especially rich domestic oil reserves. Since General American did not have Cities Service's resources, it looked as if Pickens had a good chance to succeed in this acquisition. But General American, like Cities Service, reacted with utter horror at the prospect of Pickens taking it over. The chairman of General American announced he was seeking a white knight to protect the company from Pickens. An impressive array of tactics was employed by General American to thwart Pickens, who finally responded by filing suit in federal court, charging General American with "kamikaze defensive tactics." Pickens withdrew the suit in January when Phillips Petroleum made a $1.2-billion offer for General American. General American had found its white knight, and like Cities Service, it chose dismemberment within an oil giant rather than a takeover by Pickens. Pickens had failed again, but Mesa was well rewarded; this time it made a $25-million profit on an investment of just $32 million.

The question began to emerge as to why these oil companies reacted so negatively when Pickens announced a takeover. He was, after all, a practical oil man himself, not a freebooting, divestiture expert like Irwin Jacobs. The answer, according to Eric Allison, was that Pickens was too much of a renegade: "He was a pirate, an outsider, despite his credentials, because he was engaged in *hostile* takeovers." The chairman of Aztec Oil concurred, "Engaging in hostile takeovers like this is buccaneering of the worst kind." Perhaps even more revealing, George Keller, the chairman of Chevron, said, "Pickens does not break any laws doing what he does. But he breaks tradition." "Big oil," Pickens responded, "is a club." And it is a club that does not tolerate heretics. Pickens, even though he was a staunch Reagan Republican, was the ultimate heretic. In championing the rights of the small shareholder, he attacked the executives, the "club members" of Big Oil, mercilessly. "Chief executives," Pickens said, "who themselves own few shares of their companies have no more feeling for the average stockholder than they do for the baboons of Africa."

Pickens wasted no time hunting down his next prey. In early 1983 he went after Superior Oil Company. With over 1 billion barrels of oil and gas in the ground, Superior had the kind of reserves that Mesa so desperately needed. Founded by William "Bill" Keck, perhaps the greatest wildcatter of all time, Superior had become one of the best oil companies in the world. When Keck died, the firm was passed to his children, and family quarrels soon dissipated its energies. In the early 1980s a new chief executive officer began turning the company around, making it more attractive to raiders like Pickens. As soon as Pickens bought 2 percent of the company's shares, management enacted a series of anti-takeover moves. Ultimately, Pickens accepted a substantial profit—in effect, greenmail—to sell his shares back to the company, and Superior was later acquired by Mobil Oil in a friendly takeover.

Pickens saved his real firepower for late 1983 and 1984, when he announced his intention of taking over giant Gulf Oil Company. Founded by the Mellon* family of Pittsburgh, Gulf had long been one of the integrated giants of the industry, but it had also been mismanaged for many years. The fifth largest American oil company, Gulf was seventy-five times the size of Mesa, but management had made a number of errors in recent years that had cut deeply into the company's reserves. Consequently, its stock was selling at only about $40, which, from a raider's point of view, made Gulf an ideal target. It was undervalued, since asset appraisal pegged the value of the company's shares, based on assets, at $114. Gulf was too big for Pickens and Mesa to tackle alone, so he took in a number of powerful partners—Michael Boswell of Sunshine Mining, the Belzberg brothers of Canada, and a number of Texas oil men. After a short time, Mesa and the Mesa-affiliated Gulf Investors Group had bought 12.1 percent of Gulf stock for $790 million. Ultimately, they planned to buy about 15 percent of Gulf's stock for a cost of $1.1 billion, and Mesa was responsible for supplying $700 million of that.

Pickens proposed that Gulf set up a royalty trust and then spin off its oil and gas properties into the trust, whose shares could then be traded like stock. This would allow a large and immediate profit to be paid to Gulf shareholders, one that avoided dual taxation. The predictions were that this would make Gulf attractive enough to raise its share price immediately to about $70. The management of Gulf did not appreciate what they viewed as his "meddling," and they vowed to fight Pickens all the way. Harold Hammer, Gulf's executive vice president, who was made point man in the war against Pickens, announced that Pickens' idea of a royalty trust was "a dumb idea that would mutilate Gulf Oil." In January 1984, Pickens offered Gulf's stockholders $55 a share for all outstanding Gulf stock. At that point, another bidder emerged—Atlantic Richfield Company (Arco). Arco's chairman, Robert O. Anderson, offered $70 a share for Gulf, for a total package of $11.7 billion.

Pickens knew that he had to increase his bid, but he needed additional funds to do so. He sold $300 million worth of Mesa to Penn Central Corporation to help finance a counteroffer. Pickens then tendered for 13.5 million Gulf shares at $65. Gulf's board called Pickens' offer "unfair and inadequate" and asked for alternative bids from other sources. Ultimately, Standard Oil of California (SoCal) won the bidding with an offer of $80 a share, a figure far too rich for Pickens' blood. The new company was renamed Chevron, and Pickens and his partners walked away from this "failure" with a profit of $760 million. Every time Pickens lost a takeover attempt, he ended up with such enormous profits that he had more money to tackle even larger targets the next time. His next target was Phillips Petroleum, Pickens' first employer—the "mother company."

In December 1984, Pickens proposed a tender offer for 15 percent of Phillips outstanding shares at $60 a share. He already owned 5.7 percent of the company. Phillips, whose stock was selling at just a little over $40 at the time, was another company ripe for takeover. It had $1 billion in cash in its treasury, and the breakup value of the company was somewhere between $70 and $80 a share. Phillips, like the other Big Oil companies, had no intention of allowing Pickens to take it over. But Pickens had new allies. In his quest for Gulf Oil, Pickens had turned to Michael Milken[†] of Drexel Burnham Lambert, who had astounded Wall Street by raising $1.7 billion for Pickens in the space of a few days through junk-bond financing. Pickens knew he had discovered a new source of enormous, perhaps almost unlimited, capital. Rather than submit to Pickens, however, Phillips resorted to what is called the "poison pill" defense—that is, it put together a recapitalization plan that doubled the firm's long-term debt, making the takeover cost prohibitive for Pickens. Phillips then offered to buy back Pickens' shares for a pretax profit of $75 million, plus $25 million for expenses. Pickens agreed, and he abandoned his raid on Phillips. It appeared to most people to be a classic case of greenmail, and it further tarnished Pickens' reputation in the oil industry. On Wall Street, however, there was "unqualified admiration" for Pickens' "ability to come out ahead—and improve the lot of all Phillips' shareholders in the process."

Soon after Pickens walked away from the Phillips takeover attempt with large profits, he made a raid on Unocal, the thirteenth largest oil company in the United States. By early March 1985, Mesa and Pickens had accumulated 10 percent of the company's stock, and Unocal's chairman, Fred Hartley, reacted with typical Oil Patch hostility. Appearing before a congressional committee investigating oil firm takeovers, Hartley launched into an impassioned attack on Pickens: "Mr. Pickens has somehow created a speculative frenzy that has convinced his camp followers that there's easy money to be made attacking oil companies and to hell with tomorrow." That was not all: "Too many fine oil companies have already been destroyed, or nearly so, by Mr. Pickens and his ilk," said Hartley. "The beneficiaries of Pickens' actions are not America's energy consumers, America's security, or even small shareholders, but rather only a handful of shareholders—and, of course, Mr. Pickens."

Pickens was not fazed; he offered $55 a share for 64 million shares of Unocal. Hartley rejected Pickens' bid as "grossly inadequate," and he countered with an offer to buy all outstanding Unocal stock, except Pickens', for $72. Pickens brought suit, but the Delaware Supreme Court upheld Unocal's unorthodox plan. To cut his losses, Pickens had to strike a deal with Hartley. He managed to get an agreement from Hartley to buy two-thirds of Pickens' shares for $72, but industry analysts estimated that Pickens and Mesa suffered a pretax loss of $100 million. Pickens' immediate reaction was to say, "You can't hit a home run every time you come to bat." Later it was clear that Pickens had been stung not only by the loss, but also by the vehemence of the personal attack on him. He commented to *Barron's* about Hartley,

He called me a Commie, a barbarian, all kinds of stuff. I mean, that was his thanks to somebody that had put a billion dollars in his company. I wouldn't consider doing that, even if somebody I didn't like came in and bought a billion-dollars worth of Mesa stock.

Despite the loss, Pickens did not give up his hunt for oil firms. In January 1986, he made a hostile offer for KN Energy Incorporated (after its board rejected his earlier friendly overtures), a natural gas distribution company, and about a month later he announced plans for a friendly takeover of Pioneer Corporation, an oil and gas producer in Amarillo. For a change, management in this case welcomed Pickens' bid. As Allison wrote, "Those who wrote off Pickens after Unocal have another think [sic] coming." In 1987, Pickens offered $2 billion in cash for Diamond Shamrock, only to be turned down flatly by that firm's board of directors. Pickens also attempted to diversify Mesa in 1987 by taking positions in Newmont Mining Corporation, the Singer Company, and—in a move that profoundly shocked Wall Street—the Boeing Company.

Pickens made his next takeover attempt in the oil industry in 1988, when he bid for 15 percent of giant Texaco, in conjunction with Carl Icahn,[†] who already owned 15 percent of its stock. Texaco, the nation's third largest oil company, faced an uncertain future in 1988. No one knew for sure where Pickens and Mesa Oil were heading, but an executive of a longtime opponent of his in his takeover attempts, Morgan Stanley Bank, said that "he's a very smart guy and somehow he always lands on his feet." Pickens fancies himself as the savior of American capitalism. In an interview with *Reason*, Pickens said;

Right now, you've got these same crybabies around in Washington telling about how they're under so much pressure from takeovers. They say they have rusting-out plants and everything else because they have had to have quarter-by-quarter comparisons and they couldn't rebuild. That's hogwash. They've had great opportunities to rebuild their plants and modernize. But they haven't done it, because they are very greedy personally, and they've let their employee count go down. (*Fortune*, August 5, 1985)

The implication is clear: American CEOs better watch out; the wolf is waiting just outside their doors. (**A.** T. Boone Pickens, *Boone*, 1987. **B.** *New York Times*, June 7, December 21, 1982. March 5, 1985, February 19, 1988; *Business Week*, April 15, 1983, June 3, 1985, February 27, 1989; *Fortune*, November 14, December 26, 1983, January 21, May 13, August 5, 1985; *Financial World*, December 31, 1983; *Barron's*, June 18, December 31, 1984; *Current Biography* 1985; *Harper's*, January 1985; *Time*, January 14, March 4, 1985; *Forbes*, April 8, 1985; Eric W. Allison, *The Raiders of Wall Street*, 1986; Moira Johnston, *Takeover: The New Wall Street Warriors*, 1986; *Who's Who in America* 1986–87; *Reason*, August/September 1987.)

POPE, GENEROSO PAUL, JR. (January 13, 1927–October 2, 1988). Publisher, *National Enquirer*. Gene Pope, a cautious, conservative man who drove a five-year-old Caprice, worked seven days a week, and never took a vacation, introduced America to such newspaper headlines as "Mom Uses Son's Face for an Ashtray!" and "Mom Boiled Her Baby and Ate Her!" in his *National Enquirer,* the best-selling publication in America after *TV Guide*. Although Pope did not invent the lurid tabloid, he brought to it a certain respectability when his tabloid invaded the supermarket checkout and became a staple of the average American household. Few people ever admit they buy *National Enquirer*, mentioning instead that they had "just happened to notice a story in the paper" while waiting in line to pay for their groceries. With a weekly circulation of 4.5 million in 1988, however, it was clear *somebody* was buying *National Enquirer*.

Pope was born in the Bronx, the son of Generoso Pope, an Italian immigrant who arrived in New York in the early years of the century with just $4 in his pocket. The elder Pope worked his way up from water boy to president of the city's leading sand and gravel company. To consolidate his considerable political clout, he bought *Il Progresso*, the largest Italian language newspaper in the United States, and radio station WHOM. In the turbulent Italian-American community of the 1930s, Gene Pope's father became a power in the New York Italian community, and, until the fall of Mussolini, he was an obedient Fascist. The elder Pope became embroiled in a bitter feud with Carlo Tesca, an Italian-born anarchist editor, who was shot to death on a New York street in 1943. Although the murder was never solved, community suspicion often pointed toward Pope and his Fascist cronies.

Gene Pope graduated from the Massachusetts Institute of Technology with a degree in engineering, and at the age of nineteen he was given charge of the newspaper, which he edited from 1947 until his father's death in 1950. The elder Pope's will left his entire $6-million fortune to a foundation, to be run by his three sons. Shortly thereafter, Gene Pope's brothers forced him out of the firm. Pope then left New York for Washington, D.C., where he got a job as an intelligence officer for the Central Intelligence Agency's psychological warfare unit. He left that position after a year, and he returned to New York, where he heard that the struggling *New York Enquirer* was for sale. Pope borrowed $20,000 from friends to use as a deposit on the $75,000 purchase price, and he began to publish the paper with only one other full-time staff member. The *Enquirer* had been founded in 1926 by William Griffin, who built a circulation of 50,000 by campaigning for Irish independence from England, and by providing lurid headlines focusing on crime and corruption in the city.

Over the next six years, Pope poured $250,000 into the paper, most of which had been borrowed from influential friends like Mayor Paul O'Dwyer, Roy Cohn, and racketeer Frank Costello. None of this did much, however, to build the paper's circulation. The turning point came in 1958, when Pope decided that gore had a greater appeal than crime. Selling mostly to males at newsstands and corner candy stores, Pope built the *Enquirer's* circulation to 1 million by 1968.

At that point, he decided a change was in order. Circulation had been stalled at 1 million for several years, and, besides, many of the newsstands and corner stores where the *Enquirer* was sold were going out of business. Pope wanted to reach a larger market, and to do so, he was going to have to distribute his product through supermarkets and drug chains. But to persuade the executives of such operations to carry his paper, he had to clean up the gore and violence on which it was based. Since the average buyer was targetted to be a middle-class suburban housewife, rather than a working-class urban male, the *Enquirer*'s contents had to be completely revamped.

To do so, Pope says, "I went back and read some old *Reader's Digests* of the 1930s, when the *Digest* was having its greatest growth. . . . The most important element [in these stories] was that most of it was *uplifting.*" He took this inspirational formula and combined it with gossip about movie, television, and society celebrities, stories on ESP and UFOs and other psychic phenomena, various consumer topics, and a new "easy" diet plan almost every week. The change was almost immediately successful, and circulation soon rocketed to 2.6 million.

This success came not only from the transformation of editorial content, but also from a highly sophisticated sales and distribution network. The key in supermarkets and drug chains is shelf space, and the competition has always been fierce. Furthermore, many chains were not receptive to giving over this space to the *Enquirer*, due to its rather unsavory past. But Pope used every trick in the books, including his considerable political influence and savvy, to get them to sign up. Within three years, he had locked up all the major supermarket chains in the country. Once they agreed, they soon discovered that the *Enquirer* was a massive cash machine for them. When it sold for 35 cents, 8 cents went to the retailer, and a little over 5 cents went to the wholesaler. In addition, Pope's company gave the retailers "retail space allowances" of $13 annually for each checkout display. To ensure that no checkout counter was ever without an *Enquirer*, Pope employed 205 full-time and 650 part-time employees to verify that the *Enquirer* was always prominently displayed and that the racks were always full. Just as with any other manufacturer who depends on supermarkets for sales, their job was to fight for shelf space and keep the merchandise moving. To reflect the paper's enhanced national distribution, it was renamed the *National Enquirer*.

In the mid–1970s, the *National Enquirer* provided $22 million in profits for retailers. In fact, among the thousands of items sold in supermarkets, the *Enquirer* and *TV Guide* were consistently among the ten most profitable. Circulation continued to rise during the early 1970s, until it reached nearly 6 million. It was a mammoth market, it was remarkably profitable, and Gene Pope had it all to himself. This situation, of course, could not last, and did not. Rupert Murdoch, the Australian publishing mogul, who owned over 100 newspapers, magazines, and broadcasting properties in that country and Great Britain, brought out a competitor to the *National Enquirer* in 1974. Called the *Star*, it was ushered in with great fanfare and advertising, and it soon built its circulation to 3.3 million.

Murdoch spent $10 million in a television advertising blitz, and, most dramatically, made lavish use of color in the newspaper, making the *Star* look more like a magazine. The *Enquirer* had always been printed in black and white, but for supermarket sales, color was an important advantage. So, Pope had to respond. He spent $6 million in advertising, but gained little in circulation and no additional advertising. Although the *Enquirer* was able to hold its own against the *Star*, Murdoch cut deeply into Pope's immense profits. Pope also had to begin bringing out his newspaper in color. To do so, he planned to build a new $15-million plant in Florida. But local officials demanded extensive pollution control monitoring devices, so he scrapped his plans for the plant and contracted to have most of his color printing done in a plant in Buffalo, New York, which again increased his costs.

Then, in the early 1980s, the *Enquirer's* circulation began to decline. The decline was partly due to the *Star*, which had increased its circulation to 4 million, but even more it was due to the *Globe* and the *National Examiner*, tabloids published by Canadian Mike Rosenbloom, which had a combined circulation of 3 million. Since these three papers tended to be more lurid and sensationalist than the *Enquirer*, Pope decided to take his paper farther upscale. Increasing the price of the paper a hefty 20 cents to 65 cents an issue, he rebuilt its circulation to 5.1 million with a massive $30-million advertising campaign. Gross revenues went up 54 percent, to $140 million. This quest for greater respectability was also partly a result of the $1.6-million judgment against the newspaper from a libel suit brought by television personality Carol Burnett. As a result of these changes, the *Enquirer* began to view itself in a class with *People* magazine rather than the *Star, Globe*, and *Examiner*. Its former competitors, however, were not impressed with the transformation. As *Globe* executive Tony Miles commented, ''*People* magazine would be heavy going for a lot of *Enquirer* readers.''

Pope, who *Forbes* magazine estimates was worth over $150 million in 1985, was a hands-on publisher. He rewrote headlines, directed investigative projects, and constantly pushed for a better product. On Saturdays he often showed up at the office in swim trunks and slippers, and on Sundays he took work home to his comfortable house in the West Palm Beach area. He demanded a great deal from his employees, and he was known as a difficult and arbitrary boss. But he also paid the highest salaries in the industry, and he handed out large payments for news stories and tips. From all accounts, Pope loved his work. As a former employee commented, ''He's like a little kid with a new train set. He loves it. He approves every comma, quotation mark, sentence and headline in the newspaper. It's his whole life.'' Pope died suddenly of a heart attack at his home in October 1988. (**B**. *Newsweek*, April 14, 1952;.*Time*, February 21, 1972; *Forbes*, October 16, 1978, March 19, 1979, March 14, 1983; Toronto *Globe and Mail, Report on Business Magazine*, July 1987; Dorothy Gallagher, *All the*

Right Enemies: The Life and Murder of Carlo Tesca, 1988; *New York Times*, October 3, 1988.)

PRITZKER FAMILY: ABRAM NICHOLAS PRITZKER (January 6, 1896– February 8, 1986), **JACK NICHOLAS PRITZKER** (January 6, 1904–October 31, 1979), **JAY ARTHUR PRITZKER** (August 26, 1922–), **ROBERT ALAN PRITZKER** (June 30, 1926–), **DONALD NICHOLAS PRITZKER** (October 31, 1932–May 9, 1972), **NICHOLAS J. PRITZKER** (1945–), **THOMAS JAY PRITZKER** (June 6, 1950–). Entrepreneurs and financiers, Pritzker & Pritzker, Marmon Group, Hyatt Hotels, Hyatt International, Braniff Airlines, Dalfort, and many others. The Pritzker family wealth is massive and private. Over the years, three generations of the family have worked assiduously to build an enormous empire of firms in older "smokestack" industries, upscale luxury hotels, a doomed airline, real estate, and a number of other ventures. A quiet, dignified family, they seem to be nearly universally respected by all those who know them. They have regarded estimates of their wealth, which range between $3.5 billion and $4.5 billion, as "tawdry" and "gauche." Although they are not reclusive, they do not like to talk to the press. Jay Pritzker once said reporters made him feel like a "trapped animal." Part of the reason for this nervousness about the press is the collective manner in which the Pritzker family fortune is managed. The family operates without official titles or clear lines of authority. They have managed a massive fortune in the interests of a large family without ugly court fights or other family feuds. When reporters did visit their offices they were struck by the way in which the Pritzkers gathered together, all talking at once, finishing one another's sentences without ever interrupting each other. This is a close-knit family, whose closeness extends beyond the business world. They socialize in each others' homes, play tennis with one another, and live in close proximity in an affluent enclave on Chicago's lakefront known as the Gold Coast.

The Pritzkers got their start in America in 1881, when nine-year-old Nicholas Pritzker left Kiev, Russia, with his parents for a new life. Nicholas went to work upon his arrival in America, where he did almost any odd job he could find— shining shoes, selling newspapers, anything. At the same time, the energetic and ambitious young man did not forget his studies. By the time he was a young man he had qualified to become a pharmacist. This in itself was quite an accomplishment, but for Nicholas it was merely a stepping-stone. While working as a pharmacist, he went to Northwestern University and then the law school at De Paul University. In 1901, at the age of twenty-nine, he founded the law firm which became the basis of the family business—Pritzker & Pritzker. Over the succeeding years, his three sons, Harry, Abe, and Jack, all joined him at the law firm. Nicholas, who died in 1957, had a streak of iconoclasm which has characterized the activities of his descendants. Born and raised an orthodox Jew, he became an atheist and rejected the tenets of his ancestral religion, and he instilled a sense of questioning in his sons and grandchildren.

The two driving forces in changing the focus and scope of the Pritzker family were Abram and Jack Pritzker. Abe Pritzker was born in Chicago, grew up in relative comfort, and attended Northwestern University in 1913–1914, but got his bachelor of philosophy degree at the University of Chicago in 1916. After graduating, Abe went into the navy during World War I and mustered out as a chief petty officer. He went to Harvard Law School, from which he graduated in 1920. At that point, Abe returned to Chicago, where he taught accounting at Northwestern for a time before joining his father's law firm. He began to practice law, but found he was more intrigued with real estate and finance. Before he reached his thirtieth birthday, Abe Pritzker had accumulated a tidy little fortune in Chicago real estate, but he participated in the great Florida land boom during those years and lost most of his money.

Jack Pritzker was also born in Chicago and got his bachelor's degree from the University of Michigan in 1916. A year later he received his law degree from Northwestern. Upon joining the family's law firm, he became involved with his older brother in his real estate and other ventures. In fact, as the Pritzker interests increasingly advanced beyond real estate into finance, it was Jack who remained most closely involved with real estate. As the depression settled over Chicago and the rest of America in the 1930s, Abe and Jack Pritzker established their reputations. They invested in Chicago real estate at rock-bottom prices, and then they patiently waited for these parcels to rise in value. Abe also began to invest in small companies in the Chicago area during the 1930s, and in hotels in far-flung locations. By 1936, having become so successful in their outside ventures, they left their father's law practice. That was also the last year the law firm accepted any outside clients; their only client from then on was the rapidly expanding Pritzker financial empire.

During the 1930s Abe Pritzker made an important decision. He transferred most of his assets to a series of trusts he set up to avoid paying taxes. He later boasted that "between me and my friends we saved between $100 million and $200 million in taxes." The trusts also became one of the principal units of business operation for the Pritzker family over the next half-century. Most, though not all, of the family's fortune was retained in these trusts. "There are more than 1,000 of them," said someone familiar with the Pritzker holdings. In this manner, they were able to own all of their interests collectively, but still function individually. This strategy became one of the secrets of the Pritzker family's success over the years.

Something disturbing began to surface in the 1930s—rumors of the Pritzker familys' involvement with organized crime figures in Chicago. Most of the stories were based on innuendo—after all, they were accumulating a massive fortune in Chicago in the 1920s and 1930s, when the underworld was rampant in the city. How could they not have had ties to gangsters? However, what little evidence exists that Abe or Jack Pritzker might have been involved with organized crime is either secondary or tertiary. One of Abe's good friends and business associates was Arthur "Art" Greene. Although Greene was never convicted of anything, he was accused by the Chicago Crime Commission in 1944 of being the "brains of all Chicago rackets. He is said to be the financial advisor to Jack 'Greasy Thumb' Guzik and the entire Capone Syndicate." They also had the misfortune, for a number of years, of having Stanford Clinton as an associate in their law firm of Pritzker, Pritzker & Clinton. Clinton represented a number of Capone mobsters in their scrapes with the law. Many years later, Abe Pritzker testified before the New Jersey Gaming Commission concerning his association with Clinton: "When [in the early 1960s] I started hearing about the type of clients he had, which included some infamous hoodlums, I asked him to move out of our office. We gave him a free ride pretty good." The Pritzkers may have rubbed shoulders with some hoodlum associates over the years, but despite extensive Federal Bureau of Investigation and police investigations of their past when the family applied for gambling licenses in Nevada and New Jersey, no one has ever uncovered anything more than that outlined above.

The big turning point for the Pritzker family fortunes came in 1942, when Abe negotiated the purchase of the troubled Cory Corporation, a maker of coffee percolators and small appliances. Abe negotiated an agreement for the company, which entailed paying $25,000 in cash and $75,000 in notes. He then submitted the agreement to a prestigious Chicago law firm for assessment before finalizing the agreement. The law firm examined the contract and, as Abe later recalled, "disagreed with everything in the contract." But he went ahead anyway. Cory was bought in partnership with James W. Alsdorf, and, over the next quarter-century, with Alsdorf managing, it was a consistent money-maker; it churned out profits of from $3 million to $4 million a year in the 1960s. For estate reasons, however, Alsdorf felt he had to sell out. The Pritzkers tried to hang onto it, but ultimately agreed to sell it to the Hershey Corporation for $27.5 million. Abe commented in the 1980s that he still could not see anything wrong with the original purchase agreement. With a profit like that, neither could anybody else.

As the 1950s opened, Abe's sons, Jay and Robert, began to play increasingly larger roles in the operation. Then, in the 1960s, came the short and spectacular influence of Donald, the youngest son. As his three sons began to expand the influence of the Pritzker family farther and farther afield, Abe began to recede somewhat into the background; yet he always remained an important stabilizing influence on their operations. He always leavened the serious demeanor of their business with a dose of wry humor. Abe had very early in his business career established a strong working relationship with the First National Bank of Chicago, a relationship that would stand his sons in very good stead as they commenced their expansion. Abe commented, "On Saturdays, a good Catholic goes to confession. I go to the First of Chicago." When his sons moved the family business offices to the thirtieth floor of Two First National Plaza, just across the street from the First National Bank of Chicago, Abe quipped that it was done so "they can keep an eye on their money there." In 1975, when he was seventy-nine years old, Abe went on a junket sponsored by the navy, whereupon he was given a cruise on an aircraft carrier. While aboard, Abe eagerly agreed to accompany the pilot of a fighter plane when it was catapulted into flight from the deck. He is probably the oldest man to undertake such a breathtaking, jet-propelled ride.

As his three sons increasingly took over the running of the business, Abe was given responsibility for the Pritzker philanthropies. Although Abe was no more religious than his father, he did belong to a synagogue, and he supported a large number of Jewish organizations. "I pay my dues," he once said, "even if I don't go, there are others who want to go to synagogue and I want to make it possible for them." Similarly, he was not a Zionist; Israel was not his country, America was. Nonetheless, he bought $500,000 worth of Israeli bonds each year, and then he gave the bonds back to Israel, forfeiting the interest. The family set up the Pritzker foundation, which Abe managed until his death at age 90. In 1968, they gave $12 million to the medical school at the University of Chicago, which was renamed after the family. In all, Abe Pritzker was responsible for the disbursement of about $4.5 million a year from the foundation. Still, on the eve of his ninetieth birthday in 1986, he complained to a reporter from the Chicago *Sun-Times* that he did not have enough to do. "My sons think I should retire because I'm 90, but I like to work. That's all I like to do. I don't like to sit around on my can." He died peacefully in Michael Reese Hospital in Chicago about a month later. Michael Reese Hospital in 1881 gave Abe's father, a ten-year-old penniless immigrant, a $9 overcoat. A year before his death, Abe Pritzker commented: "Best investment they ever made, I paid them back for that coat—about a million times."

Jay, Robert, and Donald Pritzker were raised in affluence. They attended Francis W. Parker School, a small private day school in the city, but they found their father to be the most valuable source of knowledge and provider of educational experience. He discussed his business deals with them around the dinner table when they were young, and he posed mathematical problems to them to sharpen their wits. Grandfather Nicholas Pritzker also participated in these discussions, although he favored debating biblical concepts with them. Jay, the eldest, was taken out of school when he was eleven to tour Russia, the Middle East, and Europe in 1934. A brilliant student, he finished high school when he was fourteen, and he enrolled at Northwestern University. As had happened with his father, however, the outbreak of war interrupted his studies. Jay became a navy flight instructor during World War II, stationed first in Pensacola, Florida, and then at the Glenview Naval Air Station near Northwestern. As a result, he was able to finish law school while serving in the military. Jay got his law degree in 1947 and passed his bar exams the same year. Because his academic record at Northwestern had been so brilliant, Jay was offered a job with a federal agency in Washington, D.C., that ran foreign-owned companies whose assets had been seized during the war. As Jay observed the operation, he became convinced that the government had no business running these companies, and he advocated divestiture. The other decision makers, all men in their sixties with much business experience, derided his judgment. Jay resigned from the government and returned home to join his father's business. The government, by the way, eventually sold the businesses.

Jay Pritzker did not want to be just his father's assistant—he wanted to be an entrepreneur—to begin making his own decisions and taking calculated risks. Abe not only gave him the latitude to do this, but also opened up his vast line of credit for Jay at the First National of Chicago. Years later, Jay recognized the importance of this: "Because of Dad I could get anything from the bank, even if the request was unreasonable." His first independent venture came, according to Jay, by way of a "ridiculous fluke." Bertrand Goldberg, an eminent architect, had developed a new lightweight plywood freight car. Jay agreed to back him. "Someone," said Jay, "suggested we buy a plywood mill. It was like starting a cookie factory and deciding you needed to buy a wheat farm." But he did. He got money from the First National to invest in a lumber and plywood operation in Eugene, Oregon, where he and his wife moved for a year to oversee its operation. This became a highly profitable operation. The mill was expanded over the years, and brought the Pritzkers into the lumber business. By the mid–1980s, they owned about 500,000 acres of timberland in the United States and Costa Rica.

With the success of the lumber operation, Jay returned to Chicago. In 1953, Jay bought the Colson Company, a small, struggling manufacturer of bicycles, industrial casters, and rocket parts. The company, with sales of $5 million a year, cost Jay several million dollars to purchase, and the First National of Chicago gave him 95 percent of the purchase price. By this time, Jay, at thirty-one, was emerging as the financial genius of the company, and he could not afford the time to go to Elyria, Ohio, where the plant was located, to turn it around. He turned this job over to his younger brother, Bob, then twenty-six.

Bob Pritzker was an engineer, and a good one. As he later commented, "I am the oddball, the operating partner who is also a member of the family," most of whom were lawyers. After high school, Bob had gone to the Illinois Institute of Technology, from which he graduated in 1946. He did postgraduate work in business administration at the University of Illinois. Upon leaving Illinois, Bob acquired six years of practical production experience outside the family business. When he took over Colson in 1953, he jettisoned the rocket parts and bicycle divisions. Concentrating on the caster business, Bob made it into a success. He then acquired a number of other small companies that fit into the caster business and integrated them with Colson; he also built a new plant in Arkansas for caster production to make the company more efficient and competitive.

As soon as Bob got Colson back on its feet, Jay purchased another small manufacturing company for Bob to turn around with his production genius. This became the pattern of the two brothers during the 1950s. Jay sought out small, smokestack industry concerns that he felt were undervalued but could be resurrected. He purchased them, and Bob brought them back to life. That accomplished, they moved on to another. These companies, after a time, were united into the Marmon Group, which ultimately comprised sixty firms picked up over the years at bargain rates. These companies included one of the nation's largest railroad tank car manufacturers, a firm which did a large-scale trading business with East Asia, companies that made gloves, refined copper, leased cranes, and did many other things.

The Pritzker family trademark has always been the incomparable teamwork of family members, and this was certainly true of Jay and Bob in the 1950s and 1960s. Although Jay was the financial wizard and deal maker and Bob was the hardheaded operations man ("Walk in with a bunch of metal in your hand, and he will grab for it"), the two worked closely on all the deals. As Bob explained, "You need a lawyer and an operator to negotiate a deal." Although they made some mistakes, most of their acquisitions were highly profitable for the company. An analyst from Salomon Brothers in the 1970s said that the Pritzker brothers had a "fundamentalist approach" to their deal making. What he meant was "they go back to classic Graham and Dodd analysis, looking at assets, liquidity, and cash flow . . . they always concentrate on the basics." Another deal man who works with the Pritzkers said, "Jay will know either the industry or the company right away" when he would call about a deal. "He likes to buy for 80 cents on the dollar and will turn down nine of ten deals on the phone, saying the price is too high . . . . He always pays cash and has a pool of borrowed capital he can tap when he finds what he wants." Not everyone, however, was impressed. One rival said, "They have a new-money, Sammy Glick smell about them."

The Marmon Group comprised companies that were not sexy, not state-of-the-art kinds of businesses. Instead, they were mundane, basic manufacturing concerns. "High technology is not for us," Jay explained. "It's terrible when bad, sky-high when good, and besides, we don't understand it anyway." But these prosaic companies generated revenues of about $3 billion a year in the 1980s, a huge increase from the $200 million Marmon had earned in the 1970s. Certainly Jay's negotiating ability and sense of value were important in this, but even he agreed that the key to Marmon's success lay with Bob. "The deals I make," said Jay, "create a lot of problems for Bob. But he is a master at finding a way to make sick companies work." Bob's approach, like the Marmon companies, is basic and straightforward. "I tell my people, 'Don't play games. Don't lie to me. Don't lie for me. Don't do me any favors. Play it straight."

Bob Pritzker invests in the latest and best equipment for his plants; he spent about $100 million annually on such investments in the 1980s. "Marmon has outdone most of the smokestack companies by striving to be No. 1 or No. 2 in each of the businesses," said Robert M. James, a management professor at the University of Chicago, "and by pouring money into equipment to make itself the low-cost producer." Bob spends much of his time either in the air, flying coach class to visit his far-flung plants, or on the phone in his office discussing problems with his managers. But Bob is not a hands-on manager, he cannot be, with about sixty companies to run. Instead, he operates in a highly decentralized fashion, letting his general managers operate with little or no interference. As he noted, "We need to respect and to be sensitive to each other. I'm always clear about what I want in terms of risk and return." Marmon's managers, in turn, regard their independence as a source of both motivation and reward. "It's like having my own company," said one manager, "but having the Pritzkers' bankroll a phone call away." The approach has helped make Marmon exceptionally profitable. Its return on equity in the decade from 1978 to 1987 averaged 20.2 percent compared to an average of 13 percent for *Fortune* 500 companies over the same period. Profits of the Marmon Group in 1987 were a robust $145 million—as much as Hershey Foods or Cray Research. And yet Marmon has never been spectacular. It has been the embodiment of Bob Pritzker's favorite slogan: "We just try to keep marching ahead, putting one foot in front of the other."

While Bob was busy building Marmon into a quiet, industrial behemoth, Jay continued to acquire a myriad of other properties for the family. In the early 1960s they joined with the Murchison* family of Texas to build Centex Park in suburban Chicago, the nation's largest industrial park. In 1973, Jay bought *McCall's Magazine* from Norton Simon Incorporated for $8 million. "It was peanuts as a deal," Jay said, but it gave the Pritzker family their first taste of fame. *McCall's Magazine* was an old and respected magazine, and when the Pritzkers bought it, they became mini-celebrities. "People ask me where I've been," Jay said. "We've been here all the time, but nobody paid any attention until we bought that magazine." In any event, the Pritzkers were not after fame, but profits. They told the McCall's people to do what they thought needed to be done to make the magazine profitable again. Page size was reduced, as was excess circulation. Advertising and subscription rates were adjusted, and the magazine began to attract more ads and to make a healthy profit.

The Pritzkers' most glittering possession, however, is the Hyatt Hotel chain: Eighty Hyatt hotels and eleven resorts with revenues of about $1.8 billion in 1987 in the United States, Canada, and the Caribbean. Most of these profits, however, went to investors. Although Hyatt was purchasing a larger number of its own hotels, it ran most of those in North America for a management fee tied to total revenues and an incentive fee linked to profits. In addition, there is Hyatt International, which manages forty-four hotels and resorts with annual sales of $530 million. The hotel chain got its start in a typical, offhand, Pritzker manner. In 1957 Jay Pritzker had flown into Los Angeles on an overnight, "red-eye" flight. Arriving in the city too early for his appointment, he went into a hotel near the airport for some breakfast. He was impressed with the general ambience of the hotel, and he asked for the name of its owner, which was Hyatt Von Dehn. Jay made him an offer of $2.1 million for the hotel, Von Dehn accepted, and the Hyatt hotel chain was a step closer to reality.

Jay Pritzker had a vision of creating a small chain of first-class airport hotels in cities around the United States. But, as usual, he was too busy with the family's financial affairs and deal making to actualize this vision. And Bob was too absorbed with the Marmon Group. To create the Hyatt chain, Jay turned to his youngest brother, Donald Pritzker. Don, who had also been born in Chicago, graduated cum laude from Harvard in 1954. He went to law school at the University of Chicago, from which he graduated in 1959. Different from his brothers, where they were slim and reserved, Don was overweight and gregarious, with a sense of humor said to rival that of a stand-up comedian. He took over the Hyatt hotel in Los Angeles, and began his plans to build more. Number two in the chain was built in Burlingame, California, near the San Francisco airport, and by 1961 he had put together a small chain of six hotels.

Operating out of Los Angeles rather than Chicago, Don Pritzker exercised more independence from his brothers than the family had experienced in the past. But he was successful, and somehow the family always managed to operate as an effective unit, regardless of distance. Don Pritzker's most important step came in 1966, when he visited a large, new downtown hotel being built in Atlanta, Georgia. Designed by the eminent architect, John Portman, it signalled a number of important new trends for the future. It was one of the first of the new luxury hotels to be built in the downtown core of cities. Before this time, downtown hotels were grand old hotels mostly built before the 1920s, which were becoming frayed and careworn. New hotels, like the earlier Hyatt ventures, were built in the suburbs, near airports and expressways. The still unfinished hotel, called the Atlanta Regency, represented a dramatic departure in hotel design. In the center was an enormous atrium—thousands and thousands of square feet of potentially usable hotel-room space was taken up by a large shaft of air and light vaulting upward for several stories in the middle of the lobby. The concept scared off the original investors, and in 1967 Jay Pritzker was able to buy the hotel, renamed the Hyatt Regency, for $18.9 million. The Atlanta hotel was not only a great success, but the atrium concept became Hyatt's signature for most of its new hotels, an increasing number of which were erected in downtown areas.

Don Pritzker also created a signature image for the Hyatt hotels with a young, innovative staff that mirrored the exuberant styling of the hotels themselves. By 1972, with twenty-seven hotels, Don had built one of the most exciting and fastest growing operations in the United States. Don went to Honolulu to attend the opening of Del Webb's Kuilima hotel-resort complex, where, at the age of thirty-nine, he died of a heart attack while playing tennis. The family and the Hyatt hotel chain were thrown into profound shock. Control of Hyatt was passed to Hugo ''Skip'' Friend, Jay's brother-in-law. Five years later, Friend was found to have used over $300,000 of company money for personal expenses—an inexcusable incident for a family firm that prided itself on its integrity. Jay demoted Friend and put Nicholas Pritzker, son of his uncle Jack, in charge of the operation. Jay also moved its headquarters to Chicago, where he could watch over its operations more closely.

Nick Pritzker, like his father, had a knack for the business of real estate. When he moved into the management structure at Hyatt in the 1970s, he spotted a potential problem. Most of the chain's hotels were run on management contracts, but they were owned by real estate developers and other investors. These groups were beginning to demand that the hotel management companies assume some of the risks of ownership in exchange for their contracts. So Nick began putting more and more of Hyatt's assets into the ownership of hotels, ensuring that the chain would be able to continue growing in the future. He became president of Hyatt's development division, and he pushed the chain toward the goal of a series of large, mega-resorts. The Hyatt Regency Waikoloa, developed in Hawaii with a consortium of investors, was, at $360 million, the most expensive hotel ever built when it opened in September 1988. Nick, a gregarious sort like his cousin Don, is the only member of the family to have a company named after him—Nick's Aqua Sports—which rents windsurfing boards and sports gear at a number of resort hotels.

The man who finally had the greatest influence on the Hyatt hotel chain in the 1980s, however, was yet another Pritzker—Thomas Jay, son of Jay. Born in Chicago, Thomas graduated from Claremont Men's College in Claremont, California, in 1971, got his MBA from the University of Chicago in 1972, and got his law degree there in 1976. In the meantime, he began to work for the Hyatt chain; he became president and chairman of its executive committee in 1986. Tom Pritzker was also the heir apparent to his father. In the 1980s he spent about half his time running the Hyatt operations and the other half attending to the diversified business interests of Pritzker & Pritzker. Like his father in the early 1950s, Tom has moved increasingly to make his own deals and acquisitions. As a family associate has noted, "Jay has become increasingly interested in the larger, sexier acquisitions like Pan Am, while Tom looks for almost any deal that makes sense."

The Pritzkers' most troubled investment, by far, has been its acquisition of Braniff International Airlines. The airline had been severely crippled by deregulation of the airline industry in the late 1970s; it was losing oceans of money and was heavily in debt. Nonetheless, in 1983 Jay Pritzker offered $70 million for 80 percent of the company. The deal for Braniff was a very un-Pritzker-like deal. First of all, it was a huge gamble, and Jay Pritzker did not usually take gambles like that. As a banking associate of his said, "There are no deals he shouldn't have done but did." But that was before Braniff. Also, Jay's style of negotiating was to size up an operation, make an offer he thought was fair for the property, and still leave room for profits to be made in the future. If the offer was refused, Jay would simply walk away, and not counteroffer. In the Braniff case, however, he upped his offer several times, spurred on by a comment from a representative of one of the banks which was holding Braniff's notes: "He's trying to steal the goddamn airline."

The main attraction, perhaps, of Braniff to the Pritzkers was that its bankrupt shell brought with it $325 million in tax benefits, along with a profitable airline maintenance division. Upon acquisition of the company, Jay cut its fleet of planes and employees in half, and he proceeded to run a scaled-down, and hopefully profitable, operation. Then, to take further advantage of the tax benefits, he acquired Conwood Company, a producer of snuff and chewing tobacco and put all the operations into a new company, Dalfort. But with monthly losses at the airline running at $8 million, Jay came close to shutting down the entire operation several times. And he probably might have if it had been some other kind of industry. But airlines, by definition, catered to the traveling public, as do hotels, and therein lay a difficult problem for the Pritzkers. "Pritzker can't walk away from Braniff," said Richard M. Incandela, head of IVI Travel. "He couldn't jeopardize the Hyatt name in the travel community." Finally, however, in June 1988, the Pritzkers were able to unload Braniff to an investor group called BIA Acquisitions in a $111-million leverage buyout. BIA was run by several former executives of Piedmont Air, who thought they had the expertise to turn the supremely troubled airline around. The Pritzkers were just happy to be rid of it.

But Braniff was a rare gaffe for the Pritzkers, and they began to look for other investments. They bought 7.2 percent of Ramada Inns and made a bid for all its outstanding shares. "When you've got this much money, you've got to do something with it." In an age when corporate raiders dominate the American business scene, the Pritzkers sometimes find themselves tarred with that appellation, but they reject it vehemently. They view themselves as builders and creators, not paper entrepreneurs. As Jay commented, "Our philosophy is that we don't buy companies to strip them of their assets. The key to us is the people who run them." Bob Pritzker put it in another way, "The American businessman has always been pictured as a materialistic dynamo with the social conscience of the saber-toothed tiger. This may have had some validity in 1890 but there's no truth to the concept today." The Pritzkers may be in for the long haul, but they folded *The Chicagoan*, a local Chicago magazine, after just eight issues, and they sold *McCall's* and Braniff. They may not be raiders, but neither are they altruists. They have been remarkably successful in making firms successful, but when their magic fails, they do not hesitate to pull out. As Tom Pritzker's generation moved in to take control of the vast family empire, Tom commented, "The breadth of what we're taking on is humongous, staggering."

What set the Pritzkers apart from so many other family empires in the 1980s, though, was their down-to-earth nature, especially as exemplified by Bob Pritzker. After he had gone on a tour of a factory in Eastern Europe, the tour guide remarked that of all the senior executives who had ever visited the plant, Bob Pritzker was the first one who understood it and was interested in it. Bob Pritzker replied, "It makes you feel good. That's the kind of respect I want, not whether your name is on the *Forbes* Four Hundred list, which is the sort of thing you're a little embarrassed about." (**B.** *Who Was Who*, vols. V, VII; *New York Times*, May 9, 1972, November 1, 1979, February 26, 1984, February 9, 1986; *Business Week*, March 5, 1975, October 6, 1980, March 7, September 9, October 31, 1983; *Maclean's*, September 19, 1983; *Forbes*, June 4, 1984, October 24, 1988; *Fortune*, October 1, 1984, October 12, 1987, April 25, October 24, 1988; *Contemporary Newsmakers*, 1986; Edwin

Darby, *The Fortune Builders*, 1986; Ovid Demaris, *The Boardwalk Jungle*, 1986; *Industry Week*, January 6, 1986; *Los Angeles Times*, February 9, 1986; *Chicago Tribune*, February 10, 1986; *Newsweek*, February 17, 1986; *Time*, February 17, 1986; *Who's Who in America*, 1986–87; Toronto *Globe & Mail*, June 27, 1988.)

R

REVSON, CHARLES HASKELL (October 11, 1906–August 24, 1975). Cosmetics manufacturer, Revlon, Incorporated. The American cosmetics industry has been dominated by strong-willed, tyrannical leaders such as Helena Rubinstein,* Elizabeth Arden,* Max Factor, and Estée Lauder,[†] but Charles Revson had the reputation of being the biggest megalomaniac of them all. His motto was emblazoned in needlepoint in his dining room: "O Lord, give me a bastard with talent," and his approach was characterized by his desire, every time the Revlon offices were redecorated during the 1950s, to replace the receptionists with new ones whose hair matched the decor. Adman Jerry Della Femina[†] commented on Revson's management style, "Revlon executives had a uniform in the fifties and early sixties: Charcoal black suit, black tie, pink or blue shirt—and a look of terror in their eyes."

Charles Revson was born in Boston, the son of a Jewish immigrant cigar wrapper from Russia. He was brought up and educated in Manchester, New Hampshire, and he came to New York City when he was seventeen. His first job was selling dresses on Seventh Avenue, and later he was put in charge of the company's piece-goods department. A few years later, while he was still in his early twenties, Revson entered the beauty business. He was working for Elka Company, which made the only kind of nail polish then available—a thin, transparent coating in a few basic colors—but, when he was refused the job of national distributor, Revson left Elka in 1932. Later that year, Revson and his older brother Joseph met Charles Lachman, a chemist who had produced a formula for a creamy, opaque, nonstreak nail polish. The three men pooled their resources (which amounted to just $300) and went into business manufacturing nail polish in a room on Manhattan's West Side. They called the firm Revlon Nail Enamel Corporation, with the L standing for Lachman.

Revson did not have enough capital during these early months and years, so he borrowed money from loan sharks, paying an interest of 2 percent a month to keep the company going. With no money to advertise, Revson went after the only market available to him: beauty salons, which were then in the midst of the permanent wave boom. To make sales, the young Revson often serviced the salons with his own fingernails painted with the different Revlon colors. Revlon soon dominated the salon trade, and even after it was sold to drug and department stores in 1937, beauty salons remained Revson's main focus. The dominance that was built up in the 1930s remained until Revson's death in the mid–1970s.

Charles Revson's objective from the very beginning was to sell quality products, thus he refused to sell to cut-rate outlets. He sold premium products at premium prices, even during the depression. As he once put it himself, "I don't ship shit." Revlon expanded into the lipstick market in 1939 in a typically flamboyant fashion. Charles Revson was recognized in his later years as a marketing genius, and that skill showed clearly in the campaign he developed for the firm's lipstick products. Developing the famous slogan, "Matching lips and fingertips," he coordinated lip and nail color in the industry for the first time. Revson had an exceedingly good eye for color, and he developed sharper, more imaginative, more fashionable colors. Just as important, he pioneered the practice of using innovative names for his colors. Prior to Revson, colors were identified in prosaic ways, like dark red. Revlon sold nail polish and lipstick in colors with suggestive names, like Fatal Apple and Kissing Pink. The firm's most ingenious campaign came in 1951, when it introduced the "Fire and Ice" line with advertisements now considered classics in the cosmetics industry.

In these ads, and others, Revson established the company's trademark—seductive sexuality. At a time when America was downright prudish, Revlon snubbed conventions and anticipated the sexual revolution. A competitor, tired of competing with these ads, commented sourly, "Charles Revson thought that every woman secretly wanted the excitement of being the mistress in the Fifth Avenue apartment; his advertising reflected it." While the competition pushed the girl-next-door look, Revlon's ads were so frankly sexual that they bordered on bad taste. In the "Fire and Ice" campaign in 1951, at a time when domesticity, marriage, and the family were considered the paramount virtues of American life, Revlon's campaign challenged these very virtues. Featuring an alluring, seductive model, the copy made an appeal to passion, and promoted sex for its own sake, not for marriage. It was a startling ad for its time. A 1953 ad went even farther. Depicting a woman dressed demurely in gingham, the copy said, "Who knows the *black lace* thoughts you think while shopping in a gingham frock?" Ads in the 1960s and 1970s, when America became more sexually cognizant, were even more explicit. A 1969 ad for lipstick, showing a gorgeous, languid model with a rabbit—a symbol of fecundity—over her pelvic area, called attention in the copy to her "sweet, suggestive mouth." Revlon's competitors never did quite grasp this approach. When Revlon introduced its "Touch and Glow" liquid makeup with the line, "Now the fabulous flattery of candlelight captured in a face makeup," Coty developed a rival campaign in which it stressed the "natural look," which most people interpreted to mean how you looked when you first woke up. It did not sell. Revlon's advertising budget, which stood at $7.5 million in 1955, had grown to $52 million by 1973.

For Charles Revson, marketing was warfare, with no quarter asked, and none given. His product competition with other manufacturers became bitter, personal feuds. The rivalry between Estée Lauder and Revson was so intense that people knew never to invite them to the same party. Elizabeth Arden simply referred to Revson as "that man"; Helena Rubinstein called him "that nail man." Their contempt was scarcely concealed. But Revson was not intimidated. As Andrew Tobias quoted in his biography of Revson,

In terms of marketing, you've got to have the will to win. You've got to see the blood running down the street. You've got to be able to take it. You've got to be able to shove it. If you're not, you're nobody. You never will be.

Revson's marketing genius carried over into its expansion overseas. Revson did not enter the international scene until the late 1950s, after many others were already established there. But quickly making up for lost time, he approached advertising and marketing with his typical arrogance and boldness. Whereas other American companies overseas attempted to adapt their selling style to local tastes, Revlon was blatantly American in its approach. Featuring a Western look in Japan, Revlon products took that country by storm in 1962, to the point that all other cosmetic companies copied Revlon's approach. By the time Revson died in 1975, Revlon had the broadest based international operation of any U.S. cosmetics firm, with ninety-seven companies in over 100 countries, which grossed nearly $170 million.

Revlon was rocketed to the front ranks of cosmetic manufacturers by a bit of luck in the mid–1950s. Revson had reluctantly agreed to sponsor a new CBS-TV program called "The $64,000 Question." He watched the first show and was terribly upset: "It's a turkey," he announced. But he was wrong. From the day the program went on the air, Revlon was swamped with dealer demand. Sales rose 54 percent, earnings went up almost 200 percent, and Revlon shares, which had just been offered to the public at $12 a share, shot up to $30 in three months. By 1959, when the show went off the air in the midst of a scandal (which never affected Revlon), Revlon's sales had quadrupled to $125 million, and earnings had increased eight times to $10.8 million.

Over the next several years, Revson's use of bold advertising and new products pushed Revlon to the top of the industry. Cosmetics, skin-care products, shampoos and hair sprays, fragrances, and men's products, in a wide range of prices, poured out of the factory. By 1960, however, Revson realized that he had to diversify the company's basic product line. Although he was successful, he felt he was taking the company down a narrow cul-de-sac defined by its upper-middle-class image. He wanted to broaden his scope, that is, to sell more things to more people, in both the upper and lower brackets. Taking his cue from Alfred Sloan,* the legendary head of General Motors (GM), Revson wished to make Revlon the "General Motors of the beauty industry." To this end, he split the company into "houses," patterned after GM's divisions, each with a unique image and price range. Ultimately, seven houses were set up, ranging from Princess Marcella Borchese and Ultima II at the upper end, to Charlie at the lower end. As a result of this segmentation, which was unique in the industry, Revlon products were sold in 10,000 outlets, compared to just 2,000 for arch rival Estée Lauder. Even though Revlon products were not sold to discounters or supermarkets, Revlon was the second largest cosmetics firm in America (after Avon), and it commanded around 11 percent of all U.S. cosmetic sales at the time of Revson's death.

Revson had other great successes during this period. One of the most impressive was the introduction of Norell, considered by many to be the first great American perfume. His introduction of Charlie, developed to counter Estée (introduced by Estée Lauder) and named after himself, was a less expensive scent targeted at a younger market. It soon became the best-selling perfume in the world, and, furthermore, it seemed to capture the modern woman's purposeful new self-image. Charles Revson, who actually had little respect for women— (he once commented, "A man gets his strength from a woman, and then he goes on from there")—always seemed to be able to predict trends in the feminine consciousness. When most image makers were stressing women's innocence, Revson accented their sexuality. When his competitors picked up on the sexual revolution, Revson, a step ahead was focusing on the new independence and freedom of working women in the 1970s.

Not everything Revson touched turned to gold. Various attempts at diversification in the 1950s and 1960s were failures. He branched out into related fashion fields, such as shoe polish, plastic flowers, Evan Picone sportswear, and a controlling interest in the Schick electric razor company, all of which failed. Revson, though, did manage to sell all of them at a small profit. More embarrassing was his blunder in attempting to introduce a male genitalia deodorant called Private. That failure was all part of his baffling inability to understand the male psyche. He attempted to compete with Estée Lauder's Aramis brand with Braggi, Top Brass, Bill Blass, and others, but none was successful. Sales of Aramis were about five times greater than those of Revlon's male products.

Nor could Revson beat his arch rival Lauder in the lucrative hypo-allergenic market. Revlon introduced its Etherea line at about the same time Lauder introduced its Clinique brand. Revlon spent vastly more money advertising its line, but by the time of Revson's death, the Clinique line had sales of $25 million, compared to just $5 million for Etherea. Beyond that, many analysts felt that Revson's obsession with the success of Estée Lauder in the upper end of the market, and the huge amount of money he spent trying to combat her influence there, caused Revson to neglect his cheaper cosmetic group. The result was that Revlon lost business to Cover Girl and Maybelline. Revlon's profits were high during this period, but largely because of the terribly high markup on cosmetics (the cost of ingredients in a tube of lipstick amounts to about 8 percent of the sales price). Many errors in marketing and management in Revson's later years were hidden by these high margins. One of Revson's shrewdest moves, however, came in 1965, when he purchased the U.S. Vitamin and Pharmaceutical Corporation for $66 million in stock, renamed it USV Pharmaceutical, and built a mammoth health care division around it. By the time of his death ten years later, it accounted for 22 percent of Revlon's sales and 27 percent of its profits.

Through success and failure one thing remained constant at Revlon—Charles Revson's autocratic and obsessive management style. He lived only for Revlon, and he never lost contact with the office. He was aware of the smallest details within the organization, and he was blunt in expressing his opinion and criticism. As one ex-executive commented, "He chewed up executives the way some people chew vitamins." As a result, the Revlon corporate headquarters was dubbed "one big revolving door." Revson never understood what all the fuss was about. "All I demand is perfection," he said once by way of explanation for his actions. Nor did advertising agencies and executives escape his wrath. Kay Daly, who developed the enormously successful Fire and Ice ad, along with most of the other Revlon ads, said that when Revson first saw the Fire and Ice ad (which he actually loved), he smiled and said, "Who wrote this crap?" He simply had little respect for creative people: "Creative people are like a wet towel. You wring them out and pick up another one." He changed advertising agencies seven times in three years. Nor did he treat workers at lower levels any better. Revson was forced to sign a contract with the Distributive Workers of America in the 1940s simply because, as Andrew Tobias relates, "It was worth the money to get those workers to stop slipping little 'fuck you' notes into the compacts." Of course, Revson was not the first or the only tough boss. Jerry Della Femina put the whole issue into perspective: "Revson was like Harry Cohn and Louis B. Mayer. They were all bastards, but they made things happen. Wheels moved because of them, people made fortunes because of them, and people had breakdowns because of them."

By 1974, Revlon's product range had grown to more than 3,500 individual items, sold in eighty-five countries. Sales were in excess of $600 million, and net earnings were at nearly $50 million. But Charles Revson was sixty-eight years old, was scheduled for major cancer surgery, and had not chosen a successor. It was clear by this time that Revlon, which had been a rather idiosyncratic operation for some time, needed a "numbers man," a professionally trained manager, if it was to grow and survive after Revson left the firm. To that end, just before his operation, Revson chose Michael G. Bergerac, the president of ITT Europe as president of Revlon.

Michael Bergerac received an unheard of $1.5-million signing bonus to join Revlon. Over the next five years, Bergerac turned around the giant cosmetics and health care company. In 1979, Revlon, for the first time, passed Avon as the largest seller of cosmetics in the world, and it pushed USV Pharmaceuticals and other health care acquisitions until they made up nearly 35 percent of the firm's sales and profits. Revenues had nearly tripled by 1979 to $1.7 billion, and profits stood at $150 million, also a threefold increase. To accomplish these ends, Bergerac did a number of things. First of all, he replaced Revson's one-man rule with what he called "controlled decentralization," an attempt to apply simultaneous "loose/tight" principles to the sprawling firm. He also pushed for the introduction of a new fragrance, and he came up with another market winner—Jontue—which soon became the world's second largest seller, behind Revlon's Charlie. Bergerac greatly increased Revlon's already huge advertising budget, doubling it to $140 million in 1979. These advertisements were also more precisely targeted at different consumer segments than ever before.

By the mid–1980s, however, Revlon was in trouble. From 1981 to 1984 the firm floundered, with particularly flat cosmetic sales. The health care division made up an increasingly larger percentage of both sales and profits, so that by 1985 it accounted for 54 percent of sales and 66 percent of earnings. The once great cosmetic company was fading rapidly. As a result, *Newsweek* commented, "The cosmetics empire built by the masterful Charles Revson now seems destined for oblivion. Even in the corporate world, beauty fades." Because of this lack-lustre performance, Revlon became a takeover target. Pantry pride, Incorporated, headed by Ronald O. Perelman, made a nearly $2-billion hostile takeover of Revlon in late 1985, and Perelman replaced Bergerac as chief executive and used Revlon as the base for further acquisitions. By the end of 1987, Revlon had sales of $2.4 billion, an increase of just 2.8 percent over the previous year, but its profits of $166 million were up 20 percent over 1986. Revlon's future remained clouded.

Revson, who was married three times, developed an opulent life-style. To compete with Estée Lauder, he increasingly pursued a frenetic social pace, and he spent a good deal of time aboard his 257-foot yacht, the Ultima II, which he bought from Daniel Ludwig.* He had opulent homes in Manhattan and Westchester County, a chauffered Rolls Royce, tailors, and barbers. It was said that Revson's personal expenses in these later years amounted to $5,000 per day; even his custom-made undershorts cost $26.50 a pair. Yet there was a certain tragic tawdriness to all of this. His daily lunch, eaten off a gold plate, usually consisted of an overdone hamburger patty, Jell-O, and a Fresca. He satisfied his strong sex drive with prostitutes who were sent to his office. *Across the Board*, in summing up Charles Revson's life said, "Revson perfectly matches the stereotype of the super tycoon who, for all his achievement and the prizes that money can buy, is a pathetic human being. In a moment of self pity . . . he remarked, 'If it weren't terrible, it wouldn't be my life.' " (**B**. *Fortune*, April 1956, December 31, 1979; *Cosmopolitan*, June 1960; *Vogue*, April 1973, October 1975; *New York Times*, August 25, 1975; *Forbes*, September 15, 1975; Andrew Tobias, *Fire and Ice: The Story of Charles Revson, the Man Who Built the Revlon Empire*, 1976; *Advertising Age*, March 8, 1976; *Across the Board*, December 1976; *Dun's Review*, December 1979; Milton Moskowitz et al., *Everybody's Business*, 1980; *Business Week*, September 2, 1985, April 18, 1986; *Newsweek*, October 14, 1985.)

RICH, MARC (December 18, 1934–). Metals and commodities trader, Marc
Rich & Company. The United States government was locked in a ferocious battle
with Marc Rich and his partner, Pincus "Pinky" Green. The two men had been
hit with a sixty-five-count indictment which included tax evasion, fraud, and
racketeering, but they refused to hand over key documents concerning the trading
activities of Marc Rich & Company to the government. In response, the courts
levied fines of $50,000 a day, which Rich and Green gladly paid out of their
firm's enormous profits. Then, they secretly sold the firm to their Zug, Switzerland, business partner, Alexander Hackel, who renamed it Clarendon. In response, the court froze Clarendon's bank accounts in the United States. Finally,
in August, Marc Rich & Company agreed to hand over the records. Soon after,
however, U.S. customs agents at Kennedy Airport stopped a plane attempting
to ferry two large steamer trunks full of secret corporate documents from Rich's
New York office to the safety of Switzerland. Because of the extreme secrecy
in which metal traders operate, it was reported that one London aluminum trader,
upon hearing of the seizure, urinated in his trousers while walking off the floor
of the Exchange. Another broker commented, "The last thing we want is the
U.S. poring over records that might outline our activities. We don't want people
to *understand* how we operate."

In the shadowy, secret world of commodities traders, Marc Rich had no peer.
He was known as the Metal Man, what author Copetas called "the Grand Dragon
of a daring and tightly knit lodge of 2,000 men." The same men were referred
to as "barbarians" by Michael Brown, chairman of the London Metal Exchange.
Rich himself was often called El Matador because of his talent and enthusiasm
for killing bull markets when they did not suit the designs of his global empire.
Other appellations used for Marc Rich have included "ruthless tycoon," "vengeful businessman," and "scheming marketeer." Often called the most corrupt
man in this fraternity of freebooting capitalists, Rich was also among the most
secretive. One fellow trader commented that "Marc gave paranoia a bad name."
He was also a cold and calculating businessman, so much so that associates
often commented on it. "He was so damned cold," one said, "He'd walk into
a room and people froze."

Marc Rich was born in Antwerp, Belgium, the son of David Reich and Paula
Wang. David Reich had come to Antwerp from Frankfurt, Germany, during the
early 1930s, joining the Belgian city's thousands of Jewish merchants. A low-
level trader, David Reich bought and sold anything that would turn a profit.
Traders like these were often referred to as rag-and-bone men, who operated in
a heartless, vulgar market in which survival was the only criterion of success.
Marc Rich grew up in this environment, leading a lonely childhood under the
direction of strict parents. With the advance of German armies, David Reich
and his family fled Belgium. In 1941 they came to the United States, arriving
first in Philadelphia, and then settling in Missouri, where they Americanized
their surname to Rich.

In 1944 they moved to Kansas City, where the French-speaking Marc was enrolled in a public elementary school. He had little to do with his classmates there, and a few years later moved on to attend junior high school. In 1947 Marc Rich became an American citizen, and in 1949–1950 he attended Southwest High School in Kansas City. Rich was a quiet, rather mediocre student there, and few of his classmates had any recollection of him later on. His father, meantime, in 1946 opened a costume jewelery outlet in Kansas City. Two years later, he converted it into a wholesale jewelry distribution center.

By the late 1940s, the Rich family was beginning to experience some material success. They bought a home in Kansas City, but in 1950, they sold it and moved to Queens, New York. There, David Rich went into a business making burlap bags, a business venture that became the foundation of a successful series of business interests. Ultimately he formed a diversified overseas trading corporation which became quite successful. Marc Rich did not do as well. He got poor marks while attending Forest Hills High School, whereupon his parents enrolled him in Manhattan's Rhodes School, a school known for its wealthy clientele and undemanding standards. It was what was known as a "rich man's reformatory." Upon graduation in 1952, Rich enrolled in the four-year marketing program at New York University, but he dropped out after two years. He wanted to be a trader, and he got that opportunity in early 1954.

Philipp Brothers, the world's largest raw material trading firm at the time, was looking for bright young men they could mold into apprentice traders. The man in charge of finding these prospects was Henry Rothschild, who had done business with Marc Rich's father. That, combined with his impression of young Rich, landed the young man a job. As Rothschild recalled, "Marc wanted to learn the business and he came from a family that understood trading. It was a good hire. Marc had the patience to learn." Rich's first job at Philipp Brothers was not impressive—he was put in the mailroom. Philipp Brothers, which later absorbed the securities firm of Salomon Brothers in 1981 to become Philbro-Salomon, was an extraordinarily tight-knit group of German-Jewish immigrants in the 1950s, who had little interest in the academic credentials of their employees, but stressed the work ethic. It was a world made for Marc Rich.

Turning out to be a superb student of metal markets, Rich soon graduated from the mailroom to the telex-driven world of the traffic department. Marc Rich was even more driven than the department he entered. One of his colleagues in the department recalled that "he was not the kind of fellow you'd ask out to lunch. Marc always felt he was brighter than us, that his shit didn't smell. And he never talked about anything but business." But if Rich did not appeal to his young colleagues, he did catch the eye of Ludwig Jesselson, one of the firm's partners. What alienated his peers made him attractive to his bosses: "Marc's great strength from the day he came here was his incredible impudence," an executive at Philipp Brothers said. "The man never hesitated to ask for anything; the kind of person you'd throw out the front door and he'd go around and crawl back in through an open window like a sneak." Others viewed him as "aloof,

frosty, occasionally irrational, dangerously irritable.'' But these were the traits
that made him a good trader. To Jesselson, Marc Rich was like a son, and he
treated him as such.

Under Jesselson's tutelage, Rich learned the volatile world of tin prices by
traveling to Bolivia to deal with the military junta. Rich also became an expert
in an exotic substance—mercury—a little-traded, highly volatile commodity.
Rich was able to "make a market" in mercury because he knew that there was
a demand for it. When mercury prices skyrocketed, Rich made significant profits
for Philipp Brothers in the early 1950s, which further enhanced his position in
the firm.

After his success with mercury, Rich was sent to Havana, Cuba, to continue
his "education." Cuba was unsettled at that time. The Batista government had
just fallen, and Fidel Castro had come to power. Here Rich operated in a massive
grey area in terms of legalities and moralities. A former associate in Havana
commented, "Marc cut his teeth in Havana, and the experience shaped his
character because it taught him that being illegal was okay under certain conditions." A friend of Rich's agreed, "Cuba was Marc's first taste of the illegal.
He saw the potential." From Cuba, Rich traveled to all parts of the world as
Philipp Brothers' key representative, establishing friendships in the international
industrial community. He also became a remarkably astute trader. Craig Copetas
commented:

The trading community admired Rich because he was able to dismantle the sticky web
of mercantile regulations and restrictions that hobble the wealth of nations and their
corporations. Like the old junk dealers who left no garbage heap unturned in their search
for discarded lead batteries, zinc cathodes, or copper pipes, Rich explored and took quiet
advantage of every opportunity that would add to his power, influence, and prosperity.

Soon, Jesselson put Rich in charge of the firm's Madrid, Spain, office, a
highly strategic location which allowed him to extend his influence into Europe,
Africa, and the Middle East. In Madrid in the 1960s, copper was the "hot"
metal, and Rich became one of the metal's best traders. He was able to supply
large quantities of metals to the world's industrial nations at opportune times.
The trading pressure took a terrible toll on Rich during this time—he began to
drink heavily and looked decades older than he was. Then, in the early 1970s,
the industrial world began to collapse, a fragmentation and chaos made worse
by the Arab oil embargo established by the Organization of Petroleum Exporting
Countries (OPEC). Philipp Brothers had never traded in oil, and, for that matter,
there was no real oil-trading industry. Traditionally, producing countries had
sold virtually their entire supply to major oil companies, which in turn traded it
among themselves. But now the Arabs were withholding oil from the majors,
industrial nations were thirsting for oil, and producing nations were beginning
to market oil to independent traders.

Rich saw the value in oil. Even though Jesselson was not keen on the idea of trading in it, Rich proceeded. He began to develop intimate associations with a number of highly placed officials in the Iranian government, especially with members of the Shah Pahlavi family. The Iranian royal family controlled all the country's oil, and they supplied Rich with important information on new oil structures, which enabled him to get in on the ground floor. Moving oil, however, was much more complex and difficult than moving minerals, so Rich allied himself with Pinky Green, a native of Brooklyn. They were the first to develop a sophisticated system for dealing in spot oil, and they became Philipp's leading crude dealers. During the Arab oil embargo, Rich's ability to fine tune the supply of Middle East oil with the demands of industrial nations generated enormous profits for his company, and made Philipp Brothers the world's largest spot oil trader.

Their independent ways of operating, however, led to disagreements with top management of the firm. On their own authority in 1973, Rich and Green contracted to purchase large quantities of Iranian oil. They agreed to pay well over $5 a barrel, which was significantly above the spot price at the time. This frightened the New York brass, who urged Rich and Green to sell out in a hurry. They reluctantly agreed, and sold it for a small profit. But they were furious when spot prices surged to $13 a barrel a few months later. At around the same time, Rich and Green verbally agreed to buy a Greek oil tanker. Again, top management intervened, forcing them to welch on the deal. Jesselson reflected on that whole situation:

The world changed in 1973. The old ways of trust were gone. Everybody started breaking contracts. Prices were changing too quickly for people to keep their word. The value system I had built the business on had changed. Trading has never been the same since then. Everyone got greedy.

By the end of 1973, Rich and Green were irritated at the timidity of top management at Philbro, they were mortified at having to renege on a verbal agreement, and they were tired of being paid peanuts while they were generating huge profits for the company. They thought they could do much better on their own. So, in the view of many in the company, Rich and Green decided to "bushwhack" Jesselson. It was a tradition at Philbro for the traders to haggle for their year-end performance bonuses with Jesselson, who was notoriously tightfisted. In light of the profits of from $4 to $5 million they had generated in oil alone, Rich and Green each demanded $400,000 in bonuses from Philbro. When Jesselson refused, they both resigned from the company, determined to start their own firm—and to wreak vengeance on Jesselson and Philbro. According to one Philbro director, "They left here with a desire to build up an organization bigger and more important than Philipp Brothers, and that's understandable. It was the way he did it that we all grew to loath. It was patricide, you know. That's really it. Marc Rich committed patricide." Another trader put it more colorfully: "There is one rule in this business, when you've been fucked over by another trader you retaliate in kind." And Marc Rich did just that.

Persuading three other Philbro traders to join them, Rich and Green established Marc Rich & Company AG with an initial capital of $350,000. The new firm ransacked Philbro for traders, telex operators, and secretaries. Rewarding his own network of traders with huge incentive bonuses, Marc Rich's new firm grew very rapidly and became a formidable competitor on the world trading scene. In one commodity after another, Marc Rich stole business away from Philbro. And he used any means he could to succeed. A trader who observed one of Rich's raiding parties recalled,

Rich wanted to get his hands on a Jamaican aluminum trader who had some sort of Philbro connection. The trader was flown from Kingston to London, driven to his penthouse suite in a Rolls, and arrived to find naked hookers prancing around the room. Women, cocaine, cash—it didn't matter as long as Philbro was put out of business.

In the mid–1970s, Rich seized control of the copper business formerly controlled by Philbro in the Philippines, and he became the largest aluminum trader in the world by buying and selling bauxite, the metal's raw material. Rich began to court new oil contacts, particularly in Latin America and Africa, but the key to his oil business, as ever, was Iran. Copetas commented that "by the mid–1970s Rich seemed to appear like a Saudi sheik wherever there was an oil deal to be made, often to the embarrassment of the American oil companies."

Profits for his first five years of operation were enormous. His firm made $14 million in 1974, $50 million the next year, and over $200 million in both 1976 and 1978. During this time, the bulk of his profits came from charging enormous premiums to oil companies short on their production quotas. The minimum oil deal Rich would touch was 100,000 tons, and that was rare. Another trader commented about Rich during this time, "Marc went everywhere chainsmoking Monte Cristo torpedo Havanas, the fattest and most expensive cigars in the world. He was on top of the heap. It was magic." But success demanded a relentless work pace from Rich. His typical business day started no later than 7 A.M., and often went until late in the evening, and his pace of work was even more relentless. One associate commented, "He was a business machine." It also demanded a large number of payoffs to grease the wheels of this lucrative engine of commerce. Rich always walked a tightrope between the profits of business and the powers of politics, and he did it very successfully. By the early 1980s, Rich had forty offices in thirty countries with over 1,000 employees, and his was the dominant trading firm in a number of commodities, especially oil, copper, and aluminum. The firm was worth about $1.5 billion, and traders there estimate that sales were in the $12-billion range. In 1979 and 1980, according to Swiss tax records, Marc Rich AG made a total of $367 million in pretax earnings—and this was just the money that was filtered through the Zug, Switzerland, headquarters. That money, in turn, flowed into big investments.

One of these was the movie studio, 20th Century Fox. Rich had known Marvin Davis,[†] the wealthy American oil wildcatter who was planning to buy 20th Century. Davis had taught Rich many of the refinements of the oil industry in the 1960s, and now Davis recommended 20th Century as a good tax shelter. Also, there was some political advantage to this, as the firm's directors included former President Gerald Ford and former Secretary of State Henry Kissinger. So, Rich agreed to invest if he could remain a silent partner. A deal was struck in which Rich put up $175 million in cash, and arranged for a line of credit of $550 million through a group of eight banks. When it finally leaked out that Rich was a part owner in Fox, foreign oil officials beseiged him with requests for videocasettes, and Rich soon realized that buying the film company was one of the smartest things he had ever done. As another trader said, "Everybody loves the movies."

But Rich's great success and unsurpassed connections during this time also proved to be his undoing. Much of his success in the world oil market in the 1970s came because he was willing and able to deal with anyone. When Angola ousted the Portuguese colonists in 1975 and installed a Marxist government, most of the major oil companies were loath to deal with them. Not Marc Rich. He rapidly moved in to make a lucrative deal to market that country's oil. When the Iranian revolution took place in 1979–1980, an event which choked off oil supplies for practically everyone else, Rich was able to exploit his long-nurtured contacts there to fullest advantage. Because of the Iranian hostage-taking incident, the United States barred American companies from virtually all trade with the Khomeini regime. And the new Iranian government itself had banished U.S. and European oil companies as oil-trading partners.

Thus, Iran needed buyers for its oil, and Rich had kept his office in Tehran open, despite the tensions in the area. His persistence paid off in 1980 with a huge oil contract from Iran. One of Rich's managers said,

You would have thought we had our own pipeline into Iranian wellheads. We bought millions and millions of barrels from Iran during the hostage crisis. When the price of oil went up to $40 a barrel in the fourth quarter of 1980 we were paying about half the world price in Iran. Rich got more excited than I had ever seen him.

Although Rich operated out of New York, the money flowed to Iran to purchase the oil from Switzerland, which he felt absolved him from any culpability. And he might have gotten away with it, in the opinion of London traders, had he not gotten involved in another, blatantly illegal, scheme.

At the same time he was dealing with Iran, Rich was also taking oil from old domestic wells in the United States. Called "old" oil, U.S. law required it to be sold at lower rates than "new" or "stripper" oil. With price controls holding its rate at about $5 a barrel, Rich supplied the oil to West Texas Marketing (WTM) of Abilene and Listo Petroleum of Houston. The government later claimed that both companies were allied with Rich in what was, in effect, a scam to cheat the government. WTM and Listo sent the $5-a-barrel oil on a daisy chain, putting the oil through a series of shady transactions through which it finally sold for $20 a barrel. At that point, the Texas companies sold the oil back to Rich's company. Rich then sold the inflated-price oil to a number of domestic petroleum companies at the highest possible spot price. This allowed Rich & Company and the two Texas firms to make an extra profit of some $70 million on the oil. The taxes on these profits were effectively evaded when the Texans transferred them to Rich's parent Swiss company, a foreign concern protected by Swiss secrecy laws. As a result, the Justice Department undertook an eighteen-month investigation which resulted in an indictment which ran to fifty-one counts in its original form, and later was increased to sixty-five counts.

It is impossible to recapitulate the entire indictment, but the main issues are as follows. First, the government alleged that in 1980 alone, Rich poured at least $20 million in taxable cash into offshore operations. Second, the indictment alleged that in 1980 Marc Rich International bought $345 million worth of crude oil from Marc Rich AG and sold it at a loss of $110 million, which was done to create a price gap in deals between New York and Zug to give the impression of a loss to avoid paying taxes. Third, the government wanted to get Rich for the hundreds of millions of dollars he made from selling Persian oil to the United States during the Iranian hostage crisis, which was in direct violation of a presidential order. Fourth, Rich was also liable for $34 million in profits made in spurious oil transactions, plus an additional $71 million in domestic profits which were shifted offshore. Fifth, the indictment further charged Rich's Swiss company with selling discounted foreign oil to Charter Oil Company, while Marc Rich International bought controlled American oil from Charter. This oil then went into Rich's WTM daisy chain.

In September 1983, the government issued warrants for the arrest of Rich and Green, but by this time the two men were safely ensconced in Switzerland, which has a treaty with the United States that does not allow extradition for tax crime. Although many in America were scandalized by Marc Rich's abuse of the law and by his arrogance concerning his duties as an American citizen, few others viewed it that way. The Swiss, for their part, viewed Marc Rich as a model citizen; and an executive of British Petroleum, which had had extensive dealings with Rich, said the case was "an attempt to push U.S. laws on the rest of the world. This line of action does nothing but handicap companies in their worldwide dealings, and it robs the market of a major player."

Five years later, Marc Rich was still at large, living in a palatial $9.5-million villa on Spain's posh Costa del Sol. The government in 1984 settled all charges against Rich's company, since it pleaded guilty to tax evasion and paid the government a whopping $172 million. But the sixty-five-count criminal case against Marc Rich and Pinky Green was still open, and they still face a possible 325 years in prison if convicted. Rich and his massive trading firm, however, just got bigger and richer. Estimates of his personal net worth have ranged as high as $750 million, and his company, with offices in thirty-five countries, does a business of around $13 billion a year. It ranked second in 1987 only to Cargill (see MacMillan family) among the world's diversified trading companies. Rich had become so dominant in metals trading that a competitor said, "In metals it's now Marc Rich and the 40 dwarfs." He has also become the world's most powerful factor in the aluminum market.

But Marc Rich cannot come back to America. Despite a high-powered legal team, consisting of Leonard Garment and Edward Bennett Williams (since deceased), the indictments still hang over his head. Sandy Weinberg, the government attorney responsible for pursuing the case has promised, "I wanted those boys [Rich and Green] in jail. But they can't come back into the United States as free men. Never." Marc Rich seems to understand that. Once, when asked where he had been traveling lately, Rich shot back, "Not to the U.S. That would be a one-way trip." (**B**. *Business Week*, September 5, 1983; *Harper's*, January 1984; *Fortune*, January 23, 1984, August 1, 1988; *Barron's*, October 15, 1984; *Economist*, October 20, 1984; *Newsweek*, October 22, 1984; A. Craig Copetas, *Metal Men: Marc Rich and the 10-Billion-Dollar Scam*, 1985; *Forbes*, October 27, 1986.)

RICH, ROBERT E., SR. (1913–   ). Food processor, Rich Products Corporation. You would have thought they were an organized crime outfit, that they were dealing in cocaine, or distributing pornography. When Rich Products brought out its Coffee Rich nondairy coffee creamer in 1960, the company was hit by a deluge of lawsuits. Dairy interests in various states brought over forty different cases against the company, including several in Wisconsin, the self-styled "America's Dairyland." Rich Products tenaciously fought each of these cases, arguing that their products were, in fact, not imitations but functionally superior products. Robert Rich, Jr., commented, "It was necessary to stand up immediately to these challenges and not accept some of the alternatives some of those people attempted to impose on us—like coloring Coffee Rich pink or green, as one state would have us do!"

The man who was responsible for upsetting America's dairy industry so much, Robert Rich, Sr., was, ironically, born into a dairy family. Born in Buffalo, New York, Robert Rich, Sr.'s, father owned a major milk company and later became an ice-cream manufacturer in the city. Young Rich attended city schools and graduated from the University of Buffalo. After graduation, in about 1935, he took over a small dairy operation in the city and had built it into a major entity by the time of World War II. At that point, he was called to Washington, D.C., as an alternate administrator of the ice cream order section of the War Food Administration. Later, he was sent to Detroit, Michigan, as milk order administrator for that state.

While in Detroit, a representative of the city's Ford Hospital called Rich in an attempt to secure more ration points for butter. Rich checked into the situation, but found it was impossible. As a consolation, Rich said he would try to increase the hospital's milk quota. Upon checking, he was amazed to learn that the hospital had not been using milk or cream at all. In fact, their entire supply of dairy products was a simulated product made from soybeans by a process developed at the George Washington Carver Laboratories. The process had been known for some time, but prior to World War II milk was cheap and plentiful, and a substitute was unnecessary. The outbreak of war, however, changed the situation, and created a demand for a cheap, synthetic product. Rich was fascinated with the new process, and he visited the Carver Laboratories to view the operation. There he found the substitute had several limitations, including the fact that it could not be whipped. As long as the war was still on, Rich thought no more about it.

Three years later, in 1945, when his government service ended, Rich returned to Buffalo to resume his dairy operations. At the same time, he began to examine the possibilities of producing a soybean-based whipping cream. He hired the Buffalo research laboratory of Spencer, Kellogg & Sons to work with various emulsifying agents in hopes of developing one that would whip into soy milk. Rich also had to develop another extraction system, since the Carver Laboratories were protective of their process. Rich called in a dairy engineer who invented a different, and superior, method of doing the same thing. By April 1945, Robert Rich had perfected his product and was ready to do business.

He soon found, however, that the product was not as easy to sell as he had anticipated. The government lifted restrictions on dairy products sooner than he had thought, making whipping cream readily available and fairly cheap. Furthermore, Rich's product was just as perishable as fresh cream, so it was difficult to transport it long distances or to store it for any length of time. Nonetheless, Rich was determined to make a success of it. One day, he had an appointment with a potential distributor in Long Island, New York. He and his party decided to travel there by train, and to protect their unstable product from spoilage, they wrapped it in paper packed in dry ice. Upon arriving in Long Island, Rich found, to his dismay, that the product had been too thinly wrapped and that it had frozen solid. He was sure his presentation was ruined—when dairy cream was frozen, it broke down the emulsion, making whipping impossible. Out of desperation, Rich mashed up the frozen soybean topping, and, as he later recalled, "it whipped to perfection."

Robert Rich had a new product, and it was the beginning of an important new industry—that of frozen nondairy products. Now Rich had a product with a difference—since it could be frozen, it had a much longer shelf life than real whipping cream and, since it could be easily transported large distances, it could become a nationally distributed product. That single advantage got Robert Rich's foot in the door. Rapidly, he developed other consumers to buy his Rich's Whip Topping: it gave twice the yield of whipped topping as regular cream, since it tripled its bulk when whipped; it remained stiffer much longer; it was a virtually sterile product, with a far lower bacterial count than milk or cream; it was cheaper than dairy products; and it was far more convenient for the consumer to use and store.

With that as the basis, Robert Rich began to create a whole new industry in 1945. Total sales of frozen nondairy products for the entire industry that year were just $28,000, and that was all Rich's products. His plant had a total work force of four, including himself. But the business grew rapidly. In 1946, sales reached $126,000. The retail market received a big boost in the early 1950s, when Rich introduced frozen aerosol cans for his whipped topping. This made the product even easier for the consumer to use, and it was a major breakthrough for the firm on the retail side. Rich Products, however, had achieved major success earlier in the institutional market. In 1946, Rich took his products to the American Dietetic Convention in Boston, and made his first institutional sale when Ohio State University bought a case of Whip Topping. The product was much cheaper and easier for institutions to use, and expansion in this area occurred rapidly.

Rich next gained a foothold in the bakery industry. There he found bakers quite resistant and suspicious about his product. Frozen whipped pies made with dairy cream continually ran into bacterial buildup problems, but Rich's ran a series of tests in which it showed that its product could be easily and safely substituted. The baking industry was finally convinced, and Rich's Whip Topping became the basis of the whole frozen cream pie business. It was also used as the "cream" filling in eclairs and a number of other products later on. By the early 1980s, market surveys showed that real dairy whipped products accounted for only about 5 percent of the institutional market; with nondairy substitutes, led by Rich's Whip Topping, accounting for the remainder.

In 1960, Rich brought out his Coffee Rich, a nondairy coffee "whitener" made from soybeans. Again, Robert Rich moved into virgin territory, creating a product to compete with the dairy industry, and in the process he developed another whole new industry. Despite legal problems and lawsuits from the dairy industry, Coffee Rich grew very rapidly. As Robert Rich commented,

The advantage we had in starting the non-dairy creamer industry was that we had no competition. We could pick out the best distributors in every market—we had national distribution in our first three years—and then, when we decided to go into other products, we had a terrific distribution system already established.

Coffee Rich again had a number of advantages over milk or cream—it could be sold at a lower price, it could be sold frozen and distributed nationally, it could be put up in individual servings, it did not form a scum around the container, it flowed without clotting in vending machines, and, like Whip Topping, it had a very low bacterial content. It could be used by people who had allergies to dairy products, or who suffered from lactose intolerance. Finally, since it was a nondairy creamer, it was given the Parve seal and was therefore free of any religious dietary restrictions for Jews. Coffee Rich quickly became the largest selling frozen nondairy creamer in the world.

The tremendous success of Coffee Rich, coupled with the continuing strong sales of Whip Topping, transformed Rich Products into a large-scale enterprise. Deciding to build on that foundation, Robert Rich in 1969 sold his dairy operations and began to purchase a number of smaller frozen-food companies. He bought Elm Tree Baking of Appleton, Wisconsin, makers of frozen baked goods in 1969, and two years later he acquired Palmer Frozen Foods of Easton, Pennsylvania, makers of frozen dough. These two companies were placed into a new Bake-Off division, and by the end of the 1970s, over 4,000 supermarkets were handling Rich's dough and bakery products. Rich continued to buy various other small, largely family-owned concerns, adding them to Rich Products. Since Rich Products remained a completely private, family-owned operation itself, Robert Rich was always cautious never to expand too quickly, or to dilute the ownership or cash base of his own operations.

By the early 1980s, Rich Products had become a large food-service packer, with a range of over 200 products, with twenty-one plants in the United States and one in Ontario, Canada. It had sales of over $350 million annually. By then, the company had three divisions: creamers, toppings, and icings; desserts; and bakery products. Their latest technological breakthrough in the industry was something called "Freeze Flo," which allowed liquids to be chilled to temperatures as low as 60 degrees below zero without solidifying. Marketed to consumers as Bettercreme, it was used as a nondairy filling and icing for cakes, cream horns, and donuts. Like Rich's other product innovations, this was an enormous success, and sales of Bettercreme in its first three years equaled Rich Products' total sales volume in its fifteenth year.

By the late 1980s, Rich Products had sales of about $600 million annually, and the company itself, wholly family owned, was worth at least $500 million. Although Robert Rich, Sr., remained chairman of the concern, he turned the day-to-day management of Rich Products over to his son, Robert Rich, Jr. The younger Rich had become vice president of marketing and sales in the mid–1960s, and he moved up to the presidency in 1978. Young Robert and his father continued to operate Rich Products as an effective team.

The Riches also dedicated themselves to refurbishing the city of Buffalo. Robert Rich, Sr. once said, "I'd like to see us be to Buffalo what Procter & Gamble is to Cincinnati." They have been good to their word. They paid $1.5 million to attach the family and company name to the Buffalo Bill's National Football League stadium in suburban Amherst. Robert Rich, Jr., became vice chairman of the Buffalo Sabres of the National Hockey League, and he also bought the double-A minor league baseball team, the Bisons, for $1 million in 1983. After nursing the team through a number of difficult years, it completed its final season with a record gate of 200,000. Rich then traded his double-A franchise for a triple-A team, which he also turned into a successful operation. Robert, Jr., was part of a group that persuaded the state to put up a sparkling $22.5-million baseball stadium, named Pilot Stadium, in downtown Buffalo, which he planned to use as a magnet to attract a major league baseball club.

When it set a minor league attendance record of $1.2 million in 1988, establishing itself as the "Cadillac" of minor AAA baseball, Buffalo became a leading candidate for such a team. Young Rich explained, "This is my home, that's why I want to see major-league baseball here." His son, and Robert Rich, Sr.'s, grandson, Robert E. Rich III, also made a bit of a name for himself when he was just seventeen. He landed the role of Robert Redford's son in the movie *The Natural*. The biggest name of all, though, was reserved for Robert Rich, Sr. With a net worth estimated at over $300 million by *Forbes* in 1988, Rich was the "Father of the Frozen Non-Dairy Products Industry." (**B**. *Quick Frozen Foods*, December 1976, August 1980, August 1982, August 1983, November 1984; *Business Week*, July 8, 1985, July 18, 1988; *Who's Who in America*, 1986–1987; *Forbes*, October 20, 1986, October 24, 1988.)

RUDKIN, MARGARET FOGARTY (September 14, 1897–June 1, 1967). Bakery executive, Pepperidge Farms. Margaret Rudkin was forty years old in 1937. A society woman, she and her stockbroker husband lived in a massive Tudor mansion on a 125-acre estate called Pepperidge Farm near Fairfield, Connecticut. During the 1920s, they had lived the kind of privileged life F. Scott Fitzgerald wrote about—riding to the hunt, showing horses at shows, and flitting from New York to Fairfield on a regular basis. With the onset of the depression of the 1930s, however, things began to change. Margaret Rudkin's husband was seriously injured in a polo accident in 1931, and he could not leave the estate for months. And then the economic downturn affected them all adversely. Margaret sold four of their five cars, dismissed all the servants, and began to look for ways to make money with their farm. She tried raising turkeys, and that was marginally successful, but in 1937, when her son came down with an asthma condition, fortune smiled again on the Rudkins.

When Margaret Rudkin took her son to the doctor he advised that the boy either be taken to the hot, dry climate of Arizona, or that he be fed rich home-baked bread. The doctor felt that the additives in commercially baked bread might be aggravating the boy's condition. At that point, the Rudkin family could hardly afford to move to Arizona, but Margaret Rudkin had never involved herself in cooking or baking. She had no choice but to try to bake some bread. As she later recalled,

They say life begins at forty—well, that's how old I was when I baked that first loaf. I just turned to the reliable *Boston Cookbook,* and started following directions. And then, suddenly, I seemed to remember the way my grandmother did it when I was six years old. (*Current Biography*)

Her first loaf of stone-ground whole wheat bread was not very successful: it was "hard as a rock and about one-inch high." She persevered, and later loaves were not only tasty, but also alleviated her son Mark's allergic condition. At that point, the allergist asked Margaret Rudkin to make the bread for other patients, which she did. When some neighbors asked for loaves, she made bread for them, too. Everyone raved about the bread and told her she should make it on a commercial basis. Taking their advice, in the summer of 1937, Margaret Rudkin went into business. In August of that year, she sold her first batch of loaves wholesale to a grocer in Fairfield. The grocer began to stock it regularly, and soon Mrs. Rudkin moved the baking operation out of her kitchen and into an abandoned stable on her Pepperidge Farm estate and hired a neighbor to help her bake. This was the beginning of a multimillion dollar business, and the creation of one of the most famous and well-regarded brand names in American foods—Pepperidge Farms.

Margaret Rudkin was born Margaret Fogarty in New York City. She claimed her mother had "never even learned to boil an egg," but until Margaret was twelve, they lived with her grandmother in a narrow, four-storied brownstone in the Tudor City area of Manhattan. During these years, living with her grandmother, Mrs. Rudkin picked up many of the rudiments of food preparation and baking that she later applied to her Pepperidge Farm Products. After her grandmother died, Margaret moved with her parents and four brothers and sisters to Flushing, Long Island. There, she attended public schools, and graduated valedictorian of her high school class. During the four years after her graduation from high school, Margaret worked as a bookkeeper at a bank in Flushing, the first woman to be hired there. During this time she prepared herself for a career in business.

With her work in the bank as background, Margaret Rudkin next got a job as a " customer's woman" for the brokerage firm of McClure, Jones & Company. It was a good job, at least for a woman in the 1920s, and Margaret enjoyed dealing with the public. During her four years there, she met Henry Albert Rudkin, a partner in the firm, who was twelve years her senior. They were married in 1923, and for the next five years lived in New York City, where the first two of their three sons were born. In 1928, because of Henry's great prosperity on Wall Street, the Rudkins built their magnificent estate in Fairfield County. A year later, their youngest son was born there. During these years, Margaret Rudkin lived the life of a proper young society matron. With servants to attend to household needs and no further interest in a business career, she was able to live a leisured existence with the "horsey set" of Fairfield County. All of this changed with the depression and with Margaret's development of what came to be known as Pepperidge Farm bread.

Mrs. Rudkin's big breakthrough came when she decided to enter the New York City market. Packing a basket with a loaf of Pepperidge Farm bread and some farm-fresh butter, she took a train to New York City. There she met with the manager of the exclusive Charles & Company, a famous specialty food store in the city. When he tasted the buttered, home-baked bread, the manager was so impressed he ordered twenty-four loaves a day, which Henry Rudkin took with him on the 7:38 "broker's special" to the city every morning. A Red Cap would meet him at Grand Central Station to take the bread to Charles & Company, while Mr. Rudkin continued on to his Wall Street office by subway. Within a few months, the bread had become so popular that Mrs. Rudkin hired a truck to transport it to the city.

The popularity of Pepperidge Farm bread is at first difficult to fathom. In the price-conscious depression years, the fact that it was selling for twice as much as its competitors in the late 1930s would seem to have been an insurmountable handicap to many. But Mrs. Rudkin's bread was made with fresh, expensive ingredients like butter and whole milk, and no yeast foods or commercial shortenings were ever used. The result was a bread with a unique, old-fashioned taste and texture that caught the public's imagination. Mrs. Rudkin was also aided by a great deal of free publicity. An article in the *New York Journal and American* in November 1937 featuring her bread alerted the public to its existence, as did a series of other articles in newspapers and magazines, which praised its wholesome quality. Her most significant breakthrough came in 1939. Benjamin Sonnenberg, the famous public relations man, arranged to have *Reader's Digest* run an article entitled "Bread, de Luxe," which made readers across North America aware of it. As a result, orders poured in from all over the United States and Canada. Mrs. Rudkin repaid Sonnenberg not only by employing him on his usual fee basis, but also by giving him a 5-percent share of the business. By 1960, his share was worth more than $1 million.

With the great prestige and popularity of her bread, Mrs. Rudkin decided it was time to expand the operation. Borrowing $15,000 in 1940, she moved the bakery from the Pepperidge Farm stable to a former auto showroom in Norwalk, Connecticut. Before long, sales exceeded 50,000 loaves a week, with white bread the leading item. Whole wheat bread, however, continued to be produced, and she also began to add a number of other bakery items; the first additions were melba toast and pound cake. As she expanded the business, Mrs. Rudkin had to find suppliers for many of the items she needed for her baked goods. She contracted to use the facilities of several mills to grind flour, and she went to Minneapolis to obtain her own wheat. When she built a new plant at Downers Grove, Illinois, there were no old grist mills in the area, so Mrs. Rudkin built a mill there, using large buhrstones and constructing it on the principles of the older mills. All the whole wheat flour was ground at these mills; they used slow-aged unbleached white flour for the white bread. The dough was then mixed in small batches, and cut and kneaded by hand. The bread loaf was wrapped by machines, but it was only after much persuasion that Margaret Rudkin allowed bread slicing machines to be used, since she felt old-fashioned bread should be cut in the home, just before it was eaten. But the realities of modern consumerism dictated that she acquiesce on that matter.

As the popularity of her bread spread farther afield, Mrs. Rudkin opened more plants, and Pepperidge Farm soon grew to be a major national firm. By 1960, in fact, it was the largest independent bakery in America. Its expansion was aided by the television image of Mrs. Rudkin herself, when she appeared in a number of the firm's commercials during the 1950s. As Maggie Rudkin, she became familiar to millions of Americans in the homespun commercials. With this geographic expansion also came expansion of the product line. Mrs. Rudkin in 1956 made an agreement with a Belgian firm to market a line of luxury cookies from recipes highly regarded in that country. To manufacture the cookies, Mrs. Rudkin added a wing to her Downington, Pennsylvania, plant, and she imported a 150-foot oven from Belgium. She also entered the frozen-food field in 1958 when she bought a frozen pastry line from a small company in New Hampshire. Internal product expansion also took place. Since Pepperidge Farm bread contained no preservatives, company policy dictated it could stay on store shelves for only two days. As a result, a lot of unsold bread was returned to the plant for disposal everyday. Margaret Rudkin came up with a typical housewife's solution to this business problem—she made it into poultry stuffing, and Pepperidge Farm soon became one of the nation's leading stuffing makers. She also brought out a line of brown-and-serve rolls.

By 1960, Pepperidge Farm was an exceptionally successful family operation, with the Rudkin family owning 80 percent of the stock. Margaret Rudkin, as president, handled all production aspects; her husband Henry was responsible for marketing and finance as chairman of the company. As the firm's business expanded during the 1950s, Henry gradually cut back on his Wall Street operations, and ultimately retired from stock brokerage. Later, when people asked him if he was still in the Street, he would quip; "No, I'm in the dough." Two of their sons have served as vice presidents of the firm. With sales of over $32 million in 1960, and profits of $1.3 million, the firm employed 1,000 people, mostly women. In that year the Rudkins were approached by Campbell Soup Company, which wished to purchase the company. After some negotiation, a merger was completed. In the deal, the Rudkins got $28 million worth of Campbell Soup stock, and Margaret Rudkin became a director of the soup company. Most important, the family was allowed to continue running Pepperidge Farm as an autonomous unit in the Campbell company. Mrs. Rudkin remained president until 1962, when she succeeded her husband as chairman, and their son William became president. In 1966, Henry Rudkin died, and Margaret became increasingly ill with breast cancer. She resigned from the chairmanship and died in June 1967. By that time, the Pepperidge Farm division had sales of $50 million annually.

Margaret Rudkin won a number of awards during her busy life. In 1955, she was presented with an award by the 32nd Women's International Exposition of the Women's National Institute. During an era in which women were expected to remain in the home, a time when what Betty Friedan called the "Feminine Mystique" was in full flower, when women in business were perceived as a threat to the very basis of American civilization, Margaret Rudkin had achieved success. And she did this without incurring the wrath of American culture. This is largely because she achieved her success in a field considered to be feminine— baking—and because her own personal image always reiterated her domestic commitment. This image was further enhanced in 1963, when she brought out the *Margaret Rudkin Pepperidge Farm Cookbook*, which became a best-seller. When *Current Biography* wrote an essay on Margaret Rudkin in 1959, they commented, "For recreation Mrs. Rudkin enjoys baking bread and pies in her home and testing new recipes. She collects antique bread boards." She may have created a $50-million company, but Mrs. Rudkin was still "just mom" in the eyes of the public. (**A.** Margaret Rudkin, *The Margaret Rudkin Pepperidge Farm Cookbook*, 1963. **B.** *Time*, July 14, 1947, March 21, 1960; *New Yorker*, May 22, 1948, November 16, 1963; *American Home*, April 1951; *Coronet*, August 1953; *Current Biography*, 1959; *New York Times*, June 2, 1967; *Who Was Who*, vol. 4; Eugenia Kaledin, *American Women in the 1950's: Mothers and More*, 1984; *Notable American Women*, vol. IV.)

S

SCHWAB, CHARLES (1938?–). Founder, discount stock brokerage firm, Charles Schwab & Company. On May 1, 1975—called "May Day" on Wall Street—the Securities and Exchange Commission (SEC) deregulated the securities industry. They discarded the old fixed-rate system for buying and selling securities in favor of one in which investors were free to negotiate with brokers over commissions. The intention of the SEC was to lower rates for the individual investors, but at first it did not work that way. The old-line, full-service Wall Street firms were forced to slash the commissions charged to large institutional customers, but they made up for the shortfall by drastically raising the fees charged to the smaller investors. "That left the little guy out in the cold," said Charles Schwab, and it opened up a golden opportunity for him. Schwab, who often shopped at K mart, began to visualize himself as the K mart of the stock brokerage business. He had been running a small, mom-and-pop, traditional stock brokerage operation. In his view, he was running a Kresge's—trying to be all things to all people. Now he was determined to become a K mart, to drop all the usual frills associated with the brokerage business—research, hand-holding, hot tips, and all the rest—and simply execute buys and sells for the customer at a discount price. Like K mart, his firm would make its money not on markup but on volume.

Charles Schwab was born in Sacramento, California, and he grew up in nearby Woodland, the son of a local lawyer and district attorney. Educated in local schools, he evidently displayed an entrepreneurial bent at an early age (his folksy, *How to Be Your Own Stockbroker* tends to portray a Horatio Alger image). As a young boy, he supposedly gathered English walnuts in the woods around his home and sold them for $5 a pound. Woodland was a farm community, and Schwab found many ways to make money in the area. The most successful of these was his chicken business, which, according to legend, he developed as a vertically integrated enterprise at age twelve. *Inc.* states, "Not content with just selling eggs, as many enterprising youngsters do, he also sold chicken droppings to the neighbors to fertilize their gardens. When the chickens got too old to lay eggs, he sold fryers.''

About this time the family moved to Santa Barbara, and Schwab channeled his energy into playing golf on the high school team and caddying to earn extra money. After graduating from high school, he went to Stanford, where he got his bachelor's in economics in 1959. Schwab remained at Stanford to get his MBA, and in 1961 he joined Investment Indicators, an investment advisory firm in the San Francisco area. There he spent several years studying growth stocks and market cycles, the results of which were published in the firm's newsletter. Eventually, Schwab branched out to manage a mutual fund during the last heady growth years of the late 1960s. Shortly thereafter, the fund got caught in the massive market collapse at the end of the decade. To make matters even worse, the state of Texas charged Schwab and his firm with selling shares in that state without being registered there. He fought them in the courts but was unsuccessful, and he came out of the whole affair about $100,000 in debt because of legal fees. Schwab extricated himself from these financial difficulties in 1973 when he arranged the sale of some timberland for his uncle, earning a large enough fee to pay off the rest of his debts and put $100,000 into his own brokerage firm.

He had opened his investment firm, Charles Schwab & Company, in 1971, which he ran as a fairly marginal operation for a number of years. Frustrated by his lack of success, Schwab was continually searching for a niche in the market. Finally, a friend from high school, Hugo Quackenbush (later a vice president at Charles Schwab & Company) suggested that he investigate the possibilities of discount brokerage because the SEC was planning a limited trial period for discounting. Charles Schwab & Company participated in that experiment. When the SEC decided to make discounting a permanent part of the brokerage scene in May 1975, Schwab was ready to take full advantage of the opportunity.

Schwab, from his single office in San Francisco, quickly set up a toll-free number to take orders nationwide, something no one else was capable of doing at the time. At that point, the company was considered little more than a mere ''gnat on an elephant's rump'' by the old-line, full-service brokerage firms, according to Quackenbush, but Schwab soon made his company a force to be reckoned with. As the larger firms lowered rates to large institutional investors and raised them to the small investors, Schwab had his opening. As he recalled in his 1984 book, ''If they'd lowered their rates, there'd be no such thing as a discount brokerage industry today. But to many people it was an insult.'' But even as Charles Schwab & Company began to emerge as a major factor in the discounting field, conventional wisdom held that it, along with all the other discounters, would fail. Schwab recalled that many of his own friends were convinced that ''nobody *buys* stocks, they're only *sold* stocks'' by high-powered broker-salesmen who earn high commissions.

But Schwab was certain he had the right idea. He paid his brokers straight salaries, without commissions, and his firm dispensed no investment advice or research; most important, Schwab's transaction fees were far lower than those of the retailers. To make his service more appealing to the small investor, Schwab used a clever advertising technique. His own photo was included in all the firm's advertising, providing a personal link between the company and the customers. A former Schwab executive commented on its effectiveness: "We'd interview customers, and they'd talk about 'Chuck' or 'Charlie.' It gave them a human being to relate to." By the end of his first full year of discounting, Schwab drew sales of $1.3 million, and although his firm was still small, it was clear that discounting was a permanent factor on the scene.

As a result, the major brokerage firms, according to Schwab, did everything they could to keep him and his discounting cohorts from becoming a further threat. Schwab and others found it difficult to buy seats on the stock exchanges, or to get leases in prime downtown buildings. The Crocker Bank broke off a fourteen-year relationship with Schwab, and the Bank of America twice denied him a loan. The concept of discount brokerage was a threat to the established interests, and they reacted with predictable antagonism. But that just made Schwab all the more determined. Although he is primarily a successful entrepreneur, there is also a bit of the crusader in him. According to *Business Week*, "[B]y all accounts, Schwab's populist sentiments are genuine," and he continually advises people on how to "keep your income from becoming [the broker's] income." That was unusual advice from somebody with a stock brokerage house in the 1970s, but that was the essence of discounting. Schwab began to offer his customers deep discounts on securities transactions, sometimes slashing them to only 30 or 40 percent of their former levels. Discounting became an enormous success, to the point that about 20 percent of all stock transactions in the late 1980s were placed through discounters. And Charles Schwab & Company was by far the largest of these discount firms. With over 100 branch offices in the United States and elsewhere, Schwab had sales of $465 million in 1987, and over 1.6 million customers—five times as many as its closest discount competitor, Quick & Reilly Group.

The key to Charles Schwab & Company's remarkable growth was its willingness to open branch offices at a breakneck pace. "More than anything else," said *Business Week*, "it was the decision to build branch offices that set Schwab & Company . . . apart from the pack of fledgling discounters." When his San Francisco office began to prosper, Schwab sought capital from banks, private investors, and customers to expand into other areas. His first branch office was in Sacramento, and his second came in 1976 in Los Angeles. Both offices boomed, and soon Schwab's offices began to sprout all over the nation. As the number of offices grew, it became apparent that the old, time-honored manual methods of taking and filling orders was no longer efficient enough. Therefore, Schwab & Company became one of the first brokerage firms to automate all processing of orders in each of its branches. The automation began in 1978, and was completed in 1980. By the mid–1980s, every one of the firm's 1,800 employees, with the single exception of Charles Schwab himself, had a computer terminal on his or her desk. The heart of the system was a huge data processing center at the San Francisco headquarters which runs twenty-four hours a day, seven days a week. This, in turn, allowed Schwab to offer twenty-four-hour service to his customers, the first to do so in the brokerage industry. This practice was also a tremendous success, and it helped to further establish the company's reputation as a firm highly responsive to the customers' needs. Assessing his achievements, Schwab said, "There was a tremendous advantage in not being part of Wall Street. They had been doing things the same way for years."

All of this, however, cost a great deal of money, and although Schwab & Company's growth rates were excellent, its profits were meager. As a result, it was hard to attract the capital needed for further expansion. Therefore, when Samuel H. Armacost, of BankAmerica, approached Schwab in late 1981 about a takeover, Schwab agonized over the offer for several weeks; ultimately, he accepted. BankAmerica offered Schwab $53 million in BankAmerica stock for Schwab & Company. Schwab himself, who owned 38 percent of the firm (he had earlier sold 20 percent to United Financial Corporation for $4.5 million, and the rest belonged to an employee stock option plan and key employees), received 850,000 shares of BankAmerica stock, then worth about $18.7 million. He was also allowed to remain as head of the brokerage subsidiary, he got a seat on the parent company's board, and he had his own, fairly independent board at Charles Schwab & Company.

There were both benefits and drawbacks to the sale. On the one hand, Schwab & Company got access to badly needed capital for vigorous expansion. The bank loaned the brokerage operation $50 million in much-needed capital, and Schwab's association with the prestigious bank added luster to the formerly downscale image of discount brokers. As a result, the company—which had sales of $41 million the year before they sold out to BankAmerica, with forty branch offices, 600 employees, and 220,000 customers—had ninety-three branches, including one in Hong Kong, 1.6 million customers, and sales of $308 million, by the end of 1986. It also moved its headquarters into plush offices in a twenty-eight-storied San Francisco high rise during this time. But Schwab had a number of problems with his banking association.

First of all, although Charles Schwab & Company's profits soared after the transaction, the bank's profits tumbled, and its stock prices declined along with the profits. This represented a threat to Schwab's individual fortune, and it got him into trouble with the SEC. When Schwab received his 850,000 shares, they were selling at $22. Shortly thereafter, Bank America's stock prices began to fall. In 1985, Schwab sold about 403,000 BankAmerica shares during a two-week period in June. During the same period, his wife also disposed of 143,000 shares of the stock. Each sold their stock at prices ranging between $18 and $19, a significant loss over what they were worth in 1982. But shortly after the sale, Bank-America reported a dismal $338 million loss on bad loans in that quarter. As a result, the bank's stock plunged on the exchanges to $15. Altogether, the

Schwabs had saved about $2.2 million by selling when they did, but the SEC investigated him for taking advantage of insider information, which he denied having done. Schwab claimed that the sales were made upon advice to diversify their investment portfolio and had had nothing to do with any impending losses at BankAmerica.

That was only part of his problem with the bank, however. Over the years, a power struggle developed between Schwab and Armacost over how rapidly Schwab & Company should be expanding. Armacost, quite understandably, considering the bank's heavy losses, wanted to go slowly, whereas Schwab wanted to pursue a more reckless game plan. Schwab took his case to the bank's board of directors, but could not interest them in his plans. "I felt like the Lone Ranger," he told an associate. Other programs also died because of friction between the staffs of Schwab & Company and BankAmerica. "Schwab's people ask tough questions," said a former bank official, and "a lot of BankAmerica people consider that rude." Schwab began to pressure Armacost into selling Schwab & Company back to him, but Armacost was at first uninterested. With nearly $5 billion in bad loans, however, BankAmerica had a desperate need for cash, and this was Schwab's opening.

Finally, in early 1987, Schwab and BankAmerica announced that he was buying back the brokerage company for $230 million, plus a 15-percent participation in equity growth. Several weeks later, Schwab took his firm public in order to raise capital to pay down the firm's $200-million debt, and also to provide additional capital for Schwab's mighty ambitions. He wanted to increase the number of branch offices in 1987 by 30 percent, to around 120, and eventually to open offices in London, West Germany, and Japan. Ethical and legal problems continued to cause Schwab and his firm problems. On November 14, 1988, *Business Week* revealed that Charles Schwab & Company had engaged in unauthorized trading in customer securities over a number of years. Hugo Quackenbush admitted that the firm had done so, and he promised to return the proceeds, some $1 million to $2 million to customers whose funds had been used. The rebate took a substantial bite out of the firm's profits, which had been calculated at just $9 million before the disclosure.

Schwab was also facing an increasingly critical situation in the brokerage market. He had found a lucrative market niche by providing discount brokerage to the sophisticated individual investor who did not need much hand-holding. But, he could not compete for the large institutional investor, nor for the small, first-time investor who needed a lot of guidance and advice. So, although Schwab had found and developed an important market, it was a limited one, and he felt the need to find ways of expanding his offerings. He decided to branch into selling term life insurance and in-house mutual funds as a way of broadening his product line, and he began to look for other outlets. "Chuck is positioning his firm between the wire houses and the barebones discounters," said one of his executives. But some competitors felt he was trying to do too much. "Schwab wants to be everything to everybody," said an executive at Quick & Reilly.

"That's hard to do." But Schwab, who was described in *Management Review* as having "an archetypal American countenance: WASPy, clean-cut good looks, quiet but confident, smiling," relishes a challenge. Having created the K mart of the stock brokerage industry, he seemed determined to make it as a major player in the field. As *Forbes* (June 15, 1987) commented, "Look out Shearson, Fidelity, Merrill and all the rest of you fat cats," Charles Schwab is on his way. (**A.** Charles Schwab, *How to Be Your Own Stockbroker*, 1984. **B.** *Forbes*, January 21, 1980, January 18, 1982, June 15, 1987; *Institutional Investor*, December 1981; *Time*, February 15, 1982; *Fortune*, March 22, 1982, January 1986; *Business Week*, August 2, 1982, November 7, November 14, 1988; *Money*, December 1982; *Banker*, June 1983; *New York*, August 26, 1985; *Inc.*, October 1985; A. David Silver, *Entrepreneurial Megabucks*, 1986; *Management Review*, September 1986.)

SEARLE, JOHN GIDEON (March 18, 1901–January 21, 1978). Pharmaceutical manufacturer, G. D. Searle & Company. It would make a fascinating and perplexing case study for a business school class. Take a pharmaceutical company, a solid, stable firm about seventy-five years old in the late 1950s. During the next quarter-century, this company would develop two products that would be in great demand, and since it would have a virtual monopoly on those markets for a number of years, the profitability of those products would be staggeringly high. Normally such inventiveness and profitability are the stuff of which legends are made. Yet in this case, the pharmaceutical concern, G. D. Searle & Company, was the perennial problem child of the industry—plagued by bad management. How and why could this firm snatch defeat from the jaws of victory? Not once, but twice?

G. D. Searle & Company was founded in Omaha, Nebraska, in 1888 by Gideon Daniel Searle and his son, Claude H. Searle. Two years later they moved the firm to Chicago, and Claude Searle, who had been educated as a physician, became president of the company. His son, John G. Searle, was born in Sabula, Iowa, and educated in the public schools of Wilmette, Illinois. After serving in the U.S. Naval Reserve during World War I, John Searle graduated from the University of Michigan in 1923. Upon graduation, he became a buyer for his father's pharmaceutical firm. A year later he became office manager, and in 1926 was named treasurer and head of the laboratory and office. In 1931 John Searle became vice president and general manager, and in 1936, upon the death of his father, he advanced to president and general manager, positions he retained for the next thirty years.

Prior to 1936, G. D. Searle was a small, but fairly profitable firm. With just ninety-five employees that year, working in a leased building, the company had sales of just over $1 million. Under John Searle's guidance, the company, which focused on manufacturing ethical pharmaceuticals for physicians, grew and prospered during the next quarter-century. Sales and profits increased impressively, until 1,100 employees were working in seven buildings in Searle's own industrial complex. Sales in that year amounted to nearly $33 million. The most important drugs John Searle developed during these early years were Dramamine, an antinauseant for motion sickness, which the firm brought out in 1949; Alidase, a hydrolytic enzyme for reducing barriers to the absorption of fluids; and Vallestril, an estrogen with reduced side effects for menopausal symptoms and suppression of lactation.

The big breakthrough for Searle came in 1957, however, when it developed Enovid, the first oral contraceptive—"The Pill." When the Food and Drug Administration (FDA) approved Enovid in May 1960, sales of the drug rocketed G. D. Searle's profits into the stratosphere, and the drug itself helped change the sexual mores of an entire generation. For an expenditure of about $10 a month and the discipline required to take twenty pills according to a rigidly prescribed monthly schedule, the pill was a safe, effective, and nearly 100-percent-certain method of contraception. Women, especially young women, rushed to their doctors to get prescriptions for the pill, and since Searle had a monopoly on the product for many years, the demand resulted in an enormous boom for the firm. Searle would never be the same again, and neither would America.

Female sexual activity, which had always been inhibited by the fear of unwanted pregnancies, a fear that helped sustain a double standard in sexual morality, was suddenly given new freedom and spontaneity. Although the sexual revolution among American women in the 1960s has undoubtedly been overemphasized, and although the role of the pill within that revolution has also probably been overstated, Enovid nonetheless stands as one of the few medical and commercial products that has had such a dramatic and profound cultural impact. The effect on G. D. Searle was equally impressive—between 1960 and 1964, Searle's earnings soared from $7.4 million to $24.2 million. Sales, which had grown steadily over the years under John Searle's guidance, and stood at $37 million in 1960, four years later had increased 137 percent to $87 million. Enovid was an extraordinarily profitable product, and during the first few years Searle had the market to itself. Inevitably, other pharmaceutical firms began to market their own oral contraceptives. Prices began to drop, and profits dipped along with them. In 1965, although Searle's sales were up, profits were off by about $1 million.

Searle had prided itself during John Searle's administration as being a strongly research-oriented organization. Disdaining the "me-too" approach to pharmaceuticals, Searle had deliberately sought profitable niches in drugs to control heart and circulatory diseases, the central nervous system, and mental disorders. About 20 percent of all Searle employees were engaged in research in the 1950s and 1960s, and the company poured 10 percent of its sales back into research, which was then one of the highest percentages in the drug industry. By risking the move into unexplored territories, Searle had often jumped far ahead of its competitors, as its success with Dramamine and Enovid attested. But the phenomenal success of Enovid created problems for Searle. As sales and profits in the product began faltering in the mid–1960s, John Searle was uncertain what to do.

By the end of 1964, G. D. Searle had total assets of $73 million, and almost half of that ($35 million) was in cash and marketable securities. With virtually no long-term debt and only $7 million in current liabilities, G. D. Searle was theoretically in a position to write its own ticket for the future. But John Searle, uncertain about what to do next, did nothing. His major decision was to treble the dividend, to $1.30 a share between 1962 and 1965, making an exceptionally generous payout of more than 70 percent. In 1963, John Searle attempted to arrange a merger with Chicago's Abbott Laboratories. He and the head of Abbott, George B. Cain, were good friends and the merger talks seemed to be amicable. Suddenly, at the last moment, negotiations were canceled. The reason for this has never been revealed, but rumor at the time laid the blame on the huge stock holdings of John Searle's two sons, Daniel Crow Searle and William Searle, along with his son-in-law Wesley Dixon. Since these relatives owned about 50 percent of Searle's stock, Abbott's executives were said to be worried about the amount of influence these men would have on the merged company. Given what happened to G. D. Searle after John Searle retired, they had cause to be concerned.

Unable to chart a course for his company, John Searle moved up to honorary chairman of the board in 1972, and Daniel Searle became president and chief operating officer. Born in Evanston, Illinois, in 1926, Daniel graduated from Harvard Business School before joining the family firm. William Searle, John's other son, became vice president of marketing. The Searle siblings decided to embark upon a diversification program for G. D. Searle. In short order, they acquired the Nuclear-Chicago Corporation, which made some 350 products, largely in nuclear instrumentation and medical electronics. They also began moving into the field of veterinary medicine, buying the tiny Curtiss Breeding Company, which developed Syncro-mate for sheep and cows. Searle also made several other small acquisitions. In addition, the long-time director of research at Searle, Dr. Albert L. Raymond, retired, and a new research director and legions of young researchers were hired to find new products for the struggling drug company. Many in the pharmaceutical industry were skeptical of Searle's program. They were particularly critical of the company's family rule. As one critic scoffed, "Outside of Searle, there are no one-man shows left in the pharmaceutical industry because no individual can be aware of all the problems." By the end of the 1960s, Searle had ceased to grow, but it still had an enormous cash balance of some $46 million. Unable to part with more of the company's huge cash assets, Daniel Searle practiced a policy of severe restraint.

The restraint paid no dividends. By the late 1970s, the once cash-rich company was in deep trouble. All of Daniel Searle's acquisitions, despite the caution he had exercised in selecting them, turned out to be disasters. As one industry analyst commented, "Few matched Searle in picking losers." As a result, Searle had to take $95 million in write-offs in the late 1970s, which put the company deeply in debt. Searle also came under investigation by the FDA, the agency's biggest investigative effort ever. The televised hearings ended in a decision that affected all of Searle's products. Two of its top-selling drugs—Aldactone and Aldactazide—were mandated to carry warning labels about potential cancer danger. Although Searle's sales increased throughout this period, reaching $844 million in 1977, its return on equity slipped from 50 percent to 11 percent. Once the most profitable drug company, it had become the least profitable. Its stock, which sold at 40 in 1973, had collapsed to 13 by 1977. Stockholders took a paper loss of $1.4 billion. The biggest loser was, by far, the Searle family, which still owned one-third of the stock.

The company's research efforts did not bear fruit. It not only failed to develop any significant new products, but it also lost the lead it once had in contraceptives. Even worse, the one new product which seemed to have some potential—Aspartame, an artificial sweetener discovered by accident—was delayed by the FDA for further study in the late 1970s. A major problem was that Searle submitted what the FDA termed "sloppy research data" to back up the safety claims of the product, and, given Searle's poor record with the agency, it was given little leeway. Daniel Searle finally faced the inevitable—he was incapable of running the family firm. He hired Donald H. Rumsfeld, a former congressman and secretary of defense in the Nixon administration, to take over the company. Daniel Searle moved up to chairman of the firm, and Rumsfeld became president and chief executive officer. William Searle and Wesley Dixon were given the honorary titles of vice chairman, but they were stripped of all managerial powers. Because the Searle family still owned such a huge block of stock, however, an industry analyst commented when Rumsfeld took over, "The No. 1 question is going to be who's really in control at Searle." It did not take long to find out.

Within a year, all the members of the Searle family had been removed from their offices in the Skokie, Illinois, headquarters, and Rumsfeld was in complete control. He trimmed Searle's bloated head office staff, and he inspected all Searle's facilities in the United States and abroad. He also announced that Searle would take massive write-offs to end its money-losing operations. Within a short period of time, he sold off twenty sickly Searle concerns, and he began a new diversification campaign for the firm. Rumsfeld's most optimistic asset at that time was a line of retail optical stores, called Vision Centers. The one profitable unit from Daniel Searle's earlier acquisition binge, it had over 300 stores when Rumsfeld assumed control. He expanded the number of stores rapidly, and by 1978 they represented revenues of $91 million. As Rumsfeld said, "It's certainly the most promising area of growth in the company." *Business Week* agreed with him, "The retail eyewear outlets are Searle's best bet for improving their performance."

Rumsfeld also emphasized consumer products, an area in which only the laxative Metamucil had been significant among Searle's offerings. The biggest hope was still Aspartame, despite the FDA's relentless obstruction. Rumsfeld finally managed to introduced it in Canada, where its sales were impressive. The key for Rumsfield and Searle, however, was the election of Ronald Reagan in 1980. Just after the election, an industry analyst predicted big things for Searle:

Take the fact that Don Rumsfield, Searle's chairman, is a big Republican—former Secretary of Defense under Nixon. Add to that George Bush, who used to be on the board of Eli Lilly and understands drug companies. Then consider that the FDA has held up the introduction of Aspartame, Searle's artificial sweetener, since 1974. If that product gets full approval, it could add from $1.25 to $1.75 annually to per share earnings within four years and become a solid competitor to saccharine. (*Forbes*, December 8, 1980)

He was right on target. Rumsfield's strong Republican connections, together with the Reagan administration's pro-business, antiregulatory attitude, brought about swift approval of Aspartame.

By 1982, G. D. Searle and Donald Rumsfield were in clover. The oceans of red ink of 1977 had become a profit of more than $120 million in 1982; sales had risen by more than one-third, exceeding $1 million. Although Rumsfield continued to look for acquisitions, he was ebullient about the company's future, saying, "We don't need to acquire companies to survive or do well." Yet Murphy's Law continued to plague Searle—whatever could go wrong, would go wrong. In 1983, the company suffered a severe decline in earnings, caused largely by a huge slump in their sales of prescription drugs. In order to save the floundering drug business, Rumsfield had to make a tough decision: he sold the 1,100-unit Pearle Vision Center Chain, which had had earnings of $34 million in 1982. Despite Rumsfield's enthusiasm for the optical group, and despite its profitability, it did not fit well with the drug company's other businesses. Rumsfield took $300 million from the sale to shore up the drug business, stating that "the biggest problem in the drug group is poor management."

Research and development continued to be a problem at Searle, and Daniel Azarnoff, whom Rumsfield chose as president of research and development in 1978, did not solve the problems. As the firm's financial officer admitted, "Searle's R&D pipeline hasn't been productive the last two or three years in terms of turning out new product." Rumsfield's solution was to cut and run. Forsaking its old image as a research company, Rumsfield decided that Searle would focus on marketing drugs developed by others. It would become a classic me-too drug company. But Searle's great promise continued to be Aspartame. Marketed as a tabletop sweetener under the name Equal, Searle also sold it as the ingredient NutraSweet for use in cold cereals, drink mixes, and other products. Sales of those two products, which were just $13 million in 1981, soared to $74 million in 1982, and over $200 million in 1983.

An enormous breakthrough with Aspartame came in 1983, when the FDA finally gave its approval for its use in carbonated drinks. Executives at Searle were so elated with the decision that one of them stated, "About all we have to do is hang out our shingle and say we're open for business.'' This approval came just about the same time the great weight and diet consciousness hit America. Suddenly everyone wanted to be thin and fit, and sugar was out. Diet drinks, especially diet colas, became enormously popular, and Searle rode that popularity to great profit. By 1983, sales of Aspartame topped $300 million, fully one-third of the stripped-down Searle's $946 million in sales. More than half the company's $151 million in profits came from the sweetener, and the bonanza had just begun.

The Searle family, in an attempt to diversify the family fortune, had sold $388 million worth of its stock in 1985 back to the company, greatly reducing its share in the company. They still, however, held nearly $600 million worth of the firm's stock, and they were anxious to dispose of that. The key for them was the fact that Aspartame was at the peak of the market. It was bringing exceptional profitability to G. D. Searle, and the Searle family did not want to experience a repeat of the birth control pill fiasco. They wanted to sell their stock while their stock was at its peak valuation. Therefore, a search commenced to find a buyer both for G. D. Searle and for the Searle family stock. But the price was terribly high, and they found it difficult to find a party willing to pay the price they demanded: $75 a share, or a total of $3.7 billion.

Finally, at the end of 1985, a buyer came forward—the mammoth Monsanto Chemical Company. Agreeing to pay a total of $2.8 billion for G. D. Searle, the Searle family got $578 million for their 7 million shares. This gave the descendants of John Searle a tidy fortune of $800 million to share. G. D. Searle itself, however, continued to have problems. Shortly after the sale to Monsanto, Searle's Copper-7 and Tatum-T intrauterine devices were the subject of lawsuits brought against the firm in early 1986. Although both products had been declared safe by the FDA, several plaintiffs complained of pelvic infection and infertility. Some 775 lawsuits were filed that year, and Searle had to spend $150 million defending itself. Even though they won eight of the ten cases tried, and were granted dismissals of 150 more, the lawyers' fees were staggering. Enraged, Monsanto stockholders also filed suit, charging that Searle failed to inform them of the suits. When they demanded the withdrawal of the contraceptives from the market, Searle complied. But the problems would not go away.

On September 9, 1988, a St. Paul, Minnesota, court, in a landmark decision, awarded $8.7 million to a woman who claimed she became infertile using Searle's Copper-7 device. The $8.7 million itself was no great problem, but many feared it would set a precedent for other huge judgments against Searle and Monsanto. As a result, Monsanto's share dropped from 78 to 71 on September 12, a paper loss of over half a billion dollars for investors in a single day. The only bright spot for Searle and Monsanto was NutraSweet. After buying Searle, Monsanto backed a large, aggressive advertising campaign for the product, with great success. NutraSweet's sales for the first half of 1988 were up 39 percent, to $694 million, and its red and white, peppermint swirl trademark was becoming famous the world over. When John Searle retired in 1966, he reportedly did not think much of his sons as businessmen. But he turned the firm over to them anyway, probably hoping for the best. Twenty years later, G. D. Searle had ceased to exist as an independent company, his heirs had become members of the rentier class, and the company itself had been reduced to virtually one product—NutraSweet. One has the feeling that that was not at all what crusty old John Searle had had in mind. (**B**. *NCAB*, 1:425; *Business Week*, November 5, 1966, May 2, 1977, March 19, 1979, July 4, July 18, 1983, January 30, October 15, 1984, February 18, 1985, February 17, February 24, 1986, September 26, 1988; *Forbes*, September 15, 1969, February 6, 1978, December 16, 1980, November 7, 1983, October 24, 1988; *Fortune*, September 3, 1984; *Who Was Who*, vol. VII; *Wall Street Journal*, April 26, 1985; *Who's Who in America*, 1986–87; Michael Patrick Allen, *The Founding Families*, 1987.)

SHAPIRO, IRVING SAUL (July 15, 1916–   ). Chemical company executive, business association leader, E. I. Du Pont de Nemours & Company and Business Roundtable. The business press was shocked when Irving Shapiro was named chairman and chief executive officer (CEO) of Du Pont in 1974. Du Pont, after all, was the quintessential family company, and it represented the apogee of old family money in America. Irving Shapiro was the second nonfamily member to run the company (Charles B. McCoy, his predecessor, was the first), but he was the first who had no connections either to the Du Pont hierarchy or to the Wilmington aristocracy (McCoy's father had been a Du Pont executive). Most of all, Shapiro was a Jew who had been picked to head a company whose founding family had never been renowned for their sympathy toward Jews. As Leonard Mosley said in *Blood Relations,* his book on the du Ponts, "There were still members of the family prejudiced enough to suspect a deep, dark Jewish plot when Irving Shapiro . . . began to rise in the organization." And Shapiro was an avowedly liberal Democrat in a staunchly conservative Republican company. Finally, he was a lawyer who had never operated a manufacturing plant in his life, in a company known for promoting stolid types who had risen through the ranks of finance or engineering. As Mosley wrote, Shapiro's appointment was momentous for Du Pont in many ways:

It was the beginning of the end of Du Pont as a family company. By the mid–1970s, with Irving Shapiro as chairman of the board, there were two thousand du Ponts living in and around Wilmington, but not a single one was on the board of directors or a member of the planning committees. They who had once been the owners of Du Pont were now its *rentier* class, living on the dividends earned for them by other men.

Irving Shapiro was born in Minneapolis, Minnesota, the son of Lithuanian immigrants. Sam Shapiro worked as a pants presser. After he married Frieda Lane, the middle-aged couple took in boarders to make ends meet, especially when three sons were born in six years, of whom Irving was the oldest. In 1924, when Irving was eight years old, Sam Shapiro borrowed $500 to open his own cleaning plant five miles from their home. Irving's younger brother, Jonas, still ran it in the 1970s.

The cleaning business was not lucrative, but as Irving's mother later said, "We were very poor, but we had a lot of respect, and so we'd forget that we had no money." Sam Shapiro was determined that Irving fulfill his father's ambition—that he become a lawyer. So, although Irving preferred accounting, he enrolled in the prelaw course at the University of Minnesota and went to law school there. While there, Shapiro was the editor of the law review, and in 1941 he graduated fourth in his class. Shapiro's education was a family venture; everyone pitched in to pay tuition, books, and other living expenses for the eldest son. Irving Shapiro also claimed that some of the money for school came from his winnings in a weekly poker game in the Shapiro living room.

After he was admitted to the Minnesota bar, Irving hung out his shingle with a local tax lawyer, who gave him office space in return for services. Within months, however, World War II broke out, and the entire world changed for Irving Shapiro. Classified 4-F because of an asthma condition, he was denied entrance into the armed services, and one of his law school professors found him a job with the newly established Office of Price Administration (OPA) in Washington, D.C. The new organization was desperate for lawyers to help it establish wartime rationing and price-control rules, and many young men just out of law school were brought in. Occupying the desk next to Shapiro was another young lawyer, Richard Nixon, who later left to join the U.S. Navy.

In 1942, after Shapiro went home briefly to Minneapolis to marry, he and his wife returned to Washington, but Shapiro soon became bored with his activities at the OPA. In June 1943 he transferred to the criminal division of the Justice Department, where he was assigned to the appellate section. Shapiro soon developed a reputation as a superb writer of briefs, and he gained admittance to the Supreme Court bar in 1944. In 1945, Shapiro's reputation was made in a difficult case, with little prospect of victory, that no one else at Justice wanted. In the words of Irving Shapiro, "they decided to let the kid from Minnesota take his raps with it and maybe learn something in the process." The government lost the case, but by less of a margin than they had expected. Many of the nation's top lawyers, who had been present in the courtroom during the government's case, were very impressed with Shapiro's ability.

Shapiro's next big case came in 1948, when he joined the five-man prosecution team for the famous "Dennis trial" of eleven communist leaders before Judge Harold Medina in New York. Ultimately, the government's case was upheld by the Supreme Court in 1951. It was the height of the Cold War period, and Shapiro became a hero for many anticommunists, among them the du Pont family. As Gerard Colby Zilg pointed out in *Du Pont: Behind the Nylon Curtain,* many du Pont family members had long been ardent anticommunists, and they had followed the Dennis trial very closely. As a result, they a came to respect Shapiro's ability in this complicated case. Oscar Provost, who had been Shapiro's boss at Justice, was by then one of Du Pont's lawyers, and he recommended hiring Shapiro. Although there was some opposition to this because Shapiro was a Jew, his unquestioned ability became the overriding factor.

Since Shapiro felt his advancement with the government had reached its limit, and because Du Pont offered a higher salary, he accepted, and he joined the legal department of E. I. Du Pont de Nemours & Company in Wilmington, Delaware, in 1951. With 130 lawyers, the Du Pont legal department was one of the largest in the nation. Shapiro was immediately assigned to its antitrust section. This was a whole new area for Shapiro, but before long he found himself deeply immersed in the General Motors (GM) divestiture case, one of the decade's major antitrust cases, which dragged on for nearly ten years before it was settled. Beginning as just one of many lawyers assigned to the case, by the time of its conclusion Shapiro had emerged as Du Pont's chief antitrust expert, and he was one of the most influential lawyers on its payroll.

The relationship of Du Pont, the du Pont family, and General Motors had long been a subject of governmental inquiry. At issue was Du Pont's ownership of 63 million shares of General Motors stock, about 23 percent of the total. The relationship was first investigated in 1927 by the Department of Justice and the Federal Trade Commission. In 1957, the court finally ruled against Du Pont, declaring that the interlocking ownership arrangement was in violation of the antitrust laws. The focus of the trial then switched to the issue of how Du Pont would divest itself of the GM stock. They wanted to be able to spin off the GM stock without too great a tax liability being incurred by their stockholders. Shapiro was put in charge of finding a solution to this problem.

Shapiro's answer was to have a bill introduced by Senator Frear of Delaware in 1959. The bill, applicable to this case only, was to amend the Internal Revenue Code to allow tax relief. Unfortunately for the du Ponts and Shapiro, even the usually compliant voters in Delaware were unwilling to comply with such blatant special-interest politics, and Frear was defeated for reelection. Shapiro's job became more complicated, but he responded by organizing a massive lobbying campaign in Washington. Described as "one of the most successful corporate lobbying efforts in history," it cost several million dollars in lobbyists' fees and other expenses, and it clearly demonstrated Shapiro's unique ability to manipulate the corridors of power in Washington. The end result was that the Frear Bill was finally passed by the Senate in January 1962 and signed into law by President Kennedy. Mosley commented that the bill was "said to have been so carefully and brilliantly constructed that it saved the du Pont family nearly a billion dollars in stock it might otherwise have had to sell." Shapiro denied that, saying,

It was not nearly as good a settlement for the du Ponts as you might suppose, and as rumor has it. We got a substantial amount of relief for the ordinary stockholders, du Pont among them. But a substantial amount of the burden was picked up by the stockholders of Christiana. . . . In a very real sense, the members of the du Pont family took a substantial tax load in order to take care of other shareholders in the company. . . . They willingly gave up tax benefits in order to protect ordinary stockholders.

Although Shapiro may have saved the du Pont family fortunes by this maneuver, it cost them something more important—the power to control the family company. And this led, if somewhat circuitously, to Shapiro's heading the firm.

During these same years, Shapiro came to be increasingly relied upon by members of the du Pont family for advice on legal and business matters. In addition , executives at Du Pont itself turned to him for advice. As a Du Pont official told the *Wall Street Journal*, "He'd tell them *how* they could do things, not *why* they couldn't." As a result, Shapiro became known as a "can do" lawyer, and his influence soon transcended his actual position in the company. In 1965, he was advanced over several senior lawyers (among them Pierre "Pete" du Pont) to become assistant general counsel. Continuing to expand his influence among corporate and family members, in September 1970, Shapiro skipped past the post he had long coveted—general counsel of the company—to become a vice president and director of the company, and a member of its executive committee. Shapiro's advancement came as a great surprise to the business community, since, in the words of *Business Week*,

The executive committee is the pinnacle of Du Pont. The men on it have traditionally spent their working lives at Du Pont and have proved their merit as general managers of an operating department before being allowed to guide corporate policy and oversee the operating departments.

Clearly, a star had been born at Du Pont.

With his new position, Shapiro inherited a number of problems and responsibilities. A major problem concerned Corfam, a synthetic substitute for leather. Corfam might have died an early death, but for the fact that it was championed in the early 1960s by Lammot du Pont Copeland, the last of the family members to run the giant Du Pont firm. No one challenged him, and, as a result, the company poured more than $150 million into the product. Shapiro was asked to analyze the situation, and his report minced no words. "What would Wilmington Dry Goods do with a losing item?" he asked. "Wouldn't they get rid of it?" In retrospect, Shapiro a few years later said, "We should have put the knife to it sooner."

In 1972, McCoy appointed Shapiro senior vice president and gave him the leading role in negotiating the terms of the proposed merger into Du Pont of Christiana Securities, the family holding company which owned 28 percent of Du Pont's stock. Again, this was an extremely touchy, even explosive issue. By diluting the family's voting power, it made Du Pont more fully a public corporation, but it also benefited family members because Christiana had a lower market value than Du Pont. The challenge for Shapiro was to devise a settlement which was fair to both sides. Ultimately, he devised a taxfree exchange of 1.123 shares of Du Pont for each share of Christiana common. Shapiro's proposal was accepted by the family and by Du Pont's board, but it was held up by a court decision. An appeal to the Supreme Court, however, resulted in a decision favorable to Du Pont.

In 1973, Shapiro was named vice chairman of Du Pont, a move which clearly indicated he would succeed Charles McCoy as chairman and CEO, which, in fact, he did a year later. Edward R. Kane, a chemist and operating man, was named vice chairman. What soon evolved was what commentators called a case of "Mr. Outside" and "Mr. Inside." Kane was given primary responsibility for internal operating matters at Du Pont; Shapiro was primarily responsible for Du Pont's relations with the outside world, especially the government. The company Shapiro took over was a massive operation. Begun in 1801 by Irénée du Pont de Nemours* as a gunpowder plant, it had been run by a succession of du Pont family* members over the years. Credited with having "invented" the modern corporation, the du Ponts also pioneered the "family-tree" style of organizational chart, delegating authority to various levels of managers and committees within the company. In the 1920s the firm began to diversify into chemicals, paints, and other areas; by the time Shapiro took over it had 113,000 employees, 224 plants in twenty-seven countries, and worldwide sales of over $5 billion. It was the nation's largest chemical company, Delaware's largest employer, the largest producer of synthetic fibers, and the leading producer of gell explosives in the United States.

Du Pont was also besieged by problems in the early 1970s. The worldwide depression of the early 1970s had severely affected its volume of business, and the energy crisis, which greatly affected the cost and availability of energy, took a heavy toll on its profits. About 40 percent of Du Pont's sales were to the textile industry, which was suffering greatly in the early 1970s. Since most of Du Pont's products were petroleum based and since the price of oil had skyrocketed, Du Pont had been more adversely affected by the rise in petroleum prices than most firms. Furthermore, top management at Du Pont had tended for years to be inbred, parochial, and narrow-minded. As Shapiro recognized, "There was a reliance around here on historical ways. There was some paternalism. There was a sense that Du Pont was different from any other company. It took a period of pain before people recognized that you can't play that way anymore."

During his first years of running Du Pont, Shapiro emphasized integration and profitability rather than growth and expansion. He also took some deep cuts in key areas, he reduced employment, and, in his most daring move, he cut back on research and development. Long a sacred cow at Du Pont, which regarded itself as a premier research company, Shapiro instead stressed the development of a limited range of new products, adopted aggressive new marketing techniques, and junked the vaunted Du Pont decentralized administration system, establishing a more centralized organization in its stead. Shapiro recognized that one of the firm's key weaknesses lay in the area of raw materials. It had long been Du Pont policy to buy raw materials and concentrate its capital on more profitable specialty chemicals. But the energy crisis had changed all that. Oil-based raw materials were by then far too expensive, and this had been a major cause of the company's poor profitability in 1974 and 1975. Shapiro decided to take Du Pont into basic chemicals, making it the first fiber maker to make a major move in that direction. Shapiro characterized his administration as "lean and tough," and some of his methods drew criticism from several quarters in the early years, but by the end of the 1970s, it was clear the methods had positive results.

Fortune, in a 1979 article, said, "Going into the 1980's, Du Pont is a smarter company than it was at the start of the 1970's." Reducing Du Pont's dependence on synthetic fibers (although that still remained its largest single product), Shapiro increased the firm's market share in specialty products such as agricultural chemicals, electronic connectors, blood analyzers, and photo systems—all high-technology products. By 1979, more than one-third of Du Pont's net earnings came from sales of such products. Shapiro said, "We've regained the momentum, now we can restore ourselves as the premier company in this industry." Although Du Pont spent over $400 million on research and development in 1978, which was still twice as much as Dow, its nearest competitor, it represented just 3.6 percent of sales, compared to 6.8 percent before Shapiro took over.

A major reason for Shapiro's choice as CEO in 1974, however, concerned the kind of relations he would be able to forge with the outside world, especially the government. Virtually unknown outside of Wilmington when he was appointed, by 1980 *Industry Week* reported that "Mr. Shapiro is as close as any U.S. businessman to being a household name." After Shapiro was appointed, he was extremely effective in guiding the company through a round of Federal Trade Commission hearings on the titanium pigments issue, and with the successful conclusion of that, he began to expand his influence. A speech he gave to the New York Board of Trade in 1975 particularly attracted attention. Calling for social progress in a number of areas, he urged business to provide safer, more useful products, and to give more attention to the whole question of ethics in business. Partially as a result of this, he was named president of the Business Roundtable and served from 1976 to 1978.

The Business Roundtable had been organized in the early 1970s, at the insistence of U.S. Steel's Roger Blough.* An association of over 150 top officials from *Fortune* 500 corporations, it was described by *Business Week* in 1976 as "the most powerful voice in business." Working largely behind the scenes prior to 1976, it had developed a reputation as "the most effective invisible lobby on Capitol Hill." Under the stewardship of such men as John Harper of Alcoa, Fred Borch and Reginald Jones of General Electric, and Shapiro, the Roundtable for some years was a personification of Shapiro's approach. As Ralph Nader and William Taylor commented in *The Big Boys*,

One of the architects of the Roundtable was former Du Pont chairman Irving Shapiro, and the organization reflected his approach to politics: a distaste for public controversy and a preference for operating quietly on Capitol Hill, a bipartisan attitude that did not exclude co-operation with pro-business Democrats, and a willingness to compromise on thorny legislative issues.

The Roundtable was, as Don Girvitz said, "the supreme spokesmen for the American business community."

With Jimmy Carter's ascension to the White House, it made sense for the Business Roundtable to have a Democrat at its helm, and Shapiro was the ideal choice. He was able to give the business community unusually close access to the White House and federal policy-making. As a White House spokesman said,

No businessman is closer to us than Irving Shapiro. He talks with Anne Wexler, Stu Eizenstat, or our office on every major business issue. And the President seeks his counsel often. He's straightforward, not reticent in voicing his views, and a man with tremendous respect by his peers in business.

Although some other businessmen were critical of what they saw as Shapiro's excessive involvement with government, Shapiro defended himself eloquently: "Government is a silent, unrecruited partner, and it's essential for CEO's to communicate with it and understand it. In no way can they do that without getting involved with the government."

The biggest change Shapiro brought to the Business Roundtable was to bring its operations and voice more into the open. "The fundamental change I made was to take it public. I felt that a group of businessmen should not operate in secret, for it would be misunderstood." With his strong interest in public policy, Shapiro was viewed by many as one of the 1970s generation of CEOs. It was part of a policy to get business executives more involved with the outside world. As Shapiro said in an interview in *Harvard Business Review*, "The whole function of the Roundtable in a sense is to educate chief executives about the outside world, to get them involved in public policy issues, to get them to understand what motivates people in government and how they approach problems." It was a stance, however, which did not survive the 1970s; the 1980s brought the onslaught on American productivity and profitability by the Japanese, and at the same time the Reagan administration stressed the removal of government from the regulatory arena. Both actions stimulated a new era of selfishness and disdain for public affairs.

By then, however, Irving Shapiro had retired; he stepped down as Du Pont chairman in 1981. The firm had $13.7 billion in sales in 1980—an increase of about 250 percent from 1973. Earnings continued to rise, reaching $716 million in 1980, a 22-percent increase over the previous year. By 1987, Du Pont's sales stood at $30.5 billion, and profits were $1.8 billion. With 140,000 employees, it was by far the largest chemical company in America. But, its sales had grown slowly since 1983, and annual profits, on an average, gained only 13 percent during these years. Irving Shapiro had provided Du Pont with a golden age, one many had not expected would come again. He justified the confidence Irénée du Pont had shown in him at the time of his appointment. The highest ranking of the eight family members working for the company at the time, du Pont had said, "Shapiro has a confidence about him and a willingness to talk to anybody who has a problem." Far from being upset over not being offered the top job, du Pont said,

As a stockholder, I wouldn't vote for me. This company must be run by the best people able to run it. . . . It would be a remarkable quirk if among the blood relations there were several candidates with the immense mental ability needed to run this company. (Mosley, *Blood Relations*)

All agreed, Irving Shapiro had just that ability. (**B**. Max Dorian, *The Du Ponts: From Gunpowder to Nylon*, 1962; Ralph Nader, *The Corporate State*, 1971; *Time*, May 3, 1971, July 30, 1973; *Wall Street Journal*, December 14, 1973; *Business Week*, December 15, 1973; Gerard Colby Zilg, *Du Pont: Behind the Nylon Curtain*, 1974; *Fortune*, January 1974, September 10, 1979; *Forbes*, July 1, 1975, March 5, 1979; *Current Biography*, 1976; *Harvard Business Review*, March-April 1978; *Chemical and Engineering News*, March 12, 1979; *Financial World*, March 15, 1979; Milton Moskowitz et al., *Everybody's Business*, 1980; Leonard Mosley, *Blood Relations*, 1980; *Industry Week*, October 27, 1980; Roger Shook, *CEO's*, 1981; Don Girvitz, *The New Entrepreneurs*, 1984; Graham D. Taylor and Patricia E. Sudnick, *Du Pont and the International Chemical Industry*, 1984; Ralph Nader and William Taylor, *The Big Boys*, 1986; *Who's Who in America*, Supplement, 1987–88.)

SHAVER, DOROTHY (July 29, 1897–June 28, 1959). Retailer, Lord & Taylor. At 9:30 A.M. each working day, a long, sleek black limousine eased to a halt outside the 39th Street entrance of the dignified Lord & Taylor department store in New York City. When the door opened, a tall, handsomely dressed woman carrying a delicate lace handkerchief emerged from the car and swept into the store. Her status was apparent; salesgirls, service managers, and elevator starters all greeted her with a deferential "Good morning, Miss Shaver." She took the elevator to the ninth floor, where in a luxurious island off the lamp department she eased herself behind a $3,000 Chippendale desk. In this comfortable, bright, elegant room Dorothy Shaver ruled the fortunes of Lord & Taylor with an iron fist for nearly forty years. Although she did not become president of the firm until 1945, she had clearly been its dominant and driving force since the 1920s.

   Dorothy Shaver was born in the tiny Arkansas town of Center Point, the daughter of James D. and Sallie (Borden) Shaver. Her father was a lawyer and chancery court judge in the nearby town of Mena, where the family moved shortly after Dorothy's birth. There she grew up, sang in the Episcopal Church choir, and graduated with honors from high school. At that point she was preparing to marry a law student, but her father disapproved of the relationship, and he sent her away to school at the University of Arkansas. After two years there, Shaver went to the University of Chicago, where she majored in English. Her younger sister, Elsie, who had an artistic bent, was planning to go to New

York City in 1920, hoping to seek her fortune as an illustrator. Dorothy decided to tag along "for the ride," but soon after arriving, she convinced her sister to make up some impish-looking rag dolls with which she felt they could make their fortune. Elsie created five different doll characters, which Dorothy called the "Five Little Shavers" and began to market. In this attempt, Dorothy and Elsie were aided by a combination of pluck and good fortune.

The good fortune came in the person of a distant cousin, Samuel Wallace Reyburn, president of Lord & Taylor and founder of its parent company, Associated Dry Goods Corporation. Mr. Reyburn was, in Dorothy Shaver's words, "from our part of the land, knew my parents, and was a kind friend." He made a family call on the Shavers one day, and at the end of his visit, Dorothy displayed the pluck that aided her rise in the business world. As Reyburn rose to leave, Dorothy said, "Show Mr. Reyburn your dolls, Elsie." The next morning four Lord & Taylor executives were at the Shavers' home, arranging to put the dolls into production for sale in the store. Patented as the "Little Shavers," the dolls became a great fad in the early 1920s, and women carried them in public as mascots. This earned the sisters a sizable income for six years. By 1924, however, Elsie had become tired of making the dolls, and Dorothy began her career with Lord & Taylor as a comparison shopper.

Lord & Taylor had been founded in 1826 in lower Manhattan near the docks and horse ferry. Here Samuel Lord and George Washington Taylor established their dry-goods store. Over the years, New York's shopping districts flourished and died in several places, and Lord & Taylor moved five times before arriving at their store on Fifth Avenue in 1914. In that same year, Samuel Reyburn came to New York from Arkansas to become treasurer of Lord & Taylor, and at the same time formed Associated Dry Goods out of Lord & Taylor and several other financially troubled stores in the city. Reyburn became president of both concerns in 1916, positions he held for nearly twenty years.

Dorothy Shaver's first job was as a comparison shopper, checking prices in competitive stores. After several months, she wrote a report in which she recommended elimination of the position, arguing, "Why not forget about our competitors and concentrate on improving our products?" Her suggestion was accepted, her career as a retail executive was launched, and her idea set the tone of Lord & Taylor's development as a tony department store for a new kind of customer. New York previously had department stores like Macy's and Gimbels, which catered to the working-class and lower-middle-class subway riders, and the uptown establishments like Henri Brendel, Hattie Carnegie, and Bergdorf Goodman, which catered to the wealthy shopper. Shaver carefully and painstakingly selected a specific kind of customer she wished to attract to Lord & Taylor—the wives and daughters of successful men—upper-middle-class women who were emerging in greater numbers in the 1920s, both in the city and in the newly created suburbs. These women wanted quality clothing with good fashion lines presented in pleasant, even slightly luxurious, surroundings. Dorothy Shaver provided that kind of clothing in precisely that sort of environment at

Lord & Taylor. It was a combination often referred to simply as "the Shaver touch."

In 1925, Dorothy Shaver became director of interior decoration and fashion. In that position, she established a board of fashion advisors who worked directly with designers and producers to improve the quality of the store's merchandise. This innovation was the first of its kind in an American department store, but soon it became an essential part of the business. After she was elected to the store's board of directors in 1927, Shaver imported a $100,000 collection of modern art and decorative objects from Paris with great fanfare. This brought fame and profit to the store, and also started a craze in modern decoration all over the country. As a result of these successes, Miss Shaver in 1931 was named vice president in charge of advertising, publicity, and the bureau of fashion, with an expanding influence in the retail sphere.

Dorothy Shaver used this position to enhance her influence in a daring manner in the 1930s—she invented something she called the "American look," and she began to focus on American designers and fashion. Her efforts helped to make New York the center of the fashion world. Throughout the 1920s, Paris was the fashion capital of the world, and *Vogue* had decreed as an article of faith during this time that only Paris could make a gown. But with Shaver's own concept of selling fashion to upper-middle-class women it made sense to promote practical, quality clothing from American designers. They just needed someone with the panache to carry it off. The advertising techniques Shaver pioneered at Lord & Taylor during these years sedately plugged one fashion idea at a time, rarely mentioned price, and always stressed the store. The whole purpose, as Shaver said, was "not to sell a specific item. It [was] to plant the idea that we know fashion." A number of other subtle touches also promulgated this concept: red-felt cushions for the customers to rest their elbows on while trying on gloves; tiny little seed pearls free to every prospective bride who shopped for her trousseau there; a complimentary pink or blue rattle with every layette purchased at Lord & Taylor; a soup bar in the men's shop; gay rabbits and papier-mâché cows leading the way to the children's department—all of this was part of the Shaver touch.

From her sponsorship of American designers and creative artists developed the annual Lord & Taylor American Design Awards begun in 1938. During the 1930s, Shaver pioneered a number of other innovations. Lord & Taylor became famous for the window displays she promoted. This was especially true at Christmas, when no merchandise was displayed in the windows, but music was piped to the outside from gold bells. She also changed the store's colorful awnings with each season. One of the most eagerly awaited signs of summer was the appearance of Lord & Taylor's bright rose-covered awnings in the first days of the season. One of her most successful innovations was the creation of the first fashion department devoted to teenagers. All of these innovations were highly successful, and although Associated Dry Goods paid no dividends throughout the depression, Lord & Taylor did show a profit in every year except 1933.

During the early 1940s, Dorothy Shaver was given charge of the store's branch store program, and she established a store in Manhasset, Long Island, in 1941. During the war years, she also served as a general consultant to the Office of the Quartermaster General and volunteered in various other positions. Then, in 1945, she was appointed president of Lord & Taylor at a salary of $110,000, succeeding Walter Hoving, who left to run his own chain of department stores. Upon her appointment, Dorothy Shaver became one of the very few women presidents of a department store. (Beatrice Fox Auerbach[†] was the only other woman to achieve that status at the time.)

Miss Shaver became head of Lord & Taylor at a significant point in the store's history. The company, with large-scale expansion designs on the drawing board, planned to open a large, new, main store farther up Fifth Avenue, between 52nd and 53rd Streets, and also to open several more suburban branches. Shaver's greatest ambition when she became president, however, was to push the store's annual gross sales, which stood at $29 million when she took over, to $60 million. These results were achieved in a dizzying fashion. During her presidency, five new suburban stores were opened, and a sixth was under construction in Washington, D.C. Store sales reached $50 million in 1951, and had topped $100 million by the time she died from a stroke in 1959. By 1980, there were thirty-three Lord & Taylor stores mostly in the Northeast, but scattered in several other states also. It remained one of the most successful units of the struggling Associated Dry Goods chain. In 1986, Associated Dry Goods was purchased by May Company, one of the so-called "power retailers" of the 1980s. Its mission was to bring Lord & Taylor into the modern age. As late as the 1980s, sales slips were still written out by hand at Lord & Taylor, and stuffed into old-fashioned cash drawers. When May Company took over, it installed computerized cash registers and sophisticated new management systems. An executive at the Liz Claiborne[†] firm remarked, "Lord & Taylor was in Neanderthal times, now there's an entire sophisticated system to give merchants up-to-the-minute sales trends."

Dorothy Shaver was a tough, demanding boss, but by all accounts she was well liked, and certainly deeply admired, by her employees. Most even felt that it was fun to work for her, since she had such drive and creativity (as she once said, "I like to stir things up"). As a manager, she stressed fundamentals, such as the basic rules of stock control, a long-range buying policy, turnover rate, and the management of the store's prima donnas. But once these essentials had been mastered, Miss Shaver liked to let creativity flow. As she said, "Learning to run a store is like learning to play a piano. Master the fundamentals, as one masters the scales, then let yourself go."

The world of retail sales, especially in department stores, is a tight, cutthroat one. To rise to the top, whether male or female, one must be able to compete intensively every waking day from the moment one enters the firm at the ground floor. And the pressure and competition increase in intensity as one moves up the ranks. That Dorothy Shaver made it to the top is significant. That she was a woman who made it to the top when that was a rarity is even more significant. That she made it to the top without evoking the typically misogynist reactions is truly exceptional. The stereotype of the career woman in the 1940s and 1950s was of a hardbitten, bitter, rasping harpy. Dorothy Shaver, though, cleverly hid her iron fist in a soft velvet glove. As *Life* magazine (May 12, 1947) commented at the time, she belonged to the "Little Women School." That is, she was always quintessentially feminine, often making a "feminine fuss over thunderstorms." She was an expert at manipulating the male ego, with her philosophy that "the best way to sell an idea is to make the other person think he thought of it first." Once, when asked how she got along with men, Dorothy Shaver answered demurely, "The best answer to that is that I have survived three changes of management and got a promotion each time." In 1976, as part of Lord & Taylor's 150th anniversary celebration, one of her American Design Awards was re-vived—an annual Dorothy Shaver Rose Award for "an outstanding individual whose creative mind has brought new beauty and deeper understanding to our lives." (**B**. *Time*, December 31, 1945, May 2, 1953; *Current Biography*, 1946; *New York Times*, January 5, 1947, June 29, 1959; *Life*, May 12, 1947, June 29, 1959; *Notable American Women; National Cyclopaedia of American Biography*, 56:507–8; *Business Week*, December 21, 1987.)

SHERMAN, NATHAN H. (1898?–July 29, 1980) and **GORDON B. SHER-MAN** (1927–May 8, 1987). Muffler company founders, Midas International. Gordon Sherman was president of Midas International in the 1960s. The company made mufflers. For automobiles. Gordon began to give money from the Midas Foundation to Ralph Nader, who had announced that he wished to eliminate the internal combustion engine. That would also eliminate mufflers. When Midas' dealers and board of directors heard about this, they were not happy. Some thought Gordon ought to have his head examined; the rest just wanted him to resign. Gordon's father, Nate Sherman, agreed, and what ensued was a bitter proxy fight for control of the giant muffler company. Gordon lost and went off to save the world through his involvement in a number of organizations. Nate, who was seventy-three when he regained control of Midas, tried to run it for a few years, but ultimately he had to sell the company. *Time*, saying it had all the overtones of a Greek tragedy, called the affair the "Ambush at Generation Gap."

Nate Sherman was running a moderately successful auto parts distribution company in Chicago. Called International Parts Corporation, it was similar to any number of like concerns across the nation. Gordon Sherman, who was born in Omaha, Nebraska, and later moved to Chicago with his parents, was educated at the University of Chicago, from which he graduated in 1950 with a B.A. Gordon joined his father's auto parts firm. It is difficult to know just how the idea for Midas Muffler evolved, since in later family disputes both father and son claimed credit for it. The weight of available evidence, however, indicates that it was Gordon's idea. Fresh out of college and always full of innovative ideas, Gordon began to develop the concept of a specialty store for mufflers—one that would be franchised and would be far different from anything that had existed before. In March 1956, father and son organized Midas, Incorporated. Since International Auto Parts had the capital, personnel, and contacts to get Midas started, little new capital was needed. Nate Sherman became the majority stockholder of the new company and also the president. Gordon, who officially had the title of executive vice president, often called himself president of the firm, and every newspaper and magazine article covering Midas in the 1950s and early 1960s assumed he was running the company. Gordon later claimed he actually had functioned as chief executive of the firm for years before he was officially given the title.

Without trying to unravel who actually ran the company during these years, it is clear that there was some sort of synergism that had a highly beneficent effect on Midas' growth. Gordon Sherman was the idea man in the company, although some of his ideas no doubt could be dismissed as slightly fanciful. Gordon liked to pipe Bach chamber music into Midas' Chicago offices through hidden loudspeakers, while technicolored finches chirped in a giant cage. He was known occasionally to hold executive meetings at a zoo, or in the office by candlelight. "A certain truth," he explained, "comes out at night that doesn't come out in the board room." He didn't like to hire men with business training or MBAs. Instead, he preferred psychologists and sociologists, whom he recruited through ads in the *Saturday Review* and *Psychology Today*. Gordon Sherman felt it was essential for his executives to be able to communicate: "You can take a so-called good businessman, but you can't necessarily teach him to communicate," he said. "But if you take a man who somehow has learned to excel in the skills of communication, put him in a business suit and pay him a fair salary, then in short order he'll learn to read a financial statement." If all of this might have been viewed as somewhat eccentric by other businessmen, none could argue with Sherman's other ideas for creating Midas Muffler.

First of all, Gordon wanted to create a chain of shops that sold nothing but mufflers and did only exhaust-system repairs and replacements. This specialization would give the company a clear focus. He was determined to make his muffler shops more comfortable and accessible to the average customer than traditional auto repair shops. Midas mechanics, for example, were not allowed to use uncouth expressions in front of the customer. "Nudie" calendars were not allowed on the walls. The customers were invited to come back into the shop and watch the muffler being installed. Many shops had playpens to occupy the children while work was being done. Gordon Sherman had grasped a significant demographic fact almost before it happened—as America moved to the suburbs, it was the wife who had the car, who was responsible for having it repaired. In response, Gordon established a muffler repair environment that was congenial to women.

Midas did not sell its mufflers on price—never did they claim to be "cheaper than" or even "as cheap as" the competition. Instead, they stressed fast service, quality installation, and durability of product. Customers were promised an average time in the shop of fifteen minutes, a far cry from the usual auto shop, where customers were told to leave their cars all day. Sherman recognized that the car was the lifeblood of suburban America; it could not easily be left all day, and women were not comfortable spending hours in a repair shop. So, by stressing how quickly the muffler could be repaired, Sherman made it a less daunting experience for people who had never had their cars repaired before. In addition, the muffler was guaranteed for life. When a woman took the car in to have the muffler replaced, this was her safety valve. She did not know mufflers, but she did understand a lifetime guarantee—how could she go wrong? Sherman had the mufflers painted a gold color, which did not affect performance in any way but did make the product look better, classier. "The customer may only see that gold color for a minute or so during installation," Gordon Sherman said, "but that's enough. He knows then he's getting something extra—for a competitive price." Again, this was a crafty recognition that packaging was equally important to this new generation of consumers. Finally, Gordon Sherman used extensive radio and magazine advertising for Midas, advertising that was aimed specifically at the housewife. Two years after the firm was started, he was spending $2 million annually on advertising.

Gordon Sherman also developed an important innovation with his "field counselors," who acted as management consultants to the shops. These individuals, who were recruited very carefully, were generally found through advertisements placed in college alumni magazines. They were not from traditional business backgrounds. About half were recruited from the teaching profession and were what Gordon called "the central concept on which we succeed or fail. . . . Counselors are an extension of our leadership." He carried forward some of these same ideas in the selection of dealers also. Since he was trying to merchandise the idea of mufflers in a very different way, Gordon Sherman was not satisfied to just sign on dealers who had a background in auto repair, or who simply had enough money to start a dealership. Rather, he developed a special technique for screening applicants. Gordon set aside one day a week in which he personally interviewed prospective dealers. If he liked their looks, they were interviewed further in a group by a clinical psychologist.

If prospective dealers passed those tests, the other requirements at Midas were relatively light. A dealer in the early years needed only about $15,000 to start a shop. He paid no lump sum for the franchise, and no royalties to Midas on his business. He simply had to agree to sell only mufflers, agree that they would only be Midas, and abide by the other rules outlined above. Midas made its money solely from the sales of mufflers and exhaust parts, which were sold directly to the dealers without any commissions to jobbers or wholesalers. Gordon Sherman felt it was important for the dealers to feel as if they were independent businessmen. Although Midas gave advice on a number of matters, usually decisions were left in the hands of the dealers. He expressed his philosophy on this at one point:

By its nature, franchising is an organizing force, taking a lot of people who have nothing to do with each other and organizing them into some kind of structured situation—whether it be by product, or service, or image, or distribution—and that's why franchising is so powerful today. You don't dominate the franchisees as if you're their boss; and yet you're not intimidated by them as if they are your customers. It is a beautiful balanced program of human relationships which imposes all kinds of responsibilities on the franchisor no matter what the nature of the franchisor or franchisee might be. (Kursh, *The Franchise Boom*)

Gordon Sherman uttered these words in the mid–1960s, at a time when franchising had become a rather well-known phenomenon in American life. But it is imperative to recognize that in 1956 there were few franchises, and not many people were familiar with the concept. When Gordon and Nate Sherman set up their franchising operation, they had few guidelines. Even in 1965, when Paul Rand Dixon, chairman of the Federal Trade Commission, attempted to define franchising, he had to say:

The so-called franchise boom is a relatively recent development on the American economic scene . . . [and] the many varieties of franchise systems differ among themselves so widely that any attempt to state applicable rules to all such systems must either be so broad as to approach the meaningless or [be] tailored with numerous qualifications in order to fit all varieties of franchises. (Kursh, *The Franchise Boom*)

Although franchising had a rather long history in the United States, dating back at least into the nineteenth century when Cyrus McCormick* franchised dealers for his farm implements, and Coca-Cola sold its products through franchised bottlers in the early twentieth century, it did not really become a common feature on the American economic landscape until after World War II. The trend began slowly in the 1950s, when the Shermans started their muffler business, and then boomed in the 1960s and beyond. By 1967, sales made by franchised businesses accounted for about 10 percent of the GNP in the United States. The boom slowed somewhat in the 1970s, and then took off again in the 1980s. In 1980, there were about 442,000 franchise outlets in the United States, and they generated $336 billion in sales. But in 1956, when the Shermans started Midas Muffler, few of these large franchise operations were visible. Ray Kroc* had just begun to peddle McDonald's franchises; Henry Winokur had just barely started his Mr. Donut chain, with just four regional stores; and later franchise giants like Holiday Inn, Kentucky Fried Chicken, and Radio Shack were not even off the drawing boards.

Nate Sherman also played a role in the early development of the Midas chain. According to one account of Midas' operations, Gordon Sherman's loosely structured franchising system worked because tough, crusty Nate Sherman was there to ride herd on the dealers. Possessed of a fiery temper, Nate Sherman was also regarded as fair and honest to a fault with the dealers. He was, in a phrase, "a benevolent dictator." As a result of the Shermans' joint efforts,

Midas grew rapidly. Within eighteen months after its inception, the company had 200 dealers nationwide, and revenues were around $20 million. It was an exceptionally rapid expansion for the early years of a franchise operation. Midas had 100 stores after its first year—Mr. Donut had four. The Shermans had obviously hit upon a winning idea.

But the friction between Gordon Sherman and his father escalated during the 1960s. Gordon was, in fact, running the company, and he wanted to have the official title that went with the responsibility. Finally, in May 1967, he persuaded his father to step up to chairman of the board to allow Gordon to become president and chief executive officer. At that point, however, things began to unravel for the Sherman family and Midas Muffler. Gordon, who had always marched to a slightly different drummer, got caught up in the radical political tides of the late 1960s. He became a prominent financial backer of Saul Alinsky, who had radical ideas for the transformation of the American economic and social system. Sherman also became prominently involved in Business Executive Move for Vietnam Peace; he backed a liberal journal which lambasted the press in Chicago; and he entertained Jerry Rubin, Abbie Hoffman, and other leaders of the Yippie movement during the trial of the Chicago Seven. Gordon did not just entertain them quietly in his home; he took them to lunch at the Standard Club, long a bastion of rock-ribbed respectability for Chicago's German-Jewish elite.

All of these activities alienated and infuriated many of Midas' dealers and other members of the business community, but none of it compared to Gordon's $100,000 donation to consumer crusader Ralph Nader. Nader was not only a nettlesome presence for American business, and for the auto industry in particular, but he made no secret of his plans to eliminate the internal combustion engine, which would also eliminate the need for mufflers. Midas' franchisees thought this was carrying idealism a touch too far. When reporters questioned Nader about all this, he replied: "I told him [Gordon Sherman] candidly of my efforts to eliminate mufflers. But he has a legitimate concern for the abuses of our society and puts that ahead of his company's interest." That hardly mollified Midas' dealers. Nor did Gordon's weak rejoinder: "I told Nader it was O.K. if he put us out of business so long as he put all of our competitors out of business, too."

With complaints from dealers mounting, Nate Sherman began pressuring Gordon to resign his post, but his son refused. Nate explained to *Business Week*, "His humanity has a place, even in industry, but when you are catering to the public, you have to keep a spotless image." Nate controlled the largest block of shares in the company, somewhere around 20 percent of the 2.9 million outstanding shares. With that clout, and with the support of many of the dealers and some of management, Nate was able to oust Gordon from the presidency in 1970. But Gordon, along with his mother and two sisters, controlled a block of shares amounting to about 27 percent of the total. Beatrice Sherman, Nate's wife, had moved out of the family home a month after Gordon resigned, took an apartment in downtown Chicago, and allied herself with her son against her husband.

Father and son began a proxy fight for control of the company—with the voters of the outstanding 1.5 million nonfamily shares holding the key to the final outcome.

Gordon fought a bitter fight with his father for control of Midas. When he resigned, he sent a letter which said that working for his father was "harmful to my health and degrading to my self respect." He also pointed to the sales and profit records of Midas during the years of his presidency, and he begged his father to retire, saying that he was "living in the 19th century." He argued that Nate Sherman's "management is attuned to a small wholesale auto-parts distribution company." Nate Sherman responded that when Gordon was running the company "he had people around him who were not qualified businessmen, people who never sold anything in their lives and never bought anything except clothes and food." A sense of impending doom for Gordon Sherman came a week before the proxy election—Beatrice Sherman returned home to Nate—he would have her vote after all. As a result, Gordon Sherman lost the election. Shortly afterward, he left Chicago for Marin County, California, where he continued to work for liberal causes, especially a public-interest law firm called Businessmen for the Public Interest.

Nate Sherman had won control of Midas Muffler, but he could not run the company. He was too old, and perhaps he had never been as involved in its operation as Gordon. In any event, he immediately began negotiations for sale of the company to Illinois Central Industries (IC). IC was the holding company for the old Illinois Central Railroad and a number of other interests. It offered some $75 million for Midas in November 1971. Midas had sales of $67 million in 1970, and at that time had fifteen manufacturing plants in the United States and Canada and about 1,800 employees. After the sale, Midas continued to grow rapidly. By 1973 sales passed the $100 million mark, and in 1976 they were $226 million. Profits also doubled during these years. From 1971 to 1973, Midas, which was still reorganizing itself, added just thirty new muffler shops. From 1974 to 1977, however, 244 were opened, which brought the total number of shops to 911. By 1980, Midas had an annual volume of $330 million with 1,049 outlets, and it had expanded outside of North America to Europe, England, and Australia. Its shops also began expanding beyond mufflers, handling brakes, shock absorbers, and related items. Virtually unnoticed that year was the death of Midas' founder, Nate Sherman.

By the mid–1980s, Midas was still the muffler industry leader with over 1,415 franchised shops in the United States and 400 more outside the country. Midas itself generated revenues of about $300 million, while their franchise operations had sales of $649 million. It was large and highly successful, but, as the editor of *Muffler Digest* commented, "Midas is a leader, of course, but there are plenty of competitors. It by no means has a stranglehold on the business." When Gordon Sherman died in 1987, only small notices appeared in the newspapers. The fact that he had pioneered a new concept, and created a highly successful business empire around it, was barely noted. Instead, it was his social concerns that were of interest. Maybe Nate's comment about his son was right. He said Gordon was "delightful and brilliant," but that maybe he was not cut out for the business world. (**B**. *Advertising Age*, March 31, 1958, May 16, 1985; *Fortune*, July 1958; *New York Times*, May 30, 1967, April 11, September 20, November 4, 1971, May 9, 1987; Harry Kursh, *The Franchise Boom*, 1968; *Business Week*, October 10, 1970, April 17, 1971; *Time*, May 3, 1971; *Industry Week*, February 28, 1977; *Automotive News*, April 9, 1979, May 19, 1980; *Who Was Who*, Vol VII; *Forbes*, July 18, 1983; Stan Luxenberg, *Roadside Empires*, 1985.)

SHOEN, LEONARD SAMUEL (February 29, 1916–   ). Trailer and truck rental company founder, Amerco Systems, U-Haul Rental System. The scenario reminded *Forbes* of King Lear. The old king, betrayed by family and friends, rails helplessly at the injustice. In this case, we see a man who built an empire from scratch, nurtured that empire carefully over the decades, and then decided to share it with his twelve children. Over a period of time, he, in effect, gave the entire empire to them. They, in turn, kicked him out unceremoniously, and he went into isolation in the desert. This did not happen in England in bygone days, and the man was not a king. It happened in Phoenix, Arizona; the empire was U-Haul, the largest one-way truck and trailer rental business in the United States; and the man was Leonard Samuel "Sam" Shoen.

Sam Shoen was born on a farm near McGrath, Minnesota. The second of seven children, his father was, in Shoen's words, a "jack of all trades . . . . He [was] not awed by the new and the different." In 1923, when young Sam Shoen was seven years old, the family moved to Oregon. At an early age, Sam helped his father in his many business ventures, most of which were unsuccessful. As he entered his teens, Shoen also began working at local farms and nearby stores. After graduating from high school, Sam Shoen worked for a few years, but finally decided to enter the premedical program at Oregon State University in 1937. To pay his way through school, Shoen learned how to be a barber, and soon he opened his own barbershop. By his second year of college, Shoen had four other barbers working for him, and with the cash flow from this operation, he opened a second shop in Albany, Oregon; later the following year, he opened yet another shop. When World War II began, however, Shoen lost all his barbers to the draft, so he closed his shops and put the equipment in storage.

Despite his heavy work load and extensive business obligations, Shoen earned good grades and was admitted to medical school at the University of Oregon in 1941. He remained there until 1944, when he was expelled for covering for a lab partner. At that point Shoen enlisted in the navy, but before he got involved in any action, he was felled by a bout of rheumatic fever. Hospitalized for five months, it was the first period of forced inactivity in Shoen's life. But his mind remained active, and, during this time, he began to conceive of a whole new business and industry in America. With the war coming to an end, Shoen realized that returning servicemen were going to be relocating and moving, and money would be scarce. Recognizing further that Americans were a nation of do-it-yourselfers, he hit upon the idea of one-way trailer rental.

What Shoen foresaw was that, after the war, Americans would be relocating over longer distances than had been true in the past, as returning servicemen went to college and took new jobs in parts of the country far from their homes. They needed to be able to transfer their still relatively meager possessions, to move them cheaply, but they would not be able to return the rented trailer when they were finished. Shoen's new business, if all the incredibly complicated logistics could be masterminded, was a natural for the highly mobile postwar American scene.

In 1945, upon his release from the navy, Shoen visited various trailer rental lots around Los Angeles, and he found that trailers, which were renting for $2 a day, were generally cheap vehicles made of old automobile parts which would deteriorate after minimal use. In addition, all the trailers had to be returned to the original rental lot. So Shoen decided he would buy new, more substantial trailers and devise a one-way trailer rental system. His problems, though, were manifold. He had no capital to buy the trailers and no network of dealers to allow for a one-way rental system to operate on even a regional, let alone national, basis. Shoen had a great idea, but no capital and no organization. It was then that Shoen used his ingenuity to stimulate the operation.

In 1945, Shoen had life savings of $5,000, was just married, and wanted to start a brand new business. In his autobiography, he described the situation he faced:

Since my fortune was just about enough to make a downpayment on a home and furnish it, and knowing that if I did this we would be sunk, we started the life of nomads by putting our belongings in a trailer and living between in-laws and parents for the next six months. I barbered part-time and bought trailers of the kind I thought we needed to rent from anybody who happened to have one at a price I thought was right. By the fall of 1945 I was in so deep into the trailer rental deal economically that it was either make it or lose the whole thing.

Before long, when Shoen had reached the limit of his own resources for buying trailers, he hit upon a clever method to finance further expansion; one that allowed him to retain all equity in the company. Shoen, after purchasing the trailers, sold them to family, friends, and other investors, and then leased them back for rental purposes, giving the investors a share of the rental revenue. In this manner, Shoen could build an ever-expanding fleet of trailers (and later trucks) without selling shares in the company itself. As U-Haul expanded, Shoen put together larger packages of equipment, shares of which were sometimes even sold on the stock exchanges, but he never gave up equity in the parent company, Amerco. It was an innovative way to leverage his capital equipment needs, but it did not solve Shoen's other major problem—establishing a nationwide network of dealerships. He addressed this problem in an equally ingenious manner.

Shoen began to allow renters to take his U-Haul trailers to cities in various parts of the United States where there were no U-Haul dealers. There they could leave the trailers, if the renter promised to try to persuade a local gas station operator to accept the trailer and open a U-Haul dealership. Although Shoen lost a few trailers this way, it was a remarkably effective and inexpensive way to develop a network of U-Haul dealers quickly. Within a relatively short time, Shoen had established a vast network of dealers, at virtually no cost to the parent company. Since the gasoline stations were already existing operations, and the U-Haul rentals just took up a corner of the station's lot, U-Haul did not have to pay for land and buildings to develop its network. Nor did it have to incur the vast labor costs, since the existing labor at the service stations handled the sporadic rental business. The new U-Haul dealers, of course, got a share of the rentals, but it was a remarkably simple way to build a vast nationwide network of dealers, virtually overnight.

Shoen also faced the problem of advertising. Since he was developing a nationwide business, would it not make sense to set up a national advertising campaign? But such a campaign would cost more money than the young, intricately leveraged U-Haul company could afford. Again, Shoen had a brilliant idea. His trailers and trucks were traveling on highways across America; why not make them into moving billboards? So all U-Haul trucks and trailers were painted a distinctive orange, silver, and white, with the name "U-Haul" in large letters, followed by various catchy slogans and mottos. Ultimately the slogan that stuck, and was emblazoned on all the equipment, was "Adventure in Moving." Shoen had, in effect, found a way to make the customer do the advertising for U-Haul, simply by pulling its trailers or driving its trucks along America's highways.

Sam Shoen's practical, instrumental approach to things even compelled him to return to school in the mid–1950s. During a time when his business was expanding rapidly, Shoen decided that a knowledge of the law would be beneficial. Most corporate executives would simply go out and hire a lawyer. Not Shoen. He ran his business during the day and attended Lewis and Clark College in Portland, Oregon, at night. He earned his law degree in 1955, but, along the way, he also taught himself welding, accounting, and engineering when he thought it would be useful. As he commented, "If you want to employ others and get the job done right, you should first learn to do it yourself."

In the 1960s, Shoen moved U-Haul's base of operations from Portland to Phoenix, and he began to recruit his children into the business while they were still young. Each of his twelve children had a steady job from childhood—painting U-Haul equipment—which gave rise to the family joke that all of Shoen's children had orange blood. By the end of the 1960s, the Shoen family controlled about 95 percent of the stock in U-Haul's parent company, and U-Haul rental outlets blanketed the nation, numbering some 14,000. Although it had a few competitors, like Ryder Trucks and Jartran Rentals, the conventional wisdom was that no one could ever overcome the massive advantage Sam Shoen had built up with his enormous network of gasoline-station dealerships. Unexpectedly, Shoen's empire began to self-destruct in the 1970s.

The oil crisis of 1973 and subsequent gasoline price hikes killed off a large number of gas stations during the decade, liquidating an extraordinarily large number of U-Haul's dealerships in the process. This opened the way for Ryder and Jartran to compete more effectively, and they slashed their prices to take business away from U-Haul, the industry giant. Sam Shoen was caught in a difficult situation. He desperately needed new locations for his rental outlets, but now he had to buy them *and* cut prices to meet the competition. At first it appeared that he had hit upon another characteristically brilliant game plan. Chrysler, which had suffered horrible times in the mid–1970s, put about 1,000 of its dealership buildings up for sale, which Shoen promptly bought at bargain prices. By the late 1970s, Shoen had poured a massive amount of money into buying these huge new retail dealer centers, taking on a very large, long-term debt for the first time.

Shoen viewed all of this as a great opportunity. The ex-Chrysler showrooms were far larger than anything U-Haul had occupied before, so he decided to turn them into vast rental supermarkets, handling recreational vehicles (RVs), trench diggers, VCRs, windsurfing boards, mobile homes, and virtually everything else. This further increased the company's debt, but did not significantly increase rentals. By the mid–1980s, U-Haul was in deep trouble, and family squabbles surfaced. By the late 1970s, Sam Shoen had turned over 88 percent of Amerco's stock to his children, but he continued to run the company with his characteristically iron hand. As long as U-Haul was doing well, the children meekly submitted to their father's autocratic management style. Richard Detmer, director of member services for the American Rental Association later said; "It's very, very tough for a business to pull off on a large scale, and what U-Haul did was an enormous undertaking."

By the end of 1984, U-Haul and Sam Shoen were in a precarious position. U-Haul still had an enormous fleet of trucks and trailers (some 165,000 in all) parked in gas stations around the country. And it had 1,275 U-Haul rental centers, crammed full of all kinds of merchandise, so that the company was worth a little over $1 billion. Sales were about $750 million, with a net income of some $42 million that year. But debt stood at a rather staggering $479 million, $80 million more than the year before. If earnings began to slip, it was questionable whether U-Haul could successfully meet its huge interest payments. And competition, especially in the form of Ryder Trucks, was intensifying almost daily.

By 1986, U-Haul's earnings plunged to just $8.6 million on stagnant sales of $783 million. Long-term debt by that point exceeded $586 million, and stood at 45 percent of capital. At about the same time, family warfare broke out at U-Haul. In late 1985, Sam Shoen removed seven of his children from the board of directors because he felt that they were not sufficiently interested in the company. Although the children had voting control of the board and the company, they meekly left. The only son remaining at the firm was the eldest, Samuel W.

Shoen, who was made president of U-Haul, while his father retained control of the entire operation as chairman of the holding company. Family directors and officers were replaced by loyal, but ineffectual, dealers and blue-collar workers in the company. In November 1986, as U-Haul's financial situation worsened, Sam Shoen's children (with the exception of young Sam) banded together and ousted their father from the company. The elder Sam Shoen, by then seventy-one years old, left for Las Vegas. When his son, Edward "Joe" Shoen, who took over Amerco, was asked if his father left willingly, he commented; "He had to retire and be run off simultaneously."

Now in control of the U-Haul empire, the children could not agree on how to proceed. Samuel Shoen, who was still president of the U-Haul division, wanted to continue his father's program of diversification; Joe Shoen wanted to return to the basic business of renting trucks and trailers. Many analysts were suspicious of Joe Shoen's credentials for running the giant rental empire. Although he had a law degree and an MBA from Harvard, his only previous business experience had been running a paint store. Joe Shoen responded by stating that "I didn't just fall off a turnip truck." Ultimately, Joe Shoen won the power struggle with his brother, ousted him from the presidency of U-Haul, and began to turn U-Haul away from RVs, surfboards, and trench diggers and to upgrade U-Haul's aging fleet of 60,000 trucks to compete more effectively with Ryder's newer trucks, many of which had air-conditioning and automatic transmissions.

The problem with Joe Shoen's strategy was that it was inordinately expensive, and U-Haul was already deeply in debt. The company lost money in the next year, and found itself mired even more deeply in debt. At that point, old Sam Shoen, his son Samuel, and six other Shoen children joined forces to fight Joe Shoen and the rest of the Shoen children who were running U-Haul. One of the dissidents commented, "It was inevitable. We're concerned about love among us, and what this will do to us. But I chalk it up to an inevitable power struggle." "We're very frustrated," said Samuel Shoen. "We're entitled to be heard." Joe Shoen, who had already spent $410 million in 1987 to upgrade U-Haul's fleet, wanted to spend another $1 billion in 1988. Although most industry analysts felt the spending was necessary for U-Haul to fight off the challenge from Ryder, the Shoen dissidents were unconvinced. Meanwhile, profitability slowly returned to U-Haul, with a sixfold increase of profits in 1988 to $13.2 million. Company officials said they expected profits to reach $39 million in 1989.

As a result, both sides in the dispute entertained the idea of selling the company, and at various times meetings have been held with Coca-Cola, Texaco, and Firestone. It seemed rather tragic to most observers. As *Business Week* commented, "So, U-Haul may very well go the way of many family empires that can't seem to be passed from generation to generation. The patriarch's dream would end in a family nightmare, and his progeny would go their separate ways." (**A.** Leonard S. Shoen, *You and Me*, 1980. **B.** *Forbes*, Fall 1983, February 11, 1985, February 23, 1987, October 24, 1988; A. David Silver, *Entrepreneurial Megabucks*, 1985; *Who's Who in America*, 1986–87; *Newsweek*, September 14,

1987; *Business Week*, March 28, August 29, 1988; Toronto *Globe & Mail*, February 2, 1989.)

SIMON, NORTON WINFRED (February 5, 1907–   ). Food processor, conglomerate organizer, Hunt Foods, Norton Simon, Incorporated. It was a classic confrontation in the 1960s—an old, stodgy, conservative American business is suddenly confronted by a raider, an aggressive, acquisitive representative of the postwar American business mentality. W.W. Holloway of Wheeling Steel represented the old business establishment. His grandfather had founded a steel mill just across the Ohio River from Wheeling Steel in the nineteenth century. His father-in-law, Alexander Glass, had founded Wheeling Steel itself. W.W. Holloway himself had served as president and chairman of the firm, and he had been a director since 1927. By 1965 he was seventy-eight years old, and he was accustomed to a traditional, unhurried way of running the venerable company.

For as long as Holloway could remember, meetings of the board of directors had begun at 10:30 A.M., had followed an agreeable and leisurely routine, and had broken up after less than two hours. The members then ambled through Wheeling's streets to the old Ft. Henry Club, where they enjoyed a pleasant lunch together. Since 1963, however, a new director of the firm had caused much unpleasantness. He had been openly critical of the inbred nature of Wheeling's management. When Holloway reached the boardroom at 10:30, he found the meeting had started a half hour earlier, and the new director had assumed the chairman's seat. Before long, the new director informed the group that he had taken control of the company, and he asked Holloway and the other old directors for their resignations. The new director was Norton Simon, and a new age was dawning at Wheeling Steel. What happened there was typical of what happened to many American companies during the great conglomerate binge of the 1960s.

Norton Simon was born in Portland, Oregon, the son of the owner of a moderately successful department store in the city. Young Simon was educated in the city's schools until 1921, when his father's business was forced into bankruptcy by the postwar recession, and his family moved to San Francisco, where he attended high school. While still in school, Norton Simon began buying bags and other paper products from a manufacturer and selling them to San Francisco stores. In this manner, he accumulated a tidy little fortune of $3,000. He briefly enrolled in the University of California at Berkeley, but he was far more interested in business than ideas, so he dropped out after several months.

Simon began to work for an export company; at the same time, he invested his savings and a portion of each paycheck in the stock market. At twenty years of age, he started his own steel distributing company, the Los Angeles Steel Products Company. Meanwhile, Simon had developed such an ingenious system of hedging in the stock market that, when the crash occurred in 1929, he emerged with $35,000. In 1931, he invested $7,000 with some others in a bankrupt California fruit company, Gold Brands, Incorporated, which bottled orange juice.

The following year, Simon bought out his partners and began to overhaul operations at Gold Brands. He changed its name to Val Vita Foods, broadened the product line to include tomatoes, and began canning rather than bottling the product. Canning was a less expensive process, and when he added his own can-making plant to the operations he cut costs even further. By 1936, despite the depression, Simon had pushed sales, which had been a paltry $43,000 when he took over, past the $1 million mark. By the end of the decade, sales stood at $9 million.

In 1941, Simon began buying stock in Hunt Brothers Packing Company in San Francisco, which had been a leading food processor in the area since 1890. A year later, in what became an almost patented Simon move, he sold Val Vita Foods to Hunt Brothers for over $3 million, and then used the proceeds to take control of Hunt Brothers. Upon seizing control of the firm, Simon began what he called "unblocking" it. He sold off unprofitable properties, reduced the number of can sizes, mechanized production lines, centralized operations, and revised the accounting system. He also pulled Hunt out of the private label business and began advertising the brand nationally for the first time, with a product that had never before been marketed nationally—tomato sauce. In 1945 and 1946, he bought several other (mostly Western) companies, and added them to the Hunt organization. In this way, Simon was able to expand without the risk of launching new products. In 1945, perhaps seeming a bit starry-eyed, the thirty-eight-year-old Simon told *Time* that someday he hoped to control a food processing empire comparable to Standard Brands. By 1946, Hunt's sales rose to over $48 million from $14 million in 1942. By the mid 1950s they were over $100 million. In 1979, Norton Simon, Incorporated surpassed Standard Brands in sales, $2.7 billion to $2.6 billion. By then, however, Norton Simon had long been retired from active business.

Much of Hunt's growth during these years was accomplished through the adroit use of advertising. To win customers for Hunt's tomato sauce, Simon instituted a $1.5-million magazine and outdoor-advertising campaign in 1947, with great success. The following year, he nearly doubled those expenditures, and bought the then largest, single, magazine advertising campaign ever devised to back a single product. He ran a full-color ad in *Life* magazine every week, supplemented by space in five other national magazines. Simon also inaugurated a $7-million modernization and expansion plan for Hunt to be completed by 1950. One of his most important innovations was borrowed from his old Val Vita plant—he set up can-making machinery right in the food processing plant, so that cans and fruit flowed in mutually coordinated production lines.

In the 1940s, Simon began to use Hunt Foods' assets to invest in other companies. Keeping 9.5 percent of the firm's assets free for investment, over a period of two decades, he spent $34 million on outside stock that attained a market value of $39 million. He especially liked to buy stock in companies whose holdings were widely dispersed and undervalued. In that way, he could purchase a small number of shares in order to gain access to the company's offices. Then, if his investigation showed the firm was worth an increased investment, Simon would buy up to 10 percent of the stock to secure control. One of the first of the "hostile takeover" artists, Simon was often successful despite incumbent management's violent objections to his raids. Professional managers derisively called Simon a raider, but like later counterparts, Simon defended himself by asserting that he was protecting the rights of shareholders and that he was only concerned with seeing that companies were astutely managed to generate high profits. He often won support from workers by promising to institute a more enlightened labor policy.

One of Simon's first acquisitions was the Ohio Match Company. He began to invest Hunt money in Ohio Match in 1944; by 1946, he was in control of the firm as president. At that point the net worth of the match company was $7 million, but it was woefully outmoded. Upon taking control, Simon instituted a major reorganization. He replaced the firm's aging executives with young men, he got rid of the horse-drawn railcars in the firm's lumber yards, and he modernized accounting methods. Within ten years, Ohio Match's sales had gone from $9 million to $20 million, and the firm was worth $24 million. Ohio Match was useful to Hunt Foods in other ways. Simon put recipes featuring Hunt's tomato sauce on the matchbook covers, which was a very effective form of ubiquitous advertising for the firm.

It was for similar reasons that Simon decided to purchase McCall's Corporation in the early 1950s. A big advertiser in *McCall's* and *Redbook* magazines, it was useful for him to control that important outlet also. By 1956 he controlled one-third of the stock and secured a majority on the board of directors. He then began making changes: he discontinued publication of *Blue Book* and *Better Living*; he spent heavily to build up the image of *McCall's*; and he purchased *Saturday Review* for $3 million in 1960. By 1965, *McCall's* circulation had increased 60 percent, and corporate earnings had risen 550 percent. The firm at that point was Norton Simon's most profitable investment.

During this same period, Simon was also investing diversely. Through Ohio Match, he bought into Wesson Oil and Snowdrift Company. In the late 1940s, he bought Atlas Imperial Diesel Engine, which he converted to food machinery, and he also purchased a number of can-making operations. In 1950, he consolidated several of these operations into the United Can & Glass Company, which by 1955 had an annual sales volume of $35 million. In 1957, he changed the name of his umbrella corporation to Hunt Foods & Industries, which had a total sales volume of about $120 million. This firm included Hunt Foods, Ohio Match, United Can & Glass, and a lumber division. Still outside were Harbor Plywood, which he picked up in 1956, with sales of about $22 million; Wesson Oil & Snowdrift, with sales of $165 million; McCall's Corporation, with sales of $60 million; and a sprinkling of smaller investments which Simon himself controlled.

During the 1960s, however, Simon's golden touch became somewhat tarnished. A major defeat for Simon occurred at Wheeling Steel. Although he moved successfully into the steel industry with his takeover of Crucible Steel in

1966, Simon's dealings with Wheeling Steel were far less remarkable. Simon stirred so much resentment, so much hostility, in his takeover of Wheeling that he was never able to recover. After he took over the company, he prepared to perform his usual reorganization of the company, but his lack of tact worked to his detriment. At a stockholders' meeting soon after Simon took control, he castigated the recently ousted chairman of the firm, a man revered by the Wheeling establishment, as "not even a good vice president" and termed his $140,000 salary "preposterous." Even one of Simon's own lawyers winced. He sent Simon a note pleading, "Norton, turn on the charm!"

Wheeling Steel was, indeed, in dreadful shape. Simon hired the consulting firm of Coverdale & Colpitts to conduct a survey. Their conclusions were devastating—Wheeling Steel, they said, was "far behind the steel industry in terms of modern facilities, operating efficiency, quality of products, costs, and personnel utilization and practices." The firm was so backward, in fact, that it still used kerosene lamps on its railroad switches, and had a staff of seven lamplighters to trim the wicks and snuff them out. (U.S. Steel had laid off their lamplighters eighteen years before.) Action was obviously essential, but Simon's approach was brusque and undiplomatic, and the cozy, inbred ranks of steel company executives resented this interloper from the food industry telling them how to run their business. When he heaped public scorn on Wheeling's ousted president, William A. Steele, fellow steel executives were outraged and rallied to his defense. As *Fortune* (July 1967) said, Simon became known "not only as a brash outsider but as a man without respect for experienced steelmen."

Simon installed Bob Morris, a vice president of Monsanto, as the new president of Wheeling Steel, but the other steel executives refused to associate with either Simon or Morris. At a meeting of the American Iron & Steel Institute (AISI), the chief executive officer (CEO) of another steel company, flush with wine, told Morris, "We don't like you or Simon because we don't want any outsiders in this industry. You won't get any help from us in any way. Even a magician can't cure Wheeling's problems in five years, and you won't get five years to try." Morris was the first Wheeling CEO to be left off the board of directors of AISI. By 1967, Simon had had enough. He began negotiations with Pittsburgh Steel, and sold Wheeling Steel to them in 1967. Hunt lost about $700,000 on the sale, but Simon continued to run Crucible Steel as a successful operation, with sales of $320 million in that year.

Simon committed other errors during the 1960s. In 1964 and 1965 he tried to take over American Broadcasting Company–Paramount Theaters Incorporated. But that firm successfully resisted his attempt by engaging International Telephone and Telegraph (IT&T) as a "white knight." IT&T bought up a larger share of stock, and forced Simon out of the race. He also tried to take over Swift & Company, the meat-packing firm, during this time, but he was unsuccessful. A more successful acquisition was Canada Dry Corporation, in which Hunt Foods bought a 22-percent interest, which Simon later increased to 34 percent. By the end of 1967, Hunt Foods & Industries had sales of $523 million, with profits of $15.4 million.

In 1968, Simon consolidated all his enterprises into a new organization, called Norton Simon, Incorporated, and then, in a move that surprised virtually everyone, he walked away from it. He decided to devote himself to his massive art collection and to politics, and he turned Norton Simon, Incorporated over to David Mahoney, whom Simon had recruited as president of Canada Dry in 1966. Since 1954, Simon had assembled one of the world's largest and finest private art collections. Some of Simon's paintings were kept in his home, some in his office, and some at the Norton Simon Foundation. Many were at the Los Angeles County Museum of Art. Most art experts were greatly impressed with the extraordinary level of quality of his collection, and Simon over the years put a great deal of study into the subject. He also tried to make his impression in politics, but he was not terribly successful. Simon ran for the Republican nomination for the Senate in California in 1970, but after spending $2 million of his own money, he was defeated. He tried very hard to unseat the conservative Reagan-wing of the party in that state, but was unsuccessful.

As time went on, Simon became increasingly withdrawn and reclusive. When he left Norton Simon, Incorporated, he commented that "I felt possessed rather than possessing." He went on, "I was looking for a way out for 13 years. The bureaucracy had me." In retirement, he began to guard his privacy closely, spending much time with his new wife, actress Jennifer Jones. Complex, aloof, and fickle, he was a constant mystery to those who dealt with him. A writer for the *New York Times* in 1979 called him "a brooding figure of American business"; a *Forbes* reporter called him a "classic pessimist," who seemed "more like an embittered intellectual than a builder of corporate empires." He became a committed philanthropist, and Franklin Murphy, then chancellor of the University of California, Los Angeles, said of Simon, "He's not interested in leaving a huge fortune. He thinks each generation should take care of its own. He has extracted his wealth from society and he intends to give it back."

Norton Simon, Incorporated, under the direction of the outgoing and loquacious David Mahoney, has witnessed both success and failure since its founder walked out. In recent years, the actions of the firm have become as mysterious and secretive as those of Norton Simon himself. Norton Simon's sales were $1.2 billion when Mahoney took it over, and profits were marginally acceptable, but he felt the firm needed to be restructured. He particularly wanted to emphasize the kind of nationally distributed, brand-name products with which he was familiar, and which he felt could be marketed successfully. He sold off about thirty of Norton Simon's businesses, including all the publishing and printing plants, Ohio Match, and the soft-drink bottling facilities. In their place, he picked up such consumer products as Max Factor, Old Fitzgerald bourbon, Halston, and Avis. During his first ten years as head of the company, Mahoney managed to double the firm's sales and to triple the profits. But this was not accomplished without some trauma.

Mahoney's biggest mistake was the purchase of Max Factor cosmetics company in 1973 for a staggering $463 million worth of Norton Simon stock. Most analysts felt, at the time, he had paid too much for it, and then, over the next several years, the company was horribly mismanaged and lost money at a breathtaking clip. Balancing that mistake, however, was Mahoney's most impressive acquisition—Avis rent-a-car. Purchased for a paltry $174 million in cash in 1977, it became a big money-maker for Norton Simon during the next several years. The other Norton Simon divisions managed to hold their own under Mahoney's leadership, but that was all. By the early 1980s, earnings at Norton Simon had dropped significantly, and Avis, which had been such a winner in the late 1970s, became Norton Simon's weakest division.

Mahoney began quietly buying back Norton Simon shares on the open market, in a move that confounded analysts. Some thought that he might be planning to go private; others thought that the firm had some major acquisition in mind. The company itself denied the first possibility, and analysts felt the second was farfetched, considering Norton Simon's deteriorating financial situation. (In 1982, Norton Simon's sales had been stagnant at $3 billion, profits dropped sharply, and Mahoney had paid out a whopping $460 million to buy back stock.) A few analysts speculated that Norton Simon might be trying to ward off a takeover, but *Fortune* (March 7, 1983) discounted that, saying, "the proposition implies that Norton Simon is a desirable property, and not too many parties seem to think it is." The only thing most commentators could agree upon was that Mahoney was grossly overpaid, at $1.85 million annually, for the job he was doing.

Then, on June 6, 1983, Mahoney dropped a bombshell, one that was to reverberate throughout the American corporate structure for well over a year, and one which set off what was perhaps the most dramatic series of mergers and acquisitions in the history of American business. Mahoney announced that he and a group of unidentified investors (most subsequently turned out to be Norton Simon executives, along with the backing of the investment firm of Drexel Burnham Lambert) were offering $29 a share in cash and preferred stock for the firm. He would also assume the company's long-term debt and supply working capital, which brought the bid to a total of $1.6 billion. The immediate reaction of Wall Street was that Mahoney was foolish. His bid was only very slightly above book value, and as a result, the New York investment firm, Kohlberg, Kravis Roberts, (see Henry R. Kravis and George R. Roberts) which was closely allied with Donald P. Kelly, head of Esmark, offered $33 a share for the company on June 14. At that point, Mahoney dropped his bid and left with a profit of about $40 million.

When the dust settled in the late summer of 1983, Esmark—the old Swift & Company that Norton Simon had tried to take over in the 1960s—was the owner of Norton Simon. Wall Street reacted with howls of derision; no one could imagine how the purchase of the ailing Norton Simon could aid Esmark's stockholders, and Esmark's stock after the purchase dropped from $72 to $68. Then, in what seemed a twinkling of an eye, Esmark was itself the target of takeover. In May 1984, Beatrice Foods, the massive food conglomerate, bid $2.5 billion for Esmark, in order to create the largest foods and household goods group in the United States. Beatrice's powerful CEO, James L. Dutt, said he was attracted by Esmark's national marketing network for Hunt-Wesson/Swift products, and that the acquistion would change Beatrice into more of a marketing company than a food company. Beatrice ultimately got control of Esmark, paying $2.8 billion for it. This worked out to about $60 a share, about fifteen times Esmark's earnings—a very high price for a troubled firm. Wall Street was dumbfounded, and it criticized Beatrice and Dutt for the purchase. Beatrice had to assume Esmark's massive $1.3-billion debt, which raised Beatrice's total debt to $5 billion, and most analysts felt the acquisition was a big gamble. As a result, Beatrice's stock fell below $30 a share, from the $50 to $55 it had been before the acquisition.

By mid–1985, executives were leaving Beatrice in droves, including many of Esmark's top people. As a result, Dutt was fired by the board of directors in September of that year. Then, in a stunning turnabout, Donald Kelly, ex-head of Esmark, allied himself with Kohlberg, Kravis Roberts and in November 1985, he offered to take Beatrice private with a $4.91-billion leveraged buyout offer. The offer was accepted by the board, and Kelly became the new chairman and CEO, and a whole group of ex-Esmark managers moved in to take control. A holding company, BCI Holdings, was set up in April 1986 to control the sprawling empire.

David Mahoney, glorying in his new-found wealth, paraded his accomplishments for all to admire in an autobiography appropriately entitled, *Confessions of a Street-Smart Manager*, but five years after leaving Norton Simon, he did not have an executive position in the corporate world. For a man who was always a joiner, a hail-fellow-well-met sort, it must have been difficult. Norton Simon had said of him several years earlier, "I owned only 10 percent or 20 percent of the company but I always acted like I owned 100 percent—and people assumed it was true. That meant I never had to socialize with the business establishment like Mahoney does." Mahoney told William Safire that he considered the sale of Norton Simon, Incorporated a failure.

While all of those earth-shaking transformations of corporate America were taking place, with Norton Simon, Incorporated at the epicenter, Norton Simon himself, whose fortune, including his vast collection of art, was reported to be worth in excess of $200 million, made no comment. But it must have been a curious sensation for him. He was, after all, the first big corporate raider, the first to pursue hostile takeovers, to do leveraged buyouts, to unblock companies after he bought them to pay back his accumulated debt. Had he created a monster that finally swallowed his own namesake firm? He did not say, but his comments on the business world in 1979 seemed germane: "Competition in business became destructive. Today it's gimmicks, gimmicks, gimmicks. Everyone is performing a service that nobody wants." Another time he said that "acquisitiveness is a

disease." A disease, perhaps, of which Norton Simon has been cured. (**B**. *Time*,
October 8, 1945, June 4, 1965, May 24, 1968; *Business Week*, October 30,
1948, April 13, 1957, April 11, December 26, 1964, November 26, 1966,
November 18, 1972, July 27, 1981, May 21, June 20, 1984, June 3, November
4, 1985; *Fortune*, December 1953, June 1965, July 1967, November 1972, July
12, 1982, March 7, July 11, October 5, 1983, October 28, 1985; *Newsweek*,
February 11, 1957, December 15, 1969, June 1, 1970; *New York Times*, January
13, 1966, May 31, 1970; *Current Biography*, 1968; *Dun's Review*, October
1970; *Forbes*, August 20, 1979; Milton Moskowitz et al., *Everybody's Business*,
1980; *Advertising Age*, May 23, July 4, 1983, March 24, 1984, March 11, 1985;
Economist, June 11, 1983, May 26, 1984; *Institutional Investor*, January 1984,
January 1986; *Wall Street Journal*, February 22, 1984; *MARG*, vol. 38, no. 1,
1986; *Who's Who in America Supplement*, 1987–88; David Mahoney with Richard Conarroe, *Confessions of a Street-Smart Manager*, 1988.)

SIMON, WILLIAM EDWARD (November 27, 1927–   ). Conglomerate entrepreneur and government official, Wesray Corporation, Secretary of the Treasury, Chairman, Energy Policy Council. To some, Bill Simon is the quintessential
contemporary businessman. An avid believer in the free market and a foe of big
government, Simon became a uniquely successful bond trader who moved on
to Washington, D.C., where he became one of the most powerful men in government. After leaving his Washington post, Simon returned to the market system
he loved and built a huge fortune with the capitalist's favorite toy of the 1980s—
the leveraged buyout. To his detractors, Simon was a dinosaur, a man who made
his money by trading on his government service and contacts, an utterly un-
creative empire builder whose only contribution to his own wealth making was
his huge network of contracts, his ruthless personality, and his sense of the
political jugular. Whatever the assessment, all agree that Bill Simon, in a short
space of time after he left government service, managed to become one of the
richest and most successful men in American business.

Bill Simon was born in Patterson, New Jersey, the son of an insurance broker.
Like most self-made businessmen in the postwar period, Simon's story is hardly
one of rags to riches. His grandfather, an immigrant from the Alsatian area of
France, had founded the National Silk Dyeing Company and had amassed a
small fortune. As a result, during Bill Simon's early years, the family lived quite
comfortably. The depression, however, was rough on the family. His mother
died when he was eight, and his father spent most of the family fortune just to
survive the depression. The family moved from Patterson to Spring Lake, on
the Jersey shore, and Simon was educated at Blair Academy and Newark Academy. He was a good athlete and popular with his classmates, but he was not
much of a student. Upon graduating from Newark Academy in 1946, Simon
joined the U.S. Army and served with the occupation army in Japan until 1948.

When Simon returned to America, he enrolled in tiny Lafayette College in
Pennsylvania, where he took a prelaw course and specialized in economics. At

Lafayette, according to reports, he "liked partying and sports a bit more than studying." When Simon graduated from Lafayette in 1952, by which time he was married and had one child and another on the way, his GI Bill funds had run out, and he had lost all interest in law school. Instead, he headed to Wall Street, looking for a job, where he did not exactly find a seller's market. His degree from Lafayette did not impress many people; in fact, it closed more doors than it opened. Finally, by virtually camping out in the waiting room of Union Securities Company, Simon managed to get a $75-a-week job in the municipal bond department. By the 1980s, trading in stocks and bonds had become the most sought-after profession for hotshot young "B-school" grads, but such was not the case in 1952. As Simon recalled, "It's funny, but when I first came into this business, trading was not a respectable profession." Simon got the job largely because the high-demand people thought it beneath them.

But Bill Simon made the most of this opportunity. He soon proved to be an especially adept municipal bond trader, and two years after joining Union Securities he became the youngest officer in the firm and the head of its municipal department. He advanced quickly because he was able to make those split-second decisions, often the correct ones, that meant the difference of millions of dollars in a person's portfolio. After five years at Union, Simon left for Weeden and Company as a vice president where he stayed through 1963. The following year he left that firm to join Salomon Brothers, and after nine months he was made a partner in that large and venerable firm and was put in charge of federal bonds and securities. Salomon Brothers retained a patina of establishment decorum that befit its status as one of the most eminent of the Wall Street firms. But Bill Simon brought an entirely new élan to his department, one that was not always appreciated by the other partners.

Simon employed little tact or decorum in the way he ran the government desk, or in the way he ran the municipal department, which he also took over five months later. "No, Bill was not popular outside his department," said William Salomon, the company's managing partner, "but I liked that. A certain amount of hostility is part of the chemistry of an aggressive, competitive firm." For his part, Simon remarked, "I never hired a B-School guy on my desk in my life. I used to tell my traders, 'If you guys weren't trading bonds, you'd be driving a truck. Don't try to get intellectual when you're in the marketplace. Just trade."

The years of the late 1960s and early 1970s were ones of spectacular growth for Salomon Brothers, and by 1970 Simon was a senior partner in the company, a member of the executive committee, a consultant to the U.S. Treasury Department, and Salomon's representative to the Federal Home Loan Bank Board. By this point, Simon was recognized throughout the financial world as one of the most brilliant bond experts, and he had also acquired a reputation as a workaholic. Putting in sixteen-hour days at a time when most Wall Street traders considered theirs a leisured profession, Simon was making between $2 and $3 million a year. At that point, however, in the view of many of his colleagues, Simon became afflicted with a serious case of "marble fever," that is, the belief that his great success in business made it imperative for him to go to Washington to, in the words of the *New York Times,* "instruct the nation, and to guide its destiny."

In December 1972, as President Richard Nixon was preparing to start his second term, Treasury Secretary George Shultz contacted Simon and asked him to become his deputy. Simon accepted, and he took up his new position in January 1973. In that position, Simon was responsible for the day-to-day running of the Treasury Department. He was also appointed chairman of the Interagency Oil Policy Committee, which suddenly became a position of high visibility in the Nixon administration. When the Arab countries in 1973 declared an embargo on oil shipped to the United States, Simon was confronted with an enormous problem. President Nixon at first had created a Federal Energy Office in July 1973, with former Colorado governor John Love as head, to deal with the problem. When Love began to push for gasoline rationing, Nixon eased him out and replaced him in December 1973 with Simon, a noted free-market operator.

Simon and his team were given three weeks to devise a system of gasoline allocation. Bill Simon handled the assignment with his characteristic brisk dispatch. Declaring that he was determined that fuel shortages not cause mass unemployment, Simon said industry would get all the fuel it needed. The second priority was home heating. As a result, Simon ordered refiners to cut their gasoline production by 5 percent. The result was a small, but critical, cutback on the amount of fuel available to the nation's automobile drivers. Long lines resulted at America's service stations, and howls of complaints emanated from millions of average Americans. Simon responded in his usual undiplomatic fashion: "We have become a nation of great energy wastrels. We have been accustomed to an overabundance of cheap energy. That day is over." He also joked later that "I'm the guy that caused the lines at the gas stations."

The longer he served as America's energy "czar," the more criticism Simon attracted. Increasingly, the major oil companies joined in the chorus of complaints raised about his policies and the roughshod manner in which they were enforced. Even worse, however, was the infighting that erupted within the Nixon administration itself over Simon's policies. In February 1974, when Budget Director Roy Ash* publicly described the energy crisis as short-lived, Simon was livid, and he told Ash to "keep his cotton-pickin' hands off energy policy." Later that month, Simon criticized statements by the Shah of Iran as "irresponsible and reckless." Since the Shah was a trusted friend of the United States, the State Department was greatly agitated over Simon's comments. Later that year, probably at least partly to remove him from an increasingly explosive situation, Simon succeeded George Shultz as secretary of the treasury.

By this point, Nixon had resigned from the presidency because of the Watergate scandal, and Gerald Ford was the new president. Simon's work at the Treasury Department hardly did anything to enhance President Ford's popularity over the next three years. Whatever Simon tried as treasury secretary seemed to backfire. His attempt at tax reform went nowhere, neither did his feeble attempts to balance the federal budget. At one point, when he was deadlocked with Congress, Simon deliberately let the government run out of money. Just a symbolic gesture, nothing of great substance, it nevertheless caused many to turn against Simon. Simon's Waterloo, however, was the fiscal crisis in New York City. Although he recommended to President Ford that the federal government help New York City stave off bankruptcy, Simon felt it should be done in such a way that the city would be severely punished, so that no other municipality would ever again spend its way into bankruptcy. A sensible enough idea, perhaps, but Simon should have remembered that the national media is headquartered in New York City and is very protective of the city. As a result, Simon was crucified by most of the nation's media for his actions. "Then came the New York fiscal crisis," he said later, "and I was Genghis Khan." This action helped bring about Ford's defeat in 1976. As a consequence, Simon was also out of office in January 1977, and he had no desire to return, calling Washington "a city with so many 180-IQ idiots."

Government service for businessmen is a curious phenomenon. Failure at an appointed task does not seem to matter; in fact, it almost seems to enhance the businessman's attraction to the business community. Government, in the minds of many free-market businessmen, is the enemy, so if a businessman goes to Washington and fails to perform successfully, it is never his fault, but rather the fault of the leviathan's hated bureaucracy. Thus it was that Simon left Washington to return to private life as a respected and much sought-after business consultant, and a darling of the rising new right with which Ronald Reagan would ride into office in 1980. Simon's great attraction for many firms were his political connections, which would normally imply one was talking about someone with great political instincts. Yet, Simon's relative failure in Washington actually worked in his favor; it proved he wasn't "too" political—he was still "one of us"—he had not caught "Potomac Fever."

When he left Washington, Simon at first thought he would waltz back in as managing director of Salomon Brothers. He was soon disabused of that notion. Although Simon was offered a position with the firm, it was not one he considered commensurate with his abilities. Furthermore, it became clear that he was not to take over management of the firm, probably because Simon's brusque manner was not to their liking. Simon also discovered he had another problem. When he entered government service Simon had put his fortune, estimated at $5 million, in a blind trust. When he got out, he found it had dwindled to less than $2.5 million, most of which was represented by the equity in his two homes. His trust managers had terribly mismanaged Simon's holdings. To take full advantage of the prestige of his previous government work, Simon offered himself out as a consultant to a number of companies, while playing the market on his own. The latter efforts did not turn out well,—he lost a quick $1 million on the commodities market—but the former turned out to be a gold mine.

Early in 1977, Simon signed on with Blyth Eastman Dillon, with Booz, Allen & Hamilton, and with Allstate Insurance for annual fees of from $150,000 to

$200,000 a year each. At the same time, he was left relatively free to take short-term consulting jobs, for which he often charged as much as $50,000 and he began giving speeches to sellout crowds. Pitching the free-market, entrepreneurial brand of conservatism that Ronald Reagan popularized, Simon did exceptionally well. Frank L. Mansell of Blyth Eastman commented, ''It was unbelievable how popular he was. He'd have standing-room crowds when he spoke.'' His popularity prompted Simon to write a book. With the aid of Edith Efron as a ghostwriter, Simon produced *A Time for Truth*. In it, Simon presented an unbridled conservatism of the type Barry Goldwater had brought forth in his *Conscience of a Conservative* in 1960. The success of Simon's book, which sold a whopping 150,000 copies in hardcover, was one of the first tip-offs that the nation was turning to the right, and that Ronald Reagan stood a good chance of being elected president in 1980. Simon produced a second book in 1980, entitled *A Time for Action*, which was, in large measure, a campaign broadside for Reagan's economic program. Simon worked during this period as part of Reagan's campaign brain trust. As a reward, Simon expected to be named secretary of the treasury by Reagan, but he was disappointed. According to a number of reports, Simon's appointment was torpedoed by Senator Robert Dole and ex-president Ford. Others, including Simon, blamed Reagan's advisers, Michael Deaver and Edwin L. Meese III. Whatever or whoever the cause, Simon was not invited to return to the ''city of 180-IQ idiots.''

With that rejection, it seemed that Simon finally had decided to devote himself totally and passionately to the business world. Not that he had done badly during the intervening four years, since his wealth escalated from $2.5 million to about $35 million. But he was ready to try something else, to get involved in the real action of the 1980s—leveraged buyouts. He had earlier met Raymond Chambers, a former tax accountant and nursing-home financier, who had formed a firm called Hampshire Capital to do small leveraged buyouts. Simon liked Chambers' track record, and the two decided to form Wesray Corporation (from Simon's initials and Chambers' first name) to enter the leveraged buyout field in a major way. In their first year of operation, they bought three companies, each time investing a relatively small amount of their own capital and using borrowed funds to raise most of the purchase price. Their biggest coup, and the one that really got them started, was their acquisition of Gibson Greeting Card Company.

Gibson, the third largest firm in the greeting card industry, with sales exceeding $200 million annually, was owned by RCA. RCA had picked up Gibson in 1980 when it acquired CIT Financial Corporation. Deciding that Gibson did not fit well with its other operations, RCA agreed to sell it to Wesray for $80 million. That, in itself, was not remarkable. What did catch the attention of Wall Street was the way in which Simon and Chambers financed the purchase. Putting up very little of their own capital, they raised the bulk of additional funds by selling off much of Gibson's assets. They sold off its real estate for $35.4 million, and immediately leased it back. They then mortgaged the company's machinery, for which they got $13 million. Next they negotiated a $100-million line of credit secured by Gibson's inventories. Most of the latter amount went to finance the purchase; the rest was used to pay for operations. In 1984, Wesray took Gibson public and sold about one-third of the stock for $27 a share. Each partner made fabulous profits on the stock they had purchased for practically nothing. Simon had put up $330,000 of his own money, and ended up owning stock in Gibson worth about $70 million by 1984.

Other deals followed in short order: Heekin Can, Anchor Glass, Wearever-Proctor Silex, Atlas Van Lines, and, in 1986, the giant Wilson Sporting Goods Company. Each of these was done in a similar manner: the partners put up little of their own money and leveraged the rest, much as they did with Gibson. Simon and Chambers' tactic was to watch for America's conglomerates to get restive with their properties, and then to move in for the kill. "America is seeing a deconglomeratization," said Simon. "Companies that were going in 50 directions are cutting back." Although not all their purchases were successful, most were, and Simon was worth over $300 million by 1987.

But things were not all roses and violins at Wesray. Tensions were rapidly building to the breaking point. Some of it may have had to do with the fact that many felt Simon was getting all the credit for Wesray's deals when, in many people's mind, Chambers was the one primarily responsible for the firm's success. According to one Wall Street investor:

Gibson wasn't Simon's deal and neither were any of the others. It was Chambers and his partners who figured out those deals. Simon's job—his only job—was to use the contacts he'd built up while he was in Washington to get them the capital to pull it off. (*New York Times Magazine*)

For his part, Simon readily conceded that his main function at Wesray was as a "door opener." These contacts, however, were not insignificant. As a former Salomon Brothers executive commented, "I'm surprised he didn't call Wesray William E. Simon Co. . . . Simon's name is worth millions." One of Simon's friends concurred: "Bill uses his previous associations. He has lots of connections. He hears about deals. And there's nothing wrong with that. He's just using the system."

Increasingly, for whatever reason, Chambers and Simon were at each others' throats during late 1985 and early 1986. This was probably at least partly due to Simon's rough, often brutal manner with associates. Possessing a terrible temper and demanding as much of his associates and subordinates as he did of himself, Simon was infamous for his verbal assaults at Wesray. Witnesses of the situation at Wesray reported that his attacks on secretaries at the firm were so vicious, and so destructive of their self-esteem, that they had to be moved to different areas of the company and given special moral support to help them "recover" from Simon's assaults. It became increasingly evident that Simon's role in the company was being cut back—and he did not like it one bit. Simon began to threaten Chambers that he was going to leave the firm. Ultimately, the two decided to part company in late 1986.

Cashing out of Wesray with a huge fortune, Simon was able to tackle new frontiers. He began to assemble what he visualized as a massive banking empire based on the Pacific Rim. Allying himself with a corps of investors in Italy, Australia, and the United States, Simon began to pick up ailing savings and loans (known in the trade as thrifts) in late 1986 and early 1987. In just four months, the investors amassed more than $4.4 billion in thrift assets, along with a few other firms and some real estate. Simon told reporters he envisioned an empire that "in a decade . . . could include insurance, mortgage, banking, real estate, savings and loans, commercial banking, and anything to do with trade facilitation." An awesome vision, but where did Simon get the idea? Simon told L. J. Davis, in a *New York Times Magazine* article, that he got the idea from James Clavell's *Noble House*, a best-seller about a great Scottish conglomerate based in Hong Kong in the 1960s. Simon said it was his ambition to become *taipan*, the "supreme and undisputed leader of a great, ocean-spanning trading company." Much of the nation's business press was agog at the prospect, but some industry analysts were less impressed. James Beneson, Jr., a highly successful takeover artist on Wall Street, commented on Simon's *Noble House* dream: "It's a good thing he didn't read Caesar's *Gallic Wars*. If he's buying those banks just because of a potboiler, it's silly."

The problem with Simon's plan, in many people's minds, was that these thrifts were terrible investments. The American savings and loan (S&L) industry had been rocked with a large number of S&L failures during this period of time, and many experts were wondering whether they had any chance at all of surviving. With the bulk of their assets tied up in fixed-rate home mortgages, many S&Ls suffered terribly during the inflation of the 1970s and 1980s, and several ended up in receivership. And there was Bill Simon and his group buying Honolulu Savings and Loan, Hawaii's largest, Bell Savings and Loan in San Mateo, California, and Southern Savings and Loan in Beverly Hills. The latter two, in fact, had been taken over by the Federal Home Loan Bank Board (on which Simon used to sit) and were assigned to the new owners. Simon's group also picked up several other healthy thrifts. Simon countered all the talk of gloom about thrifts by claiming they were wonderful investments. The main reason for his optimism was their cheap price. As Simon's partner, Gerald L. Parsky, told the *Los Angeles Times*, "You could buy a healthy S&L for under book value." For "bottom pickers," they were a cheap way to build a huge financial empire. Whether a stable empire could be built with thrifts as a foundation, only time will tell.

As early as 1983 many people in the financial world thought Bill Simon had reached his peak. "Bill is a crusader," said James J. Lowrey, formerly of Salomon Brothers, "and being a crusader takes a lot of time. I think he's reached his point of frustration. He's realized he can't change the world and he's getting too old to try." Of course, Simon went on from there to build a huge fortune from his deals at Wesray, and then to turn his hand to the Pacific Rim thrift empire. Friends of Bill Simon have always told critics never to count him out: "He's a gorilla," said one. (**A.** William E. Simon, *A Time for Truth*, 1978, *A Time for Action*, 1980. **B.** *New York Times*, December 17, 1972, December 5, 1973, August 8, 1983; *Current Biography*, 1974; *Time*, January 21, 1974, September 7, 1987; *Fortune*, May 3, 1982, July 21, 1986; *Newsweek*, August 8, 1983; *Business Week*, June 3, 1985, March 9, 1987; *U.S. News & World Report*, September 22, 1986; *Los Angeles Times*, September 27, 1987; *New York Times Magazine*, December 27, 1987; *Who's Who in America*, 1987–88; *Bankers Monthly*, February 1988; *Forbes*, October 24, 1988.)

SIMPLOT, JOHN RICHARD "JACK" (January, 1909–   ). Potato and frozen-food processor, agricultural conglomerate owner, J. R. Simplot Corporation. "Jack" Simplot is an icon of America's past. A rugged, plain-spoken country boy, he has been called a "good ole' boy," a "rich edition of Li'l' Abner," and a "child of nature." Simplot does not dispute these epithets. His license plate reads "MR SPUD," and he has described himself as just a "gol-durn potato farmer." All that might well be true, but Jack Simplot is a down-home potato farmer whose business is worth a cool $1.1 billion. His own share of that enterprise has been difficult for *Forbes* and *Fortune* to assess in analyses of American wealth, since all of Simplot's companies are privately held. In 1988 *Forbes* reassessed his wealth at $400 million, after having dropped him off their list the year before. Yet, as early as 1983, when *Forbes* figured his holdings were worth $200 million, Simplot snorted that "I wouldn't sell for that, that's for sure."

Most sources state that Simplot was born in Declo, Idaho, although one publication insists he was born in Iowa. Wherever, it is clear that Simplot was raised in the small (there were about ten families there at the time) town of Declo in southern Idaho, where he lived most of the time in a one-room cabin. His father ran a 120-acre farm, and times were rough when Jack Simplot was growing up. His father was a stern, no-nonsense kind of man, and he demanded that Simplot spend much of his youth in hard labor on the farm, pulling out rocks and sagebrush by hand. To make extra money, Simplot took a paper route in town and worked as a caddy at the golf course. By the time Simplot was in eighth grade in the town's tiny four-room schoolhouse, he was ready to drop out of school. He was fourteen, he fought with his father incessantly, and, as he recalled, "I had to stop, I didn't get along in school. I just didn't like it."

From age fourteen, for all intents and purposes, Jack Simplot was on his own. He did almost anything to survive. He started out sorting potatoes for a local firm of potato brokers, and he earned extra money by ballasting the area canals with rocks. At the same time, he rented forty acres of potato land from his father. With the money he saved from these ventures, Simplot bought some sow hogs and commenced to raise litters of hogs the next year. A year later, however, most other hog farmers in the area, fearing a surplus, decided to slaughter their animals. Simplot decided that he could not and would not do that. All his savings had been invested in the hogs, and he could not afford to destroy them. He determined that he would collect and feed the hogs and wait until the market was in short supply. Yet, he also knew he could not afford to keep feeding the hogs indefinitely or he too would go broke. Simplot found an ingenious solution. At this time, thousands of wild horses still roamed the Idaho plains. Simplot figured he could feed his litters of pigs a mash of horse meat, cull potatoes, and a little barley, at virtually no cost to himself.

So Simplot built hog pens on the Marsh Creek, planted potatoes, and rigged a huge iron vat to cook the slops, and, whenever he needed meat, he galloped into the hills and brought down some horses with a lasso or shot. By the time he was seventeen, he had 500 hogs; and when the price of hogs went to 7 1/2 cents a pound he sold out the entire spread for $7,500. Simplot had made his first entrepreneurial foray, and he had made a profit. With the money he made from his hogs, Simplot bought three teams of horses, some farm machinery, a secondhand Star Durant to drive around in, and a big supply of seed potatoes. He then rented some land on which to grow potatoes.

Simplot was on his way to a career of remarkable success and great wealth, but it involved many more years of hard, tough labor. Once, while visiting one of his potato processing plants in the late 1960s, Simplot became wistful. He spied a number of old potato cellars at the plant, heaped over with a deep layer of earth to protect them from the summer's heat and winter's cold. "I dug those cellars when I was starting out," he said. "I kept addin' to them, one or two new ones every year. An' they are still mine. I used to be tougher than a boot. I could toss those damn sacks of potatoes around like they were bags of peanuts."

In 1928, when Simplot was nineteen, he had already run his own successful farming enterprise for a number of years. Times were hard in agricultural America during the 1920s, and Simplot struggled to learn how to survive on sparse land and in difficult times. In that year, however, he heard of an electrically driven potato sorter that a local machine shop had invented. The device cost around $300, and Simplot did not have enough money to buy one, so he convinced a friend, a much older farmer in the area, to put up half the money. With this machine, Simplot could not only sort the whole of his own output, but also that of his partner, and, for a fee, those of several other area farmers as well. Simplot had passed an important milestone with that development—he was no longer just a farmer trying to make money with his crops, he was an entrepreneur acting as a middleman for a number of other farmers.

When he and his partner got into an argument over the business, they flipped a coin to see who would own the sorter, and Simplot won. He was then free to go out on his own in the potato sorting business in a big way. In the early 1930s, a number of elements were working in Simplot's favor. First, in 1931, he married the daughter of a wealthy hardware merchant in a nearby city. Second, the onset of the Great Depression, although it created tough times for agriculture generally, actually greatly increased the demand for potatoes, since they were a cheap, healthful food. As the Irish had learned long before, a diet of potatoes and milk, however dull, was healthy and nutritious, and it was cheaper than almost anything else. So, as the demand for potatoes grew, Simplot's potato business expanded. At the same time, he was one of the first of Idaho's potato farmers to recognize that the Bureau of Reclamation's massive work on the Snake River, which flows through the state, would provide a dependable supply of water that would be a boon to the state's potato industry.

By 1940, Simplot owned nearly 30,000 acres of farm and grazing land in various parts of Idaho. As both a jobber and a grower, he was shipping 10,000 carloads of potatoes annually, and he had also branched out into large-scale onion farming. It was the onion, rather than the potato, that first brought Simplot into the food processing business. A customer for his cull onions was a man in Berkeley, California, who was drying and processing them for the spice and condiment market. By the spring of 1940, he owed Simplot $8,400, so Simplot decided to get in his pickup truck and drive to Berkeley to find out why he had not been paid. When he arrived, the man's secretary told Simplot the boss was not in. Simplot said he would wait. After several hours an older man came in, but he was also looking for the boss, since he had failed to deliver on an order of onion flakes and powder. Simplot and the man talked for a few hours, and then they went to lunch together. Over lunch, Simplot said to the man, "You want onion powder and flakes, I've got onions. I'll dry 'em and make powder and flakes in Idaho." They drew up a contract on the back of an envelope, shook hands on the deal, and parted company. There was just one problem—Simplot had no idea how to dry and process onions.

Simplot drove out into the California countryside where his onion customer did his drying and processing. He examined the operation, saw what kind of dryers were used, and ordered the same equipment for his farm in Idaho. He then set up the entire operation on his farm, sinking $85,000 into it, most of which was borrowed. "I've always been pretty good around machinery," he said. "I don't exaggerate when I say that I literally assembled the plant myself, with a hammer and a blowtorch." He also installed a vertical hammer mill and a shaker to produce the powder and flakes. By September 1940, Simplot had 80 acres covered with cull onions; by November, he had poured them through the dryers and processors at his plant, causing an unpleasant odor to pervade the entire county. But he cleared $50,000 on the operation in just the first year. Simplot knew he was onto something. "But," he said, "I can tell you I've never pulled leather like I did in that first year."

Having succeeded with dried onions, Simplot learned that other foods could be dried as well, and what better candidate than the millions of pounds of potatoes that passed through his plant each year. In 1941, there were only five vegetable-dehydrating plants in the United States, and none of them performed particularly well with the potato. A potato is about 80 percent water, and not one of those processors knew how to dry and squeeze the water out without mashing the cell structure. Nor did they know how to avoid getting a gray, dull, desiccated product. At the same time, it became clear that America was going to be drawn into World War II, and that the army's demands for dried potatoes would be enormous. Simplot began to design a plant for processing potatoes: "The plant," he said, "was me. I designed it with a piece of chalk on the floor of a machine shop in Caldwell [Idaho]. It didn't do too well at first."

Simplot's major problem was that in the peeling process he was losing too much of the potato when the skin was removed. Simplot devised a procedure that revolutionized the entire potato processing business. He soaked the potatoes in a superheated lye wash which softened the skin to a point where it could be rubbed off, with little loss of the potato itself, by high-pressure jets of water and slowly rotating brushes. When the army viewed Simplot's spanking new operation, it was highly impressed, and gave him large orders. Between 1942 and 1945, Simplot produced an average of 33 million pounds of dried potatoes annually, which was about one-third of the U.S. Army's consumption. With 2,000 employees, Simplot could proclaim that, "I was the world's master potato peeler." To fulfill these enormous demands for potatoes, Simplot bought more and more farm land during the war, greatly increasing his agricultural empire in the area.

Simplot's empire also began to spread in less obvious ways. During the war, for example, when he found he could not get enough wooden boxes to fulfill his enormous and ever-growing demands, he used his federal priorities to commandeer machinery and material with which to build a large box plant alongside his processing plant in Caldwell. When he found lumber in short supply for his box plant, Simplot bought some sawmills in Idaho, and then bought a half-interest in the Cal-Ida Lumber Company, which operated a sawmill in Downieville, California. These acquisitions brought Simplot into the general sawmill business; and, by the late 1960s, he owned three sawmills, which had the capacity for more than 100 million board feet of lumber annually, which produced about $8.6 million in sales.

Simplot's potato operations also brought him into the cattle industry. During the war, he found that endless mountains of skins, eyes, and other offal were piling up outside the plant. He learned, however, that the offal, when mixed in a slop with alfalfa, barley, and several chemical supplements, could be made into a nutritious feed. So, Simplot built a small feedlot across the street from his Caldwell plant. Like almost everything else Simplot attempted, this also turned out well. He was running 4,500 cattle a year through the feedlot in 1945, which grew to 150,000 a year by 1968. Only two or three feedlots in the United States ran bigger operations than Simplot's.

A similar situation brought Simplot into the fertilizer industry. Simplot's intensive potato farming during the war depleted the soil on his farms, and then, because of wartime shortages, he was unable to secure a dependable supply of fertilizer from Anaconda in Montana. With a government loan, Simplot built a million-dollar phosphate processing plant in Pocatello, but then he discovered that Anaconda would not even supply him with the phosphate rock. Simplot had to find his own supply. He recalled seeing phosphate rocks lying around on the ground at the nearby Fort Hall Indian Reservation. As he recalled after investigating the situation further, "Damned if I didn't latch onto the biggest phosphate deposit west of Florida." He made an agreement with the tribal council on the reservation by which they leased him 2,500 acres of phosphate beds. Over the next quarter century, Simplot's fertilizer business continued to grow; by 1968, his investments in fertilizer plants exceeded $80 million, and his sales of the product brought in about $65 million annually. This was enough to give him about 15 percent of the market, and he was reputed to be one of the few people in the industry who was making a profit at the time. *Fortune* estimated his fertilizer earnings at about $2 million in 1967.

Because of the way in which Simplot craftily used government monies and his status as an essential supplier of materials to the armed forces to expand his empire, people in Idaho began referring to him by the end of the war as the "Henry J. Kaiser* of the Rocky Mountains." Kaiser was the dynamic businessman on the West Coast who used a similar situation to create a vast empire in steel, shipbuilding, automobiles, and construction during the war. But, Simplot's empire building during the war was significantly different from Kaiser's in one respect. Until Simplot came along, virtually all of Idaho's wealth and resources were held by out-of-state companies. Simplot was the first native resident of the state to build a great economic empire based within the state itself. It was an important step toward economic maturity for the young Western state. Simplot early emblazoned that idea on all the packages that left his plant: each bore the motto, "A Chance to Grow in Idaho."

Simplot's next big breakthrough came in 1946, when he innovated a process to freeze-dry French fries. Again, this process had eluded other potato processors. Simplot set up a small research group at his Caldwell plant, and gave them a green light to try every means to produce a proper product. They soon found a way to freeze the product successfully in small batches, but commercial production was another matter. Ultimately, however, through the invention of several devices, especially the continuous fryer, Simplot and his research team were able to lick the problem. Simplot had assumed that the principal market for his product would be restaurants and institutions, but he found the demand there was relatively limited. So, in 1950, his company refocused production to concentrate on the retail grocery market and the suburban housewife. Here, it found that demand far outstripped expectations. At first, Simplot just sold the product in Idaho, but soon orders were pouring in from outside the state. Simplot could not keep up with the demand, and the next great challenge was to find ways in which to increase production to meet this demand. From 1955 onward, the Caldwell plant was expanded several times to meet the demand, and soon a second Caldwell plant was built.

By 1950, the Caldwell plant was consuming more than half the total potato crop of Ada, Payette, Gem, and Canyon counties in Idaho. To continue to fulfill his other orders for potato products, Simplot had to buy another plant at Burley,

Idaho, and then a third plant at Heyburn, Idaho. By 1960, these three plants were processing the equivalent of 12,000 carloads of potatoes annually, about 16 percent of the entire Idaho potato crop. To meet increasing demand, that same year, Simplot made a deal with one of the leading New York potato distributors, Jules Salzbank, to build a potato processing plant in Presque Isle, Maine, which processed potatoes from the famous Aroostook Valley. This, like everything else Simplot did during these years, was highly profitable, with sales of $25 million from that plant alone in 1967, compared to $60 million from the three Idaho plants combined.

Simplot's biggest breakthrough with his frozen French fries came in the mid–1960s, however, when he convinced Ray Kroc* of McDonald's to replace his fresh French fries with Simplot's frozen variety. As McDonald's grew at an exponential rate, Simplot's potato processing business grew apace. Whereas he had targeted sales of 10 million pounds a year in the 1950s, with the McDonald's orders they had exploded to 550 million pounds annually by the late 1960s. By the late 1980s, Simplot was selling over 700 million pounds of frozen French fries a year to McDonald's, and his total business in the product was over one billion pounds. McDonald's sales accounted for about 40 percent of all of Simplot's business by that point, and he had added Burger King and a number of other fast-food outlets to his list of customers.

Simplot's business continued growing during the 1970s, although he ran into occasional problems. One of these involved what *Time* called "The Great Potato Bust" in 1976. It was a volatile potato market that year, and Simplot had been selling short in the potato futures market. He had made a lot of sales when the market was high, and he had bought back some of the contracts when the market began to fall, but he miscalculated and did not have enough potatoes to fulfill the contracts he had sold. The result was a shortfall of 50 million pounds of potatoes. This caused the biggest default in the 104-year history of the New York Mercantile Exchange, and it resulted in a government investigation of the whole situation. Ultimately, however, Simplot, who emerged from the imbroglio with little damage, paid a relatively minor $50,000 fine in 1978. That same year, Simplot also moved beyond his basic agricultural interests for the first time. He invested $20 million for a 20.5-percent stake in Micron Technology, Incorporated, a manufacturer of dynamic random-access chips (DRAMs). By 1988, *Forbes* estimated that investment to be worth about $100 million.

In the 1980s, Simplot continued to expand his empire in new directions. He established Western Power Company, which proposed to set up a 600-mile, $700-million power line to Nevada. This line would ship power south from 100 or so plants in Idaho, which would burn the coal from the great open-pit mines in Wyoming, with the Snake River providing the needed water. Environmentalists were staunchly opposed to the project, but Simplot was not deterred. "We've got something big here," he said. "A thousand megs of electricity is a big investment, and if someone doesn't say or do something about it, it won't get done."

Simplot in his business dealings over the years has won respect from his competitors as a "hard but fair dealer." His employees are often less generous, stressing the "hard" part over the "fair." He is renowned for "moving people out if they don't produce," and he himself admitted he was difficult: "You've got to be tough," he said. Nonetheless, his managers are given a portion of the profits, and many of them have done very well working for Simplot. There are no fancy organizational charts, no staff meetings, none of the accoutrements of most billion-dollar enterprises in Simplot's operation. Simplot, a blunt and direct man, also tried for years to learn the first names of all his employees. As the total exceeded 4,000 in the 1950s, this became impossible, but he still strode through his plants giving a cheery "Hi!" to all within earshot of his voice— which was reputed to have the cutting power of a laser beam. Simplot tended to play down his astuteness in building his empire. "The only smart thing I've ever done," he claimed, "is hang on." (**B**. *Saturday Evening Post*, June 19, 1948; *Fortune*, December 1951, August 1968, October 12, 1987; *Business Week*, January 22, 1955; *Time*, June 7, 1976; *Quick Frozen Foods*, June 1977; *Forbes*, Fall 1983, Fall 1985, July 11, 1988, October 24, 1988; George Gilder, *The Spirit of Enterprise*, 1984; A. David Silver, *Entrepreneurial Megabucks*, 1985.)

SINGLETON, HENRY EARL (November 27, 1916–   ). Conglomerate founder, Teledyne, Incorporated. In 1978, *Forbes* referred to Henry Singleton as "The Sphinx." Others have called him aloof, arrogant, taciturn, and tight-lipped. In an unguarded moment in 1966, however, Singleton was positively loquacious with an editor from *Forbes*. In an interview, he outlined his ambitions for Teledyne, his six-year-old company—"General Motors, AT&T, U.S. Steel, Du Pont—I want to build a company of that type." Well, he did not quite make it, but what he did achieve was almost as impressive. Singleton created a truly massive company, one of the first conglomerates, virtually from nothing. An aggregation of 130 operating concerns, with additional massive stockholdings in other firms, Teledyne by 1987 had sales of $3.2 billion, with a work force of 44,000. It had become the 134th largest firm on the *Fortune* 500 list (in the late 1970s, in fact, it had been the sixty-eighth largest), but it was still well behind first place General Motors, eighth place AT&T, ninth place Du Pont, and even twenty-third place USX (formerly U.S. Steel). It was not a firm that grew because of a particular product, market, or technology, it grew as the reflection of Singleton's own personality and indomitable will.

Henry Singleton was born in Hastel, Texas, the son of John B. Singleton, a prosperous rancher. After high school, Singleton went to the U.S. Naval Academy at Annapolis for a time, but got his bachelor of science and master's degrees at the Massachusetts Institute of Technology (MIT) in 1940. His studies were interrupted by World War II, during which he worked in the U.S. Navy ordnance laboratories; after the war, he learned research at the General Electric research labs. Singleton returned to MIT to get his doctorate in electrical engineering in 1950. Moving from there to Hughes Aircraft, Singleton came in contact with a

group of men called the "Whiz Kids"—men like Charles B. "Tex" Thornton*
and Roy Ash*—who had earlier reorganized Ford Motor Company, and later
started Litton Industries. After a few years at Hughes in the early 1950s, Singleton
moved on to North American Aviation, where he was put in charge of engineering
for navigation systems.

In 1954, Singleton joined Litton Industries, where he eventually became the
general manager of the electronics equipment division. During his six-year stint,
Singleton built division sales from virtually nothing to $80 million. In 1960, he
left to form his own company, Teledyne, which represented, in many respects,
the third generation of California electronics firms. The first generation was
Hughes Aircraft, which dominated the industry from 1947 to 1953, when many
of its leading personnel left in a management dispute to form a number of other
companies. One of these second-generation firms was Litton Industries. Then,
in the 1960s, firms like Teledyne began to spin off from such second-generation
firms as Litton, creating a third generation of electronics firms.

Singleton left Litton for one basic, glaring reason—a disagreement about
whether the firm should produce its own semiconductors. Singleton felt very
strongly that they should, but both Thornton and Ash adamantly disagreed. They
believed the field was too crowded and competitive, and that Litton would be
better off buying their components from others. In retrospect, it was probably
a wise decision, but Singleton was determined to get into the action on semiconductors, so he resigned from Litton. He joined a fellow Litton employee,
Dr. George Kozmetsky, to found Teledyne in 1960. While Singleton had superior
technical training, Kozmetsky was a management whiz who had taught at Harvard
Business School. Each put up $225,000 of his own money, and then they turned
to Arthur Rock, the premier venture capitalist of California's electronics and
computer industries, and persuaded him to invest $1 million in the infant venture
with his partner, Tommy J. Davis.

When Singleton established his company, he first created what he called simply
"a place to work." In 1960, he bought a nearly defunct company called Amelco.
It consisted, in Singleton's words, of "a plant, some equipment, and a handful
of people." It was an inauspicious beginning of a great business empire. A few
days after acquiring Amelco, Teledyne bought Handley, Incorporated, a small
company employing four or five persons, which made potentiometers, and Mercury Transformer Corporation. The total sales of the three companies in the first
year was about $1 million. But Singleton's major goal early on was to enter the
semiconductor field. To that end, in February 1961, he set up the Amelco
Semiconductor Division in the firm, and he hired Dr. Jay Last from Fairchild
Semiconductor to run it.

Singleton continued to pick up small electronics companies in 1961 and 1962—
Palmer Instruments, Linair Engineering, Crittenden Transformer Works, and
American Systems, Incorporated. At the end of 1961, Teledyne's sales were
$4.5 million; by the end of 1962, they stood at $10.5 million. But Singleton
had just begun. Pushing forward with a variety of small acquisitions in 1963

(Aerial Control Geotronics, Control Dynamics, Quantatron, Ordnance Specialties, Electro Development, Sprague Engineering, Kiernan Optics, Optical Products, Imperial Thermal Systems, and Aircraft Fitting), revenues jumped to $32
million. But few people at the time could figure out what Singleton was doing,
or where he was going. To finance these acquisitions, Teledyne had to float a
private stock issue in 1960, and then went public in 1961. Most of the companies
were acquired in the early years through an exchange of stock. It seemed to
many in the investment community that Singleton was almost fanatical about
growth—that it had become like a religion to him—all he and Kozmetsky seemed
to want to do was to create a large company, and they would acquire almost
any firm to achieve that end. One executive, who was asked to join Teledyne
in these early years but refused Singleton's job offer, said later, "Singleton and
Kozmetsky scared me to death." The head of a competing electronics firm was
also puzzled: "I figured Henry had built a house of cards." There seemed to
be no grand design, no purpose to the acquisitions. What were Singleton and
Kozmetsky planning?

The public found out soon enough. Singleton had had an idea in his mind for
some time. As he said in 1967,

The single advantage of being small is that you can move fast. We started out from zero
and could take advantage of the rapid evolution in electronics technology. . . . We thought
we might as well project the technology and use a little daring. So it seemed a dreamy
idea to design an airborne computer around integrated circuits. (*Business Week,* December
30, 1967)

But the government was interested in developing a new military flight control
system called the Integrated Helicopter Avionics System (IHAS) and, in response, Singleton put the brilliant Kozmetsky to work with a team of scientists
to design an airborne computer system that would enable helicopters to fly in
formation and to fire even under zero-visibility conditions. Teledyne at this time,
in 1964, was still a tiny, but brash new firm competing against industry giants
like International Business Machines and Texas Instruments. Its proposal survived the first round of the contract contest, and finally, in 1965, Teledyne
emerged as the prime contractor. An astounding achievement, it immediately
sent Teledyne's stock soaring from 15 to 65.

This was the breakthrough Singleton needed, and he used the great increase
in Teledyne's stock price and the government's developmental funds to begin
acquiring many additional firms. No longer restricted to small firms, Singleton
began to pick up significant companies in the electronics, controls, and aircraft
fittings businesses. Then, just about the time everyone figured that Singleton
was trying to build an electronics conglomerate, he changed his tactics. In 1966,
he began to acquire metals companies, such as Vasco Metals, which specialized
in titanium, molybdenum, beryllium, and vanadium alloys, and Wah Chung, a
leading producer of tungsten, hafnium, zirconium, and other exotic metals.

Singleton also picked up several other metals firms, like Edgecomb Steel and Firth-Sterling Steel. Many people were puzzled as to why Singleton would move into metals, but to him it was quite clear and sensible: "I knew that the semiconductor business was a thing where the proficiencies were in the areas of physics, chemistry, and metallurgy. Later, it became apparent that the metallurgical end was of *great* importance."

These acquisitions drove up Teledyne's revenues, from $87 million in 1965, to $257 million in 1966, and $451 million in 1967. Suddenly, from out of nowhere, the seven-year-old firm was among the "big boys." In 1968, it topped all 414 companies listed in *Forbes* Annual Report on American Industry in growth of both sales and earnings. As a result, Teledyne boasted a combined market value of its common stock and convertible securities of $1.4 billion. By that point, Teledyne had become a pure conglomerate. There was no pretense anymore that it was hewing to some technological consistency. The acquisition in 1967 of United Insurance had dispelled that notion. Purchased because of its large asset holdings, United Insurance set a pattern for Singleton, who became positively enamored of insurance companies over the next several years. In any event, by 1968 Teledyne was made up of 130 companies in a wide variety of areas. It was a true conglomerate. And Henry Singleton, as *Business Week* (December 30, 1967) commented, "wrote the book" on how to manage a diverse conglomeration of companies.

"We don't try to manage our companies," he asserted. "We can't be looking over the shoulders of our managers. We can only tell a man to do his best, and have to trust and believe he'll do it." What Singleton did (by this time, Kozmetsky had left to become dean of the school of business at the University of Texas) was to set up a strict financial reporting system, whereby each of the 130 companies was measured weekly by its performance against plan. The parent company's corporate staff consisted of just about twenty people, some of whom had as many as ten companies reporting to them. The key at Teledyne, as president George Roberts explained in 1979, was high margins.

Forget products, here's the key: we create an attitude toward having high margins. In our system a company can grow rapidly and its manager be rewarded richly for that growth if he has high margins. If he has low margins, it's hard to get capital from Henry and me. So our people look and understand. Having high margins gets to be the thing to do. No one likes to have trouble getting new money. (*Forbes,* July 9, 1979)

The goal, then, was to turn Teledyne into a huge money machine, one geared to pursue Singleton's great growth religion. In pursuing this single-minded objective, Teledyne earned a reputation as being one of the heartless conglomerates of the time for its participation in what was often referred to as "corporate rape." For instance, after it acquired Firth-Sterling, Teledyne abolished its steel division, throwing 800 people out of work, even though the division had increasing sales and earnings per share. For almost two decades, however, Singleton's policies were extraordinarily successful. To pursue his goal of continual growth, Singleton even refused to issue cash dividends.

Forbes commented in 1976:

There is, of course, another little gimmick—a "financial thing"—that other entrepreneurs have tried from time to time. It is a quaint old custom called the "cash dividend." . . . . We asked him when he planned to declare such a dividend. "Never!" he said. "First it would be taxed outside again. Why ship our money out to be taxed when it's taxed once already? More important, why give it to stockholders when there is no other company they can buy that can give them as good a return as we can give them by reinvesting here internally at Teledyne? We can always find ways to spend it." (*Forbes*, May 1, 1976)

An old friend mused about Singleton: "Henry is the most stubborn man I've ever met. We've explained to him a hundred times why he should declare a dividend. He just won't change his mind."

Throughout the 1960s, growth was the key word at Teledyne, and Singleton squeezed out every penny he could to acquire more firms and build a larger empire. And he was extremely successful. By 1969, Teledyne had sales of $1.3 billion, with profits of $58 million. Then, just as quickly as he started, Singleton stopped buying other companies—not a single one was purchased over the next several years. During the early 1970s, Singleton had Teledyne buy up its own stock. As each tender offer was oversubscribed, Singleton took every share they offered. As Teledyne's stock went down during these years, he just kept buying it, and from 1972 to 1976 he reduced the company's outstanding common stock 64 percent, from 32 million shares to 11.4 million. Most Wall Street experts thought he was crazy.

But Singleton turned out to be correct again. During the years that Teledyne's stock prices plummeted and Singleton bought up the shares, the company's revenues continued to climb, and did so solely through internal growth. Revenues, which were $1.2 billion in 1970, were $1.7 billion in 1974 and $1.9 billion in 1976. By the end of the 1970s, sales exceeded $2.5 billion. That represented an internal growth rate during those years of about 7 percent per year. By that point, Teledyne had become the sixty-eighth largest company in the United States, and its stock, which Singleton had bought back for as little as $14, soared to $130. This earned Singleton the sobriquet, "the sultan of the buybacks."

With a great cash flow in the late 1970s, Singleton again changed his strategy—moving often in the opposite direction from everyone else. He began to buy stocks with Teledyne's revenues. Turning the conglomerate into, at least partially, a portfolio manager, he bought large, but not controlling, shares in a number of firms. His biggest move during this time was to buy 27 percent of Litton Industries for $130 million. Within a short time, Litton's stock shot up on the market, and the Teledyne share was valued at a staggering $270 million.

A Wall Street analyst commented, "A fabulous gain, but when Henry first put all of that in one stock I thought he'd gone crazy." Singleton also put Teledyne's money into a 52-percent ownership of Curtiss-Wright, 33 percent of Brockway Glass, 21 percent of the investment firm of Walter Kidde & Company, 16 percent of International Harvester, 14 percent of National Can, 22 percent of Reichhold Chemical, and holdings in about seventy-five other firms. The total market value of these holdings by the end of 1981 was nearly $3 billion.

But, in the early 1980s, this massive empire began to get a bit frayed around the edges. Many of its largest portfolio investments began tumbling in value, losing some $380 million in 1981 alone, and its various manufacturing operations, which had long been squeezed for cash by Singleton so that he could pursue his dreams of growth and empire, were taking a severe drubbing in many of their markets. As a result, the Teledyne cash cow, which was so lucrative for two decades, began drying up. Singleton, when pressured about Teledyne's problems by the press, appeared unconcerned. When pressed for a strategy to deal with it, he responded that Teledyne had never had a plan, and further, "My only plan is to keep coming to work every day."

During the next five years, Singleton's "planless plan" seemed to work. Teledyne's revenues went up only gradually, to $3.2 billion in 1987, but profits in that year shot up an amazing 58 percent to $377 million. Still spending little on research and development (only 2.7 percent, about average for a conglomerate, but very low for the electronics field), Singleton evidently continued to drain revenues from his operating companies to create the profits to fuel further growth and development. Then, in January 1988, Singleton did something that shocked everyone. Teledyne announced a cash dividend to shareholders of $1 per share—the first time the firm had paid a dividend in its twenty-seven years of existence. Singleton also began to spin off some of Teledyne's holdings, selling Argonaut Corporation and a few others. He also talked about the possibility of selling back to Litton a huge chunk of its shares, for over $300 million, and he began to liquidate parts of the company's vast investment portfolio to pay down Teledyne's debt. No one on Wall Street knew quite what to make of all this, but as *Forbes* once commented, Singleton's management style has been to "watch the thundering herd, then frequently to trot off in his own direction." Owning 14 percent of Teledyne, along with a number of other investments, Singleton was worth, according to *Forbes* (February 20, 1978), over $590 million by that time. (**B**. *Business Week*, January 11, 1964, December 30, 1967, November 22, 1976, May 31, 1982, March 14, June 20, 1988; *Forbes*, April 1, 1966, January 15, 1968, May 1, 1976, February 20, 1978, July 9, 1979, July 1, 1985, March 9, 1987, October 24, 1988; Ralph Nader and Mark J. Green, eds., *Corporate Power in America*, 1973; A. David Silver, *Entrepreneurial Megabucks*, 1985; *Who's Who in America*, 1986–87; Michael Allen, *Founding Families*, 1987; *Financial World*, June 16, 1987; *Fortune*, April 25, 1988.)

SMITH, FREDERICK WALLACE (August 11, 1944–   ). Transportation company founder, Federal Express Corporation. It's a story so resonant with irony and retribution that many assume it is just a myth, a modern myth for postcapitalist America. But it is true, all true. In 1965 Fred Smith was a junior at Yale University, majoring in economics. He wrote a paper for an economics course, in which he proposed an idea to transport small packages to cities throughout the United States with the promise of overnight delivery. Smith's professor was unimpressed, and he gave the paper a "C." Just seven years later, Smith took that very same idea and parlayed it into a billion-dollar corporation, in fact, the first corporation in American business history to reach the billion-dollar plateau in less than a decade without resorting to mergers or acquisitions. To many, it just confirmed their suspicions about the bad judgment of Ivy League professors—closeted in their ivory towers, they were terribly out of touch with the reality of America in the 1970s and 1980s. Fred Smith, however, was not so sure. He later told a reporter, "to a ne'er-do-well student like myself, the grade was acceptable." To another he commented, "I was a crummy student— like Winston Churchill."

Fred Smith was born into wealth in Marks, Mississippi, to Frederick Smith and his fourth wife, Sally Wallace Smith, who were inspecting one of the elder Smith's many farm properties in northern Mississippi at the time. The elder Smith was a character. Robert A. Sigafoos, in his biography of young Fred Smith, called his father, "an outgoing, flamboyant individual; he was the southern son of Horatio Alger. Failure in life was not possible for him; it simply was not one of the options he allowed himself." The son of a riverboat captain, Fred Smith, Sr., had founded the Dixie Greyhound Bus Lines, which he built into one of the largest in the South by the time he sold it to Greyhound Bus Lines. During the 1930s, with an older son, Fred Smith, Sr. also started the Toddle House Restaurants, which specialized in Southern cuisine and became a national chain. By the time the elder Smith died at the age of fifty-three, in 1948, he was a wealthy man; but he was very concerned that his youngest son, who was just four at the time, might squander the many millions he would inherit. His father's greatest fear was that young Fred might become part of the idle rich he despised. To this end, a family trust, Frederick Smith Enterprise Company, Incorporated, managed by the National Bank of Commerce of Memphis, Tennessee, was established. The trust was to be shared by young Fred Smith and his two half-sisters; Fred's share would amount to 38.5 percent. In the intervening years between the elder Smith's death and Fred Smith's twenty-first birthday the family trust grew larger. Fred Smith's brother continued to develop the Toddle House chain after his father's death, and he sold it to Squibb-Beechnut Company in 1961 for a reported $22 million in stock. Part of this money also went into the family trust. By the time young Fred Smith came of age, there were 164,800 shares of Squibb-Beechnut in the trust, valued at about $13.3 million, which would play a major role in providing backing for Smith's ventures. Whatever young Fred Smith's other talents, he was not a "southern son of Horatio Alger."

Fred Smith was raised in Memphis by his young mother (she was just twenty-seven when the elder Smith died). Nurtured in the bosom of an affluent family, Fred Smith did not lack for creature comforts. But he had his own hurdles to overcome. He was fatherless after the age of four, and he had been born with a birth defect—a bone socket disorder called Calves-Perthes disease—which forced him to use braces and crutches during grammar school. His mother did not want him to succumb to the disease, so she encouraged him to participate in as many sports and extracurricular activities as possible. As a result, as Smith outgrew the disease in high school, he was already well integrated into a sports and social network. In Memphis, he attended a private preparatory school, Memphis University School, where he excelled in the classroom, on the athletic field, and as a leader. He did so well, he was voted "Best All-Around Student" in his senior year. Smith also began to manifest his entrepreneurial spirit during this time. With some friends he set up the Ardent Record Company, a garage-studio operation to record local rock and roll bands. The company recorded "Rock-House" and "Big Satin Mama" in its first year and broke even. Smith withdrew his involvement when he went to Yale in 1962, but the record company was still operating in the mid–1980s.

At Yale, Smith was not, by his own admission, a "great student." Far more interested in the social scene there, he worked as a campus disc jockey, revitalized the Yale Flying Club, which had been started after World War I by Juan Trippe,* the founder of Pan Am (Smith had gotten his private pilot's license when he was fifteen), and was elected to Skull and Bones, the prestigious secret senior honors society. Most important for Smith's future was the term paper he wrote as a junior. An analysis of the air freight industry had shown Smith that few packages were sent directly to their destination by existing carriers. Instead, these packages were sent "hippety-hopping around the country from city to city and from airline to airline before reaching their destination." This, Smith reasoned, wasted not only money, but also time—the very reason the packages had been sent airmail or special delivery in the first place. The conclusion of his paper suggested there might be a market for a company that moved high-priority, time-sensitive goods, such as medicines and electronic components. Smith's professor was not impressed with his logic. Although he conceded there was some merit to the argument, he pointed out that federal regulation would preclude such a service, and even if that hurdle were overcome, competition from well-entrenched airlines would impede success.

But Smith had recognized a fundamental change in postindustrial American society. As he later commented,

The professor didn't understand how the goddamn world worked . . . that America was spreading out technologically . . . that the efficacy of our society is to be smarter, not to work harder. This meant the creation of a host of new productivity-improving equipment with innumerable complex parts . . . .And that's what we're all about—reacting to the needs of today's society, which wants things done fast, or should I say faster. (*Esquire*, August 15, 1978)

Because of the shift to services and lightweight high-technology products, along with greater use of electronics, there had been a great dispersal of manufacturing facilities after 1960. No longer dependent upon proximity to raw materials, companies manufacturing these new lightweight, valuable products tended to locate facilities in places where they could attract technicians, scientists, and managers, who had become the scarcest commodity in the new economy. With this greater dispersal of people and products, a new problem was created: transmittal of information and goods. While some of this could be achieved electronically, much could not; yet, it was often necessary to deliver these goods more quickly and dependably than the postal service or freight companies could manage. An important niche was, therefore, developing in the marketplace for a firm that could guarantee overnight delivery. Since the goods were valuable, and speed was of the essence, companies would be willing to pay a premium for delivery. This seems obvious in the late 1980s, but twenty years earlier, as attested by Smith's economics professor, it was not so clear. It was Fred Smith's particular genius not only to recognize this opportunity, but also to have the courage and fortitude to carry it out, in the face of many of the obstacles his economics professor had predicted.

Before Smith ever confronted those challenges, he had other rivers to cross. The first of those was Vietnam. After graduating from Yale in 1966, the Yale preppie, who had been in the Reserve Officer Training Program, was commissioned a second lieutenant in the U.S. Marine Corps and sent to Vietnam. Made a platoon leader when he went over, Smith became a company commander. During his first tour of duty, Smith was involved in twenty-seven named operations. For his second tour, he went to flight school, and flew more than 200 ground-support missions in Quang Tri Province. When he left the marines in July 1969, Smith had risen to the rank of captain, and he had won the Silver Star, the Bronze Star, and two Purple Hearts. As Smith later recalled, his Vietnam experience provided him with some valuable lessons: it exposed him to deprivation and danger in a way his sheltered life had not previously; it provided him with a toughness to deal with the possibility of business failure; it taught him how to manage and motivate people; and, finally, it gave him a strong drive to create something. "I got so sick of destruction and blowing things up—on people I had nothing against—that I came back determined to do something constructive."

When Smith returned to America in 1969, he was determined to start a business based upon his love for flying. To this end, he used part of his family trust fund to purchase a controlling interest in Arkansas Aviation Sales, a Little Rock–based concern engaged in providing maintenance service to turbo-prop and corporate jet airplanes. The business had not been doing well, with revenues of $1 million a year and chronic losses. Smith decided to change the focus of the company, making it a clearing house to purchase and sell used jets. Revenues soon increased to $9 million a year, and within two years it yielded a profit of $250,000. Yet, Smith was not satisfied. The business was successful and profitable, but he had not been innovative or constructive. Besides, he kept mulling over his old idea of delivering small packages overnight. Was there a market for such a service? Or had his Yale professor been right? Smith finally decided to commission two consulting firms to study the situation.

At the time the study was conducted, package services were provided by the United States Postal Service, the giant United Parcel Service (UPS), and the smaller Emery Air Freight and Flying Tiger services. Only the latter two, each with revenues of over $100 million, provided a service even remotely similar to Smith's idea. The consultants confirmed Smith's suspicions that he could offer an improved service. They reported that customers were generally dissatisfied with existing freight services, since the deliveries were erratic and often late. They agreed that there was, indeed, a market for the kind of service Fred Smith was suggesting. He decided to proceed with his idea; he incorporated Federal Express Corporation in June 1971 and pursued a contract with the Federal Reserve System. He had hypothesized that the Federal Reserve would be a prime customer because he felt that he could save it $3 million a day in float with his service by hauling its checks from bank to bank. That, in fact, was the reason he called his new business "Federal" Express in the first place. He invested a large chunk of his own funds into the new venture, and he borrowed $3.5 million from the bank to buy two Dassault Falcon 20 fan jets from Pan Am. A few weeks later, the Federal Reserve Board rejected his application because the individual district banks in the system could not agree on the proposal. Smith was left with two jets and a partially formulated business plan.

In 1972 and early 1973, Smith continued his market research to devise a business plan. The research uncovered an existing need for an air cargo service to be provided to a network of 100 cities. The network had to establish a priority air service and ground links to offer service between the shipper and the consignee. This new business plan was far more complex and expensive than the original, yet Smith remained undeterred. His next step was to plunge into the canyons of Wall Street, seeking additional funds beyond the $6.25 million of Smith Enterprise Company funds and $2.5 million of Smith's own funds. With great persistence, Smith raised $96 million from various venture capitalists, banks, and corporations. Among his early backers were New Court Securities (later Rothschild, Incorporated), General Dynamics, Heizer, Allstate Insurance, Prudential Insurance, and Citicorp Venture Capital.

Next, Smith had to set up his system. The key to the future success of his operation was the establishment of what was called a "hub and spoke" system. That is, all packages would be flown at night, when the air lanes were uncluttered, to a central location. There, they would be sorted, tagged, and rerouted to their intended destinations the next day, for morning delivery. By separating small freight delivery from passenger systems, and by integrating air transport with ground transport through the use of small trucks, Smith set up an enviable system, one which recognized that packages, unlike people, do not have to be shipped in a lineal pattern.

Although he had originally set up Federal Express in Little Rock, Smith moved its operations to his hometown of Memphis because of its ideal weather conditions, its more central location, and its more ample facilities. Next, he had to buy more planes. Again he chose the Dassault Falcon, since it was small enough to slip underneath the Civil Aeronautics Board's (CAB's) certification requirements. He ordered thirty-three of them, thereby getting a 25-percent discount. His consulting firms supplied Smith with a corps of managers familiar with the airline business, and in April 1973, he was ready for business. What followed during the next several years was an entrepreneur's nightmare come true. Smith's simple idea demanded not only a massive initial capital investment, but an extraordinarily sophisticated operations procedure, political acumen, and advertising daring.

Opening with service to twenty-five cities, Federal Express' first night shipment included only 186 packages, a devastating disappointment. And things did not improve for some time. In its first twenty-six months of operation, Federal Express lost $29.3 million, and it owed its lenders $49 million. Federal Express teetered dangerously close to bankruptcy because of these fiscal and managerial difficulties, causing some of Smith's early backers to pull out. An especially poignant story concerns Smith's attempt in July 1973 to get some emergency extra financing from General Dynamics. Smith met with the board, and was turned down. Deeply disappointed, Smith, while waiting for a plane to take him from Chicago to Memphis, on impulse took one instead to Las Vegas. There he took a few hundred dollars to the blackjack tables and parlayed it into $27,000. He sent the winnings back to company headquarters to meet the payroll, averting another crisis.

To make ends meet, Smith sold his private plane and gave up virtually all of his equity in the company (which he eventually recaptured in large measure through later refinancings). Stories of employee sacrifice to save the company also became legion. Couriers often left their wristwatches for security against gasoline purchases, and cars and planes were hidden when the sheriff came to repossess them. Fred Smith had an uncanny ability to motivate his employees, to win a sense of trust and dedication from them that was unique in the annals of American business. One employee commented, "This company should have died five or six times in its first three or four years, but Fred refused to give up. Boy, was he tenacious. With sheer bull and courage he pulled off a miracle. That's the only way to express what he did." The firm's first general counsel had similar recollections, "He (Smith) was a fantastic motivator of people, I have not worked since in an environment so intense and so free of politics."

But the troubles continued to mount. To keep the company afloat, Smith had taken increasingly large amounts of money out of the family trust fund without consulting his sisters. When his sisters found out, they were furious, and in January 1975, Smith was indicted by a federal grand jury in Little Rock for forging loan documents on behalf of the Enterprise Company. Smith admitted he had done so but pleaded that "I felt at the time that I was the Enterprise Company. It's as simple as that. And I felt that both of the sisters felt the same way." Smith was finally acquitted in December 1975, but this did not settle a civil suit his sisters had also brought against him. The latter was finally settled in December 1978, in an out-of-court settlement, in which he agreed to buy out his sisters' stock in Enterprise Company and guarantee any loss. By this point, as shall be shown, he could afford to make this promise.

By 1974, there were strong pressures on Fred Smith to step down as chief executive officer of Federal Express. Several of his financial backers felt that someone else could do a better job than he of getting the company off the ground. His management team, however, remained fiercely loyal, as did his employees. As a result, one of his strongest backers, Arthur Bass, told the board that if they replaced Smith, there would be a mass resignation of Federal Express' key officers. The board reluctantly stayed with Smith, and in 1975, a turnaround began. Then Smith's luck could not be beaten. If during the first few years everything had gone wrong, for the next decade everything came up roses for him and Federal Express.

In July 1975, Federal Express had its first profitable month, netting $55,000, and realizing a net income of $3.6 million for the year, on revenues of $75 million. It was on its way. By that time, however, Federal Express had outgrown its fleet of Dassault Falcons, and applied to the CAB for permission to use five DC–9s on longer routes. In December of that year the CAB responded that it did not have the authority to grant the request under the Federal Aviation Act of 1938. Smith then took command of an eighteen-month lobbying effort in Washington, D.C., for passage of what was called the "Federal Express Bill." It was opposed by the Teamsters, the Air Transport Association, and the head of the Flying Tigers; and Smith was denied passage. When Jimmy Carter became president in 1977, he let it be known he favored deregulation of the airline and air freight industries, and he signed into law PL 95–163, which deregulated the air cargo industry. Free to act as it wished, Federal Express purchased Boeing 727s with a lift capacity of 42,000 pounds, and its future as a large-scale growth company was assured. To make this mammoth purchase, more money was needed, and in 1978 Federal Express became a publicly held company, with its shares listed on the New York Stock Exchange.

The success of Federal Express was due to two factors other than Smith's own drive and charisma: an organizational system that virtually guaranteed speed and reliability, and an ingenious and aggressive advertising campaign. Federal Express, by the mid–1980s, was an organizational triumph. Six nights a week, fleets of distinctively painted planes roar into Memphis. There, the planes are unloaded, and the packages are sorted and rerouted by 2,700 well-paid, part-time employees, many of them college students, who work between the hours of 11 P.M. and 3 A.M. (By 1987, Federal Express employed 13,000 people in Memphis—3.2 percent of the work force there.) These workers organize close to half a million pieces of freight each night, assisted by twenty-six miles of conveyor belts with electronic scanners that read bar codes on the packages indicating the ZIP code of the ultimate destination. They are then shipped off in the early morning hours on the same fleet of planes. Upon arrival at the airport of destination, the packages are again sorted and placed in an appropriate van for delivery that morning to the final customer. It sounds deceptively simple, but Smith understood clearly what he was doing:

We're a freight service with 550-mile per hour delivery trucks. This company is nothing short of being the logistics arm of a whole new society that is building up our economy— a society that isn't built around automobile and steel production, but that is built up instead around service industries and high technology endeavors in electronics and optics and medical science. It is the movement of these support items that Federal Express is all about. (*Sobel and Sicilia, The Entrepreneurs*)

The second key was advertising and image-making. This was important not only to attract customers, but also to retain the loyalty of investors, large and small. Trucks and planes were painted a distinctive orange, purple, and white; and full-page advertisements appeared in magazines and major dailies, and thirty-second television commercials appeared on the air—all of them pushed the company's ingenious slogan: to deliver packages "absolutely, positively overnight." Federal Express' advertising agency's research had shown that what people feared most was the possibility of a package not arriving on time, and the ads exploited that fear particularly by focusing on the competition's shortcomings. By 1984, the use of Federal Express had become such an accepted business practice that a *Newsweek* article called it "the middle-management equivalent of ordering up the corporate jet."

Of course, the success of Federal Express was not all due to Fred Smith or due to great organization or innovative advertising—luck played a part, too. Federal came into being just as the airline industry was being deregulated, which greatly increased general industry traffic. Total industry revenues, which stood at $7.2 billion in 1970, had risen to $19.9 billion by 1977. Since commercial carriers were suddenly in high demand, major delivery services were no longer catering to the smaller cities as they had before. That created a significant gap in the market that Fred Smith was able to exploit. Then, too, there was a long UPS strike in 1974, followed soon after by the collapse of REA Express, both of which provided additional opportunities for Federal Express. In 1977, Federal Express had revenues of $160 million, and earnings of $20 million. By 1980, revenues had exploded to $590 million, with earnings of an impressive $60 million. Prices of Federal's stock, which had been issued in 1978 at $3 a share, were up to $24. By this point, Smith had become rather contemptuous of his competitors. Dismissing the venerable Emery Freight, he said,

Emery's been in business thirty-three years and has about 12 percent of the market, and in just six years we have nearly twice that. They offer the same competition a four-legged jackass would if it ran for president. We've relegated Emery to an also-ran because they just don't seem to care. (*Esquire*)

By 1984, Federal Express and Fred Smith were on top of the world. In that year, the firm's revenues exceeded $1.4 billion, profits were high, and Federal Express seemed unstoppable. But Fred Smith had a new idea. And it seemed like a good one. People had doubted him the first time, but this time how could he be wrong? Smith came up with something called ZapMail, an electronic mail service. Promising delivery of facsimile copies of documents anywhere in the United States within two hours, Smith invested an enormous amount of money in the new project—$100 million in just the first year. Federal Express' claims for the new system were breathless: "In just seconds . . . a law firm in New York could transmit a brief via facsimile to a client in Phoenix." But it just did not work that way. Smith had hired Tandem Computers and Harris Corporation to put together the ZapMail system, with thirteen satellite earth stations supplied by Harris linked to more than thirty Tandem computer switching centers around the country. ZapMail customers leased a ZapMailer, a state-of-the-art facsimile machine made by Japan's NEC Corporation. But customers balked at what they felt was an excessively high charge of $35 for up to ten pages of transmission, and they were impatient with the system's innumerable technical problems. Then, too, ZapMail's main selling point—that it could send documents in seconds that took conventional facsimile machines minutes—was hardly compelling to many customers. After all, that was not really the same thing as promising delivery overnight rather than in several days. Customers would pay for the overnight service, but few needed the ZapMail service.

By 1986, ZapMail had lost $300 million. Although Smith had announced when he started the program that he was prepared to accept $1 billion in losses to get it going, in October of that year he pulled the plug on it. In dropping ZapMail, Smith said, "It was not in the best interests of our shareholders, employees, or customers to continue on the present course." A number of industry analysts, however, felt that he had made an enormous, and uncharacteristic, mistake by pulling out so early. One analyst said, "Killing ZapMail was foolish. If you look at the delivery industry over the next ten years, [Federal will] have to use something like [ZapMail] or they'll be dead." Another analyst agreed, "I saw major losses, near-term. But I thought strategically it made sense." Federal Express' problems in 1987 would seem to indicate that the analysts may have been right and Smith wrong. Although revenues were up 24 percent in 1986, to $3.2 billion, and although Federal continued to gain market share in the core overnight letter and package segments of the market, many consultants felt that they were losing up to 30 percent of their business to the ever-booming facsimile machines and electronic mail.

But Smith had no intention of returning to fax-technology. Instead, he changed the direction of Federal Express. Rather than focusing on letters, he shifted the emphasis to packages. He also put Federal Express in the warehousing business. Featuring what is called just-in-time inventory procedures, Federal Express began managing inventories for customers at its sorting hubs in Memphis, Oakland, California, and Newark, New Jersey. Among its early customers was International Business Machines, for whom Federal Express warehoused parts for workstations. Smith also made plans to extend Federal's influence into the still booming foreign markets, even though its eighty-nine country international service division had yet to turn a profit by 1987. But with revenues in that area at over $350 million, and growing by 60 percent annually, it was the largest, single growth field left for Federal.

Federal Express, unlike some firms run by charismatic employers, remained a good place to work even after it became big and profitable. Rated as one of the top ten companies to work for in the United States, the authors of *The 100 Best Companies to Work for in America* cited it as the "quintessential contemporary company," terming it very much a "people company" with its guaranteed fair treatment policy, a five-step grievance procedure. Other policies include no layoffs, top wages, profit sharing, stock options for managers, and open-door policies. By all accounts, Federal Express had managed to keep its 31,000 nonunion employees happy. And that was good for Memphis, formerly a very depressed city. As Smith commented about his home city in 1978,

Memphis is a horrible place . . . . You have a massive underemployed black population, and it's not because the jobs aren't there or the blacks don't want to work. The real problem is that powerful interests in this city want the status quo maintained. . . . It's a backwater town that's not very progressive in either business relations or race relations. (*Esquire*)

Federal Express has changed that, at least somewhat. An employee in August 1987 told *Fortune*, "The first thing people do when they move to Memphis is apply for a job at Federal Express. Then they go get another job till one opens up here."

One of America's fastest growing companies of all time, Federal Express continued its impressive growth in the late 1980s. With revenues of over $3.5 billion in 1987, it had an average growth rate of 35 percent per year from 1983 to 1987. But profits were no longer as strong as they had been in earlier years. With $176 million in earnings in 1987, it represented a drop of 6 percent from the year before. Yet the firm was an unprecedented success when measured by any other yardstick. Charles L. Lea, of Rothschilds, Incorporated, who was one of Smith's earliest and most loyal backers, reflected on the significance of the success of Smith and Federal Express. The overnight package industry might still have been born, and some other company might have ridden to fortune with it, but, Lea pointed out, "If Federal Express had crashed and Amdahl (Corp.)

had crashed, we would not have seen the ebullience in venture capital we have seen. There still would have been a venture capital market, but it would be much more modest.'' Federal Express, if nothing else, gave venture capitalists the profits and the confidence to plow money into a variety of other concerns in the 1980s which did a great deal to fuel the bull market of those years.

Fred Smith stunned the business world again in February 1989, when he announced the purchase of Federal Express' main competitor on international routes, Flying Tiger International. Flying Tiger was the world's largest air cargo hauler, and as such was, in most analysts' view, a perfect fit with Federal Express' small package service. Federal Express had been losing money on its international routes, but the acquisition allowed it to become a powerful force in the international cargo field. As one analyst commented, "Federal Express was getting killed flying small packages abroad in big planes. Now Federal can pack its little parcels around Tiger's big cargo and bring the DC–10's it has been using overseas back into its high-volume domestic routes." It was, however, an expensive gamble, which cost Federal Express $880 million, and came at a time when Smith's company had already lost $50 million for the year. As a result, some critics thought he had gotten in over his head. But, as *Business Week* commented, " 'Czar' may be out of the question, but if Smith can tame Tiger he has a legitimate shot at 'Lord of the Skies.' ''

When Fred Smith was asked in 1986 what it felt like to be in the limelight, he responded,

I am absolutely bound and determined not to be portrayed as something that I am not. I mean, I am just one human being that happened to have a lot of luck, and be in the right place at the right time . . . what I object to most is the heroic way in which journalists like to paint the entrepreneur, the innovator, when in fact the efforts of many, many people—not just of one person—have made the success. (*Inc.*, October 1986)

Worth nearly $395 million in 1988, Fred Smith was prouder of the fact that he had made a lasting contribution to the economic structure of America. Fred Smith is one Vietnam vet who has made a difference. (**B**. *Business Week*, November 3, 1973, March 31, 1980, December 17, 1984, October 13, 1986, November 9, 1987, November 7, 1988, February 13, 1989; *Newsweek*, December 10, 1973, February 7, 1983, January 9, 1984, October 13, 1986; *Forbes*, November 15, 1975, March 1, 1977, June 6, 1983, October 28, November 4, 1985, October 24, 1988; *New York Times*, December 3, 1977, January 7, 1979; *Esquire*, August 15, 1978; *Financial World*, March 15, 1979, August 1, 1982; *U.S. News & World Report*, December 24, 1979, October 6, 1980, December 20, 1982; *Fortune*, June 15, 1981, August 17, 1987; *Nation's Business*, November 1981; *Time*, February 15, 1982, December 17, 1984; Robert A. Sigafoos, *Absolutely, Positively Overnight*, 1983; *Inc.*, April, June 1984, October 1986; *Contemporary Newsmakers*, 1985; Robert Levering et al., *The 100 Best Companies to Work for in America*, 1985; A. David W. Silver, *Entrepreneurial*

Megabucks, 1986; Robert Sobel and David B. Sicilia, *The Entrepreneurs*, 1986; *Industry Week*, January 6, 1986; *Who's Who in America*, 1986–87; *Barron's*, March 13, 1978, February 8, 1988; *Business Month*, March 1989.)

SMITH, ROGER BONHAM (July 12, 1925–   ). Auto company executive, General Motors. John Z. DeLorean, in his scathing attack on General Motors (GM) published in 1979, blamed the corporation's problems on the "bean counters," the gray, colorless, financial men and bureaucrats from the fourteenth floor of the auto giant's headquarters in Detroit. DeLorean believed that they had taken control from the engineers, the automotive people—the men who knew something about cars, consumers, and production. Another former GM executive told automotive writer Brock Yates similar tales of the clannishness of this financial group: "They live together, they work together, they drink together, they play golf together." Another observer noted,

It's like entering the priesthood. They get out of college and go into the system at the zone level. From then on the Corporation takes care of everything: it sells their houses when they move, invests their income, provides them with new cars every few thousand miles, gets them memberships in the right clubs and so on. They even retire together in GM colonies in the South and Southwest. You talk about a cradle-to-grave welfare state. They simply have no concept of the real world. (Nader and Taylor, *The Big Boys*)

When Roger Smith was appointed chairman and chief executive officer (CEO) of General Motors on January 1, 1981, the announcement was greeted with a collective yawn. Another bean counter, another inbred bureaucrat, a financial man who had worked for GM all his life, risen the ladder colorless step after colorless step. He would, in the minds of most observers, be just another caretaker for the enormous automotive monolith. A rather slight man with graying red hair and a squeaky voice, Roger Smith did not look or sound like what most people thought the head of the world's largest corporation should. In fact, a *New York Times* reporter said Smith possessed an "uncanny physical and vocal resemblance to the comedian George Gobel." *Time* said Smith "cultivates a deceptive aw-shucks manner and punctuates conversation with his favorite expression: 'Holy Toledo.' " He did not seem a dynamic leader of men—he did not even look like a *distinguished* bean counter. Nobody expected much from Roger Smith. And when he assured his colleagues that he would be very surprised if there were any major changes during his decade-long tenure, most people took that as confirmation of Smith's caretaker status. How wrong they were! Not since the days of Billy Durant* and Alfred P. Sloan, Jr.,* has anyone taken GM through such dizzying change, angered and dismayed so many people, and generated such a wide variety of comment as Roger Smith. It is premature to assess whether his achievements at GM will rank him among the immortals, or whether he will go down in history as the man who destroyed a great corporation.

Roger Smith's first seven years as chairman can be divided into almost perfect thirds. After the initial few months of uncertainty, general public sentiment viewed him mercilessly. Due to numerous blunders, Smith was lambasted from all sides. As he later conceded, "I was probably the most unpopular chairman ever when I began." Then, as he made a series of dramatic moves, public sentiment turned 180 degrees; by 1984 and 1985, he was lauded by nearly everyone, and he was chosen 1984 Man of the Year by *Automotive Industries* magazine and top chairman of 1984 by *Automotive News*. In 1985 *Financial World* honored Smith as the top CEO in American business.

Then, nearly as suddenly as it had begun, the adulation ceased. In 1986 and 1987, the cheers became boos and sullen murmers. Virtually all the media representatives and industry analysts who had praised Roger Smith several months earlier now castigated him roundly. In 1986 the *New York Times* conducted a "case study" of General Motors to assess its problems. The study's participants analyzed the problems, and most singled out to Roger Smith as the main culprit. Ralph Nader bluntly stated, "The first thing GM should do is retire Roger Smith. He's a finance man who doesn't know how to focus on improving the quality of the product." Others took a similar approach. After two years of criticism, in early 1988, favorable opinion cautiously reemerged. Probably no business leader in recent memory has excited more controversy, or caused more people to change their minds so dramatically about him, so many times as Roger Smith. Why is this?

Roger Smith was born in Columbus, Ohio, into a family that traced its roots to the Mayflower. His father, Emmett Quimby Smith, was president of the small bank he owned. The Smith family lived well, and their home was characterized by privilege and discipline. This comfortable, secure family was shaken when Mr. Smith's bank failed as a result of the depression, but he was a resourceful, inventive man, and the family moved to Detroit, where he joined the Bundy Tubing Company, an auto parts supplier, as comptroller. Before long, Quimby Smith had worked his way up to vice president and part owner of the firm. In addition, he established his own company on the side—Agalloy Metal Tubing— which made parts for the atomic bomb and parachute hand rings during World War II. Part of the elder Smith's success came from his inventive nature. As Roger Smith recalled, "Dad invented systems and methods and even invented some parts on machines." The Smiths lived well in Detroit; they settled in the stately home of ex-governor Wilbur Brucker in the fashionable Indian Village neighborhood and sent young Roger to University School.

Roger was an excellent student, and during the summers he worked in his father's tubing plant. His favorite course was auto mechanics, but he showed his greatest ability in business and had a natural aptitude for numbers. In 1942, he went to the University of Michigan, following the traditional route of his predecessors as GM chairman. Roger tried working part time at his father's company while going to school, but when his grades suffered, his father fired him. He did well in school, but from 1944 to 1946 he took a hiatus from college to serve in the U.S. Navy as a radioman on the light cruiser USS *Montpelier* in the South Pacific.

After the war, Smith returned to get his bachelor's degree at the University of Michigan, which he earned in 1947. Two years later, he received his MBA in accounting from the same university. Upon graduation, Roger Smith had stars in his eyes—he wanted to go to sunny California and get a job in the glamorous aerospace industry. His father, though, had more practical advice. He counseled Roger to apply at General Motors, calling it "the finest-managed company in the land." Roger did it just to placate his father. To celebrate his graduation and his glowing future, the twenty-four-year-old Smith bought himself a brand-new 1949 Ford, and he drove to GM to apply for a job. When he came out, he had a job, and a ticket for overtime parking. The General Motors Roger Smith entered had a golden past, a glowing present, and a robust future.

Founded by William "Billy" Durant, a self-made man and a supersalesman, GM by the 1920s, then under the brilliant direction of Alfred P. Sloan, Jr., had become the dominant automobile firm in America. Using innovative management systems and marketing techniques, Sloan propelled GM past Ford during these years. Throughout the depression years, GM remained a profitable, successful firm. GM used its profits during these years to diversify, to make it less vulnerable to the vicissitudes of the auto market. It became a major factor in the diesel engine field, and also a large-scale aircraft manufacturer.

World War II brought even greater expansion to GM. Bringing in Charles E. Wilson* as president and operating chief, the giant auto firm made a major contribution to the war effort, and expanded its facilities enormously. During the five years of war production, GM churned out $12.3 billion worth of military supplies. The postwar world looked bright—wages were high, unemployment had been eliminated, people had not been able to buy new cars for a number of years—there was a massive pent-up demand for cars at the end of the war. Sales took off after the war, surpassing the 1929 level in 1949, the year Roger Smith joined GM. General Motors, with 38 percent of the domestic car market in 1946, had expanded its share to 43 percent by 1949. Ford and Chrysler in 1949 both had about a 21 percent share; the rest was divided by a number of other domestic producers and a very few foreign companies. GM was a smoothly functioning machine, still imbued with Sloanism.

Yet there were already signs of ossification. Peter Drucker, the management guru, in 1946 wrote his *Concept of the Corporation,* based on his observations of Sloan's management system at GM. In the book, Drucker largely lionized Sloan, praising his decentralized management system, which granted autonomy to the car divisions, allowing for innovation and creativity. Yet, Drucker had been critical of some aspects of the organization, to which GM executives responded chillingly. When a new edition of the book was released in 1972, Drucker noted in an epilogue that he was resoundingly criticized within GM for daring to question the corporation's organization, which resulted in Drucker becoming persona non grata there. That episode set the tone for General Motors during the years that Roger Smith was assimilated into the organization—smug, powerful, wealthy, and unreceptive to outside advice. It was, as John DeLorean noted, a world unto itself—a cocoon in which executives were created and protected from the realities of the outside world.

Roger Smith nestled comfortably into this cocoon. Starting in the general accounting section of the Detroit general office, Smith was, as he put it, "just another runner in the pack." But he had the insight or luck to early choose a rising star on whom to peg his career. That star was Thomas A. Murphy, then an accountant in the New York office. Ten years Smith's senior, Murphy cleared a path to the top for his junior colleague. When Murphy moved up the ladder, Smith, in lock-step fashion, moved with him. Receiving a raft of routine assignments in the early years, Smith worked day and night, in an effort to impress his bosses. At first, however, advancement was slow. It took him nine years to become director of his section in 1958. He then assembled a staff that resembled him—compulsive workers who were "so gung-ho," in Smith's words, that "we used to go out and tackle things we didn't even know anything about."

In 1960, Murphy summoned Smith to the New York office, where he became director of the financial analysis section. At that point, Smith entered the fast track at GM, and advancements came more rapidly as he formed an even closer bond with Murphy. Smith soon advanced to the post of assistant treasurer, and when Murphy went to Detroit as comptroller in 1967, he summoned Smith there a year later as his assistant. Two years later, Smith became treasurer, replacing Murphy, who moved up to vice president and group executive for the Car and Truck Group. Another two years passed, and Murphy became vice chairman. Then, in 1975, he became chairman and CEO of General Motors. Smith chugged right along behind him, becoming vice president in charge of financial staff and a member of the administrative committee in 1971. A year later, Smith finally left the financial section and became vice president of the nonautomotive and defense group. During that time, Smith disposed of two of GM's most unprofitable operations, the Frigidaire appliance division and Terex, a maker of earth-moving equipment. In 1974, Smith became executive vice president of GM and a member of the board of directors.

Smith's first twenty-five years at GM were generally halcyon years for the corporation. GM's market share continued to climb, going above 50 percent in 1954, and remaining at that level for three years. It then dropped back to about 45 percent until 1962, when it climbed to 52 percent for two years. Ford remained in the low 20s during the early years of the 1950s, and then spurted to over 30 percent in 1954. It dropped slightly in succeeding years, but remained between 26 percent and 29 percent until the late 1960s. Chrysler, which had a little over 20 percent of the market in the early 1950s, was devastated after 1954, a year in which they garnered a meager 13-percent share. Although Chrysler's sales climbed as high as 18 percent in one year, it generally had between 10 percent and 15 percent of the market during these years. Smaller car manufacturers, like Nash, Kaiser-Frazer, and Studebaker, were hit even harder. Moving up in market share during these years, but barely noticed by most Americans, were imports, especially Volkswagen, which increased market share from less than 1 percent in 1953 to 10 percent in 1959, before falling off in the early 1960s.

After 1953, when the Korean War ended, the American auto industry took off for the first time in twenty-five years. The economy was flourishing, and the automobile was the veritable symbol of American affluence. The Big Three held about 90 percent of the American market for automobiles, and General Motors was the pricing leader. Competing in an oligopolistic marketplace on the basis of styling changes, Detroit made large cars with comfortable profit margins and paid scant attention to technological innovation. The last major development in that line came at the beginning of World War II, when the automatic transmission was introduced. Robert Sobel has called this period "Detroit Baroque." Like the GM executives themselves, Detroit's Big Three during the 1950s and 1960s were competing in a highly insulated environment, which had lulled them into a false sense of security. They thought they were actually competing when, in fact, they coexisted in a stable and comfortable oligarchy. That mind-set opened the way for Japanese imports to make extensive inroads into the American marketplace in the 1970s.

General Motors, as the largest and most successful of the American auto-makers, had perfected these attitudes to the highest degree. These attitudes were symbolized most graphically with the coming of Frederick G. Donner to the post of chairman and CEO in 1958. Donner served until 1967, and was, in the words of David Cole, an automotive analyst and son of ex-GM president Ed Cole, "an ultimate financial guy." During the first half-dozen years of his administration, Donner progressively trimmed the authority of the automotive divisions to design their own cars, insisting that the corporate level perform this work and that the divisions share as many parts as possible. Donner centralized GM, undoing one of the main tenets of Sloanism. When Peter Drucker examined GM again in the late 1960s, he concluded that "Sloan's principles had become fuzzy beyond recognition." And his criticisms went to the bone:

GM has been all along a "managerial" company rather than an "innovative" one. . . . But we will need to understand increasingly how to organize and to manage innovative organizations. And for this the GM model is not adequate and may not even be appropriate. The failure of GM as an institution—for failure it is—is to a large extent the result of . . . an attitude which says: "We are the experts and within our area of competence, we make the decisions. Other areas are not our business. They are the business of other people."

But GM was successful and profitable, and GM executives felt it was foolhardy to tamper with success.

As a result, GM became an increasingly ossified organization, one whose corporate culture operated to stultify innovation. Thomas J. Peters and Robert H. Waterman, Jr., in their best-selling *In Search of Excellence,* identified a major ingredient for innovative companies: "A special attribute of the success-oriented, positive, and innovating environment is a substantial tolerance for failure." But this was the very antithesis of the situation at GM. A company task force in the 1980s was given the job of determining why GM was losing market share to the Japanese. The report said, in part, "It didn't pay to take chances in the General Motors culture, because the penalties of failure were too severe." It was culture that rewarded caution and conservatism, and this was made even worse by a bureaucratic structure that was incredibly cumbersome and time-consuming. As a reporter for the *New York Times* stated,

In essence, GM management had become a vast white-collar assembly line; even minor questions had to travel from one end to the other, through layer after layer of supervisors, before a decision could be reached. In the end, nobody was fully responsible for anything, and buck-passing was rampant. (*New York Times Magazine*)

Roger Smith in the 1970s looked like a typical, conservative bean counter from finance, and this helped him advance up the ladder. Most outsiders, however, did not realize that Smith was actually anything but conservative. As Albert Lee stated in his scathing biography of Smith, "He was a visionary and dreamer with both the energy and imagination to work his way around obstacles in a bureaucratic system to achieve personal goals. Roger was, in essence, an entrepreneur like his father." But his dreams and innovations in the early years were more organizational than charismatic. For example, his greatest innovation before he became chairman was to institute strategic planning at GM. Incredible as it may seem, the obsession at GM was with sixty- and ninety-day reporting; little attention was paid to long-term goals. Initially, Smith ran up against brick walls when he tried to get long-range planning accepted at GM; when he called it something else, his strategy was adopted. This established Smith's reputation at GM, but it did not impress many of the corporation's critics. As Harvard management professor Robert Hayes stated, "Planning's top-down orientation has emphasized the development of grandiose leaps, rather than the patient, day-to-day improvements that are difficult for competitors to copy." But it fit the culture of an elitist, top-center organization like GM. Smith was a dreamer and a visionary, maybe even an entrepreneur, but decisions were to stay where they belonged—on the fourteenth floor of the GM building—with the bean counters.

In the meantime, the world that GM and Alfred Sloan had built disintegrated in the 1970s. Despite the great success the auto industry experienced during the 1950s and 1960s, there was one nagging problem—imports, first from Germany, then increasingly from Japan. In the late 1960s and 1970s, sales of imported cars began moving upward relentlessly. By 1971, they reached 15 percent; in 1979, 22.6 percent. American automakers, including GM, reacted to this invasion in the late 1960s by introducing new subcompact cars. These subcompacts, like Chevrolet's Vega, sold well, but had little impact on the rising sales of imported cars. Yet, at least prior to 1979, there was the feeling in Detroit and certainly at GM, that the domestic car manufacturers were holding their own against the imported cars, and that it was only a matter of time before GM and its brethren would roll back the tide.

Many industry analysts were less sanguine. To them, it was clear that Detroit had been hit by a massive switch in consumer demand, and that General Motors, as the largest producer of full-size autos, was saddled with the greatest losses, watching its market share drop from 52 percent in 1962 to 44 percent in 1973. In response, GM, under the direction of Thomas Murphy, began to plan the introduction of its X-cars. It was perhaps the most ballyhooed and expensive project in GM's history. Requiring a capital investment of $2.7 billion, the X-cars were a new generation of front-wheel-drive cars for GM. Somewhat smaller, and more fuel efficient than the models they were replacing, the X-cars represented what GM executives called a new line of "world cars," that is, automobiles that would be competitive not just in America, but all over the world. In other words, "Watch out, Japan! Here comes GM!"

The X-cars did sell well in 1979, largely because of the severe gasoline crisis caused by the Iranian hostage-taking incident. As a group, the X-cars accounted for 554,000 of GM's sales and 7 percent of the industry's total. As a result, GM confidently predicted that by the early 1980s these cars, along with a new J-car which was modeled after the Honda Accord, would return GM to dominance in the American and world auto markets. They could not have been more wrong. The giant auto firm suffered a disastrous year in 1980. It was humbled by losses of $760 million, the first time GM had not shown a profit in six decades. Its only other year of loses had been 1921, and Alfred Sloan, Jr., was brought in to turn the company around the following year. In 1981, another new chairman took command to turn around GM's fortunes—Roger Smith.

The corporation Smith took over in January 1981 was reeling from having tried to counterattack the Japanese auto invasion. It also dawned on GM that it was not simply fuel efficiency that made Japanese cars popular, it was also the quality of their workmanship. Lack of quality had been the downfall of the X-cars. Recall after recall had taken place, customer complaints ran high, and the vaunted J-car was a disaster. It was clear to Smith that his work was cut out for him: "All you had to do was look at that red line on the profit-and-loss sheet and know that something had to be done now." A longtime board member, John T. Conner, remarked, "Some of us on the board concluded that because of its past success GM had become fat, dumb and happy." To most observers, the ascension of Roger Smith to the chairmanship offered scant hope for the revival of GM. He was, after all, emblematic of what was wrong with the company—he was an organization man, a bean counter—a fully formed product of the corporate culture that had brought about the crisis in the first place. Compared to charismatic leaders like Lee Iacocca* or even John DeLorean, Roger Smith seemed to be a weak antidote for what ailed GM.

Management analysts, like Drucker and Peters and Waterman, stressed the importance of the charismatic role of the CEO in business. Drucker has said that

"Whenever anything is being accomplished, it is being done, I have learned, by a monomaniac with a mission." He meant that it was necessary for leadership to have a driving dream, an almost mystical sense of the imperative. A professor of human relations in Harvard's School of Business commented, "We have found that what sets the successful chief executive officer apart is that he has a strong vision and he really drives the organization toward that vision." Peters and Waterman concurred, stating that

The truly great executives are those that fundamentally shape or reshape values throughout their organizations. Through big deeds (buying and selling parts of the business, for example) and through small (reading customer complaint letters), the chief executive sends messages about his priorities to every level of the company. (*New York Times Magazine*)

Vision, and the charisma to translate that vision to others—that is what most analysts felt GM needed, and what most felt Roger Smith lacked.

Smith's actions during his first two years in office did little to disabuse his critics. Recognizing that he needed to pull the company out of the red immediately, Smith acted as quickly as possible. The day he took over, he raised prices, closed plants, and laid off workers. A total of 27,000 white-collar and 172,000 blue-collar workers were furloughed, and $3 billion was slashed from the corporate budget. Smith alienated GM's union employees by erroneously declaring during negotiations with the United Auto Workers (UAW) that labor costs would be passed on to consumers, and then, on the same day that he signed a union contract with $2.5 billion in wage and benefit concessions from the union, he disclosed a new bonus plan for 6,000 executives. These and other gaffes caused the originally skeptical opinions about Smith to turn uniformly negative. William Hoglund, then president of the Pontiac division, recalled that "the first six months on the job, Roger succeeded in upsetting just about every constituent with whom he had to work." Critics were savage, and Smith had to withstand an almost daily firestorm of abuse. One critic said of Smith that he was "brilliance unimpeded by humanity." A young executive with GM commented, "In the past, there was always a kind of reverence for the chairman. But people don't feel that way about Roger."

Then, Roger Smith began a turnaround. When he emerged from his cocoon, he realized that something more than cost cutting would be needed to turn around GM. A more radical response was required to meet the mighty Japanese challenge. In August 1981, he borrowed some money to buy a 5-percent interest in Japan's Suzuki Motor Company. In exchange, Suzuki agreed to develop a minicar (to be called the Chevrolet Sprint) for export to GM. Next, Smith turned to another Japanese company, Isuzu, in which GM had held an interest since 1971, and he invested $200 million to have it develop a second import, the Chevrolet Spectrum. Finally, as the third leg of his Asian strategy, Smith signed an agreement with the Korean conglomerate, Daewoo Group, to establish a joint manufacturing venture to produce front-wheel-drive subcompacts to be sold in the United States and Korea. Many experts, feeling it was a perfect match for both firms, were profoundly impressed with this deal. But the cars produced under the agreement, including the Pontiac LeMans, were distinct disappointments. At the time, however, nearly everyone was impressed with Smith's acumen.

But Smith was not finished with his *entente cordiale* with Japan. He began discussions with Toyota, Japan's most efficient and popular carmaker. Import restrictions had severely limited Toyota's access to the American market, and GM had found it virtually impossible to build its own subcompact cars in America. So GM and Toyota made a deal. GM had an idle plant in Fremont, California—one that had been closed because of continual labor unrest and a poor record of productivity—where Toyota and GM could produce the car. Toyota recruited Japanese managers and used Japanese managerial techniques and work rules. The product was a new Chevrolet Nova, an upscale subcompact based on the hugely popular Toyota Corolla. The deal allowed GM to provide 240,000 additional subcompacts a year at a low price, and simultaneously gave them an insight into Japanese management techniques. Roger Smith said, "These were golden apples," and by this time the critics began to take notice.

Along with these momentous changes, Smith also made a deal which set GM on the path toward large-scale technological automation and robotics. In June 1982, he created the GMF Robotics Corporation, in partnership with Fujitsu Fanuc, Limited, a leading Japanese manufacturer of robots. This allowed GM to restructure its manufacturing environment, and, most significantly in Smith's mind, to reduce the large labor cost differential between American and Japanese cars. When Smith took over at GM, it had 300 robots in operation—by his retirement in 1990, he hoped to have 14,000. And these were to be state-of-the-art robots. To ensure that these robots functioned as part of a coordinate manufacturing environment, Smith established a set of universal communications standards, called manufacturing automation protocol (MAP). This, he was confident, would allow GM to create the ultimate factory of the future.

But Roger Smith's emerging vision went beyond these moves. He also realized that the entire corporate culture at GM needed revamping. Smith brought in the consulting firm of McKinsey & Company, which conducted a two-year soul-searching examination of the entire corporation. They concluded that the corporation had become risk-adverse and that the many levels of bureaucracy tended to stifle creativity and, in fact, made the whole decision-making process incredibly cumbersome. The commission proposed, and Smith accepted, a radical transformation of the administrative structure of the company. The five car divisions, along with the Canadian division, were reorganized into two large groups, each of which would take on total responsibility for the cars it produced. The assembly division and the Fisher Body division were disbanded and subsumed into two larger groups. It was an attempt to undo the centralization that had been intensified under Donner, and to return GM to the decentralized ethic, if not the structure, that Alfred Sloan had established earlier.

Designed to loosen the chain of command, and to increase decision making at every level of the organization, subordinates were given more direct access to their bosses. Another aspect of the program, called "participative management," was designed to give lower-level workers, especially assembly-line workers, a larger role in reaching decisions. It was an attempt to copy an aspect of the Japanese management structure known as quality circles. It was a dramatic and courageous attempt to revamp the corporate culture at GM. One GM executive commented, "Most people here didn't believe the reorganization would take place. The fact that it did was one of the strongest signals we could give to the organization that things were very different now."

But it would not be easy. By 1982, GM was making money again, and car sales were up. Many wondered, "Why go through a wrenching reorganization? Why fix something that wasn't broken?" Smith said people told him, "You're crazy. Why don't you let it alone? You can sit back and play golf or whatever it is you're supposed to be doing, but don't tear the place up. Take a couple of years and enjoy what you've got." But Smith had a vision, and he pushed forward with all his considerable energy to achieve his objective. And the giant company began to turn around. It began to loosen up, and the elements of creativity that analysts had found so sadly lacking began to appear. Smith commented in 1984 that

I think there's more freedom of expression on the executive committee right now than I've ever seen in my 35 years at General Motors. Going way back, I knew guys on it who had an idea that they were *afraid to express*. . . . I'd say, "Why don't you bring it up to the executive committee?" And they'd say, "Oh God no. They'd laugh at that." Well, today we get some crazy things we talk about at the executive committee and *nobody laughs. (New York Times Magazine)*

In all of this Roger Smith was the catalyst, the one who tried to translate his vision of the GM of the future to all his employees. But he was not always able to instill this in others. One top executive at the company commented, "I think what Roger means by participative management is, 'Give me your ideas and *I'll* decide.' "

By 1984, Smith's vision of the factory of the future—that wonder of computer-aided, robotic manufacturing methods—was achieving reality in a new plant in Saginaw, Michigan. Smith was becoming positively entranced with the possibilities of the new machine technology. His new robots were indeed fantastic creatures. "I know this is going to sound crazy to you," Smith told a *New York Times* reporter, "but do you know what really impresses me? I saw a robot pick up an egg! You show me a robot that can pick up an egg and I'll show you. . . . Well, its fabulous! Picking up an egg! You know, most robots go *squish*."

Next, Smith announced the Saturn project. With the goal of overtaking the Japanese in small car production, all of Smith's new ideas in management techniques and technological, computer-aided manufacturing would be brought to fruition in this venture. Established as a separate, free-standing corporation within GM, the Saturn was to be GM's first new automobile since the Pontiac, and it would, according to Smith, show the world that GM and America were still the world's best at producing automobiles. In January 1985, the Saturn project was given its own headquarters and management, and $5 billion was earmarked for the new car's development. A revolutionary labor agreement was worked out with the UAW in July 1985, in which the union's work rules and job classifications were made less restrictive for the new Saturn venture. The new plant, to be built in Tennessee, would use new modular construction techniques, instead of the old assembly-line process, and it would establish the kind of participatory worker-management techniques that GM had installed at their Fremont plant with Toyota.

To bring this to fruition, Roger Smith took another bold move in 1985. At just about the same time he unveiled the Saturn project, Smith also purchased Electronic Data Systems (EDS) for $2.5 billion. EDS, the world's largest data processing firm, had been founded by H. Ross Perot,[†] who is generally recognized as one of America's most charismatic CEOs, one who had instilled a powerful entrepreneurial ethic at EDS. The acquisition, solely Smith's idea, was opposed by the executive committee. Operating as an independent subsidiary, EDS absorbed 10,000 of GM's data processing employees, and set about to provide uniformity to the firm's data processing operations. EDS was to become the "central nervous system" at GM, linking engineers with designers, robots with computers, salesmen with executives, and so forth. Equally important, EDS would play a crucial role in the new Saturn project, as the entire system, in Smith's vision, would be computerized, from the sale in the showroom, to the assembly in the plant, to the final delivery to the consumer. The computer system, in conjunction with the plant robotics, Smith confidently assured the public, would allow GM to produce the car for $2,000 less than it cost to make it in 1984.

The critics were agog over what Roger Smith was doing by this time. *Newsweek*, in a feature story in 1985 on Smith, Perot, and the Saturn project, said that they "have set out to lead a second industrial revolution: a thorough redesign of the systems used to manufacture durable goods." They concluded the article by saying, "If Perot and Smith can make that attitude work throughout the company, the General Motors of the future will be awesome to behold." Other former critics were equally impressed. *Financial World* voted Roger Smith their Gold Award as the top CEO in 1985, saying, "In a mere four years he has made a bigger impact on the world's largest manufacturing company than any of his predecessors since Alfred Sloan." *Automotive News* commented, "He has turned the industry upside down so much that it will never be the same." In recognition, they named Smith chairman of the year, and *Automotive Industries* voted him Man of the Year.

Roger Smith was on top of the world. To cap it all off, in December 1985, he took over Hughes Aircraft Company for $5 billion and merged it into an independently managed subsidiary called GM Hughes Electronic Corporation.

This made GM the leading maker of missiles, satellites, and radar and sonar equipment; it also brought them technology that would aid in their development of automated quality-control systems for auto manufacturing. Smith made some other, nonautomotive acquisitions in that year, including the $11-billion mortgage portfolio of Norwest Corporation and the $7.4-billion interest of the Colonial Group of Corestates Financial Corporation. These were integrated into General Motors Acceptance Corporation, making it the second largest provider of mortgage services in the country.

Then, just as suddenly as they had lionized Smith, the critics in 1986 and 1987 turned savagely against him. Things got so bad that Smith earned the distinction of being placed on both the *Forbes* and *New York Times* lists of the ten worst CEOs for 1986, and he was given the lowest ranking in the annual awards dinner of the *Gallagher Report*. There were several reasons for this. In November 1986, with the introduction of the 1987 models, the industry as a whole experienced a boom in sales, but GM's sales fell. Then came results from the third quarter of that year, and it was learned the company had suffered an operating loss of $338 million. These were crushing disappointments for Smith and for GM, but the biggest problem of all, and the one that seemed to trigger most of the negative press for the giant automaker, was the debacle with Ross Perot and EDS.

Smith's great ambition to absorb Perot and the entrepreneurial culture of EDS at GM, to infuse the giant firm with the heroism and enthusiasm of the smaller company, was an utter failure. Perot, who was supposed to be a roving ambassador of entrepreneurial enthusiasm, soon became pointedly critical of what he found at GM. And, in violation of the entire code of corporate ethics at GM, he began telling the press what he found there. Asking the rhetorical question, "You want to know how to teach an elephant to tap-dance?" he asked, "You find the soft spots and start poking." Every aspect of GM came under his withering attack: "The whole problem is at the top. Only in America can you blame the guy on the factory floor. It's the GM system that produces the inability to make good products." Further: "You've got to move Roger and the rest of those people out of the fourteenth floor of the GM building and down to the real places where people are doing the real work of building cars." But the comment that most caught the public's imagination was Perot's comparison of GM and EDS: "The first EDSer to see a snake kills it. At GM, first thing you do is organize a committee on snakes. Then you bring in a consultant who knows a lot about snakes. . . . Then you talk about it for a year." Finally, Smith began firing broadsides back at Perot. It soon became clear to him that he had to get the loose cannon off his deck, and he was willing to pay almost anything to do it. The end result was that he paid Perot $700 million for his share of GM stock. Smith had bought Perot's shares for $51 a share—at a time when it was selling on the market for $26—a terribly expensive buyout.

The reaction was immediate. Maryann Keller, an esteemed auto industry analyst, commented, "If the price of harmony is also conformity, then you lose the uniqueness of EDS—and all that money was wasted.'' Most publications praised Perot and lambasted Smith. The consensus was that Smith and GM were running a shell game—talking a lot about creativity and openness, while at the same time complaining that there was no money for profit-sharing or higher wages. Then, when somebody is openly critical of GM, and tries to stimulate creativity, the coffers open up and buy him out with money they claimed did not exist. The *New York Times* said of Smith, ''Few executives in recent years have been longer on vision and more plagued by reality.''

The critics in 1987 descended on Roger Smith and GM in full force. *Business Week* (March 16, 1987) ran a major story, saying,

The company that was once the prototype for mass production and mass marketing now has the highest costs of the Big Three. Its integrated factories . . . have become a high-cost problem. Many of its expensive, high-tech plants are hardly more efficient than the old ones. And its cars look so much alike that many buyers are balking.

GM and Roger Smith staked the corporation's future on its ability to outspend competitors. Spending about $40 billion on new plants and machinery during the 1980s was supposed to restore market share and to return the company to its former profitability. The results were dismal. GM's share of the domestic auto market by 1986 had plunged to 41 percent, down from 48 percent eight years earlier. Despite the fact that GM's market share had dropped to 37 percent by 1987, Smith kept his plants running full tilt, trying desperately to recover the firm's former dominance. As a result, by 1989, GM had larger inventories of cars than any other maker, and many forecast severe losses for the company. Productivity, despite all the robotics, could not keep pace with Ford, and, as a result, GM's profits lagged behind those of its main competitor, Ford.

Business Week (March 16, 1987) asked, ''What Went Wrong?'' After cataloging a number of problems, it laid the blame squarely at Smith's feet. GM, it said, needed a CEO who could inspire workers and convince unions to go along with the pain of reorganization. Smith, however, was usually antagonistic; he was seldom able to inspire anyone, even his fellow executives. Also, it was not clear whether the much vaunted Saturn project would ever leave the launch-pad. The car, which had been ticketed at the low end of the market, was changed to a mid-priced auto. The car itself also got bigger on the design boards. The result of all of this was that many analysts felt the car was doomed even before it was ever produced—that it would be the Edsel of the 1990s. A former GM executive commented, ''The faster they admit it's a mistake, the better.''

Smith's response was to come out fighting. He argued that GM had been paying its dues in terms of developing new models and new factories to make them, and this had caused a downturn in sales and put a drain on the company's profits. He felt, however, that the benefits would become increasingly apparent by the end of the 1980s. ''People will see our new products and they'll appreciate the quality,'' he said, ''but they won't know what we've done on costs.'' But many in the industry felt that Smith and GM were suffering from hubris—that they could not admit that their dominant position in the car industry was no longer. As one Chrysler executive said, "They have failed to comprehend that their market share is gone forever, forever, forever—even if they do everything right."

Nonetheless, in 1988, opinion about Roger Smith and GM began to become cautiously optimistic again. *Financial World,* entitling their article "Tortoise Gains on Hare," argued that Smith had pushed plant-floor technology to the utmost and that he had fallen prey to what they called the "magic wand syndrome," the idea that technology would solve all problems. Complicating the problem was poor people management on the part of Smith, especially his clumsy relations with the union. But the magazine felt that Smith had learned his lessons, and that, further, new quality control systems were in place that would allow the firm to finally begin producing a product that lived up to the claims made in their ads. A short time later, *Fortune* ran another article on GM and Roger Smith. Although it recognized that many problems still remained, it saw promise for the future. *Fortune* was particularly optimistic about the Saturn project, although Lee Iacocca, in his book, *Talking Straight,* derided Saturn as just "another Chevy for 1990."

So the future remained clouded for Roger Smith and GM in 1989. It all seemed to boil down, as Smith predicted years before, to the success of the Saturn project. The greatest irony will be if, as *Fortune* said, "By the time Roger Smith climbs down from the driver's seat in 1990, the rest of GM could be so far advanced that it has largely caught up with Saturn. The bold, visionary venture will then look for all the world like just another car division." Does that mean that Roger Smith, the man who shook GM and the auto industry to the core, will look just like another GM bean counter to future historians? (**B.** Peter Drucker, *Concept of the Corporation,* 1946, 1972; Emma Rothschild, *Paradise Lost,* 1973; Jerry Flint, *The Dream Machine: The Golden Age of American Automobiles, 1946–1965,* 1976; J. Patrick Wright, *On a Clear Day You Can See General Motors,* 1979; Ed Cray, *The Chrome Colossus,* 1980; Milton Moskowitz et al., *Everybody's Business,* 1980; *Fortune,* October 6, 1980, July 8, 1985, August 1, 1988; Thomas J. Peters and Robert H. Waterman, Jr., *In Search of Excellence,* 1982; Brock Yates, *The Decline and Fall of the American Automobile Industry,* 1983; Alan Altshuler et al., *The Future of the Automobile,* 1984; John B. Rae, *The American Automobile Industry,* 1984; Robert Sobel, *The Car Wars: The Untold Story,* 1984; *Automotive Industries,* February 1984; *Industry Week,* February 20, 1984, January 6, 1986; Harry C. Katz, *Shifting Gears,* 1985; *Financial World,* April 3–16, 1985, February 23, 1988; *New York Times Magazine,* April 21, 1985; *Newsweek,* June 17, 1985, September 7, 1987, February 20, 1989; *Time,* June 17, 1985; *Current Biography,* 1986; Ralph Nader and William Taylor, *The Big Boys,* 1986; *New York Times,* December 7, 1986; *Who's Who in America,* 1986–87; Davis Dyer et al., *Changing Alliances,* 1987; Douglas K. Ramsey, *The Corporate Warriors,* 1987; Toronto *Globe & Mail,*

March 10, 1987; *Business Week*, March 16, September 7, 1987, March 7, September 12, 1988, February 13, March 6, 1989; Albert Lee, *Call Me Roger*, 1988.)

STEINBERG, SAUL PHILLIP (August 13, 1939–   ). Computer leasing company founder, corporate raider, and entrepreneur, Leasco and Reliance Group. Saul Steinberg has probably been the most hated and feared man in corporate America over the past two decades. The feeling has been so intensely negative toward the man that *Fortune* in 1980 wrote an article on him entitled "Fear and Loathing in the Boardrooms." Yet, Steinberg was a pioneer, and it was largely that aspect of him that frightened and infuriated the corporate establishment in the United States. He virtually created the technique known as "greenmail" before the word was coined. Over the years, he has used it more successfully than any other corporate raider. He also engineered one of the first highly visible hostile takeovers of a major corporation undertaken by a raider. Although it was unsuccessful, it set a pattern for many to follow. Steinberg also perfected the techniques of the leveraged buyout. He was a prototype for the corporate raiders who followed in the 1980s. T. Boone Pickens,[†] Carl Icahn,[†] and others were just following precedents and techniques established earlier by Steinberg. With few friends in the American corporate establishment, Steinberg is widely recognized as the epitome of the corporate raider.

Steinberg was born in Brooklyn, New York, the son of the owner of a plastics factory in the borough. By the time he was in high school, Steinberg was reading the *Wall Street Journal* from cover to cover every day, and had decided that he was going to become a millionaire before he was thirty years old. Many undoubtedly scoffed at Steinberg's puffery at that time, but when he reached his twenty-ninth birthday, he was worth $50 million. And he had only just begun. *Forbes* proclaimed in 1969 that "Steinberg has made more money on his own than any other person now under 30 in America." Not that we have a classic, rags-to-riches, Horatio Alger story here. There was no poverty for Steinberg when he was growing up; no standing out on freezing street corners peddling newspapers to help feed his family. Steinberg's father was comfortable, but not wealthy. The plastics business was not large, but it provided a decent standard of living for the family. As Saul Steinberg later remarked, his father "was unusual in that he was always satisfied with what he had and he never wanted more." That statement probably reveals more about Saul Steinberg than about his father—Steinberg thought it was highly unusual for someone to be satisfied with having achieved a comfortable life. The son would never be satisfied; he would always want more. And that desire has been frightening corporate America for years.

After graduating from high school, Steinberg went to the Wharton School at the University of Pennsylvania. There he was just an average student, whose concerns were centered more on the practical aspects of money making than the theoretical aspects of management. He demonstrated that graphically in his senior year, when he pulled off his first raid and collected his first greenmail. Steinberg began buying shares in a small firm called O'Sullivan Rubber, and soon he controlled 3 percent of the stock. At that point he began demanding that the company diversify into auto parts, and when it refused, he threatened a proxy fight. This frightened O'Sullivan's management, so they bought Steinberg out for three times what he had paid for the stock. Although the term had yet to be invented, it was a classic case of what came to be known in the 1980s as greenmail. Greenmail is the practice of buying a substantial portion of a corporation's stock and threatening a takeover or a proxy fight solely in order to persuade the threatened company to buy back the stock at a profit to the greenmailer. Blackmail, of course, is illegal; greenmail is not. But many people in the 1980s came to believe that greenmail was immoral and unethical. Not Saul Steinberg.

Having made a nice profit on his first greenmail escapade, Steinberg turned his attention to graduating. That posed a bit of a hurdle, because at Wharton one has to write a senior thesis to graduate. In 1959, in consultation with his advisor, Steinberg began to research his chosen topic—"The Decline and Fall of IBM." His nascent thesis was that IBM had sown the seeds of its own destruction, which would come about in the 1960s. As Steinberg did his research, he realized that just the opposite was true—IBM had perfected a fabulous money machine. In the process of his research, however, Steinberg discovered something else. He found, first of all, that IBM always leased, rather than sold, its machines. But he also found that in 1956 the firm had been forced to sign an antitrust consent decree agreeing to sell computers to anyone who wanted to buy them. Not only did a new thesis begin to take form in Steinberg's fertile mind but also a highly lucrative business possibility.

Steinberg figured he could buy a computer from IBM, and then lease it himself to customers. IBM charged very high leasing rates, and depreciated its computers over four years. Steinberg figured he could depreciate his computers over eight years, undercut IBM's prices, and still make a nice profit. So Steinberg changed his thesis topic to "The Economics of Computer Leasing." He got his degree and went to work for his father for two years. During this time, he also worked out the fine points on the economics of leasing, so that he would be prepared for every contingency when he entered the marketplace. In 1961, Steinberg's father lent him $25,000, and the young man started the Ideal Leasing Corporation in partnership with his father and uncle. He soon changed the name to Leasco Data Processing Equipment Corporation. Their first year of operation was tough; they made just $56,000. In 1962, it dropped to $45,000. But the companies were signing five-year leases with Leasco, and it took the first five years to cover the cost of the machine. Eventually the profits would begin to roll in.

The profits came. And came perhaps more quickly and in larger amounts than even Steinberg thought possible. In August 1965 he took Leasco public, just four years after its founding, with assets of $5.4 million. Leasco was on its way. The 1960s were hot years for all kinds of computer stocks, and Leasco was one of the hottest. At times during the late 1960s, its stock was selling for 50 times earnings. With that kind of multiple, Steinberg could easily do what others did in that situation—take over smaller companies—build a mini-conglomerate. Within a short space of time, Steinberg had bought ten small companies, paying for them with Leasco stock and cash. But Steinberg's big move came in 1968, when he went after a bigger company, a much bigger company.

Reliance Insurance was a venerable 150-year-old Philadelphia company, nearly ten times the size of Leasco with $700 million in assets. Having made a $52-million public offering with Leasco early that year, Steinberg used the proceeds to pursue Reliance. He purchased 3 percent of the insurance company's stock on the open market. Then, putting together a package of warrants and convertible preferred stock, Steinberg tendered some $400 million for the rest of Reliance's stock. Nobody knew quite what to make of it. Reliance's chief executive officer (CEO) just said they had to study the offer. There was no sense of emergency and anger as there would be with later Steinberg takeover attempts; just a rather bemused attitude. Nearly a month later, Reliance announced it was exploring a merger with a different company, and shortly thereafter declared that they would fight Steinberg's takeover "with all the resources at our command." Steinberg upped his offer, however, and they ultimately accepted it. The two companies were merged, and Steinberg became the CEO. He was now captain of a major American corporation with assets of some $400 million. Steinberg was in the big leagues now, or so he thought.

A year later, Steinberg rocked the financial community to its foundations, and he caught its full wrath in a manner that truly surprised and wounded him. Steinberg's great genius was not that he got into computer leasing and made some money at it; his genius was in knowing when to get out. And he knew to get out when the market was still hot in the 1960s. He wanted to create an integrated financial empire, and the acquisition of the lucrative cash surplus and assets at Reliance was just his first step. His vision embraced a fully integrated financial service company; to do that, he decided he needed a bank. So, Steinberg went after Chemical Bank of New York, the sixth largest commercial bank in the United States. If his run at Reliance resulted in bemused silence, his raid on Chemical generated a massive outpouring of hate and fear. Chemical Bank, which had assets of nearly $9 billion, was regarded as one of the pillars of the financial establishment. Steinberg began buying stock in Chemical, and soon he owned some 300,000 shares. Chemical Bank was a classic takeover target: asset rich, it was a mediocre performer on the stock market, so it could be bought cheaply.

Steinberg seemed blissfully unaware of the fear he had struck in the heart of America's establishment. The *New York Times* ran a story announcing that Chemical was going to fight Steinberg's takeover attempt. Within a short period of time, White, Weld, Leasco's investment banker, pulled out of the deal, piously announcing that they would not participate in a hostile takeover. Other investment bankers also refused to ally themselves with Steinberg. Nelson Rockefeller,* governor of New York, and brother of Chase Manhattan's David Rockefeller,* called for legislation to stop bank takeovers, and similar legislation was introduced into Congress. Steinberg was caught in a whirlwind of protest and angry denunciation. Bank trust departments began dumping Leasco stock, and it plummeted on the markets. Leasco stock, which had increased 5,400 percent since 1965, tumbled 33 percent in just days. Finally, on February 20, only three weeks after it all began, Steinberg publicly capitulated.

Badly shaken and humiliated, Steinberg could not understand why there had been such a ruckus. "I'm no takeover artist," he told *Forbes* in 1969. "My wife and I, we're decent people. We like tennis, art, music. We have three children. We're not really bad at all." But *Business Week* saw the whole affair in perspective; it knew that the corporate establishment regarded Steinberg as the ultimate outsider. He was "young, sometimes brash, a johnny-come-lately, and Jewish to boot." Later, Steinberg regretfully came to agree with *Business Week*: "I always knew there was an establishment. I just used to think I was part of it." He ate humble pie in his Chemical Bank defeat, and unctuously proclaimed, "Hostile takeovers of money-center banks are against the best interest of the economy because of the danger of upsetting the stability and prestige of the banking system and diminishing public confidence in it." Never again. Steinberg would bide his time, but never again would he apologize for his actions. He also found that he had made a tidy profit of $36 million on his failed attempt at Chemical. He licked his wounds and became a consummate raider.

Later that same year, Steinberg tried to take over Pergamon Press in Britain. The British establishment reacted with the same hostility that Steinberg had encountered in America. This time, though, he did not care. When he backed down, it was not because of the pressure, it was because he found that Pergamon was not as attractive a target as he had thought. He abandoned his takeover attempt, and London was left shaking after the raid of Steinberg, the enfant terrible. Steinberg might have participated in more takeover activities during the 1970s except for two things—a number of troublesome lawsuits and the increasing financial difficulties of Reliance Insurance.

The lawsuits can be handled in a summary fashion. In one, he had promised to give $375,000 to the Woodmere Academy on Long Island to build a library and computer center named after his wife. He was supposed to pay the money in 1972, but when the time came, he gave only $175,000, promising the rest in 1973. A year later, Steinberg still claimed he did not have the money, and the school took him to court. In 1977 the New York Court of Appeals made Steinberg pay the balance of the money. He also was accused by the Securities and Exchange Commission of violating securities laws in the sale of stock in Pulte Home Corporation. Steinberg signed a consent decree on that charge. More damaging was his involvement in the New York City bus-shelter scandal in 1975–1976. Steinberg had formed a company to erect bus shelters in New York, and was accused of using political influence and bribery to take the city contract away from the firm which was supplying the shelters. Nothing was ever proved, and Steinberg took the Fifth Amendment when asked about his involvement during a subsequent investigation.

Most damaging, however, was the divorce action his second wife filed against him in 1980. This was not one of the world's most amicable divorces. She was not only Steinberg's wife, but also a major stockholder in Reliance. She filed a stockholder's suit against Steinberg, making sensational charges against him. She claimed Steinberg used the company jet "exclusively" for his private enjoyment and that he spent corporate funds on his Park Avenue apartment and other things. She charged that he took $100,000 from Reliance to bribe a city official, and, most sensational of all, she said Steinberg was a "heavy user" of narcotics who "as a consequence of his drug addiction . . . failed to attend many corporate meetings and to perform certain corporate duties." She claimed he had spent over $190,000 of Reliance's money on cocaine and other drugs. The headlines were murderous: "Wife Pins Coke Rap on Top Exec." Devastated, Steinberg replied, "Everything she has said so far is a goddamn lie. . . . I'm dealing with an outraged and vengeful woman." Although investigators said they could find no truth to the allegations, many of Steinberg's associates were shaken. One said, "It's a tragedy, he is a genius who has led a notorious and sleazy life." Another said, "I assume that Saul will self-destruct." He did not. When the Steinbergs' divorce settlement was reached, the ex-wife received alimony of $10,000 a month. She dropped her stockholder suit, stating, "I was hurt, upset, and confused. All of the charges and lawsuits that I instituted were untrue."

In addition to all these suits, Steinberg had serious problems to attend to at Reliance. The firm had been hit very hard by the recession of 1974–1975, and its net worth, which stood at $205 million in 1973, had plunged to just $65 million by 1975. Realizing that he had to take action, Steinberg realigned top management and took over much of the day-to-day operations of the company himself. He did a remarkable job of turning the company around; by 1978, its earnings were $55 million, and by 1980, $103 million. A key component of this success was a subsidiary that Steinberg had started from scratch—CTI International—which he built into the world's biggest container leasing company. He expanded the container fleet by an average of 24 percent per year, and boosted its revenues by 33 percent annually after 1973. During this same period, its profits increased 67 percent.

Having brought Reliance back to profitability by 1978, Steinberg, who owned 12 percent of the company, began to buy back Reliance's stock. Over the next several years, he spent $300 million of Reliance Group's money to repurchase its own stock. By 1981, the Steinbergs owned over 15 percent of the stock in Reliance Group. They also owned a majority of the stock in another corporation that owned 25 percent of Reliance's stock. Then, the Steinberg family acquired the remaining stock in Reliance Group, financing the bulk of the purchase by issuing $434 million worth of debentures and preferred stock in a new company, Reliance Group Holdings. The new company had a very heavy debt load, but was by then under the total control of Steinberg and his relatives, who held all of its common stock. In 1986, Steinberg took Reliance public yet again, although he retained a large portion of the shares. By then, with the stock market flying high, it was estimated that Steinberg's holdings were worth $650 million. The stock market crash in October 1987, however, hit Reliance very hard, and *Forbes* estimated Steinberg's net worth in 1988 to be about $400 million.

In the late 1970s, Steinberg became a raider again. Lomas & Nettleton, a giant mortgage-banking house, became his first major takeover target. With assets of $350 million, but an undervalued stock, it was an ideal prize for Steinberg. Reliance bought about 25 percent of Lomas' stock, some 1.7 million shares, for $22 million. Steinberg then launched into his patented greenmail strategy. Telling Lomas' board that they could get a better return if they spread the company's money around to a larger number of banks, Steinberg insisted that Reliance people be made board members. Lomas became frightened, and soon agreed to pay Reliance $38 million for its stock, a tidy 70 percent increase in just a few months. When *Forbes* (December 25, 1978) asked Steinberg if what he had done was not blackmail, he replied, "Absolutely not." It was, of course, greenmail, but the term had not yet been invented. Steinberg also became involved in a complicated takeover fight for UV Industries, and he made a run at Penn Central. In both cases, his attempts at a takeover were beaten back, but Reliance emerged from the fray with healthy greenmail payments of about $20 million.

None of these maneuvers caused a great stir because they were all somewhat marginal companies in terms of the national consciousness. But in 1980 Steinberg made headlines again with his curious half-run at the *New York Times*. He bought up something over 5 percent of the newspaper's stock, but had little chance of acquiring the company, because the Ochs and Sulzberger families had a dominant stock holding. Nonetheless, the *Times* became extremely agitated over the possibility of Steinberg's involvement with its paper. *Business Week* (November 17, 1980) said, "The newspaper regards itself as the organ of the Eastern Establishment, and Steinberg has been seen as an upstart by the Establishment ever since he tried to take over Chemical Bank in 1969." A few months later, however, Steinberg sold his *Times* stock for a small profit. Perhaps he was just tweaking the nose of the Establishment.

During the decade of the 1980s Steinberg and Reliance became much more active in the takeover scene. Steinberg bought 8 percent of Chris-Craft Industries, which he later sold back to the company for a profit of $15 million. He actually took over some companies, such as Frank B. Hall, which was engaged in various kinds of insurance; Wickes Companies, which dealt in retail lumber, building materials, food, and drugs; and Zenith National Insurance, which handled workman's compensation insurance. Reliance also had a dominant position in Federal Paper Board, Imperial Corporation of America, and Midwestern Distributing, among others. But Steinberg's most highly publicized takeover bid in the 1980s came when he tried to gain control of Walt Disney Productions.

Allying himself with Michael Milken[†] of Drexel Burnham Lambert, Steinberg raised a war chest of $1.3 billion through junk-bond financing for his run at Disney. Once one of Hollywood's most profitable and fabled studios, Disney had fallen on lean times, and it had the classic raider's profile: a rich asset base and undervalued stock because of poor profitability. Steinberg, through MM Acquisitions, bought an 11-percent interest in Disney, and then made a tender offer for another 37.9 percent of the outstanding shares. Disney management reacted as did so many other firms when Steinberg began circling—they panicked. After extensive acrimonious negotiations, Disney agreed to pay Steinberg $325 million to buy out his stock, giving him a profit of between $30 and $60 million on his stock, plus another $28 million for out-of-pocket expenses. The general consensus was that Disney had paid an enormously high price to escape Steinberg's clutches. Some stockholders were so angry they even went to court to void the settlement. In the meantime, Steinberg orchestrated several other raids, sometimes gaining control of a company, sometimes just collecting a healthy greenmail payment.

By 1988, with corporate raids having become the norm in American business and with raiders having achieved a modicum of social respectability, nobody seemed to think Saul Steinberg was so bad anymore. Press coverage of Steinberg was rather friendly, and he seemed to have become respectable. Lisa Birnbach, author of the best-selling *The Official Preppy Handbook*, interviewed Saul Steinberg for a new book she was writing. In the interview, Steinberg revealed, for the first time, his boyhood hero—Howard Hughes. Steinberg, Birnbach reported, had just one goal in life—to make money, to become as rich as billionaire Howard Hughes. By 1988, Steinberg was not even halfway to a billion dollars but by then, he was cultivating a new image. Steinberg had long tried to present himself as a corporate statesman: "You're not in business to make money. You do what interests you. What excites you. The money is incidental. It just comes. It isn't any longer something you think about for itself." Had Steinberg mellowed? Or was he just softening up the Establishment for his next raid? (**B**. *Newsweek*, February 24, 1969, June 5, 1978, December 3, 1979; *Business Week*, April 16, 1969, November 17, 1980, March 16, 1981, October 18, 1982, June 25, 1984; *Forbes*, May 15, 1969, April 1, 1975, December 25, 1978, June 4, 1984; *Time*, October 24, 1969, March 4, 1985; Lawrence A. Armour, *Young Millionaires*, 1973; *New York Times Magazine*, April 16, 1978; *Financial World*, July 1, 1978; *Who's Who in America*, 1979–80; *Fortune*, December 15, 1980; Katherine D. Fisher, *The Computer Establishment*, 1981; *Economist*, June 16, 1984; *Dun's Business Monthly*, July 1984; *Barrons*, November 12, 1984; Eric W. Allison, *The Raiders of Wall Street*, 1986; Michael Allen, *Founding Families*, 1987; John Taylor, *Storming the Magic Kingdom: Wall Street, the Raiders, and the Battle for Disney*, 1987; *Institutional Investor*, April, June, 1987; *U.S. News & World Report*, July 6, 1987; *Inc.*, September 1988.)

STERN, LEONARD (March, 1938–   ). Pet food manufacturer, real estate developer, publisher, Hartz Mountain Corporation, Hartz Group Incorporated, *Village Voice*. Canaries. Thousands of singing canaries. The roots of great American fortunes are diverse, but perhaps none have more unusual origins than Leonard Stern's. Stern is the sole owner and virtual dictator of Hartz Mountain Corporation, a billion-dollar empire built on birdseed, flea collars, and cat litter. The Hartz Mountain company was founded in Germany in the early 1920s by Leonard's father, Max Stern. Max originally was a textile manufacturer who got into the pet business by accident. He had loaned $30,000 to a friend who sold canaries bred in Germany's Harz Mountain region. When his friend went broke and could not repay the loan, he suggested to Max that the two of them try to sell some of the canaries in America. What a sight it must have been: Max and his friend took a steamer to New York accompanied by 2,100 canaries. There they opened a shop and sold all the birds within six months. Recognizing he was on to something, Max imported more birds and later diversified into birdseed and cages.

Max was a master marketer. Despite his status as a newcomer in America, he exploited new advertising approaches with the aplomb of a seasoned native. During the 1930s and 1940s, he ran radio ads featuring the Hartz Mountain Master Singing Canaries, which sang lustily to the delight of his potential customers and lured them into the stores. Using advertising as a means to move toward national distribution, Max Stern began mass merchandising his pets through chain stores like F. W. Woolworth and W. T. Grant. As Gigi Mahon in *New York* has noted, "He undercut his competition on the price of the birds, then made his real money on the seed and cages." Max Stern ran the company until the 1950s, when he turned ownership of the firm over to his son Leonard.

Young Leonard Stern was born in New York, attended Yeshiva, and received his undergraduate degree from New York University in 1956. Three years later, he got his MBA from the same school. By that time, Leonard was twenty-one, and was the only one of Max's children who was interested in entering the family business. Max Stern had given the company's stock to all three children in the late 1950s, but Leonard bought out his brother and sister over the next few years. The company Leonard inherited, however, was floundering. It was deeply in debt, and sales were slipping badly. Leonard realized that he needed to take dramatic steps to correct the sad state of affairs. He was astute enough to recognize that America was on the verge of undergoing a "pet revolution," and that Hartz Mountain could be ideally placed to take advantage of this. To do so, however, it was imperative for Hartz Mountain to diversify beyond birds. Accordingly, Leonard Stern turned the firm around by expanding into dog and cat supplies—the big growth areas of the pet industry. By the mid–1960s, the company's distinctive orange packages could be found in supermarkets, pet shops, and discount stores nationwide. In 1972, Leonard Stern took the company public, selling a portion of it for $40 million. Seven years later, Stern took Hartz private again, at a price significantly below the price the original shareholders had paid.

Although Max Stern had created a profitable business, and even though it had achieved a semblance of national distribution by the 1950s, it was still a small manufacturer of a limited range of pet supplies. Leonard Stern transformed it into a major, professionally managed corporation. As Stern told *Fortune* in 1973, "I took Hartz from canaries to pet supplies, from sixty products to twelve hundred products, from eighteen people to four hundred in the field, from packaging to integrated manufacturing, from being a debtor to a lender." But this was not achieved without a touch of ruthlessness. As a business acquaintance of Stern's has commented: "He could be tough, mean, and nasty. He's not always a very nice person. I always got the feeling that you could wrestle with him and he could get you down and pin you, but it wouldn't be enough. He still wants to stick the shiv in." Reactions like that have dogged Stern throughout his business career. His notoriety became so great by 1981 that "60 Minutes" did a story on him. In the segment, Mike Wallace said about Stern, "Along with his money, he may have made more enemies than most tycoons." Even his staunchest supporters cannot deny that.

In 1966, with his father's approval, Leonard Stern got Hartz Mountain into real estate. Neither Leonard nor the company had much capital at that point, and they could not afford to invest in New York real estate. As Leonard Stern told Gigi Mahon, "With a little money, you could buy a little building in New Jersey. With a little money you can't build *any* building in New York. So we went the poor man's route." But Stern did not buy just any land in New Jersey. He bought swampland—swampland—it almost sounds like a cruel joke. He paid $9.75 million for 750 acres of swampland and pig farms just across from midtown Manhattan, and the smart money thought he was crazy. Called the Meadowlands, over the years, Stern developed it into a flourishing site of industrial parks, office buildings, and condominiums. By 1988, the land alone was estimated to be worth about $500,000 an acre. With the developments, it is worth billions, and Stern has invested an estimated $1 billion in it.

With the success of his Meadowlands project, Stern expanded his real estate interests. Along with about thirty projects that he has going on in New Jersey at any given time, Stern expanded into the "yuppie" haven of Westchester County, New York, and in 1986 he put up a twenty-four-storied office building at the corner of Madison Avenue and 61st Street in New York City. The latter may not make him any more money, but it is a hallmark of Stern's arrival of status as a real estate man. There were lots of developers in New Jersey and in the suburbs, but Manhattan is reserved for the big-time players, like William Zeckendorf* and Donald Trump.† There was no longer any question that Stern was in the big leagues in real estate.

As Hartz Mountain and Stern both flourished, reactions to his business tactics resulted in a number of lawsuits and government investigations. The troubles have pretty well run the gamut that could befall an industrial firm. In the early

1970s, Hartz tried to force independent distributors to stop handling competitors' products. When many refused, Stern and Hartz Mountain used a variety of tactics to stop the practice. The Federal Trade Commission investigated, and Hartz ultimately signed a consent decree, whereby a company admits no wrongdoing, but promises not to do it in the future. Over the next few years, Hartz Mountain simply bought out most of the distributors, which eliminated the problem.

In 1977, a Hartz executive was convicted of fraud against the company, and, in 1979, Hartz Mountain paid $42.5 million to settle an antitrust suit brought by A.H. Robins, maker of Sergeant's pet products. The latter was a particularly nasty affair. Robins accused Hartz of the worst forms of monopoly practice, claiming that Hartz resorted to bribery, coercion, and kickbacks to distributors. Leonard Stern responded by reminding everyone that "[t]hese are the people with the Dalkon Shield. . . . These people stood by while their customers died." It was of no avail; Hartz had to settle the case out of court and had to pay Robins an enormous sum.

All of this is fairly nasty fare, but neither Stern nor Hartz Mountain was the first to experience such charges. In most cases, the business press accepts it with an urbane shrug. Not so with Leonard Stern. *Forbes*, which calls itself a "capitalist tool," is not renowned for its trenchant criticism of business leaders. Yet it has mounted a veritable crusade against Leonard Stern over the years, equating him with the worst of the "robber barons" of the late nineteenth century. The magazine reported that Stern's office sports a sign proclaiming, "Once you've got them by the balls, their hearts and minds will follow." According to *Forbes*, "That kind of attitude wouldn't have been out of place 50 years ago and more— 'the public be damned.' It does seem quite out of place in 1979." Other business organs were hardly any more charitable. In 1983, the *Wall Street Journal* ran an article with a three-column headline: "Hartz Owner Made a Prime Target of a Big Grand Jury Investigation." A year later, *The American Lawyer* published a scathing indictment of Stern and his company.

These accusations all resulted from the obstruction of justice charges leveled against Hartz Mountain as a result of the Robins case. Three Hartz sales managers reported that two company vice presidents had ordered them to commit illegal acts, including the destruction of files. The vice presidents, who were fired by Hartz, both pleaded guilty to obstruction of justice. They also testified that higher-ups in the company, including Leonard Stern, had given them the order to destroy the files. Consequently, the grand jury made Leonard Stern a prime target of its investigation. In March 1984, Hartz made an agreement with the government by which they pleaded guilty to obstruction of justice and encouraging perjury, but no Hartz executives were charged. That hardly satisfied the barons of the business press. *Forbes* sniffed that Stern was "at least as much Jimmy Hoffa . . . as Horatio Alger," and he was characterized by the publication as an almost totally ruthless man.

All of this finally seemed to affect Stern. The legal troubles he and his company were experiencing he called "incredibly painful," and he began to exhibit a more liberal, less ruthless image. He became a highly public philanthropist; NYU was his major beneficiary. Among other things, he gave the school money to erect Leonard Stern Hall on Washington Square. Stern also developed a plan to house homeless mothers and children in New York City, which called for the construction of a series of garden apartment–like buildings in vacant lots in several of the boroughs, where he plans to give shelter to some 4,000 homeless families. As a result, Stern was named "Citizen of the Year" by the Legal Aid Society of New York City. Nevertheless, even these benefactions have not changed the minds of many Stern-haters. Some have branded him a "public relations" philanthropist; others have imputed more sinister behavior to him. It is true that Stern was advised in all these actions by an astute public relations man, Howard Rubenstein, but Stern denied that all of this was part of a conscious effort.

As part of his transformation as a "nice guy" and a liberal, Stern bought the *Village Voice*, the ultraliberal New York weekly, from Rupert Murdoch for $55 million in 1985. Many staffers at the *Voice* panicked when Stern purchased the paper, but, by all reports, he has been a model owner. From the very beginning, he promised not to meddle in editorial affairs, and he has remained generally true to his word.*Voice* publisher and editor in chief, David Schneiderman, said of Stern, "He is very supportive of what we are doing here and of me personally." Yet, neither is Stern an absentee owner; he devotes five or six hours a week to the paper. Under his stewardship, the *Voice* has thrived as never before, and it has become highly profitable. As many have commented, Leonard Stern seemed to have the "Midas touch." Stern also embraced feminism at about the same time, and he gave $10,000 to help fund a *Ms* magazine film on incest.

As Stern went through a public transformation, many asked which was the "real" Leonard Stern. Was it the charming, liberal supporter of worthy causes? Or was it the supremely ruthless businessman? Many observers have claimed that both are accurate; that Stern has a dual personality. While friends like Saul Steinberg,[†] Gloria Steinem, and Malcolm Forbes (Malcolm Forbes?) profess to see a warm, almost puppylike Stern, others continue to view him as a "vicious bastard." Whatever else anyone says of him, Stern remains a tough competitor. As the president of Conagra Pet Products has said, "We battle them every day, and it's trench warfare."

None of this philanthropy and good works, however, seems to have dulled the ego of Leonard Stern. In an interview with Lisa Birnbach, Stern waxed eloquently on the "virtues" of being a leader, saying, "if I start smoking a cigar, other people start smoking a cigar. If I wear brown suits, so will they. Being a leader is interesting." Nor did he have much sentiment about families: "I have one rule when I buy a family company: they leave with the check . . . [the family heirs] pontificate on everything. . . . They're assholes, and I don't make apologies for them." Stern evidently plans to make sure that doesn't happen with his own family. He announced that he intended to give away most of his $1.4-billion fortune. "It's either that," he said, "or ruin your kids." (**B**. *Fortune*,

September 1973, September 28, 1987, September 12, 1988; *Forbes*, February 15, 1974, April 2, November 26, 1979, October 24, 1988; *Business Week*, July 5, 1985; *New York*, May 5, 1986; *Manhattan, Inc.*, September 1988, February 1989; Lisa Birnbach, *Going to Work*, 1989.)

STEVENS FAMILY: STEVENS, JOHN PETERS, JR. (1897?–November 15, 1976), **ROBERT TEN BROECK STEVENS** (July 31, 1899–January 31, 1983), **WHITNEY STEVENS** (1926–   ). Textile manufacturers, J. P. Stevens & Company. In the spring of 1988, J. P. Stevens & Company, the world's oldest, diversified textile company, after more than 175 years of continuous management by members of the Stevens family, was acquired in a hostile take-over by a rival manufacturer, West Point-Pepperell Incorporated of West Point, Georgia, and its two associates in the venture, Bibb Company of Macon, Georgia, and Odyssey Partners, a Wall Street investment firm. Few in America mourned the loss. J. P. Stevens & Company had acquired an unenviable reputation as one of the most ruthless and stubborn antiunion employers in America. In fact, most Americans' familiarity with the firm came neither from reading the financial pages of their local newspaper nor from purchases at their local retailer. It came, instead, from *Norma Rae,* a 1979 hit movie, which indelibly etched the image of J. P. Stevens in the public's mind. Based on an actual incident involving a Stevens employee by the name of Crystal Lee Jordan, the movie had an enormous impact on American popular culture. When Norma Rae, played by Sally Field, leaped up on a table in the mill, and held up a sign imploring her fellow workers to join the union, members of the audience often began to chant "union, union" along with her. The film not only won an Academy Award for Miss Field, it also intensified a boycott against J. P. Stevens' goods, and it was a factor leading to the company's grudging settlement with the union in 1983.

The genesis of the $1.6-billion J. P. Stevens textile empire came in 1813, when Nathaniel Stevens built a small woolen mill at North Andover, Massachusetts. One of fourteen children of a farmer who had fought against the British in the Revolutionary War, "Captain Nat" Stevens had shipped out at twenty-two on a merchant vessel. Later he clerked in a general store and showed an aptitude for trade. When the War of 1812 cut off British textile imports, Nat Stevens, like many other enterprising Americans, began to produce woolens. Borrowing money from his father, Nat bought a grist mill and converted it to woolen manufacture. When the war ended, English imports again flooded the American market, and Captain Nat's fledgling enterprise was sorely tested. In response, he converted from broadcloth to flannel and became the first to successfully produce that item in the United States. He improved his mill over the years, and even operated it through the Panic of 1837, when every other mill in the area shut down for at least a time. He succeeded by driving both himself and his employees very hard, putting them through six-day, seventy-six-hour weeks for $4.50, plus board of $2.

In 1850, his son, Moses Stevens, became a partner in the thriving enterprise; within a short time, George and Horace, younger sons, also joined the firm. Soon thereafter, when the family acquired a second mill in Haverhill, Massachusetts, they became the first family in the state to operate more than one flannel mill. The Civil War gave great impetus to the firm's business, as sales of flannel blankets to the Union Army kept the mill at peak production levels. In 1865, Nat Stevens died, and Moses succeeded him as head of the firm. The introduction of a blended fabric, which was 60-percent wool and 40-percent cotton, helped the firm weather successfully the long depression of the 1870s; and the family acquired two more mills at bargain rates in the process. Horace and George died during the 1880s, and Moses continued to run the enterprise himself; he changed the name to M. T. Stevens, and his son, Nathaniel Stevens II, quit school and helped his father run the enterprise.

During this time, one of the Stevens' progeny entered the textile business in a different vein. John P. Stevens, son of Horace, was born in North Andover in 1868, and left Phillips Academy at Andover in 1884 when his father died. He entered the office of Faulkner, Page & Company in Boston, a commission dry-goods firm that handled the output of the Stevens mills, and remained there for a year. Then he entered the firm's New York office, where he learned to sell and establish credit risks. Having gained this valuable experience, and having a blood tie to the manufacturing end of the business, John Stevens established his own commission house. On August 1, 1899, with capital of $25,000 and twenty-one employees, he opened the doors of J. P. Stevens & Company in New York's textile district. Handling the product of the Stevens mills, and numerous other textile mills in New England and the South, J. P. Stevens soon became a leading house in the field.

The Stevens manufacturing concerns, meanwhile, were expanding and diversifying. Moses Stevens' three sons joined him in the business, and his mills soon became the largest woolen manufacturer in the state. More important, the firm branched into cotton during these years. John P. Stevens was a key factor in this latter diversification, since he traveled extensively in the South developing ties for his commission house. When he happened upon likely mill sites and prosperous mills, he invested in them. The combined Stevens operation was already highly diversified when Moses died in 1907.

By the outbreak of World War I, the Stevens mills, which were manufacturing primarily cotton, were selling the output of nine mills. After the war, they acquired five more mills, and began to experiment with rayon, a new synthetic fiber in the 1920s. At this time J. P. Stevens' sons, Robert and John P., Jr., entered the family business. John Jr. graduated from Phillips Academy in 1915, and entered Yale University. When the United States entered World War I, he interrupted his studies to serve as a second lieutenant of field artillery. He joined the firm at the end of the war, became a company director in 1923, and held a number of administrative positions with the firm during the 1920s and 1930s. When his father died two days before the great stock market crash in 1929, however, it was John, Jr.'s younger brother, Robert Ten Broeck Stevens, who assumed the presidency.

Robert Stevens also attended Phillips Academy and graduated in 1917. He then served as a second lieutenant in the field artillery until the end of the war. Upon his release from military duty, Robert Stevens entered Yale University, and graduated in 1921. He entered the firm as a salesman and worked his way up the ranks until he succeeded his father in 1929. The depression years were difficult for the textile industry. Rather than cut back during this time, however the Stevens brothers chose to expand the firm by acquiring nine additional mills during the decade. They also made significant advances in the production of synthetic products and erected two new plants designed to manufacture synthetic fibers. As a result, they hustled the firm to a volume of $100 million annually, despite the hard times. World War II brought explosive expansion for the entire industry, and the J. P. Stevens firm naturally grew along with it. As a result of acquisitions and other investments, it had become a sprawling empire by the end of the war. During part of the war years, Robert Stevens served as a colonel in the Office of the Quartermaster General, where he aided in textile procurements. While so engaged, John P. Stevens, Jr., served as president of the company.

By 1946, a crisis had been reached. The J. P. Stevens commission house by then dwarfed the family's mill operations and was in dire need of access to capital markets to consolidate and continue its growth. Further, Moses' son, Nathaniel, who had run the mill operations since 1907, died in that year at the age of eighty-six. As a result, his estate needed cash to settle with the tax collector. It was clear to both Robert and John P., Jr., that extensive changes were necessary in the organization and structure of the venerable company. The key factor involved uniting the manufacturing and selling ends of the business, merging them with eight other companies, and then taking the entire organization public. Robert Stevens became chairman and chief executive officer (CEO) of the new concern, and John Stevens, Jr., became president. Within two years, the family sold 375,000 shares on the New York Exchange.

Robert Stevens then reorganized the giant company. The 1946 merger had created an unwieldy entity with fourteen divisions operating twenty-nine mills. Robert Stevens applied the important lessons he had learned about efficient systems management and large-scale organization while in the army to his company. Within a few years, the company was reduced to three fiber-based divisions. Meanwhile, the textile industry boomed in the immediate postwar years, and J. P. Stevens experienced large profits in 1946 and 1947. However, sales and profits slumped for two years following, only to be revived by the Korean War boom.

Robert Stevens was well aware that the long-term outlook for the textile industry was not bright, and he proposed to make significant alterations in J. P. Stevens' operations. Most important was his decision to move the bulk of the firm's woolen and worsted operations from the North to the South. One of the first textile firms to make this move, Stevens felt the reasons were obvious. The northern mills were old, the costs were high, and the labor unions were well entrenched. During the 1950s, J. P. Stevens closed four northern mills, opened two mills in the North, and opened eight mills in the South. The strategy succeeded in lessening union influence and the high wages unionization entailed. By the early 1960s, the company paid an average hourly wage of $1.55 in the South, compared to $1.72 in New England. While this move south strengthened the company and improved its market situation, it also created a long festering labor problem in the South, which sorely tested the firm's resolve after 1963.

J. P. Stevens' innovations during these years went well beyond a simple move south and an antiunion philosophy. During this time, it also built a very different business than it had had prior to the war. Finishing operations, which formerly had been done by outsiders, were integrated into the company, in an automated cotton-finishing plant built at Wallace, South Carolina, in 1950. The firm also endeavored to eliminate many of the steps in the long distribution channel from the manufacturer to the retailer. Attempting to control its goods through as many of the processes as were profitable, it operated with the aim of moving closer to the consumer during these years. Their most ambitious move in this direction was the purchase of Utica & Mohawk Cotton Mills, a leading producer of sheets and pillowcases. It took years for Utica-Mohawk to become a solid moneymaker, but a new mill built at Clemson, South Carolina, in 1952 helped it achieve this goal.

At the same time, J. P. Stevens moved aggressively into synthetic fabrics. A notable experiment came with glass fiber, which had great market potential but was extremely difficult to weave. Although a very time-consuming and costly project for the firm, the glass fiber plant at Slater, South Carolina (the largest combined glass fiber weaving and finishing installation in the world), was doing a volume of about $35 million by the early 1960s. In the midst of all this change and expansion, Robert Stevens abruptly left the company in 1953 to become secretary of the army, and to engage in a titanic battle with Senator Joseph McCarthy.

In 1952, Charles E. Wilson, secretary-designate of defense, recommended to president-elect Dwight Eisenhower that Robert Stevens be appointed secretary of the army. Although he had had limited experience in Washington, D.C., and little political savvy, Stevens accepted without hesitation: ''I went to Washington for one reason, a shooting war was going on and kids were getting killed.'' As a condition of office, Stevens was forced to sell his 42,800 shares of stock in J. P. Stevens. Stevens competently handled the administrative details of the army during his tenure of office, but it was his unexpected confrontation with Senator McCarthy that overshadowed all else. The army had charged that McCarthy had used undue influence in favor of G. David Schine, and the senator had responded by alleging communist influence in the army. Stevens, who seemed to have little understanding of what was going on at first, instructed army personnel to ignore the McCarthy committee's subpoenas. Ultimately, he was compelled to appear before the Senate committee, and for thirteen days, with the help of Joseph N. Welch, a Boston lawyer, he fended off a barrage of accusations from McCarthy, while at the same time quietly criticizing the senator's tactics. The hearings, which were carried over the new medium of television, captivated Americans, and led to the downfall of the junior senator from Wisconsin. On December 2, 1954, the Senate voted to condemn McCarthy to censure proceedings. By 1955, Stevens had had enough of the political infighting of Washington, retired from his army post, and returned to the family firm.

In the meantime, John P. Stevens, Jr., had taken over the company reins; he served as chairman from 1953 until his retirement in 1962. When Robert Stevens returned in 1955, he assumed the post of president, and together the two brothers dealt with a difficult situation. Expansion to accommodate two wars had left the American textile industry with overcapacity and a glut of inventory. In addition, after the mid–1950s, a number of foreign competitors entered the American market, which created an intensified price competition. In the eight years after the end of the Korean War, cotton system spindles declined by 17 percent, and woolen and worsted looms decreased by a whopping 52 percent. J. P. Stevens' profits were plummeting with the end of the war, but, just as in earlier times of crisis, the firm was eager to continue its expansion, and it purchased several New England textile firms.

More important was Robert and John Stevens' decision to radically change the way in which the company conducted its business. Realizing that the old production-based textile industry of the past, which supplied staple goods to huge markets, was becoming obsolete, they recognized that the textile industry of the future was going to have to live by merchandising. This meant new fabrics and fashions had to be developed continually, and that J. P. Stevens had to diversify further. To achieve this, the firm undertook an extensive program of research and development. The textile industry in the United States has generally been one of the least progressive in terms of expenditures on research and development, spending just one-tenth of 1 percent of sales on research during the 1950s, compared with 2 percent for U.S. industry as a whole. J. P. Stevens resolved to spend $3 million annually, or about one-half of 1 percent. Much of this money went into research in organic chemistry, which brought about new developments in wash and wear finishes, among other products. The firm also gained a lot of business from automotive companies, by developing improved one-piece tufted and molded carpets. Also, in association with the Kimberley-Clark Corporation, J. P. Stevens began to produce various nonwoven fiber products, such as disposable aprons and pillowcases, and hospital gowns. It also joined with a division of Humble Oil and Refining to buy the National Plastic Products Company, which was involved in the development and manufacture of polypropylene, a by-product of petroleum refining.

To control his increasingly large and diverse company, Robert Stevens in 1957 installed a sophisticated $500,000 data processing system. Although many industry traditionalists were at first aghast at this, by the early 1960s the system was saving the firm $300,000 a year. By the early 1960s, J. P. Stevens & Company had 1,200,000 spindles and nearly 30,000 looms, which poured out more than 800 million linear yards of fabric. In a largely fragmented industry consisting of some 5,500 companies, it was an awesome giant, employing 35,000 workers in fifty-five plants in eight states from Maine to Georgia. It had record sales of $586 million in 1962, surpassed only by Burlington Industries, the world's first billion-dollar textile company. In most respects, the future looked bright for J. P. Stevens in 1963. It had diversified beyond simple textiles, modernized its facilities and increased the efficiency of its plants, installed a state-of-the-art electronic data processing system, and engaged in extensive vertical integration, bringing it closer to the consumer. But at that time labor problems, which had been festering under the surface, emerged, and they were to bedevil the company in the future.

For a number of years, J. P. Stevens had run unfettered by union opposition in the South. The Textile Workers Union (TWU) was a fading brotherhood with an aging membership, and the political, social, and cultural situation in the South was not conducive to union organization. Greenville, South Carolina, housed the manufacturing, personnel, and purchasing headquarters of J. P. Stevens, along with eighteen of its eighty-five plants in the late 1970s. The history of the textile industry in the area, as well as the relationship of the labor unions to the industry, is instructive for understanding the problems at J. P. Stevens in the 1970s and 1980s.

In the 1870s, cotton mill operations began moving into the Greenville area, when the Vardy Mill was erected by a coalition of Boston textile men. Other mills followed in the 1870s and 1880s, as part of the whole drive for a "New South." Establishing "mill villages" with company-owned houses, stores, and churches sprouted up in the Greenville area, and by 1882 there were 1,250 cotton mill hands in the county. The hegemony of the mill owners was challenged in 1886, when the Knights of Labor came to the area. The mill owners responded by firing union sympathizers, and using policies of racial segregation and discrimination to tie the white mill workers to the mills. By promising to hire only white labor, the mill owners' racism became an important lynchpin in a new form of Southern paternalism (which provided a number of welfare elements) for the workers. During the next several decades, the number of mills in the Greenville area expanded rapidly, and more workers were on the payroll, but the fundamental labor system remained static. By 1950, the town of Greenville had 58,000 inhabitants, of which 21,000 were employed in the mills. Gradually changes were made, and the mill owners began to lose their grasp on the growing community. An important element of the system began changing in the 1960s, when blacks began to be hired. By 1968, 17 percent of the workers were black, and by 1978 this number had climbed to 30 percent. An important element of the paternalist facade had been undermined.

In the meantime, the fledgling labor movement in the South began to stir. The TWU launched its first drive to recruit textile workers. Its first mistake occurred when it tackled the Deering-Milliken Company. Rather than negotiate with the union, Roger Milliken,[†] head of the company, simply shut down his Darlington, South Carolina, plant. The union had also been beaten off by Cannon Mills, Burlington Mills, and Harriet & Henderson Mills. At that point, the TWU concentrated on J. P. Stevens, which was expected to be a rather soft adversary. The union could not have been more mistaken. Robert Stevens, who had been confronted by the wild accusations of Joseph McCarthy, was not a man to turn away from a challenge made by a weak and disorganized union. Many years later, Sol Stein, the union's former president admitted, "Very truthfully, I never imagined the company would carry on the way it has."

Robert Stevens dug in his heels; the union would never be allowed to organize the J. P. Stevens plants in the South. He refused even to admit it was an issue for years: "We have no labor problem. We have a relationship with our people that is unusually fine for any industry. And we feel there is no need for a third party to come between us and our people to spoil that relationship." As a result, Stevens fought the union with every weapon at his disposal, including several which crossed the boundary between legality and illegality. When the union arrived in 1963 to begin organizing J. P. Stevens' Roanoke Rapids seven-plant manufacturing complex, it was confronted by a company notice to employees that said: "Our positive intention is to oppose this union and by every proper means keep it from coming in here. It is our sincere belief that if this union gets in here, it would operate to your serious disadvantage." This attitude, at the very least, led plant-floor supervisors to conclude that they should be tough on pro-union activity. As a result, supervisors accosted employees over the slightest evidence of union activity, fining, disciplining, and even firing them.

But the union had certain sources of strength, even in the early years, particularly the nation's labor laws and the National Labor Relations Board (NLRB). The union repeatedly took J. P. Stevens before the NLRB and the courts during the 1960s and early 1970s, and won virtually every confrontation. In December 1967, the U.S. Supreme Court refused to hear J. P. Stevens' appeal of these rulings, and the company was forced to rehire many of the fired workers. Robert Stevens and the company remained unrepentant. When confronted with union charges of terrorist tactics at its plants, charges which were upheld by the courts, Robert Stevens commented, "We can't prevent the union from making irresponsible statements"; he felt it was unfortunate that "the union's position makes news while ours doesn't." When asked why then these charges were upheld by the courts, a company spokesman replied, "The law is pro-union." Although it lost case after case during the first fifteen years of confrontation with the union, the union made few gains within the plants themselves, and J. P. Stevens refused to budge an inch in its attitudes or tactics.

A major change came in 1976, when the TWU merged with the Amalgamated Clothing Workers of America to become the ACTWU. The head of the new union was a skilled labor lawyer, and its general counsel was Arthur M. Goldberg, the nation's leading authority on labor law, a man extraordinarily well connected in Democratic politics. The confrontation moved to a new level at that time. By this time, however, Robert Stevens, who had stepped down in 1974, had retired from active management, and the fight against the union was carried on by chairman James D. Finley and by Whitney Stevens, Robert's son, who had become president.

While continuing to pressure J. P. Stevens legally, the ACTWU began a nationwide boycott against Stevens. Garnering the support of the National Association for the Advancement of Colored People, the National Council of Churches, and a number of women's and student's groups, the boycott aroused media and congressional sentiment against the giant textile firm. Although the boycott did not affect Stevens' goods at the retail level, it was successful in painting the firm as a villain and a lawbreaker. This severely disadvantaged the company in terms of public relations and its relations with the rest of the business community, which often treated them as a pariah. On January 1, 1980, when James D. Finley stepped down as chairman and CEO, he was succeeded by Whitney Stevens.

Whitney Stevens, like his father and grandfather, was educated at Phillips Academy, and he graduated from Princeton in 1947. He joined the newly public J. P. Stevens firm the following year as a trainee learning to erect textile machinery for making synthetic fabrics. He then moved to a sales position in New York. He was elected vice president in 1958, executive vice president in 1964, and president in 1969. Upon assuming the chairmanship in 1979, Whitney Stevens assured the press that he would not dilute the militancy of the company's position in labor relations. As he said, "The real issue is what do people in our plant want, our ultimate objection is to the forcing of people into joining the union. Naturally, we'd rather not have a union. We think it not necessary, not desirable, and certainly not in our employees' interest." Several months later, he was even blunter in his language: "We openly and strongly oppose the union in its efforts to organize our employees and we will continue to do so with every legal and proper means." Just three months later, however, Whitney Stevens did the previously unthinkable—he signed an agreement with the union. Murray Finley, president of the union, called the settlement "the successful conclusion of the most protracted labor dispute in history." Whitney Stevens, less sanguine, promised that J. P. Stevens would "continue to oppose the unions."

What Whitney Stevens had done in October 1980 was to agree to collective bargaining contracts covering just 3,000 workers in the Roanoke Rapids plants and 500 more workers in other plants. Over 40,000 other J. P. Stevens workers in some seventy plants remained nonunion. Clearly, the company had made major concessions to the union, but the great battle was far from over. Having put the worst of the labor unpleasantness behind him, Whitney Stevens determined to take the J. P. Stevens firm in new directions in the 1980s.

Stevens took the most important step in September 1983, when he announced that he had joined forces with designer Ralph Lauren,[†] to create a luxury collection of home furnishings, from 100-percent pima cotton Oxford cloth sheets to crystal stemware and sterling silver, and even items of wood furniture. The decision represented a major departure for the conservative grande dame of the textile industry, and a major public relations counteroffensive against the damage done to its image by its union-bashing tactics of the 1960s and 1970s. The new collection appeared in thirty-four of America's top retailers, including Bullock's, J.W. Robinson, Marshall Field, Neiman Marcus, I. Magnin, and Bloomingdale's. Declaring that J. P. Stevens was the first to create a "total home environment," Whitney Stevens made plans for the firm to become a major supplier of decorative home furnishings to department stores within the following five years.

A great attraction of the new home furnishing lines was the potential profitability. By the early 1980s, J. P. Stevens was earning just 2.9 percent on equity, the lowest among the ten largest textile firms. Further, although sales were $1.4 billion in 1979, profits were just $6.2 million. By contrast, the natural-fibers-only Ralph Lauren line was decidedly upscale in terms of quality and price. The potential for high profit was enormous. To help ensure this profitability, J. P. Stevens spent $1 million to advertise the line in 1983, although its name did not appear on the goods. The move was extraordinarily successful. Coupled with a decision to close many inefficient plants, lay off workers, and concentrate on profitable lines of goods, Whitney Stevens brought J. P. Stevens to new levels of profitability. Even though overall sales dropped during this period, profits grew from just $11 million in 1984 to $56 million in 1987 on sales of $1.6 billion. A key factor was Stevens' home furnishing lines for Ralph Lauren and Laura Ashley, which accounted for 61 percent of sales in the 1987. As competitor E. Erwin Maddrey II, head of Delta Woodside Industries commented, "They've been the industry leader in restructuring." In addition, union relations, which had been such a thorn in the company's side for years, had greatly improved under Whitney Stevens. By 1988 the union represented 15 percent of the 23,000 workers still in the Stevens plants, and Bruce Raynor, the union's director in the South, said that relations there were better than the industry norm.

Whitney Stevens' successful restructuring of J. P. Stevens, however, made it an attractive target for the aggressive arbitragers of the late 1980s. In 1984, Stevens had paid $24.3 million to buy back shares from the famed raider Carl C. Icahn,[†] but he found it was continually under siege from other investors, and the firm was forced to spend $175 million on stock buy backs, reducing the number of outstanding shares by 24 percent. Nonetheless, by early 1988, management owned just 2.5 percent of the stock, and needed almost $700 million in financing to take the firm private. It was unsuccessful in its quest. In February 1988, management announced that they would take J. P. Stevens private at $43 a share. Needing help to fight off a hostile takeover from West Point-Pepperell, Whitney Stevens allied with the Wall Street investment firm, Odyssey. Odyssey, however, soon joined forces with West Point-Pepperell, and in April 1988, the three-month battle for control of J. P. Stevens ended, and West Point-Pepperell secured control of its giant competitor. Furthermore, they announced that they would not retain Whitney Stevens, the fifth generation of his family to control the firm, as chairman, adding that he would "float out on his golden parachute."

The 175-year-old textile dynasty had ended, and one of the oldest continuing firms in America had been absorbed by the frantic merger and acquisition mania of the 1980s.

In 1963, writing in *Fortune* on the occasion of J. P. Stevens' one-hundred-fiftieth anniversary, Richard J. Whalen commented that

In the whole history of U.S. business there has never been anything quite like Stevens. . . . Over the century and a half, the management of the firm has passed from father to son in a direct line. . . . Among some one hundred families who started woolen mills in the U.S. in the years 1800 to 1815, the Stevenses are the sole survivors. And generation after generation of Stevenses has shown the industry how to survive and prosper by sinuously working around obstacles, by unsentimentally jettisoning outmoded traditions— in short, by adapting to the world's constant changes.

But change finally caught up with the Stevens family at the end of the 1980s. It was not the demands of technology, markets, imports, or even unions that caused their demise, but the acquisitiveness of a blatantly materialistic era. Staunch Republicans for over 125 years, it was Reaganomics and the accompanying greed that ended the Stevens dynasty. (**B**. Broadus Mitchell, *Rise of Cotton Mills in the South*, 1921; *National Cyclopaedia of American Biography*, vol. 27: 441; *Who Was Who*, vol. VIII: 381; *Time*, January 12, 1953; *Current Biography*, July 1953; *Fortune*, August 1957; April 1963, June 19, 1978, October 22, 1979; *Business Week*, March 23, 1963, March 20, 1978, September 19, 1983, February 22, May 2, 1988; *Textile World*, April 1968; Milton McLaurin, *Paternalism and Protest*, 1971; *New York Times*, November 16, 1976, February 1, 1983; *Southern Exposure*, Spring 1979; *Textile Industries*, October 1979; Milton Moskowitz et al., *Everybody's Business*, 1980; *The Economist*, July 5, October 25, 1980; Toronto *Globe and Mail*, April 26, 1988.)

T

TANDY, CHARLES DAVID (May 15, 1918–November 4, 1978). Electronics and computer manufacturer and retailer, Tandy Corporation. Charles Tandy found success by catering to America's burgeoning leisure-time and hobby activities. His secret, as he once declared, was that "I sell fun." Yet Charles Tandy himself was a bit of an anomaly—he had no hobbies and he engaged in no sports with the exception of swimming a few laps in his pool. His passion, his great love, was always his business, and his hobby was making money—mountains of it. As one of his associates commented, "He liked the constant activity, he had no hobbies, no children. He ate, drank, and slept business, from dawn until as late as anyone was willing to talk about *his* business with him." That pace and obsession with business probably also killed him. After suffering a severe heart attack at the age of fifty, he had a serious gall bladder problem four years later. At just sixty years of age, he lay down for a nap one Saturday afternoon (a very unusual thing for him to do) and never got up—Charles Tandy was dead of a heart attack.

Tandy was born in Brownsville, Texas, the son of David L. Tandy, owner of the Hinkley-Tandy Leather Company, a Ft. Worth concern that had been started in 1899. The elder Tandy had become half-owner shortly after his son's birth in 1918. Hinkley-Tandy was a wholesale leather goods firm that sold leather soles and other supplies to shoe repair shops throughout Texas. Charles Tandy was educated in Ft. Worth, went to Rice University in 1935, but dropped out, worked for a time for his father, and then graduated from Texas Christian University in 1940. Tandy spent a year at the Graduate School of Business at Harvard, until he left in 1941 to enter the U.S. Navy.

While serving in Hawaii, Charles Tandy noticed something that changed the nature of his family business forever. In 1943, Charles had been selling war bonds for the navy, and, in so doing, was impressed with how many disabled sailors worked at leather crafts as part of their rehabilitation programs. He wrote to his father, urging him to supply hospitals with leather craft goods for their programs. The elder Tandy agreed and had modest success with the leather goods line during the war. When Charles Tandy came home from the navy in 1947, he developed the leather goods line into a highly successful operation. He and his father bought out the other owners in 1950 and established it as the Tandy Leather Company.

During these early years, Tandy was primarily a mail-order business. From servicing veterans' hospitals, the company was supplied with ready-made lists for direct selling and at first 90 percent of their orders came that way. They then branched from hospitals to prisons, schools, and summer camps. The first leather-working kits were simple, designed for ill or disabled amateurs, but as their market expanded, Tandy said, "people wanted something more creative," so they concocted even more complicated kits, grading them for age, skill, and even sex. As the 1950s opened, and Americans increasingly stressed leisure-time activities, the hobby craze took off. When it did, Tandy Leather grew along with it.

Charles Tandy next moved into retail store operations. Although he retained the mail-order interest, he wanted to bring it into a fifty-fifty ratio with retail operations. He, therefore, opened company-owned retail outlets. This was done with extensive planning, according to a number of clear principles: low overhead, inexpensive fixtures (often secondhand), low labor costs, and highly motivated store managers. The idea was to operate the stores profitably even on a volume as low as $100,000 a year. Thus store rentals had to be very cheap—no more than $300 a month in the early 1950s. The key to each store's success, however, was the manager. He was given a relatively low salary (often about $300 a month), but he was given 10 percent of the profits and a 25-percent equity in the store, in return for a $250 investment and a $2,250 loan. This gave the manager the incentive to work the twelve hours or more a day that Charles Tandy demanded.

The number of stores grew gradually in the early years. Fifteen were added in 1951 and 1952, and sixteen were added in 1953, but then expansion was more rapid and there were 140 stores by 1962. Tandy orchestrated his first acquisition during these early years—American Handicrafts—which had three stores and made do-it-yourself kits. This concentration on the craft and hobby trade was profitable for Tandy Leather. In 1953 it earned a substantial 11 percent after taxes on sales of $2.9 million, a very high return in the retail trade. At that point, however, Charles Tandy blundered.

Wanting to diversify his company even further, in 1955 Charles Tandy sold Tandy Leather to American Hide & Leather Company, which had been troubled for a number of years, but whose executives told Tandy that they no longer suffered losses. But, Tandy recalled, "in each of the two months after we joined them they lost a couple of hundred thousand." It soon became clear that Tandy Leather was the parent company's only profitable division, and Tandy tried to buy his company back. Chemical Bank, American Hide & Leather's chief cred-itor, flatly refused, fearing the loss of its only chance for repayment. So Tandy had only one recourse: to purchase control of the parent company. This was completed in 1959, and three of the five divisions were sold off. He changed the name to Tandy Corporation. He had rescued the family firm, but it was still swimming in red ink, with losses of $267,000 in 1960.

By 1962, Tandy had finally worked its way back into the black, with profits of just under $1 million. Selling about $18 million worth of goods in that fiscal year, Charles Tandy carried his hobby marketing a step further with the opening of the Tandy Craft & Hobby Mart, a supermarket for the hobbyist and amateur craftsman, in Ft. Worth. Tandy owned five of the seventeen stores in the Mart; the rest were leased to pet store owners, exotic goods shops, a science shop, and others. Tandy had visions of a whole chain of these hobby marts, but he found relatively little outside interest in the project. Charles Tandy, an energetic builder and developer, was unsatisfied with the relatively stable but low-level returns from his chain of hobby shops. Longing to get into the big time, he began shopping for new acquisitions. He wanted something that would be compatible with his leather and hobby lines, but also something that would make money. To this end, Tandy explored opportunities in the photography and home-improvement industries, but finally turned his attention to consumer electronics.

In 1961, Tandy had talked with the officials of the Boston-based Radio Shack, a small chain of nine consumer electronics stores that was losing money. Because of this, Tandy backed off, but two years later, Radio Shack's executives and creditors approached him with an offer he could not refuse. Tandy would take over operating control of Radio Shack in return for lending the troubled company $300,000. For another $5,000, Tandy would also get options to buy out its controlling stockholders at book value. Within a matter of months, Tandy Corporation owned a majority of the shares. In retrospect, this seems like a fantastic bargain, but at the time it was a colossal gamble. In fact, Tandy might not have taken the plunge had he realized the state Radio Shack was in. There was a stack of unpaid bills, totaling $800,000, even when discounted, and most of the accounts receivable were uncollectable. Further, Tandy had inherited Radio Shack's $4.5-million debt to the First National Bank of Boston. It looked as if bankruptcy was imminent. If that were the case, Tandy would lose $350,000, but the bank would lose its $4.5 million. Tandy convinced the bank to advance him an immediate $600,000 to move beyond this difficult period. With the immediate crisis under control, Tandy proceeded to turn Radio Shack into a winning proposition.

Tandy first fired many Radio Shack employees and hired a team of 900 collection lawyers in an aggressive campaign to settle accounts receivable. Tandy streamlined the firm's merchandise lines. Using the same principles he had developed for his hobby stores, he eliminated many of the 25,000 items carried in the Radio Shack stores. He retained those items that could be stocked by a store of relatively modest size, which had substantial gross profit margins. At the same time, Tandy undertook an aggressive store-expansion program. The prudent businessman would have logically waited until the small chain was making money before doing this, but Tandy was convinced that more stores were needed to generate the sales volume necessary to solve the chain's problems.

When he undertook this expansion program, Tandy followed closely the pattern he had established with Tandy Leather Company. The new stores were small, averaging about 3,300 square feet, and designed to be run by a manager and two or three salespeople. He always leased, never bought, his retail space, to keep asset turnover high. He always stocked only items with extremely high gross margins, demanding margins of from 50 to 60 percent, which he was used to in his leather goods business, rather than the 32-percent average for electronics retailers. He cut the inventory to a manageable stock of high turnover items, and he advertised very heavily. This latter point was a major factor. Tandy budgeted an awesome 8 to 9 percent of sales for advertising, compared with the usual retail expenditure of 3 or 4 percent, and he plowed all the earnings back into growth.

The results were impressive. During the first two years after he took over the chain, Tandy opened an average of one new store per working day, totaling 530 by 1969. Then, in 1973, this average leaped to two stores per working day; by the end of that year, the chain had more than 2,800 stores. The Radio Shack stores benefited from an enormous expansion in the consumer-electronics business; sales in the United States grew 300 percent between 1962 and 1975, to a total of $10 billion. During the 1960s, sales for Tandy Corporation overall increased 700 percent, and earnings went up 800 percent, so that by 1969 it had sales of $189 million, and net profits of $7.7 million. The company's stock, which was virtually worthless in 1963, climbed to 8 in 1966 and 65 in 1969. Radio Shack's success came not from a lot of inventive new techniques and products, but from the speed, boldness, and scale of its operation. During the 1960s, Tandy also tried to become a conglomerate, and picked up Wolfe Nurseries, Color Tiles, and Leonard's Department store in Ft. Worth. Most of these were not terribly successful, and Tandy spun off most of them to stockholders in the 1970s.

One of Charles Tandy's most important decisions came in the late 1960s, when he began to manufacture many of his own products. From the beginning, Tandy had sold its own privately labeled brands in the stores—with names like Realistic, Micronta, and Archer. Tandy found that most American manufacturers were unwilling to produce privately labeled goods for him, so he turned to Japanese manufacturers. In his desire to retain a greater share of the profits, however, Tandy moved in the late 1960s to begin manufacturing many of his own items. Tandy thus became the first electronics retailer to integrate backward into manufacturing. In 1968, he set up a factory in Ft. Worth to make electronics kits, and a short time later he set up a plant in Japan to manufacture intercoms. By the late 1970s, Tandy Corporation had sixteen factories in North America, a small plant in Japan, and a large plant in Korea. By that time, the company was making about 40 percent of the items it sold in its stores in the United States and Canada, reducing the wholesale cost of such goods by 22 percent on the average. The plants, all nonunion, paid significantly lower wages than union plants. Charles Tandy's hardfisted labor tactics often had the company in hot water, especially in Canada, where the Ontario Labour Relations Board condemned the firm for "persistent and flagrant unfair labour practices." These included bright red T-shirts distributed by the company to nonstriking workers with the inscription: "I'm a company fink, and proud of it."

This was testimony to the fact that Charles Tandy was, by all accounts, a tough and demanding boss, but one who rewarded amply those who met his expectations. To his executives he was often heard to say, "If you can't get your work done in five days, do it in seven." He insisted that the corporate headquarters open Saturday mornings from 9 A.M. to 1 P.M., and all executives were expected to be on hand. Executives were also expected to answer their own phones, unless they were in a meeting. Even top-level executives in the firm suffered under Tandy's withering critique. Bill Nugent, a Tandy vice president, said, "Very seldom does he give a compliment, he always has something to criticize." Yet, Tandy was famous for the fact that he very rarely ever fired anyone; he reassigned incompetent executives to less demanding tasks.

Just as Tandy paid low wages to his factory workers, he also paid relatively low salaries to executives and store managers, relying instead upon the incentive system. All these people, including Charles Tandy himself, got relatively small salaries and no pension plans or frills, but they were given large bonuses and shared in the profits if they achieved satisfactory results. For example, in 1974 Tandy and his two highest paid executives received $75,000 each in salary, but the two executives earned over $255,000 each in bonuses; Charles Tandy's bonuses totaled $539,000. Store managers also shared in the profits, often earning from $30,000 to $35,000 a year in the mid–1970s. Tandy calculated in the late 1970s that his company had produced more than fifty millionaires through its profit-sharing and bonus programs.

By the time of his death in 1978, Tandy had built a billion-dollar company. With over 7,000 stores worldwide, its sales in 1978 were $1.06 billion, and net income was $66.2 million, with assets of about $400 million. During his final years as head of the firm, Tandy had brought Radio Shack into a number of profitable and important new areas. The first of these was the citizen's band radio, or CB, which became an enormous craze in the mid–1970s. Tandy early identified with the fad, and CBs soon became the firm's largest selling item, and they accounted for about one-fourth of all CBs sold in America. In 1977, however, the CB craze suddenly ended, and widespread price-cutting caused a slight drop in Tandy's large gross margins. The company's profits declined 4.2 percent between 1977 and 1978—not a pleasant phenomenon for a company accustomed to relentless growth and success. At that point, however, Tandy introduced its microcomputer, which profoundly changed the face of Tandy Corporation, Radio Shack, and the computer industry.

For Radio Shack to become a pioneer in the microcomputer industry was not something one would expect. The firm had never been a leader in new electronics technology, preferring to stick instead to a stable of safe, profitable, time-tested products. Further, computers had historically been sold by salesmen who called on customers, an enormously expensive operation that was a direct contradiction of the principles Charles Tandy had used to attain success with Radio Shack. Radio Shack's stores, in fact, were generally unimpressive in appearance and were often staffed by inexperienced salespeople. This was not the sort of operation that could normally expect to succeed in the computer business. For this reason, when Donald French, a computer hobbyist who was a merchandise buyer at Radio Shack, assembled working models of minicomputers from electronics kits and tried to interest top management in the product, they were uninterested.

In late 1976, however, it was clear to Charles Tandy that the CB craze was peaking, and that Radio Shack needed new products. So, he gave his merchandise buyers a pep talk, and urged them to develop new products. At that point French pushed Tandy to test his pet project. Tandy agreed to a demonstration of French's home-built computer, was impressed, and ordered the company to develop a production prototype. Their plans were modest. Sales of the computer over its entire life were pegged at just 1,000 units, so a very cheap machine with limited capabilities was developed. They built a compact, portable unit by consolidating all the basic circuitry on one board, which greatly reduced the size of the power supply. Dubbed the TR–80, the basic computer system was priced at an exceedingly low $599.95, with additional memory capacity and other items available for a total cost of only about $900, a price still well below that of even the cheapest minicomputer, which sold for from $10,000 to $15,000. Sales of the new product skyrocketed.

Tandy and his executives had visualized the TR–80 as appealing to the hobbyist. The idea was for the customer to be able to walk into a store and walk out with a computer small enough to fit on a desk top. More than 100,000 TR–80s were sold between September 1, 1977, and June 1, 1979. Ironically, they found that it was small businessmen, rather than home hobbyists, who were purchasing the bulk of the computers. As a result, they introduced a second model in 1979, the TRS–80 Model II, which was twice as fast with a much larger memory. The basic Model II sold for $3,450; with all the peripherals, the final price was about $7,500. This model was very successful, and computers by then accounted for more than 8 percent of Radio Shack's total sales.

When Charles Tandy died in late 1978, he was replaced as head of Tandy Corporation by his right-hand man, Phil North. It was clear that North was only an interim chief executive officer. As he himself stated at the time, "All I know about electronics is that the funny end of the battery goes into the flashlight first." Three years later, in 1981, John Roach, who had been primarily responsible for developing Radio Shack's early computers as vice president of production, became chief executive. But Radio Shack during the 1980s had a difficult time. In 1980 it was the leader in microcomputers, with 30 percent of the market. Only Apple Computer provided any competition. By 1984, its share of personal computers had fallen to less than 10 percent. During those years, Radio Shack faced a multipronged attack on its dual position as manufacturing and retail sales leader in home computers.

The first big shock was the entry of International Business Machines (IBM) into the personal computer market with its IBM-PC. Radio Shack's computers were not compatible with the IBM-PC or the Apple, and it refused to advertise name-brand software for its own computers. By 1983 software writers were switching to Apple and IBM, and were no longer writing programs for Radio Shack computers. Also, a number of new computer supermarkets had entered the retail scene, such as ComputerLand, Entré, and Computercraft, which made their reputations on service by offering more hand-holding and staffing their stores with experienced sales personnel. Finally, the Radio Shack name itself on its computers was no advantage in the more sophisticated computer market of the 1980s, since it conjured up images of nerdy computer hobbyists. Its status in computers had fallen so low by 1985, that Steve Jobs,[†] chairman of Apple Computer, declared it "totally out of the picture."

Roach thus had to institute important changes at Radio Shack during the first few years he ran the firm. In 1983, he brought out the Tandy 1200, the first of the firm's computers without the Radio Shack name and the first to be virtually 100-percent compatible with the IBM PC/XT. John Roach proudly called it "really an XT clone," allowing it to use virtually all the IBM software. (The 1200 was priced at $1,000 below the XT.) Roach also opened a large number of separate Tandy Computer Centers, to go along with the computer department in Radio Shack stores. These new stores did not have the Radio Shack name, and they provided the kind of service normally associated with computer chains— hand-holding, class instruction, and the provision of free phone numbers for immediate assistance. By 1986, Tandy was finally doing well in computers again. Its new IBM-compatible PCs, especially the low-priced home version, restored the company's place in the computer market. At that point, Tandy decided to emulate IBM and build a 1,500-person outside sales force to pitch Tandy computers directly to large corporations, an area formerly the exclusive preserve of IBM. By 1987, sales of computers had jumped 30 percent, and Tandy was battling Compaq and Olivetti to be the world's number three personal computer maker, behind IBM and Apple. But the direct-sales approach was unsuccessful, and in 1987 Tandy closed 103 computer centers and consolidated its outside sales force under the most effective managers. By the end of the 1987 fiscal year, Tandy's computer sales reached $950 million, but only 4 percent was to large businesses, along with 4 percent to the government. The bulk of its sales continued to be to home-computer buyers (40 percent), small businesses (32 percent), and educational institutions (20 percent).

In other areas, Tandy fared less well. Roach totally miscalculated the strength of the videocassette recorder (VCR) market, so that when the VCR boom hit, Radio Shack almost completely missed the massive market, which grew from 805,000 units in 1980 to 7.6 million in 1984. Tandy got only 1 percent of that market in 1984. The firm moved far more aggressively into cellular telephones and satellite dishes, stereo television sets, and compact disc players, which have been more successful. In 1988, Tandy introduced an erasable, reusable compact disk that many analysts predicted would have a dramatic impact on the recording industry. It also brought out its first personal computer, the Tandy 5000 MC, to compete head to head with IBM's PS/2. Priced well below IBM's entry, Tandy hoped it would allow it to make a larger dent in the business market. The result of all of this is that Tandy, a $1-billion corporation when Charles Tandy died in 1978, had sales of $3.65 billion nine years later. It earned profits of nearly $290 million on these sales.

All of this growth is a great monument to the vision and energy of Charles Tandy. The small, family-owned leather company he took over after World War II had become a retailing and manufacturing giant in electronics and computers. And Tandy himself before his death had become the uncrowned prince of Ft. Worth. Tandy Corporation and its subsidiaries dominated the city's business life, just as the massive, twin, seventeen-storied business towers of the eight-square-block Tandy Center dominated the landscape. In a fitting tribute, a *Forbes* writer recorded, on driving into Ft. Worth from the airport, "you see the old cow town's new skyline lit up before you, and one whole side of it is the two Tandy buildings, the name in lights carrying for miles through the darkness." (**B**. *Business Week*, September 8, 1962, April 17, 1978, August 31, 1987, March 14, 1988; James L. West, *Tandy Corporation: "Start on a Shoe String,"* 1968; *Forbes*, November 15, 1969, September 1, 1975, March 5, 1979, November 24, 1980, April 11, 1983, November 5, 1984; *Financial World*, March 15, 1976, March 15, 1978; *Fortune*, December 1976, November 12, 1979, April 29, 1985; *New York Times*, November 6, 1978; Milton Moskowitz et al., *Everybody's Business*, 1980; *Duns Business Month*, December 1981; Paul Freiberger and Michael Swaine, *Fire in the Valley: The Making of the Personal Computer*, 1984; Stephen D. McClellan, *The Coming Computer Industry Shakeout*, 1984; *Management Today*, October 1984; A. David Silver, *Entrepreneurial Megabucks, 1985; Robert Sobel, IBM vs. Japan*, 1986; James W. Cortada, *Historical Dictionary of Data Processing Organizations*, 1987; *Toronto Star*, April 22, 1988; Toronto *Globe & Mail*, April 26, 1988; *New York Times*, April 27, 1988.)

THOMPSON FAMILY: JOE C. "JODIE" THOMPSON, JR. (1901–June 11, 1961), **JOHN P. THOMPSON** (November 2, 1925–   ), **JERE WILLIAM THOMPSON** (January 18, 1932–   ), Convenience store chain founder and executives, Southland Corporation. When the automobile became ubiquitous in the 1920s, it set in motion a series of important changes. By increasing geographic mobility, it enhanced the distance people were willing to travel to work each day, which promoted the development of the first suburbs during that decade. As the suburbs blossomed, so too did a new kind of store—the supermarket. Taking advantage of cheaper land in the suburbs, new larger markets with ample available parking space were being built. As these supermarkets became increasingly dominant on the food scene in America, they drove many of the older mom-and-pop grocery stores in the center cities out of business. Customers were simply willing and able to travel farther to take advantage of the lower prices supermarkets were able to offer because of their discount buying and high volume. The supermarkets, however, left a lacuna in the market—the person who wanted to buy just a pack of cigarettes, a candy bar, a magazine, or a six-pack of beer and was unwilling to stand in long supermarket lines for his or her purchase. Recognition of that fact by Joe C. "Jodie" Thompson in 1927 led to the growth of the vast 7-Eleven convenience store chain, which numbered more than 8,000 stores by the mid–1980s. They became the modern world's version of the old mom-and-pop grocery store.

Jodie Thompson was born in Waxahachie, Texas, but he moved to Dallas with his family before he was a year old. The Thompson family was hardworking but had little money, so all members of the family had to pitch in and help out with finances. Jodie Thompson was educated in public schools, and soon he became a favorite of a next-door neighbor, J. O. Jones. Mr. Jones was vice president and general manager of Consumers Ice Company, where Jodie began to work after school and on weekends, grooming and feeding the horses used for ice delivery. During summer vacations from Oak Cliff High School in Dallas, Jodie worked for the ice company, loading ice into wagons. It was hard and heavy work, but Jodie took to it naturally, and by the time he graduated from high school, he was helping keep the company's books in addition to his other chores.

At that point, Jodie Thompson went to Austin to attend the University of Texas, where he majored in business administration. Serving as student manager of the basketball team and the freshman football team, Thompson was named class president in his senior year. In 1922 he graduated from the university and headed back to Dallas where he accepted a full-time job with Consumers Ice Company. Not all Consumers' ice was delivered; much of it was sold to customers from ice docks. Jodie came up with a new idea: to sell chilled watermelons from the docks. It was a huge success. These were the first chilled watermelons to be sold in Dallas, and Jodie earned a nice bonus of $2,300 for his idea, which enabled him to get married that year.

In 1926 Jodie Thompson became secretary-treasurer of Consumers Ice, which by then had five ice plants and sixteen retail ice docks in the Oak Cliff section of Dallas. The following year, a competitor, Southern Ice Company, began to express an interest in taking over Consumers. Southern had been founded in Denison, Texas, in the 1890s by a member of the Dawley family. One of the first ice manufacturing plants in the Southwest, it grew rapidly, and by 1920 had forty plants throughout the area. Claude S. Dawley joined his father's business at around that time, and in 1926 he set up his own firm to acquire the assets of existing ice plants. A number of friends joined him in the venture, and in 1927 they began to investigate acquisitions. Consumers Ice was one of four they decided to pursue. Needing additional capital to come up with the requisite

$1.4 million to purchase the properties, Dawley went to Chicago where he got backing from Martin and Samuel Insull,* heads of a mammoth public utility empire. In the 1920s, ice was considered a utility, and the Insulls' firm, Middle West Utilities, owned a number of them throughout the nation. With the Insulls' commitment in hand, Dawley went to the North Texas National Bank in Dallas, where he secured a $1.1-million loan to purchase the ice companies (which was at that time an enormous transaction in Dallas banking circles).

The newly merged firm was called Southland Ice Company, and Jodie Thompson, with 2,500 shares bought at $10 a share, was named a director. During that first summer of Southland's operation, one of the ice dock managers, a man named John Jefferson (Uncle Johnny) Green, was doing a bustling business keeping his ice dock open sixteen hours a day. Anxious to service his customers as well as possible, Green responded to their wishes by carrying other items, like bread and milk. At first he financed this sideline out of his own pocket, but when it proved to be a big success, he offered the service regularly. By the next spring, Green had accumulated $1,000 in extra profits with his sideline. When he presented that money to Thompson, the latter instantly recognized a good thing. "At that moment," according to the official company history, *O, Thank Heaven!,* "the convenience store business was born."

In early 1927, Thompson became secretary-treasurer of Southland Ice, and he began to play an increasingly important role in its operations. The first item of business on Southland's agenda was acquisition, and by early 1928 the company had twelve ice plants, totaling about 20 percent of the ice business in Dallas and San Antonio. Meanwhile the convenience store idea spread and became increasingly popular. Recognizing this popularity, Southland renamed their ice docks Tote'm Stores (which was a rather cute play on words). Customers "toted" away their purchases from the stores, each of which featured a large Indian totem pole.

The introduction of the convenience store framework for Southland Ice was fortuitous. By the late 1920s, mechanical refrigeration was being introduced into American homes, lessening the need for block ice. Southland was servicing a constantly dwindling market in its main endeavor, whereas the convenience stores, started as a sideline, were expanding exponentially. As the market for ice contracted, the ice manufacturers in Dallas and elsewhere engaged in "ice wars" in the late 1920s. To end the price cutting that accompanied the ice wars, Southland, the area's largest operator, began to buy up several of its competitors in 1928 and 1929. At about this time Thompson also took another, less successful, step toward diversification—he built gasoline stations at five of his stores. It did not work out, and the stations were closed; fifty years later, Southland tried the concept again, with not much more success.

As the depression hit with full fury in 1929 and 1930, Dawley and several of Southland's other major stockholders became skittish about keeping their shares. They decided to sell out to the Insulls, who paid them twice what they had originally paid for their stock. Upon the sale, Dawley resigned as president in

1931 and was succeeded by the thirty-year-old Jodie Thompson. Thompson had also served for several years as president of the Oak Cliff–Dallas Commercial Association, a chamber of commerce type of organization, and a week after becoming president of Southland he was elected to the Dallas City Council. Jodie Thompson had become a man to be reckoned with in his home community, and he would bring Southland Ice through some very hard times to become one of the leading grocery firms in the city, state, and nation.

Just about a year after Thompson assumed the presidency of Southland, it was rocked by the bankruptcy of the Insull empire in June 1932. The collapse of the Insull's Middle West Utilities took Southland by surprise. It occurred in the midst of an expansion program of its Tote'm Stores, which had a rosy future despite the depression. Thompson continued to run Southland under the jurisdiction of the federal government, but the company was suffering. Thompson sought protection from the company's creditors, and in December 1932, Southland declared bankruptcy. Jodie Thompson was named receiver and was ordered to operate the company under the receivership. These were dark times for Thompson and Southland Ice, but relief was near at hand from an unexpected source.

At the end of 1933, the Prohibition Amendment was repealed, and since most beer drinkers preferred their beverage chilled, a new market opened up for Southland's Tote'm Stores. This gave a great boost to sales and profits at an opportune time for the company. By December 1934, the situation had improved so much that Southland was able to get out of receivership, and a new firm, still called Southland Ice Company, was incorporated in Delaware. During the next two years, Southland retained its share of the ice business (about 14 percent of the market) and turned an acceptable profit. But Thompson recognized that for Southland to survive in the long run, further diversification was necessary. Tote'm Stores had become the largest retailers of dairy products in the Dallas area, and Thompson decided that it was imperative for the company to acquire its own dairy operation. Accordingly, in May 1936, it founded Oak Farms Dairies, which lost money during its first year, but became profitable in subsequent years.

By 1939, Southland had sixty retail locations, mostly in the Dallas–Ft. Worth area. Profits at the Tote'm Stores by then surpassed the earnings from ice operations for the first time by a wide margin. The outbreak of World War II, however, greatly increased the need for ice. Camp Hood, a large military training base in the area, needed great quantities of ice. To meet these needs, Southland bought additional ice plants. The business in the Tote'm Stores also boomed, since the large numbers of servicemen who flooded into the Dallas–Ft. Worth area were frequent customers, who bought beer, cigarettes, candy, and other pickup items. The war had brought about great and rapid growth for the company, but the postwar period posed greater opportunities and challenges. In recognition of this, in 1945, Thompson changed the name of the company to The Southland Corporation. Ice making had increased rapidly during the war, and great profits were made from those operations, but Thompson was astute enough to recognize that the days of the commercial ice plant were numbered. Expansion was necessary if the firm was to survive.

Thompson realized that the growth area for the company was the convenience store operation. There were seventy stores, all open front and drive in. They were open from early in the morning until late at night. All sold ice, cold drinks, groceries, and drug sundries, and all were giving curb service to their customers. Because a number of the stores had been acquired by purchase of other ice companies during the war, they did not all have the same name. It would have been easy enough to just call them all Tote'm Stores, a well-known, established name, but Thompson wanted to begin a large-scale advertising campaign for his stores, using newspaper, radio, and point-of-sale approaches. So he directed his advertising agency to come up with a new name. Ultimately, the agency suggested that, if the stores would all agree to stay open from 7 A.M. to 11 P.M., they could be called, 7-Eleven Stores. Thompson liked the idea and the name, and a new logo—a four leaf clover with the number "7" and the word "Eleven"—was designed. In January 1946, the name on the stores was changed amidst great fanfare, and the modern convenience store era had now begun.

During 1947, Thompson opened more 7-Eleven Stores, expanded their ice making and dairy operations, and diversified into a new area. Thompson started the Ice Bottling Company, a soft-drink bottler, to supply bottled soft drinks for 7-Eleven. This venture was not particularly successful, and after a short time it was sold to Royal Crown Cola so that more time and money could be devoted to store expansion. By the end of 1947, Southland was a highly diversified entity. There were seventy-four 7-Eleven Stores, large-scale ice operations, and a major dairy business. Thompson merged them all into one corporate structure—a newly incorporated Southland Corporation—and in 1949 he set up profit-sharing and trust plans for his employees. Store sales by 1949 increased enormously. A decade earlier they had amounted to just $834,000. In 1949 they were $9.7 million, and operating profits for the entire operation amounted to $429,000. Jodie Thompson, on his own, had created a large-scale, profitable operation. Since Tote'm/7-Eleven was the first convenience store operation, it was a trail blazer and could only learn from its own mistakes. But Thompson was a great innovator, and many of his ideas were winners during this period.

As the 1950s opened, Thompson expanded 7-Eleven's operations out of the north Texas area, where there were eighty stores. Thompson first went into Austin, and then into Houston. Although it was difficult at first to gain acceptance in these two areas, Thompson ultimately succeeded. In 1952 Southland was twenty-five years old, and it had become a statewide operation. As the chain's operations expanded, Thompson realized that it was important to begin standardizing architecture, store design, mechandising, employee training, advertising, and sales promotion. Southland was among the first to use television advertising in the Dallas–Ft. Worth area, and it developed a popular animated commercial which featured the "7 A.M. Rooster" and the "11 P.M. Owl." This spurred even greater expansion, and in 1952 the chain had a red-letter day, when it opened its 100th store.

Two years later, Southland took another significant step—it expanded beyond Texas for the first time. The first store, in Miami, Florida, was placed in a separate operation. In 1961, under a legal challenge from several Southland stockholders, the Florida operations were consolidated into the parent company. The 7-Eleven Stores were the only convenience stores in Florida, and they were a big success. Soon, more 7-Eleven Stores were opened in the state. Thompson also tried a hardware store operation during this time, but it was not a success. Nonetheless, by the end of 1954, Southland had reached yet another important milestone—operating profits reached $1 million. With successful operations in Florida and elsewhere in the South, Thompson decided to expand out of the warm-weather states for the first time in 1957, and he opened a 7-Eleven Store in Washington, D.C. At this time, Southland was opening about one store a month, and in June 1958, the 300th 7-Eleven Store opened its doors.

Jodie Thompson was innovative, and many of his ideas worked, although some, like the bottling company and the hardware store chain, did not. Similarly, not every 7-Eleven Store was successful. But Thompson was able to turn even failures to his advantage. Since he used a great deal of fanfare to open each store, Thompson decided to announce his first failure in a similar manner. In August 1954, Southland had opened a 7-Eleven Store in Richmond Hills, a suburb of Ft. Worth, which turned out to be a poor location. On January 4, 1956, the store was closed, and Thompson placed a huge sign in front of the shuttered store announcing: "Opened by Mistake." The sign caused quite a stir and garnered a lot of free media attention. A Southland official told the local newspaper, "We really made a mistake on this one," and he added that the store had been expected to set all sorts of records when it opened—and it did, but they were records of the wrong kind.

Failures like this were few, and by the end of the 1950s, Southland had greatly expanded its operations. By that time it had a total of 490 convenience stores, 274 of which were in Texas, Louisiana, and the East Coast; 151 were 7-Eleven's in Florida; and 65 were Cabell's Minit Markets, a major competitor in the Dallas area that Thompson had purchased earlier that year. Two years later, a malignant tumor was found on Jodie Thompson's neck. In March 1961 he moved up to chairman of the board of Southland, and in June of that year he died. Thompson's death shocked his family, friends, and business associates. As the Waco, Texas, *News-Tribune* commented:

The death of Joe C. Thompson in Dallas took from the American scene one of the most imaginative and energetic merchandisers of this century. His career is a textbook example of what the free enterprise system is all about. . . . It is probably an understatement to say that Jodie Thompson had more impact than any other individual on the shopping habits of America during his lifetime.

Thompson had not only created a successful business, he had also created an entirely new industry, the convenience food store. The convenience store concept was obviously a child of the great suburban expansion of the 1950s, and Southland evolved rapidly as American suburbs boomed. But hindsight may obscure the extent to which Jodie Thompson was a prophet of great significance in American retailing.

Although the convenience store is a ubiquitous sight on the American landscape in the 1980s, it was a strange phenomenon indeed in the 1940s and 1950s. Americans were accustomed to grocery stores and supermarkets, but Thompson's convenience stores were not grocery stores in any conventional sense. They did not sell fresh meats, fruits, or vegetables, but instead emphasized items that people wanted to pick up in a hurry. They sold beer, cigarettes, magazines, milk and dairy products, eggs, and a number of other items. The average purchase was small, and the average amount of time spent in the store was short. Thompson was wise enough to recognize that these were the strengths of his operation. Rather than attempting to carry broader lines of goods to convince people to do more of their shopping in the 7-Eleven's and thereby create longer lines and negate the convenience store advantage, Thompson instead continually looked for items with a high volume and high markup to improve the profitability of the operation.

When Jodie Thompson died, his two eldest sons moved into positions of control and responsibility in Southland's operations. John Thompson was elected president of the company and Jere Thompson vice president in 1961. Both young men had graduated in business administration from the University of Texas, John in 1948 and Jere in 1954. Both also joined Southland immediately after graduation and worked their way up through various departments in the company. John Thompson's leadership style was strongly influenced by his father. As he recalled,

When I was a child, I can remember that he worked very long hours. It was usually after seven o'clock in the evening when he got home. Many, many times we had dinner without him. Of course, he always worked on Saturdays and Sundays until the last few years of his life, when he started taking Saturdays off to go to his ranch. He believed if you worked longer and harder than your competition, you couldn't help but out-perform them.

Both his sons inherited that philosophy.

With the rise of increasingly giant supermarkets in the 1960s, and the consequent demise of the last of the mom-and-pop grocery stores, another void was created that Southland determined to fill with its convenience stores. As a result, John and Jere Thompson undertook a program of extremely rapid expansion during the 1960s. When their father died in 1961, Southland had 600 stores. By 1963, the number stood at 1,000; two years later, it passed 1,500. By the end of the decade, there were 3,500 7-Eleven Stores, nearly 3,000 more than when they took over; Southland's store operations had been expanded by a phenomenal

600 percent. This expansion brought Southland into new markets, and some of the rapid growth was accomplished by the acquisition of small, existing companies, which were immediately converted to 7-Eleven's.

Revenues and profits grew apace during the 1960s. In 1963, revenues passed $200 million for the first time, with profits of $2.6 million, the largest in the company's history. During the decade, Southland recorded an annual revenue growth rate of nearly 24 percent and its profits grew at an annual rate of 20 percent. By 1969, revenues had mushroomed to over $800 million, almost a tenfold increase over sales in 1959, and profits were $12 million. Operations were extended into Canada during this time, so that by the end of the decade there were Southland operations in thirty-eight states, three provinces in Canada, and the District of Columbia. During this time, Southland took an important new step in product development. Several Dallas inventors had created something they called an "Icee"—a frozen, carbonated drink that came in various flavors. Southland investigated the concept in 1965 and began to install machines to make it in their convenience stores. By changing the name of the product to Slurpee and promoting it with an intensive advertising campaign, Southland created a very popular and profitable drink. As a Southland executive recalled, "The sales were just astronomical in all of the markets and it really put 7-Eleven on the map in the minds of a lot of people, especially many of the radio folk." This was the beginning of a brisk business for 7-Eleven in prepared food and drink, especially coffee, hot chocolate, and sandwiches.

Southland's most important step during the 1960s involved expansion into California. The Thompsons had avoided California for over a decade because of the state's high labor costs and because most of the convenience store chains in the state were franchised, a business strategy never practiced by Southland. By 1963, however, John Thompson knew the huge California market could no longer be ignored. He decided that the best way to enter the market was through acquisition, and so he purchased the 100 plus stores of Speedee Mart. These were all franchise operations, and brought Southland into the center of perhaps the most dynamic retail development of the 1960s and 1970s. Building on the Speedee framework, Southland developed its own basic franchise agreement.

Franchising for Southland, as for most other convenience store and fast-food outlets, became the major means of expansion during the next twenty-five years. But not all franchises were thrilled with the Southland contract. One franchise owner complained to *Business Week*, "Running one of these stores can be absolute murder"; another told *Forbes*, "They've got you by the short hairs; they control the accounting, and if they say you're out $2,000, there's nothing you can do." Others, however, more enthusiastic, pointed out, "Where else could you put up $5,000 and have your own business? Their accounting operation is one of the finest; the [supervisory] group in there now is fantastic."

As the 1970s dawned, other important changes transpired in the 7-Eleven's. When the chain was started, opening at 7 A.M. and closing at 11 p.m. had represented dramatically extended hours. But America was changing rapidly.

The population was younger, there were far more two-income families, and there was an increasing demand for goods and services at all hours of the day. As a result, Southland began to experiment with twenty-four-hour stores. As these proved to be successful, the Thompsons expanded the twenty-four-hour concept to more and more stores. Southland also diversified in some new and important ways during the late 1960s and early 1970s. In 1968 they took over the prestigious Gristede Bros. grocery chain in New York City, and they picked up the Chief Auto Parts chain of more than 100 stores in Southern California. In 1969 they picked up Barricini, a chain of candy stores based on the East Coast. This was followed a short time later by the purchase of the Loft's candy store chain on the West Coast.

In 1971 Southland had its first billion-dollar year, when revenues totaled $1,085,107,334. Profits reached $17.3 million, and earnings per share were the highest in the company's history. By this time, Southland had over 4,000 7-Eleven stores, 207 candy stores, 130 Gristede's stores, and nine Bradshaw's supermarkets. It also opened its first regional distribution center in that year, located in Orlando, Florida. This was the first of a small chain of centers to be opened by Southland. Previously, the company had purchased products from local distributors, but as it expanded, and as business became more complex, it became necessary to set up its own computerized distribution system. As Joseph S. Hardin, the man who designed the system, commented, "Convenience stores have unique requirements because they need ones and twos of things." The new distribution center in Florida, and those that followed, were designed to fill that need. Because it could deliver small orders to individual stores, it eliminated the problem of split cases, and saved each store about $3,500 a year in unnecessary inventory. Finally, Southland expanded its operations into Europe at the beginning of the decade, by purchasing a half-interest in an ailing grocery chain in England, and an interest in a specialty chain in England and Scotland. In 1972, Southland's common shares were listed on the New York Stock Exchange for the first time.

Although Southland grew rapidly in the early 1970s, it did not happen without significant problems. Most particularly, it faced increased competition on numerous fronts. Southland had pioneered the convenience store concept and extended hours, but by the early 1970s many others were infringing on this territory. Supermarkets, which had long ignored convenience shoppers, started courting them with longer hours and Sunday shopping. In addition, other convenience store chains had emerged, the largest of which were Phoenix, Arizona's, Circle-K Corporation and the Atlanta, Georgia-based Munford, Incorporated. Each had about 1,000 stores in operation. Also, oil companies were beginning to set up small convenience store operations at their stations, selling the kinds of items that had long been 7-Eleven's stock in trade. The Thompson's strategy in dealing with this competition was to focus on their best-selling, most profitable products—the old Jodie Thompson idea.

As 1974 opened, Southland reached another milestone—its 5,000th store was opened. By this time, the 7-Eleven operations had become highly systematized and sophisticated. The stores remained small, averaging about 2,400 square feet, and served an average of 600 customers a day, totaling about three million customers daily for the chain. The average shopper spent just about three and a half minutes in the store, and the typical purchase was just over $1. Unlike other food stores, most of 7-Eleven's customers were male, and about 75 percent were under the age of thirty-five. Tobacco, beer and wine, and soft drinks were the three most profitable single-product lines; general grocery items still made up the largest category of purchases. These statistics allowed Southland to target its chain's potential customers with some exactitude, and it was one of the reasons for its success. By this time, 42 percent of the Southland stores were franchise operations.

As Southland grew, so did many of its problems. The violence in America became more prevalent in the late 1960s and 1970s, and since most 7-Eleven stores observed the twenty-four-hour format, they were ripe targets for burglary and armed robbery. Southland took action: it set up a crime-prevention committee and adopted various crime-prevention techniques. Because of the crime that plagued the twenty-four-hour 7-Elevens, however, many communities began to oppose the opening of stores in their areas. At the end of the 1970s, Southland tried selling gasoline, something Jodie Thompson tried in the 1930s. By 1977, 1,250 of its stores sold discount gasoline, and it also purchased a number of Phillips Petroleum stations on the West Coast. Since diversification into candy shops and department stores did not work out well for the company, the Thompsons were banking on the new gasoline outlets as a means of growth. By 1979, Southland had sales of $3.9 billion and profits of $67.5 million. With over 7,000 stores and 37,000 employees, it was not only the largest convenience store chain in the world, but also the sixth largest food retailer in the United States.

The 1980s were a critical time for Southland and the Thompson family. As the decade opened, Southland's gasoline venture was working well. Fully 40 percent of its outlets had gasoline pumps, and it cost the company relatively little to install the pumps. Since the personnel were already on hand, little additional expense was involved for the company to service the pump sales, and, since the drivers had to go into the stores to pay for their purchases, they often picked up other items while they were inside. Although some industry analysts were critical of the move, most seemed to believe that Southland had made another shrewd decision. Another part of this strategy was equally shrewd. As large numbers of gasoline stations closed in the late 1970s, they left some of the choicest corner locations available. Southland moved from its traditional mid-block location to the corners, opened up gasoline and convenience store operations there, and found they were doing 50 percent more business than before.

In the early 1980s, the Thompsons made a fateful decision—they decided that Southland, since it had become the nation's largest gasoline retailer, could no longer afford to buy its gas on the wholesale market, but that it should control its own crude oil and refining operations. It should, in other words, move what is called "upstream" in the petroleum business—they should integrate backward. As a result, in 1983 they agreed to pay an estimated $780 million in cash and stock to acquire Citgo's refining, marketing, and transportation businesses from Occidental Petroleum. Although an executive for Southland called the acquisition "a beautiful fit," petroleum industry analysts were not so sure. Alan Gaines, an oil industry expert, told *Financial World* that Southland had paid too much for Citgo's Lake Charles refinery, and felt the entire company might be dragged down by the volatility of the refining industry. A rival gasoline refiner said Southland would "rue the day they got into the refining business."

By 1985 it was clear that Gaines had been correct. Falling demand and over-capacity in the refining business caused Southland's Citgo subsidiary to post a $50-million loss in 1984, and it was obvious to most observers that Southland had chosen the worst possible time to venture into the refining end of the industry. It cost the company more to refine its own gasoline than to buy it on the spot market, and it very nearly closed the Lake Charles refinery. To help solve these problems, the Thompsons hired Ron Hall from Gulf Oil. By the end of 1985, Citgo had achieved a remarkable turnaround, earning $71 million for the year. The company, however, had a number of other problems. Two of the firm's vice presidents were indicted by the Internal Revenue Service (IRS) for con-spiracy to defraud, although they were later acquitted. There were also charges of payoffs being made to public officials by Southland officers, and John Thomp-son was named an "unindicted co-conspirator" in the case.

In 1987, the Thompsons decided to take the giant Southland firm private. The decision was prompted by an attempt on the part of the Belzberg family of Canada to take over the company. The Thompsons, along with other top man-agement, made a $5.1-billion bid to buy the company. By this time, the chain had 8,222 convenience stores in forty-nine states and Canada and revenues of $8.6 billion. Earnings in 1986, however, had fallen 6 percent, to $200 million. To pay for their leveraged buyout, the Thompsons planned to sell the company's auto parts retailer and dairy division, but to keep the convenience store and Citgo gasoline operations. Their desire to take the firm private also stemmed from a desire to step out of the limelight. In 1986, the Attorney General's Commission on Pornography accused the chain of selling pornography. Southland had always been the biggest single outlet for *Playboy* and *Penthouse*, but the Thompsons, deeply religious Roman Catholics, were stung by the accusations. As a result, they pulled those and all other "Skin" magazines out of their stores. The man-agement buyout, which was financed by the sale of $1.5 billion worth of junk bonds, was approved by the stockholders in December 1987, by which the Thompsons acquired about 75 percent of Southland's shares.

The 1980s had been difficult years for the Thompsons. The company had suffered through heavy losses with their petroleum operations, and much criticism from the financial community for their purchase. Several of the firm's officers and employees had been put on trial, and the Thompson brothers themselves had been dragged through several legal proceedings. In 1984, the company was convicted and fined $10,000 for conspiring to defraud the IRS. Through it all, however, they have tried to maintain a wholesome image. Most dramatic and most visible of their commitments has been their support of Jerry Lewis' Labor Day Telethon for the Muscular Dystrophy Association. For nearly two decades, they have raised some $4 million a year for the association, much of which comes from displays in each store near the cash register urging customers to "Let Jerry Keep the Change for His Kids."

The Thompson family and 7-Eleven stores have played a major role in the homogenization of America since 1945. This new America has not been appreciated by everyone. Stan Luxenberg, in his *Roadside Empires*, commented,

A nation where one town is indistinguishable from the next, where mediocrity rules, is likely to have a deadening effect on its citizens, particularly the young. The eighteen-year-olds I interviewed could not remember when they first ate in a McDonald's. For them Holiday Inns had always been the main hotel in town, the 7-Eleven the best place to pick up a six-pack, and Radio Shack offered the latest electronic miracles. Immersed in a world dominated more and more by large impersonal corporations, the current high school generation may be more susceptible to feelings of powerlessness that contribute to a host of psychological problems.

And to think the Thompsons thought they were just selling cigarettes and Slurpees. (**B**. *New York Times*, June 12, 1961, January 6, 1987; *Business Week*, October 28, 1972, March 21, 1977, April 11, November 1, 1983, July 1, December 23, 1985, July 20, 1987; *Chain Store Age*, November 1972, May 1976; *Forbes*, September 15, 1974, August 4, 1980, March 23, 1987; Allen Liles, *Oh, Thank Heaven! The Story of the Southland Corporation*, 1976; Milton Moskowitz, et al., *Everybody's Business*, 1980; *Financial World*, October 1, 1980, April 3–16, 1985; *Fortune*, November 1, 1982, December 7, 1987; Stan Luxenberg, *Roadside Empires*, 1985; *National Petroleum News*, November 1985, March 1988; The Southland Corporation, *Annual Report*, 1986; *Dun's Business Month*, August 1986; Toronto *Globe & Mail*, July 7, December 9, 1987; *Newsweek*, September 21, 1987.)

TISCH, LAURENCE ALAN (March 5, 1923–) and **PRESTON ROBERT TISCH** (April 29, 1926–). Founders, hotel and resort chain and conglomerate, broadcasting executive, public official, Tisch Hotels, Loews Corp., CBS. It was quite a night. Many of the glittering celebrities of New York's media world were at a party in honor of CBS correspondent Mike Wallace and his new wife, Mary Yates, on September 10, 1986. At about 7:30, a call came informing them that Thomas Wyman, the chief executive officer (CEO) of CBS, had been told to clean out his desk by the board of directors. He had been bested in a struggle for control of the corporation by Laurence Tisch. The rank and file at CBS News, long the crown jewel of the network, were elated. Wallace recalled the evening,

The call with the news came about 7:30. Soon, [Tom] Brokaw, then [Peter] Jennings and [Dan] Rather arrived, talking about it. [Walter] Cronkite came—and people got him off in a corner, very excited. Then Larry [Tisch] walked in. . . . It was just a happy, happy night. (*Newsweek*, September 22, 1986)

The sense of elation, however, might have been tempered if the newspeople had been aware of what had happened a few months before.

In April 1986, CBS held its annual shareholders meeting in Philadelphia. The meeting had not gone well; CBS was struggling with losses and attempting to ward off takeover attempts. The one bright spot at the meeting was the brilliant trumpet performance by CBS Records' star Wynton Marsalis, who was the only individual to win Emmys in both the classical and jazz fields. Hoping to make small-talk with Laurence Tisch on the train ride back to New York, young record executive Christine Reed asked him if he had enjoyed Marsalis' trumpet playing. Tisch nodded, then paused and said to Reed, "Tell me, do you know if the margins are higher on his jazz recordings or on his classical records?" Reed was flabbergasted—*the margins?*— after a moment she blurted out, "Classical. They were higher on classical." Overhearing the conversation, Walter Yetnikoff, president of CBS Records, muttered to an aide, "The guy is a goddamn machine." Those words would be heard over and over again in the months after Tisch took control of CBS. CBS had always been a glamour company—part Hollywood glitter, part Washington power politics, and part New York intellectual literati. Now executives in the company asked pointed questions about their new boss: "Is there anything more to him than the ruthlessly efficient businessman, the money machine? Was he simply going to milk the company— 'cash out'—as the winner in just another business deal?" Larry Tisch, one of the wealthiest and most powerful men in America, head of Loews Corporation, which was three times the size of CBS, suddenly had nationwide visibility. Who was this man? And what were his plans for CBS, that important icon of American culture and national identity?

Larry Tisch was born in Bensonhurst, New York, the son of Al Tisch, a former All-American basketball player, and coowner with his wife of a garment manufacturing business in Manhattan and two summer camps in New Jersey. Larry, the oldest son, was put to work in the family enterprises at an early age, as was his younger brother, Preston, known as "Bob." Both boys went through the elementary schools of the neighborhood and graduated from DeWitt Clinton High School. Larry had gone through both high school and college in an accelerated program, and he graduated cum laude from the School of Commerce at New York University in 1941, when he was just eighteen. He then went on to the University of Pennsylvania's Wharton School of Finance, where he got his MBA. Larry then went into the U.S. Army, where he served three years in the Office of Strategic Services, the forerunner of the Central Intelligence Agency. After the war, he spent one semester at Harvard Law School, where he discovered that he had absolutely no interest in law.

In January 1946 Larry Tisch left Harvard and joined his father in business. But Larry was twenty-three years old and impatient. He wanted to start his own business. The family's two summer camps and garment business were liquidated for a total of $125,000, and Al Tisch turned the entire amount over to his son, trusting him to find a good business opportunity. In April 1946, Larry spotted an advertisement in the *New York Times* concerning the sale of a hotel in New Jersey called Laurel-in-the-Pines. Larry and his father drove down to New Jersey to inspect the resort. The price was $375,000, and they only needed $175,000 down. A family friend put up another $50,000 for a one-quarter interest, and the hotel was theirs.

Upon taking possession, the Tisches established a pattern that would be characteristic of their hotel careers. They poured money into hotel improvements: they added an indoor swimming pool and an outdoor skating rink, and they raised the rates. The hotel was an instant success, and by the end of the first year they had made enough money to buy out their partner. Two years later, after graduating from the University of Michigan, Bob Tisch joined the family hotel business. Before going to Michigan, Bob had attended Bucknell College and had spent some time in the army. Larry and Bob Tisch were to prove a nearly unbeatable combination on the business scene. Larry was an introverted, quiet financial and strategic genius—a perfect "Mr. Inside"—Bob—"Mr. Outside"—a gregarious glad-hander, was in his element at cocktail parties, hotel openings, and all sorts of public affairs.

The year Bob Tisch joined the firm, they bought their second hotel, the Grand Hotel, a summer resort in New York's Catskill Mountains. At this time they also worked out the division of labor which would be so successful for them and their business. Bob handled personnel and client relations, while Larry stayed more in the background, keeping the books, making purchases, and watching for new investment opportunities. In 1950 they bought their third hotel, the old 575-room Traymore Hotel in Atlantic City, New Jersey. The Traymore had revenues of nearly $3 million a year, but it was losing oceans of money. Hours after they took over the venerable old hotel, most of the key personnel resigned, possibly because Larry and Bob Tisch were Jewish, and none of the major hotels in Atlantic City had ever been owned by Jews. Bob recalled, "We felt pretty lonely standing there in that huge lobby." Nonetheless, they rapidly overhauled the hotel's management, cut the staff, recruited less expensive entertainment, and improved the quality of the food. At the end of the first year, they had turned the hotel around and realized a small profit. Having gotten over that hurdle, the Tisches raised the room rates by 25 percent, did even more business the following year, and made a million dollars each year over the next five years.

The Tisches then embarked on two more Atlantic City ventures. In 1951 they leased the 700-room Ambassador Hotel for thirty years. This hotel had also had a recent history of steady losses. Within two years, the Tisches had it making a $750,000 profit. In 1954, they bought the decrepit Brighton Hotel. They had it knocked down, and opened the 275-room Colony Hotel in its place. In 1956, the brothers sold the Traymore for $15 million (it had cost them $4.3 million), but, at the same time, negotiated a contract that left them in charge of its management. In addition, they retained a parcel of Traymore's land, which they leased out for about $25,000 a year. Years later, they were able to sell the land for a fortune when the great casino boom hit Atlantic City. In the meantime, however, the Tisches were rapidly expanding their little hotel empire.

Moving into the Manhattan real estate and hotel market, the brothers applied the same formulas there that had brought them success in New Jersey. Their first big deal was to lease the massive 1,500-room McAlpin Hotel at Broadway and 34th Street. During the next year or so, they invested about $1 million in renovations, raised its room rates 30 percent, and watched its occupancy rate increase 20 percent. At that point, the hotel became attractive to other interests, and the owners sold it to the Sheraton chain for $9 million. The Tisches made $1.5 million during the thirty-six months they ran the McAlpin, and they used $500,000 of it to buy two office buildings adjacent to the McAlpin. Again, those little parcels, seemingly just an incidental part of all the negotiations, were worth many millions several years later. Their next venture was the Belmont Plaza in New York, which they also leased. Located across the street from the Waldorf Astoria, the brothers felt they could pick up much of that hotel's convention overflow if they spruced up the Belmont. The pattern was familiar. After making the hotel a success, the Tisches sold their twenty-year lease in 1956 for $1.7 million, most of which was clear profit.

Up to this point, the Tisches were relatively small-time operators. They effectively turned around second-line hotels, but hardly anybody paid any attention to them. This changed in 1956 when they began to build their first hotel from the ground up. And what a hotel it was. By this point, the Tisch brothers were together worth perhaps $30 million, but they wanted something more than fast-buck turnarounds. In 1955, they had paid $1.35 million in cash to buy ten acres of ocean-front property at Bal Harbour, Florida—about four miles from the string of luxury hotels in Miami Beach. In early 1956, they began to construct the Americana Hotel on the property. They hired the famous hotel architect, Morris Lapidus, who had created the fabulous (and rather garish) Fontainebleau in Miami. Larry moved with his family to Florida to supervise the whole operation personally, while Bob ran the northern end of the business.

Larry wanted a fabulous luxury hotel, and he was willing to pay almost any price. The finished hotel was lavish, and, in some people's minds a testimonial to poor taste. But it had been designed to cater to the convention trade, something the other Miami hotels ignored. Larry Tisch reasoned that he could keep the occupancy up all year round if he built extensive convention facilities. The Americana cost $17 million to build, and the Tisches paid for it in cash without a mortgage. When it was ready to open, on schedule, in December 1956, Bob Tisch flew in for the grand opening, and he put on a gala affair that attracted many celebrities and much media coverage. The 780-room hotel did $12 million worth of business in its first year, and in 1962 the *Miami Herald* called it "one of the most profitable businesses in the state."

By the end of the 1950s, the Tisch brothers were worth about $65 million, and were looking for new investment opportunities. In 1959, they began buying shares in Loews Corporation. They intended to take advantage of an antitrust decree that forced MGM to divest itself of its Loews Theaters division. In September 1959, Larry won a seat on the board of directors of Loews and became chairman of the finance committee, while Bob was made head of the executive committee. By 1960, they controlled 25 percent of Loews stock, and in January 1961 they gained complete control of the company. The first thing they did was to oust the president and CEO Eugene Picker in a dispute over diversification. The Tisches were now in control of a magnificent, if decaying, old theater chain which had been founded by Marcus Loew* many years before. The firm's chief assets were about 100 once-magnificent old theater palaces that, by 1960, stood half empty due to the influence of television.

When Larry and Bob Tisch looked at Loews, they saw something else—they saw real estate, lots of prime, downtown real estate. As Larry recalled a few years later, "The company had tremendous assets in real estate, a lot of cash, and offered a great potential." Soon after taking control, Larry and Bob began to close Loews downtown theaters and to lease the sites or buildings on them. At the same time, they began to open new theaters in the suburbs. They also used the money to take Loews into the hotel and motel business, building or modernizing in one frenzied twenty-six-month period a total of seven hotels, six of which were in New York. "We opened 6,500 rooms in one stretch," said Bob, "but it all went without a hitch." Among those built in New York City was the Summit, the first new hotel built in Manhattan in thirty years, which was designed by Morris Lapidus, and which many New Yorkers said "should have stayed in Miami Beach." They also built the Americana with 2,000 rooms and fifty stories, the world's tallest hotel when it was completed in 1962. Like its namesake in Florida, it was built to attract the convention trade, and it became a formidable competitor in that field.

By 1969, Loews had become the nation's third largest hotel operator, with a volume of more than $120 million annually. In addition to the hotels built in the early 1960s, they had acquired and renovated the Drake and Warwick in New York, the two Ambassadors in Chicago, and the Mark Hopkins in San Francisco. As these hotels were stabilized by the end of the 1960s, Bob handled their management, and Larry looked for new investment opportunities. By 1968, the two brothers had built Loews assets to $273 million, by a conservative estimate, with revenues of $167 million. With that money, Larry wanted to acquire another asset-rich company that could be bought cheaply and made more profitable. Larry honed in on Baltimore's Commercial Credit Corporation, a stodgy finance firm with nearly $3 billion in cash reserves. When Tisch made a tender offer, Commercial Credit recoiled in horror, and found a "white knight," Control Data, to take them over. It was the first time Larry Tisch had been bested in a takeover, and he was rather shocked at the reaction. But he did make a nice profit of $28 million on the stock he sold.

Tisch was hardly ready to give up his quest. A few months later, Felix Rohatyn* of Lazard Frères introduced him to the head of Lorillard, the fifth largest cigarette company in the United States. Lorillard had major assets, but had been floundering since 1964, and its stock price was quite low. Larry and Bob began an examination of the company and found a host of problems. Nonetheless, they thought they could make a go of the company, so they offered to take it over. The acquisition immediately quadrupled Loews assets and revenues, and made it a major conglomerate by the end of the decade.

But Lorillard, a company that had been around since 1760, was tradition-bound. When the Tisches began slashing costs and housecleaning, they created a tremendously hostile environment. Many rival executives in the clubby tobacco circle were very critical of the Tisches' ulterior motives, but they were placated when a respected tobacco man was hired to run Lorillard. Despite the size of Loews after the merger—it had revenues of $700 million in 1970—Larry and Bob continued to run it in a bare-bones, unostentatious manner. Jerry Snyder, a California home builder who worked with Loews, said; "The Tisches are true entrepreneurs, and they run the company just like a little store." But it was a well-managed "little store."

Their success with Lorillard was followed by another excellent acquisition—in 1974 they gained control of CNA Financial Corporation, a Chicago-based insurance company. Although its earnings were severely depressed, Larry felt the company could be turned around. After taking it over, he brought in a seasoned insurance professional to run it. Employment was cut from 12,000 to 10,500, and within a short period of time, the company was converted into a money-maker, with an asset base of $16.5 billion. One former Tisch associate discussed that acquisition, "They picked CNA out on the verge of bankruptcy and defeated the old management, and put in their own people, while gradually increasing their holdings from 5 percent to 80 percent." In 1985, CNA made $4.8 billion for Loews, 71 percent of the company's total revenue. It was a classic "cash-cow." It also illustrated the time-worn Tisch acquisition technique—buying a company on the verge of bankruptcy. "We're bottom dwellers," Larry has said.

Other acquisitions in the 1970s and early 1980s, however, did not turn out quite as well. They bought the Bulova Watch Company in 1979 just when the Japanese were invading the American watch market. Although they did well with the company the first few years, they have since seen the watch market contract substantially. Not until 1984 and 1985 was Bulova able to put two consecutive profitable years together. It was not a classic Tisch acquisition. There were other mistakes also, especially Franklin National Bank. The Tisches bought a controlling interest in the bank, and then bailed out when it became overextended. Their holdings were purchased for $40 million by Michael Sindona, an Italian financer, who then looted the bank of its assets. Loews ultimately signed a consent decree and paid a $1.2-million fine, without admitting any wrongdoing in the case. They also missed out on the big Wall Street boom of the early 1980s. As classic "bottom-pickers," Larry felt the market was overpriced in 1982 and refused to buy. The market, of course, continued rising to dizzying heights until the crash in October 1987. By that time Loew revenues had gone from just over $100 million in 1970 to over $3 billion. Larry and Bob Tisch might have missed a trick or two along the way, but they had built a staggeringly large and profitable financial empire. But, as far as most of the public was concerned, the Tisches' business career really did not begin until 1986, when they took control of CBS.

CBS was a troubled firm. The once-proud network, which had been founded by William S. Paley* in the 1920s had lost its way. In 1985–1986, it was jolted when NBC replaced it as the number-one network in the ratings. After having led for twenty-five of the past thirty years, this sag in popularity hit CBS's advertising revenues; and profits, which had been $408 million in 1984, dipped to $360 million the following year. Even worse, Senator Jesse Helms in early 1985 announced that his right-wing group, Fairness in Media, was planning to start a proxy fight for control of CBS to overcome the network's "liberal bias." Helms boasted he wanted to become "Dan Rather's boss." Larry Tisch, a centrist Democrat of long standing, who was also a liberal contributor to Jewish causes, was concerned about the impact the Helms attempt might have on the network's treatment of Israel in its broadcasts.

It is not clear just who contacted whom (Tisch says that Thomas Wyman, CEO of CBS, "came up to see me about some of his problems," while Wyman says that Tisch came to him out of concern over CBS's continued independence on such issues as "civil rights, Israel, and South Africa"); in any event, Tisch bought 5 percent of CBS' stock. Tisch was to be what is called a "white squire" in the investment community; that is, someone who takes a large position in a threatened company's stock to prevent acquisition by a hostile suitor. Tisch soon increased his holdings to 24.9 percent, buying his stock at an average of $127 a share, a price that would later prove to be a bargain. Tisch did not buy any more stock, because at 25 percent Wyman's lucrative and expensive "golden parachute" provisions came into play. But Tisch, Wyman, and other CBS directors experienced a state of siege over the next year or so.

In April 1985, the feared corporate raider Ivan Boesky purchased 8.7 percent of CBS. Wyman and CBS took Boesky to court for alleged violation of securities laws, and they settled out of court when Boesky agreed to reduce his holdings to 4.3 percent. In the meantime, however, Ted Turner,[†] the Atlanta cable television and superstation entrepreneur, announced his plans to obtain a controlling interest in CBS by using probably the "junkiest" junk-bond financing ever devised. That, too, was beaten off by Wyman, and in October 1985, he offered Tisch a seat on the board of directors, better to fight off the unwanted suitors. In March 1986, Marvin Davis,[†] the Denver oilman and head of Twentieth Century-Fox, made a $3.75 bid for CBS, which the board rejected. All of this activity greatly increased CBS' debt load.

Then, Tisch announced that he intended to oust Wyman from control of CBS and take over the company himself. The white squire had become a raider. Wyman, in a panic, tried to sell CBS to any bidder he could find. He tried Coca-Cola, Philip Morris, and Westinghouse, among others. One source said, "The whole thing smacked of desperation." Paley had announced he was supporting Tisch, and since he and Tisch together controlled 33 percent of CBS' stock, under New York State law, it meant they had enough to block any sale. Even worse, Wyman's attempt to sell CBS to Coca-Cola, without even consulting the rest of the board, destroyed much of his former support on the board. As a result, on September 10, 1986 they asked for Wyman's resignation, and Larry Tisch was asked to serve as temporary CEO. One of the first things Tisch did was to fire CBS News Division president Van Gordon Sauter, a close ally of Wyman's who had been under increasing attack from his own division. That was Tisch's last popular move for a long, long time.

When Larry Tisch took over CBS, the questions began: "What does he want with CBS? What will happen to the network?" "Would this money machine change a hallowed American institution beyond recognition?" Tisch hastened to assure them that he would not. "I'm really wearing two hats," he told *Time*. "My first obligation is to do what's best for the network and to ensure quality programming. My secondary role is as a businessman to manage the company in a way that is right for the stockholders." But many skeptics felt that pious intonations of "public trust" were just the necessary platitudes that went with Tisch's new position. They warned that once Tisch got rolling, he would be a ruthlessly efficient businessman who would not care about traditions. After all, just that spring, Tisch had sold off Loews' chain of movie theaters. What did that say about tradition?

The company Tisch took over was rich in tradition, and poor in management. As *Manhattan, Inc.,* commented, "Paley created an empire devoted to culture—both popular ("I Love Lucy") and elite (the New York Philharmonic on CBS). The founder's aesthetic . . . influenced the entire American corporate culture. . . . Whether or not CBS really was 'the Tiffany network,' it certainly had the right packaging." It was composed of the network, which itself was composed of the news, entertainment, and sports divisions. It had CBS Records, a division Paley himself had created in the 1920s. And it had a large publishing division, composed of book publishing with Holt, Rinehart & Winston and W. B. Saunders, and a large magazine publishing operation that included *Woman's Day, Field and Stream, Yachting,* and a number of others.

But this glorious empire, "America's tastemaker," had fallen on hard times. The great profitability of the three major television networks for years had depended on their comfortable oligopoly status. Although they competed with one another for ratings, it was a cozy battlefield, and one in which there was plenty of room for all to profit. Even ABC, the perennially third ranked network most of these years, made nice profits. But in the late 1970s and early 1980s, cable television and a burgeoning number of independent stations created what were referred to as a fourth and fifth network, and greatly increased the competition for ad revenues. This was exacerbated by the fact that, to cope with inflation, the networks from 1975 to 1985 increased the average number of commercials per week on the airwaves from 3,500 to 5,100. Soon, advertisers were complaining about "network clutter," and began shopping for alternatives. These alternatives were cable and independent networks like that of Fox, Incorporated and Turner Broadcasting. In 1979–1980, network television reached 90 percent of American homes; by 1985 it had dropped to 76 percent. In addition, they also had to face the challenge of videocassettes and a revived movie industry. Things were not good in the television industry.

In response to these industry changes, both ABC and NBC were taken over by concerns that wanted a bigger chunk of the communications industry. In January 1986, Capital Cities Communication acquired ABC for $3.5 billion, and in June, of that same year, General Electric took over RCA and its subsidiary, NBC, for $6.3 billion. Each of those networks under new management launched extensive austerity programs to recover profitability in an age of declining ad revenues. When Tisch took over CBS there was not much question that he would do the same; indeed, he had to do the same. The big question really was how would he go about it, and what would be spared the accountant's scalpel?

When Tisch joined the CBS board in October 1985, he was shocked when he toured the company's operations. To Tisch, *Manhattan, Inc.*, said, "CBS seemed more than fat; it seemed as if it were a self-contained society, a pampered university, or some Skinneresque version of corporate utopia." There were layers of management that boggled Tisch—"What do they all do?"—he inquired of an associate. Almost immediately he began slashing what he perceived as fat at CBS. The procedure soon became known as "Tisching," as "nonessential jobs" were eliminated in every department. Tisch had often done this before—at Loews, at Lorillard, and at CNA. In each case, he had taken an old, overstaffed, nearly catatonic corporation and made it a profit maker. A lot of the cutting— in public relations people, investor relations staff, security guards, medical staff, librarians, researchers, and gourmet chefs—was recognized by most observers as appropriate. All told, 1,000 people had been let go by the end of 1986. But would Tisch dare touch the crown jewel—the venerated News Division? That was the acid test.

Tisch had risen to power partially by exploiting the dissatisfactions of the news department. But as he began his cost-cutting crusade, many at CBS reminded him of the "Edward R. Murrow Traditions," traditions that had made CBS the premier news broadcaster for over forty years. Soon, some in the newsroom began muttering that they had "replaced the shah with the ayatollah." They began to feel they were right after Tisch traveled to CBS' foreign bureaus— the very heart of the "Murrow traditions"—and demanded that extensive cuts be made there. At the same time, he wanted a leaner, trimmer news operation at home. Then, on May 13, 1986, the hammer fell with a force heard 'round the world—on that day, Friday the 13th—"Black Friday"—about 200 people, 15 percent of the news division, were laid off. When Tisch was questioned about it, he sounded incredibly cruel and heartless: "A lot of these people are lucky to be laid off right now because there are other jobs available." Dan Rather, in an Op-Ed piece for the *New York Times* wondered publicly whether Tisch had not condemned the CBS news operation to mediocrity.

The firings set off a firestorm of reaction. The three networks and major newspapers pounced on the story. Again, Tisch was seen as callous in his response, "*The New York Times* is not going to run CBS News," he said. By early 1988, however, Tisch began to pour money back into the news division. *Business Week* was so surprised that they asked facetiously if "Larry Tisch [has] been visited by the ghost of Edward R. Murrow?" After having cut the News Division's budget by 10 percent in 1987, he increased it 27 percent in 1988. In addition to boosting the News Division, he emphasized developing hits for the network and poured more money into their development than had been spent in the past few years. Finally, he called for a stronger marketing approach, budgeting $1 million on advertising. Many of the news people, though, were not sure this largesse would last. "Whenever I think its safe to go in the water," said news president Howard Stringer, "I still see a dorsal fin out there." Most analysts felt that Tisch had not suddenly "got religion," but that he had no other choice. In the eighteen months since he had taken over, Tisch had sold off just about everything but the network itself. If he did not get that growing and making profits, then it meant he was just "cashing it out" after all. But more on that later.

While Larry Tisch was busy taking over CBS, his brother Bob found an important new job also. In the fall of 1986 he became the new postmaster general of the United States, a massive 700,000-person bureaucracy with deeply entrenched unions and a tradition of poor customer service. Bob, in large measure, did what he was brought in to do: he made important changes in the pace of automation, in the delivery of mail, and in customer service, all of which enhanced the reputation of the post office. Most important, he managed to negotiate a union contract that had eluded his predecessors for a dozen years. In May 1988, having achieved that, he resigned the position and returned to run Loews. Other Tisches were also filtering their way to the top. Larry's son Andrew runs the Bulova Watch division, and his brother is a vice president there. Another of Larry's four sons is a managing director at Salomon Brothers, and Tom runs an investment trust. Bob's son, Jonathon, is president of Loews Hotels. His brother Steve became a top-flight Hollywood producer.

Larry Tisch's primary strategy after taking over CBS, even more than the cost cutting, was divestiture—getting rid of the records, music, book and magazine publishing divisions. The first to go was the music publishing division, which was sold to SBK Entertainment World in November 1986 for $125 million. A month later, the book publishing division was spun off to Harcourt Brace Jovanovich for $500 million. Then, in October 1987, the magazine publishing operation was sold to Diamanids Communications for $650 million. The big prize, however, was the record division. CBS Records, almost as much as the News Division, was an important part of the CBS tradition. Tisch did not seem to care. In December 1986, he brought before the board a proposal to sell the record division, which at that time had Bruce Springsteen's live album riding at the top of the charts. Not long before, Tisch had said the records division was an "integral part of this company. It's been here a long time. It's got great management, it's got a great position in the industry, and we've certainly given no thought whatsoever to separating it from CBS." The board members, especially Paley, were stunned. Paley told reporters testily, "To start pulling [this company] apart now would be terrible. We fought other people to prevent that." The board voted against the sale. Several months later, Tisch came back with another offer for CBS Records, over $2 billion from Sony, the Japanese electronics manufacturer. The board resisted for a time, but Tisch reminded them of their obligations to the stockholders—and he, of course, was the largest stockholder. So, in January 1988, the records division was sold to Sony for $2 billion. Tisch had collected $3.75 billion for CBS' coffers, but many questioned the wisdom of his actions.

For one thing, it ruined Tisch's already deteriorating relations with the board. They, and many industry analysts, felt that selling the records division was a foolish move. At a time when most communications companies were seeking to broaden their offerings, to become larger players in the field, Tisch narrowed CBS' scope. Just when other companies were busy buying video companies, production studios, and record firms, Tisch pulled out. He had always achieved success by being a contrarian in the market—buying when others were selling, and selling when others were buying. One analyst said, "He is the essence of someone who buys straw hats in the dead of winter." But most experts were puzzled and concerned with his moves. One director said, "We're not happy. Tisch has dismantled the company in a piecemeal fashion, and it's too late to stop him. We've asked for a plan or a strategy. But it's not in his nature to lay out a strategy." The director ended his comments by saying, "We've got an accountant running a creative company."

Shortly after the board voted to sell the record division to Sony, its president Walter Yetnikoff, visited the eighty-six-year-old Paley at his home. *Business Week* recounted the meeting: "Sitting in his wheelchair, Paley talked about how he'd bought the record company in the 1930's, how it had recorded *My Fair Lady* and Isaac Stern, how it was a part of American culture. Paley's eyes filled with tears." *Manhattan, Inc.*, said of Tisch and CBS,

For a long time CBS was the best of networks. It put on the best shows and had the best news division. It was a prestigious, fun place to work, and, not coincidentally, it made more money than its competitors. That was and remains Paley's legacy. It's understandable if Larry Tisch tires of hearing about it. But hear about it he will unless he makes it his legacy too.

"Bottom-Line Larry" may have taken on more than he bargained for at CBS. (**B**. *Fortune*, January 1960, May 1971, November 24, 1986, January 5, 1987, October 24, 1988; *New York Times*, September 6, 1968; *Business Week*, April 12, 1969, July 25, 1988; *Forbes*, June 1, 1979, April 13, October 5, 1987, February 22, March 14, June 22, July 25, 1988; John Train, *The Money Masters*, 1980; *New York Times Magazine*, June 8, 1986; *New York*, September 1, December 26, 1986; *Newsweek*, September 15, September 22, November 24, 1986; *Time*, September 22, 1986; *Who's Who in America*, 1986–87; *Current Biography*, February 1987; *U.S. News & World Report*, July 6, 1987; *Manhattan, Inc.*, November 1987; Peter J. Boyer, *Who Killed CBS?*, 1988.)

TRUMP, DONALD JOHN (August 1946–   ). Real estate developer, financier, Trump Organization. Donald Trump is a phenomenon of the 1980s. A self-proclaimed billionaire deal maker, he has captured the attention of the nation's media like no businessman since Howard Hughes, Jr.* Barely a week goes by that his real estate deals, his mansions, his wife, his helicopter, his confrontations with political figures or with tenants in his buildings, do not make news. To top it all off, not only was a biography published about him in December 1987, but at about the same time he brought out his autobiography, which promptly soared to the top of the *New York Times* best-seller list, where it stayed for well over six months. Why such a fascination with Donald Trump? In 1988, after all, he was only the twenty-seventh largest real estate developer in the United States, not even the biggest in New York. In fact, he has built only three buildings in Manhattan. Nor, despite some highly publicized takeover attempts, did he rank with the great white sharks among corporate raiders, Thomas Boone Pickens[†] and Carl Icahn.[†] In fact, although Trump claimed to be worth more than $3 billion, neither *Fortune* nor *Forbes* thought he was worth even $1 billion in 1987.

Why, then, all the fuss about Donald Trump? He is a master at media hype, and he functions in the communications center of the world, New York City. As many have commented previously, a double in Yankee Stadium rates bigger headlines than a home run in Wrigley Field. And Trump has, in the words of *Fortune*, "simply seduced the media." Part of this seduction has derived from Trump's own sense of self-importance, his penchant for exaggeration. An equal part has come from the negative reactions of many elements in the media to Trump's vulgar self-aggrandizement. Jonathon Yardley in the *Washington Post* dismissed Trump as a parvenu who lacked taste. *Spy* magazine of New York, more bluntly, continually refers to Trump as a "short-fingered vulgarian." But in many respects, that was Trump's key and he knew it. America was hungry for heroes in the early 1980s, and he sold himself as the richest, brightest, smartest businessman in America to the media and the American people. Trump commented, "The man on the street, the little guy, digs the limo, the helicopter, the 727." He had become, as Julia Reed commented in *U.S. News & World Report*, "The populist billionaire whose tacky opulence makes him the hero they would all like to be."

Donald Trump was born with a silver spoon in his mouth. His father, Fred C. Trump, was a highly successful real estate developer in the New York boroughs and elsewhere. Fred Trump's father, a Swedish immigrant, and hard-drinking restaurant owner, died when Fred was eleven. As a consequence, Mrs. Trump had to take in work as a seamstress in order to make ends meet. It was a harsh, tough existence for them. Fred Trump became a carpenter; at the same time, he attended Pratt Institute in Brooklyn, where he studied mechanical drawing and blueprint reading. In 1923, when he was just eighteen, Fred Trump's mother signed legal documents to grant him permission to start his own construction company. Investing $4,000, Trump built a small one-family home in Queens, which at that time was developing as one of New York City's first suburban areas. Selling the house for $7,500, he used the profit to build two others. Before long, he was building the houses in batches of fifteen and twenty, all uniquely styled "modern" brick houses. Creating whole little communities with his clustered arrangement of homes, Fred Trump brought a higher quality home to the city's wage earners than had been available to them previously. The depression of the 1930s put a crimp in Fred Trump's plans, but in the middle of the decade, he shifted his attention to the lower end of the economic spectrum and built $3,900 houses in the East Flatbush section of Brooklyn. At about the same time, he got married and began to raise a family.

With the outbreak of World War II, Fred Trump had already built about 2,500 homes in the New York area; now he began to build housing for the military. At the end of the war, he returned his attention to the building of tasteful, private homes. At the same time, in 1946, his second son, Donald, was born. Fred Trump began building houses to appeal to the burgeoning suburban middle class in the postwar years, creating one- and two-family brick homes for from $9,500 to $12,500. But in 1948 Fred Trump changed his focus from single-family homes to apartment buildings. Receiving backing in the form of Federal Housing Administration loans, he built his first complex, the 1,400-unit Shore Haven Apartments in the Bensonhurst section of Brooklyn. Apartment buildings became Trump's major interest over the next few decades. By the late 1960s, he may have owned as many as 20,000 units in the metropolitan New York area.

Donald Trump grew up in luxury, but his father was determined that his children not be soft—he wanted them to be tough and competitive. "Life's a competition," Fred Trump told *New York Magazine*, "I brought my kids up in a competitive environment." Donald Trump responded in kind; he became the toughest and most competitive of the lot. "I used to fight back all the time," he said, "my father was one tough son-of-a-gun. My father respects me because I stood up to him." But Donald Trump was almost too tough, too independent. He attended Kew Forest School, a private school, and he was constantly in trouble with the teachers for minor infractions, most of which stemmed from his exuberance. Fred Trump determined that the boy "had to be reined in," and he enrolled him for high school in New York Military Academy at Croton-on-Hudson in 1959. There, according to the senior Trump, "they straightened him out real good." Donald Trump was an honor cadet three of his four years there, captain of the baseball team, and captain of a student regiment. His baseball coach remembered him as "a real leader."

In the meantime, Donald Trump came to live and breathe real estate. From the time he was a small boy, he loved trooping with his father over the construction sites, playing in the mud, driving nails into boards, and so forth. When he finished high school, Donald wanted to join his father's business and start a career in construction and real estate development, but Fred Trump insisted he go to college. Donald chose Fordham, which was nearby, but he soon found the Jesuit discipline intolerable; in mid-year he transferred to the University of Pennsylvania's Wharton School of Commerce, which he heard had a good real estate program. Here, Trump was bored because the real estate courses focused not on major projects, but on single-family homes, and he felt he had already learned more about that from his father. Donald did just enough to get by at Wharton, and he placed his major interest on Philadelphia real estate projects during his off-hours. Even then, a college friend remembered, "Donald always used to talk about changing the Manhattan skyline."

Trump graduated from Wharton in 1968, but did not even stay long enough for his class picture. Although he later told writers that he had contemplated going into the oil business, it is difficult to imagine that anything other than real estate had ever occupied his interest. He hurried back to New York and joined his father in the Trump Organization. Donald Trump was burning with ambition and vision, and although he admired his father very much, he felt he was too parochial in his plans. Other than his father, Donald Trump had a great hero, William Zeckendorf,* the flamboyant New York City real estate developer. Zeckendorf was not just a builder; he was a builder with style and flair. Fred Trump had been successful building ordinary homes and apartments for average people; Zeckendorf had dreamed grand dreams, and he was a showman as much as he was a businessman. He was, as Jerome Tucille has said, "the Mike Todd of the real estate world." Donald Trump worshipped Zeckendorf, and considered him his role model. So, as Donald Trump began playing a larger role in his father's business, he inevitably began to push him toward grander projects, especially to enter Manhattan. Fred Trump had built in all the boroughs except Manhattan. But that was where the action was, as far as Donald Trump was concerned. One building in Manhattan could get your name in the headlines; ten buildings in Brooklyn brought you anonymity.

Donald Trump first convinced his father to refinance the houses and apartment buildings the Trump Organization owned. Tens of millions of dollars were tied up in these properties, which had been mortgaged when the market price was much lower, and many had, in fact, been paid for in full. He urged that they be refinanced at from 90 to 100 percent of their current market value. Fred was unsure. This involved debt and risk, and the late 1960s were difficult times for the New York real estate market. But Donald convinced his father that the cash flow from the rents would pay the interest, and that since they already had all their money out of the buildings, they would lose nothing if they defaulted. So Fred Trump conceded, thereby freeing up an enormous pile of cash with which the Trumps could pursue further development.

"I gave Donald free rein," his father later said. "He has great vision and everything he touches seems to turn to gold. As long as he has this great energy in abundance, I'm glad to let him do it. He's the smartest person I know." With this new capital, Donald and his father built apartment buildings farther and farther afield—in Florida, California, Virginia, Maryland, and Washington, D.C. But Donald still could not convince his father to venture into Manhattan. By 1973, the Trump Organization owned apartments and houses worth about $200 million, and it was receiving rental income of about $50 million annually. The company's assets had grown 500 percent during the five years Donald had been working with his father, and much of this increase had been due to his daring.

In that same year, the Trump Organization was sued by the Justice Department for discriminating against blacks in its apartment rentals. Donald Trump came to the fore in this dispute, establishing his toughness and negotiating ability. He vehemently denied the charges, claiming that from 5 to 10 percent of their units were rented to blacks. What kept many blacks out of the Trump apartments was their refusal to rent to anyone on the welfare rolls. The Lefrak organization, run by Samuel Lefrak,* another large owner of apartments in New York, had been hit with similar charges, but caved in to government demands, agreeing to open up a certain percentage of units to people on welfare. Donald adamantly refused. Not only that, he filed a $100-million countersuit against the government and accused them of making "irresponsible and baseless charges against the realty company." This tactic—lawsuits—became a patented Trump business practice in later years. "He sues almost everybody," said an attorney for a tenants' organization. Trump explained, "You can't let people push you around." It is an extremely effective tactic. Although his suit against the government was thrown out by the judge as a "waste of time and paper," in 1974, it did accomplish its purpose. Donald still refused to rent to people on welfare, but he did agree to give the Union League a list of weekly vacancies, and to allow them to provide lists of qualified blacks for 20 percent of the units in certain buildings.

During this time, Donald Trump finally pushed his father into Manhattan development. They acquired a site on the East Side of Manhattan where they planned to build an apartment building. Neither the site nor the building was anything spectacular, and garnered no media attention. But it was a start. In 1975, everything began to come together for Donald Trump, and he slowly began to be recognized as a force to be reckoned with on the Manhattan real estate scene. What had opened the city for Trump's development schemes had

been several important political changes. Fred Trump had been stymied throughout the 1960s by the Lindsay administration, which had thwarted many of his
development proposals. In November 1973, however, Abraham Beame, a Democrat and close ally of the Trumps, was elected mayor of New York. This
resulted in a more sympathetic ear for their proposals at City Hall. To operate
on an expanded level, however, they required financial support from the federal
government, whose funds were largely administered through the state. There,
again, the Nelson Rockefeller and Malcomb Wilson Republican administrations
had not been kind to the Trumps. Thus, in 1974, they supported Hugh Carey,
the Democratic candidate, who won the election handily. Now both the city and
the state governments were in the hands of individuals and parties who had
received a great deal of campaign money from the Trumps, and with whom they
had cordial relations. To put the icing on the cake, Donald hired Louise Sunshine,
the former chairman of Carey's finance committee, and treasurer of the state
Democratic party, as a key member of the Trump Organization. They were ready
to roll.

Donald, just twenty-eight years old in the spring of 1975, acquired options
on two huge tracts of Manhattan real estate owned by the Penn Central Transportation Company. Penn Central at that time was bankrupt, and badly in need
of cash. Trump acquired the parcels for $62 million, but did not have to put up
a cent of cash. Under the terms of the deal, the payments were due in installments
as the land was developed. It was a masterstroke—Trump now controlled two
of the largest undeveloped properties in Manhattan—and he had not had to put
up any cash for them. Other developers were beginning to take notice of this
brash, boastful, young man. But he was hardly done. A few months later, in
partnership with the Hyatt hotel chain, he purchased the money-losing fifty-nine-
year-old Commodore Hotel from Penn Central. Located next to Grand Central
Terminal on 42nd Street, it was one of Manhattan's choicest properties—and
Trump got it for $10 million. Of this amount, $6 million went to the city for
back taxes. Penn Central did two deals with Trump, gave up some of their best
land holdings, and came up with $4 million in cash, along with a lot of promises
of riches in the future.

Fred Trump had opposed the purchase of the Commodore. "This is like trying
to buy a ticket on the Titanic," he told Donald. But Donald did not listen. He
sold the Commodore to the Urban Development Corporation (UDC) for $1 so
they could use the UDC's condemnation powers to evict holdout tenants. The
UDC then leased it back to Trump and Hyatt for ninety-nine years. The real key
to the deal, however, was a forty-year abatement on real estate taxes that Donald
had secured from City Hall. Although Trump agreed to pay the city amounts
that would escalate from $250,000 annually to $2,775,000 in lieu of taxes, the
deal ultimately could amount to a $400-million profit for Trump, and a corre-
sponding loss for the city. Critics pounced on the agreement, and Trump, for
the first time, became notorious in the city. To be fair, Trump had vision in
1975. New York City was teetering on the brink of bankruptcy, real estate prices

were severely depressed, and most developers were abstaining from building, fearing a major depression was near at hand. Donald Trump had faith in the city, and he had vision—as a result, he was able to negotiate an exceptionally lucrative set of deals with Penn Central, and the city and state governments. A short time later, the Commodore was torn down, and in its place rose the magnificent Grand Hyatt, which opened in 1980, just as New York began booming again. Room prices, which had been $35 a night in the late 1970s, were $175 for the cheapest room at the Hyatt in 1987, and that was with the corporate discount. Some people in New York began calling Trump the " William Zeckendorf of bad times." It must have given him no end of pleasure.

By 1976, people were beginning to refer to Donald Trump as the "boy wonder." And Trump did not disappoint them. It soon became clear what he wanted to do with the Penn Central parcels. He proposed that the city build its new convention center there. At that time, the city and state were considering two different locations. All of a sudden, Trump, with Louise Sunshine, went to work on city and state officials. Ultimately, they were successful in getting them to agree to build the New York convention center on Trump's land. The lands were purchased for $12 million, and for his efforts in this deal Trump got a $500,000 commission, plus $88,000 in expenses. He later claimed he would have dispensed with the commission if officials had agreed to name the convention center after his father. Peter Solomon, who was then deputy mayor for economic development, said, "What really got me was his bravado. I think it was fantastic. It was unbelievable. He almost got us to name the convention center after his father in return for something he never really had to give away."

By this point, Donald Trump had become a major player in the city's real estate and political circles, and his next deal, for Trump Tower, displayed his talents for negotiation and self-aggrandizement in full flower. Trump was convinced that the three cardinal rules of real estate were "location, location, location." Further, Trump said that "if you go to Paris, if you go to Duluth, the best location is called the 'Tiffany location.' That is the standard real estate phrase." What, then, could be more ideal for the location of a luxury apartment building than next door to the real Tiffany's store in New York? Louise Sunshine introduced Trump to David Evins, a powerful Carey supporter, and a major stockholder in Genesco, which owned Bonwit Teller, a department store next to Tiffany's. Bonwit Teller leased the land from the Equitable Life Assurance Company, and had turned down several other offers for the lease. But it accepted Trump's offer. He then lined up the necessary credit from Chase Manhattan Bank and worked out a "roughly fifty-fifty partnership" with Equitable, which also provided mortgage financing.

With those elements in place, Trump turned to the city for a tax abatement for the luxury condominiums he planned to build there. The city turned him down, claiming the abatement was not to be used for luxury units. At that point, Roy Cohn, Trump's attorney and friend, appealed the case to the courts, and the state Supreme Court Appellate Division awarded Trump a $50-million tax abatement. Many city officials and members of the media were upset over what appeared to be another example of Trump favoritism. Sentiment was building against Trump, whom many viewed as an arrogant bully. One of the concerns that arose as he made plans to demolish the Bonwit Teller buildings related to the art deco frieze and ornate grillwork. These had long been admired, and many city groups requested their preservation. Trump offered to contribute them to the Metropolitan Museum of Art, but when he found that it would take too much time and cost too much money, he simply had them demolished. There was a tremendous outcry over this, but Trump dismissed the artwork as "junk." For Trump, the outcry provided free publicity. Overnight, famous celebrities and wealthy individuals were calling for apartments. Before the condominiums even opened, Sophia Loren, Johnny Carson, David Merrick, and King Khalid of Saudi Arabia had purchased multimillion dollar suites. Trump boasted that prices climbed as high as $1,400 a square foot.

Trump Tower, at fifty-eight storeys when it opened in 1982, was the tallest and most expensive reinforced concrete structure in the city. It was a glittering spectacle of glass, brass, and marble. The first building to bear the Trump name, it was also Donald's first exercise in self-indulgence. When a writer from the *New Yorker* visited Trump Tower soon after it opened, he said, "Inside, the first thing we noticed was two thick and highly polished bronze T's, about four feet high, close together but not aligned." There were 263 condominiums in the building, priced from $600,000 to $10 million each. And Trump sold them with ease. The condos were sold for $277 million, which paid off the mortgage and provided a tidy profit; and six levels of retail space and thirteen floors of offices remained to be rented. The annual rents for the retail outlets, which include some of the most prestigious and priciest stores in the city, ran as high as $1 million.

It was Trump Tower that made Donald Trump a media celebrity of the first order. Trump Tower, is, for example, the only building constructed in lower Manhattan in the past decade that has become a tourist attraction. Part of the reason for this was the building's staggering, some said, overstated, opulence. With cascading waterfalls, a lobby of Breccia Perniche marble, and all the other acoutrements, it was a natural attraction for those who wished to see how "the other half lived." But much of its prominence and popularity stemmed from the Trump name itself, and he engaged shamelessly in exaggeration and self-promotion about the building. The apartments, according to Trump, are "[t]he finest apartments, in the top building in the best location in the hottest city in the world." This manner of hyperbole, which came to be known as "Trump-speak," was highly effective. Increasingly, Trump came to be known as the "P. T. Barnum of real estate." *Newsweek* (September 28, 1987) believed this was one of the keys to his success: "Trump has created one of the most profitable public empires in the most public of fashions. His high profile, in fact, has been central to his success. 'The aura of the Trump name . . . is a big asset.' 'For the new rich,' says a New York real-estate broker, the name is 'synonymous with status.' ''

When Trump Tower opened, Trump turned reflective for a moment, ''I'll be thirty-six years old when Trump Tower opens, and I'll have done everything I can do, and sometimes I think, maybe it was a mistake to have raced through it all so fast.'' But Trump was hardly finished or even ready to slow down. If anything, his pace of acquisition and accomplishment over the next five years became even more frenetic. He had bought the Barbizon-Plaza Hotel and an adjacent apartment building in 1980 for just $13 million. Two months later, he took out a mortgage on it for $65 million, and five years later the property had increased tenfold in value. One rival developer said, ''Donald has the uncanny ability to smell blood in the water.'' During this same period, he was also building Trump Plaza in New York, a cooperative apartment complex with a celebrity clientele. It cost $125 million, but most observers felt he had gotten his money back on it before the building ever opened, so everything earned subsequently was pure profit.

With success, however, came increasing criticism of Trump and his methods. One of his more publicized forays came in 1982, when, during a rent dispute with tenants of a building he owned on Central Park South, Trump offered to shelter some of the city's homeless in the vacant apartments. Trump's problem with the building was that it was filled with people living in apartments covered by New York's rent-control laws. He wanted them to move so that he could redevelop the building. So, he tried to make life unpleasant for them. Besides offering to shelter the homeless there, Trump had the windows of empty apartments covered with tin to make the building look more run-down. When the tenants filed suit against Trump, he countersued, using laws usually reserved for prosecuting organized crime. His action, however, was thrown out by the judge, who termed it ''ridiculous.''

It was not just Trump's tenants who were critical of him. Others in New York viewed Trump as a reincarnation of Citizen Kane; *Newsweek* (September 28, 1987) even ran a feature story on him called ''Citizen Trump.'' Citizen Kane was, according to *Newsweek*, ''an arrogant tycoon whose insatiable ambition leads him to seek political power.'' An episode which fed fears that Trump had political ambitions concerned an ice skating rink in Central Park, of all things. The city had been trying since 1980 to repair the rink without success. When Trump in 1986 read a short article in the paper about yet another failure to repair it, he decided to step into the breech. He wrote to Mayor Ed Koch, and promised to complete the rink in six months. And he did—he brought it in a month before the deadline, and $750,000 under budget. When Trump then ''trumpeted'' his success, to the embarrassment of city officials, Koch struck back. ''Donald Trump has gotten a lot of wonderful publicity for not a lot of money,'' he said. He then challenged Trump to open up his pocketbook and provide housing for the homeless. From that point on, Trump insulted Koch every chance he got, and Koch returned the insults in kind. The apex of all of this came in 1987, when Gary Trudeau, creator of the "Doonesbury" comic strip, featured Trump testing the waters as a presidential candidate. In response, Trump said, "I'm not running for president, but if I did . . . I'd win. There, I said it. I didn't think I would, but I did."

Nor is Trump immune from criticism from other developers. "He's incredibly arrogant, the epitome of egotism," said one broker. "He comes into a meeting and takes over like he's king." Another developer said that Trump "does business through intimidation. It's bravado and shock. Intimidate until they collapse. Ask for the moon and you will get something." Trump saw it differently, "If people are fair to me, I'm fair to them. If people screw me, I screw them back in spades."

The bitterness between Koch and Trump reached epic proportions in the summer of 1987. In November 1985, Trump had announced plans to erect a 150-storied tower, to be the tallest building in the world, as a centerpiece of a city within a city called Television City. Meant to contain apartment buildings, shopping centers, and television studios, it would have 8,000 apartments, 1.7 million square feet of retail space, forty acres of parks and open spaces, and more than 3 million square feet for television studios, offices, and technical areas. The major participant in this new enterprise was expected to be NBC. Almost from the instant he announced the plan, Trump met with a firestorm of opposition from local community groups. The whole project ground to a standstill for about two years. When NBC that year threatened to join other corporations in an exodus from New York, Trump offered to sell his $95-million parcel of land to the city for $1, with the understanding that he would lease back the property for ninety-nine years. In addition, his Television City project would be converted to a state project that would not be subject to New York City taxes or zoning review. NBC, the key tenant, would then be given extremely favorable terms to locate there. Koch turned down the proposal. Trump revised it, and Koch turned it down again. At that point, Trump called Koch's response "ludicrous and disgraceful," and he called the mayor a "moron." The mayor then characterized Trump's request for a tax abatement as "piggy, piggy, piggy," and the two continued to hurl insults at each other over the next several months. In the meantime, the Television City project remained stalled.

But Trump was not stalled permanently. In 1984 Trump had tackled Atlantic City, New Jersey, and had become the largest casino and hotel owner in the gambling mecca almost overnight. Trump properties at the beginning of 1984 were worth just over $1 billion. During that year he increased their value by almost 50 percent. In 1982, Trump had obtained a casino license in New Jersey. At the same time, he sent a number of people to Atlantic City to buy up parcels of land for future development. In his first casino, to be called Harrah's Trump Plaza, Trump went into partnership with Holiday Inn Corporation in a fifty-fifty venture. In May 1984, the casino opened to great fanfare, but within six months, Trump and Holiday Inn were at each other's throats. The casino was not doing nearly as well as Trump had hoped, and he blamed it on Holiday Inn/Harrah's association with low-budget gamblers and slot machines. Ultimately, Harrah's name was removed from the casino and it became known as Trump Plaza Casino Hotel. With 614 rooms, seven restaurants, a health club, a 750-seat showroom, and a 60,000-square-foot casino floor with 123 gaming tables and 1,734 slot machines crammed into a 2.6-acre tract, it was Atlantic City's tenth casino. In 1985, Trump made a deal with the Hilton Hotel chain to buy its nearly finished hotel casino. He paid $325 million for it, and promptly renamed it Trump Castle. The name was chosen, an associate said, because "Mr. Trump felt that Castle was the most appropriate name for such a beautiful, vast and majestic facility. The name 'Trump Castle' gives us a distinct identity yet benefits from the strength of the success of Trump's name on the Boardwalk." Holiday Inn thought otherwise, and sued Trump for using the Trump name on his new casino. The case went to trial, and Trump emerged victorious.

Then, in 1987, Trump bid $100 million for Resorts International, which owned one casino in Atlantic City, was building another enormous casino there, and had casino holdings in the Caribbean. Forced to sell because of the sudden death of its founder, James Crosby, Resorts was in a bind, and Trump knew it. Buying up the Class-B voting shares in the company, Trump gained control of Resorts for a relatively small cash outlay. Then he was ambushed by an ex-band singer, Merv Griffin[†] who had made a fortune developing game shows. Griffin decided to buy up the Class-A, nonvoting shares in Resorts, with the intention of taking over the company. After months of tense, heated negotiations, Trump finally agreed to sell Resorts to Griffin. Griffin agreed to pay $200 million to holders of Resorts' Class-A stock, and $100 million to Trump for his Class-B stock. Then, Trump agreed to pay Griffin $230 million for the new 1,250-room hotel casino (called the Taj Mahal) that Resorts was building in Atlantic City. Griffin got control of the existing Resorts' casino and other properties in Atlantic City, plus the Paradise Island operations in the Bahamas. It was a surprising development, and many felt it was the first time Trump had ever been bested in a deal, but he still became the largest casino operator in Atlantic City as a result of it. His 1988 projected cash flow in Atlantic City was for over $150 million, and he said, "I'm breaking every record in the history of Atlantic City."

Trump's latest coup involved the purchase of the Eastern Shuttle service from Eastern Airlines and Texas Air Corporation. Francisco Anthony "Frank" Lorenzo,[†] who had battled Eastern's unions for years, and who was trying to find a way to stem staggering losses at the airline, agreed to sell the lucrative New York–Washington shuttle service to Trump for $365 million. Trump, of course, announced that he would call it Trump Air, and that his name would be emblazoned on each plane's tail fin. For his purchase, Trump got seventeen Boeing 727s that had earned Eastern over $20 million on the shuttle route in 1987. Eastern's unions announced they would challenge the deal in the courts, but Trump was undaunted.

When Trump's semiautobiographical *The Art of the Deal* came out in 1987, it was roundly criticized and satirized by most of the business press and other elements of the media. Nonetheless, it became an overnight best-seller, and it remained so for months on end. Sydney Schanberg of New York's *Newsday* said that his autobiography should be entitled "The Self-Importance of Being Donald," and said further, "Imagine what his official biography will say when he grows up." Gary Belis, reviewing Trump's book for *Fortune*, paraphrased Joseph Mankiewicz's line for Orson Welles, and applied it to Trump: "There, but for the grace of God, goes God." William Thorsell, in the *Toronto Globe & Mail* said, "All this suggests a man oddly insecure in his own right, driven toward money and attention, not by instinct, but by needs he will neither acknowledge nor confront." Perhaps the second volume of his autobiography should be entitled, "Donald Trump: A Legend in His Own Mind." (**A.** Donald J. Trump and Tony Schwartz, *The Art of the Deal*, 1987. **B.** *New York Times*, November 1, 1976, August 26, 1980, August 7, 1983, April 8, 1984; *New York Daily News Magazine*, August 10, 1980; *New York*, May 19, November 17, 1980; *New York*, October 10, 1983; *Current Biography*, 1984; *New York Times Magazine*, April 8, 1984; *Barron's*, August 6, 1984; *Manhattan, Inc.*, September, November 1984, September 1988; *Business Week*, July 22, 1985, November 4, 1986, February 29, 1988; *Forbes*. October 28, 1985, October 24, 1988; *Fortune*, December 23, 1985, January 4, September 12, 1988; Ovid Demaris, *The Boardwalk Jungle*, 1986; Jerome Tuccille, *Trump*, 1987; Toronto *Globe & Mail*, March 10, 1987, May 12, October 12, October 14, 1988; Toronto *Globe & Mail, Report on Business*, June 1987, June 1988; *Newsweek*, June 29, July 20, September 28, 1987; *People Weekly*, December 7, 1987, December 28, 1987, January 4, 1988; *Los Angeles Times*, May 28, 1988; *Toronto Star*, June 5, 1988.)

TURNER, ROBERT EDWARD "TED" (November 19, 1938–). Broadcasting and media executive, Turner Communications, Atlanta Braves. In May 1980, Ted Turner made the cover of *Success* magazine. He later recalled holding the magazine to the sky and saying to his dead father, "Well, Dad, is this enough?" He has now been on the cover of more than fifty magazines, including *Time, Newsweek*, the *Saturday Evening Post*, and *Sports Illustrated*. But was it ever enough? It never seemed to be. Turner, a driven man, took over his father's failing outdoor-advertising company shortly after his father had committed suicide, and he built it into a billion-dollar media empire. In the process, he became a rather quixotic American folk hero. Known as the "Mouth from the South" and the "Mouth that Roared," Turner was disdained by older elites, especially after he took yachting's most prestigious trophy away from them. But what made him persona non grata to the establishment made Turner attractive to the average man. Turner broke the rules, he thumbed his nose at the rule makers—and he got away with it. According to *Barron's*, Turner "was the boy-hero of a movie by Spielberg or Disney, the child who breaks all the adult's rules, and, in the end, proves himself right." But Turner might have taken one step too many. In 1988, the walls were closing in, and no one, Turner included, seemed to know what the future would bring.

Turner was born in Cincinnati, Ohio, the son of Ed Turner, a native of Mississippi who became a salesman after his family lost their cotton farm during the depression. Turner's father was a stern disciplinarian, but, nevertheless, Ted was a mischievous child with a great deal of energy. The elder Turner, however, had a method in his discipline. Ted Turner's first wife said, "He wanted Ted to be insecure, because he felt that insecurity breeds greatness. If Ted was insecure then he would be forced to compete." This may have also accounted for Turner's seeming sense of insecurity during his business career, and his need to continually prove himself to his deceased father.

Turner was educated in the public schools of Cincinnati until he was nine, when the family moved to Savannah, Georgia. Ed Turner had bought an outdoor-advertising company there (Turner Advertising Company), and Ted went to school in Savannah and worked full time for his father in the summers, cutting grass and creosoting poles. He made $50 a week, and his father charged him $25 a week for room and board. When Ted complained, his father told him that if he could find cheaper accommodations, he should take them. During high school, Turner attended the George Military Academy near Atlanta and the McCallie School near Chattanooga, Tennessee. He hated the latter school, where he earned the nickname "Terrible Ted." He did, however, become a champion debater there, and after graduating he enrolled at Brown University. His father wanted Ted to prepare for a business career there, but instead he first majored in classics. Under unrelenting pressure from his father, Turner finally switched to economics. At Brown, Turner continued to excel at debating, and he also became an expert sailor.

Turner's love of sailing brought another conflict with his father. One year, while he was at Brown, the Noroton Yacht Club in Connecticut offered Ted a job for the summer, with the chance to race Lightning boats, but Ed Turner insisted Ted return to Savannah to work in the family business. Turner gave in, and became an account executive for the firm. At about the same time, Turner's parents were involved in divorce proceedings, and it was a difficult time for him all around. He reacted by becoming a reincarnation of "Terrible Ted" at Brown, getting drunk, engaging in rowdy pranks, and getting suspended from college. At that point, Ed Turner sent his son on a six-month tour of duty with the Coast Guard. Ted then returned to Brown, but he was caught in a woman's dorm room and expelled for the final time.

Turner served with the Coast Guard again that summer, and then he joined Turner Advertising as general manager of the Macon, Georgia, branch in 1960. Several years later, his father purchased The General Outdoor Advertising Company, in Atlanta, the largest firm of its kind in America. When Ed Turner became overextended, in early 1963, he committed suicide with a pistol in the bedroom of the Turner plantation in South Carolina. Just before his suicide, Ed Turner and his son had argued strenuously over the father's plans to sell the family enterprise. Upon his father's death, Ted Turner halted the proposed sale of the family business and, instead, sold off their two plantations in South Carolina and Georgia to help pay real estate taxes. With what was left over, Turner tackled the advertising company's problems with tremendous zeal and energy. As president and chief executive officer, Turner had transformed them into highly profitable entities by 1970.

Up to that point, Ted Turner had been aggressive, but conventional. He had created a solid, substantial business out of the debt-laden hulk he had inherited. But Turner could never be satisfied with what others might view as conventional success. He had larger dreams and grander visions. And he had to show his father his true mettle. So in 1970, over the loud protests of his financial advisors, Turner bought the financially troubled WTCG-Channel 17, an independent Atlanta-based UHF station, for $3 million. The station was losing $50,000 a month, but even that was not a big enough gamble. Shortly afterward, Turner also bought Channel 36 in Charlotte, North Carolina, which was losing $30,000 a month and was bankrupt. This was a tremendous, nearly foolhardy risk. Will Saunders, a Turner Broadcasting executive, recalled,

It could have sunk our ass, that TV business. We were really in it. Our purchase contract included all the debts. There was no way to cut it loose if it didn't work. We all said he was crazy, but Ted is an incredible salesman and debater. . . . That and the fact that he is in control overwhelms you. (*Esquire*)

At the end of the first year Turner had lost $2 million. Only his substantial billboard revenues kept the company afloat. The key to survival in the early years was in Atlanta. At the time, there were two independent television stations in the city, and everyone knew that only one could survive. The question was whether it would be Turner's Channel 17 or the station owned by U.S. Communications. By the spring of 1971, Turner had sunk every dollar he had into the Atlanta station, and it was still running fifth among five stations in the city. Then, without warning, the other independent station folded, and Turner had the independent field to himself. It was the big breakthrough. Turner juggled the station's format and began to run a steady diet of syndicated situation comedies, old movies, and local sporting events. The formula worked; Channel 17 soon had 16 percent of the viewing market. By 1973, Turner's station was one of the first independents to show a substantial profit.

The road to success had a number of important milestones for Turner. One of his first big breaks came when the local ABC affiliate was forced by the network to pick up the 6 P.M. network news, which they had not been running. About 25 percent of the audience does not watch the news, so Turner scheduled "Star Trek" to run at 6 P.M., and immediately he garnered high ratings. Turner himself personally selected the station's movies and sitcoms, choosing lighthearted fare. "We're essentially an escapist station," he said. "I felt the people of Atlanta were entitled to something different than a whole lot of police and crime shows with murders and rapes going on all over the place." Nor did he run much news; he restricted the station to the forty minutes per day mandated by the Federal Communications Commission (FCC).

Another big break for Turner came when WSB-TV, Atlanta's NBC affiliate, and then the city's top station, refused to pick up five network shows. Turner immediately bought them and ran ads on his billboards all over town: "The NBC network moves to Channel 17." This move also garnered Turner a great deal of free publicity in the newspapers, and it increased the visibility of Channel 17. At about the same time, Turner shelled out $2.5 million for the television rights to broadcast the Atlanta Braves baseball games for five years. "Signing the Braves did a lot for our image," said a Turner executive. "It changed our image from that of a kiddy station. It forced people to tune us in." At about the same time, Turner brought wrestling to Channel 17. At that time, stations were almost embarrassed to run wrestling programs, which were often associated with television's infant days in the early 1950s. But there was a huge potential audience out there, and it increased as the years went on. "There is no prestige to wrestling," said Garry Hogan, sales manager at Channel 17. "But you can't beat it as a rating success. It has more viewers than football or the Braves or the Hawks."

Throughout all this, however, Turner was increasingly interested in the possibilities of cable television (CATV). UHF stations had notoriously weak signals and were hard to tune in on normal television sets. It was obvious to Turner that cable could increase his station's reception. Until 1975, however, FCC regulations severely limited the access of independent stations to the cumbersome common-carrier cable systems. In that year, two important events occurred. The first was the launching of RCA's first American satellite (SAT COM I). The satellite had been originally planned for telephone purposes, but in the fall of 1975 Home Box Office (HBO), a subscriber movie service owned by Time, Incorporated, was the first to use the satellite to beam its programs back to earth stations around the country. With the relaxation of the FCC's restrictions, Turner's Channel 17 was also allowed to use the satellite, and eight days before Christmas, 1976, Turner joined HBO in space. Beaming its signal to the satellite, Channel 17 was able to reach more than two million homes in forty-seven states, and he added about 50,000 homes a month. With an audience of this size, Turner was able to attract national advertisers, and his station was soon worth $40 million.

Realizing that he needed some attractions that transcended old movies and sitcoms, which local independent stations were running anyway, Turner in 1976 bought the Atlanta Braves, guaranteeing that he would always be able to air their games on his new superstation. Billing them as "America's Team," Turner tied promotions around their appeal. To provide a similar appeal in the winter months, he bought the Atlanta Hawks, of the National Basketball Association, in 1976. He also purchased the broadcast rights to the Atlanta Flames, of the National Hockey League. He acquired the rights to over 2,700 old movies and to many old television shows, as a means to fill the airways twenty-four hours a day, seven days a week. In 1979, the programming was expanded to include news, special events, prime-time adult programs, and children's shows.

Soon, Turner's superstation was reaching into the remotest corners of North America. *Maclean's* magazine in Canada told of the tiny mining town of Faro, 220 miles north of Whitehorse in the frozen Yukon. For years, the 1,600 residents of the town had been dependent upon the Canadian cultural offerings of the state-owned Canadian Broadcasting Corporation. With the advent of cable, they could get Turner's station, and it became hugely popular. *Maclean's* commented, "It's hardly surprising that at the end of an eight-hour shift mining lead and zinc, when it's–48 [degrees] C outside, the labourers prefer 'I Love Lucy' to the Toronto symphony or a documentary on weaving." Even though it was illegal in Canada to bring in Turner's signal, since the government feared its impact on Canadian culture, they turned a blind eye to the situation in Faro because of its popularity.

By 1980, Turner had made himself a force to be reckoned with in national television, but he had made few friends among the media moguls. With his brash and antagonistic style, he had repeatedly criticized network television offerings over the years, calling them "crappy programs." Thus, when Turner announced in June 1980, that he was introducing the Cable News Network (CNN), a twenty-four-hour commercial information enterprise, the networks were derisive. After all, Turner's stations had hardly paid any attention to the news in the past, and they were going to try tackling "national" news, the sort of stuff the Edward R. Murrow–inspired legions of newsmen at the major networks had a lock on. Finally, everybody knew there was no money in the news; it was a public service, run grudgingly by the networks and affiliated stations to prove their "public service" commitment to the FCC. Turner was going to run news, twenty-four hours a day, with nonnetwork news personnel, and he was expecting to make a profit? What a joke this was going to be! Mike Dann, program advisor at ABC commented, "The days of Turner's clear sailing are over."

The first three years were terrible for CNN. It lost oceans of money; ultimately, it carried a $24-million working deficit before Turner was able to convince Manufacturers Hanover Trust Company and Citicorp to loan TBS $50 million for three years. To get the loan, Turner had to pay three points over prime (a $3-million fee) and tie up TBS' advertising accounts receivable for three years. It was a huge risk, but it indicated Turner's single-minded commitment to the enterprise. By 1983, the risk was beginning to pay off. In that year CNN was being piped into 26 million households, which amounted to 71 percent of all homes with cable, and 30 percent of all homes with television. Another service, CNN Headline News, had 10 million homes after buying out Satellite News Channel owned by ABC and Westinghouse. Turner gloated over the victory: "On a level playing field, ABC and Group W got their brains kicked out; and they had resources at least 100 times of ours."

Most galling to the networks, however, was that CNN was successful because it was good, not because it adopted some nitwit "happy news" framework.

During the presidential campaign and the conventions in 1984, CNN, because of its twenty-four-hour framework, was able to give extensive coverage to nearly every aspect. Veteran television and political observers were impressed. Walter Cronkite told *USA Today*, "I've been watching CNN during this convention, and to a political buff it's fascinating because you're getting all the issues, even the less important ones." Other print media concurred. The *Los Angeles Times* wrote, "When it came to *real* news, ABC, CBS, and NBC largely stiffed the public . . . and Cable News Network proved its value."

Turner next took on MTV, the music video cable channel. Unveiling his "Night Tracks" in June 1983, which was to play a "pop top–40 light" series of videos, in contrast to the controversial hard-rock and sexually suggestive videos that were the staple of MTV. Turner, like his friend Jerry Falwell of the Moral Majority, viewed MTV as a moral corrupter of youth. As he told *Rolling Stone*,

I was really disturbed with some of the clips they [MTV] were showing. You can take a bunch of young people and you can turn them into Boy Scouts or into Hitler Youth, depending on what you teach them, and MTV's definitely a bad influence. My wife used the word 'Satanic' to describe them. I think in the last analysis good's going to win out over evil.

But, by the fall of 1985, Turner had to admit defeat. His company sold its assets to its arch enemy MTV. Turner had suffered his first significant setback, but it hardly slowed him down.

In 1985, Turner decided to take over CBS. His friends Jerry Falwell and Senator Jesse Helms had announced their intention of taking over the network to end its "liberal bias." Turner's bid was ambitious, if nothing else. At the time, CBS was worth $4.5 billion, while TBS' revenues were just $225 million. Further, Turner tried to do it through junk-bond financing and he was using the "junkiest" bonds anyone had ever encountered. Ultimately, the bid failed, and CBS was taken over by Laurence Tisch,[†] who had originally entered the fray as a "white squire" to protect the network from "dangerous upstarts" like Turner. CBS chairman, Thomas Wyman, had asserted that Turner did not have the "conscience" to own a network, and he asked for government intervention to stop the takeover. It turned out, however, that the main problem was that Turner did not have enough money.

Undaunted, Turner next set his sights on Hollywood, and he began to negotiate with the wily Kirk Kerkorian to buy MGM, which had recently been merged with United Artists. Like a lamb being led to slaughter, Turner agreed to pay what Kerkorian asked—$29 a share, or twice what the stock was trading. Entertainment industry analysts were dumbfounded; one stated that the movie studio was worth that amount only if "Turner's found oil on the MGM backlot." He did not; instead, he wound up with $1.3 billion in high-cost debt that put him in such a cash bind that he was forced to sell the studio back to Kerkorian for less than what he paid for it. Turner only got to keep MGM's library of over 4,000 films. In that transaction, Turner retained many high-quality, high-profile films, such as *Gone with the Wind, The Wizard of Oz,* and *Singin' in the Rain,* but he did not get some of the most marketable films, such as *Rocky* and *Annie Hall,* which were in the UA library and remained in Kerkorian's hands. The other vintage MGM films had limited appeal for television, partially because they were in black and white. So, Turner began to "colorize" these film classics, which aroused a tremendous amount of opposition in Hollywood and among film buffs. Turner could not understand what all the fuss was about—"Women put on makeup don't they? That's coloring, isn't it? Nothing wrong with that. Besides, when was the last time someone took photos in black and white? I know, Ansel Adams—but he's dead too."

Besides being an aesthetic flop, which offended the Hollywood establishment, colorization did not provide the financial relief that Turner hoped it would. It was a tremendously expensive—about $18,000 a minute—and very time-consuming process, so that he could barely do one film a month. By the time Turner sold most of the MGM assets back to Kerkorian in 1987, it was generally conceded that Turner had been taken, and taken good. As *Newsweek* reported, "In Hollywood Turner is almost universally regarded as 'a pigeon.' " "He took a bath," said a Hollywood analyst. "He came to town fully clothed and left in a barrel." Other things were also going wrong for Turner at about this time. He lost $25 million sponsoring the "Good Will Games" in Moscow, saw his home burn in a fire, was aggressively audited by the Internal Revenue Service, and left his wife of twenty-three years for his former pilot. His wife sued him for divorce, asking for a settlement of $50 million. "Captain Bodacious," the reckless risk taker, was in deep trouble.

By early 1987, Turner needed help. In January he turned to Kerkorian. In Hollywood, it is generally recognized that when one turns to Kerkorian for help, there is no way that person can come out ahead. In any event, in alliance with fourteen other cable television companies, Kerkorian injected a badly needed $550 million in Turner Broadcasting. In return, the investment group got five seats on the board at TBS, and the ability to veto large expenditures. As one TBS executive put it, Turner's "play days are over." Turner thought that scenario somewhat exaggerated, but he admitted, "My power will be somewhat diminished." The money was a lifesaver for Turner. TBS, because of the staggering debt from the MGM purchase, lost $200 million in 1986, and Wall Street began to worry about Turner's ability to make interest payments on his huge debt load. Although selling assets back to Kerkorian helped, it did not solve the problem. Turner had badly overextended himself.

Besides the money, TBS got access to a built-in market of more than half the 43 million cable-subscribing American homes because of its alliance with John Malone, president of Tele-Communications, Incorporated, and one of the leaders of the investment group. Malone had quietly become the dominant force in the American cable industry, while Turner was noisily tilting at various windmills.

Often called the "Godfather of Cable," Malone had clearly become TBS' god-father by 1988. Malone and Turner were developing plans to relieve TBS of its heavy $1.4-billion debt load. One plan was to refinance TBS, but it was also necessary to sell off much of Turner Broadcasting's real estate. The lavish CNN Center in Atlanta was put on the block. Although they hoped to sell it for $175 million, it was widely recognized as a "white elephant." To alleviate personal financial problems caused by his divorce settlement, Turner in July 1988, was forced to sell another 3 million shares in TBS to several of his earlier investors. The walls, as *Forbes* noted, were closing in around Turner, but he still had 66 percent of the voting control in the company, and he was still worth an estimated $535 million.

In 1977, Ted Turner was on top of the world. His new cable television empire was beating the pants off the networks. Everything he tried, no matter how audacious, no matter how much everyone tried to convince him it would fail, turned to gold. Turner seemed to have the "Midas touch." In that year Turner piloted his yacht, the *Courageous*, to victory in the America's Cup, the world's most prestigious yachting trophy. It also brought him the title of Yachtsman of the Year for an unprecedented third straight time. The American establishment, which regarded yachting as their preserve, was outraged. At the televised con-ference after the race, Turner appeared roaring drunk, and he crawled under the table in full view of the television cameras. The establishment blanched and vowed Turner would get his comeuppance, but in 1979 he won the Fastnet Race off the southern tip of Ireland in which a storm took fifteen lives and caused $4.5 million in damages to yachts. Was there no stopping him? Was there no justice in the world, the old blue bloods asked? Then Turner's reach exceeded his grasp, and his empire began to unravel. The stress showed on Turner. His hair greyer, his faced lined, he began to withdraw from the limelight he had once craved. In the summer of 1988, *Barron's* referred to his plight as "Captain Courageous and the Albatross." But one cannot count Turner out. During an interview, the sparkle returned to his eyes and he began weaving his old magic: "But I do believe that, within the next 10 years, we'll be showing a $250 million operating profit. NBC made $300 million this year, CBS and ABC made next to nothing. We'll be the most profitable company in the business." Stay tuned. (**A.** Ted Turner and Gary Jobson, *The Racing Edge*, 1979. **B.** *Time*, April 26, 1976, June 9, 1980; *Newsweek*, June 7, 1976, September 7, 1977, June 16, 1980, February 9, 1987; *Sports Illustrated*, July 19, 1976, August 21, 1978; Roger Vaughn, *Ted Turner: The Man behind the Mouth*, 1978; *New York Times*, June 5, 1978; *Playboy*, August 1978; *Esquire*, October 10, 1978, February 1983; *Current Biography*, 1979; *Maclean's* February 26, 1979; *Broadcasting*, May 19, 1980; *Sales & Marketing Management*, June 14, 1980; *Saturday Evening Post*, October 1980; *USA Today*, November 1980; *Forbes*, August 31, 1981, October 24, 1988; *Fortune*, June 25, 1984, August 5, 1985, January 5, 1987;

A. David Silver, *Entrepreneurial Megabucks*, 1985; *Financial World*, April 3–16, 1985; *Business Week*, August 19, 1985, June 1, October 26, 1987, July 11, 1988; R. Serge Denison, "Ted Turner's Crusade: Economics vs. Morals," *Journal of Popular Culture*, 21, no. 1 [Summer 1987]; *Barron's*, July 11, 1988.)

W

WACHNER, LINDA JOY (February 3, 1949–   ). Clothing company executive, Max Factor & Company, Warnaco, Incorporated. Linda Wachner to many people seemed to be Joan Crawford incarnate—that old Crawford image from the 1930s and 1940s, in such films as *Daisy Kenyon* and *Mildred Pierce*. Dressed in a severely tailored suit with shoulder pads, Joan Crawford had a cold, brittle exterior in these movies. She was the successful businesswoman who let nothing stand in her way. Historian Molly Haskell describes Crawford in *Daisy Kenyon* as "having left the two men at her country cabin to await her decision [as to which one she will choose], driving eighty miles an hour through the woods, her chin jutting, her eyes glaring into the middle distance of her own absorption, in a narcissistic trance." Fairly or unfairly, people have described Linda Wachner in similar terms. For some, this comparison is the height of praise: "Magnificent," said David Yunich, her former boss at R.H. Macy. "Dynamic, very hard-working, and very demanding," he concluded. Those who had to work for her, however, have generally been less kind. "A disaster," said one of her peers at Max Factor. "Absolutely the worst manager I have ever encountered. She is extremely political and extremely bad in people skills." A former competitor, who may be regarded as somewhat more neutral, said, "She got tarred with this shark-eater image, but in reality she had no choice."

Linda Wachner was born in New York City and educated in the public schools of the city. At eleven years of age, she had to spend a year encased in a plaster cast from her head to her knees, as the first step in a surgical procedure to correct severe curvature of her spine. According to Wachner, it was during this time that she made plans for her eventual success in business. She determined that she would someday cross the Triborough Bridge in a Cadillac limousine, and that she would have a career. She would be a businesswoman—she would own her own company. Perhaps many young girls had similar dreams, but Linda Wachner seemed to bring a particular dedication to her vision. Since her father was a fur buyer and her uncle a clothing manufacturer, she decided that her future would be in the garment industry.

Despite the time spent at home and in the hospital because of her disability, Wachner graduated from high school at the age of sixteen. She then secured a summer job as a salesperson for Best & Company, a former Manhattan department store. She learned a great deal from this experience. Wachner then went to the University of Buffalo, where she earned a degree in business administration in 1966. Every summer, and during holiday breaks, she worked in various department stores to earn money and gain experience. After graduation, she got a job as assistant market representative with Associated Merchandising Corporation. Despite her grand title, she was actually little more than a buyer's gofer in the early years. But Wachner used the job as valuable work experience, and she learned important work-related habits that she carried throughout her career. After a year with Associated, Wachner got a job as an assistant buyer at Foley's department store in Houston, Texas. There she learned other important lessons from Milton Berman, then president of the firm. The most important of these was the custom of "holy hours," in which Berman decreed that all personnel were required to be on the floor during the lunchtime rush. Berman kept on top of the business by quizzing salespeople and customers about what was moving and what was wanted. This habit stayed with Wachner throughout her career, as she continually darted into stores when she was a top executive with Max Factor or Warnaco to grill the sales help and customers about her products. During her two years at Foley's, Linda Wachner impressed executives there and elsewhere with her acumen.

As a result, David Yunich of Macy's heard of Linda, and he hired her as the firm's bra and girdle buyer. At the age of twenty-two, Wachner became one of the youngest buyers in the history of Macy's. While working at Macy's, Wachner met her husband, Seymour Applebaum, who was thirty-two years her senior and an executive in a dressmaking company. Wachner took over as bra and girdle buyer from a woman who had been "the dean of that particular industry," and something of a legend. But at Macy's Wachner made her presence very evident, and she advanced rapidly through the ranks to positions of increasing authority. Finally, in 1974, at the still-tender age of twenty-eight, Wachner moved from the retailing to the manufacturing side of the apparel industry. In that year she took a job with Warner's, the lingerie division of Warnaco.

At that time, the market for lingerie had slumped badly in the United States. Bras and girdles had become passé by the late 1960s and early 1970s. Young women simply didn't wear them any longer. It was clear to Wachner that the girdle situation could not be corrected because panty hose had rendered them virtually obsolete. But the situation with brassieres was somewhat different. "Women didn't burn their bras as a social protest," she told *Working Woman*. "It was a fashion protest. They wanted to feel and look like women and wanted bras that let them do just that." To meet this need she introduced new soft, free-form bras, and displayed them on hangers in the stores for the first time, so customers could see and touch them. Wachner's innovations revived Warner's business and became standard practices throughout the undergarment industry.

Wachner, who had come to Warner's as the advertising director, was made vice president within a year and served in that position until 1977.

After her whirlwind career at Warner's, Wachner moved on to Caron International, a New York City manufacturer of yarn and crafts in 1977. Wachner was appointed vice president of corporate marketing there, and she worked for two years to develop the company's popular line of Columbia Minerva craft, stitchery, and latch-hook rug kits. In 1979, however, David Mahoney hired Wachner to help rejuvenate the United States division of Max Factor, Incorporated. At that point the U.S. division was losing about $16 million a year, but Wachner turned these losses around in her first year. By the end of the second year, she was producing a $5-million profit. This was not, however, accomplished without a good deal of pain. Wachner recognized that Max Factor would have to return to the basics to become successful again. "In a burst of energy," *Working Woman* said, "she trimmed unnecessary staff, cut unproductive product lines, and reined in a runaway promotion budget." But she did not make many friends. By 1982, Wachner had performed so magnificently that she was promoted—over the heads of many men who thought they would get the position—to president and chief operating officer of the entire company.

Max Factor was doing poorly, so Wachner performed her customary surgery. In her first year as president, the company lost several million dollars, partially because of some large write-offs, but she brought it into the black in the second year. To do this, she presided over two major rounds of firings that alienated a large number of people at the company. *Ms* magazine noted that some of Wachner's employees criticized her for her demeaning requests, her scapegoating, her hoarding of credit, and her unreasonable workaholism. Wachner defended herself by saying, "If you have to get a company turned around before it bleeds to death, you have to have a certain posture in the way you go about things. I'm tough, but I'm fair." Others at Max Factor were not so certain. Peter Chiarella, chief financial officer at the company while Wachner was there, and perhaps one of those whose nose was out of joint when she was made president, said in regard to the firings: "One of Linda's problems is feeling uncomfortable with competent people around her." David Mahoney, then head of Norton Simon, Incorporated, which owned Max Factor, remained Wachner's champion: "She may have been hard to get along with," he said, "but most companies that are losing millions of dollars a year will find their CEO's hard to get along with." Further, he said that "she did an excellent job. Extravagance and waste had to be cut down. You don't win any popularity contests doing that."

It should be noted that Mahoney pressured Wachner to churn out short-term profits. If she didn't produce, and produce quickly, she would be out of a job. Produce she did. Besides cutting back costs, Wachner drew raves in the industry for introducing Le Jardin de Max Factor, a new fragrance that was a huge commercial success. In 1984, it won three of the Fragrance Foundation's awards, the highest award given in the industry. During this period, however, things became increasingly chaotic at Max Factor. In 1983, Beatrice Foods bought Norton Simon, Incorporated, and thus became the parent company of Max Factor. Then, about a year later, Esmark took over Beatrice. At that point, Wachner decided, evidently with some encouragement from senior management at Beatrice, to take over Max Factor in a leveraged buyout. She established a management group and allied herself with Peterson, Jacobs & Company, a New York investment banking firm, to put together a $280-million package to buy the company. The bid fell through, due, according to insiders, to internal jealousy on the part of several former associates. As a result, Wachner resigned from Max Factor. "I allowed myself to pout a little, but not long," she told *Working Woman*.

Wachner immediately set her sights on even bigger game. Three months after joining the firm of Adler & Shaykin as managing director, she identified Revlon, Incorporated, the giant cosmetics firm, as her next target. Deciding to try a leveraged buyout of Revlon's cosmetic division, she put in a bid of $905 million for the company. At that point, Revlon's cosmetic division had annual sales of about $1 billion. In the midst of her attempt, however, the entire Revlon company was taken over by Pantry Pride in November 1985. Wachner still pushed her takeover bid, but Revlon's new owner, Ronald Perelman, one of the great corporate raiders of the 1980s, was not receptive. Nor was there much support for her takeover from the staff at Revlon cosmetics. As *Fortune* (1986) reported, "Wachner's controversial management style continues to haunt her. Her sometimes rough ways, her disrespect for other people's schedules, her habit of placing international calls without regard to time zones seem to have spooked many Revlon employees." In the end, her takeover attempt at Revlon was rebuffed. Some thought Wachner sealed her fate when she conjured up the spirit of Revlon founder Charles Revson.[†] "It's just that a lot of spirit needs to be restored from the days of Charles," she said. One former associate groused, "She's read *Fire and Ice* [Andrew Tobias' biography of Revson] three times too often." To many at Revlon, Wachner's fiery temper, imperious habits, and single-minded determination reminded them a bit too much of Revson.

Wachner, however, did not dwell on the loss of Revlon. Within four months she had formed a shell company, W Acquisition Corporation with a partner, Andrew Galef, and she set her sights on Warnaco. When management there resisted, she decided to pursue a hostile takeover. Warnaco management, perhaps goaded by the same fears of Wachner's management style as the executives at Revlon, engineered what was called "the first real junk-bond defense" to frustrate the takeover. But Wachner, too, fought back with junk bonds, employing the investment firm of Drexel Burnham Lambert to raise $500 million in cash commitments for the raid. Ultimately, Wachner acquired Warnaco for $46.50 a share. In April 1986, Wachner stepped in as president of the 113-year-old company, and she became one of the very few women to head a *Fortune* 500 company.

Warnaco, with sales in 1986 of $575 million, had not been performing up to potential. Possessing a number of valuable brand names (Christian Dior, Geoffrey Beene, and Chaps by Ralph Lauren,[†] along with Hathaway shirts, Pringle sweaters, and Olga bras), the brands were run like autonomous little fiefdoms. Wachner was determined to put an end to that. She also felt the companies paid more attention to manufacturing than to marketing. So she installed her own management in the divisions, and she reorganized the firm into just seven divisions. In that way, she achieved a $12-million savings. She also weeded out a number of slow-selling lines, which saved another $30 million. Within the first year after her leveraged buyout, Wachner had reduced Warnaco's debt from $550 million to $475 million. She also boosted operating earnings more than 35 percent, to more than $65 million. In 1987, sales were $609 million, but the company lost nearly $11 million. Wachner, who said, "I'm having a wonderful time" in 1986, probably had less fun in 1987.

Success is not certain for Wachner at Warnaco. But one can be sure she will push herself and her associates to their utmost in pursuit of that goal. She will take out her dreaded spiral notebooks. As *Fortune* commented,

She uses them to take minutes of every meeting, then quotes from them at the next to see how her instructions were followed. She insists the books help her keep tabs on assignments, pledges, and performances. Some say the books bring out her worst. At Max Factor these follow-up sessions were known as "flash meetings"—dreaded marathons up to two days long where, says one ex-associate, "she saved up criticism or reports of failure until that public moment and let the culprit have it." (*Fortune*, 1986)

Heads will not rest easy at Warnaco until Linda Wachner has made it a success. "I risked everything I had to buy [Warnaco]," she told *Ms* "I put my money down the line. The Warnaco experience has been the proudest of my life—it proves you can go home again." (**B**. *Fortune*, January 6, 1986, January 5, 1987; *Business Week*, April 14, 1986; *Ms*, January 1987; *Working Woman*, January 1987; *New York Times*, April 22, 1987; *Contemporary Newsmakers*, 1988.)

WALLACE, DWANE L. (October 29, 1911–   ). Aircraft company executive, Cessna Aircraft Company. Dwane Wallace has been called the "Henry Ford of the light-plane industry" because he took an industry, which was largely in the handicraft stage in the mid–1930s, and converted it into a wonder of mass production. By the time he retired in 1975, he had churned out over 150,000 light planes in his Wichita, Kansas, plant, and Cessna aircraft had sales of over $200 million. With more than twice the sales of its two chief competitors (Beech and Piper) combined, Cessna was far and away the most dynamic firm in the light-plane industry. But Wallace was more than a production man, he was an authentic pioneer of the aviation industry. A lean, leathery man, he looked just like the barnstorming pilot he had been. A member of the Aviation Hall of Fame, he was described in 1977 by *Flying,* "If Dwane Wallace were running for Sage of his industry, he would win."

Wallace, who was born in Belmont, Kansas, was the nephew of Clyde Cessna, one of the early pioneers of aviation. Cessna had been born in Iowa in 1879, the son of a farmer and telegrapher. The family moved to Kansas, where Cessna was educated. Cessna early on displayed a marked mechanical ability, and he started his business career by selling cars; but in February 1911, he attended an air show in Oklahoma City, and from that time on his interest was riveted on airplanes. Cessna built his first plane, a wooden monoplane with spruce wings, in 1911, but he was an impatient man, and never took flying lessons. As a result, Cessna crashed fourteen times, collecting an assortment of broken bones before he finally completed his first flight at an exhibition in Jet, Oklahoma.

During the next fourteen years, Cessna managed the family farm in Kansas, while at the same time making exhibition flights at fairs in the summers. During these years, he became a skilled builder of light planes, and in 1916 he was offered free space at J. J. Jones auto factory in Wichita in return for allowing Jones to use a reliable airplane as an advertising platform. His newly formed Cessna Aircraft Company lasted only a year, when Cessna went back to farming full time. Then, in 1925, he joined with Walter Beech* and others to organize the Travel Air Company in Wichita. During the time Cessna served as president of this firm, he also worked privately on developing a four-seater cabin plane.

In the late 1920s, Cessna and Beech test-flew the cabin plane, but in 1927 Cessna sold his interest in Travel Air to form his own company. In 1928 his Cessna Aircraft Company began to manufacture the first cantilevered plane in the country, a plane without struts or wires to anchor the wing to the fusilage. An extraordinary success, it won several races and secured a lucrative contract from Curtiss Flying Service, which operated planes from coast to coast. The depression of 1929, however, forced Curtiss Flying Service into bankruptcy, and Cessna was unable to collect the vast sums of money he was owed. As a result, Cessna Aircraft also was closed down in 1931. In 1934, Cessna's nephew, Dwane Wallace convinced his uncle to reopen the plant. Cessna did so, but shortly thereafter he sold out his interest to Wallace and retired to his farm, where he died in 1954.

In 1921, Wallace, at nine years of age, took his first flight with his uncle. Over the next few years, Wallace flew in airplanes hand-built by friends of his uncle, and, even though many of these planes crashed with other pilots, Wallace was undeterred. Becoming utterly bewitched by aircraft, Wallace worked his way through Wichita University to get a degree in aeronautical engineering, not exactly a highly sought-after specialty in the depression years. Wallace had always dreamed of joining his uncle's aircraft business, but by the time he graduated, the plant was closed. With no other options in sight, Wallace took a job at Beech Aircraft. A short time later, when he was just twenty-two years old, Dwane Wallace convinced his uncle to reopen his Wichita aircraft plant, at which time Wallace was named manager of the plant, without a salary. Armed with the latest in aeronautical technology, Wallace designed the C–34, a high-wing, four-place cabin monoplane, with a 145-horsepower Warner Super-Scarab engine. The plane was entered in the 1935 *Detroit News* trophy race, essentially a test of efficiency that included an evaluation of economy, speed, and landing and takeoff handling, as well as general comfort and appearance. The C–34 won the race handily, which helped establish Cessna's reputation as a small-plane builder.

A year later, Clyde Cessna retired, and Wallace took over the company. Having virtually no money to operate the business, Wallace kept it going in the early years by winning prize money in flying contests. These victories also enhanced the prestige of the Cessna aircraft, which were aeronautical marvels due to Wallace's engineering expertise. By 1936, Wallace had catapulted Cessna aircraft into the front ranks of plane manufacturers, and in 1937 he came out with the C–37, an improved version of the C–34. Over the next several years, Wallace added models that were produced by his company, and also began to work on what was to become the T–50. The T–50 was a light trainer/utility airplane that was easy to fly and not sophisticated to build. That factor enabled Wallace to establish production-line techniques for building it, allowing him to reduce the price significantly. By 1939, the T–50 was tested and flying, but the situation was looking rather grim for the young aircraft manufacturer.

Although Wallace had an impressive plane, its development had taken every penny the company had in its treasury. But Wallace, ever the optimist, was undaunted. Late that year he traveled to New York City, where he made a presentation to the wartime British Purchasing Commission. They were impressed with the plane, but were concerned about the company's stability. Wallace was very young, and the company, just five years old, was hardly one of the giants of a shaky industry. Concerned, they inquired into the firm's assets. Wallace stated that, at present, the company had a cash balance of just $3, but, without batting an eye, he assured the assembled members that he had a good line of credit. Rather amazingly, Wallace went home with a contract for $6.8 million for 640 RAF Cranes (which were modified Cessna T–50s). This was followed by orders from the Canadian government and the U.S. Army.

This order was the turning point for Cessna. During the next decade and a half, the firm turned out more than 21,000 planes for civilian and military pilots, and after the war it became the nation's largest light-plane manufacturer. During World War II, the firm rang up impressive profits making 5,360 twin-engined T–50 trainers for the U.S. Army. Sales reached $71 million in 1943, and Cessna made a profit of $2 million. Wallace used these profits in the early postwar years to guide the company into the building of commercial private aircraft.

At first, Wallace was intrigued by the idea of making what he called the "Family Car of the Air," an expensive gamble that would have tried to put a "plane in every garage." Realizing the folly of this, Wallace staked the company's postwar fortunes on something more utilitarian. He brought out a series of planes called the 120/140, which were strong and simple single-engined planes. They were followed by the 190/195 series, and both of these helped Cessna survive the postwar shakeout in the industry. By 1947, Cessna Aircraft was one of the few airplane builders in the country making a profit, with earnings of over $300,000 a year for 1946 and 1947. By 1948, Cessna's sales had climbed back to $14 million.

By the early 1950s, Cessna Aircraft had already established itself as one of the leaders in the light-plane industry, and Wallace was determined that Cessna would not only be the biggest general aviation manufacturer in America, but also the best. Focusing on the recreational, Sunday flyer, Wallace brought out three models of a high-wing single-engined monoplane that could fly at speeds of from 120 to 140 mph. But Wallace was also convinced that Cessna had to have a model of aircraft for every need, so he began to expand the line. In addition, he set up a strong and aggressive dealer network, and he priced his models competitively. In addition, the outbreak of the Korean War in 1950 brought further military orders to Cessna, so that over the next few years Wallace had to double employment in his plant. By 1953, the firm's assets reached $21 million, and sales in that year exceeded $43 million. By then, the company had three plants with 4,000 employees manufacturing both civilian and military aircraft and parts.

From 1955 to 1959, even without military contracts, Cessna's business increased 112 percent. By 1958, Wallace and Cessna were able to mark a momentous event—they passed Beech Aircraft as the largest builder of private aircraft in the United States—when they delivered 6,416 planes. In 1959, Cessna sold more planes than the next four competitors combined. As Wallace looked forward to the 1960s, he felt confident that his biggest market would be in planes for business use rather than pleasure. As he noted in an article in *Flying* in 1960, "Big business will be utilizing aircraft in increasing numbers as the best means of transportation for middle management, sales personnel, and technicians between plants and around the country."

But during the 1960s, despite impressive continued growth by Cessna, Wallace made a number of critical mistakes. First of all, he wasted ten years trying to sell helicopters to an uninterested public. He had proclaimed in 1960 that "we foresee an increasing market for helicopters," but it never materialized. Wallace finally pulled Cessna out of that market in the early 1960s. He also deeply involved Cessna in a business jet program. Intent on developing a jet plane called the Citation, by the early 1970s, it had cost the firm millions of dollars. The Citation came out in 1972, and Wallace predicted far larger sales than ever materialized. His estimate that they would sell 100 jets was pared down to 30. But Wallace refused to back down on the program. He had already sunk millions into the project. As he said, "Shutting down the jet program is the furthest thing from my mind," and he "was not losing any sleep" over the losses Cessna was incurring with the program. Many analysts agreed that he had a good product. The Citation cost just $795,000, and like all of Wallace's products, was of high quality.

However, Cessna's sales, which had been so explosive from the 1940s through the 1960s, leveled off in the 1970s. Part of the problem was that, with a commanding 53 percent of the light-plane market in 1972, there was no place left for Cessna to go. Making forty-four different planes, its broad market coverage even troubled Cessna executives. One of them said frankly, "We've about covered the field. We're having trouble seeing where new light planes might fit in." Thus, Wallace's jet program, with its Citation planes, was the only area of potential growth for Cessna in 1972, but it was a struggle to get it off the ground. Wallace declared, "I believe in this plane. It'll sell itself. Are you with me?" And he predicted he would sell a thousand of them in a decade. *Forbes* (1972) mockingly stated, "All he needs is a scarf around his neck and the Red Baron in his sights. Trouble is the longer sales stay down, the more he sounds like an old-time Wichita barnstormer flying by the seat of his pants."

By 1974, Wallace's faith in the Citation jet was largely vindicated. At that time it was outselling the competition by a wide margin, and Wallace claimed it had been profitable for over a year. Furthermore, Wallace's prediction that Cessna would make 1,000 Citations in a decade also came true. In January 1982, just a decade later, the 1,000th Citation was delivered to an electronics supply firm in Utica, New York. By 1985, the Citation was the best-selling business jet in America, with sales of 95 in that year. In the following year, sales exceeded 100 for the first time. *Forbes*, admitting that its earlier skepticism was misplaced, by 1982 said that Cessna's success could be laid directly to Wallace's unswerving confidence in the Citation program. It advised investors that Cessna was "worth a flier." By then, however, it was too late for Dwane Wallace—he had retired in 1975.

In late 1974, Wallace, who was always excessively optimistic, was convinced that Cessna's sales and profits would turn upward, and that the Citation would rescue the company. But the company, which had shipped nearly 15,000 planes in 1966, had sold just half that number in 1974, and although he predicted sales of 9,000 planes in 1975, most industry analysts viewed that prediction as too optimistic. In any event, Wallace retired soon afterward, and although he remained a director of the company for a time, he no longer played a significant role in its management.

Cessna after Wallace experienced both success and failure. A new Cessna model, its first turboprop plane, crashed; Wallace's vaunted production lines ran into snags; and there was a major recall of 3,700 of the firm's profitable, hot-selling Skyhawk planes because of engine problems. All of this caused profits to drop 43 percent in early 1978. At that time Russell W. Meyer, Jr., an ex-Grumman American Aviation executive who joined Cessna in 1974, became chief executive officer (CEO). Introducing a new aircraft line in 1979, Meyer returned Cessna to profitability. But he promised dealers that still more would be done. He added 2,600 workers to the employment rolls, giving the firm over 20,000 employees for the first time, to arrest production delays.

Despite this early success, however, Cessna again ran into trouble in 1983, when deliveries fell off, and the firm suffered a loss of $18.8 million. As a result, Meyer decided to sell 500,000 shares of Cessna to General Dynamics in that year. This was the beginning of a friendly takeover of the small aircraft firm by the giant defense contractor. In 1985, General Dynamics paid $594 million to gain a majority interest in Cessna, and a year later the firm was merged into General Dynamics as a wholly owned subsidiary. General Dynamics was interested in Cessna because 90 percent of General Dynamics' $7.84 billion in sales in 1984 was defense related, and Cessna allowed them to diversify. Cessna, however, again had a loss in 1984, this time of $51 million, on sales of $801 million. By 1987, Cessna, which had over 50 percent of the general aviation market fifteen years before, had to settle for 40 percent. Meyer made out just fine in the new arrangement, continuing as CEO of the Cessna subsidiary. But Wallace was a forgotten man. One of the pioneering greats in aviation, he did not have even an honorary position with either Cessna or General Dynamics. Sitting on the boards of the Coleman Company, the Wichita camping equipment manufacturer, and the Fourth National Bank in the city, Wallace seemed to be a "prophet with honor" at his own firm. (**B**. *Business Week*, December 13, 1947, June 5, 1978; *Fortune*, April 1952, June 1, 1981, October 14, 1985; *Time*, August 9, 1954, April 27, 1959; *New York Times*, November 22, 1954; *Flying*, July 1960, September 1977; Gerald Deneau, *An Eye on the Sky*, 1962; C.R. Rosenberg, *The Challenging Skies*, 1966; *Forbes*, April 1, 1972, December 15, 1974, January 18, 1982; *Who's Who in Aviation*, 1973; *National Cyclopaedia of American Biography*, 41:561; *Who's Who in Finance and Industry*, 1974–75; *Who's Who in America*, 1978; *Aviation Week & Space Technology*, December 3, 1979, October 31, 1983; Bill Gunston, *The Planemakers*, 1980; Joseph J. Fucini and Suzy Fucini, *Entrepreneurs*, 1985; *Moody's Manual of Industrials*, 1985; *Dun's Business Month*, August 1986; *Standard & Poor's Register of Directors and Executives*, 1988.)

WALTON, SAMUEL MOORE (March 1918–   ). Retail chain owner, Wal-Mart Stores, Incorporated. In 1983, residents of the tiny Ozark town of Bentonville, Arkansas, wanted to honor their most famous citizen. At the same time, they could not resist ribbing their longtime neighbor. Thus, prominent among the ten floats in the parade was a wrecked car welded to the back of a Wal-Mart truck. This memorialized Sam Walton, who was once so busy counting the cars in a Wal-Mart parking lot, as he was leaving, that he smashed his car into the back of a Wal-Mart truck. Sam Walton exudes an image of a folksy, downhome, "good ole' boy," driving around in a legendary, battered 1978 pickup truck; but beneath that benign exterior beats the soul of a driven businessman. His fraternity brothers at Zeta Phi fraternity at the University of Missouri recognized that fact when they called him "Hustler Walton" in a profile they did on him in a fraternity newspaper in 1940.

Sam Walton was born in the small town of Kingfish, Oklahoma, but he grew up in Columbia Missouri, where his father scraped through the depression by trading anything he could get his hands on. Young Sam Walton paid his way through the hometown University of Missouri by operating a paper route. While at college Walton was an athlete, a member of a number of clubs, and renowned for his friendliness and community spirit. His fraternity biography gushed: "There is little limit to the number of things Sam has done." Originally he planned to go to graduate school and then to sell insurance, but because he was impatient to enter the business world, Sam Walton joined J. C. Penney at its Des Moines, Iowa store as a trainee in 1940 for $85 a month. During the next two years, Walton received a thorough training in retailing from the Penney organization. In 1942, he was drafted into the army, and he spent the balance of the war stateside with the military police.

After the war, Walton went to Newport, Arkansas, where he opened a Ben Franklin variety store. Little in Walton's operation in the early years forecast his staggering success later on. In fact, when his landlord refused to renew his lease in 1950, Walton was forced to move across the state to Bentonville, where he opened another Ben Franklin. This store proved to be a success, and with the help of his younger brother, James L. "Bud" Walton, Sam began creating a regional chain of Ben Franklin stores. By 1962 he had sixteen Ben Franklin outlets, all in towns with fewer than 5,000 inhabitants, and he was the most successful operator of Ben Franklin stores in the country. Operating as a small, virtually independent regional chain, Walton says, "We had our own buying office, used a Ben Franklin warehouse and co-ordinated buying and marketing. Things were running so smoothly we even had time for our families." At that time, rural America was pretty much ignored by the nation's retailers. Perceived as a dying backwater within a dynamic, progressive urban nation, few national retailing chains paid much attention to the small-town market if it was beyond the hinterland of a major metropolitan area. Sam Walton found success by focusing on the small towns others passed by. As he later noted with some satisfaction, "At the time, people thought that it wouldn't work," but "there was a lot more business in those towns than people ever thought."

By the late 1950s, Sam Walton became convinced that small-town retailing was on the verge of a revolution. He noticed that discount stores were spreading throughout the East and he took a trip to New England to observe the situation at close hand. By 1962, Walton was certain that Ben Franklin's days as a successful variety store operation were numbered. He went to Chicago to plead his case, arguing that he "could see that the variety store was gradually dying because there were giant supermarkets and then discounters coming into the picture." When Ben Franklin executives did not heed his argument, Walton decided to open his own chain of discount stores.

In 1962, Sam Walton opened his first Wal-Mart Discount City in adjacent Rogers, Arkansas. A spartan, linoleum-floored operation that stocked an impressive range of name-brand goods at discount prices, the new store was an instant success. During the next eight years, with his headquarters in Bentonville, Walton opened thirty stores. At that point, needing capital to engage in more vigorous expansion, Walton took his firm public. After that, he never looked back. By 1977, Wal-Mart had 190 stores and was opening new stores at the rate of 30 or 40 a year; sales had leaped from $44 million to $650 million; and earnings had gone from 15 cents a share to $1.45. What were the keys to Walton's success in what seemed such an unlikely venture—building a great retail chain of discount stores in small towns in America's hinterland?

One key was the principle of warehousing developed by Sam Walton. He started with a giant 525,000-square-foot warehouse, and set up his first stores around it. The major operating principle was that the boundaries of his retailing empire were to be set by one-day truck routes from the warehouse in Bentonville. Eighty percent of the chain's goods passed through that warehouse facility, a percentage well above that achieved by K mart or Sears. This warehousing concept solved the major problem most retailers had with operating stores in small, out-of-the-way locations. His warehouse allowed him to achieve the same low-cost, efficient delivery methods as the big city operators. The volume discounts he got by having goods sent to his warehouse instead of to his stores and then doing his own trucking, ran between 2 and 5 percent, a very important margin for a discounter.

By 1977, the first warehouse had reached capacity, and the second, this one highly mechanized, was set up at Searcy, Arkansas, 250 miles to the southeast. This not only eased the load of the existing territory, but it allowed further expansion by the Wal-Mart chain. By the early 1980s there were five giant warehouses, and no store was more than a six-hour drive from one of them. By 1982, Walton had over 500 stores in thirteen contiguous states, and he had $2.5 billion in annual revenues. By the late 1980s Wal-Mart's warehouses remained a key ingredient. Up to 150 stores were clustered around a warehouse, so that distribution remained as fast and inexpensive as it had been in the early days. By the mid–1970s, it became clear that this massive distribution network could no longer operate efficiently without the aid of computers. So computer terminals were installed in each store, and the chain's computer system by the mid–1980s was state-of-the-art, able to do everything from tracking inventory to planning new stores. It was also linked to over 200 vendors, making deliveries even faster.

Another key to Wal-Mart's success lay in the small towns where the stores were located. Wal-Mart placed more than 80 percent of its units in towns with fewer than 10,000 residents. Consequently, the chain's stores were able to dominate the market in most areas where they were placed. Their market position was so strong that, in many of the locations, according to an executive at Merrill Lynch, "Wal-Mart commands 10 percent to 20 percent of total retail sales, including food and automobiles." At the same time that Wal-Mart was establishing a dominance in these markets, a remarkable resurgence in small towns, especially those in the Sunbelt, was occurring as industry began to establish plants there. There were also other advantages to these small-town locations, as

Sidney A. McKnight, former president of Montgomery Ward, a longtime small-town operator, noted, "Occupancy fees, advertising costs, payroll, and taxes are all lower than in the big cities, (and) you get a work force that is likely to be more stable and the instant identity of being the biggest store around."

In the early years, Walton did not have to worry much about competition. In most towns, there was a Penney's store, which did not provide much competition, since Wal-Marts had a wider merchandise mix with more hard goods. The major competitor was K mart, which was beginning to move into Wal-Mart's territory in the late 1970s and 1980s. Well over one-third of the K mart stores in the late 1970s were set up in small towns or on the fringes of metropolitan markets, so that they were going head to head with Wal-Mart in about 120 locations by 1982. Wal-Mart, for its part, stayed out of the larger cities, but it began to move into the outlying suburbs of some cities. Wal-Mart's biggest impact, though, has been on the old-line variety stores. When a Wal-Mart opens in a town, it usually devastates the small competitor. Ed Zapalac, who ran a small variety store in Sealy, Texas, commented, "Stores like mine aren't selling enough," as he gazed wistfully at his nearly bare shelves.

Most of the early Wal-Mart stores from 50,000 to 55,000 square feet in size were barn-like environments quite bare and spartan. Merchandise was displayed in plastic bins and on bare pipe racks. The decor was a harsh blue and white, and the floors were covered in linoleum. In the early 1980s, Walton began to revamp the chain's image. Nevertheless, the main item at the Wal-Mart stores remained the merchandise, not the decor. The Wal-Mart concept was to unite a friendly, general-store atmosphere with high-quality, brand-name goods at low prices. The merchandise mix in the chain's stores stressed rock-bottom-priced goods, with emphasis on hard goods. Brand names are one of the big drawing cards at Walton's stores, not such trendy names as Calvin Klein[†] or Gloria Vanderbilt, but the trusted staples—Wrangler jeans and Champion Western shirts in apparel, and Remington, Cannon, Coleman, Pioneer, and Revlon in hard goods. Wal-Mart's top sellers included budget cosmetics, motor oil, and velour tops. To attract customers, Wal-Mart spends a significant amount on direct mail, radio, and local newspaper advertising. But word-of-mouth probably best promotes Wal-Mart's values. As one customer said, "They've usually got the best selection and prices and they take back merchandise without question."

These marketing ingredients made Wal-Mart a retailing phenomenon of the post–World War II years. With over 800 stores by the mid–1980s, it had sales of $6.4 billion. But its growth in the late 1980s was virtually exponential. With 1,035 stores, in just the *first quarter* of 1987, Wal-Mart had sales of $4.5 billion. Sales for the entire year were a staggering $14 billion, a 30-percent increase over the previous year. Yet Sam Walton was not content with even this explosive growth. In 1983, he turned to deep discounting through the wholesale club business. Begun as a way to penetrate the big city, Walton established Sam's Wholesale Clubs to compete with Price Company, the pioneering membership discounter. Again, Sam Walton found success. By the end of 1986 there were

Sam's Wholesale Club stores in forty-nine cities, and they contributed $11.9 billion, or 14 percent of the chain's total revenues. Then Walton took yet another daring step. He introduced a series of "hypermarket" stores. Based on a European model, the first opened in Garland, Texas, a suburb of Dallas, in December 1987. Called Hypermart USA, these 220,000-square-foot monster stores sold groceries, television sets, hardware, patio furniture, jewelry, clothing, and practically every other kind of merchandise under one roof, and one checkout area served all. As with the Wal-Mart stores, only national brands were stocked, and the chain's policy of aggressive price-cutting was retained. Only time will tell whether this venture will be as successful for Sam Walton as the others have been.

Most analysts agree that one major factor is responsible for the massive growth of the Wal-Mart chain—the gifted leadership of Sam Walton. From the very beginning, he took an intensely personal role in the management of the chain. His management style brought him into constant contact with hundreds of store managers, thousands of employees, and millions of customers. Walton, in fact, knew the names of thousands of these employees, and he was able to develop deep bonds of loyalty among them, through his unrelenting travels to visit store locations. With a twin-engined Piper Aztec, he flew from small town to small town, often visiting four stores in a day, spending several hours at each, visiting managers, employees, and customers. And he did not just talk; he listened. He took their ideas to heart. As he told *Forbes* in 1977, "We like to let folks know we're interested in them and that they're vital to us. Cause they are. Those department heads are the only ones who really know what's going on out there in the field, and we've got to get them to tell us." Sam Walton seemed to have perfected what was called the "loose-tight" principles of management, relying on a very fine balance between central controls and local decision making.

One word describes Sam Walton's value to Wal-Mart—charisma. It has been noted by some that he runs his mammoth chain like a larger version of his original dime store. He relies on seat-of-the-pants judgments, and he does not use fancy teams of consultants to advise him on operations. He drives himself and his company with an evangelical fervor; at store openings, Sam Walton leads his employees in cheers that begin "Give me a W, give me an A." He is, in the words of another discounter, Herbert Fisher of Jamesway Corporation, "a living legend." But living legends are almost impossible to replace, and the same ingredients that gave Wal-Mart its impetus to grow may work against it once Walton is gone. Although he insists his chain is not a "one-man company," when he tried to retire as early as 1975 he soon found himself drawn back in, and his successor left the firm.

On the other hand, everyone in the industry agrees that Walton has assembled a highly talented staff, from the store managers up. The fact is, although Walton pinches pennies in many areas, he does not stint on rewarding his sales managers and executives. Wal-Mart store managers could keep 10 percent of the unit's pretax profits, which brought them average salaries of from $40,000 to $50,000 in the early 1980s. Walton also encouraged employee stock purchases, so that about 8 percent of the chain's stock in 1982 was owned by employees. Finally, there was a corporate profit-sharing plan, in which 22,000 of the 41,000 employees in 1982 were participants. As one analyst commented, "They're like Tandy Corporation in terms of incentives, Wal-Mart wants everyone working for the company instead of against it as they do in some companies."

But Sam Walton was also very old-fashioned in many respects. For years, the chain would not hire older workers, and, by the mid–1980s, there were no women in the senior executive ranks at the firm. Company policy also forbade employees, even single ones, to date one another without authorization from the executive committee. Despite urgings from several of his executives, Walton has refused to name a woman to the board of directors. One of those executives noted, "Sam is really pretty prudish."

All of this has made Wal-Mart an exceedingly profitable concern. While most other retailers struggled in the late 1970s and early 1980s, Wal-Mart regularly posted 35 percent annual sales gains, and profits increased an average of 37 percent yearly for the dozen years after 1975. This profitability has made Wal-Mart the darling of Wall Street. Wal-Mart shares, which sold for $16.50 when first issued in 1970, were worth $900 fifteen years later. As a result, Sam Walton was able to make repeated overtures to the equity markets, raising a total of $123 million during these years.

This great success also made Sam Walton extremely rich—perhaps the richest man in America in the late 1980s. In 1987, *Forbes* estimated that Walton was worth $4.5 billion. When the panic hit on October 19, 1987, analysts estimated he lost about $500 million. Walton took it all philosophically, "It was paper when we started, and it's paper afterward." Perhaps Walton's most memorable trait is his down-to-earth, folksy charm. By all accounts, Walton is a sincere, humble, Southern gentleman, who is most comfortable among the residents of his small hometown. He drives an old pickup truck, enjoys hunting and fishing and only once in his life has traveled first class on an airplane. This lack of pretention was reflected in his office at Wal-Mart. His original office was a small room above the Bentonville store, with a desk jerry-built from two filing cabinets and a piece of plywood. His later office was also modestly sized and decorated. In 1988, *Forbes* still called Walton the richest man in America, estimating his wealth at $6.7 billion. Walton himself detested all that talk, saying, "It's just paper—all I own is a pickup truck and a little Wal-Mart stock."

But if Sam Walton was modest in some respects, in others he was bizarre. This was particularly reflected in the way he ran his chain, and the camaraderie he often developed with his employees. A few years ago, Walton bet his employees that they could not push the chain's pretax profits past 8 percent. When they responded to his challenge and won the bet, he paid off as he had promised: Sam Walton donned a grass skirt and danced a hula on Wall Street to commemorate the achievement. (**B.** *New York Times*, June 29, 1976, January 22, 1979, July 1, 1984, April 10, October 15, 1985; *Forbes*, December 1, 1977, January

4, August 16, 1982, October 24, 1988; *Business Week*, November 5, 1979, October 14, 1985, December 21, 1987, March 14, 1988; *Chain Store Executive*, March 1981; *Dun's Business Month*, December 1982; *Time*, May 23, 1983; *Fortune*, August 8, 1983; *Financial World*, April 4–17, 1984, April 15, 1986; A. David Silver, *Entrepreneurial Megabucks*, 1985; *People Weekly*, October 14, 1985; *Wall Street Journal*, October 15, 1985; *U.S. News and World Report*, December 2, 1985; *Contemporary Newsmakers*, 1986; *Newsweek*, November 2, 1987; Toronto *Globe & Mail*, December 28, 1987.)

WANG, AN (February 7, 1920–   ). Electronics, office systems, and computer company founder, Wang Laboratories. An Wang found himself stranded in America. A native of China, he was in his Ph.D. program in applied physics at Harvard when it became clear to him that the Communist forces of Mao Tse Tung were going to emerge victorious in the raging civil war with ruling Nationalist China. He rapidly finished his doctorate, and then looked for "a way to be useful." Securing a position as a research fellow at Harvard's Computational Laboratory, Wang was given an assignment that involved finding a way to store and read data in the cumbersome new computers emerging at the time. He invented the components of the magnetic-core memory, a doughnut-shaped device that became essential to the computer industry for the next two decades. It made Wang's reputation, and allowed him to enter the electronics industry. The next forty years amounted to a virtual fairy-tale success story for the Chinese immigrant to America. In recognition of that, Wang was one of twelve outstanding naturalized citizens who were awarded Medals of Liberty by President Reagan at the relighting of the Statue of Liberty on July 3, 1986.

Wang was born in Shanghai, China. His father taught English in a private elementary school in Kun San, and he also practiced traditional Chinese medicine. An Wang grew up in both Shanghai and Kun San, about thirty miles away. He began to learn English when he was about five years old, and he began his formal education at the age of six in the third grade. Progressing rapidly through school, he entered Shanghai's Chiao Tung University, the so-called "MIT of China," when he was just sixteen. Wang immersed himself in electrical engineering, with an emphasis on communications, and he also edited a scientific digest, in which he translated articles from American magazines like *Popular Science* and *Popular Mechanics* into Chinese. During this period, however, Japan was bombing Shanghai, and in 1937 war broke out between the two countries. Yet the university remained a relative island in a storm of conflict. As Wang recalled in his autobiography, "The war was close by, but it was not there, and that made all the difference in the world."

Wang graduated from the university in 1940, and he took a job as a teaching assistant in electrical engineering at the university. In the summer of 1941, he went into the interior of China to help design and build transmitters and radios for government troops fighting the Japanese there. He remained an engineer for the Central Radio Works until 1945, when, as part of a program sponsored by the Chinese government, he was sent, along with several hundred other engineers, to the United States as a technical observer.

Upon his arrival in America, Wang immediately determined that he would learn more if he undertook graduate study. Enrolling in Harvard University in September 1945, he was granted his master's degree in 1946. He next signed on with the Chinese government supply agency in Ottawa, Canada, for three tedious months before returning to Harvard to begin his Ph.D. program in applied physics in February 1947. A year later, he defended his thesis on nonlinear mechanics. Deciding not to return home, he recalled his emotions in his autobiography, *Lessons*, in 1986: "I . . . knew myself well enough to know that I could not survive under a totalitarian Communist system. I had long been independent, and I wanted to continue to make my own decisions about my life."

Although Wang's graduate studies had nothing to do with computer science, he signed on as a research fellow in the Harvard Computation Laboratory after completing his Ph.D. Working there until 1951, Wang had the great fortune to be accidentally hooked up with Howard Aiken, one of the legendary figures of the early computer age. Aiken gave Wang what many regarded as a virtually impossible problem in data storage. Wang's task was, in his own words, "to find a way to record and read magnetically stored information without mechanical motion within the computer." Wang, in effect, developed the concept of rewriting information almost the instant it was erased as the machine read it. He patented his invention, and after working with Aiken a bit longer on the Mark IV computer at Harvard, Wang left when the university began to phase out its computer research.

By this time, Wang was a recognized authority in digital electronics, and he decided to open his own firm to manufacture and sell memory cores. He had just $600 in savings, but cashed in his Harvard pension for $2,000 and rented space in a loft in Boston and concentrated his efforts on devising a series of commercial applications for his memory core. Total sales in the first year were just $15,000, but volume grew at a 42-percent annual rate over the next three decades as a result of Wang's technological innovations. One of his early coups was the first digital scoreboard at New York's Shea Stadium. Wang's big breakthrough financially came in 1956. At that time, his annual business income was still only about $10,000, and International Business Machines (IBM) approached him to buy his patent for the memory core. The company used rough negotiating tactics on Wang, assuming that his relative poverty and lack of success would make him an easy mark. But it was this confrontation that really proved Wang's mettle. Bearing down, and recognizing that he had IBM over a barrel, since it was just moving toward control of the computer market, Wang drove a hard bargain. He finally settled for $400,000 for his patent. Suddenly wealthy, An Wang could now pursue business in a constructive, profitable manner.

Wang set up a plant in Tewksbury, near Lowell, Massachusetts, and began to produce electronic counters, machine tool controls, encoders, telecoder generators, and the first electronic justifying typesetter system, which revolutionized the newspaper industry. The firm's biggest breakthrough, however, came in 1964, when it introduced its first electronic desk calculator, called LOCI. Selling for $6,500, it was easier to operate than a computer, and it could do some of the work formerly done by a slide rule. The LOCI was followed by the Model 300, which was even simpler to use and cost one-quarter as much. These two products amounted to a major consumer breakthrough for Wang Laboratories, and it captured the major portion of the calculator market in America. Sales reached $2.5 million in 1965, $3.8 million in 1966, and $6.9 million in 1967. In 1967, Wang established an international division, and the firm was taken public. Its stock shot up rapidly on the exchange and became the hottest of that year's "hot stocks," achieving a staggering market value of $79 million. By 1970, Wang's sales stood at $25 million, a 1000-percent increase in five years.

An Wang decided that his company's mission would be to make jobs easier by introducing digital electronics into the workplace. His first step in this direction was to move into computers. In 1968, the 700 Model computer was introduced, the last to use his magnetic-core memory for data storage. In 1972, when Wang brought out its 600 series of computers, it had semiconductor-based random access memory (RAM) chips from Intel Corporation installed in them—the first firm whose computers offered that advanced technology. Wang may have invented the magnetic core, but when it came to business and technology he was not sentimental. One of the great hallmarks of Wang Laboratories in the 1970s and 1980s was the extent to which it remained on the leading edge of technological innovation and market strategy.

Despite its late start, Wang had become a leader in the computer field by the 1980s, producing some of the most sophisticated minicomputers on the market. Despite this success, it was in word processing that An Wang made his presence most dramatically felt. This was a sector of the market that had formerly been controlled almost solely by IBM, but in 1972 Wang Labs brought out the 1200 Word Processing System. It was a daring move, and many within the company opposed it, but An Wang was determined to make the challenge. It was a success, and it was followed in 1975 by the Wang Computer System (WCS), which was priced below the competing IBM system. This was also successful, but the big breakthrough came the following year, when Wang Labs launched the WPS, a word processing system with a video display screen the size of a television set on which the user could manipulate text. Along with the screen came a high-speed printer, giving Wang Labs a truly revolutionary product. Now called the "Word Processing Company" by the media, Wang Labs sales continued to explode exponentially.

An Wang continued to introduce new products, and the firm maintained its spectacular growth, with a string of twenty-six record growth quarters. In 1977, it introduced the VS line of computers, which allowed programs normally run only on large, mainframe machines to be run on smaller Wang computers. Several years later, An Wang launched the Office Information Systems (OIS) series, which was designed to link word processing and data processing. In 1981,

Alliance, a third generation of the OIS, was unveiled, which united all the key technologies and, simultaneously, WangNet, a network which allowed the concurrent transmission of all types of office information, whether text, voice, or video, was introduced.

By 1981, Wang Labs sales had reached a dizzying $1 billion, and profits were in excess of $100 million. During the previous five years, annual growth had averaged 55 percent. It seemed that everything An Wang touched turned to gold. Then, just as suddenly, just about everything went sour. First of all, IBM, Hewlett-Packard, American Telephone and Telegraph, and Digital Equipment Corporation all entered the office automation market. They began introducing newer, more innovative features in their systems, and Wang had difficulty in meeting the challenge. The microcomputer had also been introduced. First Apple popularized it with home buyers and small businesses, and IBM, when it introduced its personal computer (PC) in 1982, took a large chunk of the office automation market. Now much of the word processing and data processing, which had been done on large systems, could be performed at individual desks with personal computers hooked up in networks with one another and to a powerful minicomputer. Wang brought out its own PC, called the Professional Computer, but it did not do well in the market. A few months later, Wang had a technological breakthrough with the first Professional Image Computer (PIC), which could store photographic images. But it was plagued with bugs, and repeatedly malfunctioned. Ultimately, Wang Labs had to recall it. By 1983, a market researcher commented, "It is not clear that Wang is in the mainstream of the office anymore." Patricia Seybold, a Boston automation consultant, wrote, "The perception is that Wang's product line is a little tired and expensive."

This sudden downturn in Wang Labs' fortunes brought out the worst in everyone there. An Wang had stepped up to the position of chairman in 1981, handing over management of the firm to a committee composed of his son Frederick Wang and John F. Cunningham, whom Wang's wife referred to as "our American son." Management by committee did not work well, and in January 1983, An Wang made Cunningham president and CEO of the company. It looked for a while like Cunningham would turn the firm around. Earnings in fiscal 1984 shot up 31 percent, and revenues went to $2.2 billion. Craig Symons, a computer analyst with a high-technology research firm, said, "The financial success of Wang represents the high confidence customers have in the company. You can't go from $1 billion to $2 billion in two years unless you have something superior." Suitably impressed, *Dun's Business Month* tagged Wang Labs as one of the "five best managed companies" of 1984. In the following year, revenues rose to $2.8 billion, and earnings were up to $261 million. Then, in 1985, revenues plunged again, to $2.35 billion, and the company suffered a loss of $54 million. In response, Cunningham resigned from the firm, and An Wang came out of retirement to take charge of the firm; he laid off 1,600 workers and instituted a rigid cost-cutting program. In 1986, sales edged back up to $2.6 billion, with a small profit of $55.9 million.

It seemed that the old master had not lost his touch, but the apparent turnaround masked a number of problems. Many industry analysts felt that Wang Labs was plagued by a top-heavy management structure, which resulted in staff jobs becoming havens for "aging mediocrity." Many of these managers were closely aligned with the founder, and they simply supported his pet projects without question. The marketing side of the company often complained that those projects were either unworkable or unmarketable. Conversely, Wang Labs also developed a reputation for promising more than it could deliver. As one customer complained, "They're totally sales-driven."

In January 1986, Wang landed the biggest contract in its history, selling $480 million worth of minicomputers to the U.S. Air Force, and at about the same time it introduced enhanced products in the VS line. This was part of An Wang's strategy to reposition the company as a diversified minicomputer vendor. To run the company, An Wang chose his son, Fred, who was then thirty-seven years old. This did not generate enthusiasm in the industry. It was rumored that many people in the company disliked Fred because of his short temper and demanding nature. One analyst had even predicted shortly before Fred was named president that, "He can't become president of the company if everybody's gunning for him." Another analyst commented after Fred Wang was appointed, "The computer companies are the best managed in the country. Fred will be up against John Akers (IBM) and Kenneth [Harry] Olsen[†] (DEC)." The results in 1987 were not encouraging. Sales for the year totaled a healthy $2.8 billion, a modest 7.3-percent increase over the previous year, but it lost nearly $71 million on these revenues. The great growth firm, with a rate of growth that averaged 42 percent annually from 1951 to 1981, and at times averaged 55 percent, had its sales grow by just 19 percent from 1983 to 1987, hardly enough to cover inflation. With over 30,000 employees, the company had assets of $2.8 billion, and spent $222 million on research and development in 1987. To most industry experts, this state of affairs at Wang Labs was perplexing. Until the mid-1980s, the company was famous for its "uncanny ability to be in the right market at the right time with the right product." During the later 1980s, the firm floundered. Despite massive research and development, the company and its founder had trouble finding the right product mix for the rapidly changing marketplace. One of Wang's responses was to acquire a number of high-technology companies, such as Telenova, Incorporated and also to enter into joint ventures with a number of firms. By 1989, it was not clear what the future of Wang Labs would be.

An Wang, on the other hand, has become an important and successful philanthropist. With a net worth reported at $1.6 billion, the man known affectionately as "the Doctor" continued to live a quiet, family-oriented life. But he has been receptive to requests for aid. When Boston's Tremont Street Performing Arts Theater was about to close, he rescued it with a $4-million gift (it was renamed the Wang Performing Arts Center). He has also given money to hospitals and funded student exchanges between the United States and China. In 1985, An Wang donated a computer network to New York City's shelter for the homeless, and he built a $15-million computer assembly plant to provide jobs in Boston's Chinatown. With all of his donations, he has a philosophy that he follows, the belief that he is not just giving money, but is helping a community help itself. As he commented, "It's not just an act by one individual. It's an attempt to create a spirit of awareness in which everyone can participate." Walter Pierce, executive director of the Wang Performing Arts Center, appreciates what Wang has done, "Dr. Wang's an incredible person. Without him, I am convinced the [Wang] center would be an empty building. He's done wonders for Boston." (**A.** An Wang, with Eugene Linden, *Lessons*, 1986. **B.** *Business Week*, November 13, 1971, March 21, 1977, June 4, 1979, July 28, December 15, 1980, May 17, 1982, October 17, 1983, June 10, August 5, 1985, April 18, 1986, June 20, 1988; *Datamation*, March 1976, November 1977; *Forbes*, October 15, 1976, January 7, 1980, February 15, 1982, October 24, 1988; *Financial World*, August 15, 1977, September 15, 1981; *New York Times*, February 24, April 9, 1980, May 5, October 14, 1984; *Fortune*, June 14, 1980, February 3, 1986, April 25, 1988; *Time*, November 17, 1980; Stephen McClellan, *The Coming Computer Industry Shakeout*, 1984; *Wall Street Journal*, November 6, 1984; *Dun's Business Monthly*, December 1984; Joseph J. Fucini and Suzy Fucini, *Entrepreneurs*, 1985; A. David Silver, *Entrepreneurial Megabucks*, 1985; *MIS Week*, October 30, 1985; *Contemporary Newsmakers*, 1986; *Industry Week*, October 13, 1986; *Current Biography*, January 1987; *U.S. News & World Report*, July 6, 1987.)

WEXNER, LESLIE (1937–   ). Retailer, The Limited. *Forbes* magazine in 1984 called The Limited "the fastest-growing, most profitable specialty apparel retailer in the country." Milton Petrie, owner of the Petrie Stores, a large chain of women's specialty shops, called Wexner "the greatest merchandising talent in America." *Fortune* magazine in 1985 proclaimed that "Leslie Wexner knows what women want." With stores that featured a bright, irreverent European flair to their clothing, Wexner, a bachelor, had succeeded remarkably in understanding and catering to the taste of millions of American women. Explaining this uncanny ability, Wexner claimed he had learned from Charles Revson,[†] founder of Revlon:

Revson said all women hope they get laid, and I agree. They're sensuous. They're different from men. They dress to please men. You're not selling utility. That's why uptight women stockbrokers will put on a G-string when they get home. Like Revson said, we're selling hope in a bottle. (*Fortune, 1985*)

Leslie Wexner was born in Dayton, Ohio, the son of a Russian immigrant who managed clothing stores for the Miller-Wohl chain. During those years, his father was transferred often, so Leslie had grown up shifting from city to city, lacking any sense of roots until his father left Miller-Wohl and opened his own women's clothing store in Columbus. Young Wexner did not do well in school, and at least twice the principal of the school had to remind him of his intelligence and what a disappointment he was to everyone. From the recollections of his classmates, one gets the sense that Wexner was a bit of a "nerd" and a "wall-flower" when he was young. The captain of his high school football team remembered, "He wasn't very visible. . . . He didn't go out to parties. He's more distinguished-looking today than he was then."

Leslie Wexner graduated from Ohio State University, and he attended law school there but dropped out after two years and began to work in his parents' store, called Leslie's after their son. He soon became disillusioned with the work there. The small store sold a full line of women's clothing, and Leslie Wexner felt his parents should specialize in sportswear, which was the best-selling item. "I thought it would improve business if we only sold sportswear, because it was the only profitable thing. If you made money in chocolate ice cream, why sell other flavors?" His father disagreed, telling him; "You'll never be a merchant."

So Leslie left, determined to start his own outlet. He convinced his aunt to lend him $5,000 to set up a shop that sold only sportswear. He opened the store in Columbus in 1963, and since it was limited to sportswear, he decided to call it The Limited. It soon became clear that his father was wrong—Leslie Wexner was, indeed, a merchant. In just its first year of operation, the store surpassed his parents' store, with sales of $165,000. Soon his parents closed their store and joined Leslie in his successful operation. But it was a difficult struggle in the early years. Wexner worked with great attention to detail, fussing over the color schemes, cleaning the windows with vinegar and ammonia himself in order to save $50 a week, and doing his own books because he could not afford a bookkeeper.

By 1969, when The Limited went public, the chain had six stores. Wexner's old marketing professor had advised against going public, but Wexner was eager to intensify the firm's growth, and he needed the additional capital. And the growth was phenomenal. By 1976 there were 100 stores, and just three years later, there were 300 Limited stores across the nation. Despite his success, however, Wexner was having trouble finding a coherent and agreeable image for his stores. The first stores looked like British pubs with brick fronts and mullioned windows. Later stores had burlap-covered walls. Finally, Alfred Taub-man, the real estate and shopping mall developer, in whose malls several of the Limited's stores were located, summoned Wexner to Detroit. Wexner recalled,

He didn't say a word to me. We had coffee and then got in his helicopter, which was waiting out back, but he still hadn't talked. He flew me to three shopping centers and stopped at my stores, and then finally he turned to me and said, "Do you wonder why I called you? Your stores are a *blight* on my shopping centers." (*New York*)

That was all it took. Wexner, at great expense, redesigned his stores with a newer, cleaner, and more sophisticated look. The transformation was so successful that, by the 1980s, Wexner's stores were recognized as the industry leader in store presentation. But 1979 was a difficult year. Wexner had expanded too rapidly, and day-to-day operations got out of hand, causing a 55-percent drop in earnings, the only year between 1967 and 1987 in which earnings did not rise. As a result, Wexner appointed Robert Morosky as vice chairman to handle the details of the business, while Wexner concentrated on expansion. While he was building more Limited stores, Wexner was also purchasing chains from others. In 1982, he picked up the 222-store Lane Bryant chain, which grew to 360 stores three years later. Shortly thereafter, he bought and greatly expanded a small chain of sexy lingerie stores called Victoria's Secret. Recognizing that men made up about half the customers in these stores, he gave them a bordello look. In 1985, Wexner bought the large 764-unit chain of Lerner stores, paying $297 million for a business that was, in his words, "essentially bankrupt when we got it." Wexner also started a chain of stores for younger buyers called Limited Express, which had 186 stores by the mid–1980s. The result of these acquisitions was a chain of women's stores that covered a broad spectrum of the market: "That means sports clothes (The Limited), fat clothes (Lane Bryant), young clothes (The Limited Express), cheap fat clothes (Sizes Unlimited), catalog clothes (Brylane), and the teddies and garter belts of Victoria's Secret."

The Wexner approach was demonstrated very well when he took over Lane Bryant. "He eliminated tall sizes," said a retail industry analyst, "the business is just too small." He also eliminated the largest sizes, reasoning: "Size 52 women don't get out much." Recognizing that about 40 percent of all women are size 14 or larger, Wexner offered sizes 14 through 20 in the Lane Bryant stores. Most important, he changed the look of the Lane Bryant clothes. Clothing for larger women had traditionally been frumpy, or stressed loud fabrics not used for smaller sizes. Wexner thought this was all wrong: "Big women are just like every other woman. They read the same books, watch the same TV, and fall in love with Burt Reynolds just as fast. They want to look like their smaller friends." As a result of putting in higher fashion clothes, sales at Lane Bryant stores increased at the rate of 20 percent annually in the first few years after he took them over.

Wexner's success was such that The Limited exceeded $1 billion in sales in 1983, went over $2 billion in 1985, and topped the $3 billion mark in 1986. In 1987 they were $3.5 billion. Profits went up nearly as rapidly, rising at compound annual rates of about 60 percent between 1980 and 1986. About $10 million in 1980, they were $70 million in 1983, $145 million in 1985, $228 million in 1986, and $260 million in 1987. This made Leslie Wexner a very wealthy man, worth well over $1 billion in 1988. His mother, Belle Wexner, was given 10 percent of the company at an early stage, and she was worth about $400 million. Leslie Wexner's sister, Susan Wexner, was worth about $300 million. He also made over fifty of his employees millionaires, primarily by granting stock options. One hundred shares of Limited stock purchased for $750 when it went public in 1969 were worth $500,000 by the mid–1980s.

What has been the secret of Wexner's success? A number of factors have contributed, not the least of which was his uncanny merchandising ability. But there were other factors as well. Wexner, a workaholic, has a large ego, with a great deal of arrogance. These traits have manifested themselves in the Limited's corporate culture. The result, as *Forbes* noted in 1987, was "a corporate arrogance built around an almost religious reverance for Wexner and an unshakable belief that the Limited can do no wrong." All of Wexner's stores, no matter how different from the outside, are operated by a similar set of principles. The stores usually stock tightly edited "programs" rather than apparel separates. That means they stock complementary groups of easy-to-match clothing. Then, too, Wexner and his people are very adept at spotting new trends and developments and at "knocking off" copies for the private label merchandise they largely sell in their stores.

Wexner has also been a master at creating a kind of ersatz chic for the masses. The Limited buyers created a synthetic European look that they called Forenza, but marketed as if Forenza were a real designer. They also brought out an Outback Red line, which was supposed to represent some sort of Australian bush clothing. Both of these attempts were successful, although many of the things the Limited tried were not, but that is all right with Wexner. He wants his people to be adventuresome, and he expects there will be a certain number of mistakes. As a result, the Limited dumps tons of clothing into the off-price and basement markets every year. But Wexner simply shrugs and says, "When you eat like an elephant, you s— like an elephant." To get the best prices, Wexner buys more than 50 percent of his merchandise overseas, and he buys from some 6,000 suppliers and factories.

A major reason for Wexner's success has been his uncanny ability to spot trends, even before they become trends. He has done this successfully not only with his merchandise, but also with his company's organizational structure. During the early years of The Limited's growth, bigness was the order of the day in corporate America. As long as that was the case, The Limited expanded rapidly under a tightly centralized structure. One winter day in 1987, however, as Wexner was approaching his firm's massive headquarters in Columbus, he began to worry about his organization's flexibility and agility. With revenues of nearly $4 billion, The Limited was no longer the sleek, small, and fast retailer of the 1960s and early 1970s. It had become a behemoth, and profit margins were slipping. Wexner began to wonder if The Limited had become too big to manage. He phrased the question at a series of meetings over the next several weeks: "The Limited is beginning to look like General Motors. Do we act like them?"

The answer was a disconcerting "yes," so Wexner swung into action. Carrying out a major overhaul of his firm's organization, in early 1988 he decentralized the company along divisional lines, gave more authority to lower-level managers, and gave his stores yet another face-lift. As a result, sales, margins, and, most gratifying to Wexner, profits, have begun returning to former levels. Wexner had simply grasped early what management guru Thomas J. Peters has been preaching to packed houses on the lecture circuit: Big Business is inefficient, and smaller is generally better. "Size has become a paramount issue," said

Peters, "and somewhat smaller is apparently becoming much more beautiful everywhere."

But, such success has a price. The Limited has become legendary in the retail industry for its burnout and turnover rate among middle-level managers. One former executive refers to the company as a "meatgrinder." Yet, *New York* magazine said Wexner had a dybbuk, a private demon who wakes him up each morning and pushes him to accomplish ever more. It noted that Wexner is not about to rest, and has little sympathy for people who cannot keep up with him. He attempted a hostile takeover of the Carter Hawley Hale chain (see Edward Carter) in 1984 and was rebuffed, but he vowed that someday he would return, and would be victorious. As Wexner reflected,

I got great pleasure, *almost sensual pleasure,* from our attempt to merge with Carter Hawley Hale. The punishment would have been never to be able to try. Everyone says I must be doing this for the power or the money. Not at all. I don't want to be blocked from trying my ideas, from being creative.

Once, when asked what his dybbuk looked like, Wexner replied, "Me." But others are not so sure. His former professor had a different idea: "He's the enigmatic but energetic leader. He's the product of a female-dominated childhood—his mother, assertive, effervescent, bright, and action-oriented. His dad was contemplative and rather shy, uncertain of himself." Belle Wexner, whose office is right next to bachelor Leslie's in Columbus, remained a force in the firm into the late 1980s, as Leslie discussed business tactics with her once or twice a week. An executive recalled, "[Wexner] finished a speech once and came right down into the audience and kissed his mother and asked, 'How did I do?' He's like a little kid: 'Look Ma—no cavities.' " (**B.** *Chain Store Age Executive,* September 1981, March 1985; *Business Week,* April 16, 1984, February 25, 1985, October 5, December 21, 1987, March 14, 1988, March 27, 1989; *Barron's,* May 6, 1985; *New York,* August 5, 1985; *Fortune,* August 19, 1985, October 12, 1987, May 23, 1988; *Newsweek,* December 30, 1985; *Who's Who in America,* 1986–87; *Forbes,* April 6, 1987, October 24, 1988.)

AMERICAN BUSINESS LEADERS ACCORDING TO INDUSTRY

I. Extractive Industries: Petroleum and Gas Extraction

Davis, M.

Hess, L.

Kerr, R.

McGee, D.

Pickens, T. B.

II. Food and Allied Products Manufacturing and Processing

A. General Food Processors

Cummings, N.

Harper, C. M.

Holman, C.

MacMillan Family

Paulucci, J.

Perdue, F.

Rich, R.

Simon, N.

Simplot, J.

B. Meat Packers

Harper, C. M.

Holman, C.

C. Soft Drink Industry

Goizueta, R.

Kendall, D.

Llewellyn, J. B.

Steele, A.

D. Wine and Beer

Gallo, E & J.

Coors Family

E. Grain and Cereal Miller

MacMillan Family

F. Candy Manufacturer

Mars, F.

G. Bakers

Amos, W.

Fields, D. & R.

Rudkin, M.

III. Textile and Apparel Manufacturers

A. Textile Mill Products

Milliken, R.

Stevens Family

B. Apparel Manufacturing

Claiborne, L.

Haas Family

Klein, A.

Klein, C.

Lauren, R.

Schwartz, B.

Wachner, L.

C. *Footwear*

Fireman, P.

Knight, P.

IV. *Health and Beauty Aids*

Ash, M. K.

Gardner, E.

Lauder, E.

Revson, C.

Searle, J. G.

V. *Primary Metal Manufacture—Iron and Steel*

Iverson, K.

VI. *Equipment Manufacturers*

A. *Automobile*

Petersen, D.

Smith, R.

B. *Agricultural and Construction Equipment*

Caterpillar Tractor

C. *Instrument Makers*

Hewlett, W.

Packard, D.

D. *Electronics Manufacturers*

Galvin, P. & R.

Hewlett, W.

Packard, D.

Singleton, H.

E. *Aircraft Manufacturer*

Wallace, D.

F. *Computers and Business Machines*

Blumenthal, M.

Hewlett, W.

Jobs, S.

Norris, W.

Olsen, K.

Packard, D.

Palevsky, M.

Tandy, C.

Wang, A.

G. *Silcon Chips and Semiconductors*

Galvin, P. & R.

Moore, G.

Noyce, R.

H. *Miscellaneous Manufacturing*

Blumenthal, M.

Fisher, H.

Handler, E. & R.

Hassenfeld, S.

McKnight, W.

Price, I.

Pritzker Family

Shapiro, I.

Stern, L.

VII. *Transportation*

A. *Airlines*

Burr, D.

Icahn, C.

Lorenzo, F.

Pritzker Family

B. *Express*

Smith, F.

VIII. *Real Estate Developers*

Crow, T.

DeBartolo, E.

Griffin, M.

Pritzker Family

Tisch, L. & P. R.

Trump, D.

AMERICAN BUSINESS LEADERS ACCORDING TO COMPANY

Amerada Hess Corporation: Hess, L.

Amerco Systems: Shoen, L.

Amway Corporation: De Vos, R. & Van Andel, J.

Apple Computer, Incorporated: Jobs, S.

Atlanta Braves: Turner, T.

Ballantine Books: Ballantine, I.

Bantam Books: Ballantine, I.

Bendix Corporation: Blumenthal, M.

Berkshire Hathaway Incorporated: Buffett, W.

Block, H & R, Incorporated: Bloch, H. & R.

Braniff Airlines: Pritzker Family

Broadway Hale Stores: Carter, E.

Burnett, Leo Company Incorporated: Burnett, L.

Burrell Advertising, Incorporated: Burrell, T.

Burroughs Corporation: Blumenthal, M.

Business Roundtable: Shapiro, I.

Cargill Incorporated: MacMillan Family

Carter, Hawley, Hale: Carter, E.

Caterpillar Tractor: Blackie, W.; Morgan, L.; Neumiller, L.; Schaefer, G.

Cessna Aircraft Company: Wallace, D.

Chun King Foods: Paulucci, J.

Citizens & Southern National Bank: Lane, M.

Claiborne, Liz, Incorporated: Claiborne, L.

Coca-Cola Bottling Company of Philadelphia: Llewellyn, J. B.

Coca-Cola, Incorporated: Goizueta, R.

Columbia Broadcasting System (CBS): Tisch, L. & P. R.

ComputerLand Corporation: Millard, W.

Conagra Incorporated: Harper, C. M.

Consolidated Foods: Cummings, N.

Consolidated Grocers: Cummings, N.

Continental Airlines: Lorenzo, F.

Control Data Corporation: Norris, W.

Coors, Adolph Brewing Company: Coors Family

Crow, Trammell and Company: Crow, T.

Davis Oil Company: Davis, M.

DeBartolo, Edward J., Corporation: DeBartolo, E.

Deering, Milliken and Company: Milliken, R.

Della Femina and Travisano: Della Femina, J.

Desilu Productions: Arnaz, D.

Digital Equipment Corporation: Olsen, K.

Domino's Pizza: Monaghan, T.

Doyle Dane Bernbach: Bernbach, W.

Drexel Burnham Lambert: Milken, M.

Du Pont & Walston: Perot, H. R.

Du Pont, E. I. de Nemours and
Company: Shapiro, I.

Du Pont Glore & Forgan: Perot, H. R.

Eastern Airlines: Lorenzo, F.

Electronic Data Systems: Perot, H. R.

Essence Communications Incorporated:
Lewis, E.

Fairchild Semiconductor, Incorporated:
Moore, G. & Noyce, R.

Famous Amos Chocolate Chip Cookie
Company: Amos, W.

Fedco Stores: Llewellyn, J. B.

Federal Express Corporation: Smith, F.

Federated Department Stores: Lazarus, F.

Fisher-Price Toy Company: Fisher, H. &
Price, I.

Food Manufacturers, Incorporated:
Mars, F.

Ford Motor Company: Petersen, D.

Fox, G. & Company: Auerbach, B.

Gallo, E & J. Winery: Gallo, E. & J.

Gannett Company: Neuharth, A.

General Motors: Perot, H. R. & Smith,
R.

Griffey, Dick Productions: Griffey, D.

Griffin Company: Griffin, M.

Griffin Productions: Griffin, M.

Hartz Group, Incorporated: Stern, L.

Hasbro Toys, Incorporated: Hassenfeld,
S.

Hess Oil Company: Hess, L.

Hewlett-Packard Company: Hewlett, W.
& Packard, D.

Hunt Foods: Simon, N.

Hyatt Hotels: Pritzker Family

Hyatt International: Pritzker Family

Hyatt Legal Services: Bloch, H. & R.

Icahn & Company: Icahn, C.

International Data Group: McGovern, P.

Iowa Beef Processors: Holman, C.

Jeno's Frozen Pizza: Paulucci, J.

K mart: Cunningham, H.

Kelly Girl Services: Kelly, W.

Kelly Services, Incorporated: Kelly, W.

Kerr-McGee Oil Industries, Incorporated:
Kerr, R. & McGee, D.

Klein, Anne & Company: Klein, A.

Klein, Calvin, Incorporated: Klein, C. &
Schwartz, B.

Kohlberg, Kravis Roberts & Company:
Kravis, H. & Roberts, G.

Lauder, Estée, Incorporated: Lauder, E.

Leasco: Steinberg, S.

Levi Strauss & Company: Haas Family

Lillian Vernon Corporation: Katz, L.

Limited, The: Wexner, L.

Lord and Taylor: Shaver, D.

MCI Communications Corporation:
McGowan, W.

Marmon Group: Pritzker Family

Mars, Incorporated: Mars, F.

Mary Kay Cosmetics: Ash, M. K.

Mattell, Incorporated: Handler, E. & R.

Mesa Petroleum Company: Pickens,
T. B.

Metromedia: Kluge, J.

Microsoft, Incorporated: Gates, W.

Midas International: Sherman, G. & N.

Milliken & Company: Milliken, R.

Minnesota Mining & Manufacturing
(3-M): McKnight, W.

Motorola, Incorporated: Galvin, P. & R.

Mrs. Fields Cookies: Fields, D. & R.

National Enquirer: Pope, G.

Neiman-Marcus Company: Marcus, S.

AMERICAN BUSINESS LEADERS BY PLACE OF BUSINESS

Arizona

Phoenix: Shoen, L.

Arkansas

Bentonville: Walton, S.

California

Beverly Hills: Milken, M.

Cupertino: Jobs, S.

Hawthorne: Handler, E. & R.

Los Angeles: Amos, W.; Arnaz, D.;
Carter, E.; Griffin, M.; Palevsky,
M.; Singleton, H.

Modesto: Gallo, E. & J.

Oakland: Millard, W.

Palo Alto: Hewlett, W. & Packard, D.

San Francisco: Haas Family; Roberts,
G.; Schwab, C.

Santa Clara: Moore, G. & Noyce, R.

Colorado

Denver: Davis, M.

Golden: Coors Family

Connecticut

Bridgeport: Wachner, L.

Hartford: Auerbach, B.

Norwalk: Rudkin, M.

Delaware

Wilmington: Shapiro, I.

District of Columbia

Washington: Blumenthal, M.;
McGowan, W.

Florida

Manalapan: Pope, G.

Orlando: Paulucci, J.

Georgia

Atlanta: Goizueta, R.; Lane, M.;
Turner, T.

Savannah: Lane, M.

Idaho

Boise: Simplot, J.

Illinois

Chicago: Burnett, L.; Burrell, T.;
Cummings, N.; Galvin, P. & R.;
Gardner, E.; Hefner, C. & H.;
Mars, F.; Pritzker Family; Searle,
J.; Sherman, G. & N.;

Peoria: Blackie, W.; Morgan, L.;
Neumiller, L.; Schaefer, G.

Kansas

Wichita: Wallace, D.

Maryland

Salisbury: Perdue, F.

Massachusetts

Avon: Fireman, P.

Lowell: Wang, A.

Maynard: Olsen, K.

Michigan

Ann Arbor: Monaghan, T.

Dearborn: Petersen, D.

Detroit: Smith, R.

Grand Rapids: De Vos, R. & Van Andel, J.

Troy: Cunningham, H.; Kelly, W.

Minnesota

Duluth: Paulucci, J.

Minneapolis/St. Paul: McKnight, W.; MacMillan Family; Norris, W.

Missouri

Kansas City: Bloch, H. & R.

Nebraska

Dakota City: Holman, C.

Omaha: Buffett, W.; Harper, C. M.

New Hampshire

Nashua: McGovern, P.

New Jersey

Harrison: Stern, L.

Morristown: Simon, W.

Newark: Burr, D.

Rochelle Park: Lazarus, C.

New York

Buffalo: Llewellyn, J. B.; Rich, R.

East Aurora: Fisher, H.; Price, I.

Mt. Vernon: Katz, L.

New Rochelle: Llewellyn, J. B.

New York City: Ballantine, I.; Bernbach, W.; Claiborne, L.; Della Femina, J.; Guccione, R.; Hess, L.; Icahn, C.; Klein, A.; Klein, C.; Kravis, H.; Lauder, E.; Lauren, R.; Lewis, R.; Ogilvy, D.; Revson, C.; Rich, M.; Schwartz, B.; Shaver, D.; Simon N.; Steinberg, S.; Stevens Family; Tisch, L. & P. R.; Trump, D.

Purchase: Kendall, D.; Steele, A.

Rochester: Neuharth, A.

North Carolina

Charlotte: Iverson, K.

Ohio

Cincinnati: Lazarus, F.

Columbus: Wexner, L.

Youngstown: DeBartolo, E.

Oklahoma

Oklahoma City: Kerr, R. & McGee, D.

Oregon

Beaverton: Knight, P.

Portland: Shoen, L.

Pennsylvania

Blue Bell: Blumenthal, M.

Rhode Island

Pawtucket: Hassenfeld, S.

South Carolina

Spartanburg: Milliken, R.

Greenville: Stevens Family

Tennessee

Memphis: Smith, F.

Texas

Amarillo: Pickens, T. B.

Dallas: Ash, M. K.; Crow, T.; Marcus, S.; Perot, H. R.; Thompson Family

Ft. Worth: Tandy, C.

Houston: Lorenzo, F.

Utah

Park City: Fields, D. & R.

Virginia

Charlottesville: Kluge, J.

Washington

Seattle: Gates, W.

Outside the United States

Zug, Switzerland: Rich, M.

AMERICAN BUSINESS LEADERS BY PLACE OF BIRTH

Arkansas

Center Point: Shaver, D.

California

General: Fields, R.; Jobs, S.;
Milken, M.; Millard, W.

East Oakland: Fields, D.

Sacramento: Schwab, C.

San Francisco: Hess Family,
Koshland, D.; Moore, G.

San Mateo: Griffin, M.

Colorado

Denver: Coors, P.

Golden: Coors, W. & J.

Pueblo: Packard, D.

Connecticut

Bridgeport: Olsen, K.

Hartford: Auerbach, B.

South Windsor: Burr, D.

District of Columbia

Washington: Lazarus, C.

Florida

Tallahassee: Amos, W.

Georgia

Savannah: Lane, M.

Idaho

Declo: Simplot, J.

Illinois

Aledo: Morgan, L.

Chicago: Burrell, T.; Gardner, E.;
Hefner, C. & H.; Palevsky, M.;
Pritzker, A. & J.

Downers Grove: Iverson, K.

Harvard: Galvin, P.

Peoria: Neumiller, L.

Iowa

Denmark: Noyce, R.

Sioux City: Holman, C.

Kansas

Belmont: Wallace, D.

Humboldt: McGee, D.

Kentucky

Covington: Schaefer, G.

Maryland

General: Carter, E.

Baltimore: Lewis, R.

Salisbury: Perdue, F.

Massachusetts

Boston: Revson, C.

Brockton: Fireman, P.

Worcester: Price, I.

Michigan

Ann Arbor: Hewlett, W.;
Monaghan, T.

Grand Rapids: DeVos, R.; Van Andel, J.

Lansing: Harper, C. M.

St. John: Burnett, L.

Minnesota

General: Mars, F.

Aurora: Paulucci, J.

McGrath: Shoen, L.

Minneapolis/St. Paul: MacMillan, W.; Shapiro, I.

Pipestone: Petersen, D.

Mississippi

Marks: Smith, F.

Missouri

Kansas City: Bloch, H. & R.

Nebraska

Innovale: Norris, W.

Omaha: Buffett, W.; Searle, J.; Sherman, G.

New Jersey

General: Davis, M.

Asbury Park: Hess, L.

Fanwood: Stevens, J. & R.

Paterson: Simon, W.

South Plainfield: Stevens, W.

New York

Bronx: Klein, C.; Lauren, R.; Lewis, E.; Pope, G.; Schwartz, B.

Brooklyn: Della Femina, J.; Guccione R.; Klein, A.; Steinberg, S.

Buffalo: Rich, R.

Harlem: Llewellyn, J. B.

New York City: Ballantine, I.; Bernbach, W.; Icahn, C.; Lauder, E.; Lorenzo, F.; Milliken, R.; Rudkin, M.; Stern, L.; Tisch, L. & P. R.; Trump, D.; Wachner, L.

Ohio

Cincinnati: Turner, T.

Columbus: Smith, R.; Lazarus, F.

Dayton: Wexner, L.

Youngstown: DeBartolo, E.

Oklahoma

General: Kravis, H.; Roberts, G.

Ada: Kerr, R.

Holdenville: Pickens, T. B.

Kingfisher: Walton, S.

Oregon

Portland: Knight, P.; Simon, N.

Pennsylvania

Ashley: McGowan, W.

Home Camp: Cunningham, H.

Philadelphia: McGovern, P.

Unionville: Fisher, H.

Rhode Island

Providence: Hassenfeld, S.

South Dakota

Eureka: Neuharth, A.

White: McKnight, W.

Tennessee

Nashville: Griffey, D.; Steele, A.

Texas

Brownsville: Thompson, J.

Dallas: Crow, T.; Marcus, S.; Thompson, J. P.& J. W.

Ft. Worth: MacMillan, J.

Hastel: Singleton, H.

Hot Wells: Ash, M. K.

Texarkana: Perot, H. R.

Washington

Seattle: Gates, W.

Sequim: Kendall, D.

Wisconsin

Marshland: Galvin, R.

Outside the United States

Belgium

Antwerp: Rich, M.

Brussels: Claiborne, L.

Canada

St. John's New Brunswick:
Cummings, N.

British Columbia: Kelly, W.

China

Shanghai: Wang, A.

Cuba

Havana: Goizueta, R.

Santiago: Arnaz, D.

England

West Horsley: Ogilvy, D.

Germany

Berlin: Blumenthal, M.

Chemnitz: Kluge, J.

Leipzig: Katz, L.

Russia

Kiev: Pritzker, N.

Scotland

Glasgow: Blackie, W.

BLACK AND WOMEN AMERICAN BUSINESS LEADERS

Black Business Leaders

Amos, W.

Burrell, T.

Gardner, E.

Griffey, D.

Lewis, E.

Lewis, R.

Llewellyn, J. B.

Women Business Leaders

Ash, M. K.

Auerbach, B.

Claiborne, L.

Fields, D.

Handler, R.

Hefner, C.

Katz, L.

Klein, A.

Lauder, E.

Rudkin, M.

Shaver, D.

Wachner, L.

INDEX

Note: bold face entries are biographical subjects of this compilation.

About the Authors

JOHN N. INGHAM is a Professor of History at the University of Toronto. A prolific author, he has written a score of scholarly articles and book reviews, as well as serving as an editor for two anthologies. He is the author of two books, the *Biographical Dictionary of American Business Leaders* (a four-volume set) and *Iron Barons: A Social Analysis of the American Elite, 1987–1965* (Greenwood Press 1983, and 1978).

LYNNE B. FELDMAN is a freelance researcher and editor. Previously, she worked for the Gage Publishing Company as an editor.